BOSCH

Automotive Handbook
5th Edition

Comprehensive information made easy

Automotive electrics and electronics

Vehicle electrical systems, Symbols and circuit diagrams, EMC/interference-suppression, Batteries, Alternators, Starting systems, Lighting technology, Comfort and convenience systems, Diesel-engine management systems, Gasoline-engine management systems.

3rd updated edition, 314 pages.
ISBN 0-7680-0508-6

Gasoline-engine management

Combustion in the gasoline (SI) engine, Exhaust-gas control, Gasoline-engine management, Gasoline-fuel-injection system (Jetronic), Ignition, Spark plugs, Engine-management systems (Motronic).

1st edition, 370 pages.
ISBN 0-7680-0510-8

Diesel-engine management

Combustion in the diesel engine, Mixture formation, Exhaust-gas control, In-line fuel-injection pumps, Axial piston and radial-piston distributor pumps, Distributor injection pumps, Common Rail (CR) accumulator injection systems, Single-plunger fuel-injection pumps, Start-assist systems.

2nd updated and expanded edition, 306 pages.
ISBN 0-7680-0509-4

Driving-safety systems

Driving safety in the vehicle, Basics of driving physics, Braking-systems basics, Braking systems for passenger cars, ABS and TCS for passenger cars, Commercial vehicles – basic concepts, systems and schematic diagrams, Compressed-air equipment for commercial vehicles, ABS, TCS, EBS for commercial vehicles, Brake testing, Electronic stability program (ESP).

2nd updated and expanded edition, 248 pages.
ISBN 0-7680-0511-6

Automotive terminology

4,700 technical terms from automotive technology, in German, English and French, assembled from the above Bosch Technical Books:
"Automotive Electrics and Electronics",
"Diesel-engine management",
"Gasoline-engine management" and
"Driving-safety systems".

1st edition, 378 pages.
ISBN 0-7680-0338-5

Automotive Handbook

Imprint

Published by:
© Robert Bosch GmbH, 2000
Postfach 30 02 20,
D-70442 Stuttgart.
Automotive Equipment Business Sector,
Department KH/PDI 2
Product-Marketing software products,
technical publications.

Editor-in-Chief:
Dipl.-Ing. (FH) Horst Bauer.

Editorial staff:
Dipl.-Ing. Karl-Heinz Dietsche,
Dipl.-Ing. (BA) Jürgen Crepin,
Dipl.-Holzw. Folkhart Dinkler.

Translation:
Editor-in-Chief: Peter Girling
Translated by:
STAR Deutschland GmbH
Member of STAR Group

Technical graphics:
Bauer & Partner GmbH, Stuttgart.

Editorial closing: 30.09.2000

All rights reserved.

Printed in Germany.
Imprimé en Allemagne.
5th revised and extended edition,

Distribution:
SAE Society of Automotive Engineers
400 Commonwealth Drive
Warrendale, PA 15096-001
USA

ISBN 0-7680-0669-4

The brand names given in the contents serve only as examples and do not represent the classification or preference for a particular manufacturer. Trademarks are not identified as such.
The following companies kindly placed picture matter, diagrams, and other informative material at our disposal:
Audi AG, Ingolstadt;
Bayerische Motoren Werke AG, Munich;
Behr GmbH & Co, Stuttgart;
Brose Fahrzeugteile GmbH & Co. KG, Coburg;
Continental AG, Hanover;
DaimlerChrysler AG, Stuttgart;
Eberspächer KG, Esslingen;
Filterwerk Mann + Hummel, Ludwigsburg;
3K-Warner Turbosystems GmbH, Frankenthal;
Mannesmann Kienzle GmbH, Villingen-Schwenningen;
Pierburg GmbH, Neuss;
RWE Energie AG, Essen;
Volkswagen AG, Wolfsburg;
Zahnradfabrik Friedrichshafen AG, Friedrichshafen.
Source of information for motor-vehicle specifications:
Automobil Revue Katalog 1999.

Foreword to the 5th Edition

The "Automotive Handbook", a reliable guide full of up-to-date and concise information, has grown over a period of six decades from a calendar supplement of 96 pages to a 960-page reference work. In that time, over a million copies have been produced worldwide and the text translated into numerous languages.

The 5th edition, in common with its predecessors, is supported by two main pillars: the expertise of the technical staff at our company and in the automotive industry. They have fully revised the contents of this manual and brought it completely up to date. Thanks are due to all those involved.

This book is intended primarily as a source of important facts and figures and as a review of present-day technology for the automotive engineer and technician, but also for anyone else with an interest in technical matters. Accordingly, the automotive technology content is restricted to passenger cars and commercial vehicles, and the remaining content to that required for practical purposes.

Within the framework of a pocketbook it is impossible to present detailed coverage of individual technical subjects. On the other hand, bearing in mind the very wide range of readers, we do not want to dispense with generally applicable topics and data. However, we have dispensed with the "Conversion Tables" as the calculator is now an everyday item of equipment and any figure required can easily be calculated using the conversion formulas provided. The chapter "Road Traffic Legislation (Germany)" has also been deleted due to the international usage of the booklet.

These deletions have made way for new and updated topics which have added an extra 70 pages to the book.

We recommend readers to scan through the "Automotive Handbook" in order to gain an overall impression before using it.

The Editors

For your information

The following topics have been updated/extended since the 4th edition:
Vibration ● Acoustics ● Electronics (integrated circuits, micromechanics, mechatronics, sensors) ● Statistics● Reliability ● Closed and open-loop control systems ● Materials technology (basic principles, materials, lubricants, fuels, consumables) ● Corrosion ● Hardness ● Calculating fuel consumption ● Vehicle dynamics.
Internal-combustion engines (direct fuel injection, diesel combustion systems) ● Engine cooling (cooling-module technology, thermomanagement, exhaust cooling) ● Turbochargers and superchargers (multistage) ● Engine management on gasoline engines (mixture control, fuel-injection systems, fuel injectors, spark plugs, ME-Motronic, exhaust gases) ● Engine management on diesel engines (axial/radial-piston pumps, injectors, exhaust gases, start-assist systems).
Electric drive units ● Drivetrain (transmission, traction control systems (TCS) for passenger cars and commercial vehicles) ● Steering ● Braking systems (ABS for passenger cars, ABS and EBS for commercial vehicles) ● Bodywork, commercial vehicles ● Lighting systems (stepped reflectors, Bi-Litronic, headlamps and lights). Car radios ● Park Pilot systems ● Navigation systems ● Vehicle information systems ● Mobile phones ● Safety and security systems (impact detection, interior-movement detection) ● Automotive hydraulics (electric proportional control valves).
Circuit diagrams and symbols ● Vehicle electrical system (batteries, battery testers, water-cooled alternators, electromagnetic compatibility (EMC))
Passenger-car specifications.

The following topics have been introduced:
Fuel filters ● MED-Motronic ● Natural gas operation (spark-ignition engines) ● Fuel cells ● EHB for passenger cars ● Automatic Cruise Control (ACC) ● Instrumentation ● Traffic telematics ● Car radios (DAB) ● Connectors ● Cartronic.
and the following have been dropped:
Conversion tables ● Road traffic legislation (Germany).

6 Contents

Contents

8 Contents

Authors of the 5th Edition[1])

Quantities, units
Dipl.-Ing. G. Brüggen
Vibration and oscillation
Dipl.-Ing. J. Bohrer
Mechanics
Dipl.-Ing. G. Brüggen
Strength of materials
Dr.-Ing. M. Bacher-Höchst
Acoustics
Dr. rer. nat. W. Keiper
Heat
Dipl.-Ing. W. Daniel
Electrical engineering
Dr. rer. nat. W. Draxler,
Dipl.-Ing. B. Wörner
Electronics
Dr. rer. nat. U. Schaefer;
Dr. rer. nat. P. Egelhaaf;
Dr. rer. nat. U. Goebel;
Dr.-Ing. F. Piwonka; Dr.-Ing. J. Marek;
Dr. rer. nat. A. Zeppenfeld;
Dipl.-Ing. F. Raichle
Sensors
Dr.-Ing. E. Zabler
Actuators
Dr.-Ing. R. Heinz
Electrical machines
Dr.-Ing. R. Schenk
Technical optics
Dr.-Ing. F. Prinzhausen;
Dr. rer. nat. H. Sautter

Mathematics
Dipl.-Ing. G. Brüggen
Quality
Dipl.-Ing. M. Graf
Engineering statistics/measuring techniques
Dipl.-Math. H.-P. Bartenschlager
Reliability
Dr. rer. nat. E. Dilger; Dr. rer. nat. H. Weiler
Data processing in the motor vehicle
Dr. rer. nat. V. Denner
Control engineering
Dr. techn. R. Karrelmeyer

Materials
Dr. rer. nat. J. Ullmann;
Dr. rer. nat. W. Draxler; Dr.-Ing. D. Wicke;
Dipl.-Ing. D. Weidemann,
DaimlerChrysler AG, Sindelfingen;
Dr. rer. nat. H.-J. Spranger;
Dr. rer. nat. H. P. Koch;

Dipl.-Ing. R. Mayer;
Dipl.-Ing. G. Lindemann;
Dipl.-Ing. (FH) W. Hasert; R. Schäftlmeier;
Dipl.-Ing. H. Schneider;
Dipl.-Chem. Dr. W. Reckordt,
BASF Coatings AG, Münster;
Dr. rer. nat. G. Dornhöfer;
Dr. rer. nat. B. Blaich; Dr. rer. nat. D. Welting
Corrosion
Dipl.-Chem. B. Moro
Heat treatment, hardness
Dr.-Ing. D. Liedtke

Tolerances
Ing. (grad.) J. Pfänder
Sliding bearings and rolling bearings
Dr.-Ing. R. Heinz
Spring calculations
Dipl.-Ing. O. Krickau
Gears and tooth systems
Dipl.-Ing. U. v. Ehrenwall
Belt drives
C. Hansen
Basic principles of threaded fasteners
Dipl.-Ing. O. Krickau; Dipl.-Ing. M. Nöcker

Joining and bonding techniques
Dr.-Ing. M. Witt,
Volkswagen AG, Wolfsburg

Sheet-metal processing
Ing. W. Gertler, Volkswagen AG, Wolfsburg; Dr.-Ing. M. Witt, Volkswagen AG, Wolfsburg

Tribology, wear
Dipl.-Ing. H. Schorr

Road-going vehicle requirements
Prof. Dr. K. Binder, DaimlerChrysler AG, Stuttgart; Dipl.-Ing. G. Moresche, DaimlerChrysler AG, Stuttgart

Motor-vehicle dynamics
Dipl.-Ing. G. Moresche,
DaimlerChrysler AG, Stuttgart;
Prof. Dr.-Ing. habil. E.-C. v. Glasner,
DaimlerChrysler AG, Stuttgart;
Dr.-Phys. H. Böckenhoff,
DaimlerChrysler AG, Stuttgart;
Dr.-Ing. H. Steinkampf, Institut für Betriebstechnik der FAL, Braunschweig

---

[1]) Unless otherwise stated, the above are all employees of Robert Bosch GmbH.

Environmental stresses
Dipl.-Ing. G. Adalbert

Internal-combustion (IC) engines
Prof. Dr. K. Binder,
DaimlerChrysler AG, Stuttgart;
Dr.-Ing. H. Hiereth,
DaimlerChrysler AG, Stuttgart

Engine cooling
Dipl.-Ing. (FH) J.Wolf,
Behr GmbH & Co, Stuttgart

Fuel and air filters
Dr.-Ing. G.-M. Klein, Filterwerk
Mann und Hummel, Ludwigsburg;
Dr.-Ing. M. Tumbrink, Filterwerk
Mann und Hummel, Ludwigsburg

Turbochargers and superchargers
Dipl.-Ing. A. Förster, AG 3K-Warner
Turbosystems GmbH, Frankenthal

Exhaust systems
Dipl.-Ing. W. Steinle,
Eberspächer KG, Esslingen

**Engine management for gasoline
engines**
Dipl.-Ing. J. Gerhardt
Ignition
Dipl.-Ing. R. Schleupen; Dipl.-Ing. D. Betz;
Dipl.-Ing. E. Breuser; Dipl.-Ing. W. Häming
**Fuel supply and delivery, mixture
formation**
Dipl.-Ing. A. Gerhard; Dipl.-Ing. J. Gerhardt
Carburetors
Dr.-Ing. D. Großmann, Neuss
Gasoline fuel-injection systems
Dipl.-Ing. G. Felger;
Dipl.-Ing. M. Lembke;
Ing. (grad.) L. Seebald;
Dipl.-Ing. H. Deichsel

**Combined ignition and fuel-injection
system (Motronic)**
Dipl.-Ing. J. Gerhardt

Gasoline engines for alternative fuels
J. van der Weide,
TNO Road-Vehicles Research Institute,
Delft, Netherlands;
(FH) T. Allgeier;
.) L. Seebald;
M. Klenk

**Exhaust emissions from gasoline
engines**
Dr. rer. nat. M. Streib; Dr.-Ing. G. König;
Dipl.-Ing. E. Schnaibel

Engine management for diesel engines
Dr.-Ing. L. Schulze, Otto-von-Guericke
University (IMKO), Magdeburg;
Dipl.-Ing. K. Hummel; Dr.-Ing. W. Fuchs;
Dr.-Ing. R. Maier, Dr.-Ing. H. Stutzenberger
Start-assist systems
Dipl.-Ing. C. Kern; Dr. rer. nat. H.-P. Bauer
Exhaust emissions from diesel engines
Dr.-Ing. L. Schulze, Otto-von-Guericke
University (IMKO), Magdeburg

Starting systems
Dipl.-Ing.(FH) W. Rühle

Electric drives
Dr.-Ing. B. Sporckmann,
RWE Energie AG, Essen

Hybrid drives
Prof. Dr.-Ing. C. Bader,
DaimlerChrysler AG, Stuttgart
Fuel cells
Dr. rer. nat. U. Alkemade;
Dr. rer. nat. A. Häbich
Drivetrain
Dipl.-Ing. P. Köpf, Zahnradfabrik
Friedrichshafen AG ;
Dr. rer. nat. M. Schwab, Zahnradfabrik
Friedrichshafen AG;
Dr.-Ing. G. Schmidt; Dr.-Ing. H. Schramm

Suspension, suspension linkage
Dipl.-Ing. P. Dick;
Dipl.-Ing. J. Wimberger,
Dipl.-Ing. A. Mrotzek;
Dipl.-Ing. H. Stein,
all authors Bayerische Motoren Werke AG,
Munich

Wheels
Dipl.-Ing. R. Braun,
DaimlerChrysler AG, Stuttgart;
Prof. Dr.-Ing. habil. E.-C. v. Glasner,
DaimlerChrysler AG, Stuttgart

Tires
Dipl.-Ing. B. Meiß,
Continental AG, Hanover;
Prof. Dr.-Ing. habil. E.-C. v. Glasner,
DaimlerChrysler AG, Stuttgart

Steering
Ing. (grad.) D. Elser, Zahnradfabrik
Friedrichshafen AG, Schwäbisch Gmünd
Braking systems
Dr. rer. nat. J. Bräuninger; Prof. Dr.-Ing.
habil. E.-C. v. Glasner, DaimlerChrysler
AG, Stuttgart; Dipl.-Ing. (FH) K.-H. Röß,
DaimlerChrysler AG, Stuttgart;
Dr.-Ing. G. Schmidt; Dr.-Ing. H. Schramm;
Dipl.-Ing. W. Brühmann

Electronic Stability Program (ESP)
Dr.-Ing. A. van Zanten; Dipl.-Ing. G. Pfaff;
Dr.-Ing. R. Erhardt
Adaptive Cruise Control (ACC)
Dr. rer. nat. H. Winner;
Dr. rer. nat. H. Olbrich

Road-vehicle systematics
Dipl.-Ing. D. Weidemann, DaimlerChrysler
AG, Sindelfingen

Vehicle bodies, passenger cars
Dipl.-Ing. D. Weidemann, DaimlerChrysler
AG, Sindelfingen
Vehicle bodies, commercial vehicles
Dr.-Phys. H. Böckenhoff,
DaimlerChrysler AG, Stuttgart

Lighting
Dr.-Ing. M. Hamm; Dipl.-Ing. D. Boebel;
Dipl.-Ing. T. Spingler
Signaling devices and alarm systems
Dipl.-Betriebsw. C. Giek;
Dipl.-Ing.(FH) H. Hennrich

Windshield and headlamp cleaning
Dr.-Ing. J.-G. Dietrich

**Heating, ventilation and air-condition-
ing (HVAC)**
Dipl.-Ing. G. Schweizer,
Behr GmbH & Co, Stuttgart

Instrumentation
Prof. Dr. P. Knoll, Dr.-Ing. B. Herzog
Car radios, DAB
S. Rehlich; Dipl.-Ing. G. Spreitz

Parking systems
Dipl.-Ing. (FH) H. Arnold

Trip recorders
Mannesmann Kienzle GmbH,
PR-Abteilung, Villingen-Schwenningen

Navigation systems, traffic telematics
Dipl.-Ing. E. P. Neukirchner
Mobile radio
Dr.-Ing. J. Wazeck
Motor-vehicle information systems
Dr. rer. nat. D. Elke

**Safety, comfort and convenience
systems**
Dipl.-Ing. B. Mattes;
Dipl.-Ing. R. Kurzmann;
Dr.-Ing. G. Hartz; A. Walther

Automotive hydraulics
Dipl.-Ing. H. Lödige;
Dipl.-Ing. K. Griese;
Ing. (grad.) D. Bertsch;
Dipl.-Ing. W. Kötter;
Dipl.-Ing. M. Bing;
Dipl.-Ing. (FH) W. Steudel;
Dipl.-Ing. G. Bredenfeld

Automotive pneumatics
Ing. (grad.) P. Berg

Symbols, conductor-size calculations
The editorial staff

Plug-in connections
Dipl.-Ing. W. Gansert

Power supply
Dipl.-Ing. F. Meyer

Starter batteries
Dr.-Ing. G. Richter

Alternators
Dr.-Ing. H.-P. Gröter

Controller Area Network (CAN)
Dr.-Ing. M. Walther

CARTRONIC
Dr. rer. nat. J. Maier

Electromagnetic compatibility (EMC)
Dr.-Ing. W. Pfaff

Testing technology
Dr. rer. nat. W. Stöffler; R. Heinzmann;
L. Vogel; Dipl.-Ing.(FH) F. Zauner

Passenger-car specifications
R. Helfer

Quantities and units

SI units

SI denotes "Système International d'Unités" (International System of Units). The system is laid down in ISO 31 and ISO 1000 (ISO: International Organization for Standardization) and for Germany in DIN 1301 (DIN: Deutsches Institut für Normung – German Institute for Standardization).

SI units comprise the seven base SI units and coherent units derived from these base SI units using a numerical factor of 1.

Base SI units

Base quantity and symbols	Base SI unit Name	Symbol
Length	l	meter	m
Mass	m	kilogram	kg
Time	t	second	s
Electric current	I	ampere	A
Thermodynamic temperature	T	kelvin	K
Amount of substance	n	mole	mol
Luminous intensity	I	candela	cd

All other quantities and units are derived from the base quantities and base units. The international unit of force is thus obtained by applying Newton's Law:

force = mass $\times$ acceleration
$$F = m \cdot a$$

where m = 1 kg and a = 1 m/s^2, thus F = 1 kg · 1 m/s^2 = 1 kg · m/s^2 = 1 N (newton).

Definitions of the base SI units

1 meter is defined as the distance which light travels in a vacuum in 1/299,792,458 seconds (17th CGPM, 1983[1]). The meter is therefore defined using the speed of light in a vacuum, c = 299,792,458 m/s, and no longer by the wavelength of the radiation emitted by the krypton nuclide ^{86}Kr. The meter was originally defined as the forty-millionth part of a terrestrial meridian (standard meter, Paris, 1875).

1 kilogram is the mass of the international prototype kilogram (1st CGPM, 1889 and 3rd CGPM, 1901[1]).

1 second is defined as the duration of 9,192,631,770 periods of the radiation corresponding to the transition between the two hyperfine levels of the ground state of atoms of the ^{133}Cs nuclide (13th CGPM, 1967.[1])

1 ampere is defined as that constant electric current which, if maintained in two straight parallel conductors of infinite length, of negligible circular cross-sections, and placed 1 meter apart in a vacuum will produce between these conductors a force equal to 2 x 10^{-7} N per meter of length (9th CGPM, 1948.[1])

1 kelvin is defined as the fraction 1/273.16 of the thermodynamic temperature of the triple point[2] of water (13th CGPM, 1967.[1])

1 mole is defined as the amount of substance of a system which contains as many elementary entities as there are atoms in 0.012 kilogram of the carbon nuclide ^{12}C. When the mole is used, the elementary entities must be specified and may be atoms, molecules, ions, electrons, other particles, or specified groups of such particles (14th CGPM[1]), 1971.

1 candela is the luminous intensity in a given direction of a source which emits monochromatic radiation of frequency 540 x 10^{12} hertz and of which the radiant intensity in that direction is 1/683 watt per steradian (16th CGPM, 1979.[1])

Decimal multiples and fractions of SI units

Decimal multiples and fractions of SI units are denoted by prefixes before the name of the unit or prefix symbols before the unit symbol. The prefix symbol is placed immediately in front of the unit symbol to form a coherent unit, such as the milligram (mg). Multiple prefixes, such as microkilogram (μkg), may **not** be used.

---

[1]) CGPM: Conférence Générale des Poids et Mesures (General Conference on Weights and Measures).

[2]) Fixed point on the international temperature scale. The triple point is the only point at which all three phases of water (solid, liquid and gaseous) are in equilibrium (at a pressure of 1013.25 hPa). This temperature of 273.16 K is 0.01 K above the freezing point of water (273.15 K).

Prefixes are not to be used before the units angular degree, minute and second, the time units minute, hour, day and year, and the temperature unit degree Celsius.

Prefix	Prefix symbol	Power of ten	Name
atto	a	10^{-18}	trillionth
femto	f	10^{-15}	thousand billionth
pico	p	10^{-12}	billionth
nano	n	10^{-9}	thousand millionth
micro	μ	10^{-6}	millionth
milli	m	10^{-3}	thousandth
centi	c	10^{-2}	hundredth
deci	d	10^{-1}	tenth
deca	da	10^{1}	ten
hecto	h	10^{2}	hundred
kilo	k	10^{3}	thousand
mega	M	10^{6}	million
giga	G	10^{9}	milliard[1])
tera	T	10^{12}	billion[1])
peta	P	10^{15}	thousand billion
exa	E	10^{18}	trillion

Legal units

The Law on Units in Metrology of 2 July 1969 and the related implementing order of 26 June 1970 specify the use of "Legal units" in business and official transactions in Germany.[2])
Legal units are
– the SI units,
– decimal multiples and submultiples of the SI units,
– other permitted units; see the tables on the following pages.

Legal units are used in the Bosch Automotive Handbook. In many sections, values are also given in units of the technical system of units (e.g. in parentheses) to the extent considered necessary.

Systems of units not to be used

The physical system of units
Like the SI system of units, the physical system of units used the base quantities length, mass and time. However, the base units used for these quantities were the centimeter (cm), gram (g), and second (s) (CGS System).

The technical system of units
The technical system of units used the following base quantities and base units:

Base quantity	Base unit Name	Symbol
Length	meter	m
Force	kilopond	kp
Time	second	s

Newton's Law, $F = m \cdot a$, provides the link between the international system of units and the technical system of units, where force due to weight G is substituted for F and acceleration of free fall g is substituted for a.

In contrast to mass, acceleration of free fall and therefore force due to weight depend upon location. The standard value of acceleration of free fall is defined as g_n = 9.80665 m/s² (DIN 1305). The approximate value
$$g = 9.81 \text{ m/s}^2$$
is generally acceptable in technical calculations.
1 kp is the force with which a mass of 1 kg exerts pressure on the surface beneath it at a place on the earth. With
$$G = m \cdot g,$$
thus
$$1 \text{ kp} = 1 \text{ kg} \cdot 9.81 \text{ m/s}^2 = 9.81 \text{ N}.$$

---

[1]) In the USA: 10^9 = 1 billion, 10^{12} = 1 trillion.
[2]) Also valid: "Gesetz zur Änderung des Gesetzes über Einheiten im Meßwesen" dated 6 July 1973; "Verordnung zur Änderung der Ausführungsverordnung" dated 27 November 1973; "Zweite Verordnung zur Änderung der Ausführungsverordnung" dated 12 December 1977.

Quantities and units

Overview (from DIN 1301)

The following table gives a survey of the most important physical quantities and their standardized symbols, and includes a selection of the legal units specified for these quantities. Additional legal units can be formed by adding prefixes (see P. 13). For this reason, the column "other units" only gives the decimal multiples and submultiples of the SI units which have their own names. Units which are not to be used are given in the last column together with their conversion formulas. Page numbers refer to conversion tables.

Quantity and symbol	Legal units SI	Others	Name	Relationship	Remarks and units not to be used, incl. their conversion
1. Length, area, volume (PP. 19 ... 20)					
Length l	m		meter		1 µ (micron) = 1 µm 1 Å (ångström) = 10^{-10} m 1 X.U. (X-unit) ≈ 10^{-13} m 1 p (typograph. point) = 0.376 mm
		nm	international nautical mile	1 nm = 1852 m	
Area A	m²		square meter		
		a	are	1 a = 100 m²	
		ha	hectare	1 ha = 100 a = 10^4 m²	
Volume V	m³		cubic meter		
		l, L	liter	1 l = 1 L = 1 dm³	
2. Angle (P. 21)					
(Plane) angle α, β etc.	rad[1])		radian	1 rad = $\dfrac{1\ \text{m arc}}{1\ \text{m radius}}$	1 ∟ (right angle) = 90° = $(\pi/2)$ rad = 100 gon 1^g (centesimal degree) = 1 gon 1^c (centesimal minute) = 1 cgon 1^{cc} (centesimal second) = 0.1 mgon
		°	degree	1 rad = 180°/π = 57.296° ≈ 57.3° 1° = 0.017453 rad 1° = 60' = 3600" 1 gon = $(\pi/200)$ rad	
		'	minute		
		"	second		
		gon	gon		
Solid angle Ω	sr		steradian	1 sr = 1 m² spherical surface 1 m² sphere radius²	
3. Mass (PP. 22 ... 23)					
Mass (weight)[2]) m	kg		kilogram		1 γ (gamma) = 1µg 1 quintal = 100 kg 1 Kt (karat) = 0.2 g
		g	gram		
		t	ton	1 t = 1 Mg = 10^3 kg	

---

[1]) The unit rad (P. 21) can be replaced by the numeral 1 in calculations.
[2]) The term "weight" is ambiguous in everyday usage; it is used to denote mass as well as weight (DIN 1305).

Quantity and symbol	Legal units SI	Others	Name	Relationship	Remarks and units not to be used, incl. their conversion
Density ϱ	kg/m³			1 kg/dm³ = 1 kg/l	Weight per unit volume γ (kp/dm³ or p/cm³).
		kg/dm³		= 1 g/cm³	Conversion: The numerical
		kg/l		= 1000 kg/m³	value of the weight per unit vol-
		g/cm³			ume in kp/dm³ is roughly equal to the numerical value of the density in kg/dm³
Moment of inertia (mass moment, 2nd order) J	kg·m²			$J = m \cdot i^2$ i = radius of gyration	Flywheel effect $G \cdot D^2$. Conversion: Numerical value of $G \cdot D^2$ in kp·m² = 4 x numerical value of J in kg·m²

4. Time quantities (P. 28)

Time, duration, interval t	s		second[1]		
		min	minute[1]	1 min = 60 s	In the energy industry, one year is calculated at 8760 hours
		h	hour[1]	1 h = 60 min	
		d	day	1 d = 24 h	
		a	year		
Fre-quency f	Hz		hertz	1 Hz = 1/s	
Rota-tional speed (frequency of rotation) n	s⁻¹			1 s⁻¹ = 1/s	min⁻¹ and r/min (revolutions per minute) are still permissible for expressing rotational speed, but are better replaced by min⁻¹ (1 min⁻¹ = 1 r/min = 1 min⁻¹)
		min⁻¹ 1/min		1 min⁻¹ = 1/min = (1/60)s⁻¹	
Angular frequency $\omega = 2\pi f$ ω	s⁻¹				
Velocity υ	m/s	km/h		1 km/h = (1/3.6) m/s	
		kn	knot	1 kn = 1 nm/h = 1.852 km/h	
Accel-eration a	m/s²			acceleration of free fall g P.13	
Angular velocity ω	rad/s²[2]				
Angular accele-ration α	rad/s²[2]				

5. Force, energy, power (PP. 24 ... 25)

Force F Force due to weight G	N N		newton	1 N = 1 kg·m/s²	1 p (pond) = 9.80665 mN 1 kp (kilopond) = 9.80665 N ≈ 10 N 1 dyn (dyne) = 10⁻⁵ N

---

[1] Clock time: h, m, s written as superscripts; example: 3ʰ 25ᵐ 6ˢ.
[2] The unit rad can be replaced by the numeral 1 in calculations.

Quantity and symbol	Legal units SI	Others	Name	Relationship	Remarks and units not to be used, incl. their conversion
Pressure, gen. p	Pa		pascal	$1\ Pa = 1\ N/m^2$	1 at (techn. atmosphere) = $1\ kp/cm^2$
Absolute pressure p_{abs}		bar	bar	$1\ bar = 10^5\ Pa$ = $10\ N/cm^2$ $1\ \mu bar = 0.1\ Pa$ $1\ mbar = 1\ hPa$	= 0.980665 bar ≈ 1 bar 1 atm (physical atmosphere) = 1.01325 bar[1] 1 mm w.g. (water gauge)
Atmospheric pressure p_{amb}					= $1\ kp/m^2 = 0.0980665\ hPa$ ≈ 0.1 hPa
Gauge pressure p_e $p_e = p_{abs} - p_{amb}$	Gauge pressure etc. is no longer denoted by the unit symbol, but rather by a formula symbol. Negative pressure is given as negative gauge pressure. Examples:				1 torr = 1 mm Hg (mercury column) = 1.33322 hPa $dyn/cm^2 = 1\ \mu bar$
	previously now 3 atg p_e = 2.94 bar ≈ 3 bar 10 ata p_{abs} = 9.81 bar ≈ 10 bar 0.4 atu p_e = −0.39 bar ≈ −0.4 bar				
Mechanical stress σ, τ	N/m^2			$1\ N/m^2 = 1\ Pa$	$1\ kp/mm^2 = 9.81\ N/mm^2$ ≈ $10\ N/mm^2$
		N/mm^2		$1\ N/mm^2 = 1\ MPa$	$1\ kp/cm^2 ≈ 0.1\ N/mm^2$
Hardness (P. 274)	Brinell and Vickers hardness are no longer given in kp/mm^2. Instead, an abbreviation of the relevant hardness scale is written as the unit after the numerical value used previously (including an indication of the test force etc. where applicable).				Examples: previously now HB = 350 kp/mm^2 350 HB HV30 = 720 kp/mm^2 720 HV30 HRC = 60 60 HRC
Energy, work E, W	J		joule	$1\ J = 1\ N \cdot m = 1\ W \cdot s$ = $1\ kg\ m^2/s^2$	1 kp · m (kilopondmeter) = 9.81 J ≈ 10J 1 HP · h (horsepower-hour) = 0.7355 kW · h ≈ 0.74 kW · h
Heat, Quantity of heat (P. 25) Q		W · s	watt-second		
		kW · h	kilowatt-hour	$1\ kW \cdot h = 3.6\ MJ$	1 erg (erg) = 10^{-7}J 1 kcal (kilocalorie)
		eV	electron-volt	$1\ eV = 1.60219 \cdot 10^{-19}$J	= 4.1868 kJ ≈ 4.2 kJ 1 cal (calorie) = 4.1868 J ≈ 4.2 J
Torque M	N · m		newton-meter		1 kp · m (kilopondmeter) = 9.81 N · m ≈ 10 N · m
Power P Heat flow Q, (P. 25) Φ	W		watt	$1\ W = 1\ J/s = 1\ N \cdot m/s$	$1\ kp \cdot m/s = 9.81\ W ≈ 10\ W$ 1 HP (horsepower) = 0.7355 kW ≈ 0.74 kW 1 kcal/s = 4.1868 kW ≈ 4.2 kW 1 kcal/h = 1.163 W

6. Viscosimetric quantities (P. 27)

Quantity	SI	Others	Name	Relationship	Remarks
Dynamic viscosity η	Pa · s		Pascal-second	$1\ Pa \cdot s = 1\ N\ s/m^2$ = $1\ kg/(s \cdot m)$	1 P (poise) = 0.1 Pa · s 1 cP (centipoise) = 1 mPa · s
Kinematic viscosity ν	m^2/s			$1\ m^2/s$ = $1\ Pa \cdot s/(kg/m^3)$	1 St (stokes) = $10^{-4}\ m^2/s = 1\ cm^2/s$ 1 cSt (centistokes) = $1\ mm^2/s$

[1] 1.01325 bar = 1013.25 hPa = 760 mm mercury column is the standard value for atmospheric pressure.

Quantity and symbol	Legal units SI	Others	Name	Relationship	Remarks and units not to be used, incl. their conversion

7. Temperature and heat (P. 26)

Quantity and symbol		Legal units SI	Others	Name	Relationship	Remarks and units not to be used, incl. their conversion
Temperature	T	K		kelvin		
	t		°C	degree Celsius	$t = (T - 273.15 \text{ K}) \dfrac{°C}{K}$	
Temperature difference	ΔT	K		kelvin	$1 \text{ K} = 1 \text{ °C}$	
	Δt		°C	degree Celsius		
		In the case of composite units, express temperature differences in K, e.g. kJ/(m · h · K); tolerances for temperatures in degree Celsius, e.g. are written as follows: $t = (40 \pm 2)$ °C or $t = 40\,°C \pm 2\,°C$ or $t = 40\,°C \pm 2$ K.				

Refer to 5. for quantity of heat and heat flow.

Quantity and symbol		Legal units SI	Others	Name	Relationship	Remarks and units not to be used, incl. their conversion
Specific heat capacity (spec. heat)	c	$\dfrac{J}{kg \cdot K}$				$1 \text{ kcal/(kg · grd)}$ $= 4.187 \text{ kJ/(kg · K)}$ $\approx 4.2 \text{ kJ/(kg · K)}$
Thermal conductivity	λ	$\dfrac{W}{m \cdot K}$				$1 \text{ kcal/(m · h · grd)}$ $= 1.163 \text{ W/(m · K)}$ $\approx 1.2 \text{ W/(m · K)}$ $1 \text{ cal/(cm · s · grd)}$ $= 4.187 \text{ W/(cm · K)}$ 1 W/(m · K) $= 3.6 \text{ kJ/(m · h · K)}$

8. Electrical quantities (P. 60)

Quantity and symbol		Legal units SI	Others	Name	Relationship	Remarks and units not to be used, incl. their conversion
Electric current	I	A		ampere		
Electric potential	U	V		volt	$1 \text{ V} = 1 \text{ W/A}$	
Electric conductance	G	S		siemens	$1 \text{ S} = 1 \text{ A/V} = 1/\Omega$	
Electric resistance	R	Ω		ohm	$1 \, \Omega = 1/\text{S} = 1 \text{ V/A}$	
Quantity of electricity, electric charge	Q	C		coulomb	$1 \text{ C} = 1 \text{ A · s}$	
			A · h	ampere-hour	$1 \text{ A · h} = 3600 \text{ C}$	
Electric capacitance	C	F		farad	$1 \text{ F} = 1 \text{ C/V}$	
Electric flux density, displacement	D	C/m^2				
Electric field strength	E	V/m				

Quantity and symbol	Legal units SI	Others	Name	Relationship	Remarks and units not to be used, incl. their conversion

9. Magnetic quantities (P. 60)

Quantity and symbol		Legal units SI	Others	Name	Relationship	Remarks and units not to be used, incl. their conversion
Magnetic flux	Φ	Wb		weber	1 Wb = 1 V · s	1 M (maxwell) = 10^{-8} Wb
Magnetic flux density, induction	B	T		tesla	1 T = 1 Wb/m²	1 G (gauss) = 10^{-4} T,
Inductance	L	H		henry	1 H = 1 Wb/A	
Magnetic field strength	H	A/m			1 A/m = 1 N/Wb	1 Oe (oersted) = $10^3/(4\,\pi)$ A/m = 79.58 A/m

10. Photometric quantities and units (P. 137)

Quantity and symbol		Legal units SI	Others	Name	Relationship	Remarks and units not to be used, incl. their conversion
Luminous intensity	I	cd		candela[1])		
Luminance	L	cd/m²				1 sb (stilb) = 10^4 cd/m² 1 asb (apostilb) = $1/\pi$ cd/m²
Luminous flux	Φ	lm		lumen	1 lm = 1 cd · sr (sr = steradian)	
Illuminance	E	lx		lux	1 lx = 1 lm/m²	

11. Quantities used in atom physics and other fields

Quantity and symbol		Legal units SI	Others	Name	Relationship	Remarks and units not to be used, incl. their conversion
Energy	W		eV	electron-volt	1 eV= 1.60219 ·10^{-19}J 1 MeV= 10^6 eV	
Activity of a radioactive substance	A	Bq		becquerel	1 Bq = 1 s⁻¹	1 Ci (curie) = 3.7 · 10^{10} Bq
Absorbed dose	D	Gy		gray	1 Gy = 1 J/kg	1 rd (rad) = 10^{-2} Gy
Dose equivalent	Dq	Sv		sievert	1 Sv = 1 J/kg	1 rem (rem) = 10^{-2} Sv
Absorbed dose rate	$\dot{D}$				1 Gy/s = 1 W/kg	
Ion dose	J	C/kg				1 R (röntgen) = 258 · 10^{-6}C/kg
Ion dose rate	$\dot{\jmath}$	A/kg				
Amount of substance	n	mol		mole		

---

[1]) The stress is on the second syllable: the can<u>de</u>la.

Conversion of units

Units of length

Unit		X U	pm	Å	nm	µm	mm	cm	dm	m	km
1 XU	≈	1	10^{-1}	10^{-3}	10^{-4}	10^{-7}	10^{-10}	10^{-11}	10^{-12}	10^{-13}	—
1 pm	=	10	1	10^{-2}	10^{-3}	10^{-6}	10^{-9}	10^{-10}	10^{-11}	10^{-12}	—
1 Å	=	10^{3}	10^{2}	1	10^{-1}	10^{-4}	10^{-7}	10^{-8}	10^{-9}	10^{-10}	—
1 nm	=	10^{4}	10^{3}	10	1	10^{-3}	10^{-6}	10^{-7}	10^{-8}	10^{-9}	10^{-12}
1 µm	=	10^{7}	10^{6}	10^{4}	10^{3}	1	10^{-3}	10^{-4}	10^{-5}	10^{-6}	10^{-9}
1 mm	=	10^{10}	10^{9}	10^{7}	10^{6}	10^{3}	1	10^{-1}	10^{-2}	10^{-3}	10^{-6}
1 cm	=	10^{11}	10^{10}	10^{8}	10^{7}	10^{4}	10	1	10^{-1}	10^{-2}	10^{-5}
1 dm	=	10^{12}	10^{11}	10^{9}	10^{8}	10^{5}	10^{2}	10	1	10^{-1}	10^{-4}
1 m	=	—	10^{12}	10^{10}	10^{9}	10^{6}	10^{3}	10^{2}	10	1	10^{-3}
1 km	=	—	—	—	10^{12}	10^{9}	10^{6}	10^{5}	10^{4}	10^{3}	1

Do not use XU (X-unit) and Å (ångström)

Unit		in	ft	yd	mile	n mile	mm	m	km
1 in	=	1	0.08333	0.02778	–	–	25.4	0.0254	–
1 ft	=	12	1	0.33333	–	–	304.8	0.3048	–
1 yd	=	36	3	1	–	–	914.4	0.9144	–
1 mile	=	63 360	5280	1760	1	0.86898	–	1609.34	1.609
1 n mile[1])	=	72 913	6076.1	2025.4	1.1508	1	–	1852	1.852
1 mm	=	0.03937	$3.281 \cdot 10^{-3}$	$1.094 \cdot 10^{-3}$	–	–	1	0.001	10^{-6}
1 m	=	39.3701	3.2808	1.0936	–	–	1000	1	0.001
1 km	=	39 370	3280.8	1093.6	0.62137	0.53996	10^{6}	1000	1

in = inch, ft = foot, y = yard, mile = statute mile, n mile = nautical mile

Other British and American units of length
1 µin (microinch) = 0.0254 µm,
1 mil (milliinch) = 0.0254 mm,
1 link = 201.17 mm,
1 rod = 1 pole = 1 perch = 5.5 yd = 5.0292 m,
1 chain = 22 yd = 20.1168 m,
1 furlong = 220 yd = 201.168 m,
1 fathom = 2 yd = 1.8288 m.

Astronomical units
1 l.y. (light year)
= $9.46053 \cdot 10^{15}$ m (distance traveled by electromagnetic waves in 1 year),
1 AU (astronomical unit)
= $1.496 \cdot 10^{11}$ m (mean distance from earth to sun),

1 pc (parsec, parallax second)
= 206 265 AU = $3.0857 \cdot 10^{16}$ m
(distance at which the AU subtends an angle of one second of arc).

Do not use
1 line (watch & clock making)
= 2.256 mm,
1 p (typographical point) = 0.376 mm,
1 German mile = 7500 m,
1 geographical mile = 7420.4 m
(≈ 4 arc minutes of equator).

---

[1]) 1 n mile = 1 nm = 1 international nautical mile
≈ 1 arc minute of the degree of longitude.
1 knot = 1 n mile/h = 1.852 km/h.

Units of area

Unit		in²	ft²	yd²	acre	mile²	cm²	m²	a	ha	km²
1 in²	=	1	–	–	–	–	6.4516	–	–	–	–
1 ft²	=	144	1	0.1111	–	–	929	0.0929	–	–	–
1 yd²	=	1296	9	1	–	–	8361	0.8361	–	–	–
1 acre	=	–	–	4840	1	0.16	–	4047	40.47	0.40	–
1 mile²	=	–	–	–	6.40	1	–	–	–	259	2.59
1 cm²	=	0.155	–	–	–	–	1	0.01	–	–	–
1 m²	=	1550	10.76	1.196	–	–	10000	1	0.01	–	–
1 a	=	–	1076	119.6	–	–	–	100	1	0.01	–
1 ha	=	–	–	–	2.47	–	–	10000	100	1	0.01
1 km²	=	–	–	–	247	0.3861	–	–	10000	100	1

in² = square inch (sq in),
ft² = square foot (sq ft),
yd² = square yard (sq yd),
mile² = square mile (sq mile).

Paper sizes
(DIN 476)

Dimensions in mm

A 0	841 x 1189	**A 6**	105 x 148
A 1	594 x 841	**A 7**	74 x 105
A 2	420 x 594	**A 8**	52 x 74
A 3	297 x 420	**A 9**	37 x 52
A 4	210 x 297[1])	**A 10**	26 x 37
A 5	148 x 210		

Units of volume

Unit		in³	ft³	yd³	gal (UK)	gal (US)	cm³	dm³(l)	m³
1 in³	=	1	–	–	–	–	16.3871	0.01639	–
1 ft³	=	1728	1	0.03704	6.229	7.481	–	28.3168	0.02832
1 yd³	=	46656	27	1	168.18	201.97	–	764.555	0.76456
1 gal (UK)=		277.42	0.16054	–	1	1.20095	4546.09	4.54609	–
1 gal (US)=		231	0.13368	–	0.83267	1	3785.41	3.78541	–
1 cm³	=	0.06102	–	–	–	–	1	0.001	–
1 dm³ (l) =		61.0236	0.03531	0.00131	0.21997	0.26417	1000	1	0.001
1 m³	=	61023.6	35.315	1.30795	219.969	264.172	10⁶	1000	1

in³ = cubic inch (cu in),
ft³ = cubic foot (cu ft),
yd³ = cubic yard (cu yd),
gal = gallon.

Other units of volume

Great Britain (UK)
1 fl oz (fluid ounce) = 0.028413 l
1 pt (pint) = 0.56826 l,
1 qt (quart) = 2 pt = 1.13652 l,
1 gal (gallon) = 4 qt = 4.5461 l,
1 bbl (barrel) = 36 gal = 163.6 l,

Units of dry measure:
1 bu (bushel) = 8 gal = 36.369 l.

---

[1]) Customary format in USA: 216 mm x 279 mm

United States (US)
1 fl oz (fluid ounce) = 0.029574 l
1 liq pt (liquid pint) = 0.47318 l
1 liq quart = 2 liq pt = 0.94635 l
1 gal (gallon) = 231 in^3 = 4 liq quarts = 3.7854 l
1 liq bbl (liquid barrel) = 119.24 l
1 barrel petroleum[1]) = 42 gal = 158.99 l

Units of dry measure:
1 bushel = 35.239 dm^3

Volume of ships
1 RT (register ton) = 100 ft^3 = 2.832 m^3;
GRT (gross RT) = total shipping space, net register ton = cargo space of a ship.
GTI (gross tonnage index) = total volume of ship (shell) in m^3.
1 ocean ton = 40 ft^3 = 1.1327 m^3.

Units of angle

Unit[2])	°	′	″	rad	gon	cgon	mgon
1° =	1	60	3600	0.017453	1.1111	111.11	1111.11
1′ =	0.016667	1	60	–	0.018518	1.85185	18,5185
1″ =	0.0002778	0.016667	1	–	0.0003086	0.030864	0.30864
1 rad[2]) =	57.2958	3437.75	206265	1	63.662	6366.2	63662
1 gon =	0.9	54	3240	0.015708	1	100	1000
1 cgon =	0.009	0.54	32.4	–	0.01	1	10
1 mgon =	0.0009	0.054	3.24	–	0.001	0.1	1

Velocities

1 km/h = 0.27778 m/s,
1 mile/h = 1.60934 km/h,
1 kn (knot) = 1.852 km/h,
1 ft/min = 0.3048 m/min

1 m/s = 3.6 km/h,
1 km/h = 0.62137 mile/h,
1 km/h = 0.53996 kn,
1 m/min = 3.28084 ft/min,

x km/h $\triangleq \dfrac{60}{x}$ min/km $\triangleq \dfrac{3600}{x}$ s/km, $\qquad$ x mile/h $\triangleq \dfrac{37.2824}{x}$ min/km $\triangleq \dfrac{2236.9}{x}$ s/km.

x s/km $\triangleq \dfrac{3600}{x}$ km/h.

The **Mach number** Ma specifies how much faster a body travels than sound (approx. 333 m/s in air). $Ma = 1.3$ therefore denotes 1.3 times the speed of sound.

Fuel consumption

1 g/PS · h = 1.3596 g/kW · h,
1 lb/hp · h = 608.277 g/kW · h,
1 liq pt/hp · h = 634.545 cm^3/kW · h,
1 pt (UK)/hp · h = 762.049 cm^3/kW · h,

1 g/kW · h = 0.7355 g/PS · h,
1 g/kW · h = 0.001644 lb/hp · h,
1 cm^3/kW · h = 0.001576 liq pt/hp · h,
1 cm^3/kW · h = 0.001312 pt (UK)/hp · h,

x mile/gal (US) $\triangleq \dfrac{235.21}{x}$ l/100 km, $\qquad$ x l/100 km $\triangleq \dfrac{235.21}{x}$ mile/gal (US),

x mile/gal (UK) $\triangleq \dfrac{282.48}{x}$ l/100 km. $\qquad$ x l/100 km $\triangleq \dfrac{282.48}{x}$ mile/gal (UK).

---

[1]) For crude oil.
[2]) It is better to indicate angles by using only one of the units given above, i. e. not $\alpha = 33° 17′ 27.6″$ but rather $\alpha = 33.291°$ or $\alpha = 1997.46′$ or $\alpha = 119847.6″$.

Units of mass
(colloquially also called "units of weight")

Avoirdupois system (commercial weights in general use in UK and US)

Unit	gr	dram	oz	lb	cwt (UK)	cwt (US)	ton (UK)	ton (US)	g	kg	t
1 gr =	1	0.03657	0.00229	1/7000	–	–	–	–	0.064799	–	–
1 dram =	27.344	1	0.0625	0.00391	–	–	–	–	1.77184	–	–
1 oz =	437.5	16	1	0.0625	–	–	–	–	28.3495	–	–
1 lb =	7000	256	16	1	0.00893	0.01	–	0.0005	453.592	0.45359	–
1 cwt (UK)[1] =				112	1	1.12	0.05	0.05	–	50.8023	–
1 cwt (US)[2] =				100	0.8929	1	0.04464	0.05	–	45.3592	–
1 ton (UK)[3] =				2240	20	22.4	1	1.12	–	1016.05	1.01605
1 ton (US)[4] =				2000	17.857	20	0.8929	1	–	907.185	0.90718
1 g =	15.432	0.5644	0.03527	–	–	–	–	–	1	0.001	–
1 kg =	–	–	35.274	2.2046	0.01968	0.02205	–	–	1000	1	0.001
1 t =	–	–	–	2204.6	19.684	22.046	0.9842	1.1023	10^6	1000	1

Troy system (used in UK and US for precious stones and metals) and Apothecaries' system (used in UK and US for drugs)

Unit	gr	s ap	dwt	dr ap	oz t = oz ap	lb t = lb ap	Kt	g
1 gr =	1	0.05	0.04167	0.01667	–	–	0.324	0.064799
1 s ap =	20	1	0.8333	0.3333	–	–	–	1.296
1 dwt =	24	1.2	1	0.4	0.05	–	–	1.5552
1 dr ap =	60	3	2.5	1	0.125	–	–	3.8879
1 oz t = 1 oz ap =	480	24	20	8	1	0.08333	–	31.1035
1 lb t = 1 lb ap =	5760	288	240	96	12	1	–	373.24
1 Kt =	3.086	–	–	–	–	–	1	0.2000
1 g =	15.432	0.7716	0.643	0.2572	0.03215	0.002679	5	1

UK = United Kingdom, US = USA.

gr = grain, oz = ounce, lb = pound, cwt = hundredweight.
1 slug = 14.5939 kg = mass, accelerated at 1 ft/s² by a force of 1 lbf.

1 st (stone) = 14 lb = 6.35 kg (UK only),
1 qr (quarter) = 28 lb = 12.7006 kg (UK only, seldom used),
1 quintal = 100 lb = 1 cwt (US) = 45.3592 kg,
1 tdw (ton dead weight) = 1 ton (UK) = 1.016 t.
The tonnage of dry cargo ships (cargo + ballast + fuel + supplies) is given in tdw.

s ap = apothecaries' scruple,
dwt = pennyweight,
dr ap = apothecaries' drachm (US: apothecaries' dram),
oz t (UK: oz tr) = troy ounce,
oz ap (UK: oz apoth) = apothecaries' ounce,
lb t = troy pound,
lb ap = apothecaries' pound,
Kt = metric karat, used only for precious stones[5].

1) Also "long cwt (cwt l)".
2) Also "short cwt (cwt sh)".
3) Also "long ton (tn l)".
4) Also "short ton (tn sh)".
5) The term "karat" was formerly used with a different meaning in connection with gold alloys to denote the gold content: pure gold (fine gold) = 24 karat; 14-karat gold has 14/24 = 585/1000 parts by weight of fine gold.

Mass per unit length

SI unit kg/m
1 lb/ft = 1.48816 kg/m, 1 lb/yd = 0.49605 kg/m
Units in textile industry (DIN 60905 and 60910):
1 tex = 1 g/km, 1 mtex = 1 mg/km,
1 dtex = 1 dg/km, 1 ktex = 1 kg/km
Former unit (do not use):
1 den (denier) = 1 g/9 km = 0.1111 tex, 1 tex = 9 den

Density

SI unit kg/m³
1 kg/dm³ = 1 kg/l = 1 g/cm³ = 1000 kg/m³
1 lb/ft³ = 16.018 kg/m³ = 0.016018 kg/l
1 lb/gal (UK) = 0.099776 kg/l, 1 lb/gal (US) = **0.11983** kg/l

°Bé (degrees Baumé) is a measure of the density of liquids which are heavier (+°Bé) or lighter (−°Bé) than water (at 15°C). Do not use the unit °Bé.

$\varrho = 144.3/(144.3 \pm n)$
ϱ Density in kg/l, n hydrometer degrees in °Bé.
°API (American Petroleum Institute) is used in the USA to indicate the density of fuels and oils.
$\varrho = 141.5/(131.5 + n)$
ϱ Density in kg/l, n hydrometer degrees in °API.

Examples:

−12 °Bé = 144.3/(144.3 + 12) kg/l = 0.923 kg/l
+34 °Bé = 144.3/(144.3 − 34) kg/l = 1.308 kg/l
28 °API = 141.5/(131.5 + 28) kg/l = 0.887 kg/l

Units of force

Unit		N	kp	lbf
1 N (newton)	=	1	0.101972	0.224809
Do not use				
1 kp (kilopond)	=	9.80665	1	2.204615
1 lbf (pound-force)	=	4.44822	0.453594	1

1 pdl (poundal) = 0.138255 N = force which accelerates a mass of 1 lb by 1 ft/s^2.
1 sn (sthène)* = 10^3 N

Units of pressure and stress

Unit[1]	Pa	μbar	hPa	bar	N/mm^2	kp/mm^2	at	kp/m^2	torr	atm	lbf/in^2	lbf/ft^2	tonf/in^2
1 Pa = 1 N/m^2	1	10	0.01	10^{-5}	10^{-6}	–	–	0.10197	0.0075	–	–	–	–
1 μbar	0.1	1	0.001	10^{-6}	10^{-7}	–	–	0.0102	–	–	–	–	–
1 hPa = 1 mbar	100	1000	1	0.001	0.0001	–	–	10.197	0.7501	–	0.0145	2.0886	–
1 bar	10^5	10^6	1000	1	0.1	–	1.0197	10197	750.06	0.9869	14.5037	2088.6	–
1 N/mm^2	10^6	10^7	10000	10	1	0.10197	10.197	101972	7501	9.8692	145.037	20886	0.06475
Do not use													
1 kp/mm^2	–	–	98066.5	98.0665	9.80665	1	100	10^6	73556	96.784	1422.33	–	0.63497
1 at = 1 kp/cm^2	98066.5	98066.5	980.665	0.98066	0.0981	0.01	1	10000	735.56	0.96784	14.2233	2048.16	–
1 kp/m^2 = 1 mmw.g.	9.80665	98.0665	0.0981	–	–	10^{-6}	10^{-4}	1	–	–	–	0.2048	–
1 torr = 1 mmHg	133.322	1333.22	1.33322	–	–	–	0.00136	13.5951	1	0.00132	0.01934	2.7845	–
1 atm	101325	–	1013.25	1.01325	–	–	1.03323	10332.3	760	1	14.695	2116.1	–
British and American units													
1 lbf/in^2	6894.76	68948	68.948	0.0689	0.00689	–	0.07031	703.07	51.715	0.06805	1	144	–
1 lbf/ft^2	47.8803	478.8	0.4788	–	–	–	–	4.8824	0.35913	–	–	1	–
1 tonf/in^2	–	–	–	154.443	15.4443	1.57488	157.488	–	–	152.42	2240	–	1

lbf/in^2 = pound-force per square inch (psi), lbf/ft^2 = pound-force per square foot (psf), tonf/in^2 = ton-force (UK) per square inch
1 pdl/ft^2 (poundal per square foot) = 1.48816 Pa
1 barye* = 1μbar; 1 pz (pièce)* = 1 sn/m^2 (sthène/m^2)* = 10^3 Pa
Standards: DIN 66 034 Conversion tables, kilopond – newton, newton – kilopond, DIN 66 037 Conversion tables, kilopond/cm^2 – bar, bar – kilopond/cm^2, DIN 66 038 Conversion tables, torr – millibar, millibar – torr

[1] See PP. 15 and 16 for names of units * French units.

Units of energy
(units of work)

Unit[1])	J	kW · h	kp · m	PS · h	kcal	ft · lbf	Btu
1 J =	1	$277.8 \cdot 10^{-9}$	0.10197	$377.67 \cdot 10^{-9}$	$238.85 \cdot 10^{-6}$	0.73756	$947.8 \cdot 10^{-6}$
1 kW · h =	$3.6 \cdot 10^{6}$	1	367098	1.35962	859.85	$2.6552 \cdot 10^{6}$	3412.13
Do not use							
1 kp · m =	9.80665	$2.7243 \cdot 10^{-6}$	1	$3.704 \cdot 10^{-6}$	$2.342 \cdot 10^{-3}$	7.2330	$9.295 \cdot 10^{-3}$
1 PS · h =	$2.6478 \cdot 10^{6}$	0.735499	270000	1	632.369	$1.9529 \cdot 10^{6}$	2509.6
1 kcal[2]) =	4186.8	$1.163 \cdot 10^{-3}$	426.935	$1.581 \cdot 10^{-3}$	1	3088	3.9683
British and American units							
1 ft · lbf =	1.35582	$376.6 \cdot 10^{-9}$	0.13826	$512.1 \cdot 10^{-9}$	$323.8 \cdot 10^{-6}$	1	$1.285 \cdot 10^{-3}$
1 Btu[3]) =	1055.06	$293.1 \cdot 10^{-6}$	107.59	$398.5 \cdot 10^{-6}$	0.2520	778.17	1

ft lbf = foot pound-force, Btu = British thermal unit,
1 in ozf (inch ounce-force) = 0.007062 J, 1 in lbf (inch pound-force) = 0.112985 J,
1 ft pdl (foot poundal) = 0.04214 J,
1 hph (horsepower-hour) = $2.685 \cdot 10^{6}$ J = 0.7457 kW · h,
1 thermie (France) = 1000 frigories (France) = 1000 kcal = 4.1868 MJ,
1 kg C.E. (coal equivalent kilogram)[4]) = 29.3076 MJ = 8.141 kWh,
1 t C.E. (coal equivalent ton)[4]) = 1000 kg C.E. = 29.3076 GJ = 8.141 MWh.

Units of power

Unit[1])	W	kW	kp m/s	PS*	kcal/s	hp	Btu/s
1 W =	1	0.001	0.10197	$1.3596 \cdot 10^{-3}$	$238.8 \cdot 10^{-6}$	$1.341 \cdot 10^{-3}$	$947.8 \cdot 10^{-6}$
1 kW =	1000	1	101.97	1.35962	$238.8 \cdot 10^{-3}$	1.34102	$947.8 \cdot 10^{-3}$
Do not use							
1 kp · m/s =	9.80665	$9.807 \cdot 10^{-3}$	1	$13.33 \cdot 10^{-3}$	$2.342 \cdot 10^{-3}$	$13.15 \cdot 10^{-3}$	$9.295 \cdot 10^{-3}$
1 PS =	735.499	0.735499	75	1	0.17567	0.98632	0.69712
1 kcal/s =	4186.8	4.1868	426.935	5.6925	1	5.6146	3.9683
British and American units							
1 hp =	745.70	0.74570	76.0402	1.0139	0.17811	1	0.70678
1 Btu/s =	1055.06	1.05506	107.586	1.4345	0.2520	1.4149	1

hp = horsepower,
1 ft · lbf/s = 1.35582 W,
1 ch (cheval vapeur) (France) = 1 PS = 0.7355 kW,
1 poncelet (France) = 100 kp · m/s = 0.981 kW,
Continuous human power generation ≈ 0.1 kW.

Standards: DIN 66 035 Conversion tables, calorie – joule, joule – calorie,
DIN 66 036 Conversion tables, metric horsepower – kilowatt,
kilowatt – metric horsepower,
DIN 66 039 Conversion tables, kilocalorie – watt-hour,
watt-hour – kilocalorie.

---

[1]) Names of units, see P. 16.
[2]) 1 kcal ≈ quantity of heat required to increase temperature of 1 kg water at 15 °C by 1 °C.
[3]) 1 Btu ≈ quantity of heat required to raise temperature of 1 lb water by 1 °F. 1 therm = 10^{5} Btu.
[4]) The units of energy kg C.E. and t C.E. were based on a specific calorific value H_u of 7000 kcal/kg of coal.
* Metric horsepower

Units of temperature

°C = degree Celsius, K = Kelvin,
°F = degree Fahrenheit, °R = degree
Rankine.

Temperature points

$$T_K = (273.15\,°C + t_C)\,\frac{K}{°C} = \frac{5}{9}\,T_R$$

$$T_R = (459.67\,°F + t_F)\,\frac{°R}{°F} = 1.8\,T_K$$

$$t_C = \frac{5}{9}\,(t_F - 32°F)\,\frac{°C}{°F} = (T_K - 273.15\,K)\,\frac{°C}{K}$$

$$t_F = (1.8\,t_C + 32°C)\,\frac{°F}{°C} = (T_R - 459.67\,°R)\,\frac{°F}{°R}$$

t_C, t_F, T_K and T_R denote the temperature
points in °C, °F, K and °R.

Temperature difference
1 K = 1 °C = 1.8 °F = 1.8 °R

Zero points: 0 °C ≙ 32 °F, 0 °F ≙ −17.78 °C.
Absolute zero:
0K ≙ −273.15 °C ≙ 0 °R ≙ −459.67 °F.

**International practical temperature
scale:** Boiling point of oxygen −182.97 °C,
triple point of water 0.01 °C[1], boiling point
of water 100 °C, boiling point of sulfur (sulfur point) 444.6 °C, setting point of silver
(silver point) 960.8 °C, setting point of
gold 1063 °C.

---

[1] That temperature of pure water at which ice,
water and water vapor occur together in equilibrium (at 1013.25 hPa). See also Footnote [2] on
P. 12.

Units of viscosity

Legal units of kinematic viscosity v
$1\ m^2/s = 1\ Pa \cdot s/(kg/m^3) = 10^4\ cm^2/s$
$= 10^6\ mm^2/s$.

British and American units:
$1\ ft^2/s = 0.092903\ m^2/s$,
RI seconds = efflux time from Redwood-I viscometer (UK),
SU seconds = efflux time from Saybolt-Universal viscometer (US).

Do not use:
St (stokes) = cm^2/s, cSt = mm^2/s.

Conventional units
E (Engler degree) = relative efflux time from Engler apparatus DIN 51560.
For $v > 60\ mm^2/s$, $1\ mm^2/s = 0.132\ E$.

At values below 3 E, Engler degrees do not give a true indication of the variation of viscosity; for example, a fluid with 2 E does not have twice the kinematic viscosity of a fluid with 1 E, but rather 12 times that value.

A seconds = efflux time from flow cup DIN 53 211.

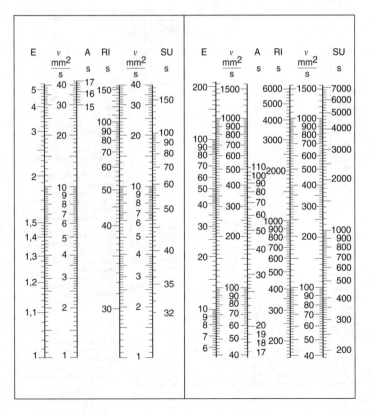

Units of time

Unit[1]		s	min	h	d
1 s[2] (second)	=	1	0.01667	0.2778 x 10⁻³	11.574 x 10⁻⁶
1 min (minute)	=	60	1	0.01667	0.6944 x 10⁻³
1 h (hour)	=	3600	60	1	0.041667
1 d (day)	=	86 400	1440	24	1

1 civil year = 365 (or 366) days = 8760 (8784) hours (for calculation of interest in banking, 1 year = 360 days),
1 solar year[3] = 365.2422 mean solar days = 365 d 5 h 48 min 46 s,
1 sidereal year[4] = 365.2564 mean solar days.

Clock times
The clock times listed for the following time zones are based on 12.00 CET (Central European Time)[5]:

Clock time	Time-zone meridian	Countries (examples)	Clock time	Time-zone meridian	Countries (examples)
	West longitude			East longitude	
1.00	150°	Alaska.	12.00	15°	**Central European Time (CET):** Austria, Belgium, Denmark, France, Germany, Hungary, Italy, Luxembourg, Netherlands, Norway, Poland, Sweden, Switzerland, Spain; Algeria, Israel, Libya, Nigeria, Tunisia, Zaire.
3.00	120°	West coast of Canada and USA.			
4.00	105°	Western central zone of Canada and USA.			
5.00	90°	Central zone of Canada and USA, Mexico, Central America.			
6.00	75°	Canada between 68° and 90°, Eastern USA, Ecuador, Colombia, Panama, Peru.	13.00	30°	**Eastern European Time (EET):** Bulgaria, Finland, Greece, Romania; Egypt, Lebanon, Jordan, Sudan, South Africa, Syria.
7.00	60°	Canada east of 68°, Bolivia, Chile, Venezuela.			
8.00	45°	Argentina, Brazil, Greenland, Paraguay, Uruguay.	14.00	45°	Western Russia, Turkey, Iraq, Saudi Arabia, Eastern Africa.
			14.30	52.5°	Iran.
11.00	0°	**Greenwich Mean Time (GMT)[6]:** Canary Islands, Great Britain, Ireland, Portugal, West Africa.	16.30	82.5°	India, Sri Lanka.
			18.00	105°	Cambodia, Indonesia, Laos, Thailand, Vietnam.
			19.00	120°	Chinese coast, Philippines, Western Australia.
			20.00	135°	Japan, Korea.
			20.30	142.5°	North and South Australia.
			21.00	150°	Eastern Australia.

---

[1] See also P. 15.
[2] Base SI unit, see P. 12 for definition.
[3] Time between two successive passages of the earth through the vernal equinox.
[4] True time of revolution of the earth about the sun.
[5] During the summer months in countries in which daylight saving time is observed, clocks are set ahead by 1 hour (from approximately April to September north of the equator and October to March south of the equator).
[6] = UT (Universal Time), mean solar time at the 0° meridian of Greenwich, or UTC (Coordinated Universal Time), defined by the invariable second of the International System of Units (P. 12). Because the period of rotation of the earth about the sun is gradually becoming longer, UTC is adjusted to UT from time to time by the addition of a leap second.

Vibration and oscillation

Symbols and units

Quantity		Unit
a	Storage coefficient	
b	Damping coefficient	
c	Storage coefficient	
c	Spring constant	N/m
c_α	Torsional rigidity	N · m/rad
C	Capacity	F
f	Frequency	Hz
f_g	Resonant frequency	Hz
Δf	Half-value width	Hz
F	Force	N
F_Q	Excitation function	
I	Current	A
J	Moment of inertia	kg · m²
L	Self-inductance	H
m	Mass	kg
M	Torque	N · m
n	Rotational speed	1/min
Q	Charge	C
Q	Resonance sharpness	
r	Damping factor	N · s/m
r_α	Rotational damping coefficient	N · s · m
R	Ohmic resistance	Ω
t	Time	s
T	Period	s
U	Voltage	V
v	Particle velocity	m/s
x	Travel/displacement	
y	Instantaneous value	
$\hat{y}$	Amplitude	
$\dot{y}$ ($\ddot{y}$)	Single (double) derivative with respect to time	
y_{rec}	Rectified value	
y_{eff}	Effective value	
α	Angle	rad
δ	Decay coefficient	1/s
Λ	Logarithmic decrement	
ω	Angular velocity	rad/s
ω	Angular frequency	1/s
Ω	Exciter-circuit frequency	1/s
ϑ	Damping ratio	
ϑ_{opt}	Optimum damping ratio	

Subscripts:

0	Undamped
d	Damped
T	Absorber
U	Base support
G	Machine

Terms
(see also DIN 1311)

Vibrations and oscillations
Vibrations and oscillations are the terms used to denote changes in a physical quantity which repeat at more or less regular time intervals and whose direction changes with similar regularity.

Period
The period is the time taken for one complete cycle of a single oscillation (period).

Amplitude
Amplitude is the maximum instantaneous value (peak value) of a sinusoidally oscillating physical quantity.

Frequency
Frequency is the number of oscillations in one second, the reciprocal value of the period of oscillation T.

Angular frequency
Angular frequency is 2π-times the frequency.

Particle velocity
Particle velocity is the instantaneous value of the alternating velocity of a vibrating particle in its direction of vibration. It must not be confused with the velocity of propagation of a traveling wave (e.g. the velocity of sound).

Fourier series
Every periodic function, which is piecewise monotonic and smooth, can be expressed as the sum of sinusoidal harmonic components.

Beats
Beats occur when two sinusoidal oscillations, whose frequencies do not differ greatly, are superposed. They are periodic. Their basic frequency is the difference between the frequencies of the superposed sinusoidal oscillations.

Natural oscillations
The frequency of natural oscillations (natural frequency) is dependent only on the properties of the oscillating system.

Damping
Damping is a measure of the energy losses in an oscillatory system when one form of energy is converted into another.

Logarithmic decrement
Natural logarithm of the relationship between two extreme values of a natural oscillation which are separated by one period.

Damping ratio
Measure for the degree of damping.

Forced oscillations
Forced oscillations arise under the influence of an external physical force (excitation), which does not change the properties of the oscillator. The frequency of forced oscillations is determined by the frequency of the excitation.

Transfer function
The transfer function is the quotient of amplitude of the observed variable divided by the amplitude of excitation, plotted against the exciter frequency.

Resonance
Resonance occurs when the transfer function produces very large values as the exciter frequency approaches the natural frequency.

Resonant frequency
Resonant frequency is the exciter frequency at which the oscillator variable attains its maximum value.

Half-value width
The half-value width is the difference between the frequencies at which the level of the variable has dropped to $1/\sqrt{2} \approx 0.707$ of the maximum value.

Resonance sharpness
Resonance sharpness, or the quality factor (Q-factor), is the maximum value of the transfer function.

Coupling
If two oscillatory systems are coupled together – mechanically by mass or elasticity, electrically by inductance or capacitance – a periodic exchange of energy takes place between the systems.

Wave
Spatial and temporal change of state of a continuum, which can be expressed as a unidirectional transfer of location of a certain state over a period of time. There are transversal waves (e.g. waves in rope and water) and longitudinal waves (e.g. sound waves in air).

Interference
The principle of undisturbed superposition of waves. At every point in space the instantaneous value of the resulting wave is equal to the sum of the instantaneous values of the individual waves.

Standing waves
Standing waves occur as a result of interference between two waves of equal frequency, wavelength and amplitude traveling in opposite directions. In contrast to a propagating wave, the amplitude of the standing wave is constant at every point; nodes (zero amplitude) and antinodes (maximum amplitude) occur. Standing waves occur by reflection of a wave back on itself if the characteristic impedance of the medium differs greatly from the impedance of the reflector.

Rectification value
Arithmetic mean value, linear in time, of the values of a periodic signal.

$$y_{rec} = (1/T) \int_0^T |\, y \,|\, dt$$

For a sine curve:
$y_{rec} = 2\hat{y}/\pi \approx 0.637\,\hat{y}.$

Effective value
Quadratic mean value in time of a periodic signal.

$$y_{eff} = \sqrt{(1/T) \int_0^T y^2\, dt}$$

For a sine curve:
$y_{eff} = \hat{y}/\sqrt{2} \approx 0.707\,\hat{y}.$

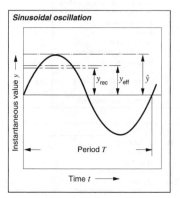

Sinusoidal oscillation

Instantaneous value y — ; y_{rec}; y_{eff}; $\hat{y}$

Period T

Time t —

Form factor = y_{eff}/y_{rec}
For a sine curve:
$y_{eff}/y_{rec} \approx 1.111$.

Peak factor = $\hat{y}/y_{eff}$
For a sine curve:
$\hat{y}/y_{eff} = \sqrt{2} \approx 1.414$.

Equations
The equations apply for the following simple oscillators if the general quantity designations in the formulas are replaced by the relevant physical quantities.

Simple oscillatory systems

	Mechanical		Electrical
	Translational	Rotational	
	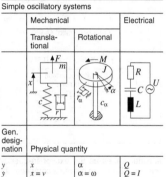		

Gen. designation	Physical quantity		
y	x	α	Q
$\dot{y}$	$\dot{x} = v$	$\dot{\alpha} = \omega$	$\dot{Q} = I$
$\ddot{y}$	$\ddot{x} = v$	$\ddot{\alpha} = \dot{\omega}$	$\ddot{Q} = \dot{I}$
F_Q	F	M	U
a	m	J	L
b	r	r_α	R
c	c	c_α	$1/C$

Free oscillation and damping

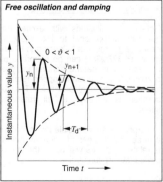

Differential equations
$a\ddot{y} + b\dot{y} + cy = F_Q(t) = \hat{F}_Q \sin \Omega t$
Period $T = 1/f$

Angular frequency $\omega = 2\pi f$

Sinusoidal oscillation
(e. g. vibration displacement) $y = \hat{y} \sin \omega t$

Free oscillations $(F_Q = 0)$
Logarithmic decrement
$\Lambda = \ln(y_n/y_{n+1}) = \pi b/\sqrt{ca - b^2/4}$

Decay coefficient $\delta = b/(2a)$

Damping ratio $\vartheta = \delta/\omega_0 = b/(2\sqrt{ca})$

$\vartheta = \Lambda/\sqrt{\Lambda^2 + 4\pi^2} \approx \Lambda/(2\pi)$
(low level of damping)

Angular frequency of undamped oscillation $(\vartheta = 0)$ $\omega_0 = \sqrt{c/a}$

Angular frequency of damped oscillation $(0 < \vartheta < 1)$ $\omega_d = \omega_0 \sqrt{1 - \vartheta^2}$
For $\vartheta \geq 1$ no oscillations but creepage.

Forced oscillations
Quantity of transfer function

$\hat{y}/\hat{F}_Q = 1/\sqrt{(c - a\Omega^2)^2 + (b\Omega)^2}$
$= (1/c)/\sqrt{(1 - (\Omega/\omega_0)^2)^2 + (2\vartheta\Omega/\omega_0)^2}$
Resonant frequency $f_g = f_0\sqrt{1 - 2\vartheta^2} < f_0$

Resonance sharpness $Q = 1/(2\vartheta\sqrt{1 - \vartheta^2})$

Oscillator with low level of damping $(\vartheta \leq 0.1)$:

Resonant frequency $f_g \approx f_0$

Resonance sharpness $Q \approx 1/(2\vartheta)$

Half-value width $\Delta f = 2\vartheta f_0 = f_0/Q$

Vibration reduction

Vibration damping
If damping can only be carried out between the machine and a quiescent point, the damping must be at a high level (cf. "Standardized transmission function" diagram).

Vibration isolation

Active vibration isolation
Machines are to be mounted so that the

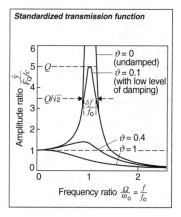

Standardized transmission function

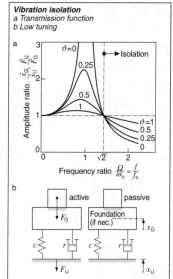

Vibration isolation
a Transmission function
b Low tuning

forces transmitted to the base support are small. One measure to be taken: The bearing point should be set below resonance, so that the natural frequency lies below the lowest exciter frequency. Damping impedes isolation. Low values can result in excessively high vibrations during running-up when the resonant range is passed through.

Passive vibration isolation
Machines are to be mounted so that vibration and shaking reaching the base support are only transmitted to the machines to a minor degree. Measures to be taken: as for active isolation.

In many cases flexible suspension or extreme damping is not practicable. So that no resonance can arise, the machine attachment should be so rigid that the natural frequency is far enough in excess of the highest exciter frequency which can occur.

Vibration absorption

Absorber with fixed natural frequency
By tuning the natural frequency ω_T of an absorption mass with a flexible, loss-free coupling to the excitation frequency, the vibrations of the machine are completely absorbed. Only the absorption mass still vibrates. The effectiveness of the absorp-

tion decreases as the exciter frequency changes. Damping prevents complete absorption. However, appropriate tuning of the absorber frequency and an optimum damping ratio produce broadband vibration reduction, which remains effective when the exciter frequency changes.

Absorber with changeable natural frequency
Rotational oscillations with exciter frequencies proportional to the rotational speed (e.g. orders of balancing in IC engines, P. 397/398) can be absorbed by absorbers with natural frequencies proportional to the rotational speed (pendulum in the centrifugal force field). The absorption is effective at all rotational speeds.

Absorption is also possible for oscillators with several degrees of freedom and interrelationships, as well as by the use of several absorption bodies.

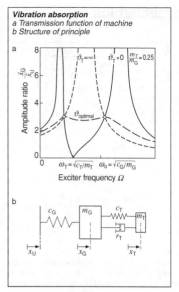

Vibration absorption
a Transmission function of machine
b Structure of principle

The modal model not only describes the actual state but also forms the basis for simulation calculations: In response calculation, the response of the structure to a defined excitation, corresponding, for instance, to test laboratory conditions, is calculated. By means of structure modifications (changes in mass, damping or stiffness) the vibrational behavior can be optimized to the level required by operating conditions. The substructure coupling process collates modal models of various structures, for example, into one overall model. The modal model can be constructed analytically. When the modal models produced by both processes are compared with each other, the modal model resulting from an analytical modal analysis is more accurate than that from an experimental modal analysis as a result of the greater number of degrees of freedom in the analytical process. This applies in particular to simulation calculations based on the model.

Modal analysis

The dynamic behavior (oscillatory characteristics) of a mechanical structure can be predicted with the aid of a mathematical model. The model parameters of the modal model are determined by means of modal analysis. A time-invariant and linear-elastic structure is an essential precondition. The oscillations are only observed at a limited number of points in the possible oscillation directions (degrees of freedom) and at defined frequency intervals. The continuous structure is then replaced in a clearly-defined manner by a finite number of single-mass oscillators. Each single-mass oscillator is comprehensively and clearly defined by a characteristic vector and a characteristic value. The characteristic vector (mode form, natural oscillation form) describes the relative amplitudes and phases of all degrees of freedom, the characteristic value describes the behavior in terms of time (damped harmonic oscillation). Every oscillation of the structure can be artificially recreated from the characteristic vectors and values.

Analytical modal analysis
The geometry, material data and marginal conditions must be known. Multibody-system or finite-element models provide characteristic values and vectors. Analytical modal analysis requires no specimen sample, and can therefore be used at an early stage of development. However, it is often the case that precise knowledge concerning the structure's fundamental properties (damping, marginal conditions) are lacking, which means that the modal model can be very inaccurate. As well as this, the error is unidentified. A remedy can be to adjust the model to the results of an experimental modal analysis.

Experimental modal analysis
Knowledge of the structure is not necessary, but a specimen is required. Analysis is based on measurements of the transmission functions in the frequency range in question from one excitation point to a number of response points, and vice versa. The modal model is derived from the matrix of the transmission functions (which defines the response model).

Basic equations used in mechanics

See PP. 14 ... 18 for names of units

Symbol	Quantity	SI unit
A	Area	m²
a	Acceleration	m/s²
a_{cf}	Centrifugal acceleration	m/s²
d	Diameter	m
E	Energy	J
E_k	Kinetic energy	J
E_p	Potential energy	J
F	Force	N
F_{cf}	Centrifugal force	N
G	Weight	N
g	Acceleration of free fall (g = 9.81 m/s², see P. 13)	m/s²
h	Height	m
i	Radius of gyration	m
J	Moment of inertia (second-order moment of mass)	kg · m²
L	Angular momentum	N · s · m
l	Length	m
M	Torque	N · m

Symbol	Quantity	SI unit
m	Mass (weight)	kg
n	Rotational frequency	s⁻¹
P	Power	W
p	Linear momentum	N · s
r	Radius	m
s	Length of path	m
T	Period, time of one revolution	s
t	Time	s
V	Volume	m³
v	Velocity	m/s
	v_1 Initial velocity	
	v_2 Final velocity	
	v_m Mean velocity	
W	Work, energy	J
α	Angular acceleration	rad/s² [1]
ε	Wrap angle	rad[1]
μ	Coefficient of friction	–
ϱ	Density	kg/m³
φ	Angle of rotation	rad[1]
ω	Angular velocity	rad/s[1]

Relationships between quantities, numbers

If not otherwise specified, the following relationships are relationships between quantities, i.e. the quantities can be inserted using any units (e.g. the SI units given above). The unit of the quantity to be calculated is obtained from the units chosen for the terms of the equation.

In some cases, additional numerical relationships are given for customary units (e.g. time in s, but speed in km/h). These relationships are identified by the term "numerical relationship", and are only valid if the units given for the relationship are used.

Rectilinear motion

Uniform rectilinear motion

Velocity
$$v = s/t$$

Uniform rectilinear acceleration

Mean velocity
$$v_m = (v_1 + v_2)/2$$

Acceleration
$$a = (v_2 - v_1)/t = (v_2^2 - v_1^2)/(2s)$$

Numerical relationship:
$$a = (v_2 - v_1)/(3.6\, t)$$
a in m/s², v_2 and v_1 in km/h, t in s

Distance covered after time t
$$s = v_m \cdot t = v_1 \cdot t + (a \cdot t^2)/2$$
$$= (v_2^2 - v_1^2)/(2a)$$

Final velocity
$$v_2 = v_1 + a \cdot t = \sqrt{v_1^2 + 2a \cdot s}$$

Initial velocity
$$v_1 = v_2 - a \cdot t = \sqrt{v_2^2 - 2a \cdot s}$$

For uniformly retarded motion (v_2 smaller than v_1) a is negative.

For acceleration from rest, substitute $v_1 = 0$. For retardation to rest, substitute $v_2 = 0$.

---

[1] The unit rad (= m/m) can be replaced by the number 1.

Force
$F = m \cdot a$

Work, energy
$W = F \cdot s = m \cdot a \cdot s = P \cdot t$

Potential energy
$E_p = G \cdot h = m \cdot g \cdot h$

Kinetic energy
$E_k = m \cdot v^2/2$

Power
$P = W/t = F \cdot v$

Lifting power
$P = m \cdot g \cdot v$

Linear momentum
$p = m \cdot v$

Rotary motion

Uniform rotary motion
Peripheral velocity
$v = r \cdot \omega$
Numerical relationship:
$v = \pi \cdot d \cdot n/60$
v in m/s, d in m, n in min^{-1}
$v = 6 \cdot \pi \cdot d \cdot n/100$
v in km/h, d in m, n in min^{-1}

Angular velocity
$\omega = \varphi/t = v/r = 2\pi \cdot n$
Numerical relationship:
$\omega = \pi \cdot n/30$
ω in s^{-1}, n in min^{-1}

Uniform angular acceleration

Angular acceleration
$\alpha = (\omega_2 - \omega_1)/t$
Numerical relationship:
$\alpha = \pi (n_2 - n_1)/(30t)$
α in 1/s^2, n_1 and n_2 in min^{-1},
t in s

Final angular velocity
$\omega_2 = \omega_1 + \alpha \cdot t$

Initial angular velocity
$\omega_1 = \omega_2 - \alpha \cdot t$

For uniformly retarded rotary motion (ω_2 is smaller than ω_1) α is negative.

Centrifugal force
$F_{cf} = m \cdot r \cdot \omega^2 = m \cdot v^2/r$

Centrifugal acceleration
$a_{cf} = r \cdot \omega^2$

Torque
$M = F \cdot r = P/\omega$
Numerical relationship:
$M = 9550 \cdot P/n$
M in N $\cdot$ m, P in kW, n in min^{-1}

Moment of inertia (see P. 38)
$J = m \cdot i^2$

Work
$W = M \cdot \varphi = P \cdot t$

Power
$P = M \cdot \omega = M \cdot 2\pi \cdot n$
Numerical relationship:
$P = M \cdot n/9550$ (see graph, P. 40)
P in kW, M in N $\cdot$ m (= W $\cdot$ s), n in min^{-1}

Energy of rotation
$E_{rot} = J \cdot \omega^2/2 = J \cdot 2\pi^2 \cdot n^2$
Numerical relationship:
$E_{rot} = J \cdot n^2/182.4$
E_{rot} in J (= N $\cdot$ m), J in kg $\cdot$ m^2, n in min^{-1}

Angular momentum
$L = J \cdot \omega = J \cdot 2\pi \cdot n$
Numerical relationship:
$L = J \cdot \pi \cdot n/30 = 0.1047\, J \cdot n$
L in N $\cdot$ s $\cdot$ m, J in kg $\cdot$ m^2, n in min^{-1}

Pendulum motion

(Mathematical pendulum, i.e. a point-size mass suspended from a thread of zero mass)

Plane pendulum
Period of oscillation (back and forth)
$T = 2\pi \cdot \sqrt{l/g}$
The above equation is only accurate for small excursions α from the rest position (for $\alpha = 10°$, the error is approximately 0.2 %).

Conical pendulum
Time for one revolution
$T = 2\pi \cdot \sqrt{(l \cos \alpha)/g}$
Centrifugal force
$F_{cf} = m \cdot g \cdot \tan \alpha$
Force pulling on thread
$F_z = m \cdot g/\cos \alpha$

Throwing and falling

(see P. 34 for equation symbols)

Body thrown vertically upward (neglecting air resistance). Uniform decelerated motion, deceleration $a = g = 9.81$ m/s²	Upward velocity	$v = v_1 - g \cdot t = v_1 - \sqrt{2g \cdot h}$
	Height reached	$h = v_1 \cdot t - 0.5 \, g \cdot t^2$
	Time of upward travel	$t = \dfrac{v_1 - v}{g} = \sqrt{\dfrac{2 \cdot h}{g}}$
	At highest point	$v_2 = 0; \quad h_2 = \dfrac{v_1^2}{2g}; \quad t_2 = \dfrac{v_1}{g}$
Body thrown obliquely upward (neglecting air resistance). Angle of throw α; superposition of uniform rectilinear motion and free fall	Range of throw (max. value at $\alpha = 45°$)	$s = \dfrac{v_1^2 \cdot \sin 2\,\alpha}{g}$
	Duration of throw	$t = \dfrac{s}{v_1 \cdot \cos \alpha} = \dfrac{2 v_1 \cdot \sin \alpha}{g}$
	Height of throw	$h = \dfrac{v_1^2 \cdot \sin^2 \alpha}{2g}$
	Energy of throw	$E = G \cdot h = m \cdot g \cdot h$
Free fall (neglecting air resistance). Uniform accelerated motion, acceleration $a = g = 9.81$ m/s²	Velocity of fall	$v = g \cdot t = \sqrt{2g \cdot h}$
	Height of fall	$h = \dfrac{g \cdot t^2}{2} = \dfrac{v^2}{2g} = \dfrac{v \cdot t}{2}$
	Time of fall	$t = \dfrac{2h}{v} = \dfrac{v}{g} = \sqrt{\dfrac{2h}{g}}$
Fall with allowance of air resistance Non-uniform accelerated motion, initial acceleration $a_1 = g = 9.81$ m/s², final acceleration $a_2 = 0$	The velocity of fall approaches a limit velocity v_0 at which the air resistance $F_L = \varrho \cdot c_w \cdot A \cdot v_0^2 / 2$ is as great as the weight $G = m \cdot g$ of the falling body. Thus:	
	Limit velocity	$v_0 = \sqrt{2m \cdot g / (\varrho \cdot c_w \cdot A)}$ (ϱ air density, c_w coefficient of drag, A cross-sectional area of body).
	Velocity of fall	$v = v_0 \cdot \sqrt{1 - 1/\varkappa^2}$ The following abbreviation is used $\varkappa = e^{g \, h / v_0^2}; \; e = 2.718$
	Height of fall	$h = \dfrac{v_0^2}{2g} \, \ln \dfrac{v_0^2}{v_0^2 - v^2}$
	Time of fall	$t = \dfrac{v_0}{g} \, \ln \left(\varkappa + \sqrt{\varkappa^2 - 1} \right)$

Example: A heavy body (mass $m = 1000$ kg, cross-sectional area $A = 1$ m², coefficient of drag $c_w = 0.9$) falls from a great height. The air density $\varrho = 1.293$ kg/m³ and the acceleration of free fall $g = 9.81$ m/s² are assumed to be the same over the entire range as at ground level.

Height of fall m	Neglecting air resistance, values at end of fall from indicated height would be			Allowing for air resistance, values at end of fall from indicated height are		
	Time of fall s	Velocity of fall m/s	Energy kJ	Time of fall s	Velocity of fall m/s	Energy kJ
10	1.43	14.0	98	1.43	13.97	97
50	3.19	31.3	490	3.2	30.8	475
100	4.52	44.3	980	4.6	43	925
500	10.1	99	4900	10.6	86.2	3690
1000	14.3	140	9800	15.7	108	5850
5000	31.9	313	49 000	47.6	130	8410
10 000	45.2	443	98 000	86.1	130	8410

Drag coefficients c_w

Body shape		c_w	Body shape		c_w
→ |	Disc, plate	1.1	Long cylinder		
			$Re < 200\,000$		1.0
→ ⌒	Open dish, parachute	1.4	$Re > 450\,000$		0.35
→ ◯	Sphere		Long plate		
	$Re < 200\,000$	0.45	$l:d = 30$		
	$Re > 250\,000$	0.20	$Re = 500\,000$		0.78
			$Re = 200\,000$		0.66
→ 🝕	Slender rotating body $l:d = 6$	0.05	Long airfoil		
			$l:d = 18$		0.2
			$l:d = 8$	$Re \approx 10^6$	0.1
			$l:d = 5$		0.08
			$l:d = 2$	$Re \approx 2 \cdot 10^5$	0.2

Reynolds number

$Re = (v + v_0) \cdot l / v$

v Velocity of body in m/s,
v_0 Velocity of air in m/s,
l Length of body in m (in direction of flow),
d Thickness of body in m,
v Kinematic viscosity in m²/s.

For air with $v = 14 \cdot 10^{-6}$ m²/s (annual mean 200 m above sea level)

$Re \approx 72\,000 \, (v + v_0) \cdot l$ with v and v_0 in m/s
$Re \approx 20\,000 \, (v + v_0) \cdot l$ with v and v_0 in km/h

The results of flow measurements on two geometrically similar bodies of different sizes are comparable only if the Reynolds number is of equal magnitude in both cases (this is important in tests on models).

Gravitation

Force of attraction between two masses
$F = f \, (m_1 \cdot m_2) / r^2$
r Distance between centers of mass
f Gravitation constant
$= 6.67 \cdot 10^{-11}$ N · m²/kg²

Discharge of air from nozzles

The curves below only give approximate values. In addition to pressure and nozzle cross section, the air discharge rate depends upon the surface and length of the nozzle bore, the supply line and the rounding of the edges of the discharge port.

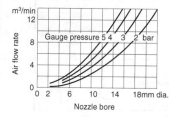

Lever law

$F_1 \cdot r_1 = F_2 \cdot r_2$

Moments of inertia

See P. 34 for symbols; mass $m = V \cdot \varrho$; P. 149 for volumes of solids V; PP. 15, 186 for density ϱ; P. 49 for planar moments of inertia.

Type of body	Moments of inertia J_x about the x-axis[1]), J_y about the y-axis[1])
Rectangular parallele-piped, cuboid	$J_x = m \dfrac{b^2 + c^2}{12}$ Cube with side length a: $J_y = m \dfrac{a^2 + c^2}{12}$ $J_x = J_y = m \dfrac{a^2}{6}$
Regular cylinder	$J_x = m \dfrac{r^2}{2}$ $J_y = m \dfrac{3\,r^2 + l^2}{12}$
Hollow regular cylinder	$J_x = m \dfrac{r_a^2 + r_i^2}{2}$ $J_y = m \dfrac{r_a^2 + r_i^2 + l^2/3}{4}$
Circular cone	$J_x = m \dfrac{3\,r^2}{10}$ Envelope of cone (excluding end base) $J_x = m \dfrac{r^2}{2}$
Frustrum of circular cone	$J_x = m \dfrac{3\,(R^5 - r^5)}{10\,(R^3 - r^3)}$ Envelope of cone (excluding end faces) $J_x = m \dfrac{R^2 + r^2}{2}$
Pyramid	$J_x = m \dfrac{a^2 + b^2}{20}$
Sphere and hemisphere	$J_x = m \dfrac{2\,r^2}{5}$ Surface area of sphere $J_x = m \dfrac{2\,r^2}{3}$
Hollow sphere r_a outer sphere radius r_i inner sphere radius	$J_x = m \dfrac{2\,(r_a^5 - r_i^5)}{5\,(r_a^3 - r_i^3)}$
Cylindrical ring	$J_x = m \left(R^2 + \dfrac{3}{4}r^2\right)$

---

[1]) The moment of inertia for an axis parallel to the x-axis or y-axis at a distance a is $J_A = J_x + m \cdot a^2$ or $J_A = J_y + m \cdot a^2$.

Friction

Friction on a horizontal plane
Frictional force (frictional resistance):
$$F_R = \mu \cdot m \cdot g$$

Friction on an inclined plane
Frictional force (frictional resistance):
$$F_R = \mu \cdot F_n = \mu \cdot m \cdot g \cdot \cos \alpha$$

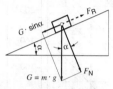

Force in direction of inclined plane[1]
$$F = G \cdot \sin \alpha - F_R = m \cdot g (\sin \alpha - \mu \cdot \cos \alpha)$$
Acceleration in direction of inclined plane[1]
$$a = g (\sin \alpha - \mu \cdot \cos \alpha)$$

Velocity after distance s
(or height $h = s \cdot \sin \alpha$)
$$v = \sqrt{2g \cdot h (1 - \mu \cdot \cot \alpha)}$$

[1] The body remains at rest if $(\sin \alpha - \mu \cdot \cos \alpha)$ is negative or zero.

Belt-wrap friction
Tension forces:
$$F_1 = F_2 \cdot e^{\mu \varepsilon}$$

Transmittable peripheral force:
$$F_u = F_1 - F_2 = F_1 (1 - e^{-\mu \varepsilon}) = F_2 (e^{\mu \varepsilon} - 1)$$
$e = 2.718$ (base of natural logarithms)

Coefficient of friction
The coefficient of friction μ always denotes a system property and not a material property. Coefficients of friction are among other things dependent on material pairing, temperature, surface condition, sliding speed, surrounding medium (e.g. water or CO_2, which can be adsorbed by the surface) or the intermediate material (e.g. lubricant). The coefficient of static friction is often greater than that of sliding friction. In special cases, the friction coefficient can exceed 1 (e.g. with very smooth surfaces where cohesion forces are predominant or with racing tires featuring an adhesion or suction effect).

Power and torque

See P. 35 for equations

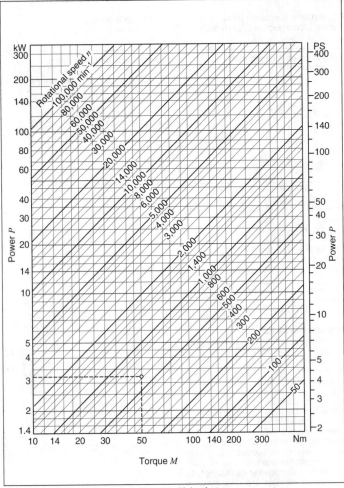

The same multiple of P corresponds to a multiple of M or n.

Examples: For $M = \quad 50$ N $\cdot$ m and $n = 600$ min^{-1}, $P = 3.15$ kW (4.3 PS)

For $M = \quad \; 5$ N $\cdot$ m and $n = 600$ min^{-1}, $P = 0.315$ kW (0.43 PS)

For $M = 5000$ N $\cdot$ m and $n = \; 60$ min^{-1}, $P = 31.5$ kW (43 PS *)

* PS = Pferdestärke = metric horsepower

Fluid mechanics

Symbol	Quantity	SI unit	Symbol	Quantity	SI unit
A	Cross-sectional area	m²	p	Fluid pressure	Pa[2]
A_b	Area of base	m²		$p_1 - p_2$ differential pressure	Pa
A_s	Area of side	m²	p_e	Gauge pressure	Pa
F	Force	N[1]		compared with	
F_a	Buoyancy force	N		atmospheric pressure	
F_b	Force acting on bottom	N	Q	Flow rate	m³/s
F_s	Force acting on sides	N	V	Volume	m³
G	Weight	N	υ	Flow velocity	m/s
g	Acceleration of free fall	m/s²	ϱ	Density	kg/m³
	$g = 9.81$ m/s²			Density of water[3]	
h	Depth of fluid	m		$\varrho_w = 1$ kg/dm³	
m	Mass	kg		$= 1000$ kg/m³	

Fluid at rest in an open container

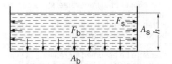

Force acting on bottom $F_b = A_b \cdot h \cdot \varrho \cdot g$
Force acting on sides $\quad F_s = 0.5 A_s \cdot h \cdot \varrho \cdot g$
Buoyancy force $\quad\quad\quad F_a = V \cdot \varrho \cdot g$
= weight of displaced volume of fluid.
A body will float if $F_a \geq G$.

Hydrostatic press

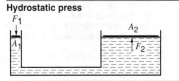

Fluid pressure $\quad p = \dfrac{F_1}{A_1} = \dfrac{F_2}{A_2}$

Piston forces $\quad F_1 = p \cdot A_1 = F_2 \cdot \dfrac{A_1}{A_2}$

$\quad\quad\quad\quad\quad\quad F_2 = p \cdot A_2 = F_1 \cdot \dfrac{A_2}{A_1}$

Flow with change in cross section

Flow rate

$$Q = A_1 \cdot \upsilon_1 = A_2 \cdot \upsilon_2 = \sqrt{\frac{2}{\varrho} \cdot \frac{p_1 - p_2}{1/A_2^2 - 1/A_1^2}}$$

Discharge from vessels

Discharge velocity
$\upsilon_a = \psi \cdot \sqrt{2\,g \cdot h + 2 p_e/\varrho}$

Discharge rate
$Q_a = \varkappa \cdot A \cdot \upsilon_a$
$= \varkappa \cdot \psi \cdot A \cdot \sqrt{2\,g \cdot h + 2 p_e/\varrho}$

Coefficient of contraction $\varkappa$ with sharp edge: 0.62 ... 0.64; for slightly broken edge: 0.7 ... 0.8; for slightly rounded edge: 0.9; for heavily rounded, smooth edge: 0.99.
Discharge coefficient $\psi = 0.97 ... 0.998$.

[1] 1 N = 1 kg m/s² (see P. 12).
[2] 1 Pa = 1 N/m²; 1 bar = 10⁵ Pa;
1 at (= 1 kp/cm²) = 0.981 bar ≈ 1 bar (see P. 24 for units of pressure).
[3] See P. 190 for densities of other fluids.

Strength of materials

Symbols and units
See PP. 14 ... 18 for names of units

Quantity		Unit
A	Cross-sectional area	mm²
E	Modulus of elasticity	N/mm²
F	Force, load	N
G	Modulus of elasticity in shear	N/mm²
I_a	Axial planar moment of inertia (P. 49)	mm⁴
I_p	Polar planar moment of inertia (P. 49)	mm⁴
l	Length	mm
M_b	Bending moment	N · mm
M_t	Torque; turning moment	N · mm
q	Knife-edge load	N/mm
R	Radius of curvature at neutral axis	mm
R_{dm}	Compression strength	N/mm²
R_e	Yield point	N/mm²
R_m	Tensile strength	N/mm²
$R_{p0.2}$	0.2 % yield strength[1]	N/mm²
S	Safety factor	–
s	Maximum deflection	mm
W_b	Section modulus under bending (P. 49)	mm³
W_t	Section modulus under torsion (P. 49)	mm³
α_k	Stress concentration factor (notch factor)	–
β_k	Fatigue-strength reduction factor	–
γ	Elastic shear	rad
δ, A	Elongation at fracture	%
ε	Elastic elongation or compression, strain	%
ν	Poisson's ratio	–
σ	Stress	N/mm²
σ_{zdw}	Reversed-bending fatigue strength	N/mm²
σ_{gr}	Limit stress	N/mm²
σ_D	Endurance limit = fatigue limit	N/mm²
σ_W	Endurance limit at complete stress reversal	N/mm²
σ_a	Stress amplitude	N/mm²
σ_{bB}	Bending strength	N/mm²
σ_{bF}	Elastic limit under bending	N/mm²
σ_{bW}	Fatigue limit under reversed bending stresses	N/mm²
τ	Shear stress	N/mm²
τ_t	Torsional stress	N/mm²
τ_{gr}	Torsional stress limit	N/mm²
τ_{tB}	Torsional strength	N/mm²
τ_{tF}	Elastic limit under torsion	N/mm²
τ_{tW}	Fatigue limit under reversed torsional stresses	N/mm²
ψ	Angle of rotation	rad

The equations in this section are general equations of quantities, i.e. they are also applicable if other units are chosen, except equations for buckling.

Mechanical stresses

Tension and compression
(perpendicular to cross-sectional area)

Tensile (compression) stress $\sigma = \dfrac{F}{A}$

Compression strain $\varepsilon = \dfrac{\Delta l}{l}$

Δl Increase (or decrease) in length
l Original length

Modulus of elasticity $E = \dfrac{\sigma}{\varepsilon}$ ²)

Long, thin bars subjected to compressive loads must also be investigated with regard to their buckling strength.

Bending
The effects of a transverse force can be neglected in the case of long beams subjected to bending stress. In calculating bending stresses (resulting from bending moments without transverse force) it can therefore be assumed for reasons of symmetry (the axis of the beam becomes circular) that plane cross sections remain plane. With these assumptions as given, the neutral axis passes through the center of gravity of every conceivable cross section.

The following equation thus applies:

$M_b = \dfrac{E \cdot I}{R}$

Edge stress $\sigma_b = \dfrac{M_b}{I} \cdot e = \dfrac{M_b}{W}$

if $W = \dfrac{I}{e}$

I Axial moment of inertia: the sum of the products of all cross-sectional elements by the squares of their distances from the neutral axis.

W Section modulus of a cross section: indicates, for the edge stress 1, the inner moment with which the cross section can resist an external bending load.

Q Transverse force: the sum of all forces acting vertically on the beam to the left or right of a given cross section; Q subjects the beam to shearing stress. In the case of short beams, the shearing stress caused by Q must also be taken into account.

e Distance between the neutral-axis zone and the outer-surface zone.

Table 1. Loading cases under bending

$F_A = F$ $M_{b\,max} = l \cdot F$	$s = \dfrac{l^3}{3} \cdot \dfrac{F}{E \cdot I_a}$	
$F_A = \dfrac{b}{l}F$; $F_B = \dfrac{a}{l}F$ $M_{b\,max} = \dfrac{a \cdot b}{l}F$	$s = \dfrac{a^2 \cdot b^2}{3l} \cdot \dfrac{F}{E \cdot I_a}$	
$F_A = q \cdot l$ $M_{b\,max} = \dfrac{q \cdot l^2}{2}$	$s = \dfrac{l^4}{8} \cdot \dfrac{q}{E \cdot I_a}$	
$F_A = F_B = \dfrac{q \cdot l}{2}$ $M_{b\,max} = \dfrac{q \cdot l^2}{8}$	$s \approx \dfrac{l^4}{77} \cdot \dfrac{q}{E \cdot I_a}$	

Buckling

In bars which are subjected to compression, the compressive stress $\sigma = F/A$ must always be less than the permissible buckling stress

$$\sigma_{kperm} = \sigma_k/S$$

otherwise the bar will buckle.

Depending upon the centricity of the applied force, a factor of safety $S \geq 3 ... \geq 6$ must be selected.

Slenderness ratio $\lambda = l_k / \sqrt{I_a / A}$

l_k Free buckling length (see diagram)

Buckling stress $\sigma_k = \pi^2 \dfrac{E}{\lambda^2} \approx 10 \dfrac{E \cdot I_a}{l_k^2 \cdot A}$

The above equation for σ_k (Euler's formula) only applies to slender bars with the following slenderness ratios:

$\lambda \geq 100$ for St 37 steel,
$\lambda \geq \pi\sqrt{E / R_e}$ for steels whose R_e values are different from that of St 37,
$\lambda \geq 80$ for GG 25 gray cast iron,
$\lambda \geq 100$ for coniferous wood.

According to Tetmajer, the following is valid for lower values of λ:
– for St 37 steel $\sigma_k = (284 - 0.8\,\lambda)$ N/mm²,
– for St 52 steel $\sigma_k = (578 - 3.74\,\lambda)$ N/mm²,

Loading cases under buckling

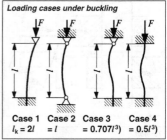

Case 1	Case 2	Case 3	Case 4
$l_k = 2l$	$= l$	$= 0.707l$[3]	$= 0.5l$[3]

– for GG 25 gray cast iron
 $\sigma_k = (760 - 12\,\lambda + 0.05\,\lambda^2)$ N/mm² and
– for coniferous wood $\sigma_k = (29 - 0.19\,\lambda)$ N/mm².

[1] 0.2 % yield strength: that stress which causes permanent deformation of 0.2 %.

[2] Hook's Law applies only to elastic deformation, i.e. in practice approximately up to the elastic limit (yield point, elastic limit under bending, elastic limit under torsion; see also P. 45.

[3] Applies to ideal clamping point, without eccentricity of the top fixing points. Calculation in accordance with Case 2 is more reliable.

Shear

Shearing stress $\tau = F/A$

τ = shear force per unit area of the cross section of a body. The stress acts in the direction of the plane element. Shear strain γ is the angular deformation of the body element as a result of shear stress. Shear modulus (modulus of rigidity) $G = \tau/\gamma^{1})^{2})$.

Torsion (twisting)

Torsional stress $\tau_t = M_t/W_t$,

See P. 49 for section moduli W_t.

Torque M_t = torsional force · lever arm.

The torque generates the illustrated shearing-stress distribution in every cross-sectional plane on every diameter.

Angle of rotation $\psi = \dfrac{l \cdot M_t}{G \cdot I_p} = \dfrac{l \cdot W_t \cdot \tau}{I_p \cdot G}$

The angle of rotation ψ is the angle of twist in rad of a bar of length l (conversion: 1 rad $\approx 57.3°$, see P. 21).

See P. 49 for polar planar moments of inertia I_p.

Notch effect

The equations cited above apply to smooth rods and bars; if notches are present, these equations yield the following nominal stresses (referred to the residual cross section):

$\sigma_{zn} = F/A$ under tension (see diagram) or compression,

$\sigma_{bn} = M_b/W_b$ under bending,

$\tau_{tn} = M_t/W_t$ under torsion.

Notches (such as grooves and holes) and changes in cross section (shoulders and offsets) as well as various clamping methods give rise to local stress concentrations σ_{max}, which are usually far in excess of the nominal stresses:

$\sigma_{max} = \alpha_k \cdot \sigma_n$

See P. 48 for the stress concentration factor α_k.

Notches reduce the endurance strength and fatigue limit (see P. 47, Fatigue strength of structure), as well as the impact strength of brittle materials; in the case of tough materials, the first permanent (plastic) deformation occurs earlier. The stress concentration factor α_k increases with the sharpness and depth of the notch (V notches, hairline cracks, poorly machined surfaces). This also holds true the more sharp-edged the changes in cross section are.

---

[1] See footnote 2 on P. 43.

[2] The relationship between the shear modulus G and the modulus of elasticity E is:

$G = \dfrac{E}{2(1 + \nu)}$ with ν = Poisson's ratio

For metallic materials with $\nu \approx 0.3$, $G \approx 0.385\,E$; see P. 193f for values of E.

Shear

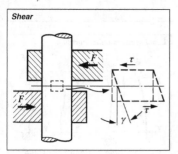

Torsion

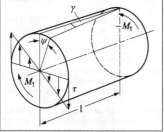

Notch effect caused by grooves and holes

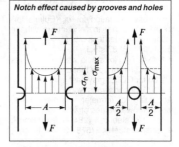

Permissible loading

The equations in the sections "Mechanical stresses" and "Notch effect" apply only to the elastic range; in practice they permit calculations approximately up to the elastic limit or up to 0.2% yield strength (see footnote 1, P. 43). The permissible loading in each case is determined by materials testing and the science of the strength of materials and is governed by the material itself, the condition of the material (tough, brittle), the specimen or component shape (notches) and the type of loading (static, alternating).

R_m Tensile strength. For steel up to $\varepsilon \approx 600$ HV
R_m (in N/mm²) ≈ 3.3 times · the HV value; see P. 193 and P. 275.

R_e Stress at the elastic limit (under tension this σ_s is the yield point).

δ (or A) elongation at fracture.

Table 2. Limit stresses σ_{gr}, τ_{gr} under static loading

Generally speaking, the limit stresses σ_{gr} and τ_{gr}, at which failure of the material occurs (permanent deformation or fracture), should not be reached in practice (s. below and P. 46). Depending upon the accuracy of the loading calculation or measurement, the material, the type of stress, and the possible damage in the event of failure, allowance must be made for a safety factor $S = \sigma_{gr}/\sigma_{perm}$ (σ_{perm} is the maximum permissible stress in service). For tough materials, S should be 1.2...2 (...4), and for brittle materials $S = (1.2...)$ 2...4 (...10).

The following must be the case: $\sigma_{max} \leq \sigma_{perm}$ (σ_{max} maximum stress, stress peak in service).

Limit stress	Tough materials	Brittle materials
Under tension	σ_{gr} = yield point R_e ($\approx$ limit of elastic elongation). For steel up to approx. R_m = 600 N/mm² and cold-rolled metals, R_e = 0.6...0.8 R_m. σ_{gr} = 0.2 yield strength $R_{p0.2}$ (see footnote 1, P. 43). For metals without a marked yield point such as steels with $R_m \geq$ 600 N/mm², Cu, Al.	σ_{gr} = tensile strength R_m
Under compression	σ_{gr} = compressive yield point σ_{dF} (limit of elastic compression, roughly corresponding to R_e).	σ_{gr} = compression strength R_{dm}.
For compression with danger of buckling	σ_{gr} = buckling strain σ_k.	σ_{gr} = buckling strain σ_k.
Under bending	σ_{gr} = elastic limit under bending σ_{bF} (limit of elastic deflection). σ_{bF} is approximately equal to yield point R_e under tension. Permanent curvature if σ_{bF} is exceeded.	σ_{gr} = bending strength $\sigma_{bB} \approx R_m$. For gray cast iron GG 40, however, σ_{bB} = 1.4...2.0 R_m since $\varepsilon = \sigma/E$ does not apply since the neutral axis is displaced
Under torsion	τ_{gr} = elastic limit under torsion τ_{tF} (limit of elastic twist). Torsional limit $\tau_{tF} \approx 0.5...0.6 R_e$. If exceeded, twist becomes permanent deformation.	τ_{gr} = torsional strength τ_{tB}. τ_{tB} = 0.5...0.8 σ_B, but for gray cast iron up to GG 25 τ_{tB} = 1...1.3 σ_B.
Under shear	τ_{gr} = elastic limit under shear $\tau_{sF} \approx 0.6 \sigma_s$.	τ_{gr} = shear strength τ_{sB}.

When minimal plastic deformations can be accepted, it is permissible to extend the loads on tough materials beyond the limits of elastic compression and deflection. The internal areas of the cross section are then stressed up to their yield point while they provide support for the surface-layer zone. The bending force applied to an angular bar can be increased by a maximum factor of 1.5; the maximum increase in torsional force applied to a round torsion bar is 1.33.

Limit stresses under pulsating loads

If the load alternates between two stress values, different (lower) stress limits σ_{gr} are valid: the largest stress amplitude, alternating about a given mean stress, which can be withstood "infinitely" often without fracture and impermissible distortion, is called the fatigue limit or endurance limit σ_D. It is determined experimentally by applying a pulsating load to test specimens until fracture occurs, whereby with the reduced load the number of cycles to fracture increases and yields the so-called "Wöhler" or stress-number (S/N) curve. The Wöhler curve is nearly horizontal after 2...10 million load cycles for steel, and after roughly 100 million cycles for non-ferrous metals; oscillation stress = fatigue limit in such cases.

If no additional factors are present in operation (wear, corrosion, multiple overloading etc.), fracture does not occur after this "ultimate number of cycles". It should be noted that $S \cdot \sigma_a \leq \sigma_W$ or in the case of increased mean stresses $S \cdot \sigma_a \leq \sigma_D$; safety factor $S = 1.25...\geq 3$ (stress values have lower-case subscripts, fatigue-strength values have upper-case subscripts). A fatigue fracture generally does not exhibit permanent deformation. With plastics, it is not always possible to give an "ultimate number of cycles" because in this case extensive superimposed creepage becomes effective. With high-tensile steels, the internal stresses resulting from production processes can have a considerable effect upon the fatigue-strength values.

Fatigue-limit diagram

The greatest "infinitely" often endurable stress amplitude can be determined from the fatigue limit diagram (at right) for any minimum stress σ_u or mean stress σ_m. The diagram is produced using several Wöhler curves with various mean stress factors.

Special cases of fatigue limit

Fatigue limit under completely reversed stress σ_W

The stress alternates between two opposite limit values of the same magnitude; the mean stress is zero.

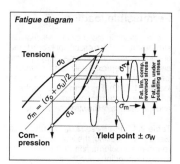

Fatigue diagram

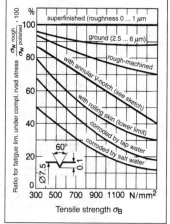

Effect of surface quality finish on fatigue limit during bending and tension-compression stresses

The fatigue limit σ_W is approximately:

Load	Steel	Non-ferrous metals
Tension/compression	0.30...0.45 R_m	0.2...0.4 R_m
Bending	0.40...0.55 R_m	0.3...0.5 R_m

Fatigue limit under pulsating stress σ_{sch}

Defines the infinitely endurable number of <u>double amplitudes</u> when the minimum stress is zero (see Fatigue diagram above).

Table 3. Relaxation for various materials

Material	Part	σ_a N/mm²	Initial stress N/mm²	Temperature °C	Time h	Relaxation %
GD-Zn Al4 Cu 1	Thread	280	150[1])	20	500	30
GD-Mg Al8 Zn 1	Compression test specimen	157	60	150	500	63
GD-Al Si12 (Cu)		207	60	150	500	3.3
Cq35	Bolt	800	540	160	500	11
40Cr Mo V 47	Bar under tension	850	372	300	1000	12

Permissible alternating loading of notched machine parts

The fatigue limit of notched parts is usually higher than that calculated using stress concentration factor α_k (see P. 48). Also, the sensitivity of materials to the effect of a notch in case of (alternating) fatigue loading varies, e.g., spring steels, highly quenched and tempered structural steels, and high-strength bronzes are more sensitive than cast iron, stainless steel and precipitation-hardened aluminum alloys. For (alternating) fatigue loading, fatigue-strength reduction factor β_k applies instead of α_k so that e.g. at $\sigma_m = 0$ the effective stress amplitude on the structural member is $\sigma_{wn}\beta_k$ (σ_{wn} the nominal alternating stress referred to the residual cross section). The following must hold true:

$$\sigma_{wn}\beta_k \leq \sigma_{wperm} = \sigma_w/S$$

Attempts have been made to derive β_k from α_k where e.g. Thum introduced notch sensitivity η_k and established that

$$\beta_k = 1 + (\alpha_k - 1)\,\eta_k$$

However η_k is not a material constant, and it also depends upon the condition of the material, the component geometry (notch acuity) and the type of loading (e.g. alternating or dynamic).

Fatigue limit values under reversed stress

σ_w for various materials is given on P. 193/198.

Stress concentration factors

α_k for different notch configurations is given on P. 48.

Fatigue strength of structure

For many component parts, it is difficult or even impossible to determine a stress concentration factor α_k and thus a fatigue-strength reduction factor β_k. In this case the fatigue limit of the entire part (fatigue strength of structural member, e.g., pulsating loads in N or moment of oscillation in N·m) must be determined experimentally and compared with test results given in literature. The local stressing can continue to be measured, using foil strain gauges for instance. As an alternative, or for preliminary design purposes, the finite-element method can be applied to calculate numerically the stress distribution and to compare it with the respective limit stress.

Creep behavior

If materials are subjected for <u>long periods of time</u> to loads at <u>increased temperatures</u> and/or to <u>high stresses</u>, creep or relaxation may occur. If resulting deformations (generally very small) are not acceptable, allowance must be made for the material's "creep behavior".

<u>Creep:</u>
Permanent deformation under constant load, and (at least approximately) constant stress (example: turbine blades).

<u>Relaxation:</u>
Reduction of the tension forces and stresses, whereby the initially applied (usually purely elastic) deformation remains constant (see Table 3 for examples).

In the case of alternating loads (where $\sigma_a \geq 0.1\ \sigma_B$) and maximum stresses and temperatures such as are encountered in static relaxation tests, the same deformations and losses of force only occur after a period of load which is approximately 10 times (or more) as long as that of the static relaxation tests.

---

[1]) In the stress area of a steel bolt.

Stress concentration factor a_k for various notch configurations

Stress concentration factors for flat bars

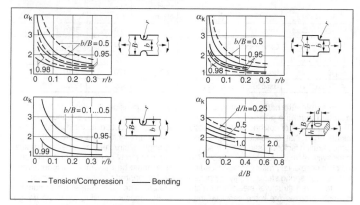

––– Tension/Compression ——— Bending

Stress concentration factors for rods

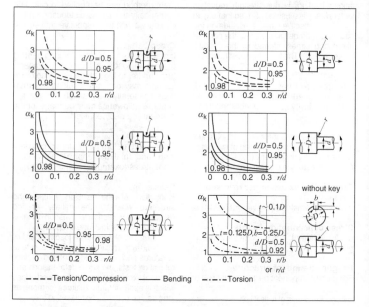

––– Tension/Compression ——— Bending —·—·— Torsion

Section moduli and geometrical moments of inertia

NL = "neutral axis"   See P. 38 for mass moments of inertia

	Section modulus W_b under bending W_t under torsion	Planar moment of inertia I_a axial, referred to NL I_p polar, referred to center of gravity
Circle (d) NL	$W_b = 0.098\, d^3$ $W_t = 0.196\, d^3$	$I_a = 0.049\, d^4$ $I_p = 0.098\, d^4$
Hollow circle (d_0, d) NL	$W_b = 0.098\,(d^4 - d_0^4)/d$ $W_t = 0.196\,(d^4 - d_0^4)/d$	$I_a = 0.049\,(d^4 - d_0^4)$ $I_p = 0.098\,(d^4 - d_0^4)$
Ellipse (a, b) NL	$W_b = 0.098\, a^2 \cdot b$ $W_t = 0.196\, a \cdot b^2$	$I_a = 0.049\, a^3 \cdot b$ $I_p = 0.196\, \dfrac{a^3 \cdot b^3}{a^2 + b^2}$
Hollow ellipse (b, a_0, a, b_0) NL	$W_b = 0.098\,(a^3 \cdot b - a_0^3 \cdot b_0)/a$ $W_t = 0.196\,(a \cdot b^3 - a_0 \cdot b_0^3)/b$	$I_a = 0.049\,(a^3 \cdot b - a_0^3 \cdot b_0)$ $I_p = 0.196\, \dfrac{n^3 (b^4 - b_0^4)}{n^2 + 1}$ $\dfrac{a}{b} = n \geq 1$ $\dfrac{a_0}{b_0} = n$ for
Square (diagonal) (a) NL	$W_b = 0.118\, a^3$ $W_t = 0.208\, a^3$	$I_a = 0.083\, a^4$ $I_p = 0.140\, a^4$
Rectangle (b, h) NL	$W_b = 0.167\, b \cdot h^2$ $W_t = x \cdot b^2 \cdot h$ (In the case of torsion, the initially plane cross sections of a rod do not remain plane.)	$I_a = 0.083\, b \cdot h^3$ $I_p = \eta \cdot b^3 \cdot h$
Hexagon (across flats) (d) NL	$W_b = 0.104\, d^3$ $W_t = 0.188\, d^3$	$I_a = 0.060\, d^4$ $I_p = 0.115\, d^4$
Hexagon (across corners) (d) NL	$W_b = 0.120\, d^3$ $W_t = 0.188\, d^3$	$I_a = 0.060\, d^4$ $I_p = 0.115\, d^4$
Trapezoid (b, a) NL	$W_b = \dfrac{h^2 (a^2 + 4a \cdot b + b^2)}{12\,(2a + b)}$	$I_a = \dfrac{h^3 (a^2 + 4a \cdot b + b^2)}{36\,(a + b)}$
I / C section (b, h_0, h, b_0) NL	$W_b = \dfrac{b \cdot h^3 - b_0 \cdot h_0^3}{6\, h}$	$I_a = \dfrac{b \cdot h^3 - b_0 \cdot h_0^3}{12}$
Cross / H section (h_0, h, b, b_0) NL	$W_b = \dfrac{b \cdot h^3 + b_0 \cdot h_0^3}{6\, h}$	$I_a = \dfrac{b \cdot h^3 + b_0 \cdot h_0^3}{12}$

Rectangle torsion factors:

$h : b$	x	η
1	0.208	0.140
1.5	0.231	0.196
2	0.246	0.229
3	0.267	0.263
4	0.282	0.281

Acoustics

Quantities and units
(see also DIN 1332)

Quantity		SI unit
c	Velocity of sound	m/s
f	Frequency	Hz
I	Sound intensity	W/m²
L_i	Sound intensity level	dB
L_{Aeq}	Equivalent continuous sound level, A-weighted	dB (A)
L_{pA}	Sound pressure level, A-weighted	dB (A)
L_r	Rating sound level	dB (A)
L_{WA}	Sound power level, A-weighted	dB (A)
P	Sound power	W
p	Sound pressure	Pa
S	Surface area	m²
T	Reverberation time	s
v	Particle velocity	m/s
Z	Specific acoustic impedance	Pa · s/m
α	Sound absorption coefficient	1
λ	Wavelength	m
ϱ	Density	kg/m³
ω	Angular frequency (= $2\pi f$)	1/s

General terminology
(see also DIN 1320)

Sound
Mechanical vibrations and waves in an elastic medium, particularly in the audible frequency range (16 to 20,000 Hz).

Ultrasound
Mechanical vibrations above the frequency range of human hearing.

Propagation of sound
In general, sound propagates spherically from its source. In a free sound field, the sound pressure decreases by 6 dB each time the distance from the sound source is doubled. Reflecting objects influence the sound field, and the rate at which the sound level is reduced as a function of the distance from the sound source is lower.

Velocity of sound c
The velocity of sound is the velocity of propagation of a sound wave.

Sound velocities and wave lengths in different materials.

Material/medium	Velocity of sound c m/s	Wavelength λ m at 1000 Hz
Air, 20 °C, 1014 hPa	343	0.343
Water, 10 °C	1440	1.44
Rubber (according to hardness)	60 ... 1500	0.06 ... 1.5
Aluminum (rod)	5100	5.1
Steel (rod)	5000	5.0

Wavelength $\lambda = c/f = 2\pi c/\omega$

Particle velocity v
Particle velocity is the alternating velocity of a vibrating particle. In a free sound field: $v = p/Z$. At low frequencies, perceived vibration is approximately proportional to the particle velocity.

Sound pressure p
Sound pressure is the alternating pressure generated in a medium by the vibration of sound. In a free sound field, this pressure equals $p = v \cdot Z$. It is usually measured as the RMS value.

Specific acoustic impedance Z
Specific acoustic impedance is a measure of the ability of a medium to transmit sound waves. $Z = p/v = \varrho \cdot c$. For air at 20 °C and 1013 hPa (760 torr) $Z = 415$ Ns/m³, for water at 10 °C $Z = 1.44 \cdot 10^6$ Ns/m³ = $1.44 \cdot 10^6$ Pa · s/m.

Sound power P
Sound power is the power emitted by a sound source. Sound power of some sound sources:

Normal conversation, average	$7 \cdot 10^{-6}$ W
Violin, fortissimo	$1 \cdot 10^{-3}$ W
Peak power of the human voice	$2 \cdot 10^{-3}$ W
Piano, trumpet	0.2 ... 0.3 W
Organ	1 ... 10 W
Kettle drum	10 W
Orchestra (75 musicians)	up to 65 W

Sound intensity I
(Sound intensity) $I = P/S$, i.e. sound power through a plane vertical to the direction of propagation. In a sound field,
$I = p^2/\varrho \cdot c = v^2 \cdot \varrho \cdot c$.

Doppler effect

For moving sound sources: If the distance between the source and the observer decreases, the perceived pitch (f') is higher than the actual pitch (f); as the distance increases, the perceived pitch falls. The following relationship holds true if the observer and the sound force are moving along the same line: $f'/f = (c - u')/(c - u)$.
c = velocity of sound, u' = velocity of observer, u = velocity of sound source.

Interval

The interval is the ratio of the frequencies of two tones. In the "equal-tempered scale" of our musical instruments (introduced by J. S. Bach), the octave (interval 2:1) is divided into 12 equal semitones with a ratio of $\sqrt[12]{2} = 1.0595$, i.e. a series of any number of tempered intervals always leads back to a tempered interval. In the case of "pure pitch", on the other hand, a sequence of pure intervals usually does not lead to a pure interval. (Pure pitch has the intervals 1, 16/15, 9/8, 6/5, 5/4, 4/3, 7/5, 3/2, 8/5, 5/3, 9/5, 15/8, 2.)

Sound spectrum

The sound spectrum, generated by means of frequency analysis, is used to show the relationship between the sound pressure level (airborne or structure-borne sound) and frequency.

Octave band spectrum

The sound levels are determined and represented in terms of octave bandwidth. Octave: frequency ranges with fundamental frequencies in a ratio of 1:2. Mean frequency of octave $f_m = \sqrt{f_1 \cdot f_2}$.
Recommended center frequencies: 31.5; 63; 125; 250; 500; 1000; 2000; 4000; 8000 Hz.

Third-octave band spectrum

Sound levels are determined and represented in terms of third-octave bandwidth. The bandwidth referred to the center frequency is relatively constant, as in the case of the octave band spectrum.

Sound insulation

Sound insulation is the reduction of the effect of a sound source by interposing a reflecting (insulating) wall between the source and the impact location.

Sound absorption

Loss of sound energy when reflected on peripheries, but also for the propagation in a medium.

Sound absorption coefficient α

The sound absorption coefficient is the ratio of the non-reflected sound energy to the incident sound energy. With total reflection, $\alpha = 0$; with total absorption, $\alpha = 1$.

Noise reduction

Attenuation of acoustic emissions: Reduction in the primary mechanical or electrodynamic generation of structure-borne noise and flow noises; damping and modification of sympathetic vibrations; reduction of the effective radiation surfaces; encapsulation.

Low-noise design

Application of simulation techniques (modal analysis, modal variation, finite-element analysis, analysis of coupling effects of airborne noise) for advance calculation and optimization of the acoustic properties of new designs.

Quantities for noise emission measurement

Sound field quantities are normally measured as RMS values, and are expressed in terms of frequency-dependent weighting (A-weighting). This is indicated by the subscript A next to the corresponding symbol.

Sound power level L_W

The sound power of a sound source is described by the sound power level L_W. The sound power level is equal to ten times the logarithm to the base 10 of the ratio of the calculated sound power to the reference sound power $P_0 = 10^{-12}$ W. Sound power cannot be measured directly. It is calculated based on quantities of the sound field which surrounds the source. Measurements are usually also made of the sound pressure level L_p at specific points around the source (see

DIN 45635). L_w can also be calculated based on sound intensity levels L_I measured at various points on the surface of an imaginary envelope surrounding the sound source. If noise is emitted uniformly through a surface of $S_0 = 1 \text{ m}^2$, the sound pressure level L_p and the sound intensity level L_I at this surface have the same value as the sound power level L_w.

Sound pressure level L_p
The sound pressure level is ten times the logarithm to the base 10 of the ratio of the square of the RMS sound pressure to the square of the reference sound pressure
$$p_0 = 20 \text{ μPa. } L_p = 10 \log p^2/p_0^2$$
or
$$L_p = 20 \log p/p_0.$$
The sound pressure level is given in decibels (dB).

The frequency-dependent, A-weighted sound pressure level L_{pA} as measured at a distance of $d = 1 \text{ m}$ is frequently used to characterize sound sources.

Sound intensity level L_I
The sound intensity level is equal to ten times the logarithm to the base ten of the ratio of sound intensity to reference sound intensity
$$I_0 = 10^{-12} \text{ W/m}^2. \ L_I = 10 \log I/I_0.$$

Interaction of two or more sound sources
If two independent sound fields are superimposed, their sound intensities or the squares of their sound pressures must be added. The overall sound level is then determined from the individual sound levels as follows:

Difference between 2 individual sound levels	Overall sound level = higher individual sound level + supplement of:
0 dB	3 dB
1 dB	2.5 dB
2 dB	2.1 dB
3 dB	1.8 dB
4 dB	1.5 dB
6 dB	1 dB
8 dB	0.6 dB
10 dB	0.4 dB

Motor-vehicle noise measurements and limits

The noise measurements employed to monitor compliance with legal requirements are concerned exclusively with external noise levels. Testing procedures and limit values for stationary and moving vehicles were defined in 1981 with the promulgation of EC Directive 81/334.

Noise emissions from moving vehicles
The vehicle approaches line AA, which is located 10 m from the microphone plane, at a constant velocity. Upon reaching line AA, the vehicle continues under full acceleration as far as line BB (also placed 10 m from the microphone plane), which serves as the end of the test section. The noise-emissions level is the maximum sound level as recorded by the microphone 7.5 m from the middle of the lane.

Passenger cars with manual transmission and a maximum of 4 forward gears are tested in 2nd gear. Consecutive readings in 2nd and 3rd gear are employed for vehicles with more than 4 forward gears, with the noise emissions level being defined as the arithmetic mean of the two maximum sound levels.

Separate procedures are prescribed for vehicles with automatic transmissions.

Noise emissions from stationary vehicles
Measurements are taken in the vicinity of

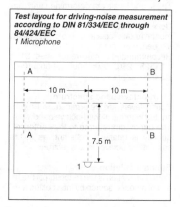

Test layout for driving-noise measurement according to DIN 81/334/EEC through 84/424/EEC
1 Microphone

A ————— B
|←— 10 m —→|←— 10 m —→|

A ————— B
7.5 m
1

Limits and tolerances in dB(A) for noise emission from motor vehicles

Vehicle category	92/97/EEC since Oct. 1995 dB (A)
Passenger cars	
With spark-ignition or diesel engine	74 + 1
– with direct-injection diesel engine	75 + 1
Trucks and buses	
Permissible total weight below 2 t	76 + 1
– with direct-injection diesel engine	77 + 1
Buses	
Permissible total weight 2 t ... 3.5 t	76 + 1
– with direct-injection diesel engine	77 + 1
Permissible total weight above 3.5 t	
– engine power output up to 150 kW	78 + 1
– engine power output above 150 kW	80 + 1
Trucks	
Permissible total weight 2 t ... 3.5 t	76 + 1
– with direct-injection diesel engine	77 + 1
Permissible total weight above 3.5 t (FMVSS/CUR: above 2.8 t)	
– engine power output up to 75 kW	77 + 1
– engine power output up to 150 kW	78 + 1
– engine power output above 150 kW	80 + 1

Higher limits are valid for off-road and 4WD vehicles.
Supplementary noise limits apply for engine brakes and pneumatic equipment.

the exhaust muffler in order to facilitate subsequent testing of motor-vehicle noise levels. Measurements are carried out with the engine running at $3/4$ the speed at which it develops its rated power output. Once the engine speed levels off, the throttle valve is quickly returned to its idle position. During this procedure, the maximum A-weighted sound-pressure level is monitored at a distance of 50 cm from the outlet at a horizontal angle of $(45 \pm 10)°$ to the direction of exhaust flow. The recorded level is entered in the vehicle documentation in dB(A) with the suffix "P" (making it possible to distinguish between this figure and levels derived using earlier test procedures). No legal maxima have been specified for standing noise levels.

Interior noise level
There are no legal requirements pertaining to interior noise levels. The interior noise is measured, e.g. at constant speed or when gradually accelerating in the range from 60 km/h or 40 % of the maximum driving speed, as the A-weighted sound pressure level and then plotted as a function of the driving speed. One series of measurements is always to be made at the driver's seat; other measurement locations are selected in accordance with the passenger seating arrangement inside the vehicle. There are no plans to introduce a single value for indicating inside noise levels.

Quantities for noise immission measurement

Rating sound level L_r
The effect of noise on the human being is evaluated using the rating sound level L_r (see also DIN 45645). This is a measure of the mean noise immission over a period of time (e.g. 8 working hours), and with fluctuating noises is either measured directly with integrated measuring instruments or calculated from individual sound-pressure-level measurements and the associated periods of time of the individual sound effects (see also DIN 45641). Noise immission parameters such as pulsation and tonal quality can be taken into account through level allowances (see table below for reference values).

The following guideline values for the rating sound level (Germany; Technical Instructions on Noise Abatement, 16 July 1968) are measured outside the nearest residential building (0.5 m in front of an open window):

	Day	Night
Purely industrial areas	70 dB (A)	70 dB (A)
Areas with predominantly industrial premises	65 dB (A)	50 dB (A)
Mixed areas	60 dB (A)	45 dB (A)
Areas with predominantly residential premises	55 dB (A)	40 dB (A)
Purely residential areas	50 dB (A)	35 dB (A)
Health resorts, hospitals etc.	45 dB (A)	35 dB (A)

Equivalent continuous sound level L_{Aeq}

In the case of noises which fluctuate in time, the mean A-weighted sound pressure level resulting from the individual sound pressure levels and the individual exposure times, equals the equivalent continuous sound level if it describes the mean sound energy over the entire assessment time period (see DIN 45641). The equivalent continuous sound level in accordance with the German "Aircraft Noise Abatement Law" is arrived at in a different manner (see DIN 45643).

Perceived noise levels

The human ear can distinguish approximately 300 levels of acoustic intensity and 3000 ... 4000 different frequencies (pitch levels) in rapid temporal succession and evaluate them according to complex patterns. Thus there is not necessarily any direct correspondence between perceived noise levels and (energy-oriented) technically-defined sound levels. A rough approximation of subjective sound-level perception is provided by A-weighted sound levels, which take into account variations in the human ear's sensitivity as a function of frequency, the phon unit and the definition of loudness in sone. Sound-level measurements alone do not suffice to define the nuisance and disturbance potential of noise emanating from machinery and equipment. A hardly-perceptible ticking noise can thus be perceived as extremely disturbing, even in an otherwise loud environment.

Loudness level L_s

The loudness level is a comparative measure of the intensity of sound perception measured in phon. The loudness level of a sound (pure tone or noise) is the sound pressure level of a standard pure tone which, under standard listening conditions, is judged by a normal observer to be equally loud. The standard pure tone is a plane sound wave with a frequency of 1000 Hz impinging on the observer's head from the front. A difference of 8 to 10 phon is perceived as twice or half as loud.

Phon

The standard pure tone judged as being equally loud has a specific sound pressure level in dB. This value is given as the loudness level of the tested sound, and has the designation "phon". Because human perception of sound is frequency-dependent, the dB values of the tested sound for notes, for example, do not agree with the dB values of the standard pure tone (exception: reference frequency 1000 Hz), however the phon figures do agree. See the graph below for curves of equal loudness level according to Fletcher-Munson.

Loudness S in sone

The sone is the unit employed to define subjective noise levels. The starting point for defining the sone is: How much higher or lower is the perceived level of a particular sound relative to a specific standard.

Definition: sound level $L_s = 40$ phon corresponds to loudness $S = 1$ sone. Doubling or halving the loudness is equivalent to a variation in the loudness level of approx. 10 phon.

There is an ISO standard for calculating stationary sound using tertiary levels (Zwicker method). This procedure takes into account both frequency weighting and the screening effects of hearing.

Pitch, sharpness

The spectrum of perceptible sound can be divided into 24 hearing-oriented frequency groups (bark). The groups define perceived pitch levels. The loudness/pitch distribution (analogous to the tertiary spectrum) can be used to quantify other subjective aural impressions, such as the sharpness of a noise.

Technical acoustics

Measuring equipment for acoustics
- Sound-pressure recording with capacitor microphones, e.g. using sound-level meters in dB(A).
- Artificial-head recordings with ear microphones for faithful sound reproduction (with headphones).

– Measuring rooms for standard sound measurements are generally equipped with highly sound-absorbent walls.
– Vibrations, structure-borne sound: acceleration sensor (mass partly under 1 g), e.g. according to piezoelectric principle; laser vibrometer for rapid non-contact measurement according to Doppler principle.

Calculating methods in acoustics

Vibration/oscillation: FE modeling and natural-oscillation calculation, adjustment with experimental modal analysis. Modeling of forces acting during operation enables calculation of operational vibration shapes. Thus optimization of design with regard to vibrational behavior.

Air-borne noise, fluid-borne noise: Sound-field calculation e.g. of cabinet radiation or in cavities using FEM (finite-element method) or BEM (boundary-element method).

Acoustic quality control

This is the evaluation, predominantly by human testers, of noise and interference levels and the classification of operating defects based on audible sound or structure-borne noise as part of the production process, e.g. in the run-up of electric motors. Automated test devices are used for specialized applications, but they are at present still unable to achieve human levels of flexibility, selectivity and learning ability. Advances have been made through the use of neural networks and combined evaluation of sound properties.

Noise design

Specific configuration of operating noises by means of design measures; subjective aural impressions and psychoacoustics are taken into consideration. The objective is not primarily to reduce noise but rather to achieve a general sound quality, to embody specific features (e.g. sporty exhaust sound by way of rough sounds) or company-specific noises (e.g. a particular door-closing noise in passenger cars, "corporate sound").

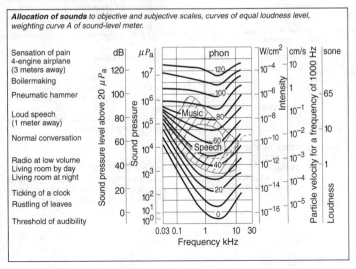

Allocation of sounds to objective and subjective scales, curves of equal loudness level, weighting curve A of sound-level meter.

Heat

Symbols and units

See PP. 12 ... 18 for names of units, P. 26 for conversion of heat units and P. 180 for thermal expansion, heat of fusion, heat of evaporation.

Quantity		SI unit
A	Area, cross-section	m^2
c	Specific heat capacity	J/(kg · K)
	c_p Isobaric (constant pressure)	
	c_v Isochoric (constant volume)	
H	Enthalpy (heat content)	J
k	Heat transmission coefficient	W/(m^2 · K)
m	Mass	kg
p	Pressure	Pa = N/m^2
Q	Heat	J
$\dot{Q}$	Heat flow = Q/z	W
R_m	Molar gas constant	J/(mol · K)
	= 8.3145 J/(mol · K)	
	(same for all gases)	
R_i	Special gas constant	J/(kg · K)
	$R_i = R_m/M$ (M = molecular	
	weight)	
S	Entropy	J/K
s	Distance	m
T	Thermodynamic temperature	K
	$T = t + 273.15$	
ΔT	Temperature difference	K
	$= T_1 - T_2 = t_1 - t_2$	
	T_1, t_1 higher temperature	
	T_2, t_2 lower temperature	
t	Celsius temperature	°C
V	Volume	m^3
v	Specific volume	m^3/kg
W	Work	J
z	Time	s
α	Heat transfer coefficient	W/(m^2 · K)
	α_a external, α_i internal	
ε	Emissivity	–
λ	Thermal conductivity	W/(m · K)
	(see P. 17 for values)	
ϱ	Density	kg/m^3

Conversion from outdated units
(see also PP. 16 and 17)
1 kcal (kilocalorie) = 4186.8 J
$\approx$ 4200 J $\approx$ 4.2 kJ
1 kcal/(m · h · grd) = 1.163 W/(m · K)

Enthalpy (heat content)

$$H = m \cdot c \cdot T$$

Enthalpy difference (ΔH) is the quantity of heat released (Q) as a result of a change in temperature ($\Delta T = T_1 - T_2$)

$$\Delta H = H_1 - H_2 = Q$$
$$= m \cdot c \cdot \Delta T = V \cdot \varrho \cdot c \cdot \Delta T$$

Heat transfer

Heat is transferred in three different ways:
Thermal conduction: Heat is conveyed inside a solid, liquid or gaseous body by contact between the particles.
Convection: Heat is conveyed by the particles of a moving liquid or gaseous body. In natural or free convection, the state of motion is brought about by the effect of buoyancy; in forced convection, however, the motion is maintained artificially.
Radiation: Heat is transferred from one body to another by electromagnetic waves without a material carrier.

Thermal conduction

The heat flow in a body of constant cross section A between two parallel cross-sectional planes separated by a distance s at a temperature difference ΔT is

$$Q = \frac{\lambda}{s} \, A \cdot \Delta T$$

Thermal radiation

Empty space and air are pervious to thermal radiation. Solid bodies and most liquids are impervious to thermal radiation, as are various gases to certain wavelengths.

The thermal radiation emitted by the area A at temperature T is

$$Q = \varepsilon \cdot \sigma \cdot A \cdot T^4$$

where $\sigma = 5.67 \cdot 10^{-8}$ W/(m^2 · K^4) is the radiation constant of the black-body radiator[1] and ε is the emissivity of the surface area (see table on opposite page).

Emissivity ε
up to a temperature of 300 °C (573 K)

Black-body radiator[1]	1.00
Aluminum, unmachined	0.07
Aluminum, polished	0.04
Ice	0.90
Enamel paint, white	0.91
Glass	0.93
Cast iron, rough, oxidized	0.94
Cast iron, turned	0.44
Wood, smooth	0.90
Lime mortar, rough, white	0.93
Copper, oxidized	0.64
Copper, polished	0.05
Brass, matt	0.22
Brass, polished	0.05
Nickel, polished	0.07
Oil	0.82
Paper	0.80
Porcelain, glazed	0.92
Soot	0.93
Silver, polished	0.02
Steel, matt, oxidized	0.96
Steel, polished, oil-free	0.06
Steel, polished, oiled	0.40
Water	0.92
Bricks	0.93
Zinc, matt	0.23
Zinc, polished	0.05
Tin, polished	0.06

Transmission of heat through a wall
The heat flow through a wall of area A and thickness s at a temperature difference ΔT is:

$$\dot{Q} = k \cdot A \cdot \Delta T$$

The heat transmission coefficient k is calculated as follows:

$$1/k = 1/\alpha_i + s/\lambda + 1/\alpha_a$$

Thermal resistance
Thermal resistance is composed of the thermal resistance of the individual layers of the wall:

$$s/\lambda = s_1/\lambda_1 + s_2/\lambda_2 + ...$$

See P. 186 for the thermal conductivity λ of various materials.

Heat transfer coefficients α
(convection + radiation)

Type of material, wall surface etc.	α_i or α_a W/($m^2 \cdot$ K)
Natural air movement in a closed room:	
Wall surfaces, interior windows	8
Exterior windows	11
Floors, ceilings:	
from bottom upwards	8
from top downwards	6
Forced air movement on a flat wall	
Mean wind velocity $w = 2$ m/s	15
Mean wind velocity $w > 5$ m/s	$6.4 \cdot w^{0.75}$
Water on a flat wall	
Still	500 ... 2000
Moving	2000 ... 4000
Boiling	2000 ... 6000

Thermal resistance of air layers s/λ
(conduction + convection + radiation)

Position of air layer	Thickness of air layer mm	Thermal resistance s/λ $m^2 \cdot$ K/W
Vertical air layer	10	0.14
	20	0.16
	50	0.18
	100	0.17
	150	0.16
Horizontal air layer Heat flow from bottom upwards	10	0.14
	20	0.15
	50	0.16
Horizontal air layer Heat flow from top downwards	10	0.15
	20	0.18
	50	0.21

[1] A "black-body radiator" completely absorbs all incident light and heat radiation directed against it; and therefore when heated radiates the maximum amount of light which can be emitted by a body. An example of a black-body radiator is the opening in a carbon tube.

Heat required to heat dwellings
50 to 60 W is required to heat each m^2 of living area.

Technical temperature measurement

(VDE/VDI Guideline 3511)

Measurement system	Measurement range	Method of operation	Examples of application
Liquid-in-glass thermometers	–200 ... 1000 °C	Thermal expansion of the liquid is visible in a narrow glass tube. Liquid: Pentane (–200 ... 30 °C). Alcohol (–100 ... 210 °C), Toluene (–90 ... 100 °C), Mercury (–38 ... 600 °C), Gallium (...1000 °C).	For liquids and gases, for monitoring steam, heating and drying systems; refrigeration equipment; media flowing through pipes.
Pressure-spring thermometers	–50 ... 500 °C	Due to its expansion pressure (mercury, toluene) or vapor pressure (ether, hexane, toluene, xylene), a liquid in an immersion vessel actuates a pointer or a recording instrument via a Bourdon tube.	For monitoring and recording temperatures (including remote applications up to 35 m) in power plants, factories, heating plants, cold rooms.
Solid expansion thermometers	0 ... 1000 °C	Different thermal expansion of two metals (rod in tube).	Temperature regulators.
Bimetallic thermometers	–50 ... 400 °C	Curvature of a strip consisting of two different metals.	Temperature regulators.
Resistance thermometers	–220 ... 850 °C	Change in resistance caused by change in temperature Platinum wires –220 ... 850 °C, Nickel wires –60 ... 250 °C, Copper wires –50 ... 150 °C, Semiconductors –40 ... 180 °C,	Temperature measurements on machines, windings, refrigeration equipment. Remote transmission possible.
Thermistors	0 ... 500 °C (2200°)	Sharp drop in electrical resistance as the temperature increases.	Measurement of minor temperature differences due to high sensitivity.
Thermocouples	–200 ... 1800 °C	Thermoelectromotive force of two metals whose junctions are at different temperatures.	Temperature measurements on and in machines, engines, etc. Remote transmission possible.
Radiation thermometers (pyrometer, infrared camera, high-speed pyrometer)	–100 ... 3500 °C	The radiation emitted by a body is an indicator of its temperature. It is sensed by using either thermocouples or photocells, or by comparing luminance values. Emissions level must be observed.	Melting and annealing furnaces. Surface temperatures. Moving objects, thermogravimetry, extremely rapid response.
Temperature-sensitive paints, temperature-indicating crayons	40 ... 1350 °C	Color changes when specific temperatures are exceeded. Paints and crayons are available with one or more color changes (up to 4). The new color remains after cooling.	Temperature measurements on rotating parts, in inaccessible places, in machining processes; warning of excessive temperature; material testing (cracks).
Suction thermometers, pyrometers	1800 ... 2800 °C	Gas is extracted from the flame.	Measurement of flame temperature (delayed display).

Other temperature-measurement methods: spectroscopy, interferometry, quartz thermometry, noise thermometry, liquid crystals, acoustic and magnetic thermometers.

Thermodynamics

First law of thermodynamics:
Energy can be neither created nor destroyed. Only the form in which energy exists can be changed, e.g., heat can be transformed into mechanical energy.

Second law of thermodynamics:
Heat cannot be completely converted to another form of energy, e.g., mechanical work. All natural and synthetic energy transformation processes are irreversible and occur in a preferred direction (according to the probable state). On its own, heat passes only from warmer to colder bodies, the reverse is possible only if energy is supplied.

Entropy S is a measure of the thermal energy in a system which is no longer capable of performing work. That proportion of energy available for work is referred to as exergy.

For reversible processes, the sum of the entropy changes is equal to zero.

The greatest efficiency in the conversion of heat to mechanical work is achieved in a reversible process. The following then applies for thermal efficiency:
$\eta_{th} = (Q_1 - Q_2)/Q_1 = (T_1 - T_2)/T_1$
(Carnot cycle)

The maximum work to be gained here is:
$W = Q_1 (T_1 - T_2)/T_1$

Changes of state for gases
(general equation of state: $p \cdot v = R_i \cdot T$)

Change of state	Characteristics	Specific heat capacity[1]	Equations (k, K are constants)[1]	Examples
Isobaric	Constant pressure	c_p	$p = k$ $v = K \cdot T$	"Constant pressure" combustion in diesel engines; heating or cooling in once-through boilers.
Isochoric	Constant volume	c_v	$v = k$ $p = K \cdot T$	"Constant volume" combustion in spark-ignition engines; heating or cooling in closed boilers.
Isothermal	Constant temperature	–	$T = k$ $p \cdot v = K$	Slow change of state (heat flows through partitions).
Adiabatic	Heat neither supplied nor dissipated	–	$P \cdot v^\varkappa = k$ $T \cdot v^{\varkappa-1} = k$	Compression or expansion stroke without cooling losses (the ideal condition which is virtually achieved in high-speed machines).
Isentropic	Adiabatic and friction-free (reversible)	–	$T^\varkappa \cdot p^{1-\varkappa} = k$	Theoretically optimum attainable comparison processes.
Polytropic	General change of state	$c = \dfrac{c_v (n - \varkappa)}{n - 1}$	$P \cdot v^n = K$ $T \cdot v^{n-1} = K$ $T^n \cdot p^{1-n} = K$	Compression and power strokes in internal-combustion engines, steam engines ($n = 1.2 \dots 1.4$).

[1] c_p, c_v and $\varkappa = c_p/c_v$ see P. 192, $n = \dfrac{\lg p_2 - \lg p_1}{\lg v_1 - \lg v_2}$

Electrical engineering

Quantities and units

Quantity		SI unit
A	Area	m^2
a	Distance	m
B	Magnetic flux density, induction	$T = Wb/m^2 = V \cdot s/m^2$
C	Capacitance	$F = C/V$
D	Electrical flux density, displacement	C/m^2
E	Electric field strength	V/m
F	Force	N
f	Frequency	Hz
G	Conductance	$S = 1/\Omega$
H	Magnetic field strength	A/m
I	Current	A
J	Magnetic polarization	T
k	Electrochemical equivalent[1]	kg/C
L	Inductance	$H = Wb/A = V \cdot s/A$
l	Length	m
M	Electric polarization	C/m^2
P	Power	$W = V \cdot A$
P_s	Apparent power[2]	$V \cdot A$
P_q	Reactive power[3]	var
Q	Quantity of electricity, electric charge	$C = A \cdot s$
q	Cross-sectional area	m^2
R	Electrical resistance	$\Omega = V/A$
t	Time	s
r	Radius	m
U	Voltage	V
V	Magnetic potential	A
W	Work, energy	$J = W \cdot s$
w	Number of turns in winding	$-$
X	Reactance	Ω
Z	Impedance	Ω
ε	Dielectric constant	$F/m = C/(V \cdot m)$
ε_0	Electric field constant $= 8.854 \cdot 10^{-12}$ F/m	
ε_r	Relative permittivity	$-$
Θ	Current linkage	A
μ	Permeability	$H/m = V \cdot s/(A \cdot m)$
μ_0	Magnetic field constant $= 1.257 \cdot 10^{-6}$ H/m	
μ_r	Relative permeability	$-$
ϱ	Resistivity[4]	$\Omega \cdot m$
σ	Specific conductance $(= 1/\varrho)$	$1/(\Omega \cdot m)$
Φ	Magnetic flux	$Wb = V \cdot s$
φ	Phase displacement angle	$°$ (degrees)
φ	(P) Potential at point P	V
ω	Angular frequency $(= 2 \cdot \pi \cdot f)$	Hz

Additional symbols and units are given in the text.

Conversion of obsolete units (see P. 17):
- Magnetic field strength H:
  1 Oe (oersted) = 79.577 A/m
- Magnetic flux density B:
  1 G (gauss) = 10^{-4} T
- Magnetic flux Φ
  1 M (maxwell) = 10^{-8} Wb

Electromagnetic fields

Electrical engineering deals with electromagnetic fields and their effects. These fields are produced by electric charges which are integral multiples of the elementary charge. Static charges produce an electric field, whereas moving charges give rise to a magnetic field as well. The relationship between these two fields is described by Maxwell's equations. The presence of these fields is evidenced by the effects of their forces on other electric charges. The force between two point charges Q_1 and Q_2 is defined by Coulomb's Law:

$$F = Q_1 \cdot Q_2/(4\pi \cdot \varepsilon_0 \cdot a^2)$$

The force acting on a moving charge in a magnetic field is expressed by the Lorentz force equation:

$$F = Q \cdot v \cdot B \cdot \sin\alpha$$

ε_0 = Electric constant, Q_1 and Q_2 = Charges, a = Distance between Q_1 and Q_2, v = Velocity of charge Q, B = Magnetic induction, α = Angle between direction of motion and magnetic field.

---

[1] The unit in common use is g/C.
[2] Apparent power is usually given in V · A rather than in W.
[3] Reactive power is usually given in var (volt-ampere reactive) rather than in W.
[4] The unit in common use is $\Omega mm^2/m$, with the wire cross-section in mm^2 and wire length in m; conversion: 1 $\Omega mm^2/m = 10^{-6}$ Ωm = 1 $\mu\Omega m$.

Electric field

An electric field can be defined by the following quantities:

Electric potential φ (P) and voltage U
The electric potential φ (P) at point P is a measure of the work required per charge to move the charge Q from a reference point to point P:
$$\varphi \text{ (P)} = W \text{ (P)}/Q$$
The voltage U is the potential difference (using the same reference point) between two points P_1 and P_2:
$$U = \varphi \text{ (P}_2) - \varphi \text{ (P}_1)$$

Electric field strength E
The electric field strength at point P depends on the location P and its surrounding charges. It defines the maximum slope of the potential gradient at point P. The following equation applies to the field strength at a distance a from a point charge Q:
$$E = Q/(4\pi \cdot \varepsilon_0 \cdot a^2)$$
The following force acts on a charge Q at point P:
$$F = Q \cdot E$$

Electric field and matter
Electric polarization M and dielectric displacement density D

In a material which can be polarized (dielectric), an electric field generates electric dipoles (positive and negative charges at a distance a; $Q \cdot a$ is called the dipole moment). The dipole moment per unit volume is called the polarization M.

The dielectric displacement density D indicates the density of the electric displacement flux, and is defined as follows:
$$D = \varepsilon \cdot E = \varepsilon_r \cdot \varepsilon_0 \cdot E = \varepsilon_0 \cdot E + M$$
where

ε: Dielectric constant of the material,
    $\varepsilon = \varepsilon_r \cdot \varepsilon_0$

ε_0:   Electric field constant (dielectric constant of vacuum)

ε_r: Relative permittivity (relative dielectric constant) $\varepsilon_r = 1$ for air, see PP. 217, 218 for other materials.

Capacitor
Two electrodes separated by a dielectric form a capacitor. When a voltage is applied to the capacitor, the two electrodes receive equal but opposite charges. The following equation holds for the received charge Q:
$$Q = C \cdot U$$
C is the <u>capacitance</u> of the capacitor. It is dependent on the geometric shape of the electrodes, the distance by which they are separated and the dielectric constant of the dielectric.

Energy content of charged capacitor:
$$W = Q \cdot U/2 = Q^2/(2 \, C) = C \cdot U^2/2$$
The force of attraction between two parallel plates (surface area A) at a distance a is:
$$F = E \cdot D \cdot A/2 = \varepsilon_r \cdot \varepsilon_0 \cdot U^2 \cdot A/(2 \, a^2)$$

Capacitance C of some conductor arrangements in F

Plate capacitor with n parallel plates	$C = (n-1) \; \dfrac{\varepsilon_r \cdot \varepsilon_0 \cdot A}{a}$	$\varepsilon_r, \varepsilon_0$ n A a	See above Number of plates Surface area of one plate in m^2 Distance between plates in m
Parallel conductors (twin conductors)	$C = \dfrac{\pi \cdot \varepsilon_r \cdot \varepsilon_0 \cdot l}{\ln\left(\dfrac{a-r}{r}\right)}$	l a r	Length of twin conductors in m Distance between conductors in m Conductor radius in m
Concentric conductor (cylindrical capacitor)	$C = \dfrac{2\pi \cdot \varepsilon_r \cdot \varepsilon_0 \cdot l}{\ln (r_2/r_1)}$	l r_2, r_1	Length of conductor in m Conductor radius in m where $r_2 > r_1$
Conductor to ground	$C = \dfrac{2\pi \cdot \varepsilon_r \cdot \varepsilon_0 \cdot l}{\ln (2 \, a/r)}$	l a r	Length of conductor in m Distance from conductor to ground in m Conductor radius in m
Sphere with respect to distant surface	$C = 4\pi \cdot \varepsilon_r \cdot \varepsilon_0 \cdot r$	r	Sphere radius in m

Direct current (DC)

Moving charges give rise to a current I, which is characterized by its intensity and measured in amperes. The direction of flow and magnitude of direct current are independent of time.

Direction of current flow and measurement

Current flowing from positive pole to negative pole outside the current source is designated as positive (in reality, the electrons travel from the negative to the positive pole).

An ammeter (A) in the current path measures current flow; voltage is measured by a voltmeter (V) connected in shunt.

Ohm's Law

Ohm's law defines the relationship between voltage and current in solid and liquid conductors.

$$U = R \cdot I$$

The constant of proportionality R is called ohmic resistance and is measured in ohms (Ω). The reciprocal of resistance is called conductance G

$$G = 1/R$$

Ohmic resistance[1]

Ohmic resistance depends upon the material and its dimensions.

Round wire $R = \varrho \cdot l/q = l/(q \cdot \sigma)$

Hollow conductor $R = \ln (r_2/r_1)/(2\pi \cdot l \cdot \sigma)$

ϱ Resistivity in $\Omega mm^2/m$
$\sigma = 1/\varrho$ Conductivity
l Wire length in m
q Wire cross section in mm^2

r_2 and r_1 Wire radii where $r_2 > r_1$

In the case of metals, resistance increases with temperature:

$$R_\vartheta = R_{20} [1 + \alpha (\vartheta - 20\,°C)]$$

R_ϑ Resistance at $\vartheta\,°C$
R_{20} Resistance at 20 °C
α Temperature coefficient[2] in 1/K (= 1/°C)
ϑ Temperature in °C

Near absolute zero (–273 °C) the resistance of many metals approaches zero (superconductivity).

Work and power

In a resistor through which current passes, the following holds for the work produced or for the quantity of heat developed:

$$W = U \cdot I \cdot t = R \cdot I^2 \cdot t$$

and thus for the power:

$$P = U \cdot I = R \cdot I^2$$

Kirchhoff's Laws

First Law

The current flowing to each junction in a circuit is equal to the current flowing away from that point.

Second Law

The algebraic sum of the voltage drops in any closed path in a circuit is equal to the algebraic sum of the electromotive forces in that path.

Current and voltage measurement
R Load, A Ammeter in circuit, V Shunt-connected voltmeter.

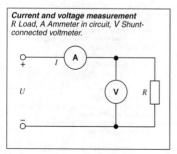

---

[1] See P. 215 for table of ϱ values.
[2] See P. 215 for table of α values.

Direct-current circuits

Circuit with load
$$U = (R_a + R_l) \cdot I$$
R_a = Load
R_l = Line resistance

Battery-charging circuit
$$U - U_0 = (R_v + R_l) \cdot I$$

U Line voltage, U_0 Open-circuit voltage[1]) of battery, R_v Series resistance, R_i Internal resistance of battery.
Condition for charging: charging voltage > battery open-circuit voltage.

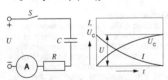

Charging and discharging a capacitor
The time constant $\tau = R \cdot C$ is the decisive factor in the charging and discharging of a capacitor.

Charging
$$I = U/R \cdot \exp(-t/\tau)$$
$$U_C = U [1 - \exp(-t/\tau)]$$

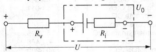

Circuit diagram, voltage and current curves

Discharging
$$I = I_0 \cdot \exp(-t/\tau)$$
$$U_C = U_0 \cdot \exp(-t/\tau)$$
U Charging voltage, I Charging current, U_C Capacitor voltage, I_0 Initial current, U_0 Voltage at start of discharge.

[1]) Formerly called emf (electromotive force).

Series connection of resistors
$$R_{total} = R_1 + R_2 + ...$$
$$U = U_1 + U_2 + ...$$
The current is the same in all resistors.

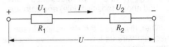

Parallel connection of resistors
$$1/R_{total} = 1/R_1 + 1/R_2 \text{ or}$$
$$G = G_1 + G_2$$
$$I = I_1 + I_2 ; I_1/I_2 = R_2/R_1$$
The voltage is the same across all resistors (Kirchhoff's second law).

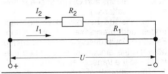

Measurement of a resistance
A resistance can be measured by measuring current and voltage, by using a direct-reading ohmmeter or a bridge circuit, e.g., Wheatstone bridge. If sliding contact D is set so that Wheatstone bridge galvanometer A reads zero, the following equations apply:
$$I_1 \cdot R_x = I_2 \cdot \varrho \cdot a/q$$
$$I_1 \cdot R = I_2 \cdot \varrho \cdot b/q$$
thus: $R_x = R \cdot a/b$

Wheatstone bridge circuit
R_x Unknown resistance, R Known resistance, AB Homogeneous measuring wire (resistivity ϱ) with same cross-section q at every point, A Galvanometer, D Sliding contact.

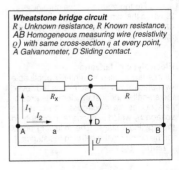

Electrolytic conduction

Substances whose solutions or melts (salts, acids, bases) conduct current are called <u>electrolytes</u>. In contrast to conduction in metals, electrolytic conduction involves chemical decomposition at the electrodes. This decomposition is called <u>electrolysis</u> and the electrodes are termed anode (positive pole) and cathode (negative pole).

When dissolved, the electrolyte dissociates into various ions which move freely. When voltage is applied, the positive ions (cations) migrate toward the cathode and the negative ions (anions) migrate toward the anode. Cations are e.g. all metal ions but also include ammonia ions (NH_4^+) and hydrogen ions (H^+). Anions comprise the ions of the non-metals, oxygen, halogens, acid radical ions and OH ions (see P. 869 for use in batteries).

The ions are neutralized at the electrodes and precipitate out of solution. Faraday's laws describe the relationship between the amount of precipitated material and the transported charge:

1. The amount of precipitate is proportional to the current and time

$$m = k \cdot I \cdot t$$

m Mass in g, I Current in A, t Time in s, k Electrochemical equivalent in g/C. The electrochemical equivalent k indicates how many g of ions are precipitated by 1 coulomb:

$$k = A/(F \cdot w) = 1.036 \cdot 10^{-5} \, A/w$$

A Atomic weight, see P. 176, w Valence (see table), F Faraday constant with the value $F = 96485$ C/g equivalent. The g equivalent is the mass in g which corresponds to the equivalent weight A/w.

2. When the same quantity of electricity is passed through different electrolytes, the masses of the precipitates are proportional to their equivalent weights.

Electrolytic polarization

Ohm's law is also essentially applicable with electrolysis. In electrolysis, however, the so-called inconstant elements precipitate out at the electrodes and create a voltage U_z which is opposite in polarity to the applied voltage. The following holds for the current in the cell with resistance R:

$$I = (U - U_z)/R$$

Electrochemical equivalent k

Substance	Valence w	Electrochemical equivalent k 10^{-3} g/C
Cations		
Aluminum Al	3	0.0932
Lead Pb	2	1.0735
Chromium Cr	3	0.1796
Cadmium Cd	2	0.5824
Copper Cu	1	0.6588
	2	0.3294
Sodium Na	1	0.2384
Nickel Ni	2	0.3041
	3	0.2027
Silver Ag	1	1.1180
Hydrogen H	1	0.01044
Zinc Zn	2	0.3387
Anions		
Chlorine Cl	1	0.3675
Oxygen O	2	0.0829
Hydroxyl OH	1	0.1763
Chlorate ClO_3	1	0.8649
Chromate CrO_4	2	0.6011
Carbonate CO_3	2	0.3109
Manganate MnO_4	2	0.6163
Permanganate MnO_4	1	1.2325
Nitrate NO_3	1	0.6426
Phosphate PO_4	3	0.3280
Sulfate SO_4	2	0.4978

The change in the electrodes is called galvanic or electrolytic polarization. It can be largely avoided through the use of oxidizing chemicals (called depolarizers), e.g. manganese dioxide to prevent the formation of H_2.

Galvanic cells

Galvanic cells convert chemical energy to electrical energy. They consist of two different metals in one or two electrolytic solutions. The open-circuit voltage of the cell depends upon the electrode materials and the substance used as the electrolyte.

Examples:

<u>Weston normal cell</u>
Electrodes: $Cd + Hg(-)$ and $Hg_2SO_4 + Hg(+)$
Electrolyte: $CdSO_4$
Voltage: 1.0187 V at 20 °C

Leclanché cell (dry cells)
Electrodes: Zn(–) and C(+)
Depolarizer: MnO_2
Electrolyte: NH_4Cl
Voltage: 1.5 V

Storage battery or battery (see P. 869).

Alternating current (AC)

Alternating current is a current whose magnitude and direction vary periodically (often sinusoidally). Its value lies in the fact that it is well suited to remote energy transmission because it can be stepped up to high voltages by means of transformers.
Standard frequencies for alternating-current power lines:
Africa: 50 Hz; most of Asia: 50 Hz; Australia: 50 Hz; Europe: 50 Hz; North America: 60 Hz; South America: 50/60 Hz.
Railroad power lines: Austria, Germany, Norway, Sweden, Switzerland: $16^2/_3$ Hz; USA: 20 Hz.

Electrolytic (galvanic) mean of sinusoidal alternating current.
This value is the arithmetic mean, i.e.

$I_{galv} = 2\ \hat{i}/\pi = 0.64\ \hat{i}$
$U_{galv} = 2\ \hat{u}/\pi = 0.64\ \hat{u}$

and has the same electrolytic effect as a direct current of this magnitude.
Root-mean-square values of sinusoidal alternating current:

$I\ (= I_{rms}) = \hat{i}/\sqrt{2} = 0.71\ \hat{i}$
$U\ (= U_{rms}) = \hat{u}/\sqrt{2} = 0.71\ \hat{u}$

These equations indicate the magnitude of direct current which will generate the same amount of heat.
There are three kinds of power specified in an alternating-current circuit:

Active power	$P = U \cdot I \cdot \cos\varphi$
Reactive power	$P_q = U \cdot I \cdot \sin\varphi$
Apparent power	$P_s = U \cdot I$

The power factor $\cos\varphi$ indicates what percentage of the apparent power is useful as actual power. The remainder, called reactive power, is useless, and oscillates between the source and the load, and loads the lines.
In order to reduce the necessary size of the lines, the phase displacement angle φ is kept as small as possible, usually by using phase shifters (e.g. capacitors).

Alternating-current circuits

Alternating-current circuit with coils
A coil of inductance L (see P. 73) acts as a resistance of magnitude $R_L = \omega \cdot L$ (inductive resistance). Because it consumes no energy, it is also called reactance. The induced countervoltage U_L (see P. 72 for law of induction) lags the current by 90°, which in turn lags the applied voltage by 90°.

Alternating-current diagram
T Duration of one complete oscillation (period) in s, f Frequency in Hz ($f = 1/T$), $\hat{i}$ Peak value (amplitude) of current, $\hat{u}$ Peak value (amplitude) of voltage, ω Angular frequency in $1/s$ ($\omega = 2\pi \cdot f$), φ Phase displacement angle between current and voltage (phase-displaced means: current and voltage reach their peak values or cross the zero axis at different times).

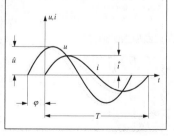

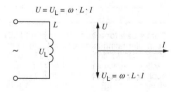

$$U = U_L = \omega \cdot L \cdot I$$

$$U_L = \omega \cdot L \cdot I$$

Inductance of coils connected in series and parallel:

Coils connected in series	Coils connected in parallel
$L_{total} = L_1 + L_2$	$\dfrac{1}{L_{total}} = \dfrac{1}{L_1} + \dfrac{1}{L_2} + \dots$

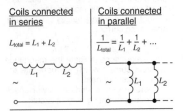

Alternating-current circuit with capacitor

A capacitor of capacitance C acts as a resistance of magnitude $R_C = 1/(\omega \cdot C)$ (capacitive reactance); it also consumes no power (reactance). The countervoltage U_C across the capacitor leads the current by 90°, which in turn leads the applied voltage U by 90°.

$$U = U_C = I/(\omega \cdot C)$$

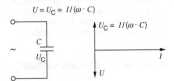

Capacitance of capacitors connected in series and parallel:

Capacitor connected in series	Capacitor connected in parallel
$1/C_{total} = 1/C_1 + 1/C_2$	$C_{total} = C_1 + C_2 + \dots$

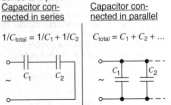

Ohm's Law for alternating current (AC)

In an alternating-current circuit with ohmic resistance (R), coil (inductance L) and capacitor (capacitance C), the same laws apply to the electrical parameters of resistance, voltage and current as in a direct-current circuit.

In calculating the total resistance, the voltage and the current in the circuit, however, phase angle must also be considered, i.e. the vectors of the values must be added together. Vector diagrams are often used for this purpose.

Series connection

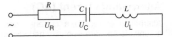

Vector diagrams for determining U, Z and φ

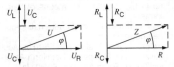

Ohm's law states that $U = Z \cdot I$

Z is termed impedance and is the vector sum of the individual resistances.

$$Z = \sqrt{R^2 + X^2}$$

R Ohmic resistance, X Reactance
$$X = \omega \cdot L - 1/(\omega \cdot C)$$
$\omega \cdot L$ is the inductive and $1/(\omega \cdot C)$ the capacitive component of reactance.

The following equation defines the phase displacement φ between current and voltage:
$$\tan\varphi = [\omega \cdot L - 1/(\omega \cdot C)]/ R$$

The maximum possible current ($I = U/R$) flows when the circuit resonates; the circuit will resonate if:
$$\omega^2 \cdot L \cdot C = 1 \text{ (i.e. } X = 0)$$

Parallel connection

Vector diagrams for determining I, Y and φ

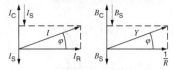

Current is determined by the following equation (Ohm's Law):
$$I = U \cdot Y$$
Y is the complex admittance,
$$Y = \sqrt{G^2 + B^2}$$

$G \, (= 1/R)$ is the conductance
$B \, [= \omega \cdot C - 1/(\omega \cdot L)]$ is the susceptance

The following equation describes the phase displacement between current and voltage:
$$\tan\varphi = R \cdot [\omega \cdot C - 1/(\omega \cdot L)]$$

As in the case of series connection, the circuit will resonate (minimum current flows in the main winding) if:
$$\omega^2 \cdot L \cdot C = 1 \ (\text{i.e. } B = 0)$$

Three-phase current

Three-phase alternating current in which the phases differ by 120° is called three-phase current. Three-phase current is generated by three-phase generators which have three mutually independent windings which are displaced relative to one another by two-thirds of a pole pitch (120°).

The number of conductors carrying voltage is reduced from six to either three or four by linking the component voltages; customary conductor configurations are the star (Y) and delta connections.

Star (Y) connection

$$I = I_p$$
$$U = \sqrt{3} \cdot U_p$$

Delta connection

$$I = \sqrt{3} \cdot I_p$$
$$U = U_p$$

I Line current, I_p Phase current, U Line voltage, U_p Phase voltage.

The transmitted power is independent of the type of connection, and is determined by the following equations:

Apparent power:
$$P_s = \sqrt{3} \cdot U \cdot I = 3 \, U_p \cdot I_p$$

True power:
$$P = P_s \cdot \cos\varphi = \sqrt{3} \cdot U \cdot I \cdot \cos\varphi$$

Star (Y) connection

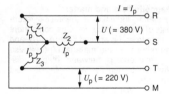

Delta connection

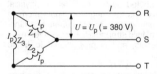

Magnetic field

Magnetic fields are produced by moving electric charges, current-carrying conductors, magnetized bodies or by an alternating electric field.

They can be detected by their effect on moving electric charges (Lorentz force) or magnetic dipoles (like poles repel, and unlike poles attract).

Magnetic fields are characterized by the vector of the <u>magnetic flux density</u> B (induction). This vector can be determined by measuring either force or voltage, because a voltage is induced in a loop of wire by a changing magnetic field (see P. 72 for law of induction):
$$U = \Delta (B \cdot q)/t$$

$\Delta (B \cdot q)$ Change in the product of magnetic induction (in T) and area of the conductor loop (in m²), t Time (in s). The following equations show the relationships between induction B and the other field parameters:

Magnetic flux Φ
$\Phi = B \cdot q$
q = Cross-sectional area in m²

Magnetic field strength H
In a vacuum:
$B = \mu_0 \cdot H$
$\mu_0 = 1.257 \cdot 10^{-6}$ H/m, magnetic field constant.

Magnetic field and matter
In matter, induction B theoretically consists of two components. One component comes from the applied field ($\mu_0 \cdot H$), and the other from the material (J) (see also the relationship between electric displacement density and electric field strength).
$B = \mu_0 H + J$
J is the magnetic polarization and describes that component of flux density contributed by the material. In physical terms, J is the magnetic dipole moment per unit volume, and is generally a function of field strength H. $J \ll \mu_0 \cdot H$ for many materials, and is proportional to H, so that:
$B = \mu_r \cdot \mu_0 \cdot H$
μ_r Relative permeability. In a vacuum, $\mu_r = 1$.

Materials are divided into 3 groups according to their relative permeability values:

Diamagnetic materials ($\mu_r < 1$)
(e.g. Ag, Au, Cd, Cu, Hg, Pb, Zn, water, organic materials, gases)
μ_r is independent of magnetic field strength and smaller than 1; the values are in the range
$(1 - 10^{-11}) > \mu_r > (1 - 10^{-5})$

Paramagnetic materials ($\mu_r > 1$)
(e.g. O_2, Al, Pt, Ti)
μ_r is independent of magnetic field strength and greater than 1; the values are in the range
$(1 + 4 \cdot 10^{-4}) > \mu_r > (1 + 10^{-8})$

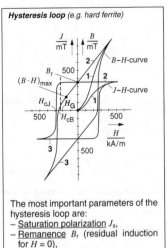

Hysteresis loop (e.g. hard ferrite)

The most important parameters of the hysteresis loop are:
– Saturation polarization J_s,
– Remanence B_r (residual induction for $H = 0$),
– Coercive field strength H_{cB} (demagnetizing field strength where B becomes equal to 0) or
– Coercive field strength H_{cJ} (demagnetizing field strength where J becomes equal to 0; of significance only for permanent magnets),
– Limiting field strength H_G (a permanent magnet remains stable up to this field strength),
– μ_{max} (maximum slope of the rise path; significant only for soft magnetic materials),
– Hysteresis loss (energy loss in the material during one remagnetizing cycle, corresponds to the area of the B–H hysteresis loop; significant only for soft magnetic materials).

Ferromagnetic materials ($\mu_r \gg 1$)
(e.g. Fe, Co, Ni, ferrites)
The magnetic polarization in these materials is very high, and its change as a function of the field strength H is non-linear; it is also dependent on hysteresis. Nevertheless, if, as is usual in electrical engineering, the relationship $B = \mu_r \cdot \mu_0 \cdot H$ is chosen, then μ_r is a function of H and exhibits hysteresis; the values for μ_r are in the range $5 \cdot 10^5 > \mu_r > 10^2$

The hysteresis loop, which illustrates the relationship between B and H as well as J and H, is explained as follows:

If the material is in the unmagnetized state ($B = J = H = 0$) when a magnetic field H is applied, the magnetization of the material follows the rise path (1). From a specific, material-dependent field strength, all magnetic dipoles are aligned and J reaches the value of saturation polarization (material-dependent) which can no longer be increased. If H is now reduced, J decreases along section (2) of the curve and at $H = 0$ intersects the B or J axis at the remanence point B_r or J_r (in which case $B_r = J_r$). The flux density and polarization drop to zero only upon application of an opposing field whose field strength is H_{cB} or H_{cJ}; this field strength is called the coercive field strength. As the field strength is further increased, saturation polarization in the opposite direction is reached. If the field strength is again reduced and the field reversed, curve (3), which is symmetrical to curve section 2, is traversed.

Ferromagnetic materials

Ferromagnetic materials are divided into soft and permanent magnetic materials. The chart on P. 211 shows a comparison of the range of magnetic characteristic values covered by the technically conventional, crystalline materials and the direction in which the materials are developed. What must be emphasized is the immense range of 8 powers of ten covered by the coercive field strength.

Permanent-magnet materials
Permanent-magnet materials have high coercive field strengths; the values lie in the range

$$H_{cJ} > 1 \ \frac{kA}{m}$$

Thus high demagnetizing fields H can occur without the material losing its magnetic polarization. The magnetic state and operating range of a permanent magnet lie in the 2nd quadrant of the hysteresis loop, on the so-called demagnetization curve. In practice, the operating point of a

permanent magnet never coincides with the remanence point because a demagnetizing field is always present due to the intrinsic self-demagnetization of the magnet which shifts the operating point to the left.

The point on the demagnetization curve at which the product $B \cdot H$ reaches its maximum value, $(B \cdot H)_{max}$, is a measure for the maximum attainable air-gap energy. In addition to remanence and coercive field strength, this value is important for characterizing permanent magnets.

AlNiCo, ferrite, FeNdB (REFe), and SeCo magnets are currently the most important types of permanent magnets in terms of technical applications; their demagnetization curves exhibit characteristics typical of the individual magnet types (see P. 209 for characteristics of permanent-magnet materials).

Soft magnetic materials
Soft magnetic materials have a low coercive field strength ($H_C < 1000$ A/m), i.e. a narrow hysteresis loop. The flux density assumes high values (large μ_r values) already for low field strengths such that in customary applications $J \gg \mu_0 \cdot H$, i.e. in practice, no distinction need be made between $B(H)$ and $J(H)$ curves (see P. 203 for characteristics).

Due to their high induction at low field strengths, soft magnetic materials are used as conductors of magnetic flux. Because they exhibit minimal magnetic loss (hysteresis), materials with low coercive field strengths are particularly well-suited for application in alternating magnetic fields.

The characteristics of soft magnetic materials depend essentially upon their pretreatment. Machining increases the coercive field strength, i.e. the hysteresis loop becomes broader. The coercive field strength can be subsequently reduced to its initial value through material-specific annealing at high temperatures (magnetic final annealing). The magnetization curves, i.e. the $B–H$ relationships, are set out below for several important soft magnetic materials.

Remagnetization losses

In the table below, P1 and P1.5 represent the remagnetization losses for inductions of 1 and 1.5 tesla respectively, in a 50 Hz field at 20 °C. These losses are composed of hysteresis losses and eddy-current losses. The eddy-current losses are caused by voltages which are induced (law of induction) in the magnetically soft circuit components as a result of changes in flux during alternating-field magnetization. Eddy-current losses can be kept low by applying the following measures to reduce electric conductivity:
– lamination of the core,
– use of alloyed materials (e.g. silicon iron),
– use of insulated powder particles (powdered cores) in the higher frequency range,
– use of ceramic materials (ferrites).

The magnetic circuit

In addition to material equations, the following equations also determine the design of magnetic circuits:
1. <u>Ampère's law</u> (equation of magnetic voltage).
The following equation holds true for a closed magnetic circuit:

$$\sum_i H_i \cdot l_i = V_1 + V_2 + ... + V_i = I \cdot w \text{ or } 0,$$

depending upon whether or not the circuit includes a power source.

$I \cdot w = \Theta$ ampere-turns,

$H_i \cdot l_i = V_i$ magnetic voltage

($H_i \cdot l_i$ is to be calculated for circuit components in which H_i is constant).
2. <u>Law of continuity</u> (equation of magnetic flux).
The same magnetic flux flows in the indi-

Type of steel sheet	Nominal thickness mm	Specific total loss W/kg P1	P1.5	B (for H = 10 kA/m) T
M 270 – 35 A	0.35	1.1	2.7	1.70
M 330 – 35 A	0.35	1.3	3.3	1.70
M 400 – 50 A	0.5	1.7	4.0	1.71
M 530 – 50 A	0.5	2.3	5.3	1.74
M 800 – 50 A	0.5	3.6	8.1	1.77

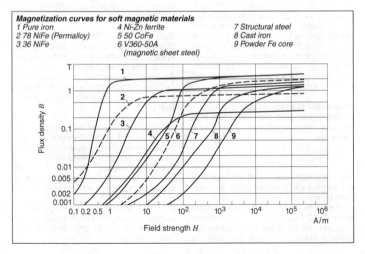

Magnetization curves for soft magnetic materials
1 Pure iron
2 78 NiFe (Permalloy)
3 36 NiFe
4 Ni-Zn ferrite
5 50 CoFe
6 V360-50A (magnetic sheet steel)
7 Structural steel
8 Cast iron
9 Powder Fe core

Demagnetization curves for various permanent-magnet materials

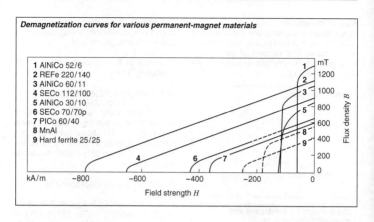

1 AlNiCo 52/6
2 REFe 220/140
3 AlNiCo 60/11
4 SECo 112/100
5 AlNiCo 30/10
6 SECo 70/70p
7 PlCo 60/40
8 MnAl
9 Hard ferrite 25/25

vidual components of the circuit

$\Phi (= B \cdot A)$:
Φ = const or $\Phi_1 = \Phi_2 = ... = \Phi_i$

The quality of a circuit is determined by the amount of flux available in the air gap. This flux is called <u>useful flux</u>; the ratio of useful flux to total flux (flux of the permanent magnet or electromagnet) is called the <u>leakage coefficient</u> σ (practical values for σ are between 0.2 and 0.9). The leakage flux – the difference between the total flux and the useful flux – does not pass through the air gap and does not add to the power of the magnetic circuit.

Magnetic field and electric current

Moving charges generate a magnetic field, i.e. conductors through which current flows are surrounded by a magnetic field. The direction in which the current flows ($\otimes$ current flow into the page, $\odot$ current flow out of the page) and the direction of the magnetic field strength form a right-handed screw. See the table on Page 73 for the magnetic field H of various conductor configurations.

Two parallel conductors through which

current flows in the same direction attract each other; if the current flows in opposite directions, they repel each other. The force acting between two conductors of length l separated by distance a and carrying currents I_1 and I_2 is governed by the equation:

$$F = \frac{\mu_0 \cdot \mu_r \cdot I_1 \cdot I_2 \cdot I}{2\pi \cdot a} \text{ [1]}$$

In air, the approximate force is given by the equation:

$$F \approx 0.2 \cdot 10^{-6} \cdot I_1 \cdot I_2 \cdot l/a \text{ [1]}$$

In a magnetic field B, a force is exerted on a current-carrying conductor (current I) of length l; if the conductor and the magnetic field form an angle of α, the following applies:

$$F = B \cdot I \cdot l \cdot \sin\alpha \text{ [1]}$$

The direction of this force can be determined using the right-hand rule (when the thumb is pointed in the direction of current flow, and the index finger is in the direction of the magnetic field, the middle finger indicates the direction of force).

[1] F Force in N; I_1, I_2 and I Current in A; l and a Length in m; B Inductance in T.

Law of induction

Any change in the magnetic flux Φ around which there is a conducting loop, caused for example by movement of the loop or changes in field strength, induces a voltage U_i in the loop.

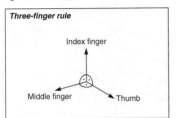

Three-finger rule

Index finger

Middle finger   Thumb

Current-carrying conductors and associated lines of force (H)
a) A single current-carrying conductor with magnetic field. b) Parallel conductors attract each other if current flows in the same direction. c) Parallel conductors repel each other if current flows in opposite directions. d) A magnetic field (B) exerts a force on a current-carrying conductor. The direction in which force is exerted is determined using the three-finger rule.

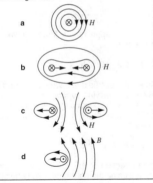

a

b

c

d

Induction. B Magnetic field, C Direction of moving conductor, U_i Induced voltage.

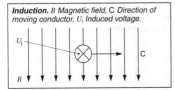

U_i

B   C

A voltage U_i going into the page is induced in a conductor moving in direction C through a magnetic field:

$$U_i = B \cdot l \cdot v$$

U_i in V, B in T, l Conductor length in m, v Velocity in m/s.

In a <u>direct-current machine</u>
$$U_i = p \cdot n \cdot z \cdot \Phi/(60a)$$
U_i in V, Φ Magnetic flux generated by the excitation (field) winding in Wb, p Number of pole pairs, n Rotational speed in min^{-1}, z Number of wires on armature surface, a Half the number of parallel armature-winding paths.

In an <u>alternating-current machine</u>
$$U_i = 2.22 f \cdot z \cdot \Phi$$
U_i in V, Φ Magnetic flux generated by the excitation winding in Wb, f Frequency of alternating current in Hz $= p \cdot n/60$, p Number of pole pairs, n Rotational speed in min^{-1}, z Number of wires on armature surface.

In a <u>transformer</u>
$$U_1 = 4.44 f \cdot w \cdot \Phi$$
U_1 in V, Φ Magnetic flux in Wb, f Frequency in Hz, w Number of windings on the coil which surround the flux Φ.

The terminal voltage U is smaller (generator) or larger (motor) than U_i by the ohmic voltage drop in the winding (approx. 5%). In the case of alternating voltage, U_i is the rms value.

Self-induction

The magnetic field of a current-carrying conductor or a coil changes with the conductor current. A voltage proportional to the change in current is induced in the conductor itself and counteracts the current change producing it:

$$U_s = -L \frac{dI}{dt}$$

The inductance L depends upon the relative permeability μ_r which is constant and practically equal to 1 for most materials with the exception of ferromagnetic materials (see P. 69). In the case of iron-core coils therefore, L is highly dependent upon the operating conditions.

Field strength H of several conductor configurations

Circular conductor	$H = I/(2\,a)$ at center of circle	H Field strength in A/m I Current in A a Radius of circular conductor in m
Long, straight conductor	$H = I/(2\pi \cdot a)$ outside conductor $H = I \cdot a/(2\pi \cdot r^2)$ inside conductor	a Distance from conductor axis in m r Conductor radius in m
Cylindrical coil (solenoid)	$H = I \cdot w/l$	w Number of turns on coil l Length of coil in m

Inductance L of several conductor configurations

Cylindrical coil	$L = \dfrac{1.257\,\mu_r}{10^6} \cdot \dfrac{w^2 \cdot q}{l}$	L Inductance in H μ_r Relative permeability w Number of turns q Coil cross-section in m² l Coil length in m
Twin conductor (in air, $\mu_r = 1$)	$L = \dfrac{4\,l}{10^7} \cdot \ln\,(a/r)$	l Length of conductors in m a Distance between conductors in m r Conductor radius in m
Conductor to ground (in air, $\mu_r = 1$)	$L = \dfrac{2\,l}{10^7} \cdot \ln\,(2a/r)$	l Length of conductor in m a Distance from conductor to ground in m r Conductor radius in m

Energy of the magnetic field

$$W = L \cdot I^2/2$$

Electric effects in metallic conductors

Contact potential between conductors
Contact potential occurs in conductors, and is analogous to the triboelectricity or contact emf in insulators (e.g. glass, hard rubber). If two dissimilar metals (at the same temperature) are joined to make metal-to-metal contact with one another and are then separated, a contact potential is present between them. This is caused by the different work functions of the two metals. The magnitude of contact potential depends upon the element positions in the electrode-potential series. If more than two conductors are so joined, the resulting contact potential is the sum of the individual contact potential values.

Contact potential values

Material pair	Contact potential
Zn/Pb	0.39 V
Pb/Sn	0.06 V
Sn/Fe	0.30 V
Fe/Cu	0.14 V
Cu/Ag	0.08 V
Ag/Pt	0.12 V
Pt/C	0.13 V
Zn/Pb/Sn/Fe	0.75 V
Zn/Fe	0.75 V
Zn/Pb/Sn/Fe/Cu/Ag	0.97 V
Zn/Ag	0.97 V
Sn/Cu	0.44 V
Fe/Ag	0.30 V
Ag/Au	− 0.07 V
Au/Cu	− 0.09 V

Thermoelectricity

A potential difference, the galvanic voltage, forms at the junction of two conductors due to their dissimilar work functions. The sum of all galvanic voltages is zero in a closed conductor loop (in which the temperature is the same at all points). Measurement of these potentials is only possible by indirect means as a function of temperature (thermoelectric effect, Seebeck effect). The thermoelectric potential values are highly dependent upon impurities and material pretreatment. The following equation gives an approximate value for thermoelectric potential in the case of small temperature differences:

$$U_{th} = \Delta T \cdot a + \Delta T^2 \cdot b/2 + \Delta T^3 \cdot c/3$$

where U_{th} Thermoelectric voltage

$\Delta T = T_1 - T_2$ Temperature difference
a, b, c Material constants

The thermoelectric series gives the differential thermoelectromotive forces referred to a reference metal (usually platinum, copper or lead). At the hot junction, current flows from the conductor with the lower differential thermoelectromotive force to that with the higher force. The thermoelectromotive force η of any pair

Thermoelectric series
(referred to platinum)

Material	Thermoelectric voltage 10^{-6} V/°C
Selenium	1003
Tellurium	500
Silicon	448
Germanium	303
Antimony	47 ... 48.6
Nickel chromium	22
Iron	18.7 ... 18.9
Molybdenum	11.6 ... 13.1
Cerium	10.3
Cadmium	8.5 ... 9.2
Steel (V2A)	7.7
Copper	7.2 ... 7.7
Silver	6.7 ... 7.9
Tungsten	6.5 ... 9.0
Iridium	6.5 ... 6.8
Rhodium	6.5
Zinc	6.0 ... 7.9
Manganin	5.7 ... 8.2
Gold	5.6 ... 8.0
Tin	4.1 ... 4.6
Lead	4.0 ... 4.4
Magnesium	4.0 ... 4.3
Aluminum	3.7 ... 4.1
Platinum	±0
Mercury	−0.1
Sodium	−2.1
Potassium	−9.4
Nickel	−19.4 ... −12.0
Cobalt	−19.9 ... −15.2
Constantan	−34.7 ... −30.4
Bismuth ⊥ axis	−52
Bismuth ‖ axis	−77

(thermocouple) equals the difference of the differential thermoelectromotive forces.

The reciprocal of the Seebeck effect is the Peltier effect, in which a temperature difference is created by electrical energy (heat pump).
If current flows through an A-B-A sequence of conductors, one thermojunction absorbs heat while the other produces more heat than can be accounted for by the Joule effect. The amount of heat produced is governed by the equation:

$$\Delta Q = \pi \cdot I \cdot \Delta t$$

π Peltier coefficient,
I Current, Δt Time interval

Thermocouples in common use[1]

Material pair	Temperature
Copper/constantan	up to 600 °C
Iron/constantan	up to 900 °C
Nickel-chromium/constantan	up to 900 °C
Nickel-chromium/nickel	up to 1200 °C
Platinum-rhodium/platinum	up to 1600 °C
Platinum-rhodium/platinum-rhodium	up to 1800 °C
Iridium/iridium-rhodium	up to 2300 °C
Tungsten/tungsten-molybdenum[2]	up to 2600 °C
Tungsten/tantalum[2]	up to 3000 °C

[1] In addition to their use for measuring temperature, thermocouples are used as thermal generators. Efficiencies hitherto achieved: approx. 10 % (application in satellites).
[2] In reducing atmosphere.

Hall effect
B Magnetic field, I_H Hall current, I_V Supply current, U_H Hall voltage, d Thickness of conductor.

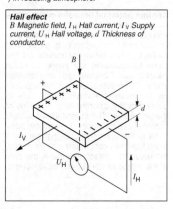

The relationship between Peltier coefficient and thermoelectromotive force η is as follows:

$$\pi = \eta \cdot T$$

where T is temperature

Current flowing through a homogeneous conductor will also generate heat if a temperature gradient $\Delta T/l$ is maintained in the conductor (<u>Thomson effect</u>). Whereas the power developed by the Joule effect is proportional to I^2, the power developed by the Thomson effect is as follows:

$$P = -\sigma \cdot I \cdot \Delta T$$

σ Thomson coefficient, I Current, ΔT Temperature difference

The reciprocal of the Thomson effect is the <u>Benedicks effect</u>, in which an electric potential is produced as a result of asymmetrical temperature distribution (particularly at points where there is a significant change in cross-sectional area).

Galvanomagnetic and thermomagnetic effects

Such effects are understood to be changes caused by a magnetic field in the flow of electricity or heat within a conductor. There are 12 different recognized effects which fall into this category, the most well-known of which are the Hall, Ettingshausen, Righi-Leduc and Nernst effects.

The <u>Hall effect</u> is of particular significance in technical applications (see P. 99 for a discussion of the Hall-effect sensor). If a voltage is applied to a conductor located in a magnetic field perpendicular to the direction of applied voltage, a voltage is produced which is perpendicular to both the flow of current and the magnetic field. This voltage is called the Hall voltage U_H:

$$U_H = R \cdot I_V \cdot B/d$$

R Hall constant, I_V Supply current, B Magnetic field, d Thickness of conductor

The Hall constant can be used to determine particle density and movement of electrons and holes. In ferromagnetic materials the Hall voltage is a function of magnetization (hysteresis).

Gas and plasma discharge

Gas discharge describes the process that occurs when electric current travels through a space containing a gas or vapor atmosphere.

The free charge carriers present in the gas accelerate within the field between the two charged electrodes, producing charge-carrier cascades due to impact ionization. This, in turn, results in the actual current discharge, which ignites with voltages of up to 100 million volts (atmospheric lightning), depending upon the type of gas, the pressure and the gap between electrodes. Self-discharge occurs when the excitation energy from the discharge frees electrons at the cathodes; the current flow is maintained at sharply reduced arc voltages. Glow discharge generally takes place at low gas pressures.

The characteristic radiation of light is determined by the transport and reaction zones produced by field forces and ionic diffusion at low current densities. At higher currents, thermal ionization in the plasma concentrates the current flow, i.e. the discharge contracts.

Thermal electron emission from the cathode results in the transition to arc discharge. The current increases (limited by the external circuit). At temperatures of up to 10^4 K, intense light is then emitted around the electrodes and from the bow-shaped (due to convection) plasma column located between them. The arc voltage drops to just a few volts. The discharge is terminated when voltage drops below the characteristic extinction potential for the specific momentary condition.

Technical applications: Spark-discharge gap as switching element, arc welding, spark ignition for combustion of gases, discharge lamps, high-pressure arc lamps.

Electronics

Fundamentals of semiconductor technology

Electrical conductivity in solid bodies

An individual material's capacity for conducting electricity is determined by the number and mobility of the free charge carriers which it contains. The disparities in the electrical conductivities displayed by various solid bodies at room temperature extend through a range defined by 10 to the 24th power. Accordingly, materials are divided into three electrical classes (examples):

Conductors, metals	Semi-conductors	Non-conductors, insulators
Silver Copper Aluminum	Germanium Silicon Gallium-arsenide	Teflon Quarz glass Aluminum-oxide

Metals, insulators, semiconductors

All solid bodies contain approximately 10^{22} atoms per cm³; these are held together by electrical forces.

In metals the number of free charge carriers is extremely high (one to two free electrons per atom). The free carriers are characterized by moderate mobility and high conductivity. Conductivity of good conductors is 10^6 siemens/cm.

In insulators the number of free charge carriers is practically nil, resulting in negligible electrical conductivity. Conductivity of good insulators is 10^{-18} siemens/cm.

The electrical conductivity of semiconductors lies between that of metals and insulators. The conductivity response of the semiconductor varies from that of metals and insulators in being extremely sensitive to factors such as variations in pressure (affects the mobility of the charge carriers), temperature fluctuations (number and mobility of the charge carriers), variations in illumination intensity (number of charge carriers), and the presence of additives (number and type of charge carriers).

Because they respond to changes in pressure, temperature and light intensity, semiconductors are suitable for application in sensors.

Doping (controlled addition of electrically active foreign substances to the base material) makes it possible to define and localize the semiconductor's electrical conductivity. This procedure forms the basis of present-day semiconductor components. Doping can be used for technically assured production of silicon-based semiconductors with conducting capacities ranging from 10^4 to 10^{-2} siemens/cm.

Electrical conductivity of semiconductors

The following discussion focuses on the silicon-based semiconductor. In its solid state, silicon assumes the form of a crystal lattice with four equidistant contiguous atoms. Each silicon atom has 4 outer electrons, with two shared electrons forming the bond with the contiguous atoms. In this ideal state silicon has no free charge carriers; thus it is not conductive. The situation changes dramatically with the addition of appropriate additives and the application of energy.

N-doping:

Because only 4 electrons are required for bonding in a silicon lattice, the introduction of foreign atoms with 5 outer electrons (e.g. phosphorus) results in the presence of free electrons. Thus each additional phosphorus atom will provide a free, negatively charged electron. The silicon is transformed into an N conductor: N-type silicon.

P-doping:

The introduction of foreign atoms with 3 outer electrons (e.g. boron) produces electron gaps ("holes") which result from the fact that the boron atom has one electron too few for complete bonding in the silicon lattice. This gap in the bonding pattern is also called a hole.

As the latter designation indicates, these holes remain in motion within the silicon; in an electric field, they migrate in a direction opposite to that of the electrons. The holes exhibit the properties of a free positive charge carrier. Thus every additional boron atom provides a free, positively-charged electron gap (positive hole). The silicon is transformed into a P conductor: P-type silicon.

Intrinsic conduction

Heat and light also generate free mobile charge carriers in untreated silicon; the resulting electron-hole pairs produce intrinsic conductivity in the semiconductor material. This conductivity is generally modest in comparison with that achieved through doping. Increases in temperature induce an exponential rise in the number of electron-hole pairs, ultimately obviating the electrical differences between the p and n regions produced by the doping procedure. This phenomenon defines the maximum operating temperatures to which semiconductor components may be subjected:

Germanium   90...100 °C
Silicon   150...200 °C
Gallium arsenide   300...350 °C

A small number of opposite-polarity charge carriers is always present in both n-type and p-type semiconductors. These minority carriers exert a considerable influence on the operating characteristics of virtually all semiconductor devices.

The pn-junction in the semiconductor

The area of transition between a p-type and an n-type zone within <u>the same</u> semiconductor crystal is referred to as the pn-junction. The properties of this area exercise a major influence on the operating properties of most semiconductor components.

pn-junction without external voltage

The p-type zone has numerous holes (○), and the n-type zone has only very few. On the other hand, there are only an extremely limited number of electrons in the p-type zone, while in the n-type zone there are a very large number (●). Each type of mobile charge carrier tends to move across the concentration gradient, diffusing into the opposed zone (diffusion currents).

The loss of holes in the p-type zone results in a negative charge in this area, while electron depletion in the n-type zone produces a positive charge in this region. The result is an electrical potential (diffusion potential) between the p and n-type zones. This potential opposes the re-

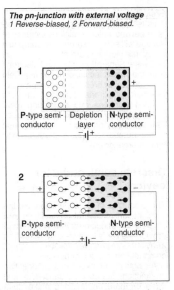

The pn-junction with external voltage
1 Reverse-biased, 2 Forward-biased.

1

P-type semi- | Depletion | N-type semi-
conductor | layer | conductor

2

P-type semi- | N-type semi-
conductor | conductor

spective migration tendencies of the charge carriers, ultimately bringing the exchange of holes and electrons to a halt.

Result: An area deficient in mobile charge carriers is produced at the pn-junction. This area, the space-charge region or depletion layer, is characterized by both severely attenuated electrical conductivity and the presence of a strong electrical field.

pn-junction with external voltage

Reverse state: The negative pole at the p-type zone and the positive pole at the n-type zone extends the space charge region. Consequently, the flow of current is blocked except for a minimal residual current (reverse current) which stems from the minority charge carriers.

Forward state:

With the positive pole at the p-type zone and the negative pole at the n-type zone, the depletion layer is reduced and charge carriers permeate the pn-junction, resulting in a large current flow in the normal direction of conductance.

Breakdown voltage:
This is the level of reverse-direction voltage beyond which a minimal increase in voltage will suffice to produce a sharp rise in reverse blocking current.

Cause: Separation of bonded electrons from the crystal lattice, either by high field strength (Zener breakdown), or due to accelerated electrons colliding with the bonded electrons and separating them from their valence bonds due to impact. This ultimately produces a dramatic rise in the number of charge carriers (avalanche breakdown).

Discrete semiconductor devices

The properties of the pn-junction and the combination of several pn-junctions in a single semiconductor-crystal wafer (chip) provide the basis for a steadily increasing array of inexpensive, reliable, rugged, compact semiconductor devices.

A single pn-junction forms a diode, two pn-junctions are used for transistors, and three or more pn-junctions make up a thyristor. The planar technique makes it possible to combine numerous operating elements on a single chip to form the extremely important component group known as integrated semiconductor circuits. These combine the device and the circuitry in a single unit.

Semiconductor chips measure no more than several square millimeters and are usually installed in standardized housings (metal, ceramic, plastic).

Diodes
The diode is a semiconductor device incorporating a single pn-junction. An individual diode's specific properties are determined by the distribution pattern of the dopant in the crystal. Diodes which conduct currents in excess of 1 A in the forward direction are referred to as power diodes.

Rectifier diode
The rectifier diode acts as a form of current valve; it is therefore ideally suited for rectifying alternating current. The current in the reverse direction (reverse current) can be approximately 10^7 times lower than

the forward current. It rises rapidly in response to increases in temperature.

Rectifiers for high reverse voltages
At least one zone with low conductivity is required for high reverse voltages (high resistance in forward direction results in generation of excessive heat). The insertion of a weakly doped zone (I) between the highly doped p- and n-type zones produces a PIN rectifier. This type of unit is characterized by a combination of high reverse voltage and low forward-flow resistance (conductivity modulation).

Switching diode
These devices are generally employed for rapid switching between high and low impedances. More rapid switching response can be achieved by diffusing gold into the material (promotes the recombination of electrons and holes).

Zener diode
This is a semiconductor diode which, once a specific initial level of reverse voltage is reached, responds to further increases of reverse voltage with a sharp rise in current flow. This phenomenon is a result of a Zener and/or avalanche breakdown. Zener diodes are designed for continuous operation in this breakdown range.

Variable-capacitance diode (varactor)
The space charge region at the pn-junction functions as a capacitor; the dielectric element is represented by the semiconductor material in which no charge carriers are present. Increasing the applied voltage extends the depletion layer and reduces the capacitance, while reducing the voltage increases the capacitance.

Schottky barrier diode (Schottky diode)
A semiconductor diode featuring a metal-to-semiconductor junction. Because the electrons move more freely from the n-type silicon into the metal layer than in the opposite direction, an electron-depleted region is created in the semiconductor material; this is the Schottky barrier layer. Charges are carried exclusively by the electrons, a factor which results in extremely rapid switching, as the minority carriers do not perform any charge storage function.

Photodiode
This is a semiconductor diode designed to exploit the photovoltaic effect. Reverse voltage is present at the pn-junction. Incident light releases electrons from their lattice bonds to produce additional free electrons and holes. These increase the reverse current (photovoltaic current) in direct proportion to the intensity of the light.

Photovoltaic cell
(See Solar cell)

LED (light-emitting diode)
See "Technical optics", P. 143.

Transistors
Two contiguous pn-junctions produce the transistor effect, a feature employed in the design of components used to amplify electrical signals and to assume switching duties.

Bipolar transistors
Bipolar transistors consist of three zones of varying conductivity, the configuration being either pnp or npn. The zones (and their terminals) are called: emitter E, base B and collector C.

There are different transistor classifications, depending on the fields of application: small-signal transistors (power dissipation up to 1 watt), power transistors, switching transistors, low-frequency transistors, high-frequency transistors, microwave transistors, phototransistors etc. They are termed bipolar because charge carriers of both polarities (holes <u>and</u> electrons) are active. In the npn transistor, the base current's <u>positive</u> charge carriers (holes) control their number of 100 times their number in <u>negative</u> charge carriers (electrons) from the emitter to the collector.

Operation of a bipolar transistor
(explanation based on the npn transistor)
The emitter-base junction (EB) is forward biased. This causes electrons to be injected into the base region.

The base-collector junction (BC) is reverse biased. This induces the formation of a space-charge region with a strong electrical field. Significant coupling (transistor effect) occurs if the two pn-junctions

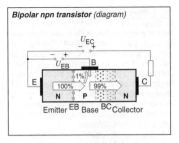

Bipolar npn transistor (diagram)

Emitter EB Base BC Collector

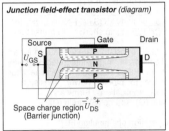

Junction field-effect transistor (diagram)

Space charge region U_{DS}
(Barrier junction)

lie in close proximity to each other (in silicon ≈ 10 μm). The electrons injected at the EB then diffuse through the base to the collector. Upon entering the BC's electrical field, they are accelerated into the collector region, whence they continue to flow in the form of collector current. Thus the concentration gradient in the base is retained, and additional electrons continue to migrate from the emitter to the collector. In standard transistors 99 % or more of all the electrons emanating from the emitter reach the space-charge region and become collector current. The few missing electrons are caught in the electron gaps while traversing the p-doped base. Left to their own devices, these electrons would produce a negative charge in the base; almost immediately (50 ns), repulsive forces would bring the flow of additional electrons to a halt. A small base current comprised of positive charge carriers (holes) provides partial or complete compensation for this negative charge in the transistor. Small variations in the base current produce substantial changes in the emitter-collector current. The npn transistor is a bipolar, current-controlled semiconductor amplifier.

Field-effect transistors (FET)

In these devices, control of the current flow in a conductive path is exercised essentially by an electric field. The field, in turn, is generated with voltage applied at the control electrode, or gate. Field-effect transistors differ from their bipolar counterparts in utilizing only a single type of charge carrier (electrons or holes), giving rise to the alternate designation "unipolar transistor". They are subdivided into the following classifications:
– Junction-gate field-effect transistors (junction FET, JFET).
– Insulated-gate field-effect transistors, particularly MOS field-effect transistors (MOSFET), in short: MOS transistors.

MOS transistors are well suited for application in highly-integrated circuitry. Power FETs represent a genuine alternative to bipolar power transistors in many applications. Terminals:
gate (G), source (S), drain (D).

Operation of a junction FET

(applies to the n-channel FET)
DC voltage is present at the ends of an n-type crystal. Electrons flow from the source to the drain. The width of the channel is defined by two laterally diffused p-type zones and by the negative voltage present within them. Raising the negative gate voltage causes the space-charge regions to extend further into the channel, thereby constricting the current path. Thus the current between source S and drain D is governed by the voltage at the control electrode G. Only charge carriers of one polarity are required for FET operation. The power necessary for controlling the current is virtually nil. Thus the junction FET is a unipolar, voltage-controlled component.

Operation of an MOS transistor

(applies to the p-channel enhancement device)
MOS represents the standard layer configuration: Metal Oxide Semiconductor. If no voltage is applied at the gate electrode, then no current will flow between the source and the drain: the pn-junctions remain in the blocking mode. The application of negative voltage at the gate causes

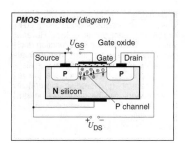

PMOS transistor (diagram)

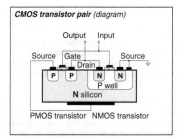

CMOS transistor pair (diagram)

the electrons in the adjacent n-type region to be displaced toward the interior of the crystal, while holes – which are always present in n-type silicon in the form of minority charge carriers – are pulled to the surface. A narrow p-type layer forms beneath the surface: this is called the P channel. Current can now flow between the two p-type regions (source and drain). This current consists exclusively of holes. Because the gate voltage is exercised through an insulating oxide layer, no current flows in the control circuit: no power is required for the control function. In summary, the MOS transistor is a unipolar, voltage-controlled component.

PMOS, NMOS, CMOS transistors

If a p-channel MOS transistor (PMOS transistor) is doped with a donor impurity rather than an acceptor impurity, it becomes an NMOS transistor. Because the electrons in the NMOS transistor are more mobile, it operates more rapidly than the PMOS device, although the latter was the first to become available due to the fact that it is physically easier to manufacture.

It is also possible to employ complementary MOS technology to pair PMOS and NMOS transistors in a single silicon chip; the resulting devices are called Complementary MOS, or CMOS transistors. The specific advantages of the CMOS transistor: extremely low power dissipation, a high degree of immunity to interference, relative insensitivity to varying supply voltages, suitability for analog signal processing and highly-integrated applications.

BCD hybrid technology
Integrated power structures are becoming increasingly important. Such structures are realized by combining bipolar and MOS components on a single silicon chip, thereby utilizing the advantages of both technologies. The BCD hybrid process (Bipolar/CMOS/DMOS) is a significant manufacturing process in automotive electronics and also facilitates the manufacture of MOS power components (DMOS).

Thyristors
Three consecutive pn-junctions provide the thyristor effect, which is applied for components which act as snap switches when triggered by an electrical signal. The term "thyristor" is the generic designation for all devices which can be switched from the forward (conducting) state to the reverse (blocking) state (or vice versa). Applications in power electronics: Control of frequency and min^{-1}; rectification and frequency conversion; switching. In specialized usage, "thyristor" is understood to mean a reverse-blocking triode thyristor.

Four-layer diode
DIN definition: A reverse-blocking diode thyristor. A semiconductor device with two terminals (anode A, cathode K) and switch characteristics. It has four layers of alternating doping. This device's electrical response is best understood by visualizing the four-layer structure as representing two transistor paths T_1 and T_2. Increasing the current between A and K induces a rise in the reverse currents of both transistors. At a specific voltage value of U_{AK} (switching voltage), the reverse current of the one transistor increases to such a degree that it begins to exert a slight bias effect on the other transistor, resulting in conduction. Meanwhile, the second transistor operates in the same fashion. The mutual bias effect exerted by the two transistor units reaches such an intensity that the four-layer diode begins to act as a conductor: this is the thyristor effect.

Thyristor with control terminal
DIN definition: Triode thyristor (also SCR, silicon-controlled rectifier), a controllable device with switching characteristics. It consists of four zones of alternating conductivity type. Like the four-layer diode, it has two stable states (high resistance and low resistance). The switching operations between the respective states are governed via the control terminal (gate) G.

GTO thyristor
DIN definition: Gate turn-off (acronym: GTO) switch activated by positive trigger pulse, with deactivation via a negative trigger pulse at the same gate.

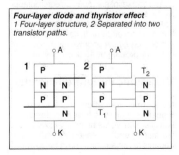

Four-layer diode and thyristor effect
1 Four-layer structure, 2 Separated into two transistor paths.

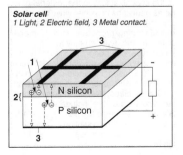

Solar cell
1 Light, 2 Electric field, 3 Metal contact.

Triac
DIN definition: Bidirectional triode thyristor (triac = triode alternating current switch), a controllable thyristor with three terminals. It maintains essentially identical control properties in both of its two switching directions.

Photovoltaic solar cells

The photovoltaic effect is applied to convert light energy directly into electrical energy.

Solar cells, consisting largely of semiconductor materials, are the basic elements of photovoltaic technology. Exposure to light results in the creation of free charge carriers (electron-hole pairs) in the semiconductor material due to the "internal photo-electric effect". If the semiconductor incorporates a pn-junction, then the charge carriers separate in its electric field before proceeding to the metal contacts on the semiconductor's surface. Depending on the semiconductor material being used, a DC voltage (photovoltage) ranging between 0.5 and 1.2 V is created between the contacts. Connection of a load resistor results in a current flow (photocurrent) of e.g. 2.8 A for a 100 cm^2 Si solar cell at 0.58 V.

The efficiency level with which radiated light energy is converted into electrical energy (indicated in percent) depends both upon how well the semiconductor material is suited to the light's spectral distribution, and the efficiency with which the generated free charge carriers can be isolated and conducted to the appropriate surface contacts.

The paths within the semiconductor should be short (thin layers from several μm to 300 μm) to prevent the free charge carriers from recombining. The structure of the crystal lattices in the material must be as perfect as possible, while the material itself must be free of impurities. The manufacturing processes include procedures of the type employed for microelectronics components. Silicon is the most commonly used material for solar cells. It is used in single-crystal, polycrystalline and amorphous modification. Typical efficiency levels achieved under laboratory conditions include:

Silicon	– single crystal	24 %
	– polycrystalline	19 %
	– amorphous	13 %
CdTe		16 %
CuInSe$_2$		18 %
GaAs[1]		28 %
Si/GaAs tandem[1]		37 %.

[1] Concentrated sunlight.

Average efficiency levels obtained from mass-produced solar cells are approximately one third lower. The "tandem cells" achieve their high efficiency by incorporating two solar cells – made of different materials – in consecutive layers; the unit is thus capable of converting light from various spectral ranges into charge carriers.

The individual solar cells are interconnected within a circuit to form solar modules. The output is always DC voltage; an inverter can be used for the conversion to AC (e.g., for discharge into mains electrical supply). The characteristic data of a module are its output voltage and power output in W_P referred to full solar exposure ($\approx$ 1000 W/m^2).

The ultimate objective is to develop inexpensive processes allowing the manufacture of large-area solar cells. Proven procedures include extracting crystals from molten mass, or cutting cast crystals into individual wafers and blocks. Research is now extending into new areas such as strip pulling, foil casting and separation of thin semiconductor layers. Although the energy generated by photovoltaic processes is still more expensive than that provided by convential power stations, improvements in cell manufacturing techniques, increases in efficiency, and large-scale production will combine to allow further reductions in cost. For applications involving isolated systems (consumers without external electrical connections) and minimal power requirements (watches, pocket calculators), photovoltaics already represents the best solution. With a worldwide installed power output of 1 GW$_P$, the photovoltaics market is currently growing by 16 % every year.

Monolithic integrated circuits

Monolithic integration

Planar technology is based on the oxidation of silicon wafers being a relatively simple matter, and the speed with which the dopants penetrate into silicon being exponentially greater than that with which they enter the oxide – doping only occurs at those locations where openings are present in the oxide layer. The specific design requirements of the individual integrated circuit determine the precise geometric configuration, which is applied to the wafer in a photolithographic process. All processing procedures (oxidizing, etching, doping and separation) progress consecutively from the surface plane (planar).

Planar technology makes it possible to manufacture all circuit componentry (resistors, capacitors, diodes, transistors, thyristors) and the associated conductor strips on a single silicon chip in a unified manufacturing process. The semiconductor devices are combined to produce monolithic integrated circuits: IC = Integrated Circuit.

This integration generally comprises a subsystem within the electronic circuit and increasingly comprises the entire system: <u>System on a Chip.</u>

Integration level
Either the number of individual functional elements, the number of transistors, or the number of gates on a single chip. The following classifications relate to the level of integration (and chip surface):
– <u>SSI</u> (Small-Scale Integration).
  Up to roughly 100 function elements per chip, mean chip surface area 3 mm², but can also be very much larger in circuits with high power outputs (e.g. smart power transistors).
– <u>MSI</u> (Medium-Scale Integration).
  Roughly 100 to 1000 function elements

per chip, mean chip surface area 8 mm².
– <u>LSI</u> (Large-Scale Integration).
  Up to 100000 function elements per chip, mean chip surface area 20 mm².
– <u>VLSI</u> (Very-Large-Scale Integration).
  Up to 1 million function elements per chip, mean chip surface area 30 mm².
– <u>ULSI</u> (Ultra-Large-Scale Integration).
  Over 1 million function elements per chip, surface area up to 300 mm², smallest structure sizes 0.25 µm.

Computer-aided simulation and design methods (CAE/CAD) are essential elements in the manufacture of integrated circuits. Entire function blocks are used in VLSI and ULSI as otherwise the time expenditure and failure risk would make development impossible.

Classifications for integrated circuitry
– According to transistor engineering:
  Bipolar, MOS, mixed (bipolar/MOS, BiCMOS, BCD).
– According to circuit engineering:
  Analog, digital, mixed (analog/digital, mixed signal).
– According to component families:
  Analog, microcomponents, memories, logic circuits.
– According to application:
  Standard IC, application-specific IC (ASIC)

Integrated analog circuits
– Basic structures:
  Stabilized-voltage supply, stabilized-current supply, differential amplifier

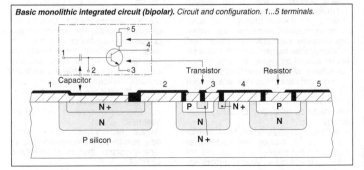

Basic monolithic integrated circuit (bipolar). Circuit and configuration. 1...5 terminals.

components, switching elements, potential shift, output stages.
– Application-oriented classes:
Operational amplifiers (OP), voltage regulators, comparators, timers, converters, interface circuits.
– Special analog ICs:
Voltage references, wideband amplifiers, analog multipliers, function generators, phase-lock circuits, analog filters, analog switches.

Integrated digital circuits
The scale ranges from LSI (logic chips) through to ULSI (memories, microcomponents).
Several conditions must be met before logic chips can be combined within a single system: The voltage supply, logic level, the circuit speed and the signal transit time must all be identical. This requirement is met within the respective circuit families. The most important are:
– Various bipolar types: TTL (Transistor-Transistor-Logic), Schottky TTL, Low-Power Schottky TTL, ECL (Emitter-Coupled Logic) and I^{2}L (Integrated Injection Logic),
– MOS logic, especially CMOS logic.
MOS and CMOS chips make up 97% (and the trend is rising) of the production of integrated digital circuits.

Semiconductor memories
Data storage includes the following operations: Recording (writing, entering), storage (data storage in the narrow sense), retrieval and readout. The memory operates by exploiting physical properties that facilitate unambiguous production and recognition of two opposed states (binary information). In semiconductor memories, the states produced are "conductive/non-conductive" or "charged/discharged"; the latter state relies on special properties in the silicon/silicon oxide or silicon nitride/metal junction.
Semiconductor memories are divided into the two main categories of "volatile" and "non-volatile". Virtually all of them are manufactured according to CMOS technology.
– Volatile memories (short-term memories) can be read out and written over an unlimited number of times, and are thus referred to as RAMs (Random Access Memory). The data which they contain is lost as soon as the power supply is switched off.
– Non-volatile memory chips (long-term memories) retain their data even when the power supply is switched off; they are also referred to as ROMs (Read-Only Memory).

The chart shows the relationships and classification of the most common types of memory.

Microprocessors and microcomputers
The microprocessor represents the integration of a computer's central processing unit on a single chip. Microprocessor design seeks to avoid individualization in the face of large-scale integration, and the units can be programmed to meet the varied requirements associated with specific operating conditions. There are two different main groups of processor:
– For use in PCs (personal computers), CISC processors are used (CISC: Complete Instruction Set Computing). These processors are very versatile and user-programmable.
– In WS (work stations), RISC processors are usually used (RISC: Reduced Instruction Set Computing). These processors are very much faster for the specific tasks frequently associated with WS use, but are significantly slower for all other tasks.

A microprocessor cannot operate by itself: it always acts as part of a microcomputer.
The microcomputer consists of:
– Microprocessor serving as CPU (central processing unit). The microprocessor contains the controller, and the arithmetic and logic unit. The arithmetic and logic unit performs the operations indicated by its name, while the controller ensures implementation of the commands stored in the program memory.
– Input and output units (I/O), which control data communication with the peripherals.
– Program memory which provides permanent storage for the operating program (user program), thus ROM, PROM or EPROM.

Overview of semiconductor memory devices

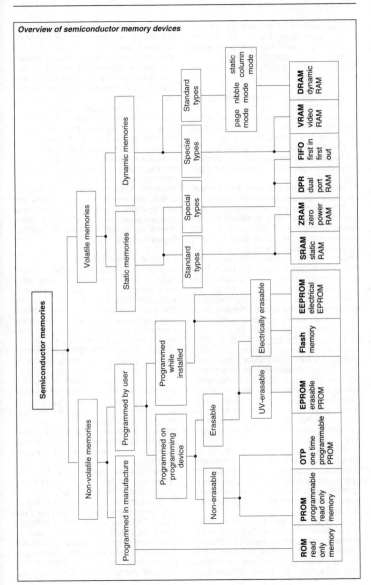

– Data memory for the data being run at any given time. These data change continually; thus the storage medium for this application is the RAM.

– Clock generator and power-supply system.

The <u>bus system</u> links the individual elements of the microcomputer.

A <u>clock generator</u> ensures that all the operations in the microcomputer take place within a specified timeframe.

Chips for special applications, e.g. for interrupting a program, inserting an intermediate program etc., are called <u>logic circuits</u>.

Input and output devices and external memories are classed as <u>peripherals</u>.

The main components of a microcomputer are normally combined as separate components on printed-circuit boards. For simpler tasks, such as e.g. in wireless communications in the case of Internet access, single-chip computers are increasingly being used which integrate the above-mentioned functions on a single silicon chip (system on a chip). The performance of these highly integrated systems is limited by the relatively small amount of RAM which can be accommodated at viable expense on the chip.

The <u>microcontroller</u> combines the CPU function, read-only memory (as ROM, EPROM or EEPROM), input/output capability (I/O) and read/write memory (RAM) on a single chip. In contrast to the microcomputer, the controller reacts with a pre-specified program which provides particular output values depending on the input information. It is used to control self-regulating systems such as e.g. engine management.

The <u>transputer</u> is a special type of microprocessor which is especially useful for building parallel computer networks. In addition to the standard microprocessor components, the chip is also equipped with communications and processing hardware.

It has at least four bidirectional serial transmission channels (links) allowing extremely rapid communication (500 Mbit/s per link) with many other transputers. Because communications are completely asynchronous, distributed networks do not require a common clock circuit. Each link has its own DMA controller; once initialized by the CPU, it can carry out data transmission on its own. Thus processing and communications are essentially parallel operations. Of particular significance are the extremely short process switchover and interrupt response times of $\ll 1$ µs. The transputer does not need a real-time operating system for this; instead it has the necessary processing commands directly in its command set.

The transputer operates as a communications node within the parallel network, meaning that it serves as both computer and communications interface. The transputer can therefore be employed to avoid one of the gravest liabilities of many parallel systems, which is the inherent need to share a common bus. Maximum-performance computers are therefore built using transputers.

Application-specific ICs

Application-specific ICs (ASICs: Application-Specific Integrated Circuits) differ from standard ICs in that they are conceived to fulfill a single purpose. They are the result of fruitful cooperation between users, with their specialized system experience, and manufacturers, who enjoy access to the requisite technology. The essential advantages of ASICs: fewer components, lower system costs, increased reliability, more difficult to copy.

The ASIC family is generally classified according to the development method which has been selected: chip-mounted circuitry, constructed from individual function elements (<u>full-custom IC</u>), provides the best results with regard to operation and packaging density. It is, however, only suited for large-series applications (time and expense).

Standardized basic circuit functions (developed and tested in advance) represent one step towards rationalizing the development process. The circuits are incorporated in elements of varying sizes (ROM, RAM, computer core, or individualized, application-specific circuit groups). Depending upon the number of available user-specific elements, this method can be employed to reduce development times without sacrificing efficient exploitation of the chip surface.

The next stage is the use of standardized, relatively complex basic functions which are developed in advance in standard cells of the same height and variable width. They are available in the form of cell libraries. These standard cells are automatically placed in series and then automatically connected with polysilicon and aluminum conductors. A dual or triple-layer metallic coating can be applied to achieve even better utilization of the surface area.

Gate arrays are predeveloped as far as the transistor/gate connection, and are manufactured in advance, leaving only the final masking operations for later completion. The connection with the application-specific circuitry is then automatic. Rationalization is achieved by providing standard circuits for frequent basic computer functions (similar to a cell library). Special gate arrays designed for specific applications have particular advantages (e.g. pure computer-oriented digital circuits under the general conditions usual for computers).

Programmable logic devices (PLDs) – completely preassembled transistor arrays – are programmed by the user in the same way as a special-application PROM. PLDs thus provide system developers with the option of producing silicon breadboard circuits within a short period of time. The production of complex systems in silicon is becoming increasingly important, as it allows the production of practical working models in the development phase.

Smart-power ICs

Automotive and industrial systems rely upon electronics to govern numerous final-control elements and other loads. The power switches must be capable of assuming auxiliary functions extending beyond the control of circuit power: driver circuits for activating switching transistors, protective circuits for excess current, voltage and temperature, fault acknowledgments in case of incorrect operation. Such bipolar or MOS-technology power ICs are generically termed smart-power ICs.

Film and hybrid circuits, MCM

Film circuits

The integrated film circuit features passive circuit elements – these include capacitors and inductors, as well as conductor tracks, insulators and resistors. An integrated film circuit is produced by applying the layers which contain these elements to a substrate carrier. The terms "thin-film" and "thick-film" circuit derive from the fact that the film thickness was originally the determining factor for tailoring to specific performance characteristics; present technology employs a variety of manufacturing techniques to achieve the same end.

Thin-film circuits

Integrated film circuits on which the individual layers are applied to glass or ceramic substrata, usually in a vacuum coating process. Advantages: fine structures (to approx. 10 µm) provide high circuit-element density, extremely good HF characteristics and low-noise resistor elements. On the minus side are the relatively high manufacturing costs.

Thick-film circuits

Integrated film circuits in which the layers are usually applied to ceramic carriers in a silk-screening process before being fused on. Advantages: Multi-layer construction provides high circuit-element density and good HF characteristics. A high degree of manufacturing automation is possible for large-scale production.

Multilayer ceramic substrates

The base material for the multilayer ceramic substrate is the unfired ceramic foil to which conductor tracks are applied in a silk-screening process. In the next step, a number of these foils are laminated together to form a multilayer substrate. This device is then sintered at high temperature (850 ... 1600 °C) to form a hard ceramic device featuring integrated conductive paths. A metal paste is applied to the orifices between the individual foils to form the interlayer electrical connections. Special materials are employed to

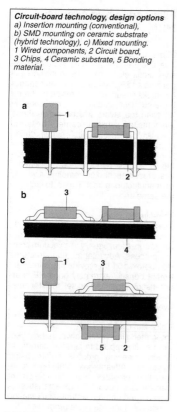

layer ceramic substrate can be used to achieve extremely small hybrid control devices (microhybrids). Advantages: The good thermal dissipation allows high installation temperatures, while compact construction provides good vibration resistance along with good HF response characteristics. Hybrid circuits are especially well-suited for automotive applications and for telecommunications.

MCM

MCM (Multi-Chip Module) is used to identify an electronic component consisting of numerous "unpacked" integrated semiconductors (ICs). The basic element is the carrier substrate with its internal circuits. The ICs are unpacked and contacted by means of bonding or TAB or flip-chip soldering. An MCM can also contain resistors and capacitors as required.

Classification is according to the selected substrate material:
– MCM-C multilayer ceramic substrate,
– MCM-D thin-layer design, generally on silicon,
– MCM-L organic multilayer laminate.
The MCM is generally selected to achieve compliance with specific operating requirements. It combines rapid switching response in processor cores with favorable EMC characteristics and extremely compact packages. The MCM is frequently employed to obtain electrical performance characteristics that would be either prohibitively expensive or downright impossible to obtain from current IC technology.

integrate resistors and capacitors in the device. This process provides for substantially higher levels of circuit density than thick-film devices.

Hybrid circuits

Integrated film circuits with additional discrete components such as capacitors and integrated semiconductor circuits (ICs) which are attached by soldering or adhesive bonding. A high component density is achieved by using unpacked semiconductor chips which are contacted by means of "bonding", or SMD components (SMD Surface Mounted Device). A multi-

Circuit-board technology, SMT

The circuitry of an electronic system can basically be implemented in accordance with semiconductor, hybrid and circuit-board technologies. Selection is contingent upon such factors as economy (cost, production-run sizes), time (development time, service life) and environmental conditions (electrical, thermal, physical).

Circuit boards represent the classical form for producing an electrical circuit. On the most basic type of circuit board, the electronic components are mounted on a

Variable	Unit	Silicon	Steel (max.)	Stainless steel
Tensile load	10^5 N/cm²	7.0	4.2	2.1
Knoop hardness	kg/mm²	850	1500	660
Elastic modulus	10^7 N/cm²	1.9	2.1	2.0
Density	g/cm³	2.3	7.9	7.9
Thermal conductivity	W/cm · K	1.57	0.97	0.33
Thermal expansion	10^{-6}/K	2.3	12.0	17.3

fiberboard or fiberglass-reinforced synthetic-resin carrier. A printing process is employed to apply the conductor tracks (copper foil) to the board (thus: printed circuit). An alternative is to etch the circuit from a copper-plated board. The components' contact pins are inserted through holes in the board and soldered into position.

The increasing IC integration level resulted in a commensurate rapid increase in the number of terminals (pins). This development initiated the transition from conventional insertion-mounting to SMT (<u>S</u>urface <u>M</u>ounting <u>T</u>echnology). In the meantime, there is a very wide range of surface-mountable components (SMD <u>S</u>urface <u>M</u>ount <u>D</u>evices) which are soldered flat to the circuit board. These SMD components and their housing configurations (SOT, PQFP, PLCC, Flat Pack etc.) are particularly suitable for processing in automatic insertion machines.

The most important application advantages provided by surface-mounting technology include:
– Efficient production of subassemblies (high insertion capacity and reliability),
– Low space requirements with the same function capacity even in the case of insertion on both sides,
– Use of normal circuit boards (e.g. laminated epoxy-resin plastic FR4),
– Omission or reduction of holes in each circuit board,
– Can be combined with wired components,
– Increased reliability due to reduction of connection points,
– Improved circuit design, coupling and reproducibility,
– Better HF characteristics.

Surface-mounting technology is much more sensitive to the combination of processing techniques than is conventional insertion mounting. The advantages of SMT are directly proportional to the care with which componentry, circuit-board layout, automatic mounting, joining techniques, testing, repair, etc., are mutually adapted for optimal performance.

Micromechanics

The term "micromechanics" is employed to designate the production of mechanical components using semiconductors (generally silicon) and semiconductor technology. This type of application exploits both the semiconductive and the mechanical properties of silicon. The first micromechanical silicon pressure sensors were installed in motor vehicles at the beginning of the 1980's. Typical mechanical dimensions can extend into the micrometer range.

The mechanical characteristics of silicon (e.g., strength, hardness and Young's modulus, see Table) can be compared to those of steel. However, silicon is lighter and has greater thermal conductivity. Single-crystal Si wafers with almost perfect physical response characteristics are used: Hysteresis and surface diffusion are negligible. Due to the brittleness of the single-crystal material, the stress-strain curve does not display a plastic range; the material ruptures when the elastic range is exceeded.

Two methods of manufacturing micromechanical structures in silicon have established themselves: bulk micromechanics and surface micromechanics.

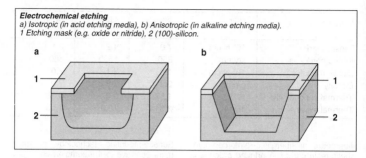

Electrochemical etching
a) Isotropic (in acid etching media), b) Anisotropic (in alkaline etching media).
1 Etching mask (e.g. oxide or nitride), 2 (100)-silicon.

Both methods use the standard procedures of microelectronics (e.g. epitaxial growth, oxidation, diffusion and photolithography) together with some additional special procedures: For the removal of material, bulk micromechanics requires anisotropic etching with or without electrochemical etch stop, while surface micromechanics requires vapor-phase etching and deep trenching. Anodic bonding and seal-glass bonding are used to hermetically join two wafers (capping, inclusion of reference vacuum).

Bulk micromechanics (BMM)
This method involves etching the entire wafer from the reverse side in order to produce the desired structure. The etching process takes place in alkaline media (caustic potash solution), in which the etching behavior of silicon demonstrates

pronounced anisotropy, i.e. the etching rate is greatly dependent on the crystal direction. It is thus possible to represent the structure very accurately in terms of depth. When silicon wafers with (100)-orientation are used, the (111)-surfaces for example remain virtually unaffected. In the case of anisotropic etching, (111)-surfaces therefore develop which form with the (100)-surface a characteristic angle of 54.74°.

In the simplest case, the etching process is stopped after a certain period of time while wafer thickness and etching rate are taken into consideration (time etching). However, for the most part, an electrochemical etch stop is engaged whereby the etching comes to a halt at the boundary of a pn-junction. BMM can be used to produce diaphragms with typical thicknesses of between 5 and 50 μm for

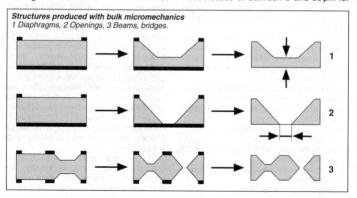

Structures produced with bulk micromechanics
1 Diaphragms, 2 Openings, 3 Beams, bridges.

applications such as pressure sensors and air-mass meters.

Surface micromechanics (SMM)

In contrast to bulk micromechanics, SMM merely uses the silicon wafer as the base material. Moving structures formed from polycrystalline silicon layers which, similar to a manufacturing process for integrated circuits, are deposited on the surface of the silicon by epitaxial growth.

When an SMM component is made, a "sacrificial layer" of silica is first applied and structured with standard semiconductor processes. An approx. 10 μm thick polysilicon layer (epipoly layer) is then applied at high temperatures in an epitaxial reactor. The epipoly obtains the desired structure with the aid of a lacquer mask and anisotropic, i.e. vertical etching (deep trenching). The vertical side walls are obtained by an alternation of etching and passivation cycles. After an etching cycle, the etched side-wall section is provided during passivation with a polymer as protection so that it is not attacked during the subsequent etching. Vertical side walls with a high representation accuracy are created in this way. In the last process stage, the sacrificial oxide layer beneath the polysilicon layer is removed with gaseous hydrogen fluoride in order to expose the structures.

Among other things, SMM is used in the manufacture of capacitive acceleration sensors with movable and fixed electrodes for capacitive evaluation, and rotation-rate sensors with quasirotatory oscillators.

Wafer bonding

In addition to structuring the silicon, joining two wafers represents another essential task for micromechanical production engineering. Joining technology is required in order for example to hermetically seal cavities (e.g. inclusion of reference vacuum in pressure sensors), to protect sensitive structures by applying caps (e.g. for acceleration and rotation-rate sensors), or to join the silicon wafer with intermediate layers which minimize the thermal and mechanical stresses (e.g. glass base on pressure sensors).

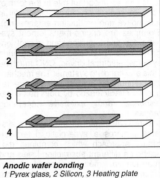

Process stages in surface micromechanics
1 Separation and structuring of sacrificial layer, 2 Separation of polysilicon, 3 Structuring of polysilicon, 4 Removal of sacrificial layer and thus creation of freely moving structures on surface.

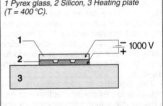

Anodic wafer bonding
1 Pyrex glass, 2 Silicon, 3 Heating plate (T = 400 °C).

With anodic bonding, a Pyrex-glass wafer is joined to a silicon wafer at a voltage of some 100 V and a temperature of approx. 400 °C. At these temperatures, the alkaline ions in the Pyrex glass move. This creates a depletion layer at the boundary to the silicon, through which the applied voltage drops. A strong electrostatic attraction and an electrochemical reaction (anodic oxidation) result in a permanent hermetic bond between the glass and the silicon.

With seal-glass bonding, two silicon wafers are contacted by way of a glass-solder layer applied in the screen-printing process at approx. 400 °C and under the exertion of pressure. The glass solder melts at this temperature and produces a hermetically sealed bond with the silicon.

Mechatronics

Mechatronics is a branch of engineering which seeks to enhance the functionality of technical systems by close integration of mechanical, electronic and data-processing components. Mechatronic systems play an important role in the form of complex control structures (especially in automotive and production engineering). Examples are engine-management systems for spark-ignition and diesel engines, ABS, TCS, stability and steering systems, electrical drives, CNC machine tools and handling systems. The mechanical components in these systems are frequently characterized by both non-linear response and extensive operating ranges.

The development of mechatronic systems requires a synergistic, interdisciplinary approach which combines modelling on different abstraction levels and inter-domain, model-supported design procedures and software engineering. Here, the classical analysis and design procedures of control engineering are being supplemented and partially replaced by real-time simulations, identification and parameter optimization with the inclusion of real components (hardware-in-the-loop).

The objective of microsystems technology is to miniaturize mechatronic systems by integrating microelectronics and micromechanics.

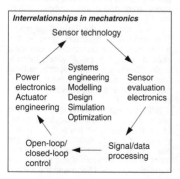

Interrelationships in mechatronics

Sensor technology

Power electronics
Actuator engineering

Systems engineering
Modelling
Design
Simulation
Optimization

Sensor evaluation electronics

Open-loop/closed-loop control

Signal/data processing

Analog/digital conversion

Analog signals are electrical quantities whose amplitude, frequency and phase convey information on physical variables or technical processes. Data registration is continuous in both time and quantity; within certain limits, analog signals can reflect any number of quantitative variations at any given point in time. Analog technology provides means for processing these signals. Initial processing, consisting of filtering and amplification, can be supplemented by mathematical operations such as addition and multiplication, as well as integration over time, etc. The operational amplifier (OP) is an integrated circuit of extreme importance in analog technology. Under ideal conditions, a relatively simple external circuit is sufficient for determining its operating characteristics (infinite amplification, no input current).

Analog units also have several disadvantages: the characteristic response curves of the various components alter with age, temperature fluctuations influence precision, and the manufacturing process must generally be supplemented by subsequent calibration.

Conversion to digital signals entails a transition to discrete monitoring of both time and intensity, i.e., the analog signal is sampled with specific periodicity (scan spots). The sampled values are assigned a numeric expression in which the number of possible values and thus the resolution are limited (quantification).

Instead of using the decimal system, digital technology uses the binary system which is easier for the computer to handle.
Example: 101 (dual) =
$1 \cdot 2^2 + 0 \cdot 2^1 + 1 \cdot 2^0 = 5$ (decimal).
The bit (position) with the greatest value is termed the MSB (Most Significant Bit), the lowest the LSB (Least Significant Bit). When represented as a two's complement, the MSB provides the prefix for the decimal number (1 $\triangleq$ negative, 0 $\triangleq$ positive). Values ranging from -4 to $+3$ can be represented with a 3-bit word.
Example: 101 =
$-1 \cdot 2^2 + 0 \cdot 2^1 + 1 \cdot 2^0 = -3$.

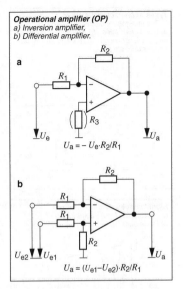

Operational amplifier (OP)
a) Inversion amplifier,
b) Differential amplifier.

a

$U_a = -U_e \cdot R_2 / R_1$

b

$U_a = (U_{e1} - U_{e2}) \cdot R_2 / R_1$

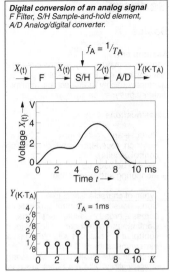

Digital conversion of an analog signal
F Filter, S/H Sample-and-hold element,
A/D Analog/digital converter.

$f_A = 1/T_A$

$T_A = 1$ ms

A word of n bits in length is able to represent 2^n different values. This is 256 for 8 bits, for 16 bits it is 65 536. An analog input voltage of ± 5 V (FSR – Full Scale Range) results in a resolution (LSB value) of 39 mV for 8 bits and 0.15 mV for 16 bits.

It is necessary to limit the bandwidth of the time signal being scanned (anti-aliasing filter). The highest signal frequency f_g must be less than half the scanning frequency f_A ($f_A > 2 \cdot f_g$). If a sample-and-hold scanning element is not employed, the maximum allowable variation in input voltage during the A/D converter's conversion period (aperture time) is one LSB.

The transfer function illustrates how a single digital value is assigned to various input voltages. The maximum amplitude of the quantification error is $Q/2$ (rounding-off error) at $Q = $ FSR/$(2^n) \triangleq$ LSB.

The quantification process results in an overlay of quantification noise which contaminates the actual data signal. If a sinus-curve signal is employed for full modulation in the A/D converter, the result is a signal-to-noise ratio which increases by about 6 dB for each additional bit of resolution. Actual A/D converters display deviations from the ideal transfer curve. These are caused by offset, amplification and linearity errors (static errors) as well as aperture inconsistency and finite settling times (dynamic error).

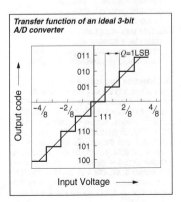

Transfer function of an ideal 3-bit A/D converter

$Q = 1$ LSB

Input Voltage

Sensors

Basics

Assignment

Sensors convert a physical or chemical (usually non-electrical) quantity into an electrical quantity (non-electrical intermediate stages may be employed).

Classifications

1. Purpose and application
- Function (open-loop and closed-loop control circuits),
- Safety and back-up,
- Monitoring and information.

2. Types of characteristic curve
- Continuous linear: Control applications across a broad measurement range,
- Continuous non-linear: Closed-loop control of a measured variable within a narrow measurement range,
- Discontinuous multi-stage: Monitoring in applications where a punctual signal is required when a limit value is reached,
- Discontinuous dual-stage (with hysteresis in some cases): Monitoring of correction thresholds for immediate or subsequent adjustments.

3. Type of output signal
Output signal proportional to:
- current/voltage, amplitude,
- frequency/periodicity,
- pulse duration/pulse duty factor.
Discrete output signal:
- dual stage (binary),
- multi-stage (irregular graduation),
- multi-stage (equidistant) or digital.

Automotive applications

In their function as peripheral elements, sensors and actuators form the interface between the vehicle with its complex drive, braking, chassis, suspension and body functions (including guidance and navigation functions) and the usually digital-electronic control unit (ECU) as the processing unit. An adapter circuit is generally used to convert the sensor's signals into the standardized form (measuring chain, measured-data registration system) required by the ECU.

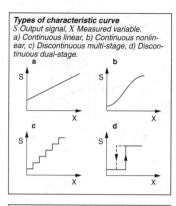

Types of characteristic curve
S Output signal, X Measured variable.
a) Continuous linear, b) Continuous nonlinear, c) Discontinuous multi-stage, d) Discontinuous dual-stage.

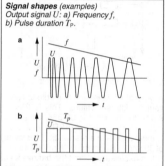

Signal shapes (examples)
Output signal U: a) Frequency f,
b) Pulse duration T_P.

In addition, system operation can be influenced by sensor information from other processing elements and/or by driver-operated switches.

Display elements provide the driver with information on the static and dynamic status of vehicle operation as a single synergistic process.

Main technical requirement, trends

The degree of stress to which the sensor is subjected is determined by the operating conditions (mechanical, climatic, chemical, electromagnetic influences) present at the installation location (for standard Degrees of Protection, see DIN 40 050, Sheet 9).

According to application and technical

requirements, automotive sensors are assigned to one of three <u>reliability classes</u>:
Class 1: Steering, brakes, passenger protection,
Class 2: Engine, drivetrain, suspension, tires,
Class 3: Comfort and convenience, information/diagnosis, theft deterrence.

<u>Miniaturization</u> concepts are employed to achieve compact unit dimensions:
– Substrate and hybrid technology (pressure and temperature sensors),
– Semiconductor technology (monitoring rotational speed, e.g., with Hall sensors),
– Micromechanics (pressure and acceleration sensors),
– Microsystem technology (combination of micromechanics, micro-electronics, can also include micro-optics).

Integrated "intelligent" sensors

Systems range from hybrid and monolithic integrated sensors and electronic signal-processing circuits at the measuring point, all the way to complex digital circuitry, such as A/D converters and microcomputers (mechatronics), for complete utilization of the sensor's inherent precision. These systems offer the following benefits and options:
– Reduction of load on the ECU,
– Uniform, flexible, bus-compatible communications links,
– Multiple application of sensors,
– Multi-sensor designs,
– By means of local amplification and demodulation, very small quantities and HF signals can be processed,

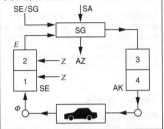

Automotive sensors
Φ Physical quantity, E Electrical quantity, Z Influencing quantities, AK Actuator, AZ Display, SA Switch, SE Sensor(s), SG Control unit (ECU).
1 Measuring sensor, 2 Adapter circuit, 3 Driver, 4 Actuators.

– Correction of sensor deviations at the measuring point, and common calibration and compensation of sensor and circuit, are simplified and improved by storage of the individual correction information in PROM.

Fiber-optic sensors

Various physical factors can be employed to modify the intensity, phase (coherent laser light) and polarization of the light conducted in the optical fibers. Fiber-optic sensors are impervious to electromagnetic interference; they are, however, sensitive to physical pressure (intensity-modulation sensors), and, to some degree, to

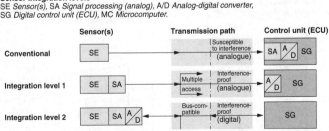

Sensor integration levels
SE Sensor(s), SA Signal processing (analog), A/D Analog-digital converter, SG Digital control unit (ECU), MC Microcomputer.

	Sensor(s)	Transmission path	Control unit (ECU)
Conventional	SE	Susceptible to interference (analogue)	SA A/D SG
Integration level 1	SE SA	Multiple access / Interference-proof (analogue)	A/D SG
Integration level 2	SE SA A/D	Bus-compatible / Interference-proof (digital)	SG
Integration level 3	SE SA A/D MC	Bus-compatible / Interference-proof (digital)	SG

contamination and aging. Inexpensive plastic fibers are now available for application within some of the temperature ranges associated with automotive applications. These sensors require special couplers and plug connections.

<u>Extrinsic sensors</u>: The optical conductor generally conducts the light to an end point; it must emerge from the conductor to exert an effect.
<u>Intrinsic sensors</u>: The measurement effect occurs internally within the fibers.

Sensor types

Position sensors (displacement/angle)
Position sensors employ both contact wipers and non-contacting (proximity) designs to register displacement and angle.

Directly monitored variable quantities:
- Throttle-valve position,
- Accelerator-pedal position,
- Seat and mirror position,
- Control-rack travel and position,
- Fuel level,
- Travel of clutch servo unit, vehicle obstruction,
- Steering (wheel) angle,
- Tilt angle,
- Vehicle-course angle,
- Brake-pedal position.

Indirectly monitored variable quantities:
- Sensor-flap deflection angle (flow rate/FLR),
- Deflection angle of a spring-mass system (acceleration),
- Diaphragm deflection angle (pressure),
- Suspension compression travel (headlamp vertical-aim adjustment),
- Torsion angle (torque).

Wiper or film potentiometers
The wiper potentiometer measures travel by exploiting the proportional relationship between the length of a wire or film resistor (conductor track) and its electrical resistance. This design currently provides the most economical travel and angle sensors.

The voltage on the measurement track is usually routed through smaller series resistors R_V for overload protection (as well as for zero and progression-rate adjustments). The shape of the contour across the width of the measurement track (including that of individual sections) influences the shape of the characteristic curve.

The standard wiper connection is furnished by a second contact track consisting of the same material mounted on a low-resistance substrate. Wear and measurement distortions can be avoided by minimizing the current at the pickup ($I_A <$ 1 mA) and sealing the unit against dust.

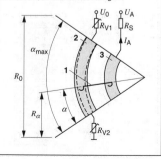

Wiper potentiometer
1 Wiper, 2 Resistor track, 3 Contact track.
U_0 Supply voltage, U_A Measurement voltage, R Resistor, α Measurement angle.

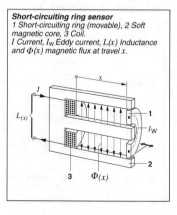

Short-circuiting ring sensor
1 Short-circuiting ring (movable), 2 Soft magnetic core, 3 Coil.
I Current, I_W Eddy current, $L(x)$ Inductance and $\Phi(x)$ magnetic flux at travel x.

Short-circuiting ring sensors

Short-circuiting ring sensors consist of a laminated soft-magnetic core (straight/curved U- or E-shape), a coil and a moving, highly-conductive short-circuiting ring made of copper or aluminum.

When an AC voltage is applied at the coil, a current I is created which is dependent on the inductance of the coil. The eddy currents thereby created in the short-circuiting ring limit expansion of the magnetic flux to the area between the coil and the ring itself. The position of the short-circuiting ring influences the inductance and thus the coil current. The current I is thus a measure of the position of the short-circuiting ring. Virtually the entire length of the sensor can be utilized for measurement purposes. The mass to be moved is very low. Contouring the distance between the sides influences the shape of the characteristic curve: Reducing the distance between the sides toward the end of the measuring range further enhances the good natural linearity. Operation is generally in the 5...50 kHz range, depending on material and shape.

Half-differential sensors employ a moving measuring ring and a stationary reference short-circuiting ring to meet exacting demands for precision (on diesel fuel-injection pumps, the rack-travel sensor for in-line units, and angular-position sensors in the injected-fuel-quantity actuator of distributor-type injection pumps); they measure by acting as

- inductive voltage dividers (evaluation L_1/L_2 or $(L_1-L_2)/(L_1+L_2)$), or as
- frequency-definition elements in an oscillating circuit, producing a signal proportional to frequency (excellent interference resistance, easy digital conversion).

The measuring effect is fairly substantial, typically $L_{max}/L_{min} = 4$.

Other sensor types

Solenoid plunger, differential-throttle and differential-transformer sensors operate based on the variation in the inductance of an individual coil and the proportional relationship of voltage dividers (supplied either directly or via inductive coupling) with moving cores. The overall length is often considerably greater than the measurement travel. This disadvantage is avoided by using a multistage winding in chambers of different dimensions. With this sensor, for angular measurement, the angle of rotation must be mechanically converted to a linear movement.

HF eddy-current sensors (electronics at the measuring point) are suitable e.g. for non-contact measurement of the throttle angle and the accelerator-pedal position. Here, the inductance of mostly nonferrous coils is modified by the approach of conductive shaped parts (spoilers) or by variable overlapping with them. Because of the frequently high operating frequency (MHz range), the signal electronics is mostly accommodated directly on the

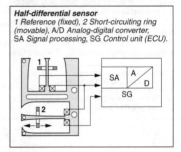

Half-differential sensor
1 Reference (fixed), 2 Short-circuiting ring (movable), A/D Analog-digital converter, SA Signal processing, SG Control unit (ECU).

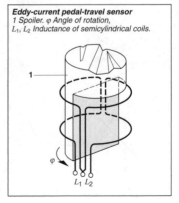

Eddy-current pedal-travel sensor
1 Spoiler. φ Angle of rotation, L_1, L_2 Inductance of semicylindrical coils.

sensor. This is the case for example when two coils are wound onto a common cylinder (differential sensor) for measuring the throttle angle. The same principle is used on sensors incorporating single lateral coils to measure clutch positions (70 mm measurement range) at substantially lower frequencies (approx. 7.5 kHz). The first of the above sensor types features a cylindrical aluminum spoiler with special recesses and is designed to pivot over the coil winding. The second concept monitors the penetration depth of an aluminum short-circuit tube within the sensor coil.

Integrated Hall ICs

The Hall effect is a galvanomagnetic effect and is evaluated mainly by means of thin semiconductor chips. When such a current-carrying chip is permeated vertically by a magnetic induction B, a voltage U_H proportional to the field can be picked off transversely to the current direction (Hall effect) while the chip resistance simultaneously increases in accordance with a roughly parabolic characteristic (Gaussian effect, magnetoresistor). When Si is used as the base material, a signal-conditioning circuit can at the same time be integrated on the chip, which makes such sensors very economical.

A disadvantage in the past proved to be their sensitivity to the mechanical stress which was inevitable due to packaging and resulted in an unfavorable offset temperature coefficient. This disadvantage has been overcome by the application of the "spinning-current" principle. This now made Hall ICs well suited for analog sensor applications. Mechanical interference (piezoresistive effects) is suppressed by rapid, electronically controlled rotation of the electrodes or cyclical switching of the electrodes and averaging of the output signal.

Such integrated Hall ICs are mainly suitable for measuring limited travel ranges in that they register the fluctuating field strengths of a permanent magnet as a function of the magnet's distance from the IC. Larger angles up to 360° (e.g. for recording the camshaft position) can be

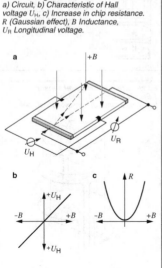

Galvanomagnetic effects
a) Circuit, b) Characteristic of Hall voltage U_H, c) Increase in chip resistance.
R (Gaussian effect), B Inductance,
U_R Longitudinal voltage.

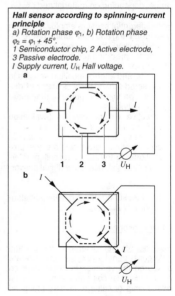

Hall sensor according to spinning-current principle
a) Rotation phase φ_1, b) Rotation phase $\varphi_2 = \varphi_1 + 45°$.
1 Semiconductor chip, 2 Active electrode, 3 Passive electrode.
I Supply current, U_H Hall voltage.

measured e.g. with the configuration shown in the illustration: The two Hall-effect sensors arranged at right angles supply sinusoidal/cosinusoidal signals which can be converted by means of the arctan function into the angle of rotation φ. In principle, the configuration can also be integrated in planar form with VHDs (Vertical Hall Devices).

It is also possible with a rotating magnet ring and some fixed soft-magnetic conductors to obtain a linear output signal directly for larger angle ranges without conversion. In this case, the bipolar field of the magnet ring is passed through a Hall-effect sensor arranged between semicir-cular flux concentrating pieces. The effective magnetic flux through the Hall-effect sensor is dependent on the angle of rotation φ.

The disadvantage here is the persisting dependency on geometrical tolerances of the magnetic circuit and intensity fluctuations of the permanent magnet.

The simplest Hall ICs ("Hall-effect switches") also permit – in conjunction with a small working-point magnet – the construction of digital angle sensors up to 360°. For this purpose, for an n-bit resolution, n Hall-effect switches are arranged equidistantly in a circle. A soft-magnetic code disk blocks the field of the individual

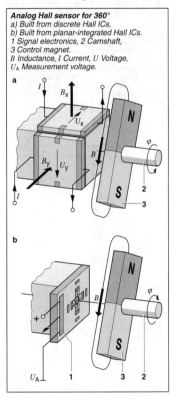

Analog Hall sensor for 360°
a) Built from discrete Hall ICs.
b) Built from planar-integrated Hall ICs.
1 Signal electronics, 2 Camshaft,
3 Control magnet.
B Inductance, I Current, U Voltage,
U_A Measurement voltage.

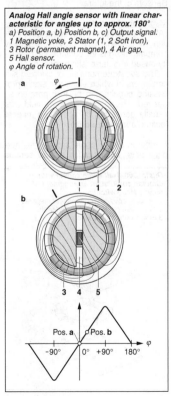

Analog Hall angle sensor with linear characteristic for angles up to approx. 180°
a) Position a, b) Position b, c) Output signal.
1 Magnetic yoke, 2 Stator (1, 2 Soft iron),
3 Rotor (permanent magnet), 4 Air gap,
5 Hall sensor.
φ Angle of rotation.

overlying permanent magnets, or enables it, so that when the disk is rotated further the Hall-effect switches in succession generate n different code words. The Gray code is used to avoid large indication errors in intermediate states. To implement a steering-wheel angle sensor, for example, the code disk is connected to the steering spindle while the rest of the sensor is connected to the chassis. Multiple rotations can be recorded with an additional, simple 3-bit configuration whose code disk is moved by means of a reduction gear. The resolution of such configurations is mostly no better than 2.5°.

Sensors of the future

Magnetoresistive NiFe thin-film sensors (AMR – anisotropic magnetoresistive thin-film NiFe, permalloy) provide extremely compact designs for contactless, proximity-based angular-position sensors.

The substrate consists of oxidized silicon layers in which electronic signal-processing circuits can be incorporated as desired. The magnetic control field B is usually generated by a pivoting magnet located above the sensor.

Magnetoresistive angle sensors in "barber's pole" configuration display serious

limitations in both precision and measurement ranges (max. ±15°). Operation is based on the detuning of a magnetoresistant voltage divider consisting of longitudinal permalloy resistors with high-conductance lateral strips in gold.

Magnetoresistive angle sensors in "pseudo-Hall" configuration utilize the inherent precision in the sinusoidal pattern of signals monitored at the output terminals of a quadripolar planar sensor structure. A second element installed at 45° generates a supplementary cosinusoidal signal. From the mutual relationship of the two signal voltages, it is possible (e.g. using the arctan function) to determine the angle α (e.g. with a microcontroller or

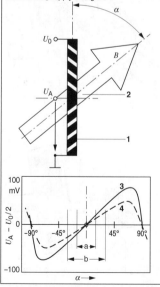

Magnetoresistive angle sensor (barber's pole configuration)
1 AMR, anisotropic magnetoresistive element (barber's pole), 2 Rotating permanent magnet with control inductance B, 3 Response curves for low, and, 4 for high operating temperature. a Linear, b Effective measurement range. α Measurement angle, U_A Measurement and U_0 supply voltages.

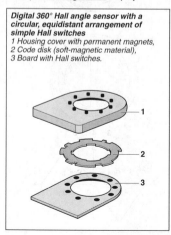

Digital 360° Hall angle sensor with a circular, equidistant arrangement of simple Hall switches.
1 Housing cover with permanent magnets, 2 Code disk (soft-magnetic material), 3 Board with Hall switches.

ASIC) with great accuracy over a range of 180°, largely irrespective of fluctuations in temperature and magnetic-field intensity (distance, aging).

The task of measuring various rotations of a rotating part (e.g. steering spindle) is solved with a dual configuration of "pseudo-Hall angle sensors". Here the two associated permanent magnets are moved by the rotating part via a step-up gear train. However, as the two smaller driving gears differ to the tune of one tooth, their mutual phase angle is a clear measure of the absolute angular position. Each individual sensor also offers an indeterminate fine resolution of the angle of rotation. This configuration provides a resolution more precise than 1° for e.g.

the entire steering-angle range of four full rotations.

Systems for monitoring vehicle to vehicle distances can use ultrasonic transit-time processes (close-range, 0.5...5 m), as well as processes based on transit-time and triangulation principles using short-range infrared light (lidar: mid-range measurements extending up to 50 m). Another option is electromagnetic radar (long-range operation, up to 150 m).

ACC systems (Adaptive Cruise Control) with just such a long-range radar sensor are vehicle-speed controllers with automatic detection of vehicles which are driving in front in a lane and where braking may be required. A working frequency of 76 GHz (wavelength approx. 3.8 mm) permits the compact design required for automotive applications. A Gunn oscillator (Gunn diode in the cavity resonator) feeds in parallel three adjacently arranged patch antennas which at the same time also serve to receive the reflected signals. A plastic lens (Fresnel) set in front focuses the transmitted beam, referred to the vehicle axle, horizontally at an angle of ±5° and vertically at an angle of ±1.5°. Due to the lateral offset of the antennas, their reception characteristic (6 dB width 4°) points in different directions. As well as the distance of vehicles driving in front

---

Magnetoresistive angle sensor (pseudo-Hall version)
a) Measurement concept,
b) Sensor structure.
1 Thin NiFe layer (AMR sensor), 2 Pivoting permanent magnet with inductive control B, 3 Hybrid, 4 ASIC, 5 Electrical connection.
I_V Supply current, U_{H1}, U_{H2} Measurement voltages, α Measurement angle.

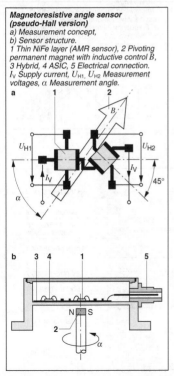

AMR steering-angle sensor
1 Steering spindle, 2 Gear with $n > m$ teeth, 3 Gear with m teeth, 4 Gear with $m+1$ teeth, 5 Magnets.
φ, ψ, θ Angle of rotation.

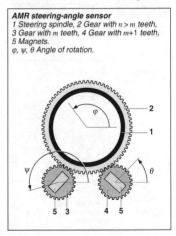

and their relative speed, it is thus also possible to determine the direction under which they are detected. Directional couplers separate transmitted and received reflection signals. Three downstream mixers transpose the received frequency down to virtually zero by admixing the transmit frequency (0...300 kHz). The low-frequency signals are digitized for further evaluation and subjected to a high-speed Fourier analysis to determine the frequency.

The frequency of the Gunn oscillator is compared continually with that of a stable reference oscillator DRO (Dielectric Resonance Oscillator) and regulated to a pre-specified setpoint value. Here the supply voltage to the Gunn diode is modulated until it corresponds again to the setpoint value. This control loop is used for measurement purposes to increase and reduce the Gunn-oscillator frequency every 100 ms briefly in a saw-tooth manner by 300 MHz (FMCW Frequency Modulated Continuous Wave). The signal reflected from the vehicle driving in front is delayed according to the propagation time (i.e. in a rising ramp by a lower frequency and in a falling ramp by a frequency higher by the same amount). The frequency difference Δf is a direct measure of the distance (e.g. 2 kHz/m). If however there is additionally a specific relative speed between the two vehicles, the received frequency f_e

is increased on account of the Doppler effect in both the rising and falling ramps by a specific, proportional amount Δf_d (e.g. 512 Hz per m/s), i.e. there are two different difference frequencies Δf_1 and Δf_2. Their addition produces the distance between the vehicles, and their difference the relative speed of the vehicles. This method can be used to detect and track up to 32 vehicles.

Magnetic-field sensors (saturation-core probes) can monitor the vehicle's direction of travel for general orientation and application in navigation systems.

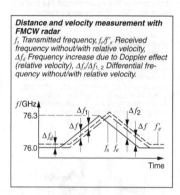

Distance and velocity measurement with FMCW radar
f_s Transmitted frequency, f_e/f'_e Received frequency without/with relative velocity, Δf_d Frequency increase due to Doppler effect (relative velocity), $\Delta f_s/\Delta f_{1,2}$ Differential frequency without/with relative velocity.

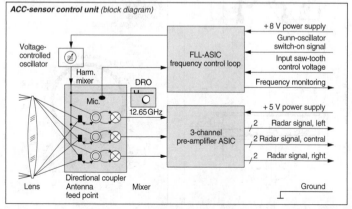

ACC-sensor control unit (block diagram)

RPM and velocity sensors

A distinction is made between absolute rotating velocity in space and relative rotating velocity between two parts.

An example of absolute rotating velocity is the vehicle's yaw rate about its vertical axis ("yaw velocity"); this is required for vehicle-dynamics control. Examples of relative rotating velocity are the crankshaft and camshaft speeds, the wheel speeds (for ABS/TCS) and the speed of the diesel injection pump. Measurements are mainly taken with the aid of an incremental sensor system comprising a gear and an min^{-1} sensor.

<u>Newer applications:</u>
– Bearing-integrated min^{-1} sensors (wheel bearings, Simmer shaft-seal module on the crankshaft),
– Linear velocity,
– Vehicle yaw rate about the longitudinal axis ("roll velocity" for rollover protection).

<u>Inductive sensors</u>
The inductive sensor consists of a bar magnet with a soft-magnetic pole pin supporting an induction coil with two connections. When a ferromagnetic ring gear (or a rotor of similar design) turns past this sensor, it generates a voltage in the coil which is directly proportional to the periodic variation in the magnetic flux. A uniform tooth pattern generates a sinusoidal voltage curve. The rotational speed is reflected in the periodic interval between the voltage's zero transition points, while the amplitude is also proportional to rotating speed.

The air gap and the tooth dimensions are vital factors in defining the (exponential) signal amplitude. Teeth can still be detected without difficulty up to air-gap widths of one half or one third of a tooth interval. Standard gears for crankshaft and ABS wheel-speed sensors cover gaps ranging from 0.8 to 1.5 mm. The reference point for the ignition timing is obtained either by omitting a tooth or by bridging a gap between teeth. The resulting increase in distance between zero transitions is identified as the reference point and is accompanied by a substantial increase in signal voltage (the system registers a larger tooth).

<u>Hall-effect sensors/vane switches</u>
Semiconductor sensors utilize the Hall effect (P. 75) in the form of Hall-effect vane switches, e.g. as ignition triggering sensors in ignition distributors (P. 490). The sensor and the electronic circuitry for supply and signal processing are integrated on the sensor chip.

This "Hall IC" (with bipolar technology for sustained temperatures of up to 150°C and direct connection to the vehicle electrical system) is located within an almost completely insulated magnetic circuit consisting of permanent magnet and pole elements. A soft-magnetic trigger wheel (e.g. camshaft-driven) travels through the

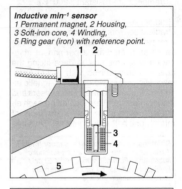

Inductive min^{-1} sensor
1 Permanent magnet, 2 Housing,
3 Soft-iron core, 4 Winding,
5 Ring gear (iron) with reference point.

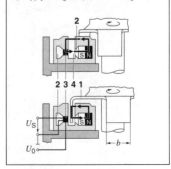

Hall-effect vane switch (ignition distributor)
1 Vane with width b, 2 Soft-magnetic conductors, 3 Hall IC, 4 Air gap.
U_0 Supply voltage, U_S Sensor voltage.

gap. The trigger-wheel vane interrupts the magnetic field (that is, it deflects it around the sensor), while the gap in the trigger wheel allows it to travel through the sensor unimpeded.

The differential Hall-effect sensor of a system with electronic ignition distribution picks off the camshaft position at a special, soft-magnetic segment disk.

Newer sensors

Sensors of the future should satisfy the following criteria:
– static monitoring (e.g. zero min⁻¹),
– larger air gaps,
– independence from air-gap fluctuations (temperature-resistant ≤ 200 °C).

Gradient sensors

Gradient sensors (e.g., based on Hall, differential, or differential magnetoresistive sensors) incorporate a permanent magnet on which the pole surface facing the gear is homogenized with a thin ferromagnetic wafer. Two galvanomagnetic elements (generic term for Hall sensors and magnetoresistors) are located on each element's sensor tip, at a distance of roughly one half a tooth interval. Thus one of the elements is always opposite a gap between teeth when the other is adjacent to a tooth. The sensor measures the difference in field intensity at two adjacent locations on the circumference. The output signal is roughly proportional to the diversion of field strength as a function of the angle at the circumference; polarity is therefore independent of the air gap.

Gauss-effect <u>magnetoresistors</u> are magnetically controlled, bipolar semiconductor resistors (indium antimonide) with a design similar to that of the Hall sensor. In the standard application range their resistance is essentially proportional to the square of the field strength. The two resistors of a differential sensor assume the function of voltage dividers in the electrical circuit; for the most part, they also compensate for temperature sensitivity. The substantial measurement effect makes it possible to dispense with local electronic amplifiers (output signal 0.1...1 V). Magnetoresistors for automotive applications withstand temperatures ≤ 170 °C (brief peaks ≤ 200 °C).

Tangential sensors

The tangential sensor differs from its gradient-type counterpart by reacting to variations in polarity and intensity in the components of a magnetic field located tangentially to the periphery of the rotor. Design options include AMR thin-film technology (barber's pole) or single permalloy resistors featuring full- or half-bridge circuitry. Unlike the gradient sensor, the tangential unit does not need to be adapted for variations in tooth distribution patterns, and thus permits semi-punctiform configuration. Although the intrinsic measurement effect exceeds that of the silicon-based Hall sensor by a factor of approx. 1...2, local amplification is still required.

In the case of a bearing-integrated crankshaft speed sensor (Simmer shaft-seal module), the AMR thin-film sensor is mounted together with an evaluation IC on a common leadframe. For the purposes of space saving and temperature protection, the evaluation IC is bent at an angle of 90° and also located further away from the sensor tip.

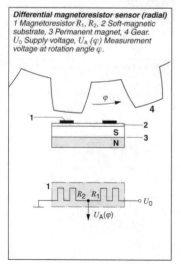

Differential magnetoresistor sensor (radial)
1 Magnetoresistor R_1, R_2, 2 Soft-magnetic substrate, 3 Permanent magnet, 4 Gear.
U_0 Supply voltage, $U_A (\varphi)$ Measurement voltage at rotation angle φ.

Oscillation gyrometers

Oscillation gyrometers measure the absolute yaw rate Ω around the vehicle's vertical axis (yaw axis), e.g. in systems for controlling a vehicle's dynamic behavior (ESP, Electronic Stability Program) and for navigation. They are similar in principle to mechanical gyroscopes and for measurement purposes utilize the Coriolis acceleration that occurs during rotational motions in conjunction with an oscillating motion.

Piezoelectric yaw-rate sensors

Two diametrically opposed piezo-ceramic elements (1-1') induce radial resonant oscillation in an oscillatory metallic hollow cylinder. A second piezoelectric pair (2-2') governs the cylinder to a constant oscillation amplitude with four axial nodes (45° offset to direction of excitation).

The nodes respond to rotation at the rate Ω about the cylinder axis with a slight peripheral displacement, inducing forces proportional to min^{-1} in the otherwise force-free nodes. This state is detected by a third pair of piezoelectric elements (3-3'). The forces are then processed back to a reference value $U_{\text{ref}} = 0$ by a fourth ex-

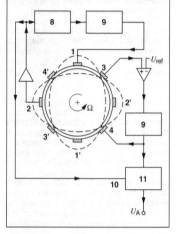

Piezoelectric yaw-rate sensor
Operating concept.
1...4 Piezoelectric elements, 8 Control circuit (fixed phase), 9 Bandpass filter, 10 Phase reference, 11 Rectifier (selective-phase).
U_A Measurement voltage, Ω Yaw rate, $U_{\text{ref}} = 0$ (normal operation), $U_{\text{ref}} \neq 0$ ("built-in" test).

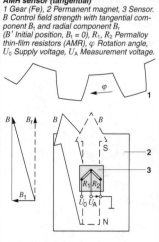

AMR sensor (tangential)
1 Gear (Fe), 2 Permanent magnet, 3 Sensor. B Control field strength with tangential component B_t and radial component B_r (B' Initial position, $B_t = 0$), R_1, R_2 Permalloy thin-film resistors (AMR), φ Rotation angle, U_0 Supply voltage, U_A Measurement voltage.

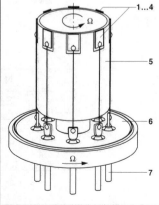

Piezoelectric yaw-rate sensor
Structure.
1...4 Piezoelectric element pairs, 5 Oscillating cylinder, 6 Baseplate, 7 Connection pins. Ω Yaw rate.

citing pair (4-4′) in a closed-loop operation. After careful filtering using synchronized-phase rectification, the required control value provides an extremely precise output signal. A controlled temporary change of the setpoint value to $U_{ref} \neq 0$ provides a simple means of testing the entire sensor system ("built-in" test).

Complex compensation circuitry is required to deal with the temperature sensitivity of this sensor. Because the piezoceramic elements' response characteristics also change with age, careful pretreatment (artificial aging) is also required.

Micromechanical silicon yaw-rate sensors provide an inexpensive and compact alternative to today's intricate mechanical sensors. A combined technology is used to achieve the high precision needed in vehicle-dynamics systems: two thicker mass boards worked from the wafer by means of bulk micromechanics (P. 90) oscillate in push-pull mode at their resonant frequency, which is determined by their mass and their coupling-spring stiffness (> 2 kHz). Each of them is provided with an extremely small surface-microme-

chanical, capacitive acceleration sensor which measures Coriolis acceleration in the wafer plane vertical to the oscillation direction when the sensor chip rotates about its vertical axis at the yaw rate Ω. They are proportional to the product of the yaw rate and the oscillation velocity which is electronically regulated to a constant value. For drive purposes, there is a simple printed conductor on the relevant oscillation board which is subjected to a Lorentz force in a permanent-magnetic field vertical to the chip surface. A similarly simple, chip-surface-saving conductor is used to measure the oscillation velocity directly and inductively with the same magnetic field. The different physical natures of the drive and sensor systems prevent unwanted crosstalking between the two parts. In order to suppress external accelerations (common-mode signal), the two opposing sensor signals are subtracted from each other (summation however can also be used to measure the external acceleration). The precise micromechanical structure helps to suppress the influence of high oscillation acceleration with regard to the Coriolis acceleration that is lower by several powers

---

Micromechanical yaw-rate sensor with electrodynamic drive in combined technology form
(bulk and SMM micromechanics)
1 Oscillation direction, 2 Oscillating body, 3 Coriolis acceleration sensor, 4 Retaining/guide pin,
5 Direction of Coriolis acceleration, Ω Yaw rate, υ Oscillation velocity.

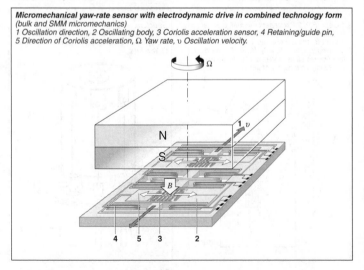

of ten (cross sensitivity well below 40 dB). The drive and measuring systems are mechanically and electrically isolated in rigorous terms here.

If the Si yaw-rate sensor is manufactured completely in accordance with surface micromechanics SMM (P. 90), and the magnetic drive and control system is replaced at the same time by an electrostatic system, this isolation can be realized less consistently: Using "comb" structures, a centrally mounted rotary oscillator is electrostatically driven to oscillate at an amplitude which is constantly regulated by means of a similar capacitive pick-off. Coriolis forces force a simultaneous "out-of-plane" tilting motion whose amplitude is proportional to the yaw rate Ω and which is detected capacitively with electrodes located under the oscillator. To prevent this motion from being excessively damped, it is essential to operate the sensor in a vacuum. The smaller chip size and the simpler manufacturing process do indeed reduce the cost of such a sensor, but the reduction in size also diminishes the already slight measuring effect and thus the attainable accuracy. It places higher demands on the electronics. The influence of external accelerations is already mechanically suppressed here.

Radar sensors
Research focuses on simple (low-cost) Doppler radar systems for measuring the vehicle's linear velocity.

Acceleration/vibration sensors
These sensors are suitable for triggering passenger-protection systems (airbags, seatbelt tensioners, rollover bars), for knock detection and control in internal-combustion engines, and for registering lateral acceleration rates and velocity changes in four-wheel-drive vehicles fitted with ABS.

Hall-effect acceleration sensor
In ABS-equipped vehicles with four-wheel drive and modern cars with vehicle-dynamics control, the wheel-speed sensors are supplemented by a Hall-effect acceleration sensor to monitor lateral and longitudinal acceleration rates. Deflection

levels in the spring-mass system used in this application are recorded using a magnet and a Hall-effect sensor (measuring range: 1 g). The sensor is designed for narrow-band operation (several Hz) and features electrodynamic damping.

Piezoelectric sensors

Piezoelectric bimorphous spring elements/two-layer piezoceramics, are used in applications such as triggering seatbelt tensioners, airbags and rollover bars.

Typical acceleration rates in automotive applications:

Application	Range
Knock control	1...10 g
Passenger protection	
Airbag, seat-belt tightener	50 g
Rollover bar	4 g
Seatbelt inertia reel	0.4 g
ABS, ESP	0.8...1.2 g
Suspension control	
Structure	1 g
Axle	10 g

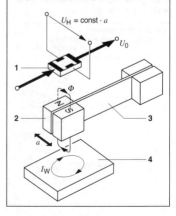

Hall acceleration sensor
1 Hall sensor, 2 Permanent magnet (seismic mass), 3 Spring, 4 Damping plate (Cu).
a Acceleration, I_W Eddy currents, U_H Hall voltage, U_0 Supply voltage, Φ Magnetic flux.

$U_H = \text{const} \cdot a$

Their intrinsic inertial mass causes them to deflect under acceleration to provide a dynamic (not DC response pattern) signal with excellent processing characteristics (typical frequency limit of 10 Hz).

The sensor element is located in a sealed housing shared with the initial signal-amplification stage. It is sometimes encased in gel for physical protection.

The sensor's actuating principle can also be inverted: An additional actuator electrode makes it easy to check the sensor (on-board diagnosis).

<u>Longitudinal elements (knock sensors)</u>
Longitudinal elements are employed as knock sensors (acceleration sensors) for ignition systems that feature knock control (P. 496). They measure (with low directional selectivity) the structure-borne noise at the engine block (measuring range approx. 10 g at a typical vibration frequency of 5...20 kHz). An unencapsulated, annular piezo-ceramic ring element measures the inertial forces exerted upon a seismic mass of the same shape.

<u>New sensor concepts</u>

Capacitive silicon acceleration sensors
The first generation of micromechanical sensors relied on anisotropic and selective etching techniques to fabricate the required spring-mass system from the full wafer (bulk silicon micromechanics) and produce the spring profile.

Capacitive pick-offs have proven especially effective for the high-precision measurement of this seismic-mass deflection. This design entails the use of supplementary silicon or glass wafers with counter-electrodes above and below the spring-held seismic mass. This leads to a 3-layer structure, whereby the wafers and their counterelectrodes also provide overload protection.

A precisely metered air cushion in the hermetically-sealed oscillating system provides an extremely compact yet efficient and inexpensive damping unit with good temperature response characteristics. Current designs almost always employ a fusion bonding process to join the three silicon wafers directly.

Due to variations in the thermal expansion rates of the different components, it is necessary to mount them on the casing baseplate. This has a decisive effect upon the desired measuring accuracy. Virtually straight-line mounting is used, with free support in the sensitive range.

This type of sensor is usually employed for low-level accelerations ($\leq 2\ g$) and relies upon a three-chip concept: (sensor chip + CMOS processing chip + bipolar protection IC). Conversion for extended signal evaluation triggers an <u>automatic reset</u>, returning the seismic mass to its base position and supplying the positioning signal as initial value.

For higher acceleration rates (passenger-protection systems), <u>surface-micromechanical sensors</u> with substantially more compact dimensions (typical edge lengths approx. 100 μm) are already in use. An additive process is employed to construct the spring-mass system on the surface of the silicon wafer.

In contrast to the bulk silicon sensors with capacitance levels of 10...20 pF, these sensors only have a typical capacitance of 1 pF. The electronic evaluating circuitry is therefore installed on a single chip along with the sensor (usually position-controlled systems).

Pressure sensors
Pressure measurement is direct, by means of diaphragm deflection or force sensor. Typical applications:

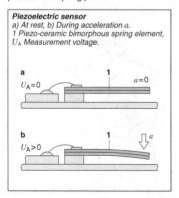

Piezoelectric sensor
a) At rest, b) During acceleration a.
1 Piezo-ceramic bimorphous spring element,
U_A Measurement voltage.

a
$U_A = 0$ 1 $a = 0$

b
$U_A > 0$ 1 a

- intake-manifold pressure (1...5 bar),
- braking pressure (10 bar), electropneumatic brakes,
- air-spring pressure (16 bar), for vehicles with pneumatic suspension,
- tire pressure (5 bar absolute), for monitoring and/or adjusting tire pressure,
- hydraulic reservoir pressure (approx. 200 bar), ABS, power steering,

- shock-absorber pressure (+ 200 bar), chassis and suspension-control systems,
- refrigerant pressure (35 bar), air-conditioning systems,
- modulator pressure (35 bar), automatic transmissions,
- brake pressure in master- and wheel-brake cylinders (200 bar), automatic yaw-moment compensation, electronically controlled brake,
- positive/vacuum pressure in fuel tank (0.5 bar) for on-board diagnostics (OBD),
- combustion-chamber pressure (100 bar, dynamic) for ignition miss and knock detection,
- diesel pumping-element pressure (1000 bar, dynamic), electronic diesel injection,
- common-rail pressure (1500 to 1800 bar), diesel engines, and
- common-rail pressure (100 bar) for spark-ignition (gasoline) engines.

<u>Thick-film pressure sensors</u>

The measurement diaphragm and its strain-gauge resistors (DMS) both use thick-film technology to measure absolute pressures of up to approx. 20 bar with a K factor (relative variation in resistance/expansion) of K = 12...15.

When the respective coefficients of expansion for the ceramic substrate and the ceramic cover film are correct, the diaphragm will form a dome-shaped bubble

---

Micromechanical-surface acceleration sensor
1 Elementary cell, 2, 3 Fixed wafers,
4 Movable wafers, 5 Seismic mass,
6 Spring shoulder, 7 Anchor.
a Acceleration, C Measurement capacitors.

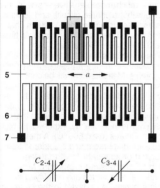

Bulk silicon acceleration sensor
1 Si upper wafer, 2 Si center wafer (seismic mass), 3 Si oxide, 4 Si lower wafer, 5 Glass substrate.
a Acceleration, C Measurement capacitors.

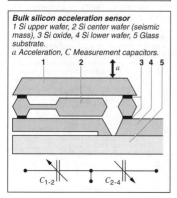

Pressure measurement
a) Direct, pressure-sensitive resistor (3),
b) with force sensor (1), c) via diaphragm deformation/DMS (2). p Pressure.

upon cooling after being bonded-on during manufacture. The result is a hollow chamber ("bubble") approx. 100 μm in height, with a diameter of 3...5 mm. After the application of additional thick-film strain-gauge resistors, the unit is hermetically sealed with another ceramic glass coating. The residual gas remaining in the "bubble" provides partial compensation for temperature changes in the sensor.

The signal-amplification and correction components are separate from the measurement medium, but are located directly adjacent to the sensor on the same substrate.

The "bubble sensor" principle is not suitable for extremely high or low pressures; versions for these applications generally incorporate flat ceramic diaphragms.

Semiconductor pressure sensors

The pressure is exerted against a Si diaphragm incorporating pressure-sensitive resistors, manufactured using micromechanics technology. The K factor of the resistors diffused into the monocrystalline silicon is especially high, typically K = 100. Up to now the sensor and the hybrid circuitry for signal processing have been located together in a single housing. Sensor calibration and compensation can be continuous or in stages, and are performed either on an ancillary hybrid chip (a second Si chip providing signal amplification and correction) or on the same sensor chip. Recent developments have seen values, e.g. for zero and lead cor-

rection, being stored in digital form in a PROM.

Integrated single-chip sensors with fully electronic calibration are suitable for use as load sensors for electronic ignition and fuel-injection systems. Due to their extremely compact dimensions, they are suitable for the functionally more favorable installation directly on the intake manifold (earlier designs were mounted either in the relevant ECU or at a convenient location in the engine compartment). Frequently applied are reverse assembly techniques in which the measured pressure is conducted to an electronically passive cavity recessed into the side of the sensor chip. For maximum protection, the – much more sensitive – side of the chip with the printed circuits and contacts is enclosed in a reference-vacuum chamber located between the housing's base and the soldered metal cap.

These sensors will also be available for application in tire-pressure monitoring systems. Measurement will be continuous and non-contacting (transformer concept). A virtually identical sensor chip can also be used as a combustion-chamber pressure sensor. This is provided that the Si chip is not directly exposed to high temperatures (max. 600 °C). A metallic insulation diaphragm and a soldered transfer rod of adequate length (several mm) furnish the desired protection. Micromechanical techniques are employed to apply a miniature pedestal to the center of the diaphragm, effectively converting the unit to a force sensor. The rod transmits

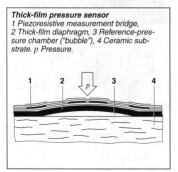

Thick-film pressure sensor
1 Piezoresistive measurement bridge,
2 Thick-film diaphragm, 3 Reference-pressure chamber ("bubble"), 4 Ceramic substrate. p Pressure.

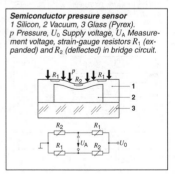

Semiconductor pressure sensor
1 Silicon, 2 Vacuum, 3 Glass (Pyrex).
p Pressure, U_0 Supply voltage, U_A Measurement voltage, strain-gauge resistors R_1 (expanded) and R_2 (deflected) in bridge circuit.

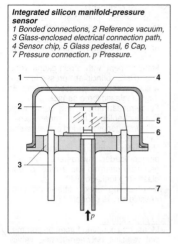

Integrated silicon manifold-pressure sensor
1 Bonded connections, 2 Reference vacuum, 3 Glass-enclosed electrical connection path, 4 Sensor chip, 5 Glass pedestal, 6 Cap, 7 Pressure connection. p Pressure.

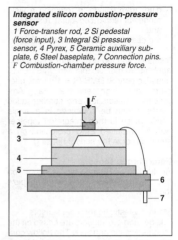

Integrated silicon combustion-pressure sensor
1 Force-transfer rod, 2 Si pedestal (force input), 3 Integral Si pressure sensor, 4 Pyrex, 5 Ceramic auxiliary sub-plate, 6 Steel baseplate, 7 Connection pins. F Combustion-chamber pressure force.

the forces registered at the front diaphragm through the pedestal and into the sensor chip with a minimum of distortion. This remote installation position means that the chip is only subjected to operating temperatures below 150 °C.

New sensor concepts

Piezoelectric sensors

Piezoelectric sensors provide dynamic pressure measurement. On electronically controlled diesel fuel-injection pumps, for determining port opening and port closing (end of pump delivery and start of pump delivery respectively) only changes of pumping-element pressure are registered by the sensor. A thin intermediate diaphragm is employed for direct or indirect pressure transmission to a cylindrical or rectangular piezo-ceramic pellet. Because extreme precision is not required in this application, deviations resulting from hysteresis, temperature and aging are not a major consideration. An amplifier featuring a high-resistance input circuit is frequently installed in the sealed housing. This unit decouples the signal locally to prevent shunts from producing measurement errors.

High-pressure sensors with metal diaphragm

Sensors are also required to monitor extremely high pressures, e.g., in the common rails of diesel injection systems to provide data for closed-loop control. Here, diaphragms made of high-quality spring steel and featuring a DMS pick-up furnish much better performance than systems designed to monitor manifold pressure. These units
– use uncomplicated and inexpensive designs to insulate the measured medium

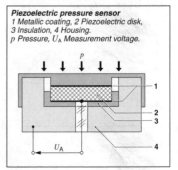

Piezoelectric pressure sensor
1 Metallic coating, 2 Piezoelectric disk, 3 Insulation, 4 Housing.
p Pressure, U_A Measurement voltage.

– differ from silicon in retaining a yield range for enhanced burst resistance, and
– are easy to install in metallic housings.

Insulated sputtered (vacuum-evaporation application) metallic thin-film DMS (K = 2) and also poly-Si DMS (K = 40) units offer permanently high sensor accuracy. Amplification, calibration and compensation elements can be combined in a single ASIC, which is then integrated together with the required EMC protection on a small carrier in the sensor housing.

Force/torque sensors

Applications: Bearing-pin sensors on tractors in systems for controlling plow force.

<u>Magnetoelastic bearing-pin sensors</u>
The bearing-pin sensors are based on the magnetoelastic principle. The hollow coupling pin contains a magnetic field coil. Positioned at a 90° angle to this is a measuring coil to which no magnetic flux is applied when no forces are present. However, when the ferromagnetic material in the pin becomes anisotropic under force, a flux proportional to the force permeates the measuring coil, where it induces electrical voltage. The supply and amplification electronics integrated in a chip are likewise located inside the pin.

<u>New sensor concepts</u>
– Eddy-current principle: eddy-current torsional-force sensor, radial and axial torsion-measurement spring, radial and axial slotted-disk and coil configuration.
– Measurement with strain-gauge resistors (DMS principle): pressed-in and welded-in sensors, pressed-in elements.
– Magnetoelastic force sensor.
– Force-measurement ring using thick-film technology: force measurement with orthogonally loaded pressure-sensitive resistors.
– Hydrostatic pressure measurement in plunger-loaded hydrostatic cylinders, generally charged with rubber or gum elastic (no leakage risk).
– Microbending effect: fiber-optic compressive-stress sensor.

<u>New applications:</u>
– Measuring coupling forces on commercial vehicles between towing vehicle and trailer/semitrailer for controlled, force-free braking.
– Measuring damping forces for electronic chassis and suspension-control systems.
– Measuring axle load for electronically-controlled braking-force distribution on heavy commercial vehicles.
– Measurement of pedal force on electronically-controlled braking systems.

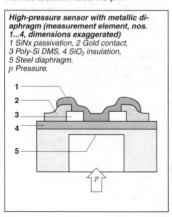

High-pressure sensor with metallic diaphragm (measurement element, nos. 1...4, dimensions exaggerated)
1 SiNx passivation, 2 Gold contact, 3 Poly-Si DMS, 4 SiO₂ insulation, 5 Steel diaphragm.
p Pressure.

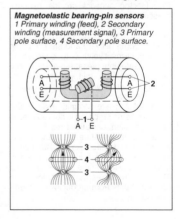

Magnetoelastic bearing-pin sensors
1 Primary winding (feed), 2 Secondary winding (measurement signal), 3 Primary pole surface, 4 Secondary pole surface.

- Measurement of braking force in electrically actuated and electronically controlled braking systems.
- Non-contact measurement of drive and braking torque.
- Non-contact measurement of steering/power-steering torque.
- Finger-protection for electric power windows and sunroofs.

In the case of the cross-ductor principle used in <u>magnetoelastic tension/compressive-force sensors</u>, no voltage is induced in the secondary transformer coil on account of the right-angled offset in the rest state ($F = 0$). A voltage is only established in the coil when under the application of force the relative permeability of the magnetoelastic sensor material used (special steel) becomes anisotropic. This sensor principle can also be applied for higher operating temperatures (up to 300 °C) (e.g. for installation in proximity to the brakes).

Torque measurement:
There are essentially two different ways of measuring torque: angle- and stress-measuring methods. In contrast to stress-measuring methods (DMS, magnetoelastic), angle-measuring methods (e.g. eddy current) require a particular length of torsion shaft over which the torsion angle (approx. 0.4...4 °) can be picked off. The

mechanical stress proportional to the torque σ is directed at an angle of under 45° to the shaft axis.

Stress-measuring torque sensor:
The mechanical stress is measured with a strain-gauge bridge. The bridge is powered via a transformer and the supply is air-gap-independent due to rectifier and control electronics accommodated on the shaft. Further local electronic components on the shaft enable the measurement signal to be amplified and converted into an air-gap-invariant alternating-current waveform (e.g. analogous to frequency) which is likewise decoupled by a transformer. For larger quantities, the required electronics can be integrated on the shaft in a single chip. The strain-gauge resistors can be inexpensively accommodated on a premanufactured round steel

Basic principles of torque measurement
1 Torsion bar. ϕ Torsion angle, σ Torsional stress, M Torque, r Radius, l Rod length.

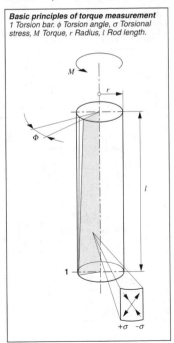

Magnetoelastic compression-tension force sensor according to cross-ductor principle
1 Supply coil, 2 Measuring coil, 3 Magnetic yoke, 4 Magnetoelastic force-sensing element, 5 Phase-selective rectifier. F Force.

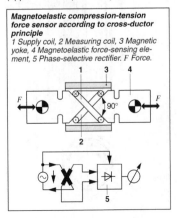

plate (e.g. in thin-film form, P. 87) and then welded with the round plate onto the shaft. High precision levels can be achieved with such a configuration in spite of reasonable manufacturing costs.

Angle-measuring torque sensor:
Concentrically engaged slot sleeves are flanged at each end over a sufficient length of the measurement shaft. The sleeves have two rows of slots which are arranged in such a way that, when the shaft is subjected to torsion, an increasingly larger view of the shaft is exposed in the one row while the view is increasingly blocked off in the other row. Two fixed high-frequency coils (approx. 1 MHz) arranged over each row are thus increasingly or decreasingly damped or varied in terms of their inductance value. In order to achieve sufficient precision, it is essen-

tial for the slot sleeves to be manufactured and mounted to exacting standards. The associated electronics are appropriately accommodated very near to the coils.

Flow meters

Flow quantities in automotive applications:
– <u>Fuel flow</u> rate, i.e., amount of fuel actually consumed by the engine, is based on the difference between forward and return flow rates.

On spark-ignition engines featuring electronically-controlled fuel-metering systems using air intake as a primary control parameter, this figure is already available in the form of a calculated metering value; thus measurement for control of the combustion process is redundant. However, fuel-flow measurement is re-

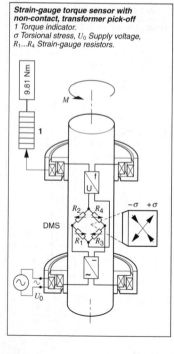

Strain-gauge torque sensor with non-contact, transformer pick-off
1 Torque indicator.
σ Torsional stress, U_0 Supply voltage, $R_1...R_4$ Strain-gauge resistors.

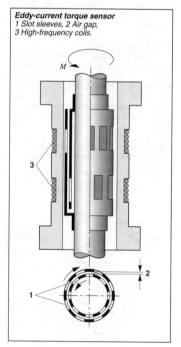

Eddy-current torque sensor
1 Slot sleeves, 2 Air gap,
3 High-frequency coils.

quired to determine and display fuel consumption on engines not equipped with electronic control systems.
– <u>Air flow</u> in the engine's intake manifold: The mass relationships are the salient factors in the chemical process of combustion, thus the actual objective is to measure the mass flow of the intake or charge air, although procedures employing volume and dynamic pressure are also applied.

The maximum air-mass flow to be monitored lies within a range of 400...1000 kg/h, depending upon engine output. As a result of the modest idle requirements of modern engines, the ratio between minimum and maximum air flow is $1:90...1:100$.

Flow measurement

A medium of uniform density ϱ at all points flows through a tube with a constant cross-section A at a velocity which is virtually uniform in the tube cross-section ("turbulent" flow):
– Volume flow rate $Q_V = v \cdot A$ and
– Mass flow rate $Q_M = v \cdot A$

If an orifice plate is then installed in the duct, forming a restriction, this will result in a pressure differential Δp in accordance with Bernoulli's Law. This differential is an intermediate quantity between the volume and mass flow rates:
$$\Delta p = const \cdot \varrho \cdot v^2 = const \cdot Q_V \cdot Q_M$$
Fixed-position orifice plates can only cover measurement variables within a range of $1:10$; variable flaps are able to monitor variations through a substantially greater ratio range.

Volume flow sensors

According to the principle of the <u>Karman vortex path</u>, whirls and eddies diverge from the air stream at a constant distance behind an obstruction. Their periodicity as measured (e.g., monitoring of pressure or acoustic waves) at their periphery (duct wall) provides an eddy frequency in the form of a signal ratio:
$$f = 1/T = const \cdot Q_V.$$

Disadvantage: Pulsation in the flow can result in measuring errors.

The <u>ultrasonic flow-measurement procedure</u> can be employed to monitor the propagation time t of an acoustic pulse as it travels through the medium to be measured (e.g. air) at angle α (see Fig.). One measurement is taken upstream and one downstream using the same measurement path l. The resulting transit-time differential is proportional to the volumetric flow rate.

Pitot-tube air-flow sensors

Pivoting, variable-position pressure flaps leave a variable section of the flow diameter unobstructed, with the size of the free diameter being dependent upon the flow rate. A potentiometer monitors the characteristic flap positions for the respective flow rates. The physical and electrical design of the air-flow sensor, e.g., for

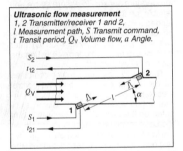

Ultrasonic flow measurement
1, 2 Transmitter/receiver 1 and 2,
l Measurement path, S Transmit command,
t Transit period, Q_V Volume flow, α Angle.

L-Jetronic (P. 471), is such as to ensure a logarithmic relationship between flow rate and output signal (at very low flow rates the incremental voltage variations referred to the flow-rate variation are substantially greater than at high flow rates). Other types of automotive air-flow sensors are designed for a linear characteristic (KE-Jetronic, P. 469). Measuring errors can occur in cases where the flap's mechanical inertia prevents it from keeping pace with a rapidly pulsating air current (full-load condition at high engine speeds).

Air-mass meters

Air-mass meters operate according to the hot-wire or hot-film principle; the unit contains no moving mechanical parts. The closed-loop control circuit in the meter's housing maintains a constant temperature differential between a fine platinum wire or thin-film resistor and the passing air stream. The current required for heating provides an extremely precise – albeit non-linear – index of mass air flow. The system's ECU generally converts the signals into linear form as well as assuming other signal-processing duties. Due to its closed-loop design, this type of air-mass meter can monitor flow rate variations in the millisecond range. However, the sensor's inability to recognize flow direction can produce substantial measuring errors when strong pulsation occurs in the manifold.

The platinum wire in the <u>hot-wire air-mass meter</u> functions both as the heating element and as the heating element's temperature sensor. To ensure stable and reliable performance throughout an extended service life, the system must burn-off all accumulated deposits from the hot-wire's surface (at approx. 1000 °C) after each phase of active operation (when the ignition is switched off).

The <u>hot-film air-mass meter</u> combines all measuring elements and the control electronics on a single substrate. In current versions, the heating resistor is located on the back of the base wafer, with the corresponding temperature sensor on the front. This results in somewhat greater response lag than that associated with the hot-wire meter. The temperature-compensation sensor (R_K) and the heating element are thermally decoupled by means of a laser cut in the ceramic substrate. More favorable flow characteristics make it possible to dispense with the hot-wire meter's burn-off decontamination process.

Extremely compact <u>micromechanical hot-film air-mass meters</u> also operate according to thermal principles. Here the heating and measuring resistors are in the form of thin platinum layers sputtered onto the base Si chip. Thermal decoupling from the mounting is obtained by installing the Si chip in the area of the heater resistor H on a micromechanically thinned section of the base (similar to a pressure-sensor diaphragm). The adjacent heater-temperature sensor S_H and the air-temperature sensor S_L (on the thick edge of the Si chip) maintain the heater resistor H at a constant overtemperature. This method differs from earlier techniques in dispensing with the heating current as an output signal. Instead, the signal is derived from the temperature differential in the medium (air) as monitored at the sensors S_1 and S_2. Temperature sensors are located in the flow path upstream and downstream from the heater resistor H. Although (as with the earlier process) the response pattern remains nonlinear, the fact that the resulting signal also indicates the flow direction represents an improvement over the former method using the heating current.

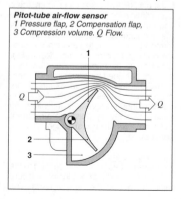

Pitot-tube air-flow sensor
1 Pressure flap, 2 Compensation flap,
3 Compression volume. Q Flow.

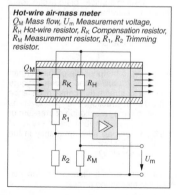

Hot-wire air-mass meter
Q_M Mass flow, U_m Measurement voltage,
R_H Hot-wire resistor, R_K Compensation resistor,
R_M Measurement resistor, R_1, R_2 Trimming resistor.

Micromechanical hot-film air-mass meter
1 Dielectric diaphragm, H Heating resistor, S_H Heater-temperature sensor, S_L Air-temperature sensor, S_1, S_2 Temperature sensors (upstream and downstream), Q_{LM} Mass air flow, s Measurement point, t Temperature.

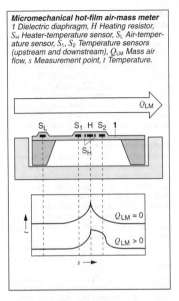

O_2 sensor response curve
λ Excess-air factor, U_S Sensor voltage.

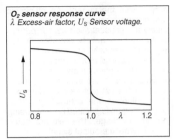

occurs at $\lambda = 1$.

Electrically-heated sensors are especially well-suited for measurements in the lean range, and already come into operation in the warm-up phase.

For the wide lean range, flat and smaller "wafer sensors" of multilayer ceramic design (wide-band lambda sensors) are used; these sensors can also be used in diesel engines. A sensor of this type is essentially a combination of a conventional concentration cell which acts as a galvanic cell (Nernst sensor) and a limit-current or "pump" cell. A voltage is applied from an external source to the pump cell, which is of the same design as a conventional concentration cell. If the voltage is high enough, a "limit current" sets in which is proportional to the difference in oxygen concentration at both ends of the sensor. Oxygen atoms are transported – depending on the po-

Concentration sensors

Virtually all chemical concentration sensors run the risk of being poisoned during the necessary direct contact with the measured medium, i.e. irreversibly damaged by harmful foreign substances. For instance, electrolytic oxygen-concentration sensors (lambda oxygen sensors) can be rendered useless by lead that may be present in the fuel or exhaust gas.

Oxygen-concentration sensor
(lambda oxygen sensor)

The fuel-metering system employs the exhaust-gas residual-oxygen content as measured by the lambda sensor to very precisely regulate the air-fuel mixture for combustion to the value λ (lambda) = 1 (stoichiometric combustion, P. 458).

The sensor is a solid-state electrolyte made of ZrO ceramic material. At high temperatures, this electrolyte becomes conductive and generates a characteristic galvanic charge at the sensor connections; this voltage is an index of the gas' oxygen content. The maximum variation

O_2 sensor in exhaust pipe
1 Ceramic sensor, 2 Electrodes, 3 Contact, 4 Housing contacts, 5 Exhaust pipe, 6 Protective ceramic coating (porous).

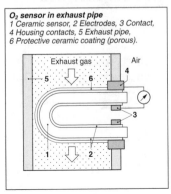

larity – with the current. An electronic control circuit causes the pump cell to supply the concentration sensor permanently through a very narrow diffusion gap with precisely enough oxygen to maintain a status of $\lambda = 1$ at the sensor. I.e. oxygen is pumped away in the event of excess air in the exhaust gas (lean range); in the event of a low residual-oxygen content in the exhaust gas (rich range), oxygen is pumped in by reversing the pump voltage. The relevant pump current forms the output signal.

Humidity sensors:
Areas of application:
– Monitoring of air drier for pneumatic brakes,
– Monitoring of outside air humidity for slippery-ice warnings,
– Calculation of dew point in vehicle interior (air-quality sensing, climate control, misting over of vehicle windows).

Capacitive sensors are mostly used to determine relative humidity. A sensor of this type is composed of a thin-film polymer with a metal coating on both sides. The capacitance of this capacitor is considerably but reversibly modified by the adsorption of water. The time constant is typically approx. 30 s. The dew point can also be determined by additionally measuring the air temperature (NTC).

When installed e.g. in an air-quality ECU, a Teflon diaphragm protects the sensor against harmful substances. Generally speaking, the air-quality ECU also contains above all <u>CO and NO_x sensors</u>, mostly in the form of thick-film resistors (SnO_x), which modify their electrical resistance in a wide range (e.g. 1...100 kohm) by adsorption of the measured media.

Temperature sensors
Temperature measurements in motor vehicles are conducted almost entirely by exploiting the sensitivity to temperature variation found in electrical resistance materials with a positive (PTC) or negative (NTC) temperature coefficient as <u>contact thermometers</u>. Conversion of the resistance variation into analog voltage is performed predominantly with the aid of supplementary temperature-neutral or inversely-sensitive resistors as voltage dividers (also providing increased linearity). <u>Non-contact (pyrometric) temperature sensing</u> has recently come into consideration for passenger safety (passenger observation for airbag activation) and also for passenger comfort (climate control,

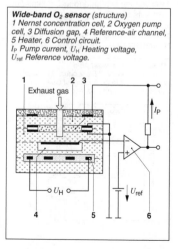

Wide-band O_2 sensor (structure)
1 Nernst concentration cell, 2 Oxygen pump cell, 3 Diffusion gap, 4 Reference-air channel, 5 Heater, 6 Control circuit.
I_P Pump current, U_H Heating voltage, U_{ref} Reference voltage.

Exhaust gas

I_P

U_H

U_{ref}

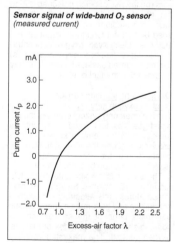

Sensor signal of wide-band O_2 sensor (measured current)

Pump current I_P / mA

Excess-air factor λ

prevention of window misting); this has been made economically viable by the introduction of microsystems technology. The following temperatures occur in motor vehicles:

Location	Range	°C
Intake air/charge air	−40 ...	170
Outside atmosphere	−40 ...	60
Passenger compartment	−20 ...	80
Ventilation & heating air	−20 ...	60
Evaporator (AC)	−10 ...	50
Engine coolant	−40 ...	130
Engine oil	−40 ...	170
Battery	−40 ...	100
Fuel	−40 ...	120
Tire air	−40 ...	120
Exhaust gas	100 ...	1000
Brake calipers	−40 ...	2000

At many locations, temperature is also measured in order that it can be compensated for in those cases in which temperature variations trigger faults or act as an undesirable influencing variable.

Sintered-ceramic resistors (NTC)

Sintered-ceramic resistors (heat conductors, thermistors) made of heavy-metal oxides and oxidized mixed crystals (sintered in pearl or plate-form) are included among those semiconductive materials which display an inverted exponential response curve. High thermal sensitivity means that applications are restricted to a "window" of approx. 200 K; however, this range can be defined within a latitude of −40 ... approx. 850 °C.

Thin-film metallic resistors (PTC)

Thin-film metallic resistors, integrated on a single substrate wafer together with two supplementary, temperature-neutral trimming resistors, are characterized by extreme precision, as they can be manufactured and then "trimmed" with lasers to maintain exact response-curve tolerances over long periods of time. The use of layer technology makes it possible to adapt the base material (ceramic, glass, plastic foil) and the upper layers (plastic molding or paint, sealed foil, glass and ceramic coatings) to the respective application, and thus provide protection against the monitored medium. Although metallic

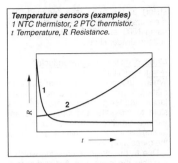

Temperature sensors (examples)
1 NTC thermistor, 2 PTC thermistor.
t Temperature, R Resistance.

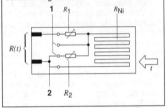

Metallic-film thermistor
1 Auxiliary contacts, 2 Bridge, R_{Ni} Nickel-plated resistor, $R(t)$ Resistance relative to temperature t, R_1, R_2 Temperature-independent trimming resistors.

layers are less sensitive to thermal variations than the ceramic-oxide semiconductor sensors, both linearity and reproducibility are better:

Sensor material	Temperature coefficient TC	Measurement range
Ni	$5.1 \cdot 10^{-3}/C$	−60...320 °C
Cu	$4.1 \cdot 10^{-3}/C$	−50...200 °C
Pt	$3.5 \cdot 10^{-3}/C$	−220...850 °C

With
$$TC = [R(100\,°C) - R(0\,°C)]/[R(0\,°C) \cdot 100\,K]$$

Thick-film resistors (PTC/NTC)

Thick-film pastes with both high specific resistance (low surface-area requirement) and positive and negative temperature coefficients are generally employed as temperature sensors for compensation purposes. They have non-linear response characteristics (without, however, the extreme variations of the massive NTC resistor) and can be laser-trimmed. The measurement effect can be enhanced by using NTC and PTC materials to form voltage-divider circuits.

Monocrystalline Si-semiconductor resistors (PTC)

When monocrystalline semiconductor materials such as Si are used to manufacture the temperature sensor, it is possible to integrate additional active and passive circuitry on the sensor chip (allowing initial signal conditioning directly at the measuring point).

Due to the closer tolerancing which is possible, these are manufactured according to the spreading-resistance principle. The current flows through the measuring resistor and through a surface-point contact before arriving at the Si bulk material. It then proceeds, widely distributed, to a counterelectrode covering the base of the sensor chip. As well as the highly reproducible material constants, the high current density after the contact point (high precision achieved through photolithographic manufacture) almost exclusively determines the sensor's resistance value.

The measurement sensitivity is virtually twice that of the Pt resistor (TC = $7.73 \cdot 10^{-3}$/K). However, the temperature-response curve is less linear than that of a metallic sensor.

Thermopile sensors

For non-contact measurement of the temperature of a body, the radiation emitted by this body is measured; this radiation is preferably in the infrared (IR) range (wavelength: 5...20 µm). Strictly speaking, the product of the radiated power and the emission coefficient of the body is measured. The latter is material-dependent but mostly close to 1 for materials of technical interest (also for glass). However, for reflective or IR-permeable materials (e.g. air, Si), it is << 1. The measuring point is reproduced on a radiation-sensitive element which thus heats up slightly with respect to its environment (typically 0.01...0.001 °C). This small temperature difference can be effectively measured with thermocouples many of which are connected in succession to increase the measuring effect (thermopile). It is possible to manufacture just such a thermopile sensor at low cost using micromechanical techniques. All the "hot" points are located on a thermally well insulated, thin diaphragm while all the cold points are located on the thicker chip edge (temperature sink). The sensor's settling time is typically approx. 20 ms. A "single-pixel sensor" of this type is ideal for e.g. determining the surface temperature of the windshield so as to prevent it from misting over should the temperature drop below the dew point.

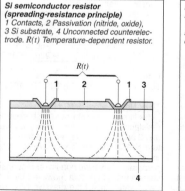

Si semiconductor resistor (spreading-resistance principle)
1 Contacts, 2 Passivation (nitride, oxide), 3 Si substrate, 4 Unconnected counterelectrode. R(t) Temperature-dependent resistor.

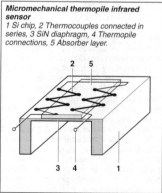

Micromechanical thermopile infrared sensor
1 Si chip, 2 Thermocouples connected in series, 3 SiN diaphragm, 4 Thermopile connections, 5 Absorber layer.

If several pixels are arranged on a chip to form an <u>array</u> (e.g. 4 x 4), rough imaging is thus already possible. However, there should not be too much insensitive surface area between the pixels and the pixels themselves must be thermally well insulated against each other. As all the pixels can optionally respond electrically, the chip has a large number of terminals. For a TO5 housing, the ASIC for instance must be located near the sensor to pre-amplify and serialize the signal. To determine the absolute temperature of the pixels, this ASIC also contains in most cases a reference temperature sensor with which object temperatures can be determined to an accuracy of approx. ±0.5 K.

In order to reproduce a scene thermally on the sensor array, the array requires an IR optical imaging unit. The highly inexpensive arched mirror must mostly be ruled out for reasons of available space. Glass lenses are impervious to IR light and plastic lenses are only adequate for operating temperatures up to approx. 85 °C. Si lenses however are very well suited to heat radiation and can be micromechanically manufactured at low cost as diffraction (Fresnel) or refraction lenses with diameters of up to approx. 4 mm. When inserted into the cover of a TO5 housing, they serve at the same time to protect the sensor against direct damage. Although filling the housing with insert gas increases crosstalk between the pixels somewhat, on the other hand it also reduces their response time.

Sensors for other applications

<u>Dirt sensors</u>
The sensor measures the level of contamination on the headlamp lens to furnish the data required for automatic lens cleaning systems.

The sensor's photoelectric reflected-light barrier consists of a light source (LED) and a light receiver (phototransistor). The source is positioned on the inside of the lens, within the cleansed area, but not directly in the light beam's path. When the lens is clean, or covered with rain droplets, the infrared measurement beam emitted by the unit passes through the lens without being obstructed. Only a minuscule part is reflected back to the light receiver. However, if it encounters dirt particles on the outer surface of the lens, it is reflected back to the receiver at an intensity that is proportional to the degree of contamination and automatically activates the headlamp washer unit once a defined level is reached.

<u>Rain sensors</u>
The rain sensor recognizes rain droplets on the windshield, so that the windshield wipers can be triggered automatically. The unit thus frees the driver to concen-

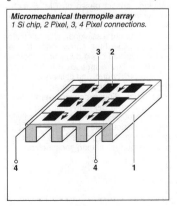

Micromechanical thermopile array
1 Si chip, 2 Pixel, 3, 4 Pixel connections.

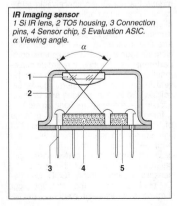

IR imaging sensor
1 Si IR lens, 2 TO5 housing, 3 Connection pins, 4 Sensor chip, 5 Evaluation ASIC.
α Viewing angle.

trate on other tasks by making the various control operations used to activate conventional wiper systems redundant. For the time being the driver can still use the manual controls; if desired, the automatic system must be manually selected when the vehicle is started.

The sensor consists of an optical transmission and reception path (similar to the dirt sensor). In this application, the light is directed toward the windshield at an angle. A dry outer surface reflects (total reflection) it back to the receiver, which is also mounted at an angle. When water droplets are present on the outer surface, a substantial amount of the light is refracted outward, thus weakening the return signal. This system also responds to dirt once the activation threshold is exceeded.

Imaging sensors

With imaging sensors, attempts are now being made to reproduce the superior capability of the human eye and the associated mental recognition faculties (albeit at present only to a very modest extent). It is certain that in the foreseeable future the costs of imaging sensors and the high-power processors needed for interpreting a scene will drop to levels that will be viable for automotive applications. In contrast to the human eye, current imaging sensors are also sensitive in the close IR range (wavelength approx. 1 µm). This means that for all the conceivable applications in an automobile, night-time operation becomes possible using invisible IR illumination. Imaging sensors could in future find a variety of uses in motor vehicles for monitoring the passenger compartment (seat position, forward displacement in event of a crash etc.) and the vehicle environment (lateral guidance, collision avoidance, parking and back-up assistance, road-sign recognition etc.).

Imaging sensors are a special instance of "multisensor structures" composed of light-sensitive elements (pixels) which are arranged in line or matrix form and receive their light from a conventional optical imaging system. With the Si imaging sensors available today (CCD Charge-Coupled Devices), the incident light through a transparent electrode gener-

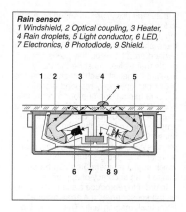

Rain sensor
1 Windshield, 2 Optical coupling, 3 Heater, 4 Rain droplets, 5 Light conductor, 6 LED, 7 Electronics, 8 Photodiode, 9 Shield.

ates charge carriers in proportion to the intensity and exposure time. These are then collected in a "potential pot" (Si-SiO$_2$ boundary layer). Using further electrodes, these charges are transferred into an opaque zone and further transported in "analog" shift registers (bucket-brigade principle) in lines into an output register which is serially read out at a higher clock-pulse rate.

While CCD sensors are only of restricted use in motor vehicles on account of their limited light/dark dynamic response (50 dB), their readout time and their temperature range (< 50 °C), newer ("smart") imaging sensors based on CMOS technology are appearing which are fully suitable for automotive applications. The logarithmic brightness/signal characteristic curve possible here corresponds to the human eye and has a dynamic response of 120 dB. This dispenses with the need for e.g. glare control and delivers constant contrast resolution over the entire brightness range. These sensors permit random access to the individual pixels with simultaneously increased sensitivity (higher readout rate). Even the first signal-preprocessing processes are already possible on the imaging-sensor chip.

Future measurement applications:
- Steering-wheel torque sensing (electromotive power steering, "steer-by-wire" system)
- Drive-torque sensing (misfire detection, load signal)
- Passenger safety: AOS (Automotive Occupancy Sensing, Out-of-Position Sensing)
- Measuring wheel forces and friction-co-efficient potential
- Fluid sensors
- Sensors for monitoring the vehicle environment (imaging sensors etc.) for autonomous driving and detection of an imminent impact.

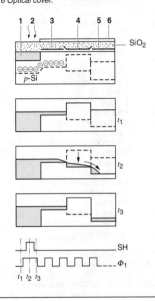

CCD principle (charge-coupled devices)
1 Photodiode, 2 Light, 3 Storage electrode, 4 Shift gate, 5 Transfer electrode, 6 Optical cover.

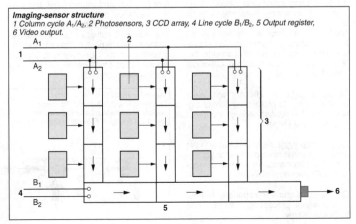

Imaging-sensor structure
1 Column cycle A_1/A_2, 2 Photosensors, 3 CCD array, 4 Line cycle B_1/B_2, 5 Output register, 6 Video output.

Actuators

Quantities and units

Quantity		Unit
A	Pole face; piston surface area	mm²
B	Magnetic induction or magnetic flux density	T
F	Force	N
I	Electric current	A
l	Length of conductor in field	mm
M	Torque	N · m
p	Pressure	Pa
Q	Volume rate of flow	l/min
Q_{Heat}	Heat flow	W
s	Distance, piston travel	mm
V	Volume	mm³
V_{th}	Displaced volume per rotation	mm³
α	Angle between current flow direction and magnetic lines of force	°
δ	Air-gap length	mm
μ_0	Permeability constant	
φ	Rotation angle	°

Actuators (final-control elements) form the junction between the electronic signal processor (data processing) and the actual process (mechanical motion). They convert the low-power signals conveying the positioning information into operating signals of an energy level adequate for process control. Signal converters are combined with amplifier elements to exploit the physical transformation principles governing the interrelationships between various forms of energy (electrical – mechanical – fluid – thermal).

Transistor actuator: Element with electronic circuitry for processing control signals. Includes auxiliary energy input and energy output stages.

Servo component: As above, but with the ability to process nonelectrical control signals. Transistor actuator + servo component = Final-control element.

Converter: Control component without control-signal processing, receives and transfers energy.

Actuator: Control chain comprising servo component and converter.
The term actuator is also employed as a general-purpose designation for servo components without converters on their own.

Electromechanical actuators

This type of energy conversion represents one option for classifying electromechanical actuators. The energy emanating from the source is transformed into magnetic or electrical field energy, or converted to thermal energy. The individual force-generation principle is determined by these forms of energy, and bases upon either field forces or certain specific material characteristics. Magnetostrictive materials make it possible to design actuators for application in the micropositioning range. This category also includes piezoelectric actuators, which are built according to a multilayer design similar to ceramic capacitors and are potential actuators for fast-acting fuel injectors. Thermal actuators depend exclusively upon the exploitation of characteristics of specific materials.

Actuators in a motor vehicle are mostly electro-magneto-mechanical transformers and by extension electrical servomotors (P. 132) and translational and rotational solenoid actuators. An exception is the pyrotechnical airbag system (P. 803). The solenoid actuators can themselves be the servo element, or they can assume a control function by governing a downstream force-amplification device (e.g. mechanical-hydraulic).

Actuator chain
1 Information, 2 Actuator, 3 Transformer, 4 Control element, 5 Losses, 6 External electrical energy, 7 External hydraulic energy.

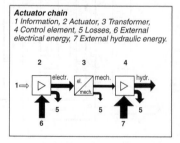

Electromechanical actuators (system)

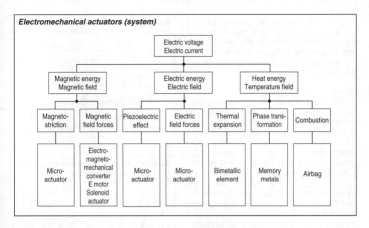

Force generation in the magnetic field

The distinction between the electrodynamic and the electromagnetic actuator principles stems from the manner in which forces are generated in the magnetic field. Common to both principles is the magnetic circuit with soft-magnetic material and the coil for excitation of the magnetic field. A major difference lies in the force which can be extracted from the unit under technically-feasible conditions. Under identical conditions, the force produced through application of the electromagnetic principle is greater by a factor of 40. The electrical time constant for this type of actuator is comparable to the mechanical time constants. Both force-generation principles are applied in linear and rotary drive mechanisms.

Electrodynamic principle

Electrodynamic designs are based on the force exerted on mobile charges or charged conductors within a magnetic field (Lorentz force). An excitation coil or a permanent magnet generates a constant magnetic field. The electrical energy destined for conversion is applied to the moving armature coil (plunger or immersion coil). A high degree of actuator precision is achieved by designing the armature coil with low mass and low inductivity. The two accumulator elements (one on the fixed and one on the moving component) produce two active force directions via current-direction reversal in the armature and excitation coils.

The secondary field produced by the armature current flows in an open mag-

---

Electrodynamic and electromagnetic transformers

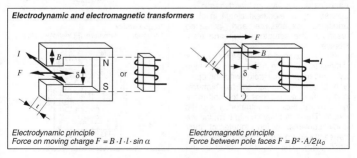

Electrodynamic principle
Force on moving charge $F = B \cdot I \cdot l \cdot \sin \alpha$

Electromagnetic principle
Force between pole faces $F = B^2 \cdot A / 2\mu_0$

netic circuit, thereby diminishing the effects of saturation. Approximately speaking, the force (torque) exerted by an electrodynamic actuator over its setting range is proportional to current and independent of travel.

Electromagnetic principle

The electromagnetic principle exploits the mutual attraction displayed by soft ferrous materials in a magnetic field. The electromagnetic actuator is equipped with only one coil, which generates both the field energy and the energy to be transformed. In accordance with the operating principles, the excitation coil is equipped with an iron core to provide higher inductance. However, as the force is proportional to the square of the density of the magnetic flux, the unit is operative in only one direction. The electromagnetic actuator thus requires a return element (such as a mechanical spring or a magnetic return mechanism).

Dynamic response

The dynamic response of an electromechanical actuator, i.e. the activation and deactivation operations, is defined by the equation of mechanical motion, the differential equation of electrical circuits and Maxwell's equations of dynamics. The current- and position-dependent force follows from Maxwell's equations.

The most basic electrical circuit consists of an inductor with an ohmic resistor. One means of enhancing the dynamic response is through over-excitation at the instant of activation, while deactivation can be accelerated with a Zener diode. In each case, increasing the dynamic response of the electrical circuit involves additional expenditure and increased losses in the actuator's triggering electronics.

Field diffusion is a delay effect which is difficult to influence in actuators with high dynamic response. Rapid switching operations are accompanied by high-frequency field fluctuations in the soft-magnetic material of the actuator's magnetic circuit. These fluctuations, in turn, induce eddy currents, which counteract their cause (build-up and decay of the magnetic field). The resultant delay in the

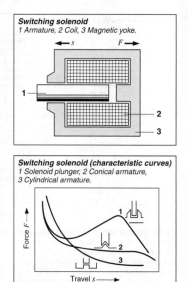

Switching solenoid
1 Armature, 2 Coil, 3 Magnetic yoke.

Switching solenoid (characteristic curves)
1 Solenoid plunger, 2 Conical armature,
3 Cylindrical armature.

Force F ⟶

Travel s ⟶

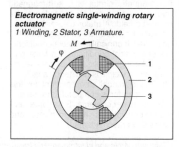

Electromagnetic single-winding rotary actuator
1 Winding, 2 Stator, 3 Armature.

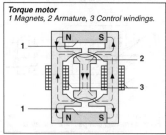

Torque motor
1 Magnets, 2 Armature, 3 Control windings.

build-up or reduction of forces can only be reduced by selecting appropriate materials with low electrical conductivity and permeability.

Design
Design selection is essentially determined by operating conditions (e.g., installation space, required force-travel curve and dynamic response).

Electromagnetic actuators
A typical form for <u>translational</u> electromagnetic actuators is the switching solenoid with a force/travel curve which falls as a function of the square of positioning travel. The precise shape of the curve is determined by the type of working gap (e.g., conical or immersion armature).

<u>Rotational</u> electromagnetic actuators are characterized by a defined pole arrangement in stator and rotor. When current is applied to one of the coils, the rotor and stator poles respond with mutual attraction, and in doing so generate a torque.

The <u>single-winding rotary actuator</u> incorporates a pair of poles in each of the two main sections, as well as a coil in the stator. Its maximum positioning range is approx. 45°.

The <u>torque motor</u> is a bidirectional electromagnetic rotary actuator featuring a stable working point and without counterforces. The rotor is maintained in a stable position by the excitation field of the permanent magnet in the stator. The magnetic field generated by one or two stator windings produces torque and provides unilateral compensation for the excitation field. This type of layout is suitable for applications in which substantial forces are required over small angles. The relationship between the applied current and the torque motor's force is roughly linear. The torque-motor principle is also employed in translational actuators.

Electrodynamic actuators
In a pot magnet (immersion-coil actuator), a cylindrical immersion coil (armature winding) is set in motion in a working gap.

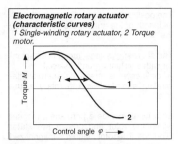

Electromagnetic rotary actuator (characteristic curves)
1 Single-winding rotary actuator, 2 Torque motor.

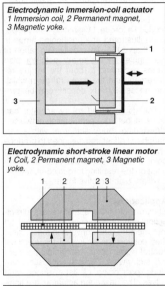

Electrodynamic immersion-coil actuator
1 Immersion coil, 2 Permanent magnet, 3 Magnetic yoke.

Electrodynamic short-stroke linear motor
1 Coil, 2 Permanent magnet, 3 Magnetic yoke.

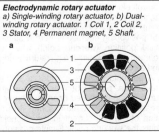

Electrodynamic rotary actuator
a) Single-winding rotary actuator, b) Dual-winding rotary actuator. 1 Coil 1, 2 Coil 2, 3 Stator, 4 Permanent magnet, 5 Shaft.

The positioning range is limited by the axial length of the armature winding and by the gap.

The <u>short-stroke linear motor</u> is an actuator with a virtually round disk coil.
A distinction is made between single-winding and dual-winding rotary actuators.

Both types include a permanent magnet within the rotor and one or two stator windings. The rotor magnet is magnetized at both ends to produce magnetic flux in the rotary magnet's working gap, which combines with the armature current to produce a torque. Originating from the position illustrated, the positioning range is less than ±45°. The positioning range of the <u>single-winding rotary actuator</u> also varies according to both the torque requirement and the angle range in which the necessary flux density can be provided.

The <u>dual-winding rotary actuator</u> can be described as a combination of two single-winding rotary actuators with a 90° peripheral offset and designed to produce opposed torque flows. A stable working point is achieved at the zero transition point on the resulting torque curve without auxiliary counteractive forces.

Applications

Electromechanical actuators are direct-action control elements, and without an intermediate ratio-conversion mechanism they convert the energy of the electrical control signal into a mechanical positioning factor/work. Typical applications include positioning of flaps, spools and valves. The described actuators are final-control elements without internal return mechanisms, i.e. without a stable working point. They are only capable of carrying out positioning operations from a stable initial position (working point) when a counterforce is applied (e.g., return spring and electrical control).

A solenoid plunger provides a stable static bias point when its force-travel curve is superimposed upon the characteristic response of a return spring. A variation of the coil current in the solenoid shifts the working point. Simple position-

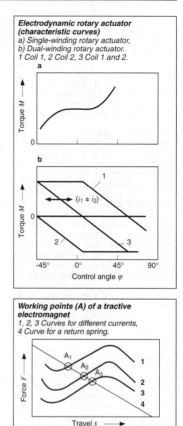

Electrodynamic rotary actuator (characteristic curves)
a) Single-winding rotary actuator,
b) Dual-winding rotary actuator.
1 Coil 1, 2 Coil 2, 3 Coil 1 and 2.

Working points (A) of a tractive electromagnet
1, 2, 3 Curves for different currents,
4 Curve for a return spring.

ing is achieved by controlling the current. However, particular attention must be paid here to the nonlinearity of the force-current characteristic and the positioning system's sensitivity to interference factors (e.g. mechanical friction, pneumatic and hydraulic forces). The temperature sensitivity of the coil resistance results in positioning errors, making corrective current control necessary. A high-precision positioning system with good dynamic response must incorporate a position sensor and a controller.

	Hydraulic actuators	Pneumatic actuators
Medium	– Fluid, mostly oil – Supply from tank, oil sump – Virtually incompressible – Self-lubricating – Viscosity heavily temperature-dependent	– Gas, mostly air – Supply from surrounding air – Compressible – Independent lubrication required – Viscosity fluctuations virtually irrelevant
Pressure range	– to approx. 30 MPa (200 MPa for diesel fuel injectors)	– to approx. 1 MPa or greater (approx. 0.05 MPa for vacuum actuators)
Line connections	– Supply and return connection (possible leakage connection)	– Pressure connection only, return directly to environment
Applications	– Positioning applications with high load rigidity, demanding requirements for syn- chronization and positioning precision in closed-loop control system	– Actuators with lower power require- ment, positioning by mechanical stops, in open control loop

Fluid-mechanical actuators

Hydraulic and pneumatic actuators utilize similar principles for the conversion and regulation of energy (see "Automotive hydraulics" P. 816 and "Automotive pneumatics" P. 832). The table shows the differences in characteristics and applications.

In most applications, fluid-mechanical actuator drives are in the form of <u>hydrostatic energy converters</u>. These operate according to the displacement principle, converting the pressure energy of the fluid medium into mechanical work and vice versa.

In contrast, <u>hydrodynamic transformers</u> operate by converting flow energy (kinetic energy of the moving fluid) into mechanical work (example: hydrodynamic coupling, P. 591).

Losses during energy conversion stem from leakage and friction. Fluid-thermal losses are caused by flow resistance, in which throttle action transforms the hy-

draulic energy into heat. A portion of this heat is dissipated into the environment, and some of it is absorbed and carried away by the fluid medium.

$$Q_{\text{Heat}} = Q_1 \cdot p_1 - Q_2 \cdot p_2$$

With incompressible fluids

$$Q_{\text{Heat}} = Q_1 \cdot (p_1 - p_2)$$

The flow develops into turbulence at restrictions. The flow rate of the fluid is then largely independent of viscosity. On the other hand, viscosity does play a role in the case of laminar flow in narrow pipes and apertures (see "Automotive hydraulics").

Fluid-mechanical amplifiers control the transition of energy between fluid and mechanical states. The regulating mechanism must be designed for control with only a very small proportion of the energy required for the ultimate positioning operation.

Switching valves open/close the orifice governing the flow to/from a fluid-mechanical energy converter. Provided that the control-element opens suffi-

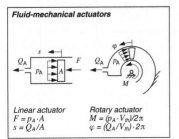

Fluid-mechanical actuators

Linear actuator
$F = p_A \cdot A$
$s = Q_A / A$

Rotary actuator
$M = (p_A \cdot V_{\text{th}})/2\pi$
$\varphi = (Q_A / V_{\text{th}}) \cdot 2\pi$

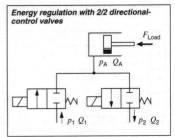

Energy regulation with 2/2 directional-control valves

ciently, the throttling losses remain negligible. Pulse-width-modulated opening and closing can be applied to achieve quasicontinuous control of the fluid-mechanical conversion process with virtually no losses. In practice, however, pressure fluctuations and mechanical contact between the valve elements result in undesirable vibration and noise.

Actuator performance data

The table below compares performance data for nine different actuator types.

It contains data based on components with lengths of 50...100 mm and diameters ranging from 20...50 mm.

Comparisons between rotation motors and linear actuators are based on a conversion mechanism consisting of a mechanical spindle with nut (1 mm pitch). Spindle length and motor length are identical.

Expansion
Expansion is the stroke relative to the length of the inner actuator where energy is generated, e.g., piezoelectric-stack

length, coil length, internal length of hydraulic cylinder. The effective stroke (70 % of specified spindle length) is assumed as the expansion for rotation motors.

Mechanical stress
Mechanical stress is the lift force relative to the force-generating area, e.g. cross-sectional area of piezoelectric devices, coil gap surface (end face or lateral surface), inner surface of hydraulic cylinder. The peripheral force at the rotor and the rotor lateral surface are used to calculate the shear stress in electric motors.

Velocity
The velocity is defined as the control-stroke travel divided by the control time. On rotating motors, it is the peripheral velocity of the rotor.

Mean control-force density
The mean control-force density is the thermally permissible control force relative to unit volume.

Control-force density per stroke
The control-force density per stroke is the

Performance data

No.	Actuator type	Expansion %	Mechanical stress N/mm²	Velocity m/s	Control-force density per stroke W/cm³	Mean control-force density mW/cm³	Efficiency %
1	Hydraulic cylinder	30	21	0.25	9	3020	92
2	Pneumatic cylinder	76	1	1	3.5	1180	88
3	DC Motor	70	0.007[2]	6[3]	0.8	791	50
4	Ultrasonic motor	70	0.06[2]	0.35[3]	0.13	133	16
5	Piezoeffect actuator	0.09	30	2[4]	15.6	61	7
6	Memory wire	4	50	0.002	0.32	53	0.3
7	Valve solenoid[1]	0.8	2.2	0.5	8	44	5
8	Magnetostriction actuator	0.09	22	1.5	1.6	5.4	5
9	Solenoid 5 % ON	21	0.1	0.16	0.12	4.1	5

[1] Fuel cooled, [2] Shear stress in rotor gap/friction gap,
[3] Rotor peripheral velocity, [4] Theoretical limit.

transitional maximum control force for one stroke relative to the unit volume. A spindle (1 mm pitch) with a length equal to the motor length is specified for motors.

Efficiency

The efficiency is the supplied energy divided by the energy transmitted to the actuator, not including losses associated with electronic or other control assemblies. Options for energy recycling (i.e., with piezoelectric actuators) are not considered.

Characteristics

Extremely high performance levels in the areas of expansion, mechanical stress and velocity make hydraulic actuators the preferred design for extended heavy-duty applications.

In electric motors, high peripheral velocities compensate for low magnetic-field forces, allowing these motors to provide high levels of force density in continuous operation.

Despite their limited expansion, piezoelectric actuators are capable of generating high force levels and are thus suitable for providing brief bursts of high energy.

Linear solenoids suffer from substantial thermal losses at the coil; with adequate cooling they achieve moderate force-density ratings, comparable to those of solid-body actuators.

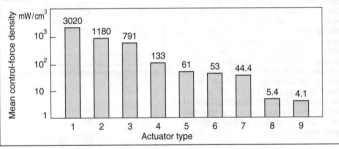

Mean control-force density of selected actuators
1 Hydraulic cylinder, 2 Pneumatic cylinder, 3 DC motor, 4 Ultrasonic motor, 5 Piezoeffect actuator, 6 Memory wire, 7 Valve solenoid actuator, 8 Magnetostriction actuator, 9 Solenoid actuator 5 % on-time.

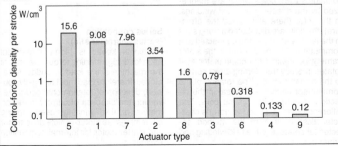

Control-force density per stroke of selected actuators
1 Hydraulic cylinder, 2 Pneumatic cylinder, 3 DC motor, 4 Ultrasonic motor, 5 Piezoeffect actuator, 6 Memory wire, 7 Valve solenoid actuator, 8 Magnetostriction actuator, 9 Solenoid actuator 5 % on-time.

Electrical machines

Operating concept

Electrical machines are used to convert electrical and mechanical energy. An electric motor converts electrical energy into mechanical energy, a generator converts energy in the opposite direction. Electrical machines consist of a stationary component (the stator) and a rotating component (the rotor). There are special designs which depart from this configuration such as linear machines which produce linear motion. Permanent magnets or several coils (windings) are used to produce magnetic fields in the stator and rotor which cause torque to develop between these two machine components. Electrical machines have iron stators and rotors in order to control the magnetic fields. Because the magnetic fluxes change over time, stators and rotors must consist of stacks of individual laminations which are insulated with respect to one another. The spatial arrangement of the coils and the type of current used (direct current, alternating current or three-phase current) permit a number of different electrical machine designs. They differ from one another in the way they operate, and therefore have different applications.

Direct-current machines

The stator of a direct-current machine contains salient poles which are magnetized by the direct-current field windings. In the rotor (here also called the armature), the coils are distributed among slots in the laminated stack and connected to a commutator. Carbon brushes in the stator frame wipe against the commutator as it rotates, thereby transferring direct current to the armature coils. The rotation of the commutator causes a reversal in the direction of current flow in the coils. The different rotational speed vs. torque characteristics result from the method selected for connecting the field winding and armature:

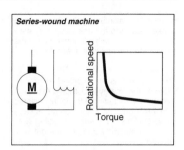

Series-wound machine

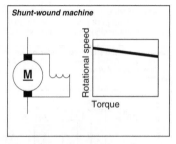

Shunt-wound machine

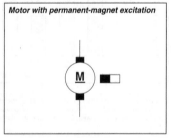

Motor with permanent-magnet excitation

Series connection (series characteristic)

Rotational speed is highly dependent upon load; high starting torque; "racing" of the machine if the load is suddenly removed, therefore load must be rigidly coupled; direction of rotation changed by reversing the direction of current in the armature or field winding; used, among other things, as motor-vehicle drive motor and starter motor for internal-combustion engines.

Parallel (shunt) connection (shunt characteristic)

Rotational speed remains largely constant regardless of load; direction of rotation is changed by reversing the direction of the current in the armature or field winding; used for instance, as drive motor for machine tools and as direct-current generator. A shunt characteristic can also be obtained by using a separate power supply for the field winding (separate excitation) or by using permanent-magnet excitation in the stator. Applications for permanent-field motors in motor vehicles: starter, wiper, and small-power motors for various drives. If the motor incorporates both series and shunt field windings (compound-wound motor), intermediate levels in the rotational speed/torque characteristic can be obtained; application: e.g. large starters.

All direct-current machines are easily capable of speed control over a wide range. If the machine incorporates a static converter which allows adjustment of the armature voltage, the torque and therefore the rotational speed are infinitely variable. The rotational speed can be further increased by reducing the field current (field weakening) when the rated armature voltage is reached. A disadvantage of direct-current machines is carbon-brush and commutator wear which makes regular maintenance necessary.

Three-phase machines

A three-phase winding is distributed among the stator slots in a three-phase machine. The three phases of current produce a rotating magnetic field. The speed n_0 (in min^{-1}) of this rotating field is calculated as follows:

$$n_0 = 60 \cdot f / p$$

f = frequency (in Hz), p = number of pole pairs.
Three-phase machines are either synchronous or asynchronous, depending upon rotor design.

Asynchronous machines

The laminated rotor contains either a three-phase winding, as in the stator, or a

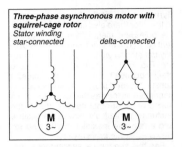

Three-phase asynchronous motor with squirrel-cage rotor
Stator winding
star-connected   delta-connected

bar winding. The three-phase winding is connected to slip rings which are short-circuited either directly or via series resistors. In the case of the bar winding, the bars are connected to one another by two short-circuiting rings (squirrel-cage rotor). As long as the rotational speed of the rotor deviates from n_0, the rotating stator field induces current in the rotor windings, thereby generating torque. Deviation of the rotational speed of the rotor n from n_0 is termed slip s:

$$s = (n_0 - n) / n_0$$

Continuous operation is only economical in the vicinity of n_0 because losses increase as slip increases (nominal slip ≤ 5%). In this range the asynchronous machine has a shunt characteristic. The machine operates as a motor when $n < n_0$, and as a generator when $n > n_0$. The direction of rotation is changed by reversing two of the phases.

The asynchronous machine is the most frequently used electric motor in the field of drive engineering. With a squirrel-cage rotor it is easy to operate, and requires little maintenance.

Examples of rotating-field speeds

No. of poles (2 p)	Frequency		
	50 Hz	150 Hz	200 Hz
	Rotating-field speed in min^{-1}		
2	3000	9000	12 000
4	1500	4500	6000
6	1000	3000	4000
8	750	2250	3000
10	600	1800	2400
12	500	1500	2000

Synchronous machines

In the rotor (here also called the inductor), the poles are magnetized by direct-current coils. The magnetizing current is usually transferred via two slip rings to the rotor. The inductor can be made of solid steel, because the magnetic flux remains constant over time. Constant torque is generated as long as the rotor rotates at a speed of n_0. At other speeds, the torque fluctuates periodically between a positive and a negative maximum value, and excessively high current is produced.

For this reason, a synchronous machine is not self-starting. The synchronous machine also differs from the asynchronous machine in that the reactive power absorption and generation are adjustable. The synchronous machine is most frequently used as a generator in electric power plants. Synchronous motors are used in cases where constant motor speed based on constant line frequency is desired, or where a reactive power demand exists. The automotive three-phase alternator is a special type of synchronous machine.

The rotational speed of all three-phase machines is determined by the stator frequency. Such machines can operate over a wide range of speeds if used in conjunction with static converters which vary the frequency.

EC motors

The "electronically-commutated direct-current" or "EC" motor is becoming increasingly popular. It is essentially a permanent-magnet synchronous machine, and thus dispenses with a slip ring. The EC motor is equipped with a rotor-position sensor, and is connected to the DC power source through its control and power electronics. The electronic transfer circuit switches the current in the stator winding according to rotor position – the magnets which induce the excitation current are attached to the rotor – to provide the interdependence between rotational speed and torque which is normally associated with a separately excited DC machine. The respective magnetic functions of the stator and rotor are the opposite of what they would be in a classical direct-current machine.

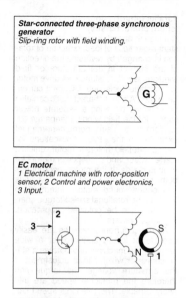

Star-connected three-phase synchronous generator
Slip-ring rotor with field winding.

EC motor
1 Electrical machine with rotor-position sensor, 2 Control and power electronics, 3 Input.

The EC motor's potential applications are a result of the advantages which this drive principle provides: Commutator and carbon brushes are replaced by electronic circuitry, dispensing with both brush noise and wear. EC motors are maintenance-free (long service life) and can be constructed to meet high degrees of protection (see below). The electronic control feature makes it easy for drive units with EC motors to incorporate auxiliary functions such as infinitely-variable speed adjustment, direction reversal, gradual starts and lock-up protection.

The main areas of automotive application are in the HVAC (Heating/Ventilation/Air-Conditioning) sectors, and for pumps and servo units. In the area of production machinery, EC motors are chiefly employed as precision drive units for feed-control in machine tools. Here the decisive advantages are freedom from maintenance, favorable dynamic properties and consistent torque output with minimal ripple.

Single-phase alternating-current machines

Universal motors

The direct-current series-wound motor can be operated on alternating current if a laminated rather than a solid iron stator is used. It is then called a universal motor.

When operated on alternating current, a torque component at twice the frequency of the current is superposed on the constant torque component.

Single-phase asynchronous motors with squirrel-cage rotor

The simplest design of a single-phase asynchronous motor is a three-phase asynchronous machine in which alternating current is supplied to only two stator phases. Although its operation remains largely the same, the power and the maximum torque are reduced. In addition, the single-phase asynchronous machine is not self-starting.

Machines which are intended only for single-phase operation have only a single-phase main winding in the stator, as well as auxiliary starting circuits. The stator also contains an auxiliary winding connected in parallel with the main winding for this purpose. The necessary phase shift of the auxiliary winding current can be achieved through increased winding resistance (low breakaway torque) or by means of a capacitor connected in series with the auxiliary winding (somewhat greater starting torque).

The auxiliary winding is switched off after the motor starts. The direction of rotation of the motor is changed by reversing the two auxiliary or main winding connections. A motor which has a capacitor in series with the auxiliary winding is called a capacitor motor. Capacitor motors with a starting and running capacitor also operate continuously with capacitor and auxiliary winding. Optimum operation for a specific working point can be achieved by correct selection of capacitor. An additional capacitor is often used in order to increase the starting torque; this capacitor is then disconnected after the motor starts.

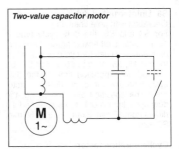

Two-value capacitor motor

Duty-type ratings for electrical machines
(VDE 0530)

S1: Continuous-running duty
Operation under constant load (rated output) of sufficient duration for thermal equilibrium to be reached.

S2: Short-time duty
Operation under constant load is so brief that thermal equilibrium is not reached. The rest period is so long that the machine is able to cool down to the temperature of the coolant.

Recommended short-time duty periods: 10, 30, 60 and 90 min.

S3 to S5: Intermittent duty
Continuous alternating sequence of load and idle periods. Thermal equilibrium is not reached during the load period or during the cooling period of one duty cycle.
S3 Intermittent duty without influence of starting on temperature.
S4 Intermittent duty with influence of starting on temperature.
S5 Intermittent duty with influence of starting and braking on temperature.

S6: Continuous operation with intermittent loading
Operation with intermittent loading. Continuous alternating sequence of load periods and no-load periods, otherwise as S3.

S7: Uninterrupted duty
Operation with starting and braking.

S8: Uninterrupted duty

Operation with pole-changing.
For S3 and S6, the duty cycle time is 10 min unless otherwise agreed; and recommended values for cyclic duration factor are 15, 25, 40 and 60%. For S2, S3 and S6, the operation time or the duty cycle time and the cyclic duration factor are to be specified after the rating; the duty cycle time is only to be specified if it differs from 10 min. Example: S2 – 60 min, S3 – 25%.

Cyclic duration factor

The cyclic duration factor is the ratio of the loading period, including starting and braking, to the cycle time.

Winding temperature

The mean temperature t_2 of the windings of an electrical machine can be determined by measuring the resistance (R_2) and referring it to an initial resistance R_1 at a temperature t_1:

$$t_2 = \frac{R_2 - R_1}{R_1} \ (\tau + t_1) + t_1$$

where

$$\tau = \frac{1}{\alpha} - 20 \text{ K}$$

α = Temperature coefficient.

Degrees of protection for electrical machines
(DIN 40 050)

Examples:

Degree of protection IP 00
No protection against accidental contact, no protection against solid bodies, no protection against water.

Degree of protection IP 11
Protection against large-area contact by the hand, protection against large solid bodies, protection against dripping water.

Degree of protection IP 23
Protection against contact by the fingers, protection against medium-size solid bodies, protection against water sprayed vertically and obliquely up to an angle of 60° to the vertical.

Degree of protection IP 44
Protection against contact by tools or the like, protection against small solid bodies, protection against splash water from all directions.

Degree of protection IP 67
Total protection against contact, dustproof, protection against entry of dangerous quantities of water when immersed in water under conditions of defined pressure and for a defined period of time.

Explosion protection Ex
(VDE 0170/0171)

Symbol d:	Explosion-containing enclosure;
Symbol f:	Separate ventilation;
Symbol e:	Increased safety;
Symbol s:	Special protection, e.g. for machines operating in flammable liquids.

Technical optics

Photometric quantities and units

See P. 18 for names of units

Quantity		Unit
A	Area	m^2
	A_1 Radiating area (surface)	
	A_2 Irradiated area (surface)	
E	Illuminance	lx = lm/m²
I	Luminous intensity	cd
L	Luminance	cd/m²
M	Luminous emittance	lm/m²
P	Power	W
Q	Luminous energy	lm · s
r	Distance	m

Quantity		Unit
t	Time	s
ε_1	Incident angle of radiation (with respect to surface normal)	°
ε_2	Angle of refraction	°
ε_3	Angle of reflection	°
η	Luminous efficiency	lm/W
Φ	Luminous flux	lm
Ω	Solid angle	sr
λ	Wavelength	nm

Electromagnetic radiation

Propagated at speed of light. Wave nature. Not deflected by electric or magnetic fields.
Wavelength $\lambda = c/f$, c = light speed ≈ $3 \cdot 10^8$ m/s = 300 000 km/s, f = frequency in Hz.

Designation	Wavelength range	Origin and/or creation	Application examples
Cosmic radiation	< 0.1 pm	Bombardment of Earth's atmosphere by cosmic elementary particles.	Nuclear-physics tests.
Gamma radiation	0.1...10 pm	Radioactive decay.	Nuclear physics, isotope technology.
X-radiation	10 pm...10 nm	X-ray tubes (bombardment of anticathode by high-energy electrons).	Materials tests, medical diagnosis.
Ultraviolet radiation	10...380 nm	Gaseous-discharge lamps, lasers.	Skin therapy, photolithography in IC manufacture.
Visible radiation	380...780 nm	Gaseous-discharge lamps, filament lamps, lasers.	Technical optics, photography, automotive lighting.
Infrared radiation	780 nm...1 mm	Thermal radiators, infrared diodes, lasers.	Therapy, motor-vehicle distance measurement.
EHF waves	1...10 mm		
SHF waves	10...100 mm		
UHF waves	100 mm...1 m		
VHF waves	1...10 m	Space-charge-wave tubes, resonant circuits, quartz oscillators.	Satellite communications, microwave heating, traffic radar, television, radio broadcasting, radio.
HF waves	10...100 m		
MF waves	100 m...1 km		
LF waves	1...10 km		
VLF waves	10...100 km		

Geometrical optics

In many cases, the geometrical dimensions of the media in which optical radiation propagates are large in comparison to the wavelength of the radiation. In such cases, the propagation of radiation can be explained in terms of "light rays", and can be described by simple geometrical laws.

An incident beam of light is split into a refracted beam and a reflected beam at the interface between two media.

The law of refraction applies to the refracted beam:

$$n_1 \cdot \sin \varepsilon_1 = n_2 \cdot \sin \varepsilon_2$$

The indices of refraction n_1 and n_2 of a vacuum and the so-called dielectric media (e.g. air, glass and plastics) are real numbers; for other media they are complex numbers. The indices of refraction of media are a function of the wavelength (dispersion). In most cases, they decrease as the wavelength increases.

The reflected beam behaves according to the following equation:

$$\varepsilon_3 = \varepsilon_1$$

The ratio of the intensity of the reflected beam to the intensity of the incident beam (degree of reflection) depends upon the incident angle and the indices of refraction of the adjacent media. In the case of a beam of light passing through air ($n_1 = 1.00$) into glass ($n_2 = 1.52$) at an angle of 90° ($\varepsilon_1 = 0$), 4.3% of the energy of the beam is reflected.

If the beam emanates from the optically denser medium ($n_1 > n_2$), total reflection can occur if the angle of incidence ε_1 is equal to or exceeds the limiting angle of total reflection ε_{1max}. According to the law of refraction:

$$\sin \varepsilon_{1max} = n_2/n_1$$

Indices of refraction n_D (for yellow sodium light, wavelength $\lambda = 589.3$ nm).

Medium	n_D
Vacuum, air	1.00
Ice (0 °C)	1.31
Water (+20 °C)	1.33
Silica glass	1.46
Standard glass for optics (BK 7)	1.51673
Window glass, glass used for headlamp lenses	1.52
Polymethyl methacrylate	1.49
Polyvinyl chloride	1.54
Polycarbonate	1.58
Polystyrene	1.59
Epoxy resin	1.60
Gallium arsenide (according to doping level)	approx. 3.5

Components

Cylindrical lenses
Parallel rays are made to converge in a focal line by a cylindrical lens.

Prisms
Prismatic elements are used for the purpose of deflecting a beam of light by a desired angle. Parallel rays remain parallel after deflection by a prism.

In the motor-vehicle headlamp, cylindrical lenses and prismatic elements are used in order to more favorably direct the light emanating from the reflector.

Reflectors
The function of motor-vehicle lamp reflectors is to reflect as much light as possible from the headlamp bulb, to achieve as great a range as possible, and to influence the distribution of light on the road in such a way that the requirements of legislation are met. Additional demands are placed on the headlamps as a result of

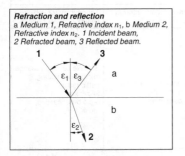

Refraction and reflection
a *Medium 1, Refractive index n_1*, b *Medium 2, Refractive index n_2*. 1 *Incident beam,* 2 *Refracted beam,* 3 *Reflected beam.*

the design (for instance, when fitted into the bumper).

Whereas in the past paraboloids were almost exclusively used as reflectors, the above-mentioned requirements, which are in some cases mutually contradictory, can today only be met by the use of stepped reflectors, free-formed areas or new headlamp designs (PES = Poly-ellipsoid System, see P. 705).

In general, the larger the lens aperture area, the greater the headlamp's range. On the other hand, the greater the solid angle achieved by the reflector, the greater the luminous efficiency.

Color filters

Motor-vehicle lamps must meet precise specifications with regard to chromaticity coordinates depending upon their intended functions (turn-signal lamps, stop lamps). These specifications can be met through the use of color filters which weaken the light emitted in certain parts of the visible spectrum.

Light sources

The outer electron shells of atoms of certain materials can absorb varying levels of energy. The transition from higher to lower levels may lead to the emission of electromagnetic wave trains.

The various types of light source can fundamentally be distinguished by the nature of electron excitation (energy supply).

Cylindrical lens element of a headlamp lens

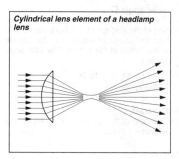

Thermal radiators

In the case of this light source, the energy level is increased by the addition of heat energy. The emission is continuous across a broad wavelength range. The total radiation capacity is proportional to the power of 4 of the absolute temperature (Stephan Boltzmann's Law) and the distribution curve maximum is displaced to shorter wavelengths as the temperature increases (Wien's Displacement Law).

Incandescent lamps

Incandescent lamps, with tungsten glow filament (melting temperature 3660 K), are also thermal radiators. The evaporation of the tungsten and the resulting blackening of the bulb restrict the service life of this type of lamp.

Halogen lamps

The halogen lamp allows the filament temperature to rise to close to the melting point of the tungsten. It has a halogen filler gas (iodine or bromine). Close to the hot bulb wall the evaporated tungsten combines with the filler gas to form tungsten halide. This is gaseous, conductive for light beams and stable in the temperature range 500 K to 1700 K. It reaches the filament by means of convection, decomposes as a result of the high filament temperature, and forms an even tungsten deposit on the filament. In order to maintain this cyclic process, an external bulb temperature of approx. 300 °C is necessary. To achieve this the bulb, made of silica gel, must closely surround the filament. A further advantage of this measure is that higher filling pressure can be used, thereby providing additional resistance to tungsten evaporation. A disadvantage of these lamps is among others their low luminous efficiency.

Gaseous-discharge lamps

Gaseous-discharge lamps are distinguished by their higher luminous efficiency. A gaseous discharge is maintained in an enclosed, gas-filled bulb by applying a voltage between two electrodes. The excitation of the atoms of the emitted gas is effected by collisions between electrons and gas atoms. The atoms excited in the process give off their energy in the form of luminous radiation.

Examples of gaseous-discharge lamps are sodium-vapor lamps (street lighting), fluorescent lamps (interior illumination), and motor-vehicle headlamps ("Litronic", P. 744).

Light and the physiology of vision

Because the range of sensitivity to visible radiation varies from person to person, a general brightness sensitivity function has been established for photometric calculations and measurements and is contained, in table form for example, in DIN 5031, Part 3. This function $V(\lambda)$ was determined with test personnel under daylight conditions ("light-adapted eye"), and can be used to calculate unambiguously the photometric values from the objective physical values (see Fig.).

Definition of photometric quantities and units:

Luminous flux Φ

The radiant power emitted by a source of light assessed on the basis of spectral brightness sensitivity.

$$\Phi = K_m \cdot \int P_\lambda \cdot V(\lambda) d\lambda$$

K_m Maximum value of luminous efficacy of radiation for photopic vision $K_m = 683$ lm/W.
$V(\lambda)$ Spectral luminous efficiency for a 2° field of vision according to DIN 5031, Part 3.
P_λ Spectral distribution of radiant energy.

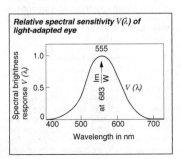

Relative spectral sensitivity $V(\lambda)$ of light-adapted eye

Spectral brightness response $V(\lambda)$

1.0

0.5

0

555

lm / W

at 683

$V(\lambda)$

400   500   600   700

Wavelength in nm

Luminous energy Q

The spectral radiation energy assessed on the basis of $V(\lambda)$. The following equation applies for temporally constant luminous flux:

$$Q = \Phi \cdot t$$

Luminous intensity I

The ratio of luminous flux to a radiation-penetrated solid angle.

$$I = \Phi/\Omega$$

Illuminance E

The ratio of the incident luminous flux to the area of the illuminated surface.

$$E = \Phi/A_2$$

Luminance L

The ratio of the luminous intensity to the apparent (projected) area of the surface from which it is emitted.

$$L = I/(A_1 \cdot \cos \alpha)$$

where α is the angle between the beam direction and the surface normal.

Luminous emittance M

The ratio of the luminous flux emitted by a luminous surface to the area of that surface.

$$M = \Phi/A_1$$

Luminous efficiency η

The ratio of the emitted luminous flux to the power absorbed.

$$\eta = \Phi/P$$

Luminous efficiency can never exceed the maximum value for "luminous efficacy of radiation" $K_m = 683$ lm/W at a wavelength of $\lambda = 555$ nm.

Solid angle Ω

The ratio of the radiation-penetrated portion of the surface of a sphere concentric with the source of radiation to the square of the radius of the sphere. The total solid angle is

$$\Omega = 4\pi \cdot sr \approx 12.56 \cdot sr$$

sr Steradian

Contrast

The ratio of the luminance values of two adjacent surfaces.

Laser technology

Compared to other light sources, the laser has the following characteristic properties:

– High luminance, concentration of radiation on a diameter of a few light wavelengths,
– Low beam expansion,
– Monochromatic radiation,
– Can be used for coherent measuring technology (high radiation coherence length),
– High power (in laser tools).

Light generation in the laser is effected by induced emission in a specific laser material, which is brought to a state of excitation by the addition of energy (usually light). A resonator influences the beam geometry as required. The laser radiation emerges at the end of the resonator via a semi-transparent mirror.

Examples of lasers in common use are:

Laser type	Wavelength	Examples of application
Helium-neon laser	633 nm	Measuring technology
CO_2 laser	10.6 µm	Material processing
YAG laser	1064 nm	Material processing
Solid-state laser	e.g. 670 nm e.g. 1300 nm	Measuring technology Telecommunications

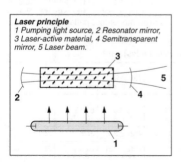

Laser principle
1 Pumping light source, 2 Resonator mirror, 3 Laser-active material, 4 Semitransparent mirror, 5 Laser beam.

With laser measuring technology the non-contact, non-interacting testing of production tolerances of precision-machined surfaces (e.g. fuel-injection valves) is possible. With interferometric methods, resolutions in the nm range are achieved. Further laser applications in technology are holography (spatial image information), automatic character recognition (barcode scanners), information recording (CD scanning), material processing/machining, microsurgery and transmitters for data transfer on optical fibers.

Specific regulations are to be observed when handling laser products. Laser products are classified according to potential hazards. For details, see DIN 0837, "Radiation Safety of Laser Products".

Optical fibers/waveguides

Design

Optical fibers transmit electromagnetic waves in the ultraviolet (UV), visible and infrared (IR) ranges of the spectrum. They are made of quartz, glass or polymers, usually in the form of fibers or in channels created in transparent materials with a core of which the index of refraction is higher than that of the cladding. Thus incident light entering the core zone is retained in that area by means of refraction or total reflection. Depending on the refractive index profile, a distinction is made between three types of fiber (see diagram):

– The step-index optical fiber, with a sharply-defined border between the core and the cladding,
– The graded-index optical fiber, with parabolic refractive index curve form in the core zone,
– The monomode fiber with a very small core diameter.

Step-index and graded-index fibers are multimode fibers, that is, lightwaves can be propagated in them at varying trajectories, generally at an oblique angle to the fiber axis. In the monomode fiber, propagation is only possible in the principal mode.

Polymer fibers are always step-index fibers.

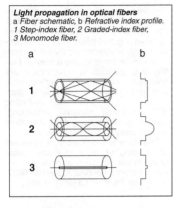

Light propagation in optical fibers
a Fiber schematic, b Refractive index profile.
1 Step-index fiber, 2 Graded-index fiber,
3 Monomode fiber.

a   b

1

2

3

Properties

Glass optical fibers have a high degree of transparency in the range UV to IR. Attenuation is particularly low at the wavelengths 850 nm, 1300 nm and 1550 nm. Synthetic fibers absorb above 850 nm and below 450 nm.

They can only absorb light from a restricted angular range Θ. The numerical aperture $NA = SIN (\Theta/2)$ serves as a basis for calculating this range (see table).

The differences in dispersion and propagation time of the various modes cause an increasing widening of light pulses as the length of the fiber increases, and thus restrict the bandwidth.

Optical fibers can be used in the temperature range $-40\,°C$ to $135\,°C$; special versions can be used up to $800\,°C$.

Areas of application

The main area of application is data transmission. Synthetic fibers are preferred for use in the LAN (Local Area Network) field. Graded-index fibers are the most suitable for medium ranges. Only monomode fibers are used for long-distance data transmission. In fiber-optic networks, optical-fiber structures manufactured according to planar techniques serve as distributors, filters or switches ("integrated optics") and erbium-doped fibers serve as optical amplifiers. Optical fibers are becoming more and more significant in the field of sensor technology. Fiber-optic sensors generate neither stray fields nor sparks, and are themselves non-sensitive to that kind of disturbance. They are currently employed in potentially explosive environments, in medicine and in high-speed trains (ICE).

Energy transport is at the forefront in the area of material processing with laser beams, in microsurgery and in lighting engineering.

Holography

In conventional image recording (photography, video cameras) a three-dimensional image is reduced to a two-dimensional representation. The spatial information contained in the image is lost when the image is stored. Spatial impressions gained when looking at the picture are based on sensory illusions.

With holography, three-dimensional information can be stored and also reproduced. For recording, coherent lightwave trains are necessary. In hologram imaging, a beam splitter divides the laser beam into object and reference beams. The resulting object and reference waves form an interference pattern on the record-

Characteristics of optical fibers (optical waveguides)

Fiber type	Diameter Core µm	Diameter Cladding µm	Wavelength nm	Numerical aperture NA	Attenuation dB/km	Bandwidth MHz·km
Step-index fiber						
Quartz/glass	50...1000	70...1000	250...1550	0.2...0.87	5...10	10
Polymer	200...>1000	250...2000	450...850	0.2...0.6	100...500	<10
Graded-index fiber	50...150	100...500	450...1550	0.2...0.3	3...5	200...1000
Monomode fiber	3...10	100...500	850...1550	0.12...0.21	0.3...1	2500...15000

ing medium (hologram plate) where the latter is stored as a diffraction grating.

The expanded beam of a laser illuminates the hologram plate and reconstructs the hologram. The diffraction grating on the hologram deforms the laser wave to such an extent that the observer has the impression that the holographically captured object is present behind the hologram plate.

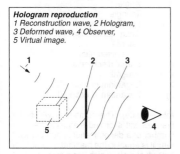

Hologram reproduction
1 Reconstruction wave, 2 Hologram,
3 Deformed wave, 4 Observer,
5 Virtual image.

Typical applications
– Registration of minute path deviations,
– Measurement of deformations and vibration amplitudes far below the wavelength of light by means of holographic interferometry,
– Holographic measuring and testing methods in precision manufacturing (e.g. fuel-injection components),
– Production of forgery-proof documents,
– Use of holographic elements for illustration purposes.

Display elements

The most important optical information displays are liquid crystal and light-emitting diode displays.

Liquid crystal display

The liquid crystal display, or LCD, is a passive display element. The contrast differences created are made visible by additional illumination. The most widely used type of LCD is the twisted nematic cell, or TN cell.

The liquid crystal substance is held between two glass plates. In the area of the display segments these glass plates are covered with a transparent conducting layer to which a voltage can be applied: an electric field is created between the layers. An additional orientation layer causes the plane of polarization of light passing through the cell to rotate. When polarizers acting at right angles to one another are added to both outside surfaces, the cell is initially transparent. In the area of the two opposed electrodes the liquid crystal molecules are aligned in the direction of the electric field by applying voltage. Rotation of the plane of polarization is now suppressed and the display area becomes opaque.

Numbers, letters and symbols are indicated in separately activated segment areas.

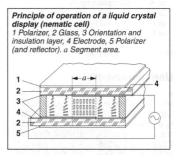

Principle of operation of a liquid crystal display (nematic cell)
1 Polarizer, 2 Glass, 3 Orientation and insulation layer, 4 Electrode, 5 Polarizer (and reflector). a Segment area.

Light-emitting diodes

The light-emitting diode, or LED, display is an active (self-luminous) display. It consists of a semiconductor element with PN junction. The charge carriers (free electrons and holes) recombine during operation in forward direction. With certain semiconductor materials, the energy which is released as a result is converted into electromagnetic radiation energy.

Frequently used semiconductor materials are: gallium arsenide (infrared), gallium arsenide phosphide (red to yellow) and gallium phosphide (green).

Mathematics

Mathematical signs and symbols

$\approx$	Approximately equal to
$\ll$	Much less than
$\gg$	Much greater than
$\triangleq$	Corresponds to
. . .	and so forth, to
$=$	Equal to
$\neq$	Not equal to
$<$	Less than
$\leq$	Less than or equal to
$>$	Greater than
$\geq$	Greater than or equal to
$+$	Plus
$-$	Minus
$\cdot$ or $\star$ or $\times$	Multiplied by
$-$ or $/$ or $:$	Divided by
Σ	Sum of
Π	Product of

Useful numbers

e	= 2.718282[1])	$\sqrt{\pi}$	= 1.77245
e^2	= 7.389056	$1/\pi$	= 0.31831
$1/e$	= 0.367879	π^2	= 9.86960
lg e	= 0.434294	$180/\pi$	= 57.29578
$\sqrt{e}$	= 1.648721	$\pi/180$	= 0.017453
$1/\lg e$	= 2.302585	$\sqrt{2}$	= 1.41421
ln 10	= 2.302585	$1/\sqrt{2}$	= 0.70711
$1/\ln 10$	= 0.434294	$\sqrt{3}$	= 1.73205
π	= 3.14159		

Number systems

Number systems are employed to form numerals in cases where the number of digits is to be less than the quantity of individual units being described. This type of notation requires the use of a single symbol (digit) for collective representation of more than one element.

Today's denominational number systems differ from former additive systems in employing groups which increase in uniform increments. The position of the digit within the numeral corresponds to the size of the unit

$\sim$	Proportional to
$\sqrt{}$	Square root of ($\sqrt[n]{}$ n^{th} root of)
$n!$	n factorial (e.g. 3! = 1 · 2 · 3 = 6)
$\lvert x \rvert$	Absolute value of x
$\rightarrow$	Approaches
∞	Infinity
i or j	Imaginary unit, $i^2 = -1$
$\perp$	Perpendicular to
$\parallel$	Parallel to
$\sphericalangle$	Angle
$\triangle$	Triangle
lim	Limiting value
Δ	Delta (difference between two values)
d	Total differential
δ	Partial differential
$\int$	Integral
ln	Logarithm to base e[1])
lg	Logarithm to base 10

(place value). The number at which the first new unit is formed is equal to the base number of a denominational number system; it is equal to the maximum number of individual digits which are available. Most frequently used is the decimal system (base 10). In information technology/computer science, the dual system (base 2) using the digits 0 and 1, and the hexadecimal system (base 16) using the digits 0 through 9 and A through F, are also employed. A real number a is represented in the denominational number system by:

$$a = \pm \sum_{i=-\infty}^{\infty} Z_i \cdot B^i$$

i Position, B Base, Z_i Natural number ($0 \leq Z_i < B$) at position i. A comma is inserted between the positions i < 0 and i = 0.

Roman number system (addition system)	Decimal system (base 10)	Dual system (base 2)
I	1	1
X	10	1010
C	100	1100100
M	1000	1111100110
II	2	10
V	5	101
L	50	110010
D	500	111110010
MIM or MDCCCCLXXXXIX	1999	11111001111

(In the Roman system, a smaller numeral is subtracted from a larger subsequent numeral when it directly precedes it.)

[1]) e = 1 + 1/1! + 1/2! + 1/3! + ...
(base of natural logarithms).

Preferred numbers

Preferred numbers are rounded-off terms in geometric series whose increments (the ratio of a term to its predecessor) are as follows:

Series	R 5	R 10	R 20	R 40
Increment	$\sqrt[5]{10}$	$\sqrt[10]{10}$	$\sqrt[20]{10}$	$\sqrt[40]{10}$

They are used for selecting preferred size and dimension increments.

In addition to the principal series, DIN 323 also contains the exceptional series R 80 as well as series of rounded numbers.

Electrical components such as resistors and capacitors are rated in increments in accordance with the E Series:

Series	E 6	E 12	E 24
Increment	$\sqrt[6]{10}$	$\sqrt[12]{10}$	$\sqrt[24]{10}$

Preferred numbers (DIN 323)

Principal series				Exact values			E series (DIN 41 426)		
R 5	R 10	R 20	R 40		lg		E 6	E 12	E 24
100	1.00	1.00	1.00	1.0000	0.0		1.0	1.0	1.0
			1.06	1.0593	0.025				1.1
		1.12	1.12	1.1220	0.05			1.2	1.2
			1.18	1.1885	0.075				1.3
	1.25	1.25	1.25	1.2589	0.1		1.5	1.5	1.5
			1.32	1.3335	0.125				1.6
		1.40	1.40	1.4125	0.15			1.8	1.8
			1.50	1.4962	0.175				2.0
1.60	1.60	1.60	1.60	1.5849	0.2		2.2	2.2	2.2
			1.70	1.6788	0.225				2.4
		1.80	1.80	1.7783	0.25			2.7	2.7
			1.90	1.8836	0.275				3.0
	2.00	2.00	2.00	1.9953	0.3		3.3	3.3	3.3
			2.12	2.1135	0.325				3.6
		2.24	2.24	2.2387	0.35			3.9	3.9
			2.36	2.3714	0.375				4.3
2.50	2.50	2.50	2.50	2.5119	0.4		4.7	4.7	4.7
			2.65	2.6607	0.425				5.1
		2.80	2.80	2.8184	0.45			5.6	5.6
			3.00	2.9854	0.475				6.2
	3.15	3.15	3.15	3.1623	0.5		6.8	6.8	6.8
			3.35	3.3497	0.525				7.5
		3.55	3.55	3.5481	0.55			8.2	8.2
			3.75	3.7584	0.575				9.1
4.00	4.00	4.00	4.00	3.9811	0.6				
			4.25	4.2170	0.625		10.0	10.0	10.0
		4.50	4.50	4.4668	0.65				
			4.75	4.7315	0.675				
	5.00	5.00	5.00	5.0119	0.7				
			5.30	5.3088	0.725				
		5.60	5.60	5.6234	0.75				
			6.00	5.9566	0.775				
6.30	6.30	6.30	6.30	6.3096	0.8				
			6.70	6.6834	0.825				
		7.10	7.10	7.0795	0.85				
			7.50	7.4989	0.875				
	8.00	8.00	8.00	7.9433	0.9				
			8.50	8.4140	0.925				
		9.00	9.00	8.9125	0.95				
			9.50	9.4409	0.975				
10.0	10.0	10.0	10.0	10.0000	1.0				

Trigonometric functions

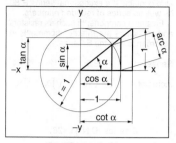

$\varphi =$	$\pm \alpha$	$90 \pm \alpha$	$180 \pm \alpha$	$270 \pm \alpha$
$\sin \varphi =$	$\pm \sin \alpha$	$\cos \alpha$	$\mp \sin \alpha$	$-\cos \alpha$
$\cos \varphi =$	$\pm \cos \alpha$	$\mp \sin \alpha$	$-\cos \alpha$	$\pm \sin \alpha$
$\tan \varphi =$	$\pm \tan \alpha$	$\mp \cot \alpha$	$\pm \tan \alpha$	$\mp \cot \alpha$
$\cot \varphi =$	$\pm \cot \alpha$	$\mp \tan \alpha$	$\pm \cot \alpha$	$\mp \tan \alpha$

Sine α	side opposite α/hypotenuse
Cosine α	side adjacent to α/hypotenuse
Tangent α	side opposite α/side adjacent to α
Cotangent α	side adjacent to α/side opposite α
Arc $\alpha = \widehat{\alpha}$	radian measure of α in circle of radius 1
inv α	involute function

$\sin 0° = \cos 90° = 0$
$\cos 0° = \sin 90° = 1$
$\tan 0° = \cot 90° = 0$
$\cot 0° = \tan 90° = \infty$
$\sin 30° = \cos 60° = 0.5$
$\cos 30° = \sin 60° = 0.5 \sqrt{3}$
$\tan 30° = \cot 60° = \sqrt{3/3}$
$\cot 30° = \tan 60° = \sqrt{3}$

$\widehat{\alpha} = \text{arc } \alpha = \dfrac{\pi \cdot \alpha}{180°} \text{ rad} = \dfrac{\alpha}{57.3°}$

$\widehat{1°} = \text{arc } 1° = \dfrac{\pi}{180} = 0.017453$

$\text{arc } 57.3° = 1$

$\text{inv } \alpha = \tan \alpha - \text{arc } \alpha$

$\cos^2 \alpha + \sin^2 \alpha = 1$

$\tan \alpha = \dfrac{\sin \alpha}{\cos \alpha} = \dfrac{1}{\cot \alpha}$

$1 + \tan^2 \alpha = \dfrac{1}{\cos^2 \alpha}$

$1 + \cot^2 \alpha = \dfrac{1}{\sin^2 \alpha}$

$\sin \alpha \approx \widehat{\alpha} - \dfrac{\widehat{\alpha}^3}{6}$

Error < 1 % at $\alpha < 58°$

$\sin \alpha \approx \widehat{\alpha}$
Error < 1 % at $\alpha < 14°$

$\cos \alpha \approx 1 - \dfrac{\widehat{\alpha}^2}{2}$
Error < 1 % at $\alpha < 37°$

$\cos \alpha \approx 1$
Error < 1 % at $\alpha < 8°$

$\sin 2\alpha = 2 \sin \alpha \cdot \cos \alpha$
$\cos 2\alpha = \cos^2 \alpha - \sin^2 \alpha$
$\tan 2\alpha = 2/(\cot \alpha - \tan \alpha)$
$\cot 2\alpha = (\cot \alpha - \tan \alpha)/2$
$\sin 3\alpha = 3 \sin \alpha - 4 \sin^3 \alpha$
$\cos 3\alpha = 4 \cos^3 \alpha - 3 \cos \alpha$

$\sin (\alpha \pm \beta) = \sin \alpha \cdot \cos \beta \pm \cos \alpha \cdot \sin \beta$
$\cos (\alpha \pm \beta) = \cos \alpha \cdot \cos \beta \mp \sin \alpha \cdot \sin \beta$

$\tan (\alpha \pm \beta) = \dfrac{\tan \alpha \pm \tan \beta}{1 \mp \tan \alpha \tan \beta}$

$\cot (\alpha \pm \beta) = \dfrac{\cot \alpha \cdot \cot \beta \mp 1}{\cot \beta \pm \cot \alpha}$

$\sin \alpha \pm \sin \beta = 2 \sin \dfrac{\alpha \pm \beta}{2} \cdot \cos \dfrac{\alpha \mp \beta}{2}$

$\cos \alpha + \cos \beta = 2 \cos \dfrac{\alpha + \beta}{2} \cdot \cos \dfrac{\alpha - \beta}{2}$

$\cos \alpha - \cos \beta = -2 \sin \dfrac{\alpha + \beta}{2} \cdot \sin \dfrac{\alpha - \beta}{2}$

$\tan \alpha \pm \tan \beta = \dfrac{\sin (\alpha \pm \beta)}{\cos \alpha \cdot \cos \beta}$

$\cot \alpha \pm \cot \beta = \dfrac{\sin (\beta \pm \alpha)}{\sin \alpha \cdot \sin \beta}$

Euler's formula
(basis of symbolic calculation):

$e^{\pm ix} = \cos x \pm i \sin x$

$\sin x = \dfrac{e^{ix} - e^{-ix}}{2i} \; ; \; \cos x = \dfrac{e^{ix} + e^{-ix}}{2}$

where $i = \sqrt{-1}$

Equations for plane and spherical triangles

Plane triangle

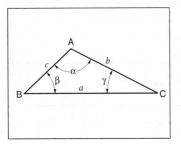

Spherical triangle

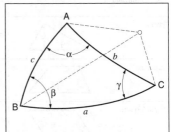

$\alpha + \beta + \gamma = 180°$

Sine law
$a : b : c = \sin \alpha : \sin \beta : \sin \gamma$

Pythagorean theorem (cosine law)
$a^2 = b^2 + c^2 - 2\, bc \cos a$
for right-angle triangle
$a^2 = b^2 + c^2$

Sine law
$\sin a : \sin b : \sin c = \sin \alpha : \sin \beta : \sin \gamma$

Cosine law for sides
$\cos a = \cos b \, \cos c + \sin b \, \sin c \, \cos \alpha$

Cosine law for angles
$\cos \alpha = -\cos \beta \, \cos \gamma + \sin \beta \, \sin \gamma \, \cos a$

Equations often used

Solution of quadratic equation
$ax^2 + bx + c = 0$

$$x = \frac{-b \pm \sqrt{b^2 - 4\, ac}}{2a}$$

Golden section (continuous division)

$1 : x = x : (1 - x)$, from which $x = 0.618$

|────────────1────────────|
|──── x ────|── $1 - x$ ──|

Conversion of logarithms

$\lg N = 0.434294 \cdot \ln N$
$\ln N = 2.302585 \cdot \lg N$

Geometric series
$a + aq + aq^2 + aq^3 + \ldots$

n^{th} member $= aq^{n-1}$

for $q > 1$: $\underset{n}{\Sigma} = a\,(q^n - 1)/(q - 1)$

for $q < 1$: $\underset{n}{\Sigma} = a\,(1 - q^n)/(1 - q)$

for n $\to \infty$ becomes $q^n = 0$
$$\underset{n \to \infty}{\Sigma} = a/(1 - q)$$

Arithmetic series

$a + (a + d) + (a + 2d) + (a + 3d) + \ldots$
n^{th} member $= a + (n - 1)\, d$

$$\underset{n}{\Sigma} = \frac{n}{2}\,[2a + (n - 1)\, d]$$

Areas of plane surfaces

Type of surface		Area A
		$\pi \approx 3.1416$
Triangle		$A = \dfrac{a \cdot h}{2}$
Trapezoid		$A = \dfrac{a + b}{2}\, h$
Parallelogram		$A = a \cdot h = a \cdot b \cdot \sin \gamma$
Circle		$A = \dfrac{\pi \cdot d^2}{4} = 0.785\, d^2$ Circumference $U = \pi \cdot d$
Annulus		$A = \dfrac{\pi}{4}\,(D^2 - d^2) = \dfrac{\pi}{2}\,(D + d)\, b$
Sector	φ in degrees	$A = \dfrac{\pi \cdot r^2 \cdot \varphi}{360°} = 8.73 \cdot 10^{-3} \cdot r^2 \cdot \varphi$ Arc length $l = \dfrac{\pi \cdot r \cdot \varphi}{180°} = 1.75 \cdot 10^{-2} \cdot r \cdot \varphi$
Segment	φ in degrees	$A = \dfrac{r^2}{2}\left(\dfrac{\pi \cdot \varphi}{180°} - \sin\varphi\right) \approx h \cdot s\left[0.667 + 0.5\left(\dfrac{h}{s}\right)^2\right]$ Chord length $s = 2\, r \cdot \sin \dfrac{\varphi}{2}$ Arc height $h = r\left(1 - \cos\dfrac{\varphi}{2}\right) = \dfrac{s}{2}\tan\dfrac{\varphi}{4} = 2\, r \cdot \sin^2\dfrac{\varphi}{4}$
Hexagon		$A = \dfrac{\sqrt{3}}{2}s^2 = 0.866\, s^2$ Width across corners $e = \dfrac{2s}{\sqrt{3}} = 1.155\, s$
Ellipse		$A = \pi \cdot D \cdot d/4 = 0.785\, D \cdot d$ Circumference $U \approx 0.75\,\pi\,(D + d) - 0.5\,\pi\,\sqrt{D \cdot d}$
Pappus theorem for surfaces of revolution	Centroid — Axis of rotation	The area of a surface of revolution is equal to the length l of the generatrix line multiplied by the distance traveled by the centroid $A = 2\pi \cdot r \cdot l$

Volume and surface area of solids

Type of solid		Volume V, surface S, lateral area M $\pi \approx 3.1416$
Regular cylinder		$V = \dfrac{\pi \cdot d^2}{4}\, h = 0.785\, d^2 \cdot h$ $M = \pi \cdot d \cdot h,\ S = \pi \cdot d\, (d/2 + h)$
Pyramid $\quad$ A Area of base $\qquad\qquad h$ Height		$V = \dfrac{1}{3} A \cdot h$
Circular cone		$V = \dfrac{\pi \cdot d^2 \cdot h}{12} = 0.262\, d^2 \cdot h$ $M = \dfrac{\pi \cdot d \cdot s}{2} = \dfrac{\pi \cdot d}{4}\sqrt{d^2 + 4h^2} = 0.785\, d \cdot \sqrt{d^2 + 4h^2}$
Truncated cone		$V = \dfrac{\pi \cdot h}{12}\,(D^2 + D \cdot d + d^2) = 0.262\, h\,(D^2 + D \cdot d + d^2)$ $M = \dfrac{\pi\,(D + d)\,s}{2} \quad s = \sqrt{\dfrac{(D - d)^2}{4} + h^2}$
Sphere		$V = \dfrac{\pi \cdot d^3}{6} = 0.524\, d^3$ $S = \pi \cdot d^2$
Spherical segment (spherical cap)		$V = \dfrac{\pi \cdot h}{6}\,(3\,a^2 + h^2) = \dfrac{\pi \cdot h^2}{3}\,(3r - h)$ $M = 2\,\pi \cdot r \cdot h = \pi\,(a^2 + h^2)$
Spherical sector		$V = \dfrac{2\,\pi \cdot r^2 \cdot h}{3} = 2.094\, r^2 \cdot h$ $S = \pi \cdot r\,(2h + a)$
Spherical segment of two bases	r Radius of sphere	$V = \dfrac{\pi \cdot h}{6}\,(3\,a^2 + 3b^2 + h^2)$ $M = 2\,\pi \cdot r \cdot h$
Torus ring		$V = \dfrac{\pi^2}{4} \cdot D \cdot d^2 = 2.467\, D \cdot d^2$ $S = \pi^2 \cdot D \cdot d = 9.870\, D \cdot d$
Ellipsoid $\quad$ d_1, d_2, d_3 Length $\qquad\qquad$ of axes		$V = \dfrac{\pi}{6}\, d_1 \cdot d_2 \cdot d_3 = 0.524\, d_1 \cdot d_2 \cdot d_3$
Circular cask D Diameter at bung $\quad\ d$ Diameter at base $\quad\ h$ Distance between bases		$V \approx \dfrac{\pi \cdot h}{12}\,(2\,D^2 + d^2) \approx 0.26\, h\,(2\,D^2 + d^2)$
Pappus theorem for solids of revolution	Centroid Rotation axis	The volume of a body of revolution is equal to the generatrix area A multiplied by the distance traveled by the centroid $V = 2\,\pi \cdot r \cdot A$

Quality

Quality is defined as the extent to which the customer expectations are fulfilled or even exceeded. The desired quality is determined by the customer. With his demands and expectations, he determines what quality is – in both products and services. Because competition leads to increased customer expectations, quality remains a dynamic quantity. Quality is defined through product- and service-related factors which are susceptible to quantitative or qualitative analysis. The preconditions for achieving high quality are:

Quality policy: The company commitment to quality as a top-priority corporate objective,

Leadership: Employee-motivation measures,

Quality assurance.

Quality management

Quality system

All elements in a quality system and all quality-assurance measures must be systematically planned. The individual assignments and the areas of competence and responsibility are to be defined in writing (Quality-Assurance Handbook). Quality systems are also described in international standards, such as DIN ISO 9001 – 9004.

Increased requirements for defect-free products (zero-defect target) and economic considerations (defect prevention in place of sorting and reworking, or scrapping) make it imperative that preventive quality-assurance measures be applied. These serve the following objectives:

– To develop products that are insensitive to production fluctuations.
– To establish production processes to ensure that quality requirements are maintained within the specified limits.
– To apply methods which identify the sources of defects at an early stage, and which can be applied to rectify the manufacturing process in good time.

Three types of "audit" are employed in the regular monitoring of all elements in a quality system:

– System audit: Evaluation of the effectiveness of the quality system regarding its comprehensiveness and the practical application of the individual elements.
– Process audit: Evaluation of the effectiveness of the quality-management (QM) elements, confirmation of quality capability, of adherence to and suitability of particular processes, and the determination of specific measures for improvement.
– Product audit: Evaluation of the effectiveness of the QM elements performed by examining the final products or their components.

Quality management in development

At the outset, every new product which must fulfill the customer's quality and reliability demands is allocated a project specifications manual.

As early as the definition phase, its contents serve as the basis for the planning of all sample and endurance tests required to verify the new product's serviceability and reliability.

Quality assessment

At the conclusion of specific development stages, all the available data regarding quality and reliability are subjected to a quality-assessment procedure, leading to initiation of the required corrective measures. Responsible for the quality assessment are staff members from development, production engineering, and quality assurance; these, in turn, receive support from the specialists in the specialist departments.

Failure Mode and Effects Analysis (FMEA)

This cost-reduction and risk-prevention procedure is suitable for investigating the types of defects which can occur in system components and their effects on the system (for details, see "Reliability", P. 165).

Quality management during procurement

This aspect must extend beyond the receiving inspection; it must comprise an entire system. This system must ensure that the components purchased from suppliers contribute to the reliable fulfillment of the Technical Specifications defined for the finished product.

Example of application of Failure Mode and Effects Analysis (FMEA)

⊕ BOSCH QUALITY ASSURANCE

FMEA
Actuator 9 319 150 342
Part 6: Parts production and assembly of bushing holder

DEPT. FVB 75
FMEA 1289940001
PAGE 10
DATE 10.10.88

NO.	COMPONENT PROCESS	FUNCTION PURPOSE	DEFECT TYPE	DEFECT EFFECT	DEFECT CAUSES	DEFECT PREVENTION	DEFECT DETECTION	S	I A	E	SxE RZ	MEASURES V/T:
1110	Assemble bushing holder	Prepare parts for soldering process	Damaged sealing surfaces	Actuator leaking to surroundings → gasoline vapors in engine compartment	Swarf in assembly device	Wash before assembly, clean tools regularly	100% visual inspection of soldering; surface check; 100% visual inspection prior to packing	10	2	1	20	
1180	Solder bushing holder	Hold parts together	Part not soldered		No solder	Scan solder feed	100% visual inspection of soldering; 100% visual inspection of surface; 100% leak test	10 (10	2 2	2 1	40 (20)	100% leak test of bushing-holder assembly V: FVB2 T: 01.89
		Ensure leak-tightness	Part leaking (bubbles)		Insufficient solder	Scan solder feed	100% visual inspection of soldering	10 (10	4 3	6 2	240 (60)	100% leak test V: FVB2 T: 01.89 + Design improvement at soldering joint V: EVA3 T: 03.89

S = Severity of fault
V = Department responsible

A = Probability of occurrence
T = Deadline for introduction
E = Probability of detection

RZ = Risk number = S x A x E
Copyright 1987 Robert Bosch GmbH Stuttgart

It is imperative that suppliers' quality capabilities be supported by modern, preventive quality-assurance techniques (e.g. SPC Statistical Process Control or FMEA). All individual requirements for the product must be specified in a clear and unambiguous manner in order to allow the subcontractor to achieve and competently evaluate comprehensive compliance with the individual quality requirements for the product. These guidelines generally are in the form of drawings, order specifications, standards, formulas, etc.

For example, the actual manufacturer of the supplied product performs the first initial sample inspection. This inspection must be reproduced by the purchaser when the product is received (with particular emphasis on the interrelationships involving manufacturing processes and the finished product), and confirmed by means of an incoming inspection.

The supplier's final or shipping inspection can take the place of the purchaser's incoming inspection in those cases where the subcontractor possesses special knowledge and/or the technical equipment necessary for carrying out specific forms of quality testing. The supplier confirms the relevant quality inspections on the products in quality certificates in accordance with DIN 55 350 or material test certificates in accordance with DIN 50049. The test results obtained must be forwarded to the purchaser.

Quality management in production engineering

The preconditions for supplying assured quality are established in the production-planning phase. Compliance with the following conditions is required:
– Planning of the production process and material flow.
– Planning of resources requirements.
– Selection and acquisition of suitable production methods and production equipment, as well as the requisite test stands (e.g. for SPC).
– Examination of manufacturing methods, production equipment and machines to determine machine and process capability.
– Documentation of the production procedure in the production-sequence plan.
– Determination of the necessary level of employee qualification.
– Preparation of technical drawings and parts lists.

The Process FMEA provides a means of methodically anticipating potential faults in the manufacturing process and of assessing their effects on the quality of the attribute or the product. The Process FMEA is employed to discover the sources of defects, and to avoid the defects or minimize their effects. This makes it possible to initiate the necessary production and test-engineering procedures required for defect prevention.

FMEA working group

Area of operation	Product FMEA	Process FMEA	FMEA contribution
FMEA moderator		▓	Coordination Methods
Construction (Ⓥ = Responsibility)	Ⓥ	▓	Construction
Testing	☐	▓	Functionality
Endurance testing	☐		Durability Climate resistance
Technical marketing	☐		Project specifications
Customer service		▓	Customer service
Pre-production (Ⓥ = Responsibility)	☐	Ⓥ	Manufacturing verifiability procedures
Quality services	☐	▓	Quality and reliability assurance
Production	☐	▓	Production
Materials		▓	Subcontractor supply
Miscellaneous			

Inspection planning comprises the following points:
- Analysis of the functions to be tested.
- Determination of the test criteria.
- Selection of suitable inspection methods and measuring and inspection equipment.
- Determination of the extent and frequency of the inspection.
- Documentation of the test procedure in the inspection plan.
- Planning of recording and documentation of quality data (e.g. in quality-control charts for SPC).
- Planning for control of inspection, measuring, and test equipment.
- Possible planning of quality-data documentation.

The specified inspection criteria must always include all essential characteristics of the finished products.

Suitable means for compilation and evaluation of the inspection results are to be specified for assessing the quality of products and their components, and for controlling production processes. Test results are to be processed in such a manner as to be suitable for application in open-loop and closed-loop process-control systems, fault analysis and fault rectification.

Machine and process capability

The evaluation of machine capability is to confirm performance potential in the following two areas:
- The machine under examination must operate with verifiable consistency. If necessary, this consistency must be formulated with the aid of statistical quantities, e.g. as normal distribution with mean value $\bar{x}$ and standard deviation s.
- The machine must be able to maintain production within specified tolerances. This can only be confirmed using the quantification of consistency indicated above.

Testing of machine capability is restricted to a limited period, and to the investigation of the equipment-related effects on the production process. However, it should be noted that equipment-related and non-equipment-related factors (e.g. effects of material or procedures) cannot usually be separated completely. Individual tests are designed to determine whether:

- unusual process results are recognized,
- mean values and scatter range remain stable within the measurement series (the verification limits of statistical process control are employed for this examination).

If no unusual process results are present, and the mean and the scatter range are stable, then the process is considered to be fully controlled; the suitability of the equipment is then described using the familiar statistics c_m and c_{mk}. The value for c_m only reflects the scatter range for the machine; it is calculated with the following equation:

$$c_m = (OGW - UGW)/(6 \cdot \hat{\sigma})$$

On the other hand, the value for c_{mk} reflects not only the machine's scatter range, but also the position of the mean within the tolerance range. It is essential that it be calculated for the production machinery on which adjustments are either imprecise or impossible. It is calculated as follows:

$$c_{mk} = (\bar{\bar{x}} - UGW)/(3 \cdot \hat{\sigma}) \text{ or}$$
$$c_{mk} = (OGW - \bar{\bar{x}})/(3 \cdot \hat{\sigma})$$

with the lesser value being valid. The definitions are:
$\bar{\bar{x}}$ Total mean value
UGW Lower tolerance-range limit
OGW Upper tolerance-range limit
$\hat{\sigma}$ Estimate for process control

Bosch only designates production equipment as capable of ensuring that manufacture will result in the required product attributes when c_{mk} is at least 1.67.

Unusual process results, or an unstable mean or scatter range indicate that the process is not fully controlled. In this case, non-random influences (interference factors) are affecting the process. These must be eliminated or compensated for. The examination of machine capability is then repeated.

If the result of the machine-capability test is positive, it is followed by an examination of the process capability. This is intended to ensure that the production process is capable of consistently meeting the quality requirements placed upon it.

The examination of process capability extends over a longer period of time. All changes to the process (e.g. material changes, tool changes or method changes) are taken into account when the scope and intervals of sample testing are determined, and then included in the examination procedure.

Once compiled, the data are subjected to a statistical analysis comparable to that employed for determining equipment performance potentials. Particular attention is devoted to ascertaining whether the process mean and process control are stable, i.e., whether the process is fully controlled. If the process is fully controlled, then the process capability is confirmed using the known statistics c_p and c_{pk}. These statistics are calculated in the same way as those for c_m and c_{mk} where the values $\bar{\bar{x}}$ and $\hat{\sigma}$ from the process examination are used.

If the process is not fully controlled, calculation of c_p and c_{pk} is not permitted. In this case, the causes of the instability in the process must be either eliminated or compensated for. The process-capability analysis is then repeated.

Bosch designates a process as capable of ensuring the required product attributes only in cases where c_{pk} is at least 1.33.

Machine- and process-capability analysis are necessary preliminary checks prior to introduction of SPC. However, both investigations are also important for processes which are not controlled by SPC, as the required potential must be confirmed for each type of process.

Statistical Process Control (SPC)

SPC is a process-control system intended to assist in the prevention of errors and their associated costs. SPC is employed in production, being applied for attributes which are vital to operation (for details, see "Technical Statistics", P. 160).

Measuring and inspection equipment

The measuring and inspection equipment must be able to demonstrate whether the inspection features of the finished product conform to the prescribed specifications. Measuring and inspection equipment must be monitored, calibrated and maintained. Uncertainty of measurement is to be considered when using measuring and inspection equipment. It must be minimal relative to the tolerance range for the attribute being tested. With measuring and inspection equipment, attention is to be paid to:
- Defining the measurements to be performed, the required precision and the suitable measuring and inspection equipment.
- Ensuring that the measuring and inspection equipment meets precision requirements, i.e. the uncertainty of measurement is generally not to exceed 10 % of the tolerance range.
- All measuring and inspection equipment and measurement systems used for

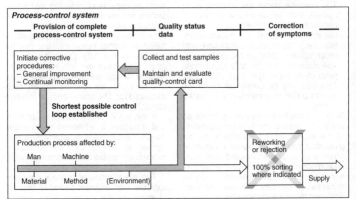

Process-control system

| Provision of complete process-control system | Quality status data | Correction of symptoms |

Initiate corrective procedures:
– General improvement
– Continual monitoring

Collect and test samples
Maintain and evaluate quality-control card

Shortest possible control loop established

Production process affected by:
Man   Machine
Material   Method   (Environment)

Reworking or rejection
100% sorting where indicated

Supply

product quality-assurance are to be specified in an inspection plan; they must be labeled, and are to be calibrated and adjusted at prescribed intervals.

– Calibration procedures must be specified. These must comprise individual data on the type of unit, its identification, application area and calibration intervals, and are also to include the steps to be taken in case of unsatisfactory results.

– Measuring and inspection equipment must be provided with appropriate identification verifying their calibration status.

– Calibration records (histories) are to be maintained.

– The appropriate environmental conditions for calibrating, testing and measurement must be maintained.

– Measuring and inspection equipment is to be carefully stored and protected against contamination in order to maintain consistent levels of precision and suitability for use.

– The measuring and inspection equipment and the software are to be protected against any influences which might invalidate their calibration.

Control of inspection, measuring, and test equipment: Type and extent

Satisfactory arrangements for monitoring test equipment embrace all measuring devices employed in development, production, assembly and in customer service. This category includes calipers, unit standards, instruments, recording devices, and special test equipment along with its ancillary computer software. In addition, the equipment, mounts and clamps, and instruments employed for process control are also monitored.

Procedures which extend to include the equipment and the abilities of the operator are employed in evaluating whether a test process is controlled. Measurement errors are compared with the quality specifications. Appropriate corrective actions are to be introduced when the requirements for precision and function in measuring and inspection equipment are no longer satisfied.

Measuring instruments subject to calibration

German legal requirements on weights and measures stipulate that calibration of measuring devices which are for use in "business transactions" be officially certified in those cases where the results of their measurements are employed to determine the price of goods or energy. This category includes equipment for measuring length, surface area, volume and mass, and thermal and electrical energy. If these conditions apply, then the calibration of the measuring instruments concerned must be officially certified. Continuing compliance must then be monitored by an official or an officially approved agency.

Relationship between measurement results, statistical analysis and process capability

Process	←Tolerance T→	Status	Process capability
Individual values		Unsure	Not calculated
Statistical analysis	σ	Result negative due to excessive variance	$C_p = \dfrac{T}{6\sigma} = 0.67$ Outside T by 4.6%
Minimum requirement	σ	Result positive, low variance Mean value maintained	$C_p = 1.33$ Outside T by 63 ppm
Mean tolerance value displaced	σ D	Result negative despite low variance	$C_p = 2.0$ but $C_{pk} = \dfrac{D}{3\sigma} = 0.67$ i.e. outside T by 2.3%

Technical statistics

Purpose of statistics

Descriptive statistics
To describe sets of similar units with specific, different characteristic values using statistical characteristics which allow objective comparisons and evaluations.

Rating statistics
To provide information on the statistical characteristics of larger sets (populations) based on relatively few individual data (samples).

Because such statements are based on the laws of chance and the theory of probability, their validity is always subject to a certain level of confidence, usually 95 % in the field of engineering.

Examples of populations:
– All products of the same type produced under constant manufacturing conditions.
– Set of all the possible results of a measurement under unchanging conditions.

There are two different types of characteristics:
– Quantitative characteristics, e.g., physical quantities (referred to as "measured values"),
– Attribute characteristics, e.g. "OK" or "Defective" etc. (referred to as "test results" in the following).

Statistical analysis methods provide valuable assistance for ensuring and improving quality standards in industrial products. Today's levels of vehicle reliability would be impossible without it.

Presentation of measured values

N Population size: the number of all items which form the basis of statistical analysis

n Number of measured values in the sample

P_A Confidence level

x Individual measured value

R Range: $R = x_{max} - x_{min}$

k Number of classes into which R is divided. $k = \sqrt{n}$ (at least 5)

w Class width

i Ordinal number of measured values (as subscript)

j Ordinal number of classes (as subscript)

x_j Midpoint of class no. j

n_j Absolute frequency of class no. j: number of measured values in class no. j

h_j Frequency in class no. j, $h_j = n_j/n$

h_j/w Frequency density

G_j Cumulative absolute frequency: absolute frequency summed up to a particular class

$$G_j = \sum_{r=1}^{j} n_r$$

H_j Cumulative frequency $= G_j/n$

$F(x)$ Distribution function: probability for values $\leq x$

$f(x)$ Frequency-density function $\dfrac{d\,F(x)}{d\,x}$

μ Arithmetic mean of population

$\overline{x}$ Arithmetic mean of a sample

$$\overline{x} = \sum_{i=1}^{n} x_i/n$$

$\overline{\overline{x}}$ Arithmetic mean of several $\overline{x}$ values

σ Standard deviation of population

s Standard deviation of sample

$$s = \sqrt{\sum_{i=1}^{n} (x_i - \overline{x})^2 / (n-1)}$$

V Variation coefficient $V = s/\overline{x}$

u Dispersion factor

X, Y, Random variable
Z

Histogram and cumulative frequency curve of an empirical distribution
The simplest way of clearly presenting a larger number of characteristic values is the histogram (frequency diagram). In the case of attributes or variables with few discrete values, bars are drawn over the characteristic values whose height is proportional to the relative frequency of the values, i.e. the frequency h_j of the attribute j in proportion from the total number of all the values $\sum_j h_j$.

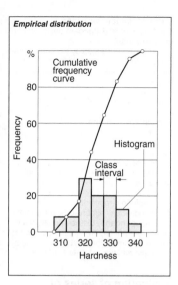

Empirical distribution

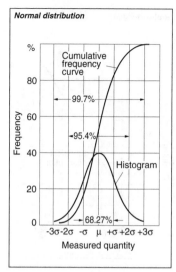

Normal distribution

In the case of variable attributes with a continuous range of values, the range is divided into k classes and the bars entered over the class midpoints. If the classes are not all the same size, the bars become rectangles whose areas are proportional to the relative frequencies of the classes. Thus, in these cases, the heights of the rectangles are also proportional to the frequency density.

If conclusions are to be drawn from the sample presentation described concerning the population, it is essential to define the classes in such a way that there are at least five values in each class.

Another way of presenting the distribution of attributes is the cumulative frequency curve. The advantage of this curve for variable attributes is that for each value or each interval the percentage of measured values below or above can easily be read off (estimate of fraction defectives outside the tolerance). The cumulative curve can be determined from the histogram by summing the relative frequencies up to the relevant value or interval. For the population, it thus represents the integral over the density function.

Distributions and statistical parameters

A random variable X is characterized by its distribution. The distribution function $F(x)$ describes the relationship between the variable value x and the cumulative frequency or probability for values $\leq x$. In empirical distributions, this function corresponds to the cumulative frequency curve. The histogram corresponds to the density function $f(x)$.

The most important parameters of a distribution are the arithmetic mean μ and the standard deviation σ.

Normal distribution

Normal, or Gaussian, distribution is the mathematically idealized limit case which always results when many mutually independent random effects are added together. The probability-density function of the Gaussian distribution clearly defined by μ and σ forms a symmetrical bell-shaped curve.

The total area under the bell-shaped curve corresponds to 1 = 100%. The standard deviation σ and its multiples allow the delimitation of specific areas with the boundaries $\mu \pm u\sigma$ in which P% of the

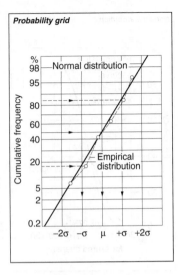

Probability grid

Sums of random variables

For the mean and standard deviation of a random variable $Z = a \cdot X + b \cdot Y$, created by the linear combination of 2 independently distributed random variables X and Y, the following apply:

$$\mu_z = a \cdot \mu_x + b \cdot \mu_y$$
$$\sigma_z^2 = a^2 \cdot \sigma_x^2 + b^2 \cdot \sigma_y^2$$

Typical applications

1. Fits.
Hole diameter: x.
Shaft diameter: y.
Clearance: $z = x - y$.
For $\sigma_x = \sigma_y$ the following applies:
$\sigma_z^2 = 2 \cdot \sigma_x^2$

2. Combined dimension.
If the individual dimensions are statistically independently distributed about their mean tolerances, the tolerance for the combined dimension can be calculated by quadratic addition (cf. DIN 7186).

values fall (Table 1). The percentages $\alpha = (100 - P)/2$ lie outside these areas on either side.

Empirical and normal distribution in probability grid

In a "probability grid", the ordinate is distorted in such a way that the S-shaped cumulative frequency curve is transformed into a straight line.

Determination of μ and σ from the probability grid:
1. Read off μ at 50 % cumulative frequency.
2. Read off abscissa values at 16 % and 84 %.
The difference corresponds to 2σ.

Evaluation of series of measurements

Random interval for $\bar{x}$ and s
(direct conclusion)

If many samples each containing n values are taken from one and the same population with the mean μ and the standard deviation σ, the mean values $\bar{x}_1, \bar{x}_2 \ldots$ of the samples are dispersed with the standard deviation

$$\sigma_{\bar{x}} = \frac{\sigma}{\sqrt{n}} \quad \text{about the true value } \mu.$$

In a similar way, random intervals can be defined for s and R.

Table 1. Value frequency P within and α outside $\pm u\sigma$

u	1.00	1.28	1.64	1.96	2.00	2.33	2.58	3.00	3.29
$P\%$	68.27	80	90	95	95.4	98	99	99.7	99.9
$\alpha\%$	15.86	10	5	2.5	2.3	1	0.5	0.15	0.05

Quantity	Random interval	
	Lower limit	Upper limit
$\bar{x}$	$\mu - u \dfrac{\sigma}{\sqrt{n}}$	$\mu + u \dfrac{\sigma}{\sqrt{n}}$
S	$D_u \cdot \sigma$	$D_o \cdot \sigma$
R	$D_u \cdot \sigma \cdot d_n$	$D_o \cdot \sigma \cdot d_n$

D_u and D_o as functions of n and P from Tables 1 and 2.

Table 2. Auxiliary constants for evaluation of measurement series

n	d_n	t values for $P =$			D_u	D_o
		90%	95%	99%	for $P = 95\%$	
2	1.13	6.31	12.7	63.7	0.03	2.24
3	1.69	2.92	4.30	9.92	0.16	1.92
5	2.33	2.13	2.78	4.60	0.35	1.67
10	3.08	1.83	2.26	3.25	0.55	1.45
20	3.74	1.73	2.09	2.86	0.68	1.32
50	–	1.68	2.01	2.68	0.80	1.20
∞	–	1.65	1.96	2.58	1.00	1.00

Confidence intervals for μ and σ (conclusion)

If only samples with x and s are known and a statement is to be made on the true mean value μ resulting from an infinite number of measurements, a so-called confidence interval can be specified which features μ with a probability of $P_A\%$. The same holds true for σ.

Quantity	Confidence interval	
	Lower limit	Upper limit
μ	$\bar{x} - t \dfrac{s}{\sqrt{n}}$	$\bar{x} + t \dfrac{s}{\sqrt{n}}$
σ	$\dfrac{s}{D_o}$	$\dfrac{s}{D_u}$

t, D_o and D_u from Table 2.

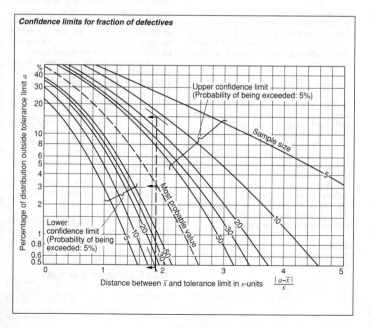

Confidence limits for fraction of defectives

Percentage of distribution outside tolerance limit a

Upper confidence limit (Probability of being exceeded: 5%)

Sample size

Most probable value

Lower confidence limit (Probability of being exceeded: 5%)

Distance between $\bar{x}$ and tolerance limit in s-units $\dfrac{|a - \bar{x}|}{s}$

Comparison of mean values

Two samples with values of n_1 and n_2 have the same standard deviations $s_1 = s_2$ but different mean values $\overline{x}_1 \neq \overline{x}_2$. The confidence interval for the difference $\mu_1 - \mu_2 = 0$ is:

$$\pm t \cdot s_A \cdot \sqrt{1/n_1 + 1/n_2} \text{ with}$$
$$s_A^2 = \left((n_1 - 1) \, s_1^2 + (n_2 - 1) \, s_2^2\right)/(n' - 1)$$

$n' = n_1 + n_2 - 1$ determines t in Table 2.

If the difference $x_1 - x_2$ is outside this confidence interval, the two samples come with confidence level P from different populations (e.g. different manufacturing conditions).

Estimation of nonconforming fractions

The percentage of parts lying outside the tolerance limit a is to be estimated based on $\overline{x}$ and s from a sample series.

Calculation procedure:
If μ and σ are known, then the percentage outside a in Table 1 or in the Figure "Confidence limits for nonconforming fractions" ("most probable value" curve) is determined by:

$$u = |a - \mu| / \sigma.$$

A value of e.g. $u = 1.65$ corresponds to a percentage of 5 %. But now only $\overline{x}$ and s of the sample are known, not the values μ and σ of the population. As these values are random, the nonconforming fraction can only be specified in terms of the confidence range in which it lies with a particular probability.

In the figure, the confidence limits can be read off as a function of $|a - \overline{x}| / s$ which are exceeded only with a probability of 5 %. Separate analyses are required for each of the two tolerance limits.

Example:

Prescribed tolerance for ground rollers $14_{-0.043}^{-0.016}$ mm.

Tested are 14 parts of 13.961 to 13.983 mm. $\overline{x} = 13.972$ mm; $R = 0.022$ mm.

Estimated value for s from R with d_n from Table 2:
$$s = 0.022/3.5 = 0.0063$$

Upper tolerance limit exceeded:

$$\frac{|a - \overline{x}|}{s} = \frac{13.984 - 13.972}{0.0063} = \frac{0.012}{0.0063} = 1.9$$

Referring to the figure:
Upper confidence limit ≈ 15 %
Most probable value $\approx 3.1\%$
Lowest confidence limit $\approx 0.5\%$

Lower tolerance limit exceeded:

$$\frac{|a - \overline{x}|}{s} = \frac{|13.957 - 13.972|}{0.0063} = \frac{0.015}{0.0063} = 2.38$$

Referring to the figure:
Upper confidence limit ≈ 9 %
Most probable value ≈ 1 %
Lowest confidence limit $< 0.5\%$

Statistical Process Control (SPC)

Quality-control charts are employed to ensure consistent quality in manufacturing processes. Small samples are tested at specified intervals; the values $\overline{x}$ and R are entered for test results while the defects are entered for attribute testing.

T_{lo}, T_{up} Lower/upper tolerance limits, T Difference between upper and lower tolerance limit (tolerance range),
$T = T_{lo} - T_{up}$, $T_m = (T_{lo} + T_{up})/2$,
$\overline{x}$, R Values from ≥ 20 samples,
$\sigma = \overline{R}/d_n$ = Standard deviation,
$c_p = T/(6 \times \sigma)$ = Process capability.

A process is considered to be "controlled" if 1) $c_p > 1$ (better: $c_p \geq 1.33$),
2) the curve displays no unusual variations (no trends, etc.),
3) $\overline{x}$ and R lie within the "action limits" of the corresponding random intervals.

Table 3 shows the approximate values for action limits as a percentage of T. The calculation is based upon the assumptions that values are:
99.7 % random intervals and $c_p = 1$.

Table 3. Action limits as % of T

n	3	4	5	6	7	8	10	12	15
$R/T < \%$	72	78	82	84	86	88	91	93	95
$(\overline{x} - T_m) < \%$	29	25	22	20	19	18	16	14	13

Weibull distribution of service lives

Weibull distribution has gained acceptance as the standard in the investigation of the service lives of technical products. Its distribution function (probability for service lives $\leq t$) is:

$$F(t) = 1 - e^{-(t/T)^b}$$

Survival probability (reliability function)

$$R(t) = 1 - F(t)$$

Failure rate (failures per unit time referred to remaining products)

$$\lambda(t) = f(t) \,/\, R(t)$$

where

T Characteristic service life,
corresponding sum of failures 63.2 %.
b Failure steepness (Weibull slope),
$b < 1$: falling (early failures)
$b = 1$: constant (random failures)
$b > 1$: rising (wear)

In the Weibull grid with abscissa $\ln t$ and ordinate $\ln (-\ln R[t])$, $F(t)$ becomes a straight line.

Evaluation of an endurance test involving n test specimens:

The diagram shows the evaluation of an endurance test involving $n = 19$ switches, of which $r = 12$ have failed. Against the service lives t ordered according to length in cycles, the sum of failures is plotted as

$$H = (i - 0.5)/n.$$

The result is:

$$T = 83 \cdot 10^3 \text{ cycles}$$
$$b = 3.2 \qquad \text{(wear)}.$$

T and b are random values like $\bar{x}$ and s. Approximate confidence intervals ($n \geq 50$) for the "true values" are provided by the formulae:

$$T \pm (u/\sqrt{n}) \cdot (T/b)$$
$$b - 0.5 \cdot (u/\sqrt{n'}) \cdot b \ldots b + (u/\sqrt{n'}) \cdot b$$

u from Table 1.

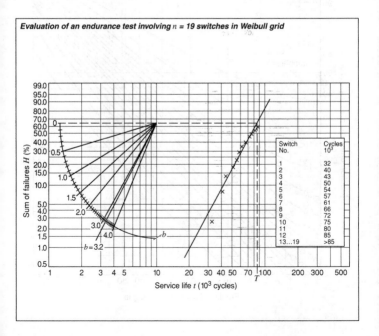

Evaluation of an endurance test involving $n = 19$ switches in Weibull grid

Switch No.	Cycles 10^3
1	32
2	40
3	43
4	50
5	54
6	57
7	61
8	66
9	72
10	75
11	80
12	85
13…19	>85

For incomplete observations ($r < n$):
$$n' \approx r \cdot \left(1 + (r/n)\right)/2$$
T, b are therefore less precisely defined by r failures at $r < n$ than at $r = n$. The proportion exceeding a specific life expectancy is estimated in the following section.

Statistical evaluation of test results

N Size of population (batch). An attribute divides the batch into two classes, e.g. "failed" and "OK".
n Number of sample units
I Number of defects in batch
i Number of defects in sample
p Defective fraction in sample
$p = i/n$
p' Defective fraction in batch
$p' = I/N$.

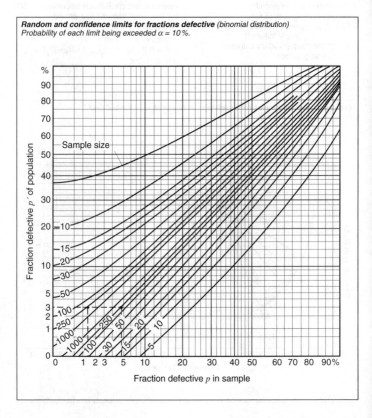

Random and confidence limits for fractions defective (binomial distribution)
Probability of each limit being exceeded $\alpha = 10\%$.

Fraction defective p' of population

Sample size

Fraction defective p in sample

Distribution of defective fraction p in random samples

The number of defectives i within the sample is a random variable. Larger batches ($N > 10 \cdot n$) are characterized by binomial distribution, expected value:
$E(i) = n \cdot p'$,

Standard deviation:
$\sigma_i = \sqrt{n \cdot p' \cdot (1 - p')}$.

Random ranges for p (p' known) and confidence intervals for p' (p known) dependent on n are provided by the diagram on P. 162 with an exceeding probability of $\alpha = 10\%$ for each limit.

For the range $p' < 5\%$, frequently encountered in practice, binomial distribution is replaced by Poisson's law of infrequent events which is exclusively dependent on $n \cdot p'$ with $E(i) = n \cdot p'$, $\sigma_i = \sqrt{n \cdot p'}$.

Examples:

1. Binomial distribution (diagram P. 162)
In endurance testing with $n = 20$ units, $i = 2$ units have failed after extended usage.

What percentage p' of the series will not achieve the corresponding service life T?

Percentage in random sample $p = {}^2\!/_{20} = 10\%$.
At $p = 10\%$, $n = 20$, the diagram provides the following figures:
$p_u' = 2.8\%$, $p_o' = 24\%$.
With constant quality, the percentage with a service life $< T$ will lie within this range.

2. Poisson distribution (Table 4)
During receiving inspection, a random sampling of $n = 500$ parts found $i = 1$ part which was out of tolerance.

What is the maximum percentage of defective parts in the batch as expressed with 90% probability?
At $i = 1$, $\alpha = 10\%$, Table 4 provides:
$np_o' = 3.89$
$p_o' = 3.89/500 = 7.78‰$.

Approximation formula for Poisson distribution

The approximate value for $i > 10$ can be derived using:

$$n \cdot p' = i + u \cdot \sqrt{i} + k$$
(see Table 4 for u, k).

Example for Poisson approximation:

In a preproduction series consisting of $n = 10\,000$ units, there were $i = 17$ warranty claims. With 97.5% probability, what is the limit for warranty claims which will not be exceeded in normal series production if identical conditions are maintained?

Inserting the values from Table 4 into the approximation formula given above provides the following:
$np_o' = 17 + 1.96 \cdot \sqrt{17} + 2 = 27.08$
$p_o' = 27.08/10\,000 = 2.7‰$.

Table 4. Confidence limits for infrequent events

Obs. no. i	Lower limit $n\,p'_u$ Probability of being exceeded		Upper limit $n\,p'_o$	
	2.5%	10%	10%	2.5%
0	—	—	2.30	3.69
1	0.025	0.105	3.89	5.57
2	0.242	0.532	5.32	7.22
3	0.619	1.10	6.68	8.77
4	1.09	1.74	8.00	10.24
5	1.62	2.43	9.27	11.67
6	2.20	3.15	10.53	13.06
7	2.81	3.89	11.77	14.42
8	3.45	4.66	12.99	15.76
9	4.12	5.43	14.21	17.08
10	4.80	6.22	15.41	18.39
u	− 1.96	− 1.28	+ 1.28	+ 1.96
k	+ 1.0	+ 0.2	+ 1.2	+ 2.0

Measurement: basic terms

Measurements can only be used as the basis for responsible decisions if their limits of error are known. Here, statistical terms are used.

Definition of terms (as per DIN 1319):

Measured variable
Physical variable which is measured (length, density, etc.).

Measured value
Particular value of the measured variables, e.g. 3 m.

Measurement result
Value calculated from one or more measured values, e.g. mean $\bar{x}$.

Measurement error $F = x_a - x_r$
x_a indicated measured value;
x_r "correct" measured value.
Causes: measured object, measurement equipment, measurement procedure, environment, observer.

Relative measurement error
Normally: F/x_r
For designation of measuring devices F/x_e, where x_e = full-scale deflection of measuring device.

Systematic measurement errors
Measurement errors which, under the same conditions, have the same magnitude and sign.
  Those systematic errors which can be detected are to be corrected $B = -F$, otherwise the measurement result is incorrect. Systematic errors which cannot be detected are to be estimated (f).

Random measurement errors
Measurement errors whose magnitudes and signs are randomly dispersed. Estimated using the standard deviation s.

Result of a series of measurements
If n measured values x_i are measured under the same conditions, the following should be specified as the measurement result:

$y = \bar{x}_E \pm u$ Confidence limits for correct measured value, where:
$\bar{x}_E = \bar{x} + B$ Corrected mean value
$u = t \cdot s/\sqrt{n} + |f|$ Measurement uncertainty.
Calculation of s P. 156,
for t, see Table 2 P. 159,
f Non-detected systematic errors.

Separation of measurement and manufacturing accuracy
On each of n products, a characteristic x_i is measured twice with measurement error f_{ik}:
$$y_{ik} = x_i + f_{ik} \quad (i = 1, \ldots n; \; k = 1.2)$$

The differences between the 2 measured values on the same product contain 2 measurement errors:
$$z_i = y_{i1} - y_{i2} = f_{i1} - f_{i2}$$
$$\sigma_z^2 = 2 \, \sigma_f^2$$
$$\sigma_y^2 = \sigma_x^2 + \sigma_f^2$$

The last two relationships can be used to determine the standard deviation σ_f of the measurement errors and the corrected standard deviation σ_x of the product characteristic x.

Standards

DIN 55 303 Statistical assessment of data
DIN 53 804 Statistical assessments
DIN 55 350 Quality assurance and statistics terms
DIN 40 080 Regulations and tables for attributive sampling
DIN 7186 Statistical tolerances
DIN/ISO 9000 Quality systems
DGQ-11-04 Quality-assurance terms and formulas (Beuth)

Literature

Graf, Henning, Stange: Formeln und Tabellen der Statistik (Formulas and tables for statistics) Springer-Verlag, Berlin, 1956;
Rauhut: Berechnung der Lebensdauerverteilung (Calculation of service life distribution) Glückauf-Verlag, Essen, 1982.

Reliability

According to DIN 40 041, reliability is the sum total of those characteristics in the unit under investigation which exert an effect on the unit's ability to achieve specified requirements under given conditions during a specified period of time. Reliability is a constituent element of quality ("reliability is quality based on time").

The essential concept here is the word dependability. Dependability comprises the terms reliability, availability, safety, security and maintainability. Dependability therefore equates to the confidence placed in a service which is to be provided by a system.

Reliability quantifies availability; it is the probability that at any given time a system will prove to be fully operational. The failure rate is the conditional probability density of a component failing before time $t+dt$ provided it has survived beyond time t. The failure rate generally has the shape of a "bathtub curve", which can be described as the superimposition of three Weibull distributions with varying failure steepness components (see Chapter "Technical statistics").

Failure in electronic components is generally spontaneous, with no advance indication of impending defects. This condition is described by a constant failure rate (middle section of the curve). Neither quality control nor preventive maintenance can prevent such failures. Failures caused by incorrect component selection,

excessive loads or abuse or manufacturing defects show a "burn-in behavior", described by a failure rate that falls with time while ageing of a component is represented by a rising failure rate (left or right section of the curve).

Reliability analysis and prediction

Mutually supplementary analysis methods are applied to determine the potential failure risk associated with a product, i.e. to discover all possible effects of operational and internal failure, as well as external interference factors (e.g. operator error); these methods are used in different phases of the product's life cycle. Mainly FMEA and fault-tree analysis are used in the development of motor vehicles.

FMEA (DIN 25448, IEC 812)

FMEA (Failure Mode and Effects Analysis) is a "bottom-up" analysis. Starting from faults at the lowest level of the system hierarchy (generally components in design FMEA, function blocks in system FMEA, work steps in process FMEA), the analysis examines the way in which they spread to higher levels. In this way, all those critical system states caused by individual failures are detected and also evaluated in relation to each other. FMEA can be used in various stages of development and production.

Design FMEA: Under the precondition that the parts are manufactured in accordance with their drawings, products/components are examined for conformity between design and specifications in order to avoid errors in system design and to facilitate detection of field risks.

Process FMEA: Under the precondition that the specifications are correct, the process of product manufacture is examined for conformity with the drawings in order to avoid manufacturing errors.

System FMEA: The system components are examined as to their correct combined operation in order to avoid errors in system design and to facilitate detection of field risks.

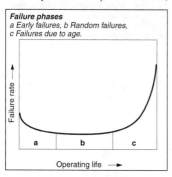

Failure phases
a Early failures, b Random failures,
c Failures due to age.

Failure rate →

Operating life →

a b c

Fault-tree analysis (DIN 25 424)

Fault-tree analysis (FTA) is a "top-down" analysis procedure, which permits quantitative assessment of probabilities. Starting from the undesirable event (top event), all the conceivable causes are enumerated, even combinations of individual failures. When the occurrence probabilities of individual failures are known, it is possible to calculate the probability of the undesirable event occurring. For this purpose, above all for electrical components, there are data collections of failure rates such as Mil Hdbk 217E or SAE 870 050. However, their suitability for use with motor vehicles must be critically checked in individual cases.

Reliability enhancement

System reliability can always be improved by avoiding errors or narrowing tolerances. Preventive measures include e.g. selecting more reliable components with higher permissible loads; or (for electronic systems), since the availability of systems declines markedly as the number of components increases, reducing the number of components and thus connections through increased integration. As a rule of thumb, purely electronic components such as transistors or integrated circuits are responsible for 10 % of failures and sensors and final controlling elements for 30 %; however the connections between components and with the outside world are responsible for 60 % of failures. If preventive measures do not prove sufficient, then fault-tolerance measures (e.g. multichannel circuitry, self-monitoring) must be implemented in order to mask the effects of a defect.

Reliability planning

In the case of products to be newly developed, the reliability growth management procedure (RG, Mil Hdbk 189) provides a planning basis for the extent of testing work required to achieve a reliability target depending on the reliability initially available.

In the course of the development of a product, its reliability improves thanks to the causes of observed failures being analyzed and eliminated as far as possible. Strictly speaking, a statistical evaluation of the reliability of a product in its final version can only be started at the end of its development. However, in the case of the service lives demanded in the automobile industry, any such evaluation requires so much time as to delay the series launch. Under certain preconditions, the RG method allows engineers to assess the reliability of a product at any stage in its development. This assessment is based on the data of earlier product versions and the effectiveness of the failure-correction measures introduced. In this way, this procedure on the one hand reduces the time needed until series launch and on the other hand increases the available data volume and thus the confidence level.

If the current average service life MTTF (Mean Time To Failure) is plotted on a log-log scale against the cumulated operating time (total test time of all the test specimens), experience shows that on average this MTTF value increases in a straight line. Depending on the product and the effort expended, the upwards gradient of this line will be between 0.35 and 0.5. This empirical relationship between testing effort and achieved reliability can be used for planning.

A comparison between planning and current status can be made at any time. As the RG program progresses, intermediate reliability targets, specified in advance, must also be met. When planning the test program, it is essential to strike an acceptable balance between testing time, testing effort and available resources, and also to make a realistic estimate of the possible reliability gains.

Control engineering

Terms and definitions (in accordance with DIN 19226)

Closed-loop control	Open-loop control

Closed-loop control
Closed-loop control is a process by which a variable, the variable to be controlled (controlled variable x), is continuously recorded, compared with another variable, the reference variable w_1, and influenced according to the result of this comparison in the sense of an adaptation to the reference variable. The ensuing action takes place in a closed control loop.

The function of closed-loop control is to adapt the value of the controlled variable to the value specified by the reference variable in spite of disturbances even if the given conditions do not allow for a perfect match.

Open-loop control
Open-loop control is the process in a system in which one or more variables as input variables influence other variables as output variables on account of the rules characteristic of that system.

This type of control is characterized by the open action via the individual transfer element or the open control loop.

The term "control" is often used not only to denote the control process itself but also the entire system in which the control function takes place.

Closed control loop
The closed control loop is formed by all the elements which take part in the closed action of the control operation.

The control loop is a closed path of action which acts in one direction. The controlled variable x acts in a circular structure in the form of negative feedback back on itself.

In contrast to open-loop control, closed-loop control takes into account the influence of all the disturbances (z_1, z_2) in the control loop.

The closed control loop is subdivided into controlled system and controlling system.

Open control loop
An open control loop is an arrangement of elements (systems) which act on each other in a chain structure.

An open control loop as a whole can be part of a higher-level system and interact in any fashion with other systems.

An open control loop can only counter the effect of the disturbance which is measured by the control unit (e.g. z_1); other disturbances (e.g. z_2) are unaffected.

The open control loop is subdivided into controlled system and controlling system.

Controlling system (open and closed loops)
The open-loop or closed-loop controlling system is that part of the control loop which acts on the controlled system via the final-controlling element as determined by the control parameters.

System boundaries
The open-loop and closed-loop controlling systems include all those devices and elements which act directly to produce the desired condition within the control circuit.

Closed control loop

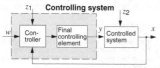

Open control loop

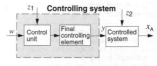

Input variables and output variable of closed-loop controlling system
The input variables to the controlling system are the controlled variable x, the reference variable w and the disturbance(s) z_1. The output variable from the controlling system is the manipulated variable y.

Input variables and output variable of open-loop controlling system
The input variables to the controlling system are the reference variable w and the disturbance(s) z_1. The output variable from the controlling system is the manipulated variable y.

Closed-loop control	Open-loop control

Controlled system (open and closed loops)
The open-loop or closed-loop controlled system is that part of the control loop which represents the area of the system to be influenced according to the function.

Input variables and output variable of closed-loop controlled system	**Input variable and output variable of open-loop controlled system**
The input variables to the controlled system are the manipulated variable y and the disturbances z_2. The output variable from the controlled system is the controlled variable x.	The input variable is the manipulated variable y. The output variable is the object variable x_A or an output variable which influences the object variable in a predetermined manner.

Transfer elements and system elements
Open- and closed-loop controls can be subdivided into elements along the control loop.

In terms of equipment design and function these are called system elements and transfer elements, respectively.

In terms of closed- or open-loop control function, only the relationship between the variables and their values which act upon one another in the system are described.

Loop, direction of control action
Both the open control loop and the closed control loop comprise individual elements (or systems) which are connected together to form a loop.

The loop is that path along which open- or closed-loop control takes place. The direction of control action is the direction in which the control function operates.

The loop and the direction of control action need not necessarily coincide with the path and the direction of corresponding energy and mass flows.

Final controlling element, control point
The final controlling element is that element which is located at the upstream end of the controlled system, and which directly affects the flow of mass or energy. The location at which this action takes place is called the control point.

Disturbance point
The disturbance point is the location at which a variable not controlled by the system acts on the loop, thereby adversely affecting the condition which the control is designed to maintain.

Manipulated variable y, manipulating range Y_h
The manipulated variable y is both the output variable of the controlling system and the input variable of the controlled system. It transfers the action of the controlling system to the controlled system.

The manipulating range Y_h is the range within which the manipulated variable can be adjusted.

Reference variable w, reference-variable range W_h
The reference variable w of an open- or closed-loop control is a variable which is not acted on directly by the control; it is input to the loop from outside the control, and is that variable whose value is to be reflected by the output variable in accordance with the control parameters.

The reference-variable range W_h is that range within which the reference variable w of an open- or closed-loop control may lie.

Disturbances z, disturbance range Z_h
Disturbances z in open- and closed-loop controls are all variables acting from outside the control which adversely affect the action of the control. In many cases, the most important disturbance is the load or the throughput through the system. The disturbance range Z_h is that range within which the disturbance may lie without adversely affecting the operation of the control.

Object variable x_A, object range X_{Ah}
The object variable x_A of an open- or closed-loop control is that variable which the control is intended to influence.

The object range X_{Ah} of an open- or closed-loop control is that range within which the object variable may lie, with full functional capability of the control.

Control methods

Transfer elements

Transfer elements are the basic modules and core elements for the control-engineering analysis and synthesis of dynamic systems. They each contain an illustration specification which allows an output variable to be clearly assigned to each input variable that is permitted for the corresponding transfer element. The general graphical representation of a transfer element is the block diagram (see illustration).

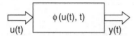

The illustration specification ϕ is often termed the operator. With the operator ϕ, the functional relationship between the input and output variables of a transfer element can be described by

$$y(t) = \phi(u(t), t).$$

A summary of the simplest transfer elements can be found in the accompanying table.

A particular position among the general transfer elements is taken up by linear time-invariant transfer elements. For these elements, the following superposition principle applies

$$\phi(u_1(t) + u_2(t)) = \phi(u_1(t)) + \phi(u_2(t))$$

together with the condition of time invariance

$$y(t) = \phi(u(t)) \rightarrow y(t-T) = \phi(u(t-T)), \; T>0.$$

With the transfer elements connected to each other by the action lines, it is possible to depict complex dynamic systems such as e.g. a DC motor, hydraulic systems, mechatronic servo-systems etc.

Controller design

A series of analytical and synthesizing processes are available for application in control engineering. Control engineers distinguish here between time-range and frequency-range procedures. A classical

and effective example of the frequency-range approach is the design of controllers using Bode diagrams. An efficient time-range procedure is the design of a state controller by means of pole specification or the Riccati controller.

Many of the problems posed by the requirements of control engineering are solved by using certain controller types which are composed as far as possible of the following four transfer elements:

– P element (proportional-action transfer element),
– I element (integral-action transfer element),
– D element (derivative-action transfer element),
– P-T_1 element (1st order time-delay element).

Parallel connection on the input side, addition of the output variables from the three transfer elements P, I, D and downstream connection of the P-T_1 element can be used to create the controller types P, I, PI, PP, PD, PID, PPD. See DIN 19226 for characteristics and system performance.

Subdivision of control modes

In control-engineering practice, distinctions are made between the individual control modes according to the following attributes: continuous-time/continuous-value, continuous-time/discrete-value, discrete-time/continuous-value and discrete-time/discrete-value. Of these four attributes, only the instances of continuous-time/continuous-value and discrete-time/discrete-value control are of significance.

Continuous-time/ continuous-value control

In continuous-time/continuous-value control, the controlled variable is recorded in an uninterrupted process and compared with the reference variable. This comparison provides the basis for continuous-time and continuous-value generation of the manipulated variable.

Continuous-time/continuous-value control is also referred to as analog control.

Table: Summary of some transfer elements

Designation	Functional relationship	Transfer function	Course of step response	Symbol
P element	$y = Ku$	K		
I element	$y = K \int_0^t u(\tau)\, d\tau$	$\dfrac{K}{s}$		
D element	$y = K\dot{u}$	Ks	Area = K	
TZ element T_1 element	$y(t) = Ku(t-T_1)$	$Ke^{-T_1 s}$		
S element	$y = u_1 \pm \ldots \pm u_p$			
$P\text{-}T_1$ element, VZ_1 element	$T\dot{y} + y = Ku$	$\dfrac{K}{1+Ts}$		
$P\text{-}T_2$ element VZ_2 element	$T^2\ddot{y} + 2dT\dot{y} + y = Ku$	$\dfrac{K}{1+2dTs+T^2s^2}$	Periodic case: $d < 1$ — Aperiodic limit case: $d \geqq 1$	

Discrete-time/discrete-value control

In discrete-time/discrete-value control, the controlled variable is recorded, quantified and subtracted from the quantified reference variable only at the sampling instants. The manipulated variable is calculated on the basis of the control difference thus created. For this purpose, an algorithm is generally used which is implemented in the form of a software program on a microcontroller. A/D and D/A converters are used as process interfaces. Discrete-time/discrete-value control is also referred to as digital control.

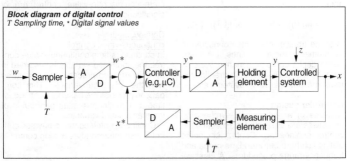

Block diagram of digital control
T Sampling time, • Digital signal values

Examples of closed-loop control systems in motor vehicles (simplified)

Control system	Object variable (x_A)	Controlled variable (x)	Reference variable (w)	Manipulated variable (y)	Disturbances (z)	Controlling system	Final controlling element	Controlled system
Lambda closed-loop control	Air/fuel ratio (λ)	O_2 content of exhaust gas	$\lambda = 1.0$ (fixed-command control)	Injected fuel quantity	Inexact pilot control, leaks, crankcase ventilation	Lambda control unit and lambda sensor	Fuel injectors	Combustion chamber; part of intake system and exhaust system up to λ sensor
Rotational-speed control in diesel engines	Engine speed		Setpoint speed (follow-up control)	Injected fuel quantity	Load	Governor	Fuel-injection pump	Mixture-formation area in engine
Antilock braking system (ABS control)	Wheel slip		Slip limit (adaptive)	Braking pressure	Road and driving conditions	Controller in ABS control unit	Pressure-control valve	Tires, road
Temperature control (passenger compartment)	Interior temperature		Setpoint temperature (follow-up control)	Hot-water flow rate or hot/cold-air mixture ratio	Engine temp., outside temp.; heat radiation; driving speed; engine speed	Temperature regulator and temperature sensor	Electromagnetic heating valve or air flap	Passenger compartment

Examples of open-loop control systems in engines

Control system	Object variables (x_A)	Reference variables (w)	Input variables of controlling system	Manipulated variable (y)	Disturbances (z)	Controlling system	Final controlling element	Controlled system
Jetronic gasoline injection	Air/fuel ratio	Air/fuel ratio (setpoint)	Engine speed, engine temperature, vehicle system voltage, air quantity, air temperature, throttle-valve position	Duration of injection	Fuel temperature, manifold-wall fuel condensation	Jetronic control unit with various measuring elements	Fuel injectors	Mixture-formation area
Electronic ignition systems	Ignition point	Ignition point (setpoint)	Engine speed, crankshaft position, intake-manifold pressure, throttle-valve position, engine temperature, vehicle system voltage	Ignition point	Condition of spark plugs, air/fuel ratio, fuel quality, mechanical tolerances	Ignition control unit	Ignition output stage	Combustion chamber in engine

Data processing in motor vehicles

Requirements

Highly sophisticated state-of-the-art open-loop and closed-loop control concepts are essential for meeting the demands for function, safety, environmental compatibility and comfort associated with the wide range of automotive subsystems installed in modern-day vehicles. Sensors monitor reference and controlled variables, which an electronic control unit (ECU) then converts into the signals required to adjust the final controlling elements/actuators. The input signals can be analog (e.g. voltage characteristic at pressure sensor), digital (e.g. switch position) or pulse-shaped (i.e. information content as a function of time; e.g. engine-speed signal). These signals are processed after being conditioned (filtering, amplification, pulse shaping) and converted (analog/digital); digital signal-processing methods are preferred.

Thanks to modern semiconductor technology, powerful computer units, with their accompanying program and data memories, and special peripheral circuitry, designed specifically for real-time applications, can all be integrated on a limited number of chips.

Modern vehicles are equipped with numerous digital control units (ECUs), e.g. for engine management, ABS and transmission-shift control. Improved performance and additional functions are obtained by synchronizing the processes controlled by the individual control units and by mutual real-time adaptation of the respective parameters. An example of this type of function is traction control (TCS), which reduces the driving torque when the drive wheels spin.

Up to now, data between the control units (in the example cited above, ABS/TCS and engine management) have been exchanged mostly through separate individual circuits. However, this type of point-to-point connection is only suitable for a limited number of signals. The data-transmission potential between the individual ECUs can be enhanced by using a simple network topology designed specifically for serial data transmission in automotive applications.

Microcomputer

The microcomputer comprises both the central processing unit (CPU) for processing arithmetic operations and logical relationships, and special function modules to monitor external signals and to generate the control signals for external servo elements. These peripheral modules are largely capable of assuming complete control of real-time operations. The program-controlled CPU could only discharge these at the price of both additional complication and curtailment in the number of functions (e.g. determining the moment at which an event occurred).

Computing capacity

Apart from the architecture (e.g. accumulator, register machine) and the word length (4...32 bits), the product of the internal clock frequency and the average number of clock pulses required per instruction determines the capacity of a CPU:
– Clock frequency: 1...40 MHz (typical),
– Clock pulses per instruction: 1...32 pulses (typical), depending on the CPU's architecture and the instruction (e.g. 6 pulses for addition, 32 pulses for multiplication).

Electronic control unit (ECU)

Digital input signals
Register a switch position or digital sensor signals (e.g. rotational-speed pulses from a Hall-effect sensor).
Voltage range: 0 V to battery voltage

Analog input signals
Signals from analog sensors (lambda sensor, pressure sensor, potentiometer).
Voltage range: several mV up to 5 V.

Microcomputer

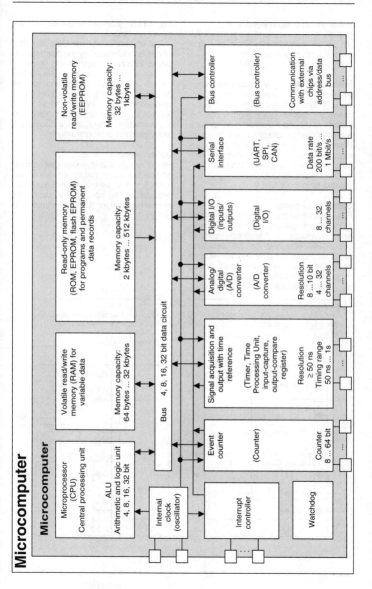

Pulse-shaped input signals
Signals from inductive min^{-1} sensors. After signal conditioning, they are processed further as digital signals.
Voltage range: 0.5 V to 100 V.

Initial conditioning of input signals
Protective circuits (passive: R and RC circuits; active: special surge-proof semiconductor elements) are used to limit the voltage of the input signals to acceptable levels (operating voltage of the microcomputer). Filters remove most of the superimposed noise from the transmitted signals, which are then amplified to the microprocessor's input voltage.
Voltage range: 0 V to 5 V.

Signal processing
ECUs generally process signals in digital form. Rapid, periodic, real-time signals are processed in hardware modules specifically designed for the particular function. Results, e.g. a counter reading or the time of an event, are transmitted in registers to the CPU for further processing. This procedure substantially reduces the CPU's interrupt-response requirements (μs range).

The amount of time available for calculations is determined by the open-loop or closed-loop control system (ms range).

The software contains the actual control algorithms. Depending on the data, an almost unlimited number of logic operations can be established and data records stored and processed in the form of parameters, characteristic curves and multidimensional program maps.

Output signals
Power switches and power-gain circuits amplify the microprocessor's output signals (0 to 5 V, several mA) to the levels required by the various final-controlling elements/actuators (battery voltage, several A).

Signal processing in ECU
1 Digital input signals, 2 Analog input signals, 3 Protective circuit, 4 Amplifier, filter, 5 A/D converter, 6 Digital signal processing, 7 D/A converter, 8 Circuit-breaker, 9 Power amplifier.

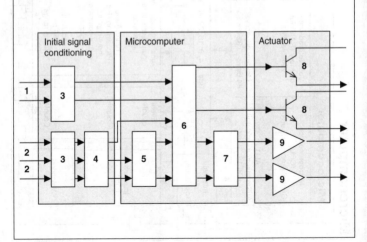

Complete system

Logistical concept (CARTRONIC)
The concept divides the total automotive electrical system into conveniently-dimensioned subsystems. Units with closely-related functions (units with a high rate of mutual data exchange) are combined in a sub-network. This logistical concept results in sub-networks with varying requirements for transmission capacity, while data transmission remains compatible.

Topology
At the logical level, all of the known communications systems developed for automotive applications are based on a single serial connection of the ECUs. The physical layout employs one-wire or differential two-wire interfaces in bus form to connect the control units with one another.

Protocol
The protocol consists of a specific collection of execution statements which are used to control data communications between the individual control units. Procedures have been laid down for bus access, message structure, bit and data coding, error recognition and response and the identification of faulty bus users (CAN, P. 884).

Transmission speed
Multiplex bus: 10 kbit/s...125 kbit/s
Drivetrain bus: 125 kbit/s...1 Mbit/s
Telecommunications bus:
10 kbit/s...125 kbit/s.

Latency time
The period that elapses between the transmitter's send request and the target station's receipt of the error-free message.
Multiplex bus: 5 ms...100 ms
Drivetrain bus: 0.5 ms...10 ms
Telecommunications bus:
5 ms...100 ms.

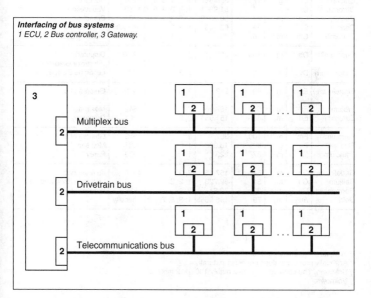

Interfacing of bus systems
1 ECU, 2 Bus controller, 3 Gateway.

Chemical elements

Element	Symbol	Type[1]	Atomic number	Relative atomic mass	Valence	Year discovered	Discoverer(s)
Actinium	Ac	m	89	227	3	1899	Debierne
Aluminum	Al	m	13	26.9815	3	1825	Oersted
Americium[2]	Am	m	95	243	2; 3; 4; 5; 6	1944	Seaborg et al
Antimony	Sb	m	51	121.760	3; 5	Antiquity	
Argon	Ar	g	18	39.948	0	1894	Ramsay, Rayleigh
Arsenic	As	n	33	74.9216	3; 5	C13	Magnus
Astatine	At	n	85	210	1; 3	1940	Corson, MacKenzie, Segré
Barium	Ba	m	56	137.327	2	1808	Davy
Berkelium[2]	Bk	m	97	247	3; 4	1949	Seaborg et al
Beryllium	Be	m	4	9.0122	2	1797	Vauquelin
Bismuth	Bi	m	83	208.9804	1; 3; 5	C15	Unknown
Bohrium[2]	Bh	m[3]	107	262	—[4]	1981	Armbruster, Münzenberg et al
Boron	B	n	5	10.811	3	1808	Gay-Lussac, Thénard, Davy
Bromine	Br	n	35	79.904	1; 3; 4; 5; 7	1826	Balard
Cadmium	Cd	m	48	112.411	1; 2	1817	Strohmeyer
Caesium	Cs	m	55	132.9054	1	1860	Bunsen, Kirchhoff
Calcium	Ca	m	20	40.078	2	1808	Davy
Californium[2]	Cf	m	98	251	2; 3; 4	1950	Seaborg et al
Carbon	C	n	6	12.011	2; 4	Antiquity	
Cer	Ce	m	58	140.116	3; 4	1803	Berzelius et al
Chlorine	Cl	g	17	35.4527	1; 3; 4; 5; 6; 7	1774	Scheele
Chromium	Cr	m	24	51.9961	1; 2; 3; 4; 5; 6	1780	Vauquelin
Cobalt	Co	m	27	58.9332	1; 2; 3; 4; 5	1735	Brandt
Copper	Cu	m	29	63.546	1; 2; 3	Antiquity	
Curium[2]	Cm	m	96	247	2; 3; 4	1944	Seaborg et al
Dubnium[2]	Db	m[3]	105	262	5 (?)	1967/70	Disputed (Flerov or Ghiorso)
Dysprosium	Dy	m	66	162.50	2; 3; 4	1886	Lecoq de Boisbaudran
Einsteinium[2]	Es	m	99	252	3	1952	Ghiorso et al
Erbium	Er	m	68	167.26	3	1842	Mosander
Europium	Eu	m	63	151.964	2; 3	1901	Demarcay
Fermium[2]	Fm	m[3]	100	257	3	1952	Ghiorso et al
Fluorine	F	g	9	18.998	1	1887	Moissan
Francium	Fr	m	87	223	1	1939	Perey
Gadolinium	Gd	m	64	157.25	2; 3	1880	de Marignac
Gallium	Ga	m	31	69.723	1; 2; 3	1875	Lecoq de Boisbaudran
Germanium	Ge	m	32	72.61	2; 4	1886	Winkler
Gold	Au	m	79	196.9665	1; 3; 5; 7	Antiquity	

[1]) m Metal, n Nonmetal, g Gas.
[2]) Artificially produced; does not occur naturally.
[3]) Unknown. The elements are presumably 100...112 metals.
[4]) Unknown.

Element	Symbol	Type[1]	Atomic number	Relative atomic mass	Valence	Year discovered	Discoverer(s)
Hafnium	Hf	m	72	178.49	4	1923	Hevesey, Coster
Hassium[2]	Hs	m[3]	108	265	−[4]	1984	Armbruster, Münzenberg et al
Helium	He	g	2	4.003	0	1895	Ramsay, Cleve, Langlet
Holmium	Ho	m	67	164.9303	3	1878	Cleve, Delafontaine, Soret
Hydrogen	H	g	1	1.0079	1	1766	Cavendish
Indium	In	m	49	114.818	1; 2; 3	1863	Reich, Richter
Iodine	I	n	53	126.9045	1; 3; 5; 7	1811	Courtois
Iridium	Ir	m	77	192.217	3; 4	1803	Tennant
Iron	Fe	m	26	55.845	2; 3; 6	Antiquity	
Krypton	Kr	g	36	83.80	0; 2	1898	Ramsay
Lanthanum	La	m	57	138.9055	3	1839	Mosander
Lawrencium[2]	Lr	m[3]	103	262	3	1961	Ghiorso et al
Lead	Pb	m	82	207.2	2; 4	Antiquity	
Lithium	Li	m	3	6.941	1	1817	Arfvedson
Lutetium	Lu	m	71	174.967	3	1907	Urbain, James
Magnesium	Mg	m	12	24.3050	2	1755	Black
Manganese	Mn	m	25	54.9380	2; 3; 4; 6; 7	1774	Grahn
Meitnerium	Mt	m[3]	109	266	−[4]	1982	Armbruster, Münzenberg et al
Mendelevium[2]	Md	m[3]	101	258	2; 3	1955	Seaborg, Ghiorso et al
Mercury	Hg	m	80	200.59	1; 2	Antiquity	
Molybdenum	Mo	m	42	95.94	2; 3; 4; 5; 6	1781	Hjelm
Neodymium	Nd	m	60	144.24	2; 3; 4	1885	Auer von Welsbach
Neon	Ne	g	10	20.1797	0	1898	Ramsay, Travers
Neptunium[2]	Np	m	93	237	3; 4; 5; 6	1940	McMillan, Abelson
Nickel	Ni	m	28	58.6934	2; 3	1751	Cronstedt
Niobium	Nb	m	41	92.9064	3; 4; 5	1801	Hatchett
Nitrogen	N	g	7	14.0067	2; 3; 4; 5	1772	Rutherford
Nobelium[2]	No	m[3]	102	259	2; 3	1958	Ghiorso, Seaborg
Osmium	Os	m	76	190.23	2; 3; 4; 5; 7; 8	1803	Tennant
Oxygen	O	g	8	15.9994	1; 2	1774	Priestley, Scheele
Palladium	Pd	m	46	106.42	2; 4	1803	Wollaston
Phosphorus	P	n	15	30.9738	3; 5	1669	Brandt
Platinum	Pt	m	78	195.078	2; 4; 5; 6	Antiquity	(Mayas)
Plutonium[2]	Pu	m	94	244	3; 4; 5; 6	1940	Seaborg et al
Polonium	Po	m	84	209	2; 4; 6	1898	M. Curie
Potassium	K	m	19	39.0983	1	1807	Davy
Praseodymium	Pr	m	59	140.9076	3; 4	1885	Auer von Welsbach
Promethium	Pm	m	61	145	3	1945	Marinsky et al
Protactinium	Pa	m	91	231.0359	4; 5	1917	Hahn, Meitner, Fajans

[1] m Metal, n Nonmetal, g Gas.
[2] Artificially produced; does not occur naturally.
[3] Unknown. The elements are presumably 100...112 metals.
[4] Unknown.

Chemical elements (continued)

Element	Symbol	Type[1])	Atomic number	Relative atomic mass	Valence	Year discovered	Discoverer(s)
Radium	Ra	m	88	226	2	1898	P. & M. Curie
Radon	Rn	g	86	222	0; 2	1900	Dorn
Rhenium	Re	m	75	186.207	1; 2; 3; 4; 5; 6; 7	1925	Noddack
Rhodium	Rh	m	45	102.9055	1; 2; 3; 4; 5; 6	1803	Wollaston
Rubidium	Rb	m	37	85.4678	1	1861	Bunsen, Kirchhoff
Ruthenium	Ru	m	44	101.07	1; 2; 3; 4; 5; 6; 7; 8	1808	Klaus
Rutherfordium[2])	Rf	m[3])	104	261	4 (?)	1964/69	Disputed (Flerov or Ghiorso)
Samarium	Sm	m	62	150.36	2; 3	1879	Lecoq de Boisbaudran
Scandium	Sc	m	21	44.9559	3	1879	Nilson
Seaborgium[2])	Sg	m[3])	106	263	−[4])	1974	Ghiorso et al
Selenium	Se	n	34	78.96	2; 4; 6	1817	Berzelius
Silver	Ag	m	47	107.8682	1; 2	Antiquity	
Silicon	Si	n	14	28.0855	2; 4	1824	Berzelius
Strontium	Sr	m	38	87.62	2	1790	Crawford
Sodium	Na	m	11	22.9898	1	1807	Davy
Sulfur	S	n	16	32.066	1; 2; 3; 4; 5; 6	Antiquity	
Tantalum	Ta	m	73	180.9479	1; 3; 4; 5	1802	Eckeberg
Technetium	Tc	m	43	98	4; 5; 6; 7	1937	Perrier, Segré
Tellurium	Te	m	52	127.60	2; 4; 6	1783	Müller
Terbium	Tb	m	65	158.9253	3; 4	1843	Mosander
Thallium	Tl	m	81	204.3833	1; 3	1861	Crookes
Thorium	Th	m	90	232.0381	2; 3; 4	1829	Berzelius
Thulium	Tm	m	69	168.9342	2; 3	1879	Cleve
Tin	Sn	m	50	118.710	2; 4	Antiquity	
Titanium	Ti	m	22	47.87	2; 3; 4	1791	Gregor
Tungsten	W	m	74	183.84	2; 3; 4; 5; 6	1783	Elhuijar
Ununbium[2]) [5])	Uub	m[3])	112	277	−[4])	1996	Armbruster, Hofmann
Ununnilium[2]) [5])	Uun	m[3])	110	270	−[4])	1994	Armbruster, Hofmann
Unununium[2]) [5])	Uuu	m[3])	111	272	−[4])	1994	Armbruster, Hofmann
Uranium	U	m	92	238.0289	3; 4; 5; 6	1789	Klaproth
Vanadium	V	m	23	50.9415	2; 3; 4; 5	1801	del Rio
Xenon	Xe	g	54	131.29	0; 2; 4; 6; 8	1898	Ramsay, Travers
Ytterbium	Yb	m	70	173.04	2; 3	1878	de Marignac
Yttrium	Y	m	39	88.9059	3	1794	Gadolin
Zinc	Zn	m	30	65.39	2	Antiquity	
Zirconium	Zr	m	40	91.224	3; 4	1789	Klaproth

[1]) m Metal, n Nonmetal, g Gas.
[2]) Artificially produced; does not occur naturally.
[3]) Unknown. The elements are presumably 100...112 metals.
[4]) Unknown.
[5]) Provisional IUPAC designation.

Periodic table of elements

Ia	IIa	IIIb	IVb	Vb	VIb	VIIb	VIIIb			Ib	IIb	IIIa	IVa	Va	VIa	VIIa	VIIIa
1 **H** 1.008																	2 **He** 4.003
3 **Li** 6.941	4 **Be** 9.012											5 **B** 10.811	6 **C** 12.011	7 **N** 14.007	8 **O** 15.999	9 **F** 18.998	10 **Ne** 20.180
11 **Na** 22.990	12 **Mg** 24.305											13 **Al** 26.982	14 **Si** 28.086	15 **P** 30.974	16 **S** 32.066	17 **Cl** 35.453	18 **Ar** 39.948
19 **K** 39.098	20 **Ca** 40.078	21 **Sc** 44.956	22 **Ti** 47.87	23 **V** 50.942	24 **Cr** 51.996	25 **Mn** 54.938	26 **Fe** 55.845	27 **Co** 58.933	28 **Ni** 58.693	29 **Cu** 63.546	30 **Zn** 65.39	31 **Ga** 69.723	32 **Ge** 72.61	33 **As** 74.922	34 **Se** 78.96	35 **Br** 79.904	36 **Kr** 83.80
37 **Rb** 85.468	38 **Sr** 87.62	39 **Y** 88.906	40 **Zr** 91.224	41 **Nb** 92.906	42 **Mo** 95.94	43 **Tc** (98)	44 **Ru** 101.07	45 **Rh** 102.906	46 **Pd** 106.42	47 **Ag** 107.868	48 **Cd** 112.411	49 **In** 114.818	50 **Sn** 118.710	51 **Sb** 121.760	52 **Te** 127.60	53 **I** 126.904	54 **Xe** 131.29
55 **Cs** 132.905	56 **Ba** 137.327	57 **La*** 138.906	72 **Hf** 178.49	73 **Ta** 180.948	74 **W** 183.84	75 **Re** 186.207	76 **Os** 190.23	77 **Ir** 192.217	78 **Pt** 195.078	79 **Au** 196.967	80 **Hg** 200.59	81 **Tl** 204.383	82 **Pb** 207.2	83 **Bi** 208.980	84 **Po** (209)	85 **At** (210)	86 **Rn** (222)
87 **Fr** (223)	88 **Ra** (226)	89 **Ac**** (227)	104 **Rf** (261)	105 **Db** (262)	106 **Sg** (263)	107 **Bh** (262)	108 **Hs** (265)	109 **Mt** (266)	110 **Uun** (269)	111 **Uuu** (272)	112 **Uub** (277)						

*

58 **Ce** 140.116	59 **Pr** 140.908	60 **Nd** 144.24	61 **Pm** (145)	62 **Sm** 150.36	63 **Eu** 151.964	64 **Gd** 157.25	65 **Tb** 158.925	66 **Dy** 162.50	67 **Ho** 164.930	68 **Er** 167.26	69 **Tm** 168.934	70 **Yb** 173.04	71 **Lu** 174.967

**

90 **Th** 232.038	91 **Pa** 231.036	92 **U** 238.029	93 **Np** (237)	94 **Pu** (244)	95 **Am** (243)	96 **Cm** (247)	97 **Bk** (247)	98 **Cf** (251)	99 **Es** (252)	100 **Fm** (257)	101 **Md** (258)	102 **No** (259)	103 **Lr** (262)

All elements are arranged sequentially according to atomic number (proton number). The horizontal rows represent the periods (or shells), while the various element groups are divided into vertical columns. The relative atomic masses are indicated below the element symbols. The values given in parentheses are the mass numbers (nucleon numbers) of the stablest isotopes of artificially produced radioactive elements.

Material terminology[1])

State of aggregation
There are three classical states of aggregation depending upon the arrangement of the elementary particles (atoms, molecules, ions): solid, liquid and gaseous. Plasma (ionized gas which has high electrical conductivity) is often considered as a fourth state of aggregation.

Solution
A solution is a homogeneous mixture of different materials which are distributed at the atomic or molecular level.

Compound
A compound is the union of two or more chemical elements whose masses are always in the same ratio with respect to one another. Compounds which have metallic characteristics are called intermetallic compounds.

Dispersion
A dispersion or disperse system consists of at least two materials; one material, called the disperse phase, is finely distributed in the other material, called the dispersion medium.

Suspension
A suspension is a disperse system in which solid particles are distributed in a liquid. Examples: graphite in oil, clay in water.

Emulsion
An emulsion is a disperse system in which droplets of one liquid are distributed in a second liquid. Examples: drilling oil, butterfat in milk.

Colloid
A colloid is a disperse system in which the particles of the disperse phase have linear dimensions ranging from roughly 10^{-9} to 10^{-6} m. Examples: smoke, latex, gold-ruby glass.

Material parameters[1])

Density
Density is the ratio of the mass to the volume of a specific amount of substance.

See DIN 1306, 1984 edition, for special density terms.

Radial crushing strength
Radial crushing strength is a strength parameter which is specified in particular for the sintered metals used for plain bearings. It is determined from the pressure test when a hollow cylinder is crushed.

For additional information see "Technical Conditions of Delivery for PM Parts (Sint. 03)", Aug. 1981 edition.

Yield strength (0.2%)
The 0.2% yield strength is that tensile stress which causes permanent (plastic) elongation of 0.2% in a solid body; it is determined from the σ-ε curve of a tensile test with a defined stress-increase rate.

Cyclic loading of a test specimen by tensile/compressive stresses with increasing amplitude yields the cyclic σ-ε curve and from this the cyclic 0.2% yield strength. When compared with the monotonic 0.2% yield strength, this value is a measure of possible softening or hardening brought about by cyclic over-stressing.

The yield strength ratio is the ratio of the cyclic to the monotonic 0.2% yield strength. $\gamma > 1$ signifies cyclic hardening, $\gamma < 1$ cyclic softening.

Fracture toughness
Fracture toughness, or K_{Ic} factor, is a material parameter of fracture mechanics. The K_{Ic} factor is that stress intensity ahead of a crack tip which leads to unstable crack propagation, and therefore to the fracture of the structural part. If the K_{Ic} factor of a material is known, the critical fracture load can be determined from crack length, or critical crack length can be determined from the given external loading value.

---

[1]) The following is a list of the most important material terms and parameters which appear in subsequent materials tables and are not defined elsewhere.

Specific heat capacity
Specific heat capacity (specific heat) is the quantity of heat in J required to raise the temperature of 1 kg of a substance by 1 K. It is dependent on temperature.

In the case of gases, it is necessary to differentiate between specific heat capacity at constant pressure and at constant volume (symbols: c_p and c_v, respectively). This difference is usually negligible in the case of solid and liquid substances.

Specific heat of fusion
The specific heat of fusion of a solid is the quantity of heat in J required to transform 1 kg of a substance at fusion temperature from the solid to the liquid state.

Specific heat of evaporation
The specific heat of evaporation of a liquid is the quantity of heat in J required to evaporate 1 kg of this liquid at boiling temperature. The specific heat of evaporation is highly dependent upon pressure.

Thermal conductivity
Thermal conductivity is the quantity of heat in J which flows in 1 s through a material sample which has a surface area of 1 m² and a thickness of 1 m if the temperatures of the two end surfaces of the sample differ by 1 K.

In the case of liquids and gases, thermal conductivity is often highly dependent upon temperature, whereas temperature is generally not significant in the case of solids.

Coefficient of thermal expansion
The coefficient of linear (or longitudinal) expansion indicates the relative change in length of a material caused by a change in temperature of 1 K. For a temperature variation ΔT, the change in length is defined as $\Delta l = l \cdot \alpha \cdot \Delta T$. The cubic or volume coefficient of expansion is defined in the same way. The volume coefficient of expansion for gases is roughly 1/273. For solids, it is roughly three times as large as the coefficient of linear expansion.

Permeability
Permeability μ or relative permeability μ_r describes the dependence of magnetic induction on the applied field:

$$B = \mu_r \cdot \mu_0 \cdot H$$

Depending on the application in which the magnetic material is used, there are roughly 15 types of permeability. These are defined according to modulation range and type of loading (direct-current or alternating-current field loading). Examples:

Initial permeability μ_a
Slope of the virgin curve for $H \rightarrow 0$. In most cases, however, the slope for a specific field strength (in mA/cm) is specified rather than this limit value. Example: μ_4 is the slope of the virgin curve for $H = 4$ mA/cm.

Maximum permeability μ_{max}
Maximum slope of the virgin curve.

Permanent permeability μ_p or μ_{rec}
Average slope of a retrograde magnetic hysteresis loop whose lowest point usually lies on the demagnetization curve.

$$\mu_p = \Delta B / (\Delta H \cdot \mu_0)$$

Temperature coefficient of magnetic polarization $TK(J_s)$
This temperature coefficient indicates the relative change in saturation polarization as the temperature changes, it is given in % per kelvin.

Temperature coefficient of coercive field strength $TK(H_c)$
This temperature coefficient indicates the relative change, in % per kelvin, of coercive field strength as the temperature changes.

Curie point (Curie temperature) T_c
The Curie point is the temperature at which the magnetization of ferromagnetic and ferrimagnetic materials becomes zero and at which they behave like paramagnetic materials (sometimes defined differently, see characteristic values of soft ferrites on P. 208).

Material groups

The materials in current industrial use can be classified according to one of four categories. Each of these, in turn, includes various subclassifications:

- <u>Metals</u>: wrought, rolled, cast etc. metals, sintered metals,
- <u>Nonmetallic inorganic materials</u>: ceramic materials, glass,
- <u>Nonmetallic organic materials</u>: natural materials, plastics and elastomers
- <u>Composite materials</u>.

Magnetic materials form an important material group with special characteristics, and will be described separately.

Metals

Metals generally exhibit a crystalline structure. Their atoms are arranged in a regular crystal lattice. The valence electrons of the atoms are not bound to a special atom, but rather are able to move freely within the metal lattice (metallic bond).

This special metal-lattice structure explains the characteristic properties of metals: high electrical conductivity which decreases as temperature increases; good thermal conductivity; low transparency to light; high optical reflectivity (metallic luster); ductility and the resulting high degree of formability. <u>Alloys</u> are metals which consist of two or more components, of which at least one is a metal.

Wrought, rolled, cast etc. metals

Apart from small flaws such as shrinkholes and nonmetallic inclusions, such metals contain no voids. Components are produced by casting, either directly (e.g. gray cast iron, diecast aluminum) or from wrought products (machined with or without cutting).

Sintered metals

Sintered metals are usually produced by pressing powder or by the injection-molding of mixtures composed of metallic powder and plastic. Following the removal of parting agents and plasticizers, the parts are then sintered to give them their characteristic properties. Sintering is a type of heat treatment in a range from 800 to 1300 °C. In addition to its chemical composition, the sintered part's properties and application are to a large extent determined by its degree of porosity. Components with complicated shapes can often be made particularly cheaply from sintered metals, either ready-to-install or requiring only little finishing.

Nonmetallic inorganic materials

These materials are characterized by ion bonds (e.g., ceramic materials), mixed (heteropolar/homopolar) bonds (e.g., glass) or homopolar bonds (e.g., carbon). These kinds of bonds, in turn, are responsible for several characteristic properties: generally poor thermal and electric conductivity (the latter increases with temperature), poor luminous reflectance, brittleness and thus almost complete unsuitability for cold forming.

Ceramics

Ceramics are at least 30 % crystalline in nature; most ceramics also contain amorphous components and pores. Their manufacture is similar to that of sintered metals, however nonmetallic powders or powder mixtures are used; sintering at temperatures generally higher than 1000 °C gives ceramics their characteristic properties. Ceramic structural parts are sometimes also shaped at high temperatures or even by a melting process, with subsequent crystallization.

Glass

Glass is viewed as under-cooled, frozen liquid. Its atoms are only in a short-range order. It is regarded as amorphous. Molten glass turns to solid glass at the transformation temperature T_g (T_g is derived from the former designation "glass formation temperature"). T_g is dependent on a variety of parameters and therefore not clearly determined (better: transformation range).

Nonmetallic organic materials

These materials consist mainly of compounds of the elements carbon and hydrogen, whereby nitrogen, oxygen and other elements are also often included in the structure. In general, these materials exhibit low thermal and electric conductivity, and are combustible.

Natural materials

The best-known natural materials are wood, leather, resin, natural rubber, and fibers made of wool, cotton, flax, hemp and silk. Most natural materials are used in processed or refined form, or serve as raw materials in the manufacture of plastics.

Plastics

A significant characteristic of plastics is their macromolecular structure. There are three different types of plastics: thermoplastics, thermosets (sometimes also called thermosetting plastics) and elastomers. The transformation temperature T_E for thermoplastics and thermosets lies above the temperature of application; the reverse is true for elastomers. T_E (comparable with the transformation temperature T_g of glass) is understood to mean that temperature below which intrinsic molecular motion ceases. The major importance of thermoplastics and thermosets lies in the fact that they can be shaped and molded without machining.

Thermoplastics

Thermoplastics soften and lose their dimensional stability at temperatures above T_E. Their physical properties are highly temperature-dependent. The effect of temperature can be somewhat reduced by using mixtures of thermoplastic polymers.

Thermosets

Thermosets retain their dimensional stability up to temperatures almost as high as the processing temperature due to closely-spaced cross-linking. Their mechanical properties are less temperature-dependent than those of thermoplastics. Fillers are usually added to thermosetting resins to counteract their inherent brittleness.

Elastomers

Elastomers are useful in many applications because of their elasticity, which is only present at temperatures above T_E. Elastomers are vulcanized (widely-spaced cross-linking) in order to stabilize their molecular bonds.

Composite materials

Composite materials consist of at least two physically or chemically different components. These components must be tightly bound together at a defined interface. The formation of the interface must have no negative effect on any of the bound components. Under these two conditions it is possible to bond many materials together. Composite materials exhibit combinations of properties which none of the components alone possesses. Different classes of composite materials are:

Particle composite materials (e.g., powder-filled resins, hard metals, plastic-bonded magnets, cermets),

Laminated composite materials (e.g., composite or sandwich panels, resin-bonded fabric),

Fiber composite materials (e.g., with fiberglass, carbon-fiber, and cotton-fiber-reinforced plastics).

Magnetic materials

Materials which have ferromagnetic or ferrimagnetic properties are called magnetic materials and belong to one of two groups: metals or nonmetallic inorganic materials. They are characterized by their ability to store magnetic energy (permanent magnets), or by their good magnetic flux conductivity (soft magnets). In addition to ferromagnets and ferrimagnets, diamagnetic, paramagnetic and antiferromagnetic materials also exist. They differ from each other in terms of their permeability μ (P. 68) or the temperature-dependence of their susceptibility $\varkappa$.[1]

$$\mu_r = 1 + \varkappa$$

---

[1] Ratio of the magnetization of a substance to the magnetic field strength or excitation.

Diamagnets: Susceptibility $\varkappa_{Dia}$ is independent of temperature.
See P. 68 for examples.
Paramagnets: Susceptibility $\varkappa_{para}$ drops as temperature increases. Curie's law: $\varkappa_{para} = C/T$

C Curie constant, T Temperature in K.
See P. 68 for examples.
Ferromagnets and ferrimagnets: Both types exhibit spontaneous magnetization which disappears at the Curie point (Curie temperature T_c). At temperatures above the Curie temperature, they behave like paramagnets. For $T > Tc$, the Curie-Weiss law is applicable to susceptibility: $\varkappa = C/(T-T_c)$

The saturation induction of ferromagnets is higher than it is for ferrimagnets, because all magnetic moments are aligned in parallel. In the case of ferrimagnets, on the other hand, the magnetic moments of the two sublattices are aligned antiparallel to one another. These materials are nevertheless magnetic, because the magnetic moments of the two sublattices have different magnitudes.

Antiferromagnets: Examples: MnO, MnS, $FeCl_2$, FeO, NiO, Cr, V_2O_3, V_2O_4.
As in the case of ferrimagnets, adjacent magnetic moments are aligned antiparallel with respect to one another. Because they are of equal magnitude, the effective magnetization of the material is zero.

At temperatures above the Néel point (Néel temperature T_N), they behave like paramagnets. For $T > T_N$, the following is applicable to susceptibility: $\varkappa = C/(T + \Theta)$
Θ Asymptotic Curie temperature

Soft magnetic materials

The following figures are from the applicable DIN Standards. Soft-magnetic metallic materials (DIN-IEC 60404-8-6).
Many material qualities defined in this standard relate to the materials in DIN 17 405 (DC relays) and DIN-IEC 740-2 (transformers and reactors).
Designation comprises a letter and number combination:
Code letter, Number 1, Number 2, – Number 3. The "code letter" indicates the main alloy constituent:

"A" pure iron, "C" silicon, "E" nickel, "F" cobalt.
Number 1 indicates the concentration of the main alloy element.
Number 2 defines the different curves: 1: round hysteresis loop, 2: rectangular hysteresis loop.
The significance of the Number 3 following the hyphen varies according to the individual alloy. It indicates the minimum initial permeability $\mu_a/1000$ in nickel alloys; with other alloys it designates the maximum coercive field strength in A/m. The properties of these materials are strongly geometry-dependent and highly application-specific. The material data quoted in extracts from the standard can therefore only provide an extremely general overview of the properties of these materials. Refer to P. 203 for material data.

Magnetic sheet steel and strip (formerly in DIN 46 400)
Designation: Code letter 1 Number 1 – Number 2 Code letter 2.
The first code letter is "M" for all varieties (indicates metallic materials). Number 1 is one hundred times the maximum magnetic reversal loss at 1.5 or 1.7 Tesla and 50 Hz in W/kg. Number 2 is the product's nominal depth in mm times one hundred.
Code letter 2 provides type data:
"A" cold-rolled electric sheets, no granular orientation, finish-annealed (DIN-EN 10 106).
Grain-oriented electric sheet, finish-annealed (DIN-EN 10 107): "N" standard magnetic reversal loss, "S" limited magnetic reversal loss, "P" low magnetic reversal loss, "D" cold-rolled electric sheet of unalloyed steel, not finish-annealed (DIN-EN 10 126), "E" cold-rolled steel-alloy electric sheet, not finish-annealed (DIN-EN 10 165). Materials data, P. 204.

Materials for transformers and reactors (DIN-IEC 740-2).
These materials comprise the alloy classes C21, C22, E11, E31 and E41 from the standard for soft-magnetic materials (DIN-IEC 60404-8-6). The standard essentially contains the minimum values for core-sheet permeability for

specified core-sheet sections (YEI, YED, YEE, YEL, YUI and YM). See P. 205 for material properties.

Materials for DC relays
(DIN 17 405); see P. 206 for material properties.
Designation:
a) Code letter "R" (relay material).
b) Code letters for identifying alloy constituents:
Fe = unalloyed, Si = silicon steels
Ni = nickel steels or alloys.
c) Code number for maximum coercive field strength.
d) Code letter for stipulated delivery state: "U" = untreated, "GB" = malleable pre-annealed, "GT" = pre-annealed for deep-drawing, "GF" = final-annealed.
DIN-IEC 60 404-8-10 essentially contains the limit deviations for magnetic relay materials based on iron and steel. The designation code defined in this standard is as follows:
– Code letter "M".
– Permitted maximum value for coercive field strength in A/m.
– Code letter for material composition: "F" = pure ferric material, "T" = steel alloy, "U" = unalloyed steel.
– Code letter for delivery state: "H" = hot-rolled, "C" = cold-rolled or cold-drawn.
Example: M 80 TH.

Sintered metals for soft-magnetic components (DIN-IEC 60 404-8-9)
Designation:
– Code letter "S": for sintered materials.
– Hyphen, followed by the identifying alloy elements, i.e. Fe plus if necessary P, Si, Ni or Co.
– The maximum coercive field strength in A/m follows the second hyphen. Refer to P. 207 for material data.

Soft-magnetic ferrite cores
(DIN 41 280)
Soft-magnetic ferrites are formed parts made of a sintered material with the general formula $MO \cdot Fe_2O_3$ where M is one or more of the bivalent metals Cd, Co, Ca, Mg, Mn, Ni, Zn.
Designation: The various types of magnetically soft ferrites are classified in groups according to nominal initial permeability, and are designated by capital letters. Additional numbers may be used to further subdivide them into subgroups; these numbers have no bearing on material quality.
The coercive field strength H_c of soft ferrites is usually in the range 4...500 A/m. Based on a field strength of 3000 A/m, the induction B is in the range 350...470 mT. Refer to P. 208 for material data.

Permanent-magnet materials
(DIN 17 410, replaced by DIN-IEC 60 404-8-1)
If chemical symbols are used in the abbreviated names of the materials, they refer to the primary alloying constituents of the materials. The numbers before the forward slash denote the $(BH)_{max}$ value in kJ/m³ and those after the slash denote one tenth of the H_{cJ} value in kA/m (rounded values). Permanent magnets with binders are indicated by a final p.

Designation by abbreviated name or material number[1]
DIN: Material number as defined in DIN 17 007, Parts 2 and 4.
IEC: Structure of material numbers;
Code letters:
R – Metallic permanent-magnet materials
S – Ceramic permanent-magnet materials
1st number:
indicates type of material, e.g.:
1 AlNiCo, 5 RECo
2nd number:
0: isotropic material
1: anisotropic material
2: isotropic material with binder
3: anisotropic material with binder.
3rd number:
indicates quality level.
Refer to P. 209 for material data.

---

[1] The designation system for permanent-magnet materials is currently undergoing extensive revision. Because the discussions were still in progress at the editorial deadline, no data or comments could be provided.

Properties of solids[8]

Substance		Density g/cm³	Melting point[1] °C	Boiling point[1] °C	Thermal conductivity[2] W/(m·K)	Mean specific heat capacity[3] kJ/(kg·K)	Melting enthalpy ΔH[4] kJ/kg	Coefficient of linear expansion[3] x10⁻⁶/K
Aluminum	Al	2.70	660	2467	237	0.90	395	23.0
Aluminum alloys		2.60...2.85	480...655	–	70...240	–	–	21...24
Amber		1.0...1.1	≈300	Decomposes	–	–	–	–
Antimony	Sb	6.69	630.8	1635	24.3	0.21	172	8.5
Arsenic	As	5.73	–	613[5]	50.0	0.34	370	4.7
Asbestos		2.1...2.8	≈1300	–	–	0.81	–	–
Asphalt		1.1...1.4	80...100	≈300	0.70	0.92	–	–
Barium	Ba	3.50	729	1637	18.4	0.28	55.8	18.1...21.0
Barium chloride		3.86	963	1560	–	0.38	108	–
Basalt		2.6...3.3	–	–	1.67	0.86	–	–
Beef tallow		0.9...0.97	40...50	≈350	–	0.87	–	–
Beryllium	Be	1.85	1278	2970	200	1.88	1087	11.5
Bismuth	Bi	9.75	271	1551	8.1	0.13	59	12.1
Bitumen		1.05	≈90	–	0.17	1.78	–	–
Boiler scale		≈2,5	≈1200	–	0.12...2.3	0.80	–	–
Borax		1.72	740	–	–	1.00	–	–
Boron	B	2.34	2027	3802	27.0	1.30	2053	5
Brass CuZn37		8.4	900	1110	113	0.38	167	18.5
Brickwork		>1.9	–	–	1.0	0.9	–	–
Bronze CuSn 6		8.8	910	2300	64	0.37	–	17.5
Cadmium	Cd	8.65	321.1	765	96.8	0.23	54.4	29.8
Calcium	Ca	1.54	839	1492	200	0.62	233	22
Calcium chloride		2.15	782	>1600	–	0.69	–	–
Cellulose acetate		1.3	–	–	0.26	1.47	–	100...160
Cement, set		2...2.2	–	–	0.9...1.2	1.13	–	–
Chalk		1.8...2.6	Decomposes into CaO and CO₂		0.92	0.84	–	–
Chamotte (fireclay)		1.7...2.4	≈2000	–	1.4	0.80	–	–
Charcoal		0.3...0.5	–	–	0.084	1.0	–	–
Chromium	Cr	7.19	1875	2482	93.7	0.45	294	6.2
Chromium oxide	Cr₂O₃	5.21	2435	4000	0.42[6]	0.75	–	–
Clay, dry		1.5...1.8	≈1600	–	0.9...1.3	0.88	–	–
Cobalt	Co	8.9	1495	2956	69.1	0.44	268	12.4
Coke		1.6...1.9	–	–	0.18	0.83	–	–
Colophonium (rosin)		1.08	100...130	Decomposes	0.32	1.21	–	–
Common salt		2.15	802	1440	–	0.92	–	–
Concrete		1.8...2.2	–	–	≈1.0	0.88	–	–
Copper	Cu	8.96	1084.9	2582	401	0.38	205	–
Cork		0.1...0.3	–	–	0.04...0.06	1.7...2.1	–	–
Corundum, sintered		–	–	–	–	–	–	6.5[7]
Cotton wadding		0.01	–	–	0.04	–	–	–
Diamond	C	3.5	3820	–	–	0.52	–	1.1
Foam rubber		0.06...0.25	–	–	0.04...0.06	–	–	–
Germanium	Ge	5.32	937	2830	59.9	0.31	478	5.6
Glass (window glass)		2.4...2.7	≈700	–	0.81	0.83	–	≈8
Glass (quartz glass)		–	–	–	–	–	–	0.5
Gold	Au	19.32	1064	2967	317	0.13	64.5	14.2
Granite		2.7	–	–	3.49	0.83	–	–

[1] At 1.013 bar. [2] At 20 °C. ΔH of chemical elements at 27 °C (300 K). [3] At 0...100 °C, see also P. 181.
[4] At the melting point and 1.013 bar. [5] Sublimed. [6] Powder form. [7] At 20...1000 °C. [8] Materials, PP. 193 ... 227.

Substance		Density	Melting point[1]	Boiling point[1]	Thermal conductivity[2]	Mean specific heat capacity[3]	Melting enthalpy ΔH[4]	Coefficient of linear expansion[3]
		g/cm³	°C	°C	W/(m·K)	kJ/(kg·K)	kJ/kg	×10⁻⁶/K
Graphite, pure	C	2.24	≈3800	≈4200	168	0.71	–	2.7
Gray cast iron		7.25	1200	2500	58	0.50	125	10.5
Hard coal (anthracite)		1.35	–	–	0.24	1.02	–	–
Hard metal K 20		14.8	>2000	≈4000	81.4	0.80	–	5...7
Hard rubber		1.2...1.5	–	–	0.16	1.42	–	50...90[5]
Heat-conductor alloy NiCr 8020		8.3	1400	2350	14.6	0.50[6]	–	–
Ice (0 °C)		0.92	0	100	2.33[7]	2.09[7]	333	51[8]
Indium	In	7.29	156.6	2006	81.6	0.24	28.4	33
Iodine	I	4.95	113.5	184	0.45	0.22	120.3	–
Iridium	Ir	22.55	2447	4547	147	0.13	137	6.4
Iron, pure	Fe	7.87	1535	2887	80.2	0.45	267	12.3
Lead	Pb	11.3	327.5	1749	35.5	0.13	24.7	29.1
Lead monoxide	PbO	9.3	880	1480	–	0.22	–	–
Leather, dry		0.86...1	–	–	0.14...0.16	≈1.5	–	–
Linoleum		1.2	–	–	0.19	–	–	–
Lithium	Li	0.534	180.5	1317	84.7	3.3	663	56
Magnesium	Mg	1.74	648.8	1100	156	1.02	372	26.1
Magnesium alloys		≈1.8	≈630	1500	46...139	–	–	24.5
Manganese	Mn	7.47	1244	2100	7.82	0.48	362	22
Marble	CaCO₃	2.6...2.8	Decomposes into CaO and CO₂		2.8	0.84	–	–
Mica		2.6...2.9	Decomposes at 700 °C		0.35	0.87	–	3
Molybdenum	Mo	10.22	2623	5560	138	0.28	288	5.4
Monel metal		8.8	1240......1330	–	19.7	0.43	–	–
Mortar, cement		1.6...1.8	–	–	1.40	–	–	–
Mortar, lime		1.6...1.8	–	–	–	0.87	–	–
Nickel	Ni	8.90	1455	2782	90.7	0.46	300	13.3
Nickel silver CuNi12Zn24		8.7	1020	–	48	0.40	–	18
Niobium	Nb	8.58	2477	4540	53.7	0.26	293	7.1
Osmium	Os	22.57	3045	5027	87.6	0.13	154	4.3...6.8
Palladium	Pd	12.0	1554	2927	71.8	0.24	162	11.2
Paper		0.7...1.2	–	–	0.14	1.34	–	–
Paraffin		0.9	52	300	0.26	3.27	–	–
Peat dust (mull), air-dried		0.19	–	–	0.081	–	–	–
Phosphorus (white)	P	1.82	44.1	280.4	–	0.79	20	–
Pitch		1.25	–	–	0.13	–	–	–
Plaster		2.3	1200	–	0.45	1.09	–	–
Platinum	Pt	21.45	1769	3827	71.6	0.13	101	9
Plutonium	Pu	19.8	640	3454	6.7	0.14	11	55
Polyamide		1.1	–	–	0.31	–	–	70...150
Polycarbonate		1.2	–	–	0.20	1.17	–	60...70
Polyethylene		0.94	–	–	0.41	2.1	–	200
Polystyrene		1.05	–	–	0.17	1.3	–	70
Polyvinyl chloride		1.4	–	–	0.16	–	–	70...150
Porcelain		2.3...2.5	≈1600	–	1.6[9]	1.2[9]	–	4...5
Potassium	K	0.86	63.65	754	102.4	0.74	61.4	83

[1] At 1.013 bar. [2] At 20 °C. ΔH of chemical elements at 27 °C (300 K). [3] At 0...100 °C. [4] At melting point and 1.013 bar. [5] At 20...50 °C. [6] At 0...1000 °C. [7] At –20...0 °C. [8] At –20...–1 °C.
[9] At 0...100 °C.

Properties of solids[12]) (continued)

Substance	Density	Melting point[1])	Boiling point[1])	Thermal conductivity[2])	Mean specific heat capacity[3])	Melting enthalpy ΔH[4])	Coefficient of linear expansion[3])
	g/cm³	°C	°C	W/(m·K)	kJ/(kg·K)	kJ/kg	x10⁻⁶/K
Quartz	2.1...2.5	1480	2230	9.9	0.80	–	8[5])/14.6[6])
Radium Ra	5	700	1630	18.6	0.12	32	20.2
Red bronze CuSn5ZnPb	8.8	950	2300	38	0.67	–	–
Red lead, minium Pb₃O₄	8.6...9.1	Forms PbO		0.70	0.092	–	–
Resin bonded fabric, paper	1.3...1.4	–	–	0.23	1.47	–	10...25[7])
Resistance alloy CuNi 44	8.9	1280	≈ 2400	22.6	0.41	–	15.2
Rhenium Re	21.02	3160	5762	150	0.14	178	8.4
Rigid foam plastic, air-filled[8])	0.015... ...0.06	–	–	0.036... ...0.06	–	–	–
Rigid foam plastic, freon-filled	0.015... ...0.06	–	–	0.02... ...0.03	–	–	–
Roofing felt	1.1	–	–	0.19	–	–	–
Rubber, raw (caoutchouc)	0.92	125	–	0.15	–	–	–
Rubidium Rb	1.53	38.9	688	58	0.33	26	90
Sand, quartz, dry	1.5...1.7	≈ 1500	2230	0.58	0.80	–	–
Sandstone	2...2.5	≈ 1500		2.3	0.71	–	–
Selenium Se	4.8	217	684.9	2.0	0.34	64.6	37
Silicon Si	2.33	1410	2480	148	0.68	1410	4.2
Silicon carbide	2.4	Decomposes above 3000°C		9[9])	1.05[9])	–	4.0
Sillimanite	2.4	1820		1.51	1.0	–	–
Silver Ag	10.5	961.9	2195	429	0.24	104.7	19.2
Slag, blast furnace	2.5...3	1300... ...1400		0.14	0.84	–	–
Sodium Na	0.97	97.81	883	141	1.24	115	70.6
Soft rubber	1.08	–	–	0.14...0.24	–	–	–
Soot	1.7...1.8	–	–	0.07	0.84	–	–
Steatite	2.6...2.7	≈ 1520	–	1.6[10])	0.83	–	8...9[11])
Steel, chromium steel	–	–	–	–	–	–	11
Steel, electrical sheet steel	–	–	–	–	–	–	12
Steel, high-speed steel	–	–	–	–	–	–	11.5
Steel, magnet steel AlNiCo12/6	–	–	–	–	–	–	11.5
Steel, nickel steel 36% Ni (invar)	–	–	–	–	–	–	1.5
Steel, sintered	–	–	–	–	–	–	11.5
Steel, stainless (18Cr, 8Ni)	7.9	1450	–	14	0.51	–	16
Steel, tungsten steel (18 W)	8.7	1450	–	26	0.42	–	–
Steel, unalloyed and low-alloy	7.9	1460	2500	48...58	0.49	205	11.5
Sulfur (a) S	2.07	112.8	444.67	0.27	0.73	38	74
Sulfur (β) S	1.96	119.0	–	–	–	–	–
Thermosets							
Melamin resin with cellulose fibers	1.5	–	–	0.35	–	–	≈ 60
Phenolic resin with asbestos fibers	1.8	–	–	0.70	1.25	–	15...30
Phenolic resin with fabric chips	1.4	–	–	0.35	1.47	–	15...30
Phenolic resin with wood dust	1.4	–	–	0.35	1.47	–	30...50
Phenolic resin w/o filler	1.3	–	–	0.20	1.47	–	80

---

[1]) At 1.013 bar.   [2]) At 20°C. ΔH of chemical elements at 27°C (300 K).   [3]) At 0...100°C.   [4]) At melting point and 1.013 bar.   [5]) Parallel to crystal axis.   [6]) Perpendicular to crystal axis.   [7]) At 20...50°C.   [8]) Rigid foam plastic from phenolic resin, polystyrene, polyethylene & similar. Values dependent on cell diameter and filler gas.   [9]) At 1000°C.   [10]) At 100...200°C.   [11]) At 20...1000°C.   [12]) Materials, PP. 193...227.

Substance		Density	Melting point[1]	Boiling point[1]	Thermal conduc- tivity[2]	Mean spe- cific heat capacity[3]	Melting enthalpy ΔH[4]	Coefficient of linear expansion[3]
		g/cm³	°C	°C	W/(m·K)	kJ/(kg·K)	kJ/kg	x10⁻⁶/K
Tantalum	Ta	16.65	2996	5487	57.5	0.14	174	6.6
Tellurium	Te	6.24	449.5	989.8	2.3	0.20	106	16.7
Thorium	Th	11.72	1750	4227	54	0.14	< 83	12.5
Tin (white)	Sn	7.28	231.97	2270	65.7	0.23	61	21.2
Titanium	Ti	4.51	1660	3313	21.9	0.52	437	8.3
Tombac CuZn 20		8.65	1000	≈1300	159	0.38	–	–
Tungsten	W	19.25	3422	5727	174	0.13	191	4.6
Uranium	U	18.95	1132.3	3677	27.6	0.12	65	12.6
Vanadium	V	6.11	1890	3000	30.7	0.50	345	8.3
Vulcanized fiber		1.28	–	–	0.21	1.26	–	–
Wax		0.96	60	–	0.084	3.4	–	–
Wood[5]	Ash	0.72	–	–	0.16		–	in
	Balsa	0.20	–	–	0.06		–	fiber
	Beech	0.72	–	–	0.17		–	direc-
	Birch	0.63	–	–	0.14		–	tion
	Maple	0.62	–	–	0.16		–	3...4,
	Oak	0.69	–	–	0.17	2.1...2.9	–	trans-
	Pine	0.52	–	–	0.14		–	verse
	Poplar	0.50	–	–	0.12		–	to fiber
	Spruce, fir	0.45	–	–	0.14		–	22...43
	Walnut	0.65	–	–	0.15		–	
Wood-wool building slabs		0.36...0.57	–	–	0.093	–	–	
Zinc	Zn	7.14	419.58	907	116	0.38	102	25.0
Zirconium	Zr	6.51	1852	4377	22.7	0.28	252	5.8

[1]) At 1.013 bar. [2]) At 20°C. [3]) At 0...100°C. [3]) At 27°C (300 K). [3]) At 0...100°C.
[4]) At melting point and 1.013 bar. [5]) Mean values for air-dried wood (moisture content: approx. 12%).
Thermal conductivity: radial. Axial conductivity is roughly twice as high.

Properties of liquids

Substance		Density[2] g/cm³	Melting point[1] °C	Boiling point[1] °C	Thermal conductivity[2] W/(m·K)	Specific heat capacity[2] kJ/(kg·K)	Melting enthalpy $\Delta_f f$[3] kJ/kg	Evaporation enthalpy[4] kJ/kg	Coefficient of volume expansion ×10⁻³/K
Acetone	$(CH_3)_2CO$	0.79	-95	56	0.16	2.21	98.0	523	-
Antifreeze-water mixture									
23 % by vol.		1.03	-12	101	0.53	3.94	-	-	-
38 % by vol.		1.04	-25	103	0.45	3.68	-	-	-
54 % by vol.		1.06	-46	105	0.40	3.43	-	-	-
Benzene	C_6H_6	0.88	+5.5[6]	80	0.15	1.70	127	394	-
Common-salt solution 20 %		1.15	-18	109	0.58	3.43	-	-	-
Diesel fuel		0.81...0.85	-30	150...360	0.15	2.05	-	-	1.25
Ethanol	C_2H_5OH	0.79	-117	78.5	0.17	2.43	109	904	1.1
Ethyl ether	$(C_2H_5)_2O$	0.71	-116	34.5	0.13	2.28	98.1	377	1.6
Ethyl chloride	C_2H_5Cl	0.90	-136	12	0.11[5]	1.54[5]	69.0	437	-
Ethylene glycol	$C_2H_4(OH)_2$	1.11	-12	198	0.25	2.40	-	-	-
Fuel oil EL		≈0.83	-10	>175	0.14	2.07	-	-	-
Gasoline/petrol		0.72...0.75	-50...-30	25...210	0.13	2.02	-	-	1.0
Glycerin	$C_3H_5(OH)_3$	1.26	+20	290	0.29	2.37	200	828	0.5
Hydrochloric acid 10 %	HCl	1.05	-14	102	0.50	3.14	-	-	-
Kerosene		0.76...0.86	-70	>150	0.13	2.16	-	-	1.0
Linseed oil		0.93	-15	316	0.17	1.88	-	-	-
Lubricating oil		0.91	-20	>300	0.13	2.09	-	-	-
Mercury[8]	Hg	13.55	-38.84	356.6	10	0.14	11.6	295	0.18
Methanol	CH_3OH	0.79	-98	65	0.20	2.51	99.2	1109	-
Methyl chloride	CH_3Cl	0.997[7]	-92	-24	0.16	1.38	-	406	-
m-xylene	$C_6H_4(CH_3)_2$	0.86	-48	139	-	-	-	339	-
Nitric acid, conc.	HNO_3	1.51	-41	84	0.26	1.72	-	-	-

[1] At 1.013 bar. [2] At 20 °C. [3] At melting point and 1.013 bar [4] At boiling point and 1.013 bar [5] At 0 °C. [6] Setting point 0 °C. [7] At -24 °C.
[8] For conversion of torr to Pa, use 13.5951 g/cm³ (at 0 °C).

Substance		Density[2] g/cm³	Melting point[1] °C	Boiling point[1] °C	Thermal conductivity[2] W/(m·K)	Specific heat capacity[2] kJ/(kg·K)	Melting enthalpy ΔH_f kJ/kg	Evaporation enthalpy[4] kJ/kg	Coefficient of volume expansion ×10⁻³/K
Paraffin oil		–	–	–	–	–	–	–	0.764
Petroleum ether		0.66	–160	> 40	0.14	1.76	–	–	–
Rape oil		0.91	± 0	300	0.17	1.97	–	–	–
Silicone oil		0.76...0.98	–	–	0.13	1.09	–	–	–
Spirit 95 %[5]		0.81	–114	78	0.17	2.43	–	–	–
Sulfuric acid, conc.	H_2SO_4	1.83	+10.5[5]	338	0.47	1.42	–	–	0.55
Tar, coke oven		1.2	–15	300	0.19	1.56	–	–	–
Toluene	C_7H_8	0.87	–93	111	0.14	1.67	74.4	364	–
Transformer oil		0.88	–30	170	0.13	1.88	–	–	–
Trichloroethylene	C_2HCl_3	1.46	–85	87	0.12	0.93	–	265	1.19
Turpentine oil		0.86	–10	160	0.11	1.80	–	293	1.0
Water		1.00[7]	± 0	100	0.60	4.18	332	2256	0.18[8]

[1] At 1.013 bar.
[2] At 20 °C.
[3] At melting point and 1.013 bar.
[4] At boiling point and 1.013 bar.
[5] Setting point 0 °C.
[6] Denatured ethanol.
[7] At 4 °C.
[8] Volume expansion on freezing: 9 %.

Water vapor

Absolute pressure bar	Boiling point °C	Evaporation enthalpy kJ/kg	Absolute pressure bar	Boiling point °C	Evaporation enthalpy kJ/kg
0.1233	50	2382	25.5	225	1837
0.3855	75	2321	39.78	250	1716
1.0133	100	2256	59.49	275	1573
2.3216	125	2187	85.92	300	1403
4.760	150	2113	120.5	325	1189
8.925	175	2031	165.4	350	892
15.55	200	1941	221.1	374.2	0

Properties of gases

Substance		Density[1] kg/m³	Melting point[2] °C	Boiling point[2] °C	Thermal conductivity[3] W/(m·K)	Specific heat capacity[3] kJ/(kg·K)		c_p/c_v	Evaporation enthalpy[2] kJ/kg
						c_p	c_v		
Acetylene	C_2H_2	1.17	–84	–81	0.021	1.64	1.33	1.23	751
Air		1.293	–220	–191	0.026	1.005	0.716	1.40	209
Ammonia	NH_3	0.77	–78	–33	0.024	2.06	1.56	1.32	1369
Argon	Ar	1.78	–189	–186	0.018	0.52	0.31	1.67	163
Blast-furnace gas		1.28	–210	–170	0.024	1.05	0.75	1.40	–
i-butane	C_4H_{10}	2.67	–145	–10.2	0.016	–	–	1.11	–
n-butane	C_4H_{10}	2.70	–138	–0.5	0.016	–	–	–	–
Carbon dioxide	CO_2	1.98	–57[4]	–78	0.016	0.82	0.63	1.30	368
Carbon disulfide	CS_2	3.41	–112	+46	0.0073	0.67	0.56	1.19	–
Carbon monoxide	CO	1.25	–199	–191	0.025	1.05	0.75	1.40	–
Chlorine	Cl_2	3.21	–101	–35	0.009	0.48	0.37	1.30	288
City/town gas		0.56...0.61	–230	–210	0.064	2.14	1.59	1.35	–
Cyanogen (dicyan)	$(CN)_2$	2.33	–34	–21	–	1.72	1.35	1.27	–
Dichlorodifluoromethane CCl_2F_2 (= Freon F 12)		5.51	–140	–30	0.010	–	–	1.14	–
Ethane	C_2H_6	1.36	–183	–89	0.021	1.66	1.36	1.22	522
Ethanol vapor		2.04	–114	+78	0.015	–	–	1.13	–
Ethylene	C_2H_4	1.26	–169	–104	0.020	1.47	1.18	1.24	516
Fluorine	F_2	1.70	–220	–188	0.025	0.83	–	–	172
Helium	He	0.18	–270	–269	0.15	5.20	3.15	1.65	20
Hydrogen	H_2	0.09	–258	–253	0.181	14.39	10.10	1.42	228
Hydrogen chloride	HCl	1.64	–114	–85	0.014	0.81	0.57	1.42	–
Hydrogen sulfide	H_2S	1.54	–86	–61	–	0.96	0.72	1.34	535
Krypton	Kr	3.73	–157	–153	0.0095	0.25	0.15	1.67	108
Methane	CH_4	0.72	–183	–164	0.033	2.19	1.68	1.30	557
Methyl chloride	CH_3Cl	2.31	–92	–24	–	0.74	0.57	1.29	446
Natural gas		≈0.83	–	–162	–	–	–	–	–
Neon	Ne	0.90	–249	–246	0.049	1.03	0.62	1.67	86
Nitrogen	N_2	1.24	–210	–196	0.026	1.04	0.74	1.40	199
Oxygen	O_2	1.43	–218	–183	0.267	0.92	0.65	1.41	213
Ozone	O_3	2.14	–251	–112	0.019	–	–	1.29	–
Propane	C_3H_8	2.00	–182	–42	0.018	–	–	1.14	–
Propylene	C_3H_6	1.91	–185	–47	0.017	–	–	–	468
Sulfur dioxide	SO_2	2.93	–73	–10	0.010	0.64	0.46	1.40	402
Water vapor at 100 °C[5]		0.60	±0	+100	0.025	2.01	1.52	1.32	–
Xenon	Xe	5.89	–112	–108	0.0057	0.16	0.096	1.67	96

[1]) At 0 °C and 1.013 bar.
[2]) At 1.013 bar.
[3]) At 20 °C and 1.013 bar.
[4]) At 5.3 bar.
[5]) At saturation and 1.013 bar, see also table "Properties of liquids".

Properties of metallic materials

Material	Standard	Abbreviation of selected types	Primary alloying constituents, mean values in % by mass	R_m[1] N/mm²	R_e[2] N/mm²	A_5[3] %	σ_{bW}[4] Ref. value N/mm²	Test bar dia.[5] mm	Properties, typical applications
Cast iron and malleable cast iron[6] E[7] in 10³ N/mm²: GG 78...143[8]; GGG 160...180; GTW and GTS 175...195									
Lamellar graphite iron (gray cast iron)	DIN EN 1561	EN-GJL-200	Not standardized	200...300	–	–	90	30	Brittle, very good machinability.
Nodular graphite iron	DIN EN 1563	EN-GJS-400-15	Not standardized	≥ 400	≥ 250	≥ 15	200	25	More ductile than gray cast iron, good machinability.
Malleable cast iron White-heart casting Black-heart casting	DIN EN 1569	GTW-40-05 GTS-35-10	Not standardized	≥ 400 ≥ 350	≥ 220 ≥ 200	≥ 5 (A_3) ≥ 10 (A_3)	– –	12 12	Ductility similar to nodular cast iron, good machinability.
Cast steel E[7] as steel	DIN 1681	GS-45	Not standardized	≥ 450	≥ 230	≥ 22	210	–	Heat-treatable.
Steel E[7] in 10³ N/mm²: unalloyed and low-alloy steel 212, austenitic steels ≥ 190, high-alloy tool steels ≤ 230									
Untreated structural steel (dia. 16...40 mm)	DIN EN 10025	S 235 JR E 360	≤ 0.19 C	340...510 670...830	≤ 225 ≥ 355	≥ 26 ≥ 11	≥ 170 ≥ 330	– –	For low-stressed parts. For higher-stressed parts.
Cold-rolled strip of soft unalloyed steels	DIN EN 10139	DC 05 LC	Not standardized	270...330	≤ 180	≥ 40 (A_{80})	≥ 130	–	For difficult deep-drawn parts.
Hot-galvanized strip and sheet	DIN EN 10142	DX 53 D	Not standardized	≤ 380	≤ 260	≥ 30 (A_{80})	≥ 190	–	For corrosion-stressed, difficult deep-drawn parts.
Free-cutting steel (dia. 16 ... 40 mm)	DIN EN 10087	11 SMn30 35 S 20	≤ 0.14 C; 1.1 Mn; 0.30 S 0.35 C; 0.9 Mn; 0.20 S	380...570 520...680	– –	– –	≥ 190 ≥ 260	– –	Soft free-cutting steel. Free-cutting heat-treatable steel.

Steel (continued)

Material Material state	Standard	Abbreviation of selected types	Primary alloying constituents, mean values in % by mass	R_m[1] N/mm²	R_e[2] N/mm²	A[3] %	σ_{bW}[4] Ref. value N/mm²	Test bar dia.[5] mm	Properties, typical applications
Heat-treatable steel, heat-treated (dia. ≤ 16 mm)	DIN EN 10083	C 45 E 34 Cr 4 42 CrMo 4 30 CrNiMo 8	0.45 C 0.34 C; 1.1 Cr 0.42 C; 1 Cr; 0.2 Mo 0.3 C; 2 Cr; 0.4 Mo; 2 Ni	700...850 900...1100 1100...1300 1250...1450	≥ 490 ≥ 700 ≥ 900 ≥ 1050	≥ 14 ≥ 12 ≥ 10 ≥ 9	≥ 280 ≥ 360 ≥ 440 ≥ 500	– – – –	← Increasing hardenability.
				Hardness HV (ref. value)					
				Surface	Core				
Case-hardened steel, case-hardened and tempered (dia. ≤ 11 mm)	DIN EN 10084	C 15 E 16 MnCr 5 17 CrNi 6-6 18 CrNiMo 7-6	0.15 C 0.16 C; 1 Cr 0.17 C; 1.5 Cr; 1.5 Ni 0.18 C; 1.6 Cr; 1.5 Ni; 0.3 Mo	700...850 700...850 700...850 700...850	200...450 300...450 400...550 400...550	In the case of hard steels – hardened and tempered, case-hardened, nitration-hardened etc. – the material characteristic values measured in the tensile test are unsuitable for dimensioning of the hard components.			High wear resistance, high vibrostability. Increasing hardenability →
Nitriding steel, heat-treated and nitration-hardened	DIN EN 10085	31 CrMoV 9 34 CrAlMo 5	0.31 C; 2.5 Cr; 0.2 Mo; 0.15 V 0.34 C; 1.0 Al; 1.15 Cr; 0.2 Mo	700...850 850...1100	250...400 250...400				High wear resistance, high vibrostability.
Rolling-bearing steel, hardened and tempered	DIN EN ISO 683-17	100 Cr 6	1 C; 1.5 Cr	Hardness 60...64 HRC					High wear resistance.
Tool steel Unalloyed cold work steel, hardened and tempered	DIN EN ISO 4957	C 80 U	0.8 C	Standard hardness 60...64 HRC					Water hardening steel.
Alloyed cold work steel, hardened and tempered	DIN EN ISO 4957	90 MnCrV 8 X153CrMoV 12 X210Cr12 12Cr	0.9 C; 2 Mn; 0.3 Cr; 0.1 V 1.53 C; 12 Cr; 0.8 Mo; 0.8 V 2.1 C; 12Cr	60...64 HRC 60...64 HRC 60...64 HR					Water/oil hardening steel. Oil hardening steel. Increasing wear resistance →

Material	Standard	Designation	Composition						Remarks
Hot work steel, hardened and tempered	DIN EN ISO 4957	X 40 CrMoV 5-1	0.4 C; 5 Cr; 1.3 Mo; 1 V	43...45 HRC			In the case of hard steels – hardened and tempered, case-hardened, nitration-hardened etc. – the material characteristic values measured in the tensile test are unsuitable for dimensioning of the hard components.		Wear-resistant at high temperature.
High-speed steel, hardened and tempered	DIN EN ISO 4957	HS6-5-2	0.85 C; 6 W; 5 Mo; 2 V; 4Cr	61...65 HRC					
Stainless steels -Ferritic steel, annealed	17440	X 6 Cr 17	≤ 0.08 C; 17 Cr	450...600	≥ 270	200...315	≥ 20		Non-hardenable. Hardness < 185 HV
-Martensitic steel, hardened and tempered	DIN EN 10088	X 20 Cr 13 X 46 Cr 13 X 90 CrMoV 18	0.20 C; 13 Cr 0.46 C; 13 Cr 0.9 C; 18 Cr; 1.1 Mo; 0.1 V	Hardness approx. 40 HRC Hardness approx. 45 HRC Hardness ≥ 57 HRC					Increasing wear resistance.
-Austenitic steel, quenched	17440	X 5 CrNi 18-10 X 8 CrNiS 18-10	≤ 0.07 C; 18 Cr; 9 Ni ≤ 0.07 C; 18 Cr; 9 Ni; 0.3 S	500...700 500...700	≥ 190 ≥ 190	≥ 45 ≥ 35	– –		Non-magnetic, non-hardenable.
Hard metals E = 440 000...550 000	–	–	W (Ti, Ta) carbide + Co	800...1900 HV					Sintered materials, extremely resistant to pressure and wear, but brittle; for machining, cutting, forming tools.
Extremely heavy metals E = 320 000...380 000	–	–	> 90 W; Ni & others	≥ 650 240...450 HV	≥ 560	≥ 2			Density 17...18.5 g/cm³; for governor flyweights, flywheel masses, counterweights.

¹) Tensile strength.
²) Yield point (or $R_{p0.2}$).
³) Elongation at fracture.
⁴) Fatigue strength under reversed bending stresses; more precise strength values are to be calculated according to FMK Guideline "Computational verification of strength for machine components".
⁵) The Fatigue limits given apply to the separately cast test bar.
⁶) The Fatigue limits of all types of cast iron are dependent on the weight and section thickness of the cast pieces.
⁷) Modulus of elasticity.
⁸) For gray cast iron, E decreases with increasing tensile stress and remains almost constant with increasing compression stress.

Steel (continued)

Spring steel

Material	DIN	Primary alloying constituents, approx. in % by mass; E and G in N/mm²	Diameter mm	R_m[1] min. N/mm²	Z[2] %	σ_b[3] N/mm²	τ_{eh}[4] N/mm²	τ_{zul}[5] N/mm²	Properties Typical applications
Spring steel wire D, patented and springy drawn[6]	17223 Sheet 1	0.8 C; 0.6 Mn; < 0.35 Si; $E = 206\,000$ $G = 81\,500$	1 3 10	2230 1840 1350	40 40 30	1590 1280 930	380[7] 360[7] 320	1115 920 675	For high maximum stresses (P. 294).
Nonrusting spring steel wire	17224	< 0.12 C; 17 Cr; 7.5 Ni; $E = 185\,000$ $G = 73\,500$	1 3	2000 1600	40 40	1400 1130	– –	1000 800	For nonrusting springs.
Heat-treated valve-spring steel wire [6]	17223 Sheet 2	0.65 C; 0.7 Mn; ≤ 0.30 Si; $E = 206\,000$ $G = 80\,000$	1 3 8	1720 1480 1390	45 45 38	1200 1040 930	380[8] 380[8] 360[8]	860 740 690	For high alternating cyclic stress.
Heat-treated, alloyed valve-spring steel wire VD Si Cr[6]	–	0.55 C; 0.7 Mn; 0.65 Cr; 1.4 Si; $E = 200\,000$ $G = 79\,000$	1 3 8	2060 1920 1720	50 50 40	– – –	430[8] 430[8] 380[8]	1030 960 860	For maximum alternating cyclic stress and higher temperatures.
Heat-treated, alloyed valve-spring steel wire VD Cr V[6]	–	0.7 C; 0.7 Mn; 0.5 Cr; 0.15 V; ≤ 0.30 S; $E = 200\,000$ $G = 79\,000$	1 3 8	1860 1670 1420	45 45 40	– – –	470[8] 470[8] 400[8]	930 835 710	For maximum alternating cyclic stress.
Spring steel strip Ck 85	17222	0.85 C; 0.55 Mn; 0.25 Si; $E = 206\,000$	h ≤ 2.5	1470	–	1270	$\sigma_{th} = 640$	–	For highly stressed leaf springs.
Nonrusting spring steel strip	17224	< 0.12 C; 17 Cr; 7.5 Ni; $E = 185\,000$	h ≤ 1	1370	–	1230	$\sigma_{th} = 590$	–	For nonrusting leaf springs.

[1] Tensile strength.
[2] Reduction of area at fracture.
[3] Permissible bending stress.
[4] Permissible lift stress for number of stress cycles $N \geq 10^7$.
[5] Permissible maximum stress for temperatures to approx. 30 °C and 1...2 % relaxation in 10 hrs.; for higher temperatures, see P. 294.
[6] See pp. 294 and 295 for fatigue-strength diagrams.
[7] 480 N/mm² for peened springs.
[8] Approx. 40 % higher for peened springs.

Vehicle-body sheet metal

Material Abbreviated name	Standard material thickness mm	$R_{p0.2}$[1] N/mm²	R_m[2] N/mm²	A_{80}[3] %	Properties Typical applications
St 12	0.6...2.5	≈ 280	270...410	≈ 28	For simple drawn metal parts.
St 13		≈ 250	270...370	≈ 32	For complicated drawn metal parts.
St 14		≈ 240	270...350	≈ 38	For very complex deep-drawn parts, outer body parts (roof, doors, fenders etc.; 0.75...1.0 mm); see also DIN 1623.
ZE 260	0.75...2.0	260...340	≈ 370	≈ 28	For highly stressed supporting parts whose degree of forming is not too complicated.
ZE 340		340...420	≈ 420	≈ 24	
ZE 420		420...500	≈ 490	≈ 20	
AlMg 0.4 Si 1.2	0.8...2.5	≈ 140	≈ 250	≈ 28	For outer body parts such as front fenders, doors, engine hood, trunk lid etc.; mostly 1.25 mm; see DIN 1745.
AlMg 4.5 Mn 0.3	0.5...3.5	≈ 130	≈ 270	≈ 28	For inner reinforcements of hinged covers; for parts which are not visible; lines of stress tolerated.

[1] Yield strength.
[2] Tensile strength.
[3] Elongation at fracture.

Nonferrous metals, heavy metals

Material Examples	Abbreviated name Examples	Composition, mean values, in % by mass	E[1] N/mm²	R_m[2] min. N/mm²	$R_{p0.2}$[3] approx. N/mm²	σ_{bW}[4] approx. N/mm²	Properties Typical applications
Wrought copper alloys (DIN EN 1652…1654, 1758, 12163…12168)							
High-conductivity copper	EN CW-Cu-FRTP	99.90 Cu	$128 \cdot 10^3$	200	120[5]	70	Very good electrical conductivity.
Brass	EN CW-CuZn 28 R370 EN CW-CuZn 37 R440 EN CW-CuZn 39 Pb3 R430	72 Cu; 28 Zn 63 Cu; 37 Zn 58 Cu; 39 Zn; 3 Pb	$114 \cdot 10^3$ $110 \cdot 10^3$ $96 \cdot 10^3$	370 440 430	320 400 250	120 140 150	Deep-drawing capability. Good cold formability. Machine parts.
Nickel silver	EN CW-CuNi 18 Zn 20 R500	62 Cu; 20 Zn; 18 Ni	$135 \cdot 10^3$	500	300	—	Corrosion-resistant.
Tin bronze	EN CW-CuSn 6 R400	94 Cu; 6 Sn	$118 \cdot 10^3$	410	300	175	Good antifriction qualities; bearing bushings, connectors.
Cast copper alloys (DIN 1705)							
Cast tin bronze	G-CuSn 10 Zn	88 Cu; 10 Sn; 2 Zn	$100 \cdot 10^3$	260[6]	140[6]	90	Corrosion-resistant, wear-resistant; gears, bearings.
Red bronze	GC-CuSn 7 ZnPb	85 Cu; 7 Sn; 4 Zn; 6 Pb	$95 \cdot 10^3$	270	130	80	
Other alloys							
Tin alloy (DIN ISO 4381)	SnSb 12 Cu 6 Pb	80 Sn; 12 Sb; 6 Cu; 2 Pb	$30 \cdot 10^3$	—	60	28	Plain bearings.
Zinc diecastings (DIN 1743)	GD-ZnAl 4 Cu 1	96 Zn; 4 Al	$85 \cdot 10^3$	280[6]	230[6]	80	Dimensionally accurate castings.
Heating-conductor alloy (DIN 17470)	NiCr 80 20 NiCr 60 15	80 Ni; 20 Cr 60 Ni; 22 Fe; 17 Cr	— —	650 600	— —	— —	High electrical resistance (P. 215).
Resistance alloy (DIN 17471)	CuNi 44 CuNi 30 Mn	55 Cu; 44 Ni; 1 Mn 67 Cu; 30 Ni; 3 Mn	— —	420 400	— —	— —	

[1] Modulus of elasticity, reference values. [2] Tensile strength. [3] 0.2 % yield strength. [4] Fatigue limit under reversed bending stress. [5] Maximum.
[6] For separately cast test rod.

Nonferrous metals, light metals

Material Examples	Composition, mean values in % by mass	R_m[1]) min. N/mm²	$R_{p0.2}$[2]) min. N/mm²	σ_{bW}[3]) approx. N/mm²	Properties Typical applications
Wrought aluminum alloys (DIN EN 458, 485, 515, 573, 754 ...), modulus of elasticity $E = 65\,000 \ldots 73\,000$ N/mm²					
ENAW-Al 99.5 O	99.5 Al	65	20	40	Soft, very good conductor, can be anodized/polished.
ENAW-AlMg 2 Mn 0.8 O	97 Al; 2 Mg; 0.8 Mn	190	80	90	Seawater-resistant, can be anodized.
ENAW-AlSiMgMn T 6	97 Al; 0.9 Mg; 1 Si; 0.7 Mn	310	260	90	Aged artificially, seawater-resistant.
ENAW-AlCu 4 MgSi (A) T 4	94 Al; 4 Cu; 0.7 Mg; 0.7 Mn; 0.5 Si	390	245	120	Precipitation-hardened, good creep rupture properties.
ENAW-AlZn 5.5 MgCuT 651	90 Al; 6 Zn; 2 Mg; 2 Cu; 0.2 Cr	525	460	140	Maximum strength.
Cast aluminum alloys[5]) (DIN EN 1706), modulus of elasticity $E = 68\,000 \ldots 80\,000$ N/mm²					
ENAC-AlSi 7 Mg 0.3 KT 6	89 Al; 7 Si; 0.4 Mg; 0.1 Ti	290	210	80	Aged artificially; highly stressed parts with good vibration strength.
ENAC-AlSi6 Cu 4 KF	89 Al; 6 Si; 4 Cu; 0.3 Mn; 0.3 Mg	170	100	60	Highly versatile, heat-resistant.
ENAC-AlCu 4 Ti KT 6	95 Al; 5 Cu; 0.2 Ti	330	220	90	Aged artificially; simple parts with maximum strength and toughness.
ENAC-AlSi 12 Cu 1 (Fe) DF	88 Al; 12 Si; 1 Cu; 1 Fe	240	140	70	Thin-walled, vibration-resistant parts.
ENAC-AlSi 9 Cu 3 (Fe) DF	87 Al; 9 Si; 3 Cu; 0.3 Mn; 0.3 Mg	240	140	70[6])	Heat-resistant; complicated diecastings.
ENAC-AlMg 9 DF	90 Al; 9 Mg; 1 Si; 0.4 Mn	200	130	60[6])	Seawater-resistant; medium-stressed parts.
Magnesium alloys (DIN 1729, 9715), modulus of elasticity $E = 40\,000 \ldots 45\,000$ N/mm²					
MgAl 6 Zn F 27	93 Mg; 6 Al; 1 Zn; 0.3 Mn	270	195	–	Parts subject to medium to high stress.
GK-MgAl 9 Zn 1 wa	90 Mg; 9 Al; 0.6 Zn; 0.2 Mn	240	150	80	Aged artificially,
GD-MgAl 9 Zn 1	90 Mg; 9 Al; 0.6 Zn; 0.2 Mn	200	150	50	Complicated diecastings.
					Chips are combustible.
Titanium alloys (DIN 17850, 17851, 17860 ... 17864), modulus of elasticity $E = 110\,000$ N/mm²					
Ti 1	99.7 Ti	290	180	–	Corrosion-resistant.
TiAl 6 V 4 F 89	90 Ti; 6 Al; 4 V	890	820	–	Corrosion-resistant, maximum strength.

[1]) Tensile strength. [2]) 0.2 % yield strength. [3]) Rotating bending fatigue strength. [4]) Maximum. [5]) Strength values apply to permanent mold castings and diecastings for separately cast test rods. Sand castings have slightly lower values than permanent mold castings. [6]) Flat bending fatigue strength.

Sintered metals[1]) for plain bearings

		Permissible ranges					Representative examples					
Material	Material code	Density ϱ	Porosity $(\Delta V/V)\cdot100$	Chemical composition % by mass	Radial breaking resistance K[2])	Hardness	Density ϱ	Chemical composition % by mass	Radial breaking resistance K[2])	Compressive yield point $\delta_{0.2}$	Hardness	Thermal conductivity λ
	Sint	g/cm³	%	%	N/mm²	HB	g/cm³	%	N/mm²	N/mm²	HB[2])	W/mK
Sintered iron	A 00	5.6...6.0	25 ± 2.5	< 0.3 C; < 1.0 Cu; < 2 others; rest Fe	> 150	> 25	5.9	< 0.2 others; rest Fe	160	130	30	37
	B 00	6.0...6.4	20 ± 2.5		> 180	> 30	6.3		190	160	40	43
	C 00	6.4...6.8	15 ± 2.5		> 220	> 40	6.7		230	180	50	48
Sintered steel containing Cu	A 10	5.6...6.0	25 ± 2.5	< 0.3 C; 1 ... 5 Cu; < 2 others; rest Fe	> 160	> 35	5.9	2.0 Cu; < 0.2 others; rest Fe	170	150	40	36
	B 10	6.0...6.4	20 ± 2.5		> 190	> 40	6.3		200	170	50	37
	C 10	6.4...6.8	15 ± 2.5		> 230	> 55	6.7		240	200	65	42
Sintered steel containing Cu and C	B 11	6.0...6.4	20 ± 2.5	0.4 ... 1.0 C; 1 ... 5 Cu; < 2 others; rest Fe	> 270	> 70	6.3	0.6 C; 2.0 Cu; < 0.2 others; rest Fe	280	160	80	28
Sintered steel containing high percentage of Cu	A 20	5.8...6.2	25 ± 2.5	< 0.3 C; 15 ... 25 Cu; < 2 others; rest Fe	> 180	> 30	6.0	20 Cu; < 0.2 others; rest Fe	200	140	40	41
	B 20	6.2...6.6	20 ± 2.5		> 200	> 45	6.4		220	160	50	47
Sintered steel containing high percentage of Cu and C	A 22	5.5...6.0	25 ± 2.5	0.5...2.0 C; 15 ... 25 Cu; < 2 others; rest Fe	> 120	> 20	5.7	2.0 C[3]); 20 Cu; < 0.2 others; rest Fe	125	100	25	30
	B 22	6.0...6.5	20 ± 2.5		> 140	> 25	6.1		145	120	30	37
Sintered bronze	A 50	6.4...6.8	25 ± 2.5	< 0.2 C; 9 ... 11 Sn; < 2 others; rest Cu	> 120	> 25	6.6	10 Sn; < 0.2 others; rest Cu	140	100	30	27
	B 50	6.8...7.2	20 ± 2.5		> 170	> 30	7.0		180	130	35	32
	C 50	7.2...7.7	15 ± 2.5		> 200	> 35	7.4		210	160	45	37
Sintered bronze containing graphite[4])	A 51	6.0...6.5	25 ± 2.5	0.5 ... 2.0 C; 9 ... 11 Sn; < 2 others; rest Cu	> 100	> 20	6.3	1.5 C[4]); 10 Sn; < 0.2 others; rest Cu	120	80	20	20
	B 51	6.5...7.0	20 ± 2.5		> 150	> 25	6.7		155	100	30	26
	C 51	7.0...7.5	15 ± 2.5		> 170	> 30	7.1		175	120	35	32

[1]) According to "Material Specification Sheets for Sintered Metals": DIN 30 910, 1990 Edition.
[2]) Measured on calibrated bearings 10/16 dia. · 10.
[3]) C is mainly present as free graphite.
[4]) C is present as free graphite.

Sinter (PM) metals[1] for structural parts

Material	Material code Sint	Permissible ranges Density ρ g/cm³	Porosity (ΔV/V)·100 %	Chemical composition % by mass %	Hardness HB	Representative examples Density ρ g/cm³	Chemical composition % by mass %	Tensile strength R_m N/mm²	Yield point $R_{p\,0.1}$ N/mm²	Elongation at break A %	Hardness HB	Elastic modulus $E \cdot 10^3$ N/mm²
Sintered iron	C 00 D 00 E 00	6.4...6.8 6.8...7.2 > 7.2	15 ± 2.5 10 ± 2.5 < 7.5	< 0.3 C; < 1.0 Cu; < 2 others; rest Fe	> 35 > 45 > 60	6.6 6.9 7.3	< 0.5 others; rest Fe	130 190 260	60 90 130	4 10 18	40 50 65	100 130 160
Sintered steel containing C	C 01 D 01	6.4...6.8 6.8...7.2	15 ± 2.5 10 ± 2.5	0.3...0.6 C; < 1.0 Cu; < 2 others; rest Fe	> 70 > 90	6.6 6.9	0.5 C; < 0.5 others; rest Fe	260 320	180 210	3 3	80 100	100 130
Sintered steel containing Cu	C 10 D 10 E 10	6.4...6.8 6.8...7.2 > 7.2	15 ± 2.5 10 ± 2.5 < 7.5	< 0.3 C; 1...5 Cu; < 2 others; rest Fe	> 40 > 50 > 80	6.6 6.9 7.3	1.5 Cu; < 0.5 others; rest Fe	230 300 400	160 210 290	3 6 12	55 85 120	100 130 160
Sintered steel containing Cu and C	C 11 D 11	6.4...6.8 6.8...7.2	15 ± 2.5 10 ± 2.5	0.4...1.5 C; 1...5 Cu; < 2 others; rest Fe	> 80 > 95	6.6 6.9	0.6 C; 1.5 Cu; < 0.5 others; rest Fe	460 570	320 400	2 2	125 150	100 130
	C 21	6.4...6.8	15 ± 2.5	0.4...1.5 C; 5...10 Cu; < 2 others; rest Fe	> 105	6.6	0.8 C; 6 Cu; < 0.5 others; rest Fe	530	410	<1	150	100
Sintered steel containing Cu, Ni and Mo	C 30 D 30 E 30	6.4...6.8 6.8...7.2 > 7.2	15 ± 2.5 10 ± 2.5 < 7.5	< 0.3 C; 1...5 Cu; 1...5 Ni; < 0.8 Mo; < 2 others; rest Fe	> 55 > 60 > 90	6.6 6.9 7.3	0.3 C; 1.5 Cu; 4.0 Ni; 0.5 Mo; < 0.5 others; rest Fe	390 510 680	310 370 440	2 3 5	105 130 170	100 130 160
Sintered steel containing P	C 35 D 35	6.4...6.8 6.8...7.2	15 ± 2.5 10 ± 2.5	< 0.3 C; < 1.0 Cu; 0.3...0.6 P; < 2 others; rest Fe	> 70 > 80	6.6 6.9	0.45 P; < 0.5 others; rest Fe	310 330	200 230	11 12	85 90	100 130
Sintered steel containing Cu and P	C 36 D 36	6.4...6.8 6.8...7.2	15 ± 2.5 10 ± 2.5	< 0.3 C; 1...5 Cu; 0.3...0.6 P; < 2 others; rest Fe	> 80 > 90	6.6 6.9	2.0 Cu; 0.45 P; < 0.5 others; rest Fe	360 380	290 320	5 6	100 105	100 130
Sintered steel containing Cu, Ni, Mo and C	C 39 D 39	6.4...6.8 6.8...7.2	15 ± 2.5 10 ± 2.5	0.3...0.6 C; 1...3 Cu; 1...5 Ni; < 0.8 Mo; < 2 others; rest Fe	> 90 > 120	6.6 6.9	0.5 C; 1.5 Cu; 4.0 Ni; 0.5 Mo; < 0.5 others; rest Fe	520 600	370 420	1 2	150 180	100 130

[1] According to "Material Specification Sheets for Sintered Metals": DIN 30 910, 1990 Edition.

Sintered metals[1] for structural parts (continued)

Material	Material code (Sint)	Permissible ranges				Representative examples						
		Density ϱ g/cm³	Porosity $(\Delta V/V)\cdot100$ %	Chemical composition % by mass %	Hardness HB	Density ϱ g/cm³	Chemical composition % by mass %	Tensile strength R_m N/mm²	Yield point $R_{p\,0.1}$ N/mm²	Elongation at break A %	Hardness HB	Elastic modulus $E\cdot10^3$ N/mm²
Stainless sintered steel AISI 316	C 40	6.4...6.8	15 ± 2.5	<0.08 C; 10...14 Ni; 2...4 Mo; 16...19 Cr; <2 others; rest Fe	> 95	6.6	0.06 C; 13 Ni; 2.5 Mo; 18 Cr; <0.5 others; rest Fe	330	250	1	110	100
	D 40	6.8...7.2	10 ± 2.5		> 125	6.9		400	320	2	135	130
AISI 430	C 42	6.4...6.8	15 ± 2.5	<0.08 C; 16...19 Cr; <2 others; rest Fe	> 140	6.6	0.06 C; 18 Cr; <0.5 others; rest Fe	420	330	1	170	100
AISI 410	C 43	6.4...6.8	15 ± 2.5	0.1...0.3 C; 11...13 Cr; <2 others; rest Fe	> 165	6.6	0.2 C; 13 Cr; <0.5 others; rest Fe	510	370	1	180	100
Sintered bronze	C 50	7.2...7.7	15 ± 2.5	9...11 Sn; <2 others; rest Cu	> 35	7.4	10 Sn; <0.5 others; rest Cu	150	90	4	40	50
	D 50	7.7...8.1	10 ± 2.5		> 45	7.9		220	120	6	55	70
Sintered aluminum containing Cu	D 73	2.45...2.55	10 ± 2.5	4...6 Cu; <1 Mg; <1 Si; <2 others; rest Al	> 45	2.5	4.5 Cu; 0.6 Mg; 0.7 Si; <0.5 others; rest Al	160	130	1	50	50
	E 73	2.55...2.65	6 ± 1.5		> 55	2.6		200	150	2	60	60

[1] According to "Material Specification Sheets for Sintered Metals": DIN 30 910, 1990 Edition.

Soft-magnetic metallic materials

Magnet type	Alloying constituents by mass %	Coercive field strength $H_{c(max)}$ in A/m Thickness in mm 0.4...1.5	>1.5	Minimum magnetic polarization in tesla (J) at field strength H in A/m 20	50	100	300	500	800	1600	4000	8000	AC test data, 50 Hz Measuring point $\hat{H}$ in A/m	Minimum amplitude permeability μ_a Sheet thickness in mm 0.30...0.38	0.15...0.20 [1])
A – 240	100 Fe	240	240				1.15	1.30			1.60			Not suitable for AC applications.	
A – 120	100 Fe	120	120				1.15	1.30			1.60				
A – 60	100 Fe	60	60				1.25	1.35			1.60				
A – 12	100 Fe	12	12			1.15	1.30	1.40			1.60				
C1 – 48	0...5 Si (typical 2...4.5)	48	48			0.60	1.10	1.20			1.50				
C1 – 12	0...5 Si (typical 2...4.5)	12	12			1.20	1.30	1.35			1.50				
C21 – 09	0.4...5 Si (typical 2...4.5)												1.60	900	750
C22 – 13	0.4...5 Si (typical 2...4.5)												1.60	1300	–
E11 – 60	72...83 Ni	2	4	0.50	0.65	0.70		0.73			0.75		0.40	40000	40000
E21	54...68 Ni	Not suitable for this thickness	10											After agreement	
E31 – 06	45...50 Ni	10		0.50	0.90	1.10		1.35			1.45		0.40	6000	6000
E32	45...50 Ni	Not suitable for this thickness	10											After agreement	
E41 – 03	35...40 Ni	24	24	0.20	0.45	0.70		1.00			1.18		1.60	2900	2900
F11 – 240	47...50 Co	60	240				1.40		1.70	1.90	2.06	2.15		As agreed between manufacturer and buyer.	
F11 – 60	47...50 Co	300					1.80		2.10	2.20	2.25	2.25			
F21	35 Co	300							1.50	1.60	2.00	2.20			
F31	23...27 Co										1.85	2.00			

[1]) Data apply to laminated rings.

Soft-magnetic metallic materials
Magnetic steel sheet and strip

Abbreviated name	Material number	Nominal thickness mm	Density ρ g/cm³	Max. cyclic magnetization loss (50 Hz) in W/kg under modulation			Magnetic polarization in tesla at field strength H in A/m min.			Static coercive field strength H_c in A/m	Permeability μ max	Properties, typical applications
				P 1.0	P 1.5	P 1.7	(B25) 2500	(B50) 5000	(B100) 10000			
M 270–35A	1.0801	0.35	7.60	1.10	2.70	–	1.49	1.60	1.70			Cyclic magnetization losses.
M 330–35A	1.0804	0.35	7.65	1.30	3.30	–	1.49	1.60	1.70			
M 330–50A	1.0809	0.50	7.60	1.35	3.30	–	1.49	1.60	1.70			
M 530–50A	1.0813	0.50	7.70	2.30	5.30	–	1.56	1.65	1.75			
M 800–50A	1.0816	0.50	7.80	3.60	8.00	–	1.60	1.70	1.78			
M 400–65A	1.0821	0.65	7.65	1.70	4.00	–	1.52	1.62	1.72			
M1000–65A	1.0829	0.65	7.80	4.40	10.00	–	1.61	1.71	1.80	≈ 100 ...300	≈ 5000	Manufacture of magnetic circuits with alternating magnetization (e.g. motors).
M 800–100A	1.0895	1.00	7.70	3.60	8.00	–	1.56	1.66	1.75			
M1300–100A	1.0897	1.00	7.80	5.80	13.00	–	1.60	1.70	1.78			
M 660–50D	1.0361	0.50	7.85	2.80	6.60	–	1.62	1.70	1.79			
M1050–50D	1.0363	0.50	7.85	4.30	10.50	–	1.57	1.65	1.77			
M 800–65D	1.0364	0.65	7.85	3.30	8.00	–	1.62	1.70	1.79			
M1200–65D	1.0366	0.65	7.85	5.00	12.00	–	1.57	1.65	1.77			
							at field strength H 800 A/m (B8)					
M 097–30N	1.0861	0.30	–	–	0.97	1.50		1.75		≈ 1	≈ 30000	
M 140–30S	1.0862	0.30	–	–	0.92	1.40		1.78				
M 111–30P	1.0881	0.30	–	–	–	1.11		1.85				
M 340–50E	1.0841	0.50	7.65	1.42	3.40	–	1.54	1.62	1.72			
M 560–50E	1.0844	0.50	7.80	2.42	5.60	–	1.58	1.66	1.76	≈ 100 ...300	≈ 5000	
M 390–65E	1.0846	0.65	7.65	1.62	3.90	–	1.54	1.62	1.72			
M 630–65E	1.0849	0.65	7.80	2.72	6.30	–	1.58	1.66	1.76			

Materials for transformers and reactors

Core-lamination permeability for alloy classes C21, C22, E11, E31 and E41 for core-lamination section YEI1.

Minimum core-lamination permeability μ_{lam} (min)

Strip 1

IEC designation	C21-09 Thickness in mm				C22-13 Thickness in mm	E11-60 Thickness in mm			
YEI1	0.3...0.38	0.15...0.2	0.1	0.05	0.3...0.38	0.3...0.38	0.15...0.2	0.1	0.05
−10	630	630			1000	14000	18000	20000	20000
13	800	630			1000	18000	20000	22400	20400
14	800	630			1000	18000	22400	25000	22400
16	800	630			1000	20000	22400	25000	22400
18	800	630			1000	22400	25000		22400
20	800	630			1000	22400			25000
22	800	630			1120				
25	800	630			1120				

(C22-13, 0.3...0.38 column additionally shows a further value 1120)

Strip 2

IEC designation	E11-100 Thickness in mm				E31-04 Thickness in mm				E31-06 Thickness in mm			
YEI1	0.3...0.38	0.15...0.2	0.1	0.05	0.3...0.38	0.15...0.2	0.1	0.05	0.3...0.38	0.15...0.2	0.1	0.05
−10	18000	25000	31500	31500	2800	2800	3150	3150	3550	4000	4500	5000
13	20000	28000	35500	35500	2800	3150	3150	3550	4000	4500	5000	5000
14	22400	28000	35500	35500	2800	3150	3150	3550	4000	4500	5000	5000
16	25000	31500	40000	35500	2800	3150	3150	3550	4500	4500	5000	5000
18	25000	31500	40000	35500	3150	3150	3550	3550	4500	4500	5000	5000
20	28000	35500		40000	3150	3150	3550	3550	4500	5000	5000	5000

Strip 3

IEC designation	E31-10 Thickness in mm				E41-02 Thickness in mm				E41-03 Thickness in mm			
YEI1	0.3...0.38	0.15...0.2	0.1	0.05	0.3...0.38	0.15...0.2	0.1	0.05	0.3...0.38	0.15...0.2	0.1	0.05
−10	5600	6300	5600	6300	1600	1800	1800	2000	2000	2240	2500	2240
13	6300	7100	6300	6300	1800	1800	2000	2000	2240	2240	2500	2240
14	6300	7100	6300	7100	1800	1800	2000	2000	2240	2240	2500	2240
16	6300	7100	6300	7100	1800	1800	2000	2000	2240	2500	2500	2240
18	7100	7100	6300	7100	1800	1800	2000	2000	2240	2500	2500	2240
20	7100	7100	6300	7100	1800	2000	2000	2000	2240		2500	2240

Materials for direct-current relays

Material type		Alloying constituents	Density[1] ρ	Hardness[1]	Remanence[1]	Permeability[1]	Specific el. resistance[1]	Coercive field strength[1]	Magnetic polarization in T (Tesla) min. at field strength H in A/m								Characteristic properties, applications
Abbreviated name	Material number	by mass %	g/cm³	HV	T (Tesla)	μ_{max}	$\Omega \cdot \frac{mm^2}{m}$ max.	A/m max.	20	50	100	200	300	500	1000	4000	
Unalloyed steels																	
RFe 160	1.1011	—	7.85	max. 150	—	—	0.15	160	—	—	—	—	—	—	—	1.60	Low coercive field strength.
RFe 80	1.1014	—	7.85	max. 150	1.10	—	0.15	80	—	—	—	—	1.15	1.30	–	1.60	
RFe 60	1.1015	—	7.85	max. 150	1.20	—	0.12	60	—	—	—	1.10	1.20	1.30	1.45	1.60	
RFe 20	1.1017	—	7.85	max. 150	1.20	≈ 20 000	0.10	20	—	—	1.15	1.25	1.30	1.40	1.45	1.60	For DC relays and similar purposes.
RFe 12	1.1018	—	7.85	max. 150	1.20	≈ 20 000	0.10	12	—	—	1.15	1.25	1.30	1.40	1.45	1.60	
Silicon steels																	
RSi 48	1.3840	2.5	7.55	130	0.50	—	0.42	48	—	—	0.60	—	—	1.10	1.20	1.50	
RSi 24	1.3843	–	–	–	1.00	≈ 20 000	–	24	—	—	1.20	—	—	1.30	1.35	1.50	
RSi 12	1.3845	4 Si	7.75	200	1.00	≈ 10 000	0.60	12	—	—	1.20	—	—	1.30	1.35	1.50	
Nickel steels and nickel alloys																	
RNi 24	1.3911	= 36 Ni	8.2	130...180	0.45	≈ 5000	0.75	24	—	0.20	0.45	0.70	0.90	1.0	1.18	—	
RNi 12	1.3926	≈ 50 Ni	8.3	130...180	0.60	≈ 30 000	0.45	12	—	0.50	0.90	1.10	1.25	1.35	1.45	—	
RNi 8	1.3927	≈ 50 Ni	8.3	130...180	0.60	30000...100000	0.45	8	—	0.50	0.90	1.10	—	—	1.45	—	
RNi 5	2.4596	70 ... 80 Ni, small quantities Cu, Cr, Mo	8.7	120...170	0.30	≈ 40 000	0.55	5	—	0.50	0.65	0.70	—	—	0.75	—	
RNi 2	2.4595	70 ... 80 Ni, small quantities Cu, Cr, Mo	8.7	120...170	0.30	≈ 100 000	0.55	2	—	0.50	0.65	0.70	—	—	0.75	—	

1) Standard values.

Sinter metals for soft-magnetic components

Material Abbreviated name	Characteristic alloying substances (except Fe) Mass proportions %	Sinter density ϱ_s g/cm³	Porosity p_s %	Maximum coercive field strength $H_{c(max)}$ A/m	Magnetic polarization in Tesla (T) at field strength H in A/m				Maximum permeability $\mu_{(max)}$	Vickers hardness HV5	Specific electrical resistance ϱ $\mu\Omega$m
					500	5000	15000	80000			
S-Fe-175	–	6.6	16	175	0.70	1.10	1.40	1.55	2 000	50	0.15
S-Fe-170	–	7.0	11	170	0.90	1.25	1.45	1.65	2 600	60	0.13
S-Fe-165	–	7.2	9	165	1.10	1.40	1.55	1.75	3 000	70	0.12
S-FeP-150	≈ 0.45 P	7.0	10	150	1.05	1.30	1.50	1.65	3 400	95	0.20
S-FeP-130	≈ 0.45 P	7.2	8	130	1.20	1.45	1.60	1.75	4 000	105	0.19
S-FeSi-80	≈ 3 Si	7.3	4	80	1.35	1.55	1.70	1.85	8 000	170	0.45
S-FeSi-50	≈ 3 Si	7.5	2	50	1.40	1.65	1.70	1.95	9 500	180	0.45
S-FeNi-20	≈ 50 Ni	7.7	7	20	1.10	1.25	1.30	1.30	20 000	70	0.50
S-FeNi-15	≈ 50 Ni	8.0	4	15	1.30	1.50	1.55	1.55	30 000	85	0.45
S-FeCo-100	≈ 50 Co	7.8	3	100	1.50	2.00	2.10	2.15	2 000	190	0.10
S-FeCo-200	≈ 50 Co	7.8	3	200	1.55	2.05	2.15	2.20	3 900	240	0.35

Soft magnetic ferrites

Ferrite type	Initial permeability[1] μ_i ±25 %	Referenced loss factor tan δ/μ[2] 10^{-6}	MHz	Amplitude power loss[3] mW/g	Amplitude permeability[4] μ_a	Curie temperature[5][6] Θ_c °C	Frequency for $0.8 \cdot \mu$[6] MHz	Characteristic properties, applications
Materials in largely open magnetic circuits								
C 1/12	12	350	100	–	–	> 500	400	Initial permeability. Compared to metallic magnetic materials, specific resistance is high: ($10^0 \dots 10^5\ \Omega \cdot$ m, metals $10^{-7} \dots 10^{-6}\ \Omega \cdot$ m), therefore low eddy-current losses. Communications technology (coils, transformers).
D 1/50	50	120	10	–	–	> 400	90	
F 1/250	250	100	3	–	–	> 250	22	
G 2/600	600	40	1	–	–	> 170	6	
H 1/1200	1200	20	0.3	–	–	> 150	2	
Materials in largely closed magnetic circuits								
E 2	60 … 160	80	10	–	–	> 400	50	
G 3	400 … 1200	25	1	–	–	> 180	6	
J 4	1600 … 2500	5	0.1	–	–	> 150	1.5	
M 1	3000 … 5000	5	0.03	–	–	> 125	0.4	
P 1	5000 … 7000	3	0.01	–	–	> 125	0.3	
Materials for power applications								
W 1	1000 … 3000	–	–	45	1200	> 180	–	
W 2	1000 … 3000	–	–	25	1500	> 180	–	

[1] Nominal values.
[2] tan δ/μ denotes the frequency-dependent material losses at a low flux density ($B < 0.1$ mT).
[3] Losses at high flux density. Measured preferably at: $f = 25$ kHz, $B = 200$ mT, $\Theta = 100$°C.
[4] Permeability when subjected to a strong sinusoidal magnetic field. Measured at: $f \leq 25$ kHz, $\hat{B} = 320$ mT, $\Theta = 100$°C.
[5] Curie temperature Θ_c in this table is that temperature at which the initial permeability μ drops to below 10 % of its value at 25 °C.
[6] Standard values.

Permanent-magnet materials

Abbreviated name	Material number DIN	IEC	Chemical composition [1] % by weight Al	Co	Cu	Nb	Ni	Ti	Fe	Density ϱ [1] g/cm³	$(BH)_{max}$ [2] kJ/m³	Remanence B_r [2] mT	Coercive field strength [2] of the flux density H_{CB} kA/m	Coercive field [2] of the polarization H_{CJ} kA/m	Rel. permanent permeability [1] μ_p	Curie temp. [1] T_C K	Temp. coeff. of polar. $TC(J_s)$ [3] %/K	Temp. coeff. of coerciv. $TC(H_C)$ [1][3] %/K	Manufacture, processing, applications
Metallic magnets																			
Isotropic																			
AlNiCo 9/5	1.3728	R 1-0-3	11…13	0…5	2…4	–	21…28	0…1	Re-	6.8	9.0	550	44	47	4.0…5.0	1030		+ 0.03	
AlNiCo 18/9	1.3756	–	6…8	24…34	3…6	–	13…19	5…9	main-	7.2	18.0	600	80	86	3.0…4.0	…	– 0.02	…	
AlNiCo 7/8p	1.3715	R 1-2-3	6…8	24…34	3…6	–	13…19	5…9	der	5.5	7.0	340	72	84	2.0…3.0	1180		– 0.07	
Anisotropic																			Manufacture: Casting or sintering. Magnets with binders are pressed or injection-molded. Processing: Grinding. Application: max. 400…500 °C.
AlNiCo 35/5	1.3761	–	8…9	23…26	3…4	0…1	13…16	–	Re-	7.2	35.0	1120	47	48	3.0…4.5	1030		+ 0.03	
AlNiCo 44/5	1.3757	R 1-1-2	8…9	23…26	3…4	0…1	13…16	–		7.2	44.0	1200	52	53	2.5…4.0				
AlNiCo 52/6	1.3759	R 1-1-3	8…9	23…26	3…4	0…1	13…15	4…6	main-	7.2	52.0	1250	55	56	1.5…3.0		– 0.02		
AlNiCo 60/11	1.3763	R 1-1-6	6…8	35…39	2…4	0…1	13…15	4…6	der	7.2	60.0	900	110	112	1.5…2.5	1180			
AlNiCo 30/14	1.3765	–	6…8	38…42	2…4	0…1	13…15	7…9		7.2	30.0	680	136	144	1.5…2.5			– 0.07	
			Pt	Co															
PtCo 60/40	2.5210	R2-0-1	77…78	20…23						15.5	60	600	350	400	1.1	800	– 0.01 … – 0.02	– 0.35	
			V	Co	Cr	Fe													
FeCoVCr 11/2	2.4570	R 3-1-3	8…15	51…54	0…4	Remain-				–	11.0	800	24	24	2.0…8.0	1000	– 0.01	≈ 0	
FeCoVCr 4/1	2.4571	–	3…15	51…54	0…6	der				–	4.0	1000	5	5	9.0…25.0				
RECo magnets of type RECo₅																			
RECo 80/80	–	R 5-1-1	Typically MMCo₅ (MM = ceramic-metal material)							8.1	80	650	500	800	1.05	1000	– 0.05	– 0.3	
RECo 120/96	–	R 5-1-2	Typically SmCo₅							8.1	120	770	590	960	1.05	1000	– 0.05	– 0.3	
RECo 160/80	–	R 5-1-3	Typically (SmPr) Co₅							8.1	160	900	640	800	1.05	1000	– 0.05	– 0.3	
RECo magnets of type RE₂Co₁₇																			
RECo 165/50	–	R 5-1-11								8.2	165	950	440	500	1.1	1100	0.03	– 0.02	
RECo 180/90	–	R 5-1-13								8.2	180	1000	680	900	1.1	1100	0.03	– 0.02	
RECo 190/70.	–	R 5-1-14								8.2	190	1050	560	700	1.1	1100	0.03	– 0.02	
RECo 48/60p	–	R 5-3-1								5.2	48	500	360	600	1.05	1000	– 0.05	– 0.3	

[1] Standard values. [2] Minimum values. [3] In the range of 273 … 373 K.

Metallic magnets (continued)

Material Abbreviated name	Material number DIN	IEC	Chemical composition [1] % by weight Al	Co	Cu	Nb	Ni	Ti	Fe	Density ϱ [1] g/cm³	$(BH)_{max}$ [2] kJ/m³	Remanence B_r [2] mT	Coercive field strength [2] of the flux density H_{CB} kA/m	of the polarization H_{CJ} kA/m	Rel. permanent permeability [1] μ_p	Curie temp. [1] T_C K	Temp. coeff. of polar. $TC(J_s)$ [3] %/K	Temp. coeff. of coerciv. $TC(H_C)$ [3] %/K	Manufacture, processing, applications
CrFeCo 12/4	–	R 6-0-1	(no data)							7.6	12	800	40	42	5.5 … 6.5	1125	– 0.03	– 0.04	
CrFeCo 28/5	–	R 6-1-1								7.6	28	1000	45	46	3 … 4	1125	– 0.03	– 0.04	
REFe 165/170	–	R 7-1-1	(no data)							7.4	165	940	700	1700	1.07	583	– 0.1	– 0.8	
REFe 220/140	–	R 7-1-6								7.4	220	1090	800	1400	1.05	583	– 0.1	– 0.8	
REFe 240/110	–	R 7-1-7								7.4	240	1140	850	1100	1.05	583	– 0.1	– 0.8	
REFe 260/80	–	R 7-1-8								7.4	260	1180	750	800	1.05	583	– 0.1	– 0.8	

Material Abbreviated name	Material number DIN	IEC	Density [1] ϱ g/cm³	$(BH)_{max}$ [2] kJ/m³	Remanence [2] B_r mT	Coercive field strength [2] of the flux density H_{CB} kA/m	of the polarization H_{CJ} kA/m	Rel. permanent permeability [1] μ_p	Curie temp. [1] T_C K	Temp. coeff. of the polarization $TK(J_s)$ %/K	Temp. coeff. of coerciv. $TK(H_C)$ %/K	Manufacture, processing
Ceramic magnets												
Isotropic												
Hard ferrite 7/21	1.3641	S 1-0-1	4.9	6.5	190	125	210	1.2	723	– 0.2	0.2 … 0.5	Manufacture: Sintering. Plastic-bound magnets are manufactured by pressing, injection-molding, rolling and extruding. Processing: Grinding.
Hard ferrite 3/18p	1.3614	S 1-2-2	3.9	3.2	135	85	175	1.1	723	– 0.2	0.2 … 0.5	
Anisotropic												
Hard ferrite 20/19	1.3643	S 1-1-1	4.8	20.0	320	170	190	1.1	723	– 0.2	0.2 … 0.5	
Hard ferrite 20/28	1.3645	S 1-1-2	4.6	20.0	320	220	280	1.1				
Hard ferrite 24/23	1.3647	S 1-1-3	4.8	24.0	350	215	230	1.1				
Hard ferrite 25/22	1.3651	S 1-1-5	4.8	25.0	370	205	220	1.1				
Hard ferrite 26/26	–	S 1-1-8	4.7	26.0	370	260	260	1.1				
Hard ferrite 32/17	–	S 1-1-10	4.9	32.0	410	160	165	1.1				
Hard ferrite 24/35	–	S 1-1-14	4.8	24.0	360	260	350	1.1				
Hard ferrite 9/19p	1.3616	S 1-3-1	3.4	9.0	220	145	190	1.1				
Hard ferrite 10/22p	–	S 1-3-2	3.5	10.0	230	165	225	1.1				

[1] Standard values. [2] Minimum values. [3] In the range of 273 … 373 K.

Permanent-magnet materials (continued)

Bosch grades [BTMT] (not standardized)

Material Abbreviated name	Density[1] ϱ g/cm³	$(BH)_{max}$[2] kJ/m³	Remanence[2] B_r mT	Coercive field strength[2] of the flux density H_{CB} kA/m	of the polarization H_{CJ} kA/m
RBX HC 370		25	360	270	390
RBX HC 380		28	380	280	370
RBX 380K		28	380	280	300
RBX 400		30	400	255	260
RBX 400 K	4.7...4.9	31	400	290	300
RBX HC 400		29	380	285	355
RBX 420		34	420	255	270
RBX 410 K		33	410	305	330
RBX HC 410		30	395	290	340
RBX 420 S		35	425	260	270
RBX HC 400 N		28	380	280	390

[1] Standard values.   [2] Minimum values.

Comparison: permanent magnets and soft magnets

Range of magnetic characteristics of some crystalline materials in widespread use.

Magnet material	Coercive field strength H_C A/m	Saturation polarization J_S T	Remanence B_r T	μ
Soft magnets	Low 0.3...400	High 0.9...2.4	Depending on application	High < 500,000
Permanent magnets	High $5 \cdot 10^4...2 \cdot 10^6$	High 0.45...1.4	High 0.4...1.25	High 1.1...5

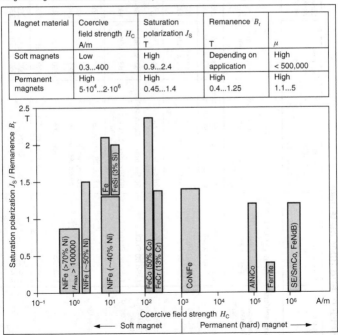

Solders and filler materials

Soft solders (selection from DIN 1707)

Type of alloy	Material code	Primary alloying constituents, mean values % (by mass)	Melting range of alloy °C	Minimum workpiece temperature °C	Properties Primary applications
Lead-base, tin-base soft solders	L-PbSn 20 Sb 3 L-PbSn 12 Sb	20 Sn; max. 3 Sb; rest Pb 12 Sn; max. 0.7 Sb; rest Pb	186 ... 270 250 ... 295	270 295	Soft soldering in motor-vehicle body construction. Soft soldering of copper in radiator construction.
	L-PbSn 40 (Sb) L-PbSn 8 (Sb)	40 Sn; max. 0.5 Sb; rest Pb 8 Sn; max. 0.5 Sb; rest Pb	183 ... 235 280 ... 305	235 305	Tin plating: soft soldering of sheet metal parts. Soft soldering; electric motors, radiator construction.
Tin-base, lead-base soft solders	L-Sn 63 Pb L-Sn 60 Pb	63 Sn; rest Pb 60 Sn; rest Pb	183 183 ... 190	183 190	Wave soldering of printed-circuit boards. Tin plating of copper and copper alloys in the electrical industry.
Tin-base, lead-base soft solders with Ag, Cu or P added	L-Sn 63 PbAg	63 Sn; max. 1.5 Ag; rest Pb	178	178	Wave soldering of printed-circuit boards.
	L-Sn 60 PbCu 2	60 Sn; max. 2 Cu; rest Pb	183 ... 190	190	Soldering (using an iron) of copper and copper alloys in the electrical industry.
	L-Sn 60 PbCuP	60 Sn; max. 0.2 Cu; max. 0.004 P; rest Pb	183 ... 190	190	Dip soldering of copper and copper alloys in the electrical industry.
Special soft solders	–	57 Bi; 26 In; rest Sn	79	79	Soft soldering of heat-sensitive components; fuses.
	L-SnIn 50 L-SnAg 5	50 Sn; rest In max. 5 Ag; rest Sn	117 ... 125 221 ... 240	125 240	Soft soldering of glass/metal. Soft soldering of copper in the electrical industry and in the installation of water pipes.
	L-SnSb 5	max. 5.5 Sb; rest Sn	230 ... 240	240	Soft soldering of copper in refrigeration engineering and in the installation of water pipes.
	L-SnCu 3	max. 3.5 Cu; rest Sn	230 ... 250	250	Soft soldering of copper in the installation of water pipes.
	L-SnZn 10 L-ZnAl 5	max. 15 Zn; rest Sn max. 6 Al; rest Zn	200 ... 250 380 ... 390	250 390	Ultrasonic soft soldering of aluminum and copper without flux.

Filler metals for brazing and high-temperature brazing (selection from DIN 8513 and ISO 3677)

Type of alloy	Material code	Primary alloying constituents, mean values % (by mass)	Melting range of alloy °C	Minimum workpiece temperature[1] °C	Properties Primary applications[1]
Aluminum-base filler metals	L-AlSi 12 L-AlSi 10 L-AlSi 7.5	12 Si; rest Al 10 Si; rest Al 7.5 Si; rest Al	575 ... 590 575 ... 595 575 ... 615	590 595 615	Brazing of Al and Al alloys with a sufficiently high melting point.
Silver-bearing filler metals Ag < 20 %	BCu 75AgP 643 L-Ag 15 P	18 Ag; 7.25 P; rest Cu 15 Ag; 5 P; rest Cu	643 650 ... 800	650 710	Brazing of Cu/Cu without flux.
	L-Ag 5	5 Ag; 55 Cu; 0.2 Si; rest Zn	820 ... 870	860	Brazing of steel, Cu, Ni and Ni alloys with flux.
Silver-bearing filler metals Ag ≥ 20 %	L-Ag55Sn L-Ag44	55 Ag; 22 Cu; 5 Sn; rest Zn 44 Ag; 30 Cu; rest Zn	620 ... 660 675 ... 735	650 730	Brazing of steel, Cu and Cu alloys, Ni and Ni alloys with flux.
	L-Ag49	49 Ag; 16 Cu; 7.5 Mn; 4.5 Ni; rest Zn	625 ... 705	690	Brazing of hard metal, steel, W, Mo and Ta with flux.
	BAg 60 CuIn 605-710 BAg 60 CuSn 600-700 L-Ag 72 BCu 58 AgNi 780-900	60 Ag; 13 In; rest Cu 60 Ag; 10 Sn; rest Cu 72 Ag; rest Cu 40 Ag; 2 Ni; rest Cu	605 ... 710 600 ... 720 780 780 ... 900	710 720 780 900	Brazing of Cu, Ni, steel in a vacuum or under shielding gas.
	BAg 68 CuPd 807-810 BAg 54 PdCu 901-950 BAg 95 Pd 970-1010 BAg 64 PdMn 1180-1200	68 Ag; 5 Pd; rest Cu 54 Ag; 21 Pd; rest Cu 95 Ag; rest Pd; 64 Ag; 3 Mn; rest Pd	807 ... 810 901 ... 950 970 ... 1010 1180 ... 1200	810 950 1010 1200	Brazing of steel, Ni and Co alloys, Mo, W, Ti in a vacuum or under shielding gas.
	L-Ag 56 InNi L-Ag 85	56 Ag; 14 In; 4 Ni; rest Cu 85 Ag; rest Mn	620 ... 730 960 ... 970	730 960	Brazing of Cr and Cr/Ni steels in a vacuum or under shielding gas.
Copper-base filler metals	BCu 86 SnP 650-700	6.75 P; 7 Sn; rest Cu	650 ... 700	690	Brazing of Cu and Cu alloys with flux. Not for Fe and Ni alloys or media containing S.

[1] Depending on the process.

Filler metals for brazing and high-temperature brazing (continued)

Type of alloy	Material code	Primary alloying constituents, mean values % (by mass)	Melting range of alloy °C	Minimum workpiece temperature[1] °C	Properties Primary applications
Copper-base filler metals (continued)	L-CuP 8	8 P; rest Cu	710 ... 740	710	Brazing of Cu/Cu without flux. Not for Fe and Ni alloys or media containing S.
	L-CuZn 40	60 Cu; 0.2 Si; rest Zn	890 ... 900	900	Brazing of steel, Cu, Ni and Ni alloys with flux.
	L-CuSn 6 L-SFCu	6 Sn max; 0.4 P; rest Cu 100 Cu	910 ... 1040 1083	1040 1100	Brazing of steel in a vacuum or under shielding gas.
	BCu 86 MnNi 970-990 BCu 87 MnCo 980-1030 BCu 96.9 NiSi 1090-1100	2 Ni; 12 Mn; rest Cu 3 Co; 10 Mn; rest Cu 0.6 Si; 2.5 Ni; rest Cu	970 ... 990 980 ... 1030 1090 ... 1100	990 1020 1100	Brazing of hard metal, steel, W, Mo, Ta in a vacuum or under shielding-gas partial pressure.
Nickel-base filler metals	L-Ni6 L-Ni1	11 P; rest Ni 3 B; 14 Cr; 4.5 Fe; 4.5 Si; rest Ni	880 980 ... 1040	925 1065	Brazing of Ni, Co and their alloys, unalloyed, low- and high-alloy steels in a vacuum or under hydrogen shielding gas.
	L-Ni5	19 Cr; 10 Si; rest Ni	1080 ... 1135	1150	
Gold-base filler metals	BAu 80 Cu 910	20 Cu; rest Au	910	910	Brazing of Cu, Ni and steel in a vacuum or under shielding gas.
	BAu 82 Ni 950	18 Ni; rest Au	950	950	Brazing of W, Mo, Co, Ni and steels in a vacuum or under shielding gas.
Active filler metals containing titanium	— — —	72.5 Ag; 19.5 Cu; 5 In; rest Ti 70.5 Ag; 26.5 Cu; rest Ti 96 Ag; rest Ti	730 ... 760 780 ... 805 970	850 850 1000	Direct brazing of non-metallized ceramics with each other or combined with steel in a vacuum or under argon protective gas.

---
1) Depending on the process.

Electrical properties

Electrical resistivity at 20 °C
(Resistance of a wire 1 m long with a cross section of 1 mm²)

Resistivity is highly dependent upon the purity of the metal concerned. The mean temperature coefficient α refers to temperatures between 0 and 100 °C whenever possible. Resistivity at a temperature t °C is $\varrho_t = \varrho_{20} [1 + \alpha (t - 20 °C)]$. For calculation of the temperature of a winding based on the increase in resistance, see P. 136.

$$1 \ \Omega \ mm^2/m = 1 \ \mu\Omega \ m, \ 1 \ S \ m/mm^2 = 1 \ MS/m \ (S = Siemens)$$

Material	Electrical resistivity ϱ $\mu\Omega m$	Electrical conductivity $\gamma = 1/\varrho$ MS/m	Mean temperature coefficient α x 10^{-3} 1/°C	Maximum operating temperature approx. °C
Aluminum, Al 99.5 (soft)	0.0265	35	3.8	–
Aluminum alloy E-AlMgSi	< 0.0328	> 30.5	3.8	–
Bismuth	1.07	0.8	4.54	–
Brass CuZn 39 Pb 3	0.0667	15	2.33	–
CuZn 20	0.0525	19	1.60	–
Bronze CuBe 0.5, age-hardened	0.04 ... 0.05	20 ... 25	–	300
Cadmium	0.068	13	–	–
Carbon brushes, unfilled	10 ... 200	0.1 ... 0.05	–	–
metal-filled	0.05 ... 30	20 ... 0.03	–	–
Copper, soft	0.01754	57	3.9	–
hard (cold-stretched)	0.01786	56	3.9	–
Gold (fine gold)	0.023	45	4	–
Gold-chromium alloy Cr2.05	0.33	3.03	± 0.001	–
Gray cast iron	0.6 ... 1.6	0.62 ...1.67	1.9	–
Heating-element alloy[1]) CrAl 20 5	1.37	0.73	0.05	1200
NiCr 30 20	1.04	0.96	0.35	1100
NiCr 60 15	1.13	0.88	0.15	1150
NiCr 80 20	1.12	0.89	0.05	1200
Lead Pb 99.94	0.206	4.8	4	–
Magnetic steel sheet I	0.21	4.76	–	–
Magnetic steel sheet IV	0.56	1.79	–	–
Mercury	0.941	1.0386	0.9	–
Molybdenum	0.052	18.5	4.7	1600[2])
Nickel Ni 99.6	0.095	10.5	5.5	–
Nickel silver CuNi 12 Zn 24	0.232	4.3	–	–
Platinum	0.106	10.2	3.923	–
Resistance alloy[3]) CuMn 12 Ni	0.43	2.33	± 0.01	140
CuNi 30 Mn	0.40	2.50	0.14	500
CuNi 44	0.49	2.04	± 0.04	600
Silver (fine silver)	0.016	66.5	4.056	–
Steel C 15	0.14 ... 0.16	7.15	–	–
Tantalum	0.124	8.06	3.82	–
Tungsten	0.056	18.2	4.82	–
Tin	0.114	8.82	4.4	–
Zinc	0.06	16.67	4.17	–

[1]) DIN 17 470.   [2]) Under shielding gas or in a vacuum.   [3]) DIN 17 471.

Insulating materials

Electrical properties

The properties of insulating materials are highly dependent upon the purity, homogeneity, processing and aging of the material, as well as moisture content and temperature. The following values are given as a guideline for non-aged test specimens at room temperature with average moisture content. 1 min test voltage at 50 Hz; specimen thickness: 3 mm.

Loss factor $\tan\delta$ = active power/reactive power; in USA: loss factor = $\varepsilon_r \cdot \tan\delta$.

Insulating material	Relative permittivity at 800 Hz ε_r (air = 1)	Loss factor $\tan\delta$ at 800 Hz $\times 10^{-3}$	Loss factor $\tan\delta$ at 10^6 Hz $\times 10^{-3}$	Volume resistivity $10^n\,\Omega m$ values of n	Dielectric strength kV_{eff}/mm	Tracking resistance according to DIN 53 480 degree
Cellulose acetates	4.7 ... 5.8	17 ... 24	48 ... 66	11 ... 13	32	–
Epoxy casting resins and molding compounds	3.2 ... 5	2 ... 30	2 ... 60	10 ... 15	6 ... 15	KA 3 b, KA 3 c
Hard porcelain	5 ... 6.5	≈ 15	6 ... 12	> 9	30 ... 40	KA 3 c
Mica	5 ... 8	0.1 ... 1	0.2	13 ... 15	60	KA 3 c
Paraffin waxes	1.9 ... 2.3	< 0.3	< 0.3	13 ... 16	10 ... 30	–
Phenolic resin molding compounds with inorganic filler	5 ... 30	30 ... 400	50 ... 200	6 ... 11	5 ... 30	KA 1
Phenolic resin molding compounds with organic filler	4 ... 9	30 ... 500	50 ... 200	6 ... 10	5 ... 20	KA 1
Polyamides	8 ... 14	20 ... 200	20 ... 200	6 ... 12	10 ... 50	KA 3 b, KA 3 c
Polycarbonates	3 ... 7	1.0	10	14 ... 16	25	KA 1
Polyester casting resins and molding compounds	2.3	3 ... 100	6 ... 60	8 ... 14	6 ... 25	KA 3 c
Polyethylene	2.3	0.2 ... 0.6	0.2 ... 0.6	> 15	≈ 80	KA 3 c
Polymethyl methacrylate	3.1 ... 3.4	40	20	> 13	30	KA 3 c
Polypropylene	2.3	< 0.5	< 0.5	> 15	–	KA 3 c
Polystyrene	2.5	0.1	0.1	> 15	40	KA 2, KA 1
Polytetrafluoroethylene	2	0.1 ... 0.5	0.1 ... 0.5	14	50	KA 3 c
Polyvinyl chloride	3.3 ... 6.5	15 ... 150	10 ... 100	13 ... 15	15 ... 50	KA 3 b
Quartz glass	3.5 ... 4.2	0.5	0.2	14 ... 16	25 ... 40	KA 3 c
Silicones	5 ... 8	4	4	10 ... 14	20 ... 60	KA 3 c
Soft rubber		0.2 ... 100	–	2 ... 14	15 ... 30	KA 1 ... KA 3 c
Steatite	5.5 ... 6.5	1 ... 3	0.3 ... 2	10 ... 12	20 ... 45	KA 3 c
Titanium ceramic	12 ... 10 000	≈ 1	0.05 ... 100	–	2 ... 30	–
Transformer oil, dry	2 ... 2.7	≈ 1	≈ 10	11 ... 12	5 ... 30	–

Properties of non-metallic materials

Ceramics

Materials	Composition	$\rho^{1)}$ g/cm³	$\sigma_{bB}^{2)}$ MN/m²	$\sigma_{bB}^{3)}$ MN/m²	$E^{4)}$ GN/m²	$\alpha_B^{5)}$ 10⁻⁶/K	$\lambda^{6)}$ W/mK	$c^{7)}$ kJ/kg·K	$\rho_D^{8)}$ Ω·cm	$\varepsilon_r^{9)}$	tan $\varrho^{10)}$ 10⁻⁴
Aluminum nitride	AlN > 97 %	3.3	250 ... 350	1100	320 ... 350	5.1	100 ... 220	0.8	> 10¹⁴	8.5 ... 9.0	3 ... 10
Aluminum oxide	Al_2O_3 > 99 %	3.9 ... 4.0	300 ... 500	3000 ... 4000	380 ... 400	7.2 ... 8.6	20 ... 40	0.8 ... 0.9	> 10¹¹	8 ... 10	2
Aluminum titanate	$Al_2O_3 \cdot TiO_2$	3.0 ... 3.2	20 ... 40	450 ... 550	10 ... 20	0.5 ... 1.5	< 2	0.7	> 10¹¹	–	–
Beryllium oxide	BeO > 99 %	2.9 ... 3.0	250 ... 320	1500	300 ... 340	8.5 ... 9.0	240 ... 280	1.0	> 10¹⁴	6.5	3 ... 5
Boron carbide	B_4C	2.5	300 ... 500	2800	450	5.0	30 ... 60	–	10⁻¹ ... 10²	–	–
Cordierite e.g. KER410, 520	$2MgO \cdot 2Al_2O_3 \cdot 5SiO_2$	1.6 ... 2.1	40 ... 200	300	70 ... 100	2.0 ... 5.0	1.3 ... 2.3	0.8	> 10¹¹	5.0	70
Graphite	C > 99.7 %	1.5 ... 1.8	5 ... 30	20 ... 50	5 ... 15	1.6 ... 4.0	100 ... 180	–	10⁻³	–	–
Porcelain e.g. KER 110 – 2 (non-glazed)	Al_2O_3 30 ... 35 % balance SiO_2 + glassy phase	2.2 ... 2.4	45 ... 60	500 ... 550	50	4.0 ... 6.5	1.2 ... 2.6	0.8	10¹¹	6	120
Silicon carbide hot-pressed HPSiC	SiC > 99 %	3.1 ... 3.2	450 ... 650	> 1500	420	4.0 ... 4.5	100 ... 120	0.8	10³	–	–
Silicon carbide pressureless-sintered SSiC	SiC > 98 %	3.1 ... 3.2	400 ... 450	> 1200	400	4.0 ... 4.5	90 ... 120	0.8	10³	–	–
Silicon carbide reaction-sintered SiSiC	SiC > 90 % + Si	3.0 ... 3.1	300 ... 400	> 2200	380	4.2 ... 4.3	100 ... 140	0.8	10 ... 100	–	–
Silicon nitride gas-pressure sintered GPSN	Si_3N_4 > 90 %	3.2	800 ... 1400	> 2500	300	3.2 ... 3.5	30 ... 40	0.7	10¹²	–	–

Ceramic materials (continued)

Material	Composition	ϱ[1] g/cm³	σ_{bB}[2] MN/m²	σ_{dB}[3] MN/m²	E[4] GN/m²	α[5] 10⁻⁶/K	λ[6] W/mK	c[7] kJ/kg·K	ϱ_D[8] Ω·cm	ε[9]	tan δ[10] 10⁻⁴
Silicon nitride hot-pressed HPSN	Si_3N_4 > 95 %	3.2	600 ... 900	> 3000	310	3.2 ... 3.5	30 ... 40	0.7	10¹²	–	–
Silicon nitride reaction-sintered RBSN	Si_3N_4 > 99 %	2.4 ... 2.6	200 ... 300	< 2000	140 ... 160	2.9 ... 3.0	15 ... 20	0.7	10¹⁴	–	–
Steatite e.g. KER 220, 221	SiO_2 55..65 % MgO 25 ... 35 % Al_2O_3 2 ... 6 % Alk. oxide < 1.5 %	2.6 ... 2.9	120 ... 140	850 ... 1000	80 ... 100	7.0 ... 9.0	2.3 ... 2.8	0.7 ... 0.9	> 10¹¹	6	10...20
Titanium carbide	TiC	4.9	–	–	320	7.4	30	–	7 · 10⁻⁵	–	–
Titanium dioxide	TiO_2	3.5 ... 3.9	90 ... 120	300	–	6.0 ... 8.0	3 ... 4	0.7 ... 0.9	–	40 ... 100	8
Titanium nitride	TiN	5.4	–	–	260	9.4	40	–	3 · 10⁻⁵	–	–
Zirconium dioxide partially stabilized, PSZ	ZrO_2 > 90 % Rest Y_2O_3	5.7 ... 6.0	500 ... 1000	1800 ... 2100	200	9.0 ... 11.0	2 ... 3	0.4	10⁸	–	–
Standards		DIN EN 623 Part 2	DIN EN 843 Part 1	pr EN 993 Part 5	DIN EN 843 Part 2	DIN EN 821 Part 1	DIN EN 821 Part 2	DIN EN 821 Part 3	DIN VDE 0335 Parts 2 and 3		

The characteristic values for each material can vary widely, depending on raw material, composition and manufacturing process. The material data relate to the information provided by various manufacturers.
The designation "KER" corresponds to DIN EN 60 672-1.

[1] Density.
[2] Flexing strength.
[3] Cold compressive strength.
[4] Modulus of elasticity.
[5] Coefficient of thermal expansion RT ... 1000 °C.

[6] Thermal conductivity at 20 °C.
[7] Specific heat.
[8] Specific electrical resistivity at 20 °C and 50 Hz.
[9] Relative permittivity.
[10] Dielectric loss factor at 25 °C and 10 MHz.

Laminates

Type	Type of resin	Filler	ϑ_G[1] °C	σ_{bB}[2] min. N/mm²	$a_{k\,10}$[3] min. kJ/m²	CTI[4] min. grade	Properties, applications
Paper-base laminates (DIN 7735, Part 2 / VDE 0318, Part 2)							
Hp 2061	Phenolic resin	Paper web	120	150	5	CTI 100	For mechanical loading.
Hp 2063	Phenolic resin	Paper web	120	80	2.5	CTI 100	For electrical loading; base material FR 2 for printed-circuit boards.
Hp 2262	Melamine resin	Paper web	90	100	–	CTI 600	Particularly resistant to tracking; decorative laminates.
Hp 2361.1	Epoxy resin	Paper web	90	120	2	CTI 100	Good electrical and mechanical properties; flame-resistant; base material FR 3 for printed-circuit boards.
Fabric-base laminates (DIN 7735, Part 2 / VDE 0318, Part 2)							
Hgw 2072	Phenolic resin	Glass-fiber fabric	130	200	40	CTI 100	High mechanical, electrical and thermal strength.
Hgw 2082	Phenolic resin	Fine-weave cotton fabric	110	130	10	CTI 100	Good workability, good sliding and wear behavior; especially good material for gears and bearings.
Hgw 2083	Phenolic resin	Superfine-weave cotton fabric	110	150	12	CTI 100	
Hgw 2372.1	Epoxy resin	Glass-fiber fabric	120	350	50	CTI 200	Optimum mechanical and electrical properties; base material FR 4 for printed-circuit boards.
Hgw 2572	Silicone resin	Glass-fiber fabric	180	125	25	CTI 400	For high service temperature.
Glass-mat-base laminates (DIN 7735, Part 2 / VDE 0318, Part 2)							
Hm 2472	Unsaturated polyester resin	Glass-fiber mat	130	200	60	CTI 500	Good mechanical and electrical properties, particularly resistant to tracking.

[1] Limit temperature according to VDE 0304, Part 2, for service life of 25,000 h.
[2] Flexural strength according to DIN 53 452.
[3] Notched impact strength in accordance with DIN 53 453.
[4] Tracking resistance according to DIN IEC 112, Comparative Tracking Index (CTI).

Plastic molding compounds

Thermoplastics (Selection from DIN 7740 ... 7749; DIN 16 771; DIN 16 781)

Chemical name	Material code (ISO 1043¹) DIN 7728)	t_G[1] °C	E[2] N/mm²	a_{kn}[3] min. kJ/m²	Resistance at 20° to[4] Gasoline	Benzene	Diesel fuel	Alcohol	Mineral oil	Properties, applications
Acrylnitrile-butadien-styrene	ABS	80	2000	5 ... 15	0	−	×		+	High gloss, some types transparent; tough housings.
Fluorinated hydrocarbons	FEP PFA	250/205 260	600 650	6) 6)	+ +	+ +	+ +	+ +	+ +	Extreme reduction in rigidity as temperature increases, resistant to chemicals; used for coatings, sliding parts and seals.
Polyamide 11, 12	PA 11, 12	140/120	1500	20 ... 40	+	+	+	0	+	Tough, hard and resistant to abrasion, low coefficient of friction, good attenuation of sound, approx. 1 ... 3% water absorption required for good toughness. PA 11/12 have much lower water absorption.
Polyamide 6	PA 6	170/120	2500	40 ... 90	+	+	+	×	+	
Polyamide 66	PA 66	190/120	2800	10 ... 20	+	+	+	×	+	
Polyamide 6 + GF⁵)	PA 6-GF	190/120	5000	8 ... 14	+	+	+	×	+	Impact-resistant machine housings.
Polyamide 66 + GF⁵)	PA 66-GF	200/120	6000	6 ... 12	+	+	+	×	+	
Polyamide 6T/6I/66 + GF45	PA 6T/6I/66 + GF45	285/185	14 000	8 ... 12	+	+	+	×	+	Rigid machine housings/components, remains rigid at elevated temperatures (engine-bay components). Lower water absorption than standard PA.
Polyamide 6/6T + GF⁵)	PA6/6T-GF	250/170	10 000	6 ... 12	+	+	+	×	+	
Polyamide MXD6 + GF50	PA MXD6 +GF50	240/170	15 000	8 ... 12	+	+	+	×	+	
Polybutylene terephthalate	PBT	160/120	1700	2 ... 4	+	+	+	+	+	Wear-resistant, chemically resistant, rigidity decreases above 60 °C, hydrolysis above 70 °C.
Polybutylene terephthalate + GF⁵)	PBT-GF	180/120	5000	5 ... 9	+	+	+	+	+	Higher rigidity than PBT without GF.
Polycarbonate	PC	130/125	2500	20 ... 30	+	−	+	0	+	Tough and rigid over wide temperature range, transparent.
Polycarbonate + GF⁵)	PC-GF	130	4500	6 ... 15	+	−	+	0	+	Very rigid structural parts.
Polyethylene	PE	80	1000	6)	×	0	+	+	+	Acid-resistant containers and pipes, films.

Material	Abbr.	Max. service temp.[1]	Modulus of elasticity[2]	Notched impact strength[3]								Properties / Applications
Polyethylene terephthalate	PET	180/120	2000	2 … 7	+	+	+	+	+	-	+	Wear-resistant, chemically resistant, rigidity decreases above 60 °C, hydrolysis above 70 °C in water.
Cyclo-olefine copolymers	COC	160	3000	1.7 … 2	+	+	-	-	-	+	-	Highly transparent, weatherproof.
Liquid crystal polymers + GF[5]	LCP-GF	300/240	15000	8 … 16	+	+	+	+	+	+	+	Highly resistant to thermal deformation, high impact strength, low bond strength, for extremely thin-walled components.
Polyethersulfon + GF[5]	PES-GF	220/180	9000	6 … 10	+	0	0	0	+	+	+	High continuous service temperature, temperature has no more than a minor influence on properties.
Polyether etherketon + GF[5]	PEEK	320/250	9000	6.5 … 10	+	+	+	+	+	+	+	High-strength components for high temperatures, good sliding characteristics and low wear.
Polyethylene terephthalate + GF[5]	PET-GF	200/120	7000	5 … 12	+	+	+	+	+	+	+	Higher rigidity than PETP without GF.
Polymethylmethacrylate	PMMA	80	3000	1.5 … 2.5	+	+	x	-	0	0	+	Transparent and in all colors, weatherproof; diffusers, lenses.
Polyoxymethylene	POM	125/120	2000	5 … 7	+	+	0	0	+	+	+	Sensitive to acid-induced stress cracking; precision moldings.
Polyoxymethylene + GF	POM-GF	140/120	6000	3 … 5	+	+	0	0	+	+	+	Resistant to hot water, flame-retardant.
Polyphenylene ether + SB[7]	PPE+S/B	120/100	2500	4 … 14	0	0	-	0	0	0	+	High resistance to heat, inherently flame-retarding; for engine-bay components.
Polyphenylene sulfide + GF 40	PPS-GF	270/240	13000	4 … 7	+	+	+	+	+	+	+	Household articles, battery cases, cover hoods.
Polypropylene	PP	130/110	1500	6 … 10	x	0	0	0	x	x	+	Fan impellers.
Polypropylene + GF[5]	PP-GF	130/110	4000	4 … 8	x	0	0	0	x	x	+	Molded parts; transparent and coated in all colors.
Polystyrene	PS	80	2500	2 … 3	-	-	-	-	0	0	x	Molded parts; transparent and coated in all colors.
Polyvinyl chloride, plasticized	PVC-P	80/70	200	6)[6]	-	0	-	-	0	0	+	Artificial leather, flexible caps, cable insulation, tubing and hosing, seals.
Polyvinyl chloride, unplasticized	PVC-U	70/60	3000	2 … 30	+	+	-	-	+	+	+	Weatherproof exterior parts, pipes, parts for galvanotechnical equipment.

[1] Maximum service temperature, short term (1 h)/long-term (5000 h).
[2] Modulus of elasticity, approx. standard values.
[3] Notched impact strength in accordance with DIN 53 453.
[2] + [3] Polyamides, saturated by air humidity at 23 °C and 50 % rel. humidity
[4] + good resistance, x limited resistance, 0 low resistance, - no resistance.
[5] GF Glass fiber (25 … 35 % by weight).
[6] No fracture.
[7] Polymer mixture of polyphenylene ether and styrene/butadiene.

Chemical name	Material code (ISO 1043/ DIN 7728)	t_G[1] °C	E[2] N/mm²	a_{k10}[3] min. kJ/m²	Resistance at 20° to[4]					Properties, applications
					Gas-oline	Ben-zene	Die-sel fuel	Alco-hol	Mi-ne-ral oil	
Styrene-acrylonitrile	SAN	90	3000	1.5 … 2.5	0	–	×	0	+	Molded parts, good chem. resistance, also transp.
Styrene-butadiene	S/B	60	1500	4 … 14	–	–	–	×	+	Tough housings for many applications.
Non-cross-linked plastics which can be processed only by molding and sintering:										
Polyimide	PI	320/290	3100	2	+	+	+	+	+	High resistance to heat and radiation, hard.
Polytetrafluorethylene	PTFE	300/240	400	13 … 15	+	+	+	+	+	Extreme reduction in rigidity as temp. rises, high resistance to heat, aging and chemicals, low coefficient of friction; for sliding parts.

[1] Maximum service temperature, short term (1 h)/long-term (5000 h).
[2] Modulus of elasticity, approx. standard values.
[3] Notched impact strength in accordance with DIN 53 453.

[2] + [3] Polyamides, saturated by air humidity at 23 °C and 50 % rel. humidity
[4] + good resistance, × limited resistance, 0 low resistance, – no resistance.

Thermosetting plastics (selection from DIN 7708, 16 911, 16 912)

Type	Type of resin	Filler	t_G[1] °C	σ_{bB}[2] min. N/mm²	a_n[3] min. kJ/m²	CTI[4] min. grade	Properties, applications
11.5	Phenol	Rock flour	200/170	50	3.5	CTI 150	For parts subject to thermal loading, high resistance to glow heat, good heat dissipation, little dimensional change in humid atmosphere. Good electrical properties for types 11.5 and 13.5.
13.5[13]		Mica	200/170	50	3.0	CTI 150	
31 and 31.5		Wood flour	160/140	70	6	CTI 125	Types 30.5 and 31.5 for parts with high electrical loads.

[1] Maximum service temperature, short-term (100 h)/continuous (20,000 h).
[2] Flexing strength.
[3] Impact strength.

[4] Tracking resistance according to DIN IEC 112 method for determining Comparative Tracking Index (CTI).
[13] Not used in new parts (asbestos ban).

Thermosetting plastics (selection from DIN 7708, 16 911, 16 912)

Type	Type of resin	Filler	$t_G^{1)}$ °C	$\sigma_{bB}^{2)}$ min. N/mm²	$a_n^{3)}$ min. kJ/m²	$CTI^{4)}$ min. grade	Properties, applications
51	Phenol	Cellulose[5]	160/140	60	5	CTI 150	Somewhat greater water absorption than types 11 ... 16. For parts with good insulating properties in low-voltage range. Type 74 has high impact strength.
71		Cotton fibers[5]	160/140	60	6	CTI 150	
74		Cotton fabric shreds[5]	160/140	60	12	CTI 150	
83		Cotton fibers[6]	160/140	60	5	CTI 150	Tougher than type 31.
–		Glass fibers, short	220/180	110	6	CTI 150	High mechanical strength, resistant to glow heat.
–		Glass fibers, long	200/180	120	7.5	CTI 150	
150	Melamine	Wood flour	160/140	70	6	CTI 600	Resistant to glow heat, high-grade electrical properties, high shrinkage factor.
181	Melamine-phenol	Cellulose	160/140	80	7	CTI 250	For parts subject to electrical and mechanical loads.
801 and 803	Polyester	Glass fibers, inorganic fillers	220/170	60	22	CTI 600	Types 801, 804: low molding pressure (large-area parts manufacture); types 803, 804 glow-heat resistant.
802 and 804		Glass fibers, inorganic fillers	220/170	55	4.5	CTI 600	
870	Epoxy	Rock flour	240/200	50	5	CTI 500	Types 870 and 871 as low-pressure plastics for encapsulating metal parts and electronic components. Low softening temperatures, low shrinkage factor.
871		Glass fibers, short	230/200	80	8	CTI 500	
872		Glass fibers, long	220/190	90	15	CTI 500	
–	Silicone	Glass fibers, short	340/180	55	2	CTI 600	High temperature resistance, high-grade electrical properties.

[1] Maximum service temperature, short-term (100 h)/continuous (20,000 h).
[2] Flexing strength.
[3] Impact strength.
[4] Tracking resistance according to DIN IEC 112 method for determining Comparative Tracking Index (CTI).
[5] With or without addition of other organic fillers.
[6] And/or wood flour.

Rubbers

Material	Code[7]	Range of application[8] °C	Shore A hardness	Tensile strength[9] N/mm²	Ultimate elongation[9] %	Resistance to[11] Weathering/Ozone	Gasoline	Diesel fuel	Mineral oil	HF[12] A	HF[12] B	HF[12] C	HF[12] D
Polyacrylate rubber	ACM	−20 ... +150	55 ... 90	5 ... 13	100 ... 350	×	–	×	+	+	×	×	–
Acrylonitrile butadiene rubber	NBR	−30 ... +120	35 ... 100	10 ... 25	100 ... 700	–[10]	×	×	+	×	×	+	–
Butyl rubber	IIR	−40 ... +125	40 ... 85	7 ... 17	300 ... 600	×[10]	–	–	–	–	–	+	×
Chloroprene rubber	CR	−40 ... +110	20 ... 90	7 ... 25	100 ... 800	×[10]	×	×	×	0	0	+	–
Chlorinated polyethylene	CM	−30 ... +140	50 ... 95	10 ... 20	100 ... 700	×	0	0	0	×	×	+	–
Chlorosulfonated polyethylene	CSM	−30 ... +140	50 ... 85	15 ... 25	200 ... 500	+	–	0	0	×	×	+	–
Epichlorohydrin rubber	ECO	−40 ... +135	50 ... 90	6 ... 15	150 ... 500	+	×	×	+	×	×	–	–
Ethylene acrylate rubber	EAM	−40 ... +185	50 ... 75	7 ... 14	200 ... 500	+	0	0	0	+	×	×	–
Ethylene propylene rubber	EPDM	−50 ... +150	20 ... 85	7 ... 17	150 ... 500	+	–	–	–	–	+	+	+
Fluorcarbon rubber	FKM	−25 ... +250	40 ... 90	7 ... 17	100 ... 350	+	+	+	+	+	+	–	+
Fluorsilicon rubber	FMQ	−60 ... +200	40 ... 70	4 ... 9	100 ... 400	+	×	+	+	+	+	–	+
Hydrogenated nitrile rubber	HNBR	−20 ... +150	45 ... 90	15 ... 35	100 ... 600	0[10]	×	+	+	+	+	+	–
Natural rubber	NR	−55 ... +90	20 ... 100	15 ... 30	100 ... 800	–[10]	–	–	–	–	–	–	–
Polyurethane elastomer	AU EU	−25 ... +80	50 ... 98	20 ... 50	300 ... 700	×	–	0	+	+	–	–	–
Silicone rubber	VMQ	−60 ... +200	20 ... 80	4 ... 9	100 ... 400	+	–	0	×	×	+	+	+
Styrene butadiene rubber	SBR	−50 ... +110	30 ... 100	7 ... 30	100 ... 800	–[10]	–	–	–	–	–	+	–

7) DIN ISO 1629.
8) Not continuous-service temperature.
9) Depending upon composition of compound.
10) Can be improved by adding protective agents.
11) + good resistance, × limited resistance, 0 low resistance, – no resistance.
12) A oil-in-water emulsion; B water-in-oil emulsion; C polyglycol-water solution; D synthetic liquids.

Material	Code[7]	Range of application[8] °C	Shore A hardness (D)	Tensile strength[9] N/mm²	Ultimate elongation[9] %	Resistance to[11] Weathering	Ozone	Gasoline	Diesel fuel	Mineral oil
Thermoplastic elastomers										
Blend/olefin with non-linked to fully cross-linked rubber	TPE-O[14]	– 40 ... + 100 (120)	45A ... 50D	3 ... 15	250 ... 600	+	+	0	0	0
Blend/styrene block polymers	TPE-S[14]	– 60 ... + 60 (100)	30A ... 90A	3 ... 12	500 ... 900	+	+	–	–	–
Polyester elastomer	TPE-E[14]	– 50 ... + 150	40D ... 80D	9 ... 47	240 ... 800	0[10]	×	×	+	+
Polyester urethane	TPE-U[14]	– 40 ... + 100	70A ... 70D	15 ... 55	250 ... 600	0[10]	+	0	×	+
Polyetherblockamide	TPE-A[14]	– 40 ... + 80	75A ... 70D	30 ... 60	300 ... 500	0[10]	+	×	+	×

[7] DIN ISO 1629.
[8] Not continuous-service temperature.
[9] Depending upon composition of compound.
[10] Can be improved by adding protective agents.
[11] + good resistance, × limited resistance, 0 low resistance, – no resistance.
[14] No ISO standard to date.

Plastics abbreviations with chemical names and trade names[3])

Code	Chemical name	Trade names
ABS	Acrylonitrile butadiene styrene	Cycolac, Novodur, Ronfalin, Terluran
ACM	Polyacrylate rubber	Cyanacryl, Hycar
EAM[1])	Ethylene acrylate rubber	Vamac
APE[1])	Ethylene propylene rubber	Arylef, APEC
ASA	Acrylate styrene acrylonitrile	Luran S
AU	Polyurethane elastomers	Urepan
CA	Cellulose acetate	Bergacell, Tenite
CAB	Cellulose acetate butyrate	Cellidor, Tenite
CM	Chlorinated polyethylene	Bayer CM, CPE
CR	Chloroprene rubber	Baypren, Neoprene
CSM	Chlorosulfonated polyethylene	Hypalon
ECO	Epichlorohydrin rubber	Herclor, Hydrin
EP	Epoxy	Araldite
EPDM	Ethylene propylene rubber	Buna AP, Dutral, Keltan, Nordel, Vistalon
EU	Polyurethane elastomers	Adiprene C
FPM	Fluorocarbon rubber	DAI-EL, Fluorel, Tecnoflon, Viton
HNBR[1])	Hydrogenated nitrile rubber	Therban, Zetpol
IR	Isoprene rubber	Cariflex IR, Natsyn
MF	Melamine-formaldehyde	Bakelite, Resinol, Supraplast, Resopal
MPF	Melamine/phenol-formaldehyde	Supraplast, Resiplast
MVQ	Silicone rubber	Rhodorsil, Silastic, Silopren
NBR	Nitrile butadiene rubber	Buna N, Chemigum, Hycar, Perbunan
PA 46[1])	Polyamide 46	Stanyl
PA 6-3-T	Amorphous polyamide	Trogamid T
PA 6	Polyamide 6 (polymers of ε-caprolactam)	Akulon, Durethan B, Grilon. Nivionplast, Perlon, Renyl, Sniamid, Technyl, Ultramid B, Wellamid
PA 66	Polyamide 66 (polymers of hexamethylene diamide and adipic acid)	Akulon, Durethan B, Grilon. Nivionplast, Perlon, Renyl, Sniamid, Technyl, Ultramid B, Wellamid
PA X[1])	X = partially aromatic polyamides	Ultramid T[4]), Amodel 1 ... 5[5]), Amodel 4 ... 6[6]), Grivory GV[7]), Grivory HTV[8]), Zytel HTN[9]), IXEF[10])
PA 11	Polyamide 11 (polymers of 11-aminoundecanoic acid)	Rilsan B
PA 12	Polyamide 12 (polymers of dodecalactam)	Grilamid, Rilsan A, Vestamid
PAI	Polyamide imide	Torlon
PAN	Polyacrylonitrile	Dralon, Orlon
PBTP	Polybutylene terephthalate	Crastin, Pocan, Ultradur, Vestodur, Celanex
PC	Polycarbonate	Makrolon, Orgalan, Sinvet, Lexan
PA 612	Polyamide 612 (polymers of hexamethylene diamine and dodecanoic acid)	Zytel
COC[1])	Cyclo-olefin copolymers	Topas
LCP	Liquid crystal polymers	Vectra, Zenite
PA 6/66	Copolyamide 6/66	Ultramid C, Technyl, Grilon TSV
SPS[1])	Syndiotactic polystyrene	Questra, Xarec
PK[1])	Polyketon	Carilon

Code	Chemical name	Trade names
LFT [1]	Long-fiber reinforced thermoplastic	Celstran
(PC + ABS)	Blend of polycarbonate + ABS	Bayblend, Cycoloy
(PC + ASA)	Blend of polycarbonate + ASA	Terblend S
(PC-PBT)	Blend of polycarbonate + PBT	Xenoy
PE	Polyethylene	Hostalen, Lupolen, Stamylan, Vestolen
PEEK	Polyether ether ketone	Victrex "PEEK"
PEI	Polyether imide	Ultem
PES	Polyether sulphone	Victrex "PES", Ultrason E
PETFE [1]	Ethylene tetrafluorethylene copolymer	Hostaflon ET, Tefzel
PETP	Polyethylene terephthalate	Arnite, Crastin, Mylar, Rynite, Impet
PF	Phenol-formaldehyde	Bakelite, Supraplast, Vyncolite
PFA	Perfluoralkoxyethylene	Teflon PFA
PFEP [1]	Fluorinated ethylene-propylene copolymer	Teflon FEP
PI	Polyimide	Kapton, Kerimid, Kinel, Vespel
PMMA	Polymethyl methacrylate	Degalan, Diakon, Lucryl, Perspex, Plexiglas, Vedril
POM	Polyoxymethylene, polyformaldehyde (a polyacetal)	Delrin, Hostaform, Ultraform
PP	Polypropylene	Daplen, Hostalen PP, Moplen Stamylan P, Starpylen, Vestolen
(PPE + SB)	Blend of polyphenylene ether + SB	Noryl, Luranyl
(PPE + PA)	Blend of polyphenylene ether + PA	Noryl GTX, Ultranyl, Vestoblend
PPS	Polyphenylene sulfide	Fortron, Ryton, Tedur
PS	Polystyrene	Edistir, Hostyren, Lustrex
PSU	Polysulphone	Udel, Ultrason S
PTFE	Polytetrafluorethylene	Fluon, Hostaflon, Teflon
PUR	Polyurethane	Lycra, Vulkollan
PVC-P	Polyvinyl chloride, plasticized	Trosiplast, Vestolit, Vinoflex
PVC-U	Polyvinyl chloride, unplasticized	Trovidur, Hostalit, Vinidur, Vestolid
PVDF	Polyvinylidene fluoride	Dyflor, Kynar, Solef
PVF	Polyvinyl fluoride	Tedlar
SAN	Styrene acrylnitrile	Kostil, Luran, Tyril
SB	Styrene butadiene	Hostyren, Lustrex
SBR	Styrene butadiene rubber	Buna Hüls, Buna S, Cariflex S
TPE-A [1]	Polyether blockamide	Pebax, Vestamid E
TPE-E [1]	TPE [2] polyester base	Arnitel, Hytrel, Riteflex
TPE-O [1]	TPE [2] olefin base	Leraflex, Santoprene
TPE-S [1]	TPE [2] styrene base	Cariflex, Evoprene, Kraton
TPE-11 [1]	Polyester urethane	Desmopan, Elastollan
UF	Urea-formaldehyde	Bakelite, Pollopas
UP	Unsaturated polyester	Keripol, Leguval, Palatal

---

[1] Material code not yet standardized. [2] TPE: Thermoplastic rubber.
[3] ISO 1043/DIN 7728 (Thermoplastics, thermosetting plastics), ISO 1629 (Rubbers).
Material codes [4] PA 6/6T [8] PA 6I/6T
[4] – [10] are standardized [5] PA 6T/6I/66 [9] PA 6T/MPMDT
 [6] PA 6T/66 [10] PA MXD 6
 [7] PA 66 + PA 6I/6T

Automotive paints, structure of solid-color coatings

Layer	Layer thickness in μm	Structure	Composition					Application
			Binders	Solvents	Pigments	Extenders	Additives and SC	
1	20...25	KTL	Epoxy resins Polyurethane	Water, small amounts of water-miscible organic solvents	Anorganic (organic)	Anorganic extenders	Surface-active substances, anti-crater agents, 20% SC	ET
2a	approx. 35	Primer	Polyester, melamine, urea & epoxy resins	Aromatic compounds, alcohols	Anorganic and organic	Anorganic solids	e.g. wetting agents, surface-active substances 58...62% SC	PZ ESTA-HR
2b	approx. 35	Water extender	Water-soluble polyester, polyurethane & melamine resins	Water, small amounts of water-miscible organic solvents			43...50% SC	PZ ESTA-HR
2c	approx. 20	Thin-film water extender	Water-soluble polyurethane & melamine resins	Water, small amounts of water-miscible organic solvents		Anorganic extenders	e.g. wetting agents, surface-active substances 32...45% SC	PZ ESTA-HR
3a	40...50	Solid-color top coat	Alkyd & melamine resins	Esters, aromatic compounds, alcohols		–	e.g. leveling & wetting agents	PZ ESTA-HR
3b	10...35 (color-specific)	Water-borne solid-color base coat	Water-soluble polyester, polyurethane, polyacrylate & melamine resins	Small amounts of water-miscible co-solvents		–	Wetting agents 20...40% SC	PZ ESTA-HR
4a	40...50	Conventional clear coat	Acrylic & melamine resins	Aromatic compounds, alcohols, esters	–	–	e.g. leveling agents and light stabilizers 45% SC	PZ ESTA-HR
4b	40...50	2C-HS	HS acrylate resin polyisocyanates	Esters, aromatic compounds	–	–	e.g. leveling agents and light stabilizers 58% SC	
4c	40...50	Powder-slurry clear coat	Urethane-modified epoxy/carboxy system	–	–	–	e.g. light stabilizers 38% SC	

Structure of metallic coatings

Layer	Layer thickness in μm	Structure	Binders	Composition			Additives and SC	Application
				Solvents	Pigments	Extenders		
1	20...25	KTL	Epoxy resin polyurethane	Water, small amounts of water-miscible organic solvents	Anorganic (organic)	Anorganic extenders	Surface-active substances, anti-crater agents, 20% SC	ET
2a	approx. 35	Extender melamine, urea & epoxy resins	Polyester, alcohols	Aromatic compounds, alcohols	Anorganic and organic	Anorganic extenders	e.g. wetting agents, surface-active substances 58...62% SC	PZ ESTA-HR
2b	approx. 35	Water extender	Water-soluble polyester, polyurethane & melamine resins	Water, small amounts of water-miscible organic solvents			43...50% SC	PZ ESTA-HR
2c	approx. 20	Thin-film water extender		Water, small amounts of water-miscible organic solvents			e.g. wetting agents, surface-active substances 32...45% SC	PZ ESTA-HR
3a	10...15	Metallic base coat		Esters, aromatic compounds	Aluminum particles, mica particles	–	15...30% SC	PZ ESTA-HR
3b	10...15	Water-soluble metallic base coat	Water-soluble polyester, polyurethane, polyacrylate & melamine resins	Small amounts of water-miscible co-solvents	Aluminum and mica particles organic and anorganic pigments	–	Wetting agent	PZ ESTA-HR
4a	40...50	Conventional clear coat	Acrylic & melamine resins	Aromatic compounds, alcohols, esters	–	–	e.g. leveling agents and light stabilizers 45% SC	PZ ESTA-HR
4b	40...50	2C-HS	HS acrylate resin, polyisocyanates	Esters, aromatic compounds	–	–	e.g. leveling agents and light stabilizers 58% SC	PZ ESTA-HR
4c	40...50	Powder-slurry clear coat	Urethane-modified epoxy/carboxy system	–	–	–	e.g. light stabilizers 38% SC	PZ ESTA-HR

Acronyms: DS High film build, ESTA-HR Electrostatic high rotation, ET Electrophoretic coating, SC (FK) Solids content or non-volatiles, KTL Cathodic deposition, PZ Pneumatic spray, 2C-HS 2-component high-solid (high levels of non-volatile matter).

Lubricants

Terms and definitions

Lubricants provide mutual insulation for components in a state of relative motion. The lubricant's function is to prevent direct contact between these components, thereby reducing wear and minimizing, or optimizing, friction. Lubricants serve as coolants, sealants and corrosion inhibitors, and can also reduce operating noise. The lubricant can be solid, consistent, liquid or gaseous in form. Specific lubricants are selected with reference to design characteristics, materials combinations, the operating environment and the stress factors encountered at the friction surface.

Additives
Additives are substances mixed into the lubricant in order to improve specific properties. These substances modify either the lubricant's physical characteristics (e.g. viscosity index improvers, pour-point depressors) or its chemical properties (e.g. oxidation inhibitors, corrosion inhibitors). In addition, the properties of the friction surfaces themselves can be modified with additives which change the friction characteristics (friction modifiers), protect against wear (anti-wear agents), or provide protection against scoring and seizure (extreme-pressure additives). Great care must be exercised in order to ensure that the additives are correctly matched with each other and with the base lubricant.

AFC (Anti-Friction-Coating)
Solid lubricant combinations which a binding agent holds in place on the friction faces.

ATF (Automatic Transmission Fluid)
Special-purpose lubricants specifically formulated to meet stringent requirements for operation in automatic transmissions.

Ash (DIN 51575, 51803)
The mineral residue which remains after oxide and sulfate incineration.

Bingham bodies
Materials whose flow characteristics differ from those of Newtonian liquids.

Bleeding (Oil separation, DIN 51817)
Separation of the base oil and the thickener in a lubricating grease.

Cloud point (DIN ISO 3015)
The temperature at which mineral oil becomes opaque due to the formation of paraffin crystals or precipitation of other solids.

Consistency (DIN ISO 2137)
A measure of the ease with which lubricating greases and pastes can be deformed.

Doped lubricants
Lubricants containing additives for improving specific properties (e.g. aging stability, wear protection, corrosion protection, viscosity-temperature characteristics).

Dropping point (DIN ISO 2176)
Temperature at which a lubricating grease attains a specified viscosity under defined conditions.

EP Lubricants (Extreme Pressure)
See high-pressure lubricants.

Fire point/flash point (DIN ISO 2592)
The lowest temperature (referred to 1013 hPa) at which a gaseous mineral product initially flashes (fire point), or continues to burn for at least 5 secs (burning point).

Flow pressure (DIN 51805)
According to Kesternich, the gas pressure required to press a consistent lubricant through a standardized test nozzle. The flow pressure is an index of a lubricant's starting flow characteristics, particularly at low temperatures.

Friction modifiers
Polar lubricant additives which reduce friction in the mixed-friction range and increase bearing capacity after adsorption on the surface of the metal. They also inhibit stick-slip behavior.

Gel-type greases
Lubricants with inorganic gelling agents (e.g. Bentonites, Aerosiles, silica gels).

Graphite
Solid lubricant with layer-lattice structure. Graphite provides excellent lubrication when combined with water (e.g. high atmospheric humidity) and in carbon-dioxide atmospheres or when combined with oils. It does not inhibit friction in a vacuum.

High-pressure lubricants
Contain additives to enhance load-bearing capacity, to reduce wear and to reduce scoring (generally provide good performance in steel-to-steel and steel-to-ceramic applications).

Induction period
The period which elapses before substantial changes occur in a lubricant (e.g. aging of an oil containing an oxidation inhibitor).

Inhibitors
Lubricant protection additives (e.g. oxidation and corrosion inhibitors).

Low-temperature sludge
Products of oil degradation which form in the engine crankcase due to incomplete combustion and condensation at low engine load. Low-temperature sludge increases wear and can cause engine damage. Modern high-quality engine oils inhibit its formation.

Metal soaps
Reaction products from metals or from their compounds with fatty acids. They are used as thickeners for grease and as friction modifiers.

Mineral oils
Mineral oils are distillates or raffinates produced from petroleum or coal. They consist of numerous hydrocarbons in various chemical combinations. Classification is according to the predominant component: paraffin-based oils (chain-shaped saturated hydrocarbons), naphthene-based oils (closed-chain saturated hydrocarbons, generally with 5 or 6 carbon atoms per ring) or aromatic oils (e.g. alkylbenzene). These substances are distinguished by major variations in their respective chemical and physical properties.

Molybdenum disulfide (MoS_2)
A solid lubricant with layer-lattice structure. Only low cohesive forces are present between the individual layers, so their mutual displacement is characterized by relatively low shear forces. A reduction in friction is only obtained when MoS_2 is applied in suitable form to the surface of the metal (e.g. in combination with a binder such as (MoS_2 anti-friction coating).

Multigrade oils
Engine and transmission oils with good resistance to viscosity-temperature change (high viscosity index VI). These oils are formulated for year-round use in motor vehicles; their viscosity ratings extend through several SAE grades.

Penetration (DIN ISO 2137)
Depth (in 10^{-1} mm) to which a standardized cone penetrates into a consistent lubricant within a defined period and at a specified temperature. The larger the number, the softer the lubricant.

Polar substances
Dipolar molecules are easily adsorbed onto metal surfaces. They enhance adhesion and bearing capacity, thus reducing friction and wear. This category includes, for example, esters, ethers, polyglycols and fatty acids.

Pour point (DIN ISO 3016)
The lowest temperature at which an oil continues to flow when cooled under defined conditions.

Rheology
Science dealing with the flow characteristics of materials. These are generally represented in the shape of flow curves.
Coordinate plotting:
Shear stress $\tau = F/A$ (N/m^2 = Pa)
  F force, A surface area
against
Shear rate $D = v/y$ (s^{-1})
(linear shear rate)
v velocity, y thickness of lubricating film.

Dynamic viscosity
$\eta = \tau/D$ (Pa $\cdot$ s)
The formerly-employed unit "centiPoise" (cP) is equal to the unit (mPa $\cdot$ s).

Kinematic viscosity
$\nu = \eta/\varrho$ (mm^2/s)
ϱ density (kg/m^3).
The formerly-employed unit "centiStokes" (cSt) is equal to the unit (mm^2/s).

Newtonian fluids
These display a linear relationship between τ and D in the shape of a straight line through zero, with the slope increasing as a function of viscosity.

All materials not characterized by this kind of flow behavior are classified as non-Newtonian fluids.

Intrinsically viscous flow behavior
Decrease in viscosity with increasing shear rate (e.g. liquid grease, multigrade oil with VI improvers).

Dilatant flow behavior
Increase in viscosity with increasing shear rate.

Plastic flow behavior
Formability of an intrinsically viscous fluid supplemented by yield value (e.g. lubricating greases).

Thixotropy
A characteristic of those non-Newtonian fluids that display an increase in viscosity proportional to shear time, and only gradually recover their original viscosity once shearing ceases.

Rheopexy
A characteristic of those non-Newtonian fluids that display a reduction in viscosity proportional to shear time, and only gradually recover their original viscosity once shearing ceases.

Stribeck curve
Portrays friction levels between two liquid- or grease-lubricated bodies separated by a narrowing gap (e.g. lubricated plain or roller bearings) as a function of sliding speed.

Solid-body friction
The height of the lubricant layer is lower than that of the roughness protrusions in the material's surface.

Mixed friction
The height of the lubricant layer is approximately equal to that of the roughness protrusons

Hydrodynamics
Complete separation between primary and opposed body (virtually frictionless condition).

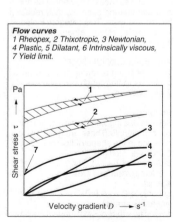

Flow curves
1 Rheopex, 2 Thixotropic, 3 Newtonian, 4 Plastic, 5 Dilatant, 6 Intrinsically viscous, 7 Yield limit.

Pa

Shear stress τ

Velocity gradient $D \longrightarrow$ s^{-1}

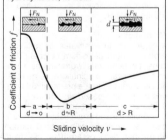

Stribeck curve
R Surface roughness, F_N Normal force, d Distance between basic and counter-body. Range a: solid friction, high wear; Range b: mixed friction, moderate wear; Range c: hydrodynamics, no wear.

Coefficient of friction f

a $d \rightarrow o$ b $d \approx R$ c $d > R$

Sliding velocity $v \longrightarrow$

Viscosity (DIN 1342, DIN 51550)
Defines the internal friction of substances. It indicates the degree of resistance (internal friction) with which the
substance's molecules oppose displacement forces (see Rheology).

Viscosity index (VI) (DIN ISO 2909)
The viscosity index VI is a mathemati-
cally-derived number expressing the
change in a mineral-oil product's viscosity
relative to its temperature. The greater the
VI, the lower the effect of temperature on
the viscosity.

Viscosity classification
Classification of oils in specific viscosity
ranges. ISO viscosity classifications
(DIN 51519, see Table 1).
SAE viscosity grades (DIN 51511,
SAE J300, DIN 51512, SAE J306c, see
Tables 2 and 3).

Yield point (DIN 13342)
The minimum shear stress at which a
substance begins to flow. Above the yield
point, the rheological characteristics of
plastic substances are the same as those
of liquids.

**Table 1. Viscosity classes for industrial
lubricating oils to ISO 3448 (DIN 51519)**

ISO viscosity class		Medium viscosity at 40 °C mm²/s	Kinematic viscosity limits at 40 °C mm²/s	
			min.	max.
ISO VG	2	2.2	1.98	2.42
ISO VG	3	3.2	2.88	3.52
ISO VG	5	4.6	4.14	5.06
ISO VG	7	6.8	6.12	7.48
ISO VG	10	10	9.00	11.0
ISO VG	15	15	13.5	16.5
ISO VG	22	22	19.8	24.2
ISO VG	32	32	28.8	35.2
ISO VG	46	46	41.4	50.6
ISO VG	68	68	61.2	74.8
ISO VG	100	100	90.0	110
ISO VG	150	150	135	165
ISO VG	220	220	198	242
ISO VG	320	320	288	352
ISO VG	460	460	414	506
ISO VG	680	680	612	748
ISO VG	1000	1000	900	1100
ISO VG	1500	1500	1350	1650

Table 2. SAE viscosity grades for engine oils/transmission lubricants (SAE J300, Dec. 95)

SAE viscosity grade	Viscosity (ASTM D 5293) mPa·s at °C max.	Limit pumping viscosity (ASTM D 4684) with no yield point mPa·s at °C max.	Kinematic viscosity (ASTM D 445) mm²/s at 100 °C		Viscosity under high shear (ASTM D 4683, CEC L-36-A-90, ASTM D 4741) mPa·s at 150 °C and 10⁶ s⁻¹ min.
			min.	max.	
0 W	3250 at −30	60000 at −40	3.8	−	−
5 W	3500 at −25	60000 at −35	3.8	−	−
10 W	3500 at −20	60000 at −30	4.1	−	−
15 W	3500 at −15	60000 at −25	5.6	−	−
20 W	4500 at −10	60000 at −20	5.6	−	−
25 W	6000 at −5	60000 at −15	9.3	−	−
20	−	−	5.6	<9.3	2.6
30	−	−	9.3	<12.5	2.9
40	−	−	12.5	<16.3	2.9 (0W−40, 5W−40, 10W−40)
40	−	−	12.5	<16.3	3.7 (15W−40, 20W−40, 25W−40, 40)
50	−	−	16.3	<21.9	3.7
60	−	−	21.9	<26.1	3.7

Table 3. SAE viscosity grades for transmission lubricants (SAE J306c, March 85)

SAE viscosity grade	Maximum temperature °C for dynamic viscosity at 150,000 mPa · s (ASTM D2983)	Kinematic viscosity mm²/s at 100 °C (ASTM D 445) min.	max.
70 W	−55	4.1	−
75 W	−40	4.1	−
80 W	−26	7.0	−
85 W	−12	11.0	−
90	−	13.5	24.0
140	−	24.0	41.0
250	−	41.0	−

Worked penetration (DIN ISO 2137)
Penetration of a grease sample after it is warmed to 25 °C and processed in a grease kneader.

Engine oils

Engine oils are employed primarily to lubricate contiguous components in relative motion within the internal-combustion engine. The oil also removes heat generated by friction, carries particles removed by friction away from the source, washes out contaminants and holds them in suspension, and protects metals against corrosion. The most common engine oils are mineral oils treated with additives (HD oils: Heavy Duty for extreme operating conditions). Higher stress-resistance requirements combined with extended oil-change intervals have led to widespread application of fully and semi-synthetic oils (e.g. hydro-crack oils). The quality of an engine oil is determined by its origin, the refining processes used on the mineral oil (except in the case of synthetic oils) and the additive composition.

Additives are classified according to their respective functions:
– Viscosity-index (VI) improvers,
– Pour-point improvers,
– Oxidation and corrosion inhibitors,
– Detergent and dispersant additives,
– Extreme-pressure (EP) additives,
– Friction modifiers,
– Anti-foaming agents.

Oil is subjected to considerable thermal and mechanical stresses in the IC engine. The data on the oils' physical properties provide information on their operating range, but are not indicative of their other performance characteristics.

There thus exist several different procedures for evaluating engine oils (see comparison of engine-oil performance categories):
– ACEA (Association des Constructeurs Européens de l'Automobile) standards, replaced the CCMC standards (Comité des Constructeurs d'Automobiles du Marché Commun) at the beginning of 1996,
– API Classification (American Petroleum Institute)
– MIL Specifications (Military),
– Manufacturer's specifications.
The approval criteria include the following:
– Sulfate-ash content,
– Zinc content,
– Engine type (diesel or spark-ignition engines, naturally-aspirated or forced-induction engines),
– Load on power-transmission components and bearings,
– Wear-protection properties,
– Oil operating temperature (in oil pan),

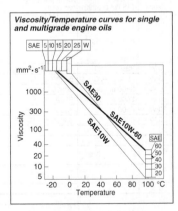

Viscosity/Temperature curves for single and multigrade engine oils

- Combustion residue and chemical stress exerted upon the oil by acidic combustion products,
- The oil's detergent and residue-scavenging properties,
- Its suitability for use with gasket and sealing materials.

ACEA (CCMC) Specifications

Engine oils for gasoline engines

A1-98: Special high-lubricity oils with reduced viscosity at high temperatures and high shear.

A2-96: Conventional and high-lubricity engine oils without any restriction on viscosity class. Higher requirements than CCMC G4 and API SH.

A3-98: Oils of this category meet higher requirements than A2-96 and CCMC G4 and G5.

Engine oils for passenger-car diesel engines

B1-98: Corresponding to A1-98 for low friction losses and, consequently, reduced fuel consumption.

B2-98: Conventional and high-lubricity engine oils compliant with the current minimum requirements (higher than those of CCMC PD2).

B3-98: Exceeds B2-98.

B4-98: Corresponds to B2-98, particularly suitable for VW TDI engines.

Engine oils for commercial-vehicle diesel engines

E1-96: Oils for naturally aspirated and turbocharged engines with normal intervals between oil changes.

E2-96: Derived from MB Specification Sheet 228.1. Primarily for engine designs predating the Euro-II standard.

E3-96: For Euro-II engines, derived from MB Specification Sheet 228.3. In comparison with the predecessor category CCMC D5, these evince a significant improvement in soot dispersion capability and a much reduced tendency to thicken.

E4-98: Currently the highest quality category for diesel engines compliant with the Euro-I and Euro-II standards and with high requirements, particularly for extended intervals between oil changes (according to manufacturer's specification). Based to a large extent on MB 228.5.

API Classifications

S Classes (Service) for gasoline engines. C Classes (Commercial) for diesel engines.

SF: For engines produced in the 80s.

SG: For engines built since 1989, with more stringent sludge test, improved oxidation stability and friction protection.

SH: Since mid-1993, corresponds to API SG quality level, but with more stringent process requirements for oil quality testing.

SJ: Since October 1996, more tests than API SH.

CC: Engine oils for non-turbocharged diesel engines with low stress factors.

CD: Engine oils for non-turbocharged and turbocharged diesels, replaced by API CF in 1994.

CD-2: API CD requirements, plus additional requirements relevant to 2-stroke diesel engines.

CF-2: Oils with special 2-stroke properties (since 1994).

CE: Oils with CD performance characteristics, with supplementary test operation in American Mack and Cummins engines.

CF: Replaced API CD in 1994. Specially for indirect injection, even if the sulfur content of the fuel is > 0.5 %.

CF-4: As API CE, but with more stringent test procedure in single-cylinder Caterpillar turbo-diesel engines.

CG-4: For diesel engines operating under very stringent conditions. Exceeds API CD and CE. Fuel sulfur < 0.5 %. Required for engines compliant with post-1994 emission-control regulations.

SAE viscosity grades

(DIN 51511, SAE J300, DIN 51512, SAE J306c)

The SAE (Society of Automotive Engineers) classifications are the internationally-accepted standard for defining viscosity. The standard provides no information on the quality of the oil. A distinction is drawn between single-grade and multigrade oils. Multigrade oils are the type in widespread use today.

Two series are employed for the designation (see Table 2) with the letter "W" (Winter) being used to define specific cold-flow properties. The viscosity grades including the letter "W" are rated according to maximum low-temperature viscosity, maximum viscosity pumping temperature and the minimum viscosity at 100 °C; viscosity grades without the "W" are rated only according to viscosity at 100 °C.

Multigrade oils
Multigrade oils are characterized by a less pronounced proportional relationship between temperature and viscosity. They reduce friction and wear, can be used all year round, and provide rapid lubrication for all engine components in cold starts.

High-lubricity oils
Lubricating oils with multigrade properties, low viscosity at low temperatures, and special anti-friction additives. Extremely low engine friction under all operating conditions reduces fuel consumption.

Transmission lubricants

Specifications for transmission lubricants are defined by the type of transmission and the stresses to which it is subjected through the entire range of operating conditions. The requirements (high pressure resistance, high viscosity stability relative to temperature, high resistance to aging, good anti-foaming properties, compatibility with gaskets and seals) can only be satisfied by lubricants treated with special additives. The use of unsuitable and qualitatively inferior oils typically results in damage to bearings and gear-tooth flanks.

The viscosity must also suit the specific application. Viscosity grades for vehicular transmissions are defined in DIN 51 512 and SAE J 306 (see Table 3).

Synthesized oils are being increasingly used to meet special requirements (e.g. poly-α-olefines). Advantages over standard mineral lubricants include superior temperature-viscosity properties and increased aging resistance.

API Classifications for transmission lubricants
GL1-GL3: Outdated, no longer of practical significance.
GL4: Transmission lubricants for moderately-stressed hypoid-gear transmissions and for transmissions which operate at extreme speeds and impact loads, high rotational speeds and low torques, or low rotational speeds and high torques.
GL5: Transmission lubricants for highly-stressed hypoid-gear transmissions in passenger cars and in other vehicles where they are exposed to impact loads at high rotational speeds, and at high rotational speeds and low torques, or low rotational speeds and high torques.
MT-1: Non-synchromeshed manual transmissions in American trucks.

Lubricants for automatic transmissions
(ATF: Automatic Transmission Fluid)
Automatic transmissions differ from their manually shifted counterparts in the way that they transfer torque; positive mechanical and hydrodynamic force transfer being supplemented by friction coupling arrangements. Thus the friction response of automatic-transmission fluids is extremely important. Applications are basically classified according to the friction characteristics:

General Motors: Superseded classifications: Type A, Suffix A, DEXRON®, DEXRON®B, DEXRON®II C, DEXRON® II D. DEXRON® II E (valid through 1994).
DEXRON® III. Valid since 1 January, 1994. Features more stringent requirements for oxidation stability and consistency in frictional coefficient.
Ford: MERCON® (valid since 1987).
Other manufacturers: In accordance with operating instructions.

Lubricating greases

Lubricating greases are thickened lubricating oils. A great advantage that greases enjoy over oil is that they do not drain from the contact location. Complicated measures designed to seal them in place are therefore unnecessary (e.g. application in wheel bearings and moving systems such as ABS, alternators, ignition distributors, windshield-wiper motors, servo motors). Table 4 provides a general overview of the components in a consistent lubricating grease as blended from three basic components – base oil, thickener and additive.

Mineral oils are usually employed as the basic oil component, although full-synthetic oils have recently become more common as a replacement (e.g. due to more stringent requirements for aging resistance, cold-flow properties, viscosity-temperature characteristics).

Thickeners are used as a binder for the base oil; metal soaps being generally employed. They bind the oil in a sponge-like soap structure (micelle) via occlusion and Van der Waals forces. The higher the proportion of thickener in the grease (depends upon the type of thickener), the greater the grease's consistency (depth of penetration of a test cone into the grease sample) and the higher the NLGI classification (see Table 5).

The additives serve to modify physical and chemical properties of the grease to achieve specific objectives (such as improvement of anti-oxidation properties, increased load capacity (EP additives), and reduction of friction and wear).

Solid lubricants (e.g. MoS_2) are also added to lubricating greases (for instance for lubricating constant-velocity joints in motor vehicles).

Specific lubricating greases are selected with reference to their physical characteristics and their effects upon the sliding surface, and to minimize interaction between the grease and the contact materials.

Example:
Mutually antagonistic effects with polymers:

– Formation of stress cracks,
– Consistency changes,
– Polymer degradation,
– Swelling, shrinkage, brittleness.

Thus, for example, mineral-oil greases and greases based on synthetic hydrocarbons should not come into contact with elastomers used together with brake fluid (polyglycol base), as this could provoke substantial swelling.

In addition, greases with varying compositions should not be mixed (changes in physical properties, grease liquefaction due to drop-point reduction).

The correct lubricating grease can substantially enhance the performance potential of products with sliding contact-surfaces (e.g. transmissions, friction and roller bearings, actuator and control systems).

Table 5. Consistency classifications for lubricating greases (DIN 51 818)

NLGI grade	Worked penetration as per DIN ISO 2137 in units (0.1 mm)
000	445 ... 475
00	400 ... 430
0	355 ... 385
1	310 ... 340
2	265 ... 295
3	220 ... 250
4	175 ... 205
5	130 ... 160
6	85 ... 150

Table 4. Composition of lubricating greases

Base oils	Thickeners	Additives
Mineral oils – Paraffinic – Naphthenic – Aromatic Poly-α-olefines Alkyl aromatics Esterols Polyalcohols Silicones Phenyletherols Perfluorpolyethers	Metal soaps (Li,Na,Ca,Ba,Al) Normal Hydroxi- Complex Polyureas PE Bentonites Silica gels	Oxidation inhibitors Fe, Cu ions, sequestering agents Corrosion inhibitors Extreme-pressure additives (EP additives) Wear-protection additives (anti-wear additives) Friction reducers (friction modifiers) Adhesion improvers Detergents, dispersants VI improvers Solid lubricants

Whatever the friction pairing, the multiplicity of lubricant components can be used to develop a high-performance lubricant.

Fuels

Characteristics

Net and gross calorific values

The specific values for the net (formerly: low) and gross (formerly: high, or combustion) calorific values, or H_u and H_o respectively, provide an index for the energy content of fuels. Only the net calorific value H_u (combustion vapor) is significant in dealing with fuels with which water is produced as a byproduct of combustion.

Oxygenates, fuel constituents which contain oxygen, such as alcohols, ether, and fatty-acid methyl ester have a lower calorific value than pure hydrocarbons, because their bound oxygen does not contribute to the combustion process. Power comparable to that achievable with conventional fuels can thus only be attained at the cost of higher consumption rates.

Calorific value of air-fuel mixture

The calorific value of the combustible air-fuel mixture determines the engine's output. Assuming a constant stoichiometric ratio, this figure remains roughly the same for all liquid gases and fuels (approx. 3500 ... 3700 kJ/m^3).

Fuels for spark-ignition engines (gasoline/petrol)

The minimum requirements for these types of fuels are contained in various national and international standards. European Standard EN228 defines the unleaded fuels which have been introduced within Europe ("Euro-Super"). DIN EN228 contains the corresponding German specifications along with supplementary descriptions of unleaded regular and super premium ("Super-Plus") fuels. In the USA, fuels for spark-ignition engines are defined in ASTM D439 (American Society for Testing and Materials). Fuels for spark-ignition engines are hydrocarbon compounds which may contain supplements in the form of oxygenous organic components or other additives to improve performance.

A distinction is made between regular and premium (super-grade) gasolines. Premium gasoline has higher anti-knock qualities and is formulated for use in high-compression engines. Volatility ratings vary according to region and whether the fuel is intended for summer or winter use.

Unleaded gasoline (EN 228)

Unleaded fuel is indispensable for vehicles equipped with catalytic converters for treating exhaust gases, as lead would damage the noble metals (e.g. platinum) in the catalytic converter and render it inoperative. It would also destroy the Lambda sensors employed to monitor exhaust gas composition for closed-loop control.

Unleaded fuels are a special mixture of high-grade, high-octane components (e.g. platformates, alkylates and isomerisates). The anti-knock qualities can be effectively increased with non-metallic additives such as methyl tertiary butyl ether (MTBE) in concentrations of 3 ... 15% and/or alcohol mixtures (methanol 2 ... 3%, and higher alcohols). As of the year 2000, the maximum lead content is limited to 5 mg/l.

Leaded gasoline

In Europe, sales of leaded gasoline are prohibited as of the year 2000, although for a transitional period it will still be available in exceptional cases.

Leaded fuel is still available in some countries, although their number is steadily decreasing.

Density

European Standard EN228 limits the fuel density range to 720 ... 775 kg/m^3. Because premium fuels generally include a higher proportion of aromatic compounds, they are denser than regular gasoline, and also have a slightly higher calorific value.

Anti-knock quality (octane rating)

The octane rating defines the gasoline's anti-knock quality (resistance to pre-ignition). The higher the octane rating, the greater the resistance to engine knock. Two differing procedures are in international use for determining the octane rat-

Table 1. Essential data for unleaded gasoline, European Standard EN 228 (valid since 1 January 2000)

Requirements	Unit	Specification
Anti-knock quality		
Premium, min.	RON/MON	95/85
Regular, min.[1]	RON/MON	91/82.5
Super Plus[1]	RON/MON	98/88
Density	kg/m³	720 ... 775
Sulfur, max.	mg/kg	150
Benzene, max.	% volume	1
Lead, max.	mg/l	5
Volatility		
Vapor pressure, summer, min./max.	kPa	45/60
Vapor pressure, winter, min./max.	kPa	60/90[1]
Evaporated vol. at 70 °C, summer, min./max.	% volume	20/48
Evaporated vol. at 70 °C, winter, min./max.	% volume	22/50
Evaporated vol. at 100 °C, min./max.	% volume	46/71
Evaporated vol. at 150 °C, min./max.	% volume	75/–
Final boiling point, max.	°C	210
VLI transitional period[3], max.[2]		1150[1]

[1]) National values for Germany, [2]) VLI = Vapor Lock Index, [3]) spring and fall.

ing; these are the Research Method and the Motor Method.

RON, MON

The number determined in testing using the Research Method is the Research Octane Number, or RON. It serves as the essential index of acceleration knock.

The Motor Octane Number, or MON, is derived from testing according to the Motor Method. The MON basically provides an indication of the tendency to knock at high speeds.

The Motor Method differs from the Research Method by using preheated mixtures, higher engine speeds and variable ignition timing, thereby placing more stringent thermal demands on the fuel under examination. MON figures are lower than those for RON.

Octane numbers up to 100 indicate the volumetric content in percent of C_8H_{18} isooctane (trimethyl pentane) contained in a mixture with C_7H_{16} n-heptane at the point where the mixture's knock-resistance in a test engine is identical to that of the fuel being tested. Iso-octane, which is extremely knock-resistant, is assigned the octane number 100 (100 RON and MON), while n-heptane, with low-resistance to pre-ignition, is assigned the number 0.

Increasing the anti-knock quality

Normal (untreated) straight-run gasoline displays little resistance to knock. Various refinery components must be added to obtain a fuel with an octane rating which is adequate for modern engines. The highest-possible octane level must also be maintained throughout the entire boiling range. Cyclic hydrocarbons (aromatics) and branched chains (iso-paraffins) provide greater knock resistance than straight-chain molecules (n-paraffins).

Additives based on oxygenous components (methanol, ethanol, methyl tertiary butyl ether (MTBE)) have a positive effect on the octane number, but can lead to difficulties in other areas (alcohols raise the volatility level and can damage fuel-system components).

Volatility

Gasolines must satisfy stringent volatility requirements to ensure satisfactory operation. The fuel must contain a large enough proportion of highly volatile components to ensure good cold starting, but the volatility must not be so high as to impair operation and starting when the engine is hot (vapor lock). In addition, environmental considerations demand that evaporative losses be held low. Volatility is defined in various ways.

EN228 defines 10 different volatility classes distinguished by various levels of vapor pressure, boiling-point curve and VLI (Vapor Lock Index). To meet special requirements stemming from variations in climatic conditions, countries can incorporate specific individual classes into their own national standards.

Boiling curve

Individual ranges on the boiling curve exercise a particularly pronounced effect on operating behavior. They can be defined according to volumetric fuel evaporation at three temperatures. The volume which evaporates up to 70 °C must be adequate to ensure good cold starting, (particularly important for old carburetor-type engines), but not so large as to promote formation of vapor bubbles when the engine is hot. The percentage of vaporized fuel at 100 °C determines the engine's warm-up qualities, as well as its acceleration and response characteristics once it has reached normal operating temperature. The vaporized volume up to 150 °C should be high enough to minimize dilution of the engine's lubricating oil, especially with the engine cold.

Vapor pressure

Fuel vapor pressure as measured at 38 °C/100 °F in accordance with prEN 13016-1 is primarily an index of the safety with which the fuel can be pumped into and out of the vehicle's tank. The Reid method is an alternative method of measuring fuel vapor pressure. All specifications place limits on this vapor pressure. Germany, for example, prescribes maxima of 60 kPa in summer and 90 kPa in winter. In the case of modern fuel-injected (EFI) engines though, when troubleshooting vapor-lock malfunctions, it is more important to know the vapor pressure at higher temperatures (80, 100 °C). Research procedures are in place, and a definitive standard is currently being prepared. Fuels to which methanol is added are characterized by a pronounced rise in vapor pressure at high temperatures.

Vapor/liquid ratio

This specification provides an index of a fuel's tendency to form vapor bubbles. It is based on the volume of vapor generated by a specific quantity of fuel at a set temperature. A drop in pressure (e.g. when driving over a mountain pass) accompanied by an increase in temperature will raise the vapor/liquid ratio and with it the probability of operating problems. ASTM D439, for example, defines specific vapor/liquid ratios for gasolines.

Vapor Lock Index (VLI)

This parameter is the sum of the Reid vapor pressure (in $kPa \times 10$), and that proportion of the fuel that vaporizes up to a temperature of 70 °C. Both components in the equation are absolute data, the latter being derived from the boiling-point curve prior to multiplication by a factor of 7. The VLI provides more useful information on the fuel's influence on starting and operating a hot engine than that supplied by conventional data.

The correlation between VLI and vapor/liquid ratio is good in the case of fuels that contain no alcohol additives.

Sulfur

Direct-injection systems for gasoline engines require fuels with a low sulfur content on account of their exhaust-emission control systems. The byproducts of sulfur combustion would render the catalytic converters inoperative. Consequently, and also on account of the target reduction in SO_2 emissions, the sulfur content of fuels will have to be further reduced in future; figures in the range < 10 ppm are desirable.

Additives

Along with the structure of the hydrocarbons (refinery components), it is the additives which determine the ultimate quality of a fuel. The packages generally used combine individual components with various attributes.

Extreme care and precision are required both when testing additives and in determining their optimal concentrations. Undesirable side-effects must be avoided. To obtain optimal results, the quantities used remain the province of the manufacturer, who can add the correct ratios in the desired concentrations when filling the tanker at the refinery. Vehicle operators should refrain from adding supplementary additives of their own.

Anti-aging additives

These agents are added to fuels to improve their stability during storage, and are particularly important when the fuel also contains cracked components. They inhibit oxidation due to atmospheric oxygen and prevent catalytic reactions with metal ions (metal deactivators).

Intake-system contamination inhibitors

The entire intake system (injectors, intake valves) must be kept free of contamination and deposits for several reasons. A clean intake tract is essential for maintaining the factory-defined A/F ratios, as well as for trouble-free operation and minimal exhaust emissions. To achieve this end, effective detergent agents should be added to the fuel.

Corrosion protection

Moisture entrained with the fuel can lead to corrosion in the fuel system. An extremely effective remedy is afforded by anti-corrosion additives designed to form a protective layer below the film of water.

Environmentally compatible gasolines

Environmental authorities and legislative bodies are imposing increasingly stringent regulations for fuels to ensure low evaporation and pollutant emissions (ecologically sound fuels, reformulated gasoline). As defined in the regulations, these fuels' salient characteristics include reduced vapor pressure along with lower levels of aromatic components, benzene and sulfur, and special specifications for the final boiling point. In the USA, additives designed to prevent deposit formation in the intake tract are also mandatory.

Diesel fuels

Diesel fuels contain a multiplicity of individual hydrocarbons with boiling points ranging from roughly 180 °C to 370 °C.

They are the product of graduated distillation of crude oil. The refineries are adding increasing amounts of conversion products to the diesel fuel; these "cracked components" are derived from heavy oil by breaking up (cracking) large molecules. Specifications for diesel fuels are defined in national standards, while European Standard EN 590 applies throughout Europe. The most important specifications in this standard are listed in Table 2.

Ignition quality, cetane number, cetane index

Because the diesel engine dispenses with an externally-supplied ignition spark, the fuel must ignite spontaneously (auto-ignition) and with minimal delay (ignition lag) when injected into the hot, compressed air in the combustion chamber. Ignition quality is an expression of the fuel's suitability for spontaneous auto-ignition in a diesel engine. The higher the cetane number, the greater the fuel's tendency to ignite. The cetane number 100 is assigned to n-hexadecane (cetane), which ignites very easily, while slow-burning methyl naphthalene is allocated the cetane number 0. The cetane number is determined using a test engine. A cetane number in excess of 50 is desirable for optimal operation in modern engines (smooth operation, emissions). High-quality diesel fuels contain a high proportion of paraffins with elevated CN ratings. Conversely, the aromatic compounds found in cracked components have a detrimental effect on ignitability.

Yet another indication of ignitabilty is provided by the cetane index, which can be calculated on the basis of density and various points on the boiling curve. In contrast to the cetane number, this index does not reflect the positive influence of "ignition enhancers" on the fuel's ignitability.

Cold-flow properties, filtration

Precipitation of paraffin crystals at low temperatures can result in fuel-filter blockage, ultimately leading to interruption of the fuel flow. Under unfavorable conditions paraffin particles can start to form at temperatures of 0 °C or even higher. Special selection and manufacturing procedures are thus necessary for winter diesel fuels in order to ensure trouble-free operation during cold seasons of the year. Normally, flow improvers are added to the fuel at the refinery. Although these do not actually prevent paraffin precipitation, they severely limit the growth of the crystals, which remain small enough to pass through the pores in the filter material. Other additives can be used to maintain the crystals in a state of suspension, extending the filtration limit downward even further.

Suitability for cold-weather operation is defined with reference to a standardized procedure for determining the "limit of filtration". This is known as the CFPP, or Cold Filter Plugging Point. European Standard EN 590 defines CFPPs for various classes. Individual classes are then selected according to the country and season (summer/winter) in which the fuel is to be used.

At one time owners frequently improved the cold response of diesel fuel by adding kerosene or regular gasoline to the contents of their vehicles' fuel tanks. Fuels conforming to modern standards have rendered this measure unnecessary, and it is no longer recommended by vehicle manufacturers.

Flash point
The flash point is the temperature at which the quantities of vapor which a combustible fluid emits into the atmosphere are sufficient to allow a spark to ignite the vapor-air mixture above the fluid. Safety considerations (transport, storage) dictate that diesel fuels must meet the requirements for Class A III (flash point $> 55\,°C$). Less than 3% gasoline in the diesel fuel is sufficient to lower the flash point to such an extent that ignition becomes possible at room temperature.

Boiling range
The boiling range affects several parameters of major importance in determining the diesel fuel's operating characteristics. Extending the boiling range downward to embrace lower temperatures improves the fuel's cold-operation properties, but at the price of a reduction in the cetane num-

ber. Particularly critical is the negative effect on the fuel's lubrication properties, with the attendant increase in the risk of wear to injection-system components. In contrast, raising the final temperature at the upper end of the boiling range, although desirable from the standpoint of efficient utilization of petroleum resources, also results in higher soot emissions as well as carbon deposits (combustion residue) in the injection nozzles.

Density
There is a reasonably constant correspondence between a diesel fuel's calorific value and its density; higher densities have a higher calorific value. Assuming constant injection-pump settings (and thus constant injection volume), the use of fuels with widely differing densities in a given system will be accompanied by variations in mixture ratios stemming from fluctuations in calorific value. Higher densities provoke increased particulate emissions, while lower densities lead to reductions in engine output.

Viscosity
Leakage losses in the injection pump result if viscosity is too low, and this in turn results in lower power, while on the other hand high viscosity has a detrimental effect on fuel atomization. The viscosity of diesel fuels, therefore, is limited to a narrow bandwidth.

Lubricity
The hydrodynamic lubricity of diesel fuels is not as important as that in the mixed-friction range. The introduction of environmentally compatible, hydrogenation-desulfurized fuels resulted in huge wear problems with distributor injection pumps in the field. Lubricity enhancers have to be added to the fuel to avoid these problems. Lubricity is tested using a high-frequency reciprocating rig (HFRR). Minimum lubricity is defined in EN 590.

Sulfur
Diesel fuels contain chemically bonded sulfur, with the actual quantities depending upon the quality of the crude petroleum and the components which are added at the refinery. Cracked compo-

nents are generally characterized by especially high sulfur contents, but these can be reduced with hydrogen treatment at the refinery. The sulfur converted to sulfur dioxide (SO_2) during combustion in the engine is undesirable due to its environmentally harmful acidic reactions. For this reason, the legal limits placed on sulfur levels in diesel fuels have been progressively tightened in recent years. As of 1 January, 2000, the European limit is 350mg/kg. Reducing particulate mass (sulfate in the soot) is another reason why vehicles with oxidation catalytic converters require fuel with a low sulfur content. The same applies in terms of avoiding damage to the converters used for removing nitrogen from the exhaust gas (NO_x treatment). Sulfur contents < 10 ppm are desirable.

Carbon-deposit index (carbon residue)
The carbon-deposit index describes the fuel's tendency to form residues on the injection nozzles. The mechanisms of deposit formation are complex and not easily described.

The components (particularly the cracking constituents) which the diesel fuel contains at the end of vaporization exercise a not inconsiderable influence on deposit formation.

Additives
Additives, long a standard feature in gasolines, have attained increasing significance as quality improvers for diesel fuels. The various agents are generally combined in additive packages to achieve a variety of objectives. As the total concentration of the additives generally lies < 0.1 %, the fuel's physical characteristics – such as density, viscosity and boiling range – remain unchanged.

Flow improvers: Flow improvers are polymers whose application is generally restricted to winter (see Cold-flow properties).

Cetane improvers: Cetane improvers are added to promote good ignition response; they are in the form of alcohol-derived esters of azotic acid. These agents improve the fuel's combustion properties, with

positive effects upon noise and particulate emissions.

Detergent additives: Detergent additives help clean the intake system to ensure efficient mixture preparation and inhibit the formation of carbon deposits on the injection nozzles.

Corrosion inhibitors: Corrosion inhibitors resist corrosion on metallic components (when fuel-borne moisture is entrained into the system).

Anti-foaming agents: Anti-foaming agents prevent the fuel foaming, so it is easier to refuel the vehicle.

Environmentally compatible diesel fuels

Some countries and regions (including Sweden and California) are promoting reductions in exhaust emissions by providing fiscal incentives for the use of "ecologically sound/environmentally compatible" fuels and/or making their use mandatory. In these fuels the final boiling point and the aromatic content are reduced, while sulfur is virtually eliminated. Introduction of these fuels was accompanied by serious problems stemming from component wear and elastomer damage in fuel-injection systems. Special additives are required to prevent this type of damage.

Alternative fuels

Coal hydrogenation
The essential raw materials are coal and coke. These emerge from initial processing in the form of water gas (H_2 + CO), while subsequent catalytic conversion produces hydrocarbons. These, in turn, provide the basic materials for the production of gasoline and diesel fuel. The byproducts are liquefied petroleum gas (LPG) and paraffin. Fischer-Tropsch synthesis has acquired particular significance in South Africa, where it is in widespread use in large industrial installations.

Properties of liquid fuels and hydrocarbons

Substance	Density kg/l	Main constituent % by weight	Boiling temperature °C	Latent heat of evaporation kJ/kg[1]	Specific calorific value MJ/kg[1]	Ignition temperature °C	Theoretical air requirement kg/kg	Ignition limit Lower	Upper % by vol. of gas in air
Spark-ignition engine fuel,									
Regular	0.715...0.765	86 C, 14 H	25...215	380...500	42.7	≈ 300	14.8	≈ 0.6	≈ 8
Premium	0.730...0.780	86 C, 14 H	25...215	–	43.5	≈ 400	14.7	–	–
Aviation fuel	0.720	85 C, 15 H	40...180	–	43.5	≈ 500	–	≈ 0.7	≈ 8
Kerosene	0.77...0.83	87 C, 13 H	170...260	–	43	≈ 250	14.5	≈ 0.6	≈ 7.5
Diesel fuel	0.815...0.855	86 C, 13 H	180...360	≈ 250	42.5	≈ 250	14.5	≈ 0.6	≈ 7.5
Crude oil	0.70...1.0	80...83 C, 10...14 H	25...360	222...352	39.8...46.1	≈ 220	–	≈ 0.6	≈ 6.5
Lignite tar oil	0.850...0.90	84 C, 11 H	200...360	–	40.2...41.9	–	13.5	–	–
Bituminous coal oil	1.0...1.10	89 C, 7 H	170...330	–	36.4...38.5	–	–	–	–
Pentane C_5H_{12}	0.63	83 C, 17 H	36	352	45.4	285	15.4	1.4	7.8
Hexane C_6H_{14}	0.66	84 C, 16 H	69	331	44.7	240	15.2	1.2	7.4
n-Heptane C_7H_{16}	0.68	84 C, 16 H	98	310	44.4	220	15.2	1.1	6.7
Iso-octane C_8H_{18}	0.69	84 C, 16 H	99	297	44.6	410	15.2	1	6
Benzene C_6H_6	0.88	92 C, 8 H	80	394	40.2	550	13.3	1.2	8
Toluene C_7H_8	0.87	91 C, 9 H	110	364	40.6	530	13.4	1.2	7
Xylene C_8H_{11}	0.88	91 C, 9 H	144	339	40.6	460	13.7	1	7.6
Ether $(C_2H_5)_2O$	0.72	64 C, 14 H, 22 O	35	377	34.3	170	7.7	1.7	36
Acetone $(CH_3)_2CO$	0.79	62 C, 10 C, 28 O	56	523	28.5	540	9.4	2.5	13
Ethanol C_2H_5OH	0.79	52 C, 13 H, 35 O	78	904	26.8	420	9	3.5	15
Methanol CH_3OH	0.79	38 C, 12 H, 50 O	65	1110	19.7	450	6.4	5.5	26

Viscosity at 20 °C in mm²/s (= cSt, P. 27); gasoline = 0.6; diesel fuel = 4; ethanol = 1.5; methanol 0.75.

[1] Values per l = values per kg × density in kg/l. See P. 25 for conversion tables.

Properties of gaseous fuels and hydrocarbons

Substance	Density at 0°C and 1013 mbar (kg/m³)	Main constituents (% by weight)	Boiling temp. at 1013 mbar (°C)	Specific calorific value Fuel (MJ/kg¹)	A/F mixture (MJ/m³¹)	Ignition temperature (°C)	Theoretical air requirement (kg/kg)	Ignition limit Lower (% by vol. of gas in air)	Upper
Liquefied gas	2.25²⁾	C_3H_8, C_4H_{10}	−30	46.1	3.39	≈ 400	15.5	1.5	15
Municipal gas	0.56..0.61	50 H, 8 CO, 30 CH_4	−210	≈ 30	≈ 3.25	≈ 560	10	4	40
Natural gas	≈ 0.83	76 C, 24 H	−162	47.7	–	–	–	–	–
Water gas	0.71	50 H, 38 CO	–	15.1	3.10	≈ 600	4.3	6	72
Blast-furnace gas	1.28	28 CO, 59 N, 12 CO_2	−170	3.20	1.88	≈ 600	0.75	≈ 30	≈ 75
Sewage gas ³⁾	–	46 CH_4, 54 CO_2	–	27.2³⁾	3.22	–	–	–	–
Hydrogen H_2	0.090	100 H	−253	120.0	2.97	560	34	4	77
Carbon monoxide CO	1.25	100 CO	−191	10.05	3.48	605	2.5	12.5	75
Methane CH_4	0.72	75 C, 25 H	−162	50.0	3.22	650	17.2	5	15
Acetylene C_2H_2	1.17	93 C, 7 H	−81	48.1	4.38	305	13.25	1.5	80
Ethane C_2H_6	1.36	80 C, 20 H	−88	47.5	–	515	17.3	3	14
Ethene C_2H_4	1.26	86 C, 14 H	−102	14.1	–	425	14.7	2.75	34
Propane C_3H_8	2.0²⁾	82 C, 18 H	−43	46.3	3.35	470	15.6	1.9	9.5
Propene C_3H_6	1.92	86 C, 14 H	−47	45.8	–	450	14.7	2	11
Butane C_4H_{10}	2.7⁷⁾	83 C, 17 H	−10; +1⁴⁾	45.6	3.39	365	15.4	1.5	8.5
Butene C_4H_8	2.5	86 C, 14 H	−5; +1⁴⁾	45.2	–	–	14.8	1.7	9
Di-methylether C_2H_6O	2.05⁵⁾	52 C, 13 H, 35 O	−25	28.8	3.43	235	9.0	3.4	18.6

¹) Values per m³ = values per kg × density in kg/m³. See P. 25 for conversion tables.
²) Density of liquefied gas 0.54 kg/l, density of liquefied propane 0.51 kg/l, density of liquefied butane 0.58 kg/l.
³) Purified sewage gas contains 95% CH_4, (methane) and has a heating value of 37.7 MJ/kg.
⁴) First value for isobutane, second value for n-butane or n-butene.
⁵) Density of liquefied dimethylether: 0.667 kg/l.

Table 2. Essential data for diesel fuels, European Standard EN 590 (valid since 1 January 2000)

Requirements	Unit	Specification
Flame point, min.	°C	55
Water, max.	mg/kg	200
Sulfur content, max.	mg/kg	350
Lubricity, "wear scardiameter" max.	μm	460
For temperate climates:		
Density (at 15 °C), min./max.	kg/m³	820/845
Viscosity (at 40 °C), min./max.	mm²/s	2/4.5
Cetane number, min.	–	51
Cetane index, min.	–	46
up to 250 °C, distilled, max.	% volume	65
up to 350 °C, distilled, min.	% volume	85
up to 360 °C, distilled, min.	% volume	95
CFPP[1]) in 6 classes A...F, max.	°C	+5...−20
For arctic climates (in 5 classes 0...4):		
Density (at 15 °C), min./max.	kg/m³	800/845...800/840
Viscosity (at 40 °C), min./max.	mm²/s	1.5/4...1.2/4
Cetane number, min.	–	49...47
Cetane index, min.	–	46...43
up to 180 °C, distilled, max.	% volume	10
up to 340 °C, distilled, min.	% volume	95
CFPP[1]), max.	°C	−20...−44

[1]) Filtration limit.

Liquefied Petroleum Gas (LPG)

The two major components of LPG are butane and propane. It is in limited use as a fuel for motor vehicles. LPG is a byproduct of the petroleum-refining process, and can be liquefied under pressure. LPG is distinguished by a high octane number (RON >100).

CNG (Compressed Natural Gas)

This usually assumes the form of compressed methane, and is suitable for obtaining ultra-low emissions from combustion engines. Due to its high H/C ratio (relative to other fuels), CNG also produces less CO_2. CNG is being tested in both diesel and spark-ignition engines. Soot production is virtually zero when this fuel is combusted in the diesel cycle. The vehicles must be specially adapted for operation on this type of alternative fuel.

Alcohol fuels

Methanol, ethanol, and their various byproducts (e.g. ether) are the main contenders as alternative fuels for spark-ignition engines, being the focus of both discussion and actual application. Methanol can be derived from the plentiful hydrocarbon reserves represented by coal, natural gas, and heavy oils, etc. In certain countries (such as Brazil, but also in the USA), biomass (sugar cane, wheat) is distilled to produce ethanol for use as an engine fuel and fuel additive.

Methanol additives ≤3 % by volume are permissible in many countries. Methanol, however, should be used only in conjunction with solubilizers. Fuels with higher concentrations (15...85 %) have been subjected to large-scale testing (flexible fuel).

Ethanol fuel mixtures are commercially available in countries with high agricultural yield (e.g. E22 in Brazil).

Both calorific value and other factors differ from those of conventional fuels, so special vehicle modifications are sometimes required.

Dimethylether (DME)

This is a synthetic product with a high

cetane number, producing little soot and reduced nitrogen oxide when combusted in diesel engines. Its calorific value is low, on account of its low density and high oxygen content. It is a gas-phase fuel, so the fuel-injection equipment has to be modified. Other ethers (dimethoxymethane, di-n-pentylether, and others) are also being tested.

Emulsions

Emulsions of water and alcohols in diesel fuels are undergoing testing by a number of different institutes. Water and alcohols (particularly methanol) are difficult or impossible to mix with diesel. Emulsifiers are required to keep the mixture stable and prevent it from de-emulsifying. Corrosion-inhibiting measures are also necessary. Soot and nitrogen-oxide emissions can be reduced by these emulsions, but to date their use has been restricted to certain fleet applications; there has been no broad-based testing for a variety of injection systems.

Fatty-acid methyl ester (FAME)

Fatty-acid methyl ester is the generic term applied to all vegetable and animal oils and greases transesterified with methanol, including rapeseed (RME), soy, and sunflower methyl esters, among others. The use of vegetable oils for combustion in diesel engines is a field of investigation because it would allow agricultural areas to be used for the production of regenerative energy. Considerable problems arise with pure vegetable oils, due to their high viscosity and severe tendency to cause nozzle coking; oils transesterified with methanol are free of these difficulties.

Fatty-acid methyl esters are used in pure form and as additives for diesel fuel ($\leq 5\%$). In concentrations as low as $1...2\%$ they boost the lubricity of the fuels. A definitive standard for these substances is now in preparation. This standard will have to lay down characteristics, stability and maximum permissible contaminants in order to ensure trouble-free operation of the injection equipment and engines. FAME fuels are uneconomical in comparison with conventional fuels and their use will require subsidization.

Antifreeze and brake fluid

Brake fluids

Brake fluid is the hydraulic medium employed to transmit actuation forces within the braking system. Compliance with stringent requirements is essential to ensure reliable brake-system operation. These requirements are defined in various standards of similar content (SAE J 1703, FMVSS 116, ISO 4925). The performance data contained in FMVSS 116 (Federal Motor Vehicle Safety Standard), mandatory in the US, also serve as an international reference. The US Department of Transportation (DOT) has defined specific ratings for salient characteristics (Table 1).

Requirements

Equilibrium boiling point

The equilibrium boiling point provides an index of the brake fluid's resistance to thermal stress. The heat encountered in the wheel cylinders (with the highest temperatures in the entire braking system) can be especially critical. Vapor bubbles can form at temperatures above the brake fluid's instantaneous boiling point, resulting in brake failure.

Wet boiling point

The wet boiling point is the fluid's equilibrium boiling point subsequent to moisture absorption under specified conditions (approx. 3.5%). Hygroscopic (glycol-based) fluids respond with an especially pronounced drop in boiling point. The wet boiling point is tested to quantify the response characteristics of used brake fluid. Brake fluid absorbs moisture, mostly by diffusion through brake-system hoses. This is the main reason why it should be replaced every $1...2$ years. The illustration shows the reductions in boiling point that result from moisture absorption in two different brake fluids.

Table 1. Brake fluids

Reference standard for testing	FMVSS 116			SAE J1703
Requirements/Date	DOT3	DOT4	DOT5	Nov. 1983
Dry boiling point min. °C	205	230	260	205
Wet boiling point min. °C	140	155	180	140
Cold viscosity at −40 °C mm²/s	1500	1800	900	1800

Viscosity
To ensure consistent reliability throughout the braking system's extended operating range (−40 °C … +100 °C), the viscosity should remain as constant as possible, with minimal sensitivity to temperature variations. Maintaining the lowest possible viscosity at very low temperatures is especially important in ABS/TCS/ESP systems.

Compressibility
The fluid should maintain a consistently low level of compressibility with minimal sensitivity to temperature fluctuations.

Corrosion protection
FMVSS 116 stipulates that brake fluids shall exercise no corrosive effect on those metals generally employed in braking systems. The required corrosion protection can be achieved only by using additives.

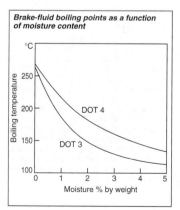

Brake-fluid boiling points as a function of moisture content

Boiling temperature °C vs. Moisture % by weight

DOT 4
DOT 3

Elastomer swelling
The elastomers employed in a particular brake system must be able to adapt to the type of brake fluid being used. Although a small amount of swelling is desirable, it is imperative that it not exceed approximately 10 %. Otherwise, it has a negative effect on the strength of the elastomer components. Even minute levels of mineral-oil contamination (such as mineral-oil-based brake fluid, solvents) in glycol-based brake fluid can lead to destruction of rubber components (such as seals) and ultimately lead to brake-system failure.

Chemical composition

Glycol-ether fluids
Most brake fluids are based on glycol-ether compounds. These generally consist of monoethers of low polyethylene glycols. Although these components can be used to produce a brake fluid which conforms to the DOT 3 requirements, their undesirable hygroscopic properties cause this fluid to absorb moisture at a relatively rapid rate, with an attendant swift reduction in the boiling point.

If the free OH (hydroxyl) groups are partially esterified with boric acid, the result is a superior DOT 4 (or "DOT4+", "Super DOT4", "DOT5.1") brake fluid capable of reacting with moisture to neutralize its effects. As the DOT 4 brake fluid's boiling point drops much more slowly than that of a DOT 3 fluid, its service life is longer.

Mineral-oil fluids (ISO 7308)
The great advantage of mineral-oil-based fluids is the fact that they are not hygroscopic, so the boiling point does not drop owing to moisture absorption. The mineral and synthetic oils for this fluid must be selected with utmost care. Viscosity-index improvers are generally added to

achieve the desired relationship between viscosity and temperature.

The petroleum industry can also supply a range of further additives to improve other brake-fluid properties. It should be noted that mineral-oil-based fluids should never be added to braking systems designed for glycol ether (or vice versa), as this destroys the elastomers.

Silicone fluids (SAE J1705)

Because silicone fluids – like mineral oils – do not absorb moisture, they formerly saw occasional use as brake fluids. The disadvantages of these products include considerably higher compressibility and inferior lubrication, both of which reduce their suitability for use as hydraulic fluid in many systems. A critical factor with brake fluids based on silicone or mineral oils is the absorption of free water in a fluid state, as the water forms vapor bubbles when it heats up to more than 100 °C and freezes when it cools to less than 0 °C.

Coolants

Requirements

The cooling system must dissipate that part of the engine's combustion heat that is not converted into mechanical energy. A fluid-filled cooling circuit transfers the heat absorbed in the cylinder head to a heat exchanger (radiator) for dispersal into the air. The fluid in this circuit is exposed to extreme thermal loads; it must also be formulated to ensure that it does not attack the materials within the cooling system (corrosion).

Owing to its high specific heat and its correspondingly substantial thermal-absorption capacity, water is a very good cooling medium. Its disadvantages include its corrosive properties and limited suitability for application in cold conditions (freezing).

This is why additives must be mixed with the water for satisfactory performance.

Table 2. Ice flaking and boiling points for water-glycol mixtures

Glycol Vol. %	Ice flaking point °C	Boiling point °C
10	−4	101
20	−9	102
30	−17	104
40	−26	106
50	−39	108

Antifreeze

It is possible to lower the coolant's freezing point by adding ethylene glycol. When glycol is added to form a mixture with water the resulting coolant no longer freezes at a given temperature. Instead, ice crystals are precipitated in the fluid once the temperature drops to the flaking point. At this temperature the fluid medium can still be pumped through the cooling circuit. Glycol also raises the coolant's boiling point (Table 2).

In their owner's manuals automobile manufacturers usually specify various optional antifreeze mixture ratios for different levels of low-temperature frost protection.

Additives

Coolants must include effective additives to protect the glycol against oxidation (with formation of extremely corrosive byproducts) and to protect metallic cooling-system components against corrosion. Common additives include:
- Corrosion inhibitors: silicates, nitrates, nitrites, metal salts of organic acids, benzthiazole derivates,
- Buffers: borates,
- Antifoaming agents: silicones.

Many of these additives are subject to aging deterioration, leading to a gradual reduction in coolant performance. The manufacturers have responded to this fact by granting official approval exclusively for coolants of proven long-term stability.

Names of chemicals

Hazard codes: E = explosive, O = oxidizing, F = readily flammable, F₊ = highly flammable, C = caustic, Xₙ = slightly toxic, Xᵢ = irritant, T = toxic, T₊ = highly toxic.

Commercial name English (hazard code)	German	French	Chemical name	Chemical formula
(Glacial) acetic acid (C)	Eisessig (Essigessenz)	Acide acétique glacial	Acetic acid	CH_3COOH
Acetic ether; vinegar naphta (F)	Essigester (Essigäther)	Ether acétique	Ethylacetate	$CH_3COOC_2H_5$
Aerosil (fumed silica)	Aerosil		Silicon dioxide in extremely fine particles	SiO_2
Ammonia liquor (Xᵢ, C)	Salmiakgeist	Ammoniaque hydroxide	Aqueous solution of ammonium hydroxide	NH_4OH in H_2O
Anon; pimelic ketone (Xₙ)	Anon	Anone	Cyclohexanone	$C_6H_{10}O$
Aqua fortis (C)	Scheidewasser	Eau forte	Nitric acid (50 % aqueous solution)	HNO_3 in H_2O
Aqua regia (C, T₊)	Königswasser	Eau régale	Mixture of nitric acid and hydrochloric acid	$HNO_3 + HCl$ (1 + 3)
Bitter almond oil (T)	Bittermandelöl	Essence d'amandes amères	Benzaldehyde	C_6H_5CHO
Bleach (C)	Chlorkalk	Chlorure de chaux	Calciumchloride-hypochlorite	$Ca(OCl)Cl$
Chloride of lime				
Blue vitriol	Kupfervitriol	Vitriol bleu	Copper sulphate pentahydrate	$CuSO_4 \cdot 5H_2O$
Borax (tincal)	Borax (Tinkal)	Borax (tincal)	Sodium tetraborate	$Na_2B_4O_7 \cdot 10H_2O$
Butoxyl	Butoxyl®		(3-methoxybutyl) acetate	$CH_3COO(CH_2)_2CH(OCH_3)CH_3$
Butter of tin (C)	Zinnbutter	Beurre d'étain	Tin tetrachloride	$SnCl_4 \cdot 5H_2O$
Calcium carbide (F)	Karbid	Carbure de calcium	Calcium carbide	CaC_2
Calomel (Xₙ)	Kalomel	Calomel	Mercury(I) chloride	Hg_2Cl_2
Carbitol acetate™ ¹)	Carbitolacetat®		Diethylene glycol ethylether acetate	$CH_3COOCH_2CH_2OCH_2CH_2OC_2H_5$
Carbitol™ ¹) (solvent)	Carbitol®; Dioxitol®	Carbitol	Diethylene glycol monoethylether	$HOCH_2CH_2OCH_2CH_2OC_2H_5$

	French	German		Formula
Carbolic acid (T)	Acide carbolique	Karbolsäure	Phenol	C_6H_5OH
Caustic potash (C)	Potasse caustique	Ätzkali	Potassium hydroxide	KOH
Caustic soda (C)	Soude caustique	Ätznatron	Sodium hydroxide	$NaOH$
Cellosolve™¹) (solvent)		Cellosolve®, Oxitol®	Ethylene glycol monoethylether	$HOCH_2CH_2OC_2H_5$
Cellosolve™¹) acetate		Cellosolveacetat®	Ethylene glycol ethylether acetate	$CH_3COOCH_2CH_2OC_2H_5$
Chalk	Craie	Kreide	Calcium carbonate	$CaCO_3$
Chloramine-T (X_n)	Chloramine-T	Chloramin T	Sodium salt of the p-toluene-sulfonic acid chloroamide	$Na[CH_3C_6H_4SO_2NCl] \cdot 3H_2O$
Chloroprene (F, X_n)	Chloroprène	Chloropren	2-chloro 1.3-butadiene	$CH_2=CClCH=CH_2$
Chlorothene™; ("1.1.1"); (X_n) Methylchloroform	Chlorothène	Chlorothene® Methylchloroform	1.1.1-trichloroethane	Cl_3CCH_3
Chromic anhydride (C, O, X_i)	Anhydride chromique	Chromsäure	Chromium trioxide (chromic acid anhydride)	CrO_3
Cinnabar	Cinabre; vermillon	Zinnober	Mercury (II) sulfide	HgS
Colophony; rosin	Colophane	Kolophonium	Naturally occurring abietic acid	$C_{19}H_{29}COOH$
Corrosive sublimate (T)	Sublimé corrosif	Sublimat	Mercury (II) chloride	$HgCl_2$
Cryolite (X_n)	Cryolithe	Kryolith	Sodium hexafluoroaluminate	$Na_3[AlF_6]$
Decalin	Décaline	Dekalin	Decahydro naphthalene	$C_{10}H_{18}$
Diane	Diane	Bisphenol A; Diphenylolpropan	Dihydroxyphenyl propane-2.2	$(CH_3)_2C(C_6H_4(OH)\text{-}4)_2$
Diisobutylene (F)	Diisobutylène	Diisobutylen	2.4.4-trimethyl pentenes 1 and 2	$(CH_3)_3CCH_2C(CH_3)=CH_2$ and $(CH_3)_3C\text{-}CH=C(CH_3)_2$
DMF (X_n)	DMF	DMF	N.N-dimethyl formamide	$HCON(CH_3)_2$
DMSO	DMSO	DMSO	Dimethyl sulfoxide	$(CH_3)_2SO$
Dry ice	Carboglace	Trockeneis	(Solid) carbon dioxide	CO_2
English red	Rouge d'Angleterre	Polierrot	Iron (III) oxide	Fe_2O_3
Epsomite, bitter salt	Epsomite	Bittersalz (Magnesiumvitriol)	Magnesium sulfate	$MgSO_4 \cdot 7H_2O$

¹) methyl-, propyl-, i-propyl-, butyl-c.: names for analogous ethers containing the above mentioned groups instead of ethyl-.

Names of chemicals (continued)

Commercial name			Chemical name	Chemical formula
English	German	French		
				Numerical characterization[2]
Fixing salt; (hypo)	Fixiersalz ("Antichlor")	Sel fixateur	Sodium thiosulfate	$Na_2S_2O_3 \cdot 5H_2O$
Fluorspar; fluorite (T)	Flußspat; Fluorit	Spath fluor; fluorine	Calcium fluoride	CaF_2
Formalin (T)	Formalin®	Formol	Aqueous solution of formaldehyde	H_2CO in H_2O
Freon™(es)	Freon®(e); Frigen®(e)	Fréon(es); Frigène(s)	Compounds of C, H, F, Cl, (Br)	Numerical characterization[2]
Glauber's salt; mirabilite	Glaubersalz	Sel de Glauber	Sodium sulphate	$Na_2SO_4 \cdot 10H_2O$
Glycol (X)	Glysantin®; Glykol	Glycol	1.2-ethanediol	$HOCH_2CH_2OH$
Golden antimony sulphide	Goldschwefel	Soufre doré d'antimoine	Antimony (V)-sulfide	Sb_2S_5
Green vitriol	Eisenvitriol	Vitriol vert; couperose verte	Iron (II) sulfate	$FeSO_4 \cdot 7H_2O$
				Numerical characterization[3]
Halone(s)	Halon(e)	Halon(s)	Compounds of C, F, Cl, Br	$(C_2F_4)_n$
Halon™	Halon®		Polymer from tetrafluoroethylene 2-bromine 2-chlorine	
Halothane	Halothan		1.1.1-tetrafluoroethane	$F_3CCHClBr$
Hartshorn salt	Hirschhornsalz	Sel volatil d'Angleterre	Ammonium hydrogen carbonate + ammonium carbonate	$(NH_4)HCO_3 + (NH_4)_2CO_3$
Hexalin	Hexalin®	Hexaline	Cyclohexanol (also: hexahydronaphthalene)	$C_6H_{11}OH$ ($C_{10}H_{14}$)
Hexone (F)	Hexon; MIBK		4-methylpentanone 2 (Methylisobutylketon)	$(CH_3)_2CHCH_2COCH_3$
Hydrochloric acid (C)	Salzsäure	Esprit de sel	Aqueous solution of hydrogen chloride	HCl in H_2O
Hydrofluoric acid (T, C)	Flußsäure	(Acide fluorhydrique)	Aqueous solution of hydrogen fluoride	HF in H_2O
Hydrogen peroxide	Perhydrol®	Eau oxygénée	Hydrogen dioxide	H_2O_2
Laughing gas (O)	Lachgas ("Stickoxydul")	Gaz hilarant	Nitrous oxide	N_2O
Lead sugar (X,)	Bleizucker	Sel de Saturne	Lead acetate	$Pb(CH_3COO) \cdot 3H_2O$

English	German	French	Description	Formula
Lead vinegar (X_n)	Bleiessig	Eau blanche; vinaigre de plomb	Aqueous solution of lead acetate and lead hydroxide	$Pb(CH_3COO)_2 \cdot Pb(OH)_2$
Libavius' fuming spirit (C)	Spiritus fumans Libavii		Tin (IV) chloride	$SnCl_4$
Lime saltpeter	Salpeter, Kalk-; Norge-	Salpêtre	Calcium nitrate	$Ca(NO_3)_2 \cdot 4H_2O$
Liquid gas (F)	Flüssiggas	Gaz liquéfié	Propane, isobutane, n-butane	$C_3H_8 + C_4H_{10}$
Lunar caustic (C)	Höllenstein; "lapis infernalis"	Pierre infernale	Silver nitrate	$AgNO_3$
Marble	Marmor	Marbre	Calcium carbonate	$CaCO_3$
Microcosmic salt	Phosphorsalz		Sodium ammonium hydrogenphosphate	$NH_4NaHPO_4 \cdot 4H_2O$
Mine gas (F)	Grubengas; Sumpfgas	Grisou; gaz des marais	Methane	CH_4
Minium	Mennige	Minium	Lead (II) orthoplumbate	Pb_3O_4 (Pb_2PbO_4)
Mohr's salt	Mohr'sches Salz	Sel de Mohr	Iron (II) ammonium sulfate	$(NH_4)_2[Fe(SO_4)_2] \cdot 6H_2O$
Mordant rouge; mordant salt[4]	Tonerde, essigsaure	Mordant d'alun	Basic aluminum acetate	$(CH_3COO)_2AlOH$
Mota (X_n)	Meta®	Alcool solidifié	Tetramethyltetroxacyclooctane (metaldehyde)	$(CHCH_3)_4O_4$
Muthmann's liquid	Muthmann's Flüssigkeit		1.1.2.2-tetrabromethane	$Br_2CHCHBr_2$
Nitroglycerin (E, F)	Nitroglycerin	Nitroglycérine	Glycerol trinitrate	$CHONO_2(CH_2ONO_2)_2$
Nitrolim; lime nitrogen	Kalkstickstoff	Chaux azotée	Calcium cyanamide	$CaCN_2$
Norway saltpeter	Salpeter, Ammon-	Nitrate d'ammonium	Ammonium nitrate	NH_4NO_3

2) Numerical codes for freons (fluorine-chlorine derivatives of methane and ethane, CH_4 and C_2H_6):
Number in hundreds column = number of carbon atoms – 1
Number in tens column = number of hydrogen atoms + 1
Number in ones column = number of fluorine atoms
The missing atoms for valence saturation are chlorine atoms. Examples: F 113 = $C_2F_3Cl_3$; F 21 = $CHFCl_2$

3) Numerical codes for halones (fully halogenated hydrocarbons):
Number in thousands column = number of C atoms
Number in hundreds column = number of F atoms
Number in tens column = number of Cl atoms
Number in ones column = number of Br atoms
Examples: halone 1211 = CF_2ClBr; halone 2402 = $C_2F_4Br_2$

4) Mordanting agent, for instance for dyeing textiles red. See Hawley's Condensed Chemical Dictionary, 11th ed. 1987, "Aluminium acetate".

Names of chemicals (continued)

Commercial name			Chemical name	Chemical formula
English	German	French		
Oleum (C)	Oleum ("Vitriolöl")	Oléum	Sulfuric acid + disulfuric acid	$H_2SO_4 + H_2S_2O_7$
Oxalic acid (X_n)	Kleesäure	Acide oxalique	Oxalic acid	$(COOH)_2 \cdot 2H_2O$
Phosgene (T)	Phosgen	Phosgène	Carbonic acid dichloride	$COCl_2$
Phosphine (T_+)	Phosphin	Phosphine (sel de phosphore)	Hydrogen phosphide	PH_3
Picric acid (T, E)	Pikrinsäure	Acide picrique	2,4,6-trinitrophenole	$C_6H_2(NO_2)_3OH$
Potash	Pottasche	Potasse	Potassium carbonate	K_2CO_3
Potash alum	Alaun, Kali-	Alun de potassium	Potassium aluminum sulfate	$KAl(SO_4)_2 \cdot 12H_2O$
Potassium chlorate (O, X_n)	Knallsalz	Sel de Berthollet	Potassium chlorate	$KClO_3$
Potassium metabisulphite	Kaliummetabisulfit	Métabisulfite de potassium	potassium disulfite	$K_2S_2O_5$
Pyrolusite (X_n)	Braunstein	Pyrolusite	Manganese dioxide	MnO_2
Quicklime; burnt lime; caustic lime	Kalk, gebrannter	Chaux vive	Calcium oxide	CaO
Red prussiate of potash	Blutlaugensalz, rotes; Kaliumferricyanid	Ferricyanure de potassium	Potassium hexacyanoferrate (III)	$K_3[Fe(CN)_6]$
Rochelle salt; salt of Seignette	Seignettesalz (Natronweinstein)	Sel de Seignette	potassium sodium tartrate	$(CHOH)_2COOKCOONa$
Sal ammoniac (X_n)	Salmiak (Salmiaksalz)	salmiac	Ammonium chloride	NH_4Cl
Saltpeter	Natronsalpeter Salpeter, Kali-	Saltpêtre	Potassium nitrate	KNO_3
Silica gel with indicator	Blaugel (Silicagel)	Gel bleu	Porous silicon dioxide with humidity indicator	SiO_2 with cobalt compound
Slaked lime	Kalk, gelöschter	Chaux éteinte	Calcium hydroxide	$Ca(OH)_2$
Soda crystals	Soda (Kristall-)	Soude (cristaux de)	Sodium carbonate	$Na_2CO_3 \cdot 10H_2O$
Soda niter; Chile saltpeter	Salpeter, Chile;	Salpêtre du Chili	Sodium nitrate	$NaNO3$

Sorrel salt; potassium binoxalate	Kleesalz	Sel d'oseille	Potassium tetraoxalate	$(HOOCCOOK) \cdot (COOH)_2 \cdot 2H_2O$
Sulphuric ether (F)	Schwefelether	Ether sulfurique	Diethyl ether	$C_2H_5OC_2H_5$
Tetrachloroethylene (X_n)	Per	Tétrachloroéthylène	Tetrachloroethylene (perchloroethylene)	$Cl_2C=CCl_2$
Tetrachloromethane (T)	Tetra ("Tetraform")	Tétrachlorométhane	Perchloromethane	CCl_4
Tetralin (O, C)	Tetralin	Tétraline	1.2.3.4-tetrahydronaphthalene	$C_{10}H_{12}$
Tin foil	Stanniol	Papier d'étain	Foil tin	Sn
Tin salt	Zinnsalz	Sel d'étain	Tin (II) chloride	$SnCl_2 \cdot 2H_2O$
TNT; trotyl (E)	TNT	TNT; tolite	2.4.6-trinitro toluene	$C_6H_2(NO_2)_3CH_3$
Trichlorethylene (X_n)	Tri	Trichloréthylène	Trichlorethene	$Cl_2C=CHCl$
Urea	Harnstoff	Urée	Carbonic acid diamide	$CO(NH_2)_2$
Urotropine	Urotropin	Urotropine	1.3.5.7-Tetra acadamantane	$(CH_2)_6N_4$
Vichy salt; baking soda	Bullrichsalz®. Natron (Natriumbicarbonat)	Sel de Vichy	Sodium hydrogen carbonate	$NaHCO_3$
Waterglass	Wasserglas (Kali- bzw. Natron-)	Verre soluble	Aqueous solution of potassium or sodium silicates	$M_2SiO_3 + M_2Si_2O_5$ (M = K or Na)
Yellow prussiate of potash	Blutlaugensalz, gelbes; Kaliumferrocyanid	Ferrocyanure de potassium	Potassium hexacyanoferrate (II)	$K_4[Fe(CN)_6]$
	GB-Ester; Polysolwan O®		Glycol acid butyl ester (hydroxic acetic acid butylester)	$HOCH_2COOC_4H_{10}$

Corrosion and corrosion protection

Corrosion is the attrition of metal as a result of electrochemical reactions with substances in the environment. As it proceeds, metal atoms oxidize to form non-metallic compounds in a process emanating from the affected material's surface. In thermodynamic terms, the process can be viewed as an entropic transition from an ordered, high-energy state into a less-ordered state of lower energy and consequently greater stability.

Corrosion processes are always interphase reactions. An example of this type of reaction is metal scaling, i.e. oxidation in hot gases. The following deals exclusively with the corrosion that occurs at the phase limit between the metal and aqueous phases, generally referred to as electrochemical corrosion.

Corrosive attack

Two distinct reactions occur in every corrosive attack: in the anodic subprocess – the directly visible corrosive effect – the difference in respective potentials causes the metal to oxidize as described in the reaction equation

$$Me \rightarrow Me n^+ + ne^-,$$

freeing an equivalent number of electrons. The metal ions thus formed can either be dissolved in the electrolyte, or can precipitate out on the metal after reacting with constituents in the attacking medium.

This anodic subprocess can continue only as long as the electrons it produces are consumed in a second process. This second subprocess is a cathodic subreaction in which oxygen is reduced to hydroxyl ions in neutral or alkaline media, in accordance with the reduction equation

$$O_2 + 2 H_2O + 4 e^- \rightarrow 4 OH^-.$$

These hydroxyl ions, in turn, are able to react with the metal ions, whereas in acidic media the hydrogen ions are reduced via the formation of free hydrogen, which escapes as a gas according to the following formula:

$$2 H^+ + 2 e^- \rightarrow H_2.$$

When two different metals moistened by the same fluid are in mutual electrical contact, the cathodic subprocess occurs at the more noble metal while the anodic subprocess progresses at the baser material. This is called contact corrosion.

However, it is also possible for both reactions to occur on the same metal in a process termed "free corrosion". Anodic and cathodic subprocesses can alternate continuously at the metal/solution interface with statistically random time and location distributions for the individual subprocesses.

Each of the individual subreactions corresponds to a partial current/voltage curve. The total current is the sum of the two currents I_a and I_c:

$$I_{total} = I_a + I_c$$

The two partial current/voltage curves combine to produce the cumulative current/voltage curve.

If no voltage is supplied externally, i.e., in free corrosion, the system assumes a state in which the anodic and cathodic partial currents are precisely balanced:

$$I_a = - I_c = I_{corr}$$

The anodic current is called the corrosion current I_{corr}, while the corresponding potential at which this current compensation

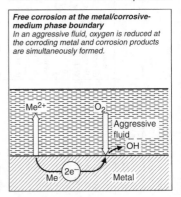

Free corrosion at the metal/corrosive-medium phase boundary
In an aggressive fluid, oxygen is reduced at the corroding metal and corrosion products are simultaneously formed.

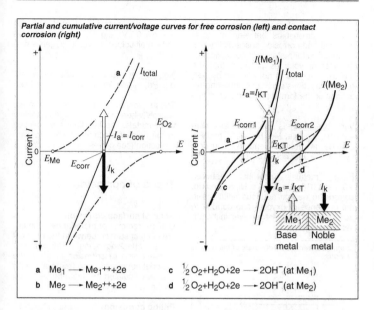

Partial and cumulative current/voltage curves for free corrosion (left) and contact corrosion (right)

a $Me_1 \longrightarrow Me_1^{++} + 2e$
b $Me_2 \longrightarrow Me_2^{++} + 2e$
c $\frac{1}{2} O_2 + H_2O + 2e \longrightarrow 2OH^-$ (at Me_1)
d $\frac{1}{2} O_2 + H_2O + 2e \longrightarrow 2OH^-$ (at Me_2)

occurs is called the "open-circuit potential" E_{corr}.

The open-circuit potential is a mixed potential in which there is no equilibrium; matter is converted continuously, as defined in the following general equation:

$$O_2 + 2 H_2O + \frac{4}{n} Me \rightarrow \frac{4}{n} Me^{n+} + 4OH^-$$

The above is essentially applicable for contact corrosion, although the interrelationships are more complicated. In addition to pairs of partial current/voltage curves for each of the two metals and the resulting two cumulative current/voltage curves, the resultant total current/voltage curve for the entire system must be considered as a value which can be measured externally.

Electrochemical series of metals

Metals are often ranked in "electrochemical series of metals" corresponding to consecutively higher "standard potentials." Here, the term "standard potential" indicates that the specified values apply to standard conditions, especially to the activities (in the electrochemically active part of the concentration) of the dissolved metal ions and hydrogen in a concentration of 1 mol/l at a hydrogen pressure of 1 bar at 25°C. Such conditions are seldom found in practice; in fact, most solutions are virtually free of ions from the metal in question.

It should be emphasized that the table ("Standard electric potentials of the metals") is limited to thermodynamic values, and does not reflect the effects of corrosion kinetics, for example as encountered in the formation of protective layers. For instance, lead is shown as a base metal; as such it should dissolve in sulfuric acid. Although the "practical" and "technical" electrochemical series of metals do not have this disadvantage, their practical application range remains restricted. In contrast, electrochemical corrosion measurements provide unambiguous data.

For general reference purposes, the following relationships between electrical potential and corrosion susceptibility can be specified for metals with no application of external voltages provided that the metal's response is not affected by secondary reactions such as complexing reactions or the formation of protective layers:

Very base metals (potential less than – 0.4 V), e.g. Na, Mg, Be, Al, Ti and Fe, corrode in neutral aqueous solutions, even in the absence of oxygen.

Base metals (potential between – 0.5 and 0 V), e.g. Cd, Co, Ni, Sn and Pb, corrode in neutral aqueous solutions in the presence of oxygen, and corrode in acids to produce hydrogen even in the absence of oxygen.

Semi-noble metals (potential between 0 and + 0.7 V), e.g. Cu, Hg and Ag, corrode in all solutions only if oxygen is present.

Noble metals (potentials above + 0.7 V), e.g. Pd, Pt and Au, are generally stable.

These response patterns can vary sharply when external voltage is applied to the metals. The variations are exploited in the field of electrochemical corrosion protection (see corresponding section).

Types of corrosion

General surface corrosion
Uniform removal of material over the entire contact surface between the material and the attacking medium. This is a very frequent type of corrosion in which the material penetration rate (removal depth) can be calculated per unit of time based on the corrosion current.

Pitting corrosion
Limited localized attack by a corrosive medium which penetrates the material by forming holes, or pits, whose depth is almost always greater than their diameter. Practically no material is removed from the surface outside the pitted areas. Pitting corrosion is frequently caused by halogenide ions.

Crevice corrosion
Corrosive attack primarily occurring in narrow crevices, caused by concentration differences in the corrosive medium, e.g., as a result of long oxygen diffusion paths. This type of corrosion generates potential differences between the crevice's extremities, leading to intensified corrosion in more poorly ventilated areas.

Stress corrosion cracking
Corrosion stemming from the simultaneous concerted action of a corrosive medium and mechanical tensile stress (which can also be present as internal stress in the object itself). Intercrystalline or transcrystalline fissures form, in many

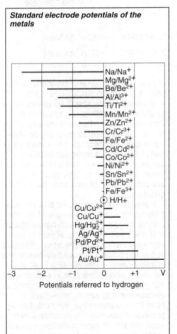

Standard electrode potentials of the metals

Na/Na$^+$
Mg/Mg^{2+}
Be/Be^{2+}
Al/Al^{3+}
Ti/Ti^{2+}
Mn/Mn^{2+}
Zn/Zn^{2+}
Cr/Cr^{3+}
Fe/Fe^{2+}
Cd/Cd^{2+}
Co/Co^{2+}
Ni/Ni^{2+}
Sn/Sn^{2+}
Pb/Pb^{2+}
Fe/Fe^{3+}
H/H+
Cu/Cu^{2+}
Cu/Cu$^+$
Hg/Hg$_2^{2+}$
Ag/Ag$^+$
Pd/Pd^{2+}
Pt/Pt$^+$
Au/Au$^+$

–3   –2   –1   0   +1   V
Potentials referred to hydrogen

cases without the appearance of visible corrosion products.

Vibration corrosion cracking
Corrosion caused by the simultaneous effects of a corrosive medium and mechanical fatigue stress, e.g., caused by vibrations. Transcrystalline fissures are formed, frequently without visible deformation.

Fretting corrosion
Corrosion caused by the simultaneous effect of a corrosive medium and mechanical friction; sometimes called frictional oxidation.

Intercrystalline and transcrystalline corrosion
Types of corrosion characterized by selective formation along the grain boundaries or roughly parallel to the deformation plane in the grain's interior.

Dezincification
Selective dissolution of zinc from brass, leaving behind a porous copper structure. Denickelification and dealuminification are analogous processes.

Rust formation
Formation of ferriferous oxide and hydroxide corrosion products on iron and steel.

Corrosion testing

Electrochemical corrosion-testing procedures
In electrochemical testing procedures, in addition to determining the relationship between potentials and object materials during the corrosion reaction, above all the corrosion currents are measured. In the case of uniform surface corrosion, these are then used for the precise definition of the periodic weight and thickness losses. The relevant conversion factors are listed in Table 2.

These electrochemical processes thus represent a valuable supplement to non-electrochemical methods.

The rate of <u>free corrosion</u> is defined based on the polarization resistance (slope of the total-current/voltage curve). Testing entails subjecting the metal to minimal, alternating anodic and cathodic pulses.

<u>Electrochemical</u> Impedance Spectroscopy (EIS) is employed to examine corrosion mechanisms. This alternating-current technique determines the AC resistance (impedance) and the phase angle of an electrochemical test object as a function of frequency. A low-amplitude sinusoidal alternating voltage is superimposed on the working electrode's potential, and the current response is measured. After measurement, the system is approximated in the form of an equivalent network. By way of example, the illustration captioned "Evaluation of EIS data" shows the equivalent network for the metal/coating/medium system.

The parameter-fit method is used to fit the equivalent networks to the experimental data. The impedance elements (resis-

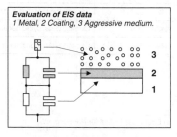

Evaluation of EIS data
1 Metal, 2 Coating, 3 Aggressive medium.

Table 1. Overview of selected standardized non-electrochemical corrosion-testing procedures

Standard	Type of corrosion-testing procedure
DIN[1]) EN ISO 196 (replaces DIN 50911)	Testing of copper and copper alloys; mercury nitrate test
DIN EN ISO 3651 (replaces DIN 50914)	Testing intercrystalline corrosion in stainless steels
DIN EN ISO 4628-3 (draft) DIN 53210	Evaluation of degradation of paint coatings, Part 3: evaluation of degree of rusting Designation of degree of rusting of paint surfaces and similar coatings (will be replaced by DIN EN ISO 4628-3)
DIN EN ISO 8565 (repl. DIN 50917-1)	Corrosion tests in atmosphere; natural weathering tests
DIN EN ISO 11306 (repl. DIN 50917-2)	Corrosion of metals; testing under natural conditions; testing in sea water
DIN 50016	Method of test in damp, alternating atmosphere
DIN 50017	Condensation water test atmospheres
DIN 50018	Testing in a saturated atmosphere in the presence of sulfur dioxide
DIN 50021	Salt spray testing
DIN 50900 -1...3	General terms, electrochemical terms, terms of corrosion testing
DIN 50905 -1...4	Corrosion testing; principles, corrosion characteristics under uniform corrosion attack, corrosion characteristics under non-uniform and localized corrosion attack without mechanical stress
DIN 50 915	Testing intercrystalline stress corrosion in non-alloy and low-alloy steels
DIN 50919	Testing contact corrosion in electrolyte solutions
DIN 50920 -1	Testing corrosion in flowing liquids
DIN 50922	Testing resistance of metallic materials against stress corrosion cracking
DIN 50928	Testing and evaluating protection of coated metallic materials against aqueous corrosive media
DIN 51213	Testing metallic wire coatings (tin, zinc)
N42AP 206	Climatic tests; testing in constant condensate climate
N42AP 209	Climatic tests; cyclic humidity tests
N42AP 213	Climatic tests; industrial-climate tests

---

1) Deutsches Institut für Normung e.V.

tances, capacitances, inductances) are assigned physical properties. Direct conclusions can then be drawn about various characteristics, such as the effectiveness of corrosion-protection measures, porosity, thickness, a coating's ability to absorb water, the effectiveness of inhibitors, the rate of corrosion of the base metal, and so on.

The <u>S</u>canning <u>R</u>eference <u>E</u>lectrode <u>T</u>echnique (SRET) is used for detecting corrosion in its early stages and for examining local corrosion processes.

Pit, gap, and intercrystalline corrosion are examples of local processes that can significantly impair mechanical properties and even result in failure in extreme cases. A high local rate of corrosion and a change in local potential are typical of these processes.

The illustration captioned "SRET principle" is a diagrammatic view of the equipotential lines at a local, active corrosion point. A sensor consisting of two offset platinum tips measuring the micropotential changes above a rotating probe is used to pick up the signal.

Data is recorded automatically on a PC using the appropriate software for analysis and presentation in the form of 2D graphics.

SRET is used to examine pitting corrosion, activation and repassivation, to detect defects in organic coatings and at welds, and to trace delamination, etc.

To measure <u>contact corrosion</u>, the current which flows between the two affected metals is measured directly with both immersed in the same corrosive medium.

The degradation rates determined through electrochemical measurements closely reflect those obtained in field testing. In addition to the small amount of corrosive medium required, another advantage of electrochemical procedures over non-electrochemical methods is that they provide quantitative data on corrosion rates.

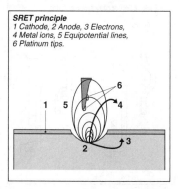

SRET principle
1 Cathode, 2 Anode, 3 Electrons,
4 Metal ions, 5 Equipotential lines,
6 Platinum tips.

Table 2. Loss of mass and thickness due to surface corrosion of various metals with a corrosion current density of 1 $\mu A/cm^2$

Metals	Relative atomic mass	Density g/cm³	Loss of mass mg/ (cm² · year)	Loss of thickness μm/year
Fe	55.8	7.87	9.13	11.6
Cu	63.5	8.93	10.40	11.6
Cd	112.4	8.64	18.40	21.0
Ni	58.7	8.90	9.59	10.8
Zn	65.4	7.14	10.70	15.0
Al	27.0	2.70	2.94	10.9
Sn	118.7	7.28	19.40	26.6
Pb	207.2	11.30	33.90	30.0

Table 3. Degree of rusting and proportion of rust penetrations and visible sub-rusting at the surface to DIN EN ISO 4628-3

Degree of rusting	Rust surface in %
R_i0	0
R_i1	0.05
R_i2	0.5
R_i3	1
R_i4	8
R_i5	40 ... 50

Non-electrochemical corrosion-testing procedures

Non-electrochemical test procedures rely on determining the weight loss by weighing, or defining the rust level. DIN EN ISO 4628-3 (formerly DIN 53210) defines 5 different rust categories according to rust coverage or surface perforation (Table 3).

The corrosion tests have been defined to reflect actual field requirements. In addition to the standard DIN corrosion-testing procedures (Table 1), processes have evolved to reflect specific requirements, e.g. motor-vehicle testing. These tests provide reliable indices of projected service life under normal operating conditions by using short-term exposure in extremely harsh conditions to simulate long-term stresses in the real world. (These tests include operating exposure to climatic factors, splash-water tests of air/fuel mixture systems).

Corrosion protection

The manifestations and mechanisms of corrosion are many and varied, so widely differing methods can be adopted to protect metals against corrosion attack. Corrosion protection means intervening in the corrosive process with the object of reducing the rate of corrosion in order to prolong the service life of the components.

Corrosion protection can be achieved by applying four basic principles:
- Measures in planning and design: the choice of suitable materials and the suitable structural design of components,
- Measures that intervene in the corrosive process by electrochemical means,

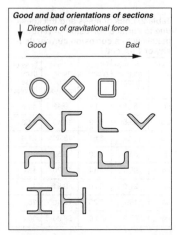

Good and bad orientations of sections

Direction of gravitational force

Good   Bad

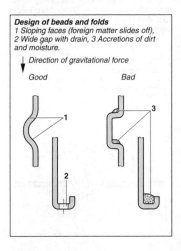

Design of beads and folds
1 Sloping faces (foreign matter slides off),
2 Wide gap with drain, 3 Accretions of dirt and moisture.

Direction of gravitational force

Good   Bad

- Measures that separate the metal from the corrosive medium by protective layers or coatings, and
- Measures that influence the corrosive medium, for example the addition of inhibitors to the medium.

Corrosion protection by means of suitable structural design

Selecting suitable materials which feature optimum resistance to corrosion under the expected conditions can be of considerable assistance in avoiding corrosion damage. When the costs that would otherwise be incurred for upkeep and repair are factored into the long-term cost of ownership equation, a more expensive material can often be the more cost-effective alternative.

Design measures, too, are of major importance. A great deal of skill and expertise goes into design, particularly regarding the connections between parts that are made of the same material or different materials.

Corners and edges of sections are difficult to protect, and this is where corrosion can easily attack. Favorable orientation can reduce corrosion.

Beads and folds can trap dirt and moisture. Suitable surfaces and drain openings can help avoid this problem.

Welds, which generally modify the microstructure for the worse, are another weak point. In order to avoid crevice corrosion, welds have to be smooth and free of gaps.

Contact corrosion can be avoided by joining same or similar metals, or by installing washers, spacers or sleeves to ensure that both metals are electrically insulated.

Electrochemical processes

The schematic current/voltage curves for a metal suitable for passivation coating show how these processes work. The current-density values arranged in ascending order on the y-axis represent anodic currents corresponding to the corrosion reaction defined in the equation

$$Me \rightarrow Me^{n+} + ne^-$$

In contrast, the descending current-density values represent cathodic currents with the reaction equation progressing from right to left. The diagram indicates that external voltage can be applied to suppress corrosion. There are two basic ways of doing this:

For <u>cathodic protection</u> the potential is shifted so far toward the left that no an-

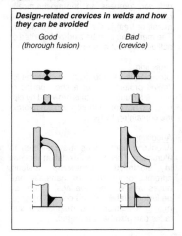

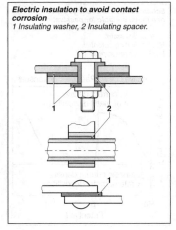

odic currents flow, leading to $U < U_a$. As an alternative to applying voltage from an external source, it is also possible to shift the potential by using a base metal to act as a "sacrificial" reactive anode.

Another option is to shift the potential of the threatened electrode into the passive range, i.e., into the potential range between U_p and U_d. This is called <u>anodic protection</u>. The anodic currents which flow in the passive range are less than those in the active range by exponential powers of between 3 and 6, depending upon the type of metal and the corrosive medium. The result is excellent protection for the metal.

However, the potential should not exceed U_d, as oxygen would be produced in this transpassive range, potentially leading to higher rates of oxidation. Both of these effects would cause the current to increase.

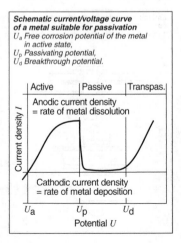

Schematic current/voltage curve of a metal suitable for passivation
U_a Free corrosion potential of the metal in active state,
U_p Passivating potential,
U_d Breakthrough potential.

Active	Passive	Transpas.

Anodic current density = rate of metal dissolution

Cathodic current density = rate of metal deposition

U_a U_p U_d

Potential U

Current density I

Coatings

Coatings inhibit corrosion by forming protective films applied directly to the metal to be protected, where they resist attack by the corrosive medium. These protective coatings should be neither porous nor electrically conductive. Because adequate application depths are also essential, considerable difficulties may be encountered when attempts are made to apply these substances in systems with close dimensional tolerances.

Inorganic nonmetallic coatings
Protective coatings can be formed interactively with the material to be protected. The formation of <u>stable oxide coatings</u> can be promoted in many metals by alloying in small amounts of foreign metals, such as silicon in the case of cast iron, or molybdenum with chrome-nickel steels. Phosphates, chromates and silicates can also produce coatings. Examples are found in the automotive industry, where these substances are employed in body panel manufacture ("phosphate coating") and in cooling systems.

<u>Diffusion process</u>
Surface treatment can be selectively combined with surface hardening by using the diffusion process to thermochemically carburize, carbonitride or chromate the metal, or treat it with boron or vanadium. The metal can also be oxidized, nitrited or sulfided without hardening.

<u>Browning</u>
Browning is used to produce coatings for limited protection over a short period of time. A ferrous material is browned by dipping it in hot concentrated sodium hydroxide containing $NaNO_2$.

<u>Anodizing</u>
Anodizing applications are restricted to aluminum. This anodic oxidation process in electrolytes containing sulfuric, chromic, or oxidic acids generally produces very durable coatings, which can be further stabilized and colored by <u>chromating</u>. Cadmium and magnesium surfaces can also be chromated.

Enameling

Enameling furnishes high levels of corrosion protection, particularly on unalloyed steel. On the negative side, enamel coatings are brittle and thus particularly susceptible to impact and thermal shock. In addition, they are subject to consistent internal compressive stress, and tensile stress factors (e.g. when the yielding point of the carrier material is exceeded) cause fissures in the relatively inflexible enamel. To improve enamel bonding, an intermediate layer consisting of a base material is first fused to the metal; this intermediate layer is then covered with the actual silica-based protective coating.

Glass ceramics

Glass ceramics do not display the disadvantages of enamel under mechanical or thermal loading. They are applied to the material in the form of a semi-crystalline coating using controlled crystallization of thermodynamically unstable glasses. Subsequent heat treatment establishes roughly 50 % crystallinity.

Metallic coatings

Numerous options are available for applying foreign metals or metal compounds to base materials. In many cases, corrosion protection is combined with enhanced wear resistance and with the formation of decorative surfaces. Standard procedures, suitable metals and application ranges are listed in Table 4. It should be noted though that not every metal is suitable for every type of protection (e.g. aluminum applied to base materials in thermal spray processes provides no protection against wear).

Electroplating (electrolytic deposition)

In electrolytic plating, metals suspended in ionized metallic-salt solutions are deposited on conductive bases in a cathodic reaction. Under controlled conditions it is possible to produce alloys and dispersion coatings (layers of finely dispersed additives) of a type not amenable to duplication in fusion processes. Most metals are deposited from suspensions in aqueous solutions. In contrast, aluminum – an extremely base metal – can only be applied using water-free organic or molten saline solutions.

Table 4. Uses of inorganic protective coatings

Method of application	Type of metal	Primarily used for
Chemical deposition	Ni (NiB, NiP, NiPCu), Cu, dispersion coatings (NiB + SiC, NiP + SiC).	Corrosion protection, protection against wear, decorative surfaces.
Vapor deposition	Al, Au, Ta.	Corrosion protection
Electroplating (external power source)	Ag, Al, Au, Cd, Cr, Ni, Sn, Zn, ZnNi, ZnNiP.	Corrosion protection, decorative surfaces
Plating	Al, Cu, Ni, Pb, Ti, Zr and their alloys, stainless steels.	Corrosion protection
Hot immersion (including "hot-dip galvanization")	Al, Pb, Sn, Zn.	Corrosion protection
Thermal spraying	Al and alloys, Cr, Ni, NiCr, NiCrBSi, Ti, borides, carbides, oxides.	Corrosion protection, protection against wear.

Chemical deposition
The basic principles are the same as in the electroplating process, but the electrons required for reduction do not come from an external power source. Instead, they are furnished by an added reducing agent (usually sodium hypophosphite or sodium boranate). This is why phosphorus and boron are present in most nickel coatings.

Hot immersion priming
The most common immersion process is the hot-dip galvanizing of iron and steel; this process is also the one most frequently used in the automotive industry. Here the pretreated (pickled and wetted with flux) material is immersed in the molten coating metal to produce alloy layers; this process progresses at the phase limit in accordance with solubility conditions in the phase diagrams. The alloy layers promote bonding between the coating and the base material. This process allows substantially greater layer depths than electroplating methods.

Evaporation
Due to its high cost, the evaporation process is limited to special applications, particularly in applying thin coatings to objects with limited surface areas (substrates). These thin layers often require additional protection from supplementary inorganic or organic coatings (example: headlight reflectors). The coating material (metal) is heated by an electric current and evaporated in an intense vacuum. It condenses on the substrate, forming a fine metal coating.

Thermal spraying
In thermal spraying, the coating material (usually in powdered form) is melted by a plasma ("plasma spraying") or an arc as it leaves the spray gun. Because this process entails accepting a certain amount of inconsistency and porosity in the final coating, thick layers (150 to 200 μm) are required to ensure effective corrosion protection.

Plating
Plating is the joining of two or more metal layers at high temperature and/or under high pressure. These metal layers do not separate under normal stress. Plating methods are divided into rolling, transfer and mechanical cladding. The materials are joined by using diffusion processes, bonding with alloying techniques, or mechanical interlocking. The application materials are several millimeters in thickness.

Organic coatings
Thermoplastics, elastomers and duromers are the primary types of organic protective coatings. They are used in the automobile industry in paints, whirl-sintered compounds, interior coatings, fiber-reinforced resins and fillers. How well these coatings protect the underlying material depends not only on the individual plastic, but also on the binder, anti-aging agent, UV stabilizers and the type of filler and pigment used. Organic coatings can be used alone or together with one of the inorganic coatings mentioned above.

Painting
Depending upon individual requirements, paint can be applied with brushes and rollers, using compressed-air or high-pressure sprays, and by immersion processes (with and without electrophoresis), and with electrostatic spray painting. An adhesion-promoting primer coat is applied to the pretreated metal surface with subsequent application of the actual protective coat on top of the primer. Solvent evaporation and/or oxygen absorption then promote formation of a homogenous, continuous surface layer.

Powder coating
Powdered plastics, which are very difficult to transform into a liquid phase at room temperature, can be applied using powder coating processes. The powder can either be fused onto the preheated parts, flame-sprayed or electrostatically sprayed. Heat treatment can be employed to form homogenous sealed layers as required. Powder coating processes are usually more economical than painting processes, while environmental and occupational safety are both less of a problem.

Internal rubber and plastic coatings

Rubber and plastic coatings are frequently used to protect the insides of transport and storage tanks, vessels and pipes. Prelinked natural and synthetic rubber, and pretreated thermoplastic films are applied with interlacing adhesives; final linkage takes place either catalytically or by applying heat after the coatings have been applied to the bare carrier materials.

Plasma polymerization

Plasma polymerization is a process in which a gaseous-discharge plasma promotes polymerization of organic monomers on the object material. This type of polymer film represents a suitable coating for any metal. The result is an organic layer without gas enclosures or the volatile components frequently found in solid polymers.

Inhibitors

Inhibitors are substances added to the corrosive medium in low concentrations (up to a maximum of several hundred ppm) for absorption at the surface of the protected metal. Inhibitors drastically reduce the rate of corrosion by blocking either the anodic or the cathodic subprocess (frequently blocking both subprocesses simultaneously). Organic amines and amides of organic acids are the most frequent inhibitors. In automotive applications, for example, inhibitors are used in fuel additives; they are also added to antifreeze in order to inhibit corrosion damage in the coolant circuit.

Vapor-phase inhibitors provide only temporary protection for metallic products during storage and shipping. They must be easy to apply and remove.

The drawback of vapor-phase inhibitors is that they are potentially injurious to health.

Vapor-phase inhibitors (VPI), or volatile corrosion inhibitors (VCI), are organic substances of moderate vapor pressure. They are frequently enclosed in special-purpose packing materials or as solvents in liquids or emulsions with oil. The inhibitors evaporate or sublimate over the course of time, and are adsorbed as monomolecules on the metal, where they inhibit either anodic or cathodic corrosion subreactions, or both at once. Dicyclohexylamin nitrite is a typical example.

For optimal effectiveness, the inhibitor should form a sealed coating extending over the largest possible surface area. This is why they are generally enclosed in packing materials such as special paper or polyethylene foil. An airtight edge seal is not required; the packing can be opened briefly for inspection of contents. The duration of the packing's effectiveness depends on the tightness of the seal and the temperature (normally approx. 2 years, but less in environments substantially hotter than room temperature).

Standard commercial vapor-phase inhibitors are generally a combination of numerous components capable of providing simultaneous protection for several metals or alloys. Exceptions: cadmium, lead, tungsten and magnesium.

Heat treatment of metallic materials

Heat treatment is employed to endow metallic tools and components with the specific qualities required either for subsequent manufacturing processes or for actual operation. The heat-treating process includes one or several time and temperature cycles. First, the parts to be treated are heated to the required temperature, where they are maintained for a specific period before being cooled back down to room temperature (or below in some processes) at a rate calculated to achieve the desired results.

The process modifies the microstructure to achieve the hardness, strength, ductility, wear resistance, etc., required to withstand the stresses associated with static and dynamic loads. The most significant industrial processes are summarized in Table 1 (see DIN EN 10 052 for terminology).

Hardening

Hardening procedures produce a martensitic microstructure of extreme hardness and strength in ferrous materials such as steel and cast iron.

The parts being treated are heated to the austenitizing, or hardening temperature, at which they are maintained until an

Table 2. Standard austenitizing temperatures

Type of steel	Quality specification	Austenitizing temperature °C
Unalloyed and low-alloy steels	DIN EN 10083-1 DIN 17 211 DIN 17 212	
< 0.8% by mass of C		780...950
≥ 0.8% by mass of C	–	780...820
Cold- and hot-working tool steels	DIN 17 350	950...1100
High-speed steels		1150...1230
Cast iron	–	850...900

austenitic structure emerges, and until an adequate quantity of carbon (released in the decay of carbides, such as graphite in cast iron) is dissolved in the treated material. The material is then quenched or otherwise cooled back to room temperature as quickly as possible in order to obtain a maximum degree of conversion to a martensitic microstructure (the time-temperature transformation chart for the specific steel in question contains the reference figures for the necessary cooling rate).

The austenitizing temperature varies according to the composition of the material in question (for specific data, consult the DIN Technical Requirements for Steels). Table 2 above furnishes reference data. See DIN 17 022, Parts 1 and 2, for practical information on hardening procedures for tools and components.

Table 1. Summary of heat-treatment processes

Hardening	Austempering	Tempering	Thermo-chemical treatment	Annealing	Precipitation hardening
Through hardening	Isothermic transformation in the bainite stage	Tempering of hardened parts	Carburizing	Stress-relief	Solution treatment and aging
Surface hardening		Hardening and tempering above 550 °C	Carbonitriding	Recrystallization annealing	
Hardening of carburized parts (case-hardening)			Nitriding	Soft annealing, spheroidization	
			Nitrocarburizing	Normalizing	
			Boron treatment	Homogenizing	
			Chromating		

Not all types of steel and cast iron are suitable for hardening. The following equation describes the hardening potential for alloyed and unalloyed steels with mass carbon contents of between 0.15 and 0.60%, and can be applied to estimate the hardness levels achievable with a completely martensitic microstructure:

Max. hardness = $35 + 50 \cdot (\%C) \pm 2$ HRC

If the microstructure does not consist entirely of martensite, then the maximum hardness will not be reached.

When the carbon content exceeds 0.6% by mass, it may be assumed that the material's structure contains untransformed austenite (residual austenite) in addition to the martensite. This condition prevents the maximum hardness from being achieved, and the wear resistance will be lower. In addition, residual austenite is metastable, i.e. there exists a potential for subsequent transformation to martensite at temperatures below room temperature or under stress, with changes in specific volume and internal stress as the possible results. Low-temperature follow-up procedures or tempering operations at over 230 °C can be useful in cases where residual austenite is an unavoidable product of the hardening procedure.

The surface and core hardnesses remain virtually identical in components with material thicknesses up to approx. 10 mm. Beyond this point the core hardness is lower; there is a hardness progression or gradient. The rate of the progression depends upon the hardening response (testing described in DIN 50 191), which is a function of the material's composition (Mo, Mn, Cr). This factor requires particular attention with parts which do not cool well (thick parts and/or slow or graduated cooling processes designed to minimize the risk of cracks and/or distortion).

DIN 50 150 defines the method for using hardness as the basis for estimating tensile strength R_m; this method can only be applied in cases where the surface and core hardnesses are virtually identical:

$R_m \approx (34...37.7) \cdot$ Rockwell C hardness number in N/mm^2 or
$R_m \approx (3.2...3.35) \cdot$ Vickers hardness number in N/mm^2.

The specific volume of the martensitic microstructure is approximately 1.0% greater than that of the original material. In addition, stresses result from the rearrangement of the microstructure and from contraction during cooling. As the latter phenomenon does not take place at a uniform rate in all sections of the part, it produces variations in shape and dimensions; tensile stresses near the surface and pressure tension at the core are the common result.

Surface hardening

The process is especially suited for integration within large-scale manufacturing operations, and can be adapted to fit the rhythm of the production line.

Heating and hardening are restricted to the surface, thereby minimizing alterations in shape and dimensions. Heating is generally provided by high- or medium-frequency alternating current (inductive hardening) or by a gas burner (flame hardening). Friction (friction hardening) and high-energy beams (e.g. electron or laser beams) can also provide the heat required for austenitizing. Table 3 provides a summary of the specific heat energies for the individual procedures.

These methods can be used to treat both linear and flat surfaces, meaning that the parts can be heated either while stationary or in motion. The heat source itself can also be moved. Rotation is the best way of dealing with radially symmetrical parts, as it ensures concentric hardening. Either immersion or spraying arrange-

Table 3. Comparison of power densities when heating with different sources

Energy source	Normal power density W/cm^2
Laser beam	$10^3...10^4$
Electron beam	$10^3...10^4$
Induction (MF, HF, HF pulse)	$10^3...10^4$
Flame heating	$10^3...6 \cdot 10^3$
Plasma beam	10^4
Molten salt (convection)	20
Air/gas (convection)	0.5

ments can be applied for quenching.

Heat rise is rapid, so the temperatures must be 50...100°C higher than those used in furnace heating so as to compensate for the shorter dwell period. The procedure is generally employed with low-alloy or unalloyed steels with mass carbon contents of 0.35...0.60% (consult DIN 17 212 for list of suitable steels). However, surface hardening processes can also be applied with alloyed steels, cast iron and rolling-bearing steels. The parts can be heat-treated to provide a combination of improved base strength and high surface hardness, making them suitable for high-stress applications (recessed edges, bearing surfaces, cross-sectional transitions).

Surface hardening generally results in internal compression stresses along the edge. This leads to increased fatigue resistance, especially when notched parts are exposed to inconstant vibration stress (see illustration).

The relationship defined above can be employed to estimate the potential surface hardness. There is a substantial reduction in hardness between the surface and the unhardened core region. The hardening depth R_{ht} – the depth at which 80% of the Vickers surface hardness is found – can be derived from the hardness progression curve (see DIN 50 190, Part 2).

Austempering

The object of this process is to achieve a bainite microstructure. This microstructure is not as hard as martensite, but does display greater ductility as well as smaller changes in specific volume.

After austenitizing (see hardening), the parts for austempering are first cooled to a temperature of 200...350°C (depending upon the exact composition of the material) at the required rate. The parts are then held at this temperature until the microstructure's transformation into bainite has been completed. The parts can then be cooled to room temperature (no special procedure required).

Austempering is an excellent alternative for parts whose geometrical configuration makes them sensitive to distortion

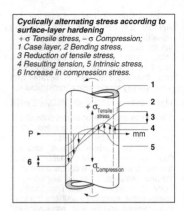

Cyclically alternating stress according to surface-layer hardening
+ σ Tensile stress, − σ Compression;
1 Case layer, 2 Bending stress,
3 Reduction of tensile stress,
4 Resulting tension, 5 Intrinsic stress,
6 Increase in compression stress.

and/or cracks, or in which high ductility is required together with substantial hardness, or which should combine hardness with a low level of residual austenite.

Draw tempering

Parts emerge from the hardening process in a brittle state; they must be tempered to increase their ductility in order to reduce the risk of damage associated with excessive internal tension, such as delayed cracking after hardening or splintering during grinding. This tempering process is based on the elimination of carbides, a phenomenon accompanied by an increase in ductility, albeit at the price of reductions in hardness.

The parts are heated in the draw to a temperature of between 180 and 650°C; they are then held there for at least one hour before being allowed to cool to room temperature. Depending upon the specific composition of the material, tempering at temperatures in excess of 230°C may result in any residual austenite being transformed into bainite and/or martensite.

Tempering at temperatures as low as 180°C is enough to reduce the hardness of unalloyed and low-alloy steels by approx. 1...5 HRC. The individual materials respond to higher temperatures with specific characteristic hardness loss. The graph at the right shows a characteristic tempering curve for typical types of steel. The graph illustrates the fact that the hardness of high-alloy steels remains constant until the temperature exceeds 550 °C, after which it drops.

The mutual relationships between tempering temperature on the one side, and hardness, strength, yield point, fracture contraction and ductility on the other, can be taken from the tempering diagrams for the various steels (see DIN EN 10083).

Tempering of hardened parts is accompanied by a reduction in specific volume. In some cases, tempering can also induce changes in the progressive variation in internal tension at different depths in the parts.

It must be remembered that steels alloyed with manganese, chromium, manganese and chromium, chrome-vanadium, and chromium and nickel should not be tempered at temperatures of 350...500 °C, as brittleness could result. When these types of materials are cooled from higher tempering temperatures, the transition through this critical range should also be effected as rapidly as possible (see DIN 17022, Parts 1 and 2 for additional information).

Quench and draw

This type of quench and draw process combines hardening and tempering at temperatures above 500 °C. This procedure is designed to achieve an optimal relationship between strength and ductility. It is applied in cases where extreme ductility or malleability is required.

Particular care must be devoted to avoiding brittleness in the quench and draw operation (see above).

Thermochemical treatment

In thermochemical treatment, the parts are annealed in agents which emit specific elements. These diffuse into the surface layer of the parts being treated and modify their composition. This results in very specific properties. Of particular importance for this process are the elements carbon, nitrogen and boron.

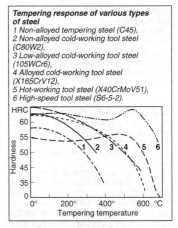

Tempering response of various types of steel
1 Non-alloyed tempering steel (C45),
2 Non-alloyed cold-working tool steel (C80W2),
3 Low-alloyed cold-working tool steel (105WCr6),
4 Alloyed cold-working tool steel (X165CrV12),
5 Hot-working tool steel (X40CrMoV51),
6 High-speed tool steel (S6-5-2).

Carburizing, carbonitriding, case hardening

Carburizing increases the carbon content in the surface layer, while carbonitriding supplements the carbon enrichment with nitrogen. This process is generally carried out in molten salt, granulate, or gas atmospheres at temperatures ranging from 850...1000 °C. The actual hardening is performed subsequently, either by quenching directly from the carburizing/carbonitriding temperature (direct hardening), or by allowing the parts to cool to room temperature (single hardening), or by allowing them to cool to a suitable intermediate temperature (e.g. 620 °C) prior to reheating (hardening after isothermic conversion). This process produces a martensitic surface layer, while the degree of martensite at the core is a function of hardening temperature, hardenability and part thickness.

Specific temperatures can be selected for either surface hardening in the upper layers with higher carbon content (case refining), or for the non-carburized core (core refining) (see DIN 17022, Part 3).

Carburizing and carbonitriding produce a characteristic carbon declivity, with levels dropping as the distance from the surface increases (carbon curve). The distance between the surface and the point at which the mass carbon content is still

0.35 % is normally defined as the carburization depth $At_{0.35}$.

The length of the carburizing or carbonitriding process depends upon the required carburization depth, the temperature and the atmosphere's carbon-diffusion properties. A reasonable approximation is possible:

$$At = K \cdot \sqrt{t} - D/\beta \text{ in mm}$$

Depending on temperature and carbon levels, K lies between 0.3 and 0.6 during carburization in a gas atmosphere, for example; the correction factor D/β is generally 0.1...0.3 mm; the time t in h must be inserted.

Generally, the objective is to achieve a carbon gradient with a concentration of at least 0.60 % mass carbon content, the ultimate goal being a surface hardness of 750 HV (corresponding to 65 HRC). Higher concentrations of carbon can lead to residual austenite and/or carbide diffusion, which could have negative effects on the performance of case-hardened parts in actual use. Control of the atmosphere's carbon level, and thus the part's ultimate carbon content, is thus extremely important.

The gradient defining the relationship between hardness and depth corresponds to the carbon concentration curve. The hardness gradient is used to define the case depth Eht. DIN 50190, Part 1 defines this as the maximum distance from the surface before the hardness drops below 550 HV.

The case-hardened part generally exhibits compression tension at the surface, and tensile stresses at the core. As with surface-hardened materials, this distribution pattern provides enhanced resistance to vibration loads.

In carbonitriding, nitrogen is also absorbed; it serves to improve the material's tempering properties, increase its durability and enhance its wear resistance. The positive effects are especially pronounced with non-alloyed steels. For additional, more detailed information on case-hardening procedures consult DIN 17022, Part 3, and Information Sheet 452 of the Steel Information Center, Düsseldorf.

Nitriding and nitrocarburizing

Nitriding is a thermal treatment process (temperature range: 500...600 °C) which can be used to enrich the surface layer of virtually any ferrous material with nitrogen. In nitrocarburizing, a certain amount of carbon is diffused into the material at the same time.

The nitrogen enrichment is accompanied by precipitation hardening. This strengthens the surface layer, enhancing the material's resistance to wear, corrosion and alternating cyclic stress.

Because the process employs relatively low temperatures, there are no volumetric changes of the kind associated with transformations in the microstructure, so that changes in dimensions and shape are minute.

The nitrided region consists of an outer layer, several millimeters in depth, and a transitional white layer, the hardness of which may be anywhere from 700 to over 1200 HV, depending upon the composition of the material. Still deeper is a softer diffusion layer extending several tenths of a millimeter. The thickness of the individual layers is determined by the temperature and duration of the treatment process. The process produces a hardness gradient (similar to that which results from surface and case-hardening); this gradient furnishes the basis for determining the nitriding depth Nht. DIN 50190, Part 3 defines this as the depth from the surface at which the hardness is still 50 HV above the core hardness.

The material's resistance to wear and corrosion is essentially determined by the white layer, which contains up to 10 mass components of nitrogen in %. The nitriding depth and the surface hardness determine the material's resistance to alternating cyclic stress (for additional details, see DIN 17022, Part 4, and Information Sheet 447 from the Steel Information Center, Düsseldorf).

Boron treatment

This is a thermochemical treatment method which employs boron to enrich the surface layer of ferrous materials. Depending upon duration and temperature (normally 850...1000 °C), an iron-boron white layer of 30 µm ... 0.2 mm in depth and with a hardness of 2000...2500 HV is produced.

Boron treatment is particularly effective as a means of protecting against abrasive wear. However, the comparatively high process temperature leads to relatively large changes in shape and dimensions, meaning that this treatment is only suitable for applications in which large tolerances can be accepted.

Annealing

Annealing can be applied to optimize certain operational or processing characteristics of parts. With this method, the parts are heated to the required temperature and maintained there for an adequate period before being cooled to room temperature. Table 1 lists the various processes used in specific individual applications.

Stress-relief
Depending upon the precise composition of the parts, this operation is carried out at temperatures ranging from 450...650°C. The object is to achieve the maximum possible reduction in internal stress in components, tools and castings by inducing physical deformation.

After an oven time of 0.5...1 h, the parts are cooled back to room temperature; this cooling should be as gradual as possible to prevent new stresses from forming.

Recrystallization annealing
Recrystallization annealing is applied with parts that have been formed using noncutting procedures. The goal is to restructure the grain pattern in order to prevent increased hardening, thereby facilitating subsequent machining work.

The temperature requirement depends upon the composition of the material and the degree of deformation: it lies between 550...730°C for steel.

Soft annealing, spheroidization
Soft annealing is intended to facilitate the machining and/or shaping of workpieces which have hardened owing to deformation processes or other heat treating procedures.

The temperature requirement is determined by the material's composition. It is in a range of 650...720°C for steel, and lower for nonferrous materials.

Spheroidizing of cementite is applied when a microstructure with a granular carbide pattern is desired. If the initial structure is martensite or bainite, the result will be an especially homogeneous carbide distribution.

Normalizing
Normalizing is carried out by heating the parts to austenitizing temperature and then allowing them to gradually cool to room temperature. In low-alloy and nonalloyed steels, the result is a structure consisting of ferrite and perlite. This process is essentially employed to reduce grain size, reduce the formation of coarse grain patterns in parts with limited reshaping, and to provide maximum homogeneity in the distribution of ferrite and perlite.

Precipitation hardening treatment
This process combines solution treatment with aging at ambient temperature. The parts are heated and then maintained at temperature to bring precipitated structural constituents into a solid solution, and quenched at room temperature to form a supersaturated solution. The aging process comprises one or several cycles in which the material is heated and held at above-ambient temperatures (hot aging). In this process, one or several phases, i.e. metallic bonds between certain base alloys, are formed and precipitated in the matrix.

The precipitated particles enhance the hardness and strength of the base microstructure. The actual characteristics are determined by the temperature and duration of the aging process (option of mutual substitution); exceeding a certain maximum will usually reduce the strength and hardness of the final product.

Precipitation hardening is mostly applied for nonferrous alloys, but some hardenable steels (maraging steels) can also be processed.

Hardness

Hardness testing

Hardness is the property of solid materials that defines their resistance to deformation. In metallic materials the hardness is used to assess mechanical properties such as strength, machinability, malleability, and resistance to wear. DIN 50150 defines guidelines for converting hardness to tensile strength. Measurement processes are practically nondestructive.

The test data are generally derived from the size or depth of the deformation produced when a specified indentor is applied at a defined pressure.

A distinction is made between static and dynamic testing. Static testing is based on measurement of the permanent impression left by the indentor. Conventional hardness tests include the Rockwell, Vickers and Brinell procedures. Dynamic testing monitors the rebound of a test tool accelerated against the surface of the test specimen.

Another option for obtaining an index of surface hardness is to scratch the surface with a hard test tool and then measure the groove width. The table (next page) compares the standard application ranges for the Rockwell, Vickers and Brinell hardness tests.

Rockwell hardness

(DIN EN 10109)

This method is particularly suitable for large-scale testing of metallic workpieces. A steel or diamond indentor is positioned vertically against the surface of the test specimen and a minor load applied prior to application of the full test pressure (major load) for a period of at least 30 s. The Rockwell hardness is the resulting penetration depth e in mm (see Table 1).

The test surface should be smooth (depending on hardness range, $R_{max} \leq$ 1.2...3.4 µm) and as flat as possible. If the specimen's radius of curvature is less than 20 mm then the results must be scaled using the correction factor for the individual resistance level.

Selection of the individual test procedures enumerated in Table 1 is based upon either the specimen's thickness or the case depth of the hardened surface layer (refer to Figs. A.1...A.3 in DIN EN 10109). The abbreviation for the selected test method should be appended to the numerical data when indicating hardness, e.g., 65 HRC, 76 HR 45 N. The Rockwell C procedure's error range is approx. ±1 HRC.

Advantages of the Rockwell test method include minimal specimen preparation and rapid measurement; this test process can also be completely automated.

Table 1. Rockwell test methods

Abbreviation	Indentor	Minor load N	Total test force N	Hardness number (e indentor penetration depth)	
HRC	Diamond cone		1471 ± 9	100 − e / 0.002	20...70
HRA		98 ± 2	588 ± 5		60 ... 881
HRB	Steel ball		980 ± 6.5	130 − e / 0.002	35 ... 100
HRF			588 ± 5		60 ... 100
HR15N HR30N HR45N	Diamond cone	29.4 ± 0.6	147 ± 1 294 ± 2 441 ± 3	100 − e / 0.001	66 ... 92 39...84 17...75
HR15T HR30T HR45T	Steel ball	3 ± 0.06	15 ± 0.1 30 ± 0.2 45 ± 0.3		50 ... 94 10 ... 84 0 ... 75

Any tester vibration, or shifting and movement of either the test probe or the specimen itself can lead to testing errors, as can an uneven support surface or a damaged indentor.

Brinell hardness (DIN EN 10003)

This procedure is used for metallic materials of low to medium hardness. The test tool (indentor) is a hard-metal or hardened-steel ball. It is applied to the surface of the specimen at an individually specified force F for at least 15 s[1]. Microscopic examination of the resulting deformation diameter d provides the basis for calculating the Brinell hardness. These data can be correlated with standard charts or calculated as follows:

$$\text{Brinell hardness} = \frac{0.204 \cdot F}{\pi \cdot D \cdot (D - \sqrt{D^2 - d^2})} \text{ HB}$$

F Force in N
D Ball diameter in mm
d Indentation diameter in mm

Test pressures range from 9.81 to 29,420 N. Results obtained using spheres of different diameters are only conditionally comparable, and any comparisons should be based on testing at identical force levels. Testing should always be performed using the largest possible spherical sphere, while load factors should be

[1] At least 30 s for lead, zinc, etc.

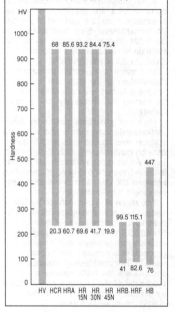

Comparison of hardness ranges for different test methods
The figures at the range extremities indicate the hardness data for the respective methods. HB test procedures with force levels 30 (1); 10 (2); 5 (3); and 1 (4)

Table 2. Application of the Brinell hardness test

Material	Brinell hardness	Load factor 0.102 F/D^2
Steel; nickel and titanium alloys		30
Cast iron [1]	< 140	10
	≥ 140	30
Copper and copper alloys	< 35	5
	35 to 200	10
	< 200	30
Light metals and their alloys	< 35	2.5
	35 to 80	5
		10
		15
	> 80	10
		15
Lead and tin		1
Sintered metals	see EN 24498-1	

[1] Ball nominal diameters of 2.5, 5 or 10 mm are specified for testing cast iron.

selected to obtain an indentation diameter of $(0.24 \ldots 0.6) \cdot D$. Table 2 lists the recommended load factors and ball diameters for a variety of materials as laid down in DIN EN 10003.

In the Brinell hardness designation the numeric data are accompanied by the procedure code, the material of the ball (W for hard metal, S for steel) and the ball diameter. The final element is the test force (in N) multiplied by a factor of 0.102. Example: 250 HBW 2.5/187.5.

To prevent test errors stemming from deformation of the ball itself, testing at hardness factors in excess of 450 HB is to be carried out exclusively with a hard-metal ball.

High test pressures producing deformations extending over a relatively wide surface area can be employed to gather data on materials with inconsistent structures. An advantage of the Brinell method is the relatively high degree of correlation between the Brinell hardness factor and the steel's tensile strength.

The range of application for the Brinell test method is limited by specifications for the thickness of the test specimen (cf. DIN EN 10003) and by the ball material. The required preparations and ensuing test procedures are more complex than those used for Rockwell testing. Potential error sources are the test's reliance on visual evaluation of the impact area's diagonal length and the possibility of inconsistencies in the impression itself.

Vickers hardness (DIN 50 133)

This test method can be used for all metallic materials, regardless of hardness. It is especially suitable for testing minute and thin specimens, while the potential application range extends to include surface and case-hardened parts as well as nitrided workpieces and parts carburized in nitrogen-based atmospheres.

The test tool is a square-based diamond pyramid with an apical angle of 136°. This is applied to the surface of the test specimen at the specified force F.

The diagonal d of the rhomboidal cavity remaining after the tool's removal is measured using a magnifying glass to obtain the basis for calculating the Vickers hardness, which can be read from tables or calculated as follows:

Vickers hardness = $0.189 \cdot F/d^2$ HV

F Applied force in N
d Diagonal of impression in mm

Table 3 gives an overview of the graduated force levels defined in DIN 50 133.

In the formula for Vickers hardness data, the actual test figure is accompanied by the abbreviation HV, the force in N (multiplied by a factor of 0.102) and, following a slash, the force application period (if other than the standard 15 s) in seconds, e.g.: 750 HV 10/25.

The test specimen's surface should be smooth ($R_{max} \leq 0.005 \cdot d$) and flat. DIN 50 133 stipulates that correction factors be used to compensate for any error stemming from surface curvature. Test pressure levels are selected with reference to either the thickness of the test specimen itself or of its hardened outer layer (cf. Fig. 2 in DIN 50 133). Practical experience indicates an error range of approximately ± 25 HV. Although the geometrical configurations are similar, hardness data vary as a function of applied-force levels.

A major advantage of this test method is that there are virtually no limitations on using it to assess thin parts or layers. It allows the use of extremely small force levels to determine the hardness of individual structural sections. The Brinell and Vickers numbers correlate up to approximately 350 HV.

However, a certain minimal degree of surface consistency is necessary to ensure accurate results. Vickers testing furnishes roughly the same accuracy levels as the Brinell method, although the mea-

Table 3. Vickers hardness force increment

Abbreviation	HV0.2	HV0.3	HV0.5	HV1	HV2	HV3	HV5	HV10	HV20	HV30	HV50	HV100
Applied force N	1.96	2.94	4.9	9.8	19.6	29.4	49	98	196	294	490	980

Correlation between hardness and strength in accordance with DIN 50 150

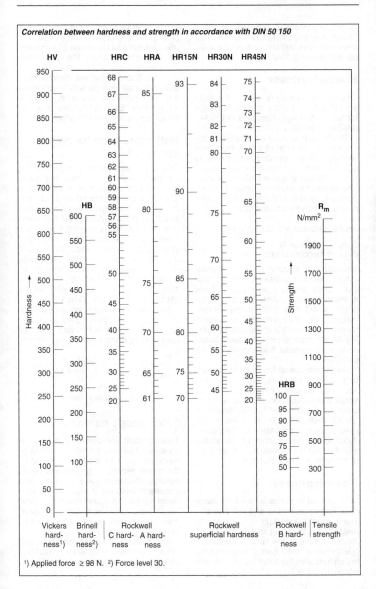

| Vickers hardness[1] | Brinell hardness[2] | Rockwell C hardness | Rockwell A hardness | Rockwell superficial hardness | Rockwell B hardness | Tensile strength |

[1] Applied force ≥ 98 N. [2] Force level 30.

surement process is extremely sensitive to movement of the test set-up. The test tools are more expensive than the balls used in Brinell testing.

Knoop hardness

This process closely resembles the Vickers procedure. It is the method of choice for testing thin-layer hardness in the Anglo-Saxon world.

The test tool is designed to leave an impression in the form of a thin, elongated rhombus. The extended diagonal d is seven times longer than the short one and is the only one that is actually measured. The applied force is less than 9.8 N. Hardness ratings are available from standard charts, or may be calculated as follows:

Knoop hardness = $1.451 \cdot F/d^2$ HK

F Applied load in N
d Long diagonal in mm

The diagonal, which is roughly 2.8 times longer than in the Vickers method, provides more accurate results with visual assessment procedures. The penetration depth is 1/3 less than in the Vickers method, allowing evaluation of surface hardness in thin parts and layers. By making Knoop impressions in different directions, even material anisotropies can be detected.

Disadvantages of this method include pronounced sensitivity to misaligned specimen surfaces, which must be absolutely perpendicular to the force-application axis, and the fact that the maximum force is restricted to 9.8 N. There are no special German standards for this procedure. Test results cannot be correlated with those of the Vickers test, on account of this lack of standardization.

Shore hardness

This method is primarily used for hardness testing on rubber and soft plastics. The test tool is a steel pin of 1.25 mm diameter; this is forced against the surface of the test specimen by a spring. The subsequent change in the spring length (spring travel) furnishes the basis for determining Shore hardness.

In the Shore D method a pretensioned spring exerts a force of 0.55 N. The tip of the steel pin has the shape of a frustrum (for testing hard rubber). The spring rate c is 4 N/mm.

In the Shore A method, measurement uses a conical steel pin with a rounded tip and no pretension. The spring rate c is 17.8 N/mm. Each 0.025 mm of spring travel corresponds to 100 Shore units.

Ball impression hardness
(DIN 53 456)

This is the standard test for determining hardness levels in plastomers, and is also employed with hard rubber substances. The test tool is a hardened steel ball 5 mm in diameter. It is applied with a minor load of 9.81 N to the surface of the test specimen which must be at least 4 mm thick. Subsequent graduated rises in force provide application pressures of 49, 132, 358 and 961 N. After 30 s the penetration depth is measured and indicated on an analog display. The test load F should be selected to provide a penetration depth h of between 0.15 and 0.35 mm.

Ball impression hardness is defined as the ratio of the applied load to the deformed area in the test surface. It can be read from tables or calculated as follows:

$$\text{Ball impression hardness} = \frac{0.21 \cdot F}{1.25 \cdot \pi \cdot (h - 0.04)} \text{ N/mm}^2$$

F Applied load in N
h Penetration depth in mm

Scleroscope hardness

This dynamic measurement method is specially designed for heavy and large metal pieces. This process is based on the measurement of the rebound height (energy of impact) of a steel indentor (hammer) featuring a diamond or hard metal tip; this is dropped from a stipulated height onto the surface of the test specimen. The rebound serves as the basis for determining the hardness.

The method is not standardized and there is no direct correlative relationship with any other hardness testing method.

Tolerances

Correlations

In the absence of special supplementary definitions, envelope analysis is mandatory for all individual form elements in prints based on standardized DIN definitions for tolerances and fits (e.g. Independence Principle from ISO 8015). The envelope concept is based on the Taylor gauge test, which specifies that maximum intolerance material mass shall not penetrate the geometric envelope at any point.

Because it is not possible to produce geometrically ideal workpieces, dimension limits (dimensional tolerances) are defined for production.

DIN 7167 includes all tolerances of form, including tolerances of parallelism, position and planar regularity as well as dimensional tolerances. The geometrical tolerance may lie anywhere within the dimensional tolerance (see diagram).

For the following tolerances of position the envelope dimension at maximum material dimension is not defined:

Tolerances of perpendicularity, slope, symmetry, coaxiality and concentricity. For these tolerances of position either direct specifications on the drawing or the general tolerances are necessary.

No generally applicable correlative data are defined for the relationship between dimensional tolerance and peak-to-valley height (general formula: $R_z \leq 0.5 \cdot T$).

ISO International Organization for Standardization.

Tolerance position
1 Actual form.
a Form tolerance, b Dimensional tolerance.

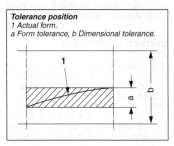

ISO system for limit allowances and fits

ISO tolerance classes are indicated by letters (for basic allowances) and numbers (for basic tolerance grades). The definitions are:
– The **letters** A to Z indicate the position of the tolerance range relative to the base line; small letters for shafts; capital letters for bores.
– The **numbers** 01 to 18 indicate the magnitude of the tolerance grade.

The ISO tolerance ranges for shafts and bores can be combined as desired to give fits; the standard bore and standard shaft systems of fits are preferred.
Standard bore: The basic allowances for all holes are identical, and different fits are obtained by selecting the appropriate shaft sizes.
Standard shaft: The basic allowances for all shafts are identical, and different fits are obtained by selecting the corresponding bore dimensions.

Most common clearance, transition and interference fits can be defined using the following selection of ISO tolerances from ISO 286.

Example for tolerance class: H7
Basic allowance ⌐ |
Tolerance grade ⌐

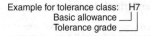

Tolerances of form and position

Tolerances of form and position should be specified only where required (e.g. in response to functional requirements, interchangeability and possible production conditions).

An element's geometrical and positional tolerances define the zone within which it must be located (surface, axis or generating line).

Within the tolerance zone the toleranced element may have any desired form or directional orientation. The tolerance applies to the entire length or surface of the toleranced element.

Symbols are employed when entering the tolerances in prints (see table).

Symbols for toleranced properties

Properties		Symbols
Straightness	1)	—
Flatness		▱
Roundness (circularity)		○
Cylindricity		⌀
Profile of any line		⌒
Profile of any surface		◠
Parallelism	2)	//
Perpendicularity		⊥
Slope		∠
Position	3)	⊕
Concentricity, coaxiality		◎
Symmetry		≡
Path	4)	↗
Overall path		↗↗

1) Tolerances of form, 2) Tolerances of direction,
3) Tolerances of location,
4) Running tolerances.

Supplementary symbols

Description		Symbols
Identification of the toleranced element	direct	↓
	with letter	A
Identification of the reference	direct	
	with letter	A A
Reference point		⌀2 / A1
Theoretically precise dimension		50
Projected tolerance zone		P
Maximum material condition		M

Geometrical deviations

The term "geometrical deviation" refers to all disparities between the actual surface and its ideal geometrical configuration.

Critical considerations may be restricted to dimensional deviations, surface irregularities or undulations, or may encompass the entire potential deviation range, depending upon the specified application. To help distinguish between the different types of geometrical deviation DIN 4760 defines a classification system including examples of deviation types and their possible sources:

1st order geometrical deviations
Formal deviations are 1st order geometrical irregularities which can be detected when an entire surface area is examined. Usually, the general relationship between formal deviation intervals and depth is > 1000:1.

2nd to 5th order geometrical deviations
Undulations, or waviness, are geometrical irregularities of the 2nd order. These essentially periodic irregularities are defined using a representative section of the actual surface area on the geometrical element under investigation.
Roughness consists of geometrical irregularities of orders 3 through 5. It is characterized by periodic or irregular formal deviations in which the deviation intervals are a relatively low multiple of their depth.

Surface parameters

Stylus instruments are employed to record sectioning planes of surface profiles, registering vertically, horizontally, and as a function of the two components in combination. The characteristics are derived from the unfiltered primary profile (P profile), the filtered roughness profile (R profile), and the filtered waviness profile (W profile). Roughness and waviness are differentiated by means of profile filters.

Profile height P_t, R_t, W_t
Maximum excursion above the centerline Z_p plus the maximum excursion below the centerline Z_v within the traversing length l_n.

The <u>traversing length</u> l_n can consist of one or more sampling lengths l_r. The value of a parameter is computed from the measured data for its sampling length. As a rule, five sampling lengths are required for computing the roughness and waviness parameters. The standardized measuring conditions are based on the maximum roughness peak-to-valley height and include, for example, limit wave length λ_c, sampling length l_r, traversing length l_n, profile length l_t, stylus-tip radius $r_{SP\,max}$ and digitizing cutoff Δx_{max}. For industrial purposes, the parameters generally employed in describing surfaces are as follows:

Arithmetic roughness average R_a
Arithmetic average of the absolute values of the ordinates of the roughness profile.

Maximum peak-to-valley height R_z
Maximum excursion above the centerline R_p plus the maximum excursion below the centerline R_v within a sampling length. As the vertical distance between the highest peak and the lowest valley, R_z is a measure of scatter of the roughness ordinates.

Material content of the roughness profile $R_{mr(c)}$
The material-content curve reflects the material content as a function of section height c. The characteristic is formed by a percentage relationship between the sum of the material lengths Ml(c) of the profile elements in a specified section height c and traversing length l_n..

Parameters of the material-content curve R_k, R_{pk}, R_{vk}, Mr_1, Mr_2
The material-content curve derived from the filtered roughness profile is divided into three sections characterized by parameters (core peak-to-valley height R_k, reduced peak height R_{pk} and reduced score depth R_{vk}). The parameters Mr_1 and Mr_2 reflect the material content at the limits of the roughness core profile.

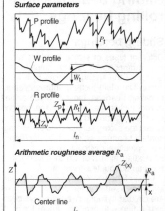

Surface parameters

Arithmetic roughness average R_a

Maximum peak-to-valley height R_z

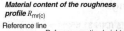

Material content of the roughness profile $R_{mr(c)}$

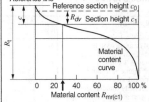

Parameters of the material-content curve R_k, R_{pk}, R_{vk}, M_{r1}, M_{r2}

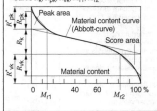

Sliding bearings and rolling bearings

Sliding bearings

Different types of sliding bearings range from bearings with usually complete separation of the sliding surfaces by a lubrication film (fluid friction), through self-lubricating bearings, most of which exhibit mixed friction i.e. some of the bearing load is transformed to solid contact between the sliding surfaces, to dry sliding-contact bearings which exhibit dry friction (i.e. completely without an effective fluid lubricating film), but which nevertheless have an adequate service life.

Most of the hydrodynamic sliding bearing types used in automotive applications are circular cylindrical radial-sleeve bearings (often with oval clearance) for holding the crankshaft and camshaft, and turbocharger bearings. Thrust bearings are usually used only as axial locators, and are not subjected to large forces.

Hydrodynamic sliding bearings

Symbols (DIN 31 652)

Designation	Symbols	Unit
Axial bearing length	B	m
Inside bearing diameter (nominal diameter)	D	m
Shaft diameter (nominal diameter)	d	m
Eccentricity (displacement between shaft and bearing centers)	e	m
Load	F	N
Min. lubricant depth	h_0	m
Local lubricant pressure	p	Pa = N/m²
Specific load $\bar{p} = F/(B \cdot D)$	$\bar{p}$	Pa
Bearing clearance $s = (D - d)$	s	m
Sommerfeld number	So	–
Relative eccentricity $2 e/s$	ε	–
Effective dynamic viscosity of the lubricant	η_{eff}	Pa · s
Relative bearing clearance $\psi = s/D$	ψ	–
Displacement angle	β	°
Hydrodynamically effective angular velocity	ω_{eff}	s⁻¹

A hydrodynamic sliding bearing is reliable in service if it remains sufficiently unaffected by the following:
– <u>Wear</u> (sufficient separation of the contact surfaces by the lubricant),
– <u>Mechanical stress</u> (bearing material of sufficient strength),
– <u>Thermal loading</u> (observance of thermal stability of bearing material and viscosity/temperature behavior of lubricant).

The dimensionless Sommerfeld number So is used when determining loadability, i.e. when assessing the formation of the lubricating film

$$So = D \cdot \psi^2/(D \cdot B \cdot \eta_{\text{eff}} \cdot \omega_{\text{eff}})$$

As the Sommerfeld number So increases, relative eccentricity ε rises and minimum lubricating-film thickness h_0 drops:
$$h_0 = (D - d)/2 - e = 0.5 \, D \cdot \psi \cdot (1 - \varepsilon)$$
with relative eccentricity
$$\varepsilon = 2e/(D - d)$$

Table 1. Orders of magnitude of the coefficients of friction for different types of friction
The coefficients of friction given below are approximate values, and are intended solely for comparison of the different types of friction.

Type of friction	Coefficient of friction f
Dry friction	0.1 ... > 1
Mixed friction	0.01 ... 0.1
Fluid friction	0.01
Friction in roller bearings	0.001

Table 2. Empirical values for maximum approved specific bearing load
(Maximum values only apply for very low sliding velocities)

Bearing materials	Maximum specif. bearing load $\bar{p}_{\text{lim}}$
Pb and Sn alloys (babbitt metals)	5 ... 15 N/mm²
Bronze, lead base	7 ... 20 N/mm²
Bronze, tin base	7 ... 25 N/mm²
AlSn alloys	7 ... 18 N/mm²
AlZn alloys	7 ... 20 N/mm²

The Sommerfeld number is also used to determine the coefficient of friction in the bearing, and thus for calculation of frictional power and thermal stress (cf. DIN 31 652, VDI Guideline 2204).

Because hydrodynamic bearings also operate with mixed friction a certain amount of the time, they must accommodate a certain amount of contamination without loss of function, and are additionally subjected to high dynamic and thermal stress (particularly in piston engines), the bearing material must meet a number of requirements, some of which are opposed to each another.
– <u>Anti-seizure performance</u> (resistance to welding),
– <u>Conformability</u> (compensation of misalignment without shortening service life),
– <u>Embeddability</u> (ability of the bearing surface to absorb particles of dirt without increasing bearing or shaft wear),
– <u>Fatigue strength</u> (under fatigue loading, particularly with high thermal stress),
– <u>Mechanical loadability</u>,
– <u>Run-in performance</u> (a combination of compatibility, resistance to wear and embeddability),
– <u>Seizure resistance</u> (bearing material must not weld to shaft material, even under high compressive load and high sliding velocity),
– <u>Wear resistance</u> (in the case of mixed friction),
– <u>Wettability by lubricant</u>.

If a bearing (e.g. piston-pin bushing) is to be simultaneously subjected to high loads and low sliding velocities, high fatigue strength and wear resistance should take precedence over resistance to seizing. Bearing materials used in such cases are hard bronzes, e.g. leaded tin bronzes (Table 3).

Since they are subjected to high dynamic loads with high sliding velocities, connecting-rod and crankshaft bearings in internal-combustion engines must fulfill a number of different requirements. In these applications, **multilayer bearings**, above all trimetal bearings, have proved themselves in practice.

The service life of crankshaft bearings can be further increased through the use of **grooved sliding bearings**. In these bearings, fine grooves have been machined into the surface in the sliding direction, and filled with a liner made of soft material (an electroplated liner similar to that found in trimetal bearings). These contact areas are separated from one another by a harder light-alloy metal.

These bearings feature low rates of wear and high fatigue strength with good embeddability regarding lubricant impurities.

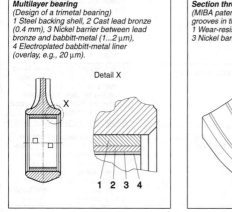

Multilayer bearing
(Design of a trimetal bearing)
1 Steel backing shell, 2 Cast lead bronze (0.4 mm), 3 Nickel barrier between lead bronze and babbitt-metal (1...2 μm), 4 Electroplated babbitt-metal liner (overlay, e.g. 20 μm).

Detail X

1 2 3 4

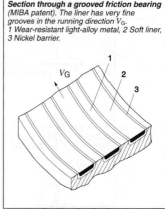

Section through a grooved friction bearing
(MIBA patent). The liner has very fine grooves in the running direction V_G.
1 Wear-resistant light-alloy metal, 2 Soft liner, 3 Nickel barrier.

V_G

Table 3. Selection of materials for hydrodynamic sliding bearings

Material	Alloy designation	Composition in %	HB hardness 20°C	HB hardness 100°C	Remarks, application examples
Tin-base babbitt metal	LgPbSn 80 (WM 80)	80 Sn; 12 Sb; 6 Cu; 2 Pb	27	10	Very soft, good conformance of contact surfaces to off-axis operation, excellent anti-seizure performance.
Lead-base babbitt metal	LgPbSn 10 (WM 10)	73 Pb; 16 Sb; 10 Sn; 1 Cu	23	9	Reinforcement necessary, e.g. as composite steel casting or with intermediate nickel layer on lead bronze.
Lead-base bronze	G-CuPb 25	74 Cu; 25 Pb; 1 Sn	50	47	Very soft, excellent anti-seizure performance, less resistant to wear.
	G-CuPb 22	70 Cu; 22 Pb; 6 Sn; 3 Ni	86	79	
Lead-tin-base bronze	G-CuPb 10 Sn	80 Cu; 10 Pb; 10 Sn	75	67	Improved anti-seizure performance by alloying with Pb. More resistant to off-axis performance than pure tin bronzes, therefore high-load Pb-Sn bronzes are preferable for use as crankshaft bearings. Composite bearings used in internal-combustion engine manufacture, piston-pins $\bar{p}$ to 100 N/mm².
	G-CuPb 23 Sn	76 Cu; 23 Pb; 1 Sn	55	53	Composite casting for low-load bearings (70 N/mm²). Also thick-wall bearing shells. Very good anti-seizure performance. Crankshaft and camshaft bearings, connecting-rod bearings.
Tin-base bronze	G-CuSn 10 Zn	88 Cu; 10 Sn; 2 Zn	85		Hard material. Friction-bearing shells can be subjected to moderate load at low sliding velocities. Worm gears.
	CuSn 8	92 Cu; 8 Sn	80 ... 220		High-grade wrought alloy. Good performance under high loads and in absence of sufficient lubrication. Steering-knuckle bearings. Particularly well suited for use as thin-wall sliding bearing bushings.
Red brass	G-CuSn7 ZnPb	83 Cu; 6 Pb; 7 Sn; 4 Zn	75	65	Tin partially replaced with zinc and lead. Can be used in place of tin bronze, but only for moderate loads (40 N/mm²). General sliding bearings for machinery. Piston pins, bushings, crankshaft and toggle-lever bearings.

Material	Alloy designation	Composition in %	HB hardness 20°C	100°C	Remarks, application examples
Brass	CuZn 31 Si	68 Cu: 31 Zn; 1 Si	90 ... 200		Zn content is disadvantageous at high bearing temperatures. Can be used in place of tin bronze; low loads.
Aluminum bronze	CuAl 9 Mn	88 Cu; 9 Al; 3 Mn	110 ... 190		Thermal expansion comparable to that of light alloys. Suitable for use as interference-fit bearings in light-alloy housings. Better wear resistance than tin bronze, but higher friction.
Aluminum alloy	AlSi 12 Cu NiMn	1 Cu; 85 Al; 12 Si; 1 Ni; 1 Mn	110	100	Piston alloy for low sliding velocities.
Rolled aluminum cladding	AlSn 6	1 Cu; 6 Sn; 90 Al; 3 Si	40	30	Liquated tin stretched by rolling, therefore high loadability and good anti-friction properties. Improved by electroplated layer.
Electro-plated liners	PbSn 10 Cu	2 Cu; 88 Pb; 10 Sn	50 ... 60		Used in modern trimetal bearings, electroplated to thickness 10 ... 30 μm, very fine grain. Intermediate nickel layer on bearing metal.

For materials, see also DIN 1703, 1705, 1716, 17 660, 17 662, 17 665, 1494, 1725, 1743.
ISO 4381, 4382, 4383.

Table 4. Sintered-metal bearing materials
Sint-B indicates 20% P (porosity) (Sint-A: 25% P; Sint-C: 15% P).

Material group	Desig-nation Sintered ...	Composition	Remarks
Sintered iron	B 00	Fe	Standard material which meets moderate load and noise requirements.
Sintered steel, containing Cu	B 10	< 0.3 C 1 ... 5 Cu Rest Fe	Good resistance to wear, can be subjected to higher loads than pure Fe bearings.
Sintered steel, higher Cu content	B 20	20 Cu Rest Fe	More favorably priced than sintered bronze, good noise behavior and $p \cdot v$ values.
Sintered bronze	B 50	< 0.2 C 9 ... 10 Sn Rest Cu	Standard Cu-Sn-base material, good noise behavior.

Sintered-metal sliding bearings

Sintered-metal sliding bearings consist of sintered metals which are porous and impregnated with liquid lubricants. For many small motors in automotive applications, this type of bearing is a good compromise in terms of precision, installation, freedom from maintenance, service life and cost. They are primarily used in motors with shaft diameters from 1.5...12 mm. Sintered-iron bearings and sintered-steel bearings (inexpensive, less likely to interact with the lubricant) are preferable to sintered-bronze bearings for use in the motor vehicle (Table 4). The advantages of sintered-bronze bearings are greater loadability, lower noise and lower friction indices (this type of bearing is used in phonograph equipment, office equipment, data systems and cameras).

The performance of sintered bearings over long periods of service is closely related to the use of optimum lubricants.
Mineral oils: Inadequate cold-flow properties, medium non-aging properties.
Synthetic oils: (e.g. esters, Poly-α olefins): Good cold-flow properties, high resistance to thermal stresses, low evaporation tendency.
Synthetic greases: (oils which include metal soaps): Low starting friction, low wear.

Dry sliding bearings
(see Table 5, P. 288)

Solid polymer bearings made of thermoplastics
Advantages: Economically-priced, no danger of seizure with metals.
Disadvantages: Low thermal conductivity, relatively low operating temperatures, possible swelling due to humidity, low loadability, high coefficient of thermal expansion.

The most frequently used polymer materials are: Polyoxymethylene (POM, POM-C), polyamide (PA), polyethylene and polybutylene terephthalate (PET, PBT), polyetheretherketone (PEEK).

The tribological and mechanical properties can be varied over a wide range by incorporating lubricants and reinforcements in the thermoplastic base material.
Lubricant additives: polytetrafluoroethylene (PTFE), graphite (C), silicone oil and other liquid lubricants.
Reinforcement additives: glass fibers (GF), carbon fibers (CF).
Application examples: windshield wiper bearings (PA and fiberglass), idle-position actuators (PEEK and carbon fiber, PTFE and other additives).

Polymer bearings made of duroplastics and elastomers
These materials, with their high levels of intrinsic friction, are seldom used as bearing materials in the motor vehicle. Duroplastics include: phenol resins (high friction, e.g. Resitex), epoxy resins (require the addition of PTFE or C in order to reduce their high intrinsic brittleness, reinforcement necessary usually by fibers), polyimides (high thermal and mechanical loadability).
Application examples: polyimide axial stop in wiper motor.

Metal-backed composite bearings
Composite bearings are combinations of polymer materials, fibers and metals. Depending upon bearing structure, they provide advantages over pure or filled polymer sliding bearings in terms of loadability, bearing clearance, thermal conductivity and installation (suitable for use with oscillating motion).
Example of bearing structure: Tinplated or copper-clad steel backing (several millimeters thick), onto which is sintered an 0.2...0.35 mm thick porous bronze layer with a porosity of 30...40%. A low-friction polymer material is rolled into this bronze layer as a liner. Liner made of a) acetal resin, either impregnated with oil or containing lubricating recesses, or b) PTFE + Pb or MoS₂ additive.

Metal-backed composite bearings are available in a number of different shapes and compositions. Metal-backed composite bearings with woven PTFE fiber inserts exhibit unusually high loadability and are suitable for use in ball-and-socket joints.

Some motor-vehicle applications for this type of bearing are: Shock-absorber-piston bearings, release-lever bearings for clutch pressure plates, brake-shoe bearings in drum brakes, ball-and-socket bearings, door-hinge bearings, bearings for seat-belt winding shafts, steering-knuckle bearings, gear-pump bearings.

Carbon-graphite bearings

Carbon-graphite bearings are members of the ceramic bearing family due to their method of manufacture and material properties. The base materials are powdered carbon; tar or synthetic resins are used as binders.

<u>Advantages</u>: Heat-resistant up to 350 °C (hard-burnt carbon) or 500 °C (electrographite), good antifriction properties, good corrosion resistance, good thermal conductivity, good thermal shock resistance. They are highly brittle, however.

Examples of carbon-graphite bearing applications: Fuel-pump bearings, bearings in drying ovens, adjustable blades in turbochargers.

Metal-ceramic bearings

Metal-ceramic bearings consist of material manufactured by powder metallurgy processes; in addition to the metallic matrix, the bearing material also contains finely distributed solid lubricant particles.

<u>Matrix</u>: e.g. bronze, iron, nickel.
<u>Lubricant</u>: e.g. graphite, MoS_2.

These materials are suitable for use under extremely high loads, and are at the same time self-lubricating.

Application example: Steering-knuckle bearings.

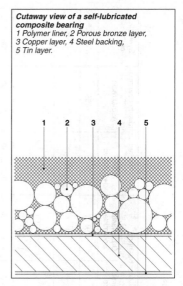

Cutaway view of a self-lubricated composite bearing
1 Polymer liner, 2 Porous bronze layer, 3 Copper layer, 4 Steel backing, 5 Tin layer.

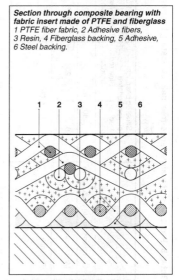

Section through composite bearing with fabric insert made of PTFE and fiberglass
1 PTFE fiber fabric, 2 Adhesive fibers, 3 Resin, 4 Fiberglass backing, 5 Adhesive, 6 Steel backing.

Table 5. Properties of maintenance-free, self-lubricating bearings

	Sintered bearings oil-impregnated		Polymer bearings		Metal-backed composite bearings	Liner	Synthetic carbons
	Sintered iron	Sintered bronze	Thermoplastic polyamide	Duroplastic polyimide	PTFE + additive	Acetal resin	
Compression strength N/mm²	80 ... 180		70	110	250	250	100 ... 200
Max. sliding velocity m/s	10	20	2	8	2	3	10
Typical load N/mm²	1 ... 4 (10)		15	50 (at 50 °C) 10 (at 200 °C)	20 ... 50	20 ... 50	50
Permissible operating temperature °C Short-term	− 60 ... 180 (depends on oil) 200		− 130 ... 100 120	− 100 ... 250 300	− 200 ... 280	− 40 ... 100 130	− 200 ... 350 500
Coefficient of friction without lubrication	with lubrication 0.04 ... 0.2		0.2 ... 0.4 (100 °C) 0.4 ... 0.6 (25 °C)	0.2 ... 0.5 (unfilled) 0.1 ... 0.4 (filled)	0.04 ... 0.2	0.07¹) ... 0.2	0.1 ... 0.35
Thermal conductivity W/(m · K)	20 ... 40		0.3	0.4 ... 1	46	2	10 ... 65
Corrosion resistance	poor	good	very good	very good	good	good	very good
Chemical resistance	none		very good	very good	conditional	conditional	good
max. $p \cdot \upsilon$ (N/mm²) · (m/s)	20		0.05	0.2	1.5 ... 2		0.4 ... 1.8
Embeddability of dirt and abraded material	poor		good	good	poor	good	poor

¹) PTFE filled

Rolling bearings

In rolling bearings, forces are transmitted by rolling elements (balls or rollers). Here, rolling is a form of movement comprising rolling and sliding. In rolling bearings a microslip (i.e. sliding) nearly always occurs in addition to the pure rolling movement. In the case of mixed friction, this sliding movement leads to increased wear.

Advantages:
Low static coefficient of friction (0.001...0.002), therefore particularly well suited to applications in which starting occurs frequently,
Low maintenance,
Suited to permanent lubrication,
Low lubricant consumption,
Small bearing width,
High precision.

Disadvantages:
Sensitive to impact loads, sensitive to dirt,
Bearing noise is too high for some applications,
Standard bearings are only 1-piece bearings.

Bearing materials

Bearing races and rolling elements are made of a special chromium-alloy steel (100 Cr6H) which has a high degree of purity and a hardness in the range of 58...65 HRC.

Depending upon application, the bearing cages are made of stamped sheet steel or brass. Cages made of polymer materials have come into recent use due to their ease of manufacture, improved adaptability to bearing geometry and other tribological advantages (e.g. antifriction properties). Polymer materials made of fiberglass-reinforced polyamide 66 can withstand continuous operating temperatures of up to 120 °C, and can be operated for brief periods at temperatures up to 140 °C.

Static loadability (ISO 76-1987)

The static load rating C_o is used as a measure of the loadability of very slow-moving or static rolling bearings. C_o is that load at which total permanent deformation of rolling elements and races at the most highly-loaded contact point amounts to 0.0001 of the diameter of the rolling element. A load equal to this load rating C_o generates a maximum compressive stress of 4000 N/mm² in the center of the most highly-loaded rolling element.

Dynamic loadability

The basic load rating C is used for calculating the service life of a rotating rolling bearing. C indicates that bearing load for a nominal bearing service life of 1 million revolutions. In accordance with ISO 281:

Service life equation $L_{10} = \left(\dfrac{C}{P}\right)^p$

L_{10} Nominal service life in millions of revolutions achieved or exceeded by 90 % of a large batch of identical bearings,
C Basic load rating in N (determined empirically),
P Equivalent dynamic bearing load in N,
p Empirical exponent of the service life equation: for ball bearings, $p = 3$, for roller bearings, $p = 10/3$.

Modified nominal service life

$$L_{na} = a_1 \cdot a_2 \cdot a_3 \cdot \left(\frac{C}{P}\right)^p$$

L_{na} Modified nominal service life in millions of revolutions,
a_1 Factor for survival probability, e.g. 90 %: $a_1 = 1$; 95 %: $a_1 = 0.62$,
a_2 Material coefficient of friction,
a_3 Coefficient of friction for operating conditions (bearing lubrication).

As the frictional coefficients a_2 and a_3 are not mutually independent, the combined coefficient a_{23} is employed.

Rolling bearings are subject to a fatigue stress. It is included, along with other influencing parameters such as contamination, in the calculation of service life (see catalogs issued by rolling-bearing manufacturers).

Spring calculations

See PP. 14 ... 16 for names of units

Quantity		Unit
b	Width of spring leaf	mm
c	Spring rate (spring constant): For leaf springs and helical springs, increase in spring force per mm of spring deflection;	N/mm
	For torsion bar springs, coiled torsion springs and flat spiral springs, increase in spring moment per degree of rotation	$N \cdot mm/°$
d	Wire diameter	mm
D	Mean coil diameter	mm
E	Modulus of elasticity: for spring steel = 206,000 N/mm², for other materials, see P. 196	N/mm²

Quantity		Unit
F	Spring force	N
G	Shear modulus: for hot-formed springs ≈ 78,500 N/mm² for cold-formed springs ≈ 81,400 N/mm²	N/mm²
h	Height of spring leaf	mm
n	Number of active coils	–
M	Spring moment	$N \cdot mm$
s	Spring deflection	mm
α	Angle of rotation	°
σ_b	Bending stress	N/mm²
τ	Torsional stress	N/mm²

Conversion of no longer permissible units:
1 kp = 9.81 N ≈ 10 N, 1 kp/mm ≈ 10 N/mm, 1 kp mm ≈ 10 N mm,
1 kp mm/° ≈ 10 N mm/°, 1 kp/mm² ≈ 10 N/mm².

Springs subjected to bending stress

Type	Bending stress	Spring rate
Rectangular cantilever spring (constant cross section) 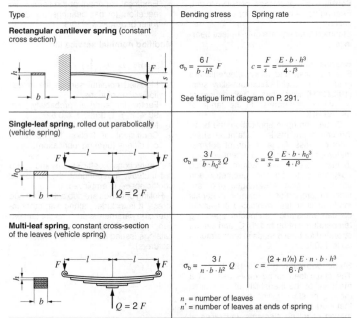	$\sigma_b = \dfrac{6\,l}{b \cdot h^2}\,F$	$c = \dfrac{F}{s} = \dfrac{E \cdot b \cdot h^3}{4 \cdot l^3}$ See fatigue limit diagram on P. 291.
Single-leaf spring, rolled out parabolically (vehicle spring) $Q = 2\,F$	$\sigma_b = \dfrac{3\,l}{b \cdot h_0^2}\,Q$	$c = \dfrac{Q}{s} = \dfrac{E \cdot b \cdot h_0^3}{4 \cdot l^3}$
Multi-leaf spring, constant cross-section of the leaves (vehicle spring) $Q = 2\,F$	$\sigma_b = \dfrac{3\,l}{n \cdot b \cdot h^2}\,Q$	$c = \dfrac{(2 + n'/n)\,E \cdot n \cdot b \cdot h^3}{6 \cdot l^3}$

n = number of leaves
n' = number of leaves at ends of spring

Type	Bending stress	Spring rate
Coil spring (DIN 2088) 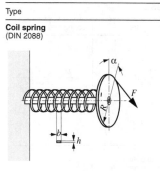	The same equations are used for torsion and spiral springs. Rectangular cross-section $$\sigma_b = \frac{6}{b \cdot h^2} M \qquad c = \frac{M}{\alpha} = \frac{E \cdot b \cdot h^3}{57.3 \cdot 12 \cdot l}$$ Circular section $$\sigma_b = \frac{32}{\pi \cdot d^3} M \qquad c = \frac{M}{\alpha} = \frac{E \cdot \pi \cdot d^4}{57.3 \cdot 64 \cdot l}$$ where $M = F \cdot R$ l = straight length of spring material = $2\pi \cdot r \cdot n$ (r mean coil radius)
Spiral torsion spring (both ends clamped) 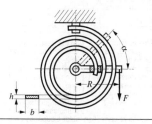	Under a pulsating load the stress increase due to curvature must be taken into consideration.	

Fatigue-limit diagram
For polished spring-steel strip (not for vehicle springs) in accordance with DIN 17 222 Ck 75 and Ck 85, hardened and tempered to 430...500 HV[1]), and Ck 85 and Ck 101, hardened and tempered to 500...580 HV.
Example (broken line in diagram):
For a leaf spring with a hardness of 430...500 HV, assuming a minimum stress of

σ_U = 600 N/mm²

the permissible stress range is

σ_{hperm} = 480 N/mm²

and the overstress is

$\sigma_O = \sigma_U + \sigma_{hperm}$ = 1080 N/mm².

For reasons of safety, the stress range selected should be approximately 30 % lower. Surface damage (corrosion pits, score marks) drastically reduces the fatigue limit.

[1]) Vickers hardness; see P. 276.

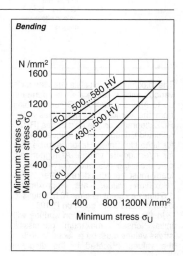

Bending

Springs subjected to torsional stress

Type	Torsional stress	Spring rate
Torsion-bar spring of circular cross-section (DIN 2091)	$\tau = \dfrac{16}{\pi \cdot d^3} M$ where $M = F \cdot R$	$c = \dfrac{M}{\alpha} = \dfrac{G \cdot \pi \cdot d^4}{57.3 \cdot 32 \cdot l}$
Helical springs made of round wire (DIN 2089) Compression spring Extension spring Above: half "German" loop, Below: hifo® hook (see P. 295)	a) In the case of a static or infrequently alternating load, allowance need not be made for the effect of the wire curvature: $\tau = \dfrac{8 \cdot D}{\pi \cdot d^3} F$ b) In the case of a pulsating load, the non-uniform distribution of torsional stresses must be taken into consideration: $\tau_k = k \cdot \tau = \dfrac{8\,k \cdot D}{\pi \cdot d^3} F$ The curvature correction factor k depends on the spring index D/d.	$c = \dfrac{F}{s} = \dfrac{G \cdot d^4}{8 \cdot n \cdot D^3}$ In the case of compression springs with only 1 ... 3 coils, the load deflection curve is no longer a straight line; spring rate c is initially smaller and then larger than the calculated rate.

D/d	3	4	6	8	10	20
k	1.55	1.38	1.24	1.17	1.13	1.06

Avoid $D/d < 3$ and > 20.

The maximum permissible stresses τ_{k0} for various wire diameters at temperatures up to approximately 40 °C can be taken from the vertical boundary lines of the RDZ diagrams on the next pages (RDZ = relaxation, fatigue limit, fatigue strength for finite life). Interpolation is to be used for intermediate values. At higher temperatures, the relaxation curves (loss of load) must be considered. After 300 h, relaxation values are approximately 1.5 times as great as after 10 h. Values for other materials are given on P. 196.

In the case of extension springs with initial tension, maximum permissible stress values must be reduced to 90 % of the values indicated in the diagrams because so-called setting is not possible here.

Explanation of the nomogram on the following page

The nomogram applies to cylindrical helical extension and compression springs made of round steel wire (shear modulus $G = 81{,}400$ N/mm²). In the case of materials with a different shear modulus G' spring deflection must be multiplied by G/G'.

The nomogram indicates the deflection s' of one coil. Total deflection s is obtained by multiplying (s') by the number of active coils n: $s = n \cdot s'$.

Nomogram for helical spring calculation

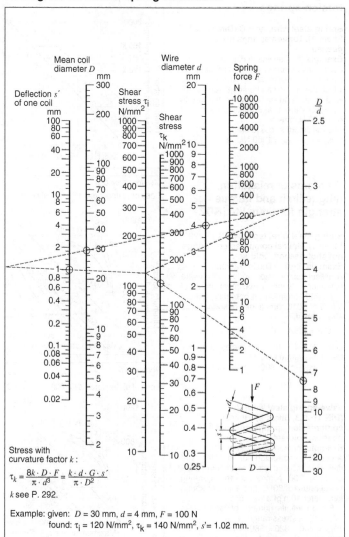

Mean coil diameter D mm

Deflection s' of one coil mm

Wire diameter d mm

Shear stress τ_i N/mm²

Shear stress τ_k N/mm²

Spring force F N

$\dfrac{D}{d}$

Stress with curvature factor k :

$$\tau_k = \frac{8k \cdot D \cdot F}{\pi \cdot d^3} = \frac{k \cdot d \cdot G \cdot s'}{\pi \cdot D^2}$$

k see P. 292.

Example: given: D = 30 mm, d = 4 mm, F = 100 N
found: τ_i = 120 N/mm², τ_k = 140 N/mm², s'= 1.02 mm.

Fatigue-limit diagram for torsion springs

Spring-steel wire, type C (DIN 17 223, Sheet 1). Torsion springs not shot-peened.
Example (broken line in diagram):
For a torsion spring with a wire diameter $d = 2$ mm, the permissible stress range to which the spring can be subjected for 10^7 load cycles and more without fracture is $\sigma_{bh} = 500$ N/mm² at a minimum stress of $\sigma_U = 800$ N/mm².
The maximum stress is then

$\sigma_O = \sigma_U + \sigma_{bh} = 1300$ N/mm².

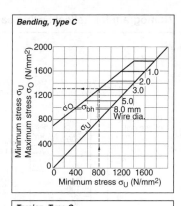

Bending, Type C

Diagrams of relaxation fatigue limit and fatigue strength for finite life (RDZ)

Spring-steel wire, type C (DIN 17 223, Sheet 1). Helical compression springs not shot-peened, cold-set.
Example (broken line in diagram):
A helical compression spring with a wire diameter of 3 mm a maximum stress of $\tau_{kO} = 900$ N/mm² at an operating temperature of 80 °C, has a loss of spring force after 10 h of

$\Delta F_{10} = 5.5\,\%$.

Given $N = 4 \times 10^5$ load cycles to failure, the stress range would be

$\tau_{kh} = \tau_{kO} - \tau_{kU} = 900 - 480 = 420$ N/mm².

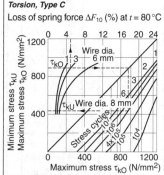

Torsion, Type C
Loss of spring force ΔF_{10} (%) at $t = 80$ °C

Valve-spring steel wire, VD (DIN 17 223, Sheet 2). Helical compression springs not shot-peened, cold-set.
Example (broken line in diagram):
A helical compression spring with a wire diameter of 3 mm and a maximum stress of $\tau_{kO} = 700$ N/mm² at an operating temperature of 80 °C, has a loss of spring force after 10 h of $\Delta F_{10} = 5\,\%$.
For an infinite number of load cycles ($N \geq 10^7$), a stress range of

$\tau_{kh} = 700 - 320 = 380$ N/mm²
is permissible.

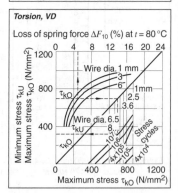

Torsion, VD
Loss of spring force ΔF_{10} (%) at $t = 80$ °C

Valve-spring steel wire, VD CrV.[1]
Helical compression springs not shot-peened, cold-set.
Example (broken line in diagram):
A helical compression spring with a wire diameter of 3 mm and a maximum stress of τ_{kO} = 700 N/mm^2 at an operating temperature of 160°C, has a loss of spring force after 10 h of ΔF_{10} = 6%.

For an infinite number of load cycles ($N \geq 10^7$), a stress range of
$$\tau_{kh} = 700 - 240 = 460 \text{ N/mm}^2$$
is permissible.

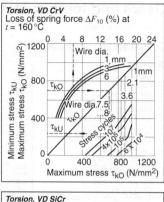

Torsion, VD CrV
Loss of spring force ΔF_{10} (%) at t = 160°C

Valve-spring steel wire, VD SiCr.[1]
Helical compression springs not shot-peened, cold-set.
Example (broken line in diagram):
A helical compression spring with a wire diameter of 3 mm and a maximum stress of τ_{kO} = 900 N/mm^2 at an operating temperature of 160°C, has a loss of spring force after 10 h of ΔF_{10} = 3.5%.

For an infinite number of load cycles ($N \geq 10^7$), a stress range of
$$\tau_{kh} = 900 - 510 = 390 \text{ N/mm}^2$$
is permissible.

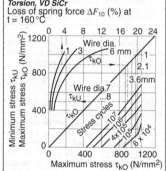

Torsion, VD SiCr
Loss of spring force ΔF_{10} (%) at t = 160°C

If the danger of natural oscillation or other additional loads is present, reduce the selected stress range by approximately 30%. Shot peening increases the permissible stress range by approximately 40%.

In the case of **compression springs**, force eccentricity is reduced as far as possible by winding the spring such that the wire end at each end of the spring touches the adjoining coil (closed ends). Each end of the spring is then ground flat perpendicular to the axis of the spring (wire end $\approx d/4$). The following values then apply:
Total number of coils $n_t = n + 2$.
The solid length from coil to coil $\leq (n + 2) \, d$.

Helical extension springs are over-stressed by roughly 50% at standard hooks and loops when the body of the spring is subjected to permissible stress ranges. Hifo® hooks (German Patent, and others) exhibit infinite fatigue strength due to internal high initial force F_O.

Due to their favorable internal stresses, twist-wound extension springs can be subjected to stresses as high as those to which compression springs are subjected, and exhibit smaller relaxation than the latter. For high initial forces F_O (= hifo), these springs can be up to 50% shorter at F_1 than standard extension springs.

---

[1] According to DIN 17 223, Part 2.

Gears and tooth systems

(with involute flanks)

Quantities and units (DIN 3960)

Quantity		Unit
a	Center distance	mm
b	Face width	mm
c	Bottom clearance	mm
d	Reference diameter	mm
d_a	Outside diameter	mm
d_b	Base circle diameter	mm
d_f	Root diameter	mm
d_w	Pitch diameter	mm
h_a	Addendum $= m \cdot h_{aP}^*$	mm
h_f	Dedendum $= m \cdot h_{fP}^*$	mm
i	Transmission ratio $= z_2/z_1$	–
j_n	Normal backlash	mm
m	Module m $= d/z$	mm
n	Rotational speed	min⁻¹
p	Pitch $p = \pi \cdot m$	mm
s	Tooth thickness (circular)	mm
W	Span measurement	mm
x	Addendum modification coefficient	–

Quantity		Unit
z	Number of teeth	–
α	Pressure angle	°
β	Helix angle	°
ε	Contact ratio	°
*	Specific value, to be multiplied by m	
Superscripts and subscripts		
1	referred to gear 1	
2	referred to gear 2	
a	referred to tooth tip	
b	referred to base circle	
f	referred to root	
n	referred to normal profile	
t	referred to transverse profile	
w	referred to operating pitch circle	
F	referred to root tooth load	
P	referred to basic rack	
W	referred to contact pressure	

Gear type and shape are determined by the position of the shafts which are joined by the gears in order to transmit forces or movements.

Cycloidal teeth: Cycloidal teeth are used primarily in the watch and clock industry. They permit small numbers of teeth without cutter interference (undercut). They are characterized by low contact pressure, but are sensitive to variations in the distance between centers.

Involute teeth: Involute teeth, on the other hand, are not sensitive to variations in the distance between centers.

They can be produced with relatively simple tools using the generating method. The automobile industry uses involute teeth almost exclusively, therefore the following information is limited to this type of gear system.

All spur gears with the same module (and the same pressure angle) can be produced using the same generating tool, regardless of the number of teeth and addendum modification. A number of modules have been standardized in order to

Parameters for spur gears (cycloidal teeth)

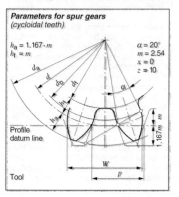

$h_a = 1.167 \cdot m$
$h_f = m$

$\alpha = 20°$
$m = 2.54$
$x = 0$
$z = 10$

Profile datum line

Tool

Effect of addendum modification at spur gear (cycloidal teeth)

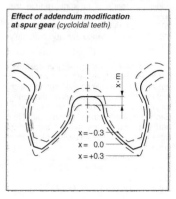

$x = -0.3$
$x = 0.0$
$x = +0.3$

Definitions

Table 1. Gear types

Position of shafts	Gear type	Properties	Examples of application in automotive engineering
Parallel	External or internal spur-gear pair with straight or helical teeth	Helical teeth run more smoothly but are subject to axial thrust	Manual transmissions
Intersecting	Bevel-gear pair with straight, helical, or curved teeth	Sensitive to fluctuations in angular and axial clearance	Differentials
Crossing	Offset bevel-gear pair with helical or curved teeth		Rear-axle drives
	Crossed helical-gear pair	For small loads	Distributor drives
	Worm-gear pair	High-ratio, single-stage transmission	Windshield wiper drives
Coaxial	Toothed shaft and hub	Sliding shaft coupling	Starters (Bendix shaft and pinion)

limit the number of such tools and the number of master gears required for gear testing:

Module for spur and bevel gears: DIN 780 (see table on P. 299), module for worms and worm gears: DIN 780, module for toothed shafts and stubs: DIN 5480. The module in the normal profile for crossed helical gears is also selected in conformance with DIN 780 in most cases. A series of modules suited to the manufacturing process is generally used for curved-tooth bevel gears.

Tooth shape
Basic rack for spur gears: DIN 867, DIN 58 400; basic rack for bevel gears: DIN 3971; basic rack for worms and worm gears: DIN 3975; basic rack for toothed shafts and hubs: DIN 5480.

The tooth shape for crossed helical gears can also be designed in conformance with the basic rack as per DIN 867. In addition to the standardized pressure angles (20° for running gears and 30° for toothed shafts and hubs), pressure angles of 12°, 14°30', 15°, 17°30', 22°30' and 25° are used.

Table 2. List of standards

Standard	Title
DIN 3960	Definitions, parameters and equations for involute cylindrical gears and gear pairs
DIN 3961...4	Tolerances for cylindrical gear teeth
DIN 3990/1...5	Calculation of load capacity of cylindrical gears
DIN 58 405/1...4	Spur gear drives for precision engineering
DIN 3971	Definitions and parameters for bevel gears and bevel gear pairs
DIN 5480	Involute spline joints
DIN 3975	Terms and definitions for cylindrical worm gears with shaft angle 90°

Table 3. Basic equations for spur gears

Designation	Straight gear ($\beta = 0$)	Helical gear ($\beta \neq 0$)
Reference-circle diameter	$d = z \cdot m$ Module m, see P. 296	$d = \dfrac{z \cdot m_n}{\cos \beta}$ Module m_n, see P. 296
	The neg. value of z is to be used for internal teeth; center distance a becomes neg.	
Base-circle diameter	$d_b = d \cdot \cos \alpha_n$	$d_b = d \cdot \cos \alpha_t$ α_t from $\tan \alpha_t = \dfrac{\tan \alpha_n}{\cos \beta}$
Center distance, no backlash; if normal backlash $j_n = 0$	$a = m\dfrac{z_1 + z_2}{2} \cdot \dfrac{\cos \alpha}{\cos \alpha_w} = \dfrac{d_{b1} + d_{b2}}{2 \cdot \cos \alpha_w}$ as per DIN 867, $\alpha = 20°$ α_w from: $\operatorname{inv} \alpha_w = \dfrac{2\,(x_1 + x_2)\sin \alpha + j_n/m}{(z_1 + z_2)\cos \alpha} + \operatorname{inv}\alpha$	$a = m_t\dfrac{z_1 + z_2}{2} \cdot \dfrac{\cos \alpha_t}{\cos \alpha_{wt}} = \dfrac{d_{b1} + d_{b2}}{2 \cdot \cos \alpha_{wt}}$ $m_t = \dfrac{m_n}{\cos \beta}$ $\cos \beta_b = \dfrac{\sin \alpha_n}{\sin \alpha_t}$ $\operatorname{inv} \alpha_{wt} = \dfrac{m_n \cdot 2(x_1 + x_2)\sin \alpha_n + j_n/\cos \beta_b}{m_t(z_1 + z_2)\cos \alpha_t} + \operatorname{inv}\alpha_t$
Involute	$\operatorname{inv} \alpha = \tan \alpha - \operatorname{arc}\alpha$ P. 146.	when $\alpha = 20°$, $\operatorname{inv} \alpha = 0.014904$
Pitch-circle diameter	$d_w = d_b/\cos \alpha_w$	$d_w = d_b/\cos \alpha_{wt}$
Root-circle diameter	$d_f = d + 2\,xm - 2\,h^*_{fP} \cdot m$	$d_f = d_b + 2\,xm_n - 2\,h^*_{fP} \cdot m_n$
	with dedendum $h^*_{fP} \cdot m$ ($h^*_{fP} = 1.167$ or 1.25 as per DIN 3972)	
Tip-circle diameter	$d_a = d + 2\,xm + 2\,h^*_{aP} \cdot m$	$d_a = d \cdot 2\,xm_n + 2\,h^*_{aP} \cdot m_n$
	with addendum $h^*_{aP} \cdot m$ ($h^*_{aP} = 1.0$ as per DIN 867)	
Bottom clearance	$c_1 = a_{min} - d_{a1}/2 - d_{f2}/2;$ $c_2 = a_{min} - d_{a2}/2 - d_{f1}/2$	$c \geq 0.15\,m_n$
Tooth thickness in pitch circle (circular)	$s = m\,(\pi/2 + 2\,x \cdot \tan \alpha)$	Normal profile $s_n = m_n(\pi/2 + 2\,x \cdot \tan \alpha_n)$ Transverse profile $s_t = s_n/\cos \beta = m_t\,(\pi/2 + 2 \cdot x \cdot \tan \alpha_n)$
Ideal number of teeth	$z_i = z$	$z_i = z\,\dfrac{\operatorname{inv} \alpha_t}{\operatorname{inv} \alpha_n}$
Number of teeth spanned	$k \approx z_i\,\dfrac{\alpha_{nx}}{180} + 0.5$ for k take the next whole number	α_{nx} from $\cos \alpha_{nx} \approx \dfrac{z_i}{z_i + 2x}\cos \alpha_n$
Base tangent length over k teeth	$W_k = \{[(k' - 0.5)\,\pi + z_i \operatorname{inv} \alpha_n]\cos \alpha_n + 2x \cdot \sin \alpha_n\}\,m_n$	
Back-reckoning of x from the base tangent	$x = \dfrac{(W/m_n) - [(k - 0.5) \cdot \pi + z_i \cdot \operatorname{inv} \alpha_n] \cdot \cos \alpha_n}{2 \cdot \sin n\alpha}$	
Transverse contact ratio for gears without allowance for cutter interference	$\varepsilon_\alpha = \dfrac{\sqrt{d_{a1}^2 - d_{b1}^2} + \dfrac{z_2}{\lvert z_2 \rvert}\sqrt{d_{a2}^2 - d_{b2}^2} - (d_{b1} + d_{b2})\tan \alpha_w}{2 \cdot \pi \cdot m_t \cdot \cos \alpha}$ (straight teeth) $\varepsilon_\alpha = \dfrac{\sqrt{d_{a1}^2 - d_{b1}^2} + \dfrac{z_2}{\lvert z_2 \rvert}\sqrt{d_{a2}^2 - d_{b2}^2} - (d_{b1} + d_{b2})\tan \alpha_{wt}}{2 \cdot \pi \cdot m_t \cdot \cos \alpha}$ (helical teeth)	
Overlap ratio	—	$\varepsilon_\beta = \dfrac{b \cdot \sin \lvert \beta \rvert}{m_n \cdot \pi}$
Total contact ratio	$\varepsilon_\tau = \varepsilon_\alpha$	$\varepsilon_\tau = \varepsilon_\alpha + \varepsilon_\beta$
	Apply only if: $\varepsilon_\tau > 1$ for $d_{a\,min}$ and a_{max}	

Addendum modification

Addendum modification (see diagram) is used to avoid undercut when the number of teeth is small, to increase tooth root strength and to achieve a specific distance between centers.

Gear pair with reference center distance

With a gear pair at reference center distance, the addendum modifications to the gear and pinion are equal but opposite, such that the distance between centers does not change. This design is preferred for crossed helical and bevel gear pairs.

Gear pair with modified center distance

The addendum modifications to the gear and pinion do not cancel each other, so the distance between centers changes.

Terms and errors

Terms and errors are explained in detail in the following standards: DIN 3960, DIN 58 405 (spur gears), DIN 3971 (bevel gears), and DIN 3975 (worms and worm gears).

Inserting $j_n = 0$ in the preceding formulas results in gearing with zero backlash. The tooth thickness and span measurement deviations required to produce backlash can be specified in accordance with DIN 3967 and DIN 58 405, taking into consideration the quality of the gears. It is necessary to ensure that the minimum backlash is great enough to compensate for tooth error (such as total composite error, alignment deviation, center-to-center distance error, etc.) without reducing the backlash to zero, and without leading to gear jamming. Other parameters for which the tolerances must be determined (with reference to the tooth errors given above in parentheses) are those for (two-flank) total composite error and (two-flank) tooth-to-tooth composite error

DIN gear qualities (DIN 3961 to DIN 3964)
Table 4. Manufacture and applications

Quality	Examples of applications	Manufacture
2	Primary-standard master gears	Form grinding (50...60% scrap rate)
3	Master gears for the inspection department	
4	Master gears for the workshop, measuring mechanisms	
5	Drives for machine tools, turbines, measuring equipment	Form grinding and generative grinding
6	As 5, also highest gears of passenger-car and bus transmissions	
7	Motor-vehicle transmissions (highest gears), machine tools, rail vehicles, hoisting and handling equipment, turbines, office machines	Non-hardened gears (carefully manufactured) by hobbing, generative shaping and planing (subsequent shaving is desirable); additional grinding is required for hardened gears
8 and 9	Motor-vehicle transmissions (middle and lower gears), rail vehicles, machine tools and office machines	Hobbing, generative shaping and planing (non-ground but hardened gears)
10	Transmissions for farm tractors, agricultural machinery, subordinate gear units in general mechanical equipment, hoisting equipment	All of the usual processes apply, plus extrusion and sintering, and injection molding for plastic gears
11 and 12	General agricultural machinery	

(DIN 3963, DIN 58 405), alignment deviation (DIN 3962 T2, DIN 3967, DIN 58 405), and distance between centers (DIN 3964, DIN 58 405).

Module series for spur and bevel gears in mm (extract from DIN 780)

0.3	1	3	10	32
0.35	1.125	3.5	11	36
0.4	**1.25**	**4**	**12**	**40**
0.45	1.375	4.5	14	45
0.5	**1.5**	**5**	**16**	**50**
0.55	1.75	5.5	18	55
0.6	**2**	**6**	**20**	**60**
0.65	2.25	7	22	70
0.7	**2.5**	**8**	**25**	
0.75	2.75	9	28	
0.8				
0.85				
0.9				
0.95				

Modules given in bold type are preferred.

Addendum modification coefficient x

Table 5. Addendum modification coefficient x **for straight-tooth gearing,** $\alpha = 20°$,
Basic rack I, DIN 3972 ($h_{fP} = 1.167 \cdot m$)

1	2	3	4
Number of teeth z, for helical teeth z_i	Tooth free from under-cut if $x \geq$	Top land width $0.2 \cdot m$ if $x \approx$	Tooth pointed if $x \geq$
7	+ 0.47	–	+ 0.49
8	+ 0.45	–	+ 0.56
9	+ 0.4	+ 0.4	+ 0.63
10	+ 0.35	+ 0.45	+ 0.70
11	+ 0.3	+ 0.5	+ 0.76
12	+ 0.25	+ 0.56	+ 0.82
13	+ 0.2	+ 0.62	+ 0.87
14	+ 0.15	+ 0.68	+ 0.93
15	+ 0.1	+ 0.72	+ 0.98
16	0	+ 0.76	+ 1.03

If the number of teeth is greater than $z = 16$, x should not be less than $x = (16 - z)/17$, for helical teeth $x = (16 - z_i)/17$.

Starter-tooth design

The system of tolerances for gears "Standard distance between centers" as specified in DIN 3961, which is customary in mechanical engineering and by which the required backlash is produced by negative tooth thickness tolerances, cannot be used for starters. Starter gear teeth require far more backlash than constant-mesh gears due to the starter engagement process. Such backlash is best achieved by increasing the distance between centers.

The high torque required for starting necessitates a high transmission ratio (i = 10 to 20). For this reason, the starter pinion has a small number of teeth (z = 8...12). The pinion generally has positive addendum modification. In the case of pitch gears, this addendum modification is expressed using the following notation outside Germany: Number of teeth, for instance = 9/10.

This means that only 9 teeth are cut on a gear blank with a diameter for 10 teeth; this corresponds to an addendum modification coefficient of + 0.5. Slight deviations of $x = + 0.5$ are quite common and do not affect the above-mentioned notation method: Number of teeth = 9/10. (This notation is not to be confused with the P 8/10 notation, see below and next page.)

Table 6. Customary starter gearing

Module m mm	Diametral pitch P 1/inch	Pressure angle of basic rack	American standard	European standard
2.1167	12	12°	SAE J 543 c	ISO 8123 1991 E
2.5	–	15°		ISO 9457–1 1991 E
2.54	10	20°	SAE J 543 c	ISO 8123 1991 E
3	–	15°		ISO 9457–1 1991 E
3.175	8	20°	SAE J 543 c	ISO 8123 1991 E
3.5	–	15°		ISO 9457–1 1991 E
4.233	6	20°	SAE J 543 c	ISO 8123 1991 E

American gear standards

Instead of the module, in the USA standardization is based on the number of teeth on 1 inch of pitch diameter = diametral pitch (P).

$P = z/d$

The conversion is as follows:
Module $m = 25.4$ mm/P

The tooth spacing in the pitch circle is called circular pitch (CP):

$$CP = \frac{1 \text{ inch}}{P} \cdot \pi$$

Pitch $p = 25.4$ mm $\cdot CP = \pi \cdot m$

Full-depth teeth

Full-depth teeth have an addendum $h_a = m$ in German standards, however the dedendum is frequently somewhat different.

Stub teeth

The formulas are the same as for full-depth teeth, however calculation of the addendum is based on a different module from that used for the other dimensions. Notation (example):

$P\ 5/7$ —— $P\ 7$ for calculation of the addendum

$P\ 5$ for calculation of all other dimensions

Notation and conversions:

Outside Diameter:
$OD = da$

Pitch Diameter:
$PD = z/P = d$ in inches

Root Diameter:
$RD = d_f$

Layout Diameter:
$LD = (z + 2x)/P$ in inches
$LD = (z + 2x) \cdot m$ in mm
$LD \approx d_w$
d_w Pitch circle diameter

Measurement over D_M-pins:
M_d = measurement over D_M pins

Table 7. Diametral pitches P and modules derived from them

Diametral pitch P 1/inch	Corresponds to module m mm	Diametral pitch P 1/inch	Corresponds to module m mm	Diametral pitch P 1/inch	Corresponds to module m mm
20	1.27000	**6**	4.23333	**2**	12.70000
18	1.41111	5.5	4.61818	1.75	14.51429
16	1.58750	**5**	5.08000	**1.5**	16.93333
14	1.81429	4.5	5.64444	**1.25**	20.32000
12	2 11667	**4**	6.35000	**1**	25.40000
11	2.30909	3.5	7.25714	0.875	29.02857
10	2.54000	**3**	8.46667	**0.75**	33.86667
9	2.82222	2.75	9.23636	**0.625**	40.64000
8	3.17500	**2.5**	10.16000	**0.5**	50.80000
7	3.62857	2.25	11.28889		

Calculation of load-bearing capacity

The following can be employed for rough estimations as an alternative to DIN 3990 "Calculation of load-bearing capacity of spur bevel gears". It applies to 2-gear pairs in a stationary transmission unit.

The quantities which appear in the following formulas are to be entered for the units given below:

Term		Unit		Term		Unit
P	Power	kW		φ	Life factor	–
P_{PS}	Metric horsepower	PS*		HB	Brinell hardness	
M	Torque	N · m		HRC	Rockwell hardness	
n	Rotational speed	min^{-1}		b_N	Effective flank width	mm
F	Peripheral force	N		k	Contact pressure	N/mm^2
u	Gear ratio	–		L_h	Service life	h

Table 8. Calculating load-bearing capacity of spur gears

Power	$P = 0.736 \cdot P_{PS}$ $P = M \cdot n/9549$ $P = F_t \cdot d \cdot n/(19.1 \cdot 10^6)$
Peripheral force in pitch circle	$F_{tw} = 2000 \cdot M/d_w = 19.1 \cdot 10^6 \, P/(d_w \cdot n)$
in reference circle	$F_t = 2000 \cdot M/d = 19.1 \cdot 10^6 \, P/(d \cdot n)$
Gear ratio	$u = z_2/z_1 = n_1/n_2$ for pairs of internal gears $u < -1$
Life factor	$\varphi = \sqrt[6]{5000/L_h}$ or from the table on P. 303
Contact pressure for the small gear	$k_{perm} = \dfrac{(HB)^2}{2560 \cdot \sqrt[6]{n}} = \dfrac{(HRC)^2}{23.1 \cdot \sqrt[6]{n}}$ or from the table on P. 303
Straight teeth	$k_{actual} = \dfrac{F_{tw}}{b_N \cdot d_{w1}} \cdot \dfrac{4 \,(u + 1)}{u \cdot \sin 2 \, \alpha_w}$
Helical teeth	$k_{actual} = \dfrac{F_{tw}}{b_N \cdot d_{w1}} \cdot \dfrac{4 \,(u + 1) \cdot \cos^2 \beta}{u \, \sin 2 \, \alpha_{wt}}$ $\cos^2 \beta$ only for full contact, otherwise = 1
Resistance to pitting	$S_w = \varphi \cdot k_{perm}/k_{IST} \geq 1$

Resistance to pitting and wear due to excessive contact pressure is provided if the equations for S_w for the smaller gear (gear 1) yield a value equal to or greater than 1. In the case of gear pairs where $z_1 < 20$, select $S_w \geq 1.2 \ldots 1.5$ on account of the greater contact pressure at the inside single engagement point. Because the contact pressure k is equal in magnitude for both gears of the pair, for k_{perm} a material can be selected for gear 2 from the table which has at least the same contact pressure as for gear 1 at rotational speed n_2.

The k_{perm}-values in the table below apply when both gears are made of steel. For cast iron on steel or bronze on steel, the values should be roughly 1.5 times higher; for cast iron on cast iron or bronze on bronze, they should be approximately 1.8 times higher. For the gear with non-hardened surfaces, 20 % higher k_{perm} values are permissible if the other gear in the pair has hardened tooth flanks. The values in the table apply to a service life L_h of 5000 hours. A different service life L_h is allowed for in the equation for resistance to pitting S_w by means of the life factor φ.

Table 9. Permissible contact pressure k_{perm} in N/mm² for a service life L_h = 5000 h

Hardness of teeth HB	HRC	Rotational speed min⁻¹ (for 1 load change per revolution)											
		10	25	50	100	250	500	750	1000	1500	2500	5000	10000
90		2.2	1.9	1.7	1.5	1.3	1.1	1.05	1.0	0.94	0.86	0.77	0.68
100		2.7	2.3	2.0	1.8	1.6	1.4	1.3	1.2	1.15	1.06	0.94	0.84
120		3.8	3.3	2.9	2.6	2.2	2.0	1.9	1.8	1.66	1.53	1.36	1.21
140		5.2	4.5	4.0	3.6	3.0	2.7	2.5	2.4	2.26	2.08	1.85	1.65
170		7.7	6.6	5.9	5.2	4.5	4.0	3.75	3.6	3.34	3.06	2.73	2.43
200		10.7	9.1	8.1	7.3	6.2	5.6	5.2	4.9	4.6	4.24	3.78	3.37
230		14.1	12.1	10.8	9.6	8.2	7.3	6.9	6.5	6.1	5.61	5.0	4.45
260		18.0	15.4	13.8	12.2	10.5	9.4	8.8	8.4	7.8	7.17	6.39	5.69
280		20.9	17.9	16.0	14.2	12.2	10.9	10.2	9.7	9.0	8.31	7.41	6.6
300		24.0	20.6	18.3	16.3	14.0	12.5	11.7	11.1	10.4	9.54	8.5	7.6
330		29.0	24.9	22.2	19.8	17.0	15.1	14.1	13.5	12.6	11.6	10.3	9.2
400		42.6	36.6	32.6	29.0	24.9	22.2	20.7	19.8	18.5	17.0	15.1	13.5
	57	96.0	82.3	73.3	65.3	56.0	49.9	46.7	44.5	41.6	38.2	34.0	30.3
	≥ 62	112	96.5	86.0	76.6	65.8	58.6	54.8	52.2	48.8	44.8	39.9	35.5

Corresponding materials are given in the table "Strength values" on P. 305.

Table 10. Life factor φ
The life factor is used to convert the values in the table (referred to a service life L_h of 5000 hours) to values which correspond to a different service life period.

Service life in hours of operation L_h	10	50	150	312	625	1200	2500	5000	10,000	40,000	80,000	150,000
Life factor φ	2.82	2.15	1.79	1.59	1.41	1.27	1.12	1	0.89	0.71	0.83	0.57

Guidelines for selection of service life: Drives in continuous operation at full load: 40,000...150,000 hours of operation; drives run intermittently at full load or only intermittently: 50...5000 hours of operation.

Teeth calculations for bending and tooth fracture

Table 11. Formulae for calculating the strength of spur gears

Peripheral velocity $v_1 = v_2$ m/s	$v_1 = \dfrac{\pi \cdot d_1 \cdot n_1}{60{,}000}$ d_1 in mm, n_1 in min^{-1}
Velocity factor f_v	Take from table below, or calculate.
Perm. root stress $\sigma_{F\,perm}$ N/mm²	Take $\sigma_{F\,lim}$ and Y_{NT} from table P. 305; estimate intermediate values. $\sigma_{F\,perm} = \sigma_{F\,lim} \cdot Y_{NT} \cdot Y_L$ $Y_L = 1$ for pulsating loads. $Y_L = 0.7$ for alternating loads.
Tooth profile factor Y_{Fa}	Take from graph below.

Root stress of tooth $\sigma_{F\,actual}$ N/mm²	For straight teeth	For helical teeth
	$\sigma_{F\,actual} = \dfrac{F_t}{b \cdot m} \cdot \dfrac{Y_{Fa}}{f_v \cdot \varepsilon_\alpha}$	$\sigma_{F\,actual} = \dfrac{F_t}{b \cdot m_n} \cdot \dfrac{Y_{Fa}}{f_v \cdot \varepsilon_\alpha} \left(1 - \dfrac{\varepsilon_\beta \cdot \beta}{120°}\right)$
	ε_α, see P. 298 m, m_n, b in mm, F_t in N see P. 302	where $\left(1 - \varepsilon_\beta \cdot \beta / 120°\right)$ must be ≥ 0.75. ε_β see P. 298, β in °

Resistance to tooth fracture S_F	$S_F = \sigma_{F\,perm} / \sigma_{F\,actual} \geq 1$

Resistance to tooth fracture is provided if the equations for S_F for the smaller gear (gear 1) yield a value greater than or equal to 1.

If a better material is selected for gear 1 than for gear 2, the calculation for bending must also be made for gear 2.

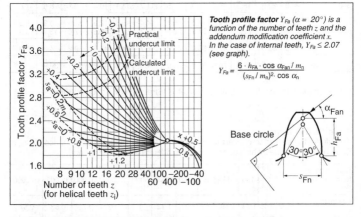

Tooth profile factor Y_{Fa} ($\alpha = 20°$) *is a function of the number of teeth z and the addendum modification coefficient x. In the case of internal teeth,* $Y_{Fa} \leq 2.07$ *(see graph).*

$$Y_{Fa} = \dfrac{6 \cdot h_{FA} \cdot \cos \alpha_{Fan} / m_n}{(s_{Fn} / m_n)^2 \cdot \cos \alpha_n}$$

Table 12. Velocity factor f_v

Materials	Peripheral velocity v m/s							Basic equation
	0.25	0.5	1	2	3	5	10	
Steel and other metals	Velocity factor f_v							$f_v = \dfrac{A}{A + v}$ [1])
	0.96	0.93	0.86	0.75	0.67	0.55	0.38	
Fabric-base laminates and other non-metals	0.85	0.75	0.62	0.5	0.44	0.37	0.32	$f_v = \dfrac{0.75}{1 + v} + 0.25$

Gear materials

Table 13. Material parameters

Material		Condition	Tensile strength R_m N/mm² min.	Fatigue strength for reversed bending stress σ_{bW} N/mm² min.	Hardness HB or HRC min.	Permissible root stress[2]) $\sigma_{F\,lim}$ N/mm²	Life factor Y_{NT}[3]) at number of load changes $N_L = L_h \cdot 60 \cdot n$				
							≥ 3·10⁶	10⁶	10⁵	10⁴	10³
Heat-treatable steel	St 60-2, C 45	annealed	590	255	170 HB	160	1	1.25	1.75	2.5	2.5
		heat-treat.	685	295	200 HB	185					
		heat-treat.	980	410	280 HB	245					
	St 70-2, C 60	annealed	685	295	200 HB	185					
		heat-treat.	785	335	230 HB	209					
		heat-treat.	980	410	280 HB	245					
	50 Cr V 4	annealed	685	335	200 HB	185					
		heat-treat.	1130	550	330 HB	294					
		heat-treat.	1370	665	400 HB	344					
	37 Mn Si 5	annealed	590	285	170 HB	160					
		heat-treat.	785	355	200 HB	230					
		heat-treat.	1030	490	300 HB	270					
Case-hardening steel	RSt 34-2, C 15	annealed	335	175	100 HB	110	1	1.25	1.75	2.5	2.5
		surf.-hard.[4])	590	255	57 HRC	160	1	1.2	1.5	1.9	2.5
	16 Mn Cr 5	annealed	800	–	150 HB	–	–	–	–	–	–
		surf.-hard.[4])	1100	–	57 HRC	300	1	1.2	1.5	1.9	2.5
	20 Mn Cr 5	annealed	590	275	170 HB	172	–	–	–	–	–
		surf.-hard.[4])	1180	590	57 HRC	330	1	1.2	1.5	1.9	2.5
	18 Cr Ni 8	annealed	640	315	190 HB	200	–	–	–	–	–
		surf.-hard.[4])	1370	590	57 HRC	370	1	1.2	1.5	1.9	2.5
Gray iron	GG-18	–		175	200 HB	50	1	1.1	1.25	1.4	1.6
	GS-52.1	–		510	140 HB	110	1	1.25	1.75	2.5	2.5
	G-SnBz 14		195		90 HB	100	1	1.25	1.75	2.5	2.5
Polyamide PA 66 Pa 66 + 30 % GF		at 60 °C	–	40	–	27	1	1.2	1.75	–	–
			140	43	–	29					
Fabric-base fine laminate coarse			–	–	–	75	1	1.15	1.4	1.65	2.0
			–	–	–	50	1	1.2	1.6	2.1	2.8

For the heat-treatable steels, two values are given in each case for the heat-treated condition. For smaller gears up to roughly module 3, the larger of the two values can be specified. With very large gears, however, only the smaller value can be achieved with certainty.

---

[1]) Values are valid for $A = 6$ (average tooth quality). With cast gears and high-precision gears, $A = 3$ and 10 respectively.
[2]) For pulsating loads with a material fatigue strength $N_L \geq 3 \cdot 10^6$. In the case of alternating loads (idler gears), take into account the alternating load factor Y_L.
[3]) Within fatigue strength of finite life, root bending stress is multiplied by the factor Y_{NT}, depending upon the number of load changes $N_L = L_h \cdot 60 \cdot n$.
[4]) Surface-hardened.

Belt drives

Friction belt drives

Units and symbols

Quantity		Unit
A	Belt cross section	mm²
F	Contact force	N
F_1	Belt force on load side	N
F_2	Belt force on slack side	N
F_F	Centrifugal force of belt	N
F_f	Centrifugal force per side	N
F_R	Frictional force	N
F_u	Peripheral force	N
F_v	Pretensioning force	N
F_w	Tensioning force of shaft	N
P	Required power transmission	kW
k_1	Pretension factor, with reference to operating conditions and wrap angle	–
k_2	Factor for centrifugal force	–
v	Belt speed	m/s
z	Number of belts (V-belt drives) or ribs (V-ribbed belts)	–
α	Groove angle	°
β	Wrap angle	°
μ	Coefficient of friction	–
μ'	Wedge coefficient of friction	–
ϱ	Mean density of belt material	g/cm³

Transmission of force

The general equation for friction

$$F_R = \mu \cdot F$$

yields the following equation for V-belt pulleys (see illustration)

$$F_R = \mu \cdot 2 \cdot F'$$

or $F_R = \mu' \cdot F$

where $\mu' = \mu/\sin(\alpha/2)$

The Eytelwein equation describes the transition from static friction to sliding friction:

$$F_1/F_2 = e^{\mu'\beta}$$

where $\mu' \approx 0.5 \pm 0.15$
according to the specifications of the V-belt manufacturers with the incorporation of various safety factors.
As long as the ratio of forces on the two belt sides is

$$F_1/F_2 \leq e^{\mu'\beta}$$

the belt will not slip during transmission of the peripheral force

$$F_u = F_1 - F_2 = P \cdot 1020/v$$

A pretensioning force F_v is required in order to transmit the peripheral force F_u; at high rotational speeds, the centrifugal force constituent F_F of the belt must be taken into consideration. The pretensioning force is

$$F_v = F_w \cdot F_F$$

where $F_w = F_u \cdot [(e^{\mu'\beta} + 1)/(e^{\mu'\beta} - 1)] \cdot \sin(\beta/2)$
$F_F = 2 \cdot z \cdot F_f \cdot \sin(\beta/2)$
$F_f = \varrho \cdot A \cdot v^2 \cdot 10^{-3}$
or in simplified form
$F_F = 2 \cdot z \cdot k_2 \cdot v^2 \cdot \sin(\beta/2)$
In practice, the following approximation process is frequently sufficient for calculating the pretensioning force (according to the Continental Co.):

$$F_v = (k_1 \cdot F_u + 2 \cdot z \cdot k_2 \cdot v^2) \cdot \sin(\beta/2)$$

The following rule of thumb can often be used for drives with 2 pulleys:

$$F_v = (1.5 \ldots 2) \cdot F_u$$

In order to check belt pretensioning, the static force applied to each side of each belt

$$F_s = F_v/[2z \cdot \sin(\beta/2)]$$

is compared with the value obtained by measuring belt deflection.

Belt drive calculations are performed in accordance with DIN 2218, or in accordance with the specifications supplied by the belt manufacturers. Manufacturer's belt performance specifications are based on a theoretical service life of 25,000 h. Computer programs are used to perform service life calculations. In properly designed drives, belt creep is less than 1 %, and belt efficiency is 94...97 %.

Belt service life is shortened if the maximum permissible belt speed and bending frequency are exceeded, if the belt pulleys are smaller than the minimum permissible pulley diameter or, in the case of V-belts, belt tensioners are used to apply force to the back of the belt.

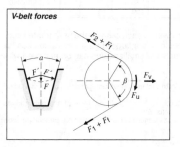

V-belt forces

Determination of the static force F_s of the side of the belt by means of belt deflection t_e produced by a test force F_e.

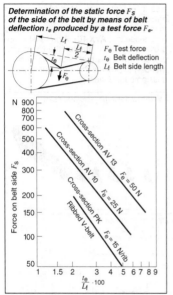

F_e Test force
t_e Belt deflection
L_f Belt side length

	Pretension factor k_1			
Belt	β		Drive	
		Light constant loads	Moderate loads	Heavy shock loads
V-belts	180°	1.5	1.7	1.9
	90°	2.6	2.8	3.0
V-ribbed belt	180°	1.8	2.0	2.2
	90°	3.3	3.5	3.7

Intermediate values for other wrap angles may be interpolated.

Belt	Cross section	Centrifugal factor k_2
V-belt	SPZ	0.07
	SPA	0.12
V-ribbed belt	K	0.02

Belt velocities up to 30 m/s and bending frequencies up to 40 s^{-1} are permissible. See DIN 2217 for corresponding pulley dimensions.

Narrow V-belts

In accordance with DIN 7753, Part 1; machine construction, motor vehicles built in the 1960s and 1970s. Ratio of top width to height: 1.2:1. The narrow V-belt is a modified version of the standard V-belt in which the central section, which in any case transmitted only limited forces, has been omitted. Higher capacity than standard V-belts of equal width. Toothed version exhibits less creep when bending around small pulleys. Belt velocities up to 42 m/s and bending frequencies up to 100 s^{-1} are permissible. (See DIN 2211 for corresponding pulley dimensions.)

Standard V-belts (classical V-belts)

In accordance with DIN 2215, for domestic appliances, agricultural machinery, heavy machinery. Ratio of top width to height: 1.6 : 1. Belt designs which use corded cable and bundled fibers as the tension members transmit considerably less power than equally wide narrow V-belts. Due to their high tensile strength and transverse stiffness, they are suitable for use under rough operating conditions with sudden load changes.

Raw-edge V-belts

Raw-edge standard V-belts in accordance with DIN 2215, and raw-edge narrow V-belts for motor vehicles in accordance with DIN 7753, Part 3 (draft). Subsurface belt fibers perpendicular to the direction of belt motion provide a high degree of flexibility while at the same time giving extreme transverse stiffness and high wear resistance. They also provide excellent support for the specially treated tension member. Particularly with small-diameter pulleys, this design increases belt capacity and provides a longer service life than wrapped narrow V-belts.

V-belt types
1 Wrapped standard V-belt
2 Wrapped narrow V-belt
3 Raw-edge narrow V-belt

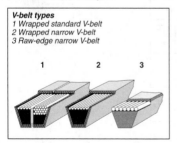

Further developments
The latest development are V-belts with tension members made of Kevlar. Kevlar has very high tensile strength with a very small degree of elongation, and is more highly temperature-resistant.

V-ribbed belts (poly-grooved belts)
In accordance with DIN 7867. Very flexible; the back of the belt may also be used to transmit power. This capability makes it possible for one such belt to be used to drive several vehicle accessories simultaneously (alternator, fan, water pump, air-conditioner compressor, power-steering pump, etc.) if the wrap angle around each driven pulley is sufficiently large. Optional cross sections include the PH, PJ, PK, PL, and PM, of which the PK cross section has been widely used in motor vehi-

cles in recent years. This allows use of narrower pulley diameters ($d_{b\,min} \approx 45$ mm) than those possible with narrow V-belts (cross-section: AVX 10). A pretension approximately 20 % greater than that employed on a narrow V-belt is recommended to provide the same force-transmission capabilities.

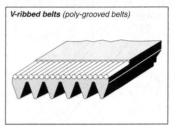

V-ribbed belts (poly-grooved belts)

Narrow V-belts for motor vehicles in accordance with DIN 7753 Part 3
Example of designation: narrow V-belt DIN 7753 AVX 10 × 750 La,
Raw-edge, toothed with belt cross-section code AVX 10 L_a = 750 mm.

Narrow V-belt		Wrapped		Raw-edge Solid cross section (V)		Toothed (G)		Dimensions in mm
Belt cross-section	Code	9.5	12.5	AVP10	AVP13	AVX10	AVX13	
	ISO code	AV 10	AV 13	AV 10	AV 13	AV 10	AV 13	
Top width	$b_0 \approx$	10	13	10	13	10	13	
Belt height	$h \approx$	8	10	7.5	8.5	8	9	
Eff. line differential	h_b	1.8	2.6	0.9				
Belt runout	$h_{a\,max}$	–		2.4				
Effective length	L_a	500 to 2550: in increments of 25 mm						

Active zone

Groove cross-section code		AV 10		AV 13	
Effective diameter	d_b	< 57	≥ 57	< 70	≥ 70
Groove angle $\alpha \pm 0.5°$		34°	36°	34°	36°
Effective width	b_b	9.7		12.7	
Groove depth	t_{min}	11		14	
Radius of curvature	r	0.8			
Distance bet. grooves e_{min}		12.6		16	

Positive belt drives

Synchronous drive belts (toothed belts) in accordance with DIN/ISO 5296
Toothed belts are used in motor vehicles as camshaft drives, and in some cases as ignition distributor drives.

Synchronous drive belts with trapezoidal or rounded teeth combine the advantages of a belt drive (any desired distance between pulley centers, quiet operation, low maintenance) with the advantages of a positive transmission (synchronous operation, low bearing stress due to low shaft load).

Synchronous drive belts must be guided on both sides to prevent them from running off. This is accomplished by using either a toothed pulley with two flanges or two toothed pulleys with one flange each on opposite sides.
See DIN/ISO 5294 for corresponding toothed-pulley dimensions.

Synchronous drive belts (toothed belts)
1 with trapezoidal teeth
2 with rounded teeth

V-ribbed belts and pulleys as per DIN 7867

Designation for a 6-ribbed V-belt, cross-section code PK and reference length 800 mm:
V-ribbed belt DIN 7867-6 PK 800.

Designation for the corresponding V-belt pulley with 90 mm reference diameter:
V-ribbed belt pulley DIN 7867-6 Kx 90.

Dimensions in mm	Belt	Groove profile
Cross-section code	PK	K
Rib or groove spacing s or e	3.56	3.56
Perm. deviation tolerance for s or e	± 0.2	± 0.05
Sum of deviation tolerances s or e	± 0.4	± 0.30
Groove angle α		40° ± 0.5°
r_k at rib / r_a at groove head	0.50	0.25
r_g at rib / r_i at groove seat	0.25	0.50
Belt height h	6	
Nominal dia. of test pin d_s		2.50
$2 \cdot h_s$ nominal dimension		0.99
$2 \cdot \delta$ (see illustration)		2.06
f (see illustration)		2.5

Belt cross-section

Groove cross-section

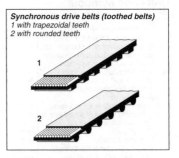

Determining effective diameter

1 Position of tension member

Belt width $b = n \cdot s$
with number of ribs $= n$

Effective diameter for K cross-section
$d_w = d_b + 2\,h_b$
$h_b = 1.6\ mm$

Basic principles of threaded fasteners

Units and symbols

Quantity	Unit
A_s Stress area of thread, see P. 312	mm²
D_{Km} Effective diameter for determining the friction torque at the fastener head or nut bearing surface	mm
F_M Installed tension force (gen.)	N
F_{sp} (Axial) installed tension force of threaded fastener at 90% of yield strength	N
M_M Tightening torque for mounting	N · m
M_{sp} Tightening torque required to load a threaded fastener to F_{sp}	N · m
P Thread pitch	mm
d Fastener diameter (major diameter of the thread)	mm
d_2 Mean flank diameter of the thread	mm
d_3 Root diameter of the thread	mm
μ_G Coefficient of thread friction (friction factor)	–
μ_{tot} Mean coefficient of friction for the fastener and head or nut bearing faces	–
μ_K Coefficient of friction for the head and nut bearing faces	–
$\sigma_{0.2}$ 0.2% yield strength of the fastener material (for low-strength fasteners, the yield point σ_s applies instead; see footnote[1]) on P. 43)	N/mm²

Basic rules

Threaded fasteners (screws, bolts, nuts) should clamp parts together with a force great enough to hold them in contact with one another without dislocation in spite of all applied operating forces. Bolts must not be subjected to shear.

A correctly preloaded fastener needs itself only to absorb a fraction of those operating forces which are applied roughly parallel to the bolt axis and which are usually dynamic in nature. When the parts to be joined are themselves as rigid as possible and elastic fasteners are used (viz. long and reduced in the body to d_3 and of property classes 8.8...12.9 with optimum tension force), the lowest fastener fatigue loading is achieved. Highly stressed joints are also the best provision against subsequent working loose (setting of the joint

after tightening). As a rule of thumb, setting of the joint reduces the installed tension force of a joint using 8.8 fasteners by 10...20% if the maximum temperature is 100 °C and the parts so joined are metals with a tensile strength of at least 300 N/mm².

The tensioned section of the threaded fastener should have a minimum threaded length of 0.5 d, the object being to achieve 1.0 d whenever possible.

The spring force of installed locking devices (spring lock washers and the like) should be as great as the tension force of the fastener! Spring lock washers are usually disadvantageous when used with screws of property classes ≥ 8.8, grip lengths > 2.5 d and metallic components (because $F \ll F_{sp}$, and joint setting in the bearing faces additionally occurs). In the case of 4.8 and 5.6/5.8 fasteners, spring lock washers are generally superfluous if grip lengths are ≥ 5 d.

The compressive load per unit area under fastener heads and nuts must not exceed the crushing yield point (corresponds to at least the 0.2% permanent elongation limit or yield strength) of the material of the joint parts (if required, use large washers or flanged hex screws).

Flange mountings using four bolts are considerably more reliable than such joints which use 3 bolts in a 120° arrangement (in the latter case, failure of one bolt leads to failure of the entire bolted joint).

Property classes

The designation system for threaded fasteners consists of two numbers separated by a decimal point. The first number represents ≈ 1/100 of the minimum tensile strength in N/mm², while the second number is 10 times the ratio of the minimum yield point (or 0.2% yield strength) to the minimum tensile strength.

The property classes of standard nuts (with nominal heights ≥ 0.8 d and width across flats ≥ 1.45 d) are indicated by a number which corresponds to 1/100 of the stress under proof load in N/mm². This stress corresponds to the minimum tensile strength of a fastener in the same property class. The ability of a nut to with-

Table 1. Threaded fasteners: Mechanical strength properties and designations
Fasteners made of steels alloyed with boron which have a low carbon content are indicated by a solid line below the numerical designation, e.g. for property class: 10.9 (see also DIN-EN 20 898, Part 1).

Property class		3.6	4.6	4.8	5.6	5.8	6.8	8.8	10.9	12.9
Tensile strength σ_B N/mm²	min	330	400	420	500	520	600	800	1040	1220
	max ≈	490	550			700		800	1000	1200	1400
Yield point R_{el} N/mm²	min	180	240	320	300	400	480	–	–	–
0.2 % yield strength $\sigma_{0.2}$	min	–	–	–	–	–	–	640	900	1080
Vickers hardness HV30	min	95	120	130	155	160	190	250	320	385
	max	250							320	380	435

stand the stress under proof load is determined using a bolt thread of greater strength (min. 45 HRC); after the stress is relieved, the nut must still be movable on the thread.

Property classes for nuts:

4	5	6	8	10	12

For nuts with limited loadability:

04	05

(e.g. flat nuts)

For thread diameters of 5 mm and larger,

- Fasteners in property class 8.8 and greater, as well as
- Nuts of all property classes

must be marked with the property class on the fastener head or nut face. If the fasteners are small, the decimal point between the two numbers can be omitted; for nuts, a code system can also be used, whereby the chamfers of the nuts are marked with notches and dots.

The fatigue limit of cold-formed steel fasteners of sizes up to M12 is $\sigma_D = \sigma_m \pm$ 50 ... 60 N/mm² (referred to the root

Table 2. Yield strength for threaded fasteners made of other materials

Material	Designation	Thread	0.2 % yield strength N/mm²
X5CrNi 1911	A2-70	≤ M20	450
CuZn37	Cu2	≤ M6	340
		M8 ... M39	250
CuSn6	Cu4	≤ M12	340
		M14 ... M39	200
AlMgSi1	Al3	≤ M39	250

cross-section), and applies up to a mean stress of $\sigma_m = 0.6 \cdot \sigma_{0.2}$ and for all property classes from 4.8 to 12.9. Fasteners of sizes up to M8 whose threads are rolled after hardening and tempering can achieve σ_D values up to 450 ± 100 N/mm², whereas gray cast iron and aluminum nuts and fasteners can achieve values of ± 120 N/mm².

Tightening of threaded fasteners

Sufficient tightening torque for threaded fasteners can be realized by hand using a screwdriver up to sizes M5 – 8.8, using a hexagon socket up to a maximum of M8 – 10.9, and using a ring wrench or box-end wrench up to a maximum of M12 – 10.9 (provided that $\mu = \mu_G = \mu_K = 0.14$).

When fasteners are tightened using (conventional) <u>torque measurement</u>, variations in tension force occur in a ratio of approx. 1:2, and are caused by
- Variations in the coefficients of friction μ_K and μ_G (for screw head or nut and thread contact surface),
- Variations in the tightening torque (when tightened by hand and using power screwdrivers).

For $\mu_G = \mu_K = 0.1$, the effective force for producing the tension force is 17 % of the complete tightening torque, whereas the corresponding figure for $\mu_G = \mu_K = 0.2$ is only 9.5 % of the complete tightening torque.

The highest possible tension forces with very small variations can be achieved with threaded fasteners using the <u>angular tightening method</u> and the <u>yield-point-controlled tightening method</u>. It must be noted that these procedures – employed to greatest advantages with grades 8.8 and above – necessitate the use of pre-calculations and empirical testing and/or special electronically-controlled wrenches. In addition, if the yield-point-controlled tightening method is used, the grip (total thickness of the bolted parts without female thread) should be at least as thick as the nominal diameter of the bolt which should be $\geq$ M4.

Basic formulas for tightening with torque measurement

The maximum permissible <u>installed tension force</u> in the fastener is limited by the effective stress (tension and torsion) which is equal to 0.9 times the minimum yield strength; this installed tension force is designated F_{sp}. The effective stress for the <u>stress area</u> is calculated according to the formula

$$A_s = \frac{\pi}{4} \cdot \left(\frac{d_2 + d_3}{2} \right)^2$$

with which the static, axial tensile stresses and the torsional stresses (generated by thread friction) can be viewed as if the fastener were a smooth component (A_s is greater than the root cross-section due to the fact that the threads inhibit deformation). Thus

$$F_{sp} = \frac{0.196 \, (d_2 + d_3)^2 \cdot 0.9 \cdot \sigma_{0.2}}{\sqrt{1 + 4.86 \left(\dfrac{P + \mu_G \cdot 3.63 \, d_2}{d_2 + d_3} \right)^2}}$$

The values given in Table 5 for the installed tension forces F_{sp} were calculated for various coefficients of thread friction μ_G using the above formula.

In determining <u>tightening torques</u> it was formerly standard practice to assume that $\mu_G = \mu_K = \mu_{tot}$ in order to arrive at the simplified formula

$$M_{sp} = F_{sp} \left[0.16 \, P + \mu_{tot} \left(0.58 \, d_2 + \frac{D_{Km}}{2} \right) \right]$$

and corresponding graphs. In the case of differing fastener head and thread coefficients of friction (see example at end of chapter), however, this formula cannot be used to correctly determine the necessary tightening torque (see also the explanation above Table 4).

A simple, practical way of calculating tightening torque in the case of differing coefficients of friction μ_G and μ_K is the <u>K method</u> (proposed by Gill, used in the USA and contained in VDI Recommendation 2230, 1977 edition):
According to this method, the installed tightening torque is

$$M_M = K \cdot F_M \cdot d$$

and for tightening to 90 % of the yield strength

$$M_{sp} = K \cdot F_{sp} \cdot d$$

where

$$K = \frac{0.16 \cdot P + \mu_G \cdot 0.58 \cdot d_2 + \mu_K \cdot D_{Km}/2}{d}$$

For differing coefficients of friction μ_G and μ_K and a wide range of fastener dimensions, K can be given independently of d in tabular form (see Table 4).

Coefficients of friction

Using Table 3 below, both the coefficient of friction for fastener head or nut (μ_K) and thread friction (μ_G) at the contact surface are determined separately and one after the other.

These coefficients of friction are significantly increased by the use of self-locking screws, washers with sharp roughly radial edges and lock nuts; connections using these fastening devices must be tightened according to special specifications.

Tightening threaded-fastener connections

Table 3.
Coefficients of friction μ_K and μ_G for various surface and lubrication conditions
$\mu_{G\,min}$ (lower value in Table 3) is used to determine tension force F_{sp} in Table 5.

Surfaces on mating party: Bearing face on part (μ_K) or *nut thread* (μ_G)		Lubrication condition	Fastener surfaces: Bearing face of head or underside of nut (μ_K) or *fastener thread* (μ_G)		
			Steel, oil-quenched or Zn-phosph. pressed rolled	turned cut	Steel zinc-plated 6 μm
Steel,	rolled		0.13...0.19	0.10...0.18	0.10...0.18
	turned, cut planed, milled		0.10...0.18	–	0.10...0.18
	ground		0.16...0.22	0.10...0.18	0.10...0.18
Gray cast iron	planed, milled, turned, cut		0.10...0.18	–	0.10...0.18
All-black	malleable iron, ground		0.16...0.22	0.10...0.18	0.10...0.18
Steel	cadmium-electroplated, 6 μm	Lightly oiled	0.08...0.16	0.08...0.16	–
	zinc-electroplated, 6 μm		0.10...0.18	0.10...0.16	0.16...0.20
	zinc-electropl. female threads		–	–	0.10...0.18
	ground, rolled, phosphated		0.12...0.20	–	–
	machined, phosphated		0.10...0.18	–	–
Al-Mg	alloy, processed, cut		0.08...0.20	–	–
Steel,	cadmium-electroplated, 6 μm	Dry	0.08...0.16	–	–
	cadm.-electropl., fem. threads		0.08...0.14	–	–
	zinc-electroplated, 6 μm		0.10...0.18	–	0.20...0.30
	zinc-electropl., female threads		0.08...0.16	–	0.12...0.20

Table 4. K-Values

The K-values apply to standard threads of sizes M1.4 to M42 <u>and</u> bolt head and nut sizes corresponding to hexagon bolts and screws in accordance with DIN 931, 933; fillister-head slotted screws in accordance with DIN 84, hexagon cap screws in accordance with DIN 912, 6912, 7984; and nuts in accordance with DIN 934.

For M16 to M42 threads, the K-value is to be reduced by 5%, because the transition from M14 to M16 represents a significant jump in the coarseness of thread pitch d/P.

Intermediate values can be interpolated with sufficient accuracy.

Note: In special cases where only μ_{tot} has been determined previously, the K-value is determined for the case in which $\mu_K = \mu_G = \mu_{tot}$ (see also "Tightening of threaded fasteners" P. 304).

		Coefficient of friction for fastener head and nut bearing face μ_K										
		0.04	0.06	0.08	0.10	0.12	0.14	0.16	0.18	0.20	0.24	0.28
Coefficient of friction for threads μ_G	0.08	0.094	0.108	0.120	0.134	0.148	0.162	0.176	0.190	0.204	0.232	0.260
	0.10	0.104	0.118	0.132	0.146	0.158	0.172	0.186	0.200	0.214	0.242	0.270
	0.12	0.114	0.128	0.142	0.156	0.170	0.184	0.196	0.210	0.224	0.252	0.280
	0.14	0.124	0.138	0.152	0.166	0.180	0.194	0.208	0.222	0.234	0.262	0.290
	0.16	0.134	0.148	0.162	0.176	0.190	0.204	0.218	0.232	0.246	0.272	0.300
	0.18	0.146	0.160	0.172	0.186	0.200	0.214	0.228	0.242	0.256	2.284	0.312
	0.20	0.156	0.170	0.184	0.198	0.210	0.224	0.238	0.252	0.266	0.294	0.322
	0.24	0.176	0.190	0.204	0.218	0.232	0.246	0.260	0.274	0.286	0.314	0.342
	0.28	0.198	0.212	0.224	0.238	0.252	0.266	0.280	0.294	0.308	0.336	0.362

Axial tension forces of bolted joints

Scope of Table 5 for installed tension forces F_{sp}

Table 5 applies only to
- Bolts with standard thread and $\dfrac{\text{shank diameter } d_1}{\text{minor diameter } d_3} \geq 1.05$
- With respect to material strength, the correct mating of nut and bolt, or female thread in housings;
- Nut height at least 0.8 x thread diameter and sufficient depth of thread in housings and the like.

Correction factors for tension forces and coefficients of friction (selection)

<u>Flat nuts</u> with a height of $0.5 \cdot d$ and the same hardness as the bolts allow a tension force of only 80% of the values given in the table. In the case of low-strength flat nuts (04) on 12.9 bolts, only 33% of F_{sp} is permissible.

In the case of <u>fastener heads and nuts with smaller or larger bearing faces</u> as well as <u>adjusting screws and locating screws</u> which do not have contact at their heads, the μ_K-value must be reduced or increased by the same ratio as the ratio of the mean friction diameter of their bearing faces to the mean friction diameter of the above-mentioned standard hexagon etc. fasteners and nuts. It is this corrected hypothetical μ_K-value which is used to determine the K-value (for this reason, Table 4 gives μ_K-values beginning with 0.04).

In the case of <u>countersunk-head screws</u>, allowance must be additionally made for the conical effect of the countersink angle as well as the greater elasticity of the outer edge of the head; thus the μ_K-value hypothetically increases by a factor of 1.25 in the case of standard countersunk screws (countersink angle: 90°).

Table 5. Tension forces F_{sp} in 10^3 N for standard threads and coefficients of friction μ_G in the threads (for 90 % utilization of $\sigma_{0.2}$ or σ_s)

Dimension (pitch)	Property class	F_{sp} (10^3 N) for coefficients of friction μ_G in the threads									
		0.06	0.08	0.10	0.12	0.14	0.16	0.18	0.20	0.24	0.28
M 4 (0.7)	4.8	2.3	2.2	2.1	2.0	1.9	1.9	1.8	1.7	1.6	1.4
	5.8	2.8	2.7	2.6	2.5	2.4	2.3	2.2	2.1	2.0	1.8
	8.8	4.5	4.4	4.2	4.1	3.9	3.7	3.6	3.4	3.2	2.9
	10.9	6.4	6.2	5.9	5.7	5.5	5.3	5.0	4.8	4.4	4.1
	12.9	7.7	7.4	7.1	6.9	6.6	6.3	6.0	5.8	5.3	4.9
M 5 (0.8)	4.8	3.7	3.6	3.5	3.3	3.2	3.1	2.9	2.8	2.6	2.4
	5.8	4.6	4.5	4.3	4.2	4.0	3.8	3.6	3.5	3.2	3.0
	8.8	7.4	7.2	6.9	6.6	6.4	6.1	5.9	5.6	5.2	4.8
	10.9	10.4	10.1	9.7	9.4	9.0	8.6	8.3	7.9	7.3	6.7
	12.9	12.5	12.1	11.7	11.2	10.8	10.3	9.9	9.5	8.7	8.1
M 6 (1.0)	4.8	5.2	5.1	4.9	4.7	4.5	4.3	4.1	4.0	3.7	3.4
	5.8	6.6	6.3	6.1	5.9	5.6	5.4	5.2	5.0	4.6	4.2
	8.8	10.5	10.1	9.8	9.4	9.0	8.6	8.3	7.9	7.3	6.7
	10.9	14.7	14.2	13.7	13.2	12.7	12.1	11.7	11.2	10.3	9.5
	12.9	17.7	17.1	16.5	15.8	15.2	14.6	14.0	13.4	12.3	11.4
M 8 (1.25)	4.8	9.6	9.3	8.9	8.6	8.3	7.9	7.6	7.3	6.7	6.2
	5.8	12.0	11.6	11.2	10.8	10.3	9.9	9.5	9.1	8.4	7.7
	8.8	19.2	18.6	17.9	17.2	16.5	15.7	15.2	14.6	13.4	12.4
	10.9	27.0	26.1	25.2	24.2	23.2	22.3	21.4	20.5	18.9	17.4
	12.9	32.4	31.3	30.2	29.0	27.9	26.8	25.7	24.6	22.6	20.9
M 10 (1.5)	4.8	15.3	14.8	14.2	13.7	13.2	12.6	12.1	11.6	10.7	9.9
	5.8	19.0	18.5	17.8	17.1	16.5	15.9	15.1	14.5	13.4	12.3
	8.8	30.5	29.5	28.5	27.4	26.3	25.3	24.2	23.2	21.4	19.7
	10.9	42.9	41.5	40.1	38.5	37.0	35.5	34.1	32.7	30.1	27.7
	12.9	51.5	49.8	48.1	46.2	44.4	42.6	40.1	39.2	36.1	33.2
M 12 (1.75)	4.8	22.2	21.5	20.8	20.0	19.2	18.4	17.7	16.9	15.6	14.4
	5.8	27.8	26.9	25.9	25.0	24.0	23.0	22.1	21.2	19.5	18.0
	8.8	44.5	43.0	41.5	40.0	38.4	36.8	35.3	33.9	31.2	28.7
	10.9	62.5	60.5	58.4	56.2	54.0	51.8	49.7	47.7	43.8	40.4
	12.9	75.0	72.6	70.0	67.4	64.8	62.2	59.6	57.2	52.6	48.5
M 14 (2.0)	4.8	30.5	29.6	28.5	27.4	26.4	25.3	24.3	23.3	21.4	19.7
	5.8	38.1	36.9	35.6	34.3	32.9	31.6	30.3	29.1	26.8	24.7
	8.8	61.0	59.1	57.0	54.9	52.7	50.6	48.5	46.5	42.8	39.5
	10.9	85.8	83.1	80.1	77.1	74.1	71.2	68.3	65.5	60.2	55.5
	12.9	103	99.7	96.2	92.6	89.0	85.4	81.9	78.5	72.3	66.6
M 16 (2.0)	4.8	41.8	40.5	39.2	37.7	36.3	34.8	33.4	32.1	29.5	27.2
	5.8	52.3	50.7	48.9	47.2	45.4	43.6	41.8	40.1	36.9	34.0
	8.8	83.6	81.1	78.3	75.5	72.3	69.7	66.9	64.2	59.0	54.4
	10.9	118	114	110	106	102	98.0	94.1	90.2	83.0	76.5
	12.9	141	137	132	127	122	118	113	108	99.6	91.9
M 20 (2.5)	4.8	65.3	63.3	61.2	59.0	56.7	54.5	52.2	50.1	46.1	42.5
	5.8	81.7	79.2	76.5	73.7	70.9	68.1	65.3	62.7	57.7	53.2
	8.8	131	127	122	118	113	109	105	100	92.3	85.1
	10.9	184	178	172	166	159	153	147	141	130	120
	12.9	220	214	206	199	191	184	176	169	156	144

In contrast to 5.8 bolts, the tension forces F_{sp} for bolts in other (nonferrous) property classes must be converted based on their yield points or their yield strengths; e.g. for M6 Cu2 fastener with $\mu_G = 0.10$, $F_{sp} = (340/400) \cdot 6.1 \cdot 10^3 \approx 5.2 \cdot 10^3$N.

Advantages of the K-method over previously used methods of determining tightening torque

– Easily takes into account the different coefficients of friction μ_K and μ_G.

The K-method therefore allows for more reliable design and greater minimum installed tension force (if the example below were calculated using $\mu_{tot} = \mu_K$, the maximum tension force would be impermissibly high, reaching a value just below the yield point. If the calculation were made using $\mu_{tot} = \mu_G$ instead, the tightening torques would be lower and the minimum tension force would be only 68 % of 14,800 N).

– In order to express the values listed in Table 3 as μ_{tot} values, more comprehensive tabular information would be required. Table 3 requires only a fraction of this information.

– The K-method is used to precisely determine the tightening torques when tightening threaded fasteners using a torque wrench, and is an advantageous replacement for the tables and somewhat complicated graphs used previously.

– Using yield point or angle-controlled tightening methods, better utilization factors can still be achieved at threaded-fastener connections (see "Tightening of threaded fasteners").

Determining tension forces and tightening torques

The maximum attainable installed tension force $F_{sp\,max}$ is determined using the smallest coefficient of friction in the threads μ_G and Table 5. (Most of the torque applied to the screw shank is used to overcome thread friction, while only the remainder is converted to tension force by the thread pitch; the maximum permissible tension force must not be exceeded even when this residual torque reaches its maximum value and μ_G its minimum value.)

The maximum permissible installed tightening torque $M_{sp\,max}$ is calculated using the K-value for the lowest values for μ_K and μ_G (because the maximum permissible tensioning force must not be exceeded even when maximum tightening torque coincides with the smallest coefficients of friction).

$$M_{sp\,max} = K_{min} \cdot F_{sp\,max} \cdot d$$

The lowest installed tightening torque $M_{sp\,min}$ is a result of the quality of the tightening process and the equipment used. If good power screwdrivers are used or the tightening process is carefully performed by hand using torque wrenches, the nominal torque can usually be achieved within a variation ±10 %. The lowest installed tightening torque is then

$$M_{sp\,min} \approx 0.8 \cdot M_{sp\,max}$$

The lowest installed clamping force $F_{sp\,min}$ which then may occur is calculated using the K-value for the maximum values of the two coefficients of friction μ_K and $_G$ as follows:

$$F_{sp\,min} = M_{sp\,min}/(K_{max} \cdot d)$$

Example: An M 10-8.8 bolt or screw (pressed and rolled, phosphated) is used to fasten a ground steel part to an AlMg housing with blind threaded holes; the parts are lightly oiled.

From Table 3: μ_K = 0.16 ...   0.22

μ_G = 0.08 ...   0.20 ⟶ for μ_G = 0.08 in accordance with Table 3: $F_{sp\,max}$ = 29,500 N

From Table 4: K_{min} = 0.176 | K_{max} = 0.280

$M_{sp\,max}$ = 0.176 · 29 500 · 0.010 = 51.9 N · m
$M_{sp\,min}$ = 0.8 · $M_{sp\,max}$ = 41.5 N · m
$F_{sp\,min}$ = 41.5/(0.280 · 0.010) = 14 800 N
(with d in m)

Threads (Selection)

ISO metric screw threads
(DIN 13, ISO 965); Nominal dimensions

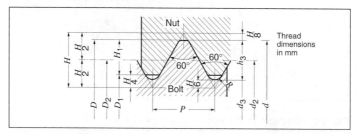

Thread
dimensions
in mm

Metric standard thread
Example of designation: M8 (nominal thread diameter: 8 mm)

Nominal thread dia. $d = D$	Pitch P	Pitch diameter $d_2 = D_2$	Minor diameter		Thread depth		Tensile stress area A_s in mm²
			d_3	D_1	h_3	H_1	
3	0.5	2.675	2.387	2.459	0.307	0.271	5.03
4	0.7	3.545	3.141	3.242	0.429	0.379	8.78
5	0.8	4.480	4.019	4.134	0.491	0.433	14.2
6	1	5.350	4.773	4.917	0.613	0.541	20.1
8	1.25	7.188	6.466	6.647	0.767	0.677	36.6
10	1.5	9.026	8.160	8.376	0.920	0.812	58.0
12	1.75	10.863	9.853	10.106	1.074	0.947	84.3
14	2	12.701	11.546	11.835	1.227	1.083	115
16	2	14.701	13.546	13.835	1.227	1.083	157
20	2.5	18.376	16.933	17.294	1.534	1.353	245
24	3	22.051	20.319	20.752	1.840	1.624	353

Metric fine thread
Example of designation: M8 x 1 (Nominal thread diameter: 8 mm; pitch: 1 mm)

Nominal thread dia. $d = D$	Pitch P	Pitch diameter $d_2 = D_2$	Minor diameter		Thread depth		Tensile stress area A_s in mm²
			d_3	D_1	h_3	H_1	
8	1	7.350	6.773	6.917	0.613	0.541	39.2
10	1.25	9.188	8.466	8.647	0.767	0.677	61.2
10	1	9.350	8.773	8.917	0.613	0.541	64.5
12	1.5	11.026	10.160	10.376	0.920	0.812	88.1
12	1.25	11.188	10.466	10.647	0.767	0.677	92.1
16	1.5	15.026	14.160	14.376	0.920	0.812	167
18	1.5	17.026	16.160	16.376	0.920	0.812	216
20	2	18.701	17.546	17.835	1.227	1.083	258
20	1.5	19.026	18.160	18.376	0.920	0.812	272
22	1.5	21.026	20.160	20.376	0.920	0.812	333
24	2	22.701	21.546	21.835	1.227	1.083	384
24	1.5	23.026	22.160	22.376	0.920	0.812	401

Pipe threads for non self-sealing joints
(DIN ISO 228-1); Parallel internal threads and external threads; nominal dimensions

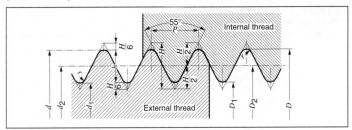

Example of designation: G 1/2 (nominal thread size 1/2 inch)

Nominal thread size	Number of threads per inch	Pitch P mm	Thread depth h mm	Major diameter $d = D$ mm	Pitch diameter $d_2 = D_2$ mm	Minor diameter $d_1 = D_1$ mm
$^1/_4$	19	1.337	0.856	13.157	12.301	11.445
$^3/_8$	19	1.337	0.856	16.662	15.806	14.950
$^1/_2$	14	1.814	1.162	20.955	19.793	18.631
$^3/_4$	14	1.814	1.162	26.441	25.279	24.117
1	11	2.309	1.479	33.249	31.770	30.291

Whitworth pipe threads for threaded pipes and fittings
(DIN 2999); Parallel internal threads and taper external threads; nominal dimensions (mm)

Parallel internal thread (Abbr. Rp)

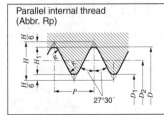

Tapered external thread (Abbr. R) (taper 1:16)

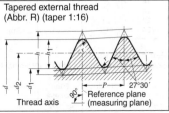

Designation		Major diameter $d = D$	Pitch diameter $d_2 = D_2$	Minor diameter $d_1 = D_1$	Pitch P	Number of threads per inch Z
External thread	Internal thread					
R $^1/_4$	Rp $^1/_4$	13.157	12.301	11.445	1.337	19
R $^3/_8$	Rp $^3/_8$	16.662	15.806	14.950	1.337	19
R $^1/_2$	Rp $^1/_2$	20.955	19.793	18.631	1.814	14
R $^3/_4$	Rp $^3/_4$	26.441	25.279	24.117	1.814	14
R 1	Rp 1	33.249	31.770	30.291	2.309	11

Areas of application: For joining pipes with parallel internal threads to valves, fittings, threaded flanges, etc. with tapered external threads.

Joining and bonding techniques

Welding

Automotive components and subassemblies are joined using a wide and highly variegated range of welding and bonding techniques. Resistance-pressure and fusion welding are among the most commonly applied welding methods. This summary concentrates on the resistance-welding procedures in standard production use (processes and symbols based on DIN 1910, Part 5).

Resistance welding

Resistance spot-welding
In resistance spot-welding, locally applied electrical current is used to melt the contact surfaces of the parts to be joined into a soft or fluid state; the parts are then joined together under pressure. The contact-point electrodes which conduct the welding current also convey the electrode force to the parts. The amount of heat required to form the welding joint is determined according to $Q = I^2 \cdot R \cdot t$ (Joule's Law).

The precise amount of heat required is a function of current, resistance and time. The following factors should be coordinated in order to achieve a good weld and adequate spot diameter d_1:

– welding current I,
– electrode force F and
– welding time t.
According to the manner in which the current is conducted, a distinction is drawn between:
– bilateral direct resistance spot-welding and
– unilateral indirect resistance spot-welding.

The electrode for a specific spot-welding operation is selected with reference to shape, outside diameter and point diameter. Before welding, the parts must always be completely free of scaling, oxides, paint, grease and oil; they therefore receive appropriate surface treatment prior to welding (where indicated).

Projection welding
Projection welding is a process in which electrodes with a large surface area are employed to conduct the welding current and the electrode force to the workpiece. The projections, which are generally incorporated into the thicker of the workpieces, cause the current to concentrate at the contact surfaces. The electrode force compresses the projections partially or completely during the welding process. A permanent, inseparable joint is produced at the contact points along the welding seam. One or more than one projection can be welded simultaneously, depending on the type of projection (round or annular) and the power available from the welding unit.

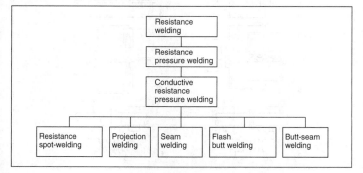

Depending on the number of spots welded, a distinction is drawn between
– single-projection welding and
– multiple-projection welding.

This technique requires high welding currents applied for short periods of time.
Applications:
– welding parts of different thicknesses,
– welding multiple projections in a single operation.

Seam welding
In this process, roller electrodes replace the spot-welding electrodes used in resistance spot-welding. Contact between the roller pair and the workpiece is limited to an extremely small surface area. The roller electrodes conduct the welding current and apply the electrode force. Their rotation is coordinated with the movement of the part.
Applications:
Production of sealed welds or seam spot welds (e.g. fuel tanks).

Flash-butt welding
In flash-butt welding, the butt ends of the workpieces are joined under moderate pressure while the flow of current at the contact surfaces produces localized heat and melting (high current density). The metal's vapor pressure drives molten material from the contact patches (burn-off) while force is applied to form an upset butt weld. The butt ends should be parallel to each other and at right angles to the direction in which the force is applied (or virtually so). Smooth surfaces are not required. A certain amount of extra length must be factored in to compensate for the losses incurred in the flash-welding process.
Result:
A weld with the characteristic projecting seam (burr).

Butt-seam welding
This process employs copper jaws to conduct the welding current to the workpieces being joined. When the welding temperature is reached, the current switches off. Constant pressure is maintained and the workpieces then weld to-

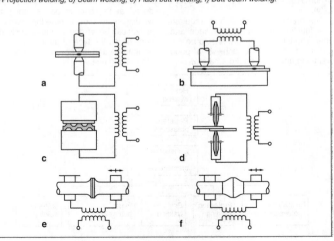

Welding techniques
a) Bilateral resistance spot-welding, b) Unilateral resistance spot-welding,
c) Projection welding, d) Seam welding, e) Flash butt welding, f) Butt-seam welding.

a
b
c
d
e
f

gether (requirement: properly machined butting faces). The result is a burr-free seam. The process does not completely displace contamination that may be present at the butt ends.

Fusion welding
The term "fusion welding" describes a process employing limited local application of heat to melt and join the parts; no pressure is applied.

Shielded (inert gas) arc welding is a type of fusion welding. The electrical arc extending between the electrode and the workpiece serves as the heat source. Meanwhile, a layer of inert gas shields the arc and the melted area from the atmosphere. The type of electrode is the factor which distinguishes between the various techniques:

Tungsten inert-gas welding
In this process, an arc is maintained between the workpiece and a stable, non-melting tungsten electrode. The shielding (inert) gas is argon or helium. Weld material is supplied from the side (as in gas fusion welding).

Gas-shielded metal-arc welding
In this process, an arc is maintained between the melting end of the wire electrode (material feed) and the workpiece. The welding current flows to the wire electrode via sliding contacts in the torch holder. Insert-gas metal-arc welding uses inert gases (slowly reacting and noble gases such as argon, helium, or combinations of the two) as protective gas. Active-gas metal-arc welding, on the other hand, employs reactive gases such as CO_2 and mixed gases containing CO_2, argon and sometimes oxygen, and is frequently referred to as CO_2 welding.

This process is employed for welding non-alloy and mild-alloy steels.
In addition, the following welding techniques are employed in the automobile industry:
– electron-beam welding,
– friction welding,
– arc pressure welding (stud welding),
– stored-energy welding (pulse welding).

Soldering

In soldering, a supplementary material (solder) is melted onto two or more parts of similar or varying metallic composition in order to produce a permanent connection between them. Flux and/or protective gas may also be used. The melting temperature of the solder is below that of the parts being joined. The solder is distributed along the join to produce the connection without the parts themselves being melted.

Soldering processes are classified by working temperature. This is defined as the lowest surface temperature at the connection between the workpieces to be joined at which the solder can be melted and distributed to form a bond.

Soft soldering
Soft soldering is employed to form permanent solder joints at melting temperatures below 450 °C (as with soldering tin). Soft solders which melt at temperatures of 200 °C and below are also known as quick solders.

Hard soldering
Hard soldering (brazing) is used to form permanent joins at melting temperatures above 450 °C (as with copper/zinc, combined copper/zinc and silver alloys, e.g. silver brazing filler). Further data on soldering materials is contained in DIN Sheets 1707, 8512, 8513 and 8516.

Fluxes (non-metallic substances) are applied to remove any film (oxidation) remaining on the surface of the parts after cleaning and to prevent a new film from forming: this makes it possible to apply a consistent coat of solder to the joint surfaces. Data on fluxes can be found in DIN 8511.

The strength of a soldered joint can be equal to that of the base material itself. This phenomenon is due to the fact that the more rigid adjoining materials limit the solder's deformation potential.

The method used for heating provides yet another criterion for the classification of soldering processes. The two standard types are: open-flame soldering and iron soldering.

Flame soldering
A hand-held burner or a gas-fired unit provides the heat. Depending on the specific soldering operation, either oxy-acetylene burners (familiar from gas welding) or soldering lamps are employed.

Iron soldering
A hand-held or mechanically guided soldering iron provides the heat. Irons can also be used to solder pretinned surfaces.

Other processes include: oven, salt-bath, immersion, resistance, and induction soldering.

Adhesive technologies

Organic or anorganic adhesives are employed to form permanent rigid connections between two metallic or non-metallic materials. The adhesive bonds under pressure, either at room temperature or with moderate heat. The bond is adhesive, in other words physical and chemical bonding forces operate at the molecular level to bond the surfaces. A distinction is drawn between single-component and two-component adhesives, referring to their as-delivered condition.

Single-component adhesives
These are components which contain all the constituents necessary to form a bond.

Two-component adhesives
The second component in an adhesive of this type is a hardener that initiates the cross-linking process. An accelerator may be added to the hardener. Metal adhesives are generally of the two-component type. The hardening (cross-linking) process is polymerization, polycondensation or polyaddition under the influence of temperature and/or time. Spatially interlinked macro-modules are the result. Depending on the hardening temperature, a distinction is drawn between cold adhesives (harden at room temperature, relatively easy to apply, and hot adhesives harden at 100 ... 200 °C).

Adhesive connections should be designed to ensure that the bond is subjected exclusively to tensile shear loads. Overlapping connections are virtually the only application for adhesives. Butt joins subjected to tensile or sliding forces should be avoided.

Metal adhesives can be employed in conjunction with spot welding. The adhesive prevents premature swelling of the sheets between the resistance-welded spots. This method is also suitable for reducing stress peaks at the edges of the weld spots and limited the number of spots required. Constructions of this nature evince enhanced structural integrity, rigidity, and damping when subjected to dynamic loads. Welding is carried out when the adhesive is still soft; otherwise the adhesive would act as an insulator.

The most significant metal adhesives include: epoxy, polyester and acrylic resins, vinyl acetate, and metal cement.

Automotive applications
Adhesive joining has become a standard technique in automotive engineering. The individual areas of application can be classified as follows.
– Body shell: Raised-seam and brace bonding for attached components.
– Painting line: Attachment of stiffeners.
– Assembly line: Attachment of insulating material, appliqués, moldings, mirror-support bracket to windshield.
– Component production: Bonding brake pads, laminated safety glass (LSG), rubber-to-metal connections to absorb vibration.

Riveting

Riveting is used to produce a permanent fixed connection between two or more components made of identical or dissimilar materials. Depending on the method and application, riveted connections are divided into the following categories:
- permanent rigid connections (interference fits, for example in mechanical and plant engineering),
- permanent, sealed connections (for example in boilers and pressure vessels) and
- extremely tight seals (for example in pipes, vacuum equipment, etc.).

In some areas such as mechanical engineering in general and in tank manufacture, riveting has largely been displaced by welding. A distinction is drawn between cold and hot riveting, depending on the temperature used. Cold riveting is employed for rivet joints up to 10 mm in diameter in steel, copper, copper alloys, aluminum, etc. Rivets with diameters in excess of 10 mm are installed hot.

The most common types of rivet are mushroom head, countersunk, tallowdrop, hollow and tubular. There are also standardized rivets for specialized applications, for example explosive rivets and pop rivets. Pop rivets are hollow and are expanded by a drift or punch. The types

of rivet and the corresponding materials are defined in DIN sheets; structural integrity and chemical composition are specified in DIN 17 111. In order to avoid the danger of electrochemical corrosion, the rivet material and the material of the parts being joined should be similar, if possible.

Advantages/disadvantages compared to other joining techniques
- Unlike welding, riveting exerts no effects such as hardening or molecular alteration on the material,
- no distortion of the components,
- suitable for joining dissimilar materials,
- riveting weakens the components,
- butt joints cannot be riveted and
- riveting is generally more expensive than welding when performed outside the factory.

Automotive applications
- Riveting joint pins (window winders, windshield-wiper linkages),
- Riveting reinforcement plates (in the course of repairs).

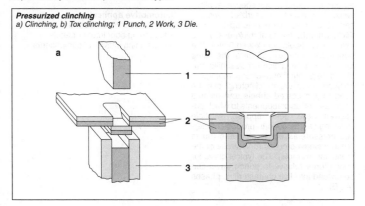

Pressurized clinching
a) Clinching, b) Tox clinching; 1 Punch, 2 Work, 3 Die.

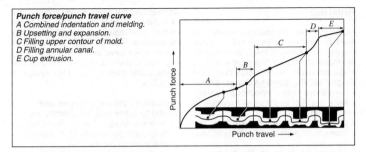

Punch force/punch travel curve
A Combined indentation and melding.
B Upsetting and expansion.
C Filling upper contour of mold.
D Filling annular canal.
E Cup extrusion.

Bonding and joining (pressurized clinching)

Pressurized clinching is a mechanical process for penetration assembly of layered materials. It combines cutting, penetration and cold upsetting in a single continuous joining operation without the application of additional heat. The basic principle is one of joining through reshaping. DIN 8593, Part 5, issued in September 1985 contains the first reference to this process as a means of joining sheet-metal panels by deformation.

The past few years have marked the advent of tox clinching as yet another joining process: it resembles penetration clinching, but does not include a cutting process. The tools employed for tox clinching are relatively small. The diameter can be varied to suit specific applications. At present, pressurized clinching can be used to join panels up to 3 mm thick, whereby the total thickness of the two sheets should not exceed 5 mm. The panels being joined can be of the same material (e.g. steel/steel) or dissimilar materials (e.g. steel/non-ferrous metal). In addition, pressurized clinching can be used to join coated sheets and painted parts, as well as components to which adhesives have been applied. Multiple clinching can be used to produce numerous pressure-assembly elements (up to 50) in a single process (one stroke of the press, for example). The typical curve for punch force relative to punch travel can be divided into five characteristic phases (A...E).

Advantages/disadvantages of pressurized clinching
– No need for noise-abatement encapsulation,
– tox clinching does not impair corrosion protection,
– when combined with a cutting operation there is a partial loss of corrosion protection,
– no heat distortion,
– painted, protected (oil, wax) and glued sheets can be clinched,
– different materials can be joined (e.g. steel/plastic)
– energy savings, no power supply required for welding and no cooling water,
– one side of the workpiece evinces a projection similar to that produced by a rivet head, while the other side has a corresponding depression.

Automotive applications
– Windshield wiper brackets,
– Fastening door interior panels,
– Positioning individual components.

Punch riveting

The punch riveting technique joins solid materials employing stamping and riveting elements (solid or semi-hollow rivets) in a combined cutting and joining operation.

The parts to be joined do not have to be predrilled and stamped, as is the case with other riveting techniques.

Punch riveting with solid rivets

The first stage in punch riveting with solid rivets is to position the work on the die plate.

The top section of the rivet unit, including the blank holder, descends and the rivet die presses the rivet through the parts to be joined in a single stamping operation.

Punch riveting with semi-hollow rivets

The first stage in punch riveting with semi-hollow rivets is to position the work on the (bottom) die plate. The rivet die descends and presses the semi-hollow rivet through the upper sheet into the lower sheet in a single stamping operation. The rivet deforms and the bottom spreads to form a securing element, usually without fully penetrating the lower sheet.

Equipment

Highly rigid hydraulic tools are used in punch riveting. Rivets can be singled from a batch feed or carried in belts with individual holders to the riveting tool.

Materials

The rivets must be harder than the materials to be joined. The most common materials are steel, stainless steel, copper and aluminum with various coatings.

Characteristics

– Used to join similar and dissimilar materials (e.g. steel, plastic or aluminum), parts of various thicknesses and strengths, and painted sheets.
– No preliminary stamping or drilling, no electrical current or vacuum extraction required.
– Approved overall material thicknesses: steel 6.5 mm; aluminum 11 mm.
– Low-heat, low-noise joining process.
– Tools have a long service life (approx. 300,000 rivet applications) with consistent quality.
– Process dependability with monitored process parameters.
– High forces have to be applied.
– Restricted jaw reach.

Applications

Punch riveting with solid rivets: joining metal sheets in automotive engineering, e.g. window winders in passenger cars. Punch riveting with semi-hollow rivets: joining materials at the body-in-white stage in automotive engineering, household appliances, joining metals to composites (heat shields).

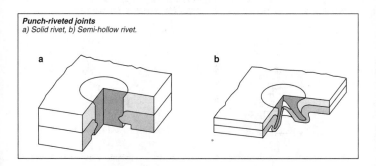

Punch-riveted joints
a) Solid rivet, b) Semi-hollow rivet.

Sheet-metal processing

Deep-drawing technology

Units and symbols

Symbols		Units
D	Section diameter	mm
d_B	Support diameter of hold-down device	mm
d_1	Stamping diameter, 1st draw	mm
d_2	Stamping diameter, 2nd draw	mm
F	Total deep-drawing force	kN
F_B	Hold-down force	kN
F_z	Deep-draw force	kN
p	Pressure of hold-down device	N/mm²
R_m	Tensile strength	N/mm²
s	Sheet thickness	mm
β_1, β_2	Individual drawing ratio	
β_{max}	Maximum possible drawing ratio	

Drawing methods

The drawing procedure employs a drawing die, punch and sheet-metal retaining device to reshape flat sections, blanks and round plates.

The variables exercising an influence on the deep-drawing of three-dimensional bodywork components are exceedingly complex; rough calculations thus do not provide a suitable basis for their definition. The finite-element method (FEM), in which powerful computers employ numerical procedures from continuum mechanics, is used to calculate deep-drawing processes. Software development has reflected the significance of specific parameters affecting the deep-drawing process, including the influence of friction, of bilateral contact, of material values which vary according to rolling direction, and additional factors.

Deep-draw simulation is of major assistance in designing deep-drawing tools, helping to optimize production times for this equipment.

Deep-drawing process

The drawing process reshapes a flat blank into a concave section. A punch, surrounded by a retaining mechanism (holding-down clamp, blank holder), pulls the sheet metal into the matrix. The clamp applies the defined force to the sheet, prevents creases from forming, and permits application of tensile force.

The maximum possible drawing ratio is determined by various factors:
– material strength,
– tool dimensions and sheet thickness,
– retention force,
– friction,
– lubrication,
– material and surface of the workpiece.

Drawing with single-action presses

This category includes all crank presses in which the ram represents the only moving component.

Deep drawing
a) With single-action press, b) With double-action press; 1 Ram, 2 Air cushion, 3 Hold-down device, 4 Matrix, 5 Punch, 6 Air pins, 7 Matrix insert, 8 Hold-down ram.

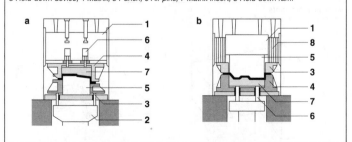

Applications: for deep-drawing flat work-pieces in simple reshaping operations to produce trimmers, arches, supports.

Drawing on double-action presses

Double-action drawing presses employ separate rams to retain the metal and to pull it. The hold-down ram is actuated mechanically via disk or toggle, or hydraulically.

Applications: for deep-drawn components of complex geometry, including fenders, wheel arches, decklids.

Calculations for the drawing process

$$F_Z = \pi \cdot (d_1 + s) \cdot s \cdot R_m$$
$$F_B = \frac{\pi}{4} \cdot (D^2 - d_B^2) \cdot p$$
$$F = F_Z + F_B$$
$$\beta_1 = D/d_1; \quad \beta_2 = d_1/d_2.$$

Example

$D = 210$ mm; $d_B = 160$ mm; $d_1 = 140$ mm; $p = 2.5$ N/mm²; $R_m = 380$ N/mm²; $s = 1$ mm; $\beta_{max} = 1.9$.

Result

Drawing ratio $\beta_1 = 1.5$; Deep-drawing force $F_Z = 112.2$ kN; Sheet retention force $F_B = 36.3$ kN; Total deep-drawing force $F = 148.5$ kN.

The diagram shows the motions of the drawing ram and the hold-down ram in the course of one cycle. The rams have differing strokes. The drawing ram, with its longer stroke, is set in motion first, while the

Material	β_1 max.	β_2 max.	Pressure of hold-down device p N/mm²
St 12	1.8	1.2	2.5
St 13	1.9	1.25	
St 14	2.0	1.3	
Copper	2.1	1.3	2.0...2.4
CuZn 37 w	2.1	1.4	
CuZn 37 h	1.9	1.2	
CuSn 6 w	1.5	–	
Al 99.5 w	2.1	1.6	1.2...1.5
AlMg 1 w	1.85	1.3	
AlCuMg 1 pl w	2.0	1.5	
AlCuMg 1 pl ka	1.8	1.3	

[1]) Valid up to $d_1/s = 300$; specified for $d_1 = 100$ mm, $s = 1$ mm. Different sheet thicknesses and punch diameters result in minor deviations from the figures given. Basic qualities are also used with galvanized surfaces. The figures can vary slightly.

shorter-stroke retention ram starts second, but is first to achieve contact.

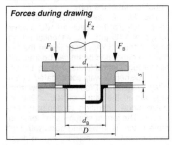

Forces during drawing

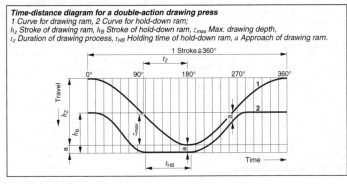

Time-distance diagram for a double-action drawing press
1 Curve for drawing ram, 2 Curve for hold-down ram;
h_Z Stroke of drawing ram, h_B Stroke of hold-down ram, z_{max} Max. drawing depth,
t_Z Duration of drawing process, t_{HB} Holding time of hold-down ram, a Approach of drawing ram.

Laser technology

Deviation mirrors are used to deflect the coherent light beam generated by the laser for concentration in a focusing device. At the focal point the laser beam has a diameter of approx. 0.3...0.5 mm, allowing intensities in excess of $10^6...10^8$ W/cm^2 to be achieved. The workpiece melts and vaporizes in milliseconds if the focal point is in its immediate vicinity, an effect which can be exploited in laser-based processing operations. According to the physical condition of the active medium, the device is classified as a solid-state, gas, semiconductor or liquid laser. The following are applied in industrial metal processing:

Solid-state laser (Nd:YAG)

Neodynium (Nd) is an element of the rare-earth group, while YAG stands for yttrium-aluminum-garnet ($Y_5Al_5O_{12}$). The crystal exhibits mechanical and thermal stability equal to that of the ruby.

The Nd:YAG laser emits light in the infrared range of the spectrum, with a wavelength of 1.06 µm. The essential advantage of the Nd:YAG laser lies in the fact that the generated beam can be transmitted through optical fibers, making it possible to dispense with complicated beam-relaying systems. Present laser power ratings are in the range of 400...1200 W; pulse-mode operation is generally employed. The foremost application for solid-state lasers is in welding parts with high requirements for precision, e.g. in precision mechanics. Welding depths depend on power and welding speed, and are in the range of tenths of a millimeter.

Gas laser (CO$_2$)

The CO$_2$ laser is among the most important gas-laser devices. Molecular gas serves as the active medium. Radiation emissions are in the medium infrared band, with wavelengths spread across a number of spectral ranges between 9.2 and 10.9 µm; the mean is 10.6 µm. This type of laser is generally used in continuous operation, with standard laser power ratings of between 2 and 5 kW. Laboratory units with up to 20 kW have already been installed.

Characteristics of the laser cutter
– Clean, burr-free edges,
– high dimensional/manufacturing precision (no subsequent processing necessary),
– minimal thermal and mechanical stresses on the workpiece during the cutting process,
– uncomplicated clamping devices,
– sheet metal of up to 10 mm can be cut (1 kW), rapid cutting (10 m/min with metal 1 mm thick).

Characteristics of laser welding
– High depth/width ratio (e.g. approx. 1 mm seam width at 5 mm seam depth),
– minimal base-material thermal stress results in narrow heat-affected zone (HAZ),
– minimal distortion,
– welding in protective-gas atmosphere,
– joint gaps must be virtually zero,
– welding with filler metals is possible (for bridging gaps and achieving specific effects at the weld),
– specialized clamping and equipment technology is required.

Applications in machine tool and automotive engineering
– Cutting and welding bodywork sheet metal,
– welding (joining) blanks of various thicknesses,
– welding (joining) of rotationally symmetrical parts (transmission components, tappets, automotive components),
– boring and perforation,
– surface hardening, e.g. in treating valve seats, etc.,
– providing surfaces with upgraded finishes, e.g. structural transformation around cylinder liners.

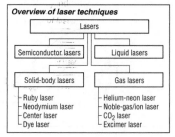

Overview of laser techniques

Tribology

Purpose and goals

Tribology is defined as "The study of the phenomena and mechanisms of friction, lubrication, and wear of surfaces in relative motion". Industrial application is directed toward gathering information for use in extending the service lives of products and maximizing utilization of resources. The specific activities are as follows:
- Analysis of friction and wear,
- Analysis and evaluation of tribological damage,
- Provision of technical recommendations on materials, lubricants and design (for damage control and in the design of new components and products),
- Quality assurance,
- Assistance in providing optimal performance,
- Service-life assessment,
- Development and selection of new materials and lubricants.

The complexity of the task renders a synergetic approach essential. The disciplines involved include materials science, physics, chemistry and mechanical engineering.

Definitions

Friction (DIN 50 281)
Friction is physical resistance to relative motion at two or more surfaces in a state of mutual contact. The most significant physical parameters for describing friction are:
Friction force: The amount of force with which a motion is resisted.
Coefficient of friction (or friction factor): Friction force relative to normal force.
Friction power: Friction force x sliding speed.
Classification of friction:
1. According to condition of friction (type of contact),
2. According to type of motion.

Condition of friction (type of contact)
Gas friction: A gas layer completely separates the base object and the opposed body from one another, thereby assuming the entire load.
Fluid friction (hydrodynamic and hydrostatic friction): A fluid layer completely separates the base object and opposed body from one another, thereby assuming the entire load.
Combination friction: The base object and the opposed body are in mutual contact at surface peaks. The load is shared by the fluid/lubricating film and by the objects in contact.
Dry or boundary friction: The lubricating film no longer performs any support function, but residue from previously absorbed lubricants continues to exercise a tribological effect.
Solid-body friction: Direct contact between the opposed surfaces.

Types of motion
Possible types of motion contact include sliding friction, rolling friction, and combinations of the two.

In many cases the effects which friction produces in machine components are undesirable, as there are negative consequences for energy consumption and/or associated temperature increases and/or changes to the material. In other cases, friction can make a necessary contribution to proper operation. This is the case with self-locking transmission devices, where the lubricant must furnish a specific coefficient of friction, and in some types of clutches in which defined levels of friction are also required.

Tribological concepts (DIN 50 323)
Tribology embraces the science and associated technology devoted to the interaction of surfaces in mutually opposed states of motion. It focuses on the entire range of friction, wear and lubrication, and also includes the effects at the contact surfaces of solids as well as those between solids and gases.

Tribo-technology (DIN 50323)
This branch is devoted to the actual technical application of tribology.

Tribological stress (DIN 50320)
The stress which results at a solid body

from contact with, and the relative motion of, an opposed body in solid, fluid or gaseous form.

<u>Tribological damage</u>
Damage resulting from tribological stress. This contrasts with the concepts of wear and wear damage as defined in DIN 50320, which always include material erosion. Here, the term "tribological damage" extends to embrace both numerous tribologically induced changes to the material's surface, as well as reductions in operational efficacy which according to DIN 50320 are not regarded as wear.

Wear (DIN 50320)
Progressive loss of material from the surface of a solid body, caused by tribological stress. Wear is characterized by the presence of abraded particles, as well as changes in both the material and structure of the surface which is exposed to tribological stress. This type of wear is generally undesirable, and impairs functionality (exception: "running-in" processes). Thus any such procedures which enhance the object's operational value are not considered as wear.

Tribological system

Wear can be regarded as a system characteristic. There exists no specific material value for "wear-resistance" as such, corresponding to, say, tensile strength in materials science. The tribological system for the contact surfaces which are the focus of the present discussion consists of:
– The material "A elements": base object, opposed body, intermediate material and surrounding medium (see illustration),
– The properties P of the elements A,
– The reciprocal influence R between the elements A.

The elements' properties and their reciprocal effects form the structure of the tribological system. As the composite stress factor (comprising forces, motion, temperature) acts upon this structure, it is transformed into useful quantities and loss quantities. The latter include friction and wear.

Because tribological stresses are surface stresses, the previously mentioned P properties must also be viewed as surface characteristics. In technical applications, there frequently exists a substantial discrepancy between the material values measured for the base material and those actually found upon examination of the surfaces. Manufacturing procedures, cleaning processes, and the operating environment can all cause changes in the surface layer, provoking attendant variations in the tribological response of the material.

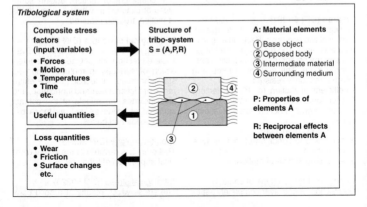

Tribological system

Composite stress factors (input variables)
• Forces
• Motion
• Temperatures
• Time
etc.

Useful quantities

Loss quantities
• Wear
• Friction
• Surface changes
etc.

Structure of tribo-system
$S = (A, P, R)$

① ② ③ ④

A: Material elements
① Base object
② Opposed body
③ Intermediate material
④ Surrounding medium

P: Properties of elements A

R: Reciprocal effects between elements A

Types of wear

Wear processes can be classified according to the type of stress and the materials involved (system structure), a classification from which the following types of wear emerge (DIN 50320):

System structure
Solid body/solid body:
Sliding → Sliding wear,
Rolling → Rolling wear,
Oscillation → Vibration wear.

System structure
Solid body/liquid:
Flow/oscillation → cavitation erosion

Manifestations of wear

The manifestations of wear as defined by DIN 50 320 apply to the surface changes resulting from abrasion, as well as to the type and shape of the resulting particles.

Wear mechanisms

Adhesion
Formation and separation of (atomic) surface bonds.

There is a transfer of material when the separation deviates from the original boundary between the base object and the opposed body.

The adhesion process starts at the molecular level, but can expand until damage on a massive scale occurs (seizing).

Abrasion
Scraping stress and microscopic scraping action, performed by the base object, the opposed body, reaction products or solid particles in the intermediate medium.

Surface fatigue
Alternating tribological loads (e.g. impact, rolling, sliding stress, cavitation) cause mechanical stresses. The resulting fissures lead to material separation (separation of wear particles).

Tribo-chemical reactions
Reaction of the base and/or opposed object with the intermediate material (and surrounding medium), caused by tribological stress.

Wear quantities

Rates of wear are defined by the so-called wear quantites. These provide direct or indirect indices of the variations in the shape or in the mass of a body which are traceable to wear (definitions based on DIN 50 321).

Coefficient of wear
The quantities by which wear is defined can only be indicated as system-specific quantities.

The wear coefficient k facilitates comparison of wear rates at varying surface pressures and speeds:

$$k = W_v/(F \cdot s) \text{ in mm}^3/(N \cdot m)$$

F Force,
W_v Volumetric wear,
s Sliding distance.

Tribological damage analysis

In cases where operation of a component results in damage or changes of a kind which could be expected to affect the component's functional integrity, DIN 50320 indicates that all stresses and characteristics occurring at the points of tribological contact should be investigated (DIN 50320, Appendix A).

The topographical and material analysis of tribological contact (base object, opposed body, intermediate material) provides information on the mechanisms causing the damage and/or wear (adhesion, abrasion, surface fatigue, tribo-chemical reaction). These investigations also provide data on accompanying phenomena and on changes in the lubricant.

The analysis must be based on the following information:
– surface structure,
– material composition of the surface,
– microstructure,

- microhardness,
- intrinsic tension,
- material composition and chemical/physical changes in the lubricant.

Tribological test procedures

DIN 50 322 divides wear testing into 6 categories:
Category I: Operational testing.
Category II: Test-stand procedure with complete machine.
Category III: Test-stand procedure with assembly or entire unit.
Category IV: Testing with unmodified component or reduced assembly.
Category V: Simulated operational stress with test specimens.
Category VI: Model test with simple test specimens.
The original production assembly is employed for testing according to Categories I through III, while the structure of the system is modified substantially from Category IV onward. It is highly advisable to integrate the tribological examinations of essential and safety-related products into a tribological test series:
- Model testing (e.g. pin and sphere, plate for sliding and vibration wear),
- Component testing,
- Product testing.

Model tests (with simple test specimens), although frequently employed in basic research, are no longer used for examining complex tribological systems. Of the various elements in the sequence of tribological tests, it is examination of the actual product itself that provides the most reliable information. Modern research procedures (such as radio-nuclide testing) make it possible to garner precise data on wear as a function of composite stress.

For radio-nuclide testing (RNT), the parts to be examined are marked radioactively. The abraded particles can then be detected "on-line" by gamma-ray measurement.

Inhibiting wear

Variations in design, materials and lubricants can all be employed to improve tribological properties.

Design
The design options include:
- Improving the surface topography,
- Reduction of surface pressures by raising the contact-surface ratio,
- Surface reinforcement,
- Improving lubrication efficiency.

Material
The materials options include:
- Skin-layer hardening,
- Skin-layer remelting,
- Surface-layer remelt alloying,
- Thermochemical processes,
- Electrical and chemical plating,
- Resurface welding,
- Thermal spraying,
- Metal coating,
- PVD/CVD layers (physical/chemical vapor deposition, e.g., TiN, TiC),
- Ion-beam treatment (e.g. ion implantation, ion-beam mixing, transition-layer mixing and ion-beam supported coating),

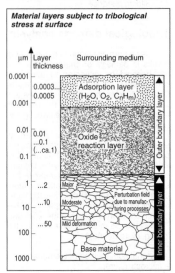

Material layers subject to tribological stress at surface

- Diamond-like carbon coatings (metallic),
- Anti-friction paints,
- Penetration coatings (soft metals prevent high local surface pressures).

There exist a multiplicity of surface treatment and coating processes. The process parameters can frequently be adjusted to focus on specific kinds of wear. The result is a wide potential field of options for applying tribology to assist products in meeting numerous requirements.

Lubricants

In many cases, selection of the appropriate lubricant (P. 230) and optimal lubrication-system design will exercise a dramatic effect on the tribological properties – the potential is frequently greater than that represented by a change in materials. The choice of lubricant is the initial response when dealing with unsatisfactory operating characteristics.

Lubricity

Lubricity testing is based on specially defined wear parameters. The test results provide a relative index of the efficiency of fluids as separating media in defined tribological systems. In evaluations under otherwise identical conditions, a fluid displays a higher lubricity than another when it produces relative reductions in wear between the opposed elements in the tribological system and/or lower generation of friction energy (DIN/ISO 12156).

It is important to distinguish between lubricity and viscosity.

Descriptions and specific numerical data on lubricity are derived from product, component and model wear testing with specifically defined stress and load parameters. The results are indicated in specific test data for wear.

The results of this type of testing are valid only for the object tribological system.

In many products the separating element in the tribological system is also a flow medium, as in hydraulic and fuel-injection systems.

The lubricity level of such a fluid must suffice to ensure reliable operation and a long service life.

Special additives can be employed to enhance lubricity.

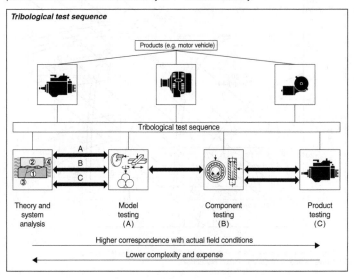

Tribological test sequence

Products (e.g. motor vehicle)

Tribological test sequence

Theory and system analysis   Model testing (A)   Component testing (B)   Product testing (C)

Higher correspondence with actual field conditions

Lower complexity and expense

Road-going vehicle requirements

Driveability

The vehicle must be capable of effecting the transition from a stationary to a mobile state. Once in motion, it must be able to ascend gradients and accelerate to the desired cruising speed with a reasonable degree of alacrity. With a given power P, ideal correspondence with these requirements is achieved when force M and the engine speed n can be varied according to the formula $P = M \cdot n$. Under these conditions, the limits on the potential field of operation are defined by P_{Nominal}, resulting in an inverse relationship between available force and vehicle speed (limit curve defined by tractive-force hyperbola).

Power density and storage density

Both the power density (W/kg) and the energy-storage density (Wh/kg) of the combined engine/energy-storage system must be high if the size of the vehicle – and with it the mass to be accelerated – are to be maintained at a modest level. Low density factors for power and energy storage would increase vehicle size and mass, with attendant escalations in the power and energy consumption which would be needed to achieve the desired performance (acceleration, speed).

Discharge or operating time of the energy-storage device

The vehicle's operating time – and thus the operating range which can be covered before the energy-storage device must be replenished (renewed/refilled/recharged) – is a function of the energy-storage density, the power requirement, and the vehicle weight; the latter, in turn, is influenced by the power-to-weight ratio of the drive system.

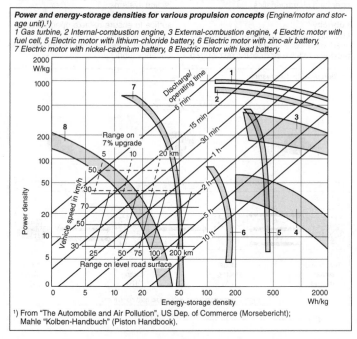

Power and energy-storage densities for various propulsion concepts (Engine/motor and storage unit).[1]
1 Gas turbine, 2 Internal-combustion engine, 3 External-combustion engine, 4 Electric motor with fuel cell, 5 Electric motor with lithium-chloride battery, 6 Electric motor with zinc-air battery, 7 Electric motor with nickel-cadmium battery, 8 Electric motor with lead battery.

[1] From "The Automobile and Air Pollution", US Dep. of Commerce (Morsebericht); Mahle "Kolben-Handbuch" (Piston Handbook).

The drive and energy-storage configuration employed for a specific application determines the relationship between power density/energy-storage density and operating time; it also exerts a decisive influence on the shape of the torque curve. Favorable power-to-weight ratios combine with high energy-storage densities (period of operation per tank of fuel) to make internal-combustion engines particularly suitable for vehicular applications. However, the torque curves provided by the standard piston powerplants (diesel and spark-ignition engines) are less satisfactory. They thus need some form of transmission unit for both the transfer and the conversion of torque. The unit must be capable of transmitting torque in the slip range (for starting off) while incorporating various torque-conversion ratios (for ascending gradients and selecting different speed ranges).

Electric and steam-driven powerplants also need a transmission due to the limitations imposed by the respective maxima for current and steam pressure.

In addition to fulfilling the basic requirements enumerated above, the powerplant and energy-storage system must also meet the following demands:

Economic efficiency, characterized by minimal fuel consumption, low manufacturing and maintenance costs, long service life;

Environmental compatibility, with low emissions levels for both pollutants and noise, sparing use of raw materials;

Flexibility in operation, including good starting from −30°C to +50°C, operation unaffected by climate and altitude, good driveoff, acceleration and braking characteristics.

Internal-combustion (IC) engines are thus the most favorable option for independent self-contained vehicles, whereby the priority assigned to the individual factors in the above list will vary according to application. Examples:

Passenger cars: High power density, low exhaust and noise emissions, low manufacturing costs,

Trucks and buses: Maximum economy, long service life, and conformity with all emissions requirements.

Special drive systems, such as those relying exclusively on electric motors, or hybrids (dual-system buses, P. 533 ff.) can represent the best, or indeed only, option for special applications and/or under certain operating conditions.

Basic requirements for fuels

Engines featuring external combustion place the least exacting demands on fuel quality, as their combustion and working gases are not identical and remain isolated from each other. In contrast, the fuel used in internal-combustion engines must burn rapidly and virtually without residue.

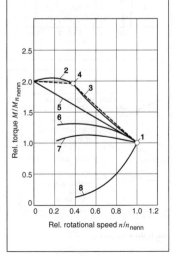

Relative torques for various power units
1 Reference point: Gas-turbine base point,
Piston engine n_{max}, 2 Steam engine,
3 Electric motor, 4 Limit curve for max. pressure/max. current, 5 Dual-shaft gas turbine,
6 Gasoline (SI) engine, 7 Diesel engine,
8 Single-shaft gas turbine.

Rel. torque $M/M_{n\,\text{nenn}}$

Rel. rotational speed n/n_{nenn}

Determining fuel consumption

The New European Driving Cycle (NEDC, 93/116/EEC) is a cycle run on a dynamometer to ascertain fuel consumption. It consists of four similarly weighted urban cycles each lasting 195 s and an extra-urban cycle lasting 400 s. The exhaust gas is collected in a sample bag and its components subsequently analyzed. CO, HC and CO_2 are factored into the calculations in accordance with the carbon analysis.

The CO_2 content of the exhaust gas is proportional to the fuel consumption. It can therefore be used as an indicator to gauge the vehicle's fuel consumption (diesel or gasoline, as appropriate).

The test mass specified for the vehicle equals the vehicle's empty mass plus a payload of 100 kg. The vehicle mass has to be simulated by finite balanced inertia masses on the dynamometer, so an inertia-mass class is assigned to the vehicle test mass.

Current legislation (EU 2) permits the engine to be started 40 s before testing commences $t = t_0$. This lead-in time will not be allowed under the more stringent EU 3 requirements.

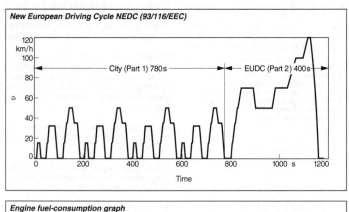

New European Driving Cycle NEDC (93/116/EEC)

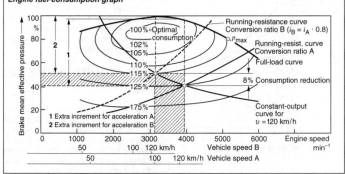

Engine fuel-consumption graph

Effect of vehicle design on fuel consumption

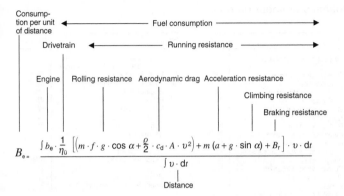

$$B_e = \frac{\int b_e \cdot \frac{1}{\eta_\ddot{u}} \left[\left(m \cdot f \cdot g \cdot \cos \alpha + \frac{\varrho}{2} \cdot c_d \cdot A \cdot v^2\right) + m\,(a + g \cdot \sin \alpha) + B_r\right] \cdot v \cdot dt}{\int v \cdot dt}$$

Symbol		Unit
B_e	Consumption per unit of distance	g/m
$\eta_\ddot{u}$	Transmission efficiency of drivetrain	–
m	Vehicle mass	kg
f	Coefficient of rolling resistance	–
g	Gravitational acceleration	m/s²
α	Angle of ascent	°
ϱ	Air density	kg/m³
c_d	Drag coefficient	–
A	Frontal area	m²
v	Vehicle speed	m/s
a	Acceleration	m/s²
B_r	Braking resistance	N
t	Time	s
b_e	Specific fuel consumption	g/kWh

The consumption equation distinguishes between three distinct groups of factors:
– Engine,
– Transmission, and
– External resistance factors.

Transmission (gearbox)
The influence of the gearbox is determined by both the power-transmission losses and the transmission (gear) ratios selected for the application. The former should be kept as low as possible; the latter determine the correspondence between vehicle speed and specific points on the engine's fuel-consumption curve.

"Long" (wide-ratio) gearing will generally move a specific operating state onto a point on the curve corresponding to lower fuel consumption (see illustration), albeit at the expense of reduced acceleration.

External resistance factors
Outside resistance to motion can be counteracted by measures such as weight reduction, improved aerodynamics and lower rolling resistance.

On an average production vehicle, 10 % reductions in weight, drag and rolling resistance result in fuel-economy improvements of roughly 6 %, 3 %, and 2 %, respectively.

The cited formula distinguishes between acceleration resistance and braking resistance, thereby illustrating with particular clarity the fact that the increased fuel consumption associated with acceleration largely stems from subsequent application of the brakes. If the brakes are not applied, then the vehicle's kinetic energy is exploited to impel it forward (retardation = negative acceleration), with attendant reductions in overall fuel consumption.

Motor-vehicle dynamics

Dynamics of linear motion

Symbol		Unit
A	Largest cross-section of vehicle[1]	m²
a	Acceleration, braking (deceleration)	m/s²
c_w	Drag coefficient	–
F	Motive force	N
F_{cf}	Centrifugal force	N
F_L	Aerodynamic drag	N
F_{Ro}	Rolling resistance	N
F_{St}	Climbing resistance	N
F_w	Running resistance	N
f	Coefficient of rolling resistance	–
G	Weight $= m \cdot g$	N
G_B	Sum of wheel forces on driven or braked wheels	N
g	Gravitational acceleration $= 9.81$ m/s² ≈ 10 m/s²	m/s²

Symbol		Unit
i	Gear or transmission ratio between engine and drive wheels	–
M	Engine torque	N · m
m	Vehicle mass (weight)	kg
n	Engine speed	min⁻¹
P	Power	W
P_w	Motive power	W
p	Gradient ($= 100 \tan \alpha$)	%
r	Dynamic radius of tire	m
s	Distance traveled	m
t	Time	s
υ	Vehicle speed	m/s
υ_0	Headwind speed	m/s
W	Work	J
α	Gradient angle	°
μ_r	Coefficient of static friction	–

Additional symbols and units in text.

Total running resistance
The <u>running resistance</u> is calculated as:

$$F_W = F_{Ro} + F_L + F_{St}$$

<u>Running-resistance power</u>
The power which must be transmitted through the drive wheels to overcome running resistance is:

$$P_W = F_W \cdot \upsilon$$

or

$$P_W = \frac{F_W \cdot \upsilon}{3600}$$

with P_W in kW, F_W in N, υ in km/h.

[1] On passenger cars $A \approx 0.9 \times$ Track $\times$ Height.

Rolling resistance
The <u>rolling resistance</u> F_{Ro} is the product of deformation processes which occur at the contact patch between tire and road surface.

$$F_{Ro} = f \cdot G = f \cdot m \cdot g$$

An approximate calculation of the rolling resistance can be made using the coefficients provided in the following table and in the diagram on page 339.

The increase in the coefficient of rolling resistance f is directly proportional to the level of deformation, and inversely proportional to the radius of the tire. The coefficient will thus increase in response to

Road surface	Coefficient of rolling resistance f
Pneumatic car tires on	
Large sett pavement	0.015
Small sett pavement	0.015
Concrete, asphalt	0.013
Rolled gravel	0.02
Tarmacadam	0.025
Unpaved road	0.05
Field	0.1...0.35
Pneumatic truck tires on concrete, asphalt	0.006...0.01
Strake wheels in field	0.14...0.24
Track-type tractor in field	0.07...0.12
Wheel on rail	0.001...0.002

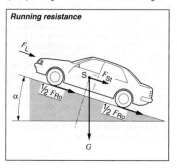

Running resistance

greater loads, higher speeds and lower tire pressure.

During cornering, the rolling resistance is augmented by the <u>cornering resistance</u>

$$F_K = f_K \cdot G$$

The coefficient of cornering resistance f_K is a function of vehicle speed, curve radius, suspension geometry, tires, tire pressure, and the vehicle's response under lateral acceleration.

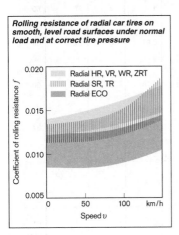

Rolling resistance of radial car tires on smooth, level road surfaces under normal load and at correct tire pressure

Coefficient of rolling resistance f (vertical axis): 0.005 to 0.020
Speed v (horizontal axis): 0 to 100 km/h

Legend:
- Radial HR, VR, WR, ZRT
- Radial SR, TR
- Radial ECO

Aerodynamic drag

<u>Aerodynamic drag</u> is calculated as:

$$F_L = 0.5 \cdot \varrho \cdot c_d \cdot A \, (v + v_0)^2$$

With v in km/h:

$$F_L = 0.0386 \cdot \varrho \cdot c_d \cdot A \cdot (v + v_0)^2$$

Air density ϱ
(at 200 m altitude ϱ = 1.202 kg/m³),
Drag coefficient c_d PP. 37 and 340.

<u>Aerodynamic drag in kW</u>

$$P_L = F_L \cdot v = 0.5 \cdot \varrho \cdot c_d \cdot A \cdot v \cdot (v + v_0)^2$$

or

$$P_L = 12.9 \cdot 10^{-6} \cdot c_d \cdot A \cdot v \cdot (v + v_0)^2$$

with P_L in kW, F_L in N, v and v_0 in km/h, A in m², ϱ = 1.202 kg/m³.

Empirical determination of coefficients for aerodynamic drag and rolling resistance

Allow vehicle to coast down in neutral under windless conditions on a level road surface. The time that elapses while the vehicle coasts down by a specific increment of speed is measured from two initial velocities, v_1 (high speed) and v_2 (low speed). This information is used to calculate the mean deceleration rates a_1 and a_2. See following table for formulas and example.

The example is based on a vehicle weighing m = 1450 kg with a cross section A = 2.2 m².

The method is suitable for application at vehicle speeds of less than 100 km/h.

	1st Trial (high speed)	2nd Trial (low speed)
Initial velocity	v_{a1} = 60 km/h	v_{a2} = 15 km/h
Terminal velocity	v_{b1} = 55 km/h	v_{b2} = 10 km/h
Interval between v_a and v_b	t_1 = 6.5 s	t_2 = 10.5 s
Mean velocity	$v_1 = \dfrac{v_{a1} + v_{b1}}{2}$ = 57.5 km/h	$v_2 = \dfrac{v_{a2} + v_{b2}}{2}$ = 12.5 km/h
Mean deceleration	$a_1 = \dfrac{v_{a1} - v_{b1}}{t_1}$ = 0.77 $\dfrac{\text{km/h}}{\text{s}}$	$a_2 = \dfrac{v_{a2} - v_{b2}}{t_2}$ = 0.48 $\dfrac{\text{km/h}}{\text{s}}$
Drag coefficient	$c_d = \dfrac{6 \, m \cdot (a_1 - a_2)}{A \cdot (v_1^2 - v_2^2)}$ = 0.36	
Coefficient of rolling resistance	$f = \dfrac{28.2 \, (a_2 \cdot v_1^2 - a_1 \cdot v_2^2)}{10^3 \cdot (v_1^2 - v_2^2)}$ = 0.013	

Drag coefficient and associated power requirements for various body configurations

	Drag coefficient c_d	Drag power in kW, average values for $A = 2$ m² at various speeds[1]			
		40 km/h	80 km/h	120 km/h	160 km/h
Open convertible	0.5...0.7	1	7.9	27	63
Station wagon (2-box)	0.5...0.6	0.91	7.2	24	58
Conventional form (3-box)	0.4...0.55	0.78	6.3	21	50
Wedge shape, headlamps and bumpers integrated into body, wheels covered, underbody covered, optimized flow of cooling air.	0.3...0.4	0.58	4.6	16	37
Headlamps and all wheels enclosed within body, underbody covered	0.2...0.25	0.37	3.0	10	24
Reversed wedge shape (minimal cross-section at tail)	0.23	0.38	3.0	10	24
Optimum streamlining	0.15...0.20	0.29	2.3	7.8	18
Trucks, truck-trailer combinations	0.8...1.5	–	–	–	–
Motorcycles	0.6...0.7	–	–	–	–
Buses	0.6...0.7	–	–	–	–
Streamlined buses	0.3...0.4	–	–	–	–

[1] No headwind ($v_0 = 0$).

Climbing resistance and downgrade force

Climbing resistance (F_{St} with positive operational sign) and downgrade force (F_{St} with negative operational sign) are calculated as:

$$F_{St} = G \cdot \sin \alpha$$
$$= m \cdot g \cdot \sin \alpha$$

or, for a working approximation:

$$F_{St} \approx 0.01 \cdot m \cdot g \cdot p$$

valid for gradients up to $p \le 20\%$, as $\sin \alpha \approx \tan \alpha$ at small angles (less than 2% error).

Climbing power is calculated as:

$$P_{St} = F_{St} \cdot v$$

with P_{St} in kW, F_{St} in N, v in km/h:

$$P_{St} = \frac{F_{St} \cdot v}{3600} = \frac{m \cdot g \cdot v \cdot \sin \alpha}{3600}$$

or, for a working approximation:

$$P_{St} \approx \frac{m \cdot g \cdot p \cdot v}{360,000}$$

The gradient is:

$$p = (h/l) \cdot 100 \% \text{ or}$$
$$p = (\tan \alpha) \cdot 100 \%$$

with h as the height of the projected distance l. In English-speaking countries, the *gradient* is calculated as follows:
Conversion:

Gradient 1 in 100/p

Example: "1 in 2".

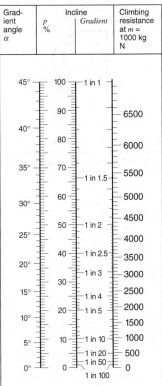

Gradient angle α	Incline p %	*Gradient*	Climbing resistance at m = 1000 kg N

Values at m = 1000 kg

Climbing resistance F_{St} N	Climbing power P_{St} in kW at various speeds				
	20 km/h	30 km/h	40 km/h	50 km/h	60 km/h
6500	36	54	72	–	–
6000	33	50	67	–	–
5500	31	46	61	–	–
5000	28	42	56	69	–
4500	25	37	50	62	–
4000	22	33	44	56	67
3500	19	29	39	49	58
3000	17	25	33	42	50
2500	14	21	28	35	42
2000	11	17	22	28	33
1500	8.3	12	17	21	25
1000	5.6	8.3	11	14	17
500	2.3	4.2	5.6	6.9	8.3
0	0	0	0	0	0

Example: To climb a hill with a gradient of p = 18%, a vehicle weighing 1500 kg will require approximately 1.5 · 1700 N = 2550 N motive force and, at v = 40 km/h, roughly 1.5 · 19 kW = 28.5 kW climbing power.

Motive force

The higher the engine torque M and overall transmission ratio i between engine and driven wheels, and the lower the power-transmission losses, the higher is the <u>motive force</u> F available at the drive wheels.

$$F = \frac{M \cdot i}{r} \cdot \eta \quad \text{or} \quad F = \frac{P \cdot \eta}{\upsilon}$$

η Drivetrain efficiency level
(longitudinally installed engine
$\eta \approx 0.88...0.92$)
(transverse engine $\eta \approx 0.91...0.95$)

The motive force F is partially consumed in overcoming the running resistance F_W. Numerically higher transmission ratios are applied to deal with the substantially increased running resistance encountered on gradients (gearbox).

Vehicle and engine speeds

$$n = \frac{60 \cdot \upsilon \cdot i}{2 \cdot \pi \cdot r}$$

or with υ in km/h:

$$n = \frac{1000 \cdot \upsilon \cdot i}{2 \cdot \pi \cdot 60 \cdot r}$$

Acceleration

The surplus force $F - F_W$ accelerates the vehicle (or retards it when F_W exceeds F).

$$a = \frac{F - F_W}{k_m \cdot m} \quad \text{or} \quad a = \frac{P \cdot \eta - P_W}{\upsilon \cdot k_m \cdot m}$$

The rotational inertia coefficient k_m, compensates for the apparent increase in vehicle mass due to the rotating masses (wheels, flywheel, crankshaft, etc.).

Motive force and road speed on vehicles with automatic transmissions

When the formula for motive force is applied to automatic transmissions with hydrodynamic torque converters or hydrodynamic clutches, the engine torque M is replaced by the torque at the converter turbine, while the rotational speed of the converter turbine is used in the formula for engine speed.

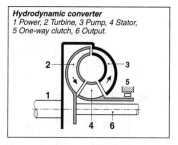

Hydrodynamic converter
1 Power, 2 Turbine, 3 Pump, 4 Stator,
5 One-way clutch, 6 Output.

The relationship between $M_{Turb} = f (n_{Turb})$ and the engine characteristic $M_{Mot} = f (n_{Mot})$ is determined using the characteristics of the hydrodynamic converter (P. 685).

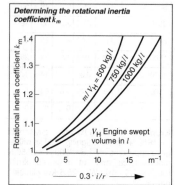

Determining the rotational inertia coefficient k_m

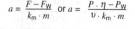

$0.3 \cdot i/r$ →

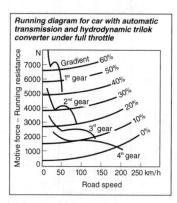

Running diagram for car with automatic transmission and hydrodynamic trilok converter under full throttle

Adhesion to road surface

Coefficients of static friction for pneumatic tires on various surfaces

Vehicle speed km/h	Tire condition	Road condition Dry	Wet: water approx. 0.2 mm	Deep rainfall: water approx. 1 mm deep	Puddles: water approx. 2 mm deep	Iced (black ice)
		Coefficient of static friction μ_{HF}				
50	new	0.85	0.65	0.55	0.5	0.1 and less
	worn[1]	1	0.5	0.4	0.25	
90	new	0.8	0.6	0.3	0.05	
	worn[1]	0.95	0.2	0.1	0.05	
130	new	0.75	0.55	0.2	0	
	worn[1]	0.9	0.2	0.1	0	

The static coefficient of friction (between the tires and the road surface), also known as the tire-road-interface friction coefficient, is determined by the vehicle's speed, the condition of the tires and the state of the road surface (see table above). The figures cited apply for concrete and tarmacadam road surfaces in good condition. The coefficients of sliding friction (with wheel locked) are usually lower than the coefficients of static friction.

Special rubber compounds providing friction coefficients of up to 1.8 are employed in racing tires.

The maxima for acceleration and uphill driving, and for retardation and downhill braking, are provided on page 345.

Aquaplaning

Aquaplaning, has a particularly dramatic influence on the contact between tire and road surface. It describes the state in which a layer of water separates the tire and the (wet) road surface. The phenomenon occurs when a wedge of water forces its way underneath the tire's contact patch and lifts it from the road. The tendency to aquaplan

is dependent upon such factors as the depth of the water on the road surface, the vehicle's speed, the tread pattern, the tread wear, and the load pressing the tire against the road surface. Wide tires are particularly susceptible to aquaplaning. It is not possible to steer or brake an aquaplaning vehicle, as its front wheels have ceased to rotate, meaning that neither steering inputs nor braking forces can be transmitted to the road surface.

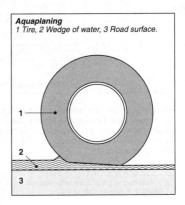

Aquaplaning
1 Tire, 2 Wedge of water, 3 Road surface.

[1] Worn to tread depth of ≥1.6 mm (legal minimum in Germany, as per para. 36.2, StVZO (FMVSS/CUR)).

Accelerating and braking

The vehicle is regarded as accelerating or braking (decelerating) at a constant rate when a remains constant. The following equations apply to an initial or final speed of 0:

	Equations for v in m/s	Equations for v in km/h
Acceleration or braking (deceleration) in m/s^2	$a = \dfrac{v^2}{2 \cdot s} = \dfrac{v}{t} = \dfrac{2 \cdot s}{t^2}$	$a = \dfrac{v^2}{26 \cdot s} = \dfrac{v}{3.6 \cdot t} = \dfrac{2 \cdot s}{t^2}$
Accelerating or braking time in s	$t = \dfrac{v}{a} = \dfrac{2 \cdot s}{v} = \sqrt{\dfrac{2 \cdot s}{a}}$	$t = \dfrac{v}{3.6 \cdot a} = \dfrac{7.2 \cdot s}{v} = \sqrt{\dfrac{2 \cdot s}{a}}$
Accelerating or braking distance[1] in m	$s = \dfrac{v^2}{2 \cdot a} = \dfrac{v \cdot t}{2} = \dfrac{a \cdot t^2}{2}$	$s = \dfrac{v^2}{26 \cdot a} = \dfrac{v \cdot t}{7.2} = \dfrac{a \cdot t^2}{2}$

Stopping distance, P. 346.
Symbols and units, P. 15.

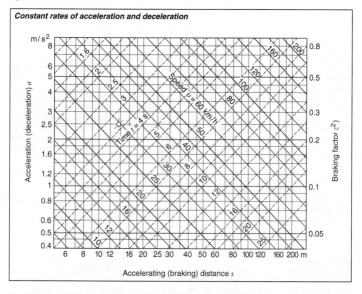

Constant rates of acceleration and deceleration

Each point on the graph represents a particular relationship between v, a or z^2), s and t. Two values must be available for all values to be determined.
Given: Vehicle speed $v = 30$ km/h, braking distance $s = 13.5$ m.
Determined: Mean deceleration $a = 2.5$ m/s^2, retardation $z = 0.25$,
Braking time $t = 3.3$ s.

---

[1] If final speed v_2 is not 0, braking distance $s = v_1 \cdot t - at^2/2$ at v_1 in m/s.
[2] Deceleration rate relative to 1 g.

Maxima for acceleration and braking (deceleration)

When the motive or braking forces exerted at the vehicle's wheels reach such a magnitude that the tires are just still within their limit of adhesion (maximum adhesion is still present), the relationships between the gradient angle α, coefficient of static friction μ_{HF}[1] and maximum acceleration or deceleration are defined as follows. The real-world figures are always somewhat lower, as all the vehicle's tires do not simultaneously exploit their maximum adhesion during each acceleration (deceleration). Electronic traction control and antilock braking systems (TCS, ABS, ESP)[2] maintain the traction level in the vicinity of the coefficient of static friction.

k = Ratio between the load on driven or braked wheels and the total weight. All wheels driven or braked: $k = 1$. At 50% weight distribution $k = 0.5$.

Example: $k = 0.5$; $g = 10$ m/s^2, $\mu_{HF} = 0.6$; $p = 15\%$
$a_{max} = 0.5 \cdot 10 \cdot (0.6 \pm 0.15)$
Braking on upgrade (+): $a_{max} = 3.75$ m/s^2, downgrade braking (−): $a_{max} = 2.25$ m/s^2

Work and power

The power required to maintain a consistent rate of acceleration (deceleration) varies according to vehicle speed. Power available for acceleration:

$$P_a = P \cdot \eta - P_W$$

where P = engine output, η = efficiency, and P_W = motive power.

Acceleration and braking (deceleration)

	Level road surface	Inclined road surface $\alpha°$; $p = 100 \cdot \tan \alpha \%$	
Limit acceleration or deceleration a_{max} in m/s^2	$a_{max} \leq k \cdot g \cdot \mu_r$	$a_{max} \leq k \cdot g \ (\mu_r \cos \alpha \pm \sin \alpha)$ approximation[3]: $a_{max} \leq k \cdot g \ (\mu_r \pm 0.01 \cdot p)$	+ Upgrade braking or downgrade acceleration − Upgrade acceleration or downgrade braking

Achievable acceleration a_e (P_a in kW, υ in km/h, m in kg)

Level road surface	Inclined road surface	
$a_e = \dfrac{3600 \cdot P_a}{k_m \cdot m \cdot \upsilon}$	$a_e = \dfrac{3600 \cdot P_a}{k_m \cdot m \cdot \upsilon} \pm g \cdot \sin \alpha$	+ Downgrade acceleration − Upgrade acceleration for $g \cdot \sin \alpha$ the approximation[3] is $g \cdot p/100$

Work and power

	Level road surface	Inclined road surface $\alpha°$; $p = 100 \cdot \tan \alpha \%$	
Acceleration or braking work W in J[4]	$W = k_m \cdot m \cdot a \cdot s$	$W = m \cdot s \ (k_m \cdot a \pm g \cdot \sin \alpha)$ approximation[3]: $W = m \cdot s \ (k_m \cdot a \pm g \cdot p/100)$	+ Downgrade braking or upgrade acceleration
Acceleration or braking power at velocity υ in W	$P_a = k_m \cdot m \cdot a \cdot \upsilon$	$P_a = m \cdot \upsilon \ (k_m \cdot a \pm g \cdot \sin \alpha)$ approximation[3]: $P_a = m \cdot \upsilon \ (k_m \cdot a \pm g \cdot p/100)$	− Downgrade acceleration or upgrade braking υ in m/s. For υ in km/h, use $\upsilon/3.6$.

---

[1] See P. 343 for numerical values.
[2] ABS: antilock braking system; P. 659, 693.
TCS: traction control system; P. 606.
ESP: electronic stability program; P. 704.

[3] Valid to approx. $p = 20\%$ (under 2% error).
[4] J = N $\cdot$ m = W $\cdot$ s; conversions, P. 16.

Stopping distance

This is the distance covered between the moment when a hazard is recognized and the time when the vehicle comes to a complete stop. It is the sum of the distances traveled during the reaction time t_r, the brake response time t_a (at constant vehicle speed υ), and the active braking time t_w. Maximum retardation a is obtained in the pressure-build-up period t_s. Alternately, half of the pressure-buildup period may be considered to be fully decelerated. The periods in which no braking occurs are combined to form the so-called lost time $t_{\upsilon z}$:

$$t_{\upsilon z} = t_r + t_a + t_s/2.$$

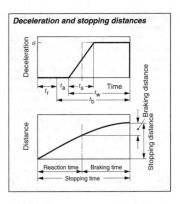

Deceleration and stopping distances

The upper limits on retardation are determined by the static coefficient of friction between tires and road surface (P. 343), while the lower extremes are defined by the legally required minima (P. 650).

The difference between the stopping time/distance and the braking time/distance is defined by $t_{\upsilon z}$ or $\upsilon \cdot t_{\upsilon z}$. The brake actuation time given on page 647 includes the times $t_a + t_s/2$.

Reaction time

The reaction time is the period which

elapses between recognition of the object, the decision to brake and the time it takes for the foot to hit the brake pedal. The reaction time is not a fixed value: it ranges from 0.3 to 1.7 s, depending upon the driver and on external factors (P. 347).

Special tests are necessary to determine individual reaction patterns (such as those performed by the Medical and Psychological Institute for Traffic Safety of the German Inspection, Testing, and Certification Authorities, Stuttgart [TÜV Stuttgart, e.V.]).

	Equations for υ in m/s	Equations for υ in km/h
Stopping time t_h in s	$t_h = t_{\upsilon z} + \dfrac{\upsilon}{a}$	$t_h = t_{\upsilon z} + \dfrac{\upsilon}{3.6 \cdot a}$
Stopping distance s_h in m	$s_h = \upsilon \cdot t_{\upsilon z} + \dfrac{\upsilon^2}{2 \cdot a}$	$s_h = \dfrac{\upsilon}{3.6} t_{\upsilon z} + \dfrac{\upsilon^2}{26 \cdot a}$

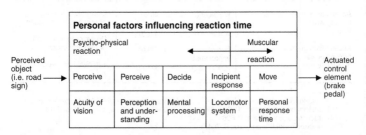

Personal factors influencing reaction time

Psycho-physical reaction				Muscular reaction	
Perceive	Perceive	Decide	Incipient response	Move
Acuity of vision	Perception and understanding	Mental processing	Locomotor system	Personal response time

Perceived object (i.e. road sign) → ... → Actuated control element (brake pedal)

Effect of personal and extraneous factors on reaction time

	Reduction down to 0.3 s	Extension up to 1.7 s
A) Personal factors	Trained, reflexive response	Inexperienced, uncoordinated response
	Good frame of mind; optimum performance potential	Poor frame of mind, e.g. fatigue
	Highly skilled driver	Lower level of driving skill
	Youth	Advanced age
	Anticipation	Inattentiveness, distraction
	Physical and mental health	Health disorders in response groups
		Panic, alcohol
B) Extraneous factors Traffic situation	Uncomplicated, easily comprehended, predictable, familiar	Complicated, difficult to comprehend, unpredictable, rarely encountered
Type of perceived object	Explicit, conspicuous	Equivocal, inconspicuous
Location of perceived object	Within field of vision	At edge of field of vision
Nature of control element	Logical layout of mechanic controls	Poor layout of mechanical controls

Brake response and pressure build-up times

The condition of the brakes at the moment at which they are applied (e.g. wet brake disks) is one factor influencing brake response time t_a and pressure build-up time t_s; others are the designs of the actuation and force-transmission mechanism and linkage. Consult ECE R13 for legal regulations concerning t_a and t_s on tightly adjusted brakes. The applicable regulation[1] for testing braking-system effectiveness uses figures of 0.36 s (vehicle class M_1) and 0.54 s (vehicle classes M_2, M_3, $N_1...N_3$) in the braking-distance equation $t_a + t_s/2$, see P. 717). The response and pressure build-up times are longer if the brake system is in poor condition. A response delay of 1 s results in a stopping distance of (see table):

---

[1] EC Directive 71J320/EEC.

Deceleration a in m/s²	Vehicle speed prior to braking in km/h												
	10	30	50	60	70	80	90	100	120	140	160	180	200
	Distance during delay of 1 sec (no braking) in m												
	2.8	8.3	14	17	19	22	25	28	33	39	44	50	56
	Stopping distance in m												
4.4	3.7	16	36	48	62	78	96	115	160	210	270	335	405
5	3.5	15	33	44	57	71	87	105	145	190	240	300	365
5.8	3.4	14	30	40	52	65	79	94	130	170	215	265	320
7	3.3	13	28	36	46	57	70	83	110	145	185	230	275
8	3.3	13	26	34	43	53	64	76	105	135	170	205	250
9	3.2	12	25	32	40	50	60	71	95	125	155	190	225

Passing (overtaking)

Symbol		Unit
a	Acceleration	m/s²
l_1, l_2	Vehicle length	m
s_1, s_2	Safety margin	m
s_H	Relative distance traveled by passing vehicle	m
s_L	Distance traveled by vehicle being passed	m
s_u	Passing distance	m
t_u	Passing time	s
v_L	Speed of slower vehicle	km/h
v_H	Speed of faster vehicle	km/h

The complete passing maneuver involves pulling out of the lane, overtaking the other vehicle, and returning to the original lane. Passing can take place under a wide variety of highly differing circumstances and conditions, so precise calculations are difficult. For this reason, the following calculations, graphs, and illustrations will confine themselves to an examination of two extreme conditions: Passing at a constant velocity and passing at a constant rate of acceleration.

We can simplify graphic representation by treating the passing distance s_u as the sum of two (straight-ahead) components, while disregarding the extra travel involved in pulling out of the lane and back in again.

Passing distance

$$s_U = s_H + s_L$$

The distance s_H which the more rapid vehicle most cover compared to the slower vehicle (considered as being stationary) is the sum of the vehicle lengths l_1 and l_2 and the safety margins s_1 and s_2.

$$s_H = s_1 + s_2 + l_1 + l_2$$

During the passing time t_u, the slower vehicle covers the distance s_L; this is the distance that the overtaking vehicle must also travel in order to maintain the safety margin.

$$s_L = t_u - v_L/3.6$$

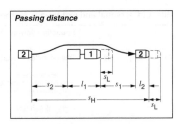

Passing distance

Safety margin

The minimum safety margin corresponds to the distance covered during the lost time t_{uz} (P. 346). The figure for a lost time of $t_{uz} = 1.08$ s (velocity in km/h) is $(0.3 \cdot v)$ meters. However, a minimum of $0.5 \cdot v$ is advisable outside built-up areas.

Passing at constant speed

On highways with more than two lanes, the overtaking vehicle will frequently already be traveling at a speed adequate for passing before the actual process begins. The passing time (from initial lane change until return to the original lane has been completed) is then:

$$t_u = \frac{3.6 \cdot s_H}{v_H - v_L}$$

The passing distance

$$s_u = \frac{t_u \cdot v_H}{3.6} = \frac{s_H \cdot v_H}{v_H - v_L}$$

t in s,
s in m,
v in km/h

Passing with constant acceleration

On narrow roads, the vehicle will usually have to slow down to the speed of the preceding car or truck before again accelerating to pass. The attainable acceleration figures depend upon engine output, vehicle weight, speed and running resistance (P. 345). These generally lie within the range of 0.4...0.8 m/s², with up to 1.4 m/s² available in lower gears for further reductions in passing time. The distance required to complete the passing maneuver should never exceed half the visible stretch of road.

Operating on the assumption that a constant rate of acceleration can be maintained for the duration of the passing maneuver, the passing time will be:

$$t_u = \sqrt{2 \cdot s_H/a}$$

The distance which the slower vehicle covers within this period is defined as $s_L = t_u \cdot v_L/3.6$. This gives a passing distance of:

$$s_u = s_H + t_u \cdot v_L/3.6 \qquad \begin{array}{l} t \text{ in s,} \\ s \text{ in m,} \\ v \text{ in km/h.} \end{array}$$

The left side of the graph below shows the relative distances s_H for speed differentials $v_H - v_L$ and acceleration rates a, while the right side shows the distances s_L covered by the vehicle being passed at various speeds v_L. The passing distance s_u is the sum of s_H and s_L.

The graph is applied as follows. First, determine the distance s_H to be traveled by the passing vehicle. Enter this distance on the left side of the graph between the Y axis and the applicable line for $(v_H - v_L)$ or acceleration. Then extrapolate the line to the right, over to the speed line v_L.

Example (represented by broken lines in the graph):

$v_L = v_H = 50$ km/h,
$a = 0.4$ m/s^2,
$l_1 = 10$ m, $l_2 = 5$ m,
$s_1 = s_2 = 0.3 \cdot v_L = 0.3 \cdot v_H = 15$ m.

Solution: Enter intersection of $a = 0.4$ m/s^2 and $s_H = 15 + 15 + 10 + 5 = 45$ m in the left side of the graph.
Indication $t_u = 15$ s, $s_L = 210$ m.
Thus $s_u = s_H + s_L = 255$ m.

Visual range

For safe passing on narrow roads, the visibility must be at least the sum of the passing distance plus the distance which would be traveled by an oncoming vehicle while the passing maneuver is in progress. This distance is approximately 400 m if the vehicles approaching each other are traveling at speeds of 90 km/h, and the vehicle being overtaken at 60 km/h.

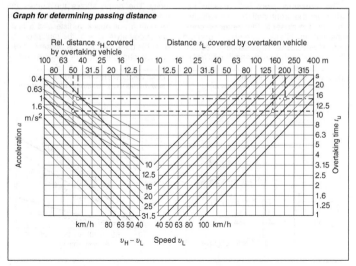

Graph for determining passing distance

Dynamics of lateral motion

Response to crosswinds
Strong crosswinds will deflect a vehicle from its lane, particularly at high speeds. Sudden crosswinds, of the kind encountered when embankments give way to open, unsheltered roads, can evoke yaw-angle changes as well as causing the vehicle to drift off course. On vehicles which are sensitive to crosswind (for reaction time see page 346), these effects are substantial and can occur before the driver has had time to react and take preventive action. It is thus essential that the relevant factors are considered in the vehicle design stage.

When wind impacts upon the vehicle from an oblique angle, aerodynamic drag is supplemented by a lateral component of the aerodynamic force. This force, which is distributed across the entire body, can be considered as a single force – the crosswind force – directed toward what is known as the pressure point. The actual location of the pressure point is determined by body shape and angle of impact.

The pressure point will usually be found on the front half of the vehicle, whereby it is closer to the center on conventional notchback ("three-box") bodies than on vehicles with a sloping tail section ("fast-backs" and aerodynamic designs).

With the latter, the pressure point may even lie forward of the front axle in extreme cases. The pressure point on notchback bodies generally remains in a specific location; on streamlined vehicles it tends to vary according to the angle of impact. All else being equal, the greater lateral forces will occur with the notchback.

As the above implies, the pressure point will hardly provide a suitable reference point for use in illustrating the effects of crosswinds, because it has no fixed location on the vehicle. At the same time, the center of gravity varies with vehicle load. It is thus useful to select a central location on the forward section of the body as a reference point, a practice which also ensures that the data remain unaffected by the variations in the relative positions of bodywork and suspension.

When the crosswind force is specified for a reference point other than the pressure point, it must be supplemented by the crosswind moment at the pressure point in question. The standard practice in aerodynamics is to replace the forces and moments with dimensionless coefficients which remain independent of air-flow velocity. The graph shows the curves for crosswind force and the yaw coefficients for both a notchback vehicle and a fastback body style. Due to the multiplicity of possible body designs, the present investigation can only provide general refer-

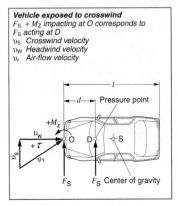

Vehicle exposed to crosswind
$F_S + M_Z$ impacting at O corresponds to F_S acting at D
v_S Crosswind velocity
v_W Headwind velocity
v_r Air-flow velocity

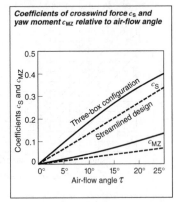

Coefficients of crosswind force c_S and yaw moment c_{MZ} relative to air-flow angle

Three-box configuration
Streamlined design
c_S
c_{MZ}

Coefficients c_S and c_{MZ}

Air-flow angle τ

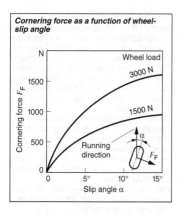

Cornering force as a function of wheel-slip angle

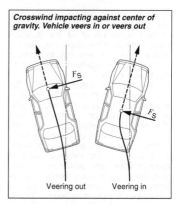

Crosswind impacting against center of gravity. Vehicle veers in or veers out

Veering out   Veering in

ence data; wind-tunnel measurements are essential for obtaining precise information on specific body shapes.

The following equations are applied to derive forces and moments from the coefficients:

Crosswind force $F_S = c_S \cdot \varrho \cdot (v_r^2/2) \cdot A_S$

Yaw moment $M_Z = c_{MZ} \cdot \varrho \cdot (v_r^2/2) \cdot A_S \cdot l$

ϱ Atmospheric density, v_r Resulting air-impact velocity, A_s Projected lateral surface of the vehicle, l Total length of the vehicle (in coherent units), c_S Coefficient of crosswind force, c_{MZ} Coefficient for crosswind-induced yaw.

The distance between the pressure point and the leading edge of the vehicle is calculated using

$$d = M_Z/F_S = l \cdot c_{MZ}/c_S$$

The crosswind force is resisted by the lateral cornering forces at the wheels. The degree of lateral cornering force which a pneumatic tire can provide depends upon numerous factors, such as wheel slip angle, wheel load, tire design and dimensions, tire pressure and the amount of traction afforded by the road surface.

The pneumatic tire's specific response characteristics mean that, at a constant slip angle, higher wheel loads will not evoke proportional increases in cornering forces. In the example (diagram), doubling the wheel load increases the corner-

ing force by a factor of only 1.5...1.7. The slip angle must also be increased if the cornering force is to be doubled. This explains why the axle supporting the greater load assumes a larger slip angle than its less heavily loaded counterpart, assuming that identical ratios of lateral (side) force to tire contact force act on both axles.

When the crosswind force impacts against the center of gravity, the distribution ratio for the required cornering forces between front and rear axles is a function of the wheel-load factors, i.e. the ratio of contact force to lateral force is the same at both axles. When the center of gravity is in the forward section of the vehicle, the crosswind force causes the vehicle to "veer-out" due to the front axle's necessarily greater wheel slip angle; when the center of gravity is at the rear, the vehicle "veers-in". In both cases, the vehicle's center of gravity is deflected downwind from the original path of travel. When the crosswind ceases, the "veering-out" vehicle will continue to deviate from its original path, while the "veering-in" vehicle will return to and indeed go beyond the original line.

The crosswind's impact point, however, will rarely coincide with the center of gravity; the distance forward from the center of the vehicle depends upon the individual body shape. Thus a vehicle which responds to impact at the center of gravity by veering inwards, will veer out when exposed to actual crosswinds. Due to the forward displacement of the pressure point, vehicles with a sloping rear section display a greater tendency to veer-out; they are thus more difficult to control than notchback vehicles.

Rear-mounted vertical stabilizer fins can be installed to move the pressure point rearward, toward the center of gravity. However, except in competition vehicles and other special applications, this option has to date rarely been applied.

Placing the pressure point in the immediate vicinity of the vehicle's center of gravity results in improved directional stability. Oversteer vehicles have a minimum tendency to deviate from their path of travel when the pressure point is forward of the center of gravity. On understeer vehicles, the best pressure-point location is just to the rear of the center of gravity.

Crosswind force is generally minimal relative to contact force, and the influence of non-linearity in the ratio of contact force to lateral force is limited when small lateral forces are applied – a vehicle's response to crosswinds is therefore not governed by tire properties alone. Other important factors include compliance in suspension and steering. Thus the suspension designer can also exercise a major influence on the vehicle's crosswind response characteristics.

Oversteer and understeer

Cornering forces can only be generated between a rubber tire and the road surface when the tire rolls at an angle to its longitudinal plane; that is, a certain wheel slip angle is required.

A vehicle is said to understeer when, as lateral acceleration increases, the slip angle at the front axle increases more than it does at the rear axle. The opposite applies for a vehicle which oversteers.

A vehicle will not necessarily display the same self-steering effect at all possible rates of lateral acceleration. Some vehicles always understeer or oversteer, and some display a transition from understeer to oversteer as lateral acceleration increases, while other vehicles respond in precisely the opposite manner.

References:
Barth, R.: "Windkanalmessungen an Fahrzeugmodellen und rechteckigen Körpern mit verschiedenem Seitenverhältnis bei unsymmetrischer Anströmung" (Wind Tunnel Measurements on Vehicle Models and Rectangular Bodies with Different Side Ratios under Asymmetrical Flow). Dissertation, Stuttgart Technical College, 1958.
Barth, R.: "Luftkräfte am Kraftfahrzeug" (Aerodynamic Forces Acting on Motor Vehicles). Deutsche Kraftfahrforschung und Straßenverkehrstechnik (German Motor Vehicle Research and Traffic Engineering), Vol. 184, Düsseldorf. VDI-Verlag, 1966.
Mitschke, M.: "Dynamik der Kraftfahrzeuge" (Dynamics of Motor Vehicles). Springer-Verlag, 1972.

Cornering behavior

Centrifugal force in curves

$$F_{cf} = \frac{m \cdot v^2}{r_K} \text{ (P. 35)}$$

or, with v specified in km/h and r_K as the radius of the curve in m

$$F_{cf} = \frac{m \cdot v^2}{12.96 \cdot r_K}$$

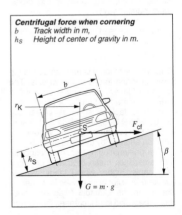

Centrifugal force when cornering
b Track width in m,
h_S Height of center of gravity in m.

Critical speeds

The concrete example provided in the table below would apply to a vehicle with a track $b = 1.5$ m, height of center of gravity $h_S = 0.6$ m; max. adhesion coefficient $\mu_r = 0.8$, curve radius $r_K = 90$ m, curve banking $\beta = 20°$.

	Flat curve	Banked curve
Speed at which the vehicle exceeds the limit of adhesion (skid)	$v \leq 11.28 \sqrt{\mu_r \cdot r_K}$ km/h	$v \leq 11.28 \sqrt{\dfrac{(\mu_r + \tan \beta) \, r_K}{1 - \mu_r \cdot \tan \beta}}$ km/h
Example:	≤ 96 km/h	≤ 137 km/h
Speed at which the vehicle tips	$v \geq 11.28 \sqrt{\dfrac{b \cdot r_K}{2 \cdot h_S}}$ km/h	$v \geq 11.28 \sqrt{\dfrac{\left(\dfrac{b}{2 \cdot h_S} + \tan \beta\right) \cdot r_K}{1 - \dfrac{b}{2 \cdot h_S} \cdot \tan \beta}}$ km/h
Example:	≥ 120 km/h ($\mu_r \geq 1.25$)	≥ 184 km/h ($\mu_r \geq 1.25$)

Body roll in curves

Roll axis

When cornering, the centrifugal force which concentrates around the center of gravity causes the vehicle to tilt away from the path of travel. The magnitude of this rolling motion depends upon the rates of the springs and their response to alternating compression, and upon the lever arm of the centrifugal force (distance between the roll axis and the center of gravity). The roll axis is the body's instantaneous axis of rotation relative to the road surface. Like all rigid bodies, the vehicle body consistently executes a screwing or rotating motion; this motion is supplemented by a lateral displacement along the instantaneous axis.

The higher the roll axis, i.e. the closer it is to a parallel axis through the center of gravity, the greater will be the transverse stability and the less the roll during cornering. However, this generally implies a corresponding upward displacement of the wheels, resulting in a change in track width (with negative effects on operating safety). For this reason, designs are sought which combine a high instantaneous roll center with minimal track change. The goal therefore is to place the instantaneous axes of the wheels as high as possible relative to the body, while simultaneously keeping them as far from the body as possible.

Determining the roll axis

A frequently-applied means for finding the approximate roll axis is based on determining the centers of rotation of an equivalent body motion. This body motion takes place in those two planes through the front and rear axles which are vertical relative to the road. The centers of rotation are those (hypothetical) points in the body which remain stationary during the rotation. The roll axis, in turn, is the line which connects these centers (instantaneous centers). Graphic portrayals of the instantaneous centers are based on a rule according to which the instantaneous centers of rotation of three systems in a state of relative motion lie on a common pole line.

The complexity of the operations required for a more precise definition of the spatial relationships involved in wheel motion makes it advisable to employ computers capable of carrying out calculations in matrix notation (vector algebra, linear geometry, etc.).

References:

E. v. d. Osten-Sacken: "Berechnung allgemein räumlicher, vielgliedriger Gelenkgetriebe"; Dissertation, Aachen Technical College, 1970.
G. Prigge: "Grundsätzliches der Ermittlung der Rollachse von Kraftfahrzeugen mit räumlichen Radführungen"; Dissertation, Braunschweig Technical University, 1972.

ISO procedures for evaluating vehicle handling

The science devoted to studying the dynamics of vehicle handling generally defines its subject as the overall behavior of the entire system represented by "driver + vehicle + environment". As the first link in the chain, the driver makes judgements on the vehicle's handling qualities based on the sum of diverse subjective impressions. On the other hand, handling data derived from specific driving maneuvers executed without driver input (open-loop operation) provide an objective description of the vehicle's handling qualities. The driver, who up to the present day still cannot be defined accurately in terms of behavior, is replaced in these tests by a specific, objectively quantifiable interference factor. The resulting vehicular response can then be analyzed and discussed.

Standardized versions of the driving maneuvers in the list (performed on a dry road surface) below have either already been defined by the ISO or are under consideration; they serve as recognized standard procedures for vehicular evaluation [1], [2]:
– Steady-state skidpad [3],
– Transient response [4], [5], [6],
– Braking during cornering [7],
– Crosswind sensitivity,
– Straight-running stability, and
– Reaction to throttle change on skidpad.

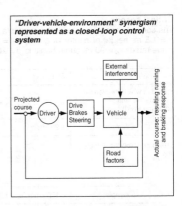

"Driver-vehicle-environment" synergism represented as a closed-loop control system

To date, it has still not been possible to arrive at comprehensive objective definitions for the dynamic characteristics associated with closed-loop operation, as adequate data on the precise control characteristics of the human element are still unavailable.

Test quantities
The main criteria employed in evaluating vehicle dynamics are:
– Steering-wheel angle,
– Lateral acceleration,
– Longitudinal acceleration and deceleration,
– Yaw speed,
– Float and roll angles.

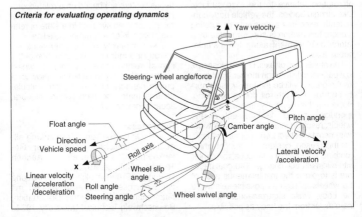

Criteria for evaluating operating dynamics

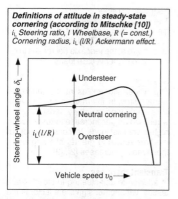

Definitions of attitude in steady-state cornering (according to Mitschke [10])
i_L Steering ratio, l Wheelbase, R (= const.)
Cornering radius, i_L (l/R) Ackermann effect.

Additional data are employed to verify and confirm the previously derived information on specific points of vehicle handling:
– Linear and lateral velocity,
– Steering angles at front and rear wheels,
– Slip angles at all wheels,
– Camber and pitch angles,
– Steering-wheel force.

Steady-state skidpad
The most important data to be derived from steady-state skidpad testing are the maximum lateral acceleration, and the manner in which individual dynamic parameters respond to the variations in lateral acceleration which occur up to the limit. This information is employed in evaluating the vehicle's self-steering response [2], [3]. Compliance in both the steering system and the suspension is represented in the current standard definition of steering response, which employs the terms "oversteer", "understeer" and "neutral steering". Several dynamic factors and their derivatives are considered in conjunction with lateral acceleration in describing vehicle handling, examples being steering-wheel angle, roll angle and float angle. Other significant vehicle parameters are steering angle and slip angle.

In the following, a light utility van (similar to a passenger car) and a heavy truck are used to provide examples of the results gathered on a dry surface.

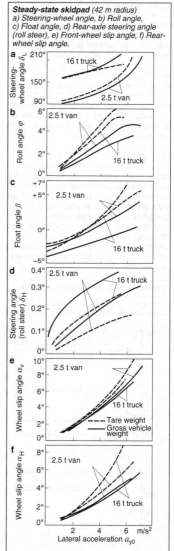

Steady-state skidpad (42 m radius)
a) Steering-wheel angle, b) Roll angle, c) Float angle, d) Rear-axle steering angle (roll steer), e) Front-wheel slip angle, f) Rear-wheel slip angle.

Steering-wheel angle
As small utility vehicles are fitted with tires similar to those used in passenger cars, and are also equipped with relatively high-power engines, they achieve high rates of lateral acceleration. Both vehicle types understeer.

Roll angle
The degree of self-steering which prevails at the axles is largely determined by the roll angle. Higher loads result in more pronounced roll angles due to the greater vehicle mass and the attendant increase in effective centrifugal force.

Float angle
The float angle encountered at high rates of lateral acceleration is regarded as an index of controllability, in other words the vehicle's response to driver input. High absolute figures or fluctuations in float angle are regarded as particularly undesirable [8].

At low rates of lateral acceleration, the float angle is a function of the radius of the driven circle, and the vehicle's center of gravity which varies along with changes in vehicle load.

Rear-axle roll steer
The relationship between the steering angle at the rear axle (roll-steer angle) and lateral acceleration illustrates how the roll-steer angle at the rear axle decreases in response to higher vehicle loads.

Slip angle
The wheel slip angles at the individual wheels provide information on the vehicle's self-steering characteristics. The wheel slip angles increase in response to higher vehicle loads, a consequence of the tires requiring greater slip angles as their loading increases [2], [9].

Transient response
In addition to self-steering in steady-state testing, yet another significant factor is the vehicle's response during directional changes (e.g. for rapid evasive maneuvers) [2]. Two test methods have become accepted internationally. These are defined according to the type of input stimulus, and illustrate both the time and frequency ranges of the vehicle's response:
– Step-input (sharp change in steering

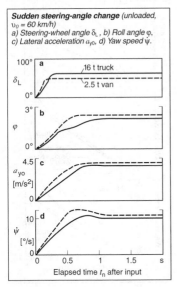

Sudden steering-angle change (unloaded, $v_0 = 60$ km/h)
a) Steering-wheel angle δ_L, b) Roll angle φ,
c) Lateral acceleration a_{y0}, d) Yaw speed $\dot{\psi}$.

a
δ_L 16 t truck 2.5 t van
$100°$ – $0°$

b
φ
$3°$ – $0°$

c
a_{y0} [m/s²]
4.5 – 0

d
$\dot{\psi}$ [°/s]
10 – 0

Elapsed time t_n after input
0   0.5   1   1.5   s

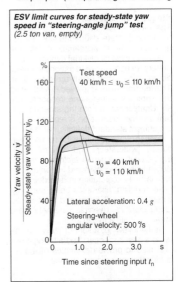

ESV limit curves for steady-state yaw speed in "steering-angle jump" test
(2.5 ton van, empty)

Yaw velocity $\dot{\psi}$ / Steady-state yaw velocity $\dot{\psi}_0$
%
Test speed 40 km/h $\leq v_0 \leq$ 110 km/h
160
120
80
40
0

$v_0 = 40$ km/h
$v_0 = 110$ km/h

Lateral acceleration: 0.4 g
Steering-wheel angular velocity: 500 °/s

Time since steering input t_n
0   1.0   2.0   3.0   s

angle),
– Sinusoidal input (sinusoidal steering-angle input).

Step input (time response)

Starting with the vehicle traveling in a straight line, the steering wheel is abruptly "pulled" to a specified angle; the vehicle's response serves as the basis for evaluation. The most important quantities to be measured are [5]:
– Steering-wheel angle,
– Yaw speed,
– Vehicle speed, and
– Lateral acceleration.

The light utility van responds to the step input with a more rapid change in lateral acceleration – and thus in yaw – than the heavy truck.

US authorities have defined a transient yaw requirement for Experimental Safety Vehicles (ESV) [11]. Those vehicles which are classified as being similar to passenger cars may exhibit relatively pronounced overswing in the initial input phase (whereby this effect must cease after a certain period).

Sinusoidal steering-angle input (frequency curve)

Permanent sinusoidal steering inputs at the steering wheel are also used to measure frequency-response characteristics. This provides yet another basis for evaluating a vehicle's transitional handling response, the intensity and phase of which varies according to the steering frequency. The most important factors for this evaluation are [6]:
– Steering-wheel angle,
– Lateral acceleration,
– Yaw speed, and
– Roll angle.

Braking in a curve

Of all the maneuvers encountered in everyday driving situations, one of the most critical – and thus one of the most important with regard to vehicle design – is braking during cornering. The vehicle's concept must be optimized so that its reaction to this maneuver is characterized by the best possible compromise between steerability, stability and retardation [2], [7]. Testing starts from a specified initial rate of lateral acceleration, and focuses upon

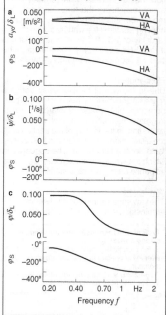

Sinusoidal steering-angle input
(16-ton truck, $v_0 = 60$ km/h, $\delta_L = 60°$).
Relative to steering-wheel angle:
a) Lateral acceleration a_{y0}/δ_L,
b) Yaw velocity $\dot{\psi}/\delta_L$ and
c) Roll angle φ/δ_L; with phase angle φ_s.

Frequency f

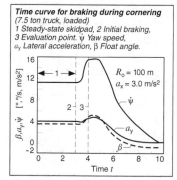

Time curve for braking during cornering
(7.5 ton truck, loaded)
1 Steady-state skidpad, 2 Initial braking,
3 Evaluation point. $\dot{\psi}$ Yaw speed,
a_y Lateral acceleration, β Float angle.

$R_0 = 100$ m
$a_x = 3.0$ m/s²

Time t

float angle and yaw speed relative to lateral deceleration as the significant factors.

The vehicle, initially in steady-state circulation at a stipulated lateral acceleration, is braked with the rate of deceleration being increased incrementally. In every test, using the time functions, the measurements are taken "1 s after initial braking" for vehicles with hydraulic brakes (a delay of 1.5...2 s after initial braking is applied for heavy-duty commercial vehicles with compressed-air brake systems).

Float angle

Due to the weight transfer away from the rear axle and the tires' response to this phenomenon, higher rates of retardation result in greater float angles. At high rates of deceleration, in the vicinity of the traction limit, the distribution of brake force is the decisive factor for the float angle. The sequence in which the wheels lock exercises a decisive influence on the vehicle's stability.

Yaw speed

The yaw speed serves as a reference in determining whether braking performance during cornering is stable or unstable. In the illustration, both vehicles' yaw-speed curves move as zero as the vehicles progress through phases of increasing deceleration up to full lockup at both axles. This indicates acceptable braking response: The vehicle remains stable.

References:
[1] Rönitz R.; Braess H.H.; Zomotor A. Verfahren und Kriterien des Fahrverhaltens von Personenwagen. (Testing procedure and evaluation of passenger-car driveability). AI 322, 1972, Volume 1.
[2] von Glasner E.C. Einbeziehung der Prüfstandsergebnissen in die Simulation des Fahrverhaltens von Nutzfahrzeugen. (Including test-stand results in driveability simulation for heavy-duty commercial vehicles). Habilitation, Universität Stuttgart, 1987.
[3] ISO. Road Vehicles – Steady-State Circular Test Procedure. ISO, 1982, No. 4138.
[4] ISO. Road Vehicles – Double Lane Change. ISO, 1975, TR 3888.
[5] ISO. Draft Proposal for an International Standard, Road Vehicles – Transient Response Test Procedure (Step/Ramp Input). ISO/TC22/SC9/N 185.
[6] ISO. Draft Proposal for an International Standard, Road Vehicles – Transient Response Test Procedure (Sinusoidal Input). ISO/TC 22/SC9/N219.
[7] ISO. Road Vehicles – Braking in a Turn. Open-Loop Test Procedure. ISO/DIS 7975.
[8] Zomotor A.; Braess H.H.; Rönitz R. Doppelter Fahrspurwechsel, eine Möglichkeit zur Beurteilung des Fahrverhaltens von Kfz? (Double Lane Change, a Method for Evaluating a Vehicle's Driveability?) ATZ 76, 1974, Volume 8.
[9] Mitschke M. Dynamik der Kraftfahrzeuge. (Dynamics of the Motor Vehicle), Springer Verlag, 1st Edition 1972, 2nd Edition 1982 and 1984, and subsequent Editions.
[10] Mitschke M. Fahrtrichtungshaltung – Analyse der Theorien. (Maintaining Direction of Travel – Analysis of the Theories). ATZ 70, 1968, Volume 5.
[11] Mischke A.; Göhring E.; Wolsdorf P.; von Glasner E.C. Contribution to the Development of a Concept of Driving Mechanics for Commercial Vehicles. SAE 83 0643.

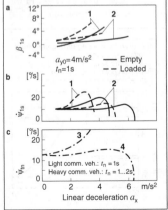

Typical yaw response when braking during cornering
a) Float angle β_{1s} and b) Yaw speed $\dot{\psi}_{1s}$ 1s after initial braking (t_n), c) Yaw speed at moment t_n.
1 16-ton truck, 2 2.5-ton van, 3 Vehicle starts to skid, 4 Vehicle remains stable.

a

β_{1s} (12°, 8°, 4°, 0°, -4°)

$a_{y0} = 4\,\text{m/s}^2$
$t_n = 1\text{s}$
— Empty
-- Loaded

b [°/s]

$\dot{\psi}_{1s}$ (20, 0)

c [°/s]

$\dot{\psi}_{tn}$ (20, 10, 0)

Light comm. veh.: $t_n = 1$s
Heavy comm. veh.: $t_n = 1...2$s

Linear deceleration a_x (0, 2, 4, 6 m/s²)

Special operating dynamics for commercial vehicles

Units and symbols

G_V	N	Front-axle load
G_H	N	Rear-axle load
G_G	N	Total weight
G_F	N	Sprung weight
U_V	N	Unsprung weight, front
U_H	N	Unsprung weight, rear
C_{DSt}	N · m/wheel	Torsional spring rate for all stabilizers
$C_{FV,H}$	N/m	Spring rates for axle springs
$C_{RV,H}$	N/m	Spring rates for tires
$S_{FV,H}$	m	Spring track
$S_{RV,H}$	m	Tire track
$m_{V,H}$	m	Instantaneous center height
h_F	m	Height of center of gravity, sprung weight
h_G	m	Height of center of gravity, total vehicle
$C_{QV,H}$	N/m	Lateral stiffness rate of tires
r	m	Radius of curve

Self-steering properties

In the development phase in which the parameters affecting a vehicle's self-steering properties are determined, empirical and test-stand measurements and computer simulations are employed in an optimization process. The major determinants are the geometry and compliance rates of the steering, the frame and the suspension.

The objects of analysis are those interference factors influencing straight-running stability and cornering behavior

Self-steering angle of a 18-ton truck cornering at 3 m/s² lateral acceleration
The self-steering angle is plotted over Y.

which can be traced to the interaction between steering and suspension, and which do not stem from driver inputs. The self-steering effect is examined at both the front and rear axles, in steady-state driving on a circular course, during braking and under unilateral spring compression.

When the springs are compressed on one side, a solid axle supported on leaf springs will tend to rotate about the vehicle's vertical axis. The degree of spring tilt exercises a major effect on this type of roll-steer effect. Neutral behavior or mild understeer, desirable from the safety point of view, are enhanced by tilting the front spring upward at the front and downward toward the rear, while the rear spring is mounted in the opposite manner, with the lowest end at the forward extremity.

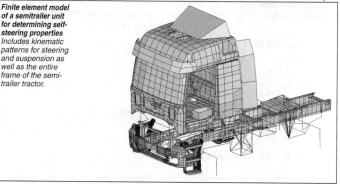

Finite element model of a semitrailer unit for determining self-steering properties
Includes kinematic patterns for steering and suspension as well as the entire frame of the semi-trailer tractor.

The wheel loads at the truck's rear axle vary dramatically, depending upon whether it is empty or loaded. This leads to the vehicle responding to reductions in load with more pronounced understeer.

On three-axle 6 x 4 vehicles, the non-steered tandem axle unit represents a constraining force around the vehicle's vertical axis, thus enhancing straight-line stability. For low speeds, the additional cornering force required at the front and rear axles is determined as follows:

Cornering forces resulting from constraint
$F_{S1} = F_{S2} - F_{S3}$ with
$F_{S2} = c_{p2} \cdot n_2 \cdot \alpha_2$
$F_{S3} = c_{p3} \cdot n_3 \cdot \alpha_3$

Slip angle
$$\alpha_2 = \frac{1}{r} \cdot \frac{c_{p3} \cdot n_3 \cdot b \cdot (a+b)}{c_{p3} \cdot n_3 \cdot (a+b) + c_{p2} \cdot n_2 \cdot a}$$

$$\alpha_3 = (b/r) - \alpha_2$$

c_p Coefficient of cornering stability from tire performance curve,
n Number of tires per axle, other designations as in illustration.

Tipping resistance
As the vehicle's total height increases, there is also an increasing tendency in a curve for it to tip over to the side before it starts to slide. Simulations of the tipping process for precise determination of the tip limit take into account both the elasticities

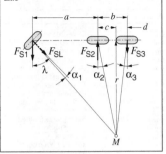

Cornering forces F_s and slip angle α on a 3-axle vehicle with non-steered tandem axle

and displacements of the center of gravity.
Achievable rates of lateral acceleration at the tip limit:

Van	$b = 6$ m/s²
Truck	$b = 5$ m/s²
Double-decker bus	$b = 3$ m/s²

Width requirement
The width requirement of motor vehicles and truck-trailer combinations is greater during cornering than when the vehicle moves in a straight line. With respect to selected driving maneuvers, it is necessary to determine the radius described by the vehicle's outer extremities during cornering, both in order to ascertain its suitability for certain applications (e.g. narrow transit routes

---

Tipping resistance
Approximation formula for critical velocities v_{tip} on a 2-axle truck (in km/h):

$$v_{tip} = 7.98 \cdot \sqrt{\frac{r \cdot (G_V \cdot S_{RV} + G_H \cdot S_{RH})}{G_G \cdot h_G + \frac{G_V^2}{C_{QV}} + \frac{G_H^2}{C_{QH}} + \frac{G_F^2 \cdot h_m^2}{C_D - G_F \cdot h_m}}}$$

with $C_D = \frac{C_{DF} \cdot C_{DR} \cdot i^2}{C_{DF} + C_{DR} \cdot i^2}$; $i = \frac{h_m}{h_m + m}$;

$h_m = h_m - m$; $m = \frac{(G_V - U_V) \cdot m_V + (G_H - U_H) m_H}{G_F}$

$C_{DF} = 1/2 \cdot (C_{FV} \cdot S_{FV}^2 + C_{FH} \cdot S_{FH}^2) + C_{DSt}$

$C_{DR} = 1/2 \cdot (C_{RV} \cdot S_{RV}^2 + C_{RH} \cdot S_{RH}^2)$

through constricted areas) and to confirm compliance with legal regulations. Evaluation is conducted with reference to the tractrix principle using electronic programs.

Handling characteristics

Objective analyses of vehicle handling are based on various maneuvers such as steady-state circulation on the skidpad, steering-angle jumps, wag frequency response, and braking in a curve.

The dynamic lateral response of truck-trailer combinations generally differs from that of rigid vehicles. Particularly significant are the distribution of loads between truck and trailer, and the design and geometry of the mechanical coupling device within a given combination.

Rotary oscillation, with the vehicle's masses turning against the tires (as compliance element) around a vertical axis, impairs straight-running stability. This phenomenon is induced by
– Rapid steering corrections associated with evasive maneuvers,
– Crosswinds, and
– Pronounced slope to the side of the road, obstacles on one side, lane grooves.
Oscillation amplitudes associated with this pendulum motion must subside rapidly if vehicle stability is to be maintained.

Below is a graphic depiction of the yaw-speed progressions for various types of truck-trailer combination. The worst case is represented by a combination, in which the towing vehicle is empty, while the center-

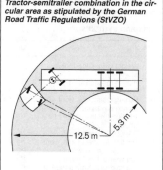

Tractor-semitrailer combination in the circular area as stipulated by the German Road Traffic Regulations (StVZO)

5.9 m

12.5 m

axle trailer is loaded. Here, the curve indicates an excessive increase in resonance. This type of combination demands a high degree of driver skill and circumspection.

With semitrailer units, braking maneuvers undertaken under extreme conditions can induce jackknifing.

This process is initiated when, on a slippery road surface, loss of lateral-force is induced by excess braking force being applied at the tractor's rear axle, or due to excess yaw moment under μ-split conditions. Installation of an antilock braking system (ABS) represents the most effective means of preventing jackknifing. This measure is mandatory for towing vehicles >18 metric tons since 1 October, 1991.

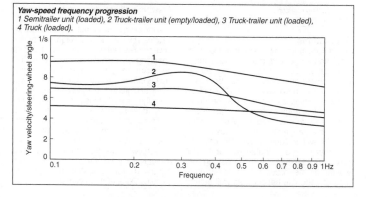

Yaw-speed frequency progression
1 Semitrailer unit (loaded), 2 Truck-trailer unit (empty/loaded), 3 Truck-trailer unit (loaded), 4 Truck (loaded).

Requirements for agricultural tractors

Units and symbols

Symbol		Unit
F	Weight (wheel load) of a wheel	N
F_R	Rolling resistance	N
F_{Rh}	Rolling resistance, rear axle	N
F_{Rv}	Rolling resistance, front axle	N
F_{St}	Climbing resistance	N
F_T	Traction (motive) force of a wheel	N
F_{Th}	Traction (motive) force, rear	N
F_{Tv}	Traction (motive) force, front	N
F_w	Soil (ground) resistance	N
F_Z	Drawbar pull of tractor	N
$F_{Zerf.}$	Drawbar-pull requirement of implement	N
P_e	Net engine power	kW
$P_{Getr.}$	Transmission power losses	kW
P_N	Rated engine power	kW
P_R	Auto-motive power requirement	kW
P_S	Slip power losses	kW
P_{St}	Hill-climbing power requirement	kW
P_Z	Drawbar power	kW
v	Vehicle speed	km/h
v_0	Peripheral velocity of a driving wheel	km/h
$\eta_{Getr.}$	Transmission/gearbox efficiency	–
η_L	Tractive efficiency at tractor wheels	–
η_T	Tractive efficiency of a single wheel	–
η_Z	Tractive efficiency of an agricultural tractor	–
λ	Engine utilization ratio	–
$\varkappa$	Coefficient of traction force	–
ϱ	Rolling resistance	–
σ	Wheel slip	%

Applications

Agricultural tractors are employed for field work and for general transport and farm-yard duties. Depending upon the type of unit, power from the engine can be transmitted through an auxiliary PTO shaft and hydraulic lines, as well as via the drive wheels. The engine outputs for farm tractors used in the Federal Republic of Germany range up to approximately 250 kW, with weights of over 120 kN.

Higher engine outputs exaggerate the problems associated with supporting the weight at the ground on large-volume tires of adequate capacity, as well as the difficulties encountered in transforming the engine's power into tractive power at acceptable tractor speeds.

Essential requirements of a tractor
– High drawbar pull, high tractive efficiency.
– The engine must combine high torque increase and low specific fuel consumption with as constant a power characteristic as possible.
– Depending upon application and the distances involved, vehicle speeds (rated speeds) up to 25, 32, 40, 50 km/h, with > 60 km/h for special-purpose tractors; multiple conversion ratios with appropriate gear spacing (especially important up to 12 km/h), suitable for shifting under load if possible.
– Power take-off (PTO) shaft and hydraulic connections for powering auxiliary equipment. Option of installing and/or powering equipment at the front of the tractor.
– Facilities for monitoring and operating auxiliary equipment from the driver's seat, e.g. with hydraulic control levers (P. 824).
– Clear and logical layout of control levers in ergonomically correct arrangement.
– On field tractors, provision for adjusting track to suit crop-row spacing.
– Driver protection against vibration, dust, noise, climatic influences and accident.
– Universal applicability.

Drawbar pull and drawbar power of a tractor in field work

The effective drawbar pull is essentially determined by the tractor's weight, the type of drive (rear-wheel or 4-wheel drive) and the operating characteristics of its tires. The operational response of the tractor's drive tires is determined by such factors as type of soil and ground conditions (moisture and porosity), tire dimensions, carcass and tread design, and tire pressure. Due to these particular operating characteristics, the farm tractor in field work develops its maximum drawbar pull only when tire slip is high, whereas the maximum drawbar power is achieved at relatively low levels of slip and drawbar pull. With the engine developing 90 % of its maximum output, the

drawbar pull of an AWD tractor will not exceed 60 % of the rated engine power, even under extremely favorable conditions.
The effective engine output is:

$$P_e = P_Z + P_R + P_S + P_{Getr.}$$
$$(+ P_{St} \text{ on gradients})$$

The drawbar power is calculated as:

$$P_Z = F_Z \cdot v$$

With rear-wheel drive, the power required to propel the tractor itself is:

$$P_R = F_{Rv} \cdot v + F_{Rh} \cdot v_o$$

The slip power losses are defined as:

$$P_S = F_T \cdot (v_o - v) = F_T \cdot \sigma \cdot v_o$$

The power losses in the transmission unit are determined with the equation:

$$P_{Getr.} = P_e \cdot (1 - \eta_{Getr.})$$

Efficiency levels:
With rear-wheel drive:

$$\eta_L = \frac{F_{Th} - F_{Rv}}{F_{Th} + F_{Rh}} \cdot (1 - \sigma)$$

With all-wheel drive (AWD):

$$\eta_L = \frac{F_{Th} + F_{Tv}}{F_{Th} + F_{Tv} + F_{Rh} + F_{Rv}} \cdot (1 - \sigma)$$

For single wheel:

$$\eta_T = \frac{F_T}{F_T + F_R} \cdot (1 - \sigma) = \frac{\varkappa}{\varkappa + \varrho}(1 - \sigma)$$

For the tractor:

$$\eta_Z = \eta_{Getr.} \cdot \eta_L = P_Z/P_e$$

The coefficients are calculated as follows:
$$\varkappa = F_T/F$$
$$\varrho = F_R/F$$
$$\lambda = P_e/P_N$$
$$\sigma = (v_o - v)/v_o$$

Drawbar-pull requirements of auxiliary equipment and trailers

At a constant speed on a flat surface, the drawbar-pull requirement depends either on the rolling resistance F_R (e.g. farm equipment) or on soil resistance F_W (e.g. the force needed to move a tool through

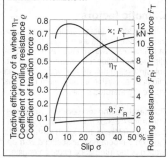

Operating characteristics of a tractor drive wheel
Tire: 16.9/14-30 AS; Wheel load: 1582 daN;
Tire pressure: 1.1 bar; Ground: loamy clay,
wheat stubble, treated with disk harrow,
moisture: 17.3...20.8 %.

the soil) or on both at the same time (e.g. beet lifter). Rolling resistance is calculated using the coefficient of rolling resistance and the sum of the weights supported at the wheels, giving:

$$F_R = \varrho \cdot \Sigma F$$

For pneumatic tires on asphalt: $\varrho \leq 0.03$
For pneumatic tires on field:

$$\varrho = 0.04...0.35$$

Soil resistance is determined by the type and condition of the soil, number and type of implements, working depth and vehicle speed. General reference figures for plowing would be a specific ground resistance of 400...600 N/dm² on moderate soils, with 600...1000 N/dm² on hard (clay) soils. On moderate ground at speeds of between 6 and 9 km/h, the soil resistance per meter of working width of a cultivator is 5500...7800 N for a working depth of 13...15 cm, and 11,000...12,500 N for a depth of 22...25 cm.

Examples of the power required by PTO-driven agricultural equipment working a 1 meter swath on moderate ground.

Implement	Required engine power kW	Working depth cm	Vehicle speed km/h
Tiller on loose soil	10.5...25	8	3...7
Vibrating harrow	8...22	8	3.5...6.5
Circular harrow	0...15	8	3.5...6.5

Environmental stresses on automotive equipment

Climatic factors

Climatic stress factors acting upon automotive components encompass the effects of the natural environment, i.e. the macroclimate, and influences stemming from the vehicle itself (such as fuel vapor) and the microclimate within a component (such as the heat generated in electrical devices).

Temperature and temperature variations
The range extends from extremely low temperatures (storage, transport) all the way to the high temperatures associated with operation of the internal-combustion engine.

Atmospheric humidity and variations
This range embraces everything from arid desert climates to tropical environments, and can even extend beyond these under certain conditions (as occur for instance when water is sprayed against a hot engine block). Humid heat (high temperatures combined with high atmospheric humidity) is especially demanding. Alternating humidity results in surface condensation, which causes atmospheric corrosion.

Corrosive atmospheres
Salt spray encountered when the vehicle is operated on salt-treated roads and in coastal areas promotes electrochemical and atmospheric corrosion. Industrial atmospheres in concentrated manufacturing regions lead to acid corrosion on metallic surfaces. When they are present in sufficient concentrations, today's increasing amounts of atmospheric pollutants (SO_2, H_2S, Cl_2 and NO_x) promote the formation of contaminant layers on contact surfaces, with the result that resistance increases.

Water
Stresses of varying intensities result from rain, spray, splash, and hose water as encountered when driving in rain, during car and engine washes, and – in exceptional cases – during submersion.

Aggressive chemical fluids
The product in question must be able to resist the chemical fluids encountered in the course of normal operation and maintenance at its particular operating location. Within the engine compartment, such chemicals include fuel (and fuel vapor), engine oil and engine detergents. Certain components are confronted with additional substances, for example, brake-system components and the brake fluid used to operate them.

Sand and dust
Malfunctions result from the friction due to sand and dust on adjacent moving surfaces. In addition, under the influence of moisture, certain types of dust layers can cause current tracking in electrical circuits.

Solar radiation
The sun's rays cause plastics and elastomers to age (a factor to be taken into account in the design of external, exposed components).

Atmospheric pressure
Fluctuations in atmospheric pressure affect the operation and reliability of differential-pressure components, such as diaphragms, etc.

Laboratory simulation of stress

Climatic and environmental conditions are simulated both according to standardized test procedures (DIN IEC 68 – Environmental testing procedures for electronic components and equipment) and in special field-testing programs designed specifically for individual cases. The goal is to achieve the greatest possible approximation of the stresses encountered in actual practice ("test tailoring").

Temperature, temperature variation and atmospheric humidity
Simulation is carried out in temperature and climate chambers as well as in climate-controlled rooms which afford access to test personnel.

The dry heat test allows evaluation of a component's suitability for storage and operation at high temperatures. Testing is not restricted to ascertaining the effects of heat upon operation; it also monitors influences on material characteristics. Depending upon the particular application (component mounted on body, engine, or exhaust system), the degree of heat can cover an extremely wide range. The stress time can be up to several hundred hours.

Testing the product's operation under <u>cold conditions</u> devotes particular attention to starting behavior and changes in materials characteristics at low temperatures. The testing range extends down to − 40 °C for operation, and to − 55 °C for storage. At less than 100 hours, the actual testing times are shorter than those employed for dry heat.

A further test simulates <u>temperature fluctuation</u> between the extremes encountered in actual operation; the temperature gradient and the dwell time also contribute to determining the degree of stress. The dwell time must be at least long enough to ensure that the sample achieves thermal equilibrium. The different levels of thermal expansion mean that the temperature variations induce both material aging and mechanical stresses within the component. The selection of appropriate test parameters makes it possible to achieve substantial time-compression factors.

<u>Atmospheric humidity</u> testing under steady-state damp heat (e.g., +40 °C/ 93 % relative humidity) is employed in the evaluation of a product's suitability for operation and storage at relatively high humidity levels (tropical climates).

Corrosive atmospheres

<u>Salt fog</u> is produced by diffusing a 5 % NaCl solution at a room temperature of 35 °C. Depending upon the intended installation location, the test times can extend to several hundred hours. <u>Cyclic salt fog</u> is a combination test comprising the following: "salt fog, dry heat and damp heat". It yields a closer correlation with field results. The <u>industrial-climate</u> test comprises up to 6 cyclical alternations between an 8-hour dwell period at 40 °C/100 % relative humidity at 0.67 % SO_2 and 16 hours at room temperature. The <u>pollutant</u> test with SO_2, H_2S, NO_X and CL_2 is performed either for single gases or as a multisubstance test. Testing is carried out at 25 °C/75 % relative humidity

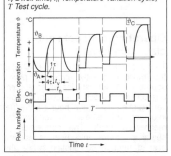

with concentrations in the ppm and ppb ranges, and lasts up to 21 days.

Water spray

A pivoting sprayer is used to simulate water spray. Water pressure, spray angle and the pivot angle can all be adjusted for different stress severity levels. The water-spray test employs high-pressure jets and standard steam-cleaners of the type used for cleaning engines.

Aggressive chemical fluids

The sample is wetted with the fluid in question for a defined period. This is followed by 24-hour storage at elevated temperature. This test can be repeated numerous times, according to the particular application.

Sand and dust

Dust simulation is carried using a device which maintains a dust density of 5 g per m³ in moving air. A mixture of lime and fly ash is one of the substances employed.

Combined tests

Combined temperature, temperature variation and humidity tests on an operating electrical product ensure a high degree of convergence with the aging effects to be anticipated under extreme operating conditions. The advantage of this test is its high level of conformity with actual practice. The disadvantage is the test duration, which is generally well in excess of that required for the corresponding individual investigations.

Internal-combustion engines

Operating concepts and classifications

The internal-combustion (IC) engine is the most frequently employed power source for motor vehicles. Internal-combustion engines generate power by converting chemical energy bound in the fuel into heat, and the heat thus produced into mechanical work. The conversion of chemical energy into heat is accomplished through combustion, while the subsequent conversion of this thermal energy into mechanical work is performed by allowing the heat energy to increase the pressure within a medium which then performs work as it expands.

Liquids, which supply an increase in working pressure via a change of phase (vaporization), or gases, whose working pressure can be increased through compression, are used as working media.

The fuels – largely hydrocarbons – require oxygen in order to burn; the required oxygen is usually supplied as a constituent of the intake air. If fuel combustion occurs in the cylinder itself, the process is called internal combustion. Here the combustion gas itself is used as the working medium. If combustion takes place outside the cylinder, the process is called external combustion.

Continuous mechanical work is possible only in a cyclic process (piston engine) or a continuous process (gas turbine) of heat absorption, expansion (production of work) and return of the working medium to its initial condition (combustion cycle).

If the working medium is altered as it absorbs heat, e.g. when a portion of its constituents serve as an oxidant, restoration of its initial condition is possible only through replacement.

This is called an open cycle, and is characterized by cyclic gas exchange (expulsion of the combustion gases and induction of the fresh charge). Internal combustion therefore always requires an open cycle.

In external combustion, the actual working medium remains chemically unchanged, and can thus be returned to its initial condition by suitable measures (cooling, condensation). This enables the

Table 1. Classification of the internal-combustion engine

Type of process	Open process			Closed process		
	Internal combustion			External combustion		
	Combustion gas $\triangle$ working medium			Combustion gas $\neq$ working medium		
				Phase change in working medium		
				No		Yes
Type of combustion	Cyclic combustion			Continuous combustion		
Type of ignition	Auto-ignition	Externally supplied ignition				
Type of machine — Engine $\triangle$ machine enclosing a working chamber	Diesel	Hybrid	Otto	Rohs	Stirling	Steam
Type of machine — Turbine $\triangle$ gas turbine	–	–	–	Gas	Hot steam	Steam
Type of mixture	Heterogeneous (in the combustion chamber)	Homogenous		Heterogeneous (in a continuous flame)		

use of a closed process.

In addition to the main process characteristics (open/closed) and the type of combustion (cyclic/continuous), the various combustion processes for internal-combustion engines can also be defined according to their air-fuel mixture formation and ignition arrangements.

In external air-fuel mixture formation, the mixture is formed outside the combustion chamber. In this type of mixture formation a largely homogenous air-fuel mixture is present when combustion is initiated, so it is also referred to as homogenous mixture formation.

In internal air-fuel mixture formation the fuel is introduced directly into the combustion chamber. The later internal combustion occurs, the more heterogeneous the air-fuel mixture will be at the time combustion is initiated. Internal mixture formation is therefore also called heterogeneous mixture formation. External ignition designs rely on an electric spark or a glow plug to initiate combustion. In auto-ignition, the mixture ignites as it warms to or beyond its ignition temperature during compression, or when fuel is injected into air whose boundary conditions permit evaporation and ignition.

Cycles

The p-V diagram

A basic precondition for continuous conversion of thermal energy into kinetic energy is a modification in the condition of the working medium; it is also desirable that as much of the working medium as possible be returned to its initial condition.

For technical applications the focus can rest on changes in pressure and the corresponding volumetric variations which can be plotted on a pressure vs. volume work diagram, or p-V diagram for short.

As the figure shows, the addition of heat and the change in condition of the working medium that accompany the progress of the process in the 1→2 phase must consume less energy than that required for the 2→1 phase. Once this condition is satisfied the result is an area corresponding to the process work potential: $L = \oint V \mathrm{d}p$.

The T-S diagram

The temperature entropy, or T-S diagram, is used to provide a similar graphic representation of the bidirectional thermal energy transfers in this cyclic process.

In the T-S diagram heat quantities can be represented as areas in the same manner that work is represented as an area in the p-V diagram. With known specific working-medium heats, the T-S diagram can be transformed into the H-S dia-

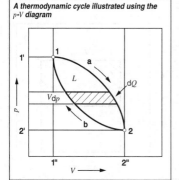

A thermodynamic cycle illustrated using the p-V diagram

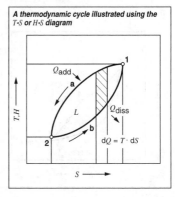

A thermodynamic cycle illustrated using the T-S or H-S diagram

gram, known as the enthalpy-entropy diagram, in accordance with the equation $dH = c_p \cdot dT$.

The cycle illustrated in the p-V diagram on page 367 shows the amount of heat added along "a"

$$Q_{add} = \int_2^1 T_a \, dS$$

and the amount of heat dissipated along "b"

$$Q_{diss} = \int_2^1 T_b \, dS, \text{ where}$$

$$Q_{add} - Q_{diss} = L = \oint V dp$$

(difference between the amount of heat supplied and the amount of heat discharged) which corresponds to the available amount of mechanical work. The diagram also shows that a thermal efficiency $\eta_{th} = (Q_{add} - Q_{diss})/Q_{add}$ can be defined based on the equality of mechanical work and the difference between the heat quantities. It also illustrates the theoretical cycle providing the maximum amount of technical work, as found in the area between two specified temperatures for the working medium.

The Carnot cycle

This cycle, described in 1824 by Carnot, consists of two isothermal [1]) and two isentropic [2]) changes in condition, which yield the maximum area in the T-S diagram between T_{max} and T_{min}. Because the Carnot cycle represents maximum process effi-

ciency between the defined temperature limits, it is the theoretical optimum for converting heat into work:

$$\eta_{thCarnot} = (T_{max} - T_{min})/T_{max}$$

Internal-combustion engines operate according to other cycles, however, because isothermal compression, i.e. a pressure increase in the working medium without an increase in temperature, and isothermal expansion are not technically feasible.

Theoretical treatment today involves the following ideal combustion cycles:
the <u>constant-volume</u> cycle for all piston engines with periodic combustion and generation of work, and
the <u>constant-pressure</u> cycle for all turbine engines with continuous combustion and generation of work.

Both cycles will be dealt with in more detail in the discussion of the corresponding machines.

---

[1]) Isothermal change in condition: temperature does not change.
[2]) Isentropic change in condition: adiabatic (heat is neither added nor dissipated) and frictionless (reversible).
[3]) Isochoric change in condition: volume does not change; see P. 369.

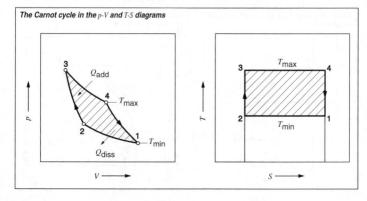

The Carnot cycle in the p-V and T-S diagrams

Reciprocating-piston engines with internal combustion

Operating concept

All reciprocating-piston engines operate by compressing air or an air-fuel mixture in the working cylinder prior to igniting the mixture, or by injecting fuel into the hot compressed air to initiate combustion. The crankshaft assembly converts the work generated in this process into torque available at the end of the crankshaft.

The p-V diagram reflects the actual power-generation process in the engine as a function of piston travel. It shows the mean effective pressures p_{mi} within the cylinder during a complete working cycle. Easier to produce are other diagrams such as the pressure vs. time (p-t) and the pressure vs. crankshaft angle (p-α) diagrams. The surfaces defined in these two diagrams do not directly indicate the amount of work generated, but they do provide a clear picture of essential data such as firing point and peak combustion pressure. The product of the mean effective pressure in the cylinder and the displacement yields the piston work, and the number of working cycles per unit of time indicates the piston power or the internal power (power index) for the engine. Here

it will be noted that the power generated by a reciprocating-piston internal-combustion engine increases as min^{-1} rises (see equations on P. 416 to P. 423).

Ideal combustion cycle for piston engines with internal combustion

For reciprocating-piston engines with internal combustion, the ideal thermodynamic combustion process is the "constant-volume process", consisting of isentropic compression, isochoric[3] heat supply, isentropic expansion and isochoric reversion of the ideal working gas to its initial condition. This cycle is only possible if the following conditions are met:

− No heat or gas losses, no residual gas,
− Ideal gas with constant specific heats c_p, c_v and
  $\varkappa = c_p/c_v = 1.4$,
− Infinitely rapid heat supply and discharge,
− No flow losses.

Because the crankshaft assembly restricts expansion to finite levels, the

The engine power cycle
1 In the p-V diagram, 2 in the p-t and p-α diagrams.

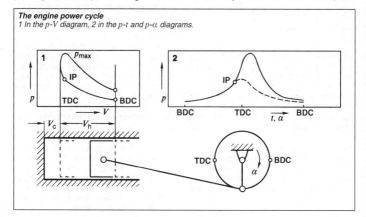

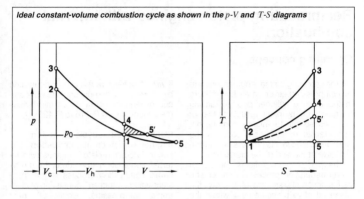

Ideal constant-volume combustion cycle as shown in the p-V and T-S diagrams

4–5–1 surface in the diagrams is not directly available for use. Section 4–5'–1, lying above the atmospheric pressure line, becomes available when an exhaust-gas turbine is connected downstream.

The efficiency of the ideal constant-volume combustion cycle is calculated in the same manner as all thermal efficiencies:

$$\eta_{th} = \eta_v = (Q_{add} - Q_{diss})/Q_{add}$$

with $Q_{add} = Q_{23} = m \cdot c_v \cdot (T_3 - T_2)$ and
$Q_{diss} = Q_{41} = m \cdot c_v \cdot (T_4 - T_1)$

Using the same $\varkappa$ for compression and expansion:

$$\eta_{th} = 1 - Q_{diss}/Q_{add} = 1 - \frac{T_4 - T_1}{T_3 - T_2} = 1 - T_1/T_2$$

if $T_1/T_2 = \varepsilon^{\varkappa - 1}$ then
$\eta_{th} = 1 - \varepsilon^{1-\varkappa}$,

where the compression ratio is defined as $\varepsilon = (V_c + V_h)/V_c$ with a displacement of V_h and a compression volume of V_c.

Real internal-combustion engines do not operate according to ideal cycles, but rather with real gas, and are therefore subject to fluid, thermodynamic and mechanical losses.

Efficiency sequence (DIN 1940)
The <u>overall efficiency</u> η_e includes the sum of all losses, and can thus be defined as the ratio of effective mechanical work to the mechanical work equivalent of the

supplied fuel:

$$\eta_e = W_e/W_B \text{ where}$$

W_e is the effective work available at the clutch and
W_B is the work equivalent of the supplied fuel.

In order to better distinguish among the different losses, a further distinction can be made:

the <u>fuel conversion factor</u> η_B provides an index of combustion quality:

$$\eta_B = (W_B - W_{Bo})/W_B, \text{ where}$$

W_B is the work equivalent of the supplied fuel,
W_{Bo} is the work equivalent of the unburned fuel.

There are no operating conditions in which complete combustion takes place. A portion of the supplied fuel does not burn (hydrocarbon constituents in the exhaust gas), or fails to combust completely (CO in exhaust).

η_B is often defined as "1" for small diesel engines at operating temperature and for comparisons.

The <u>efficiency index</u> η_i is the ratio of indicated high-pressure work to the calorific content of the supplied fuel $\eta_i = W_i/W_B$.

The <u>efficiency of cycle factor</u> η_g includes all internal losses occurring in both high-pressure and low-pressure processes. These stem from:

Table 2. Graphic representations and definitions of the individual and overall efficiencies of the reciprocating-piston engine

Pressure vs. volume diagram	Designation	Conditions	Definition	Efficiencies		
	Theoretical reference constant-volume cycle	Ideal gas, constant specific heats, infinitely rapid heat addition and dissipation, etc.	$\eta_{th} = 1 - \varepsilon^{1-\varkappa}$ Theoretical or thermal efficiency	η_{th}		
	Real high-pressure working cycle	Wall heat losses, real gas, finitely rapid heat addition and dissipation, variable specific heats	η_{gHP} Efficiency factor of the high-pressure cycle	η_g	η_i	η_e
	Real charge cycle (4-stroke)	Flow losses, heating of the mixture or the air, etc.	η_{gLW} Charge exchange efficiency			
Mechanical losses	Losses due to friction, cooling, auxiliary units	Real engine	η_m	η_m	η_m	

Real working gas, residual gas, wall heat losses, gas losses and pumping losses. For this reason, η_g is more appropriately broken down into η_{gHD} for the high-pressure portion and η_{gLW} for gas-exchange processes. The efficiency of cycle factor therefore indicates how closely engine performance approaches the theoretical ideal combustion cycle:

$$\eta_g = \eta_{gHD} \cdot \eta_{gLW} = W_i / W_{th} \text{ where}$$

W_i is the indicated work and
W_{th} is the work generated in the ideal-combustion cycle.
Mechanical efficiency η_m defines the relationship between mechanical losses – especially friction losses in the crankshaft assembly and induction/exhaust systems, and in oil and water pumps, fuel pump, alternator, etc. – and the work index:

$$\eta_m = W_e / W_i \text{ where}$$

W_e is the effective work available at the clutch and
W_i is the work index.

The efficiency chain therefore appears as follows:

$$\eta_e = \eta_B \cdot \eta_{th} \cdot \eta_{gHD} \cdot \eta_{gLW} \cdot \eta_m$$

(see Table 2).

The spark-ignition (Otto) engine

The spark-ignition engine (or SI engine) is a piston engine with external or internal air-fuel mixture formation. External mixture formation generally produces homogenous mixtures, whereas an internally formed mixture is largely heterogeneous at the instant of ignition. The time of mixture formation is a major factor influencing the degree of homogenization achievable by internal mixture formation.

In both cases, the mixture is compressed to approximately 20...30 bar (ε = 8...12) on the compression stroke, to generate a final compression temperature of 400...500 °C. This is still below the auto-ignition threshold of the mixture, which then has to be ignited by a spark shortly before the piston reaches TDC.

Since reliable ignition of homogenous air-fuel mixtures is only possible within a narrowly defined window of the air-fuel ratio (excess-air factor λ = 0.6...1.6), and flame velocity drops steeply as the excess-air factor λ increases, SI engines with homogenous mixture formation have to operate in a λ range 0.8...1.4 (best overall efficiency is achieved at 1.2 < λ < 1.3). The λ range is further restricted to 0.98...1.02 for engines with three-way catalytic converters.

On account of this narrow λ range, load has to be controlled by the quantity of mixture entering the cylinders (quantity control): this is achieved by throttling the amount of air-fuel mixture entering the cylinders under part-load operating conditions (throttle control).

Optimization of the overall efficiency of SI engines has given rise to increasing development effort directed at engines with internal heterogeneous mixture formation.

Homogenous and heterogeneous mixture formation are alike in that economic efficiency and untreated emissions depend on the combustion process which takes place after ignition. Combustion, in turn, can be influenced to a very large extent by the flows and turbulences that can

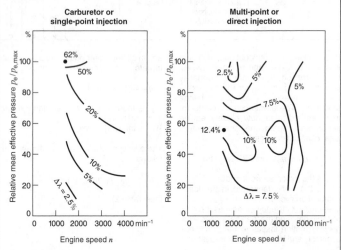

Mixture-preparation
Differences in the air-fuel (A/F) ratio in the individual cylinders as a function of load and engine speed.

Carburetor or single-point injection

Multi-point or direct injection

be produced in the combustion chamber by the geometry of the intake duct and the combustion chamber.

Homogenous mixture formation

The homogenous mixtures present at the time when ignition commences cause the fuel to vaporize fully, because only gas or gas/vapor mixtures can achieve homogeneity.

If some factor (such as low temperature during a cold start) inhibits complete vaporization of the fuel, sufficient additional fuel must be provided to ensure that the volatile, vaporizable constituent can produce an adequately rich – and therefore combustible – air-fuel mixture (cold-start enrichment).

In addition to mixture homogenization, the mixture-formation system is also responsible for load regulation (throttle regulation) and for ensuring the minimization of deviations in the A/F ratio from cylinder to cylinder and from working cycle to working cycle.

Heterogeneous mixture formation

The aim pursued in heterogeneous internal mixture formation is that of operating the engine without throttle control across the entire operating map. Internal cooling is a side-effect of direct injection, so engines of this type can operate at higher compression ratios. The conjunction of these two factors, no throttle control and higher compression, means that the degree of efficiency is higher than that attainable with a homogenous mixture. Load is controlled by means of the mass of injected fuel. Development in mixture-formation systems gave fresh impetus to the "hybrid" or "stratified-charge" techniques that were the subject of much research from about 1970 onward. The definitive breakthrough came with the high-speed fuel injectors that allowed flexibility in injection timing and could achieve the high injection pressures required.

GDI (Gasoline Direct Injection) was the generic term applied to worldwide development in "jet-directed", "wall-directed" or "air-directed" mixture-formation systems (see illustration). The positions of spark plug and injector have a major influence on mixture formation, but flows in the

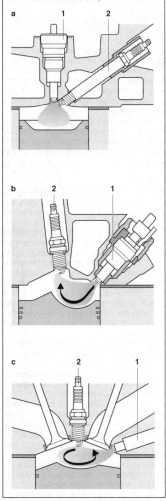

Mixture-formation systems for gasoline direct injection GDI (assisted by swirl or tumble in each case)
a) Jet-directed, b) Wall-directed,
c) Air-directed.
1 Fuel injector, 2 Spark plug.

combustion chamber are another, supporting factor. Swirl (induced by spiral or tangential channels) is primarily rotation about an axis paralleling that of the cylinder, whereas the axis of tumble, which is induced by fill channels, is normal to the cylinder's axis.

Precision positioning of the spark plug and the jet from the fuel injector is essential for jet-directed spray injection. The spark plug is under severe strain, because it is struck directly by the jet of liquid fuel. Wall-directed and air-directed configurations direct the mixture to the plug by means of the motion of the charge, so requirements in this respect are not as high.

Heterogeneous mixture formation entails excess air (unthrottled operation), so lean-burn catalytic converters have to be developed in order to reduce nitrogen-oxide emissions.

Ignition

The ignition system must reliably ignite the compressed mixture at a precisely defined instant, even under dynamic operating conditions with the attendant substantial fluctuations in mixture flow patterns and air-fuel ratios. Reliable ignition can be promoted by selecting spark-plug locations with good mixture access in combination with efficient mixture swirl patterns; these are especially important considerations for lean operation and at very low throttle apertures. Similar improvements can also be achieved by positioning the spark plug in small auxiliary "ignition chambers".

Ignition-energy requirements depend on the mixture's air-fuel (A/F) ratio. An ignition energy of 0.2 mJ is required for gasoline/air mixtures in the stoichiometric range, while up to 3 mJ may be required to ignite richer or leaner mixtures.

The ignition voltage required increases with the gas pressure at the instant of ignition. Increasing the electrode gap is one way of improving ignition reliability, but at the expense of higher ignition voltage and accelerated electrode wear.

The energy content of the mixture ignited by the spark must be sufficient to ignite the neighboring mixture. This defines the leanest possible mixture and the ear-

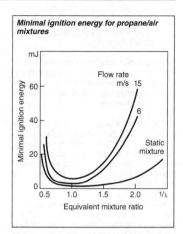

Minimal ignition energy for propane/air mixtures

liest possible instant of ignition. In engines with a compression ratio $\varepsilon = 8...12$, this range is approximately 40...50 °crankshaft before TDC.

Combustion process

The initial thermal reaction which occurs between the provision of the ignition energy by the spark and the exothermal reaction of the air-fuel mixture is the ignition phase. This phase is roughly constant over time, with mixture composition as the only influencing factor. As a result, increasing engine speeds are accompanied by proportionally higher ignition delays – referred to piston travel (°crankshaft) – which change together with excess-air factor (lambda) λ.

The moment of ignition, therefore, has to be advanced as engine speed increases and excess-air factor λ rises. Ignition advance, however, is limited by the fall-off in the mixture's energy density in the vicinity of the electrodes (see above). When this physical limit is reached, designers can resort to twin spark-plug configurations or pre-chamber ignition to improve the situation.

The heat-release transient is determined by the rate of combustion, which in turn is defined by the speed of flame propagation and the area of the flame front. The speed of flame propagation depends on diffusion processes at the flame front and reaches a peak of approximately 20...40 m · s⁻¹ in gasoline-air mixtures with approx. 10 % air deficiency ($\lambda = 0.9$). It is influenced by the excess-air factor λ and the temperature of the mixture.

The area of the flame front can be influenced by the geometry of the combustion chamber and the position of the spark plug. Folding of the flame front due to turbulence and induced flows (such as swirl and tumble) is a significant factor in this respect. The flows induced primarily by the induction process and to a lesser extent by combustion-chamber geometry in conjunction with the compression squish fold the flame front and thus accelerate the process of energy conversion. Tumble, swirl and squish increase with engine speed and consequently, folding of the flame front also becomes more pronounced. This explains why the rate of heat release increases with speed despite the fact that by definition, the rate of flame propagation must remain constant.

Although it can factor in ultra-low-turbulence processes or in tests in low-flow pressure chambers, the turbulence created by flame propagation itself is of no significance in the combustion process as it takes place in modern SI engines.

The rising pressure due to local flame propagation causes an increase in temperature throughout the mixture, including that not yet reached by the flame and known as the "end gas". On account of local heat radiation and heat conduction, however, the temperature in the flame front is higher than in the rest of the mixture. This ensures regular flame propagation. The anomaly known as combustion knock or pre-ignition, due to simultaneous combustion of the end gas, occurs when the increase in pressure causes the temperature of the end gas to exceed its ignition limits.

Low fuel consumption and high efficiency are promoted by high combustion speeds (brief duration), combined with the optimal thermal release pattern relative to piston travel. Maximum heat release should occur shortly (approx. 5...10 °crankshaft) after top dead center. If most of the heat is released too early, wall heat losses and mechanical losses (high

peak pressure) are increased. Late heat release leads to sacrifices in thermal efficiency (efficiency of cycle factor) and high exhaust-gas temperatures.

The ignition timing must be selected for optimum thermal generation curves in accordance with the:
– Air-fuel mixture ratio (λ, T),
– Effects of engine parameters (particularly load and speed) on combustion-chamber turbulence,
– Constant-duration ignition and flame propagation processes, meaning that variations in ignition timing are required as engine speed increases.

Problems and limits of combustion

In actual practice, reliable flame initiation and propagation in engines with external mixture formation and spark ignition prohibit the use of mixtures leaner than $\lambda > 1.3$, although these would be desirable for improving the levels of theoretical (polytropic exponent) and gas-exchange (low throttle losses) efficiency, along with useful reductions in wall-heat and dissociation losses (reduction in combustion temperature). Appropriate tests are undertaken with GDI engines (Gasoline Direct Injection).

Although higher compression ratios provide enhanced part-load efficiency, they also increase the risk of combustion knock (pre-ignition) under full load. Pre-ignition occurs when the entire charge of end gas reaches ignition temperature and burns instantaneously without regular flame propagation. The end gas is highly compressed and its energy density is therefore very high, so pre-ignition suddenly releases very large amounts of heat. The high local temperatures caused in this way place extreme loads on the engine components and can also damage them. The high-energy cycles also result in extreme pressure peaks. Within the combustion chamber these pressure peaks propagate at the speed of sound and can cause damage to the piston, cylinder head, and cylinder-head gasket at critical points.

The risk of combustion knock can be reduced by using fuel additives or by richer mixtures (supplementary internal cooling).

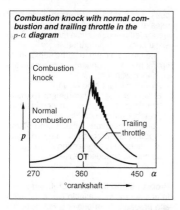

Combustion knock with normal combustion and trailing throttle in the p-α diagram

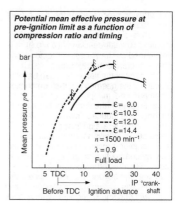

Potential mean effective pressure at pre-ignition limit as a function of compression ratio and timing

The current expedient of avoiding pre-ignition by retarding the ignition timing raises problems of its own, especially when used on high-compression engines. Because the ignition curve (mean pressure relative to ignition point) becomes increasingly steeper as compression increases, the resulting sacrifices in mean effective pressure are accompanied by extreme exhaust-gas temperatures. Reliable detection and avoidance of pre-ignition are thus vitally important in the $\varepsilon = 11...13$ compression range.

Load control

In unthrottled GDI engines with heterogeneous mixture, load is controlled by means of the quantity of fuel injected. Spark-ignition engines with homogeneous mixture formation, on the other hand, afford little latitude for operation with lean mixtures, so load control has to be implemented by adjusting the mass flow of mixture. In carburetor engines, which have lost virtually all their significance in automotive engineering, this can be achieved by throttling the mixture mass flow. In engines with intake-manifold injection, throttle control to reduce the density of the intake air is the conventional approach. This arrangement, however, increases charge-cycle losses, so development is concentrating on alternative methods of load control. Mass flow can be influenced, for example, by prematurely closing the intake valves and thus shortening the effective intake periods. This complicated means of load control, however, requires fully variable valve timing and can cause fuel condensation as the result of expansion when the intake valves are closed. This drawback can be countered with "feedback control", an arrangement in which the intake valves are not closed until the requisite mass of mixture has just had time to fill the cylinder.

Another way of reducing or even eliminating throttle losses is exhaust-gas recirculation with the intake valves open. Load can be varied across a wide range by modulating the exhaust-gas recirculation rate.

Regulating charge-air pressure is a method of accomplishing load control over wide regions of the characteristic map with supercharged spark-ignition engines.

Power output and economy

The efficiency index for engines with external mixture formation and spark ignition falls primarily in the lower portion of the map (see illustration). This is owing to combustion inefficiency (insufficient turbulence, inadequate charge density) along with an inefficient gas-exchange process.

Effective efficiency is further reduced by the low mechanical efficiency characteristic of this region of the map.

All measures for avoiding these lower sections of the map therefore contribute to improving the engine's overall efficiency.

Selective interruption of the fuel supply to individual cylinders allows the remaining cylinders to operate at higher efficiency levels with improved combustion and gas exchange. Valve deactivation provides further reductions in power loss by allowing the intake and exhaust valves for the deactivated cylinders to remain closed. Cylinder shut-off entails immobilizing the mechanical power-transmission components of the idle cylinders for further increases in mechanical efficiency.

The measures cited above vary in terms of sophistication, but engine speed reduction also enhances general efficiency while promoting effective gas exchange; simultaneous reductions in mean frictional pressure also improve mechanical efficiency.

The diesel engine

A diesel engine is a reciprocating-piston engine with internal (and thus heterogeneous) mixture formation and auto-ignition. During the compression stroke intake air is compressed to 30...55 bar in naturally aspirated engines or 80...110 bar in supercharged engines, so that its temperature increases to 700...900 °C. This temperature is sufficient to induce auto-ignition in the fuel injected into the cylinders shortly before the end of the compression stroke, as the piston approaches TDC. In heterogeneous processes the mixture formation is decisive in determining the quality of the combustion which then follows, and the effi-

Curves of indicated efficiency vs. load factor and engine speed for a spark-ignition engine with throttle control

ciency with which the inducted combustion air is utilized, and thus in defining the available mean effective pressure levels.

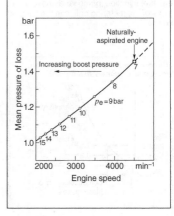

Relationship between engine speed and mean pressure of friction loss
5-liter gasoline engine, P_e = 130 kW = constant at increasing engine load, p_e Mean pressure.

Mixture formation

In heterogeneous mixtures, the air-fuel ratio λ extends from pure air ($\lambda = \infty$) in the spray periphery to pure fuel ($\lambda = 0$) in the spray core.

The figure provides a schematic illustration of the λ distribution and the associated flame zone for a single stationary droplet. Because this zone always occurs for every drop of injected mixture, load control with heterogeneous mixture formation can be performed by regulating the fuel supply. This is termed mixture-quality control.

As with homogenous mixtures, combustion takes place in the relatively narrow range between $0.3 < \lambda < 1.5$. The mass transport necessary for generating these combustible mixtures relies on diffusion and turbulence; these are produced by the mixture formation energy sources described below as well as by the combustion process itself.

Kinetic energy of the fuel spray

The spray's kinetic energy varies according to the pressure differential at the nozzle orifice. Along with the spray pattern (as determined by the nozzle geometry) and the fuel's exit velocity it determines the configuration of the space in which the air and fuel interact as well as the range of droplet sizes in the chamber. The spray energy is influenced by the delivery rate of the fuel-injection pump and the dimensions of the metering orifice in the injector nozzle.

Thermal energy

Thermal energy from the combustion-chamber walls and the compressed air vaporize the injected fuel (as a film layer on the walls and as droplets).

Combustion-chamber shape

The shape of the combustion chamber and the action of the piston can be utilized to create turbulence (squish), or to distribute liquid fuel or the fuel-air vapor jet.

Controlled air patterns (swirling action)

If the direction of fuel flow is roughly perpendicular to the direction of the vortex and droplet vaporization is taking place, a movement imparted to the combustion air inside the combustion chamber, usually in the form of solid-particle rotating flow, promotes the flow of air toward the fuel stream, and removes the combusted gases from the stream.

As the wall film evaporates, the air's swirling motion absorbs the vapor layer and provides thermal insulation between the combusted and fresh gases, while the microturbulence patterns superimposed upon the solid-particle vortex ensure rapid mixture of air and fuel. The air's controlled solid-particle swirl can be induced using special induction tract geometries or by shifting a portion of the cylinder charge into a rotationally symmetric auxiliary chamber (by transporting it through a side passage).

Partial combustion in a swirl chamber

When fuel is partially combusted in an auxiliary chamber its pressure rises above that in the main combustion chamber. This increase then propels the partially oxidized combustion gases and vaporized fuel through one or more passages into the main combustion chamber, where they are thoroughly mixed with the remaining combustion air.

The diesel combustion process makes use of at least one (but usually an appropriate combination) of these mixture formation methods.

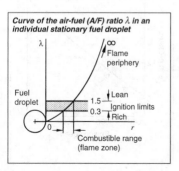

Curve of the air-fuel (A/F) ratio λ in an individual stationary fuel droplet

λ

∞ Flame periphery

Fuel droplet

1.5 ↓ Lean
↓ Ignition limits
0.3 ↑ Rich

0

r

Combustible range (flame zone)

Direct injection

This term refers to all designs with a single unified combustion chamber.

Low-swirl or static-charge spray-injection combustion

This combustion process operates virtually without swirl of the air mass in the cylinder, or even with none at all, and relies on the energy in the injection jets to ensure mixture formation. It was formerly used in large medium- and slow-speed diesels operating with high excess-air factors on account of thermal design considerations.

The combustion chamber is a wide, usually ω-shaped recess centered in the piston crown. Fuel is injected through a central, vertical multi-hole nozzle with 5...8 orifices.

Higher excess-air factors and higher injection-jet energies (resulting from higher injection pressures) are two consequences of the increasingly lower emission limits for NO$_X$ and particulates in the exhaust gas. At the same time, all modern commercial-vehicle engines with displacements down to approximately 1 *l* per cylinder are turbocharged and are fitted with governors to restrict their speed ranges for the sake of improved fuel consumption. These are the reasons why this method has become commonplace for commercial-vehicle engines, particularly since the retarded start of injection for the sake of further reductions in NO$_X$ emissions goes hand in hand with higher thermal loads in the engines themselves.

Swirl-assisted multiple-orifice nozzle combustion process

The mixture-forming energy of the injection jets alone is not enough for sufficiently uniform and rapid mixture preparation in high-revving diesels with wide operating-speed ranges and small swept volumes (in other words, the engines most frequently found in passenger cars and vans). Supportive motion of the air inside the combustion chamber is required. This is achieved by installing pistons with considerably shallower recesses. These recesses are constricted at the top in order to create highly turbulent squish from the piston gap in the vicinity of the injection-jet contact points and to accelerate the swirl of the air charge induced by the design of the inlet elements (swirl inlet ducts). The total swirl velocity of the in-cylinder air mass achieved in this way is selected to ensure that the air-fuel mixture formed over the injection period from the injection jet issuing from the nozzle, and the air swirl rotating about an axis normal to this jet, completely fills and utilizes the downflow region of the combustion chamber until the next injection jet is received.

Consequently, this method employs nozzles with a significantly smaller number of orifices, namely 4...6. In this case, too, the nozzle is positioned as close as possible to an imaginary line extending though the center of the piston recess.

If the air-fuel mixture fails to completely fill the combustion-chamber segment, both air utilization and power output will suffer. On the other hand, if there is an

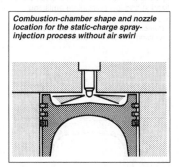

Combustion-chamber shape and nozzle location for the static-charge spray-injection process without air swirl

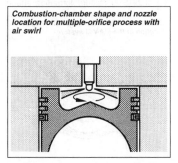

Combustion-chamber shape and nozzle location for multiple-orifice process with air swirl

overlap and the mixture extends beyond this space between the individual injection events, the resulting excessive local fuel concentration leads to air deficiencies and increased formation of soot.

M System

In the MAN wall-distribution combustion system (M system) most of the fuel is sprayed against the wall of the combustion chamber. This process supplements the energy in the injection spray by exploiting the heat from the combustion-chamber wall and the swirling action of the air to form the mixture. The single-orifice nozzle, projecting into the narrow piston-crown chamber at an angle, sprays the fuel into the swirl and against the combustion-chamber wall. Here the fuel forms a film which vaporizes and forms a very homogenous mixture with the swirling combustion-chamber air as it passes. This process combines excellent air utilization with low exhaust-gas opacity (soot emissions).

The fuel film evaporates more slowly from the combustion-chamber wall than the droplets in the compressed air, so combustion processes of this nature are no longer of practical value in terms of the requirements applicable to fuel consumption and gas-phase emissions.

Divided-chamber (two-chamber) combustion systems

Divided-chamber combustion systems are well-suited to small, high-speed diesel engines, usually installed in passenger cars. Here, very stringent requirements are placed on mixture formation speed and air utilization (potential λ). At the same time, economic considerations dictate that the use of the expensive injection equipment required to generate high injection energy be avoided.

In addition, swirl-type intake passages present difficulties with regard to volumetric efficiency.

The divided-chamber method combines rich mixtures in the auxiliary chamber with relatively lean charges in the main chamber to achieve extremely low NO_x and HC emissions.

Swirl-chamber system

This process features an almost spherical auxiliary chamber, comprising approx. 50 % of the total compression volume, located at the edge of the main combustion chamber. The connection between the auxiliary and main chambers is furnished by a passage which enters the main chamber at an angle directed toward the center of the piston. The swirl chamber houses the injector and the glow plug (starting aid). The compression stroke generates an intense air vortex in the swirl chamber. As in the M process, the fuel is injected eccentrically to converge with the swirl pattern and land against the chamber's wall. Critical factors are the design of the swirl chamber (for instance, with supplementary mixture vaporization surfaces where the injection spray contacts the wall) and the locations of the injector and the glow plug; these factors define the quality of the combustion process. This process combines very high engine speeds (> 5000 min^{-1}), with good air utilization and low particulate emissions.

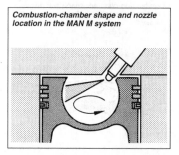

Combustion-chamber shape and nozzle location in the MAN M system

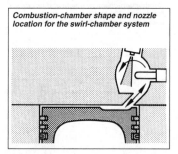

Combustion-chamber shape and nozzle location for the swirl-chamber system

Prechamber system
The prechamber system features an auxiliary chamber (prechamber) which is centrally located relative to the main combustion chamber, with 35...40 % of the compression volume. Here too, the injection nozzle and glow plug (starting aid) are located in the prechamber. It communicates with the main combustion chamber through several orifices to allow the combustion gases to mix as completely as possible with the main combustion air. One optimized prechamber concept utilizes the deflection surface below the injector nozzle to simultaneously induce rapid mixture formation and a controlled turbulence pattern (on some designs) in the prechamber. The turbulent flow meets the injection spray, which is also aimed into the swirl at an angle. The entire system, including the downstream glow plug, provides combustion with very low emissions and major reductions in particulates. The process is distinguished by a high air-utilization factor, and is also suitable for high engine speeds.

On account of the inherently high fuel consumption, prechamber combustion is becoming less and less viable for passenger-car applications. Common rail injection (P. 551) and refined turbocharging techniques for small engines have rendered direct injection increasingly commonplace in passenger-car diesel engines.

Combustion process
The start of injection (and thus the start of mixture formation) and the initiation of the exothermal reaction (start of ignition) are separated by a certain period of time, called ignition lag. The actual delay is defined by:
- the ignitability of the fuel (cetane number),
- the compression end pressure (compression ratio, boost factor),
- the compression end temperature (compression ratio, component temperatures, intercooling), and
- the fuel-management system.

The combustion process, which begins with the start of ignition, can be subdivided into three phases. In the "premixed flame" phase, the fuel injected prior to the start of ignition and mixed with the air combusts. The fuel injected once ignition has started combusts in a "diffusion flame". That portion of the combusted fuel which burns as a very rapid premixed flame is primarily responsible for the pressure rise, and thus is the primary cause of both combustion noise and oxides of nitrogen. The slower-burning diffusion flame is the main source of particulates and unburned hydrocarbons.

The third, post-injection, phase is when the soot formed primarily during the second phase is oxidized. This phase is becoming increasingly significant in modern combustion processes.

The heat release of a diesel engine depends on the combustion process itself, but also to a very large extent on the start of injection, the injection rate, and the maximum injection pressure. In direct-injection diesel engines, the number of orifices in the nozzle is another crucial factor. The injection system, moreover, requires a pre-injection capability (pilot injection) in order to reduce combustion noise and ensure that injection for the main injection phase commences as early as possible. This reduces fuel consumption for given levels of nitrogen-oxide emissions.

The diagram illustrates the thermal-release patterns which are characteristic of the various injection methods. The dual-stage combustion available with the di-

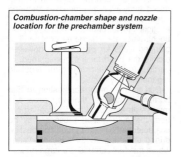

Combustion-chamber shape and nozzle location for the prechamber system

vided-chamber process provides yet another means of influencing the combustion process by allowing selection of different diameters for the passage between the auxiliary and main chambers.

Problems and limits of combustion

Because the fuel injected into diesel engines must ignite through auto-ignition, highly volatile fuel is required (cetane number CN ≈ 45...50). Since at low starting speeds compression does not begin until after intake-valve closure (that is, significantly after BDC), the effective compression ratio, and with it the compression temperature, are greatly reduced. This means that despite high compression ratios, ignition problems can occur during starting, particularly when the engine is cold.

In addition, cold engine components tend to absorb thermal energy from the compressed air (polytropic exponent: $1.1 < n < 1.2$). The equation $T_1 = T_0 \cdot \varepsilon^{n-1}$ indicates that a reduction in the effective compression or the polytropic exponent causes a reduction in the final compression temperature. At the same time, mixture formation is unsatisfactory at low engine speeds (low injection pressure, large fuel droplets) and air movement is inadequate. Extended vaporization times (in-

jection begins sooner) and an increase in the injected fuel quantity – to significantly higher levels than the full-load quantity (providing more low-boiling fuel) can only partially solve the starting problem, because the higher-boiling fuel constituents leave the engine in the form of white or blue smoke. Thus starting aids designed to increase the temperature, such as glow plugs or flame starting systems, are essential, especially in small engines.

Because a significant portion of the mixture-formation process occurs during combustion in heterogeneous processes, it is important to avoid local concentrations of excessively rich mixture in the diffusion flame, as the result would be an increase in soot emissions, even with extremely lean overall mixtures. The air-fuel ratio limits at the officially mandated tolerance level for smoke provide an index of air-utilization efficiency. Divided-chamber engines reach the smoke limit with excess air of 5...15%, while the comparable figure is 10...80% for direct-injection diesels. It should be noted that large-volume diesel engines must also be run with significant levels of excess air owing to thermal component load.

Soot is an inevitable byproduct of heterogeneous combustion, so a sootless diesel engine must inevitably remain a conditional development and will require significant improvement in soot oxidation.

It has, however, proven possible to reduce the particulate emissions from modern diesel engines to below the visibility threshold using a variety of measures. These include raising injection pressures at the nozzle, and the transition to optimized spray injection processes featuring larger combustion recesses in the piston, multiple injector orifices, exhaust-gas turbocharging, and charge-air cooling. The planned limits for particulates, however, dictate the need for the development of particulate filters employing the requisite regenerative systems.

Due to the abrupt combustion in that portion of the fuel that vaporizes and mixes with air during the ignition-lag period, the auto-ignition process may be characterized by "hard," loud combustion during operation under those conditions where this fuel comprises a large propor-

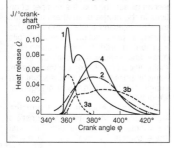

Thermal-release curves
1 Air-distributed direct fuel injection (naturally-aspirated engine tuned for maximum economy), 2 Wall-distribution direct injection (designed for minimal noise), 3 Divided-chamber process in auxiliary chamber (3a) and main chamber (3b), 4 Minimum emissions static-charge spray injection (intercooled turbocharged engine).

J/°crank-shaft cm³

Heat release $\dot{Q}$

0.10
0.08
0.06
0.04
0.02
0

340° 360° 380° 400° 420°
Crank angle φ

tion of the total. These conditions include idle, low part-throttle on turbocharged engines, and high-load operation on high-speed naturally-aspirated powerplants.

The situation can be improved by decreasing the ignition lag (preheating the intake air, turbocharging or increasing compression) and/or by reducing the injected fuel quantity during the ignition-lag period. On direct-injection engines, this reduction is usually obtained by applying pilot injection, whereas on divided-chamber engines a special injector configuration is employed (throttling pintle nozzle).

Not to be confused with the "hard" combustion inherent to the design is the "knock" to which turbulence-chamber arrangements with pintle nozzles are particularly susceptible, and which occurs primarily in the medium- and low-load areas of the diesel's operating curve. This phenomenon is traceable to inadequacies in the mixture-formation system (poor injector "chatter" or soot at the injectors), and is characterized by a pulsating metallic sound.

The diesel engine must be designed for operation with high peak pressures, and its materials and their dimensions must be selected accordingly. The reasons include:
– High compression ratios required for reliable starting and noise reductions,
– Combustion process for maximum ignition propagation for fuel economy, and
– Increasingly frequent use of turbochargers featuring higher charge pressures.

Owing to the fact that diesel engines must also operate with excess air (lean) at full throttle, they generally have lower specific outputs than their spark-ignition counterparts.

Hybrid processes

Hybrid engines share characteristics with both diesel and spark-ignition engines.

Charge stratification

In stratified-charge SI engines the mixture directly adjacent to the spark plug is enriched to ensure reliable ignition, while the rest of the combustion process proceeds in an extremely lean mixture. The objective is to combine the part-throttle economy comparable to that of a diesel with (especially important) low NO_x and CO emissions.

Research on open-chamber combustion systems with many characteristics similar to those of diesel systems (mixture quality control, high-pressure injection, etc.) is focusing on employing internal mixture formation (Texaco TCCS, Ford PROCO, Ricardo, MAN-FM, KHD-AD) to generate an ignitable mixture at the spark plug while using progressively leaner mixtures (down to pure air) in the remainder of the combustion chamber.

Processes which use internal mixture formation have an air-utilization factor comparable to that of diesel engines.

Divided-chamber combustion systems tend to resemble spark-ignition engines in their basic layout (throttle control, mixture induction, etc.). In these the spark plug is located within a small auxiliary chamber – the ignition chamber – corresponding to roughly 5...25% of the total compression volume. One or several passages connect this primary ignition chamber with the main combustion chamber.

The auxiliary combustion chamber features an additional injector which injects a portion of the fuel directly (VW, Porsche-SKS), or a supplementary valve to supply fuel-air mixture to the ignition chamber (Honda-CVCC).

A disadvantage of these processes is their more complex design and the higher HC emissions stemming from lower exhaust-gas temperatures and the attendant reductions in secondary combustion activity in the exhaust tract.

Multifuel engines

In multifuel engines, the ignitability and knock resistance of the fuel can be relatively insignificant; these engines must be able to burn fuels of varying qualities without sustaining damage. Because fuels used with multifuel engines can have a very low knock-resistance rating, external mixture formation would be accompanied by the danger of combustion knock or pre-ignition. For this reason, multifuel engines always use internal mixture formation and retarded injection timing (similar to the diesel engine). The injection pump for multifuel operation has an annular lubrication channel in the pumping element to lubricate the plungers with engine oil from the forced-feed lubrication system. This lubrication channel also prevents fuel from entering the pump's camshaft chamber. Because the low ignition quality of the fuels makes auto-ignition difficult or even impossible, multifuel engines operate with extremely high compression ratios (Mercedes-Benz, MTU: $\varepsilon = 25{:}1$). As an alternative they may be equipped with an auxiliary ignition source such as spark plugs or glow plugs (MAN-FM). At $\varepsilon = 14...15$, the compression ratio in these engines with externally-supplied ignition lies between that of spark-ignition and diesel engines.

A special type of ignition is the ignition spray process used in alcohol and gas engines (KHD, MWM), in which supplementary diesel fuel – corresponding to 5...10% of the full-throttle supply of diesel fuel – is sprayed directly into the combustion chamber to ensure ignition. In this process, the main energy source can be supplied via external or internal mixture formation.

Whereas stratified charging with new mixture-formation systems is a focus of attention within the framework of ongoing development of GDI engines, multifuel engines are of virtually no significance at this time.

Gas exchange

In combustion engines employing open processes, the gas-exchange (exhaust and refill) system must serve two decisive functions:
1. Replacement is employed to return the gas medium to its initial (start of cycle) condition, and
2. The oxygen required to burn the fuel is provided in the form of fresh air.

The parameters defined in DIN 1940 can be used to evaluate the gas-exchange process. For overall air flow (air expenditure $\lambda_a = m_g/m_{th}$) the entire charge transferred during the work cycle m_g is defined with reference to the theoretical maximum for the specific displacement. In contrast, the volumetric efficiency $\lambda_{a1} = m_z/m_{th}$ is based exclusively on the fresh charge m_z actually present or remaining in the cylinder. The difference between m_z and the total charge transfer m_g consists of the proportion of the gas that flows directly into the exhaust tract in the overlap phase, making it unavailable for subsequent combustion. The retention rate

$\lambda_z = m_z/m_g$

is an index of the residual charge in the cylinder. The scavenge efficiency

$\lambda_S = m_z/(m_z + m_r)$

indicates the volume of the fresh charge m_z relative to the existing total charge, consisting of the fresh charge and the

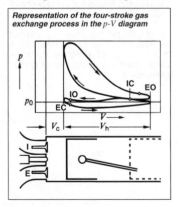

Representation of the four-stroke gas exchange process in the p-V diagram

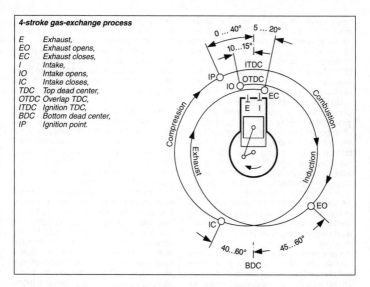

4-stroke gas-exchange process

E   Exhaust,
EO Exhaust opens,
EC Exhaust closes,
I   Intake,
IO Intake opens,
IC Intake closes,
TDC Top dead center,
OTDC Overlap TDC,
ITDC Ignition TDC,
BDC Bottom dead center,
IP Ignition point.

residual gas m_r. Here, the parameter m_r indicates the amount of residual gas from earlier working cycles remaining in the cylinder after the exhaust process.

In a 2-stroke cycle, the gas is exchanged with every rotation of the crankshaft at the end of the expansion in the area around bottom dead center. In a 4-stroke cycle, separate intake and exhaust strokes provide a supplementary gas-exchange cycle.

4-stroke process
Valve timing – and thus gas exchange – are regulated by a control shaft (camshaft) rotating at half the frequency of the crankshaft by which it is driven. The camshaft opens the gas-exchange valves by depressing them against the valve springs to discharge the exhaust gas and to draw in the fresh gas (exhaust and intake valves respectively). Just before piston bottom dead center (BDC), the exhaust valve opens and approx. 50 % of the combustion gases leave the combustion chamber under a supercritical pressure ratio during this predischarge phase. As it moves upward during the exhaust stroke, the piston sweeps nearly all of the combustion gases from the combustion chamber.

Shortly ahead of piston top dead center (TDC) and before the exhaust valve has closed, the intake valve opens. This crankshaft top dead center position is called the gas-exchange TDC or overlap TDC (because the intake and exhaust processes overlap at this point) in order to distinguish it from the ignition TDC. Shortly after gas-exchange TDC, the exhaust valve closes and, with the intake valve still open, the piston draws in fresh air on its downward stroke. This second stroke of the gas-exchange process, the intake stroke, continues until shortly after BDC. The subsequent two strokes in the 4-stroke process are compression and combustion (expansion).

On throttle-controlled gasoline engines, during the valve overlap period exhaust gases flow directly from the combustion chamber into the intake passage, or from the exhaust passage back into the combustion chamber and from there into the intake passage. This tendency is especially pronounced at low throttle openings with high manifold vacuum. This "internal" exhaust-gas recirculation can have negative effects on idle quality, but it is impossible to avoid entirely, as a compromise has to be found between adequate high-speed valve lift and a satisfactory idle.

Early exhaust valve timing allows a high degree of blowdown, and thus guarantees low residual-gas compression as the piston sweeps through its upward stroke, although at the price of a reduction in the work index for the combustion gases.

The "intake valve closes" (IC) timing exercises a decisive effect on the relationship between air expenditure and engine speed.

When the intake valve closes early (IC) the maximum charge efficiency occurs at low engine speeds, while late closing shifts the efficiency peak toward the upper end of the min^{-1} spectrum.

Obviously, fixed valve timing will always represent a compromise between two different design objectives: Maximum brake mean effective pressure – and thus torque – at the most desirable points on the curve, and the highest possible peak output. The higher the min^{-1} at which maximum power occurs, and the wider the range of engine operating speeds, the less satisfactory will be the ultimate compromise. Large variations in the valves' effective flow opening relative to stroke (i.e. in designs featuring more than two valves) will intensify this tendency.

At the same time, the demands for minimal exhaust emissions and maximum fuel economy mean that low idle speeds and high low-end torque (despite and along with high specific outputs for reasons of power-unit weight) are becoming increasingly important. These imperatives have led to the application of variable valve timing (especially for intake valves), whereby the most significant concepts (with attention focused on high-speed gasoline engines in series production) have been the following:

Variable camshaft timing by rotation: A hydraulic control mechanism rotates the intake camshaft to vary the valve timing for "intake opens" and "intake closes" as a

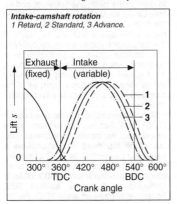

Intake-camshaft rotation
1 Retard, 2 Standard, 3 Advance.

Exhaust (fixed) | Intake (variable)

Lift s

300° 360° 420° 480° 540° 600°
TDC   BDC
Crank angle

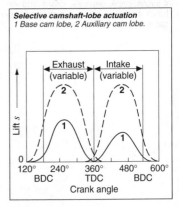

Selective camshaft-lobe actuation
1 Base cam lobe, 2 Auxiliary cam lobe.

Exhaust (variable) | Intake (variable)

Lift s

120° 240° 360° 480° 600°
BDC   TDC   BDC
Crank angle

function of engine speed (Alfa-Romeo, Mercedes-Benz).

The camshaft is set for delayed closing of the intake valve at idle and at high engine speeds. This results in a certain amount of valve overlap at overlap top dead center (OTDC) for stability at idle and enhanced output at high min⁻¹. The camshaft is rotated to close the intake valve early (IC) under full load in midrange operation, furnishing higher volumetric efficiency with correspondingly high levels of torque.

<u>Selective camshaft-lobe actuation</u>: The timing of the intake and exhaust valves is varied by alternating between separate lobes featuring two different lift profiles (Honda).

The first lobe features a profile tailored for optimum intake and exhaust timing and valve lift in the lower and middle engine-speed ranges. At high min⁻¹, a rocker arm that pivots freely at low speeds is coupled to the standard rocker arm; this rocker arm rides on a second cam lobe to provide greater lift and extended opening times.

<u>Infinitely-variable valve lift and timing</u>: Continuous modification of valve timing as a function of engine speed (Fiat).

This is the optimum concept, but it is also the most difficult to implement. It employs cam lobes with a curved three-dimensional profile and lateral camshaft shift to achieve substantial increases in torque over the engine's entire min⁻¹ range.

High-speed solenoid injectors (injection valves) have opened the way for development of electro-hydraulically actuated valve timing systems. Work is also under way on valve timing arrangements with solenoid actuation. At this time, however, solutions of this nature have not progressed as far as series production.

<u>Evaluating gas-exchange components</u>
The intake and exhaust tracts can be evaluated using stationary flow testing with flow numbers or passage efficiency levels. It is useful to evaluate the exhaust valves in the lower lift range with reference to supercritical pressures of the kind occurring in the blowdown phase.

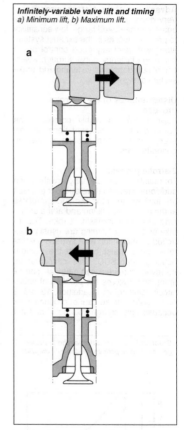

Infinitely-variable valve lift and timing
a) Minimum lift, b) Maximum lift.

a

b

Alongside assessment of the flow number and the derived parameters for swirl and tumble. Increasing use is being made of 3D computer models which, unlike the available measuring techniques, can furnish local information about flow conditions. Highly developed engine models are widely used today in the theoretical assessment of the overall gas cycle.

Advantages of the 4-stroke process:
Very good volumetric efficiency over the entire engine-speed range, low sensitivity to pressure losses in the exhaust system, along with relatively good control of the charging-efficiency curve through selection of appropriate valve timing and intake system designs.

Disadvantages of the 4-stroke process:
Valve control is highly complex. The power density is reduced because only every second shaft rotation is used to generate work.

2-stroke process
To maintain gas exchange without an additional crankshaft rotation, the gases are exchanged in the two-stroke process at the end of expansion and at the beginning of the compression stroke. The intake and exhaust timing are usually controlled by the piston as it sweeps past intake and exhaust ports in the cylinder housing near BDC. This configuration, however, requires symmetrical control times and involves the problem of short-circuit scavenging. In addition, 15...25 % of the piston stroke cannot produce work because only charge volume V_f and not

displacement volume V_h can be exploited for power generation. Because the two-stroke process lacks separate intake and exhaust strokes, the cylinder must be filled and scavenged using positive pressure, necessitating the use of scavenging pumps. In an especially simple and very frequently-used design, the bottom surface of the piston works in conjunction with a crankcase featuring a minimal dead volume to form a scavenging pump. The illustrations show a 2-stroke engine with crankcase scavenging or crankcase precompression along with the associated control processes. The processes which take place on the scavenging pump side are shown in the inner circle, while those occurring on the cylinder side are shown in the outer circle. Satisfactory cylinder scavenging is available using crossflow scavenging, loop scavenging and uniflow scavenging.

Advantages of the 2-stroke process:
Simple engine design, low weight, low manufacturing costs, better torsional force pattern.

Disadvantages of the 2-stroke process:
Higher fuel consumption and higher HC emissions (cylinder scavenging is problematic), lower mean effective pressures (poorer volumetric efficiency), higher thermal loads (no gas-exchange stroke), poor idle (higher percentage of residual gas).

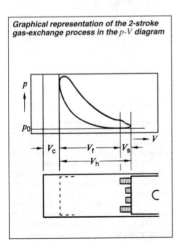

Graphical representation of the 2-stroke gas-exchange process in the p-V diagram

2-stroke gas-exchange process with crankcase compression

E Exhaust,
EO Exhaust opens,
EC Exhaust closes,
I Intake,
IO Intake opens,
IC Intake closes,
T Transfer passage, closes,
TO Transfer passage opens,
TDC Top dead center,
BDC Bottom dead center,
IP Ignition point.

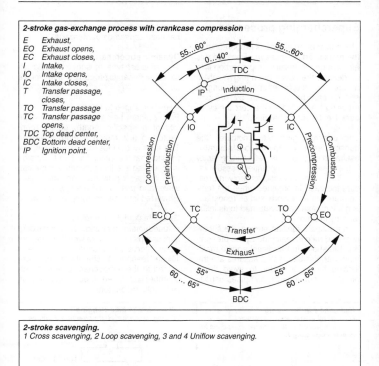

2-stroke scavenging.
1 Cross scavenging, 2 Loop scavenging, 3 and 4 Uniflow scavenging.

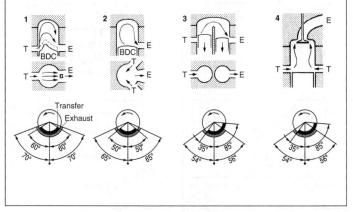

Supercharging processes

The power of an engine is proportional to the processed air mass m_z. Because this air throughput, in turn, is proportional to air density, the power of an engine, given a specific displacement and engine speed, can be increased by precompressing the air before it enters the cylinders, i.e. by supercharging.

The supercharging ratio indicates the density rise as compared to a naturally-aspirated engine. One determining factor is the system used (potential pressure ratio). The maximum ratio for a given pressure increase is obtained when the temperature of the compressed air (boost air) is not increased or is returned to its initial level by intercooling.

In the spark-ignition engine, the supercharging ratio is restricted by the pre-ignition threshold. In the diesel engine maximum permissible peak pressures are the limiting factor. In order to avoid these problems, supercharged engines usually have lower compression ratios than their naturally aspirated counterparts.

Dynamic supercharging

The simplest type of supercharging exploits the dynamic properties of the intake air.

Ram-pipe supercharging

Each cylinder has a special intake manifold of a specific length, usually connected to a common plenum chamber. The energy balance is characterized by the fact that the intake work of the piston is converted into kinetic energy in the column of gas upstream from the intake valve, and this kinetic energy, in turn, is converted into charge compression work.

Tuned-intake-tube charging

In tuned-intake charging, short ducts connect groups of cylinders with the same ignition intervals to resonance chambers. These resonance chambers are connected to the atmosphere or a common chamber by tuned tubes, and act as Helmholtz resonators.

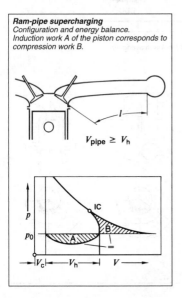

Ram-pipe supercharging
Configuration and energy balance.
Induction work A of the piston corresponds to compression work B.

$V_{pipe} \geq V_h$

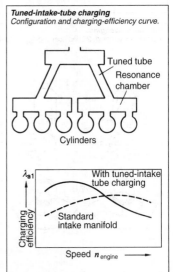

Tuned-intake-tube charging
Configuration and charging-efficiency curve.

Tuned tube
Resonance chamber
Cylinders

λ_{a1}
With tuned-intake tube charging
Standard intake manifold
Charging efficiency
Speed n_{engine}

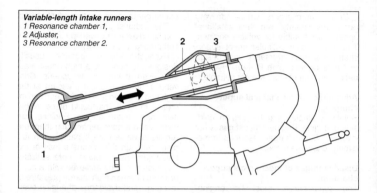

Variable-length intake runners
1 Resonance chamber 1,
2 Adjuster,
3 Resonance chamber 2.

Variable-geometry intake manifold

Several manufacturers (BMW, Citroën, Opel, Ford) have already introduced systems employing the principles of dynamic boost (including combination designs). These systems enhance charge efficiency, above all at low min⁻¹.

Switch-over in the variable-geometry system uses flaps or similar devices to connect or isolate the different groups of cylinders as a function of engine speed.

At low min⁻¹ the variable-length intake runners operate in conjunction with an initial resonance chamber. The length of the intake runners is adjusted continually as engine speed increases, the entire process culminating with the opening of a second resonance chamber.

Mechanical supercharging

In mechanical supercharging, the supercharger is powered directly by the engine, which usually drives the supercharger at a fixed transmission ratio. Mechanical or electromagnetic clutches are often used to control supercharger activation.

A clear illustration of the relationship between the engine and the supercharger is provided by the diagram for pressure vs. volumetric flow rate, in which the pressure ratio π_c of the supercharger is plotted against volumetric flow rate V.

The curves for unthrottled 4-stroke engines (diesel) are particularly descriptive because they contain sloped straight lines (engine mass flow characteristics) which represent increasing engine air-through-put values as the pressure ratio $\pi_c \triangleq p_2/p_1$ increases at constant engine speed.

The diagram shows pressure ratios which result at corresponding constant supercharger speeds for a positive-displacement supercharger and a hydrokinetic compressor.

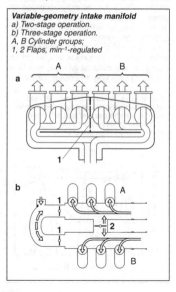

Variable-geometry intake manifold
a) Two-stage operation.
b) Three-stage operation.
A, B Cylinder groups;
1, 2 Flaps, min⁻¹-regulated

Only superchargers whose delivery rates vary linearly with their rotational speeds are suitable for vehicle engines. These are positive-displacement superchargers of piston or rotating-vane design or Roots blowers (see P. 440). Hydrokinetic flow compressors are not suitable.

Advantages of mechanical supercharging:

Relatively simple superchargers on "cold" side of engine. Engine exhaust gas is not involved. Supercharger responds immediately to load changes.

Disadvantages of mechanical supercharging:

The supercharger must be engine-powered, causing increased fuel consumption.

Exhaust-gas turbocharging

In exhaust-gas turbocharging, the energy for the turbocharger is extracted from the engine's exhaust gases. Although the process exploits energy that remains unused (owing to crankshaft assembly expansion limits) by naturally-aspirated engines, exhaust back-pressure increases as the gases furnish the power required to turn the compressor.

Current turbocharged engines employ an exhaust-driven turbine to convert the energy in the exhaust gas into mechanical energy, making it possible for the tur-bocharger to compress the induction gas.

The exhaust-gas turbocharger is a combined exhaust-driven turbine and flow compressor (see P. 442).

Exhaust-gas turbochargers are usually designed to generate a high boost pressure even at low engine speeds. Conversely, however, boost pressure at the high end of the engine min^{-1} range can increase to levels that could place excessive load on the engine. Engines with wide speed ranges in particular therefore require a waste gate bypassing the turbine, although this means a loss of exhaust-gas energy. Much more satisfactory results can be achieved with a compromise between high charge pressure at low min^{-1} and avoidance of engine overload at the high end of the min^{-1} range by employing Variable Turbine Geometry (VTG). The blading of a VTG turbine adjusts to suit the flow cross-section and thus the gas pressure at the turbine by variation of the flow cross-section.

Advantages of exhaust-gas turbocharging:

Considerable increase in power output per liter from a given configuration; improved torque curve within the effective engine-speed range; significant improvement in fuel consumption figures relative to naturally-aspirated engines with the same output power; improvement in exhaust-gas emissions.

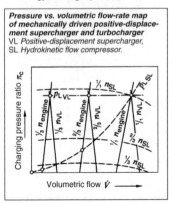

Pressure vs. volumetric flow-rate map of mechanically driven positive-displacement supercharger and turbocharger
VL *Positive-displacement supercharger,*
SL *Hydrokinetic flow compressor.*

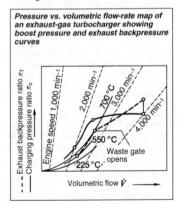

Pressure vs. volumetric flow-rate map of an exhaust-gas turbocharger showing boost pressure and exhaust backpressure curves

Disadvantages of exhaust-gas turbocharging:

Installation of the turbocharger in the hot exhaust-gas tract requiring materials resistant to high temperatures; complexity and space requirements for turbocharger and intercooler; low base torque at low engine speed; throttle response is extremely sensitive to the efficient matching of the turbocharger to the engine.

Pressure-wave supercharging

The pressure-wave supercharger uses direct energy exchange between exhaust gas and the intake air to increase the latter's density. This is accomplished by utilizing the differing speeds of the gas particles and pressure waves on the one side, and the reflection properties of these pressure waves on the other (see P. 446).

The pressure-wave supercharger consists of a cell rotor with an air casing on one side and an exhaust casing on the other. These incorporate specific timing edges and gas-pocket configurations.

Advantages of pressure-wave supercharging:

Rapid throttle response because energy exchange between exhaust gas and boost air takes place at the speed of sound; high compression at low engine speeds.

Disadvantages of pressure-wave supercharging:

Restrictions on installation flexibility owing to the belt drive and gas lines; increased quantities of exhaust gas and scavenge air; loud operation; extremely sensitive to increased resistance on the low-pressure side.

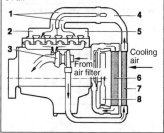

Truck diesel engine with exhaust-gas turbocharging, tuned-intake-tube supercharging and intercooler
1 Tuned tubes, 2 Resonance chamber for cylinders 4 – 5 – 6, 3 Turbocharger, 4 Balance chamber, 5 Resonance chamber for cylinders 1 – 2 – 3, 6 Radiator, 7 Intercooler, 8 Fan

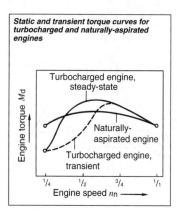

Static and transient torque curves for turbocharged and naturally-aspirated engines

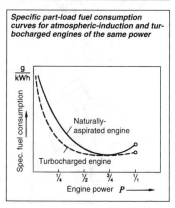

Specific part-load fuel consumption curves for atmospheric-induction and turbocharged engines of the same power

Power transfer in reciprocating-piston engines

Engine types

Single-piston-power unit
The working chamber is formed by cylinder head, cylinder liner, and piston.

In-line engine (1)
Cylinders arranged consecutively in a single plane.

V-engine (2)
The cylinders are arranged in two planes in a V configuration.

Radial engine (3)
The cylinders are arranged radially in one or more planes.

Opposed-cylinder (boxer) engine (4)
The cylinders are horizontally opposed.

Multi-piston-power unit
More than one (usually two) working pistons share a common combustion chamber.

U-engine (5)
The pistons move in the same direction.

Opposed-piston engine (6)
The pistons move in opposite directions.

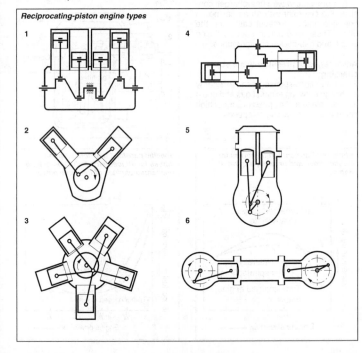

Reciprocating-piston engine types

Direction of rotation

(DIN 73 021)[1]

Clockwise rotation: as viewed looking at the end of the engine opposite the power-output end. Abbreviation: cw.

Counterclockwise rotation: as viewed looking at the end of the engine opposite the power-output end. Abbreviation: ccw.

Numbering the cylinders

(DIN 73 021)[1]

The cylinders are numbered consecutively 1, 2, 3, etc. in the order in which they would be intersected by an imaginary reference plane. As viewed looking at the end of the engine opposite the power-output end. This plane is located horizontally

to the left when numbering begins; the numerical assignments then proceed clockwise around the longitudinal axis of the engine (see figures below). If there is more than one cylinder in a reference plane, the cylinder nearest the observer is assigned the number 1, with consecutive numbers being assigned to the following cylinders. Cylinder 1 is to be identified by the number 1.

Firing order

The firing order is the sequence in which combustion is initiated in the cylinders. Engine design configuration, uniformity in ignition intervals, ease of crankshaft manufacture, optimal crankshaft load patterns, etc., all play a role in defining the firing order.

Design		Number of cylinders	Normal firing order (examples)
	Power output	4	1 3 4 2 or 1 2 4 3
		5	1 2 4 5 3
		6	1 5 3 6 2 4 or 1 2 4 6 5 3 or 1 4 2 6 3 5 or 1 4 5 6 3 2
		8	1 6 2 5 8 3 7 4 or 1 3 6 8 4 2 7 5 or 1 4 7 3 8 5 2 6 or 1 3 2 5 8 6 7 4
	Power output	4	1 3 2 4
		6	1 2 5 6 4 3 or 1 4 5 6 2 3
		8	1 6 3 5 4 7 2 8 or 1 5 4 8 6 3 7 2 or 1 8 3 6 4 5 2 7
	Power output	4	1 4 3 2

[1] Applies to motor-vehicle engines only. For internal-combustion engines for general and marine use, the reverse direction (as viewed looking at the power-output end) is standardized (ISO 1204 and 1205, DIN 6265).

Crankshaft-assembly operation and dynamic properties

The purpose of the piston, connecting rod and crankshaft assembly in the reciprocating-piston engine is to transform the gas forces generated during combustion within the working cylinder into a piston stroke, which the crankshaft then converts into useful torque available at the power-output end of the engine. The cyclic principle of operation leads to unequal gas forces, and the acceleration and deceleration of the reciprocating power-transfer components generate inertial forces. It is usual to distinguish between internal and external effects of the gas-pressure and inertial forces.

The external effects, consisting of free forces or moments, impart movement to the engine. This is then transmitted to the engine supports in the form of vibration.

In this context, the <u>smooth running</u> of an engine is understood to mean freedom from low-frequency vibration, while <u>quiet running</u> means freedom from high-frequency, audible vibration.

The internal forces induce periodically variable loads in block, piston, connecting rod, crankshaft assembly and force-transfer components. These factors must be included in calculations for defining their dimensions and fatigue resistance.

Crankshaft assembly and gas force

The crankshaft assembly of a single-cylinder powerplant comprises the piston, connecting rod (conrod) and crankshaft. These components react to gas forces by generating mass inertial forces of their own.

The gas force F_G which acts on the piston can be subdivided into the side forces F_N applied by the piston to the cylinder wall and supported by it, and the connecting-rod force F_S. The connecting-rod force, in turn, causes the tangential force F_T to be applied at the crankshaft journal. This force together with the crank radius generates the shaft torque and the radial force F_R.

These forces can be calculated as a function of the gas force using the crank angle α, the pivoting angle of the connecting rod β and the stroke/connecting rod ratio λ:

Connecting-rod force: $F_S = F_G/\cos\beta$
Piston side force: $F_N = F_G \cdot \tan\beta$
Radial force: $F_R = F_G \cdot \cos(\alpha + \beta)/\cos\beta$
Tangential force: $F_T = F_G \cdot \sin(\alpha + \beta)/\cos\beta$
where $\lambda = r/l$; $\sin\beta = \lambda \cdot \sin\alpha$;

$$\cos\beta = \sqrt{1 - \lambda^2 \cdot \sin^2\alpha}$$

All of these relationships can be represented in the form of a Fourier series, which can be useful in vibration calculations.

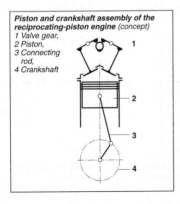

Piston and crankshaft assembly of the reciprocating-piston engine (concept)
1 Valve gear,
2 Piston,
3 Connecting rod,
4 Crankshaft

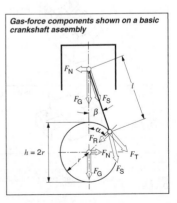

Gas-force components shown on a basic crankshaft assembly

Inertial forces and moments of inertia

The mass inertial properties of the piston, connecting rod and crankshaft assembly are a composite of the forces of the rotating masses of the crankshaft around their axis (x-axis) and the reciprocating masses in the cylinder direction (z-axis for in-line engines). With multiple-cylinder machines, free moments of inertia occur owing to different points of application for gas and inertial forces. The inertial properties of a single-cylinder engine can be determined using the piston mass m_K (exclusively oscillating mass), the crankshaft mass m_W (exclusively rotating mass) and the corresponding connecting-rod mass components (usually assumed to consist of oscillating and rotating rod masses amounting to one third and two thirds of the total mass respectively):

Oscillating mass

$$m_o = m_{Pl}/3 + m_K$$

Rotating mass

$$m_r = 2\,m_{Pl}/3 + m_W$$

The rotating inertial force acting on the crankshaft is as follows:

$$F_r = m_r \cdot r \cdot \omega^2$$

Oscillating inertial force:

$$F_o = m_o \cdot r \cdot \omega^2 \cdot (\underset{\text{1st Order}}{\cos \alpha} + \underset{\text{2nd Order}}{\lambda \cdot \cos 2\alpha} + ...)$$

The following approximations also apply:

$$F_y = r \cdot \omega^2 \cdot m_r \cdot \sin \alpha$$
$$F_z = r \cdot \omega^2 \cdot [m_r \cdot \cos \alpha + m_o \cdot (\cos \alpha + \lambda \cdot \cos 2\alpha)]$$

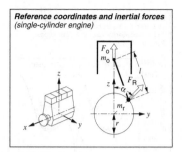

Reference coordinates and inertial forces
(single-cylinder engine)

where $\quad \lambda = r/l$

The inertial-force components are designated as inertial forces of the 1st, 2nd or 4th order, depending upon their rotational frequencies relative to engine speed.

In general, only the 1st and 2nd order components are significant; higher orders can be disregarded.

In the case of multiple-cylinder engines, free moments of inertia are present when all of the complete crankshaft assembly's inertial forces combine to produce a force couple at the crankshaft. The crankshaft assembly must therefore be regarded as a three-dimensional configuration when determining the free moments of inertia, while the inertial forces can be determined using a two-dimensional system.

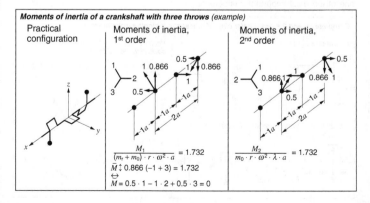

Moments of inertia of a crankshaft with three throws (example)

Practical configuration

Moments of inertia, 1st order

$$\frac{M_1}{(m_r + m_o) \cdot r \cdot \omega^2 \cdot a} = 1.732$$

$$\overset{\leftrightarrow}{M}\updownarrow 0.866\,(-1+3) = 1.732$$

$$M = 0.5 \cdot 1 - 1 \cdot 2 + 0.5 \cdot 3 = 0$$

Moments of inertia, 2nd order

$$\frac{M_2}{m_o \cdot r \cdot \omega^2 \cdot \lambda \cdot a} = 1.732$$

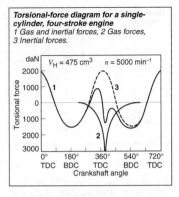

Torsional-force diagram for a single-cylinder, four-stroke engine
1 Gas and inertial forces, 2 Gas forces,
3 Inertial forces.

$V_H = 475$ cm³ $n = 5000$ min⁻¹

Torsional force (daN) vs Crankshaft angle:
0° TDC, 180° BDC, 360° TDC, 540° BDC, 720° TDC

Torsional-force diagram for the reciprocating-piston engine

If the periodic gas force acting on the piston and the periodic mass inertial forces acting on the piston, connecting rod and crankshaft assembly are grouped together, they generate a sum of tangential force components at the crankshaft journal. When multiplied by the crank radius, this yields a periodically variable torque value. If this torque value is referred to the piston surface and the crank radius, the result is a value valid for any engine size: tangential pressure. The torsional-force diagram shows the curve for this pressure as a function of crankshaft position. It is one of the most important characteristic curves in assessing dynamic engine behavior.

With multiple-cylinder engines, the tangential-pressure curves for the individual cylinders are superimposed with a phase shift in accordance with the number of cylinders, their configuration, crankshaft design and the firing order. The resulting composite curve is characteristic for the engine design, and covers a full working cycle (i.e., 2 crankshaft rotations for 4-stroke engines). It is also called a tangential-pressure diagram.

Harmonic analysis can be employed to replace the torsional-force diagram with a series of sinusoidal oscillations featuring whole-number multiples of the basic frequencies, and to obtain the "torsional harmonics". When defined according to engine speed these multiples are also called orders. When applied to a four-stroke engine this procedure generates half orders, e.g. the 0.5th order.

The cyclical fluctuations in torsional force encountered in all reciprocating-piston engines lead to variations in the crankshaft's rotation speed, the so-called coefficient of cyclic variation.

$$\delta_s = (\omega_{max} - \omega_{min})/\omega_{min},$$

An energy storage device (the flywheel) provides adequate compensation for these variations in rotation rate in normal applications.

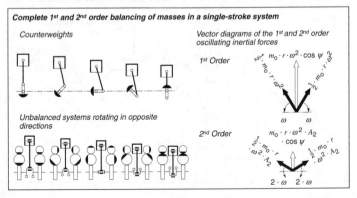

Complete 1st and 2nd order balancing of masses in a single-stroke system

Counterweights

Unbalanced systems rotating in opposite directions

Vector diagrams of the 1st and 2nd order oscillating inertial forces

1st Order $m_0 \cdot r \cdot \omega^2 \cdot \cos \psi$

ω ω

2nd Order $m_0 \cdot r \cdot \omega^2 \cdot A_2 \cdot \cos \psi$

$2 \cdot \omega$ $2 \cdot \omega$

Balancing of masses in the reciprocating-piston engine

Mass balancing encompasses a wide array of measures employed to obtain partial or complete compensation for the inertial forces and moments of inertia emanating from the crankshaft assembly. All masses are externally balanced when no free inertial forces or moments of inertia are transmitted through the block to the outside. However, the remaining internal forces and moments subject the engine mounts and block to various loads as well as deformative and vibratory stresses. The basic loads imposed by gas-based and inertial forces are shown in Table 3.

Balancing of inertial forces in the single-stroke powerplant

The simplest way to balance rotating masses is to use counterweights to generate an equal force to oppose the centrifugal force. Oscillating masses generate periodic forces. The 1st order forces are propagated at crankshaft speed, while the periodicity of the 2nd order forces is twice the crankshaft's rotation rate. Compensation for these forces is available in the form of a counterweight balance system designed for opposed rotation at a rate equal to or twice that of the crankshaft. The balance forces' magnitudes must equal those of the rotating inertial-force vectors while acting in the opposite direction.

Table 3. Forces and moments applied to the piston, connecting rod and crankshaft assembly

Forces and moments at the engine	x		z y	
Designation	Oscillating torque, transverse tilting moment, reaction torque	Free inertial forces	Free inertial moment, longitudinal tilting moment about the y-axis (transverse axis) ("pitching" moment) about the z-axis (vertical axis) ("rolling" moment)	Internal flex forces
Cause	Tangential gas forces as well as tangential inertial forces for ordinals 1, 2, 3 and 4	Unbalanced oscillating inertial forces 1st order in 1 and 2 cylinders; 2nd order in 1, 2, and 4 cylinders	Unbalanced oscillating inertial forces as a composite of 1st and 2nd order forces	Rotating and oscillating inertial forces
Design factors	Number of cylinders, ignition intervals, displacement, p_i, ε, p_z, m_0, r, ω, λ	Number of cylinders, crank configuration m_0, r, ω, λ	Number of cylinders, crank configuration, cylinder spacing, counterweight size influences inertial torque components about the y- and z-axes m_0, r, ω, λ, a	Number of throws, crank configuration, engine length, engine-block rigidity
Remedy	Can only be compensated for in exceptional cases	Free mass effects can be eliminated with rotating balancing systems, however this process is complex and therefore rare; crank sequences with limited or no mass effects are preferable		Counterweights, rigid engine block
		Shielding of the environment through flexible engine mounts (in particular for orders ≥ 2)		

Table 4. Residual 1st order inertial forces with differing balancing rates

		Balancing rate		
		0%	50%	100%
Size of counter-weight	$m_G \triangleq$	m_r	$m_r + 0.5m_0$	$m_r + m_0$
Residual inertial force (z) 1st order	$F_{1z} =$	$m_0 \cdot r \cdot \omega^2$	$0.5 \cdot m_0 \cdot r \cdot \omega^2$	0
Residual inertial force (y) 1st order	$F_{1y} =$	0	$0.5 \cdot m_0 \cdot r \cdot \omega^2$	$m_0 \cdot r \cdot \omega^2$

Balancing rate

The forces exerted by the counterweights used to balance the rotating masses can be increased by a certain percentage of the oscillating mass in order to reduce the oscillating forces acting in the direction of the cylinders (z). The percentage of this inertial force which is counteracted then appears in the y-axis. The ratio of the compensated inertial-force component in the z-axis relative to the initial value for the 1st order inertial force is termed the balancing rate (Table 4).

Balancing of inertial forces in the multi-cylinder engine

In multi-cylinder engines the mutual counteractions of the various components in the crankshaft assembly are one of the essential factors determining the selection of the crankshaft's configuration, and with it the design of the engine itself. The

Table 5. Star diagram of the 1st and 2nd order for three- to six-cylinder, in-line engines

	3-cylinder	4-cylinder	5-cylinder	6-cylinder
Crank sequence				
Star diagram 1st Order				
Star diagram 2nd Order				

inertial forces are balanced if the common center of gravity for all moving crankshaft-assembly components lies at the crankshaft's midpoint, i.e. if the crankshaft is symmetrical (as viewed from the front). The crankshaft's symmetry level can be defined using geometrical representations of 1st- and 2nd-order forces (star diagrams). The 2nd order star diagram for the four-cylinder in-line engine is asymmetrical, meaning that this order is characterized by substantial free inertial forces. These forces can be balanced using two countershafts rotating in opposite directions at double the rate of the crankshaft (Lanchester system).

Balancing of inertial and gas forces
The tangential gas forces produce yet another periodic torque; this can be detected as reaction torque in the engine block. The composite forces generated in a four-cylinder in-line engine include free mass forces of the 2nd order as well as variable torque forces from the 2nd order mass and gas forces. Compensation for 2nd order mass forces, along with a reduction in the intensity of the 2nd order force transitions, is available from two offset balance shafts.

Balancing 2nd order inertial and transitional forces in a four-cylinder, in-line engine with two offset countershafts
1 Inertial torque only; 2 Gas torque only or complete balancing of inertial torque, $z_I - z_{II} = -2\,B_2/A_2 \cdot r$; 3 Gas and inertial torque without force compensation; 4 Gas and inertial torque with half of the inertial torque balanced, $z_I - z_{II} \approx 0.5 \cdot l$.

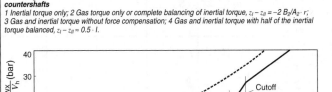

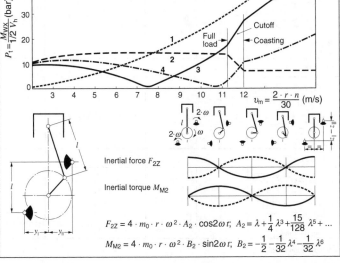

$$F_{2Z} = 4 \cdot m_0 \cdot r \cdot \omega^2 \cdot A_2 \cdot \cos 2\omega\,t; \quad A_2 = \lambda + \frac{1}{4}\lambda^3 + \frac{15}{128}\lambda^5 + \dots$$

$$M_{M2} = 4 \cdot m_0 \cdot r \cdot \omega^2 \cdot B_2 \cdot \sin 2\omega\,t; \quad B_2 = -\frac{1}{2} - \frac{1}{32}\lambda^4 - \frac{1}{32}\lambda^6$$

Table 6. Free forces and moments of the 1st and 2nd order, and ignition intervals of the most common engine designs

$$F_r = m_r \cdot r \cdot \omega^2 \qquad F_1 = m_0 \cdot r \cdot \omega^2 \cdot \cos\alpha \qquad F_2 = m_0 \cdot r \cdot \omega^2 \cdot \lambda \cdot \cos 2\alpha$$

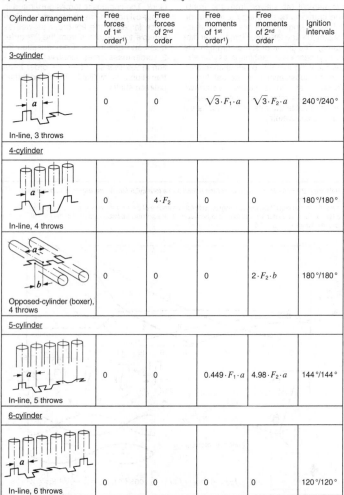

Cylinder arrangement	Free forces of 1st order[1]	Free forces of 2nd order	Free moments of 1st order[1]	Free moments of 2nd order	Ignition intervals
3-cylinder					
In-line, 3 throws	0	0	$\sqrt{3} \cdot F_1 \cdot a$	$\sqrt{3} \cdot F_2 \cdot a$	240°/240°
4-cylinder					
In-line, 4 throws	0	$4 \cdot F_2$	0	0	180°/180°
Opposed-cylinder (boxer), 4 throws	0	0	0	$2 \cdot F_2 \cdot b$	180°/180°
5-cylinder					
In-line, 5 throws	0	0	$0.449 \cdot F_1 \cdot a$	$4.98 \cdot F_2 \cdot a$	144°/144°
6-cylinder					
In-line, 6 throws	0	0	0	0	120°/120°

[1] Without counterweights.

Cylinder arrangement	Free forces of 1st order[1]	Free forces of 2nd order	Free moments of 1st order[1]	Free moments of 2nd order	Ignition intervals
6-cylinder (continued)					
 V 90°, 3 throws	0	0	$\sqrt{3} \cdot F_1 \cdot a$ [2]	$\sqrt{6} \cdot F_2 \cdot a$	150°/90° 150°/90°
 Normal balance V 90°, 3 throws, 30° crank offset	0	0	$0.4483 \cdot F_1 \cdot a$	$(0.966 \pm 0.256) \cdot$ $\sqrt{3} \cdot F_2 \cdot a$	120°/120°
 Opposed-cylinder, 6 throws	0	0	0	0	120°/120°
 V 60°, 6 throws	0	0	$3 \cdot F_1 \cdot a/2$	$3 \cdot F_2 \cdot a/2$	120°/120°
8-cylinder					
 V 90°, 4 throws in two planes	0	0	$\sqrt{10} \cdot F_1 \cdot a$ [2]	0	90°/90°
12-cylinder					
 V 60°, 6 throws	0	0	0	0	60°/60°

[1] Without counterweights.
[2] Can be completely balanced by using counterweights.

Main components of reciprocating-piston engine

Piston

Pistons in today's motor-vehicle engines must perform a wide range of functions:
- They transmit the force generated by the combustion gas to the connecting rods.
- They serve as crosstails to define the connecting rods' travel paths within the cylinders.
- They support the normal force applied against the cylinder walls while the cylinder pressure is conveyed to the connecting rod.
- Together with their sealing elements, they seal the combustion chamber from the crankcase.
- They absorb heat for subsequent transfer to the cooling system.

Both the piston's design and the wristpin configuration employed to transfer the combustion gas forces to the connecting rod are largely determined by the combustion chamber's shape, including the geometry of the piston crown, while other variables include the selected combustion process and the associated pressure maxima. The priority is to produce the lightest possible piston in a unit capable of withstanding intense forces during operation in an environment with temperatures that can approach the physical limits of the materials used in its manufacture.

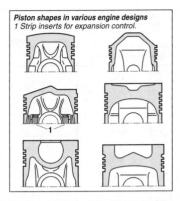

Piston shapes in various engine designs
1 Strip inserts for expansion control.

Precise definition of the dimensions for the piston, wristpin and wristpin bushings are essential for achieving this goal.

The most frequently used materials for cylinder liners and pistons are gray cast iron and aluminum. Variations in piston clearance within the cylinder must be minimized to reduce noise (piston slap) and improve sealing, notwithstanding the fact that piston and cylinder liner have different coefficients of expansion. To this end, steel strips or similar elements are sometimes cast into the piston to limit its expansion.

Piston rings form the sealing element between the combustion chamber and the crankcase. The upper two – the compression rings – serve as gas seals. At

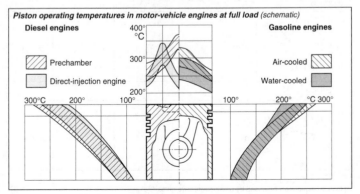

Piston operating temperatures in motor-vehicle engines at full load (schematic)

Diesel engines

- Prechamber
- Direct-injection engine

Gasoline engines

- Air-cooled
- Water-cooled

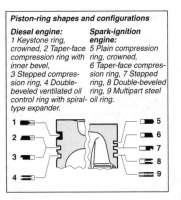

Piston-ring shapes and configurations

Diesel engine:
1 Keystone ring, crowned, 2 Taper-face compression ring with inner bevel, 3 Stepped compression ring, 4 Double-beveled ventilated oil control ring with spiral-type expander.

Spark-ignition engine:
5 Plain compression ring, crowned, 6 Taper-face compression ring, 7 Stepped ring, 8 Double-beveled ring, 9 Multipart steel oil ring.

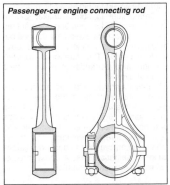

Passenger-car engine connecting rod

least one additional ring (generally of a different design), the oil control ring, is also present. This is a "scraper" ring and ensures correct lubrication of the piston and compression rings. Owing to the rings' extreme tension and the force that they exert against the cylinder walls, they are a major source of friction within the reciprocating-piston engine.

Connecting rod

The connecting rod (conrod) is the joining element between piston and crankshaft. It is subject to extreme tensile, compression and flex stresses, while it also houses the wristpin bushings and crankshaft bearings. Connecting-rod length is deter-

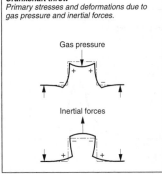

Crankshaft throw
Primary stresses and deformations due to gas pressure and inertial forces.

Gas pressure

Inertial forces

mined by the piston stroke and the counterweight radius; whereby the engine height can also be an important factor (usually the case in vehicle engines).

Crankshaft

The crankshaft with its rod extensions, or throws, converts the reciprocating motion of the pistons – conveyed to it by the connecting rods – into rotary motion, making effective torque available at the crankshaft's end. The forces acting upon the crankshaft are characterized by highly variable periodicities and vary greatly according to location. These torques and flex forces, and the secondary vibrations which they generate, all represent intense and highly complex stress factors for the crankshaft itself. As a result, its structural properties and vibrational response patterns rely upon precise calculations and carefully defined dimensions. Calculations and dimensioning though are further complicated by the fact that too many multiple journal bearings are practically always installed as a precautionary measure.

The number of crankshaft bearings is primarily determined by overall load factor and maximum engine speed. To accommodate their intense operating pressures, all diesel-engine crankshafts incorporate a main bearing journal between each crankshaft throw and at each end of the crankshaft. This arrangement is also found in high-speed spark-ignition (SI) engines designed for high specific outputs.

Crankshafts in some smaller SI engines designed for operation at lower load factors sometimes extend the interval between main bearings to 2 cylinders to reduce expense. The number of counterweights also depends upon the criteria cited above.

Stresses and load factors are also primary considerations in the selection of both materials and manufacturing processes. Highly-stressed crankshafts are usually drop-forged. In smaller and less highly stressed engines, cast crankshafts, incorporating the dual advantages of lower weight and less expense, are becoming increasingly popular.

Crankshaft vibrations

Flexural vibration is significant only on engines with a small number of cylinders, because the crankshaft and the necessary large flywheel form an oscillatory

Cast crankshaft

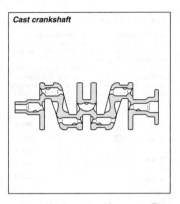

system with a low natural frequency. Flexural vibration is not a critical factor on engines of 3 cylinders or more. By logical extension, this also applies to the longitudi-

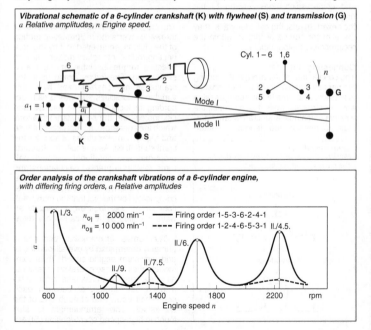

Vibrational schematic of a 6-cylinder crankshaft (K) with flywheel (S) and transmission (G)
a Relative amplitudes, n Engine speed.

Order analysis of the crankshaft vibrations of a 6-cylinder engine, with differing firing orders, a Relative amplitudes

$n_{OI} = 2000 \text{ min}^{-1}$ — Firing order 1-5-3-6-2-4-1
$n_{OII} = 10\,000 \text{ min}^{-1}$ - - - Firing order 1-2-4-6-5-3-1

nal crankshaft vibrations induced by flexural vibrations.

At the same time, the torsional vibrations of the resonant system formed by crankshaft, connecting rods and pistons become increasingly critical with higher numbers of cylinders. This system, in which the mass moments of inertia for connecting rods and pistons vary according to crankshaft angle, can be calculated by reducing it to a smooth, flexible shaft free of inertia with equivalent masses mounted on it. The oscillation reduction model makes it possible to determine both the system's inherent frequency and the intensity of the vibration forces. The oscillations emanate from the tangential forces generated by a combination of gas forces and oscillating mass forces at the crank pin. Vibration dampers are required to reduce the crankshaft's torsional vibrations to acceptable levels (e.g. bonded rubber vibration dampers or viscous vibration dampers).

Engine block and crankcase
The block and crankcase unit supports the force-transfer mechanism between cylinder head and crankshaft assembly; it bears the crankshaft assembly's support bearings, and incorporates (or holds) the cylinder sleeves. Also included in the block are a separate water jacket and sealed oil chambers and galleries. The block also serves as a mounting and support surface for most of the engine's ancillary units.

A cast block and crankcase unit is the standard configuration for automotive applications. The cylinder-head bolts oppose the gas forces to facilitate a force transfer of maximum linearity and minimal flexural tendency through transverse support walls and to the main bearings. For greater strength the crankcase is frequently extended to below the crankshaft's center axis. The pistons in spark-ignition engines almost always run in integral cylinders machined from the block casting. In diesel engines, separate dry or wet liners made of special wear-resistant materials are usually used.

Whereas, virtually all blocks for truck engines continue to be manufactured in cast iron, aluminum passenger-car blocks are becoming increasingly popular owing to their weight-savings potential.

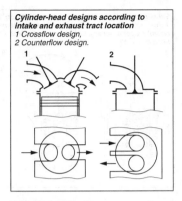

Cylinder-head designs according to intake and exhaust tract location
1 Crossflow design,
2 Counterflow design.

Cylinder head
The cylinder head seals off the upper end of the block and cylinder(s). It houses the gas-exchange valves as well as the spark plugs and/or injectors. Together with the piston, it also provides the desired combustion-chamber shape. In the vast majority of passenger-car engines, the entire valve gear is also mounted in the cylinder head. Based on the gas-exchange concepts, one differentiates between two basic design configurations:

– <u>Counterflow cylinder head</u>: Intake and exhaust passages open onto the same side of the cylinder head. This limits the space available for the intake and exhaust gas passages, but due to the short flow tracts this represents a substantial advantage in supercharged applications. This design, with the gas supply and discharge tracts on a single side, also provides practical advantages in transverse-mounted engines.

– <u>Crossflow cylinder head</u>: Intake and exhaust passages are located on opposite sides of the engine, furnishing a diagonal flow pattern for the intake and exhaust gases. This layout's advantages include more latitude in intake and exhaust-tract design as well as less complicated sealing arrangements.

In truck and large industrial engines, individual cylinder heads are often used on each cylinder for better sealing-force distribution and easier maintenance and re-

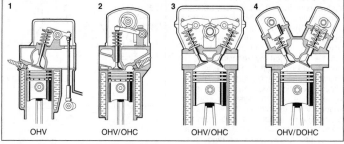

Valve-gear designs (source: Hütten "Motoren")
1 Push-rod assembly, 2 Single rocker-arm assembly, 3 Twin rocker-arm assembly, 4 Overhead bucket-tappet assembly, OHV Overhead valves, OHC Overhead camshaft, DOHC Double overhead camshaft.

OHV   OHV/OHC   OHV/OHC   OHV/DOHC

pair. Separate cylinder heads are also specified for improved cooling efficiency on air-cooled engines.

In passenger-car and low-power engines, one cylinder head is usually employed for all cylinders together. The cylinder heads on water-cooled diesel truck engines are usually made of cast iron.

Superior heat dissipation and lower weight have combined to make aluminum the material of choice in the construction of cylinder heads for air-cooled engines as well as on virtually all spark-ignition and diesel engines for passenger cars.

Valve gear

It is the function of the valve-gear assembly in a 4-stroke engine to permit and to control the exchange of gases in the IC engine (see P. 384). The valve gear includes the intake and exhaust valves, the springs which close them, the camshaft drive assembly and the various force-transfer devices.

Valve-actuation concepts

In the following widely-used designs the camshaft is located in the cylinder head:
– Overhead bucket-tappet assembly, in which a "bucket" moving back and forth in the cylinder head absorbs the cam lobe's lateral force while transferring its linear actuating pressure to the valve stem.
– Cam follower or single rocker-arm assembly actuated by an overhead cam, in which the cam lobe's lateral and lin-

ear forces are absorbed and relayed by a cylinder-head-mounted lever rocking back and forth between cam lobe and valve. In addition to transferring forces, the rocker arm can also be designed to magnify the effective lobe profile for greater valve travel.
– Twin rocker-arm assembly actuated by overhead cam, in which the rocker arm's tilt axis is located between the camshaft and the valve. Here too, the rocker arm is usually designed as a cam lift multiplier to produce the desired valve travel.

When the camshaft is installed within the block, the camshaft lobe acts against an intermediate lifter and pushrod assembly instead of directly against the valve.

Valve arrangements

The valve control arrangement and the design of the combustion chamber are closely interrelated. Today, nearly all valve assemblies are overhead units mounted in the cylinder head. In diesels and simpler spark-ignition engines, the valves are parallel to the cylinder axis, and are usually actuated by twin rocker arms, bucket tappets or single rocker arms. With increasing frequency, those current spark-ignition engines designed for higher specific outputs tend to feature intake and exhaust valves which are inclined towards each other. This configuration allows larger valve diameters for a given cylinder bore while also providing greater latitude

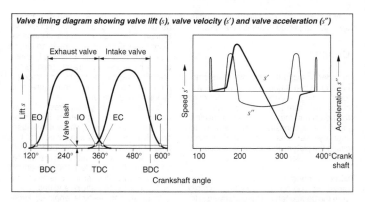

Valve timing diagram showing valve lift (s), valve velocity (s') and valve acceleration (s'')

for optimizing intake and exhaust passage design. Twin rocker-arm assemblies actuated by overhead cams are used most often here. High-performance and racing engines are increasingly using four valves per cylinder and overhead-bucket-tappet valve assemblies.

An engine's valve-timing diagram shows the opening and closing times of the valves, the valve-lift curve with maximum lift, and the valve's velocities and acceleration rates.

Typical valve acceleration rates for passenger-car OHC (overhead camshaft) valve assemblies:

$s'' = 60 ... 65$ mm $(b/\omega^2) \triangleq 6400$ m/s^2 at 6000 min^{-1} for single and twin rocker-arm assemblies,

$s'' = 70 ... 80$ mm $(b/\omega^2) \triangleq 7900$ m/s^2 at 6000 min^{-1} for overhead-bucket tappet assemblies. For heavy commercial-vehicle engines with block-mounted camshafts:

$s'' = 100 ... 120$ mm $(b/\omega^2) \triangleq 2000$ m/s^2 at 2400 min^{-1}.

Valve, valve guide and valve seat

The materials employed in manufacturing valves are heat and scale-resistant. The valve seat's contact surface is frequently hardened. A proven method for improving the thermal transfer characteristics of exhaust valves is to fill their stems with sodium. To extend service life and improve sealing, valve-rotating systems (rotocaps) are now in common use.

The valve guides in high-performance engines must feature high thermal conductivity and good antifriction properties. They are usually pressed into the cylinder head and are often supplemented by valve stem seals at their cold ends for reducing oil consumption.

Valve-seat wear is generally reduced by making the valve seats of cast or sintered materials and shrink-fitting them into the cylinder head.

Lobe design and timing dynamics

The cam lobe must be able to open (and close) the valve as far as possible, as fast as possible and as smoothly as possible. The closing force for the valves is applied by the valve springs, which are also responsible for maintaining contact between the cam lobe and the valve. Dynamic forces impose limits on cam and valve lift.

The entire valve-gear assembly can be viewed as a spring/mass system in which the conversion from stored to free energy causes forced vibration. Valve-gear assemblies with overhead camshafts can be represented with sufficient accuracy by a 1-mass system (consisting of the propelled mass, valve-gear assembly stiffness, and the corresponding damping effects).

Dual-mass systems are becoming increasingly popular for use with block-mounted camshafts and pushrods.

The maximum permissible surface pressure, usually regarded as the decisive parameter limiting cam-lobe radius and the rate of opening on the flank, currently lies between 600 and 750 N/mm², depending upon the employed material pairings.

Cooling

In order to avoid thermal overload, combustion of the lubricating oil on the piston's sliding surface, and uncontrolled combustion due to excessive component temperatures, the components surrounding the hot combustion chamber (cylinder liner, cylinder head, valves and in some cases the pistons themselves) must be intensively cooled.

Direct cooling
Direct air cooling removes heat directly from the components. The underlying principle is based on intensive air flow, usually through a finned surface. Although primarily used in motorcycle and aircraft engines, this form of cooling is also employed for some passenger-car and commercial-vehicle diesel and spark-ignition engines. Its main advantage is its high reliability and freedom from maintenance. On the negative side, the design measures required to ensure efficient heat dissipation to the cooling air increase the cost of the components.

Indirect cooling
Because water has a high specific heat capacity and provides efficient thermal transition between the materials, most contemporary vehicle engines are water-cooled. The air/water recirculation cooling system is the most prevalent system. It comprises a closed circuit allowing the use of anti-corrosion and anti-freeze additives. The coolant is pumped through the engine and through an air/water radiator. The cooling air flows through the radiator in response to vehicle movement and/or is forced through it by a fan. The coolant temperature is regulated by a thermostatic valve which bypasses the radiator as required.

Lubrication

The internal-combustion engine employs oil to lubricate and cool all of the power-transmission components. This oil is also used to remove dirt and neutralize chem-

ically-active combustion products, as well as for transmitting forces and damping vibration. The oil can only fulfill all these requirements if it is transported in adequate quantities to the engine's critical points, and if its properties are adapted to the specific requirements by appropriate measures taken during manufacture (e.g., inclusion of additives).

In total-loss lubrication (fresh-oil lubrication), a metering system supplies oil to the lubrication points, where it is subsequently consumed. A special case of this type of lubrication is mixture lubrication in which oil is either added to the fuel in a ratio ranging from 1:20 to 1:100, or metered to the engine (this process is used primarily in small two-stroke engines).

In most motor-vehicle engines, force-feed lubrication systems are used in combination with splash and oil mist lubrication. The basic force-feed system pumps pressurized oil (usually by gear pump) to all bearing points, while sliding parts are lubricated by splash lubrication systems

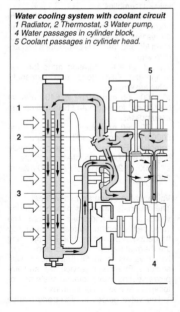

Water cooling system with coolant circuit
1 Radiator, 2 Thermostat, 3 Water pump,
4 Water passages in cylinder block,
5 Coolant passages in cylinder head.

and oil mist.

After flowing through the bearing points and sliding parts, the oil collects below the piston, connecting rod and crankshaft assembly in the oil pan (sump). The sump is a reservoir where the oil cools while the foam dissipates and settles. Engines subject to high loads are also fitted with an oil cooler. Engine service life can be prolonged dramatically by keeping the oil clean.

Oil filters

Oil filters remove solid particles from the engine oil (combustion residue, metal particles and dust) and maintain the lubricating capability of the oil in the intervals between changes. Oil-filter dimensions are governed by the degree to which impurities are generated in the engine and by the maintenance intervals prescribed by the engine manufacturer. Filter maintenance and oil changes should be performed at the same time.

Full-flow filters protect the entire oil circuit because particles which cause wear are trapped during their first pass through the circuit. Fine-mesh paper filters have proven effective as filtration elements in full-flow circuits. Their filtration is significantly finer than that furnished by strainers or disk filters. Full-flow filters must incorporate a bypass valve to prevent interruptions in oil supply should the filter get clogged. They should always be installed in the oil circuit downstream from the pressure-relief valve. Full-flow filters usually incorporate replaceable elements.

Bypass filters remove only about 5...10 % of the oil from the engine's lubricating system for subsequent return to the oil pan after filtering. Most bypass filters are of the fiber-filling type (deep-bed filter).

Such bypass filters are recommended for use only in conjunction with full-flow filters. The bypass filter can remove extremely fine particles (primarily soot) not previously extracted by the full-flow filter, reducing the concentration of micro-contaminants in the oil.

Force-feed lubrication system
1 Pressure relief valve 2 Oil filter, 3 Gear pump, 4 From main bearing to connecting-rod bearing,
5 Suction strainer, 6 Main oil-pressure line to crankshaft bearings, 7 Return flow from timing-gear
case to crankcase, 8 To camshaft bearings.

Empirical values and data for calculation

Comparisons

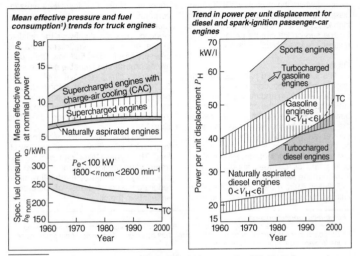

Mean effective pressure and fuel consumption[1] trends for truck engines

Trend in power per unit displacement for diesel and spark-ignition passenger-car engines

[1] See P.337 for on-the-vehicle measures influencing fuel consumption. TC = Turbo Compound.

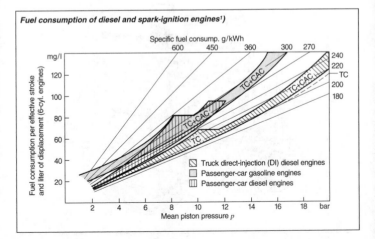

Fuel consumption of diesel and spark-ignition engines[1]

Comparative data

Engine type		Engine speed min⁻¹	Compression ratio	Mean pressure bar	Power per liter kW/l	Weight-to-power ratio kg/kW	Fuel consumption g/kWh	Torque increase %
SI engine for Motorcycles	2-stroke	4500...12000	7...9	5...12	40...100	5...0.5	600...350	5...10
	4-stroke	5000...10000	8...11	7...10	30...70	4...0.5	350...270	5...25
Pass. cars	NA[1]	4500...7500	8...12	8...11	35...65	3...1	350...250	15...25
	SC[2]	5000...7000	7...9	11...15	50...100	3...1	380...280	10...30
Trucks		2500...5000	7...9	8...10	20...30	6...3	380...270	15...25
Diesel engine for Pass. cars	NA[1]	3500...5000	20...24	7...9	20...35	5...3	320...240	10...15
	SC[2]	3500...4500	20...24	9...12	30...45	4...2	290...240	15...25
Trucks	NA[1]	2000...4000	16...18	7...10	10...20	9...4	240...210	10...15
	SC[2]	2000...3200	15...17	10...13	15...25	8...3	230...205	15...30
	CAC[3]	1800...2600	14...16	13...18	25...40	5...2,5	225...195	20...40
Special types Rotary engine		6000...8000	7...9	8...1	35...45	1.5...1	380...300	5...15
Stirling engine		2000...4500	4...6	–	–	10...7	300...240	20...40
Gas turbine		8000...70000	4...6	–	–	3...1	1000...300	50...100

[1] Naturally aspirated engine, [2] with supercharging, [3] with charge air cooling/intercooling.

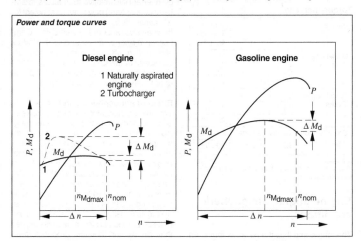

Power and torque curves

Diesel engine
1 Naturally aspirated engine
2 Turbocharger

Gasoline engine

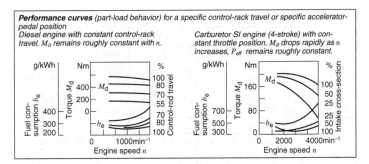

Performance curves (part-load behavior) for a specific control-rack travel or specific accelerator-pedal position
Diesel engine with constant control-rack travel. M_d remains roughly constant with n.
Carburetor SI engine (4-stroke) with constant throttle position. M_d drops rapidly as n increases, P_{eff} remains roughly constant.

Torque position

The position on the engine-speed curve (relative to min⁻¹ for max. output) at which maximum torque is developed, specified in % ($n_{Mdmax}/n_{nenn} \cdot 100$).

Useful speed range
(minimum full-load speed/nominal speed)

Engine type		Useful speed range Δn_N	Torque position %
Diesel engine for	pass. cars	3.5...5	15...40
	trucks	1.8...3.2	10...60
Spark-ignition engine		4...7	25...35

Torque increase

Engine type		Torque increase M_d in %
Diesel engine Pass. cars	Nat. asp. engine	15...20
	SC[1]	20...30
	SC[1] + CAC[2]	25...35
Diesel engine Trucks	Nat. asp. engine	10...15
	SC[1]	15...30
	SC[1] + CAC[2]	25...40
Spark-ignition engine	Nat. asp. engine	25...30
	SC[1] + CAC[2]	30...35

[1] with supercharging, [2] with charge-air cooling/intercooling.

Engine output, atmospheric conditions

The torque and thus the power output of an internal-combustion engine are essentially determined by the calorific content of the cylinder charge. The amount of air (or, more precisely, of oxygen) in the cylinder charge provides a direct index of calorific content. The change which the engine will display at full power can be calculated as a function of variations in the condition of the ambient air (temperature, barometric pressure, humidity), provided that engine speed, air/fuel (A/F) ratio, volumetric efficiency, combustion efficiency, and total engine power loss remain constant. The A/F mixture responds to lower atmospheric density by becoming richer. The volumetric efficiency (pressure in cylinder at BDC relative to pressure in ambient atmosphere) only remains constant for all atmospheric conditions at maximum throttle-valve aperture (full-throttle). Combustion efficiency drops in cold thin air as vaporization rate, turbulence, and combustion speed all fall. Engine power loss (friction losses + gas-exchange work + boost power drain) reduces the indicated power.

Effect of atmospheric conditions

The quantity of air which an engine draws in, or is inputted to the engine by supercharging, depends upon the ambient atmosphere's density; colder, heavier, denser air increases engine output. Rule of thumb: Engine power drops by approximately 1 % for each 100 m increase in altitude. Depending upon engine design, the cold intake air is normally heated to some degree while traversing the intake passages, thereby reducing its density and thus the engine's ultimate output. Humid air contains less oxygen than dry air and therefore produces lower engine power outputs. The decrease is generally modest to the point of insignificance. The warm humidity of air in tropical regions can result in a noticeable engine power loss.

Definitions of power

The <u>effective power</u> is the engine's power as measured at the crankshaft or ancillary mechanism (such as the transmission) at the specified min^{-1}. When measurements are made downstream from the transmission, the transmission losses must be factored into the equation. <u>Rated power</u> is the maximum effective power of the

engine at full throttle. <u>Net power</u> corresponds to effective power.

Conversion formulas are used to convert the results of dynamometer testing <u>to reflect standard conditions</u>, thereby negating the influences of such factors as time of day and year while simultaneously allowing the various manufacturers to provide mutually comparable data. The procedure converts atmospheric density – and thus the effective volume of air in the engine – to defined "standard conditions" for air mass.

The comparison data in the following table show the most important standards used in <u>power correction</u>.

Power correction standards (Comparison)

Standard (Date of publication)	EEC 80/1269 (4/81)	ISO 1585 (5/82)	JIS D 1001 (10/82)	SAE J 1349 (5/85)	DIN 70 020 (11/76)
Barometric pressure during testing (* vapor pressure subtracted)					
Dry p_{PT}* kPa	99	99	99	99	–
Absolute p_{PF} kPa	– –	–	–	–	101.3
Temperature during testing					
Absolute T_p K	298	298	298	298	293
Engines with spark ignition, naturally-aspirated and turbo/supercharged					
Correction factor α_a	$\alpha_a = A^{1.2} \cdot B^{0.6}$ $A = 99/p_{PT}$ $B = T_p/298$				$\alpha_a = A \cdot B^{0.5}$ $A = 101.3/p_{PF}$ $B = T/293$
Corrected power: $P_0 = \alpha_a \cdot P$ (kW) (P measured power)					
Diesel engines, naturally-aspirated and turbo/supercharged					
Atmospheric correction factor f_a	$f_a = A \cdot B^{0.7}$ ($A = 99/p_{PT}$; $B = T_p/293$) (naturally-aspirated and mechanically-supercharged engines).				as α_a for SI engines
	$f_a = A^{0.7} \cdot B^{1.5}$ ($A = 99/p_{PT}$; $B = T_p/293$) (turbocharged engines with/without charge-air cooling)				
Engine correction factor f_m	$40 \leq q/r \leq 65$: $f_m = 0.036 \cdot (q/r) - 1.14$ $q/r < 40$: $f_m = 0.3$ $q/r > 65$: $f_m = 1.2$				$f_m = 1$
$r = p_L/p_E$ Boost pressure response, with p_L absolute boost pressure, p_E absolute pressure before compressor, q spec. fuel consumption (SAE J 1349). 4-stroke engines: $q = 120,000 \, F/DN$, 2-stroke engines: $q = 60,000 \, F/DN$, with F Fuel flow (mg/s); D Effective stroke volume (l); N Engine speed (min^{-1}).					
Corrected power: $P_0 = P \cdot f_a^{fm}$ (kW) (P measured power).					
Prescribed accessories					
Fan	Yes, with electric/viscous-drive fan at max. slip				} Not defined
Emissions control system	Yes				}
Alternator	Yes, loaded with engine-current draw				Yes
Servo pumps	No				No
Air conditioner	No				No

Calculation

Quantity		Unit		Symbol		Unit
a_K	Piston acceleration	m/s²		V_c	Cylinder compression volume	dm³
B	Fuel consumption	kg/h; dm³/h		V_E	Injected quantity per pump stroke	mm³
b_e	Spec. fuel consumption	g/kWh		V_f	Charge volume of a cylinder (2-stroke)	dm³
D	Cylinder diameter $2 \cdot r$	mm				
d_v	Valve diameter	mm		V_F	Charge volume of a 2-stroke engine	dm³
F	Force	N				
F_G	Gas force in the cylinder	N		V_h	Displacement of a cylinder	dm³
F_N	Piston side thrust	N		V_H	Displacement of the engine	dm³
F_o	Oscillating inertial force	N		v	Velocity	m/s
F_r	Rotating inertial force	N		v_d	Mean velocity of the injected spray	m/s
F_s	Rod force	N				
F_T	Tangential force	N		v_g	Gas velocity	m/s
M	Torque	N · m		v_m	Mean piston velocity	m/s
M_o	Oscillating moments	N · m		v_{max}	Max. piston velocity	m/s
M_r	Rotating moments	N · m		z	Number of cylinders	–
M_d	Engine torque	N · m				
m_p	Weight-to-power ratio	kg/kW		α_d	Injection period (in °crankshaft at injection pump)	°
n	Engine speed	min⁻¹				
n_p	Injection-pump speed	min⁻¹		β	Pivot angle of connecting rod	°
P	Power	kW		ε	Compression ratio	–
P_{eff}	Net horsepower[1]	kW		η	Efficiency	–
P_H	Power output per liter	kW/dm³		η_e	Net efficiency	–
p	Pressure	bar		η_{th}	Thermal efficiency	–
p_c	Final compression pressure	bar		v, n	Polytropic exponent of real gases	–
p_e	Mean effective pressure (mean pressure, mean working pressure)	bar				
				ϱ	Density	kg/m³
				φ, α	Crank angle (φ_o = top dead center)	°
p_L	Boost pressure	bar				
p_{max}	Peak cylinder pressure	bar		ω	Angular velocity	rad/s
r	Crank radius	mm		λ	= r/l Stroke/connecting-rod ratio	–
s_d	Injection cross section of the nozzle	mm²		λ	Air/fuel (A/F) ratio	–
				$\varkappa$	= c_p/c_v Adiabatic exponent of ideal gases	–
S, s	Stroke, general	mm				
s	Piston stroke	mm				
s_f	Suction stroke of a cylinder (2-stroke)	mm				

Superscripts and subscripts

0, 1, 2, 3, 4, 5	Cycle values/main values
o	Oscillating
r	Rotating
1st, 2nd	1st, 2nd order
A	Constant
', ''	Subdivision of main values, derivations

Symbol	Quantity	Unit
s_F	Suction stroke, 2-stroke engine	mm
S_k	Piston clearance from TDC	mm
S_s	Slot height, 2-stroke engine	mm
T	Temperature	°C, K
T_c	Final compression temperature	K
T_L	Boost-air temperature	K
T_{max}	Peak temperature in combustion chamber	K
t	Time	s
V	Volume	m³

Conversion of units
(See PP. 19...28)

1 g/hp · h	= 1.36 g/kW · h
1 g/kW · h	= 0.735 g/hp · h
1 kp · m	= 9.81 N · m ≈ 10 N · m
1 N · m	= 0.102 kp · m ≈ 0.1 kp · m
1 hp	= 0.735 kW
1 kW	= 1.36 hp
1 at	= 0.981 bar ≈ 1 bar
1 bar	= 1.02 at ≈ 1 at

---

[1] Effective power P_{eff} is the effective horsepower delivered by the internal-combustion engine, with it driving the auxiliary equipment necessary for operation (e.g., ignition equipment, fuel-injection pump, scavenging-air and cooling-air fan, water pump and fan, supercharger) (DIN 1940). This power is called net engine power in DIN 70 020 (see P. 415).

Calculation equations

Mathematical relationship between quantities	Numerical relationship between quantities
Swept volume (displacement) Swept volume of a cylinder $$V_h = \frac{\pi \cdot d^2 \cdot s}{4}; \quad V_f = \frac{\pi \cdot d^2 \cdot s_F}{4} \text{ (2-stroke)}$$	$V_H = 0.785 \cdot 10^{-6} d^2 \cdot s$ V_h in dm³, d in mm, s in mm
Swept volume of engine $V_H = V_h \cdot z; \ V_F = V_f \cdot z$ (2-stroke)	$V_H = 0.785 \cdot 10^{-6} d^2 \cdot s \cdot z$ V_h in dm³, d in mm, s in mm
Compression Compression ratio $$\varepsilon = \frac{V_h + V_c}{V_c}$$ (see P. 420 for diagram) Final compression pressure $p_c = p_0 \cdot \varepsilon^v$ Final compression temperature $T_c = T_0 \cdot \varepsilon^{v-1}$	
Piston movement (see P. 421 for diagram) Piston clearance from top dead center $$S_k = r\left[1 + \frac{l}{r} - \cos\varphi - \sqrt{\left(\frac{l}{r}\right)^2 - \sin^2\varphi}\right]$$ Crankshaft angle $\varphi = 2 \cdot \pi \cdot n \cdot t$ (φ in rad) Piston velocity (approximation) $$v \approx 2 \cdot \pi \cdot n \cdot r\left(\sin\varphi + \frac{r}{2l}\sin 2\varphi\right)$$ Mean piston velocity $v_m = 2 \cdot n \cdot s$ Maximum piston velocity (approximate, if connecting rod is on a tangent with the big-end trajectory; $a_k = 0$)	**4-stroke engine** **2-stroke engine** $\varphi = 6 \cdot n \cdot t$ φ in °, n in min⁻¹, t in s $$v \approx \frac{n \cdot s}{19\,100}\left(\sin\varphi + \frac{r}{2l}\sin 2\varphi\right)$$ v in m/s, n in min⁻¹, l, r and s in mm $$v_m = \frac{n \cdot s}{30\,000} \text{ (see P. 422 for diagram)}$$ v_m in m/s, n in min⁻¹, s in mm

l/r	3.5	4	4.5
v_{max}	$1.63 \cdot v_m$	$1.62 \cdot v_m$	$1.61 \cdot v_m$

(see P. 422 for diagram)

Piston acceleration (approximation) $$\alpha_k \approx 2 \cdot \pi^2 \cdot n^2 \cdot s\left(\cos\varphi + \frac{r}{l}\cos 2\varphi\right)$$	$$a_k \approx \frac{n^2 \cdot s}{182\,400}\left(\cos\varphi + \frac{r}{l}\cos 2\varphi\right)$$ a_k in m/s², n in min⁻¹, l, r and s in mm

[1] See P. 34 for definitions of "mathematical relationships between quantities" and "numerical relationships between quantities".

Calculation equations (continued)

Mathematical relationship between quantities	Numerical relationship between quantities
Gas velocity Mean gas velocity in the valve section $$v_g = \frac{d^2}{d_v^2} \cdot v_m$$	$$v_g = \frac{d^2}{d_v^2} \cdot \frac{n \cdot s}{30\,000}$$ v_g in m/s, d, d_v, and s in mm, n in min^{-1}

The highest volumetric efficiency values are achieved at mean gas velocities of 90 ... 110 m/s (empirical values).

Fuel supply Injected quantity per injection pump stroke $$V_E = \frac{P_{eff} \cdot b_e}{\varrho \cdot n_p \cdot z}$$	$$V_E = \frac{1000 \cdot P_{eff} \cdot b_e}{60 \cdot \varrho \cdot n_p \cdot z}$$ V_E in mm^3, P_{eff} in kW, b_e in g/kW · h (or also P_{eff} in hp, b_e in g/hp · h), n_p in min^{-1}, ϱ in kg/dm^3 (for fuels $\varrho \approx 0.85$ kg/dm^3)
Mean velocity of injection spray $$v_d = \frac{2 \cdot \pi \cdot n_p \cdot V_E}{S_d \cdot \alpha_d} \quad (\alpha_d \text{ in rad})$$	$$v_d = \frac{6\, n_p \cdot V_E}{1000 \cdot S_d \cdot \alpha_d}$$ $v_d =$ in m/s, n_p in min^{-1}, V_E in mm^3, S_d in mm^2, α_d in °
Engine power $P = M \cdot \omega = 2 \cdot \pi \cdot M \cdot n$ $P_{eff} = V_H \cdot p_e \cdot n/K$ $K = 1$ for 2-stroke engine $K = 2$ for 4-stroke engine	$P = M \cdot n/9549$ P in kW, M in N · m (= W · s), $$P_{eff} = \frac{V_H \cdot p_e \cdot n}{K \cdot 600} = \frac{M_d \cdot n}{9549}$$ P_{eff} in kW, p_e in bar, n in min^{-1}. M_d in N · m
Power per unit displacement (power output per liter) $$P_H = \frac{P_{eff}}{V_H}$$	$P = M \cdot n/716.2$ P in hp, M in kp · m, n in min^{-1}
Weight-to-power ratio $$m_p = \frac{m}{P_{eff}}$$	

Calculation equations (continued)

Mathematical relationship between quantities	Numerical relationship between quantities

Mean piston pressure (mean pressure, mean working pressure)

4-stroke engine	2-stroke engine	4-stroke engine	2-stroke engine
$p = \dfrac{2 \cdot P}{V_H \cdot n}$	$p = \dfrac{P}{V_H \cdot n}$	$p = 1200 \dfrac{P}{V_H \cdot n}$	$p = 600 \dfrac{P}{V_H \cdot n}$

p in bar, P in kW, V_H in dm³, n in min⁻¹

$$p = 833 \frac{P}{V_H \cdot n} \qquad p = 441 \frac{P}{V_H \cdot n}$$

p in bar, P in hp, V_H in dm³, n in min⁻¹

$p = \dfrac{4 \cdot \pi \cdot M}{V_H}$	$p = \dfrac{2 \cdot \pi \cdot M}{V_H}$	$p = 0.1257 \dfrac{M}{V_H}$	$p = 0.0628 \dfrac{M}{V_H}$

p in bar, M in N · m, V_H in dm³

Engine torque

$M_d = \dfrac{V_H \cdot p_e}{4\pi}$	$M_d = \dfrac{V_H \cdot p_e}{2\pi}$	$M_d = \dfrac{V_H \cdot p_e}{0.12566} \qquad M_d = \dfrac{V_H \cdot p_e}{0.06284}$

M_d in N · m, V_H in dm³, p_e in bar

$M_d = 9549 \cdot P_{eff}/n$

M_d in N · m, P_{eff} in kW, n in min⁻¹

Fuel consumption[1]

B = Measured values in kg/h

$b_e = B/P_{eff}$

$b_e = 1/(H_u \cdot \eta_e)$

B in dm³/h or kg/h

V_B = Measured volume on test dynamometer

t_B = Elapsed time for measured volume consumption

$$b_e = \frac{V_b \cdot \varrho_B \cdot 3600}{t_B \cdot P_{eff}}$$

ϱ_B = Fuel density in g/cm³, t_B in s, V_B in cm³, P_{eff} in kW.

Efficiency

$\eta_{th} = 1 - \varepsilon^{1-\nu}$

$\eta_e = P_{eff}/(B \cdot H_u)$

$\eta_e = 86/b_e$

where H_u = specific calorific value 42,000 kJ/kg

b_e in g/(kW · h)

---

[1] See P. 337 for the effect of vehicle design measures on fuel consumption.

Displacement and compression area   *See P. 417 for diagram and equation.*

The diagram below applies to the displacement V_h and compression space V_c of the individual cylinder, and to the total displacement V_H and total compression space V_C.

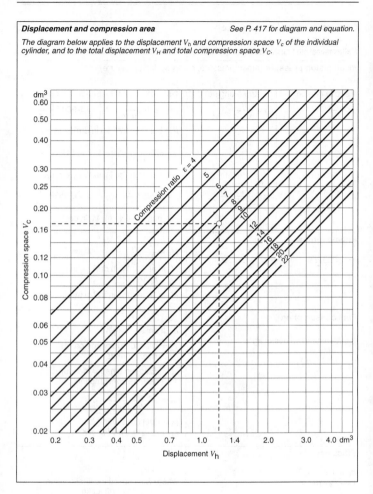

Example:

An engine with a displacement of 1.2 dm³ and a compression ratio $\varepsilon = 8$ has a compression area of 0.17 dm³.

Piston clearance from top dead center *See P. 417 for equation.*

Conversion of degrees crank angle to mm piston travel.

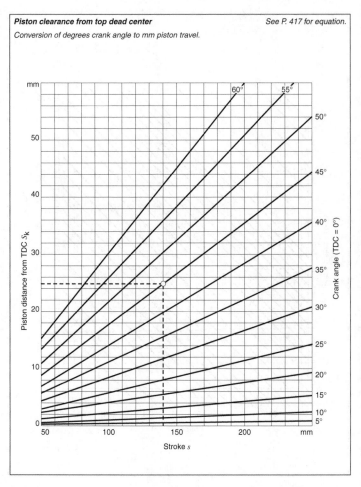

Example:

The piston clearance from top dead center is 25 mm for a stroke of 140 mm at 45° crankshaft.

The diagram is based on a crank ratio $l/r = 4$ (l connecting-rod length, r one half of the stroke length). However, it also applies with very good approximation (error less than 2%) for all ratios l/r between 3.5 and 4.5.

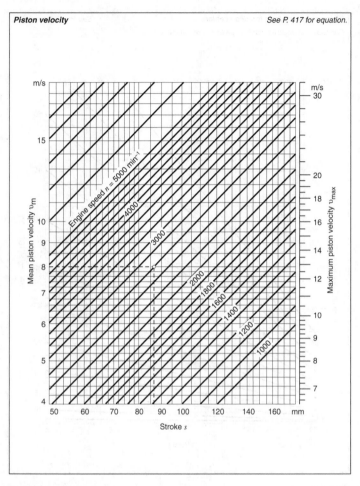

Piston velocity See P. 417 for equation.

Example:
Mean piston velocity v_m = 8 m/s and maximum piston velocity v_{max} = 13 m/s for stroke s = 86 mm and at an engine speed of n = 2800 min^{-1}.

The diagram is based on v_{max} = 1.62 v_m (see P. 417).

Charge density increase in the cylinder with turbo/supercharging

Increase in density on supercharging as a function of the pressure ratio in the compressor, the compressor efficiency and the intercooling rate for charge-air cooling (CAC).

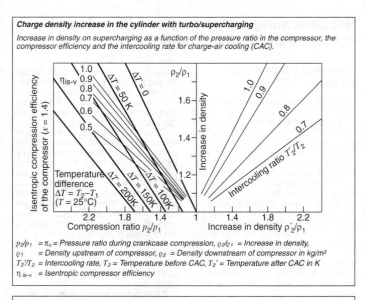

$p_2/p_1 = \pi_c$ = Pressure ratio during crankcase compression, ϱ_2/ϱ_1 = Increase in density,
ϱ_1 = Density upstream of compressor, ϱ_2 = Density downstream of compressor in kg/m³
T_2'/T_2 = Intercooling rate, T_2 = Temperature before CAC, T_2' = Temperature after CAC in K
η_{is-v} = Isentropic compressor efficiency

Final compression pressure and temperature

Final compression temperature as a function of the compression ratio and the intake temperature.

Final compression pressure as a function of the compression ratio and boost pressure.

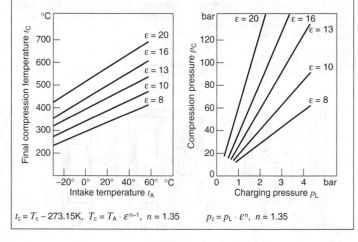

$t_c = T_c - 273.15\,\text{K}, \quad T_c = T_A \cdot \varepsilon^{n-1}, \quad n = 1.35$

$p_c = p_L \cdot \varepsilon^n, \quad n = 1.35$

Reciprocating-piston engine with external combustion (Stirling engine)

Operating concept and efficiency

Cycle sequence: In phase I, the power piston (bottom), or working piston, is at its lowest position and the displacer (top piston) is in its highest; all of the working gas is expanded in the "cold" area between the two pistons. During the transition from phase I to phase II, the power piston compresses the working medium in the cold chamber. The displacer remains in its uppermost position. During the transition from phase II to phase III, the displacer moves down to push the compressed working medium through the heat exchanger and into the regenerator (where it absorbs the stored heat) and from there into the heater (where it is heated to maximum working temperature). Because the power piston remains in its lowermost position, the volume does not change.

After being heated the gas enters the "hot" area above the displacer. During the transition from phase III to phase IV the hot gas expands; the power piston and displacer are pushed into their lowermost positions and power is produced. The cycle is completed with the transition from phase IV back to phase I, where the displacer's upward motion again propels the gas through the heater and into the regenerator, radiating substantial heat in the process. The residual heat is extracted at the heat exchanger before the gas reenters the cold area.

Thus the theoretical cycle largely corresponds to isothermal compression (the working gas is cooled back down to its initial temperature in the heat exchanger after adiabatic compression), isochoric heat addition via the regenerator and heater, quasi-isothermal expansion (the working gas is reheated to its initial condition in the heater after adiabatic expansion) and isochoric heat dissipation via the regenerator and heat exchanger.

The ideal cycle shown in the p-V and T-S diagrams could only be achieved if – as described – the movement of the power and displacer systems were discontinuous.

If both pistons are connected to a shaft, i.e., via a rhombic drive, they carry out phase-shifted sinusoidal movements leading to a rounded work diagram with the same cycle efficiency – similar to the efficiency of the Carnot cycle – but with sacrifices in power and net efficiency.

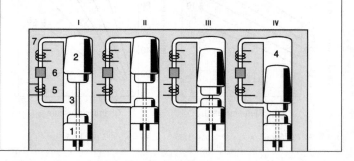

The Stirling engine cycle
Four states of discontinuous power-piston and displacer movement. 1 Power piston, 2 Displacer, 3 Cold space, 4 Hot space, 5 Heat exchanger, 6 Regenerator, 7 Heater.

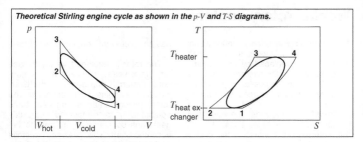

Theoretical Stirling engine cycle as shown in the p-V and T-S diagrams.

Design and operating characteristics

Modern Stirling engines are double-acting engines with (for instance) 4 cylinders operating with a defined phase shift. Each cylinder has only one piston whose top surface acts as a power piston, and whose bottom surface acts as a displacer for the following cylinder. The heat exchanger, regenerator and heater are located between the cylinders.

In order to maintain an acceptable ratio between power and displacement, the engines run at high pressures of 50 to 200 bar, variable for purposes of load control. Gases with low flow losses and high specific heats (usually hydrogen) must be used as working fluids. Because the heat exchanger must transfer all of the heat which is to be extracted from the process to the outside air, Stirling engines require considerably larger heat exchangers than IC-engines.

Advantages of the Stirling engine: very low concentrations of all the pollutants which are subject to legislation (HC, CO and NO_x); quiet operation without combustion noise; burns a wide variety of different fuels (multifuel capability); fuel consumption (in program map) roughly equivalent to that of a direct-injection diesel engine at comparable speeds.

Disadvantages: high manufacturing costs due to complicated design; very high operating pressures with only moderate power output relative to the unit's volume and weight; expensive load-control system required; large cooling surface and/or ventilation power required.

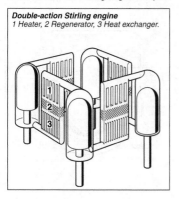

Double-action Stirling engine
1 Heater, 2 Regenerator, 3 Heat exchanger.

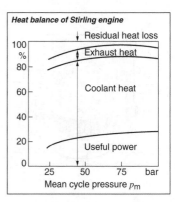

Heat balance of Stirling engine

Wankel rotary engine

The rotary engine is an unconventional piston powerplant in which the crankshaft mechanism is replaced by an eccentric drive unit operated by a rotary piston. The piston forms the combustion chambers as it proceeds through its trochoidal rotation pattern.

Viewed from the side, the rotor is a triangle with convex sides. Located within the water-cooled housing is the oval – or more precisely: hourglass shaped – piston chamber (epitrochoid). As the rotor turns, its three apices follow the wall of the housing to form three mutually-sealed, variable displacement chambers (A, B and C) spaced at 120° intervals. Each of these chambers hosts a complete four-stroke combustion cycle during each full rotation of the rotor, i.e. after one full rotation of the triangular rotor, the engine has completed the four-stroke cycle three times and the eccentric shaft has completed an equal number of rotations.

The rotor is equipped with both face and apex seals. It incorporates a concentric internal ring gear and the bearings for the engine shaft's eccentric. The rotary piston's internal ring gear runs against a housing-mounted gear: this gear runs concentrically relative to the eccentric shaft. This gear set transmits no force. Instead, it maintains the rotary piston in the trochoidal orbit pattern required to synchronize piston and eccentric shaft.

The teeth of the gear set act in accordance with a 3:2 conversion ratio. The rotor turns at two thirds of the shaft's angular velocity and in the opposite direction. This arrangement produces a relative rotor velocity that is only one third of the shaft's angular velocity relative to the housing.

Design and operating concept of the Wankel rotary engine
1 Rotor, 2 Internal gearing in rotor, 3 Spark plug, 4 Fixed pinion, 5 Running surface of eccentric.
a) Cell A takes in air-fuel mixture, cell B compresses the mixture, and the combustion gases C are exhausted from cell C. (Depressions in the rotor flanks allow gas to pass by the trochoidal restriction.)
b) Cell A is filled with fresh gas, the combustion gases expand in cell B, thereby turning the eccentric shaft via the rotor, combustion gases continue to be exhausted from cell C. The next phase of combustion is again that shown in figure a), whereby cell C has taken the place of cell A. Thus the rotor, by turning through 120° of one rotation, has carried out the complete four-stroke process at its three flanks. During this process, the eccentric shaft has made one complete rotation.

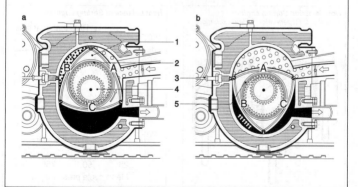

Gas exchange is regulated by the piston itself as it moves past slots in the housing. An alternative to this arrangement – with peripheral intake ports located along the apices' trochoidal path – is represented by intake ports in the side of the block (side ports).

Considerably higher gas velocities and engine speeds are made possible by the lack of restrictive gas passages and the absence of reciprocating masses. Every rotary engine can be completely balanced mechanically. The only remaining irregularity is the uneven torque flow, a characteristic of all internal-combustion engines. However, the torsional force curve of a single-rotor engine is considerably smoother than that of a conventional single-cylinder engine, due to the fact that the power strokes occur over 270° of the eccentric shaft's rotation. Power-flow consistency and operating smoothness can both be enhanced by joining several rotary pistons on a single shaft. In this context, a three-rotor Wankel corresponds to an eight-cylinder, reciprocating-piston engine. The torque curve can be made to assume the characteristics of a throttled engine or a racing engine by changing the timing (location) and shape of the intake ports.

Advantages of the rotary engine: complete balancing of masses; favorable torsional force curve; compact design; no valve-gear assembly; excellent tractability.

Disadvantages: less than optimal combustion chamber shape with long flame paths, high HC emissions, increased fuel and oil consumption, higher manufacturing costs, diesel operation not possible, high location of output shaft.

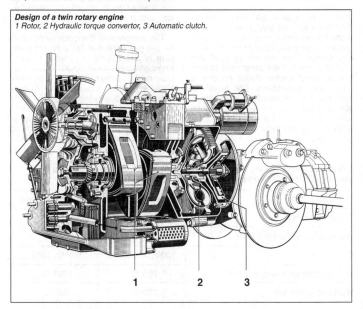

Design of a twin rotary engine
1 Rotor, 2 Hydraulic torque convertor, 3 Automatic clutch.

1   2   3

Gas turbine

In the gas turbine, the individual changes of state during the cycle take place in spatially separate components (compressors, burners and turbines), which communicate with one another via flow-conducting components (diffusers, spirals and the like). These changes of state therefore occur continuously.

Operating concept, comparative cycle and efficiency

In automotive gas turbines, the intake air is drawn in continuously through a filter and noise attenuator prior to condensation in a radial compressor and subsequent warming in a heat exchanger. The heat exchanger in current automotive units is usually designed as a rotating regenerator.

The compressed and preheated air then flows into the burner where it is directly heated through injection and combustion of gaseous, liquid or emulsified fuels. Energy from the compressed and heated gases is then transmitted to one, two or three turbine stages on one to three shaft assemblies. The radial- or axial-flow turbines initially drive compressors and auxiliary assemblies, which then relay the remaining power to the driveshaft via a power turbine, reduction gear and transmission.

The turbine usually incorporates adjustable guide vanes (AGV turbine) designed to reduce fuel consumption at idle and in part-load operation whilst simultaneously enhancing tractability during acceleration. In single-shaft machines, this necessitates an adjustment mechanism at the transmission.

After partial cooling in the expansion phase the gases flow through the gas section of the heat exchanger, where most of their residual heat is discharged into the air. The gases themselves are then expelled through the exhaust passage, whereby they can also supply heat for the vehicle's heating system.

The thermal efficiency and with it the fuel consumption of the gas turbine are largely determined by the maximum possible operating temperature (burner exit temperature). The temperatures that can be achieved using highly heat-resistant cobalt- or nickel-based alloys do not allow fuel consumption that is comparable with present-day piston engines. It will need the changeover to ceramic materials before similar or even better fuel efficiency can be achieved.

The comparative thermodynamic cycle for the gas turbine is the constant-pressure or Joule cycle. It consists of isentropic compression (process $1 \rightarrow 2$), isobaric heat addition (process $2 \rightarrow 3$), isentropic expansion (process $3 \rightarrow 4$) and isobaric heat dissipation (process $4 \rightarrow 1$). High levels of thermal efficiency are only available when the temperature increase from T_2 to $T_{2'}$, supplied by the heat exchanger, is coupled with a thermal discharge ($4 \rightarrow 4'$). If heat is completely

Characteristic operating temperatures (orders of magnitude) at various positions in metallic and ceramic automotive gas turbines at full load

Measuring point	Metal turbine	Ceramic turbine
Compressor exit	230 °C	250 °C
Heat-exchanger exit (air side)	700 °C	950 °C
Burner exit	1000 °C...1100 °C	1250 °C...1350 °C
Heat-exchanger inlet (gas side)	750 °C	1000 °C
Heat-exchanger exit	270 °C	300 °C

Thermodynamic comparative cycle as shown in the p-V and T-S diagrams.

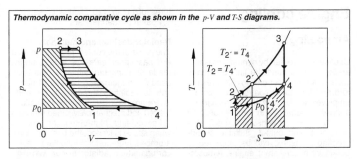

exchanged, the quantity of heat to be added per unit of gas is reduced to

$$q_{add} = c_p \cdot (T_3 - T_{2'}) = c_p \cdot (T_3 - T_4)$$

and the quantity of heat to be removed is

$$q_{rem} = c_p \cdot (T_{4'} - T_1) = c_p \cdot (T_2 - T_1).$$

The maximum thermal efficiency for the gas turbine with heat exchanger is:

$$\eta_{th} = 1 - Q_{rem}/Q_{add} = 1 - (T_2 - T_1)/(T_3 - T_4)$$

Where $p_2/p_1 = (T_2/T_1)^{\frac{\chi}{\chi-1}} = (T_3/T_4)^{\frac{\chi}{\chi-1}}$ and $T_4 = T_3 \cdot (T_1/T_2)$ it follows that

$$\eta_{th} = 1 - (T_2/T_3).$$

Current gas-turbine powerplants achieve thermal efficiencies of up to 35%.

<u>Advantages of the gas turbine</u>: clean exhaust without supplementary emissions-control devices; extremely smooth running; multifuel capability; good static torque curve; extended maintenance intervals.

<u>Disadvantages</u>: manufacturing costs still high, poor transitional response, higher fuel consumption, less suitable for low-power applications.

Gas turbine
1 Filter and silencer, 2 Radial-flow compressor, 3 Burner, 4 Heat exchanger, 5 Exhaust port, 6 Reduction gearset, 7 Power turbine, 8 Adjustable guide vanes, 9 Compressor-turbine, 10 Starter, 11 Auxiliary equipment drive, 12 Lubricating-oil pump.

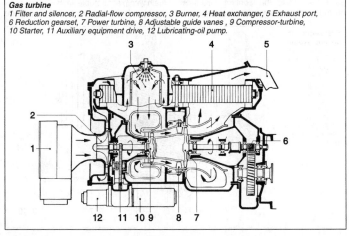

Engine cooling

Air cooling

Cooling air is routed by dynamic pressure and/or a fan around the finned external walls of the cylinder casing. Flow restrictors and fan-speed control, etc., can be employed to regulate the current in response to variations in temperature and load factor. Power consumption is 3...4% of total engine output. Suitable sound-proofing measures can be employed to obtain both consistent engine temperatures and noise levels comparable to those of liquid-cooled engines. Heat absorbed by the engine's oil is dispersed by an air-cooled oil cooler mounted at a suitable position in the air stream.

Water cooling

Water cooling has become the standard in both passenger cars and heavy-duty vehicles.

Pure water is no longer employed as coolant; today's coolants are a mixture of water (drinking quality), antifreeze (generally ethylene glycol), and various corrosion inhibitors selected for the specific application. An antifreeze concentration of 30...50% raises the coolant mixture's boiling point to allow operating temperatures of up to 120°C at a pressure of 1.4 bar in passenger cars.

Radiator designs and materials

The cores of the coolant radiators in modern passenger cars are almost always made of aluminum, which is also being used in an increasing number of heavy-vehicle radiators throughout the world. There are two basic assembly variations: brazed and mechanically joined radiators.

For cooling high-output engines, or when space is limited, the best solution is a brazed, high-performance flat-tube and corrugated-fin radiator layout with minimal aerodynamic resistance on the air-intake side.

The less expensive, mechanically-assembled finned-tube system is generally employed for applications with less powerful engines or when more space is available.

When the radiator is assembled mechanically, the cooling grid is formed by mounting stamped fins around round, oval and flat-oval tubes. The fins are corrugated and/or slotted at right angles to the direction of air flow.

Turbulators are applied in all types of radiators to enhance the thermal transfer on the coolant side (i.e. in the pipes) provided the attendant pressure losses remain within acceptable limits. On the cooling-air side, corrugations and gills provide

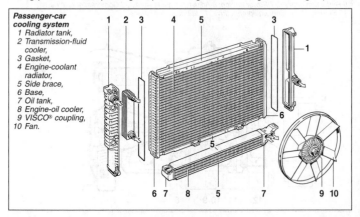

Passenger-car cooling system
1 Radiator tank,
2 Transmission-fluid cooler,
3 Gasket,
4 Engine-coolant radiator,
5 Side brace,
6 Base,
7 Oil tank,
8 Engine-oil cooler,
9 VISCO® coupling,
10 Fan.

improved thermal transfer in the fins.

The radiator tank ensures that the coolant is distributed throughout the block. These tanks are made of fiberglass-reinforced polyamides, and are injection molded with all connections and mountings in a single unit. They are flange-mounted to the radiator core.

Radiator design

Regardless of operating and environmental conditions, the radiator must continue to provide reliable thermal transfer by discharging engine heat into the surrounding air. Different methods can be applied to determine radiator capacity. The cooling capacity required for a specific radiator can be determined empirically, using comparisons with reference units of the same design, or calculations based on correlation equations for thermal transfer and flow-pressure loss can be employed.

Aside from reliable cooling, other priorities in radiator design include minimizing the power required to operate the fan and maintaining low aerodynamic drag. The mass of the cooling air stream is a decisive factor, as there is an inverse relationship between fan and radiator capacities: A more powerful fan with higher energy consumption allows a smaller radiator, and vice versa. In addition, the temperature differential between the surrounding air and the coolant should be as large as possible, an objective that can only be achieved by maximizing coolant temperature, which in turn entails a corresponding increase in system pressure.

Regulation of coolant temperature

A motor vehicle's engine operates in a very wide range of climatic conditions and with major fluctuations in engine load factors. The temperature of the coolant – and with it that of the engine – must be regulated if they are to remain constant within a narrow range. An efficient way to compensate for varying conditions is to install a temperature-sensitive thermostat incorporating an expansion element to regulate temperature independent of pressure variations in the cooling system. The thermostat responds to drops in coolant temperature by activating a valve to increase the amount of coolant bypassing the radiator. This method provides consistent operating temperatures, good vehicle-heater performance and helps lower emissions while also reducing engine wear.

Further possibilities are permitted when a map thermostat is used. An electronically controlled thermostat differs from purely expansion-element-regulated thermostats in that it has a larger logic content. When the wax element is heated in the map thermostat, which can be controlled by the engine-management sys-

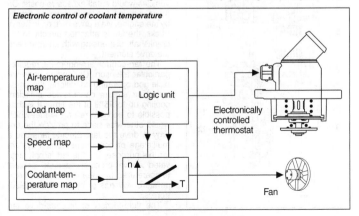

Electronic control of coolant temperature

Air-temperature map

Load map

Speed map

Coolant-temperature map

Logic unit

Electronically controlled thermostat

Fan

tem, an increased coolant temperature is simulated such that an optimum temperature level is set.

Coolant expansion tank

The expansion tank provides a reliable escape channel for pressurized gases, preventing cavitation of the kind that tends to occur on the suction side of the water pump. The expansion tank's air volume must be large enough to absorb the coolant's thermal expansion during rapid pressure buildup and prevent the coolant from boiling over.

Expansion tanks are injected-molded in plastic (generally polypropylene), although simple designs can also be inflated to shape. The expansion tank can form a single unit with the radiator tank, or the two can be joined in a flange or plug connection. It is also possible to install the expansion tank at a remote location.

The position and shape of the filler opening can be used to limit capacity, thus preventing overfilling. A sight glass or an electronic level sensor can be employed to monitor the level of the coolant, or the expansion tank can be manufactured in undyed, transparent plastic. However, colorless polypropylene is sensitive to ultraviolet rays; it is thus important that the expansion tank not be exposed to direct sunlight.

Cooling-air fan

Because motor vehicles also require substantial cooling capacity at low speeds, force-air ventilation is required for the radiator. Single-piece injection-molded plastic fans are generally employed in passenger cars; injection-molded fans with drive-power ratings extending up to 20 kW are likewise now used in commercial vehicles. Fans with more modest power ratings are mostly driven electrically by DC and EC motors (up to 600 W). Although blade design and arrangement can be selected to provide relatively quiet operation, the noise levels of such fans remain substantial due to their consistently high rotation speeds. Using electric motors for cooling in mid-size cars and larger vehicles would entail excessive costs. On these vehicles, the fan is powered directly by the engine, via a drive belt, or, in heavy trucks, the fan is attached directly to the crankshaft, dispensing with an intermediate drive element.

The fan-control arrangement requires particular attention. Depending upon vehicle and operating conditions, the unassisted air stream can provide sufficient cooling up to 95 % of the time. It is thus possible to economize on the fuel which would otherwise have to provide the energy to drive the fan. Electric fans use a multistage or continuous control system for this purpose, i.e. the fan is only activated above precisely defined coolant temperatures by means of electric temperature switches or by the engine electronics.

The fluid-friction or viscous-drive fan

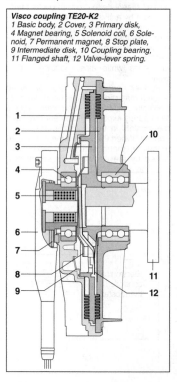

Visco coupling TE20-K2
1 Basic body, 2 Cover, 3 Primary disk,
4 Magnet bearing, 5 Solenoid coil, 6 Solenoid, 7 Permanent magnet, 8 Stop plate,
9 Intermediate disk, 10 Coupling bearing,
11 Flanged shaft, 12 Valve-lever spring.

(VISCO® coupling) is a mechanical-drive arrangement of proven effectiveness for application in both passenger cars and heavy vehicles. It basically consists of three sections: the engine-powered primary (or input) disk, the internally-activated secondary (or output) section, and the control mechanism.

Control can be effected by two methods:

– Firstly, the pure temperature-dependent, self-regulating coupling, which varies its speed infinitely through a bimetallic element, an operating pin and a valve lever by means of the amount of silicone oil located in the working chamber. The controlled variable is the temperature of the air leaving the radiator, and thus indirectly the temperature of the coolant.

– Secondly, the electrically activated coupling; this coupling is electronically controlled and electromagnetically actuated. Instead of just one controlled variable, a wide range of input variables is used for control purposes. These are usually the temperature limits of the various cooling media.

An intermediate disk divides the secondary section into a supply chamber and a working chamber through which the fluid circulates. There is no mechanical connection between the working chamber and the primary disk, which rotates freely within it. Torque is transmitted through the internal friction of the highly-viscous fluid and its adhesion to the inner surfaces. There is a degree of slippage between input and output.

Intercooling (charge-air cooling)

Cooling the boost air reduces both the thermal loads placed on the engine and the exhaust-gas temperatures, with attendant benefits in NO_x emissions and fuel consumption. It also inhibits preignition in spark-ignition engines. Basically speaking, both the engine coolant and the ambient air can be employed to cool the boost air. An air-to-coolant intercooler can be installed in virtually any location, a benefit associated with this water-cooled unit's modest dimensions. However, without an auxiliary cooling circuit, this type of system can only cool the charge air down almost to the temperature of the engine coolant.

For these reasons air-to-air intercoolers have become the configuration of choice in both passenger cars and heavy vehicles. These intercoolers can be mounted in front of, beside or above the engine radiator, or at a completely separate location. A separately-mounted intercooler can utilize either the unassisted vehicle air stream or its own fan. Extra effort is required to ensure adequate air supply when the intercooler is to be located to the front of the engine radiator. The advantage of this location lies in the fact that the fan ensures sufficient air flow across the intercooler at low vehicle speeds. A disadvantage is that the cooling air is itself heated in the process: The capacity of the engine radiator must therefore be increased accordingly.

The system of corrugated aluminum fins and tubes employed for the intercooler core is similar to that used in the radiator for the engine coolant. Wide tubes with internal fins provide superior performance and structural integrity in actual practice. Owing to the high level of thermal-transfer resistance on the charge-air side it is possible to hold the fin density on the cooling-air side to a minimum. The diffusion rate Φ is a particularly important intercooler property. It defines the relationship between boost-air cooling efficiency and the boost-air/cooling-air temperature differential:

$$\Phi = (t_{1E} - t_{1A}) / (t_{1E} - t_{2E})$$

The equation's elements are:
Φ Diffusion rate
t_{1E} Boost-air intake temperature,
t_{1A} Boost-air exit temperature,
t_{2E} Cooling-air intake temperature.
For passenger cars: $\Phi = 0.4...0.7$;
For commercial vehicles: $\Phi = 0.65...0.85$.
Whenever possible, the plenum chamber is injection-molded in fiberglass-reinforced polyamide as a single casting incorporating all connections and mounts. Plenum chambers which are subject to increased stresses, e.g. the charge-air inlet

system, are injection-molded from highly heat-resistant PPA or PPS. The plenum chamber is flange-mounted on the radiator core. Plenum chambers which feature undercut shapes or are intended for high-temperature applications are die-cast in aluminum, and welded to the core.

Oil and fuel cooling

Oil coolers are often needed in motor vehicles to cool both engine oil and gear oil. They are used when the heat losses from the engine or transmission can no longer be dissipated via the surface of the oil pan or the transmission with the result that the permitted oil temperatures are exceeded.

Fuel coolers are installed in modern diesel assemblies in order to cool down to a permissible level the excess diesel fuel from the return which heats up during the injection process.

Oil coolers generally take the form of aluminum oil-to-air or oil-to-coolant coolers, which can be installed either adjacent to the engine-coolant radiator in the cooling module or separately. Separately mounted units depend upon the unassisted air stream or an extra fan for cooling.

Oil-to-air coolers mostly consist of a system of flat tubes and corrugated fins with a high power density, or of a system of round tubes and flat fins. Turbulence inserts are soldered into flat-tube systems for strength reasons (high internal pressures).

Stainless-steel disk coolers and aluminum forked-pipe coolers are used to cool lubricating oil and engine coolant in passenger cars. However, aluminum stack designs have entered the market and proven successful over the last few years.

Disk coolers have their own casing and are mounted between the engine block and the oil filter. Forked-pipe coolers have no casing and must therefore be integrated in the oil-filter housing or in the oil pan.

Disk-stack oil coolers are made up of individual disks which are turned and arranged on top of each other. Turbulence inserts are inserted between the individual disks.

If only a modest cooling output is required (e.g. cooling of transmission fluid in automatic transmissions), aluminum flat-tube coolers can be used for passenger cars and commercial vehicles. They are installed in the outlet tank of the engine radiator.

An oil-to-air cooler is used to cool transmission fluid in more powerful heavy vehicles. The unit is mounted in front of the engine radiator in order to ensure good ventilation.

Lube oil in heavy vehicles is generally cooled by stainless-steel disk packs or aluminum disk-stack coolers which are accommodated in an extended coolant duct in the engine block. If conditions are favorable, neither a casing nor additional lines are required.

Cooling-module technology

Cooling modules are structural units which consist of various cooling and air-conditioning components for a passenger vehicle, and include a fan unit complete with drive, e.g. a hydrostatic or electric motor or a Visco® coupling.

In principle, module technology features a whole range of technical and economic advantages:
– optimum layout and alignment of the components to the fan's power output,
– thus improved efficiency in the passenger car, or smaller and more inexpensive components can be realized.

The optimum layout of the individual components and their coordination with each other are made possible by exact knowledge of the characteristic curves for the fan, the fan-drive and the heat-exchanger. This prevents e.g. the backflow of cooling air, which would reduce the effective cross-sectional area of the cooler.

Intelligent thermomanagement

Future developments are heading in the direction of operationally optimized regulation of different heat flows.

Thermomanagement involves operationally optimized cooling by means of the demand-compatible regulation and allocation of material and heat flows. Thus the cooling-air flow must be regulated by the fan and radiator-blind actuators in such a way that only the minimum throughput that is actually required for heat dissipation passes through the cooling-air system (demand-triggered regulation). This minimum throughput must then be made available by suitable routing elements to the heat exchangers which require cooling air. This philosophy is to be applied to all material flows such as coolant, cooling air, engine and gear oil, charge air and fuel. For this concept to be successfully implemented, it is essential that new actuators be used in the cooling-air system and fluid circuits such as e.g. controllable fans, pumps, valves, flaps, throttling and routing elements, and that they be incorporated in a microprocessor-controlled control system.

Exhaust-gas cooling

Because of the introduction of new, stricter exhaust-emission regulations for diesel engines, new technologies for reducing emissions have become the focus of engineers' attention.

One such technology is cooled exhaust-gas recirculation (EGR), which allows the reduction of emissions at the cost of only a minimum rise in fuel consumption.

The EGR system is accommodated in the high-pressure area of the engine. The exhaust gas to be recirculated is removed from the main flow between the cylinder and turbine, cooled by the engine coolant and then reintroduced to the fresh air after the intercooler. The EGR system consists of a valve which regulates the amount of exhaust gas to be recirculated, the exhaust lines, and the exhaust-gas-to-coolant heat exchanger.

Because of its location in the high-pressure area, the exhaust-gas heat exchanger is subject to extreme operating conditions. For instance, the exhaust-gas temperature can reach up to 400 °C for passenger cars and up to 700 °C for commercial vehicles, a fact which makes it imperative to use heat-resistant materials.

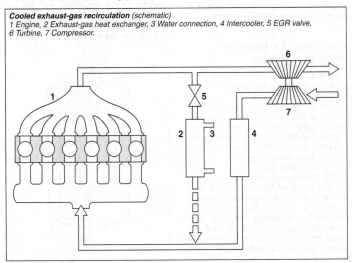

Cooled exhaust-gas recirculation (schematic)
1 Engine, 2 Exhaust-gas heat exchanger, 3 Water connection, 4 Intercooler, 5 EGR valve, 6 Turbine, 7 Compressor.

Fuel filters

Injection systems for spark-ignition and diesel engines are sensitive to the smallest impurities in the fuel. Damage can be caused above all by particulate erosion, abrasion and water corrosion. The service life of the fuel-injection system is only guaranteed by a specific minimum purity of the fuel supplied to the components exposed to wear.

The function of the fuel filter is to reduce particulate impurities. The necessary filter fineness is defined by the requirements of the fuel-injection system. As well as guaranteeing protection against wear, the fuel filter must feature an adequate particulate retention capacity. Filters with insufficient capacity to retain contaminants are liable to become clogged before the end of the official replacement interval. This will result in a reduction in fuel delivery and thus a drop in engine power. It is therefore essential to install a fuel filter that is custom-tailored to the relevant injection system. Using unsuitable filters has at best unpleasant and at worst very costly consequences (replacement of components up to and including the entire injection system).

Fuel filters for gasoline injection systems

Fuel filters for spark-ignition engines are located between the fuel tank and the fuel pump and/or on the pressure side downstream of the fuel pump. The preferred design is the in-line filter. In addition, easy-change filters screwed to a base, and housing filters with non-metal filter elements are used. Components such as the pressure control valve can be integrated in the filter head.

The filter element consists of radial or spiral vee-shaped filter media. Modern filter media for gasoline consist of mixtures of superfine pulp and polyester fibers. The filter media are always deep-bed filters where particulates are predominantly retained on the inside of the medium. The filtration efficiency in once-through operation for a particulate fraction of between 3 and 5 µm (ISO/TR 13353: 1994, Part 1) is 20...50% depending on the injection system. The structure of the mixed-fiber medium and the filter area determine the particulate retention capacity and thus the maintenance interval. The design of new fuel filters for spark-ignition engines is increasingly tending towards maintenance-free service-life concepts (e.g. filter in the in-tank fuel-pump unit).

Fuel filters for diesel injection systems

Because of the significantly higher injection pressures, considerably higher demands are placed on the wear-protection performance of modern diesel injection systems compared with gasoline injection systems. This ensures reliability, low fuel consumption and compliance with emission limits over the entire service life of the vehicle (up to 1,000,000 km for commercial vehicles). Depending on the fuel contamination and application, this requires a filtration efficiency in once-through operation for a particulate fraction of between 3 and 5 µm of 70...>95% (ISO/TR 13353: 1994, Part 1). Less se-

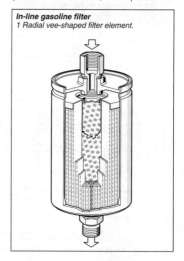

In-line gasoline filter
1 Radial vee-shaped filter element.

vere filtration stipulations apply to in-line injection pumps since they are connected to the engine lube-oil circuit.

As well as high levels of superfine particulate separation, the fuel filter is expected to feature a particulate-retention capability which will permit compliance with the maintenance intervals as stipulated by the vehicle manufacturer. This can only be achieved by using special filter mediums, e.g. in multilayer form with synthetic microfiber layers. These filter mediums apply a fine prefilter effect, and guarantee maximum particulate-retention capability by separating the particulates inside the particular filter layer.

A second essential function of the diesel filter is to separate emulsified and free water in order to prevent corrosion damage. An effective water separation of >93% at rated flow (ISO 4020) is absolutely essential for distributor injection pumps and common-rail systems. Water separation takes the form of coalescence on the filter medium. The separated water collects in the water chamber in the bottom of the filter housing. Conductivity sensors are used to monitor the water level, and the water is drained off manually via a drain plug.

Diesel fuel is more heavily contaminated than gasoline (particularly due to products which result from the aging process). Diesel filters are therefore designed as easy-change filters. Screw-on easy-change filters with radial or spiral vee-shaped filter elements are widely used. Fuel filters with aluminum/plastic and fully plastic housings are being increasingly used. Only a non-metal filter element remains as a replacement part.

If particularly exacting demands are placed on wear protection and/or maintenance intervals, there are filter systems which have a prefilter that is adapted to the fine filter. In addition to the "microfiltration" and "water separation" functions, modern diesel filters combine "fuel preheating" (using electrical, coolant, or fuel-recirculation methods) to prevent clogging due to paraffin during winter operation, maintenance indication by way of a differential-pressure measurement, and manual pumping for filling/venting after the filter is replaced.

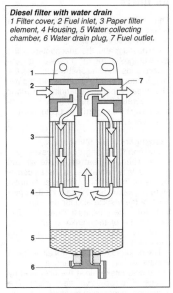

Diesel filter with water drain
1 Filter cover, 2 Fuel inlet, 3 Paper filter element, 4 Housing, 5 Water collecting chamber, 6 Water drain plug, 7 Fuel outlet.

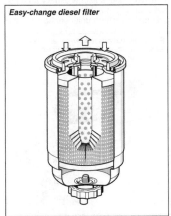

Easy-change diesel filter

Air supply

Air filters

The air filter serves to inhibit internal wear by preventing air-borne dust from being drawn into the engine.

On paved roads, the dust content of the air averages 1 mg/m³, however, on unpaved roads and on construction sites the dust content can be high as 40 mg/m³. This means that – depending on roads and operating conditions – a medium-sized engine can draw in up to 50 g of dust over 1,000 km.

Passenger-car air filters
In addition to filtering the air, passenger-car air filters preheat the intake air and regulate its temperature, as well as damping the air-intake noise. Intake-air temperature regulation is important for the operation of the vehicle and for the composition of the exhaust gases. The temperature of the intake air may differ under part-load and full-load operating conditions.

The required amount of hot air is drawn in in the vicinity of the exhaust and added to the cold intake air at the filter inlet by means of a flap-valve mechanism. The regulating mechanism is usually an automatic arrangement employing either a pneumatic vacuum unit connected to the

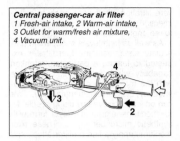

Central passenger-car air filter
1 Fresh-air intake, 2 Warm-air intake,
3 Outlet for warm/fresh air mixture,
4 Vacuum unit.

intake manifold or an expansion element. The constant regulated intake-air temperature improves engine performance and fuel consumption, and decreases the percentage of pollutants in the exhaust gases as a result of better fuel management and distribution of the air-fuel mixture. Preheating the intake air also shortens the warm-up phase of the engine after it is started, particularly in cold weather. It also prevents ice from forming in the carburetor.

Passenger-car air filters employ paper cartridges and can be mounted either centrally or at the side of the engine compartment. This type of filter is characterized by a high retention factor which, to a large extent, remains insensitive to fluctuations in load. Cartridge replacement is a simple operation performed at the intervals specified by the vehicle's manufacturer. Passenger-car air filters must be

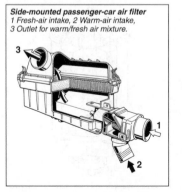

Side-mounted passenger-car air filter
1 Fresh-air intake, 2 Warm-air intake,
3 Outlet for warm/fresh air mixture.

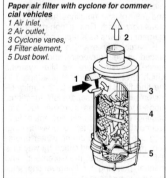

Paper air filter with cyclone for commercial vehicles
1 Air inlet,
2 Air outlet,
3 Cyclone vanes,
4 Filter element,
5 Dust bowl.

specially matched to each engine type in order to optimize power output, fuel consumption, intake-air temperature and damping.

Commercial-vehicle air filters

Most of the air filters used in heavy vehicles are of the paper-element type, although oil-bath filters are employed in some applications. Paper filters exhibit high filtering efficiency in all load ranges and increased flow resistance as the amount of dirt retained by the filter increases. To save space, a cyclone pre-filter is often integrated in the air-filter housing fitted with a paper element. The filter is serviced by either replacing the filter element or emptying the dust cup.

Paper air filters often incorporate maintenance indicators to show when the filter needs servicing.

The servicing information provided by the manufacturer of the vehicle or the equipment must be followed. Servicing can be simplified, according to the intensity of engine-air pulsation, by using specially matched automatic dust-unloading valves.

Cyclones increase filter service life and extend the maintenance intervals. The cyclone vanes rotate the air, causing the majority of dust particles to be separated from the air before reaching the downstream air filter. Cyclones can be installed upstream of both paper air filters and oil-bath air filters. They cannot be used alone as engine air filters because their filtering efficiency is inadequate.

Intake-noise damping

The intake noise of passenger-car and commercial-vehicle air filters must be damped in order to comply with legal regulations pertaining to the overall vehicle noise level. Noise damping is achieved almost exclusively by designing the air filter to act as a reflection sound absorber having the specialized shape of a Helmholtz resonator; see P. 451.

Assuming that the air filter is of sufficient size, intake noise can generally be damped by 10 to 20 dB (A). A good empirical value for 4-stroke engines is 15 to 20 times the displacement of one cylinder. In special cases in which the noise at particular frequencies is excessive, supplemental dampers must be used.

The resonance frequency of an intake damper is

$$f_0 = \frac{c}{2\,\pi} \cdot \sqrt{\frac{A_m}{l \cdot V}}$$

Where
c Speed of sound in air
l Length of the intake manifold
A_m Mean cross section of the intake manifold
V Filter volume

Intake-noise damping

Damping curves of an intake-noise damper
Damper resonance $f_0 = 66$ Hz.
1 Theoretical damping curve without taking into account pipe resonances.
2 Curve of measured damping response with low sound energy density and without parallel flow (loudspeaker measurement).
3 Measured damping response with high sound energy density and with parallel flow (measurement at the engine).

Air filter with intake pipe
l Length of intake pipe,
A_m Mean cross-section of intake pipe,
V Filter volume.

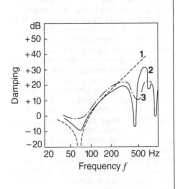

Turbochargers and superchargers for internal-combustion engines

(self-charging)

By compressing the air inducted for combustion in the internal-combustion (IC) engine, and thereby increasing its mass, charging systems also increase the output obtained for a given displacement at a given engine speed. The "compressors" generally used for IC engines are of three basic types; the mechanically-driven supercharger, the exhaust-gas turbocharger and the pressure-wave supercharger.

Mechanical superchargers compress the air using power supplied by the engine crankshaft (mechanical coupling between engine and supercharger), while the turbocharger is powered by the engine's exhaust gases (fluid coupling between engine and turbocharger).

Although the pressure-wave supercharger also derives its compression force from the exhaust gases, it requires a supplementary mechanical drive (combination of mechanical and fluid coupling).

Superchargers (mechanically driven)

These fall into two categories: mechanically-driven centrifugal superchargers (MKL) and mechanically-driven positive-displacement superchargers (MVL).

The turbo-type supercharger for the MKL corresponds to the exhaust-gas turbocharger in its essential configuration. This type of device is very efficient, providing the best ratio between unit dimensions and unit volume. However, the extreme peripheral velocities required to generate the pressure mean that drive speeds must be very high. As the secondary drive pulley (2:1 conversion ratio relative to primary drive) does not rotate fast enough to drive a centrifugal supercharger, a single-stage planetary gear with a 15:1 speed-increasing ratio is employed to achieve the required peripheral speeds. In addition, a transmission unit must be included to vary the rotational speeds if the pressure is to be maintained at a reasonably constant level over a wide range of flow volumes (~ engine speed).

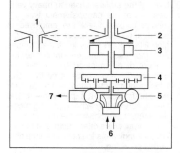

Mechanical centrifugal supercharger (MKL) (schematic)
1 Variable-speed primary pulley, 2 Variable-speed secondary pulley, 3 Solenoid clutch, 4 Step-up planetary-gear set, 5 Compressor, 6 Air intake, 7 Air outlet.

The necessity of using extreme rotational speeds, and the technical limits imposed on the transmission of drive power, mean that the centrifugal supercharger's range of potential applications is limited to medium- and large-displacement diesel and gasoline passenger-car engines. This design has not been extensively employed for mechanical superchargers.

Positive-displacement superchargers (MVL) operate both with and without internal compression. Internal-compression superchargers include the reciprocating-piston, the screw-type, the rotary-piston and the sliding-vane compressor. The Roots supercharger is an example of a unit without internal compression. All of these positive-displacement superchargers share certain characteristics as shown in the graphic illustration for a Roots supercharger.

– The curves for the constant rotational speed n_{LAD} = in the graph of p_2/p_1 against $\dot{V}$ are extremely steep, indicating that increases in the pressure ratio p_2/p_1 are accompanied by only slight reductions in the mass-flow volume $\dot{V}$. The precise extent of the drop in flow volume is basically determined by the efficiency of the gap seal (backflow losses). It is a function of the pressure ratio p_2/p_1 and of time, and is not influenced by rotational speed.

– The pressure ratio p_2/p_1 does not depend upon the rotational speed. In other words, high pressure ratios can also be generated at low mass-flow volumes.
– The mass-flow volume $\dot{V}$ remains independent of the pressure ratio, and is, roughly formulated, directly proportional to rotational speed.
– The unit retains stability throughout its operating range. The positive-displacement compressor operates at all points of the p_2/p_1-$\dot{V}$ graph as determined by supercharger dimensions.

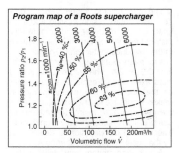

Program map of a Roots supercharger

The two twin-bladed rotary pistons of the <u>Roots supercharger</u> operate without directly contacting each other or the housing. The size of the sealing gap thus created is determined by the design, the choice of materials and the manufacturing tolerances. An external gear set synchronizes the motion of the two rotary pistons.

In the <u>sliding-vane supercharger</u>, an eccentrically-mounted rotor drives the three centrally mounted sliding vanes; the eccentric motion provides the internal compression. The extent of this internal compression can be varied for any given eccentricity by altering the position of the outlet edge A in the housing.

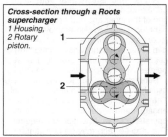

Cross-section through a Roots supercharger
1 Housing,
2 Rotary piston.

The <u>spiral-type supercharger</u> employs an eccentrically-mounted displacement element which is designed to respond to rotation of the input shaft by turning in a double-eccentric oscillating pattern. In sequence, the working chambers open for charging, close for transport and open once again for discharge at the hub. The spirals can be extended beyond the length shown in the illustration to provide internal compression.

The displacement element is driven by a belt-driven, grease-lubricated auxiliary shaft, while the input shaft is lubricated by the engine's oil circuit. Radial sealing is via gaps, while lateral sealing strips provide the axial seal.

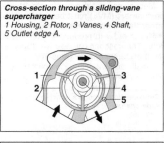

Cross-section through a sliding-vane supercharger
1 Housing, 2 Rotor, 3 Vanes, 4 Shaft, 5 Outlet edge A.

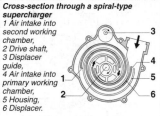

Cross-section through a spiral-type supercharger
1 Air intake into second working chamber,
2 Drive shaft,
3 Displacer guide,
4 Air intake into primary working chamber,
5 Housing,
6 Displacer.

The <u>rotary-piston supercharger</u> incorporates a rotary piston moving about an internal axis. The driven inner rotor (rotary piston) turns through an eccentric pattern in the cylindrical outer rotor. The rotor ratios for rotary-piston superchargers are either 2:3 or 3:4. The rotors turn around fixed axes without contacting each other or the housing. The eccentric motion makes it possible for the unit to ingest the maximum possible volume (chamber I) for compression and discharge (chamber III). The internal compression is determined by the position of the outlet edge A.

A ring and pinion gear with sealed grease lubrication synchronizes the motion of the inner and outer rotors. Permanent lubrication is also employed for the roller bearings. Inner and outer rotors use gap seals, and usually have some form of coating. Piston rings provide the seal between working chamber and gear case.

Superchargers on IC engines are usually belt-driven (toothed or V-belt). The coupling is either direct (continuous engagement) or via clutch (e.g., solenoid-operated clutch, actuation as required). The step-up ratio may be constant, or it may vary according to engine speed.

Mechanical positive-displacement superchargers (MVL) must be substantially larger than their centrifugal counterparts (MKL) in order to produce a given mass flow. The mechanical positive-displacement supercharger is generally applied to small- and medium-displacement engines, where the ratio between charge volume and space requirements is still acceptable.

Exhaust-gas turbochargers

The exhaust-gas turbocharger (ATL) consists of two turbo elements: a turbine and a compressor installed on a single shaft. The turbine uses the energy of the exhaust-gas to drive the compressor. The compressor, in turn, draws in fresh air which it supplies to the cylinders in compressed form. The air and the mass flow of the exhaust gases represent the only coupling between the engine and the compressor. Turbocharger speed does not depend upon engine speed, but is rather a function of the balance of drive energy between the turbine and the compressor.

Exhaust-gas turbochargers are used on engines in passenger cars, trucks and heavy-duty engines (marine and locomotive power plants, stationary power generators).

The typical engine-performance curves for this type of application are illustrated in a compression graph (P. 441), valid for all displacements, in which the surge line separates the stable operating range on its right from the instable range. It is obvious that the instable range presents no difficulties provided that the correct turbocharger is selected, as all of the points representing potential operating conditions lie either on the engine operating curves (full load) or below them (part-load operation).

Cross-section through a rotary-piston supercharger
1 Housing,
2 Outer rotor,
3 Inner rotor,
4 Outlet edge A,
5 Chamber III,
6 Chamber II,
7 Chamber I.

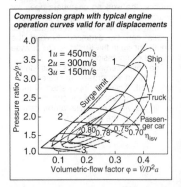

Compression graph with typical engine operation curves valid for all displacements

$1u = 450 \text{m/s}$
$2u = 300 \text{m/s}$
$3u = 150 \text{m/s}$

Pressure ratio p_2/p_1

Surge limit

Ship

Truck

Passenger car η_{isv}

0.80 0.78 0.75 0.70

Volumetric-flow factor $\varphi = \dot{V}/D^2 a$

Different applications require various configurations. However, all exhaust-gas turbochargers have practically the same major components: the turbocharger rotor and shaft assembly, which combine with the bearing housing to form the so-called core assembly, and the compressor housing. Other components such as turbine housing and control elements vary according to the specific application.

Piston rings are installed on both the exhaust and intake sides to seal off the bearing housing's oil chamber. In some special applications sealing is enhanced by trapped air or a compressor-side carbon axial face seal. Friction bearings are generally used, installed radially as either floating double plain bushings or stationary plain-bearing bushings, while multiple-wedge surface bushings provide axial support. The turbocharger is connected to the engine's lube-oil circuit for lubrication, with oil supply and return lines located between the compressor and turbine housings. No additional cooling arrangements are provided for the bearing housing on standard units. The temperatures can be maintained below critical levels using devices such as a heat shield, and by thermally isolating the bearing housing from the hot turbine housing, supplemented by incorporating suitable design elements in the bearing

housing itself. Water-cooled bearing housings are employed for exhaust-gas temperatures in excess of 850°C. The rear wall of the compressor seals the compressor side of the bearing housing.

The housing of the radial compressor is generally made of cast aluminum. A by-pass valve can be integrated in the housing for special applications. This bypass valve is used exclusively in SI-engine supercharging and prevents pumping on the compressor side when load is swiftly removed from the engine.

Turbine housings differ substantially according to intended use. Casting materials for turbine housings range from GGG 40 to NiResist D5 (depending upon exhaust-gas temperature). Exhaust-gas turbochargers for trucks incorporate a twin-flow turbine housing in which the two streams join just before reaching the impeller. This housing configuration is employed to achieve pulse turbocharging, in which the pressure of the exhaust-gas is supplemented by its kinetic energy.

In contrast, in the case of constant-pressure turbocharging, only the pressure energy of the exhaust-gas is utilized, and single-flow turbine housings can be employed. This configuration has become especially popular for use in conjunction with water-cooled turbine housings on marine engines. The exhaust-gas tur-

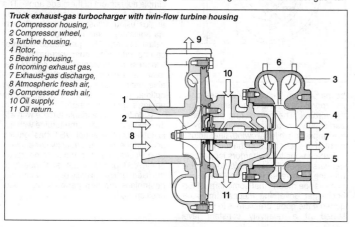

Truck exhaust-gas turbocharger with twin-flow turbine housing
1 Compressor housing,
2 Compressor wheel,
3 Turbine housing,
4 Rotor,
5 Bearing housing,
6 Incoming exhaust gas,
7 Exhaust-gas discharge,
8 Atmospheric fresh air,
9 Compressed fresh air,
10 Oil supply,
11 Oil return.

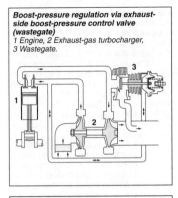

Boost-pressure regulation via exhaust-side boost-pressure control valve (wastegate)
1 Engine, 2 Exhaust-gas turbocharger, 3 Wastegate.

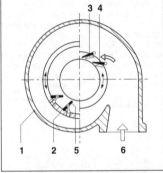

Variable turbine geometry
(schematic diagram)
1 Turbine housing, 2 Adjusting ring,
3 Control cams, 4 Adjustable guide blades,
5 Guide blades with adjusting lever,
6 Air intake.

bochargers on heavy-duty engines often incorporate a nozzle ring upstream from the turbine. The nozzle ring provides a particularly smooth and consistent flow to the impeller while allowing fine adjustment of the flow through the turbine.

Exhaust-gas turbochargers for passenger cars generally use single-flow turbine housings. However, the car engine's wide min⁻¹ range means that some form of turbocharger governing mechanism is required if the boost pressure is to be maintained at a relatively constant level throughout the engine's operating range. Standard practice presently favors regulating flow on the exhaust side, whereby a portion of the engine's exhaust gases is routed past the turbine (bypass) using a governing mechanism (wastegate) which can be in the form of a valve or a flap.

In today's production turbochargers, the wastegate is actuated pneumatically, i.e. with negative pressure or overpressure. Here the necessary control pressure is tapped off directly or in timed mode from the turbocharger or as timed negative pressure from the vehicle electrical system.

With appropriate microelectronic support, boost-pressure control can be effected as a function of the engine program maps. Future wastegates will be electrically or electronically actuated.

The available energy is exploited more efficiently by governing systems incorporating turbines with variable blade geometry. With this system, the turbine's flow resistance is modified continuously to achieve maximum utilization of the exhaust energy under all operating conditions.

Of all the potential designs, adjustable guide blades have achieved general acceptance, as they combine a wide control range with high efficiency levels.

An adjusting ring is rotated to provide simple adjustment of the blade angle. The blades, in turn, are swiveled to the desired angles using adjusting cams, or directly via adjusting levers attached to the individual blades. The pneumatic actuator can operate with either vacuum or positive pressure. Microelectronic control systems can exploit the advantages of variable turbine-blade geometry by providing optimal boost pressure throughout the engine's operating range.

Aside from the variable turbine with adjustable guide blades, the turbine with adjustable control spool VST has gained acceptance in small-capacity car engines (see illustration). The mode of operation of the VST provides that, analogously to the fixed turbine, initially one flow channel determines the ram performance (spool position 1).

When the maximum permissible boost pressure is reached, the spool opens continuously in an axial direction and exposes the second flow channel (position 2). Both channels together are configured in such a way that by far the largest part of the exhaust-gas mass flow is routed through the turbine. The remaining quantity is routed past the impeller inside the charger by further displacement of the control spool (position 3).

Multistage supercharging

Multistage supercharging is an improvement on single-stage supercharging in that the power limits can be significantly extended. The objective here is to improve the air supply on both a stationary and a non-stationary basis and at the same time to improve the specific consumption of the engine. Two supercharging processes have proven successful in this respect.

Sequential supercharging

Because of the expensive charger switching equipment, sequential supercharging is predominantly used in ship propulsion systems or generator drives. In this case, as engine load and speed increases, one or more turbochargers are cut in to the basic supercharging process. Thus, in comparison with a large supercharger, which is geared to the rated power, two or more supercharging optima are achieved.

Two-stage controlled supercharging

This supercharging process is used in motor-vehicle applications on account of its simple control response. Two-stage controlled supercharging involves the serial connection of two turbochargers of different sizes with a bypass control system and ideally a second intercooler.

The exhaust-gas mass flow from the cylinders initially passes into the exhaust manifold. From this point, there is the possibility of either expanding the exhaust-gas mass flow through the high-pressure turbine (HP) or diverting a partial mass flow through the bypass line. The entire exhaust-gas mass flow is then used again by the downstream low-pressure turbine (LP).

Operation of VST supercharger with adjustable spool
a) Spool position 1 (only left channel open),
b) Spool position 2 (both channels open),
c) Spool position 3 (both channels and bypass open).

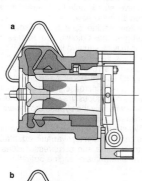

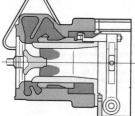

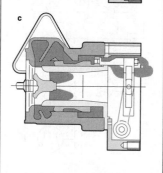

The entire fresh-air mass flow is initially precompressed by the low-pressure stage and ideally intercooled. The flow is then further compressed and intercooled in the high-pressure stage. As a result of the precompression, the relatively small HP compressor works on a higher pressure level so it is able to generate the required air mass flow.

At low engine speeds, i.e. small exhaust-gas mass flows, the bypass remains fully closed and the entire exhaust-gas mass flow expands through the HP turbine. This results in a very rapid and high build-up of boost pressure. As engine speed increases, the expansion work is continuously switched to the LP turbine whereby the bypass cross-section is enlarged accordingly.

Two-stage controlled supercharging thus enables infinitely variable adaptation on the turbine and compressor sides to the requirements of engine operation.

Pressure-wave superchargers

The pressure-wave supercharger exploits the dynamic properties of gases, using pressure waves to convey energy from the exhaust-gas to the intake air. The energy exchange takes place within the cells of the rotor (known as the cell rotor or cell wheel), which also depends upon an engine-driven belt for synchronization and maintenance of the pressure-wave exchange process.

Inside the cell rotor, the actual energy-exchange process proceeds at the speed of sound. This depends upon exhaust-gas temperature, meaning that it is essentially a function of engine torque, and not engine speed. Thus the pressure-wave process is optimally tailored to only a single operating point if a constant step-up ratio is employed between engine and supercharger. To get around this disadvantage, appropriately-designed "pockets" can be incorporated in the forward part of the housings. These achieve high efficiency levels extending through a relatively wide range of engine operating

---

Schematic structure of two-stage controlled supercharging
1 HP stage (high pressure),
2 LP stage (low pressure),
3 Intake manifold,
4 Exhaust manifold,
5 Bypass valve,
6 Bypass line.

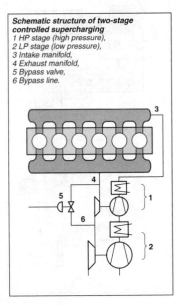

Pressure-wave supercharger
1 Engine, 2 Cell rotor, 3 Belt drive,
4 High-pressure exhaust-gas,
5 Pressurized air, 6 Low-pressure air intake,
7 Low-pressure exhaust outlet.

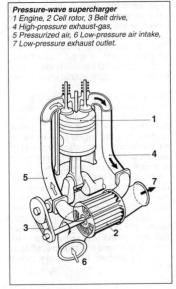

conditions and provide a good overall boost curve.

The exchange of energy occurring within the rotor at the speed of sound ensures that the pressure-wave supercharger responds rapidly to changes in engine demand, with the actual reaction times being determined by the charging processes in the air and exhaust tracts.

The pressure-wave supercharger's cell rotor is driven by the engine's crankshaft via a belt assembly. The cell walls are irregularly spaced in order to reduce noise. The cell rotor turns within a cylindrical housing, with the fresh air and exhaust-gas tracts feeding into the housing's respective ends. On one side are low-pressure air intake and pressurized air, while the high-pressure exhaust and low-pressure exhaust-gas outlet are located on the other side.

The accompanying gas-flow and state diagrams illustrate the pressure-wave process in a basic "Comprex" at full load and moderate engine speed. Developing (or unrolling) rotor and housing converts the rotation to a translation. The state diagram contains the boundary curves for the four housing openings in accordance with local conditions. The diagrams for the ideal no-loss process have been drawn-up with the assistance of the intrinsic characteristic process.

The pressure-wave supercharger's rotor is over-mounted and is provided with permanent grease lubrication, with the bearing located on the unit's air side. The air housing is of aluminum, the gas housing of NiResist materials. The rotor with its axial cells is cast using the lost-wax method. An integral governing mechanism regulates boost pressure according to demand.

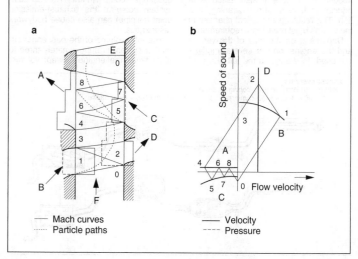

Gas-flow diagram (a) and state diagram (b) for pressure-wave supercharger
A Exhaust-gas outlet, B Exhaust-gas intake, C Air intake, D Air outlet, E Residual air, fresh air, F Direction of rotor rotation.

Exhaust systems

Exhaust-system purpose
The exhaust system reduces the pollutant constituents of the exhaust gas generated by combustion in the engine. The remaining exhaust gas is then discharged as quietly as possible at a convenient point on the vehicle. The engine power should be reduced as little as possible during the process.

Exhaust-system design
A passenger-car exhaust system serves here as our example. It consists basically of three main components (although some of these are also found in commercial-vehicle exhaust systems):

The <u>catalytic converter</u> serves as the exhaust-gas cleaning device for spark-ignition (SI) engines, and the oxidation catalytic converter for diesel engines. It is mounted as close as possible to the engine so that it can quickly reach its operating temperature and therefore be effective in urban driving. When installed as retrofit equipment it is fitted in place of the front muffler (front silencer), whose acoustical functions it also assumes in addition to its exhaust-gas cleaning function. The resulting acoustical changes in the vehicle must meet legal requirements.

Depending on the size of the vehicle and the engine, one or several <u>mufflers</u> are used. In V-engines the left and right cylinder banks are frequently run separately, each being fitted with its own catalytic converter or muffler, and only brought together at the end of the vehicle in one large muffler.

The <u>exhaust pipes</u> are the third and last component in the exhaust system. They combine the exhaust-gas outlets in the cylinder head into one or more pipes (manifolds), and also connect the catalytic converter(s) and the mufflers to each other. The length and cross-section of the pipes, as well as the type of junction used, influence the vehicle's performance characteristics and acoustic behavior. Exhaust systems for vehicles with larger swept volumes are therefore often fitted with twin pipes. The pipes, the catalytic converter and muffler are connected to the main body of the system by means of insert connections and flanges. Many original-equipment systems are welded into one complete unit for faster mounting.

The entire exhaust system is connected with the underbody of the vehicle via flexible suspension elements. The fixing points must be carefully selected, as otherwise vibration can be transmitted to the bodywork and generate noise in the passenger compartment. The exhaust-system noise at the exhaust-emission point (tailpipe) can also cause bodywork resonances.

The total volume of the passenger-car muffler system is approximately three to eight times the engine's swept volume.

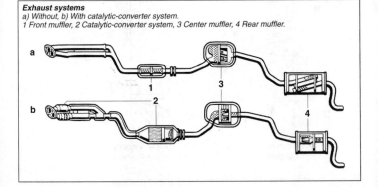

Exhaust systems
a) Without, b) With catalytic-converter system.
1 Front muffler, 2 Catalytic-converter system, 3 Center muffler, 4 Rear muffler.

Depending on swept volume and type of muffler, the exhaust system weighs between 8 and 40 kg.

Catalytic converters

The catalytic-converter housing is of heat-resistant, high-quality steel. It contains actively-coated ceramic monoliths. In order to compensate for the differing coefficients of thermal expansion of steel and ceramics, and to protect the sensitive monolith against bumps and vibrations, a flexible mounting is used. Two different types of mounting have been developed:

The <u>wire-knit mounting</u>, of highly heat-resistant stainless steel, is insensitive to extreme exhaust-gas temperatures and to pronounced gas pulsations in the high-speed range. Because of its poor heat-insulation qualities, the pipes and the body of the catalytic converter must often also be insulated.

The <u>swelling-mat mounting</u> has come to the forefront in application. This mounting is made of ceramic fiber felt, composed of aluminum silicate fibers and expanding mica particles. The two substances are combined using acrylic latex. Under the influence of temperature the matting expands and presses the monolith into an immovable position. As the swell matting is a good insulator, there is no need for additional insulation. However, if the exhaust gases cause excessive heating, the pressure on the monoliths can reach such a level that there is the danger of fracture. If the exhaust-gas temperatures are not high enough, the pressing force exerted on the monolith is insufficient, allowing the monolith to move and possibly be destroyed. Exhaust-gas pulsation may lead to erosion in the swell matting.

In order to restrict linear expansion and to achieve better mixing of the exhaust gases, several monoliths are frequently used in one catalytic converter. The shape of the inflow funnel into the catalytic converter must be designed carefully, so that the exhaust gases flow through the monolith evenly. The external shape of the ceramic body depends on the space available underneath the vehicle, and may be triangular, oval or round.

The metal catalytic converter is an alternative to the ceramic monolith. It is made of finely corrugated, 0.05 mm thick metal foil, wound and hard-soldered in a high-temperature process. As in the case of the ceramic catalytic converter, the surface is coated with catalytically effective material. As a result of its thin walls, more channels can be accommodated in the same area. That means less resistance to the exhaust gas, which is beneficial with regard to performance optimization in high-performance vehicles.

Catalytic converters also have an acoustic effect. As a result of the narrow ceramic pipes in the monolith, numerous small sound sources are formed. The

Dual-bed three-way catalytic converter
1 Lambda sensor for lambda closed-loop control, 2 Monolith, 3 Wire-knit mounting,
4 Heat-insulated double shell.

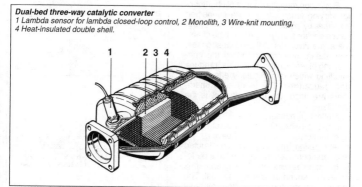

sound waves are thereby partially extinguished by interference or are damped by friction.

When designing the exhaust system, careful catalytic-converter matching is imperative, as its high level of flow resistance has a considerable influence on the system's vibration characteristics as well as on the performance of the engine (see also Catalytic Afterburning, page 521).

Mufflers

Mufflers (or silencers) are intended to smooth the exhaust-gas pulsations and make them as inaudible as possible. There are basically two physical principles involved: reflection and absorption. Mufflers also differ according to these principles. However, they mostly comprise a combination of reflection and absorption. As mufflers together with the pipes of the exhaust system form an oscillator with natural resonance, the position of the mufflers is highly significant for the quality of sound-damping. The objective is to tune the exhaust systems as low as possible, so that their natural frequencies do not excite bodywork resonances. To avoid structure-borne noise and to provide heat insulation against the underbody of the vehicle, mufflers often have double walls and an insulating layer. Depending on the space available underneath the vehicle, mufflers are produced either as "winding cups" or from half-shells.

Reflection mufflers consist of chambers of varying lengths which are connected together by pipes. The differences in the cross-sections of the pipes and the chambers, the diversion of the exhaust gases, and the resonators formed by the connecting pipes with the chambers, produce muffling which is particularly effective at low frequencies. The more such chambers are used, the more efficient is the muffler.

Reflection mufflers cause a higher exhaust-gas backpressure, as a rule have greater power loss, and are heavier.

Absorption mufflers are constructed with one chamber, through which a perforated pipe is passed. The chamber is filled with sound-deadening material. The sound enters the absorption material through the perforated pipe and is converted into heat by friction. The absorption material usually consists of long-fiber mineral wool (basalt or rock wool) with a bulk density of 120...150 g/l. The level of muffling depends on the bulk density, the sound-absorption grade of the material, and on the length and coating-thickness of the chamber. Damping takes place across a very broad band, but only begins at higher frequencies. The shape of the perforations, and the fact that the pipe passes through the wool ensures that the material is not blown out by the pulsation of the exhaust gas. Sometimes the mineral wool is protected by a layer of stainless-steel wool around the perforated pipe.

Absorption mufflers are principally used as rear mufflers.

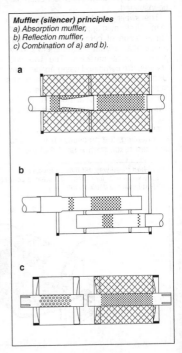

Muffler (silencer) principles
a) Absorption muffler,
b) Reflection muffler,
c) Combination of a) and b).

a

b

c

Acoustic tuning devices

A number of different components can be used to remove disturbing frequency areas of the noise emitted from the tailpipe.

The <u>Helmholtz resonator</u> damps sound in its natural frequency range and functions as a suction resonator. It is a through-flow resonator and amplifies at its natural frequency, but thereafter it has a broad damping range.

<u>Pipes perforated with holes</u> work in a similar way to a watering-can rose. The one large sound source, the pipe, is converted into many small sound points, formed by the perforations. A broad-band filter effect occurs as a result of interference and swirling of the exhaust gas.

<u>Venturi nozzles</u> damp low-frequency sound. They must be designed so that the flow speed in the nozzle throat is always below the speed of sound. The funnel must be set at a specific angle, as otherwise hissing noises occur.

Soot filters

In order to remove solid particles (particulates) from diesel-engine exhaust gas, soot filters are in development. Various kinds of filter system are used, e.g., steel-wool filters, ceramic-monolith filters, ceramic-coil filters etc.

The <u>ceramic-monolith filter</u> currently represents the best compromise with regard to the requirements made of the filter. In contrast to the flow-through catalytic-converter monoliths, the channels for the soot filter are alternatingly opened and closed, so that the particle-laden exhaust gas is forced to flow through the uncoated, porous walls of the honeycomb structure. The particles are deposited in the pores. Depending on the porosity of the ceramic body, the effectiveness of these filters ranges from 70 to 90 %.

In order to guarantee full functioning of the filters they must be regenerated at certain intervals. Two cleaning processes are possible; in both cases the soot particles are burnt away:

In the <u>chemical process</u>, additives in the fuel reduce the flammability of the soot particles to the usual exhaust-gas temperature. The secondary emissions arising as a result of the additives may have a disadvantageous effect.

In the <u>thermal process</u>, a high-power heating element is connected, which raises the exhaust-gas temperature to approx. 700 °C. The regeneration is most simply carried out with the engine switched off. The filter regeneration point is ascertained either via a time control or an aneroid box. If it is necessary to regenerate the filter while the vehicle is running, two filters can be fitted which are alternatingly either filtering or being regenerated. This is, however, very cost-intensive. A further possibility is to divert the exhaust gases via a sound muffler during regeneration, whereby the exhaust gases are emitted unfiltered for approx. 5% of the journey. Heating elements are also being developed which permit simultaneous regeneration and filtering of engine exhaust gases (full-flow regeneration).

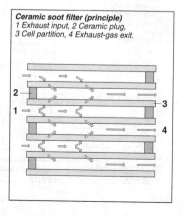

Ceramic soot filter (principle)
1 Exhaust input, 2 Ceramic plug,
3 Cell partition, 4 Exhaust-gas exit.

Engine management for spark-ignition (SI) engines

Requirements

SI-engine torques

The power output P from a spark-ignition (SI) engine is determined by the available clutch torque and the engine speed.

The clutch torque is produced from the torque generated by the combustion process, reduced by the friction torque (friction losses in the engine) and the charge-cycle losses, and the torque required for operating the auxiliary systems.

The combustion torque is generated in the power cycle and determined by the following variables:
- the air mass that is available for combustion once the intake valves have closed,
- the fuel mass available at the same time, and
- the point at which the ignition spark initiates combustion of the air/fuel mixture.

Primary function of engine management

The primary function of engine management is to adjust the torque generated by the engine. For this purpose, all the variables that influence the torque are controlled in the various engine-management subsystems.

Cylinder-charge control

In Bosch engine-management systems with an electronic accelerator pedal (EGAS), the required charging of the engine cylinders with air is determined and the throttle valve opened accordingly in the "cylinder-charge control" subsystem. In conventional injection systems, the driver directly controls the opening of the throttle valve by pressing the accelerator pedal.

A/F mixture formation

In the "mixture formation" subsystem, the associated fuel mass is calculated and from this the necessary injection time and the optimum injection point are determined.

Ignition

In the "ignition" subsystem, the crankshaft angle is determined at which the ignition spark ignites the mixture at the correct time.

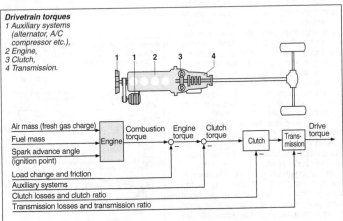

Drivetrain torques
1 Auxiliary systems (alternator, A/C compressor etc.),
2 Engine,
3 Clutch,
4 Transmission.

The objective of this management system is to make available the torque requested by the driver, and at the same time to satisfy the exacting demands placed on exhaust emissions, fuel consumption, power output, comfort and safety.

Cylinder charge

Constituent elements

The gas mixture in the cylinder after the intake valves have closed is termed the cylinder charge. This charge consists of the supplied fresh A/F mixture and residual exhaust gas.

Fresh A/F mixture

The constituent elements of the fresh mixture drawn in are fresh air and the fuel suspended in it. The majority of the fresh air flows through the throttle valve; additional fresh mixture can be drawn in through the evaporative-emissions control system (if fitted). The air supplied via the throttle valve and present in the cylinder after the intake valves have closed is the decisive factor in the work performed at the piston during combustion, and thus in the torque delivered by the engine.

Measures for increasing maximum torque and maximum engine power therefore almost always necessitate an increase in the maximum possible cylinder charge. The theoretical maximum charge is predetermined by the piston displacement.

Residual exhaust gas

The share of residual exhaust gas in the charge is formed
- by the exhaust-gas mass which remains in the cylinder and is not discharged during the period when the exhaust valve is open, and
- in systems with exhaust-gas recirculation (EGR), by the mass of the recirculated exhaust gas.

The residual exhaust-gas share is determined by the charge cycle.

The residual exhaust-gas mass does not contribute directly to the combustion process but does influence ignition and the course of the combustion process. This residual exhaust-gas share can therefore be perfectly desirable when the engine is in part-load operation.

In order for a desired torque to be generated, the reduction in the fresh-mixture volume (due to the residual-gas quantity) must be compensated for by increasing the throttle-valve opening. This reduces

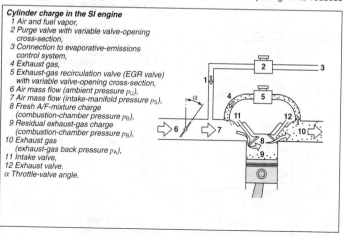

Cylinder charge in the SI engine
1 Air and fuel vapor,
2 Purge valve with variable valve-opening cross-section,
3 Connection to evaporative-emissions control system,
4 Exhaust gas,
5 Exhaust-gas recirculation valve (EGR valve) with variable valve-opening cross-section,
6 Air mass flow (ambient pressure p_U),
7 Air mass flow (intake-manifold pressure p_S),
8 Fresh A/F-mixture charge (combustion-chamber pressure p_B),
9 Residual exhaust-gas charge (combustion-chamber pressure p_B),
10 Exhaust gas (exhaust-gas back pressure p_A),
11 Intake valve,
12 Exhaust valve.
α Throttle-valve angle.

the engine's pumping losses, and fuel consumption drops as a result. A specifically introduced residual exhaust-gas share can likewise influence combustion and thus the emission of nitrogen oxides (NO_X) and unburnt hydrocarbons (HC).

Control

In a spark-ignition engine with external mixture formation, the power output is proportional to the air mass flow drawn in. In future, it will also be possible to directly control the direct-injection SI engine operating with lean A/F mixtures via variation of the injected fuel mass.

Throttle valve

The throttle valve is used when the engine power, and thus (at a specific engine speed) the engine torque, are to be controlled by means of the air mass flow. When the throttle valve is not fully open, the air drawn in by the engine is throttled, thereby reducing the torque generated. This throttling effect is dependent on the position and thus on the opening cross-section of the throttle valve.

The maximum engine torque is achieved when the throttle valve is fully open (see Fig.).

Charge cycle

The charge cycle of fresh A/F mixture and residual exhaust gas is controlled by the appropriate opening and closing of the intake and exhaust valves. The cams on the camshaft determine the points at which the valves open and close (valve timing) and the course of the valve lift. This influences the charge-cycle process and thus also the amount of fresh A/F mixture available for combustion.

The valve overlap, i.e. the overlapping of the opening times of the intake and exhaust valves, has a decisive impact on the residual exhaust-gas mass in the cylinder. This situation involves "interior" exhaust-gas recirculation. The residual exhaust-gas mass can also be increased by "exterior" exhaust-gas recirculation. In this case, an additional EGR valve connects the intake manifold and exhaust manifold. When the valve is open, the engine draws in a mix of fresh A/F mixture and exhaust gas.

Supercharging

The obtainable torque is proportional to the charge of fresh A/F mixture. It is therefore possible to increase the maximum torque by compressing the air in the cylinder by means of dynamic supercharging, mechanical supercharging, or exhaust-gas turbocharging (P. 392).

Throttle map of an SI engine
– – – Intermediate position of throttle valve.

Throttle valve fully open

Fresh A/F-mixture charge ↑

Throttle valve fully closed

min.   max.
Idle   Speed →

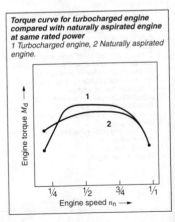

Torque curve for turbocharged engine compared with naturally aspirated engine at same rated power
1 Turbocharged engine, 2 Naturally aspirated engine.

Engine torque M_d ↑

$\frac{1}{4}$ $\frac{1}{2}$ $\frac{3}{4}$ $\frac{1}{1}$
Engine speed n_n →

Fuel delivery with electric fuel pump

Function

The electric fuel pump must deliver sufficient quantities of fuel to the engine and maintain enough pressure for efficient injection under all operating conditions. Essential requirements include:

- maintaining flow rates between 60 and 200 liters/h at the rated voltage,
- maintaining fuel-system pressures of 300...450 kPa,
- the ability to pressurize the system during operation at 50...60 % of the rated voltage, important for cold-starting response.

In addition, the electric fuel pump is increasingly being used as the presupply pump for modern direct-injection systems, both for gasoline and for diesel engines. For gasoline direct-injection systems, at times pressures of up to 700 kPa must to be provided. This, together with the very high viscosity range when pumping diesel fuel, signifies new challenges facing the hydraulic and electric systems of the electric fuel pump.

Design

The electric fuel pump consists of:

- the end cover including the electrical connections, non-return valve (to maintain system pressure) and the hydraulic discharge fitting. Most end covers also include the carbon brushes for the drive-motor commutator and interference-suppression elements (inductance coils, with condensers in some applications).
- the electric motor with armature and permanent magnets. Electronically commutated (EC) fuel pumps are being developed for use with special fuels which feature for instance marked electrolytic effects, and for use in other environments which have negative effects on carbon-brush and commutator assemblies.
- a positive-displacement or flow-type pump assembly.

Positive-displacement pump

As the positive-displacement unit's pump element rotates it draws in fluid through the suction side and through a sealed area on its way to the high-pressure side. Electric fuel pumps fall into two categories, the roller cell and the internal-gear unit. Positive-displacement pumps provide good performance in high-pressure (400 kPa and up) systems. They also perform well at low supply voltages, i.e. the flow rate curve remains relatively "flat" and constant throughout a wide range of operating voltages. Efficiency ratings can be as high as 25 %. The unavoidable pressure pulses may cause noise; the extent of this problem varies according to the pump's design configuration and mounting location. Yet another disadvantage may be encountered with hot fuel, when the unit tends to pump gas instead of fuel, leading to reduced flow rates (problem potential varies according to in-

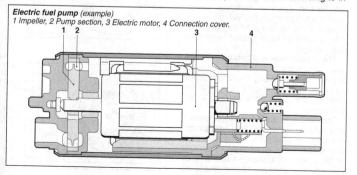

Electric fuel pump (example)
1 Impeller, 2 Pump section, 3 Electric motor, 4 Connection cover.

stallation location). Standard positive-displacement pumps usually incorporate peripheral primary circuits to deal with this problem by discharging the gas.

While the flow-type pump has to a large extent replaced the positive-displacement pump in electronic gasoline injection systems for performing the classical function of the electric fuel pump, a new field of application has opened up for the positive-displacement pump in terms of the above-mentioned presupply for direct-injection systems with their significantly increased pressure requirements and viscosity range. This is especially true for the presupply of diesel and biodiesel.

Flow-type pumps

Designs based on the principles used for the peripheral pump and the side-channel pump have become the standard for electric fuel pumps, with a slight preference for the side-channel pump as this tends to provide higher pressures and improved efficiency. An impeller equipped with numerous peripheral vanes rotates within a chamber consisting of two fixed housing sections. Each of these sections features a passage along the path of the impeller's vanes, with the openings on one end of the passage on a plane with the suction openings. From here they extend to the point where the fuel exits the pump at system pressure. Within the passage is a baffle element designed to prevent internal leakage. A small gas-discharge orifice (not necessary in diesel applications) located at a specified angular distance from the suction opening, improves performance when pumping hot fuel; this orifice facilitates the discharge of any gas bubbles which may have formed (with minimal leakage).

The pulses reflected between the impeller vanes and the fluid molecules result in pressurization along the length of the passage, inducing a spiral rotation of the fluid volume in the impellers and in the passages.

Because pressurization is continuous and virtually pulse-free, flow-type pumps are quiet in operation. Pump design is also substantially less complex than that of the positive-displacement unit. Single-stage pumps generate system pressures

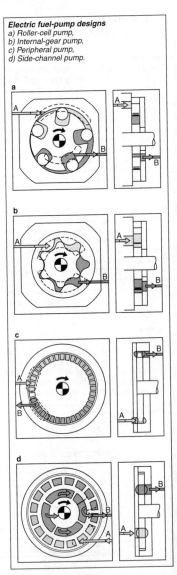

Electric fuel-pump designs
a) Roller-cell pump,
b) Internal-gear pump,
c) Peripheral pump,
d) Side-channel pump.

a

b

c

d

extending up to 450 kPa. Still higher system pressures, as will become necessary for brief periods in future for highly supercharged engines, and for engines with gasoline direct injection (see above), are possible, but under continuous-duty conditions such pressures would overload today's conventional electrical systems (permanent-magnet DC motors with conventional electromechanical commutation) and would result in a significantly reduced service life. The following remedial measures are being considered:

– High-pressure operation only when required → demand control of the electric fuel pump, e.g. with the aid of a timing module or another upstream device.
– Equipping of the fuel-pump motor with a carbon commutator in place of the conventional copper commutator so as to safeguard the service life also at high current and additionally with corrosive and/or high-viscosity fuels.
– For applications where the wide range of operating conditions and fuels place particularly high demands on the pump's versatility, work is proceeding on electronically commutated (EC) fuel-pump drives. Such an electrical system features unlimited service life.

The efficiency ranges between 10 and approx. 20%. The fuel systems of newly designed vehicles with spark-ignition engines rely almost exclusively on flow-type pumps for fuel delivery.

Electric fuel pumps: integration in injection system and in fuel tank

Whereas the first electronic fuel-injection systems almost always featured electric fuel pumps designed for in-line installation outside the tank, current and more recent applications tend to have in-tank installation as a standard feature. The electric fuel pump is one of the elements within the in-tank units now being designed to include an increasingly wide array of components such as: the suction filter, a fuel-baffle chamber to maintain delivery during cornering (usually with its own "active" supply based on a suction-jet pump or a separate primary circuit in the main electric pump), the fuel gauge sensor, and a variety of electrical and hydraulic connections.

Another advance is the returnless fuel system (RLFS), usually in the form of an in-tank unit with an integral fuel-pressure regulator designed to maintain a continuous return circuit within the in-tank assembly. A pressure-side fine-mesh fuel filter can also be incorporated in this unit. Further functions will in future be integrated in the delivery module, e.g. diagnostic devices for tank leakage, timing module for fuel-pump control.

In-tank unit: complete integrated assembly for returnless fuel systems
1 Fuel filter, 2 Electric fuel pump, 3 Suction-jet pump (regulated), 4 Fuel-pressure regulator, 5 Fuel-gauge sensor, 6 Suction strainer.

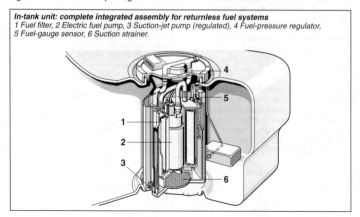

A/F-mixture formation

Influencing variables

Air-fuel (A/F) mixture

To be able to operate, a spark-ignition engine requires a specific air-fuel mixture ratio. Ideal theoretical complete combustion is available at a mass ratio of 14.7:1. This is also termed the stoichiometric ratio. I.e.: an air mass of 14.7 kg is needed to burn a fuel mass of 1 kg. Or expressed as a volume: 1 *l* fuel burns completely in roughly 9500 *l* air.

The specific fuel consumption of a spark-ignition engine is essentially dependent on the mixture ratio of the A/F mixture. It is necessary to have an excess of air in order to ensure genuine complete combustion, and thus as low a fuel consumption as possible. Limits are imposed though by the flammability of the mixture and the available combustion time.

The A/F mixture also has a decisive impact on the efficiency of the exhaust-gas treatment systems. State-of-the-art technology is represented by the three-way catalytic converter. This, though, needs a stoichiometric A/F ratio in order to operate with maximum efficiency. Such a catalytic converter helps to reduce harmful exhaust-gas constituents by more than 98 %.

The engines available today are therefore operated with a stoichiometric mixture as soon as their operating status permits this.

Certain engine operating states require mixture corrections. Specific corrections of the mixture composition are necessary e.g. when the engine is cold. The mixture-formation (carburation) system must therefore be in a position to satisfy these variable requirements.

Excess-air factor

The excess-air factor λ (lambda) has been chosen to designate the extent to which the actual air-fuel mixture differs from the theoretically necessary mass ratio (14.7:1):

λ = Ratio of supplied air mass to air requirement with stoichiometric combustion.

$\lambda = 1$: The supplied air mass corresponds to the theoretically necessary air mass.

$\lambda < 1$: There is an air deficiency and thus a rich mixture. Maximum power output at $\lambda = 0.85...0.95$.

$\lambda > 1$: There is an excess of air or a lean mixture in this range. This excess-air factor is characterized by reduced fuel consumption and reduced power output. The maximum value for λ that can be achieved – the so-called "lean-burn limit" – is very heavily dependent on the engine design and on the mixture-formation system used. The mixture is no longer ignitable at the lean-burn limit. Combustion misses occur and this is accompanied by a marked increase in uneven running.

Spark-ignition engines with manifold injection achieve their peak power output at an air deficiency of 5...15 % ($\lambda = 0.95...0.85$), and their lowest fuel consumption at an air excess of 10...20 % ($\lambda = 1.1...1.2$).

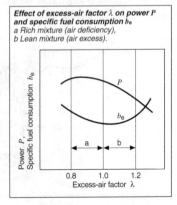

Effect of excess-air factor λ on power P and specific fuel consumption b_e
a Rich mixture (air deficiency),
b Lean mixture (air excess).

The graphs show the dependence of power output, specific fuel consumption and pollutant buildup on the excess-air factor for a typical engine with manifold injection. It can be deduced from these graphs that there is no ideal excess-air factor at which all the factors assume the most favorable value. For engines with manifold injection, excess-air factors of $\lambda = 0.9...1.1$ have proven effective in realizing "optimal" consumption at "optimal" power output.

Engines with direct injection and charge stratification involve different combustion conditions such that the lean-burn limit is significantly higher. These engines can therefore be operated in the part-load range with significantly higher excess-air factors (up to $\lambda = 4$).

For the treatment of exhaust gas by a three-way catalytic converter, it is absolutely essential to adhere exactly to $\lambda = 1$ with the engine at normal operating temperature. In order to do so, the air mass drawn in must be precisely determined and an exactly metered fuel mass added to it.

For optimum combustion in today's common manifold-injection engines, not only is a precise injected fuel quantity necessary, but also a homogeneous A/F mixture. This necessitates efficient fuel atomization. If this precondition is not satisfied, large fuel droplets will precipitate on the intake manifold or the combustion chamber walls. These large droplets cannot fully combust and will result in increased hydrocarbon emissions.

Mixture-formation systems

It is the job of fuel-injection systems, or carburetors, to furnish an A/F mixture which is adapted as well as possible to the relevant engine operating state. Injection systems, especially electronic systems, are better suited to maintaining narrowly defined limits for the mixture composition. This is advantageous with regard to fuel consumption, driving performance and power output. The result of increasingly stringent exhaust-emissions legislation in the automotive sector is that today, injection systems have completely superseded carburetors.

Today, the automotive industry almost exclusively uses systems in which the mixture formation takes place outside the combustion chamber. However, systems with interior mixture formation, i.e. where the fuel is injected directly into the combustion chamber, already formed the basis of the first gasoline injection systems. These systems are increasing in importance as they are very well suited to reducing fuel consumption even further.

Effect of excess-air factor λ on pollutant composition in untreated exhaust gas

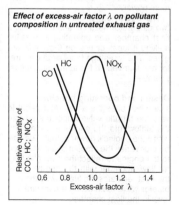

Schematic of a carburetor system
1 Fuel tank, 2 Fuel supply pump, 3 Fuel filter, 4 Carburetor, 5 Intake manifold.

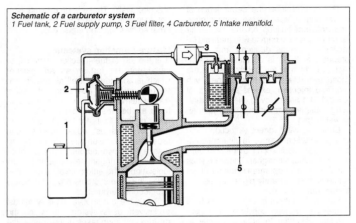

Carburetors

Carburetor systems
The fuel is transported from the fuel tank to the carburetor by a fuel pump (generally a diaphragm unit) powered by the camshaft or distributor shaft. The system is designed to limit the maximum supply pressure. A fine-mesh fuel filter can be installed upstream or downstream from the pump as required.

Carburetor types

Downdraft carburetors
Downdraft carburetors are the most common type. Designs featuring optimized float chamber and metering-jet configurations result in efficient units. These designs work in conjunction with the corresponding intake-manifold layouts for optimum mixture formation and distribution.

Horizontal-draft carburetors
Horizontal-draft carburetors (familiar as fixed-venturi and constant-depression units) are useful for minimizing engine height.

Constant-depression carburetors feature venturi cross sections which vary in size during operation to maintain essentially constant vacuum levels at the fuel outlet. The variation in intake cross section is provided by a pneumatically-actuated plunger; attached to the plunger is a needle which regulates the fuel quantity.

Venturi configurations
The single-throat carburetor with <u>one</u> venturi is the least expensive design.

The two-stage carburetor featuring <u>two</u> venturis provides convenient tuning for individual applications and has become the standard in 4-cylinder applications. The first barrel controls part-throttle operation, while the second venturi opens for maximum power.

The double-barrel carburetor features two carburetor sections sharing a single float chamber and operating in parallel, making it ideal for use on 6-cylinder engines. The two-stage four-barrel carburetor has four venturi fed from a single float chamber.

Design and operating principles
The driver uses the accelerator pedal to vary the throttle valve's aperture so that the airflow into the engine is varied and with it the engine's power output. The carburetor varies the amount of fuel metered to the engine to reflect the current intake air flow. Together with the needle valve, the float regulates the fuel flow to the carburetor while maintaining a constant fuel level in the float chamber.

Airflow is monitored by an air funnel designed to induce a venturi effect. The progressively narrower diameter increases the velocity of the air, producing a corresponding vacuum at the narrowest point. The resulting pressure differential relative to the float chamber – which can be further augmented with a boost venturi – is exploited to extract fuel from the float chamber. The jets and metering systems adapt fuel delivery to airflow.

Fuel-metering systems

Main system

The fuel is metered by the main jet. Correction air is added as a delivery aid to the fuel through side orifices in the venturi tube.

Idle and progression system

At idle, the vacuum which the air stream produces at the fuel outlet is not sufficient to withdraw fuel from the main system. For this reason, there is a separate idle system with an outlet located downstream from the throttle valve at the point of maximum vacuum. The emulsion required for idling emerges from the idle circuit after initial processing by the idle fuel and air-correction jets.

During transitions to the main metering system the throttle valve controls a series of orifices, or a slit, drawing fuel from the idle circuit.

Other systems

These basic devices are supplemented by a range of additional systems. These are designed to adapt carburetor performance for warm operation (part-throttle control, full-throttle enrichment), to compensate for fuel accumulation within the intake-manifold during acceleration (accelerator pump) and to meet the special engine requirements encountered during starting and in the warm-up phase. Other supplementary systems include lambda closed-loop mixture control and devices to deactivate the fuel supply during trailing-throttle operation.

Schematic of a two-stage carburetor
a) Primary stage, b) Secondary stage.
1 Idle cutoff valve, 2 Accelerator pump, 3 Idle circuit, 4 Choke, 5 Boost venturi,
6 Main systems with venturi tubes, 7 Full-throttle enrichment, 8 Float, 9 Fuel supply,
10 Needle valve, 11 Bypass plug, 12 Idle mixture screw, 13 Throttle valves, 14 Venturi wall,
15 Part-throttle control valve, 16 Venturi chamber.

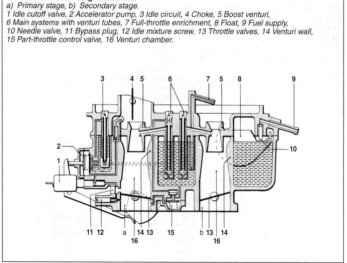

Electronically-controlled carburetor system (ECOTRONIC)

Basic carburetor
The basic carburetor is restricted to the throttle valve, float system, idle and transition systems, main system and choke. An idle-air control system with a choke-activated needle jet is also provided.

Additional components and actuators
The throttle-valve actuator is an electropneumatic servo device for controlling the cylinder charge. The actuator's plunger moves the throttle valve via a lever attached to the carburetor's throttle shaft.

The choke valve actuator is a final-control element designed to adapt the mixture in response to variations in engine operating conditions. This unit closes the choke valve to enrich the mixture by raising the pressure differential (vacuum) at the main jets while simultaneously increasing flow rates from the idle circuit.

Sensors
The throttle-valve potentiometer monitors the throttle valve's position and travel. One temperature sensor monitors the engine's operating temperature while a second sensor can be installed if necessary to monitor the temperature within the intake manifold.

The idle switch serves to identify trailing-throttle operation; it can be replaced by appropriate software in the electronic control unit (ECU).

Electronic control unit (ECU)
The ECU's input circuit converts incoming analog signals into digital form. The processor performs further operations with the input data in order to calculate output values with reference to the programmed data map. The output signals control several functions, including regulation of the servo elements that operate the choke valve and main throttle valve.

Basic functions
The basic carburetor determines the primary functions of the system. The idle, transition and full-throttle systems all contribute to matching performance to the programmed curves. The base calibrations can be intentionally "lean", as the choke-valve control can provide a corrective enrichment.

Electronic functions
Electronic open and closed-loop control circuits regulate a number of secondary operations within the ECU. Several of these are illustrated below. Further functions may include: ignition control, transmission-shift control, fuel consumption displays and diagnosis capabilities.

Schematic of an electronically controlled carburetor (ECOTRONIC)
1 ECU, 2 Temperature sensor, 3 Carburetor, 4 Throttle actuator, 5 Choke actuator, 6 Choke valve, 7 Idle switch, 8 Throttle valve, 9 Throttle potentiometer.

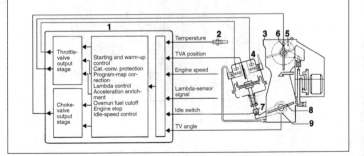

Gasoline injection systems

Systems for external A/F mixture formation

Gasoline injection systems for external mixture formation are identified by the fact that the air-fuel mixture is created outside the combustion chamber (in the intake manifold).

Single-point injection (SPI)

Single-point injection is an electronically controlled injection system in which an electromagnetic fuel injector injects the fuel intermittently into the intake manifold at a central point ahead of the throttle valve. The Bosch single-point injection systems are called Mono-Jetronic and Mono-Motronic.

Multipoint injection (MPI)

Multipoint injection creates the ideal preconditions for satisfying the demands placed on a mixture-formation system. In multipoint injection systems, each cylinder is assigned a fuel injector, which injects the fuel directly ahead of that cylinder's intake valve. Examples of such systems are KE- and L-Jetronic with their respective variants.

Mechanical injection system:

The K-Jetronic system operates without a drive and injects the fuel continuously. The injected fuel mass is not determined by the fuel injector but rather prespecified by the fuel distributor.

Combined mechanical-electronic injection system:

KE-Jetronic is based on the mechanical basic system of K-Jetronic. Thanks to the extended acquisition of operating data, this system facilitates electronically controlled supplementary functions in order to adapt the injected fuel quantity more exactly to the different engine operating states.

Electronic injection systems:

Electronically controlled injection systems inject the fuel intermittently with electromagnetically actuated fuel injectors. The injected fuel mass is determined by the injector opening time (for a given pressure drop across the injector).

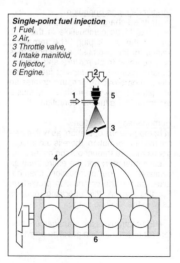

Single-point fuel injection
1 Fuel,
2 Air,
3 Throttle valve,
4 Intake manifold,
5 Injector,
6 Engine.

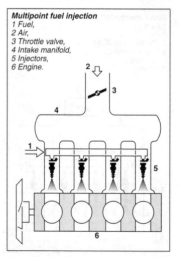

Multipoint fuel injection
1 Fuel,
2 Air,
3 Throttle valve,
4 Intake manifold,
5 Injectors,
6 Engine.

Examples: L-Jetronic, LH-Jetronic, and Motronic as an integrated engine management system.

The high standards required of a vehicle's smooth running and exhaust-emissions necessitate high demands being made on the A/F mixture composition of each working cycle. Precisely timed injection is significant as well as precise metering of the injected fuel mass in accordance with the air drawn in by the engine.

In modern multipoint injection systems, therefore, not only is each engine cylinder assigned an electromagnetic fuel injector but also this fuel injector is activated individually for each cylinder. In this way, both the fuel mass appropriate to each cylinder and the correct start of injection are calculated by the control unit (ECU). Injecting the precisely metered fuel mass directly ahead of the cylinder intake valve(s) at the correct moment in time improves mixture formation. This, in turn, helps to a large extent in preventing wetting of the intake-manifold walls with fuel, which can result in temporary deviations from the desired lambda value during transient engine operation. The advantages of multipoint injection can thus be fully exploited.

The engine intake manifolds thus carry only the combustion air and can therefore be optimally adapted to the gas-dynamic requirements of the engine.

Systems for internal A/F mixture formation

In direct-injection systems for internal mixture formation, the fuel is injected directly into the combustion chambers by electromagnetically actuated fuel injectors. Each cylinder is assigned a fuel injector. Mixture formation takes place inside the cylinder. To ensure efficient combustion, it is essential that the fuel be finely atomized when leaving the injectors.

In normal operation, a direct-injection engine draws in only air and not an air-fuel mixture, as is the case in conventional injection systems. Herein lies an advantage of this new system: no fuel can precipitate on the intake-manifold walls. With external mixture formation, the air-fuel mixture is generally present throughout the entire combustion in a homogeneous state and in a stoichiometric ratio. On the other hand, formation of the mixture in the combustion chamber permits two completely different operating modes:

Stratified-charge operation

In stratified-charge operation, the mixture only has to be combustible in the area around the spark plug. The remaining section of the combustion chamber thus only contains fresh mixture and residual exhaust gas without unburnt fuel. In the idle and part-load ranges, this creates an altogether highly lean mixture and thus a reduction in the fuel consumption.

Homogeneous operation

In homogeneous operation, as with external mixture formation, there is a homogeneous mixture throughout the entire combustion chamber; and the entire fresh air available in the combustion chamber takes part in the combustion procedure. For this reason, this operating mode is used in the full-load range.

MED-Motronic is the management system for direct-injection gasoline engines.

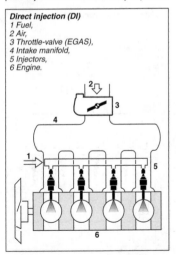

Direct injection (DI)
1 Fuel,
2 Air,
3 Throttle-valve (EGAS),
4 Intake manifold,
5 Injectors,
6 Engine.

Single-point injection systems

Single-point fuel injection has advanced beyond the compact fuel-injection system stage to become part of a comprehensive engine-management system.

The various single-point injection systems differ in the design of the central-injection unit. All systems feature an injector located above the throttle plate; they differ from multipoint injection units in that they frequently operate at low pressure (0.7...1 bar). This means that an inexpensive, hydrodynamic electric fuel pump can be used which is generally in the form of an in-tank unit. The injector is flushed continuously by the fuel flowing through it in order to inhibit the formation of air bubbles. This arrangement is an absolute necessity in such a low-pressure system. The designation "Single-Point Injection (SPI)" corresponds to the terms Central Fuel Injection (CFI), Throttle Body Injection (TBI) and Mono-Jetronic (Bosch).

Mono-Jetronic

Mono-Jetronic is an electronically controlled, low-pressure single-point injection system for 4-cylinder engines, and features a centrally located solenoid-controlled fuel injector. At the heart of the system is the central injection unit, which uses the throttle valve to meter the intake air while injecting the fuel intermittently above the throttle valve. The intake manifold then distributes the fuel to the individual cylinders. Various sensors monitor all important engine operating data, which are then are used to calculate the triggering signals for the injectors and other system actuators.

Central injection unit

The injector is located above the throttle, in the intake-air path, in order to ensure homogeneous mixtures and consistent cylinder-to-cylinder distribution. The fuel spray is directed into the sickle-shaped orifice between the housing and throttle plate, whereby fuel wetting of the intake-tract walls is inhibited to a great extent, and the high pressure differential pro-

Schematic of a Mono-Jetronic system
1 Fuel tank, 2 Electric fuel pump, 3 Fuel filter, 4 Pressure regulator, 5 Injector, 6 Air-temperature sensor, 7 ECU, 8 Throttle actuator, 9 Throttle potentiometer, 10 Canister-purge valve, 11 Carbon canister, 12 Lambda sensor, 13 Coolant-temperature sensor, 14 Ignition distributor, 15 Battery, 16 Ignition switch, 17 Relay, 18 Diagnostic connector, 19 Central injection unit.

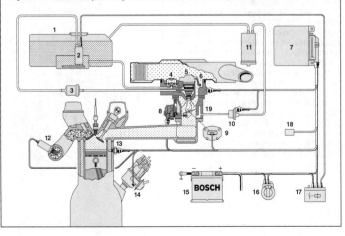

motes optimum mixture formation. The injector operates at a system pressure of 1 bar (referred to atmospheric pressure). Efficient fuel atomization ensures consistently good mixture distribution, even in the critical full-load range. Injector triggering is synchronized with the ignition pulses.

System control

In addition to the engine speed n, the main actuating variables for the injection system can include the air volume/air mass flow, the absolute manifold pressure, and the throttle position α. The (α/n) system applied with Mono-Jetronic can meet stringent emission requirements when used in conjunction with lambda closed-loop control and a 3-way catalytic converter. A self-adaptive system employs the signal from the lambda sensor as a reference to compensate for component tolerances and engine changes, thus maintaining high precision throughout the service life of the system.

Adaptation functions

The injection time is extended to provide additional fuel for cold starts and during the post-start and warm-up phases. When the engine is cold, the throttle actuator adjusts the throttle position to supply more air to the engine, thus maintaining idle speed and exhaust emissions at a constant level. The throttle potentiometer recognizes the change in throttle position and initiates an increase in the fuel quantity via the ECU. The system regulates the enrichment for acceleration and full-throttle operation in the same way. The overrun fuel cutoff provides reductions in fuel consumption and in exhaust emissions during trailing-throttle operation. Adaptive idle-speed control lowers the idle speed and stabilizes it. For this purpose, the ECU issues a signal to the servomotor to adapt the throttle-valve position as a function of engine speed and temperature.

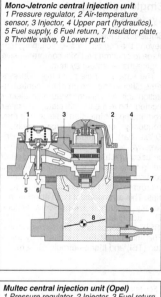

Mono-Jetronic central injection unit
1 Pressure regulator, 2 Air-temperature sensor, 3 Injector, 4 Upper part (hydraulics), 5 Fuel supply, 6 Fuel return, 7 Insulator plate, 8 Throttle valve, 9 Lower part.

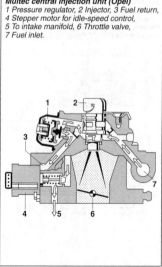

Multec central injection unit (Opel)
1 Pressure regulator, 2 Injector, 3 Fuel return, 4 Stepper motor for idle-speed control, 5 To intake manifold, 6 Throttle valve, 7 Fuel inlet.

Multipoint injection systems

K-Jetronic

Operating principle
– Continuous injection,
– Direct air-flow measurement.

K-Jetronic is a mechanical system which does not require an engine-driven injection pump. It meters a continuous supply of fuel proportional to the quantity of air being drawn into the engine.

Because of direct air-flow measurement, K-Jetronic also takes into account changes caused by the engine and permits the use of emission-control equipment, for which precise intake-air monitoring is an essential requirement.

Operation
The intake air flows through the air filter,

the air-flow sensor, and the throttle valve, before entering the intake manifold and continuing to the individual cylinders.

The fuel is delivered from the fuel tank by an electric (roller-cell) fuel pump. It then flows through the fuel accumulator and fuel filter to the fuel distributor. A pressure regulator in the fuel distributor maintains the fuel at a constant system pressure. The fuel flows from the fuel distributor to the injectors. Excess fuel not required by the engine is returned to the tank.

Mixture-control unit
The mixture-control unit consists of the air-flow sensor and the fuel distributor.

Air-flow sensor
The air-flow sensor consists of an air funnel and a pivoting air-flow sensor plate. A counterweight compensates for the weight of the sensor plate and pivot as-

---

Schematic of a K-Jetronic system
1 Fuel tank, 2 Electric fuel pump, 3 Fuel accumulator, 4 Fuel filter, 5 Warm-up regulator, 6 Injector,
7 Intake manifold, 8 Electric start valve, 9 Fuel distributor, 10 Air-flow sensor, 11 Frequency valve,
12 Lambda sensor, 13 Thermo-time switch, 14 Ignition distributor, 15 Auxiliary-air valve,
16 Throttle switch, 17 ECU, 18 Ignition switch, 19 Battery.

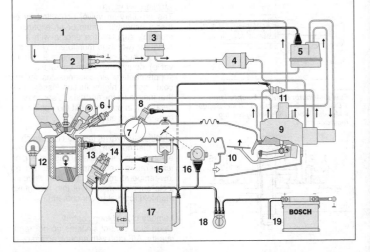

sembly. The sensor plate is displaced by the air flow, while the control plunger in the fuel distributor exerts hydraulic counterpressure to maintain the system in a balanced state. The position of the airflow sensor plate provides an index of intake air flow, and is transmitted to the fuel distributor's control plunger by a lever.

Fuel distributor
The amount of fuel supplied to the individual cylinders is regulated by varying the aperture of the metering slots in the fuel-distributor barrel. The number of rectangular-shaped metering slots in the barrel corresponds to the number of engine cylinders. The specific size of the metering-slot aperture depends on the control-plunger's position. In order to ensure constant pressure drop at the slots for various flow rates, a differential pressure regulator is located downstream of each metering slot.

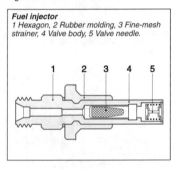

Fuel injector
1 Hexagon, 2 Rubber molding, 3 Fine-mesh strainer, 4 Valve body, 5 Valve needle.

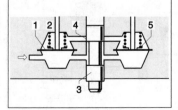

Fuel distributor in mixture-control unit
1 Diaphragm, 2 To injector, 3 Control plunger, 4 Metering slot, 5 Differential-pressure regulator.

Injector
The injector opens automatically at a pressure of approximately 3.8 bar, and has no metering function. It provides efficient mixture formation by opening and closing at a frequency of approx. 1500 Hz ("chatter").

It is held in place by a rubber molding. It is pressed, not screwed, into position. The hexagon serves to brace the injector when the fuel-supply line is screwed on.

Warm-up regulator
The warm-up regulator is controlled by an electrically-heated bimetallic element; it enriches the mixture in the warm-up phase by reducing the counterpressure (control pressure) exerted against the control plunger. A reduction in this control pressure means that the stroke of the airflow sensor plate for a given air flow increases (reflected by a correspondingly larger metering-slot aperture). The result is a richer mixture during warm-up.

Where desired, the warm-up regulator can be expanded to incorporate the following functions:
– full-throttle enrichment,
– acceleration enrichment,
– altitude compensation.

Auxiliary-air valve
The auxiliary-air valve, controlled by either a bimetallic spring or an expansion element, supplies the engine with additional air (which is monitored by the airflow sensor, but bypasses the throttle valve) during the warm-up phase. This supplementary air compensates for the cold engine's higher friction losses; it either maintains the normal idle speed or increases it in order to heat the engine and exhaust more quickly.

Electric start valve, thermo-time switch
The thermo-time switch activates the electric start valve as a function of engine temperature and elapsed time. During low-temperature starts, the start valve injects supplementary fuel into the intake manifold (cold-start enrichment).

Lambda closed-loop control
Open-loop control systems do not regulate the A/F ratio with enough accuracy to

allow compliance with stringent emissions limits.

Lambda closed-loop control is required for operation of the 3-way catalytic converter. When it is installed, the K-Jetronic system must include an electronic control unit which uses the Lambda sensor's signal as its main input variable.

A solenoid frequency valve regulates the A/F mixture ratio by controlling the pressure differential at the metering slots. However, this principle cannot be applied to meet the more stringent emissions requirements scheduled for the future.

KE-Jetronic

KE-Jetronic is an advanced version of the K-Jetronic system. KE-Jetronic includes an ECU for increased flexibility and supplementary functions. Additional components include:

– a sensor for the intake air flow,
– a pressure actuator for mixture ratio adjustment, and
– a pressure regulator which maintains system pressure at a constant level as well as providing a fuel-cutoff function when the engine is switched off.

Operation

An electric fuel pump generates the system pressure. The fuel flows through the fuel distributor, while a diaphragm regulator maintains the system pressure at a constant level. With K-Jetronic, the control circuit performs mixture corrections via the warm-up regulator. In contrast, with KE-Jetronic the primary pressure and the pressure exerted upon the control plunger are equal. The ratio is corrected by adjusting the pressure differential in all the fuel distributor's chambers simultaneously.

Schematic of a KE-Jetronic system
1 Fuel tank, 2 Electric fuel pump, 3 Fuel accumulator, 4 Fuel filter, 5 Fuel-pressure regulator, 6 Injector, 7 Intake manifold, 8 Electric start valve, 9 Fuel distributor, 10 Air-flow sensor, 11 Electrohydraulic pressure actuator, 12 Lambda sensor, 13 Thermo-time switch, 14 Coolant-temperature sensor, 15 Ignition distributor, 16 Auxiliary-air valve, 17 Throttle switch, 18 ECU, 19 Ignition switch, 20 Battery.

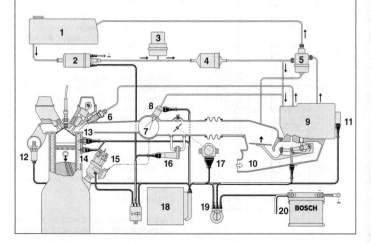

The system pressure is present upstream from the metering slots, and applies a counterpressure to the control plunger. As with K-Jetronic, the control plunger is moved by an air-flow sensor flap. A damper unit prevents the oscillations that could be induced by the forces generated at the sensor flap. From the control plunger the fuel flows through the pressure actuator, the lower chambers of the differential-pressure valve, a fixed flow restrictor, and the pressure regulator, before returning to the fuel tank. Together with the flow restrictor, the actuator forms a pressure divider in which the pressure can be adjusted electrodynamically. This pressure is present in the lower chambers of the differential-pressure valves.

A pressure drop corresponding to the actuator current occurs between the actuator's two connections. This causes variations in the pressure differential at the metering slots, and alters the amount of fuel injected. The current can also be reversed to shut down the fuel supply completely. This feature can be employed for such functions as overrun fuel cutoff and engine-speed limitation.

Electrohydraulic pressure actuator
This electrohydraulic actuator is flange-mounted on the fuel distributor. It is an electrically-controlled pressure regulator which operates using the nozzle/flapper-plate system. The mixture enrichment is directly proportional to the current flow.

Electronic control unit (ECU)
The ECU processes signals from the ignition (engine speed), temperature sensor (coolant temperature), throttle potentiometer (intake air flow), throttle switch (idle and overrun, WOT), starter switch, Lambda (O_2) sensor, pressure sensor and other sensors. Its most important functions are the control of:
– starting and post-start enrichment,
– warm-up enrichment,
– acceleration enrichment,
– full-throttle enrichment,
– overrun fuel cutoff,
– engine-speed limitation,
– idle-speed control,
– altitude compensation,
– closed-loop lambda control.

A coding switch (trim plug) makes it possible to select between operation with lambda control (with catalytic converter) and without it. This permits a choice between leaded and unleaded gasoline.

Lambda closed-loop control
The signal from the Lambda sensor is processed in the KE-Jetronic's ECU. The pressure actuator carries out the necessary adjustments.

L-Jetronic

Operating principle
– Air-flow measurement,
– Main controlled variables: air flow and engine speed,
– Intermittent injection.

L-Jetronic combines the advantages of direct air-flow measurement with the unique

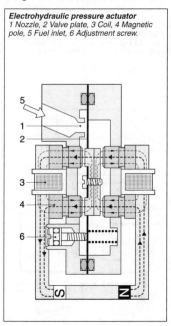

Electrohydraulic pressure actuator
1 Nozzle, 2 Valve plate, 3 Coil, 4 Magnetic pole, 5 Fuel inlet, 6 Adjustment screw.

possibilities afforded by electronics. It is similar to K-Jetronic in that it recognizes all changes in engine condition (due to wear, combustion-chamber deposits, changes in valve setting). This ensures consistently good exhaust-gas composition.

Operation

The fuel is injected through the engine's solenoid-operated injectors. A solenoid valve assigned to each cylinder is triggered once per crankshaft revolution. All of the injectors are wired in parallel to reduce the complexity of the electrical circuit. The pressure differential between fuel and intake-manifold pressures is maintained at a constant level of 2.5 or 3 bar such that the injected fuel quantity is only dependent on the opening period of the valves. For this purpose, the ECU delivers control pulses whose duration is dependent on the intake air flow, the engine speed, and the other influencing variables.

These are monitored by sensors and processed in the ECU.

Fuel supply

An electric fuel pump supplies the fuel and generates the injection pressure. The fuel is pumped from the fuel tank, through a paper filter, and into a high-pressure supply line at the other end of which there is a pressure regulator (spring-loaded diaphragm). The pressure regulator maintains a constant pressure at the metering orifice, regardless of the injected fuel quantity.

Schematic of an L-Jetronic system
1 Fuel tank, 2 Electric fuel pump, 3 Fuel filter, 4 ECU, 5 Injector, 6 Fuel-pressure regulator, 7 Intake manifold, 8 Electric start valve, 9 Throttle switch, 10 Air-flow sensor, 11 Lambda sensor, 12 Thermo-time switch, 13 Coolant-temperature sensor, 14 Ignition distributor, 15 Auxiliary-air valve, 16 Battery, 17 Ignition switch.

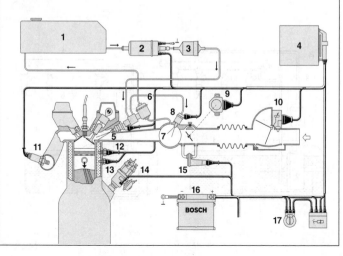

Standard system:

The fuel flows through the high-pressure line on its way to the engine-mounted fuel rail with the injectors. The pressure regulator is installed on the fuel rail. After flowing through the rail the portion of the fuel not required by the engine flows through the return line attached to the regulator and back to the tank. Because the returning fuel has been warmed on the way back from the engine, fuel temperatures within the tank rise.

Fuel vapor is generated in the tank as a function of fuel temperature. For environmental purposes these vapors are routed through the tank ventilation system for storage in an activated charcoal canister until they can be returned through the intake manifold for combustion within the engine.

Returnless system:

A returnless fuel-supply system reduces the tendency of the fuel in the fuel tank to heat up, thus making it easier to comply with the legal requirements governing vehicular evaporative emissions. The pressure regulator is located either in the fuel tank or in its immediate vicinity, which means that the return line from the engine to the fuel tank can be dropped. The amount of fuel pumped to the fuel rail is limited to the quantity being used by the injectors. The excess flow volume emerging from the pump returns directly to the tank without the round trip to the engine and back. Assuming equivalent operating conditions, and depending upon the specific vehicular application, this system can reduce in-tank fuel temperatures by up to 10 K, cutting vaporization by roughly one third.

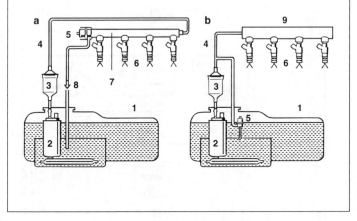

Fuel supply
a) Standard system, b) Returnless system.
1 Fuel tank, 2 Electric fuel pump, 3 Fuel filter, 4 Pressure line, 5 Fuel-pressure regulator, 6 Injectors, 7 Fuel rail (continuous flow), 8 Return line, 9 Fuel rail (no return flow).

Air-flow sensor
1 Idle-mixture adjustment screw, 2 Air-flow sensor flap, 3 Stop, 4 Compensation flap, 5 Damping chamber, 6 Air-temperature sensor.

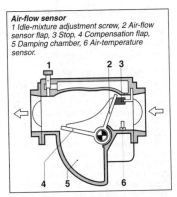

Injector
1 Pintle, 2 Needle, 3 Armature, 4 Spring, 5 Solenoid winding, 6 Electrical terminals, 7 Fuel strainer.

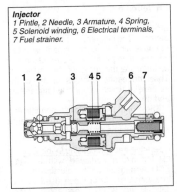

Air-flow sensor

The intake air flow deflects a sensor flap against the constant return force of a spring to a defined angular position, which is converted by a potentiometer into a voltage ratio. This voltage ratio determines the pulse length of a timing element in the ECU. A temperature sensor in the air-flow sensor indicates changes in air density caused by temperature variations.

Fuel injectors

Fuel injectors serve to meter and atomize the fuel. When the solenoid winding is energized, the nozzle needle is lifted a mere 0.05 mm off its seat.

Throttle-valve switch

This transmits a control signal to the ECU when the throttle valve is either completely closed (idle) or fully opened (full-throttle [WOT]).

Engine-temperature sensor

The engine-temperature sensor is designed as a temperature-sensitive resistor (thermistor) and controls the warm-up enrichment.

Auxiliary-air valve, electric start-valve, thermo-time switch

Design and function are similar to those of the corresponding K-Jetronic components.

Electronic control unit (ECU)

This ECU converts the engine variables into electrical pulses. Transmission intervals for these pulses are correlated with ignition timing, while their duration is basically a function of speed and intake air flow. Since all injectors are activated simultaneously, only a single driver stage is required. The temperature sensors respond to lower engine and air temperatures by increasing the injection duration. The throttle-switch signals allow mixture adaptation for idle and full-throttle operation.

Lambda closed-loop control

The ECU compares the signal from the Lambda sensor with a setpoint value before activating a two-state controller. The control adjustment is then performed, as are all corrections, by modifying the injection duration.

L3-Jetronic

L3-Jetronic incorporates functions extending beyond those provided by the L-Jetronic's analog technology. The L3 system's ECU employs digital technology to adjust the mixture ratios based on a load/engine-speed map. In order to save space, the ECU is installed in the engine compartment, directly on the air-flow sensor, where the two components form a single monitoring and control unit.

LH-Jetronic

LH-Jetronic is closely related to L-Jetronic. The difference lies in the method of intake air-flow measurement, with LH-Jetronic using a hot-wire air-mass meter to measure the mass of the intake air. Thus, the results no longer depend on the air density, which varies with temperature and pressure.

The other LH-Jetronic components and the basic system concept are to a large extent the same as those in L-Jetronic.

Operating-data processing in the ECU

LH-Jetronic is equipped with a digital ECU. Arrangements for adjusting the mixture ratio vary from those used with L-Jetronic in using a load/engine-speed map programmed for minimum fuel consumption and exhaust emissions. The ECU processes the sensor signals when calculating the injection duration that determines the injected fuel quantity. The ECU includes a microprocessor, a program and data memory, and an A/D converter. The microprocessor is provided with a suitable voltage supply and with a stable clock rate for data processing. The clock rate is defined by a quartz oscillator.

Hot-wire air-mass flow meter

The stream of intake air is conducted past a heated wire (hot wire). This wire forms part of an electrical bridge circuit. The flow of current through the wire serves to maintain it at a constant temperature above that of the intake air. This principle makes it possible to employ the current requirement as an index of the air mass being drawn into the engine. A resistor converts the heating current into a voltage signal, which the ECU then processes along with engine speed as a main input variable. A temperature sensor is mounted in the hot-wire air-mass flow meter to ensure that its output signal is not influenced by the temperature of the intake air. The A/F ratio at idle can be adjusted with a potentiometer. As contamination on

Schematic of an LH-Jetronic system

1 Fuel tank, 2 Electric fuel pump, 3 Fuel filter, 4 ECU, 5 Injector, 6 Fuel distributor, 7 Fuel-pressure regulator, 8 Intake manifold, 9 Throttle switch, 10 Hot-wire air-mass flow meter, 11 Lambda sensor, 12 Coolant-temperature sensor, 13 Ignition distributor, 14 Idle-speed actuator, 15 Battery, 16 Ignition switch.

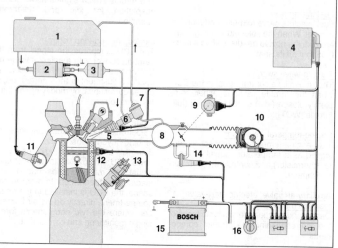

the surface of the hot wire could affect the output signal, each time the engine is shut down the wire is electrically heated for one second to burn-off any contamination. The hot-wire air-mass flow meter has no moving parts, and its aerodynamic resistance within the intake tract is negligible.

Hot-film air-mass flow meter

The operating principle of the hot-film air-mass flow meter is the same as that of the hot-wire sensor. However, in the interests of simplified design, a substantial portion of the electrical bridge circuit is installed on a ceramic substrate, in the form of thin-film resistors. In addition, there is no need to burn contaminants off the film. The contamination problem is solved by placing the areas on the sensor element which are decisive for thermal transmission at a downstream location. This prevents them from being affected by deposits on the sensor element's leading edge.

Kármán vortex volumetric flow meter

Yet another option for measuring intake air is provided by a sensor which uses the Kármán vortex principle to measure the volumetric flow rate. This meter monitors vortices generated as the intake air flows past vortex generators. The frequency of these vortices is a measure of the volumetric flow rate. This frequency is measured by emitting ultrasonic waves perpendicular to the direction of the intake-air flow. The propagation velocity of these waves as modified by the vortices is detected by an ultrasonic receiver and the resulting signals are evaluated in the ECU.

Hot-film air-mass flow meter
a Housing, b Hot-film sensor (installed in center of housing). 1 Heat sink, 2 Spacer, 3 Driver stage, 4 Hybrid, 5 Sensor element (metallic film).

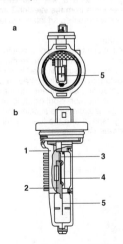

Kármán vortex volumetric flow meter
1 Oscillator, 2 Vortex generator, 3 Transmitter, 4 Ultrasonic waves, 5 Eddy currents, 6 Receiver, 7 Amplifier, 8 Filter, 9 Pulse shaper.

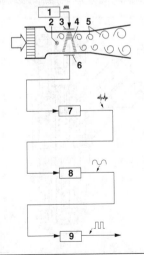

Electromagnetic fuel injectors

Design and operation

Fuel injectors essentially consist of a valve housing with current coil and electrical connection, a valve seat with spray-orifice disk and a moving valve needle with solenoid armature.

A filter strainer in the fuel feed protects the injector against contamination. Two O-rings seal the injector against the fuel-distribution pipe and the intake manifold. When the coil is de-energized, the spring and the force resulting from the fuel pressure press the valve needle against the valve seat to seal the fuel-supply system against the intake manifold (see Fig.).

When the injector is energized, the coil generates a magnetic field which attracts the armature and lifts the valve needle off of its seat to allow fuel to flow through the injector.

The injected fuel quantity per unit of time is essentially determined by the system pressure and the free cross-section of the spray orifices in the spray-orifice disk. The valve needle closes again when the field current is switched off.

Spray formation

The fuel injectors' spray formation, i.e. spray shape, spray angle and droplet size, influences the formation of the A/F mixture. Individual geometries of intake manifold and cylinder head make it necessary to have different types of spray formation.

Tapered spray:

Individual fuel sprays emerge through the openings in the spray-orifice disk. These fuel sprays combine to form a tapered spray. Tapered sprays can also be obtained by means of a pintle projecting through the injector needle tip. Tapered-spray injectors are typically used in engines with one intake valve per cylinder. The tapered spray is directed into the opening between the intake-valve disk and the intake-manifold wall.

Dual spray:

Dual-spray formation is used in engines with two intake valves per cylinder. The openings in the spray-orifice disk are arranged in such a way that two fuel sprays emerge from the injector. Each of these sprays supplies an intake valve.

Air-shrouding:

In the case of an air-shrouded injector, the pressure drop between intake-manifold and ambient pressures is used to improve mixture formation. Air is routed through an air-shrouding attachment into the outlet area of the spray-orifice disk. In the narrow air gap, the air is accelerated to a very high speed and the fuel is finely atomized when it mixes with it.

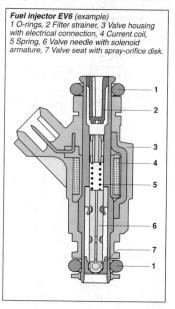

Fuel injector EV6 (example)
1 O-rings, 2 Filter strainer, 3 Valve housing with electrical connection, 4 Current coil, 5 Spring, 6 Valve needle with solenoid armature, 7 Valve seat with spray-orifice disk.

Ignition

The ignition system's function is to initiate combustion in the flammable air-fuel mixture by igniting it at precisely the right moment. In the spark-ignition (Otto) engine, this is achieved with an electrical spark, i.e. an arc generated between the spark plug's electrodes. Consistently reliable ignition under all circumstances is essential for ensuring fault-free catalytic-converter operation.

Misfiring results in damage to or destruction of the catalytic converter due to overheating during afterburning of the uncombusted mixture.

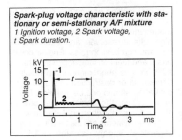

Spark-plug voltage characteristic with stationary or semi-stationary A/F mixture
1 Ignition voltage, 2 Spark voltage,
t Spark duration.

Mixture ignition

Provided the composition of the mixture is stoichiometric, an energy of approximately 0.2 mJ is required for each individual ignition of the A/F mixture via electric spark. Over 3 mJ are required for a rich or lean mixture. This energy represents only a fraction of the total energy in the ignition spark, the actual ignition energy. If sufficient ignition energy is not available, there will be no ignition, the mixture cannot ignite, and misfiring will result.

The system must therefore deliver enough ignition energy to ensure consistently reliable ignition of the mixture, even under unfavorable conditions. Igniting a small flammable mixture cloud flowing past the spark can be enough to initiate the process.

This mixture cloud ignites, the flame spreads to the remaining mixture in the cylinder, and the fuel starts to combust. Ignitability is enhanced by efficient fuel atomization and good access of the mixture to the electrodes, as well as through extended spark duration and spark length (large electrode gap).

The spark plug determines the location and length of the spark; spark duration depends upon the type and design of the ignition system, as well as on the momentary ignition conditions.

Spark generation

Adequate voltage must be present before a spark will arc from one electrode to another. At the moment of ignition, the volt-

age across the electrodes abruptly rises from zero up to the arcing (ignition) voltage and the plug fires. Once the spark has ignited, the spark-plug voltage drops to the sparking voltage. The A/F mixture may ignite at any point during the firing period of the ignition spark (spark duration). Once the spark has broken away, the voltage is damped and drops to zero.

Although intense mixture turbulence is basically desirable, it can extinguish the spark, thus leading to incomplete combustion. The energy stored in the ignition coil should therefore suffice for one or more consecutive sparks, depending on individual requirements.

High-voltage generation and energy storage

Battery-ignition systems generally employ an ignition coil to generate the high-tension voltage needed to generate the spark. The ignition coil operates as an autotransformer but within coil-ignition systems it also assumes the further important function of storing the ignition energy. When the contact breaker closes, energy from the vehicle's electrical system flows into the coil's primary winding. This energy is then stored in a magnetic field until the firing point, when the secondary winding discharges it to one of the engine's spark plugs. The ignition coil is designed to ensure that the available high-tension voltage in the coil is always well in excess of the spark plug's maximum-possible ignition-voltage requirement. Energy levels of 60...120 mJ within the coil correspond to an available voltage of 25...30 kV.

The operational reserves of high voltage and ignition energy are sufficient to compensate for all electrical losses. Inadequate maintenance reduces these high-voltage reserves, and leads to ignition and combustion miss. Engine power drops and fuel consumption increases. In addition, this phenomenon can result in damage to or destruction of the catalytic converter, should one be installed. In extreme cases, the engine either fails to start – especially when cold – or stalls.

Ignition systems are also available with capacitive energy storage (CDI or Capacitor-Discharge Ignition) for use on high-performance and racing engines. These systems store the ignition energy in the electrical field of a capacitor before a special transformer transmits it to the spark plug in the form of a high-voltage ignition pulse.

Ignition timing and adjustment

Approximately two milliseconds elapse between the mixture's initial ignition and its complete combustion. The ignition spark must therefore arc early enough to ensure that main combustion, and thus the combustion-pressure peak in the cylinder, occur shortly after piston TDC. The ignition angle should therefore move further in the advance direction along with increasing engine speed. The chosen firing point should ensure that the following requirements are met:
– maximum engine performance
– low fuel consumption
– no engine knock
– clean exhaust gas.

Since it is impossible to obtain optimal compliance with all of these requirements simultaneously, compromises must be found on a case-to-case basis. Optimal ignition timing is defined according to a variety of parameters. The most important are engine speed, engine load, engine design, fuel quality and momentary operating conditions (starting, idle and trailing throttle, etc.). In the simplest case, spark-advance mechanisms sensitive to variations in engine speed and intake-manifold vacuum adapt the ignition timing to suit the engine's current operating conditions.

In modern engine-management systems with extended functions, additional

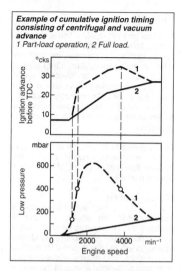

Example of cumulative ignition timing consisting of centrifugal and vacuum advance
1 Part-load operation, 2 Full load.

adjustments can be used e.g. for rapid torque adaptation or for swift heating of the catalytic converter.

All the adjustment strategies can operate either individually or simultaneously. The degree to which the ignition timing is advanced or retarded is determined by the ignition-advance curves calibrated specifically for each individual engine configuration.

At full load, the accelerator pedal is depressed fully and the throttle is wide open (WOT). Along with increasing engine speeds, ignition takes place earlier in order to maintain the combustion pressure at the levels required for optimal engine performance. The leaner A/F mixtures encountered during part-throttle operation are more difficult to ignite. Because this means that more time is required for ignition, it must be triggered earlier, with the timing being shifted further in the "advance" direction. The manifold vacuum employed to determine the necessary degree of spark advance is monitored downstream from the throttle valve. If the vacuum bore is located near the throttle valve (P. 489), the vacuum initially increases as the throttle is opened wider and begins to

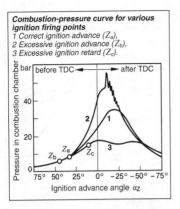

Combustion-pressure curve for various ignition firing points
1 Correct ignition advance (Z_a),
2 Excessive ignition advance (Z_b),
3 Excessive ignition retard (Z_c).

sumption. Excessive "advance" may result in extreme cases in serious damage to spark plugs or to the engine if the engine knocks. The level of exhaust emissions also increases.

Ignition and emissions

Owing to the fact that it directly affects the various exhaust-gas components, the ignition has a significant effect upon exhaust emissions. Because various – and in this context sometimes mutually antagonistic – factors such as fuel economy, driveability, etc., are also potential optimization criteria, it is not always possible to specify the ideal ignition timing for minimum emissions.

Shifts in ignition timing induce mutually inverse response patterns in fuel consumption and exhaust emissions: While more spark advance increases power and reduces fuel consumption, it also raises HC and, in particular, NO_x emissions. Excessive spark advance can cause engine knock and lead to engine damage. Retarded ignition results in higher exhaust-gas temperatures, which can also harm the engine. Electronic engine-management systems featuring programmed ignition curves are designed to adapt ignition timing in response to variations in factors such as min^{-1}, load, temperature, etc. They can thus be employed to achieve the optimum compromise between these mutually antagonistic objectives.

fall in the proximity of the full-throttle (WOT) position. The progressively wider throttle openings required to increase engine speed on the operating curve for part-throttle road operation are reflected in the relationship between vacuum and min^{-1} shown in the diagram.

Yet another diagram shows the curves for combustion-chamber pressure in a 4-stroke engine with correct and incorrect ignition timing. Even if the timing is initially correct, neglected maintenance can allow it to drift over the course of time. If the timing shifts towards a later firing point ("retard"), the result is a gradual drop in engine power and increased fuel con-

Overview of various ignition systems				
Function	Ignition system			
	CI	TI	EI[1])	DLI
Designation	Coil ignition system	Transistorized ignition system	Engine management	
			Electronic ignition system	Distributorless semiconductor ignition system
High-voltage generation	Inductive			
Ignition triggering	Mechanical	Electronic		
Ignition angle determined from engine speed and load	Mechanical		Electronic	
Spark distribution to appropriate cylinder	Mechanical			Electronic

[1]) Any desired ignition timing is not possible with EI. DLI therefore dominates with integrated engine-management systems.

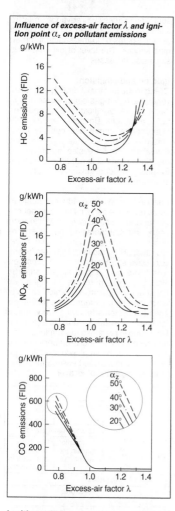

Influence of excess-air factor λ and ignition point α_z on pollutant emissions

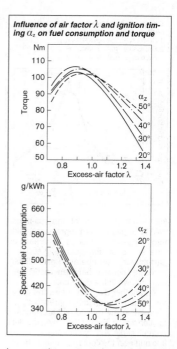

Influence of air factor λ and ignition timing α_z on fuel consumption and torque

leaner mixtures require substantially higher levels of spark energy. Excess energy, i.e., from an ignition system designed to generate a high-energy spark of extended duration (transistorized or electronic ignition) stabilizes flame propagation and reduces the fluctuations from cycle to cycle. The reduction in fluctuations results in smoother engine operation and lower HC emissions. Increased spark projection, larger electrode gaps and thin electrodes also have a positive influence on the engine's smoothness and HC emissions.

Ignition energy

The ignition system generates a high-voltage spark at the spark plug to initiate combustion. An ignition-spark energy of approx. 0.2 mJ is adequate to ignite a stoichiometric air-fuel mixture, while richer or

Ignition coil

The ignition coil functions as both an energy-storage device and a transformer. The coil, which is powered by DC voltage from the vehicle's electrical system, supplies the ignition pulses for the spark plugs at the required high voltage and discharge energy. The ignition driver stage with its defined deactivation current combines with a primary winding featuring specific resistance and inductance characteristics to determine the amount of energy stored within the ignition coil's magnetic field. The secondary winding can be designed to provide peak voltage, spark current and discharge duration in accordance with individual requirements.

The contact-breaker points used with coil ignition (CI) can only handle interrupt currents of up to approx. 5 A. TI, EI and DLI ignition systems and Motronic ECUs can handle much higher interrupt currents. The series resistors generally employed with coil ignition (they can be bypassed to increase energy during cold starts) can be omitted in electronic ignition systems. Here the electronic circuitry activates the ignition coil depending on battery voltage, engine speed and other influencing variables in such good time that full energy is available at the ignition point.

Each ignition coil is designed to meet the requirements of a particular application. It must charge quickly in order to furnish the voltages and ignition energies required at high engine speeds. Important priorities thus include low primary inductance and, in some cases, higher primary interrupt currents (for adequate energy storage).

Design and operation

Traditional ignition coils with asphalt or oil insulation enclosed in metal casings are being increasingly replaced by units featuring an epoxy-resin filler. These not only allow more latitude in the selection of geometry, type and number of electrical terminals, but also provide more compact dimensions, better vibration resistance and lower weight. The ignition coil is generally attached by way of the iron core to the engine or vehicle body. Rod-type ignition coils are installed in the cylinder-head recess above the spark plug.

The coil's synthetic materials provide good adhesion between all of the high-voltage components and the molded epoxy resin, which penetrates into all the capillary spaces. Supplementary iron cores are sometimes embedded on the inside of the synthetic molding.

The secondary winding is mostly designed as a disk or sandwich coil, with the

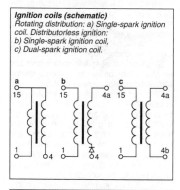

Ignition coils (schematic)
Rotating distribution: a) Single-spark ignition coil. Distributorless ignition:
b) Single-spark ignition coil,
c) Dual-spark ignition coil.

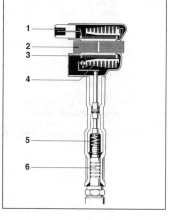

Single-spark ignition coil
1 External low-voltage terminal,
2 Laminated iron core, 3 Primary winding,
4 Secondary winding, 5 Internal high-voltage connection via spring contact, 6 Spark plug.

windings distributed among a series of segments. Even distribution of stresses among the insulating elements in all chambers combines with high dielectric strength to permit compact dimensions while at the same time making foil and paper between wire layers redundant. The winding's self-capacitance is also reduced.

Because lower breakdown voltages are required for the negative (relative to engine ground) ignition spark, the positive terminals for the primary and secondary windings are generally combined on those ignition coils used with rotating high-voltage distribution.

Single and dual-spark ignition coils are an alternative for use in ignition systems with distributorless ignition (DLI).

When a <u>single-spark coil</u> per spark plug is used, the primary current is controlled to furnish the relevant spark plug with an ignition pulse at precisely the right moment in time. High-voltage diodes are used to prevent the positive 1...2 kV high-voltage pulse generated when the primary current is activated from causing the spark plug to fire prematurely.

On the <u>dual-spark coil</u>, the secondary winding is galvanically insulated from the primary winding. Each of the two high-voltage outputs are connected to a spark plug. Ignition sparks are created at the two spark plugs when the primary current is deactivated. As with rotating high-voltage distribution, this system does not usually require any special precautions to prevent activation sparks.

Connection and installation are facilitated by combining several ignition coils in a common casing to form a single assembly. However, the individual coils continue to operate as independent units. The integration of output stages in the ignition coils means that short primary leads can be used (lower voltage drop). This arrangement also prevents power loss in the driver circuits from overheating the ECU.

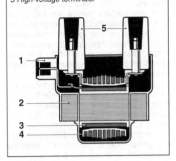

Dual-spark ignition coil (distributorless ignition)
1 Low-voltage terminal, 2 Laminated iron core, 3 Primary winding, 4 Secondary winding, 5 High-voltage terminals.

Spark plug

Function
The spark plug introduces the ignition energy generated by the ignition coil into the combustion chamber. The high voltage creates an electric spark between the spark-plug electrodes which ignites the compressed A/F mixture. As this function must also be guaranteed under extreme conditions (cold starting, full load), the spark plug plays a decisive role in the optimum performance and reliable operation of a spark-ignition engine. These requirements remain the same over the entire service life of the spark plug.

Requirements
The spark plug must satisfy a variety of extreme performance demands: It is exposed to the varying periodic processes within the combustion chamber as well as external climatic conditions. However, the combustion chamber must remain sealed.

During spark-plug operation with electronic ignition systems, ignition voltages of up to 30,000 V may occur and must not damage the insulator. This insulation capability must also be guaranteed at temperatures in the region of 1000 °C.

Because the spark plug is subjected to mechanical stresses in the form of exposure to periodic pressure peaks (up to

80 bar) within the combustion chamber, its materials must exhibit extreme resistance to thermal loads and continuous vibratory stress. At the same time, that section of the spark plug that protrudes into the combustion chamber is exposed to high-temperature chemical processes, making resistance to aggressive combustion deposits essential. Because it is subjected to rapid variations between the heat of the combustion gases and the cool A/F mixture, the spark-plug insulator must feature high resistance to thermal stresses (thermal shock). Effective heat dissipation at the electrodes and the insulator is also essential for reliable spark-plug performance.

Design

In a special high-grade ceramic insulator, an electrically conductive glass seal forms the connection between the center electrode and terminal stud. This glass element acts as a mechanical support for the components while providing a gas seal against the high-pressure combustion gases. It can also incorporate resistor elements for interference suppression and burn-off.

The connection end of the insulator is glazed for improved protection against contamination. The connection between it and the nickel-plated steel shell is gastight. The ground electrode, like the center electrode, is primarily manufactured using nickel-based alloys to cope with the high thermal stresses. It is welded to the shell. The thermal conduction properties of both the center and the ground electrodes are improved by using a nickel-alloy jacket material and a copper core. Silver and platinum, or platinum alloys, are employed as electrode material for special applications. The spark plugs have either an M4 or a standard SAE thread, depending upon the type of high-voltage connection. Spark plugs with metal shields are available for watertight systems and for maximum interference suppression.

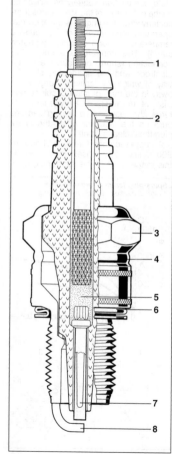

Spark plug
1 High-voltage connector (terminal nut),
2 Al_2O_3 Ceramic insulator,
3 Shell,
4 Heat-shrinkage zone,
5 Conductive glass,
6 Captive gasket,
7 Composite center electrode Ni/Cu,
8 Ground electrode.

Heat range

The operating temperature of the spark plug represents a balance between heat absorption and dissipation. The aim is to achieve a self-cleaning temperature of approx. 500 °C even at low engine power outputs.

If the temperature drops below this level, there is the danger that unburnt hydrocarbons and oil residue from incomplete combustion sequences will settle on the cold areas of the spark plugs (particularly when the engine is not at normal operating temperature, at low outside temperatures, and during repeated starts). This can create a conductive connection (shunt) between the center electrode and the spark-plug shell by way of which the ignition energy leaks away in the form of short-circuit current (risk of misfires). At higher temperatures, the residues containing carbons burn on the insulator nose; the spark plug thus "cleans" itself.

An upper temperature limit of approx. 900 °C should be observed because in this range wear of the spark-plug electrodes increases markedly (due to hot-gas corrosion) and if this limit is significantly exceeded this increases the risk of auto-ignition (ignition of the air-fuel mixture on hot surfaces). Such auto-ignition subjects the engine to extreme loads and can result in the engine's destruction within a short period of time. The spark plug must therefore be adapted accordingly in terms of its heat-absorption capability to the engine type. The identifying feature of a spark plug's thermal loading capacity is its heat range, which is defined by a code number and determined in comparison measurements with a reference standard source.

The Bosch ionic-current process presents possibilities for adapting the heat range to each engine. Characteristic changes in the combustion procedure due to increased thermal loading of the spark plugs can be detected using ionic current and used in the assessment of the auto-ignition process. The spark plug must be adapted in such a way as to preclude any possibility of premature ignition.

The use of center-electrode materials with high thermal conductivity (silver or nickel alloys with copper core) makes it possible to substantially extend the insulator nose without changing the plug's heat range, thus extending the plug's operating range downward into a lower thermal-load range and reducing the probability of fouling. These advantages are inherent in all Bosch Super (thermoelastic) spark plugs.

Reducing the likelihood of combustion miss and ignition miss – with their attendant massive increases in hydrocarbon emissions – provides benefits in exhaust emissions and fuel consumption in part-throttle operation at low load factors.

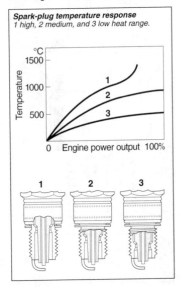

Spark-plug temperature response
1 high, 2 medium, and 3 low heat range.

Electrode gap and ignition voltage

The electrode gap should on the one hand be as large as possible so that the ignition spark activates a large volume element and thus results in reliable ignition of the air-fuel mixture due to the development of a stable flame-core.

It is frequently impossible to achieve a smooth idle when the electrode gap is too

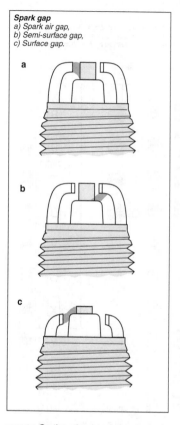

Spark gap
a) Spark air gap,
b) Semi-surface gap,
c) Surface gap.

a

b

c

and density of the gas to be ignited, also play an important role.

On today's high-compression engines, which frequently feature high charge turbulence, electrode gaps must be carefully defined in order to guarantee reliable ignition and thus misfire-free operation throughout the required service life.

Spark gap
The configuration of the arcing path is defined by the mutual arrangement of the electrodes.

Spark air gap (a):
A linear spark arcing directly between the center and ground electrodes ignites the air/fuel mixture between the electrodes.

Semi-surface gap (b):
The semi-surface gap is created by positioning the ground electrodes (at a defined distance to the insulator end face) to the sides of the center electrode. Under certain conditions, the ignition spark forms between the center electrode and the surface of the insulator tip before arcing across a gas-filled gap to the ground electrode.

Shifting a portion of the spark's propagation travel to this shunt path extends the gap across which any given voltage can produce an arc.

The increased electrode gap improves the ignition properties.

Surface gap (c):
On surface-gap spark plugs, the ground electrodes are positioned to the sides of the ceramic body. The sparks thus form over the surface of the insulator tip before arcing across a small gas-filled gap to the ground electrode. The arrangement of the ground electrode to the side of the ceramic body helps to reduce the quenching losses, i.e. the flame core can extend more effectively into the combustion chamber, thus enhancing the ignition properties of the plug.

narrow. On the other hand, the electrode gap must be narrow enough to guarantee that the ignition voltage will continue to produce a reliable arc, even at the end of the spark plug's service life and under unfavorable circumstances.

The required ignition voltage is influenced not only by the size of the electrode gap, but also by the electrodes' shape and temperature and the materials used in their manufacture. Parameters specific to the combustion chamber such as mixture composition (lambda value), flow velocity, turbulence

Designation codes for Bosch spark plugs

Individual spark-plug specifications are contained in the designation code. This code includes all vital spark-plug characteristics except the electrode gap, which is indicated on the package. Spark-plug specifications for individual engine applications are defined by Bosch and the engine manufacturers.

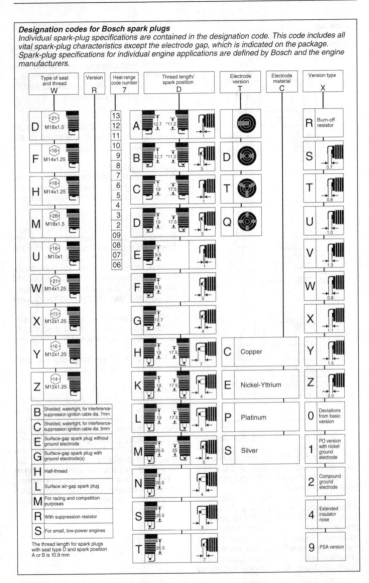

Type of seat and thread	Version	Heat-range code number	Thread length/ spark position	Electrode version	Electrode material	Version type
W	R	7	D	T	C	X

The thread length for spark plugs with seat type D and spark position A or B is 10.9 mm

Conventional coil ignition (CI)

Many vehicles are still equipped with conventional coil ignition. When the contact breaker closes with the ignition switched on, current from the battery or alternator flows through the ignition coil's primary winding, generating a powerful magnetic field in which the energy is stored. At the ignition point, the contact breaker interrupts the current, the magnetic field collapses and the high voltage necessary for ignition is induced in the secondary winding. This voltage is fed from terminal 4 to the ignition distributor via a high-tension cable and from there to the individual spark plugs.

The following is a basic definition of the relationship between the speed of a four-stroke SI engine and the number of sparks generated per minute:

$$f = z \cdot n/2$$

f Spark-generation rate, z Number of cylinders, n Engine speed.

At low engine speeds, the contact-breaker points remain closed long enough to exploit the coil's full energy-storage potential. At higher engine speeds, this contact period – the dwell angle – is shorter, and the primary current is interrupted before maximum energy can be transferred to the coil. The resulting reduction in stored energy means that less

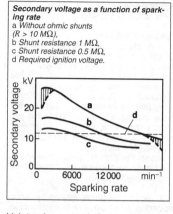

Secondary voltage as a function of sparking rate
a *Without ohmic shunts*
($R > 10$ MΩ),
b *Shunt resistance 1 MΩ,*
c *Shunt resistance 0.5 MΩ,*
d *Required ignition voltage.*

high-tension current is then available from the coil.

In response, ignition coils are designed to provide high-tension voltage well in excess of the spark plugs' requirements, even at maximum engine speeds. Contamination on the insulating components acts as a capacitive and ohmic shunt, increasing the ignition loads placed upon the system, with combustion and ignition misfiring as the ultimate consequences.

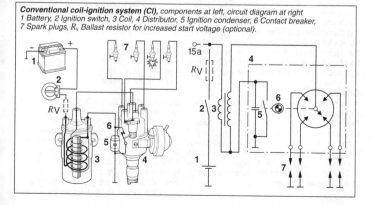

Conventional coil-ignition system (CI), components at left, circuit diagram at right
1 Battery, 2 Ignition switch, 3 Coil, 4 Distributor, 5 Ignition condenser, 6 Contact breaker,
7 Spark plugs, R_v Ballast resistor for increased start voltage (optional).

Ignition coil
Description: see P. 481.

Ignition distributor
The distributor is a separate, self-contained component within the ignition system. It has the following functions:
– it distributes the ignition pulses to the engine's spark plugs in the defined sequence (CI, TI, and electronic ignition),
– triggers the ignition pulse, either when the contact breaker interrupts the primary current, or, with breakerless systems (CI, TI, EI in some cases), using a pulse generator,
– adjusts the ignition timing with a spark-advance mechanism on conventional ignition systems (CI, TI).

In modern electronic ignition systems, operating either alone or in combination with the fuel-injection system (Motronic), the distributor generally comprises only a rotor arm connected to the camshaft and the distributor cap with high-voltage cables.

The contact-breaker points and the spark-advance mechanism perform separate functions from those of the distributor proper. They are combined with it in a single unit because they require a synchronized drive.

The ignition pulse passes through the center connection and the carbon brush or the center-tower spark gap to the distributor's rotor arm which then distributes this ignition energy by arcing it to fixed electrodes pressed into the periphery of the distributor cap. From here, the ignition pulses travel through the ignition cables to the spark plugs. A dust cover is sometimes installed to separate this high-voltage section from the rest of the unit.

Contact breaker
A cam opens the contact-breaker points to interrupt the flow of primary current to the coil for ignition. The number of cam lobes corresponds to the number of engine cylinders. The portion of the distributor shaft's rotation during which the points remain closed is the dwell angle.

The contact-breaker points are subject to three types of wear:

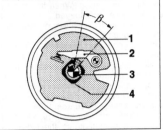

Contact breaker
1 Moving breaker-plate assembly, 2 Breaker lever, 3 Distributor shaft, 4 Distributor cam.

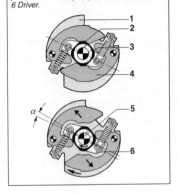

Centrifugal advance mechanism, at rest (above), in operation (below)
1 Support plate, 2 Distributor cam, 3 Contact path, 4 Advance flyweight, 5 Distributor shaft, 6 Driver.

– contact pitting,
– contact arm (rubbing-block) wear,
– plastic deformation and local compression of the contact metal.

Contact pitting stems from the breaking sparks (residual arcing) induced by induction voltage during interruption of the primary current. The ignition condenser is designed to suppress this type of arcing, but residual sparks continue to occur. Although contact wear and rubbing-block wear are mutually counteractive, the effects of the latter are generally more pronounced, resulting in a tendency for the ignition to drift in the "retard" direction, toward a later ignition point.

Spark-advance mechanism
Ignition distributors are generally equipped with two spark-advance mechanisms: a speed-sensitive centrifugal advance mechanism and a load-dependent vacuum-controlled device.

Centrifugal advance mechanism
The centrifugal advance mechanism adjusts the ignition timing in response to changes in engine speed. The support plate upon which the flyweights are mounted rotates with the distributor shaft. The flyweights move outward as engine speed increases, thereby turning the driver over the contact path to the distributor shaft in the direction of rotation. In this way, the distributor cam also turns towards the distributor shaft by the ignition advance angle α. The point of ignition is advanced by this angle.

Vacuum adjustment mechanism
The vacuum mechanism adapts the ignition timing to changes in engine output and load factor. Intake manifold vacuum is monitored or tapped off in the vicinity of the throttle valve. The vacuum acts upon two aneroid capsules.

Operation of advance mechanism
Because the air/fuel mixture combusts more slowly during operation at low load

factors, it must be ignited earlier to compensate. Meanwhile, the proportion of those residual gases which have been burned but not discharged from the combustion chamber increases, and the mixture leans out. Vacuum for the advance mechanism is tapped off immediately downstream from the open throttle valve. As the engine load decreases, the vacuum in the advance unit rises, causing the diaphragm and its control arm to move to the right. The control arm turns the breaker-plate assembly against the distributor shaft's direction of rotation; the point of ignition is advanced still further.

Operation of retard mechanism
Here the connection with the intake manifold's internal vacuum is downstream from the closed throttle. The ring-shaped vacuum retard unit reduces exhaust emissions by reducing ignition advance under specific operating conditions (e.g. idle, trailing throttle). The ring diaphragm and its control arm move to the left when vacuum is applied. The control arm rotates the breaker-plate assembly together with the contact breaker in the distributor shaft's direction of rotation.

This spark-retard system operates independently of the advance mechanism. The advance mechanism has priority: simultaneous vacuum in both units during part-throttle operation shifts the unit to its "advance" position.

Vacuum advance mechanism with ignition advance and retard units
a Advance adjustment up to stop, b Retard adjustment up to stop
1 Ignition distributor, 2 Breaker-plate assembly, 3 Diaphragm, 4 Vacuum retard unit,
5 Vacuum advance unit, 6 Vacuum unit, 7 Throttle valve, 8 Intake manifold.

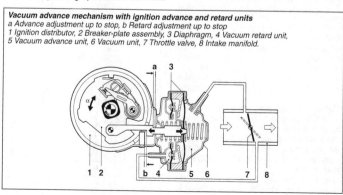

Transistorized ignition (TI)

With conventional coil-ignition systems, ignition energy and maximum voltage are restricted by various electrical and mechanical factors limiting the breaker points' switching capacity. The demands placed upon battery-ignition systems are often more than the contact-breaker assembly can satisfy in its role as a power switch. In electronic ignition systems, the points are assisted or replaced entirely by wear-free control devices. Transistorized (coil) ignition is available in both breaker-triggered and breakerless versions.

Transistorized coil ignition with contact control is especially suitable for upgrading existing coil-ignition systems (CI). Breaker-triggered transistorized coil ignition systems are no longer installed as original equipment.

Breakerless transistorized ignition

On breakerless transistorized ignition systems, the cam-actuated contact breaker is replaced by a magnetic "pulse generator". This generates current and voltage pulses magnetically (without contacts) to trigger the high-voltage ignition pulse through the system electronics. The pulse generator is installed in the ignition distributor.

These triggering devices operate according to various principles.

Induction-type pulse generators (TI-I)

The induction-type pulse generator is a permanently-excited AC generator consisting of stator and rotor. The number of teeth or arms corresponds to the number of cylinders in the engine. The frequency and amplitude of the alternating current generated by the unit vary according to engine speed. The ECU processes this AC voltage and uses it for ignition control.

Hall-effect pulse generators (TI-H)

This type of ignition-pulse generator utilizes the Hall effect. A speed-sensitive magnetic field produces voltage pulses in an electrically charged semiconductor layer to control activation of the ECU's primary current.

Ignition pulse generators (impulsers) display clear benefits over mechanical

Breakerless transistorized ignition system
1 Battery, 2 Ignition switch, 3 Coil, 4 Electronic trigger box, 5 Ignition distributor with centrifugal and vacuum advance mechanism, 6a Induction-type pulse generator, 6b Hall-type pulse generator (alternative), 7 Spark plugs.

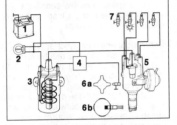

contact breakers: They do not wear, and are thus maintenance-free. They allow precise control of ignition timing with attendant benefits in engine performance.

Ignition distributor with induction-type pulse generator
1 Permanent magnet, 2 Induction winding with core, 3 Variable air gap, 4 Trigger wheel.

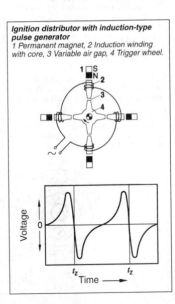

Electronic control units

Virtually all of the electronic control units (trigger boxes) in use today are equipped with primary-current regulators and closed-loop dwell-angle control.

The primary-current regulator limits the current in order to protect the ignition coil and the driver stage. When used in conjunction with a coil featuring low primary resistance, it provides high starting current at low battery voltages. This makes it possible to dispense with series resistors upstream of the coil as well as with the bridging function for starting.

Closed-loop dwell-angle control ensures that the desired primary current is obtained in the control range as far as possible at the point of ignition. This reduces the power losses in the ECU. It also compensates for battery-voltage fluctuations and ignition-coil temperature effects. Depending on system design, this dwell-angle control is effective up to medium engine speeds. At high engine speeds, the dwell angle is determined by the break time required to achieve adequate arcing durations. The residual energy remaining in the coil after the break time promotes optimal coil charging with reduced dwell times.

The sparkless closed-circuit current deactivation switches off the primary current with the ignition on and the engine off to ensure that no sparks occur at the spark plug. However, there are also TC-I systems (with induction-type pulse-generator) with intrinsic closed-circuit current deactivation.

Transistorized ignition is sometimes employed together with auxiliary devices to adjust the spark advance. An example would be the idle-speed control which is installed between the Hall generator and the ECU; below idle speed it reacts to further decreases in engine min^{-1} by advancing the ignition, thus increasing torque and preventing engine speed from dropping any further. The electronic retard device reduces ignition advance at high engine speeds to prevent knocking. It is connected in parallel with the ECU. Today, both of these functions are integrated in the electronically adjusted ignition systems within the engine-management system.

Hybrid units have become the ECU standard for transistorized ignition systems owing to their ability to combine high packaging density with low weight and excellent reliability. Hybrid technology replaces the printed-circuit board, with an Al_2O_3 substrate bearing conductor paths and resistors applied in a silk-screening process. Semiconductor devices and capacitors in chip form complete the circuit. As the Darlington power-transistor chip is mounted insulated on the metallic base plate, cooling is excellent, permitting operation at high temperatures.

Ignition coils (description on P. 481)

The performance specifications of ignition coils for conventional ignition differ from those of ignition coils with electronic circuit-breakers (transistorized ignition, see P. 490). A coil designed for one application should never be employed in the other.

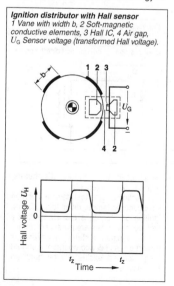

Ignition distributor with Hall sensor
1 Vane with width b, 2 Soft-magnetic conductive elements, 3 Hall IC, 4 Air gap, U_G Sensor voltage (transformed Hall voltage).

Note: Unlike with breaker-triggered ignition, terminal 1 of the systems mentioned must not be shorted to ground (e.g. during compression testing as this would overload the low-resistance primary winding of the ignition coil.

Capacitor-discharge ignition (CDI)

The operating concept behind CDI, or "thyristor ignition," as it is also called, differs from that of the ignition systems described above. CDI was developed for use with high-speed, high-output multi-cylinder reciprocating IC engines in high-performance and competition applications and for rotary-piston engines.

The salient characteristic of the CDI system is that it stores ignition energy in the electrical field of a capacitor. Capacitance and charge voltage of the capacitor determine the amount of energy which is stored. The ignition transformer converts the primary voltage discharged from the capacitor to the required high voltage. Capacitor-discharge ignition is available in both breaker-triggered and breakerless versions.

The major advantage of the CDI is that it generally remains impervious to electrical shunts in the high-voltage ignition circuit, especially those stemming from spark-plug contamination. For many applications, the spark duration of 0.1...0.3 ms is too brief to ensure that the air-fuel mixture will ignite reliably. Thus CDI is only designed for specific types of engine, and today its use is restricted to a limited application range, as transistorized ignition systems now afford virtually the same performance. CDI is not suited for aftermarket installations.

CDI can also be employed for distributorless ignition (DLI) with the installation of one ignition coil per cylinder, with energy distribution taking place at the medium-voltage level.

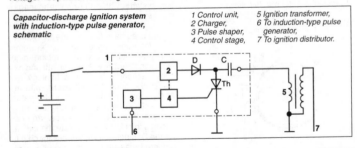

Capacitor-discharge ignition system with induction-type pulse generator, schematic

1 Control unit,
2 Charger,
3 Pulse shaper,
4 Control stage,
5 Ignition transformer,
6 To induction-type pulse generator,
7 To ignition distributor.

Accident hazard

All electronic ignition systems (including capacitor discharge, transistorized ignition and all systems with partial or comprehensive electronic control) are potentially dangerous. Always switch off the ignition or disconnect the battery before performing any service or maintenance including:
– Replacing components such as spark plugs, coils, transformers, distributors, high-tension cables, etc.
– Connecting engine test devices such as stroboscopic lamps, dwell-tach testers, ignition oscillographs etc. Dangerously high voltage levels are present throughout the ignition system whenever it is turned on. All service operations should be performed exclusively by qualified technicians.

Electronic ignition (EI and DLI)

Electronic ignition derives its name from the fact that it calculates the ignition point electronically. The characteristic curves provided by the conventional distributor's centrifugal and vacuum-advance units are replaced by an optimized electronic ignition map. Mechanical high-tension distribution is retained with EI ignition. Fully electronic distributorless semiconductor ignition (DLI) uses stationary electronically controlled components to replace the mechanical, rotating high-tension distributor.

Electronic ignition systems operate more precisely than mechanical systems, with major benefits originating in the fact that the ignition process can be triggered from the crankshaft instead of from a distributor (distributor drive tolerances are no longer a factor). The limitations which mechanical adjustment mechanisms place upon the performance curve (summation of curves for load and engine speed in a single progression) are also avoided. The number of input variables is also theoretically unlimited, usually allowing extensions in the ignition angle's adjustment range. The fixed-drive ignition distributor's limitations regarding the engine's ignition-voltage requirements and ignition-angle adjustment range are such that it has difficulty coping with larger numbers of cylinders; efficient spark distribution cannot always be guaranteed. Corrective measures include dividing the ignition into two circuits (e.g., for 8- and 12-cylinder engines) and static voltage distribution.

Electronic ignition can be combined with electronic fuel-injection (Motronic), knock control, ASR, etc., making it possible to employ sensors and/or signals from other units in more than one system. A serial bus (CAN, P. 884) further reduces the number of inputs and processing circuits on the ECU's input-side.

Schematic of an electronic ignition system (EI)
1 Ignition coil with ignition driver stage, 2 High-voltage distributor, 3 Spark plug, 4 ECU,
5 Engine-temperature sensor, 6 Knock sensor, 7 Engine-speed and reference-mark sensor,
8 Ring gear for sensor, 9 Throttle switch, 10 Battery, 11 Ignition switch.

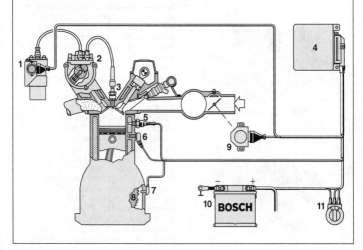

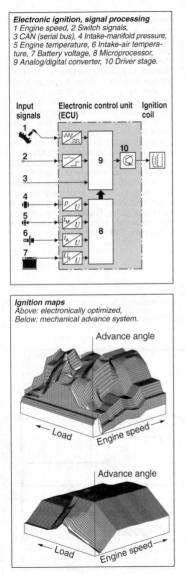

Electronic ignition, signal processing
1 Engine speed, 2 Switch signals,
3 CAN (serial bus), 4 Intake-manifold pressure,
5 Engine temperature, 6 Intake-air temperature, 7 Battery voltage, 8 Microprocessor,
9 Analog/digital converter, 10 Driver stage.

Ignition maps
Above: electronically optimized,
Below: mechanical advance system.

Operation

The engine's speed and crankshaft position are monitored directly at the ring
gear, using either a separate rotor or a
specific pin sequence employing an inductive, rod-type sensor, with two sensors
being employed on older units. Triggering
is either incremental or segmentary, according to whether the information is
taken from teeth distributed evenly
around the crankshaft or a crankshaft
segment per cylinder pair:
– Beginning of segment = maximum
  spark advance angle,
– End of segment = starting angle.

In the incremental system illustrated here,
the reference mark (shown as a tooth
gap) represents a defined crankshaft position, providing a reference for electrically monitoring crankshaft angle using
the ring-gear teeth. A distributor without
an advance mechanism can also be employed for triggering; here the control signal is provided by a Hall generator. An ab-
solute-pressure sensor in the intake manifold is the best way to monitor load. This
provides a better gauge of cylinder
charge than the spark-advance or retard
bores on the throttle valve. It is also possible to incorporate load switches, throttle-valve potentiometers or electronic load
signals from the mixture-preparation system. The microcomputer in the ECU
processes the engine-speed and load signals prior to using them to calculate the
precise ignition angle within the ignition
map. The computer can also process
other input variables, such as e.g. engine
temperature, or information on trailing
throttle or full-load operation from the
throttle-valve switch, to derive correction
values and regulate other vehicle-specific
functions as required. The dwell angle for
charging the ignition coil is also specified
by the computer. The battery voltage is
monitored here to enable voltage correction. The system responds to deviations
in battery voltage from the specified baseline by extending or reducing coil-charg-
ing times accordingly. This ensures consistent availability of maximum voltage
while at the same time limiting the accumulation of heat in ECU and coil to a minimum. At speeds below the starting

speed, the computer interrupts the current flow through the ignition coil in order to prevent overheating. The driver stage can be either integrated inside the ECU or installed externally, e.g. on the ignition coil.

Signal processing in the ECU

After initial processing the digital signals go directly to the processor. Analog signals are first converted into digital form. There are also ECU's which can transmit supplementary digital or analog signals (e.g., for overrun fuel cutoff and exhaust-gas recirculation). There exists a range of EI ignition-system versions of varying complexity. A comparison of the ignition map with the response curve of a distributor shows that it is possible to program each point in the ignition map independently from every other point. Thus the optimum ignition timing (e.g., for maximum fuel economy) can be selected for every operating condition, according to the limits imposed by factors such as exhaust emissions, pre-ignition limit and driveability. The entire system is completely

maintenance-free and does not require any adjustments during the engine's service life.

Rotating voltage distribution

A high-voltage distributor distributes the ignition pulses to the spark plugs of the individual cylinders (as described earlier). If the distributor's adjustment range is insufficient for handling a larger number of cylinders, then two ignition circuits are employed, i.e., two 4-cylinder distributors can be used for one 8-cylinder engine. Synchronization through the crankshaft can be used for "two times 4 cylinders", whereas "two times 3 cylinders" with constant ignition-angle spacing (not employed up to now) must be controlled by the camshaft.

Distributorless (stationary) voltage distribution

Systems with single-spark ignition coil
Each cylinder has its own ignition coil with driver output stage, installed either di-

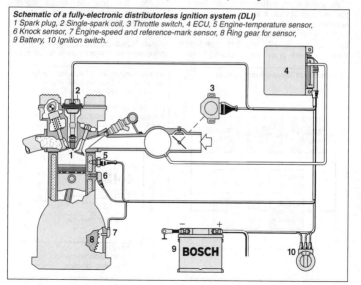

Schematic of a fully-electronic distributorless ignition system (DLI)
1 Spark plug, 2 Single-spark coil, 3 Throttle switch, 4 ECU, 5 Engine-temperature sensor,
6 Knock sensor, 7 Engine-speed and reference-mark sensor, 8 Ring gear for sensor,
9 Battery, 10 Ignition switch.

rectly above the spark plug or separately. Either synchronization with the camshaft sensor or a method for detecting the compression cylinder is required. On engines with an even number of cylinders, the system reverts to crankshaft triggering in the event of camshaft-sensor failure, although two coils are then always activated simultaneously (one of the sparks is discharged during an exhaust stroke). This system, suitable for engines with any number of cylinders, provides the greatest latitude for adjustment, as there is only one spark per cycle. All these advantages mean that the single-spark ignition coil is being increasingly used and is taking over from the dual-spark ignition coil in spite of costing more.

Systems with dual-spark ignition coil
One ignition coil is required for every two cylinders. The crankshaft can be used for synchronization. The high-voltage end of each ignition coil is connected to the spark plugs for two cylinders whose operating cycles are 360° out of phase with each other.

As there is an additional spark during the exhaust stroke, it is important to ensure that residual mixture or fresh mixture is not ignited. Furthermore, the dual-spark system is only suited for use with even numbers of cylinders. Owing to its

cost advantage relative to the single-spark ignition unit, the dual-spark ignition system is the most common distributorless ignition in use today.

Knock control

Application
Electronic control of the ignition point offers the possibility of controlling very precisely the ignition angle as a function of engine speed, load and temperature.

Nevertheless, without knock control a clear safety distance to the knock limit is required. This distance is necessary to ensure that even in the most knock-sensitive case with regard to engine tolerances, engine aging, environmental conditions and fuel quality, no cylinder reaches or exceeds the knock limit. The resulting engine design leads to lower compressions with retarded ignition points and thus worsening of fuel consumption and torque figures.

These disadvantages can be avoided through the use of knock control. Experience shows that knock control increases engine compression and significantly improves fuel consumption and torque. However, the pre-control ignition angle now no longer needs to be deter-

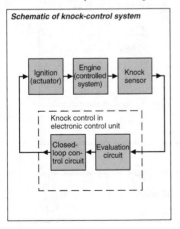

Schematic of knock-control system

Ignition (actuator) → Engine (controlled system) → Knock sensor

Knock control in electronic control unit

Closed-loop control circuit ← Evaluation circuit

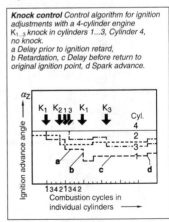

Knock control Control algorithm for ignition adjustments with a 4-cylinder engine $K_{1...3}$ knock in cylinders 1...3, Cylinder 4, no knock.
a Delay prior to ignition retard,
b Retardation, c Delay before return to original ignition point, d Spark advance.

α_Z

Ignition advance angle

K_1 $K_{2\,1\,3}$ K_1 K_3 Cyl. 4
2
3

a b c d

1 3 4 2 1 3 4 2
Combustion cycles in individual cylinders

mined for the most knock-sensitive but rather for the most insensitive conditions (e.g. engine compression at lower tolerance limit, best possible fuel quality, most knock-insensitive cylinder). Each individual engine cylinder can now be operated over its entire service life in virtually all operating ranges at its knock limit and thus at optimal efficiency.

The essential precondition for this ignition-angle configuration is reliable knock detection for each individual cylinder as from a particular knock intensity, and over the entire engine operating range.

Combustion knock

The characteristic vibrations of combustion knock are detected by knock sensors, converted into electrical signals and forwarded to the Motronic.

It is essential to work out carefully the number and installation positions of the required knock sensors. Reliable knock detection must be guaranteed for all cylinders and for all engine operating points, particularly at high engine speeds and loads. As a rule, 4-cylinder in-line engines are equipped with one knock sensor, 5- and 6-cylinder engines with two sensors and 8- and 12-cylinder engines with two or more sensors.

Knock detection, evaluation

For the purpose of knock detection, the vibrations characteristic to knocking are converted into electrical signals by one or more knock sensors mounted at appropriate positions on the engine, and then forwarded to the Motronic for evaluation. It is here that the corresponding evaluation algorithm is applied to detect knock for each cylinder and each combustion. Detected combustion knocks result in a retardation of the ignition point by a programmable amount at the cylinder in question. If knock stops, the ignition point is advanced again in stages up to the pre-control value.

The knock-detection and knock-control algorithms are matched in such a way as to eliminate any knocking that is audible and damaging to the engine.

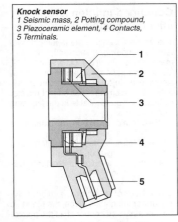

Knock sensor
1 Seismic mass, 2 Potting compound, 3 Piezoceramic element, 4 Contacts, 5 Terminals.

Adaptation

Real engine operation produces different knock limits and thus also different ignition points for the individual cylinders. In order to adapt the ignition-point pre-control values to the particular knock limit, the ignition-point retardation values individual to each cylinder and dependent on the operating point are stored.

They are stored in non-volatile maps of the permanently powered RAM covering load and engine speed. In this way, the engine can also be operated in the event of rapid load and speed changes in each operating point at optimal efficiency and without audible combustion knocks.

The engine can even be approved for fuels with lower anti-knock properties.

Combined ignition and injection system (Motronic)

The Motronic engine-management system has undergone substantial development since its introduction in 1979. Intially, integration was based on the basic gasoline-injection systems, in combination with distributorless semiconductor ignition, as were available in the following systems:
– KE-Motronic, based on KE continuous gasoline injection (P. 469),
– Mono-Motronic, based on intermittent single-point injection (P. 465),
– M-Motronic, based on intermittent multipoint injection (P. 471).

On the basis of M-Motronic, and by applying further integration steps, the Motronic system assumed control of all the manipulated variables of a spark-ignition engine that influence engine torque:
– ME-Motronic with electronic accelerator pedal (ETC) for controlling gasoline injection, ignition and fresh-air charge for manifold injection (P. 498).
– MED-Motronic with further integrated open- and closed-loop control functions for the high-pressure fuel circuit. With direct injection and realization of the various operating modes of this engine type (P. 507).

System overview
The Motronic system comprises all the sensors for recording the current engine and vehicle operating data (P. 501, Operating-data acquisition) and all the actuators for the adjustments to be carried out on the SI engine (P. 503, Operating-data processing).

Electronic control unit
The ECU employs sensors to monitor the relevant status of engine and vehicle at extremely short intervals (milliseconds).
Input circuits suppress sensor-signal interference and convert the signals to a single unified voltage scale. An analog-digital converter then transforms the conditioned signals into digital values. Further signals are received by way of a digital interface. Using this information, the microprocessor identifies the operating state desired by the driver and from it calculates for instance:
– the required torque,
– the resulting cylinder charge with the associated injected fuel quantity, and
– the correct ignition timing.

The low-level signal data from the microprocessor outputs are adapted by the driver stages to the levels required by the various actuators. A semiconductor memory chip stores all programs and performance maps, ensuring system consistency which remains completely impervious to fluctuations resulting from signal-level and component tolerances.

Digital accuracy is a function of word length, as well as of the consistency of the quartz's basic clock frequency and the types of algorithms used for the calculations. The consistency and precision of the reference voltages and the components installed in the analog input circuits influence the analog accuracy.
Program design must satisfy the engine's severe real-time demands: in an 8-cylinder engine at maximum speeds, less than 2.5 ms are available between two ignitions. All essential calculations must be completed within this period. In addition to these crankshaft-synchronous processes, there are also time-synchronous operations. Both types can be suspended by interrupts.

ME-Motronic

Design

Basic functions
In order to set the operating state desired by the driver (main function), the position of the gas pedal is converted by the microprocessor into a setpoint value for the engine torque. Then, while taking into consideration the highly varying current operating data from the ME-Motronic, these are converted into the variables for determining the engine torque:
– the charging of the cylinders with air,
– the mass of the injected fuel and
– the ignition angle.

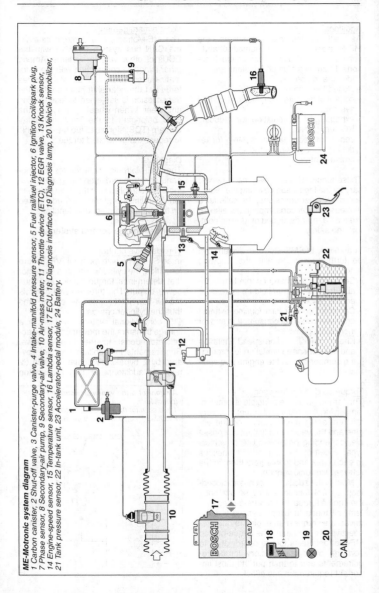

ME-Motronic system diagram
1 Carbon canister, 2 Shut-off valve, 3 Canister-purge valve, 4 Intake-manifold pressure sensor, 5 Fuel rail/fuel injector, 6 Ignition coil/spark plug, 7 Phase sensor, 8 Secondary-air pump, 9 Secondary-air valve, 10 Air-mass meter, 11 Throttle device (ETC), 12 EGR valve, 13 Knock sensor, 14 Engine-speed sensor, 15 Temperature sensor, 16 Lambda sensor, 17 ECU, 18 Diagnosis interface, 19 Diagnosis lamp, 20 Vehicle immobilizer, 21 Tank pressure sensor, 22 In-tank unit, 23 Accelerator-pedal module, 24 Battery.

Additional function

As well as the basic functions, the ME-Motronic has a large number of additional open- and closed-loop control functions. Examples of such functions are:
– idle-speed control,
– closed-loop lambda control,
– control of evaporative-emissions control system,
– exhaust-gas recirculation for reducing NO_x emissions,
– control of secondary-air system for reducing HC emissions, and
– cruise control.

These functions have been made necessary by the legislation covering the reduction of exhaust emissions, the calls for a decrease in fuel consumption but also increased demands placed on driving comfort and safety.

In addition, the ME-Motronic system can be further extended with the following functions:
– Control of turbocharger control and variable-tract intake manifold for increasing engine power output,
– Camshaft control for reducing exhaust emissions and fuel consumption and for increasing power,
– Knock control, engine-speed limitation and vehicle-speed limitation for protecting components in the engine and vehicle.

Torque-guided control concept

The torque-guidance principle is aimed at simplifying the many and sometimes very different assignments placed on the engine and the vehicle. Only then is it possible, depending on the engine or vehicle type, to determine the required functions in each case and to integrate them in the relevant Motronic version.

Most of the additional open- and closed-loop control functions likewise influence the engine torque. In a torque-guided system, all these functions behave like the driver: they request an engine torque irrespective of each other. The torque-guided ME-Motronic uses torque coordination to sort the often contradictory torque requirements and to then put the most important requirement into effect.

Vehicle management

The ME-Motronic can communicate via the CAN bus system (P. 884) with the ECUs of other vehicle systems. Among other things, in conjunction with the automatic-transmission ECU, it reduces torque at the gear-shift point so that the transmission is subjected to less loading and wear. When wheel spin occurs, the ECU belonging to the Traction Control System (TCS) signals to the ME-Motronic to reduce the generated torque.

Diagnosis

The ME-Motronic incorporates components for on-board monitoring (OBD). It therefore complies with the most stringent emission limits and the demands placed on the integrated diagnosis functions.

Cylinder-charge control systems

Throttle-valve control

In an SI engine with external A/F mixture formation, the cylinder charge is the factor that determines torque output and thus power output. The throttle valve controls the air-flow intake into the engine and thus the cylinder charge.

In conventional systems, a cable or a linkage transfers the movement of the accelerator pedal to the throttle valve. Requirements for additional air are covered by a bypass air actuator which directs an additional air flow around the

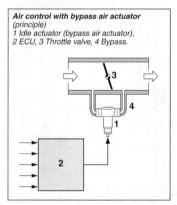

Air control with bypass air actuator
(principle)
1 Idle actuator (bypass air actuator),
2 ECU, 3 Throttle valve, 4 Bypass.

throttle valve (see Fig.), or a throttle-valve actuator alters the stop for minimum air quantity. However, the air flow required by the engine can only be electronically influenced to a limited extent (idle-speed control).

Systems with ETC (electronic throttle control, integrated in the engine control unit for ignition, injection and other auxiliary functions) detect the position of the accelerator pedal with a pedal-travel sensor (potentiometer).

Taking into account the current engine operating status, the ECU calculates how far the throttle valve needs to open and actuates the throttle-valve drive accordingly (see Fig.). A throttle-valve angle sensor (potentiometer) monitors exact compliance with the desired throttle-valve position. Two potentiometers (for redundancy reasons) at the accelerator pedal and throttle device are part of the ETC monitoring system which, while the engine is running, continually checks all the sensors and calculations which affect throttle-valve opening.

Charge-cycle control
The behavior of the gas columns flowing into and out of the cylinders changes considerably as a function, for instance, of engine speed or throttle-valve opening. With fixed valve timing, the charge cycle can

only be optimized for a specific operating range.

Camshaft control or camshaft-lobe control (P. 387) permits not only variable valve timing, and thus adaptation to various engine speeds, but also enables the residual exhaust-gas mass in the cylinder to be influenced ("internal EGR").

("External") EGR effectively reduces the temperature-dependent NO_X emissions. Exhaust gases which have already been combusted are added to the A/F mixture in order to reduce peak combustion temperatures. For this purpose, the Motronic triggers the exhaust-gas recirculation valve as a function of the engine operating point. The EGR valve then adds a partial flow of exhaust gas to the fresh mixture, thereby increasing the total charge while the fresh-air charge remains constant. In this way, the engine must be throttled less heavily in order for a specific torque to be reached (lower fuel consumption).

The achievable torque, which is proportional to the fresh-mixture charge, can be increased still further by compressing the air in the cylinder. This is the purpose of dynamic supercharging, exhaust-gas turbocharging, or mechanical supercharging (P. 390).

Operating-data acquisition

Vehicle-operator command
In the case of engine management with an electronic throttle valve (ETC), there is no longer a mechanical connection between the accelerator pedal and the throttle-valve actuator. Instead, the position of the accelerator pedal is sensed by a pedal-travel sensor or accelerator-pedal module and converted into an electrical signal. The engine-management system interprets this signal as the vehicle-operator command.

Air charge
In engine concepts with manifold injection, there is a linear relationship between the air charge and the torque generated by combustion. In the torque-guided ME-Motronic, the air charge is therefore not just one of the main factors involved in calculating the injected fuel quantity and

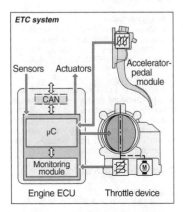

ETC system

Sensors Actuators Accelerator-pedal module

CAN

μC

Monitoring module

Engine ECU   Throttle device

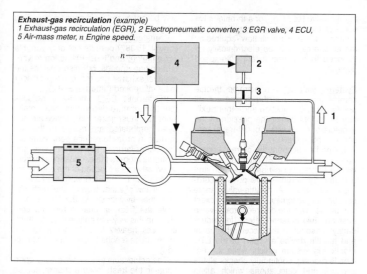

Exhaust-gas recirculation (example)
1 Exhaust-gas recirculation (EGR), 2 Electropneumatic converter, 3 EGR valve, 4 ECU,
5 Air-mass meter, n Engine speed.

ignition angle, but also serves to calculate the torque currently being delivered by the engine. The following sensors can be used for this purpose:
– Hot-film air-mass meter,
– Intake-manifold pressure sensor,
– Ambient pressure sensor,
– Boost-pressure sensor (BPS) and
– Throttle-valve sensor.

Engine speed, crankshaft position and camshaft position
A speed sensor on the crankshaft monitors the crankshaft revolutions per minute (rotational speed). It then forwards this information on the crankshaft position, that is, the piston position of all cylinders, as an important input variable to the ME-Motronic. The cylinder's piston position is used, for instance, to determine the injection and ignition points.

To trigger the single-spark ignition coils, the ME-Motronic with static voltage distribution also requires additional information on the camshaft position. This information is mostly monitored with a Hall-effect sensor and forwarded to the ECU as a switch signal.

A/F mixture composition
The lambda factor (λ) is the figure which quantifies the A/F mass ratio of the mixture. The catalytic converter only performs optimally at $\lambda = 1$. The lambda sensor measures the oxygen concentration in the exhaust gas and provides information on the current value of the excess-air factor (P. 458).

Combustion knocks
The characteristic vibrations of combustion knocks are detected by knock sensors, converted into electrical signals and forwarded to the ME-Motronic (P. 498).

Engine and intake-air temperatures
The voltage at the NTC resistor of the engine-temperature sensor is a function of the coolant temperature. It is input via the analog-digital converter and is a measure of the temperature. In the same way, a sensor in the intake port measures the temperature of the intake air.

Operating-data processing

Torque guidance
Torque guidance is a feature of the ME-

Motronic. Numerous subsystems within the Motronic (e.g. idle-speed control, engine-speed limitation), and the systems for management of the drivetrain (e.g. TCS or transmission-shift control) or of the complete vehicle (e.g. air-conditioner control), direct their torque requirements to the basic Motronic system with the aim of modifying the engine torque which has just been generated. The ME-Motronic evaluates and coordinates these requirements and implements the resulting setpoint torque using the available manipulated variables (optimum engine operation in terms of exhaust gas and fuel consumption at each operating point).

An essential precondition for torque guidance is the electronic accelerator pedal ETC with the throttle valve controlled independently of the accelerator pedal.

Calculation of setpoint torque
The basic variable for the ME-Motronic torque structure is the internal torque arising from combustion. The function of torque guidance is to set the internal torque, through appropriate selection of the manipulated engine variables, in such a way that the vehicle-operator command is satisfied, and all the losses and addi-

tional requirements are covered. Because the Motronic "knows" the optimum values for charge, injection time and ignition angle for each and every desired setpoint torque, it can ensure optimal engine operation in terms of exhaust gas and fuel consumption.

Setting of setpoint torque
For setting the internal torque, the ME-Motronic's torque converter has a slow path (cylinder-charge path, steady-state operation) for the throttle valve (ETC), and a high-speed path (ignition-angle path, dynamic operation) for variation of the ignition angle and/or injection blank-out of individual cylinders.

Calculation of cylinder charge
The air mass in the cylinder after the intake valves have closed is termed the air charge. Referring the actual air charge to the maximum obtainable charge produces a variable that is independent of the engine piston displacement: the "relative (air) charge". The associated injected fuel quantity can be calculated from the relative air charge.

The relative charge cannot be measured directly but it can be determined from the available measurement signals.

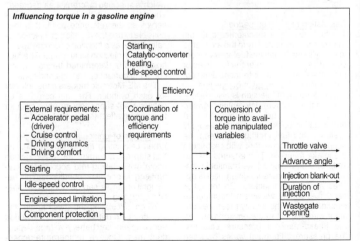

Influencing torque in a gasoline engine

For this purpose, an intake-manifold model calculation is used in which all the air-mass flows into the intake manifold and from the intake manifold to the combustion chamber are calculated. The most important measured variable in this model is either the air flow through the throttle valve (measured with a hot-film air-mass meter) or the absolute intake-manifold pressure (measured with a pressure sensor).

Starting out from this intake-manifold model, it is then also possible to determine the actual relative air charge.

Cylinder-charge control

In today's spark-ignition engines, the relative cylinder charge is also the main factor in influencing the engine torque, and is therefore used in the torque structure as a manipulated variable. The intake-manifold model is also used to control the cylinder charge by means of the throttle valve: for this purpose, a required cylinder charge is first of all calculated from the desired torque (which was calculated by ME-Motronic torque guidance). This cylinder charge is then converted into an associated throttle-valve angle and finally passed on as the setpoint value to the position controller of the throttle-valve actuator.

Calculation of injection period

The fuel mass for a stoichiometric air-fuel ratio can be calculated from the air charge in the cylinder. When the fuel-injector constant (this is a function of the fuel-injector properties) is taken into consideration, this furnishes the duration of injection.

The duration of injection is also dependent on the pressure differential between fuel-supply pressure (approx. 300 kPa) and injection back pressure. Fuel-supply systems with fuel recirculation keep the supply pressure constant with respect to the intake manifold. This ensures that, in spite of a changing intake-manifold pressure, the same pressure differential is applied at the fuel injectors. On the other hand, fuel-supply systems without fuel recirculation keep the supply pressure constant with respect to the environment. As the intake-manifold pressure changes, the pressure differential varies between

fuel supply and intake manifold. A compensation function corrects this error.

A further adaptation factor individual to each cylinder serves to accommodate fuel-pressure pulsations caused by the opening and closing of the fuel injectors.

The effective opening duration calculated in this way is valid under the precondition that the fuel injector is already open. It must therefore be extended by the opening and closing time of the injector. An additional, battery-voltage-dependent duration of injection, which is added to the valve-opening period, compensates for this effect.

If the effective injection duration is too short, the influences of the valve-opening and closing time become excessive. In order to ensure exact fuel metering, the injection duration is restricted to a minimum value. This value is below the injection duration associated with the minimum possible cylinder charge.

To ensure optimum combustion, it is necessary to precisely define the injected fuel quantity and the exact point for the start of injection. The fuel is generally injected into the intake manifold while the intake valves are still closed. The end of injection is determined by the "fuel-hold angle", which is specified in "crankshaft degrees". The point at which the intake valve closes serves as the reference point. It is then possible to use the duration of injection for calculating, as a function of engine speed, the start of injection as an angle. The fuel-hold angle is determined taking into account the current operating conditions.

The ME-Motronic triggers a fuel injector for each cylinder. The fuel can thus be held (stored) separately for each cylinder to optimum effect (sequential injection).

Calculation of ignition and dwell angles

When calculating the ignition angle, the first step is to determine the "basic ignition angle" while taking into account the current engine operating conditions. This basic ignition angle can be adapted in specific operating states.

When calculating the dwell angle, the first step is to determine the dwell period from a speed- and battery-voltage-dependent map. Once a temperature-dependent correction has been taken into account, the associated dwell angle is determined by means of a time/angle conversion.

The difference between the end of dwell (determined from the resulting ignition angle) and the dwell angle determines the start of dwell.

Operating states
In some operating states, the fuel requirement differs markedly from the steady-state requirements of an engine at normal operating temperature, with the result that corrective intervention in the mixture formation becomes necessary.

Starting
Intake-air adjustment, fuel injection and ignition are specially calculated during the starting procedure. An increased injected fuel quantity adapted to the engine temperature serves to build up a fuel film on the intake-manifold and cylinder walls and covers the increased fuel demand while the engine is running up. The ignition angle is likewise adapted to the starting procedure. The air charge while the engine is at a standstill is not affected by the throttle valve, which however is opened slightly in anticipation of the post-start phase.

Post-start
In this phase, the still increased charge and injected fuel quantity are reduced as a function of engine temperature and time at the end of the starting procedure. The ignition angle is adapted accordingly.

Warming-up
After starting at low engine temperatures, the engine's increased torque demand is covered up to a specific temperature threshold by adaptation of the charge, fuel injection and ignition.

Catalytic-converter heating
Highly retarded ignition angles generate very hot engine exhaust gas, thereby quickly bringing the catalytic converter up to operating temperature.

Idle
At idle, the engine-generated torque is just enough to permit sustained engine operation and running of the auxiliary systems. With idle-speed control, the desired idle speed remains stable under all conditions.

Full load
At full load, the throttle valve is wide open (WOT) and there are no throttling losses. The engine delivers the maximum torque relative to the current engine speed.

Acceleration and deceleration
Heavy acceleration and deceleration result in rapid changes in the intake-manifold pressure and thus in the conditions for the fuel film on the intake-manifold wall. In order to prevent leaning during acceleration, additional fuel is injected to build up the wall film. During deceleration, the injected fuel quantity is reduced accordingly.

Overrun fuel cutoff and restart
During the transition to no-combustion overrun conditions, the ME-Motronic cuts off the engine torque without jolting, and also provides for a smooth torque build-up when fuel feed starts again.

Additional closed- and open-loop control functions

Idle-speed control
Idle-speed control specifies a torque at which the desired engine speed is maintained under the given operating conditions. This torque increases as engine speed drops and decreases as engine speed rises.

Lambda closed-loop control
It is only possible to convert the noxious exhaust-gas constituents in the three-way catalytic converter in a very narrow range ("lambda window" where $\lambda = 0.99...1$). Lambda closed-loop control is essential in order to remain inside this window (P. 522).

Evaporative-emissions control system
The function of evaporative-emissions control systems is to limit the HC emissions. Such systems are equipped with a carbon canister, which accommodates

the end of the vent line from the fuel tank. Degassing fuel is retained in the canister's activated carbon. When the engine is running, a vacuum is created in the intake manifold which causes air to be drawn in from the environment through the activated carbon and into the intake manifold. The fuel vapors trapped in the canister are entrained with this air and carried to the engine for combustion. A canister-purge valve meters this "scavenging flow".

Knock control
Knock sensors convert the vibrations characteristic to knocking into electrical signals. These are used by the Motronic to adjust the ignition point in order to prevent audible knocking and knocking which could damage the engine (P. 496).

Boost-pressure control
On engines with exhaust-gas turbocharging, the setpoint value of the desired boost pressure is adjusted by electronic boost-pressure control. It is converted into a setpoint value for the desired maximum charge and then by means of torque management into a setpoint value for the throttle-valve angle and a control duty factor for the "wastegate". In the "wastegate", by means of a change in the control pressure

and stroke this signal leads to a change in the cross-section at the bypass valve.

Safety and security, comfort and convenience functions
The safety and security functions include:
– Engine-speed/vehicle-speed limitation,
– Torque/power limitation,
– Limitation of exhaust-gas temperature,
– Vehicle immobilizer.

The comfort and convenience functions include:
– Load-change damping,
– Surge-damping function,
– Cruise control.

Integrated diagnosis (OBD)
"On-board diagnosis" (OBD) is a basic feature of the ME-Motronic. During normal operation, it continually compares the system's responses with the ECU's commands, as well as comparing the various sensor signals with each other for plausibility.

During vehicle inspection, a tester connected to a standardized interface reads out the stored faults and displays them. Due to the demands of the Californian Environmental Protection Agency, an ex-

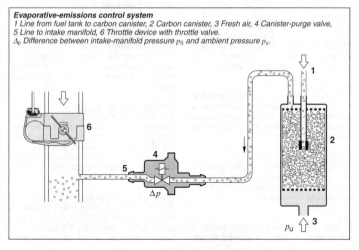

Evaporative-emissions control system
1 Line from fuel tank to carbon canister, 2 Carbon canister, 3 Fresh air, 4 Canister-purge valve,
5 Line to intake manifold, 6 Throttle device with throttle valve.
Δ_p *Difference between intake-manifold pressure p_S and ambient pressure p_u.*

panded diagnosis system (OBD II; adapted for Europe: EOBD) monitors all those components which if they fail could result in a significant increase in noxious emissions (fault indication with diagnosis lamp).

Examples of systems subject to diagnosis:
– Air-mass meter,
– ETC throttle-valve actuator,
– Combustion misses,
– Catalytic converter,
– Lambda sensor,
– Fuel supply,
– Tank system,
– Secondary-air injection,
– Exhaust-gas recirculation (EGR).

Fault memory

If exhaust-gas-related faults are detected, an entry is made in the non-volatile fault memory. Apart from the officially stipulated fault codes, each entry includes a "freeze frame", which contains additional information on the general conditions under which the fault occurred (e.g. engine speed, engine temperature). Service-related faults can also be stored.

Limp-home operation

If a fault occurs during driving (e.g. failure of a component), this leads not only to an entry in the fault memory. Substitute values and emergency functions now come into force for calculating cylinder charge, fuel injection and ignition in such a way that the vehicle can continue to be driven, albeit with restricted comfort.

For this purpose, the ETC throttle-valve actuator has a limp-home position, in which the throttle valve is held in place by spring force. The engine speed is then restricted to low values so that the vehicle can continue to be driven (with impaired functions) in spite of this important actuating device having failed.

MED-Motronic

Requirements

With gasoline direct injection in SI engines, fuel consumption can be reduced by up to 20 % when compared with con-

ventional manifold injection, and the CO_2 emissions caused by road traffic can be reduced with lasting effect.

In order for direct injection to be at all feasible, it must be possible during engine operation for coordinated alternation to take place between "charge stratification" at part load and operation with a homogeneous mixture at full load.

Essentially, the features required of the MED-Motronic engine-management system are:
– precise metering of the required injected fuel quantity,
– generation of the necessary injection pressure,
– definition of the start of injection, and
– introduction of the fuel directly and accurately into the engine's combustion chambers.

It must also coordinate the various torque demands on the engine in order then to be able to perform the required adjustments at the engine.

An important system interface delivers the internal torque from combustion. The torque-control structure is divided into the following areas of operation:
– torque demand,
– torque coordination and
– torque conversion.

The most important torque demand derives from the vehicle-operator command generated by the accelerator pedal, from the position of which the engine-management system interprets the demand to be made on the IC engine for a particular torque.

Further torque demands can also originate, for instance, from the transmission-shift control, the traction control system, or the electronic stability program.

Torque coordination is performed centrally in the engine-management system.

Design

As with manifold injection, the high-pressure direct-injection system is designed as a rail, or accumulator-type, injection system. In such systems, the fuel can be directly injected into the cylinders at any stipulated moment in time using electro-magnetic high-pressure fuel injectors.

In comparison to the ME basic ECU, the ECU for the MED gasoline direct-injection system also incorporates a driver stage for triggering the pressure-control valves.

The intake air mass can be freely adjusted by the electronically controlled throttle valve (ETC). Precision measurement of air mass is made by means of a hot-film air-mass meter. The A/F mixture is monitored by universal lambda sensors LSF and LSU in the exhaust-gas flow upstream and downstream of the catalytic converter. They serve to control $\lambda = 1$ operation and lean-burn operation, and are also responsible for the precise control of catalytic-converter regeneration. It is important to set the exhaust-gas recirculation rate exactly, particularly in dynamic operation.

Operation

Fuel delivery and injection

The MED-Motronic accumulator injection system injects the fuel stored under pressure in the rail. Injection can take place at any moment in time, whereby electromagnetically controlled fuel injectors inject the fuel directly into the combustion chamber. It thus offers the following functions:
– free selection of the injection point,
– variable system pressure.

Low-pressure circuit:

A primary pressure of 0.35 MPa (3.5 bar) is initially generated in a low-pressure circuit on the tank side which comprises an electric fuel pump with a mechanical pressure regulator connected in parallel. This feeds the high-pressure pump driven by the IC engine.

High-pressure circuit:

High-pressure pump: The function of the H.P. pump is to increase the fuel pressure

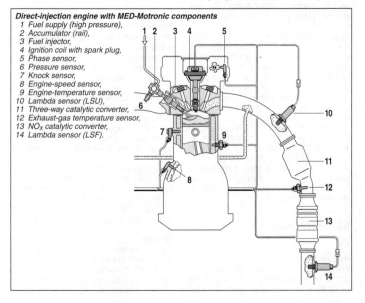

Direct-injection engine with MED-Motronic components
1 Fuel supply (high pressure),
2 Accumulator (rail),
3 Fuel injector,
4 Ignition coil with spark plug,
5 Phase sensor,
6 Pressure sensor,
7 Knock sensor,
8 Engine-speed sensor,
9 Engine-temperature sensor,
10 Lambda sensor (LSU),
11 Three-way catalytic converter,
12 Exhaust-gas temperature sensor,
13 NO_x catalytic converter,
14 Lambda sensor (LSF).

from 0.35 MPa (3.5 bar) primary pressure to 12 MPa (120 bar), to ensure that pressure fluctuations in the rail remain at a minimum, and to ensure operation exclusively with fuel (to prevent any mixing with engine oil).

Rail: The rail must on the one hand feature sufficient elasticity to damp the pressure pulsations arising from the periodic fuel-extraction processes when injection takes place, and from the fuel-delivery pulsation generated by the H.P. fuel pump. On the other hand, it must be rigid enough for the rail pressure to adapt quickly to the requirements of engine operation.

Pressure sensor: The pressure sensor (welded diaphragm of high-grade steel as sensor element with measuring resistors) serves to register the pressure level in the rail.

Pressure-control valve: The pressure-control valve adjusts the system pressure across the entire engine operating range according to the map specifications, and irrespective of the injected fuel quantity and pump delivery rate. Excess fuel is returned to the intake side of the H.P. pump.

Fuel injectors: The fuel injectors are the central components of the gasoline direct-injection system and are directly connected to the rail. Start of injection and injected fuel quantity are defined by the triggering signal for the fuel injectors.

Mixture formation and combustion

A complex engine-management system is necessary for the gasoline direct-injection system to be exploited to the full in terms of low fuel consumption and high engine power output. A distinction is made between two basic operating modes in this respect:

Lower load range

In this range, the engine is run with a heavily stratified cylinder charge and a high level of excess air in order to achieve the lowest-possible fuel consumption. Retarded injection just before the ignition point is used with the aim of achieving the ideal state of having two zones in the combustion chamber: In one zone the combustible air-fuel mixture cloud at the spark plug, embedded in the second zone in the

form of an insulating layer of air and residual exhaust gas. In this way, the engine can be run to a large extent unthrottled while gas-exchange losses are avoided. In addition, thermodynamic efficiency increases due to the avoidance of heat losses at the combustion-chamber walls.

Upper load range

As engine load and thus the injected fuel quantity increases, the stratified-charge cloud becomes increasingly richer. This would result in a deterioration in exhaust emissions, particularly with regard to soot. The engine is therefore operated with a homogeneous cylinder charge in this higher torque range.

Lambda coordination assumes the control function between $\lambda = 1$ and lean-burn operation. The fuel is injected during the intake stroke in order to ensure that fuel and air are thoroughly mixed.

Alternation between torque ranges

In the event of a switch between homogeneous and stratified-charge operation, it is crucial to control injected fuel quantity, air charge and ignition angle in such a way that the torque delivered by the engine to the transmission remains constant. The torque structure means that here also the important functions for controlling the electronic throttle valve have been transferred directly from the ME-Motronic. The throttle valve must be closed prior to the actual changeover from stratified to homogeneous operation.

Exhaust-gas treatment, catalytic-converter control

An important consideration with gasoline direct injection is that in stratified-charge operation the NO_X content in the very lean exhaust gas cannot be reduced by a three-way catalytic converter. Exhaust-gas recirculation with a high EGR rate helps to reduce the NO_X content of the exhaust gas by roughly 70 %. To comply with emissions-control legislation, it is also absolutely essential to treat the NO_X emissions. To reduce this exhaust-gas content, the NO_X accumulator-type catalytic converter offers the greatest potential.

Engine-test technology

Service and maintenance requirements for modern vehicles are declining steadily; electronic systems are essentially maintenance-free. But malfunctions can still occur. Factors such as wear, contamination and corrosion can impair the operation of engine and electronic systems, and settings can drift over time. Rapid and reliable diagnosis of malfunctions is the most important function of any service facility. It is important to distinguish between testing and diagnosis. Testing entails the determination of certain measured values for comparison with the prescribed specifications. Diagnostic procedures (e.g. engine diagnostics) attempt to correlate deviations from specified values with system functions, malfunction patterns and experience in order to determine the failure mode or to locate the defective component.

Engine diagnosis

Engine, ignition and fuel-metering systems are becoming more complex and less accessible. Universal, automated procedures, free from the effects of subjective influences, are thus essential elements of the computer-controlled testing program in the automotive service facility. These include:
– comparison of cylinder output by selective shorting of the ignition or smooth running analysis via current engine speed,
– comparison of compression via the shape of the starter current curve,
– determination of mixture distribution performed by selective measurement of the exhaust-gas HC content,
– analysis of the primary and secondary ignition-voltage patterns.

Electronic-system testing

Testing of engine-related electronic systems is carried out using test equipment specifically designed to utilize on-board engine monitoring technology.

The test connection is established by inserting a universal test adapter between the plug and socket at the junction linking the peripheral device with the ECU. If only the peripheral device (sensor, actuator, wiring and power supply) is to be tested,

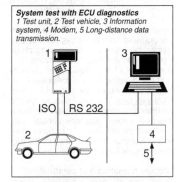

Peripheral and functional testing
1 ECU, 2 System wiring harness, 3 System adapter cable, 4 Plug connection, 5 Universal test adapter, 6 Sockets for test unit

System test with ECU diagnostics
1 Test unit, 2 Test vehicle, 3 Information system, 4 Modem, 5 Long-distance data transmission.

then it is sufficient to connect the tester to the peripheral's plug, while the ECU is also connected for tests embracing dynamic operation. The individual electronic system requires only a single interchangeable, system-specific adapter cable. The program switches on the universal test adapter are then used to establish a logical test sequence specifically tailored to the requirements of the system.

Once connected, the test unit provides a display of both measured values and of signals such as ignition and fuel-injection pulses.

When the ECU remains connected for operational testing, keys can be used to enter simulations of various operating conditions for test-unit evaluation.

ECU diagnostics

The dominant role being assumed by electronic systems in the vehicle makes it necessary to devote increased attention to the problems associated with service. In addition, because essential vehicle functions are becoming increasingly dependent upon electronics, these systems must satisfy stringent reliability requirements, while emergency default programs are required to deal with system errors.

The solution is to incorporate electronic system-diagnosis functions in the ECU. These rely on the electronic "intelligence" already in place in the vehicle to continuously monitor the system, detect faults, store the fault data and perform diagnostics.

For instance, the ECU carries out its own self-check as follows: Programmed memory chips are provided with test patterns which can be retrieved and used for comparisons. For program memories, a comparison with test sums is employed to ensure that data and programs are correctly stored. The data and address buses are included in the test program.

Sensors are tested for plausibility within specified limits, while open and short circuits are also recognized. Final-control elements can be tested during activation using current-draw limits.

The "off-board test units" used for the evaluation of "on-board diagnostics" employ a communications interface as defined in ISO 9141. The serial port can maintain communications at rates ranging from 10 baud to 10 kbaud. It is designed as a single- or two-wire port, allowing connection of several control units to a central diagnosis plug.

A stimulation address is transmitted to all of the connected ECUs, whereupon each unit recognizes its address and responds by transmitting back a baud-rate recognition word.

The test unit monitors the period between pulse flanks to determine the sender's baud rate, which it then adopts automatically. The key bytes that follow (assigned by the DIN Motor-Vehicle Committee) specify the protocol for subsequent data communications.

The programmable test unit converts the received data into diagnosis sequences and plain-text information designed specifically for the respective system.

The ECU diagnostic capabilities include:
– identification of system and ECU,
– recognition, storage and readout of static and sporadic malfunctions together with the error path, failure mode and associated parameters,
– readout of current actual values, switching conditions, specifications,
– stimulation of system functions, and
– programming of system variants.

Individual programs for the test unit are stored in plug-in modules, while updates and communications with data systems are supported by a data interface.

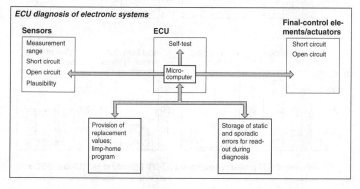

ECU diagnosis of electronic systems

Sensors
Measurement range
Short circuit
Open circuit
Plausibility

ECU
Self-test
Micro-computer

Final-control elements/actuators
Short circuit
Open circuit

Provision of replacement values; limp-home program

Storage of static and sporadic errors for read-out during diagnosis

LPG systems

Liquefied petroleum gas
Liquefied petroleum gas assumes a liquid state at pressures of 2...20 bar, depending on the propane/butane ratio and the temperature (see chapter on "Fuels", P. 238).

At the end of the '90s, LPG was being consumed by internal-combustion (IC) engines at a rate of approximately 10.3 million metric tons annually (of which 2.6 million tons were consumed in Europe). Should efforts to utilize the gas contained in petroleum succeed, then these figures could increase exponentially. The mineral-oil tax is a decisive factor in determining the profitability of liquefied petroleum gas.

Natural gas as engine fuel
Reserves of natural gas are extensive. Together with it being used nowhere near as much as crude oil, this fact makes natural gas a very interesting alternative fuel for automotive applications. Both the LPG equipment configurations and the emissions produced would be similar to those for the combination of propane and butane known as LPG (see illustration). Natural gas can be transported in the vehicle either as a high-pressure gas (160...200 bar) or in liquefied form (at −160 °C) in an insulated tank; the disadvantage of the former mode lies in its limited operating range.

The only real difference between concepts based on natural gas and LPG is the way the gas is transported in the vehicle; actual differences in operating principles are minimal.

Operation on LPG
Any vehicle equipped with an IC engine can be converted for operation on LPG. For the most part, spark-ignition (SI) engines are re-equipped for dual-fuel operation (system can be switched between gasoline and LPG). LPG-powered taxis and buses are

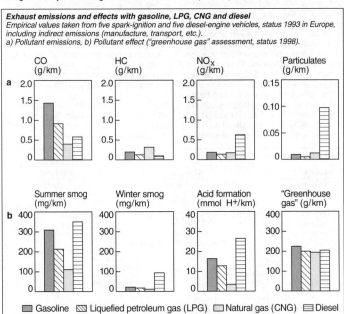

Exhaust emissions and effects with gasoline, LPG, CNG and diesel
Empirical values taken from five spark-ignition and five diesel-engine vehicles, status 1993 in Europe, including indirect emissions (manufacture, transport, etc.).
a) Pollutant emissions, b) Pollutant effect ("greenhouse gas" assessment, status 1998).

Legend: ▓ Gasoline ▨ Liquefied petroleum gas (LPG) ☐ Natural gas (CNG) ☰ Diesel generally set up for single-fuel (LPG only) operation, while regulations require this configuration on gas-powered industrial trucks intended for indoor use. When engines are converted, it should be remembered that they operate as naturally aspirated engines while running on LPG (consumption in liters increases by approx. 25% as compared to gasoline).

Exhaust emissions

Because LPG mixes well with air, emissions (of CO_2 and other components such as polycyclic aromatic hydrocarbons) are substantially lower than those produced by gasoline-burning engines, and are lower even than those produced by fuel-injection engines equipped with three-way closed-loop catalytic converters. LPG contains no lead or sulphur compounds. It's very good combustion characteristics are complemented by excellent mixture formation and distribution properties. These characteristics are even more significant at low temperatures.

Advantages
– Extremely economical for drivers who cover large distances.
– Assuming the same level of technology (electronic control systems, etc.), emissions from an LPG engine are substantially lower than those achieved with gasoline or diesel fuel.

Disadvantages
– Lower cruising ranges and increased fuel volumetric consumption compared to gasoline (although actual energy use is not higher than with gasoline, lowest with diesel engine).
– Special safety precautions are necessary, as LPG is pressurized.
– Pressurized gas cylinders require a lot of space, as the actual capacity is only 80% of cylinder volume (the remainder serving as expansion room for the gas).

LPG system
In Germany, professional installation of

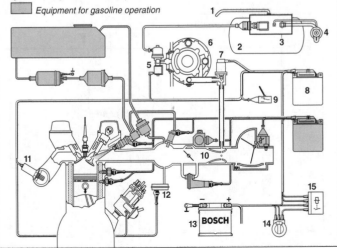

Schematic diagram of an LPG system (carburetor principle)
1 Ventilation line for tank fittings, 2 LPG tank, 3 Housing with tank fittings, 4 External filler valve (designed to interrupt refueling at 80% of container capacity), 5 Gas shut-off valve, 6 Pressure regulator for evaporator, 7 Servomotor for gas control, 8 ECU, 9 Gas/gasoline changeover switch, 10 Venturi mixing device, 11 Lambda oxygen sensor, 12 Vacuum sensor, 13 Battery, 14 Ignition/starting switch, 15 Relay.

▨ *Equipment for gasoline operation*

the LPG system in a specialist workshop is followed by a trip to the TÜV or TÜA (German inspection authorities) to secure operating approval. This inspection is based on the "Guidelines for inspecting vehicles with engines powered by liquefied gases" as issued by the Federal Minister of Transportation. Uniform regulations for Europe are being drawn up.

A modern LPG system will incorporate the following components:
– LPG tank,
– external filler valve designed to interrupt refueling at 80 % of container capacity,
– flow-interrupt valve,
– evaporator pressure regulator with cooling system,
– venturi mixing unit/injector,
– electronic control unit (ECU),
– servomotor for controlling gas flow,
– switch for alternating between LPG and gasoline operation.

The LPG flows from the LPG tank to the evaporator pressure regulator, where it is vaporized and its pressure reduced. The ECU processes the signals from the Lambda (O_2) and vacuum sensors, which serve as references for controlling the servomotor used to regulate the flow of liquefied gas to the venturi mixing unit.

The flow-interrupt valve shuts immediately when the ignition is switched off. A gasoline/LPG switch installed in the instrument panel allows the operator to alternate between the two fuels.

LPG tanks

As LPG tanks are used to store pressurized gas, they are subject in Germany to the "TRG 380" technical regulations. At the factory, each tank receives official technical approval with certification.

They are equipped with an external filler valve (designed to interrupt refueling at 80 % of container capacity) as well as an electromagnetic discharge valve, and have a capacity of 40 ... 128 l for passenger cars.

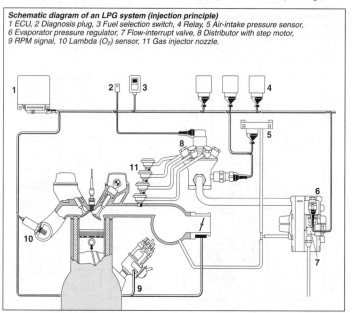

Schematic diagram of an LPG system (injection principle)
1 ECU, 2 Diagnosis plug, 3 Fuel selection switch, 4 Relay, 5 Air-intake pressure sensor,
6 Evaporator pressure regulator, 7 Flow-interrupt valve, 8 Distributor with step motor,
9 RPM signal, 10 Lambda (O_2) sensor, 11 Gas injector nozzle.

Natural-gas operation of spark-ignition engines

Against the backdrop of worldwide efforts to reduce CO_2 emissions and to comply with ever more stringent exhaust emission limits, natural gas is gaining increasing significance as an alternative fuel.

Properties and storage of natural gas

The main component of natural gas is methane (CH_4), making up 80...99%. The remainder consists of inert gases such as carbon dioxide, nitrogen and other low-order hydrocarbons. A differentiation is made between L-gas (80...90% methane) and H-gas (>90%) depending on the gas quality.

Natural gas can be stored both in liquid form at $-162\,°C$ as LNG (Liquefied Natural Gas) or in compressed form at pressures of up to 200 bar as CNG (Compressed Natural Gas). In view of the great expense involved in storing the gas in liquid form, natural gas is used in compressed form in virtually all applications. The low energy density of natural gas is a particular disadvantage, making large storage tanks necessary. Metal-hydride storage tanks represent a further storage option, although they are not used for reasons of cost.

Mixture formation

In most systems, gas is injected into the intake manifold as in conventional multipoint gasoline-injection systems. A low-pressure common rail supplies the injector valves that inject intermittently into the intake manifold. Mixture formation is simplified by the completely gaseous supply of fuel, as natural gas does not condense on the intake manifolds and does not form a film on the walls. This has a favourable effect on emissions, particularly during the warm-up phase.

The output of the natural-gas engine is approx. 10...15% lower than that of the gasoline engine due to the lower fuel mass necessary for stoichiometric combustion (17.2:1 ratio) as well as a lower volumetric efficiency due to the injected natural gas. Higher compression can boost performance while simultaneously increasing efficiency. The extremely high antiknock quality of natural gas (120 RON) enables very high compressions of approx. 13:1 (8:1 for regular gasoline). As a result, the natural-gas engine is ideally suited for turbocharging. As piston displacement decreases, efficiency increases due to additional de-throttling and reduced friction.

A further improvement in efficiency can be achieved by lean-mixture operation up to $\lambda = 1.7$. A lean mixture reduces combustion temperatures while at the same time further de-throttling the engine.

Emissions

Natural-gas vehicles are characterized by low CO_2 emissions due to the favourable hydrogen/carbon ratio (H/C ratio) of almost 4:1 (gasoline: 2.3:1) and the resulting shift in the main combustion products CO_2 and H_2O. Apart from the virtually particle-free combustion, in conjunction with a three-way closed-loop catalytic converter only very low levels of the pollutants NO_X, CO and NMHC ("non-methane hydrocarbons": the sum of all hydrocarbons minus methane) are emitted. Methane is classified as nontoxic, and is therefore not considered to be a pollutant.

In lean mixture mode the NO_X emissions are higher than in $\lambda = 1$ mode with a three-way catalytic converter. In the same way as in gasoline operation, this disadvantage can be largely eliminated by using more expensive exhaust-gas treatment methods (e.g. NO_X catalytic converter).

Natural-gas-engine applications

In view of their limited range, natural-gas engines are used almost exclusively in local public transportation fleets (e.g. buses and taxis). Bivalent systems which can be easily changed over from natural gas to gasoline operation are used primarily in passenger cars.

Operation on alcohol (spark-ignition engines)

The limited availability of fossil fuels has led to an increased effort to develop engines and injection systems capable of using alcohols such as ethanol and methanol as alternative fuels ("Alternative fuels", P. 246). Due to its non-availability, virtually the only place where ethanol is used is Brazil. In the US (and in California in particular), increasing attention is being focused on methanol, which generates lower emissions: reduced NO_x and CO_2 along with reduced ozone and smog formation.

In the absence of comprehensive methanol-distribution networks to ensure universal availability, engines and engine-control systems must be designed for flexible dual-fuel operation (ranging from pure gasoline to max. 85% methanol). Alcohol places special, particularly critical demands upon engines and fuel-delivery components. Moisture, acids and gums contained in the fuel pose a hazard to metals, plastics and rubber. Because

methanol has a high antiknock quality, engines designed to run exclusively on methanol have substantially higher compression ratios than gasoline engines, making them more efficient. On the other hand, methanol's low calorific value means that fuel consumption is almost doubled, necessitating higher fuel supply rates, greater tank volumes and special injectors.

Suitable Lambda (O_2) sensors can be employed for optimal emissions control with a catalytic converter. Special lubricants are able to maintain long-term stability in the face of this aggressive fuel and its combustion products.

Pilot control of the fuel mixture is facilitated by a fuel sensor which sends a signal to the ECU reflecting the proportion of methanol in the fuel.

Suitable programs implement the necessary mixture and ignition corrections applicable to a particular set of engine operating characteristics.

Hydrogen-powered passenger car with spark-ignition engine (BMW 735i)
LH_2 *Liquid hydrogen,* GH_2 *Gaseous hydrogen. 1 Valve block for* LH_2 *fueling and* GH_2 *supply (vacuum-insulated), 2 Hydrogen lines, vacuum-insulated, 3* LH_2 *Evaporator, 4 Metering valve for regulating power with electronic control, 5 Hydrogen injectors, 6 Overcurrent and safety valves, 7 Liquid-hydrogen tank with vacuum super-insulation, 8 Hydrogen sensors for automatic leak monitoring, 9 Throttle valve for gasoline operation with electronic control, 10 Variable-speed centrifugal supercharger.*

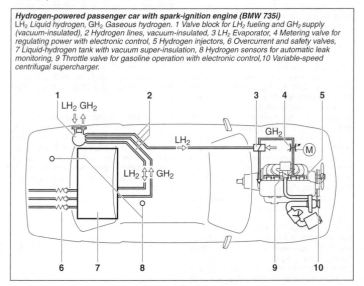

Operation on hydrogen (spark-ignition engines)

Although the production of hydrogen, the required infrastructure and refueling all pose difficult problems, technically feasible solutions are on the horizon. Producing hydrogen by means of electrolysis necessitates sufficient quantities of electrical power in the form of solar energy or nuclear power.

Storing hydrogen in the vehicle

Gaseous storage in pressurized tanks
High pressures (300 bar) are required for storage in gaseous form. This results in high weight along with safety risks.

Liquid storage (cryogenic tank)
Liquid storage represents the best alternative with regard to both weight and energy density (present operating range approx. 300 km). The extremely low temperature required (−253 °C) places substantial demands on thermal insulation. Residual heat causes loss of hydrogen via the safety valves at a rate of about 2 % per day when the vehicle is parked. An electric evaporator maintains the specified tank pressure during operation.

Metal-hydride tanks
Hydrides are produced as hydrogen is absorbed by a metallic powder. This is an exothermic process, i. e. heat must be dissipated during fueling. There are no storage losses.

The disadvantages associated with the low energy density (range: 120 km) and high materials costs are to a degree offset by uncomplicated safety technology.

Methylcyclohexanol storage
This type of storage employs a catalyst to dehydrate the hydrogenous methylcyclohexanol at 500 °C. The by-products are hydrogen and recyclable toluene.

Mixture formation

Regardless of storage mode, up to now all systems inject gaseous hydrogen into the intake manifold. Although a number of advantages could be gained by injecting extremely low-temperature hydrogen directly into the combustion chamber (improved charge for higher output, cool mixture for low NO_x emissions, no danger of backfiring), the short injector-valve service life means that this type of system is not likely to appear in production in the near future.

Current external mixture-formation concepts rely on a continuous-injection system in which a central electric metering valve and a hydrogen distributor conduct the vaporized hydrogen to the individual intake tracts.

Backfiring into the intake passage is prevented by lean mixtures or supplementary water injection. A supercharging device can be used to compensate for a portion of the power loss associated with lean operation.

One alternative, based on intermittent sequential injection of hydrogen into the intake manifold, is currently in the development stage.

This system's unlimited range of options for injection timing allows it to inhibit backfiring almost completely, even with rich mixtures.

Injector valve and electronic-control system must operate with extreme precision and short valve-opening times; the technical requirements are thus substantial.

Emissions

During combustion, pure hydrogen (H_2) oxidizes to form water (H_2O). No CO_2 is produced by the combustion process. Provided no fossil fuels are used in its production, H_2 is thus the only fuel which can be used to avoid all CO_2.

Electric drive is the only alternative which can make a similar claim. Future NO_x emission limits can be met by lean mixtures or a system for catalytic control of emissions (still to be developed).

Exhaust emissions from spark-ignition engines

Combustion products

Complete combustion
The by-products of complete gasoline combustion are carbon dioxide and water.

Incomplete combustion
Unburned hydrocarbons:
C_nH_m (paraffins, olefins, aromatic hydrocarbons)
Partially-burned hydrocarbons:
$C_nH_m \cdot CHO$ (aldehydes),
$C_nH_m \cdot CO$ (ketones),
$C_nH_m \cdot COOH$ (carboxylic acids),
CO (carbon monoxide).
Thermal crack products and derivatives:
C_2H_2, C_2H_4, H_2 (acetylene, ethylene, hydrogen, etc.), C (soot), polycyclic hydrocarbons.

Combustion by-products
From atmospheric nitrogen: NO, NO_2 (nitrogen oxide). From fuel impurities: sulfurous oxides.

Oxidants
The following oxidants are produced when exhaust gas is exposed to sunlight: organic peroxides, ozone, peroxy-acetyl-nitrates.

Properties of exhaust-gas components

Major components
The major proportion of the exhaust gas is composed of the three components nitrogen, carbon dioxide and water vapor. These are nontoxic. However, emissions of CO_2 – largely the result of fuel combustion – are becoming more and more important due to their contribution to the "greenhouse effect".

Minor components
Carbon monoxide CO: A colorless, odorless and tasteless gas. Inhalation of air with a volumetric concentration of 0.3% carbon monoxide can result in death within 30 minutes. The CO-content of the exhaust gas from spark-ignition engines is especially high at idle. It is therefore imperative that the engine never be run in a closed garage!
Nitrogen monoxide NO: A colorless, tasteless and odorless gas; in air it is gradually converted into NO_2. Pure NO_2 is a poisonous, reddish-brown gas with a penetrating odor. The concentrations found in exhaust gases and in extremely polluted air can induce irritation in mucous membranes. NO and NO_2 are generally referred to collectively as oxides of nitrogen NO_x.
Hydrocarbons are present in exhaust gases in a variety of forms. When exposed to sunlight and nitrous oxide, they react to form oxidants which irritate the mucous membranes. Some hydrocarbons are considered to be carcinogenic.
Particulates (particulate matter) in accordance with American regulatory practice, are defined as all substances (except unbound water) which under normal conditions are present in exhaust gases in a solid (ash, carbon) or liquid state.

Mixture formation

The fuel used in spark-ignition (SI) engines is more volatile than diesel fuel, while the air-fuel mixing process prior to combustion also extends over a longer period than in a diesel engine. The result is that spark-ignition engines operate on a more homogenous mixture than their diesel counterparts. Spark-ignition engines run on a mixture in the stoichiometric range ($\lambda = 1$). Diesel engines, on the other hand, always operate with excess air ($\lambda > 1$). An air deficiency ($\lambda < 1$) results in increased soot, CO and HC emissions.

Combustion characteristic

The combustion characteristic defines the combustion as a function of time, and applies the ratio of the already combusted fuel to the fuel awaiting combustion.

Here, the efficiency, the combustion temperature, and therefore the fuel consumption and NO_x emissions are particularly influenced by the position of maximum energy conversion referred to piston TDC.

In the spark-ignition engine, the ignition timing initiates the combustion process, while the start of injection initiates combustion in a diesel engine.

Emissions control

The methods used to influence the composition of the SI-engine exhaust gases are divided into two basic categories: engine-design measures and exhaust-gas treatment. The selection of procedures to be employed in any given country is determined by the legal regulations in force there. The major industrial nations, with their important markets, have been moving toward implementation of the stringent American exhaust emissions regulations (or have already implemented them). Compliance with this legislation necessitates using emission control systems which incorporate the 3-way catalytic converter, a principle which has already proven itself in the USA.

Engine-design measures

Setting the A/F ratio
The excess-air factor λ of the A/F mixture delivered to the engine has a dominating effect on the composition of the exhaust gas. The engine produces its maximum torque at approximately $\lambda = 0.9$; thus this ratio is generally programmed for full-load operation. A certain level of excess air is required for favourable fuel consumption. This coincides with the setting for low CO and HC emissions; oxides of nitrogen (NO_X) however, are at a maximum at this ratio. Excess-air factors of $\lambda = 0.9...1.05$ are selected at idle. An excessively lean mixture results in the engine's lean misfire limit (LML) being reached or exceeded, and as the mixture becomes progressively leaner, misfiring causes a rapid increase in HC emissions. For overrun (trailing-throttle) operation, it is frequently necessary to enrich the mixture ($\lambda = 0.9$) in order to maintain an ignitable mixture, while at the same time air is added to avoid excessive manifold vacuum.

Yet another option for overrun operation is to completely interrupt the fuel supply to the engine at speeds above idle (overrun

The excess-air factor λ influences:
Exhaust-gas composition (CO, NO_x, HC), torque (M) and specific fuel consumption (b). The values apply to the part-load range of a spark-ignition engine operating at a constant moderate speed and cylinder charge (λ values implemented in the vehicle engine range from approx. 0.85...1.15, depending on the operating point).

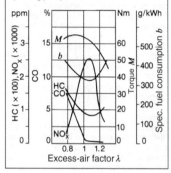

fuel cutoff). Precise mixture control (P. 465) is achieved by the use of electronic fuel-injection systems (EFI).

Mixture formation
Mixture formation embraces not only setting the correct A/F ratio, but also the quality of the A/F mixture which actually enters the combustion chamber. The fuel's homogeneity, its stratification patterns, and its temperature at the instant of ignition are all essential factors in determining combustibility and combustion characteristic, with consequent effects upon exhaust-gas composition. Homogenous mixtures and controlled stratification (rich mixture at the spark plug, lean mixture in the vicinity of the combustion-chamber walls) are examples of two different development options.

Uniform distribution
Maximum engine efficiency can only be achieved if every cylinder is operated with the same excess-air factor. This necessitates a system which ensures that both air and fuel are distributed evenly among the individual cylinders.

Exhaust-gas recirculation (EGR)

Exhaust gas can be conducted back to the combustion chamber to reduce peak combustion temperatures. Higher combustion temperatures induce an over-proportional increase in NO_x formation, and because exhaust-gas recirculation (EGR) reduces combustion temperatures, it represents a particularly effective means of controlling NO_x emissions. Extensive optimization of EGR can also lead to a reduction in fuel consumption. EGR can be implemented in either of two ways:
- Internal exhaust-gas recirculation is achieved with appropriate valve timing (overlap),
- External exhaust-gas recirculation employing controlled EGR valves.

Valve timing

Large valve overlaps (early opening of the inlet valve) increase the internal exhaust-gas recirculation, and can therefore help to reduce NO_x emissions. However, since the recirculated exhaust gas displaces fresh A/F mixture, early opening of the inlet valve also leads to a reduction in the maximum torque. In addition, excessively high exhaust-gas recirculation, particularly at idle, can lead to combustion misfire which in turn causes an increase in HC emissions. An optimum can be found with variable valve timing (P. 387), in which the valve timing is varied as a function of the operating point.

Compression ratio

It has long been recognized that the enhanced thermal efficiency associated with high compression ratios represents an effective means of improving fuel economy. However, the increase in peak combustion temperature also results in higher NO_x emissions.

Combustion-chamber design:

Low HC emissions are best achieved with a compact combustion chamber featuring a minimal surface area and no recesses. A centrally-located spark plug with short flame travel produces rapid and relatively complete combustion of the mixture, resulting in low HC emissions and reduced fuel consumption. Induced combustion-chamber turbulence also provides rapid combustion. Combustion chambers optimized in this way feature favourable HC emissions at $\lambda = 1$ and improve the engine's lean-mixture operation.

A thoroughly optimized combustion chamber design coupled with external measures (such as intake swirl) produce a <u>lean-burn engine</u> capable of running on mixtures in the range of $\lambda \approx 1.4...1.6$. Although the lean-burn engine features low exhaust emissions and excellent fuel economy, it does require catalytic exhaust-gas treatment in order to meet the most stringent emissions limits for CO, HC, and NO_x. Particularly due to the fact that developments in the aftertreatment of NO_x in lean exhaust gas are still in their infancy, the lean-burn engine has up to now only been successful in Europe and Japan, and only in the case of a few models using lean/mix concepts which compromised between emissions and fuel consumption. A new way of substantially improving the lean-running behavior of the spark-ignition engine is to inject fuel directly into the combustion chamber with stratified charge. In this case, accumulator-type catalytic converters are favoured for exhaust gas treatment.

The lean-running characteristics achieved by combustion-chamber design and induced turbulence can also be applied to implement high EGR rates for designs with $\lambda = 1$. Here, a reduction in fuel consumption can be easily achieved with exhaust-gas treatment, but not to the same degree as in lean-burn engines.

Ignition system

The design of the spark plug, its position in the combustion chamber, together with spark energy and spark duration all exercise a major influence on the ignition, the mixture's combustion characteristic, and therefore on emissions levels. The significance of these factors increases with the leanness ($\lambda > 1.1$) of the mixture. Ignition timing exerts a decisive effect on both exhaust emissions and fuel economy. Using the firing point for optimum fuel economy as a baseline, the timing is retarded to a point at which the exhaust valve opens before the combustion process is completed. Excess oxygen in the exhaust system can cause a thermal post-reaction to occur. Although this process reduces unburned hydrocarbons, it also leads to increased fuel consumption. NO_X emissions are low due to the low combustion-chamber temperatures. Fuel consumption and NO_X and HC emissions increase when the firing point is set earlier compared to the optimum.

Crankcase ventilation (blowby)
The concentration of hydrocarbons in the crankcase can be many times that found in the engine's exhaust gases. Control systems conduct these gases to a suitable point in the engine's intake tract, from where they are drawn into the combustion chamber for burning. Originally, these gases were allowed to escape untreated directly into the atmosphere; today, crankcase emission-control systems are a standard legal requirement.

Exhaust-gas treatment

Thermal afterburning
Before today's catalytic treatment of exhaust emissions became standard, initial attempts to reduce emissions utilized thermal afterburning. This method employs a specific residence time at high temperatures for burning the exhaust-gas components which failed to combust during normal combustion in the engine cylinders. In the rich range ($\lambda = 0.7...1.0$), the process must be supported with supplementary air injection (secondary air). In lean-burn engines ($\lambda = 1.05...1.2$), the residual oxygen in the exhaust gas supports the afterburning process.

In the past, mechanical pumps driven by belts directly from the engine were used for secondary-air injection. Since such air injection is only required during the engine's warm-up period, these pumps are switched using electromagnetic couplings. Lower-priced blower pumps powered by electric motors are quickly superseding the former mechanical versions.

Due to its lack of potential, particularly in maintaining low NO_X limits, thermal afterburning alone is currently considered to be of little significance. It can be used, however, to reduce emissions of HC and CO during the operating phase in which

the catalytic converter has not yet reached its operating temperature. Because it greatly reduces the time taken for the catalytic converter to reach its operating temperature, thermal aftertreatment with air injection during the engine warm-up phase in combination with catalytic aftertreatment will play a major role in achieving compliance with more stringent emission limits in the future.

Catalytic afterburning
The catalytic converter is composed of a carrier substrate, which serves as a base for the catalytic material, mounted within a housing using vibration-proof, heat-insulated supports. Granulate and ceramic or metallic monolith structures are employed as substrate materials. The suitability of the monolith structure for automotive applications has been demonstrated over the course of an extended development period. It offers the following advantages: maximum utilization of catalytic surface, durability combined with physical strength, low thermal retention and limited exhaust back-pressure. The active catalytic layer consists of small quantities of noble metals (Pt, Rh, Pd), and is sensitive to lead. For this reason, it is essential that engines with catalytic converters be run on unleaded fuel exclusively, as lead destroys the effectiveness of the active layer. The conversion rate is largely a function of operating temperature; no significant conversion of pollutants takes place below an operating temperature of approx. 250 °C. Operating temperatures of approx. 400...800 °C provide ideal conditions for maximum efficiency and extended service life.

Installing the catalytic converter directly adjacent to the engine means that it more quickly reaches operating temperature since the exhaust gases are hotter. This results in improved efficiency, but at the cost of high thermal stresses. Because the maximum permissible operating temperature lies just slightly above 1000 °C, the units are generally installed at a less critical location under the floor of the vehicle. Engine malfunctions, such as ignition miss, can cause the temperature in the catalytic converter to increase to the point where the substrate melts, resulting in destruction of the unit. This must be prevented by using reliable, maintenance-free ignition systems. <u>Oxidation-type catalytic converters</u> oxidize CO and HC either by utilizing the excess air supplied by

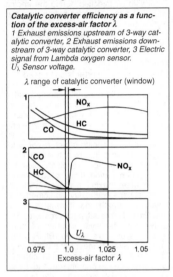

Catalytic converter efficiency as a function of the excess-air factor λ
1 Exhaust emissions upstream of 3-way catalytic converter, 2 Exhaust emissions downstream of 3-way catalytic converter, 3 Electric signal from Lambda oxygen sensor.
U_λ Sensor voltage.

λ range of catalytic converter (window)

0.975   1.0   1.025   1.05
Excess-air factor λ

Functional schematic of the Lambda closed-loop control
1 Air-mass meter, 2 Engine, 3a Lambda oxygen sensor 1, 3b Lambda oxygen sensor 2 (only if required), 4 Catalytic converter, 5 Fuel injectors, 6 ECU.
U_S Sensor voltage, U_V Injector triggering voltage, V_E Injected fuel quantity.

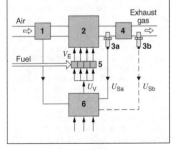

lean engine mixtures or by relying on secondary-air injection. <u>Reduction-type converters</u> on the other hand operate with air deficiency, and thus without air injection, to reduce NO_X levels.

The reduction- and oxidation-type catalytic converters can also be combined in series to produce a <u>dual-bed catalytic converter</u>. This device uses air injection between the two converters to reduce not only NO_X emissions but also HC and CO levels. Its disadvantages include a more complex design (two converters, air injection) and the need to operate the engine in a range with higher fuel consumption (λ = 0.9).

The <u>three-way</u> or <u>selective catalytic converter</u> with lambda closed-loop control has proven to be the most effective concept for exhaust-gas aftertreatment. It is capable of providing the required reduction of all three pollutants provided the engine is operated with a stoichiometric mixture. The "window" for treatment of the three toxic components is narrow; this means that an open-loop fuel-metering system cannot be used with this concept.

Lambda closed-loop control

In the US, Europe and Japan, catalytic aftertreatment of the exhaust gas using a closed-loop three-way catalytic converter has proven to be a highly effective means of meeting the current low emission limits for CO, NO_X and HC.

Approximately 14.7 kg of air are required for complete combustion of 1 kg of gasoline. The excess-air factor λ (Lambda) is used to define this A/F ratio; it is the ratio of the actual A/F ratio to the stoichiometric A/F ratio. Two main control concepts for exhaust gas optimization are used in the spark-ignition engine:

Closed-loop control for λ = 1
This concept is the most effective for minimizing pollutants. The engine must be operated within a very narrow range in which λ = 1 ±0.005 (catalytic-converter window). Such precision can only be achieved with precise closed-loop control of the A/F mixture with a Lambda oxygen sensor installed upstream of the converter. A second Lambda sensor down-

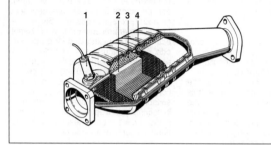

Two-bed, 3-way catalytic converter with Lambda oxygen sensor
1 Lambda oxygen sensor, 2 Ceramic monolith, 3 Wire screen, 4 Heat-resistant double shell.

stream of the catalytic converter increases the precision even further.

Closed-loop control for $\lambda > 1$ (lean-burn control)

The main advantage here lies in the reduction of fuel consumption as a result of lean-burn (non-throttled) operation. The success of this concept depends to a high degree upon the availability of catalytic converters which are able to reduce NO_X emissions during lean-burn operation. The lean-misfire limit (LML) for spark-ignition engines in the lean-burn range is reached at $\lambda \approx 1.7$ regardless of engine design measures.

Lambda oxygen sensors

Zirconium-dioxide sensor ($\lambda = 1$)

This sensor operates according to the principle of a galvanic oxygen concentration cell with solid electrolyte whose ceramic is made of zirconium dioxide and yttrium oxide. This oxide mix is a practically pure oxygen-ion conductor and separates the exhaust gas from the surrounding air.

An electrical voltage is generated across the platinum-cermet electrodes in accordance with the Nernst principle.

$$U_s = R \cdot \frac{T}{4F} \cdot \ln\left(\frac{p_{O_2}{}''}{p_{O_2}}\right)$$

R general gas constant, F Faraday constant, T absolute temperature, $p_{O_2}{}''$ oxygen partial pressure of reference load, $p_{O_2}{}'$ oxygen partial pressure in exhaust gas.

The catalytically active electrodes must be in thermodynamic balance before measurement of the oxygen concentration can be applied for reaching conclusions on the Lambda values. In this case, the sensor's characteristic shows a jump at $\lambda = 1$. When high concentrations of exhaust-gas components which are not in thermodynamic balance are incompletely converted, the sensor's characteristic shows shifts in the excess-air factor λ.

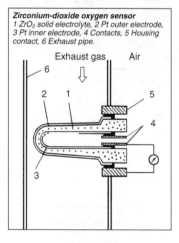

Zirconium-dioxide oxygen sensor
1 ZrO$_2$ solid electrolyte, 2 Pt outer electrode, 3 Pt inner electrode, 4 Contacts, 5 Housing contact, 6 Exhaust pipe.

These must be compensated for by design measures taken at the engine. The sensor characteristic's dependence on temperature can be minimized by heating the sensor electrically.

Resistive sensor

Due to the change in the O_2 vacancy concentration of the oxide, oxidic semiconductors such as titanium oxide or strontium titanate change their volume conductivity.

The temperature-dependency of the conductivity is superimposed upon this effect, so that the determination of the Lambda value depends upon the quality of the required temperature control – open-loop or closed-loop (by varying the amount of heat generated).

Lean sensor

In its lean range (λ in the vicinity of 1), the "voltage-jump" (zirconium-dioxide) sensor as described above has only been used to a limited extent. Special measures taken to stabilize the sensor, together with the use of a high-capacity heater (18 W) permit operation to approx. $\lambda \leq 1.5$. The lean sensor

using the limit-current principle permits the measurement of any values above $\lambda = 1$.

O_2 ions are pumped from the cathode to the anode when an external voltage is applied across two electrodes deposited on a ZrO_2 ceramic substrate. Since a diffusion barrier prevents the flow of O_2 molecules from the exhaust gas to the cathode, current saturation is reached above a given pump-voltage threshold value. By approximation, the resulting limit current is proportional to the oxygen concentration. This sensor principle is particularly suitable for lean-burn concepts. However, in lean/mix concepts in which a control setpoint $\lambda = 1$ is often desired, the broadband sensor is more suitable.

Broadband sensor

This is a combination of the lean sensor using the limit-current principle, and the zirconium-dioxide sensor (Nernst oxygen concentration cell). As a two-cell sensor, and in combination with closed-loop control electronics, this sensor generates a clear signal which rises linearly within a broad lambda range ($0.7 < \lambda < 4$).

The pump cell and the concentration cell are made of ZrO_2, and each is coated with 2 porous platinum electrodes. The cells are so arranged that there is a measuring gap of $10...50$ μm between them. This measuring gap is connected to the surrounding exhaust-gas atmosphere through an exhaust-gas opening in the solid electrolyte, and at the same time represents the diffusion barrier which determines the limit current. An electronic circuit controls the voltage applied to the pump cell so that the composition of the exhaust gas in the measuring gap remains constant at $\lambda = 1$. This corresponds to a voltage at the concentration cell of $U_N = 450$ mV. With lean exhaust gas, the pump cell pumps the oxygen from the measuring gap to the outside. On the other hand, when the exhaust gas is rich, the oxygen is pumped into the measuring gap from the surrounding exhaust gas (by decomposition of CO_2 and H_2O) and the direction of current flow is reversed. The pump current is proportional to the oxygen concentration or oxygen requirement. An integrated heater maintains an operating temperature of at least 600 °C.

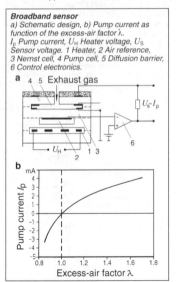

Broadband sensor
a) Schematic design, b) Pump current as function of the excess-air factor λ.
I_p Pump current, U_H Heater voltage, U_S Sensor voltage. 1 Heater, 2 Air reference, 3 Nernst cell, 4 Pump cell, 5 Diffusion barrier, 6 Control electronics.

a

4 5 Exhaust gas

$U_S \cdot I_p$

U_H 1 3   6

2

b

Pump current I_p / mA

0.8 1.0 1.2 1.4 1.6 1.8
Excess-air factor λ

Types of control

Two-step control

The zirconium-dioxide sensor as described above with its voltage-jump characteristic at $\lambda = 1$ is suitable for two-step controls. A manipulated variable composed of the voltage jump and the ramp changes its direction of control for each voltage jump which indicates a change from rich/lean or lean/rich. The typical amplitude of this manipulated variable has been set to the 2...3 % range. This results in a limited controller response which for the most part is determined by the sum of the dead times.

This sensor's typical "false measurement", caused by variations in exhaust-gas composition, can be compensated for by selective control. Here, the manipulated-variable curve is designed to incorporate an intended asymmetry, whereby the retention of the ramp value for a controlled dwell time t_v following the sensor's voltage jump is the preferred method.

Two-step control with reference sensor downstream of the catalytic converter

The effect of the disturbance on the accuracy at the voltage-jump point at $\lambda = 1$, as described above, has been minimized by a modified surface coating. Nevertheless, aging and environmental influences (poisoning) still have an effect. A sensor downstream of the catalytic converter is subjected to these influences to a considerably lesser extent. The principle of the two-step control is based upon the fact that the controlled rich or lean shift is changed additively by means of a "slow" corrective control loop.

The resulting long-term stability is of decisive importance for compliance with the exhaust-gas legislation now coming into force.

Continuous-action control with broadband sensor

The defined dynamic response of a two-step control can only be improved when the deviation from $\lambda = 1$ is actually measured. With the broadband sensor, it is possible to achieve continuous-action $\lambda = 1$ control with a stationary, very low amplitude together with high dynamic response. This control's parameters are calculated and adapted as a function of the engine's operating points. Above all, with this type of Lambda control, the unavoidable offset of the stationary and instationary pilot control can be compensated for far more quickly. If demanded by certain engine operating conditions (for instance, warm-up), further optimisation of the exhaust-gas emission applies the potential inherent in the control setpoints $\lambda \neq 1$, for instance, in the lean range. The expansion to a lean-mixture control system, with the advantages and disadvantages already dealt with, merely necessitates the definition of other control setpoints.

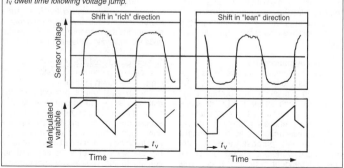

Manipulated-variable curve with closed-loop-controlled Lambda shift (two-step control)
t_v *dwell time following voltage jump.*

Testing exhaust and evaporative emissions

Test program

In order to precisely determine a passenger car's emission levels, the vehicle must be tested in an emissions test cell under conditions which accurately simulate actual driving conditions. Compared to on-road driving, operation in the test cell offers the advantage of allowing tests to be conducted at precisely predefined speeds without having to take traffic flow into consideration. This is the only means of ensuring that individual emissions tests remain mutually comparable.

The vehicle to be tested is parked with its drive wheels on rollers whose rotational resistance can be adjusted to simulate friction and aerodynamic drag. Inertial masses can be added or removed to simulate the weight of the vehicle. A blower mounted a short distance in front of the vehicle provides the necessary cooling.

The measurement of emission levels is based on a simulated driving pattern which progresses through a precisely defined driving cycle incorporating various vehicle speeds. The exhaust gases produced during this driving cycle are collected for analysis of the pollutant masses at the end of the cycle (see illustration).

The methods for collecting the exhaust gases, and the procedures for determining emissions, have largely been standardized in the various countries, but the driving cycles have not. In some countries, regulations governing exhaust emissions are supplemented by limits placed on evaporative losses from the fuel system.

Chassis dynamometer

In order to compare vehicle emissions, the speeds and forces acting on the vehicle during simulation on the chassis dynamometer and on the road must agree with respect to time. It is necessary to simulate the vehicle's moments of inertia, its rolling resistance, and its aerodynamic drag. For this purpose, eddy current brakes or DC motors produce a suitable speed-dependent retarding force. This force acts on the rollers, and must be overcome by the vehicle. Rapid couplings of various sizes are used to attach inertial masses to the rollers, thus simulating vehicle weight. It is imperative that the curve of braking load versus vehicle speed, and the required inertial masses, be maintained precisely. Deviations result in measuring errors. Ambient conditions such as atmospheric humidity, temperature and barometric pressure also influence test results.

Driving cycles

To obtain comparable exhaust-emission values, the predefined speeds on the dynamometer must agree with those on the road. Testing is based on a standardized driving cycle in which gearshifts, braking, idle phases, and standstill periods, have all been selected to provide a high level of correspondence with the velocities and acceleration that characterise typical driving in the normal traffic of a large town. Seven different test cycles are employed internationally. In Europe, the driving schedule has been abbreviated to EU Stage III (as of 01/2000; the 40 s pre-run is no longer used). The USA additionally uses the SFTP test for vehicles with air conditioning, as well as further sets of driving conditions.

Usually, a driver sits in the vehicle to maintain the speed at the levels indicated on a display screen.

Sampling and dilution procedures (CVS Method)

The European adoption of the constant-volume sampling method (CVS) in 1982 means that there is now basically a single standardized procedure in force worldwide for collecting exhaust gases.

Sampling and analysis of emissions

The dilution procedure operates according to the following principle:

The exhaust gases produced by the test vehicle are diluted with fresh air at a mean ratio of 1:10, and extracted using a special system of pumps such that the flow volume composed of exhaust gas and fresh air is maintained at a fixed ratio, i.e. the admixture of air is adjusted according to the vehicle's momentary exhaust volume. Throughout the test a constant proportion of the diluted exhaust gas is extracted for collection in one or several sample bags. The pollutant concentration in the sample bags at the end of the test corresponds precisely to the mean concentration in the total quantity of fresh-air/exhaust mixture which has been extracted. Because the total volume of the fresh-air/exhaust mixture can be defined, the pollutant concentrations can be used as the basis for calculating the pollutant masses produced during the course of the test.

Advantages of this procedure: Condensation of the water vapor contained in the exhaust gas is avoided, which would otherwise cause a substantial reduction in the NO_x losses in the bag. In addition, dilution greatly inhibits the tendency of the exhaust components (especially hydrocarbons) to continue to react with one another. However, dilution does mean that the concentration of the

pollutants decreases proportionally to the mean dilution ratio, necessitating the use of more sensitive analyzers. Standardized equipment is available for analysis of the pollutants in the bags.

Dilution systems
Either of two different but equally acceptable pump arrangements is generally used to maintain a constant flow volume for the test. In the first, a normal blower extracts the fresh-air/exhaust mixture through a venturi tube; the second arrangement makes use of a special rotary-piston blower (Roots blower). Either method is capable of measuring the flow volume with an acceptable degree of accuracy.

Test setups
a) For the US federal test (here with a Venturi system),
b) For the Europe test (here with rotary-piston blower).
1 Chassis dynamometer, 2 Inertial mass, 3 Exhaust gas, 4 Air filter, 5 Dilution air, 6 Radiator,
7 Sampling venturi tube, 8 Gas temperature, 9 Pressure, 10 Venturi tube, 11 Blower,
12 Sample bags, 13 Rotary-piston blower, 14 System outlet.
ct Emissions in transition phase, s Emissions in stabilized phase, ht Emissions during hot test

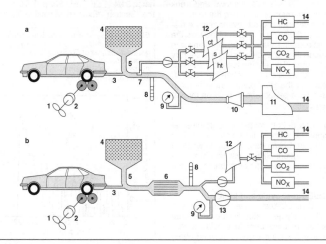

Determining evaporative losses from the fuel system
(Evaporation tests)

Apart from the combustion pollutants produced in the engine, a motor vehicle emits additional quantities of hydrocarbons (HC) through evaporation of fuel from the fuel tank and fuel system (dependent on design and fuel temperature). Some countries (e.g. the USA and Europe) have regulations which limit these evaporative losses.

<u>SHED Test</u>

The SHED (Sealed Housing for Evaporative Determination) test is the most common procedure for determining evaporative emissions. It comprises two test phases with varying conditioning processes in a gas-tight chamber.

The first part of the test is carried out with the fuel tank approx. 40 % full. The actual testing of the HC concentration in the chamber begins at 15.5 °C as the test fuel is warmed (initial temperature: 10...14.5 °C). The test concludes after one hour when the temperature of the fuel has risen by 14 °C; at this time the HC concentration is measured once again. Evaporative emissions are determined by comparing the initial and final measurements. The vehicle's windows and trunk lid must remain open during the test.

For determining the evaporative emissions in the second portion of the test, the vehicle is first warmed up by being run through the test cycle valid for the country concerned. The engine is then turned off with the vehicle in the chamber. The increase in the HC concentration is measured for a period of one hour as the vehicle cools.

The sum of both measurements must lie below the current limit value of 2 g of evaporated hydrocarbons. Meanwhile, a more stringent SHED test has been decided upon for implementation in the USA.

ECE/EC test cycle and limits

The ECE/EC test cycle incorporates a synthetically generated driving curve (see illustration) calculated to provide a reasonable approximation of driver behav-

iour in urban traffic. Since 1993, the test cycle has been supplemented by a suburban section with speeds of up to 120 km/h. This new ECE/EC test cycle is presently required by law in the following countries: Germany, Netherlands, Belgium, Luxembourg, France, Denmark, Great Britain, Ireland, Italy, Spain, Finland, Austria, Sweden, Greece and Portugal.

The exhaust emissions test is conducted as follows:

After the vehicle has been appropriately conditioned (vehicle allowed to stand with engine off at a room temperature of 20...30 °C for at least 6 hours) the actual test begins after a cold start and 40 second pre-running phase (this phase does not apply as of EU Stage III). During measurement, exhaust gas is collected in a sample bag using the CVS method. The pollutant masses determined by analysis of the contents of the bag are converted in the Europe test to the driven distance. In addition, hydrocarbons and oxides of nitrogen are combined to form a composite limit (HC+NO$_x$). These substances are considered separately as of EU Stage III.

More stringent limits have been in force since 1992 irrespective of the vehicle engine displacement. This directive designated 91/441 EEC (EU Stage I) is listed in the Section "Exhaust emission limits",

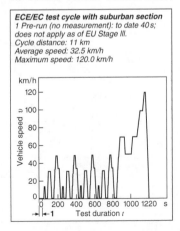

ECE/EC test cycle with suburban section
1 Pre-run (no measurement): to date 40 s;
does not apply as of EU Stage III.
Cycle distance: 11 km
Average speed: 32.5 km/h
Maximum speed: 120.0 km/h

Table 1. It also places limits on evaporative losses. A further reduction of the limits was imposed in 1996/97 by directive 94/12/EEC (EU Stage II).

Further reductions of limits are planned for Europe (Stage III and IV, 2000 and 2005):
– Cold start at –7°C (as of 2002),
– EOBD (European On-Board Diagnosis) of parts relevant to exhaust emissions,
– More stringent evaporative-emissions test,
– Durability (80,000; 100,000 km) and in-field monitoring,
– Exhaust-gas sampling immediately after start

Test cycles in the USA

FTP 75 test cycle

The FTP 75 test cycle (Federal Test Procedure), which consists of three test sections, represents actual speeds measured in the USA on the streets of Los Angeles in morning commuter traffic (see illustration 3a):

The vehicle to be tested is first conditioned (allowed to stand with engine off for 12 hours at a room temperature of 20...30°C), then started and run through the prescribed test cycle:

Phase ct: Collection of diluted exhaust gas in bag 1 during the cold transition phase.

Phase s: Changeover to sample bag 2 at the beginning of the stabilized phase (after 505 s) without any interruption in the

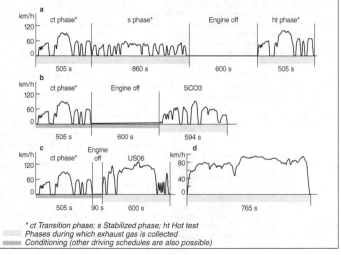

USA test cycles

Test cycle	a	b	c	d
	FTP 75	SC03	US06	Highway
Cycle distance:	17.87 km	5.76 km	12.87 km	16.44 km
Cycle duration:	1877 s + 600 s pause	594 s	600 s	765 s
Average cycle speed:	34.1 km/h	34.9 km/h	77.3 km/h	77.4 km/h
Maximum cycle speed:	91.2 km/h	88.2 km/h	129.2 km/h	96.4 km/h

* ct Transition phase; s Stabilized phase; ht Hot test
Phases during which exhaust gas is collected
Conditioning (other driving schedules are also possible)

driving cycle. The engine is turned off for a 10-minute pause immediately following the stabilized phase (after 1372 s).

<u>Phase ht</u>: The engine is restarted for the hot test (505 s in duration). The speeds used in this phase correspond directly to those in the cold transition phase. Exhaust gases are collected in a third sample bag. The bag samples from the previous phases are analyzed during the pause before the hot test, and then the samples should not remain in the bags for longer than 20 minutes.

The exhaust-gas sample in the third sample bag is analyzed once the driving sequence has been completed. The weighted sums of the pollutant masses (HC, CO and NO_x; ct 0.43, s 1, ht 0.57) from all three bags are correlated with the distance covered during the test, and then expressed as emissions per mile. The limits on pollutant emissions vary among individual countries. This test procedure is used in the USA including California ("Emission limits", Table 2) and in other countries (Table 4).

SFTP schedules

The tests in accordance with the SFTP standard will be phased-in in stages between 2001 and 2004. Together they consist of three driving schedules: the FTP 75, the SC03 and the US06 schedule.

They are intended to additionally examine the following driving patterns (see illustration, USA test cycles b and c):
– aggressive driving,
– major changes in driving speed,
– engine start and driving-off,
– frequent minor changes in driving speed,
– parking times and
– operation with the air conditioner running.

In the SC03 and US06 schedules, the ct phase of the FTP 75 test cycle is applied after preconditioning with no collection of exhaust gases, however other conditioning procedures are also possible.

The SC03 schedule is carried out at a temperature of 30 °C and 40 % relative humidity (vehicles with air conditioning only). The individual driving schedules are weighted as follows:

– Vehicles with air conditioner:
  35 % FTP 75 + 37 % SC03 + 28 % US06
– Vehicles without air conditioner:
  72 % FTP 75 + 28 % US06

The SFTP and FTP 75 test cycles must be successfully completed independently of each other (Tables 2 and 3 in the section "Exhaust emission limits").

Test cycles for determining fleet fuel consumption

Every vehicle manufacturer must determine the fuel consumption of his vehicle fleet. If a manufacturer exceeds certain limits, he is fined. He is awarded a bonus if consumption lies below certain limits. Fuel consumption is determined from the exhaust emissions produced during two test cycles: the FTP 75 test cycle (55 %) and the highway test cycle (45 %).

The highway test cycle is conducted once after preconditioning (vehicle allowed to stand with engine off for 12 hours at 20...30 °C) without measurements being conducted. The exhaust emissions from a second test run are then collected. Fuel consumption is determined based on the emissions (test cycle d).

Every new vehicle is required to comply with the limits for 50,000 miles, regardless of vehicle weight and engine displacement. Under certain conditions, the USA grants exemptions for the various model years. The legislation imposes different limits at 50,000 and 100,000 miles; permissible limits are higher at 100,000 miles (deterioration factors).

In addition to many measures designed to protect the environment, the Clean Air Act stipulated more stringent emission limits for vehicles since 1994 (Table 2). California decided to enforce the more stringent limits as early as 1993, and is planning to take further drastic steps.

Cold-start enrichment, which is necessary when a vehicle is started at low temperatures, produces particularly high emissions. These cannot be measured in current emissions testing, which is conducted at ambient temperatures of 20...30 °C. The Clean Air Act attempts to limit these emissions as well by prescribing an emissions test at −6.7 °C.

However, a limit is prescribed for carbon monoxide only.

Japanese test cycle
Two test cycles with differing hypothetical driving curves are combined to provide the complete test.

Following a cold start, the 11-mode cycle is run four times, with evaluation of all four cycles. The 10·15-mode test as a hot test is run through once (see illustration).

Preconditioning for the hot start also includes the stipulated idle emissions test, and is conducted as follows:

After warming up the vehicle at 60 km/h for approx. 15 minutes, the HC, CO and CO_2 concentrations in the exhaust pipe are measured. Following a secondary warm-up period of 5 minutes at 60 km/h, the 10·15-mode hot test is then started. In the 11-mode test as well as in the 10·15-mode test, analysis is performed using a CVS system. The diluted exhaust gas is in each case collected in a bag. In the cold test, the pollutants are specified in terms of g/test, whereas in the hot test they are correlated with the distance driven, i.e. they are converted to g/km (see Table 5 in the section "Exhaust emission limits").

The exhaust gas regulations in Japan include limits on evaporative emissions which are measured using the SHED method.

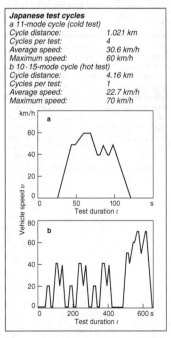

Japanese test cycles
a 11-mode cycle (cold test)

Cycle distance:	1.021 km
Cycles per test:	4
Average speed:	30.6 km/h
Maximum speed:	60 km/h

b 10·15-mode cycle (hot test)

Cycle distance:	4.16 km
Cycles per test:	1
Average speed:	22.7 km/h
Maximum speed:	70 km/h

Exhaust-gas analyzers

Legislation requires that emission testing also be carried out on vehicles which are already on the road.

In addition, exhaust-gas analyzers are also indispensable service tools in the workshop, necessary both for optimal A/F-mixture adjustment and for effective trouble-shooting on the engine.

Test procedure

In automotive service operations, the infrared method has proved to be the only efficient and reliable means for testing exhaust gases.

This method bases on the fact that individual exhaust-gas components absorb infrared light at different specific rates, according to their characteristic wavelengths. The various designs include both single-component analyzers (e. g. for CO only) and multi-component analyzers (for CO/HC, CO/CO_2, CO/HC/CO_2 etc.).

Test chamber

Infrared radiation is transmitted by an emitter which has been heated to approx. 700 °C. The beam passes through a measuring cell before entering the receiver chamber. When measuring the CO content, the sealed receiver chamber contains gas with a defined CO content which absorbs a portion of the CO-specific radiation. This absorption causes the gas temperature to increase, which in turn causes gas with a volume of V_1 to flow via a flow sensor into the compensation volume with a volume of V_2. A rotating chopper disk induces a rhythmic interruption in the beam, producing an alternating basic flow between the two volumes V_1 and V_2. The flow sensor converts this motion into an alternating electrical signal. When a test gas with a variable CO content flows through the measuring cell, it absorbs radiant energy in a quantity proportional to its CO content; the energy is then no longer available in the receiver chamber. The result is a reduction of the base flow in the receiver chamber. The deviation from the alternating basic signal is therefore a measure of the CO content in the test gas.

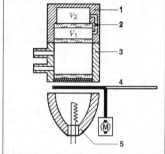

Test chamber using infrared method
(schematic diagram)
1 Receiver chamber with compensation volume V_1 and V_2, 2 Flow sensor, 3 Measuring cell, 4 Rotating chopper disk with motor, 5 Infrared emitter.

Catalytic-converter testing

A representative component can be used to obtain an indirect measurement of catalytic-converter operation on vehicles with closed-loop-controlled catalytic devices. The best-suited is CO, which must not exceed 0.3 % by volume downstream of the converter, whereby lambda must be exactly 1.00 (± 0.01). Lambda, in turn, can be determined using the composition of the exhaust gas at the catalytic converter's outlet. The exhaust-gas analyzer calculates the value for lambda using the CO, HC, CO_2 and O_2 exhaust gas components, with constants used for NO and fuel composition HC_V. The O_2 content is measured by an electrochemical probe.

Current (1998) emissions limits for gasoline engines

Table 1
EU emissions limits as measured in ECE/EU test cycle

Standards	Introduction	CO g/km	HC g/km	NO$_X$ g/km	HC+NO$_X$ g/km
EU Stage I	07.92	2.72	–	–	0.97
EU Stage II	01.96	2.2	–	–	0.5
EU Stage III	01.00	2.3	0.2	0.15	–
EU Stage IV	01.05	1.0	0.1	0.08	–

Table 2
US Federal (49 states) and California emissions limits. FTP 75 test cycle

	Model year	Standards	CO g/mile	HC g/mile	NO$_X$ g/mile
US Federal	1994	Level 1	3.4	0.25	0.4
	2004 [1]	Level 2	1.7	0.125 [2]	0.2
California	[3]	TLEV [4]	3.4	0.125 [2]	0.4
	[3]	LEV [5]	3.4	0.075 [2]	0.2
	[3]	ULEV [6]	1.7	0.04 [2]	0.2

[1] Proposal. [2] NMOG = Non Methanic Organic Gases. [3] Introduction varies according to manufacturer's NMOG fleet average (both vehicle and total fleet are certified).
[4] Transitional Low Emission Vehicles. [5] Low Emission Vehicles. [6] Ultra Low Emission Vehicles.

Table 3
US emissions limits. STFP test cycle

	NMHC[1]+NO$_X$ g/mile	CO$_{Composite}$ [2] g/mile	CO$_{SC03}$ [2] g/mile	CO$_{US06}$ [2] g/mile
up to 50,000 miles	0.65	3.4	3.0	9.0
50,000 to 100,000 miles	0.91	4.2	3.7	11.1

[1] Non Methane HC. [2] The manufacturer has the option of selecting CO$_{Composite}$ or CO$_{SC03}$ and CO$_{US06}$ limits.

Table 4
Emissions limits for Argentina, Australia, Brazil, Canada, Mexico, Norway, Switzerland, and South Korea measured with FTP 75 test cycle

Country	Introduction	CO g/km	HC g/km	NO$_X$ g/km	Evap. emissions (HC) g/test
Argentina	01.97	2.0	0.3	0.6	6.0
Australia	01.97	1.9	0.24	0.57	1.9
Brazil	01.97	2.0	0.3	0.6	6.0
Canada	01.98	2.1	THC [2] 0.25; NMHC [3] 0.16	0.24	2.0
Mexico	01.95	2.1	0.25	0.62	2.0
Norway	01.89	2.1	0.25	0.62	2.0
Switzerland [1]	10.87	2.1	0.25	0.62	2.0
South Korea	01.91 01.00	2.1	0.25	0.62 0.25	2.0

[1] EU/ECE regulations recognized since 10/95. [2] THC = Total HC. [3] NMHC = Non Methane HC.

Table 5
Japanese emissions limits measured in Japanese test cycle

Test procedure	CO	HC	NO$_X$	Evap. emissions
10·15-mode (g/km)	2.1...2.7 (0.67)	0.25...0.39 (0.08)	0.25...0.48 (0.08)	–
11-mode (g/test)	60.0...85.0 (19.0)	7.0...9.5 (2.2)	4.4...6.0 (1.4)	–
SHED (g/Test)	–	–	–	2.0

( ) planned figures

Diesel-engine management

Fuel metering

Requirements

To ensure efficient preparation of the A/F mixture, the fuel must not only be injected into the combustion chamber at a pressure of between 350 and 2000 bar, depending on the diesel combustion process, but it must also be metered with the greatest possible accuracy during each injection. In order to maintain the compromise between low fuel consumption and compliance with emission limits (exhaust gas and noise), it is necessary to precisely time the start of injection with an accuracy of approx. ± 1° crankshaft.

The start of injection is adjusted in order to control the start of combustion and compensate for the pressure-wave propagation times in the pressure lines.

In mechanical control systems, an upstream timing device uses the upper helix on the injection-pump plunger to adjust the start of injection as a function of engine speed and load.

EDC systems (Electronic Diesel Control) have an integral timing function that adjusts the injection pump's start of delivery as a function of engine speed, load and engine temperature.

The injected fuel quantity is used for load- and speed-dependent control of diesel engines; the quantity of intake air is not throttled. Because the speed of an unloaded diesel engine could therefore increase to the point of self-destruction given sufficient injected fuel, an engine-speed governor is essential. Special control devices are also required to ensure stable idle behavior.

Fuel-injection process

The fuel can no longer be regarded as incompressible, considering the high pressures and short delivery times involved. Thus the injection processes are not static (i.e. they do not conform to the geometric laws of displacement), but rather dynamic (largely in accordance with the laws of acoustics).

In the case of cam-driven systems, a camshaft driven by the engine moves the injection-pump plunger in the direction of delivery. This causes pressure to build up in the high-pressure chamber of the pump element. The increasing pressure opens the delivery valve, and a pressure wave moves through the high-pressure delivery line to the injection nozzle at the speed of sound (approx. 1400 m/s). When the opening pressure of the nozzle is reached, the needle valve overcomes the force of the nozzle spring and lifts from its seat so that it can be injected through the spray orifices into the engine's combustion chamber. Fuel delivery ends when the pressure in the high-pressure chamber collapses due to the spill port being opened by the pump-plunger helix. The delivery valve then closes and reduces the pressure in the injection line. The pressure drop to static pressure between every two injection cycles is dimensioned such that

- the injection nozzle closes quickly to provide a clean break in fuel discharge and to prevent fuel dribble,
- residual pressure oscillations in the lines are effectively dampened. On the one hand to prevent the pressure peaks from reopening the nozzle, and on the other hand to ensure that the pressure drops do not cause cavitation damage.

Fuel-injection system

The fuel-injection system supplies fuel to the diesel engine, and consists of a low-pressure stage and a high-pressure stage.

The low-pressure stage consists of the fuel tank, fuel filter, mechanical or electric delivery pump with pressure relief valve, and the fuel lines.

The high-pressure stage comprises the high-pressure pump with delivery valve which generates the fuel pressure required for injection, the fuel-injection tubing, and the fuel injectors (nozzle-holder assemblies and nozzles). EDC (Electronic Diesel Control) systems also incorporate a control valve, which in today's systems generally takes the form of a solenoid valve. In the future, however, piezovalves will also be used.

Generally speaking, current state-of-the-art technology prescribes one of the following high-pressure injection systems for automotive diesels:

In-line fuel-injection pumps with mechanical governors or electronic actuators, and integral timing devices as dictated by the specific application.

The in-line fuel-injection pump is used primarily on commercial-vehicle engines. In this pump system, a number of pumping elements (also known as plunger-and-barrel assemblies) corresponding to the number of engine cylinders are accommodated in a housing and operated by means of a common camshaft. The range of in-line fuel-injection pumps also includes the control-sleeve pump, which allows the start of delivery in addition to the injected fuel quantity to be adjusted as desired.

The distributor injection pump incorporates a mechanical governor or electronic controller, and an integrated timing device.

The axial-piston pump is used in particular on high speed IDI and DI diesel engines for passenger cars and small commercial vehicles. In this type of pump, a central plunger driven by a cam plate generates pressure and distributes the fuel to the individual cylinders. A control sleeve or solenoid valve meters the injected fuel quantity.

The radial-piston pump is primarily used on modern high speed DI diesel engines for passenger cars and small commercial vehicles. Pressure is generated and fuel delivered by two to four plungers in a radial configuration driven by a cam ring. A solenoid valve controls the injection timing and meters the fuel.

In addition to the in-line and distributor injection pumps, there are also individual injection pumps which are driven directly by the engine camshaft. These are mostly used on large marine engines, construction machinery and small engines.

Another modern fuel-injection system is the UIS (Unit Injector System), in which the injection pump and fuel injector form one unit. One unit injector per cylinder is installed in the cylinder head. The unit is driven by the engine's camshaft, either di-

rectly via a push rod or indirectly via a rocker-arm assembly.

The UPS (Unit Pump System) operates according to the same principle as the Unit Injector System. However, in this type of pump a short high-pressure delivery line is connected between the pump and nozzle. This permits more design latitude, as the camshaft can be located either in the engine block or cylinder head.

Common to all of these systems is the fact that the required injection pressure is generated at the moment each injection occurs. In the case of electronically controlled systems, however, the rate-of-discharge curve can be influenced not only by the cam contour but also by solenoid valve actuation. Nevertheless, the maximum possible pressure depends directly on engine speed and injected fuel quantity.

The injection pressure can be set independently of engine speed and load using an accumulator-type injection system. In this so-called Common Rail System (CRS), pressure generation and fuel injection are decoupled with respect to time and location. Injection pressure is generated by a separate high-pressure pump. This pump need not necessarily be driven synchronously with respect to the injection timing. The pressure can be set independently of engine speed and injected fuel quantity, and electrically operated injectors are used in place of pressure-controlled fuel injectors. The time and duration of injector actuation determine the start of injection and the injected fuel quantity. This system also offers a great deal of freedom with regard to the design of multiple or divided injection functions.

In order to achieve accurate open and closed-loop control of injected fuel quantity and start of injection, as well as minimum scatter between the individual cylinders and long service life, it is imperative that all injection systems are manufactured from high-precision, close-tolerance components.

Size P in-line fuel-injection pump
1 Delivery-valve holder, 2 Spring seat,
3 Delivery valve, 4 Pump barrel, 5 Pump
plunger, 6 Lever arm with ball head,
7 Control rack, 8 Control sleeve, 9 Plunger
control arm, 10 Plunger return spring,
11 Spring seat, 12 Roller tappet,
13 Camshaft.

In-line fuel-injection pump (PE)

Fuel-supply pump

A piston pump delivers the fuel to the injection pump's fuel gallery at a pressure of 1...2.5 bar. The cam-driven supply-pump plunger travels to TDC on every stroke. It is not rigidly connected to the drive element; instead, a spring supplies the return pressure. The plunger spring responds to increases in line pressure by reducing the plunger's return travel to a portion of the full stroke. The greater the pressure in the delivery line, the lower the delivery quantity.

High-pressure pump

Every in-line fuel-injection pump has a plunger-and-barrel assembly (pumping element) for each engine cylinder. An engine-driven camshaft moves the plunger in the supply direction, and a spring presses it back to its initial position. Although the plunger has no seal, it is fitted with such precision (clearance: 3...5 μm) that its operation is virtually leak-free, even at high pressures and low engine speeds.

The plunger's actual stroke is constant. The delivery quantity is changed by altering the plunger's effective stroke. Inclined helices have been machined into the plunger for this purpose, so that the plunger's effective stroke changes when it is rotated. Active pumping starts when the upper edge of the plunger closes the in-

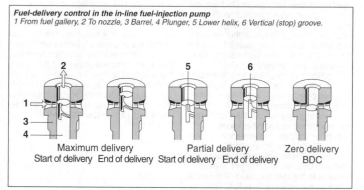

Fuel-delivery control in the in-line fuel-injection pump
1 From fuel gallery, 2 To nozzle, 3 Barrel, 4 Plunger, 5 Lower helix, 6 Vertical (stop) groove.

Maximum delivery		Partial delivery		Zero delivery
Start of delivery	End of delivery	Start of delivery	End of delivery	BDC

take port. The high-pressure chamber above the plunger is connected by a vertical groove to the chamber below the helix. Delivery ceases when the helix uncovers the intake port.

Various helix designs are employed in the plunger. On plunger-and-barrel assemblies with a lower helix only, pumping always begins at the same stroke travel, the plunger being rotated to advance or retard the end of delivery. An upper helix can be employed to vary the start of delivery. There are also plunger-and-barrel assemblies on the market which combine upper and lower helices in a single unit.

In order of their suitability for use with high injection pressures, the major <u>types of delivery valve</u> currently in use are:
– <u>Constant-volume valve</u>,
– <u>Constant-volume valve with return-flow restriction</u>,
– <u>Constant-pressure valve</u>.

The delivery valve and pressure-relief characteristics must be specially designed for the specific application. Units incorporating a return-flow restriction or constant-pressure valve have an additional throttle element to damp the pressure waves reflected back from the injection nozzle, thus preventing it from opening again. The constant-pressure valve is employed to maintain stable hydraulic characteristics in high-pressure fuel-injection systems and on small, high-speed direct-injection engines.

In fuel-injection pumps which generate moderate pressures of up to 600 bar (e.g. Size A), the plunger-and-barrel assembly is installed in the pump housing in a fixed position, where it is held in place by the delivery valve and the delivery-valve holder.

In pumps which generate injection pressures greater than approx. 600 bar, the plunger-and-barrel assembly, delivery valve and delivery-valve holder are screwed together to form a single unit, which means that the high sealing forces must no longer be accommodated by the pump housing (e.g. Sizes MW, P).

The in-line fuel-injection pump and the attached governor are connected to the engine's lube-oil system.

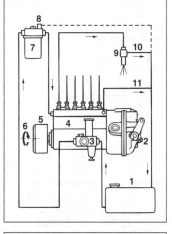

In-line fuel-injection pump with mechanical (flyweight governor)
1 Fuel tank, 2 Governor, 3 Fuel-supply pump, 4 Injection pump, 5 Timing device, 6 Drive from engine, 7 Fuel filter, 8 Vent, 9 Nozzle-and-holder assembly, 10 Fuel return line, 11 Overflow line.

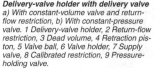

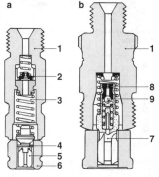

Delivery-valve holder with delivery valve
a) With constant-volume valve and return-flow restriction, b) With constant-pressure valve. 1 Delivery-valve holder, 2 Return-flow restriction, 3 Dead volume, 4 Retraction piston, 5 Valve ball, 6 Valve holder, 7 Supply valve, 8 Calibrated restriction, 9 Pressure-holding valve.

Governor characteristic curves
a Positive torque control in upper speed range, b Unregulated range, c Negative torque control.
1 Idle-speed setpoint, 2 Full-load curve, 3 Full-load curve, turbocharged engine, 4 Full-load curve, naturally-aspirated engine, 5 Full-load curve, naturally-aspirated engine with altitude compensation, 6 Intermediate engine-speed control, 7 Temperature-sensitive starting quantity.

Variable-speed governor

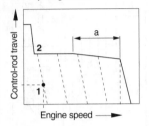

Minimum-maximum-speed governor

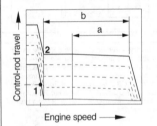

Complex governor with additional control functions

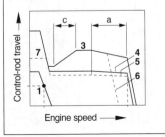

Speed governing

The main function of the governor is to limit the maximum engine speed. In other words, it must ensure that the diesel engine does not exceed the maximum min⁻¹ specified by its manufacturer. Depending upon type, the governor's functions may include maintaining specific, constant engine speeds, such as idle, or other speeds in the range between idle and maximum speed. The governor can also adjust full-load delivery in accordance with engine speed (adaptation), boost or atmospheric pressure, and it can be used to meter the extra fuel required for starting. The governor adapts the delivery quantity to these conditions by making corresponding adjustments in the position of the control rack.

Mechanical (flyweight) governors

The mechanical governor (also known as a flyweight or centrifugal governor) is driven by the engine's camshaft, and provides the performance curves described below. The flyweights, which act against the force of the governor springs, are connected to the control rack by a system of levers. During steady-state operation, centrifugal and spring forces are in a state of equilibrium, and the control rack assumes a position for fuel delivery corresponding to engine power output at that operating point. A drop in engine speed – for instance, due to increased load – results in a corresponding reduction in centrifugal force, and the governor springs move the flyweights, and with them the control rack, in the direction for increased delivery quantity until equilibrium is restored. Various functions are combined to produce the following types of governor:

Variable-speed governors

The variable-speed governor maintains a virtually constant engine speed in accordance with the position of the control lever. Applications: Preferably for commercial vehicles with auxiliary power take-off, for construction machinery, agricultural tractors, in ships and in stationary installations.

Minimum-maximum-speed governors

From the characteristic curve for the minimum-maximum-speed governor it can be seen that this type of governor is effective only at idle and when the engine reaches maximum min⁻¹. The torque in the range between these two extremes is determined exclusively by the position of the accelerator pedal. Applications: For road vehicles.

Combination governors
Combination governors are a synthesis of the two governor types described above. Depending upon the specific application, active control can be in the upper or lower engine-speed range.

Governor types
In the RQ and RQV governor, the flyweights act directly on the governor springs, and control-lever movements vary the transfer ratio at the fulcrum lever.

In the RSV, and RSF governor, the governor spring is outside the flyweights; the transfer ratio at the fulcrum lever remains essentially constant.

Speed droop
The governor's performance characteristics are essentially a function of the slope of the control curve, defined as speed droop:

$$\delta = \frac{n_{LO} - n_{VO}}{n_{VO}} \cdot 100\%$$

The smaller the difference between the upper no-load speed (n_{LO}) and the upper full-load speed (n_{VO}), the lower the speed droop, i.e. the greater the precision with which the governor maintains a specific engine speed. Variable-speed governors in small high-speed engines generally achieve a full-load speed regulation (top-end breakaway consistency) of 6...10%.

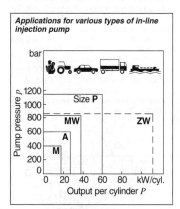

Applications for various types of in-line injection pump

RQ Minimum-maximum-speed governor
1 Pump plunger, 2 Control rack, 3 Full-load stop, 4 Control lever, 5 Injection-pump camshaft, 6 Flyweight, 7 Governor spring, 8 Sliding bolt.

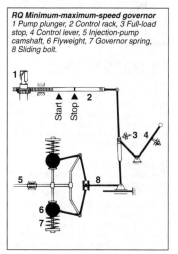

RSV Variable-speed governor
1 Pump plunger, 2 Control rack, 3 Maximum-speed stop, 4 Control lever, 5 Start spring, 6 Stop or idle stop, 7 Governor spring, 8 Auxiliary idle spring, 9 Injection-pump camshaft, 10 Flyweight, 11 Sliding bolt, 12 Torque-control spring, 13 Full-load stop.

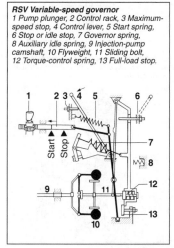

Mechanical add-on equipment

Torque control

An auxiliary spring (torque-control spring) is installed at a suitable position in the governor mechanism. The spring precisely adapts the governor's output curve to the diesel engine's full-load fuel requirements by lowering it slightly. When a given engine speed is reached, the spring compresses and causes the control rack to move in the direction for reduced fuel-delivery quantity (positive torque control). Negative torque control, which responds to increased engine speed by augmenting the fuel-delivery quantity, is also possible, albeit at the price of far more components and more complicated adjustment procedures.

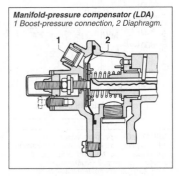

Manifold-pressure compensator (LDA)
1 Boost-pressure connection, 2 Diaphragm.

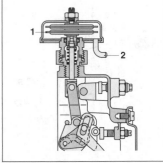

Altitude-pressure compensator (ADA)
1 Pressure capsule, 2 Atmospheric-pressure connection.

Manifold-pressure compensator (LDA)

Due to the larger air mass, turbocharged engines are capable of converting a greater amount of fuel into engine torque as the boost pressure increases; A spring-loaded diaphragm is used to make a corresponding correction in the full-load fuel-delivery quantity. Increasing boost pressure acts on the working side of the diaphragm, which is connected to the control rack in such a way that the injected fuel quantity increases as boost pressure increases

Altitude-pressure compensator (ADA)

The altitude-pressure compensator is similar to the LDA. It reduces the full-load fuel-delivery in response to the low atmospheric pressure (and low air density) encountered at high altitudes.

The unit includes a barometric capsule which displaces the control rack in the direction for lower fuel-delivery once atmospheric pressure drops by a specific increment.

Temperature-dependent starting device (TAS)

A cold engine requires a certain amount of additional fuel (enrichment) in order to start. This enrichment is not necessary on a warm engine and could lead to the emission of smoke.

The solution is TAS, which features a control-rack stop employing an expansion element to prevent enrichment during warm starts.

Rack-travel sensor (RWG)

The RWG monitors the control-rack position inductively.

After processing in an evaluation circuit, the signal can be used for such tasks as control of hydraulic or mechanical transmissions, for measuring fuel consumption, for exhaust-gas recirculation, and for diagnostics.

Port-closing sensor (FBG)

The FBG is an inductive unit which, with the engine running, monitors the point at which pump delivery starts (port closing). It can also check the timing device.

In addition, injection pumps equipped with this device can be supplied with the camshaft locked in the port-closing position. This setting facilitates simple and precise pump installation on the engine.

Timing devices

Centrifugally-controlled timing devices are positioned in the drivetrain between the engine and the injection pump. The flyweights respond to increasing engine speed by turning the injection pump's camshaft, with respect to the drive shaft, in the "delivery advance" direction. Front-mounted clutch-driven units and gear-driven in-pump devices, with an adjustment range of 3°...10° on the pump shaft are available.

Pump shutoff

A mechanical (stop lever), electric or pneumatic shutoff device is employed to shut down the diesel engine by interrupting the fuel supply.

Electronic governor (EDC)

Instead of flyweights, the electronic governor for the in-line fuel-injection pump uses a solenoid actuator with a non-contacting inductive position sensor to position the control rack. The solenoid actuator is triggered by an ECU.

The ECU microprocessor compares accelerator position, min^{-1}, and a number of additional correction factors with the program maps stored in its memory in order to determine the correct injected fuel quantity, i.e. the correct rack position.

An electronic controller compares the monitored control-rack position with the specified setpoint in order to determine the required excitation-current input to the solenoid, which operates against a return spring. When deviations are detected, the excitation current is regulated to shift the control rack to precisely the specified position.

An inductive speed sensor monitors a camshaft-mounted pulse wheel; the ECU uses the pulse intervals to calculate engine speed.

Because it can monitor a number of engine and vehicle parameters and combine them to calculate the injected fuel quantity, an electronic governor has a number of advantages over a mechanical unit:
- Engine can be switched on and off with key,
- Complete freedom in determining full-load response,

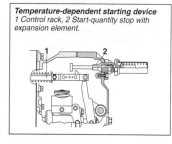

Temperature-dependent starting device
1 Control rack, 2 Start-quantity stop with expansion element.

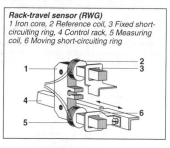

Rack-travel sensor (RWG)
1 Iron core, 2 Reference coil, 3 Fixed short-circuiting ring, 4 Control rack, 5 Measuring coil, 6 Moving short-circuiting ring

Port-closing sensor (FBG)
a) Measurement with sensor,
b) Blocking position;
1 Pump camshaft, 2 Sensor, 3 Blocking pin.

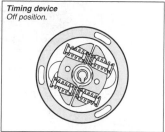

Timing device
Off position.

– Maximum injected fuel quantity can be precisely coordinated with the boost pressure in order to remain below the smoke limit,
– Corrections for air and fuel temperatures,
– Temperature-dependent start quantity,
– Engine-speed control for auxiliary power take-offs,
– Cruise-control facility,
– Regulation of maximum speed,
– Consistent, low idle speed,
– Active surge control,
– Option for intervention in traction control (TCS)/automatic transmission,
– Signal outputs for display of fuel consumption and engine speed,
– Service support through integral error diagnosis.

In-line control-sleeve fuel-injection pump

The in-line control-sleeve injection pump makes it possible to provide electronically-controlled adjustment of port closing (start of pump delivery). The spill port, which on conventional in-line pumps is in the housing and therefore immovable, is incorporated in the control sleeve which is a component in each plunger-and-barrel assembly. A control shaft with control-sleeve levers which engage the slide valves changes the positions of all sleeves at the same time.

Depending on the position of the control sleeve (up or down), the start of delivery is advanced or retarded relative to the position of the camshaft lobe. An electromagnetic actuator mechanism similar to that used in the electronically controlled in-line injection pumps turns the control shaft, albeit without position feedback.

A needle-motion sensor monitors the start of injection directly at the injection nozzle. It transmits a corresponding signal to the ECU, which compares it with the programmed value as a function of min^{-1}, injected fuel quantity, etc., in order to adjust the solenoid-excitation current to achieve congruence between the feedback and setpoint values for start of injection.

The engine-speed sensor obtains precise information on injection timing relative to TDC by monitoring pulses from reference marks on the engine's flywheel.

Electronic diesel control (EDC) for in-line fuel-injection pumps
1 Control rack, 2 Actuator, 3 Camshaft, 4 Engine-speed sensor, 5 ECU. Input/output quantities: a Redundant shutoff, b Boost pressure, c Vehicle speed, d Temperature (water, air, fuel), e Fuel-quantity command, f Engine speed, g Control-rack travel, h Solenoid position, i Fuel-consumption and engine-speed display, k Diagnostics, l Accelerator position, m Speed preset, n Clutch, brakes, engine brake.

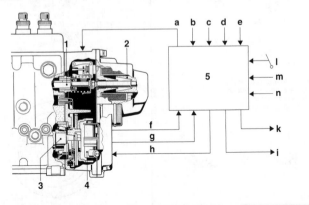

Distributor-type fuel-injection pump (VE)

Distributor-type fuel-injection pumps are used in 3-, 4-, 5- and 6-cylinder diesel engines in passenger cars, tractors and light- and medium-duty commercial vehicles which generate up to 42 kW per cylinder, depending on engine speed and combustion system. Distributor-type fuel-injection pumps for direct-injection (DI) engines achieve a peak injection pressure of 1950 bar in the nozzle at speeds of up to 2400 min^{-1}.

A differentiation is made between distributor-type fuel-injection pumps with mechanical control, and those with electronic governing available in versions with a rotating-solenoid actuator and with solenoid valve open-loop control.

Mechanically controlled axial-piston distributor pumps (VE)

These mechanically controlled axial-piston distributor pumps comprise the following major assemblies:

Fuel-supply pump

If no presupply pump is present, this integral vane-type supply pump draws fuel from the tank and, together with a pressure-control valve, generates an internal pump pressure which increases with engine speed.

High-pressure pump

The VE distributor-type fuel-injection pump incorporates only one pumping element for all cylinders. The element's plunger displaces the fuel during its stroke while at the same time rotating to distribute it to the individual outlets. During each rotation of the drive shaft, the plunger completes a number of strokes equal to the number of engine cylinders to be supplied. Via the yoke, the injection pump's drive shaft turns the cam plate and the pump plunger fixed to it. The lobes on the bottom surface of the cam plate turn against the rollers of the roller ring, causing the cam plate and plunger to make a stroke movement in addition to their rotary movement (distribution and delivery). The pump delivers fuel for as long as the spill port in the plunger remains closed off during the working stroke. Delivery ends when the spill port is uncovered by the control collar. The position of the control collar thus determines the effective stroke and the injected fuel quantity. The governor determines the position of the sliding control collar on the plunger.

Mechanical (flyweight) governor

A ball pin connects the control collar with the governor levers, which are acted upon

Plunger-and-barrel assembly with control sleeve
a) Start of delivery, b) End of delivery.
1 Control helix, 2 Control sleeve, 3 Spill port, 4 Control groove, 5 Pump plunger.

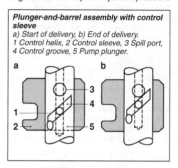

In-line control-sleeve pump
1 Pump plunger, 2 Control sleeve, 3 Control-sleeve adjustment shaft, 4 Control rack.

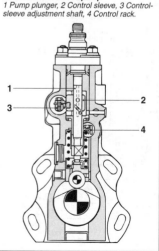

by the governor springs and the centrifugal force generated by the flyweights. Idling, transition ranges and max. engine speed can be adapted to meet engine requirements.

Speed droop, governor types: The description of speed droop and governor types (variable-speed governors, minimum-maximum-speed governors) for in-line fuel-injection pumps also applies to governors used with distributor-type fuel-injection pumps.

Load signal: On distributor fuel-injection pumps equipped with minimum-maximum speed governors, the position of the outer control lever can be monitored via microswitch or potentiometer to provide information on load.

Add-on modules:
A number of add-on modules are available to process additional operating parameters for regulation of delivery quantity (such as manifold-pressure compensator

(LDA), start quantity, hydraulic and mechanical full-load torque control) and for adjustment of the start of delivery – (e.g. cold-start accelerator, load-dependent start of delivery).

Hydromechanically controlled timing device
The speed-dependent supply-pump pressure (5...10 bar) acts on the front end of the spring-loaded timing-device plunger through a throttle bore. The plunger rotates the roller ring counter to the direction of rotation of the pump as a function of engine speed, thereby advancing the start of delivery.

Pump shutoff
An electric shutoff device (solenoid valve) shuts off the diesel engine by interrupting the fuel supply.

Electronic Diesel Control (EDC): Distributor-type fuel-injection pump with rotating-solenoid actuator
In contrast to the mechanically controlled

VE Distributor-type fuel-injection pump (basic version)
1 Vane-type supply pump, 2 Governor drive, 3 Timing device, 4 Cam plate, 5 Control collar, 6 Distributor plunger, 7 Delivery valve, 8 Solenoid-actuated shutoff, 9 Governor lever mechanism, 10 Overflow throttle, 11 Mechanical shutoff device, 12 Governor spring, 13 Speed-control lever, 14 Control sleeve, 15 Flyweight, 16 Pressure-control valve.

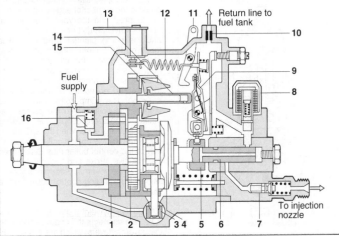

Electronic diesel control (EDC) for distributor-type fuel-injection pumps
1 Supply pump, 2 Solenoid valve, 3 Timing device, 4 Control collar, 5 Rotary actuator with sensor,
6 ECU. Inputs/Outputs: a Speed, b Start of injection, c Temperature, d Boost pressure,
e Accelerator position, f Fuel return, g To injection nozzle.

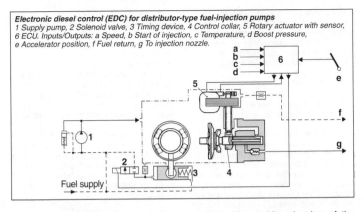

distributor-type fuel-injection pump, the EDC pump with rotating-solenoid actuator has an electronic governor and an electronically controlled timing device.

Electronic governor

An eccentrically-mounted ball pin provides the connection between the VE pump's control collar and the solenoid rotary actuator. The actuator's angular setting determines the position of the control collar, and with it the effective stroke of the pump. A non-contacting position sensor is connected to the rotary actuator. The ECU's microcomputer receives various signals from the sensors: accelerator-pedal position; engine speed; air, coolant and fuel temperature; boost pressure; atmospheric pressure; etc. It uses these input variables to determine the correct injected fuel quantity, which is then converted to a specific control-rack position with the aid of program maps stored in the unit's memory. The ECU varies the excitation current to the rotary actuator until it receives a signal indicating convergence between the setpoint and actual values for control-rack position.

Electronically-controlled timing device

In this device, the signal from a sensor in the nozzle-holder assembly, which indicates when the nozzle begins to open, is compared with a programmed setpoint value. A clocked solenoid valve con-

nected to the working chamber of the plunger in the timing device varies the pressure above the plunger and thus the position of the timing device. The actuation clock ratio of the solenoid valve is varied until the setpoint and actual values agree.

Advantages of electronic versus mechanical control:
- Improved control of injected fuel quantity (fuel consumption, engine power, emissions),
- Improved control of engine speed (low idle speed, adjustment for air conditioner, etc.)
- Enhanced comfort (anti-surge control, smooth-running control),
- More precise start of injection (fuel consumption, emissions),
- Improved service possibilities (diagnostics).

The application options extend to embrace features such as open-loop and closed-loop control of exhaust-gas recirculation, boost-pressure control, glow-plug control, and interconnection with other on-board electrical systems.

Electronic Diesel Control (EDC): Solenoid-controlled distributor pumps

In the case of solenoid-controlled distributor pumps, the fuel is metered by a high-pressure solenoid valve which directly closes off the pump's element chamber.

This permits even greater flexibility in fuel metering and in variation of the start of injection (see Figure for operating principle). The main assemblies of this new generation of distributor pumps are:
– the high-pressure solenoid valve,
– the ECU, and
– the incremental angle/time system for angle/time control of the solenoid valve using an angle of rotation sensor integrated into the pump.

The solenoid valve closes to define the start of the delivery, which then continues until the valve opens. The injected fuel quantity is determined by the length of time the valve remains closed. Solenoid-valve control enables rapid opening and closing of the element chamber irrespective of engine speed. In contrast to mechanically governed pumps and EDC pumps with a rotating-solenoid actuator, direct triggering by means of solenoid valves results in lower dead volumes, improved high-pressure sealing, and therefore greater efficiency.

The injection pump is equipped with its own, integral ECU for precise start-of-delivery control and fuel metering. Individual pump program maps and example-specific calibration data are stored in this ECU.

The engine ECU determines the start of injection and delivery on the basis of engine operating parameters, and sends this data to the pump ECU via the data bus. The system can control both the start of injection and the start of delivery.

The pump ECU also receives the injected fuel quantity signal via the data bus. This signal is generated by the engine ECU according to the accelerator-pedal signal and other parameters for required fuel quantity. In the pump ECU, the injected fuel quantity signal and the pump speed for a given start of delivery are taken as the input variables for the pump map on which the corresponding actuation period is stored as degrees of camshaft rotation.

And finally, the actuation of the high-pressure solenoid valve and the desired period of actuation are determined on the basis of the angle of rotation sensor integrated in the VE distributor pump.

The angle of rotation sensor in the pump is used for angle/time control. It consists of a magnetoresistive sensor and a reluctor ring divided into 3° increments interrupted by a reference mark for each cylinder.

The sensor determines the precise angle of camshaft rotation at which the solenoid valve opens and closes. This requires the pump ECU to convert timing data to angular position data and vice versa.

The low fuel-delivery rates at the start of injection, which result from the design of the VE distributor pump, are further reduced by the use of a two-spring nozzle holder. With a warm turbocharged engine, these low delivery rates permit low basic noise levels.

Pilot injection
Pilot injection allows the combustion noise to be further reduced without sacrificing the objects of the system's design which aim at generating maximum power output at the rated-power operating point. Pilot injection does not require additional hardware. Within a matter of milliseconds, the ECU actuates the solenoid valve twice in rapid succession. The solenoid valve controls the injected fuel quantity with a high degree of precision and dynamic response (typical pilot-injection fuel quantity: 1.5 mm^3).

Solenoid-controlled axial-piston distributor pumps
Axial-piston pumps use the same principle of pressure generation as EDC pumps with rotating-solenoid actuators. The injection pressure at the nozzle can be as high as 1500 bar, depending on the application.

By shifting the point at which delivery begins from the bottom dead center position of the pump plunger to a point within the plunger stroke, the pressure at low speeds can be increased and maximum pump torque can be substantially reduced at high speeds. For special applications, the variable start of delivery permits the start of injection to be advanced even at cranking speed.

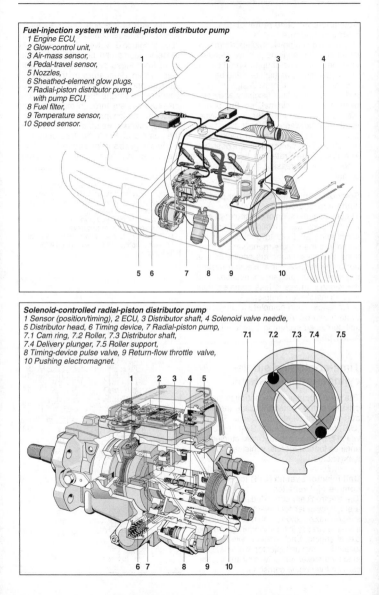

Fuel-injection system with radial-piston distributor pump
 1 Engine ECU,
 2 Glow-control unit,
 3 Air-mass sensor,
 4 Pedal-travel sensor,
 5 Nozzles,
 6 Sheathed-element glow plugs,
 7 Radial-piston distributor pump
    with pump ECU,
 8 Fuel filter,
 9 Temperature sensor,
10 Speed sensor.

Solenoid-controlled radial-piston distributor pump
 1 Sensor (position/timing), 2 ECU, 3 Distributor shaft, 4 Solenoid valve needle,
 5 Distributor head, 6 Timing device, 7 Radial-piston pump,
 7.1 Cam ring, 7.2 Roller, 7.3 Distributor shaft,
 7.4 Delivery plunger, 7.5 Roller support,
 8 Timing-device pulse valve, 9 Return-flow throttle valve,
10 Pushing electromagnet.

Solenoid-controlled radial-piston distributor pumps

Radial-piston pumps for high-performance direct-injection engines achieve element-chamber pressures of up to 1100 bar and nozzle pressures as high as 1950 bar.

Because the cam-drive design employs a direct, positive link, flexibility and compliance remain minimal, so the performance potential is greater. Fuel delivery is shared between at least two radial plungers. The small forces involved mean that steep (fast) cam profiles are possible. The fuel-delivery rate can be further increased by increasing the number of plungers.

Solenoid-controlled distributor pumps with integral ECU

The latest generation of distributor pumps are compact, self-contained systems incorporating an ECU to control both the pump and the engine-management functions. Because a separate engine ECU is no longer required, the injection system requires fewer plug-in connections and the wiring harness is less complex, thus making installation simpler.

The engine and complete fuel-injection system can be installed and tested as a self-contained system independent of vehicle type.

Time-controlled single-cylinder pump systems

The new modular, time-controlled single-cylinder pump systems include the electronically controlled "Unit Injector System" (UIS) and the "Unit Pump System" (UPS) which are used on modern direct-injection engines for commercial vehicles and passenger cars.

Unit injector system (UIS) for commercial vehicles

The electronically controlled unit injector is a single-cylinder fuel-injection pump with integral nozzle and solenoid valve which is installed directly in the cylinder head of the diesel engine. Each engine cylinder is allocated its own unit injector, which is operated by a rocker arm driven by an injection cam on the engine camshaft.

The start of injection and the injected fuel quantity are controlled by the high-speed solenoid valve. The values for these variables can be selected as desired from those stored in the program map. When de-energized, the solenoid valve is open. This means that fuel can flow freely from the fuel inlet of the low-pressure system through the pump and back into the low-pressure system in the engine cylinder head, thereby allowing the pump chamber to be filled during the pump plunger's suction stroke. Energizing the solenoid valve during the pump

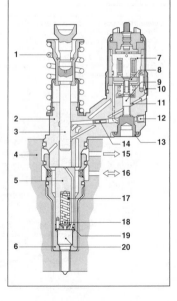

Unit Injector (UI).
1 Return spring, 2 Pump body, 3 Pump plunger, 4 Cylinder head, 5 Spring retainer, 6 Tension nut, 7 Stator, 8 Armature plate, 9 Solenoid-valve needle, 10 Solenoid-valve tension nut, 11 High-pressure plug, 12 Low-pressure plug, 13 Solenoid travel stop, 14 Restriction, 15 Fuel return, 16 Fuel supply, 17 Injector spring, 18 Pressure pin, 19 Shim, 20 Injector.

plunger's delivery stroke closes this by-pass, causing pressure to build up in the high-pressure system and fuel to be injected into the combustion chamber of the engine once the nozzle opening pressure is exceeded.

The compact design of the unit means that high-pressure volume is very small and hydraulic rigidity very high. As a result, injection pressures as high as 180 MPa (and 200 MPa in the future) can be achieved.

Such high injection pressures combined with electronic map-based control allow emission levels to be substantially reduced while simultaneously keeping fuel consumption low. The unit injector system is capable of meeting both present and future emission limits.

Electronic control enables this fuel-injection system to perform additional functions which are primarily intended to considerably improve driving smoothness.

By using adaptive cylinder matching, the complete drivetrain's rotational irregularity up to rated speed can be reduced. This ensures that the complete drivetrain runs much more smoothly. At the same time, this function can equalise the injected fuel quantity from the engine's individual injectors.

In the future, electrically controlled pilot injection (double triggering of the solenoid valve) will significantly reduce combustion noise and improve cold-starting characteristics.

In addition, the system permits the shutoff of individual cylinders. For instance, when the engine is running in the part-load range.

Unit pump system (UPS) for commercial vehicles

The unit pump system is also a modular, time-controlled single-cylinder high-pressure pump system, and is closely related to the UIS. Each of the engine's cylinders is supplied by a separate module with the following components:
– high-pressure single-cylinder pump with integral high-speed solenoid valve,
– short high-pressure delivery line
– nozzle-holder assembly

The unit pump is integrated into the diesel-engine cylinder block and operated directly by an injection cam on the engine's camshaft via a roller tappet.

The method of solenoid valve actuation is the same as that of the UIS.

When the solenoid valve is open, the fuel can be drawn into the pump cylinder during the pump plunger's suction stroke, and return during the supply stroke. Only when the solenoid valve is energized, and thus closed, can pressure build up in the high-pressure system between the pump plunger and the nozzle during the pump plunger delivery stroke. Fuel is injected into the combustion chamber of the en-

Unit Pump (UP)
1 Solenoid-valve needle-travel stop,
2 Engine block, 3 Pump body, 4 Pump plunger,
5 Return spring, 6 Roller tappet, 7 Armature plate, 8 Stator, 9 Solenoid-valve needle,
10 Filter, 11 Fuel supply, 12 Fuel return,
13 Retainer, 14 Locating groove.

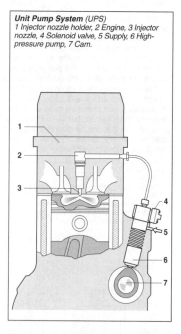

Unit Pump System *(UPS)*
1 Injector nozzle holder, 2 Engine, 3 Injector nozzle, 4 Solenoid valve, 5 Supply, 6 High-pressure pump, 7 Cam.

gine once the nozzle opening pressure is exceeded.

Solenoid-valve closure thus defines the start of injection, and valve opening the injected fuel quantity.

The unit pump system can achieve injection pressures of up to 180 MPa (200 MPa in the future). As is the case with the UIS, these high injection pressures combined with electronic map-based control enable this injection system to meet both present and future emission limits while at the same time providing for low fuel consumption. This fuel-injection system also allows implementation of additional functions such as adaptive cylinder matching, electrically controlled pilot injection, and shutoff of individual cylinders.

Unit injector system (UIS) for passenger cars

The unit injector system for passenger cars is designed to meet the demands of

modern direct-injection diesel engines with high levels of power density. It is characterized by its compact design, high injection pressures of up to 2000 bar, and mechanical-hydraulic pilot injection throughout the entire program-map range which substantially reduces combustion noise.

The unit injector system for passenger cars is also an individual-pump injection system, i.e. there is a separate unit injector (consisting of a high-pressure pump, nozzle and solenoid valve) for each engine cylinder. The unit injector is installed in the cylinder head between the valves, with the nozzle protruding into the combustion chamber. The unit injectors are operated by rocker arms driven by an overhead valve camshaft. The transverse mounting of the solenoid valve makes the unit more compact and achieves minimal high-pressure volume with correspondingly high hydraulic efficiency.

The injection system is filled during the pump-plunger suction stroke, while the solenoid valve is de-energized and thus open.

The injection period begins when the solenoid valve is energized (closed) during the pump-plunger delivery stroke. Pilot injection begins when pressure builds up in the high-pressure system and the nozzle opening pressure is reached. Pilot injection ends when a mechanical valve (bypass plunger) opens and abruptly reduces the pressure in the high-pressure chamber so that the nozzle closes. The stroke and shaft diameter of the bypass plunger determine the length of the interval, the so-called injection interval, between the end of pilot injection and the start of main injection. The movement of the bypass plunger also tensions the nozzle spring, which rapidly closes the nozzle at the end of pilot injection. Due to the strong hydraulic damping produced by a damper located between the nozzle needle and the nozzle spring, the opening stroke of the nozzle needle remains very short during pilot injection. Main injection begins when the nozzle opening pressure is reached. However, due to the additional force applied by the pretensioned nozzle spring, this pressure is twice as high as at the start of pilot injection. Injection ends when the solenoid valve is de-energized, and thus opened. The time interval between re-opening of the nozzle and opening of the solenoid valve therefore determines the quantity of fuel injected during the main-injection phase.

Electronic control allows the values for the start of injection and the injected fuel quantity to be selected as desired from those stored in the program map. This feature, together with the high injection pressures, makes it possible to achieve very high power densities combined with very low emission levels and exceptionally low fuel consumption.

The further reduction in size of the unit injectors will allow them to be used on 4-valve-per-cylinder engines in the future, thereby making it possible to reduce emissions even more. Its ability to further reduce emissions, coupled with further optimization of injection characteristics, makes the unit injector system capable of meeting future emission limits.

Electronic control unit (ECU)

The solenoid valves on the unit injector and unit pump are triggered by an ECU. The ECU analyses all of the relevant status parameters in the system relative to the engine and its environment, and defines the exact start of injection and injected fuel quantity for the operating state of the engine at any given time, thereby enabling environmentally friendly and economical engine operation. The start of injection is also controlled by a BIP signal (beginning of injection period) in order to balance out the tolerances in the overall system. Injection timing is synchronized with engine piston position by precise analysis of the signals from an incremental trigger wheel. In addition to the basic fuel-injection functions, there are a variety of additional functions for improving driving smoothness such as surge dampers, idle-speed governors, and adaptive cylinder matching. In order to meet strict safety requirements, the ECU automatically corrects and compensates for any faults and deviations that may occur in the system components and, when required, enables precise diagnosis of the injection system and the engine. The ECU communicates with other electronic systems on the vehicle such as the antilock braking system

(ABS), the traction control system (TCS), and the transmission-shift control system via the high-speed CAN data bus.

Common-rail system (CRS)

Common-rail (accumulator) fuel-injection systems make it possible to integrate the injection system together with a number of its extended functions in the diesel engine, and thus increase the degree of freedom available for defining the combustion process.

The common-rail system's principal feature is that injection pressure is independent of engine speed and injected fuel quantity.

System design

The functions of pressure generation and injection are separated by an accumulator volume. This volume is the essential feature for the functioning of this system and is made up of volume components from the Common Rail itself, as well as from the fuel lines, and the injectors.

The pressure is generated by a high-pressure plunger pump. An in-line pump is used in trucks and a radial-piston pump in passenger cars. The pump operates at low maximum torques and thus substantially reduces drive-power requirements. For the high-pressure pumps in passenger cars, the required fuel-rail pressure is regulated by a pressure-control valve mounted on the pump or the rail. High-pressure pumps in commercial vehicles have a fuel-quantity control system. The latest generation of high-pressure pumps for passenger-car use also has a fuel-quantity control system. This reduces the temperature of the fuel within the system.

The system pressure generated by the high-pressure pump flows through a pressure-control circuit and is applied to the conventional injector. This injector serves as the core of this concept by ensuring correct fuel delivery into the combustion chamber. At a precisely defined instant the ECU transmits an activation signal to the precise solenoid to initiate fuel delivery. The injected fuel quantity is defined by the injector opening period and the system pressure.

The ECU, sensors and most of the other system functions in the common-rail system are basically the same as in other time-controlled single-pump systems.

Hydraulic performance potential

This system enhances the latitude for defining combustion-process patterns by separating the pressurization and injection functions. Injection pressure can basically be selected from any point on the program map. The pressures currently used are 1350 bar in passenger-car systems and 1400 bar in commercial-vehicle systems.

Pilot injection and multiple injection can be used to further reduce exhaust and particularly noise emissions.

In the common-rail system, the movement of the nozzle needle, and thus the injection pattern, can be controlled within a defined range. The system can trigger the extremely fast solenoid several times in succession for multiple injection. Hydraulic pressure is used to augment injector-needle closing, ensuring rapid termination of the injection process.

System application engineering on the engine

No major modifications are required to adapt the diesel engine for operation with the common-rail system. A high-pressure pump replaces the injection pump, while the injector is integrated in the cylinder head in the same manner as a conventional nozzle-and-holder assembly. All of these features make the common-rail configuration yet another injection-system option.

Injection-pump test benches

Thorough testing and precise adjustment are indispensable if injection pumps and governors are to assist the diesel engine in achieving its optimal consumption and output while at the same time allowing it to maintain compliance with today's increasingly stringent emissions requirements. This is where the injection-pump test bench is essential. The basic specifications for test procedure and test bench are stipulated in ISO standards, which place especially severe demands on the rigidity and drive uniformity of the drive unit.

Common-rail accumulator injection system
1 Fuel tank, 2 Filter, 3 Presupply pump, 4 High-pressure pump, 5 Pressure-control valve,
6 Pressure sensor, 7 Fuel rail, 8 Injectors, 9 Sensors, 10 ECU.

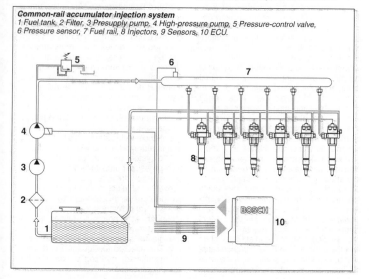

The injection pump under test is clamped to the test bench and its drive side is connected to the test-bench coupling. The test-bench drive unit comprises a special motor attached directly to the flywheel. Test-bench control is by means of a frequency converter with a vector control loop. Supply and return lines connect the injection pump to the test bench calibrating-oil supply, while pressure lines lead to the fuel-delivery measuring device. This consists of calibrating nozzles set to a precise opening pressure, which inject calibrating oil directly into the measuring system via injection dampers. The pressure and temperature of the calibrating fluid can be adjusted to comply with the test specifications.

Continuous-flow delivery-quantity measurement

Using the continuous flow method of delivery-quantity measurement, the 12 measurement inputs are connected to two precision gear pumps via a hydraulic multiplexing device. The gear pump's speed is regulated so that the quantity of calibrating oil which it pumps corresponds with the amount of calibrating oil being discharged. The pump's speed thus provides an index for the flow quantity per unit of time. A microprocessor analyzes the measurement results and converts them to bar-graph form for display on a monitor. This test method is characterized by a high degree of accuracy and consistently reproducible test results.

Delivery-quantity measurement using measuring glasses

Quantity measurement with measuring glasses (graduates) starts with the calibrating oil from the test nozzles being routed past the graduates and back to the calibrating-oil reservoir. The control unit waits until the prescribed number of strokes has been entered at the stroke counter before starting the actual test by switching the calibrating-oil flow to the graduates. The flow is interrupted again once the prescribed number of strokes has been completed. The quantity of calibrating oil which has been discharged by the test nozzles can be read from the graduates.

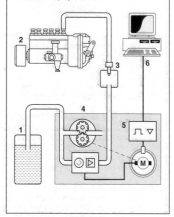

Continuous-flow delivery-quantity measurement
1 Calibrating-fluid reservoir, 2 Injection pump, 3 Test nozzle, 4 Measurement cell, 5 Pulse counter, 6 Display monitor.

"Motor testers" for diesel engines

The diesel-pump tester is used to calibrate the pump precisely to the engine's requirements. The unit monitors port closing (start of delivery) and timing adjustment at specific engine speeds without any need to open the high-pressure lines. An inductive clamp sensor is attached to the injection line for cylinder no. 1. In conjunction with a stroboscope or TDC sensor for monitoring crankshaft position, the diesel-pump tester determines the port closing and the degree of timing adjustment.

If a port-closing sensor system is used, an inductive sensor is screwed into the governor housing. The sensor receives pulses from a pin when this moves past the sensor. This pin is attached to the governors flyweight housing. These pulses trail the signals from the TDC sensor at a specific interval which is used by the unit to calculate the start of delivery.

Nozzles and nozzle holders

Functions

In a diesel-engine fuel-injection system, the nozzles connect the injection pump to the engine. Their functions are to:
– Assist in metering the fuel,
– Process the fuel,
– Define the rate-of-discharge curve,
– Seal off the combustion chamber.

In systems with separate injection pumps (inline, distributor and plug-in pumps) the nozzles are integrated in the nozzle holders. On unit injector systems (UIS) and common-rail systems (CRS), the nozzles are integral parts of the injectors.

Diesel fuel is injected at high pressure. Peak diesel fuel injection pressure can range as high as 2000 bar, a figure which will become even higher in the future. Under these conditions the diesel fuel ceases to behave as a solid, incompressible fluid, and becomes compressible. During the brief delivery period (in the order of 1 ms), the injection system is locally "inflated." For a given pressure, the nozzle cross section is one of the factors determining the quantity of fuel injected into the engine's combustion chamber.

The length and diameter of the nozzle spray hole (or orifice), the direction of the fuel jet and (to a certain degree) the shape of the spray hole affect mixture formation, and thus the engine's power output, fuel consumption, and emission levels.

Within certain limits, it is possible to achieve the required rate-of-discharge curve through optimal control of the injector's aperture (defined by the needle's stroke) and by regulating the injector needle's response. Finally, the injection nozzle must be capable of sealing the fuel-injection system against the hot, highly-compressed combustion gases at temperatures up to approx. 1000 °C. To prevent backflow of the combustion gases when the injection nozzle is open, the pressure in the injection nozzle's pressure chamber must always be higher than the combustion pressure. This requirement becomes particularly relevant toward the end of the injection sequence (when a stark reduction in injection pressure is accompanied by massive increases in combustion pressure), where it can only be ensured by carefully matching the injection pump, the injection nozzle and the nozzle needle for mutually satisfactory operation.

Designs

Diesel engines with divided or two-section combustion chambers (prechamber and whirl- (or turbulence) chamber engines) require nozzle designs differing from those used in single-section chambers (direct-injection engines).

In prechamber and whirl-chamber engines with divided combustion chambers, throttling-pintle nozzles are used which feature a coaxial spray pattern and which are generally equipped with needles which retract to open.

Direct-injection engines with single-section combustion chambers generally require hole-type nozzles.

Throttling-pintle nozzles

One injector (Type DN..SD..) and one injector holder (Type KCA for threaded socket installation) represent the standard combination for use with prechamber and whirl-chamber engines. The standard nozzle holder features M24x2 threads and uses a 27 mm wrench fitting. DN O SD.. nozzles with a needle diameter of 6 mm and a spray aperture angle of 0° are usually used; less common are nozzles with a defined spray dispersal angle (for example 12° in the DN 12 SD..). Smaller holders are used when only limited space is available (e. g., KCE holders).

As a distinctive feature, throttling-pintle nozzles vary the discharge aperture – and thus the flow rate – as a function of needle stroke. The hole-type nozzle displays an immediate, sharp rise in aperture when the needle opens; in contrast, the throttling-pintle nozzle is characterized by an extremely flat aperture progression at moderate needle strokes. Within this stroke range, the pintle (an extension at the end of the needle) remains in the spray orifice. The flow opening consists only of the small annular gap between the larger spray orifice and the throttling pintle. As needle stroke increases, the pintle completely opens the spray orifice, with an attendant substantial increase in the size of the aperture.

This stroke-sensitive aperture regulation can be employed to exert a certain amount of control on the rate-of-discharge curve (quantity of fuel injected into the engine within a specific period). At the start of injection, only a limited amount of fuel emerges from the injector nozzle, while a substantial quantity is discharged at the end of the cycle. This rate-of-dis-

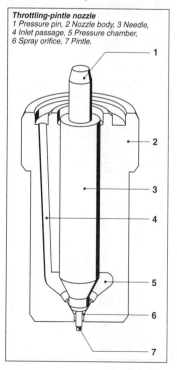

Throttling-pintle nozzle
1 Pressure pin, 2 Nozzle body, 3 Needle,
4 Inlet passage, 5 Pressure chamber,
6 Spray orifice, 7 Pintle.

charge curve has a particularly positive effect on combustion noise.

It must be remembered that excessively small apertures, i. e. excessively short needle strokes, cause the injection pump to more strongly push the nozzle needle in the "open" direction, thereby causing the needle to quickly emerge from the throttling stroke area. The injected fuel quantity per unit of time increases dramatically, and combustion noise rises accordingly.

Similarly, negative effects result from excessively small openings at the end of the injection cycle: the volume displaced by the closing nozzle needle is restricted by the narrow aperture. The result is an undesirable extension of the injection duration. Thus aperture configurations must accurately reflect both the injection-pump's delivery rate and the specific combustion conditions.

Special manufacturing processes are employed to produce spray holes to precise geometrical tolerances. During engine operation, substantial and unfortunately very irregular carbon deposits form in the throttle gap. The degree of deposit formation is determined by the quality of the fuel and the engine's operating conditions. In most cases only 30 % of the initial flow channel remains unobstructed.

Fewer and more even deposits are found on flat pintle nozzles, in which the annular opening between the nozzle body and the throttle pintle is almost zero. Here the throttle pintle utilises a machined surface to open the flow aperture. The resulting flow passage features reduced surface area relative to the flow opening, resulting in an enhanced self-cleaning effect. The machined surface is frequently parallel to the axis of the nozzle needle. Additional inclination can be employed to produce a more pronounced rise in the flat part of the flow curve, allowing a smoother transition to full nozzle opening. This expedient has a positive effect on part-load noise emissions and on operating characteristics.

Temperatures above 220 °C also promote deposit formation on injectors. Thermal shields are available to transfer the heat from the combustion chamber back to the cylinder head.

Hole-type nozzles

A wide range of nozzle-and-holder assemblies (DHK) is available for hole-type nozzles. In contrast to throttling pintle nozzles, hole-type nozzles must generally be installed in a specific position to ensure correct alignment between the orifices (which are at different angles in the nozzle body) and the engine combustion chamber. For this reason, lugs or hollow screws are usually employed to attach the nozzle-and-holder assemblies to the cylinder head while a locating device ensures the proper orientation.

Multihole nozzles are available with needle diameters of 6 and 5 mm (Size S) and 4 mm (Size P), with sac-less (vco) nozzles available in the latter size only. The nozzle springs must be suitable for use with the particular needle diameters and the normally extreme opening pressures (> 180 bar). At the end of the injection sequence there is a pronounced danger of the combustion gases being blown back into the nozzle, a development which would, in the course of time, result in destruction of the nozzle and hydraulic instability. **Nozzle shapes.** The nozzle-needle diameter

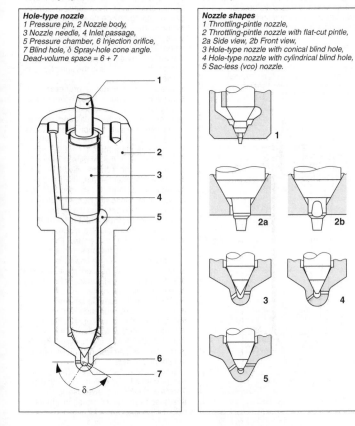

Hole-type nozzle
1 Pressure pin, 2 Nozzle body,
3 Nozzle needle, 4 Inlet passage,
5 Pressure chamber, 6 Injection orifice,
7 Blind hole, δ Spray-hole cone angle.
Dead-volume space = 6 + 7

Nozzle shapes
1 Throttling-pintle nozzle,
2 Throttling-pintle nozzle with flat-cut pintle,
2a Side view, 2b Front view,
3 Hole-type nozzle with conical blind hole,
4 Hole-type nozzle with cylindrical blind hole,
5 Sac-less (vco) nozzle.

and the compression spring are carefully matched to one another to ensure a good seal. In special cases, it is even necessary to allow for oscillation of the compression spring.

There are three different ways in which the spray orifices are arranged in the cone of the hole-type nozzle. These three designs differ in the amount of fuel which can freely evaporate into the combustion chamber at the end of the injection cycle. The designs with a cylindrical blind hole, conical blind hole, as well as the sac-less nozzle, have successively smaller fuel volumes in that order.

The engine hydrocarbon emissions decrease in the same order due to there being less residual fuel available for evaporation.

The length of the spray orifice is limited by the nozzle cone's mechanical integrity. At present, the minimum spray-orifice length is 0.6...0.8 mm for cylindrical and conical blind holes. The 1 mm minimum for sac-less (vco) nozzles is available only when special processing methods are employed to produce the spray orifices.

The tendency is toward shorter holes, as these generally allow better control of smoke emissions. Fuel flow tolerances of around ± 3.5% can be achieved in drilled hole-type nozzles. Additional hydro-erosive rounding of the inflow edges of the spray orifices can refine these tolerances to ± 2%.

Particularly for use in low-emission direct-injection diesel engines for cars, further refinement has been carried out on the injector nozzle. By optimizing the dead-volume space (see Fig. Hole-type nozzle, 6 and 7) in the nozzle body and modifying the injection-orifice geometry it has been possible to achieve maximum pressure at the injection orifice outlet in order to produce the optimum A/F mixture. In sac-less (vco) nozzles, spray-dispersal uniformity can be improved by the use of a double needle guide and a complex needle-tip geometry. The latter measure also improves performance stability throughout the nozzle's service life. These improvements required more advanced manufacturing processes, and in particular more sophisticated measuring methods.

The high-temperature strength of the material used in hole-type nozzles limits peak temperatures to approx. 300 °C. Thermal-protection sleeves are available for operation in especially difficult conditions, and there are even cooled injection nozzles for large-displacement engines.

Nozzle holders

Standard nozzle holders

The basic injector nozzle-and-holder assembly comprises the nozzle and the holder. The injector nozzle consists of two sections: the body and the needle. The nozzle needle moves freely within the body's guide bore while at the same time providing a positive seal against high injection pressures. At the bottom of the needle is a conical seal, which the nozzle spring presses against the body's correspondingly shaped sealing surface when the nozzle is closed. These two opposed conical surfaces exhibit a slight mutual variation in aperture angle, providing linear contact with high dynamic compression and a positive seal.

The diameter of the needle guide is greater than that of the seat. The hydraulic pressure from the injection pump acts against the differential surface between the needle diameter and the surface covered by the seat. The injection nozzle opens when the product of sealing surface and pressure exceeds the force of the nozzle spring in the holder. Because this process produces a sudden increase in pressurized surface area – with the seat suddenly joining the needle – a sufficiently high delivery rate will result in the injection nozzle snapping open very rapidly. It does not close again until the system has dropped from its opening pressure to below the (lower) closing pressure. This hysteresis effect is of particular significance when designing hydraulic stability into fuel-injection systems.

The opening pressure of a nozzle-and-holder combination (approx. 110...140 bar for a throttling pintle nozzle and 150...250 bar for a hole-type nozzle) is adjusted by placing shims under the compression spring.

Closing pressures are then defined by the injection nozzle's geometry (ratio of needle diameter to seat diameter).

Dual-spring nozzle holders

These nozzle holders are primarily used in direct-injection (DI) engines, where precise pilot delivery patterns are the most important factors in reducing noise levels.

Pilot injection furnishes relatively gentle pressure rises for a quiet, stable idle along with a general reduction in combustion noise.

The dual-spring nozzle holder produces this effect by improving the rate-of-discharge curve, based on precise control and definition of
– opening pressure 1,
– opening pressure 2,
– prestroke, and
– overall stroke.

Opening pressure 1 is set and tested as with the single-spring holder. Opening pressure 2 is the sum of the pretension figures for spring 1 and auxiliary spring 2. Spring 2 is supported by a stop sleeve into which has been machined the dimensions of the prestroke (see Fig. Dual-spring nozzle holder KBEL..P.., H1). During injection, opening of the nozzle needle is initially restricted to the prestroke range. Common prestroke figures are 0.03...0.06 mm. As the pressure in the nozzle holder increases, the stop sleeve is lifted, allowing the nozzle needle to move to the end of its stroke. Also designed for use in dual-spring holders are the special-purpose injector nozzles in which the nozzle needle has no pintle, and the shoulder of the needle is level with the nozzle body.

In other words, the springs in the dual-spring holder are matched such that initially only a small quantity of fuel is injected into the combustion chamber, causing a slight initial rise in combustion pressure. The resulting extension in injection duration (with the main fuel delivery following the pilot delivery) serves to smooth out the combustion process.

There are also dual-spring holders available for prechamber and whirl (turbulence) chamber engines. The setpoints are tailored to the respective injection

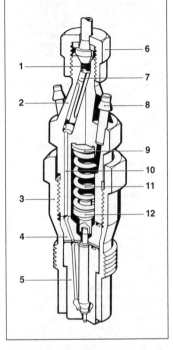

Nozzle-holder assembly with throttling-pintle nozzle.
1 Inlet, 2 Nozzle-holder body, 3 Nozzle-retaining nut, 4 Shim, 5 Injection nozzle, 6 Union nut with high-pressure line, 7 Edge filter, 8 Leak-off connection, 9 Pressure-adjusting shims, 10 Pressure passage, 11 Pressure spring, 12 Pressure pin.

system, with varying opening pressures of 130/180 bar and prestrokes of approx. 0.1 mm.

Nozzle-holder assembly with hole-type nozzle.
1 Inlet , 2 Nozzle-holder body, 3 Nozzle-retaining nut, 4 Intermediate element, 5 Injection nozzle, 6 Union nut with high-pressure line, 7 Edge filter, 8 Leak-off connection, 9 Pressure-adjusting shims, 10 Pressure passage, 11 Pressure spring, 12 Pressure pin, 13 Locating pins.

KBEL..P... **Dual-spring nozzle holder**
H_1 Prestroke, H_2 Main stroke,
$H_{tot} = H_1 + H_2$ Total stroke.
1 Holder body, 2 Shim, 3 Compression spring 1, 4 Pressure pin, 5 Guide washer, 6 Compression spring 2, 7 Pressure pin, 8 Spring seat, 9 Shim, 10 Stop sleeve, 11 Spacer, 12 Nozzle-retaining nut.

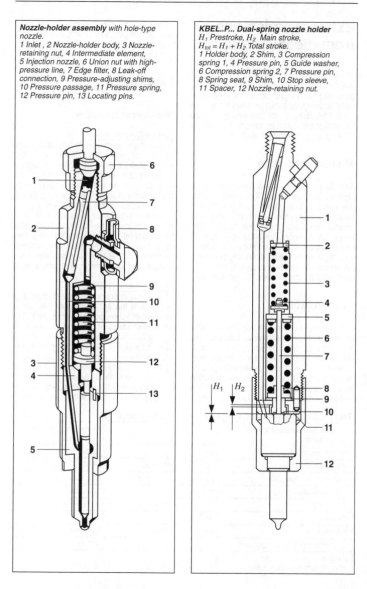

Exhaust emissions from diesel engines

The primary and secondary constituents of the exhaust gases produced by diesel engines are listed together with the emissions from spark-ignition (SI) engines beginning on P. 518. Table 1 provides information on the composition and temperature of the exhaust gases from diesel engines.

Mixture formation

The fuel used in diesel engines has a higher boiling point than that used in gasoline engines. In addition, the A/F mixture in diesel engines is formed quickly just before combustion starts and is therefore less homogeneous. Diesel engines operate with excess air ($\lambda > 1$) across their entire operating range. An insufficient quantity of excess air results in increased particulate emissions (soot), and CO and HC emissions.

Combustion

The start of injection marks the initiation of the combustion process. The engine's efficiency is determined by the start of combustion and by the combustion characteristics. The characteristics (as a function of time) of the injected fuel quantity and the injection pressure, can be applied to control the combustion characteristics.

These factors also determine the combustion temperature which, in turn, has a significant effect on the formation of nitrogen oxides (NO_x).

Emissions control

Measures at the engine

Combustion chamber
Exhaust-gas emission is affected by the design of the combustion chamber. Engines which have a divided combustion chamber (prechamber, swirl (turbulence) chamber) produce fewer nitrogen oxides than direct-injection engines, although these feature better fuel economy.

Careful adaptation of the air flow characteristics inside the combustion chamber to the fuel-jet pattern promotes better mixing of fuel and air, and thus more complete combustion. Reliable ignition requires a sufficiently high compression temperature.

Fuel injection
The start of injection, the rate-of-discharge curve, and the atomization of the fuel all have an effect on pollutant emissions. The point at which combustion starts is essentially a function of the start of injection (injection timing). Delayed injection reduces NO_x emissions, whereas excessive delay results in increased fuel consumption and HC emissions. With regard to the start of injection, a deviation of 1° (crankshaft) from the setpoint can increase NO_x emissions or

Table 1: Composition and temperature of diesel exhaust gas

Exhaust-gas components and temperature		at idle	at maximum output
Nitrous oxides (NO_x)	ppm	50...200	600...2500
Hydrocarbons (HC)	ppm C_1	50...500	<50
Carbon monoxide (CO)	ppm	100...450	350...2000
Carbon dioxide (CO_2)	Vol%	...3.5	12...16
Water vapor	Vol%	2...4	...11
Oxygen	Vol%	18	2...11
Nitrogen, etc.	Vol%	residual	residual
Smoke number, passenger cars		SZ ≈ <0.5	SZ ≈ 2...3
Exhaust-gas temperature downstream of exhaust valve	°C	100...200	550...750

HC emissions by as much as 15%.

This high degree of sensitivity means that precise injection timing is essential. Electronic control systems are capable of maintaining optimum injection timing with a high degree of precision. Such devices control the timing-device setting, or the actuation of the injection-system solenoid valve relative to a crankshaft-angle mark (start-of-delivery control). Greater precision can be achieved by measuring the start of injection directly at the fuel injector by using a needle-motion sensor to detect the movement of the needle valve (start-of-injection control). In systems with solenoid valves, the start of injection can also be controlled by means of the current applied to the valve coil.

Any fuel entering the combustion chamber after combustion has terminated could be discharged directly into the exhaust system in unburned form, thus raising hydrocarbon emissions. To prevent this, the fuel volume between the injection nozzle seat and its injection orifices is held to a minimum. Sac-less (vco) nozzles completely seal off the injection orifice. In addition, "post-injection" must be avoided at all costs.

Finely atomized fuel promotes formation of a good A/F mixture which helps to reduce hydrocarbon and particulate emissions. Fine atomization is achieved with high injection pressures and optimum injection-orifice geometry.

The maximum injected fuel quantity for a given intake air mass must be limited such that the engine does not produce visible soot emissions. This requires an excess-air factor of at least 10...20% (λ = 1.1...1.2).

Intake-air temperature

As the temperature of the intake air increases the combustion temperature increases along with it, which in turn leads to an increase in NO_x emissions. Charge-air cooling (intercooling) is an effective means of reducing NO_x formation in turbocharged engines.

Exhaust-gas recirculation (EGR)

The exhaust gases mixed with the intake air reduce the amount of oxygen in the fresh intake charge while increasing its specific heat. Both factors result in a lower combustion temperature and thus decreased NOx production, and also reduce exhaust emissions. However, too much recirculated exhaust gas results in increased particulate and carbon-monoxide emissions due to air deficiency. The quantity of recirculated exhaust gases must therefore be limited to ensure that the combustion chamber receives sufficient oxygen to support combustion.

Exhaust-gas treatment

The use of noble-metal catalytic converters in the exhaust system reduces hydrocarbon emissions by burning a portion of the gaseous hydrocarbons and those bound to the soot (particulates) using the oxygen in the exhaust gases.

The catalytic converters used to reduce the NO_x emissions produced by gasoline engines must operate with either an oxygen deficit or a precise stoichiometric mixture (λ = 1). Diesel engines, however, can only be operated with excess air ($\lambda > 1$) because of the heterogeneous A/F mixture. Thus such conventional catalytic converters cannot be used on diesel engines. However, filters can be installed in the exhaust system to reduce particulate emissions (soot).

Emissions testing

In industrialized nations, and increasingly worldwide, harmful emissions from internal-combustion engines are limited by law. Exhaust-gas emissions tests are conducted under defined conditions.

Test layout

In general, the testing of passenger-car exhaust emissions takes place on a chassis dynamometer whereas commercial-vehicle emissions are tested on an engine test bench.

The prescribed method for dynamic test cycles and particulate-emission testing is the CVS (constant volume sampling) method. In this process, the exhaust gases produced by the vehicle are diluted with filtered ambient air and extracted with a blower during a standardized test cycle.

A constant volume of gas is delivered as determined either by a positive displacement pump (PDP) or a critical flow venturi (CFV). The temperature level specified for particulate-emissions testing (max. 52 °C) must be maintained during the sampling procedure.

A sample of the diluted exhaust gas is passed through special filters whose increase in mass (determined by weighing on a microbalance before and after sampling) is used to calculate the level of particulate emissions.

A second sampling line (heated to 190 °C) leads to a flame ionization detector (FID), and a chemo-luminescence detector (CLD) for diesels, which continuously measure the hydrocarbon concentration (FID) and the nitrogen oxide concentration (CLD). A third sample is collected in exhaust-gas collection bags. Based on the contents of the bags at the end of the test, gas analyzers determine the CO, CO_2 and NO_x concentrations. The "ambient-air concentration" is determined by comparing the collected intake air with the exhaust so that the emissions originating from the engine

can be distinguished from pollution already in the atmosphere. Calculations to determine the levels of the various exhaust-gas component emissions are based on the volume of mixed gas and the concentrations of the individual components.

In the USA, the same procedures and analyzers are employed in testing emissions produced by passenger-car and truck engines. The exhaust gases are usually diluted in a two-stage procedure to enable the larger volumes of gases to be processed using reasonably-sized dilution tunnels while simultaneously ensuring compliance with the legally prescribed conditions. In the European stationary test cycle, partial-flow dilution is also approved for use in measuring particulates. Testing for particulate levels is usually followed by an additional examination of exhaust-gas opacity in both stationary and dynamic full-throttle operation.

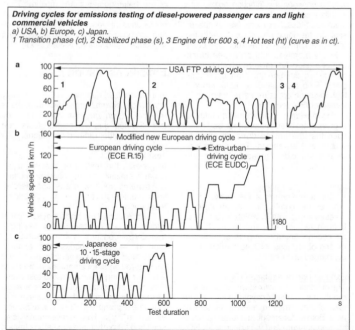

Driving cycles for emissions testing of diesel-powered passenger cars and light commercial vehicles
a) USA, b) Europe, c) Japan.
1 Transition phase (ct), 2 Stabilized phase (s), 3 Engine off for 600 s, 4 Hot test (ht) (curve as in ct).

Test cycles and exhaust-emission limits

Passenger cars and light utility vehicles

Europe

Emission-control legislation in the nations of the European Union is based on ECE Directive R15 along with EEC Directive 70/220 as revised. Existing emission limits (Euro 2) have been in effect since 1997 for production vehicles, and are expected to be lowered further in the year 2000 (Euro 3) and again in 2005 (Euro 4).

The original driving cycle according to ECE R15 has been completely replaced by the ECE R83 New European Driving Cycle (NEDC) with its non-urban component and speeds of up to 120 km/h, which in turn will be replaced beginning in the year 2000 (Euro 3) by the Modified New European Driving Cycle (MNEDC), in which the exhaust gas is collected immediately without a (40 s) delay. The entry of new nations into the European Union means that their emissions regulations will have to be revised so that they agree with EU regulations.

Japan

A 10·15 driving cycle is used to determine the concentrations of gaseous pollutants and particulates in diesel-engine exhaust gas. The driving cycle for passenger cars has been extended to include a high-speed section (similar to Europe).

USA

The FTP (Federal Test Procedure) 75 driving cycle is required for passenger cars and light commercial vehicles with a gross vehicle weight of less than 8500 lbs.

The speed curve corresponds to an urban operation cycle in the USA. Testing is performed on a chassis dynamometer, and the results are measured using the CVS method. Since it has now become enormously complex, emission-control legislation in the USA can only be described here in very abridged form. Additional test cycles have been integrated, including for instance SFTP-US 06 (maximum speed); SFTP-SC 03 (air-conditioner operation); HWFET (fuel economy) with averaging. A variety of service-life requirements, together with emission limit crediting, staggered phase-in of emission limits, and local regulations for vehicle-fleet operators in highly polluted regions of the country (California), etc. have also been incorporated.

Commercial vehicles

Europe

In Europe, until 1999 vehicles with a gross vehicle weight of > 3.5 tons and more than 9 seats were required to meet the stipulations of the 13-stage test in accordance with ECE R49. The test sequence stipulated a series of 13 different steady-state operating modes. An average emission level for both the gaseous exhaust components and the particulates was calculated by applying weighting factors to the measurements of emissions taken in the various operating modes.

Directive 91/542/EEC sets forth the limits which are currently applicable in the EU. The levels prescribed by the EURO 2 stage have been in effect since 1995. The 3rd stage (EURO 3), which will go into effect in the year 2000, also involves changes to the test cycle to bring it into agreement with the European Steady-state Cycle (ESC).

A European Transient Cycle (ETC) is planned for a further stage to begin in 2005 (EURO 4).

Japan

Pollutant emissions are measured using the Japanese 13-stage steady-state test, however the operating points, their order and their relative weighting differ from those of the European 13-stage test. Emission limits, which in Japan are still classified according to vehicle weight (over or under 12 t), are shown here for vehicles over 12 t.

USA

Since 1987, engines for heavy commercial vehicles have been tested on an engine test bench in a transient cycle, with emissions being measured according to the CVS method. The test cycle is based on highway operation under real-world conditions. The opacity of the exhaust gas

Emission limits for diesel-powered passenger cars and commercial vehicles

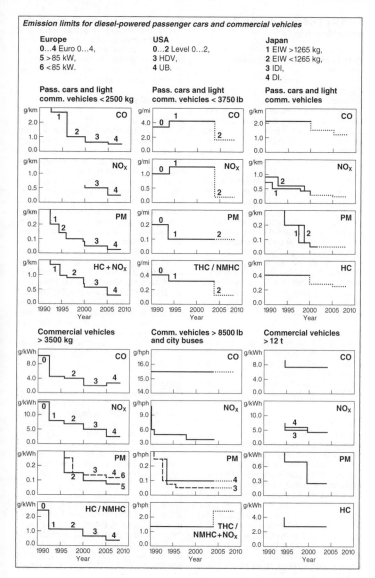

Europe
0...4 Euro 0...4,
5 >85 kW,
6 <85 kW.

USA
0...2 Level 0...2,
3 HDV,
4 UB.

Japan
1 EIW >1265 kg,
2 EIW <1265 kg,
3 IDI,
4 DI.

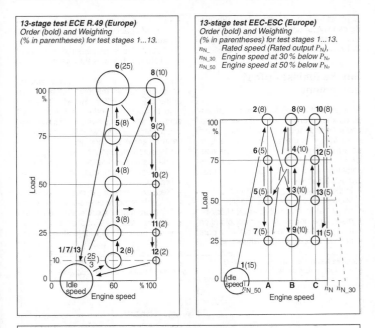

13-stage test ECE R.49 (Europe)
*Order (bold) and Weighting
(% in parentheses) for test stages 1...13.*

13-stage test EEC-ESC (Europe)
*Order (bold) and Weighting
(% in parentheses) for test stages 1...13.*
$n_{N\_}$ Rated speed (Rated output P_N),
n_{N_30} Engine speed at 30 % below P_N,
n_{N_50} Engine speed at 50 % below P_N,

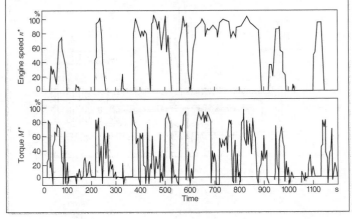

USA transient driving cycle for emissions testing of heavy commercial vehicle engines
*Both the nominal engine speed n^* and the nominal torque M^* are taken from tables specified by
legislation.*

is monitored in a further test (Federal Smoke Cycle) under transient and quasi-steady-state operating conditions. California has different emission limits.

Smoke Emission Test Equipment

An important reason for testing diesel-engine exhaust emissions in the workshop, and for monitoring them while the vehicle is actually in operation on the road, is to determine the amount of soot (particulates) produced. This is indicated by the smoke number. Two standard procedures are used:
- In the <u>filter method</u> (measurement of reflected light), a specified quantity of exhaust gas is drawn through a filter element. The degree of filter discoloration then provides an indication of the amount of soot contained in the exhaust gas.

- In the <u>absorption method</u> (measurement of opacity), the opacity of the exhaust gas is indicated by the degree to which it blocks the passage of a beam of light which shines through it.

Measurement of diesel-engine smoke emissions is relevant only if the engine is under load, since it is only when the engine is operated under load that emissions of significant levels of particulates occur. Here, as well, two different test procedures are in common use:
- Measurement under full load, e.g. on a chassis dynamometer or over a specified test course, against the vehicle brakes.
- Measurements made under conditions of unhindered acceleration with a defined amount of accelerator pedal depression and load applied by the flywheel mass of the accelerating engine.

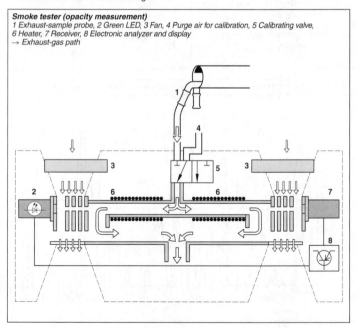

Smoke tester (opacity measurement)
1 Exhaust-sample probe, 2 Green LED, 3 Fan, 4 Purge air for calibration, 5 Calibrating valve,
6 Heater, 7 Receiver, 8 Electronic analyzer and display
→ Exhaust-gas path

As the results of testing for diesel smoke emissions vary according to both test procedure and type of load, they are not generally suitable for direct mutual comparisons.

Smoke tester (opacity measurement)

During unhindered acceleration, some of the exhaust gas is routed from the vehicle exhaust pipe via an exhaust-sample probe and sampling hose to the measuring chamber (without vacuum assistance). In particular, since temperature and pressure are controlled (Hartridge unit), this method prevents the test results from being affected by exhaust-gas back pressure and its fluctuation.

Inside the measuring chamber the diesel exhaust gas is penetrated by a beam of light. The attenuation of the light is measured photoelectrically, and is indicated as % opacity T or as a coefficient of absorption k. A high degree of accuracy and reproducibility of the test results requires that the length of the measuring chamber be precisely defined, and that the optical windows be kept free of soot (by air curtains, i.e. tangential air flows).

During testing under load, measurement and display are a continuous process. In the case of unhindered acceleration the entire test curve can be digitally stored. The tester automatically determines the maximum value and calculates the mean from several gas pulses.

Smoke tester (filter method)

The smoke tester extracts a specified quantity (e.g. 0.1 or 1l) of diesel exhaust gas through a strip of filter paper. Consistent, mutually comparable test results are achieved by recording the volume of gas processed in each test step; the device converts the results to a standardized form. The system also takes into account the effect of pressure and temperature, as well as the dead volume between the exhaust-sample probe and the filter paper.

The darkened filter paper is analyzed optoelectronically using a reflective photometer. The results are usually displayed as a Bosch smoke number or as a mass concentration (mg/m^3).

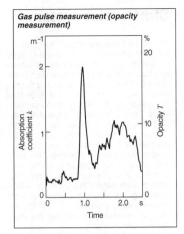

Gas pulse measurement (opacity measurement)

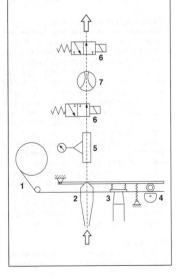

Smoke tester (filter method)
1 Filter paper, 2 Gas passage, 3 Reflective photometer, 4 Paper transport, 5 Volume measurement, 6 Changeover valve for purge air, 7 Pump.

Start-assist systems

The colder the diesel engine, the more reluctant it is to start. Higher levels of internal friction combine with blowby and thermal losses to reduce compression pressures and temperatures to such a degree as to render starting impossible without the assistance of auxiliary start-assist devices. The individual temperature threshold for starting depends upon the specific engine design. Direct-injection (DI) engines, with their single-section combustion chambers and relatively low thermal losses, start more readily than prechamber or whirl-chamber engines (two-section combustion chamber) in which glow plugs are installed which extend into the secondary chamber. On DI engines the glow element extends into the main combustion chamber.

On large-displacement DI engines a flame plug or heater is employed to preheat the air in the intake tract.

Sheathed-element glow plugs

Design and characteristics
The main component in the sheathed-element glow plug is the tubular heating element. Firm, gas-tight installation in the glow-plug shell ensures that it can resist both corrosion and hot gases. The element contains a spiral filament embedded in magnesium-oxide powder. This spiral filament consists of several elements. The two resistor elements are installed in series. The tip-mounted heater coil maintains virtually constant electrical resistance regardless of temperature, while the control coil consists of a material with a positive temperature coefficient.

Circuit continuity is provided by welding the ground side of the heater coil to the inner tip of the glow tube, and by connecting the control coil to the terminal screw. The terminal screw, in turn, connects the glow plug to the vehicle's electrical system.

Operation
The glow plug responds to the initial application of voltage by converting most of

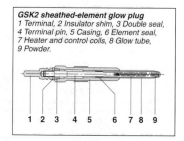

GSK2 sheathed-element glow plug
1 Terminal, 2 Insulator shim, 3 Double seal,
4 Terminal pin, 5 Casing, 6 Element seal,
7 Heater and control coils, 8 Glow tube,
9 Powder.

the electrical energy into heat within the heater coil, producing a radical increase in the tip's temperature. The control coil heats more slowly. The resulting delayed rise in resistance reduces current draw and overall heat generation within the glow plug as it approaches its continuous-operation temperature. Individual heating patterns are defined by component dimensions.

Start phase: Here the glow plug must heat to starting temperature (approx. 850 °C) as rapidly as possible. Plug locations within the combustion chamber are selected to ensure access to an ignitable mixture. Modern glow plugs heat to the required temperature in roughly 4 seconds.

Post-start phase: The glow plugs continue to operate briefly after the engine has started, improving initial engine operation while reducing blue-smoke emissions and combustion noise. The periods involved are no more than 180 s.

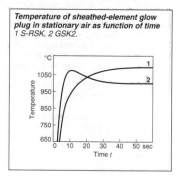

Temperature of sheathed-element glow plug in stationary air as function of time
1 S-RSK, 2 GSK2.

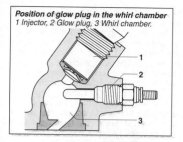

Position of glow plug in the whirl chamber
1 Injector, 2 Glow plug, 3 Whirl chamber.

GSK2 sheathed-element glow plugs
Nickel control coils are used in conventional S-RSK sheathed-element glow plugs, while second-generation GSK2 glow plugs feature coils in CoFe alloy. These plugs reach ignition temperature more quickly and have a lower steady-state temperature. As a result, the pre-heating time prior to starting is shorter and the afterglow phase becomes possible.

Internal engine temperatures
The temperature at the glow plug changes according to the engine's operating mode. The examples shown illustrate the steady-state operating temperatures at a 13.5 V glow plug in a direct-injection engine. The maximum temperatures occur at low revolutions and high load (low air throughput resulting in less efficient cooling of the glow plug). In contrast, the highest temperatures in prechamber/whirl-chamber engines occur during operation at high loads and high min⁻¹.

Glow-control unit

The complete glow-plug system incorporates not only the glow plugs themselves (only in rare cases are flame plugs used) but also a switching element for the high electrical glow-plug currents which is triggered by a special control unit. In addition, the system incorporates an indicator lamp (also controlled by the control unit) for signaling when the system is ready for engine start.

In the past, simple bi-metal switches were used but nowadays glow-plug systems have electronic control units. On more basic vehicles, independent glow-plug control units which handle all control and display functions are used. On modern vehicles, these functions are controlled by the central engine management system. Such units also perform safety and monitoring functions.

Design
The glow-control unit essentially consists of a power relay to regulate the glow-plug current, a printed-circuit board with the electronic circuitry to control glow times and triggering of the ready-to-start indicator, and the elements for the protective functions. The later generations of control units increasingly use semiconductor switches (Power MOSFET) instead of the electromechanical relay. The unit is enclosed in a plastic housing for protection against dust and water (this applies especially when it is installed in the engine compartment).

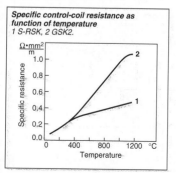

Specific control-coil resistance as function of temperature
1 S-RSK, 2 GSK2.

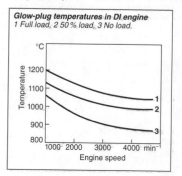

Glow-plug temperatures in DI engine
1 Full load, 2 50 % load, 3 No load.

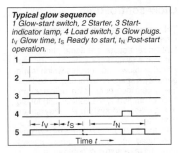

Typical glow sequence
1 Glow-start switch, 2 Starter, 3 Start-indicator lamp, 4 Load switch, 5 Glow plugs.
t_V Glow time, t_S Ready to start, t_N Post-start operation.

Operation

The preheating and starting sequence is initiated by the glow-plug and starter switch in a similar manner to starting a gasoline engine. The preheating phase begins when the key is turned to "Ignition On".

Independent glow control units

On basic units, a temperature sensor in the glow control unit controls the preheating period. This is designed to suit the specific requirements of the particular combination of engine and glow-plug so that the glow plug can reach the temperature necessary for efficient starting. At the end of the glow period, the start-indicator lamp goes out to signal that the engine can be started. The glow process continues for as long as the starter remains in operation, or until the safety override comes into effect (this limits the loads on

battery and glow plugs). A strip fuse provides protection against short circuits.

With more sophisticated independent control units, an engine-temperature sensor (coolant NTC sensor) determines the heating periods more precisely. The glow control unit takes account of differences in battery voltage by adjusting the preheating period accordingly. Current continues to flow through the glow plugs once the engine has started. An engine-load monitor is used to interrupt or switch off the glow process. Protection against overvoltage and short circuits is provided by an electronic override circuit. A monitoring circuit detects glow-plug failure and relay errors. These are then displayed using the start-indicator lamp.

EDC-controlled glow control units

This type of unit receives information on when glow-plug operation is required, and when not, directly from the engine's central ECU. That unit provides (statically or by means of a serial data protocol) the information relating to the engine operating status (coolant temperature, engine speed and load) that is required for optimum control of the glow plugs. Similarly, the glow control unit also signals any faults it detects to the engine ECU via a diagnosis line or the serial interface. There, they are stored for servicing purposes or displayed if necessary for compliance with OBD requirements.

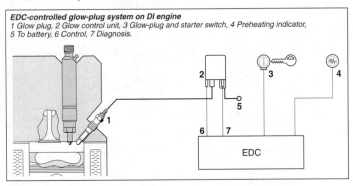

EDC-controlled glow-plug system on DI engine
1 Glow plug, 2 Glow control unit, 3 Glow-plug and starter switch, 4 Preheating indicator, 5 To battery, 6 Control, 7 Diagnosis.

Starting systems

Most starting systems for IC engines comprise a battery-driven DC motor (the actual starter motor), switchgear, control units and the associated wiring. The speeds at which an engine has to be cranked in order to start it (gasoline engines: approx. 60...100 min^{-1}; diesel engines: approx. 80...200 min^{-1}) are substantially lower than the speed at which the starter turns. The different speeds are matched to one another by the use of a suitable gearing ratio (between about $1/_{10}$ and $1/_{20}$) between the starter pinion and the engine's flywheel ring gear.

Design factors

The crankshaft torque and the minimum rotational speed required to start the engine depend among other things upon engine type, engine swept volume, number of cylinders, compression, bearing friction, additional loads driven by the engine, the fuel-management system, engine oil and temperature.

Both the torque and the rotational speed required for starting increase with declining temperatures, with the result that starter output must increase accordingly.

The battery internal resistance increases as its temperature and its state of charge drop. The battery no-load voltage decreases as temperature drops. The higher the battery output current and the lower the temperature, the lower is the battery terminal voltage. In addition, battery capacity decreases as temperature decreases and the battery discharge current increases. Therefore, the lower the temperature, the less power the battery can supply. In addition, the engine design characteristics, the minimum temperature at which the engine will start is a central factor in determining starting-system power.

Starters

A starter consists of an electric motor, a solenoid switch and a pinion-engaging drive mechanism whose functions are defined by the engine-starting sequence.

Initially, the pinion must engage the ring gear. As the engine starts and runs up to speed, it spins the pinion faster than the starter does and would eventually destroy the starter due to centrifugal force.

To prevent this, an overrunning clutch is installed between pinion and armature shaft which breaks the connection between them as soon as the engine "overtakes" the starter.

Electric motor

The advances made in present-day ferrite technology have enabled the development of permanent-magnet-energized starter motors which are proof against demagnetization. The form of energization is now virtually the standard design for car starters.

Reductions in starter weight and dimensions are achieved by operating the starter at higher speeds and lower armature torques. For such a starter to become a practical proposition, the crankshaft/starter-armature gear ratio must be increased. Since the ring-gear diameter cannot be increased, the higher gear ratio is achieved through the use of an additional transmission stage incorporated in the starter (reduction-gear starters).

On larger gasoline engines and passenger-car diesel engines, by far the most common type of starter motor is the permanent-magnet-energized reduction-gear design. For starter power in the 2.2 kW to 4 kW range, series-wound reduction-gear starters are beginning to supersede direct-drive versions.

Among the higher-power starters, as well as the direct-drive versions with a series-wound motor, there are also shunt-

Permanent-magnet reduction-gear starter
1 Engaging shift lever, 2 Engagement solenoid and solenoid switch, 3 Overrunning clutch with pinion, 4 Reduction gear (planetary gear), 5 Armature, 6 Permanent magnets.

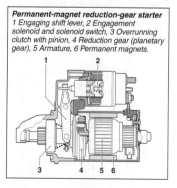

wound designs which provide smoother startup characteristics and limitation of the armature no-load speed.

Pinion-engaging systems

Inertia-drive starters

The inertia drive (as employed, e.g., in lawn mowers) is the simplest form of pinion-engaging drive. A helical spline in the shaft slides the overrunning clutch forward when the armature rotates.

When the starter is switched on, the un-loaded armature begins to rotate freely. The pinion and overrunning clutch do not yet rotate due to their inertia, and are pushed forward by the spline. As soon as the pinion makes contact with the ring gear, it is kept from rotating and pushed further forward until making contact with the stop ring. At this point, the overrunning clutch begins to transmit the armature torque to the ring gear via the pinion, and the engine is cranked.

As soon as the engine begins to rotate the pinion at a speed above armature speed, although the overrunning clutch interrupts the transmission of force, the friction of the overrunning clutch attempts to accelerate it above armature speed. This causes the overrunning clutch and pinion to slide backward in the helical spline. This pinion-disengaging operation is assisted by the return spring which also holds the pinion in the disengaged position when the starter is not running.

Pre-engaged-drive starters

In pre-engaged-drive starters, an engagement solenoid engages the pinion with the ring gear.

The engagement solenoid incorporates the switching contacts for the starter current.

When the starting switch is closed, the hold-in winding H is energized, and current flows through the series circuit comprising pull-in winding E and electric motor. The starter motor solenoid picks up and moves the overrunning clutch and pinion gear assembly forwards by means of the thrust lever and the engaging spring.

If the pinion and ring gear happen to find themselves in mutually optimal positions, then the pinion will immediately mesh with a gap in the ring gear's teeth. In this case the pinion teeth's engagement depth in the ring gear increases until the travel limit is reached and the contact bridge in the solenoid switch hits the relay contacts; at this point the full voltage is applied to the starter motor.

If the pinion teeth do not immediately mesh with the ring-gear gaps, the ring gear prevents the pinion from advancing any further. The engaging lever then compresses the meshing spring, and the main contact closes without the pinion having engaged.

The electric motor then turns the pinion which is in contact with the face of the ring gear until a pinion tooth finds a ring-gear gap and the meshing spring pushes the pinion and overrunning clutch forward.

When the solenoid winding is de-ener-

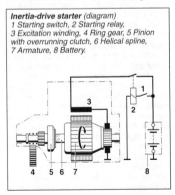

Inertia-drive starter (diagram)
1 Starting switch, 2 Starting relay,
3 Excitation winding, 4 Ring gear, 5 Pinion with overrunning clutch, 6 Helical spline,
7 Armature, 8 Battery.

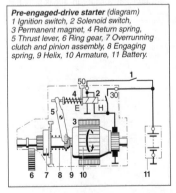

Pre-engaged-drive starter (diagram)
1 Ignition switch, 2 Solenoid switch,
3 Permanent magnet, 4 Return spring,
5 Thrust lever, 6 Ring gear, 7 Overrunning clutch and pinion assembly, 8 Engaging spring, 9 Helix, 10 Armature, 11 Battery.

gized, the return spring pushes the solenoid plunger and pinion with overrunning clutch back into the rest position.

This disengaging operation is assisted by the helix when the engine speed overtakes the starter speed.

Sliding-gear starters
The sliding-gear drive switches the starter on in two stages.

When the starting switch is closed, battery voltage is applied across the hold-in winding H of the engagement solenoid and the control relay in parallel. The control relay picks up, but is held in contact position 1 (first stage) by a tripping lever and latch. Battery voltage is applied to the

pull-in winding E of the engagement solenoid and the shunt winding of the motor which are connected in parallel with one another and in series with the armature. The starter begins to rotate, however, it can only generate low torque due to the high winding resistances in series with the armature winding. At the same time, the engagement solenoid pushes the pinion in the direction of the ring gear, so that it engages at low torque. Shortly before the end of meshing travel is reached, the engagement solenoid releases the latched control relay which immediately moves into contact position 2 (second stage). The starting current now flows through the series winding and the armature. The changeover contact on the engagement solenoid connects the shunt winding parallel to the armature and the series winding. The starter develops full torque.

Overrunning clutch types
Overrunning clutches protect the starter armature from excessive speed when "overtaken" by the engine.

Roller-type overrunning clutch
Small and medium-sized starters generally have an overrunning clutch in which rollers are pushed by springs into wedge-shaped recesses between the clutch shell and the pinion shaft. When torque is applied in the opposite direction, the rollers are forced loose and the pinion is decoupled from the engine.

Multiplate overrunning clutch
The multiplate overrunning clutch is used in large commercial-vehicle starters. The driver with the outer plates and the starter armature, and on the other side the driving shaft and the pinion are positively connected to one another. The inner plates fit in an inner clutch race which rides axially in a helical spline in the driver shaft. Under no-load conditions the plate stack is lightly compressed by the compression spring, and can only transmit low torque. As load increases, the inner clutch race is moved by the helical spline in the direction of the compression spring, which is thus more strongly compressed and presses the plates more tightly together. The multiplate overrunning clutch is therefore able

Sliding-gear starter (circuit diagram)
1 Starting switch, 2 Control relay, 3 Tripping lever, 4 Pinion, 5 Ring gear, 6 Changeover contact, 7 Engagement solenoid, 8 Series winding, 9 Shunt winding, 10 Battery.

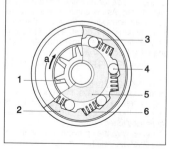

Roller-type overrunning clutch
1 Pinion, 2 Clutch shell, 3 Roller race, 4 Roller, 5 Pinion shaft, 6 Spring.
a Direction of rotation.

to transmit increasing torque as the starter load increases.

Radial-tooth overrunning clutch

The radial-tooth overrunning clutch is also used in large commercial-vehicle starters. The entire clutch system is coupled to the armature shaft, on which it slides axially (meshing), by means of spur toothing in the dirt sleeve. The outer surface of the dirt sleeve has a helical spline, and transmits the torque to a clutch nut which further transmits the torque to the pinion by means of the steep flanks of the saw-tooth-shaped radial teeth. During overrun, the pinion pushes the clutch nut backwards by means of the shallow flanks of the radial teeth, and interrupts the transmission of force. The disengaging ring is also moved backward, and held in the disengaging position by the flyweights. The

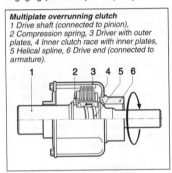

Multiplate overrunning clutch
1 Drive shaft (connected to pinion),
2 Compression spring, 3 Driver with outer plates, 4 Inner clutch race with inner plates, 5 Helical spline, 6 Drive end (connected to armature).

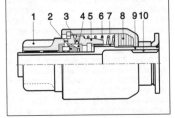

Radial-tooth overrunning clutch
1 Pinion, 2 Centrifugal weight, 3 Spur gear, 4 Thrust ring, 5 Clutch nut, 6 Spring, 7 Helix, 8 Damper, 9 Dirt sleeve, 10 Straight gear.

centrifugal force developed by the fly-weights at low pinion speeds no longer suffices to keep the overrunning clutch in its disengaged position, and the spring again pushes the clutch nut into the pinion.

Starter protection

Starter power is also a function of the size of the vehicle battery. The thermal loading of the current-carrying parts and the mechanical loading of the torque transmission parts increase as battery size increases. It is for this reason that a <u>maximum permissible</u> battery size is usually specified for each starter type. Although the starter is designed to operate for only short periods of time, its design must allow for longer cranking times and thus increased thermal load at low temperatures.

This is why extended periods of starter operation should be followed by cooling-off periods.

In the case of larger starters, excessively long operating times are prevented by built-in thermo-switches (e.g., in the carbon brushes). In remote-control starting systems (e.g., rear-engine buses, emergency power generator sets, diesel railroad cars, etc.) on the other hand, the starting procedure cannot always be monitored by the driver.

Operator errors can damage the starter or ring gear.

Start-locking relays

These prevent inadvertent engagement of the starter when the engine is running or excessive overrunning after the engine has started. The rise in alternator voltage that occurs when the engine is running is used as the variable for indicating that the engine has started. As the engine slows down after the ignition switch is turned off, the alternator no longer produces a usable voltage "signal"; in this case a timer in the start-locking relay blocks for a few seconds any repeated attempt to use the starting system.

Start-repeating relays

Start-repeating relays interrupt the starting procedure if the pinion is still unable to engage the ring gear, but the starter remains switched on.

In this way, they prevent overloading of the solenoid switch winding.

Electric drives

The electric drive is quiet, produces no exhaust emissions and is very efficient. Whereas in purely electrically powered vehicles the electric drive alone powers the wheels, hybrid vehicles have at least two different sources of drive energy, at least one of which is usually an electric drive.

In contrast to internal-combustion engine vehicles, on electric-only vehicles the energy accumulator generally determines the vehicle's performance. The capacity of the electric motor is matched to the maximum output of the energy accumulator. The energy accumulator may take the form of an electrochemical battery or a fuel cell and its associated fuel tank.

Depending on the intended application, battery-powered electric vehicles can be classified as either road vehicles or industrial trucks. Industrial trucks are used for transporting goods on company premises, and are generally not licensed for use on public roads. Their top speed is below 50 km/h. Due to the low power density of the batteries, the range of battery-powered on-road vehicles is significantly less than that of vehicles powered by internal-combustion engines. The maximum speed of such vehicles is also normally limited to around 130 km/h. Whereas more than half of all new industrial trucks are electrically powered, the percentage of electrically powered on-road vehicles is very low.

Energy supply

There is no shortage of power for electric vehicles that are recharged by plugging them into a wall socket. If electric vehicles in Germany were largely recharged at night, existing power plants could provide enough energy to charge more than 10 million vehicles. That number of electric vehicles would require less than 5 % of Germany's total electricity output.

Any household power outlet can be used to charge the batteries. However, these outlets can provide only 3.7 kW of electrical power, which means that an hour of charging would provide enough power to drive a distance of no more than about 20 km. Shorter recharging periods can be achieved by using a three-phase AC power source (as for industrial trucks). Compared to the refueling times for diesel vehicles in particular, the recharging periods required by comparable electric vehicles in order to cover the same distances are roughly 100 times longer, even in the case of very high charging capacity.

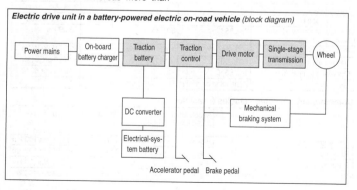

Electric drive unit in a battery-powered electric on-road vehicle (block diagram)

Batteries

Whereas costs considerations dictate that the lead-acid battery is the power source used most often in industrial trucks, in modern electric cars it is increasingly being replaced by nickel and lithium batteries.

Lead-acid battery

Although the basic design of the lead-acid battery is the same as that of the starter battery (see "Starter Battery", P. 866), the combinations of materials and the cell design are specially adapted to the particular requirements of traction operation. The batteries commonly used in industrial trucks are generally combinations of individual cells, whereas a modular design with 3 or 6 cells per module is used in most electric on-road vehicles due to the higher energy density.

Industrial trucks generally use lead-acid batteries with a liquid electrolyte which must be topped up with water on a regular basis. In the case of electric on-road vehicles, this level of maintenance is not acceptable for the vehicle's user. Consequently, maintenance-free batteries with a solid electrolyte (gel) have become standard in these applications. Under real-world conditions, vehicles equipped with lead-acid batteries have a range of 50...70 km per battery charge in city driving. The daily range of an electric vehicle can be increased through intermediate charging of the batteries when the vehicle is parked.

The amount of energy which can be drawn from a lead-acid battery decreases as battery temperature drops. This means that a battery heating system is required by electric on-road vehicles in some climates in order to prevent a reduction in vehicle range during the winter months.

Because the electrolyte takes part in the chemical reaction inside a lead-acid battery, the available capacity varies as a function of discharge time. For example, if the discharge time is reduced from two hours to one, the available capacity is reduced by roughly 20 %.

Batteries in industrial-truck applications can achieve service lives of 7...8 years with 1200...1500 cycles. Fleet experience with electric passenger cars indicates that lead-acid batteries can be expected to last for around 5 years and roughly 700 cycles. The shorter service life in electric on-road vehicle applications is primarily a result of the much greater battery load. In these vehicles the battery is discharged in an average of 2 hours or less, whereas discharge times in industrial trucks are generally in the 7...8 hour range.

Battery systems

Properties	Lead-acid system open/sealed	Nickel systems Nickel-cadmium (Ni/Cd) Nickel-metal hydride (NiMH)	Lithium systems Lithium-ion Lithium-polymer
Cell voltage	2 V	1.2 V	3...4 V
Energy density	25...30 Wh/kg	35... 100 Wh/kg	60...150 Wh/kg
Energy efficiency without heating/cooling	75...85 %	60...85 %	85...90 %
Power density	100...200 W/kg	100...500 W/kg	300...1500 W/kg
Service life in cycles	600...900	> 1000	> 1000 projected
Operating temperature	10...55 °C	–20...55 °C	–10...50 or 60 °C
Maintenance-free	Depending on design	Depending on design	yes

Commercially available vehicles (examples)

Vehicle type	Type of battery	Engine power	Acceleration 0...50 km/h	Maximum speed	Typical range per charge	Typical line-power consumption
Passenger car	Ni/Cd	21 kW	9 s	90 km/h	80 km	18 kWh/100 km
Passenger car	NiMH	49 kW	7 s	130 km/h	200 km	26 kWh/100 km
Passenger car	Lithium-ion	62 kW	6 s	120 km/h	200 km	23 kWh/100 km
Van	Lead-acid	80 kW	7 s	120 km/h	90 km	35 kWh/100 km

Nickel-based batteries

Nickel-cadmium batteries and, increasingly, nickel-metal hydride batteries with an alkaline electrolyte are now used in many electrical appliances. Because cadmium is harmful to the environment, it is likely that in the foreseeable future the nickel-cadmium system will be replaced by the nickel-metal hydride system. Whereas electrical appliances normally use sealed batteries, in traction applications open nickel-cadmium cells are often used. These cells, like open lead-acid batteries, must be refilled with water at regular intervals. Nickel-metal hydride batteries must be sealed due to the inherent characteristics of the system. The low cell voltage of only 1.2 V means that the relative density of non-active components in a 6 V nickel-cadmium module, for example, must be higher than in a lead-acid battery. A battery service life of up to 10 years or 2000 cycles has been demonstrated in a number of applications. The higher costs resulting from the use of relatively expensive materials and the complex manufacturing process are partially offset by a much longer service life than that of lead-acid batteries.

Nickel-cadmium and nickel-metal hydride batteries are cooled when used in electric on-road vehicles; heating is required only at temperatures below −20 °C. Available capacity is virtually independent of discharge time. The alkaline battery's higher energy density can be exploited both to increase the payload and to extend the vehicle's radius of action. Electric cars typically have a range of approx. 80...100 km using nickel-cadmium batteries.

In the nickel-metal hydride system, cadmium is replaced by hydrogen. This hydrogen must be stored in a multimetal medium. The nickel-metal hydride battery has a higher energy density and a somewhat longer service life than the nickel-cadmium battery. Nickel-based batteries also have a higher power density, making them particularly interesting for use in hybrid vehicles.

Lithium-based batteries

Lithium systems allow energy densities of over 100 Wh/kg and power densities of over 300 W/kg in vehicle traction batteries. They can be operated at ambient temperature or slightly higher temperatures, and are characterized by high cell voltages of over 4 V. In the demanding electrical-appliance battery market (for products such as laptops and video recorders) the lithium-ion system has already become successfully established.

Lithium systems do not show any memory effect as do nickel-cadmium systems. A disadvantage of the lithium batteries is that they require a relatively complex battery protection system. For example, each individual cell must be monitored because they are not proof against overcharging. In order to prevent endangerment of the environment, these batteries must also be specially protected against short circuits.

Lithium-ion battery

A lithium-ion battery stores lithium ions in electrically reversible form on the negative electrode in a graphite lattice. The positive electrode contains cobalt as the main component, along with lithium, making the system rather expensive. Attempts are thus being made to use more economical materials such as manganese.

Organic material is used as the electrolyte; aqueous electrolytes cannot be used because lithium reacts strongly with water.

Lithium-polymer battery

Another very promising lithium system is the lithium polymer battery. It consists of a thin lithium film, a polymer electrolyte and a positive film electrode made primarily of either vanadium or manganese. Individual cells are formed by rolling or folding the film, which has an overall thickness of approx. 0.1 mm. The working temperature is approx. 60 °C.

Drivetrains

The drivetrain in an electric vehicle generally consists of the power controller, the motor and the transmission. The power controller translates the position of the accelerator pedal into the appropriate motor current and voltage. In most cases the drive torque is a function of the accelerator pedal position, as in the case of IC engines.

The cost of the motor depends largely on the required maximum torque; thus it is advantageous to use the highest-possible step-down gear ratio between the engine and the drive wheels. The step-down gearing may consist of one or two stages, depending on the desired hill-climbing ability and the vehicle's maximum speed for the given maximum torque and variable speed range of the drive train. Modern electric cars have single-stage reduction gears.

A difference between electric drive units and combustion engines is the necessary distinction between short-term and extended-duty performance. Short-term performance is usually limited by the maximum setting of the power controller. The maximum power available over longer periods is defined by the half-hourly output in the case of on-road electric vehicles, which is generally limited by the permissible motor temperature. This distinction also applies to most batteries. Depending on the type of drive, short-term and extended-duty ratings vary by a factor of 1 to 3. Maximum drive power must therefore be monitored and adjusted, if necessary, in accordance with the characteristic thermal limits of the power controller, motor or batteries.

This distinction between short-term and half-hourly operation has among other things also led to the adoption of two maximum-speed ratings for electric on-road vehicles: maximum speed over a distance of 2 x 1 kilometer and maximum speed over a period of 30 minutes.

Series-wound direct-current drive

This type of drive unit has the simplest type of power controller. The motor voltage is set in accordance with the desired current by applying the battery voltage to the motor in a variable on/off ratio and/or chopper frequency by means of a circuit breaker (thyristor or transistor(s)).

For the recovery of braking energy, the power controller must operate as a step-up chopper, which means that additional components are needed. Because the field and armature of the motor are in se-

ries, drive power drops in proportion to the square of the motor speed with the full battery voltage applied.

Although its efficiency is relatively low, this type of drive is still used in most industrial trucks today because of its simple design and low cost. The low top speeds of these vehicles make it possible to use single-stage reduction gears.

Separately-excited direct-current drive

In this type of drive unit, the motor's magnetic excitation is provided by its own controller (field rheostat). Depending on the size of the motor, the field can be weakened in a ratio of up to approx. 1:4. Field strength starts to diminish at a nominal motor speed obtained with full motor voltage at the armature and maximum field current. During initial acceleration with maximum field current an electronic armature-control device limits the motor current until the motor reaches its nominal speed, with the full motor voltage applied to the armature. In the reduced field-strength range, consistent armature currents produce relatively constant power outputs. Because commutation becomes more difficult as the field current drops, the armature current must usually be reduced before the maximum speed is reached.

Because commutating poles are required, this design is somewhat more complex than that of a series-wound motor. The mechanical commutator limits rotational speed to roughly 7000 min^{-1}. This type of drive unit can be used with a multi-stage transmission to reduce motor cost and weight. Efficient energy recovery during braking is possible without requiring additional components.

However, very few electric cars today are being equipped with direct-current drive units. Three-phase AC asynchronous or synchronous drives are now the norm, due in part to their low maintenance requirements. The carbon brushes in DC motors must be regularly replaced, albeit at relatively long intervals.

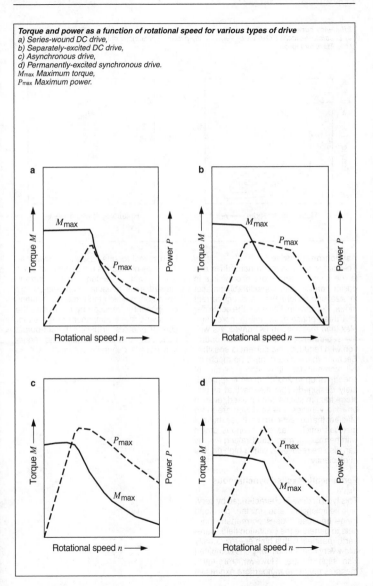

Torque and power as a function of rotational speed for various types of drive
a) Series-wound DC drive,
b) Separately-excited DC drive,
c) Asynchronous drive,
d) Permanently-excited synchronous drive.
M_{max} Maximum torque,
P_{max} Maximum power.

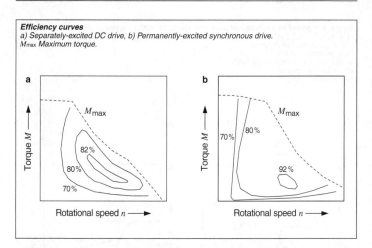

Efficiency curves
a) Separately-excited DC drive, b) Permanently-excited synchronous drive.
M_{max} Maximum torque.

a — Torque M / Rotational speed n — M_{max}, 82%, 80%, 70%

b — Torque M / Rotational speed n — M_{max}, 70%, 80%, 92%

Asynchronous drive

The motor in an asynchronous drive unit is the simplest and most economical in design, and is also considerably smaller in size and weight than a direct-current motor. In principle, however, the controller in a three-phase drive unit is more complex than that used in DC drives. As with the separately-excited DC motor, operation with reduced field current is possible. Because these motors have no mechanical commutator, they can operate at speeds of up to 20,000 min^{-1} if appropriately designed. This means that single-stage transmissions can be used, even in on-road vehicles. These drives are more efficient than direct-current drives, but not quite as efficient as synchronous drives with permanent magnets. Braking energy can also be recovered with a high degree of efficiency.

Permanently-excited synchronous drive

This type of drive is characterized by very-high efficiencies also in the part-load range because it uses permanent magnets to generate the excitation field. Rare-earth magnets with a high energy density allow very compact dimensions combined with high torque. However, rare-earth magnets make the motor more expensive than asynchronous designs, for example. This type of motor is not capable of operation with reduced field current. Nevertheless, quasi reduced-field-current operation in which the torque-generating component is reduced by increasing the reactive-current component of the stator current enables virtually constant-output operation, so that a single-stage reduction gear is generally sufficient here as well.

Hybrid drives

In the broadest sense, the term "hybrid drives" is used to denote vehicle drives with more than one drive source. Hybrid drives can incorporate several similar or dissimilar types of energy stores and/or power converters. The goal of hybrid-drive developments is to combine different drive components, such that the advantages of each are utilized under varying operating conditions in such a manner that the overall advantages outweigh the higher technical outlay associated with hybrid drives.

Classification of hybrid drives

In terms of available performance and range, the IC engine as a drive source is superior to all other drive systems. Its disadvantages – drop in efficiency at part load, and the generation of toxic emissions – led to the development of hybrid drives which incorporate the IC engine. IC engines in some hybrid drives are thus designed for use over the medium-power range, whereby the differences between generated power and the power required at any given time are made up by the additional mechanical or electrical energy store.

Hybrid drive with mechanical energy store

A hybrid drive incorporating an IC engine and flywheel, can be operated in a number of ways by engaging and disengaging the three couplings K1, K2 and K3. The IC engine can be directly coupled to the power-shift transmission or the flywheel. There are 2 kinetic-energy storage devices, the flywheel and the vehicle mass.

In addition, the internal-combustion engine can start the two kinetic-energy storage devices from standstill via the continuously variable transmission. This configuration also permits parallel operation with the two drive sources, diesel engine and flywheel. Here, only the power delivered by the flywheel is transmitted to the power-shift transmission via the loss-intensive continuously variable transmission using hydrostatic converters, whereas the engine power is fed directly to the transmission input.

Classification of hybrid drives △ *Research proposals,* ● *Prototype vehicles,* ◆ *Tested in practical applications*										
Drive source	Internal-combustion engine	●	●					◆	◆	◆
	Electric motor			●	◆	△	△	◆	◆	◆
Mechanical energy store	Flywheel	●			◆	△				◆
	Pressure accumulator		●							
Electrical energy sources	Battery			●		△	△	◆		
	Fuel cell						△			
	External supply (trolley)			●	◆				◆	
Design examples		DB MAN Gyro-bus	MAN Hydro-bus	Esslin-gen DUO-bus	Basel Neo-plan Trolley bus			DB hybrid electric bus, MB/MAN delivery truck	Essen DUO-bus	Munich Magnet motor-bus

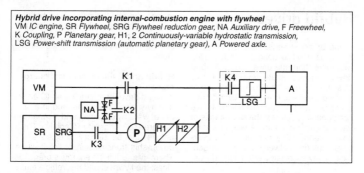

Hybrid drive incorporating internal-combustion engine with flywheel
VM *IC engine,* SR *Flywheel,* SRG *Flywheel reduction gear,* NA *Auxiliary drive,* F *Freewheel,*
K *Coupling,* P *Planetary gear,* H1, 2 *Continuously-variable hydrostatic transmission,*
LSG *Power-shift transmission (automatic planetary gear),* A *Powered axle.*

Hybrid drive with electrical energy store

Hybrid drives without IC engines which use only electrical drive components are designed to apply their hybrid components in order to avoid the disadvantages of the purely battery-powered electric drive. The useful energy stored in the battery allows only a limited driving range, and is further reduced as power demand increases.

Combining a mechanical energy store with the battery prevents it being affected by power peaks, thus contributing to more efficient utilization of the battery energy. A hybrid system which uses a combination of two different electrochemical energy sources (battery and fuel cell) separates the energy sources such that one source has a high power, and the other has good energy-storage capability. In the case of hybrid electric drives with an external supply of energy (trolley systems), the vehicle's own energy store is used as a short-time storage medium for short distances of travel without the overhead power supply. This configuration reduces the high costs associated with overhead contact wires and increase versatility in traffic.

Hybrid drive designs

Hybrid drives which combine an internal-combustion (IC) engine and an electric drive are the only hybrid drives which have warranted serious attention to date. The electric drive component of such drives is powered either by an on-board bat-

tery or via an overhead contact wire and current-collector system. The diagram at the right shows the various basic drive configurations. The battery indicated in each configuration can be replaced by the external power-supply arrangement.

The main difference among the various configurations is the series, parallel or mixed interconnection of the power sources. In the series configuration (1)

Hybrid drive configurations
1 Series configuration, 2 Parallel configuration, 3 Mixed configuration VM *IC engine,* EL *Electric drive (operated as a motor or alternator/generator),* BA *Battery or external power supply,* SG *Manually shifted transmission.*

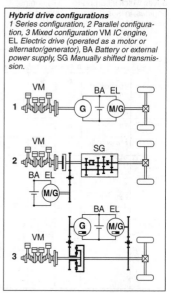

the individual drive components are connected in series, whereas in the parallel configuration (2) the drive power of both drive sources is mechanically added. The letters M and G indicate whether the electric drive is operating in "motor" or "generator" mode.

Because the diesel engine in the series configuration is mechanically decoupled from the vehicle drive, the diesel engine can be operated at a constant speed, i.e. at its optimum operating point in terms of efficiency and emissions. Despite the advantages of the series configuration, its disadvantage is that energy must be converted several times. Including battery storage efficiency, the mechanical efficiency between the diesel engine and the powered axle is hardly greater than 55%.

The parallel hybrid configuration (2) has the advantage that when operated in the mode which incorporates an IC engine, it is just as efficient as the engine in a conventional vehicle. In configuration 2, the change-speed transmission required by the diesel-engine drive is also part of the electric drive branch. In this type of drive the speed of the electric motor therefore must be varied only within a specific range above a basic speed, in a manner similar to the way in which the diesel engine is operated. Moreover, in this configuration the electric drive also

profits from the torque conversion by the downstream transmission, as a result of which the electric motor must only be dimensioned for low drive torque. This leads to an equivalent reduction in motor mass which is roughly proportional to motor torque.

The mixed configuration (3) represents a combination of configurations 1 and 2, and corresponds to a splitter transmission with an infinitely-variable transmission ratio. On the one hand, the power of the IC engine is mechanically transmitted directly to the driving wheels, while on the other, the rotation of the IC engine is decoupled from the rotation of the driving wheels by the speed overlay in the planetary gear.

The drive configuration in a hybrid electric bus is the same as that in type 1 described above. In order to obtain the low floor height required, the electric drive takes the form of wheel hub motors. Due to the low floor level, the electrical energy store – a high-temperature battery – must be mounted together with its peripherals on the roof of the vehicle.

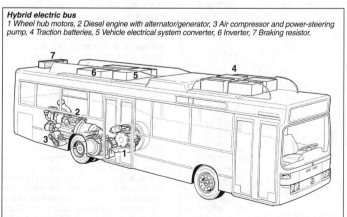

Hybrid electric bus
1 Wheel hub motors, 2 Diesel engine with alternator/generator, 3 Air compressor and power-steering pump, 4 Traction batteries, 5 Vehicle electrical system converter, 6 Inverter, 7 Braking resistor.

Fuel Cells

Fuel cells are electrochemical cells in which the chemical energy of a suitable fuel is continuously converted into electrical energy using atmospheric oxygen (O_2). The most common fuels which lend themselves to such applications are hydrogen (H_2), methanol (CH_3OH) and, to a more limited degree, methane (at very high temperatures). Because conventional fuels can not be used directly, they must be converted into H_2 in a chemical gas-reforming reaction. Fuel-cell operation is very efficient, and produces low levels of harmful emissions. They are modular in design, and can therefore be used over a wide power range from a few watts to several megawatts.

Due to those characteristics and promising new developments in the field of low-temperature fuel cells, many automobile manufacturers now see the fuel-cell drive as a serious alternative to the internal-combustion engine for automotive applications. For that reason, the major vehicle manufacturers in particular are working intensively on the development of fuel cells suitable for automotive use.

However, a realistic assessment of the fuel-cell drive in terms of its environmental and customer benefit is only possible by looking at the whole picture. As far as emissions are concerned, not only must the direct emissions from the vehicle be taken into account, but also those produced in the fuel-cell manufacturing process. The same applies to the system's efficiency, which can only be compared with other types of drive if the overall efficiency of the entire process from the primary energy source to the driving wheels is considered.

The most important application for fuel cells to date has been as a means of generating electrical energy in spacecraft and submarines.

Design variations

In contrast to combustion engines, fuel-cell operation does not require a specific (high) temperature; some fuel cells operate at room temperature, while others are designed for temperatures of up to approximately 1000 °C (Table 1). The various designs differ from one another above all in the type of electrolyte used, which depends on the temperature. Up to around 90°C the electrolyte is aqueous or contains water. For mid-range temperatures (500 ... 700 °C) molten alkaline carbonate electrolytes have become the standard, while for high temperatures (800 ... 1000 °C), only ceramic-based solid electrolytes (e.g. zirconium dioxide) can be used. Apart from the differences in the type of electrolyte used, fuel cells also differ according to their electrode materials.

Fuel cells are often referred to by the acronyms shown in Table 1.

Fuel conditioning

Although attempts have long been made to operate fuel cells directly using various fuels, the fuel cells available today must use H_2 as their energy source. At present, H_2 is generally obtained from natural gas or other fossil fuels by means of a chemical gas-reforming process. For mobile applications, H_2 must either be stored in the

---

Polymer electrolyte fuel cell (principle of operation)
1 Hydrogen, 2 Electrical load, 3 Air (oxygen),
4 Catalyst, 5 Electrolyte, 6 Bipolar plate,
7 Water vapor and residual air.

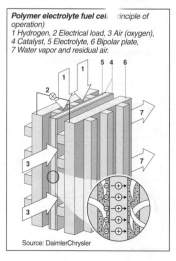

Source: DaimlerChrysler

vehicle or derived from another on-board fuel.

Hydrogen storage medium

For automotive applications, H_2 can be stored and transported in gaseous form in cylinders at pressures of up 300 bar or in liquid form in cryotanks at $-253\,°C$. For low-power applications or in submarines, hydrogen is stored in metal hydrides or even in special modified carbon compounds. If H_2 is stored as a gas under pressure or as a liquid, it must be remembered that a considerable portion of the primary energy is required simply to compress or liquefy the H_2. Furthermore, the energy density of an H_2 storage medium is less than that of a conventional fuel tank.

Methanol reforming

CH_3OH is produced from natural gas with an efficiency of approx. 65 %. Its advantage over H_2 is that it can be dispensed in liquid form similar to conventional vehicle fuels. However, a separate infrastructure must be made available to handle CH_3OH; it cannot be stored in existing fuel tanks because it is considerably more corrosive than gasoline or diesel fuel. CH_3OH can be converted into H_2, CO_2 and CO in a catalytic reforming process using water vapor at temperatures of $250...450\,°C$. The CO combines with water to produce H_2 and CO_2 in a subsequent catalytic conversion stage. The residual CO must be removed in a gas purifier because it chemically inhibits the fuel-cell electrodes.

Gasoline reforming

The advantages of gasoline are its high energy density and widespread availability through an already existing infrastructure, however it is considerably more difficult to reform gasoline into H_2 than it is to reform CH_3OH, for example. Conversion involves partial oxidation in the presence of air and water at temperatures of 800 ... $900\,°C$, producing H_2, CO_2 and CO. The CO is converted in two subsequent catalytic stages using H_2O into H_2 and CO_2. The residual CO must be separated out in a gas purifier in this case as well, because it inhibits the fuel-cell electrodes. The problems associated with gasoline reformation concern primarily the complex system which must be controlled at high temperatures, and the inhibition of the catalysts by the formation of coke.

Thermodynamics and kinetics

The electrochemical reactions which take place in fuel cells are essentially the same as those in galvanic cells (e. g. batteries), however in fuel cells only gaseous or liquid fuels are used. The oxidizing agent is generally O_2 or atmospheric oxygen. For that reason, fuel cells require special porous electrode structures.

Table 2 gives the reaction equations and the calculated fuel-cell data (theoretical cell voltage E_0 and thermodynamic efficiency η_{th}) for the two fuels of interest, H_2 and CH_3OH, at different temperatures. The first reaction equation describes the

Table 1. Types of Fuel Cells

Fuel Cell Designation		Electrolyte	Temperature °C	Cell Efficiency (Load Partial Load) %	Type of Application
Alkaline Fuel Cell	AFC	Aqueous KOH	60...90	50...60	Mobile, stationary
Polymer Electrolyte Fuel Cell	PEFC	Polymer electrolyte	50...80	50...60	Mobile, stationary
Direct Methanol Fuel Cell	DMFC	Membrane	110...130	30...40	Mobile
Phosphoric Acid Fuel Cell	PAFC	H_3PO_4	160...220	55	Stationary
Molten Carbonate Fuel Cell	MCFC	Alkaline carbonates	620...660	60...65	Stationary
Solid Oxide Fuel Cell	SOFC	ZrO_2	800...1000	55...65	Stationary

familiar electrolytic gas reaction, which in fuel cells is a controlled process ("cold combustion") rather than an explosive one. This reaction takes place in a controlled manner in fuel cells because the important reaction processes (H_2 oxidation and O_2 reduction) occur at physically separate electrodes and at a relatively low temperature (Figure and Table 1). It is therefore possible in fuel cells to directly and completely convert the chemical energy, which corresponds to the decrease in free enthalpy ΔG_R of the reaction, into electrical work A_e in accordance with Equation 1:

$$A_e = -\Delta G_R = n \cdot F \cdot E_0 \qquad \text{(Equation 1)}$$

(n Number of electrons converted per fuel molecule, F Faraday constant).

Because in this type of energy conversion the customary indirect path via the generation of heat is avoided, fuel-cell efficiency is not limited by the relatively poor efficiency of the Carnot cycle.

As shown in Table 2, the cell voltages E_0 for the two fuels are close to one another (approx. 1.2 V) and the thermodynamic efficiency η_{th} calculated according to Equation 2 is also < 1 for CH_3OH if liquid water is formed as the reaction product:

$$\eta_{th} = \Delta G_R / \Delta H_R \qquad \text{(Equation 2)}$$

At temperatures above 100 °C (if CH_3OH and H_2O are present in gaseous form), the CH_3OH/O_2 fuel cell shows that in principle fuel cells can also attain a thermodynamic efficiency of > 1.

In practice the theoretical fuel-cell figures are not reached with any of the fuels, even at high temperatures. The reasons for this are primarily to be found in the kinetic inhibition at the two electrodes (e.g. charge penetration and material transfer) as well as in the mixed potential formation at the positive electrode and the electrolyte impedance. The resulting polarization can be reduced but not completely eliminated by using noble metals (platinum, ruthenium) as catalysts, specially structured porous electrodes and small electrode gaps. This applies even in the absence of current flow when a steady-state voltage of only approx. 1 V is measured at an H_2/O_2 PEFC (see Table 1) instead of the expected 1.23 V. When a load is applied, fuel-cell voltage and efficiency drop by varying degrees, depending on the fuel, as current increases due to increasing polarization (see graph). Other variables which have a significant effect on the shape of the current/voltage characteristic of a fuel cell are temperature, gas pressure (1.5 ... 3 bar) and the noble-metal electrode coating, which is now as little as 0.1 ... 0.5 mg Pt/cm².

The typical working voltage of an H_2/air

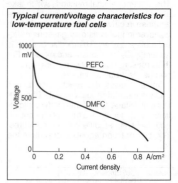

Typical current/voltage characteristics for low-temperature fuel cells

Table 2. Reaction equations and calculated data for hydrogen (H_2) and methanol (CH_3OH) as energy sources for fuel cells

Reaction equations	State of H_2O/CH_3OH	Temperature °C	E_0 V	η_{th} %
$H_2 + \frac{1}{2}O_2 \rightarrow H_2O$	Liquid	25	1.23	83
	Liquid	127	1.15	81
	Gaseous	127	1.16	92
	Gaseous	227	1.11	87
$CH_3OH + \frac{3}{2}O_2 \rightarrow CO_2 + 2\,H_2O$	Liquid/liquid	25	1.21	97
	Liquid/liquid	127	1.20	99
	Gaseous/gaseous	127	1.20	103
	Gaseous/gaseous	227	1.21	104

PEFC at rated continuous output (0.4 ... 0.5 W/cm^2 of electrode surface area) is around 0.75 ... 0.70 V (see graph) which, according to Equation 2, results in an efficiency of 51 ... 48 %. With CH_3OH as the PEFC energy source, despite the higher temperature (110 ... 130 °C), lower power density (0.1 ... 0.2 W/cm^2) and greater amount of Pt on the electrodes, a lower voltage (0.50 ... 0.35 V) and a correspondingly lower thermodynamic efficiency (41 ... 30 %) is produced than in the case of an H_2/air PEFC. However, this does not take into account the fact that, in the case of CH_3OH, its permeation through the electrolyte membrane results in a loss at the anode due to which the efficiency of a direct methanol fuel cell is even further reduced.

Fuel cells in motor vehicles

As clean, high-efficiency energy converters, from the point of view of environmental protection and conservation of resources, fuel cells represent an interesting alternative to the traditional methods of generating electrical power. Of the types of fuel cells described here, PEFCs in particular show the most promise in both fixed and mobile applications by virtue of their low operating temperature and compact and robust design. In the area of mobile applications, driven by the increasingly stringent exhaust-emission regulations in the USA and Europe, fuel-cell power units are clearly at the forefront of development efforts. In addition, however, the possibility of using PEFCs as the electrical power source in vehicles with conventional engines is also being investigated, and initial experiments have been carried out. A vehicle electrical system with a power supply independent of the engine which provides the motive power would enable implementation of desirable timer-controlled or remotely controlled auxiliary functions (e.g. preheating of the engine/catalytic converter, air-conditioner operation without the engine running).

All of the automobile manufacturers engaged in comprehensive fuel-cell development work have focused on two key problems, which in principle affect all fuel-cell applications: the high cost of PEFCs and the availability of pure H_2, which is essential for the operation of PEFCs and for which there is no infrastructure at present which could be used to supply vehicles powered by such fuel cells. An additional disadvantage of H_2 as a fuel for fuel-cell powered vehicles is the fact that its energy density is satisfactory only if it is stored in pressurized or liquefied form. For reasons of safety alone, there are serious concerns regarding the storage of H_2 in those forms in private passenger cars.

When using fuel cells as automotive drives, efficiency drops to around 30 % from the H_2 storage tank to the wheels. This loss is attributable in part to the auxiliary systems required for monitoring and operation of the fuel cells (e.g. air compressor, coolant pumps, fan cooler, control equipment and, where applicable, gas reformers). The electrical power required by the secondary loads can amount to as much as 25 % of the fuel-cell output, depending on the nature of the peripherals and the size and operating point of the fuel cell. In addition to fuel-cell efficiency, the efficiency of the electric drive unit must also be taken into consideration. When considering the entire energy chain from the primary energy source to the vehicle's powered wheels, and given the technology available at present, the overall efficiency of modern diesel and fuel-cell-powered vehicles is comparable for vehicles of equal power-to-weight ratios.

No predictions can be made at this time regarding the service life of PEFCs under the dynamic conditions of motor-vehicle operation. As in all applications involving catalysts, fuel cells can also be expected to suffer from a reduction in the catalytic action of the electrodes over time. The result is a gradual decline in the voltage and efficiency of the fuel cell which is referred to as degradation. It is assumed, however, that over the long term the service life of fuel-cell drives will be similar to that of internal-combustion engines.

Bibliography
Karl Kordesch, Günther Simander, Fuel Cells and Their Applications, VCH Weinheim 1996.

Drivetrain

Units and symbols

Quantity		Unit
a	Acceleration	m/s^2
c_w	Drag coefficient	–
e	Rotational inertia coefficient	–
f	Rolling resistance coefficient	–
g	Gravitational acceleration	m/s^2
i	Transmission ratio	–
m	Vehicle mass	kg
n	Speed of rotation	min^{-1}
r	Dynamic tire radius	m
s	Wheel slip	–
v	Road speed	m/s
A	Frontal area	m^2
D	System diameter	m
I	Overall conversion range	–
J	Moment of inertia	kg · m^2
M	Torque	N · m
P	Power	kW
α	Angle of inclination	°
φ	Overdrive factor	–
η	Efficiency	–
λ	Performance index	–
μ	Conversion	–
ρ	Density	kg/m^3
ω	Angular velocity	rad/s
v	Speed ratio	–

Subscripts:			
eng	Engine		
eff	Effective	o	Towards maximum output
tot	Total	dt	Drivetrain
hydr	Hydraulic	G	Gearbox
max	Maximum	P	Pump
min	Minimum	R	Roadwheel
fd	Final drive	T	Turbine

Assignment

The function of the automotive drivetrain is to provide the thrust and tractive forces required to induce motion. Energy in chemical (fuels) or electrical (batteries, solar cells) form is converted into mechanical energy within the power unit, with spark-ignition and diesel internal-combustion engines representing the powerplants of choice. Every power unit operates within a specific revolution range as defined by two extremities: the idle speed and the maximum min^{-1}. Torque and power are not delivered at uniform rates throughout the operating range; the respective maxima are available only within specific bands. The drivetrain's conversion ratios adapt the available torque to the momentary requirement for tractive force.

Design

The dynamic condition of an automobile is described by the motion-resistance equation. It equates the forces generated by the drive train with the forces required at the driving wheels (resistance to motion).

From the motion-resistance equation it is possible to calculate acceleration, maximum speed, climbing ability and also the overall conversion range I of the transmission.

$$I = \frac{(i/r)_{max}}{(i/r)_{min}} = \frac{\tan \alpha_{max} \cdot v_o}{(P/(m \cdot g))_{eff.} \cdot \varphi}$$

Equilibrium relation between drive forces and tractive resistance

The equation defining the equilibrium between drive forces and resistance factors is applied to determine various quantities, such as acceleration, top speed, climbing ability, etc.

Available power = Tractive resistance at drive wheels (power requirement)

$$M_{eng} \cdot \frac{i_{tot}}{r} \cdot \eta_{tot} = m \cdot g \cdot f \cdot \cos \alpha + m \cdot g \cdot \sin \alpha + e \cdot m \cdot \alpha + c_w \cdot A \cdot \frac{\rho}{2} \cdot v^2$$

Driving force applied to tyre footprint	Rolling resistance	Gravitational resistance	Acceleration	Wind resistance

Where rotational inertia coefficient $e = 1 + \dfrac{J}{m \cdot r^2}$, and mass inertia $J = J_R + i_{fd}^2 \cdot J_{dt} + i_{fd}^2 \cdot i_G^2 \cdot J_{eng}$

The overdrive factor φ is

$$\varphi = \frac{(i/r)_{min}}{\omega_o / \upsilon_o}.$$

Calculations of effective specific output should always be based on the power P which is actually available for tractive application (net power minus driven ancillaries, power losses, altitude loss). Special conditions, such as automobile trailer towing, must be factored into the weight $m \cdot g$. $\varphi = 1$ is true, when the curve for cumulative running resistance in top gear directly intersects the point of maximum output. The φ factor determines the relative positions of the curves for running-resistance and engine output in top-gear operation, it also defines the efficiency level at which the engine operates.

$\varphi > 1$ displaces operation into an inefficient engine-performance range, but also enhances acceleration reserves and hillclimbing ability in top gear. In contrast, selecting $\varphi < 1$ will increase fuel economy, but only at the price of substantially slower acceleration and lower climbing reserves. Minimum fuel consumption is achieved on the operating curve η_{opt}. $\varphi > 1$ reduces, $\varphi < 1$ increases the required transmission conversion range I.

Drivetrain configurations

The layout of the automotive drivetrain varies according to the position of the engine and the drive axle:

Drive configuration	Engine position	Driven axle
Standard rear-wheel drive	front	Rear-axle
Front-wheel drive	front. longit. or transverse	Front axle
All-wheel drive	front, occasionally rear or middle	Front-axle and rear-axle
Rear-wheel drive with rear-mounted engine	rear	Rear-axle

Drivetrain elements

The elements of the drive train must perform the following functions:
- remaining stationary even with the engine running,
- achieving the transition from a stationary to a mobile state,
- converting torque and rotational speed,
- providing for forward and reverse motion,
- compensating for wheel-speed variations in curves,
- ensuring that the power unit remains within a range on the operating curve commensurate with minimum fuel consumption and exhaust emissions.

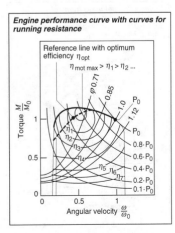

Engine performance curve with curves for running resistance

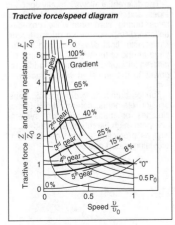

Tractive force/speed diagram

Stationary idle, transition to motion and interruption of the power flow are all made possible by the <u>clutch</u>. The clutch slips to compensate for the difference in the rotational speeds of engine and drivetrain when the vehicle is being set in motion. When different conditions demand a change of gear, the clutch disengages the engine from the transmission while the gear shift operation takes place. With automatic transmissions, the hydrodynamic torque converter is responsible for the take-up of power. The <u>transmission</u> (gearbox) modifies the engine's torque and min^{-1} to adapt them to the vehicle's momentary tractive requirements.

The overall conversion of the drivetrain is the product of the constant transmission ratio of the axle differential and the variable transmission ratio of the gearbox – assuming there are no other transmission stages involved. Gearboxes are almost always multiple fixed-ratio gearboxes though some are of the continuously variable ratio type.

Gearboxes generally fall into one of two categories: manual gearboxes with spur gears and a layshaft arrangement and load-actuated automatic transmissions with planetary gears. The transmission also allows the selection of different rotational directions for forward and reverse operation.

The <u>differential</u> allows laterally opposed axles and wheels to rotate at varying rates during cornering while providing uniform distribution of the driving forces. Limited-slip final drives respond to slippage at one of the wheels by limiting the differential effect, shifting additional power to the wheel at which traction is available.

Torsion dampers, hydrodynamic transmission elements, controlled-slip friction clutches or mass-suspension systems dissipate high vibration amplitudes, as well as protecting against overload and providing added ride comfort.

Power take-up elements

Dry-plate friction clutch

The friction clutch consists of a pressure plate, a clutch disk – featuring bonded or riveted friction surfaces – and the second friction surface represented by the engine-mounted flywheel. The flywheel and pressure plate provide the thermal absorption required for friction operation of the clutch; flywheel and pressure plate are connected directly to the engine, while the clutch disk is mounted on the transmission's input shaft.

A spring arrangement, frequently in the form of a central spring plate, applies the force which joins the flywheel, pressure plate and clutch disk for common rotation; in this state, the clutch is engaged for positive torque transfer. To disengage the clutch (e.g., for gear shifting), a mechanically or hydraulically actuated throwout bearing applies force to the center of the pressure plate, thereby releasing the pressure at the periphery. The clutch is controlled either with a clutch pedal or with an electrohydraulic, electropneumatic or electromechanical final-control element. A single- or multi-stage torsion damper, with or without a predamper, may be integrated in the clutch plate to absorb vibration.

Clutch with dual-mass flywheel
1 Dual-mass flywheel, 2 Flexible element,
3 Pressure plate, 4 Spring plate, 5 Friction plate, 6 Thrust bearing

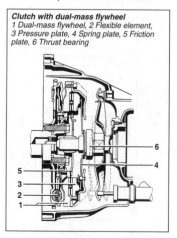

A two-section (dual-mass) flywheel featuring a flexible intermediate element can be installed forward of the clutch for maximum insulation against vibrations. The resonant frequency of this sprung mass system is below the exciter frequency (ignition frequency) of the engine at idling speed and therefore outside the operating speed range. It acts as a vibration insulating element between the engine and the other drive-train components (low-pass filter).

When used together with electronic control units, the automatic clutch can provide either gradual engagement for starting off, or it can be applied in conjunction with a servo-operated shifting mechanism to form a fully-automatic transmission unit. Traction control and disengagement of power transmission during braking are also possible.

Wet-plate friction clutch

The wet-plate friction clutch has the advantage over the dry-plate version that its thermal performance is better as oil can be passed through to assist heat dissipation. However, its drag losses when disengaged are considerably higher than with a dry clutch. Use in combination with synchromesh gearboxes presents problems due to the increased synchronous load when changing gear. The wet clutch

was introduced as a standard component on continuously variable car transmissions. It has space-saving advantages particularly when one or more friction-drive gear-shift components (multiplate clutch or clutch stop) that are present in any case can also be used for the power take-up process.

Hydrodynamic torque converter

The hydrodynamic torque converter consists of the impeller which is the driving component, the turbine which is the driven component and the stator which assists the torque converter function. The torque converter is filled with oil and transmits the engine torque by means of the viscosity of the oil. It compensates for the speed difference between the engine and the other drive-train components and is therefore ideally suited to a power take-up function. An impeller converts the mechanical energy into fluid energy; and a second transformation, back into mechanical energy, takes place at the blades within the turbine.

The impeller's input torque M_p and input power P_p are calculated as follows:

$$M_p = \lambda \cdot \rho \cdot D^5 \cdot \omega_p^2$$
$$P_p = \lambda \cdot \rho \cdot D^5 \cdot \omega_p^3$$

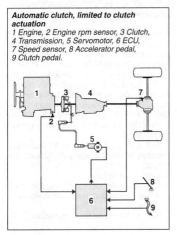

Automatic clutch, limited to clutch actuation
1 Engine, 2 Engine rpm sensor, 3 Clutch,
4 Transmission, 5 Servomotor, 6 ECU,
7 Speed sensor, 8 Accelerator pedal,
9 Clutch pedal.

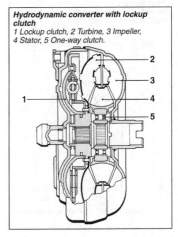

Hydrodynamic converter with lockup clutch
1 Lockup clutch, 2 Turbine, 3 Impeller,
4 Stator, 5 One-way clutch.

λ Performance index
ρ Density of medium
   (≈ 870 kg/m³ for hydraulic fluid)
D Circuit diameter in m
ω_p Angular velocity of impeller

A stator located between impeller and turbine diverts the hydraulic oil back to the input side of the impeller. This raises the torque beyond the initial engine output as exerted at the impeller. Torque conversion is then

$$\mu = -M_T/M_P$$

The factor ν is defined as the ratio of turbine speed to impeller speed; it has a determining influence on both the performance index λ and the conversion factor μ:

$$\nu = \omega_T / \omega_P.$$

The slip factor $s = 1 - \nu$ and the force conversion together determine the hydraulic efficiency:

$$\eta_{hydr} = \mu\,(1 - s) = \mu \cdot \nu.$$

Maximum torque multiplication is achieved at $\nu = 0$, i.e., with the turbine at

stall speed. Further increases in turbine speed are accompanied by a virtually linear drop in multiplication until a torque ratio of 1:1 is reached at the coupling point. Above this point the stator, which is housing-mounted with a one-way clutch, freewheels in the flow.

In motor-vehicle applications, the two-phase Föttinger torque converter with centripetal flow through the turbine, the "Trilok converter", has become the established design. The geometrical configuration of this unit's blades is selected to provide torque multiplication in the range of 1.7 ... 2.5 at stall speed ($\nu = 0$). The curve defining the hydraulic efficiency factor $\eta_{hydr} = \nu \cdot \mu$ in the conversion range is roughly parabolic. Above the coupling point, which is at 10 ... 15 % slip, the efficiency is equal to the speed ratio ν and reaches levels of around 97 % at high speeds.

The hydrodynamic torque converter is a fully automatic infinitely variable transmission with virtually zero-wear characteristics; it eliminates vibration peaks and absorbs vibration highly effectively.

However, its conversion range and efficiency, particularly at high levels of slip, are not sufficient for motor-vehicle applications so that the torque converter can only be usefully employed in combination with multi-speed or continuously variable gearboxes.

Converter lockup clutch

In order to improve efficiency, the impeller and turbine can be locked together by a converter lockup clutch once power take-up is complete. The converter lockup clutch consists of a plunger with friction surface, which is connected to the turbine hub. The transmission's valve body regulates the direction in which the fluid flows through the converter to regulate coupling engagement.

The converter lockup clutch normally requires additional means of vibration absorption such as
– a torsion damper,
– controlled-slip operation of the converter lockup clutch at critical vibration levels or
– both of the above in combination.

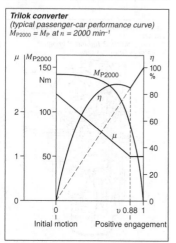

Trilok converter
(typical passenger-car performance curve)
$M_{P2000} = M_P$ at $n = 2000$ min⁻¹

Multi-speed gearbox

Multi-speed gearboxes have become the established means of power transmission in motor vehicles. Good efficiency characteristics dependent upon the number of gears and engine torque characteristics, satisfactory to good adaptation to the traction hyperbola and easily mastered technology are the essential reasons for its success.

Gear shifting on multi-speed gearboxes is performed using either disengagement of power transmission (positively interlocking mechanism) or under load by a friction mechanism. The first group includes manual and semi-automatic gearboxes while the second group encompasses automatic transmissions.

The manually-shifted transmissions installed in passenger cars and in most heavy vehicles are dual-shaft units with main and countershaft (layshaft, idler gears). Transmissions in heavy commercial vehicles sometimes incorporate two or even three countershafts. In such cases, special design features are required in order to ensure that power is evenly distributed to all countershafts.

Automatic transmissions for cars and commercial vehicles are, in the majority of cases, planetary gear transmissions and only in rare cases are countershaft designs used. The planetary gears generally take the form of a planetary-gear link mechanism. They frequently involve the use of Ravigneaux or Simpson planetary gears.

Planetary-gear sets
The basic planetary-gear set consists of the sun gear, internal ring gear and the planet gears with carrier. Each element can act as input or output gear, or may be held stationary. The coaxial layout of the three elements makes this type of unit ideal for use with friction clutches and brake bands, which are employed for selective engagement or fixing of individual elements. The engagement pattern can be changed – and a different conversion ratio selected – without interrupting torque flow; this capability is of particular significance in automatic transmissions.

As several gear wheels mesh under load simultaneously, planetary-gear transmissions are very compact. They have no free bearing forces, permit high torque levels, power splitting or power combination, and feature very good efficiency levels.

Planetary-gear set with various conversion ratios
A *Sun gear*, B *Internal ring gear*, C *Planet gears with carrier*,
Z *Number of teeth.*

Basic equation for planetary-gear sets: $n_A + (Z_B / Z_A) \cdot n_B - [1 + Z_B / Z_A] \cdot n_C = 0$

	Input	Output	Fixed	Transmission ratio	Remarks
	A	C	B	$i = 1 + Z_B / Z_A$	$2.5 \leq i \leq 5$
	B	C	A	$i = 1 + Z_A / Z_B$	$1.25 \leq i \leq 1.67$
	C	A	B	$i = \dfrac{1}{1 + Z_B / Z_A}$	$0.2 \leq i \leq 0.4$ overdrive
	C	B	A	$i = \dfrac{1}{1 + Z_A / Z_B}$	$0.6 \leq i \leq 0.8$ overdrive
	A	B	C	$i = - Z_B / Z_A$	Non-automotive with reversible direction of rotation $-0.4 \leq i \leq -1.5$
	B	A	C	$i = - Z_A / Z_B$	Non-automotive with reversible direction of rotation $-0.25 \leq i \leq -0.67$

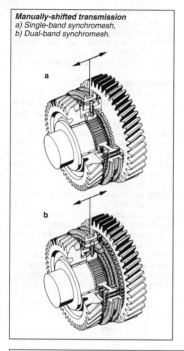

Manually-shifted transmission
a) Single-band synchromesh,
b) Dual-band synchromesh.

Manually-shifted transmissions

The basic elements of the manually-shifted transmission are:
– single or multiplate dry clutch for interrupting and engaging the power flow; actuation may be power-assisted to deal with high operating forces,
– variable-ratio gear transmission unit featuring permanent-mesh gears in one or several individual assemblies,
– shift mechanism with shift lever.

The force required for gear selection is transmitted via shift linkage rods or cable, while dog clutches or synchronizer assemblies lock the active gears to the shafts. Before a shift can take place, it is necessary to synchronize the rotating speeds of the transmission elements being joined. When the transmission incorporates dog clutches (of the type still sometimes used in transmissions for heavy commercial vehicles), the driver performs this task by double-clutching on both upshifts and downshifts, with the latter being accompanied by the application of throttle.

Virtually all passenger-car transmissions, and the majority of those in commercial vehicles, employ locking synchronizer assemblies. These include a friction

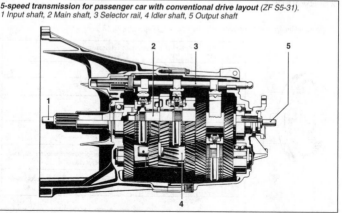

5-speed transmission for passenger car with conventional drive layout (ZF S5-31).
1 Input shaft, 2 Main shaft, 3 Selector rail, 4 Idler shaft, 5 Output shaft

coupling for initial equalization of rotating speed and a lockout mechanism to prevent positive gear engagement prior to completion of the synchronization process. By far the majority use single-cone synchromesh clutches. In cases where there are particularly high demands for performance and/or reduction of gear-shifting force, double or even triple-cone synchromesh clutches or multi-plate synchromesh clutches are used.

Most transmissions in passenger cars include 5, occasionally even 6 forward ratios. The transmission-ratio range (depending on the number of gears and closeness of the ratios) is approximately between 4 and 5.5 while the transmission efficiency can be as high as 99%. The gearbox layout depends on the vehicle's drive configuration (standard rear-wheel drive, front-wheel drive with inline or transverse engine, or four-wheel drive). Thus the input and output shafts may share a single axis, or they may be mutually offset; the final-drive and differential assembly may also be included in the unit.

Transmissions in commercial vehicles can have between 5 and 16 gears, depending upon the type of vehicle and the specific application. For up to 6 gears, the transmission consists of a single gearbox. The transmission-ratio range is between 4 and 9. Transmissions with between 7 and 9 gears are two-box transmissions in which the range-selector box is pneumatically operated. The conversion range extends to 13.

For still higher numbers of ratios – up to 16 – three transmission elements are employed: the main transmission, a splitter group and the range group, with pneumatic actuation for the latter two units. The conversion range is as high as 16.

Power take-offs (auxiliary drives)
Commercial-vehicle transmissions are fitted with a variety of power take-off connections for driving auxiliary equipment. A basic distinction is made between clutch and engine-driven PTO's. The individual selection depends upon the specific application.

Retarders
Hydrodynamic or electrodynamic retarders are non-wearing auxiliary brakes for reducing the thermal load on the road-wheel brakes under continuous braking. They can be fitted either on the drive input side (primary retarders) or the drive output side (secondary retarders) integral with the transmission, or as a separate unit between the transmission output shaft and the driving axle. The advantages of the integrated designs are com-

---

5-speed transmission for longitudinal-engine passenger car with 4wd *(Audi quattro)*
1 Input shaft, 2 Front-axle differential, 3 AWD transfer box with Torsen locking differential,
4 Rear-axle drive shaft

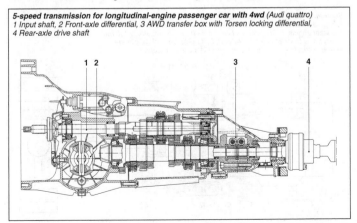

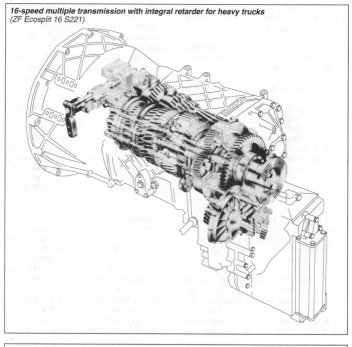

16-speed multiple transmission with integral retarder for heavy trucks
(ZF Ecosplit 16 S221)

Semi-automatic transmission *(schematic)*
1 Engine electronics (EDC), 2 Transmission electronics, 3 Transmission actuator,
4 D iesel engine, 5 Dry-plate friction clutch, 6 Clutch actuator, 7 Intarder control unit,
8 Display, 9 Gear selector, 10 ABS/TCS, 11 Gearbox, 12 Air cylinder.
——— Electrical, – – – – Pneumatic, ——— CAN communication

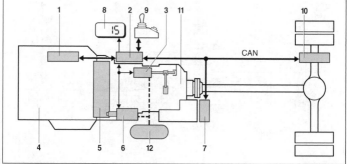

CAN

pact dimensions, low weight and fluid shared with the transmission in a single circuit. Primary retarders have specific advantages when braking at low speeds and are therefore widely used on public transport busses. Secondary retarders have particular advantages on long-distance trucks for adjustment braking at higher speeds or when traveling downhill.

Automatic transmissions

There are two types of automatic transmission (or gearbox) which are distinguished according to their effect on vehicle handling dynamics:
- <u>Semi-automatic transmissions</u> are manual gearboxes on which all operations normally performed by the driver when changing gear are carried out by electronically controlled actuator systems. In terms of vehicle dynamics, this means that a gear change always involves disengagement of a clutch and therefore of the drive to the driving wheels.
- <u>Fully automatic transmissions</u>, usually referred to simply as automatic transmissions, change gear under load, i.e. the power continues to be transmitted to the driving wheels during a gear-shift operation.

That difference in vehicle handling dynamics is the essential factor which determines the types of application for these two transmission types. Fully automatic transmissions are used in situations where disengagement of the power transmission would be associated with a significant reduction in comfort (above all on cars with powerful acceleration), or where it is unacceptable for reasons of handling dynamics (above all on off-road vehicles). Semi-automatic transmissions are found on long-distance haulage trucks, passenger coaches and more recently also on small cars, racing cars and fast production sports cars.

Semi-automatic transmissions

Partially or fully automated gear-shifting systems contribute substantially to simplifying control of the gears and increasing

economy. Particularly when used on trucks, the disadvantages inherent in the interruption of power transmission are compensated for by a number of decisive advantages:
- narrower spacing of ratios, with up to 16 gears,
- enhanced-efficiency power transfer,
- reduced costs,
- same basic transmission unit for manual and semi-automatic designs.

Operation
A positioner module on the transmission converts the electrical signals into hydraulic or pneumatic signals and controls the actuator cylinders for the gear-shift operation. The electrical control signals are generated by an intermediate ECU.

Design variations
On the simplest systems, the mechanical gear-shift linkage is simply replaced by a remote control system. The gear-shift lever then merely sends out electrical signals. Drive-engagement and clutch-operation procedures are as with a standard manually-shifted transmission. More complex versions combine these systems with a recommended shift-point function. Advantages are:
- reduced shifting effort,
- simplified installation (no shift linkage),
- prevention of incorrect operation (over-revving of engine).

On fully automated gear-shifting systems both the transmission and the drive-engagement mechanism are automated. The driver's control device consists of either a lever or pushbuttons, with an override provision in the shape of a driver-selected manual mode or +/− buttons.

Complex shift programs are required to control a multi-ratio transmission. A system which engages the gears according to a fixed pattern will not be adequate. Current running resistance (as determined by load and road conditions) must be factored in to achieve the optimal balance between driveability and fuel economy. This task is performed by a microcomputer control system along with control of synchromesh for gear changing. To that end the engine speed is adjusted by the electronic throttle-control system (ETC or EGAS) to the speed called for by the transmission control system via the data communication bus. As a result, mechanical synchromesh systems can be partly or entirely dispensed with in the gearbox.

Advantages are:

- optimum operating economy through automatic, computer-controlled shifting,
- reduced driver workload,
- lower weight and smaller dimensions,
- enhanced safety for both driver and vehicle.

Fully automatic transmissions

Fully automatic transmissions perform the drive-engagement and ratio selection (shifting) operations with no additional driver input. The power take-up unit is always a hydrodynamic torque converter which almost always has a converter lockup clutch on cars and generally does on commercial vehicles. The power-transmission efficiency of such automatic transmissions is inherently slightly lower than that of manual and semi-automatic transmissions. However, in many applications this is compensated for by shift programs designed to keep engine operation inside the maximum economy range.

The components are:

- hydrodynamic torque converter (always employed with passenger-car transmissions, while commercial vehicles generally use the Trilok design); for starting off, for torque multiplication and for absorption of harmonic vibrations.
- a number of planetary-gear sets downstream from the hydrodynamic torque converter. Number and arrangement according to number of gears and ratios.
- hydraulically-actuated multiplate clutches, plate or band brakes. Assigned to the individual elements within the planetary-gear sets to execute shifts without interrupting the flow of power.
- one-way clutches together with shift elements for optimal activation under load.
- a transmission-control system to define gear selections and shift points and to regulate demand-response shifting, as dictated by the driver-selected shift program (selector lever), accelerator

pedal, engine operating conditions and vehicle speed. The transmission control system is an electronic-hydraulic system.

- an engine-driven hydraulic-fluid pump (occasionally supplemented by a second fluid pump at the output end) provides hydraulic pressure for valve body and shift elements as well as supplying fluid to the hydrodynamic torque converter. It also supports lubrication and cooling in the transmission.

Design variations

Present-day automatic car transmissions have 4 or 5 gears while future designs will feature 6 speeds. The mechanical conversion range lies between 3.5 (4-speed transmission) and 5.0 (5-speed unit). Figures for driveoff conversion extend from 1.7 to 2.5.

Automatic transmissions in commercial vehicles can have between 3 and 6 forward gears. The mechanical conversion range extends from 2 to 8. These transmissions frequently have integral hydrodynamic retarders, as the requisite peripheral systems (fluid pump, large fluid pan, fluid cooler) are already in place.

Electronic transmission control

Automatic gearboxes are nowadays almost exclusively controlled by electronically operated hydraulic systems. Hydraulic actuation is retained for the clutches, while the electronics assume responsibility for gear selection and for adapting the pressures in accordance with the torque flow. The advantages are:

- a number of gear-shift programs,
- smoother gear shifting,
- adaptability to different types of vehicle,
- simpler hydraulic control, and
- ability to dispense with one-way clutches.

Sensors detect the transmission output-shaft speed, the engine load and speed, the selector-lever position and the positions of the program selector and the kickdown switch. The control signal

5-speed passenger-car automatic gearbox (ZF 5 HP24)
1 Input shaft, 2 Controlled-slip converter lock up clutch (GWK), 3 Hydrodynamic torque converter, 4 5-speed planetary gears with three multiplate brakes, three multiplate clutches and one one-way clutch, 5 Electronic-hydraulic transmission-shift control, 6 Output shaft

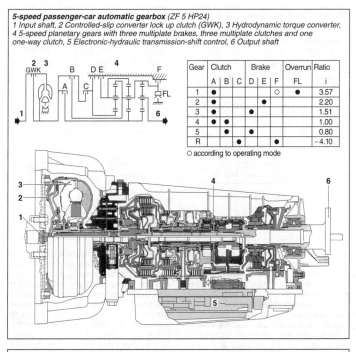

Gear	Clutch			Brake			Overrun	Ratio
	A	B	C	D	E	F	FL	i
1	●					○	●	3.57
2	●				●			2.20
3	●			●				1.51
4	●	●						1.00
5		●		●				0.80
R			●			●		– 4.10

○ according to operating mode

Automatic transmission with integral primary retarder for busses, trucks and special vehicles
(ZF Ecomat 5HP 500).
1 Hydrodynamic torque converter with lockup clutch,
2 Hydrodynamic retarders,
3 5-speed planetary gears,
4 Oil pump,
5 Transmission-shift control.

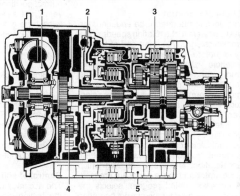

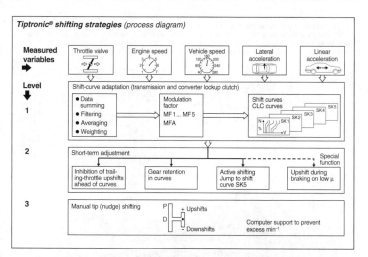

Tiptronic® shifting strategies (process diagram)

processes this information according to a predefined program and uses the results in determining the control variables to be transmitted to the gearbox. Electrohydraulic converter elements form the link between the electronic and hydraulic circuits, while standard solenoid valves activate and disengage the clutches. Analog or digital pressure regulators ensure precise control of pressure levels at the friction surfaces. A typical system includes:

Shift-point control

In selecting the gear to be engaged, the system refers to the rotating speeds of the transmission output shaft and of the engine before triggering the appropriate solenoid valves. The driver may select from among different shift programs (e. g., for maximum fuel economy or for maximum performance). In addition, the selector lever allows manual input from the driver.

"Intelligent" shift programs improve driveability by supplementing the standard transmission-control data with additional parameters such as forward and lateral acceleration, and the speed with which accelerator and brake pedal are pressed. A complex control program selects the appropriate gear for the current operating conditions and driving style using such expedients as suppressing trailing-throttle upshifts on the approach to and during corners, or automatically responding to slow throttle openings by activating a shift program for low- min^{-1} upshifts. Concepts which combine the high level of convenience of such "intelligent" gear-shift programs with facilities for active adaptation to individual driver preferences have become very widespread. In addition to the normal positions for neutral, drive and reverse, the selector levers for such systems have a second parallel channel in which one touch of the lever produces an immediate gear change (provided no engine-speed limits would be exceeded).

Converter lockup

A mechanical lockup clutch can be employed to improve the efficiency of the transmission unit by eliminating torque-converter slip. The variables employed to determine when conditions are suitable for activation of the converter lockup mechanism are engine load and transmission output-shaft min^{-1}.

Control of shift quality

The accuracy with which the pressure at the friction elements is adjusted to the level of torque being transmitted (determined with reference to engine load and min⁻¹) has a decisive influence on shift quality; this pressure is regulated by a pressure regulator. Shifting comfort can be further enhanced by briefly reducing engine output for the duration of the shift (e.g., by retarding the ignition timing); this also reduces friction loss at the clutches and extends component service life.

Safety circuits

Special monitoring circuits prevent transmission damage stemming from operator error, while the system responds to malfunctions in the electrical system by reverting to a backup mode.

Final-control elements

Electrohydraulic converter elements such as solenoid valves and pressure regulators form the link between the electronic and hydraulic circuits.

Continuously-variable transmissions

The continuously-variable transmission (CVT) can convert every point on the engine's operating curve to an operating curve of its own, and every engine operating curve into an operating range within the field of potential driving conditions. Its advantage over conventional fixed-ratio transmissions lies in the potential for enhancing performance and fuel economy while reducing exhaust emissions (e.g., by maintaining the engine in the performance range for maximum fuel economy).

The continuously variable transmission (CVT) can operate mechanically (belt or friction-roller), hydraulically or electrically. The highest level of development has been achieved with mechanical continuously variable units employing steel belts (as installed in low-output series-production cars), where the unit's offset axes make it ideal for installation in front-wheel drive cars with transverse-mounted engines. The conversion range is 5.5...6. The major elements in the continuously variable mechanical belt transmissions for passenger cars are:

– engagement mechanism for starting off (wet multiplate clutch, hydrodynamic torque converter or magnetic-particle coupling),
– primary and secondary disks with axially adjustable taper-disk sections and power transfer via steel bands (CVT)
– electronic/hydraulic transmission control,

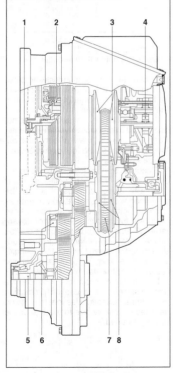

Continuously variable passenger-car transmission (ZF VT1)
1 Input shaft,
2 Reversing-wheel set with power take-up components,
3 Axial-shift cones (input side),
4 Oil pump,
5 Final drive unit with differential,
6 Intermediate shaft,
7 Linked steel belt,
8 Axial-shift cones (output side).

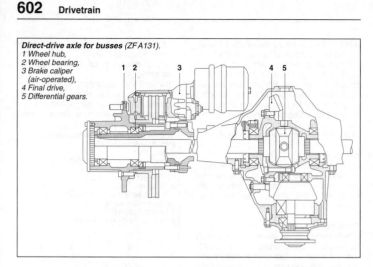

Direct-drive axle for busses (ZF A131).
1 Wheel hub,
2 Wheel bearing,
3 Brake caliper
  (air-operated),
4 Final drive,
5 Differential gears.

– reversing mode, and
– final drive unit with differential.

We can expect continuously variable transmissions (CVTs) using steel belts to be fitted on more powerful cars as well in the foreseeable future.

Friction-roller transmissions have not been used in production vehicles to date. Form the point of view of configuration, they are better suited to rear-wheel-drive vehicles.

Electrical transmissions are used on some public transport vehicles. Apart from with diesel engines, they can be combined with alternative power sources such as batteries, overhead power lines or, in the future, fuel cells. Other advantages of electrical bus transmissions on busses are non-integrated (distributed) design of the overall power train, single-wheel drive and, in particular, simpler realisation of low-floor vehicle designs.

Hydrostatic-mechanical indirect-drive transmissions are in use on production agricultural tractors. Use on road-going vehicles is unlikely due to the high noise levels produced.

Final-drive units

The overall conversion ratio between engine and drive wheels is produced by several elements operating in conjunction: a transmission with several fixed ratios (automatic or manual), an intermediate transmission in some applications (AWD transfer case) and the final-drive unit.

Longer distances between transmission and final drive are bridged by the drive shaft (in one piece or in several sections with intermediate bearings). Angular offsets resulting from non-aligned connecting drive shafts are compensated for by means of universal joints, constant-velocity joints and flexible-disk joints.

The central component of a car final drive is either a hypoid bevel-gear crownwheel and pinion (in-line engine) or a spur-gear crownwheel and pinion (transverse engine) while the layout of the components may take the form of a separate differential (on rear-wheel-drive and four-wheel-drive vehicles) or an integral gearbox and differential (on front-wheel-drive vehicles).

The chief components of a final drive differential are the crown wheel and pinion, the planetary gears, bearings, drive shaft and halfshaft flanges and differential housing. The final-drive transmission ratio is usually between 2.6 and 4.5 to 1.

The crown wheel is normally bolted to the differential case which holds the planetary gears, and the pinion shaft and differential case run in taper roller bearings. To reduce the transmission of structure-borne noise to the bodyshell, the final drive unit is attached to the vehicle frame by flexible (rubber) mountings.

In addition to its torque transmission capabilities, mechanical efficiency and weight, the noise-producing characteristics of a final drive unit have become a decisive criterion in modern automobile development. In this regard, the crown wheel and pinion are of primary significance in terms of noise generation. The quietness of the mechanism is essentially dependent on the way in which the gears are manufactured. A distinction is made between conventional manufacturing methods and grinding of the teeth whereby the imperfections produced by heat treatment (case hardening) are eliminated by appropriate grinding so that in contrast with conventional methods (e.g.

lapping) precise (i.e. maximum possible correspondence between calculated tooth-profile topography and actual geometry produced on the machine) and reproducible tooth-profile topographies are produced.

On commercial vehicles, direct-drive axles with hypoid bevel gears are most commonly used. The final-drive transmission ratio ranges between 3 and 6 to 1. In cases where smooth-running characteristics are particularly important, e.g. on busses, the gears are ground.

On public transport busses, which nowadays are almost always low-floor designs, portal (hub reduction) axles are used as they allow very low floor levels. In addition to the helical bevel-gear differential there is also an indirect-drive spur-gear reducer stage. This indirect-drive arrangement allows the required high torque levels to be transmitted with the limited reducer offset.

If there are special ground clearance requirements (e.g. construction-site vehi-

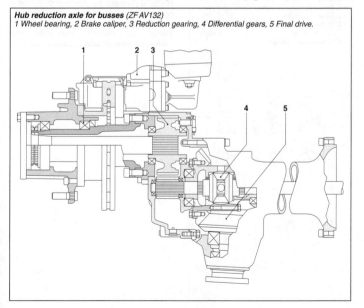

Hub reduction axle for busses (ZF AV 132)
1 Wheel bearing, 2 Brake caliper, 3 Reduction gearing, 4 Differential gears, 5 Final drive.

cles), planetary axles are used. Propeller shaft and halfshafts can be made smaller by splitting the power transmission, and the available space is increased.

Differential

The differential unit compensates for discrepancies in the respective rotation rates of the drive wheels: between inside and outside wheels during cornering, and between different drive axles on AWD vehicles.

Apart from a few special cases, bevel gears are the preferred design for differentials. The differential gears act as a balance arm to equalize the distribution of torque to the left and right wheels. When lateral variations in the road surface produce different coefficients of friction at the respective wheels ("μ-split"), this balance effect limits the effective drive torque to a level defined as twice the tractive force available at the wheel (tire) with the lower coefficient of friction. If torque then exceeds frictional resistance, that wheel will spin.

This undesirable effect can be eliminated by locking the differential either by a positively interlocking or friction mechanism. Positively interlocking differential locks are switched-in by the driver. Their disadvantage lies in the stress applied to the drivetrain which occurs during cornering. Friction-type differential locks operate automatically using friction plates, cones or a combination of worm and spur-gear drives and thus have a variable locking action depending on torque. The friction-type locking action can also be achieved with a viscous coupling and is then dependent on the differential speed.

The importance of self-locking differentials is declining. They are increasingly being displaced by electronic systems which slow down a spinning wheel by applying the brake and thereby transfer power transmission to the wheel with more grip (e.g. Traction Control System (TCS)).

Passenger-car rear-axle final-drive unit (ZF HAG 210)
1 Housing (two-piece),
2 Halfshaft flange,
3 Differential-case bearings,
4 Differential gears,
5 Crownwheel and pinion,
6 Pinion bearing,
7 Propeller-shaft flange.

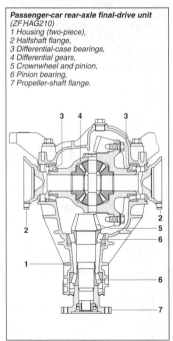

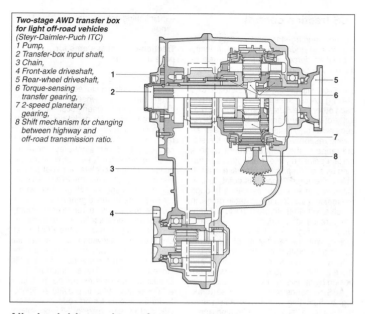

***Two-stage AWD transfer box
for light off-road vehicles***
(Steyr-Daimler-Puch ITC)
1 Pump,
2 Transfer-box input shaft,
3 Chain,
4 Front-axle driveshaft,
5 Rear-wheel driveshaft,
*6 Torque-sensing
transfer gearing,*
*7 2-speed planetary
gearing,*
*8 Shift mechanism for changing
between highway and
off-road transmission ratio.*

All-wheel drive and transfer case

All-wheel drive (AWD) improves traction on cars, off-road vehicles and commercial vehicles on wet and slippery road surfaces and rough terrain. The following types of system are available:
– Disengageable all-wheel drive with either direct transmission to front and rear axles, or with transfer box. The transfer box and final-drive differentials can also have a disengageable lock. Transfer cases for off-road vehicles incorporate an additional driver-controlled conversion range for steep gradients and low speeds.
– Permanent all-wheel drive whereby all wheels are driven at all times. Central transfer box, either non-locking or with friction-type torque-dependent locking mechanism, Torsen lock or viscous coupling. Torque distribution between front and rear axles 50:50 or asymmet-

rical. Additional crawler-gear ratios are also possible.

Designs with viscous coupling or electronically controlled multiplate clutch instead of the central all-wheel-drive transfer box also come under the umbrella of permanent all-wheel drive.

On more recent vehicles, additional locks on the AWD transfer box or axle differentials are increasingly being dispensed with in favor of intelligently controlled operation of the brakes.

TCS traction control

During standing-start and moving acceleration and under braking, the efficiency with which forces can be transferred to the road depends upon the traction available between tires and road surface. The adhesion/ slip curves for acceleration and braking display the same basic pattern as each other (see illustration). The vast majority of acceleration and braking operations entail only limited amounts of slip, allowing response to remain within the stable range in the diagram where up to a certain point any rise in slip is accompanied by a corresponding increase in available adhesion. Beyond this point, further increases in slip take the cuves through the maxima and into the instable range, in which any further increase in slip will generally result in a reduction of adhesion. Under braking, this will result in the wheel locking within a few tenths of a second. Under acceleration, one or both of the driving wheels will start to spin more and more as the drive torque exceeds the adhesion by an ever increasing amount.

ABS responds to the first case (braking) by inhibiting wheel lock. ASR reacts to the second scenario by holding acceleration slip within acceptable levels to prevent wheel spin. The system actually performs two functions:
– enhancing traction

– maintaining vehicle stability (true tracking).

Traction-control systems for passenger cars

ABS/TCS 2I (Bosch)

To provide optimal closed-loop control of torque at the drive wheels, the mechanical connection between accelerator pedal and throttle valve (or pedal and injection-pump control lever on diesel engines) is replaced by the ETC electronic throttle control (EGAS or electronic "drive-by-wire" accelerator). A sensor converts the position of the accelerator pedal into an electrical signal, which the ECU then uses to generate a control voltage. A servomotor responds to this signal by repositioning the throttle valve (or injection-pump control lever on diesels); it then transmits a position report back to the ECU. Brief, simultaneous activation of the service brakes is employed to supplement the ETC (improved tractive performance via limited-slip effect). The standard ABS hydraulic modulator is expanded to include a TCS section, both to provide additional hydraulic energy for brake-force application and for switching to TCS operation. The ABS solenoid valves in the hydraulic modulator switch between three positions – "pressure buildup", "maintain pressure" and "discharge" – to regulate the flow of

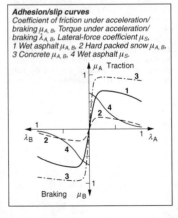

Adhesion/slip curves
Coefficient of friction under acceleration/ braking $\mu_{A, B}$, Torque under acceleration/ braking $\lambda_{A, B}$, Lateral-force coefficient μ_S.
1 Wet asphalt $\mu_{A, B}$, 2 Hard packed snow $\mu_{A, B}$, 3 Concrete $\mu_{A, B}$, 4 Wet asphalt μ_S.

μ_A Traction

λ_B λ_A

Braking μ_B

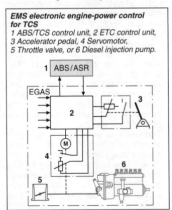

EMS electronic engine-power control for TCS
1 ABS/TCS control unit, 2 ETC control unit, 3 Accelerator pedal, 4 Servomotor, 5 Throttle valve, or 6 Diesel injection pump.

1 ABS/ASR

EGAS

ABS/TCS schematic diagram for cars

1 ABS/TCS control unit, 2 Motronic ECU, 3 ETC control unit, 4 Engine, clutch, transmission, 5 Differential, 6 TCS pressure source, 7 ABS hydraulic modulator, 8 Brake master cylinder with brake booster, 9 Wheel brakes, 10 Wheel 1, 11 Wheel 2, 12 Wheel-speed sensor, 13 Road surface, 14 Road surface, 15 Vehicle mass m_F, p Brake pressure, υ Wheel speed, υ_F Vehicle speed, λ Slip, θ_R Wheel inertia, M_A Drive force, M_B Braking force, M_R Total forces acting on drive wheel, M_S Surface forces. Indices 1, 2: Wheel 1, 2.

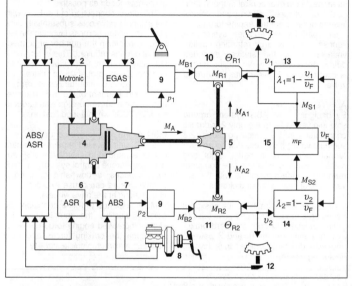

ABS/TCS system components for cars

1 Speed sensor, 2 ABS/TCS hydraulic modulator, 3 ABS/TCS control unit, 4 ETC control unit, 5 Throttle (gasoline engine)/Diesel fuel-injection pump control lever.

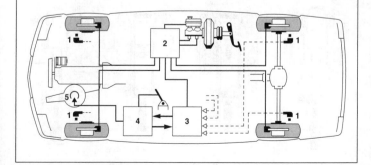

system pressure and furnish the pressure modulation required for rapid and precise control of braking force at the drive wheels.

The ETC control unit, which is connected to the ABS/TCS control unit via an interface, takes over control of the throttle or the diesel fuel-injection pump control lever in order to control engine torque.

On spark-ignition engines, system response is improved by retarding ignition timing to reduce the relatively extended delays encountered when engine torque is controlled exclusively with the throttle valve.

ABS/TCS5 (Bosch)
By designing this ABS system around solenoid valves featuring only 2 hydraulic connections and 2 switch positions (2/2 solenoid valve) it was possible to achieve further reductions in both weight and costs – while combining the complete range of standard functions with the advantages of sealed braking circuits.

Because the hydraulic unit's design is based on a modular concept, it is easy to adapt for use with both standard brake-system configurations (II and X pattern) and with different vehicle drive layouts (including all-wheel drive).

The design of the 2/2 solenoid valves allows the sealed hydraulic valve section to be inserted into its energizer coil. This considerably simplifies the design of an add-on ECU for the hydraulic modulator, and separate testing of the two components now becomes possible.

This direct connection of the ECU with the solenoid valve coils substantially simplifies the wiring-harness layout in the vehicle by reducing the number of connectors and leads required. This in turn considerably reduces susceptibility to faults and thereby the probability of failure.

The engine-control functions remain largely independent of the hydraulic system, and the current design was adopted for ABS/TCS5 without modification.

MSR engine drag-torque control
The TCS unit installed in passenger cars can be expanded to include the MSR engine drag-torque control system. On slick road surfaces, a downshift or sudden throttle closure can cause excessive engine braking at the drive wheels.

MSR responds to these conditions by gently adjusting the throttle-valve for slightly increased engine torque in order to reduce the braking forces and help maintain maximum vehicle stability.

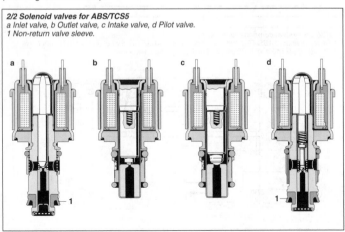

2/2 Solenoid valves for ABS/TCS5
a Inlet valve, b Outlet valve, c Intake valve, d Pilot valve.
1 Non-return valve sleeve.

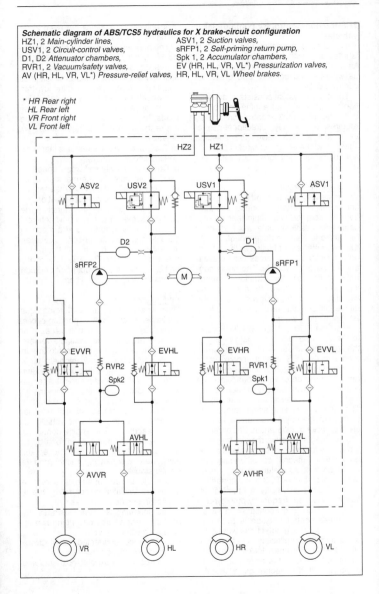

Schematic diagram of ABS/TCS5 hydraulics for X brake-circuit configuration
HZ1, 2 *Main-cylinder lines,*
USV1, 2 *Circuit-control valves,*
D1, D2 *Attenuator chambers,*
RVR1, 2 *Vacuum/safety valves,*
AV (HR, HL, VR, VL*) *Pressure-relief,*
ASV1, 2 *Suction valves,*
sRFP1, 2 *Self-priming return pump,*
Spk 1, 2 *Accumulator chambers,*
EV (HR, HL, VR, VL*) *Pressurization valves,*
HR, HL, VR, VL *Wheel brakes.*

* HR Rear right
  HL Rear left
  VR Front right
  VL Front left

TCS traction-control for commercial vehicles

This closed-loop traction-control system is integrated within the ABS control unit for shared use of ABS components such as wheel-speed sensors and pressure-control valves.

The control system consists of a brake-control circuit and an engine-control circuit. The TCS brake-control circuit also requires a two-way directional-control valve and a TCS valve (2/2 solenoid valve), and the engine-control circuit a final control element for reducing the engine torque.

Brake-control circuit

When the vehicle moves off on a low-traction or μ-split (left/right variations in traction) surface, the wheelspin that accompanies excessive throttle will frequently be limited to a single drive wheel. Due to the low coefficient of friction at this wheel, only minimal tractive forces will be available to move the vehicle. The brake controller responds to this situation by applying braking pressure to the spinning wheel; this force is conveyed through the differential and acts as drive torque at the (still) stationary wheel.

First, the ECU switches the TCS valve to the open position for initial braking at the spinning wheel. The control circuit then uses the ABS pressure-control valve to control the pressure at the wheel cylinder as a function of wheel behavior. The brake pressure is controlled in such a way that the driving wheels are synchronized. The result is a locking effect comparable to that provided by a mechanical limited-slip or locking differential. In order to achieve the same forward drive, however, the engine torque must be greater than required with a mechanical differential lock by an amount equivalent to the braking force applied by the TCS brake controller.

This is one reason why mechanical differential locks are frequently employed in difficult terrain (e. g., construction sites). The brake control function is then employed under those conditions where the driver might have difficulty in determining whether the differential lock is providing increased traction. It is often possible to dispense with the mechanical differential lock entirely on vehicles not used in demanding off-road conditions.

The benefits of the brake controller are generally felt when starting off, when accelerating, or in alpine conditions on "μ-split" surfaces. The control circuit must supply high braking forces to the low-traction wheel when a fully-loaded vehicle operates on extreme μ-split on mountain roads. To prevent excessive thermal loading of the brakes, TCS incorporates two default modes:

a) The brake controller remains inactive at speeds above 30 km/h,

b) Controller activity and wheel speed are used to estimate the thermal load at the brakes; if a defined limit is exceeded, the controller responds with deactivation.

Using the brake-control function described above, the driving wheels can also be synchronized so that a mechanical differential lock, if present, can be automatically engaged, e. g. with the aid of a pneumatic cylinder. The ABS/TCS control unit calculates the correct point and conditions for releasing the differential lock.

Engine-control circuit

Drive wheels on surfaces affording equal but limited traction will respond to excess throttle by spinning on both sides. The residual tractive force available for propelling the vehicle then shifts into the unstable section of the adhesion/slip curve with its diminishing adhesion coefficients (see Fig. "Adhesion/slip curve") Attempts to accelerate a stationary or crawling vehicle on ice or snow "polish" the surface, resulting in a further, substantial reduction of traction. At the same time vehicle stability is sacrificed. The engine-control circuit responds to these conditions by reducing the drive slip to an acceptable level, thereby enhancing traction and vehicular stability.

Both electric and pneumatic servo elements are available for controlling the reduction in engine torque.

The following section illustrates the principles involved by describing two options for electric control:

– an interface connected to electronic engine-control devices,

– direct control of an electrical servomotor.

Traction control system (TCS) for commercial vehicles with electronic injection-pump control (EDC)
1 Wheel-speed sensor, 2 Pulse ring, 3 ABS/TCS control unit, 4 Pressure control valve (single circuit), 5 2/2 Solenoid valve, 6 Two-way valve, 7 Service-brake valve, 8 Brake-pressure regulator, 9 Wheel cylinders, 10 EDC control unit, 11 Accelerator pedal, 12 Pedal-position sensor, 13 Injection pump.

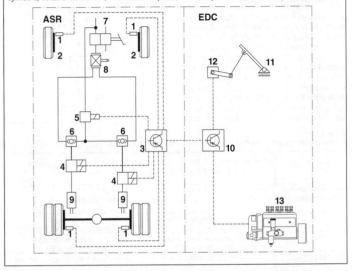

<u>Interface</u> (refer to CAN on page 884): The ABS/TCS control unit receives the signals reflecting driver commands from one of the engine-management ECUs (e.g., accelerator-pedal position or desired fuel-injection quantity). The ABS/TCS control unit consults both this signal and various other data such as wheel slip in calculating the torque reduction requirement to be implemented by the engine-management ECU. Examples of engine-management ECUs are the ETC (Engine Throttle Control) and EDC (Electronic Diesel Control) units. They incorporate all engine management functions (e.g. vehicle-speed control, engine-speed limiting, idle-speed control, etc.) and immediately carry out the TCS request to reduce engine speed with the required degree of accuracy.

<u>Servomotor</u> the ABS/TCS control unit operates the servomotor directly. The servo-

motor is a DC device with integral position feedback for precise position control; regulation thus remains unaffected by variables such as positioning forces at the injection pump and friction in the throttle linkage. The TCS can only use the linkage to reduce throttle, thereby excluding the possibility of inadvertent opening of the throttle. A vehicle-speed limiter (FGB) integrated in the ECU either holds the vehicle's road speed at a statutory speed limit (v_{max} control) or at a speed set by the driver by means of a button (v_{set} control). Here, the driver must depress the accelerator beyond the position which would otherwise correspond to the desired v_{max} or v_{set} velocity. The ABS/TCS control unit compensates for the excess throttle. These FGB limiters have been mandatory equipment on buses (AGVW > 10 metric tons) and trucks (AGVW > 12 tons) since 1 January, 1994.

Suspension

Types of oscillation

Suspension springing and damping operate chiefly on the vertical oscillations of the vehicle. Driving comfort (oscillatory loads on passengers and cargo) and operating safety (distribution of forces against the road surface as wheel-load factors fluctuate) are determined by the suspension. Several spring-damper systems will serve to illustrate the synergetic operation of the vehicle components. Driving comfort is largely determined by

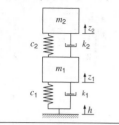

Dual-mass model as quarter-vehicle model
h Excitation amplitude, z Oscillation amplitude, c Spring resistance, k Damping constants, m Mass. Subscripts: 1 Tires and axle, 2 Body.

Table 1.
Effects of design parameters on the vehicle's vertical oscillations

Design variable	Effect at body natural frequency	Effect in intermediate frequency range	Effect at suspension natural frequency
Body specifications <u>Spring constant</u>	Large on ride comfort	Medium on ride comfort	Small on handling safety
harder	Frequency and amplitude increase, comfort decreases		Frequency increases, amplitude decreases slightly
softer	Frequency and maximum amplitude decrease, comfort increases		Amplitude increases slightly at low excitation frequencies
<u>Damper constant</u>	Major on ride comfort Optimization required		Major on wheel-load fluctuation
higher (damper harder)	Acceleration decreases	Acceleration increases	Acceleration increases, dynamic wheel-load fluctuation decreases
lower (damper softer)	Acceleration increases	Acceleration decreases	Amplitude decreases slightly, dynamic wheel-load fluctuation increases
Mass	Minor on amplification factor or wheel-load fluctuation; as payload increases, the acceleration amplification factor decreases (ride comfort is worse and relative wheel-load fluctuation higher with vehicle empty than with vehicle fully loaded)		
Wheel and tyre specifications <u>Suspension</u> (with tires getting softer)	Natural frequency and amplitude change hardly at all		Natural frequency and amplitude of body acceleration and wheel-load fluctuation decrease roughly in proportion to the reduction in vertical tire rigidity
<u>Damping</u>	Frequency and amplitude do not change with change in tire damping Due to heat generation, tire damping should be held to a minimum in order to allow long spring travel for soft tires		Amplitude with body acceleration and wheel-load fluctuation decreases minimally with harder damping
<u>Wheel mass</u>	Reducing wheel mass hardly affects ride comfort		Small wheel mass increases handling safety

the degree of body oscillation. Root mean square of vertical body acceleration:

$$\overrightarrow{\ddot{z}_2} / \overrightarrow{h}$$

Axle oscillations (and thus, indirectly, fluctuations in wheel load) are the salient factor in determining driving safety. Root mean square of vertical axle oscillations:

$$\overrightarrow{\ddot{z}_1} / \overrightarrow{h}$$

Both types of motion are characterized by specific frequency relationships in the form of amplitude ratios.

Table 1 enumerates the relative effects of parameter variations in a dual-mass model (also applicable to actual vehicles).

Body-mounted springs and dampers also affect pitch and roll of the vehicle body as well as its vertical vibration characteristics.

Pitch: Gyration around the vehicle's transverse axis, such as that encountered under acceleration from rest (front-suspension expansion and rear-suspension compression). Pitching movements under acceleration or braking are reduced by the chosen suspension kinematics (suspension-link configuration).

Roll: Gyration around a longitudinal axis

which generally runs from the lower front to the upper rear of the vehicle; roll motion occurs in response to steering inputs (suspension compresses at the outside and expands on the inside of the curve). Stabilizers (anti-roll bars) at front and rear axles reduce this effect.

Suspension design elements
(See Table 2)

Controlled suspension systems

Level-control system

Partially loaded systems
The use of soft springs (comfort) results in long spring travel, such as that encountered with the vehicle loaded. In order to maintain vehicle-body height at an acceptable level, auxiliary <u>air springs</u> or <u>hydropneumatic springs</u> are employed.

The springing element is provided by the volume of the gas, while vehicle level is monitored mechanically directly at the suspension. Valves are used to control the input or output of the air or hydraulic fluid to/from the suspension element; the

---

Effect of frequency on kinematic amplitudes
z_1 Amplitude of axle acceleration, z_2 Amplitude of body acceleration, h Excitation amplitude. 1 Natural body frequency, 2 Natural axle frequency.

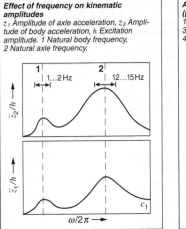

Air-suspension level-control system (partially loaded system)
1 Air connection, 2 Steel spring,
3 Auxiliary air-spring element,
4 Gas volume, 5 Shock absorber.

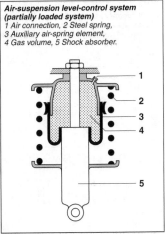

system can also incorporate intermediate electronic level-control units acting upon solenoid valves.

Advantages of the electronic system:
– Reduced energy consumption achieved by avoiding control cycles during braking, acceleration and in curves,
– System reacts to increased vehicle speed by reducing body ride height, resulting in fuel savings,
– Increase in vehicle-body ride height on poor road surfaces,
– Enhanced stability in curves achieved through lateral blocking of the suspension elements on a given axle.

Additional advantages for commercial vehicles:
– Automatic limitation of suspension travel in order to accomodate interchangeable bodies and containers,
– Vehicle-body height can be adjusted as desired, e.g., to align load floor with loading ramps,
– Control of lifting axles (ride height raised automatically when lifting axle is elevated), lowers automatically when approved drive-axle weight is exceeded, lift axle raised briefly (2...3 minutes) to increase weight on drive axle (drive-traction increase).

Hydropneumatic level-control system (partially loaded system)
1 Fluid supply, 2 Steel spring, 3 Accumulator, 4 Gas volume, 5 Rubber diaphragm, 6 Fluid, 7 Hose, 8 Shock absorber.

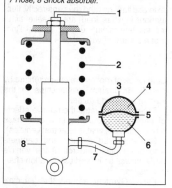

Fully loaded suspension systems

The cushioning effect is provided by the gas suspension element alone and coil springs are dispensed with. Either a single axle (generally the rear axle) or both axles of the vehicle can be controlled. If all

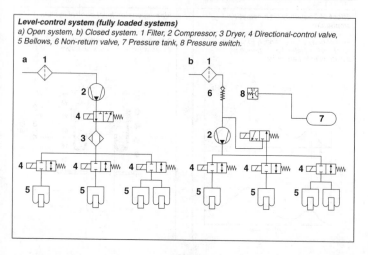

Level-control system (fully loaded systems)
a) Open system, b) Closed system. 1 Filter, 2 Compressor, 3 Dryer, 4 Directional-control valve, 5 Bellows, 6 Non-return valve, 7 Pressure tank, 8 Pressure switch.

axles are to be controlled, then the system must include an ECU with a specific control strategy which responds to factors such as fluctuations in axle load (to prevent the vehicle from tilting), while monitoring control times and recognizing system errors.

Open system:
Advantages: Relatively simple design and control.

Disadvantages: High compressor output required for brief periods of active control, air dryer required, noise during suction and blow-off.

Closed system:
Advantages: Low compressor output (minimal pressure differential between accumulator and suspension element), no problems with moisture.

Disadvantages: Relatively complicated design (accumulator, pressure switch, non-return valve).

Air-filled suspension elements weigh less than their hydropneumatic counterparts.

Active suspension

Active suspension controls both the "springing" and the "damping" functions. Various types of design concepts have been realized.

Designs incorporating hydraulic cylinder

A source of auxiliary power generates the energy needed for rapid adjustments using high-speed hydraulic cylinders, while sensors provide the link between the cylinders and the vehicle body. Sensors for wheel load, travel and acceleration transmit signals to an ECU featuring a control cycle of just a few milliseconds.

The control system achieves virtually constant wheel-load factors while maintaining a constant mean vehicle-body height. Steel springs or hydropneumatic suspension elements are employed to support the static wheel load.

Active suspension
a) Hydraulic cylinder,
b) Hydropneumatic suspension,
c) Air suspension.
1 Vehicle body, 2 Wheel-load sensor,
3 Travel sensor, 4 Accumulator, 5 Pumping circuit, 6 Servo valve, 7 Actuating cylinder, 8 Acceleration sensor, 9 Damper, 10 Valve, 11 Pressure tank, 12 Compressor, 13 Solenoid valve.

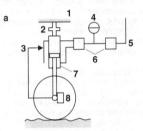

a

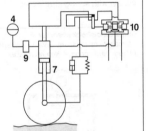

b

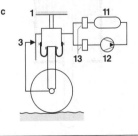

c

Designs incorporating hydropneu-matic suspension (fluid control)

Vehicle-body oscillations are compensated for by selective control of the hydraulic fluid in the hydropneumatic suspension circuit. The hydraulic fluid is either directed to the hydropneumatic element or discharged from the spring strut. In order to reduce energy requirements, the system's action is restricted to smoothing wide-spaced undulations; a gas accumulator installed adjacent to the spring strut is responsible for higher-frequency spring reaction.

The damping element can be set to concentrate on wheel movements.

Air-suspension designs

Controlled supply of compressed air to the air-spring bellows smoothes out the body vibrations. The sealed air-spring system only handles low-frequency vibrations and steering-related body roll.

Because the system compensates for transverse forces, it is also suitable for application with spring-strut axles.

Shock absorbers

Telescopic shock absorbers convert oscillations in body and suspension into heat. The resilient mountings used to attach them to body and axle also provide for noise insulation.

Single-tube shock absorbers

A sliding separating-piston and gas cushion form the gas-pressure damper in the single-tube shock absorber.

Advantages: Easy to tailor to specific applications, as the large piston diameter allows low working pressures. Sufficient room for valves and passages. Heat is dissipated directly via the outer tube. The shock absorber can be installed in any position.

Disadvantages: Length. The outer tube, which acts as a guide cylinder for the piston, is susceptible to damage from stone throw etc. Cannot be shortened in order to fit in positions where space is limited. The piston-rod seal is subjected to the damping pressure.

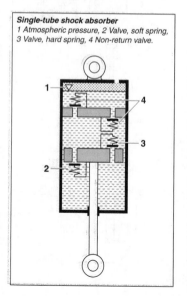

Single-tube shock absorber
1 Atmospheric pressure, 2 Valve, soft spring, 3 Valve, hard spring, 4 Non-return valve.

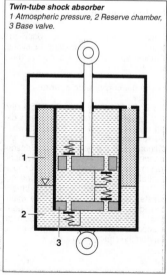

Twin-tube shock absorber
1 Atmospheric pressure, 2 Reserve chamber, 3 Base valve.

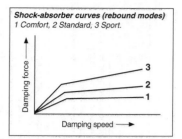

Twin-tube shock absorber

This type of damper is available either as the atmospheric or low-pressure twin-tube type.

Advantages: Insensitive to stone throw. Tube can be adapted to fit in locations where space is limited. This shock-absorber type is short, as the balance chamber is next to the working cylinder.

Disadvantages: These shock absorbers are sensitive to overloading (damping stops). Only certain specific installation positions are possible.

Damping characteristics

The damping characteristics are the result of the cumulative function of orifice damping and of the spring-loaded valve which closes the passage; the spring responds to pressure by increasing the free aperture of the outlet orifice. Piston bore and spring can be specifically tailored to provide linear to mildly degressive damping curves. An internal adjustment mechanism can be used to obtain several performance curves from a single shock absorber. The compression-stage values are frequently only 30...50 % of those for the rebound mode.

Electronically-controlled adjustable shock absorbers (active adaptation to operating conditions) can be used to enhance driving comfort and safety. Fixed damping parameters, on the other hand, result in defined relationships between comfort and safety.

The control law is frequently a semi-active "Skyhook" type, in which the shock absorber adjusts with reference to body speed.

Vibration absorber

The vibration absorber is a supplementary mass providing both springing and damping. The vibration absorber assimilates the oscillations of the main system, i.e., the main system ceases to oscillate – the motion is restricted to the vibration damper (see "Oscillations" P. 29).

Vibration dampers affect body vibrations, their effect on the suspension is minimal.

Shock-absorber curves (rebound modes)
1 Comfort, 2 Standard, 3 Sport.

Amplification function of axle acceleration
1 With absorber, 2 Without absorber.
a_1 Amplitude of z_1, h Excitation amplitude.

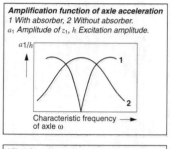

Vibration absorption
a) Installation on vehicle,
b) Mechanical equivalent system.
1 Spring and damper, 2 Damping mass,
3 Wheel mass, 4 Tire spring.

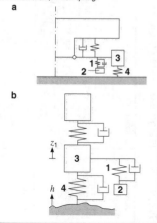

Suspension design elements (Table 2)

Suspension design elements	Diagram	Effect of vehicle load on natural frequency of body	Characteristics
Steel springs Leaf spring	Car leaf spring; Truck leaf spring with auxiliary spring		Single or multi-leaf. Is also used to determine wheel travel in some applications. Interleaf friction in some types, can be reduced with plastic inserts (noise possible). Generally without inserts in trucks, maintenance required. Good transfer of forces to chassis.
Coil spring	Barrel-shaped coil spring; Cylindrical coil spring	$\frac{v_{loaded}}{v_{empty}} = \sqrt{\frac{m_{empty}}{m_{loaded}}}$ Natural frequency decreases with increase of payload. Characteristics are generally linear.	Progressive characteristic achieved by change of pitch or conical coil. Shock absorber can be fitted inside spring. No self-damping. Spring noise possible. Advantages: Limited space requirement, low weight, maintenance-free. Disadvantages: special suspension links required.
Torsion bar			Made of round or flat-bar steel (round section is lighter). Vehicle height adjustment possible, depending on design. Wear and maintenance-free. Flat-steel bundle employed for additional flexural loads.
Air spring Roll-gaiter air spring	Element with constant gas volume. 1 Chassis frame, 2 Roll-gaiter air spring, 3 Piston, 4 Compressed air, 5 Mounting plate. Roll bellows; Toroid bellows	$\frac{v_{loaded}}{v_{empty}} = 1$ Natural frequency remains constant when vehicle loaded. Characteristics are dependent on gas properties, piston shape, direction of plies in the gaiter.	Used as suspension strut or spring particularly on commercial vehicles and busses. Increasingly widespread use in passenger cars for level control at rear axle and for suspension on all wheels. Achieves high vertical compliance (increased comfort). Wheel travel must be defined by separate suspension components. Low pressure (<10 bar) demands large volume. Low vertical spring rate not achievable due to geometry of toroid air bellows.
Toroid bellows			

Hydropneumatic suspension Hydraulic diaphragm accumulator Piston accumulator	Hydropneumatic spring element with constant gas mass. *1 Gas, 2 Oil, 3 Diaphragm, 4 Steel spring.* Hydraulic diaphragm accumulator Piston accumulator 	$\dfrac{v_{loaded}}{v_{empty}} = \sqrt{\dfrac{m_{loaded}}{m_{empty}}}$ Natural frequency increases with payload. Characteristics are progressive and dependent on initial charge pressure of reservoir.	The gas volume in a reservoir (separated from oil by a piston) determines its spring characteristics. The fluid compresses the gas according to wheel load. Damper valves are integrated in the shock absorber and the junction between suspension strut and reservoir. The rubber diaphragm requires maintenance due to gas diffusion.
Rubber springs		Natural frequency is affected by payload due to the non-linear spring characteristics.	Vulcanized rubber compression spring between metal components, increasingly with integral hydraulic damper. Used as engine/transmission mountings, suspension-arm mountings and auxiliary springs.
Stabilizer		No effect if both sides simultaneously moved in same direction. If one side moved up/down half of anti-roll bar rigidity effective, if two sides moved in opposing directions full rigidity of anti-roll bar effective.	Reduces body-roll tendency and influences vehicle cornering characteristics (over or understeer). Generally made of U-shaped bar or tube, sides frequently flattened to cope with flexural loads. Attachment points must be at extreme outside of axle to allow minimal stabilizer diameter. Suspension link fulcrums must be arranged relative to the anti-roll bar in such a way that it is subjected only to torsion and not bending.

Suspension linkage

The suspension layout employed to connect the individual wheels to the vehicle structure defines the suspension-linkage design. The linkage enables the wheel for the most part to move vertically in order to compensate for irregularities in the road surface. In addition, the front wheels are steered, together with the rear wheels in the case of rear-wheel-steered vehicles. The front and rear suspension linkage systems differ due to the special demands imposed by the steering mechanism. Appropriate design measures are taken for the suspension geometry and springing so as to limit vertical body travel while also reducing pitch and roll.

Suggested reading:
Wolfgang Matschinsky.
Radführungen der Straßenfahrzeuge.
("Suspension linkage for road vehicles").
2nd Edition; Springer-Verlag 1998.

Kinematics

The front wheels pivot around an inclined axis whose position is determined by the joints and the suspension components.

The following kinematic data are of essential importance for the wheel's response to steering input and the transfer of forces between tire and road surface:

Toe-in δ_{vs}

Toe-in is the angle between the vehicle's longitudinal axis and a plane through the center of the (steered-wheel) tire. It can also be defined as half the difference in the distance between the wheel's front and rear rim flange. Toe-in affects the straight-ahead running as well as the steering, and in the case of front-wheel-drive vehicles compensates for the resulting elastokinematic changes in track. For standard-drive vehicles the toe-in is approx. 5...20'. For FWD vehicles, the toe-out is up to −20' (to compensate for drive forces).

Deflection-force lever arm r_{st}

The deflection-force lever arm is the shortest distance between the wheel center and the inclination angle of the steering axis. On

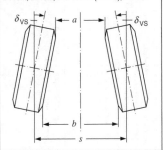

Toe-in
δ_{vs} Toe-in angle, Distance between wheels: a Front, b Rear, b–a Toe-in (in mm), s Track.

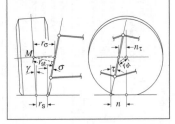

Wheel position
M Center of wheel, r_{st} Radius of deflection leverage, n_τ Caster offset, n Positive caster, τ Caster angle, r_σ Kingpin inclination offset, r_s Kingpin offset, γ Camber angle, σ Kingpin angle.

FWD vehicles, its length provides an index of the effect of the drive forces on the steering and therefore of the rolling-resistance forces.

Caster n

Positive caster is the distance between the wheel's contact point and the point at which the steering axis intersects the road as viewed from the side. Caster determines the degree of self-centering action in the steering as well as influencing straight-line stability and steering force in curves.

Caster angle τ

The caster angle is defined as the angle between the steering axis and the vertical plane as viewed from the side. In conjunction with the kingpin angle, it influences the camber change as a function of the steering angle, as well as the self-centering characteristics of the steering.

Kingpin offset r_s

The kingpin offset, or steering offset, is the distance between the point of contact between wheel and road surface, and the point at which the steering axis intersects the road surface. It is negative when the point of steering-axis intersection is between the center and the outside of the wheel. Kingpin offset combines with the effects of braking forces to generate steering motions and self-centering action at the steering wheel (driver information). Negative kingpin offset results in self-stabilizing steering angles.

Camber angle γ

Camber angle is the inclination of the wheel axis towards the road surface in the vertical plane. The camber angle is negative when the top of the wheel is inclined toward the center of the vehicle. It influences lateral control (today's vehicles generally employ moderate cambers of $-3...0°$ out of consideration for the tires).

Kingpin angle σ

The kingpin angle is the angle between the steering axis and the vehicle's longitudinal plane, as measured in the vehicle's transverse plane. It influences steering force (steering feel) along with caster angle and offset, and the steering roll radius.

Basic types

(see Tables on following pages).

Elastokinematics

The wheel's rack and camber are influenced by the kinematic properties of the suspension geometry and by the variations in kinematic properties attendant upon spring compression. The forces acting on the suspension (acceleration, deceleration, vertical and lateral forces, rolling resistance) also have an effect upon the wheel's dynamic position due to compliance in mountings and in the components themselves (kinematic response due to elastic deformation: elastokinematics). The usual objective is to aim at specific changes in wheel posi-

Wheel displacement by longitudinal force F_x due to system flexibility
F_1, F_2 Suspension-arm mounting forces, a Distance between wheel axes and suspension arm, b Suspension arm mounting separation, δ_{vs} Toe-in angle.

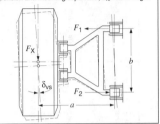

Positioning of suspension-arm mountings to counteract steering deflection due to flexibility
S_F Center of gravity (A Reduction, B Complete equalization), c_{ax}, c_{rad} Axial/radial spring constants, α Alignment angle.

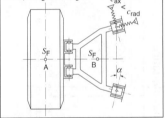

tion by employing kinematic and elastokinematic effects. To this end, kinematic and elastokinematic properties are designed into the axle which are calculated to provide a self-compensating response to force and spring action. Specially-aligned component mountings result in cardanic angles during springing. According to the design of the rubber mount they define the options for the compensation of elastokinematic effects.

Some modern rear suspensions employ elastokinematics to reduce reaction to changes in dynamic load. Differing longitudinal and vertical forces at the wheels allow the flexibly-mounted axle carrier or individual locating member to pivot, providing the wheels at the outside of the curve with more toe-in (stabilizing steering effect at the rear wheels).

Basic suspension types and their characteristics

Rigid axles

Leaf spring | A-arm / Trailing arm | Watt linkage / A-bracket | Panhard rod / A-bracket / Trailing arm | Panhard rod / Trailing arm

Used for rear axle with conventional (rear-wheel) drive; for front and rear axle on heavy and off-road vehicles

Track, toe-in, camber remain constant relative to road surface, even with body roll, good tracking

Low manufacturing costs, axle tramp, high unsprung masses, unfavorable deformation under lateral force and torsion	No lateral body movements during suspension travel, no unfavorable wheel displacement by transverse and longitudinal forces or torsion, large space requirements			
	Unrestricted choice of pitch fulcrum High cost and weight		Panhard rod causes lateral body movements when vehicle is driven	Unrestricted choice of pitch fulcrum

Semi-rigid axles

Torsion-beam axle | Torsion-beam trailing-arm axle | Trailing-arm torsion-beam axle

Employed for rear axle in conjunction with front-wheel drive

Large distance between mounts minimizes structural stresses, favorable force transfer at rigid longitudinal members, simple manufacture, two attachment points, simple assembly, extremely robust, limited kinematic possibilities

RA depends on position of Panhard rod above wheel centre	RA below center of wheel (depending on link position)	RA on road surface (all RAs aligned with vehicle center)	RA = Roll axis

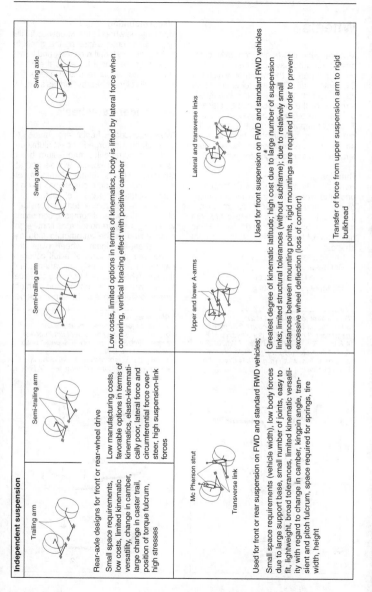

Independent suspension

Trailing arm	Semi-trailing arm	Semi-trailing arm	Semi-trailing arm	Swing axle	Swing axle

Rear-axle designs for front or rear-wheel drive

Small space requirements, low costs, limited kinematic versatility, change in camber, large change in caster trail, position of torque fulcrum, high stresses

Low manufacturing costs, favorable options in terms of kinematics, elasto-kinematically poor, lateral force and circumferential force over-steer, high suspension-link forces

Low costs, limited options in terms of kinematics, body is lifted by lateral force when cornering, vertical bracing effect with positive camber

Mc Pherson strut	Transverse link	Upper and lower A-arms	Lateral and transverse links

Used for front or rear suspension on FWD and standard RWD vehicles;

Used for front suspension on FWD and standard RWD vehicles

Small space requirements (vehicle width), low body forces due to large support base, small number of joints, easy to fit, lightweight, broad tolerances, limited kinematic versatility with regard to change in camber, kingpin angle, transient and pitch fulcrum, space required for springs, tire width, height

Greatest degree of kinematic latitude; high cost due to large number of suspension links; limited structural tolerances (without subframe); due to relatively small distances between mounting points, rigid mountings are required in order to prevent excessive wheel deflection (loss of comfort)

Transfer of force from upper suspension arm to rigid bulkhead

Wheels

Modern vehicle wheels generally comprise a rim and nave or wheel disc. The rim is that part of the wheel on which the tire is mounted. The nave joins the rim to the wheel hub. Wheel size is primarily determined by the wheel-brake diameter and by the load-bearing capacity of the tire. The most important terms are: rim width, rim diameter, center hole, hole circle diameter, number of mounting holes, countersunk and stud design, and rim offset.

Rim designs

Rims differ from one another (depending upon the type of tire) in terms of number of parts and cross-sectional rim shape. The most important rim details are: rim flange, rim bead seat and rim base. Rims have one of the following cross-sectional shapes:
- Drop center,
- Flat base,
- 5° tapered bead seat or
- 15° tapered bead seat.

Wheel mounting

Mounting the wheel to the wheel hub fulfills two requirements: Centering the wheel in order to ensure that it runs true, and transmission of the wheel forces to the wheel hub. Correct wheel mounting affects the service life of the wheel system as a whole.

Passenger-car wheels

Mass-produced wheels are made of sheet steel, with forged or cast aluminum and (less commonly) magnesium being used primarily for special wheels and aftermarket wheels. Sheet aluminum, although used in some cases, has not become popular for reasons of cost.

The wheels in particular feature considerable potential when it comes to complying with the general trend towards lightweight construction in the automobile industry. The sheet-aluminum wheel (with the wheel cap in the form of a full cover or painted in silver as a styling variant), and the split wheel derived from the classical forged wheel, are among the lightest wheel versions while at the same time be-

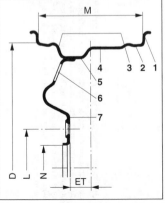

Disc wheel (e.g. 6J x 14 H 2)
1 Rim flange (e.g. "J" section), 2 5° tapered bead seat, 3 Hump (e.g. double hump H 2), 4 Rim, 5 Rim well, 6 Vent hole, 7 Wheel disc. D Rim diameter (e.g. 14"), L Hole circle diameter, M Rim width (e.g. 6"), N Center hole, ET Rim offset.

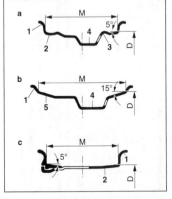

Rim designs
a) Passenger-car hump rim as per DIN 7817, b) Truck 15° sloping bead seat rim (tubeless) as per DIN 78022, c) Truck 5° tapered bead seat rim as per DIN 7820.
1 Flange, 2 5° tapered bead seat, 3 Hump, 4 Rim well, 5 15° tapered bead seat. M Rim width, D Diameter.

ing reasonably priced considering the weight savings involved.

Whereas the manufacturing process for the two-piece sheet-aluminum wheels and for the steel wheel are practically identical, a difference is made between two different versions of 1-piece split wheel:
1. An extruded section formed by a forging process. This is rolled and split at its circumference.
2. A circular blank stamped from the coil and deep-drawn.

There are further important lightweight-wheel versions on the market although these have still not become very widespread. They include the cast-aluminum wheel with pressure-rolled rim and the structured wheel which is designed primarily for maximum force transfer and less with regard to an attractive appearance. Since wheel covers in different materials, shapes and colors can be fitted, this provides a wide range of design possibilities.

The use of plastic as a material for wheels is still in the developmental stage due in particular to insufficient high-temperature strength and difficult wheel mounting and manufacture.

The disc and rim are welded together on sheet-steel wheels; in the case of forged and cast light-alloy wheels, these two components are usually manufactured in one piece. Multiple-piece designs, even those which are made of different materials (e. g., magnesium disc and aluminum rim), are available only in special cases and for racing vehicles. Car-wheel rims are almost always drop-centre rims with double humps H 2 (rarely with flat hump FH), tapered bead seats and "J" section rim flange. The lower flange shape is frequently found on smaller vehicles; the higher flange shapes JK and K are only rarely seen, and only on higher-weight vehicles.

More recent rim developments which have been put into series manufacture on a limited basis are the TR rim (with metric dimensions) developed by MICHELIN for use with matching TRX tires, which permit more room for the brakes, as well as the rim with "Denloc" groove, which also requires a matched tire. The Dunlop rim and tire combination provides improved safety in case of loss of air. The TD system (TRX-Denloc) brings together both wheel/tire systems. As opposed to common practice, in all three above designs incorporating other rim and tire versions is either not possible at all, or possible only to a very limited extent.

In a completely new development, the tire grips the outside of the rim (CONTI-NENTAL). This design enables the brake diameter to be increased considerably, although at the same time changing the way some tire/rim properties react with one another. It allows the driver to drive at reduced speed for several hundred kilometers with a flat tire or tires. This could eliminate the need for a spare tire This version has also not become popular on the market and its use is confined to special applications.

Based on American efforts to reduce the amount of space taken up by the spare tire as well as – to a very limited extent – to reduce overall vehicle weight, European vehicles are increasingly being fitted with a space-saving spare wheel, which has a matching, lower-performance tire. Opinions on the usefulness of this substandard combination vary.

Design criteria for passenger-car wheels include high component strength, efficient brake cooling, reliable wheel mounting, high concentricity, small space requirements, good corrosion protection, low weight, low cost, easy tire mounting, a good tire seat, good balance-weight attachment and aesthetically pleasing design (particularly in the case of light-alloy wheels). Recent attention has also been given to wheel designs which reduce the vehicle drag coefficient c_w.

Wheels are usually mounted to the vehicle by means of three to five wheel lugs or tug nuts whose collars have a special shape which conforms to the wheel which is usually centered. A high level of true-running is achieved by means of a central wheel mount at the wheel hub using an alignment shoulder. A central wheel mount designed as a Rudge hub or incorporating driving pins is only used with racing wheels.

Wheel trims are fixed onto the wheels with clips or (less frequently) by the wheel nuts in order to
– improve visual appearance,
– improve the drag coefficient,
– cool the wheels/and or the brakes.
Traditional materials for wheel covers are steel and aluminum. Plastics have re-

cently been used much more frequently in order to reduce weight and cost.

Commercial-vehicle wheels

The primary requirements to be met by commercial-vehicle wheels are:
- high fatigue strength and long service life in order to maximize traffic safety,
- lowest possible wheel weight because the wheel, as an unsprung, rotating mass, influences the oscillation system "vehicle",
- high load capacity via appropriate wheel shape and use of optimum materials,
- reduction in wheel-disk unevenness,
- reduction of radial and lateral run-out and wheel imbalance,
- easy assembly of tire to rim during manufacture and in practical use.

15° tapered-bead seat rim
A modern technical design is the one-piece 15° tapered-bead seat rim for tubeless commercial-vehicle tyres.

Advantages:
- The one-piece wheel allows a reduction in wheel weight of up to 10% as compared to the two-piece rim, and exhibits improved true-running and less lateral run-out,
- increased rim diameter,
- sufficient free space,
- unified valve in a precise position and at a sufficient distance from the brake drum or caliper,
- unified balance-weight shapes,
- introduction of central centering and
- use of fully- or semi-automatic tire-fitting equipment.

Radial and lateral run-out, imbalance
Radial run-out of the wheel is one of the main causes of vehicle vibrations. With today's commonly used 15° tapered-bead seat, the reduction of the permissible radial run-out to 1.25 mm (peak-to-peak) results in a marked improvement compared to the flat-bed rims. As opposed to radial run-out, lateral run-out is a less critical problem. Wheel imbalance is also not nearly as much of a problem as tire imbalance, which is of a greater magnitude.

Maximum permissible static imbalance is limited to 2000 cmg.

Wheel centering
Lug centering via spherical washers or solely via ball-seat nuts has been replaced by central centering in order to reduce excessive radial run-out; this arrangement also permits different maximum and minimum play depending upon wheel size (especially with 22.5″ wheels). This requires tolerances which are as close as possible.

Flatness of the contact surface
Any unevenness of the wheel contact surface (waviness, inclination, shielding, etc.) is transmitted to the brake drum when the wheel nuts are tightened, causing fluctuations in braking force as the wheel rotates. These fluctuations, in turn, cause vibrations in the steering system. Driving tests have led to the establishment of a maximum value for waviness of 0.15 mm and 0.2 mm for inclination from the center of the wheel outward.

Trilex wheel system
The Trilex wheel system with cast steel "spoked wheels" comprises a rim and spider. The removable rims are connected to the spider by means of clips and screws. In order to simplify mounting and dismounting of tube tires, the rim consists of three parts with transverse pitch. The same spider can be used in conjunction with the so-called Tublex rim for mounting tubeless tires.

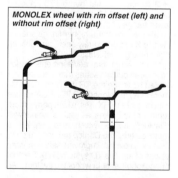

MONOLEX wheel with rim offset (left) and without rim offset (right)

A more recent development is the one-piece cast MONOLEX 15° tapered-bead seat wheel which in comparison with optimized-weight steel wheels is neutral in terms of weight effect.

Light-alloy wheels
One reason for the use of light-alloy wheels is the reduction in weight for 15° tapered-bead seat wheels. Light-alloy wheels are available with cast or forged rims. In spite of weight reduction and adequate strength characteristics, for reasons of cost, light-alloy wheels are used on commercial vehicles only in special cases.

Commercial-vehicle wheel loading

Prestress
Prestress occurs through the combination of stresses caused by assembling the wheel with those which result from inflating the tire.

Static nominal wheel stress
If the wheel is allowed to roll slowly on a perfectly flat road surface under static nominal wheel load, the stress in the wheel section in question varies periodically as the wheel rotates.

Additional dynamic stresses
These similar additional stresses are caused by dynamic wheel forces which result as the vehicle is driven straight ahead over an uneven road surface. Quasi-static wheel forces are then produced which occur during maneuvers such as cornering, steering while stationary, braking and accelerating.

The resulting group of stresses caused by the above-mentioned types of wheel loading is used today as the basis for wheel dimensioning and testing.

Significant weak points
The highly stressed parts of the wheel which are thus most susceptible to cracking are the disc flange, the venting holes, the welded joint between disc and rim, and the rim-well radius.

The flange joint is particularly susceptible. Hub-centered wheels most often crack tangentially above the centre hole.

With bolt-centered wheels, the cracks generally spread out radially from the bolt holes.

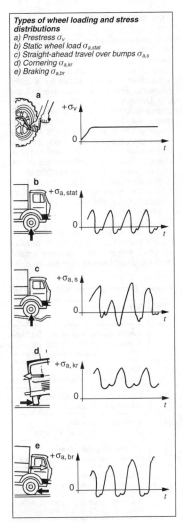

Types of wheel loading and stress distributions
a) Prestress σ_v
b) Static wheel load $\sigma_{a,stat}$
c) Straight-ahead travel over bumps $\sigma_{a,s}$
d) Cornering $\sigma_{a,kr}$
e) Braking $\sigma_{a,br}$

Tires

Tire categories

Tires are classified with reference to the respective requirements of various vehicle types and sizes, and operating conditions. The essential data – tire dimensions, load ratings, specified inflation pressures and authorized speeds – are standardized in the interests of interchangeability in the 7 tire groups or categories listed in Table 1. In addition to pneumatic tires, solid tires are also in use which are approved for speeds of up to 25 km/h (up to 16 km/h for unsprung drive wheels). The classifications in tire groups 1...4 are based upon road conditions:
– "Standard" highway (summer) tires,
– "Special" tyres for use off-road or for mixed use on and off the road,
– "M+S" (winter) tyres.
The same basic set of operating requirements applies for all tires (Table 2), although it should be noted that the emphasis shifts toward the final three criteria (esp. No. 6) on heavier vehicles.

Tire design

Today, passenger cars are equipped exclusively with radial tires. Bias-ply tires are now only fitted on motorcycles, bicycles, earthmoving equipment, and industrial and agricultural machines. For commercial vehicles they are increasingly becoming less important.

The once-dominant bias-ply tire received its name from the fact that referred to the tread, the cord threads of the tire casing run diagonally (or with a bias) so that they cross each other (cross ply). However, the more complex radial tire, with its radial design comprising two main sections, represents the only means of satisfying the increasingly variegated range of operating capabilities demanded of the tires used on today's passenger cars and heavy commercial vehicles.

The cords in the radial tire's casing layers run in the shortest and most direct path – radially – from bead to bead. A belt surrounds the relatively thin, elastic cas-

---

[1] The corresponding European standards can be found in the "Data Book of Tires and Rims" of the ETRTO (European Tire and Rim Technical Organization, Brussels).
[2] Guideline of the Economic Association of the German Rubber Industry, Frankfurt.

Table 1. Tire categories and applicable standards

No.	Tire application	German Standards (selection)[1] DIN	WdK[2]
1	**Engine-driven, two-wheeled vehicles** Motorcycles, motor scooters, motorcycles of less than 50 cm³ engine displacement, mopeds	7801, 7802, 7810	119
2	**Passenger cars** Including station wagons and special spare tires	7803	128, 203
3	**Light-duty commercial vehicles** Including delivery trucks	7804	132, 133
4	**Commercial vehicles** Including multipurpose vehicles	7805, 7793	134, 135, 142, 143, 144, 153
5	**Earthmoving machines** Transport vehicles, loaders, graders	7798, 7799	145, 146
6	**Industrial trucks** Including solid rubber tires	7811, 7845	171
7	**Agricultural vehicles and machinery** Tractors, machines, implements, trailers	7807, 7808, 7813	156, 161

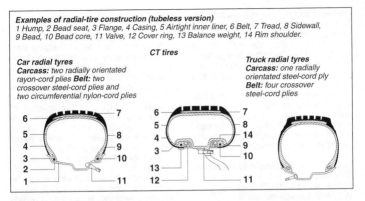

Examples of radial-tire construction (tubeless version)
1 Hump, 2 Bead seat, 3 Flange, 4 Casing, 5 Airtight inner liner, 6 Belt, 7 Tread, 8 Sidewall,
9 Bead, 10 Bead core, 11 Valve, 12 Cover ring, 13 Balance weight, 14 Rim shoulder.

CT tires

Car radial tyres
Carcass: two radially orientated
rayon-cord plies **Belt:** two
crossover steel-cord plies and
two circumferential nylon-cord plies

Truck radial tyres
Carcass: one radially
orientated steel-cord ply
Belt: four crossover
steel-cord plies

ing in order to provide sufficient stability. The "bias-belted" design, more widespread in the US than elsewhere, incorporates an additional belt outside the diagonal casing. The performance of this type of tire is nowhere near as good as that of the radials.

CT tires feature run-flat properties. When deflated, the tyre presses against the inverted bead seat and can thus be driven for several 100 km when flat.

In the TRX/Denloc System, a specially-designed protrusion in the bead fits into a corresponding groove in the wheel rim. This arrangement locks the bead in position to prevent it from slipping into the center of the wheel, and thus provides limited run-flat properties.

Tubeless tires, already popular on passenger cars, are being used with increasing frequency on heavy commercial vehicles. The essential requirement is a single-piece, airtight wheel rim, or a multi-piece rim capable of accepting the required flexible rim-seal rings. Tubeless tyres have a vulcanized-on airtight inner layer instead of an inner tube.

The bead of the tubeless tire must press more tightly against the wheel rim in order to provide the necessary seal. Special, supplementary bead seals in the form of elastomer rings are sometimes used.

Dispensing with the inner tube reduces weight and simplifies mounting procedures.

Table 2. Service requirements

No.	Main criteria	Sub-criteria
1	Ride comfort	Soft suspension, low noise, smooth running (low out-of-roundness)
2	Steering behavior	Steering-force, steering precision[3]
3	Driving stability	Straight-ahead stability[3], cornering stability[3]
4	Driving safety	Tire seat on rim, tire/road adhesion[3]
5	Durability	Structural stability, high-speed performance, bursting pressure, puncture resistance
6	Economy	Expected service life (mileage), wear pattern, sidewall wear, rolling resistance, retreadability

[3] Main criteria for driving on roads in winter.

Diameter and design of the wheel rim

With tyre types 3 and 4, non-sectional 15° tapered-bead seat rims (for tubeless tyres) have displaced the sectional 5° tapered-bead seat rim. This type of rim is identified by the diameter code (1 unit = 25.4 mm) ending in 0.5, as in 17.5, 19.5, 22.5.

Important codes for 5° tapered-bead seat rims are 16 and 20. For car tyres there are not only the normal drop-centre rims with whole-number diameter codes 10, 12, 13, etc. but also special designs with diameter measurements in mm.

Aspect ratio *H/W* (height-to-width ratio)

$H{:}W$ ratio $= (H/W) \cdot 100$

H Tire cross-sectional height
W Tire cross-sectional width

The aspect ratio (H/W = Height relative to Width) on today's standard passenger-car tires ranges between 80 and 50; the figure ranges down to 25 for sports-car tires, and is between 100 and 45 for the tires on heavy commercial vehicles.

Passenger-car tires with low H/W aspect ratios provide high levels of cornering stability. The different aspect ratios are all based on a single outside diameter in order to facilitate interchangeability. At a constant internal diameter for tire and wheel rim, a tire with a low H/W aspect ratio will be wider, with a larger contact surface, and it will be distinguished by a more impressive appearance.

A low H/W aspect ratio makes it possible to maintain the width of the footprint while increasing the internal diameter of the wheel rim; thus providing more space for the brakes. The introduction of the tapered drop-center rim for heavy commercial vehicles was only made possible by the development of a suitable tubeless tire with a low H/W aspect ratio. This was because a reduction of the rim-base diameter was impossible due to the brake-drum diameter having to remain unchanged.

Wider tires with low H/W aspect ratios also represent the only feasible option for applications where minimum tire diameters (in other words, maximum usable height) are stipulated, e.g., for container transport.

Tire designation symbols

The tire's designation is stamped on the sidewall (see Table 5), and reflects standards mandatory in a number of European countries. These include ECE Directive Number 30 for passenger-car tires; Number 54 for tires for heavy commercial vehicles (speeds of 80 km/h and above); and ECE Directive Number 75 concerning tires for motorized two-wheeled vehicles (vehicles with engine displacement exceeding 50 cm³ or attaining speeds in excess of 40 km/h).

Tires tested for compliance with ECE regulations are identified by the code molded into the sidewall adjacent to the bead. The code consists of a circle containing a large "E" followed by the code number of the responsible agency, which is in turn followed by an approval number.

Example: (E4) 020 427.

The small "e" which can be molded into the sidewall in accordance with the European guidelines 92/23 is of equal significance to the ECE marking

Example: (e4) 00321.

Appropriate European guidelines are being prepared for agricultural machinery.

The tire's width, its construction (R = Radial; "—" = Cross-ply; B = Bias-belted) and its rim diameter represent the minimum information requirement for tire designation. The diameter of the tire is also usually included on tires for industrial trucks. On tires for two-wheeled vehicles, passenger cars and heavy commercial vehicles, this information is frequently supplemented by the H/W aspect ratio in % which is appended directly behind the width information from which it is separated by a slash. ECE regulations require this information for all new tires. Although it is not stipulated by the ECE Directives, tires for passenger cars and two-wheeled vehicles may also feature a speed-rating code letter behind the H/W aspect ratio or tire width. On cross-ply tires the code letter replaces the horizontal line. On VR, VB, ZR and ZB tires, it is mandatory that the code letter forms an integral part of the tire-size designation.

The <u>PR</u> (<u>P</u>ly <u>R</u>ating) follows the tire size, and is now employed as a code to distinguish the load ratings for various versions of the same size. Originally it indicated the number of plies in the tire carcass.

The <u>service description</u> is an additional suffix combining the <u>load index</u> (LI) and the <u>speed-rating symbol</u> (GSY). ECE Directives prescribe it as a replacement for the PR number or the speed-rating letters in the tire size. Specific values are assigned to the codes in the service description (Table 4).

For passenger-car tires:
Rated speed = Top speed. On vehicles whose design only allows top speeds of 60 km/h and below, the tire load ratings may be increased as shown in the table below so that higher loads can be carried.

Table 3. Load-rating increase

km/h	Load-rating increase in %	Air pressure increase in bar
60	10	0.1
50	15	0.2
40	25	0.3
30	35	0.4
25	42	0.5

Reductions in tire load can be traded for higher top speeds on most tires for motorscooters and heavy commercial vehicles. Conversely, both types of tire may be used to carry higher loads throughout virtually the entire speed range when operated below their rated (reference) speed, provided that the vehicle be specifically designed to operate at the lower maximum speed. Again, increased maximum load ratings are approved for tires on passenger-car trailers for speeds up to 100 km/h, and on certain commercial ve-

hicles used for short-distance haulage and transportation.

The correct <u>inflation pressure</u> for a particular tire size and PR rating or service description are specified in the standards and/or the manuals provided by the tire's manufacturer (Table 1). The suffix containing the speed-rating symbol always indicates the actual rated speed.

Special passenger-car spare tires (lowweight and "space-saver" designs) are identified on the sidewall as intended for temporary use at limited speeds.

Correspondence between the speed rating for M+S tires on passenger cars, heavy commercial vehicles and motorcycles, and the respective maxima of the vehicles upon which they are mounted is not mandatory. However, a sticker indicating the lower speed for which the tires are approved must be affixed to the inside of the vehicle within the driver's field of vision. The following categories of tires may feature additional data prescribed by <u>US highway safety legislation</u>. These data, molded into the sidewall adjacent to the bead, are valid for Canada, and are also used in Israel:
– <u>FMVSS 109</u> for passenger-car tires,
– <u>FMVSS 119</u> for two-wheeled and heavy commercial vehicles.

These data are stamped adjacent to the letters "DOT", following which come the tire identification code and the date of manufacture, as well as further data on maximum load rating, maximum inflation pressure, and the cord plies which make up the casing and belts.

<u>Australian Safety Regulation ADR 23</u>, which applies to passenger-car tires, employs the identification codes from FMVSS 109 and ECE-R30.

Table 4. Service description codes (examples)

Load index

LI	50	51	88	89	112	113	145	149	157
kg	190	195	560	580	1120	1150	2900	3250	4125

Speed symbol

SS	F	G	J	K	L	M	N	P	Q	R	S	T	H	V	W	Y
km/h	80	90	100	110	120	130	140	150	160	170	180	190	210	240	270	300

Table 5. Tire identification examples

Tire category		Identification example				Example includes details of			
	Suitability	Tire designation symbols	PR[3] number	Usage code [4] LI	[5] GSY	Tyre dia. A	Tire width B	H/W %	Rim dia. d
MC	Moped	2¹/₄–16 Moped	–	–	–	–	Code	–	Code
	Small motor cycles	3–17 reinforced[2]	–	51	J	–	Code	–	Code
	Motorcycles	3.00–17 reinforced[2]	–	50	P	–	Code	–	Code
		110/80 R 18	–	58	H	–	mm	80	Code
		120/90 B 18	–	65	H	–	mm	90	Code
	Motor scooters	3.50–10	–	51	J	–	Code	–	Code
Passenger cars		165 R 14 M+S	–	84	Q	–	mm	–	Code
		195/65 R 15 reinforced[2]	–	95	T	–	mm	–	Code
		200/60 R 365	–	88	H	–	mm	60	mm
		205/60 ZR 15	–	91	W	–	mm	60	Code
		CT 235/40 ZR 475	–	–	–	–	mm	40	mm
CV	Delivery vans	185 R 14 C[1]	8 PR	102/100	M	–	mm	–	Code
	Light-duty trucks	245/70R 17.5	–	143/141	J	–	Code	–	Code
	Trucks	11/70 R 22.5	–	146/143	K	–	Code	70	Code
	Trailers	14/80 R 20	–	157	K	–	Code	80	Code
	Buses	295/80 R 22.5	–	149/145	M	–	mm	80	Code
MPV	Multi-purp. veh.	10.5 R 20 MPT[8]	14 PR	134	G	–	Code	–	Code
EM	Transporters	18.00–25 EM[9]	32 PR	–	–	–	Code	–	Code
	Loaders	29.5–29 EM[9]	28 PR	–	–	–	Code	–	Code
IT	Industrial trucks	6.50–10[6]	10 PR	–	–	–	Code	–	Code
	Carts	21 x 4[6]	4 PR	–	–	Code	Code	–	–
	Industrial trucks	28 x 9–15[7]	14 PR	–	–	Code	Code	–	Code
		300 x 15[7]	18 PR	–	–	–	mm	–	Code
AS	Tractors	480/70 R 34	–	143	A 8	–	mm	–	Code
		7.50–60 AS[10] Front	6 PR	–	–	–	Code	–	Code
	Equipment[11]	11.0/65–12 Impl.	6 PR	–	–	–	Code	65	Code

Example for passenger-car tires: **175/70R13 82S**
175 mm nominal tire width, **70** % H/W ratio, **R**adial tires, Code **13** Rim diameter
(approx. 330 mm [13 inches]), Load index **82** (475 kg), Speed symbol **S** = 180 km/h.

[1] C = light-duty truck (delivery-van) tires (also for high-load-capacity motor-scooter tires). [2] reinforced = additional designation for reinforced tires for two-wheeled motor vehicles and passenger cars. [3] PR = load-range class. [4] Load-range code for single/dual tires. [5] Speed code for vehicle nominal (reference) speed. [6] Pneumatic tires. [7] Solid rubber tires. [8] MPT = Multi-purpose tire. [9] EM = Earthmoving machinery. [10] AS = Agricultural tractor. [11] Tires for equipment and trailers.

Tire applications

Tire selection based upon the recommendations of the tire manufacturer is essential for obtaining satisfactory performance. Optimal operating characteristics can only be obtained when tires of one single design are mounted on all wheels (for instance, radial tires). This is obligatory for private cars. For commercial vehicles with a gross weight of over 2.8 t, tires on the same axle must be of identical design. During seasonal storage of the tires, inner tubes and bead bands tend to age and become brittle more rapidly when exposed to direct sunlight. Moving air promotes this process. Intact packaging is particularly important for ensuring that the tube remains in good condition. The storage area should thus be cool, dry and dark. Any contact with oil or grease is to be avoided. Particular care is required when mounting tires. They must never be mounted on anything other than undistorted, undamaged, rust-free wheel rims which show no signs of more than minimal wear. When a loose flange is used, that side should receive especially critical attention. New valves, and, where applicable, new tubes and bead bands are always to be installed with new tires. Caution is also advised when used inner tubes are refitted following repairs: Inner tubes expand during use, a condition which can result in dangerous folds forming when the tube is reinstalled. If there are any doubts at all, new tubes should be used.

Tire tread (see examples)
It is illegal to regroove the tread on tires for two-wheeled vehicles and passenger

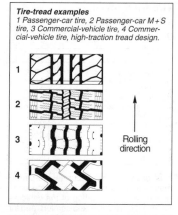

Tire-tread examples
1 Passenger-car tire, 2 Passenger-car M + S tire, 3 Commercial-vehicle tire, 4 Commercial-vehicle tire, high-traction tread design.

Rolling direction

cars; manufacturer regulations must be complied with for other tire categories.
Tire rotation is recommended to deal with variations in tread wear between axles. The less tread there is on the tire, the thinner is the protective layer covering belts and casing. This aspect should be considered when planning operation under demanding operating conditions extending over a long period of time. In addition, reduced tread depth results in a more than proportional increase in braking distances on wet road surfaces. This applies in particular to passenger cars and fast commercial vehicles. For instance, for a light FWD passenger car and a heavy rear-wheel drive car, the figures apply in Table 6 below when the vehicle is braked from 100 km/h (highly dependent upon the road surface, tire profile, and the tire's rubber mixture).

Table 6. Tread depth and braking distances (braking from 100 km/h)

Vehicle		Light passenger car with front-wheel drive					Heavy passenger car with rear-wheel drive (ABS)			
Tread depth	in mm	8	4	3	2	1	8	3	1.6	1
Braking distance	in m	76	99	110	129	166	59	63	80	97
	in %	100	130	145	170	218	100	107	135	165
Increased braking distance per mm of wear	in %	7		15		25	48	1.4	20	50

Tire traction

Units and symbols

Symbol		Unit
f	Frequency	Hz
F_B	Braking force	kN
F_R	Wheel load	kN
F_S	Side force	kN
M_R	Aligning torque	N · m
n_S	Caster	mm
p_i	Tire pressure	bar
v_0	Test velocity	km/h
α	Slip angle	°
γ	Camber angle	°
λ	Slip	–

It is essential that accurate tire-performance maps are available for the engineering and optimization of the vehicle's handling, driveability, and comfort, and for the reduction of its drivetrain vibration.

Representative tire-performance maps for passenger-cars and light commercial vehicles are already familiar and are available in various publications [1, 3, 4]. For this reason, the following will concentrate

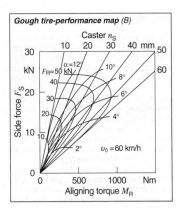

Gough tire-performance map (B)

on tires for heavy-duty commercial vehicles with the dimensions 11 R 22.5. These tires are in widespread use [2].

All data in the performance maps refer to the Michelin XZA 11 R 22.5 tire.

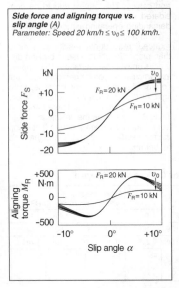

Side force and aligning torque vs. slip angle (A)
Parameter: Speed 20 km/h $\leq v_0 \leq$ 100 km/h.

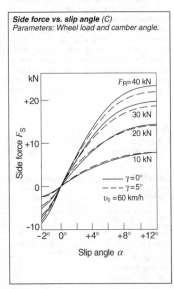

Side force vs. slip angle (C)
Parameters: Wheel load and camber angle.

Tire performance with wheel rotating freely at a given slip angle

When the tire rotates at a slip angle, side forces are generated as a function of the slip angle. These side forces are accompanied by an aligning torque (Diagram B). The Gough diagram [3] is frequently employed to illustrate this phenomenon. The side force is dependent on the slip angle and increases degressively as higher loads are applied to the wheel (Diagram C). The maximum side force is inversely proportional to speed, while the influence of speed increases as a function of wheel load (Diagram A).

When dealing with tires for passenger-cars and light commercial vehicles, the situation is thus: If a wheel rotating at a given slip angle is subjected to camber, the camber and side forces cause a parallel displacement of the side-force/slip-angle curves. Tires on heavy-duty commercial vehicles also display additional displacements of the side-force/slip-angle curves due to the side forces accompanying the camber; this phenomenon only occurs at larger slip angles. The result is

that practically all curves intersect the co-ordinate origin (Diagram C).

On dry roads, reduced tread depth results in steeper side-force/slip-angle curves, with an accompanying increase in the maximum side forces which can be transferred (Diagram D).

Tire performance under acceleration and braking with wheel rolling straight ahead

The tire's response to "slip" is similar to its reaction to slip angles (Diagram E). The maximum circumferential force will generally lie within the range of 10 to 20 % slip on a dry road surface. The coefficient of adhesion responds to higher wheel loads with a less striking, more degressive increase in the circumferential than in the lateral direction. On larger tires, the influence which speed exerts on the level of the lateral coefficient of adhesion is less pronounced in the normal speed range for heavy-duty commercial vehicles than with tires similar to those used on passenger cars (Diagram E).

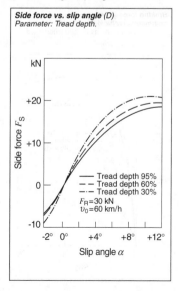

Side force vs. slip angle (D)
Parameter: Tread depth.

Side force F_S (kN) vs. Slip angle α

— Tread depth 95%
– – Tread depth 60%
–·– Tread depth 30%
$F_R = 30$ kN
$v_0 = 60$ km/h

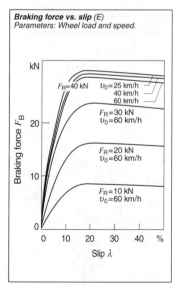

Braking force vs. slip (E)
Parameters: Wheel load and speed.

Braking force F_B (kN) vs. Slip λ

$F_R = 40$ kN $v_0 = 25$ km/h
                40 km/h
                60 km/h
$F_R = 30$ kN
$v_0 = 60$ km/h
$F_R = 20$ kN
$v_0 = 60$ km/h
$F_R = 10$ kN
$v_0 = 60$ km/h

Tire pressure has only a minimal effect on maximum circumferential forces at low wheel loads. At higher wheel loads, reduced tire pressures result in a substantially more pronounced rate of increase in the maximum circumferential force (Diagram G).

Side and circumferential forces respond to high tire loads by displaying mutually opposed reactions to variations in tire pressure (Diagrams F, G).

Tire performance at slip angles and slip
If a tire operating under circumferential forces or slip is subjected to an additional slip angle, at all slip rates the usable circumferential forces will decrease with increasing slip angle. The higher the slip angle, the more the curve for maximum circumferential force is displaced toward higher slip rates (Diagram I).

The elliptical curves for side force vs. circumferential force (braking force) vary according to wheel load (Diagram H). For a specific wheel load, on ABS-equipped vehicles this curve represents the maximum available adhesion limits for the vehicle dynamics.

The tire-performance curves resulting from measurements actually taken, indicate the propagation of side force as a function of braking force within the slip-angle range of 0...10°. The parameters for wheel load, speed and tire pressure remain constant (Diagram K).

Dynamic tire-performance curves
The illustrated tire-performance curves are based on parameters which are only subject to gradual change during the course of the measurements, i.e. quasi-static conditions. Actual operation, on the other hand, is characterized by dynamic processes. Increases in the speed at which the influencing parameters vary will induce certain maneuver-specific changes in tire response, the magnitude of which makes it imperative that they be considered.

The most significant influencing parameters are dynamic changes in:
– Slip angle,
– Trackwidth,

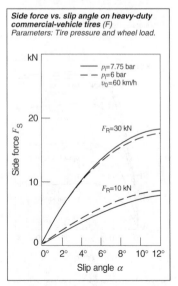

Side force vs. slip angle on heavy-duty commercial-vehicle tires (F)
Parameters: Tire pressure and wheel load.

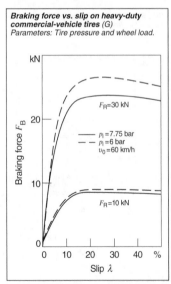

Braking force vs. slip on heavy-duty commercial-vehicle tires (G)
Parameters: Tire pressure and wheel load.

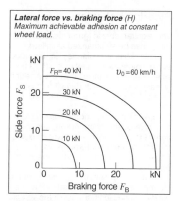

Lateral force vs. braking force (H)
Maximum achievable adhesion at constant wheel load.

Tire-performance curves measured at a wheel load of 30 kN (K)
Side force as function of braking force, Parameter: Slip angle.

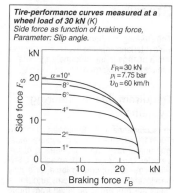

– Camber,
– Slip,
– Wheel load.

Generally, the tire's response to these rapidly changing parameters is shown graphically as a function of frequency. That is, amplitudes and phase angles of the tire forces and moments are illustrated relative to frequency, as a function of the forces acting on the tire, while including

the frequency-dependent progression of mean values for tire forces [5, 6].

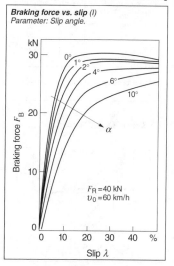

Braking force vs. slip (I)
Parameter: Slip angle.

Literature
[1] Gengenbach, W.: Experimentelle Untersuchung von Reifen auf nasser Fahrbahn (Experimental investigation of tires on wet road surface). ATZ, 1968, Hefte 3, 8, and 9,
[2] von Glasner, E.C.: Einbeziehung von Prüfstandsergebnissen in die Simulation des Fahrverhaltens von Nutzfahrzeugen (Including test-bench results in the simulation of commercial-vehicle handling). Habilitation, Universität Stuttgart, 1987.
[3] Gough, V. E.: Cornering Characteristics of Tires. Automobile Engineer, 1954, Vol. 44.
[4] Weber R.: Beitrag zum Übertragungsverhalten zwischen Schlupf- und Reifenführungskräften (Contribution concerning the transmission behavior between slip and circumferential/side forces). AI, 1981, Vol. 4.
[5] Fritz, G. Seitenkräfte und Rückstellmomente von Personenwagenreifen bei periodischer Änderung der Spurweite, des Sturz- und Schräglaufwinkels (Side forces and aligning torques of passenger-car tires under the influence of periodic change of track width, camber, and slip angle). Dissertation, Universität Karlsruhe, 1978.
[6] Weber, R.: Reifenführungskräfte bei schnellen Änderungen von Schräglauf und Schlupf (Circumferential/side forces as a function of rapid changes in slip angle and slip). Habilitation, Universität Karlsruhe, 1981.

Steering

The steering mechanism converts the driver's rotational input at the steering wheel into a change in the steering angle of the vehicle's steering road wheels.

Requirements on steering systems

In accordance with European Directive 70/311/EWG the steering system must guarantee easy and safe steering of the vehicle: The maximum permissible operating time and operating force for a fully serviceable steering system, and for a faulty system, are to be taken from these Regulations (Table). They must be complied with when the vehicle is turned into a spiral path from a straight-ahead path at a speed of 10 km/h.

Steering behavior

The requirements in terms of steering behavior can be summarized as follows:
1. Jolts from irregularities in the road surface must be damped as much as possible during transmission to the steering wheel. However, such damping must not cause the driver to lose contact with the road.
2. The basic design of the steering kinematics must satisfy the Ackermann conditions: the extensions of the wheel axes of the left and right front wheels, when at an angle, intersect on an extension of the rear axle.
3. By means of suitable directness of the steering system (particularly if rubber-elastic connections are used) the vehicle must react to minute steering corrections.
4. When the steering wheel is released, the wheels must return automatically to the straight-ahead position and must remain stable in this position.

Regulations for steering operating force

Vehicle category	Fully serviceable steering system			Faulty steering system		
	Maximum applied force in daN	Time in s	Turning radius in m	Maximum applied force in daN	Time in s	Turning radius in m
M_1	15	4	12	30	4	20
M_2	15	4	12	30	4	20
M_3	20	4	12	45	6	20
N_1	20	4	12	30	4	20
N_2	25	4	12	40	4	20
N_3	20	4	12[1]	45[2]	6	20

[1] Or steering lock in case this value is not reached.
[2] 50 daN for non-articulated vehicles, with two or more steered axles, excluding friction-steered axles.

Steering assembly (diagram)
a) Basic principle, b) Rack-and-pinion steering
1 Steering arm, 2 Drag link, 3 Idler arm, 4 Tie rod/rack, 5 Steering wheel, 6 Steering shaft,
7 Steering box, 8 Pitman arm.

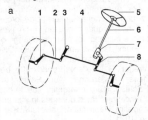
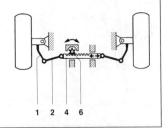

5. The steering should have as low a ratio as possible (number of steering-wheel turns from lock to lock) in order to obtain ease of handling. The steering forces involved are determined not only by the steering ratio but also by the front suspension load, the turning circle, the suspension geometry (caster angle, kingpin angle, kingpin offset), the properties of the tire tread and the road surface.

Types of steering box

A steering box must have the following qualities:
– no play in the straight-ahead position,
– low friction, resulting in high efficiency,
– high rigidity,
– readjustability.

For these reasons, only two types have become established to date:

Rack-and-pinion steering
Basically, as the name implies, the rack-and-pinion steering consists of a rack and a pinion. The steering ratio is defined by the ratio of pinion revolutions (= steering-wheel revolutions) to rack travel. Suitable toothing of the rack allows the ratio to be made variable over the travel. This lowers the actuating force or reduces the travel for steering corrections.

Recirculating-ball steering
The forces generated between steering worm and steering nut are transmitted via a low-friction recirculating row of balls. The steering nut acts on the steering shaft via gear teeth. A variable ratio is possible with this steering box.

Steering kinematics

Steering kinematics and axle design must be such that, although the driver receives feedback on the adhesion between wheels and road surface, the steering wheel is not subjected to any forces from the spring motion of the wheels or from driving forces (front-wheel drive) (see P. 620).

The steering-axis inclination causes the front section of the vehicle to lift when the wheels are at an angle. This leads to a steering-angle-dependent caster return torque.

The toe-in (toe-out) is a slip angle present even during straight-ahead driving which tensions the linkages and causes a rapid build-up of transverse forces when the wheels are at an angle.

The caster produces a lever arm for lateral forces: i.e., a speed-dependent return torque.

The steering roll radius determines the extent to which the steering system is affected by disturbance forces (brakes pulling unevenly, driving forces under traction/overrun conditions with front-wheel drive). Today, the goal is to achieve a steering roll radius which is "zero" to "slightly negative".

Rack-and-pinion steering
1 Pinion, 2 Rack.

Recirculating-ball steering
1 Steering worm, 2 Recirculating balls,
3 Steering nut, 4 Steering shaft with gear teeth.

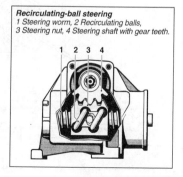

Classification of steering systems

European Directive 70/311/EEC distinguishes three types of steering system for front wheels:

- <u>Muscular-energy steering systems</u> in which the steering force is produced exclusively by the driver (see mechanical steering boxes on P. 639)
- <u>Power steering systems</u> in which the steering force is produced exclusively by an energy source in the vehicle.
- <u>Power-assisted steering systems</u> in which the steering force is produced by the muscular energy of the driver and by an energy source. Used for high-speed vehicles.

Hydraulic power-assisted steering

Energy source

The energy source consists of a vane pump (generally driven by the engine) with an integral oil-flow regulator, an oil reservoir and connecting hoses and pipes.

The pump must be dimensioned so that it generates sufficient pressure to enable rotation of the steering wheel at a speed of at least 1.5 n/s even when the engine is only idling.

The compulsory pressure-limiting valve required on hydraulic systems is usually integrated.

The pump and the system components must be designed such that the operating temperature of the hydraulic fluid does not rise to an excessive level (<100 °C) and such that no noise is generated and the oil does not foam.

On small cars, electrically powered gear or roller pumps are occasionally used as well. Such units are powered by the vehicle's electrical system and are more versatile with regard to their location, as well as facilitating modular vehicle design. An ECU achieves energy saving effects by varying the pump speed. Higher-voltage electrical systems currently under development would also allow larger cars to use this type of unit.

Control valve

The control valve provides the steering cylinder with an oil pressure which corresponds to the rotary motion of the steer-

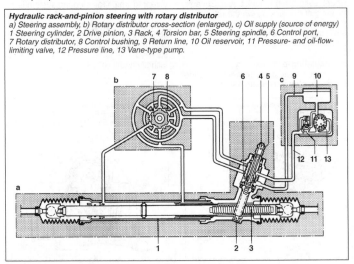

Hydraulic rack-and-pinion steering with rotary distributor
a) Steering assembly, b) Rotary distributor cross-section (enlarged), c) Oil supply (source of energy)
1 Steering cylinder, 2 Drive pinion, 3 Rack, 4 Torsion bar, 5 Steering spindle, 6 Control port,
7 Rotary distributor, 8 Control bushing, 9 Return line, 10 Oil reservoir, 11 Pressure- and oil-flow-
limiting valve, 12 Pressure line, 13 Vane-type pump.

ing wheel. A flexible torque detector (e. g. torsion bar, spiral spring, leaf spring) translates the applied torque, proportionally in most cases, precisely and without any degree of play into as small an actuator travel as possible. The control edges, which are in the form of chamfers or bevels, move as a result of the actuator travel and thus form the corresponding opening cross section for the oil flow.

Control valves are usually built according to the "open center" principle, i. e., when the control valve is not actuated, the oil delivered by the pump flows back to the oil reservoir at zero pressure.

Steering cylinder

The double-acting steering cylinder converts the applied oil pressure into an assisting force which acts on the rack and which intensifies the steering force exerted by the driver. The steering cylinder is normally integrated in the steering box. As the steering cylinder has to be extremely low-friction, particularly high demands are made on the piston and rod seals.

Parameterizable hydraulic power-assisted steering

Increasing demands regarding vehicle operating comfort and safety have led to the introduction of power-assisted steering systems with modulation capability. The electronically controlled power-assisted rack-and-pinion steering system is an example. It operates dependent on speed, i. e., the vehicle speed as measured by the electronic speedometer controls the actu-

ating force of the steering system. A control unit evaluates the speed signals and determines the level of hydraulic reaction, and therefore the actuating force on the steering wheel. This level of hydraulic reaction is transmitted to the steering-system control valve via an electrohydraulic converter, in the course of which the hydraulic reaction changes in relation to the vehicle speed. The special design of the steering characteristic means that when parking, and when moving the steering wheel while standing still, only minimal forces need be applied to the steering wheel, whilst the level of assistance is reduced as speed increases. Thus precise and accurate steering is made possible at high speeds. With this system, it is important that oil pressure and volume flow are at no time reduced, so that they can be called on immediately in emergency situations. These qualities permit outstanding steering precision and safety, while at the same time providing optimum steering comfort.

Electric power-assisted steering

The SERVOLECTRIC (Bosch/ZF designation) is currently under development for medium-sized and smaller cars. This electric power-assisted steering system features an electric motor which is powered by the vehicle's electrical system and can be fitted in one of three possible arrangements either as a steering-column, pinion-drive or rack-and-pinion drive unit.
The SERVOLECTRIC's ECU provides the

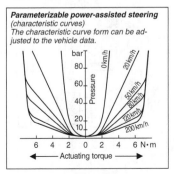

Parameterizable power-assisted steering (characteristic curves)
The characteristic curve form can be adjusted to the vehicle data.

Speed-dependent power-assisted steering with modulation capability (diagram)
1 Pressure-oil pump, 2 Steering-valve housing, 3 Electrohydraulic converter, 4 ECU, 5 Electronic speedometer, 6 Battery.

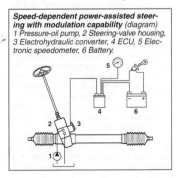

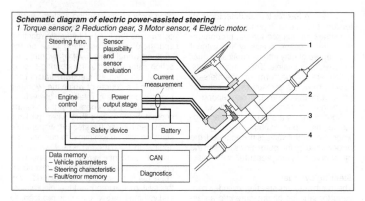

Schematic diagram of electric power-assisted steering
1 Torque sensor, 2 Reduction gear, 3 Motor sensor, 4 Electric motor.

system's programmability (e.g. dynamic handling variables), the automatic steering-axis feedback amplification, as well as offering considerable steering-energy savings potential (approx. 85% compared with hydraulic power-assisted steering with engine-driven pump).

The SERVOLECTRIC system allows the vehicle to be steered unassisted (using greater effort) in the event of failure of the power assistance.

Power-assisted steering for commercial vehicles

Power-assisted steering with all-hydraulic transmission

With "hydrostatic steering" there is no mechanical connection between steering wheel and road wheels. The steering force is hydraulically boosted and is transmitted exclusively by hydraulic means. Located in the ECU is a metering pump which supplies the steering cylinder with an oil pressure corresponding to the movement of the steering wheel. Owing to unavoidable leakage losses in the metering pump, the straight-ahead position of the steering wheel is no longer defined. This is why the use of this steering system is confined to machines.

The maximum permissible speed is 25 km/h in many European countries; in Germany it is 50 km/h and, with dual-circuit design, could be increased to 62 km/h.

Dual-circuit power-assisted steering system for heavy commercial vehicles

Dual-circuit steering systems are necessary where the actuating forces needed at the steering wheel exceed 450 N in the case of failure of the power assistance (EWG 70/311).

These steering systems are characterized by hydraulic redundancy. Both steer-

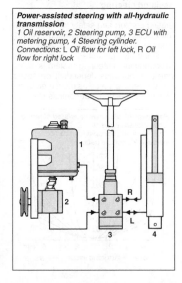

Power-assisted steering with all-hydraulic transmission
1 Oil reservoir, 2 Steering pump, 3 ECU with metering pump, 4 Steering cylinder.
Connections: L Oil flow for left lock, R Oil flow for right lock

ing circuits of such a system are functionally tested by means of flow indicators. The steering-circuit supply pumps must be driven in differing ways (e.g., engine-dependent, vehicle-speed-dependent or electrically). In accordance with legislation, if the engine or one of the steering circuits fails, the vehicle can be steered with the still functioning circuit.

Single-circuit power-assisted steering system for commercial vehicles

Commercial vehicles are usually fitted with recirculating-ball power steering. In modern systems the control valve is integrated into the steering worm, which leads to compact design and optimum weight.

Only minor modification of the control valve components is necessary, to permit the actuating force in modern recirculating-ball power-steering systems to be adjusted with the aid of control electronics to vehicle speed and to other parameters such as lateral acceleration or load condition.

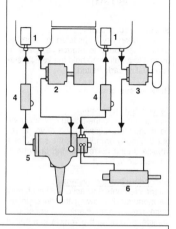

Dual-circuit power-assisted steering system
1 Oil reservoir, 2 Engine-driven pump,
3 Wheel-driven pump, 4 Flow indicator,
5 Dual-circuit hydraulic steering,
6 Steering cylinder.

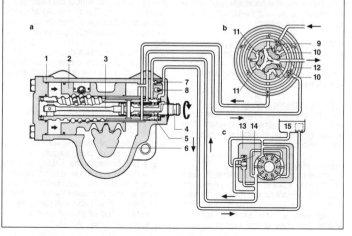

Recirculating-ball hydraulic steering system
a) Steering assembly, b) Rotary distributor cross-section (enlarged), c) Oil supply (source of energy)
1 Housing, 2 Piston, 3 Torsion bar, 4 Rotary distributor/steering spindle, 5 Control bushing/worm,
6 Sector shaft, 7 Pressure-limiting valve, 8 Replenishing valve, 9 Inlet slot, 10 Return slot,
11 Axial groove, 12 Return groove, 13 Vane-type pump, 14 Pressure and oil-flow-limiting valve,
15 Oil reservoir.

Braking systems

Definitions, Principles
(Based on ISO 611)

Braking equipment
All the braking systems fitted to a vehicle, whose function is to reduce its speed or bring it to a halt, or to hold the vehicle stationary if already halted.

Braking systems

Service braking system
All the elements, the action of which may be modulated, allowing the driver to reduce, directly or indirectly, the speed of a vehicle during normal driving or to bring the vehicle to a halt.

Secondary braking system
All the elements, the action of which may be modulated, allowing the driver to reduce, directly or indirectly, the speed of a vehicle or to bring the vehicle to a halt in case of failure of the service braking system.

Parking braking system
All the elements allowing the vehicle to be held stationary mechanically even on an inclined surface, and particularly in the absence of the driver.

Additional retarding braking system
All the elements allowing the driver directly or indirectly to stabilize or to reduce the speed of the vehicle, particularly on a long incline.

Automatic braking system
All the elements which automatically brake the towed vehicle as a result of intended or accidental separation from the towing vehicle.

Antilock braking system (ABS)
Aggregate of all devices within the service-braking system which provide automatic slip control (in the direction of rotation) for one or several wheels under braking conditions. The braking force at wheels featuring direct control is controlled using data provided by the wheel's own wheel-speed sensor, while indirectly controlled wheels rely on data provided by the wheel-speed sensor(s) at one or more of the other wheels. An ABS system with "Select High" control has directly and indirectly controlled wheels. With an ABS system with "Select Low" control, all wheels with speed sensors are directly controlled.

Constituent elements

Energy supplying device
Parts of a braking system which supply, regulate and, if necessary, condition the energy required for braking. It terminates at the point where the transmission device starts, i.e. where the various circuits of the braking systems, including the circuits of accessories if fitted, are protected either towards the energy supplying device or from each other.

The energy source is the part of the energy-supplying device which generates the energy. It may be located away from the vehicle (for example in the case of a compressed-air braking system for a trailer) and can also be the muscular strength of the driver.

Control device
Parts of a braking system which initiate the operation and control the effect of this braking system. The control signal can be conveyed within the control device by, for example, mechanical, pneumatic, hydraulic or electrical means, including the use of auxiliary or non-muscular energy.

The control device is defined as starting at that component to which the control force is directly applied, and can be operated:
- by direct action of the driver, either by hand or foot;
- by indirect action of the driver or without any action (only in the case of towed vehicles);
- by variation of the pressure in a connecting pipe, or of the electric current in a cable, between the towing and the towed vehicle at the time of operation of one of the braking systems of the towing vehicle, or in the case of a failure; and
- by the inertia of the vehicle or by its weight or that of one of its main constituent elements.

The control device is defined as ending at that point at which the braking energy is distributed, or where a portion of the energy is diverted to control braking energy.

Transmission device

Parts of a braking system which transmit the energy distributed by the control device. It starts either at the point where the control device terminates or at the point where the energy supplying device terminates. It terminates at those parts of the braking system in which the forces opposing the vehicle's movement, or its tendency towards movement, are generated. It can, for example, be of the mechanical, hydraulic, pneumatic (pressure above or below atmospheric), electric, or combined (for example hydromechanical, hydropneumatic) type.

Brake

Parts of a braking system in which the forces opposing the vehicle's movement, or its tendency towards movement, are developed, such as friction brakes (disk or drum) or retarders (hydrodynamic or electrodynamic retarders, engine brakes).

Supplementary device of the towing vehicle for the towed vehicle

Parts of a braking system on a towing vehicle which are intended for the supply of energy to, and control of, the braking systems on the towed vehicle. It comprises the components between the energy supplying device of the towing vehicle and the supply-line coupling head (inclusive), and between the transmission device(s) of the towing vehicle and the control-line coupling head (inclusive).

Definitions relating to the energy supplying device

Muscular-energy braking system

Braking system in which the energy necessary to produce the braking force is supplied solely by the physical effort of the driver.

Energy-assisted braking system

Braking system in which the energy necessary to produce the braking force is supplied by the physical effort of the driver and one or more energy supplying devices.

Non-muscular-energy braking system

Braking system in which the energy necessary to produce the braking force is supplied by one or more energy supplying devices excluding the physical effort of the driver. This is used only to control the system. Note: However, a braking device in which the driver can increase the braking force, in the total failed energy condition, by muscular effort acting on this device, is not included in the above definition.

Inertia braking system

Braking system in which the energy necessary to produce the braking force arises from the approach of the trailer to its towing vehicle.

Gravity braking system

Braking system in which the energy necessary to produce the braking force is supplied by the lowering of a constituent element of the trailer (e.g. trailer drawbar), due to gravity.

Definitions of braking systems relating to the arrangement of the transmission device

Single-circuit braking system

Braking system having a transmission device embodying a single circuit. The transmission device comprises a single circuit if, in the event of a failure in the transmission device, no energy for the production of the application force can be transmitted by this transmission device.

Multi-circuit braking system

Braking system having a transmission device embodying several circuits. The transmission device comprises several circuits if, in the event of a failure in the transmission device, energy for the production of the application force can still be transmitted, wholly or partly, by this transmission device.

Definitions of braking systems relating to vehicle combinations

Single-line braking system
Assembly in which the braking systems of the individual vehicles act in such a way that the single line is used both for the energy supply to, and for the control of, the braking system of the towed vehicle.

Two- or multi-line braking systems
Assembly in which the braking systems of the individual vehicles act in such a way that several lines are used separately and simultaneously for the energy supply to, and for the control of, the braking system of the towed vehicle.

Continuous braking system
Combination of braking systems for vehicles forming a vehicle combination. Characteristics:
– from the driving seat, the driver can operate by a single operation and with a variable degree of force a directly operated control device on the towing vehicle and an indirectly operated control device on the towed vehicle,
– the energy used for the braking of each of the vehicles forming the combination is supplied by the same energy source (which can be the muscular effort of the driver) and
– simultaneous or suitably phased braking of the individual units of a vehicle combination.

Semi-continuous braking system
Combination of braking systems for vehicles forming a vehicle combination. Characteristics:
– the driver, from his driving seat, can operate gradually by a single operation a directly operated control device on the towing vehicle and an indirectly operated control device on the towed vehicle,
– the energy used for the braking of each of the vehicles forming the combination is supplied by at least two different energy sources (one of which can be the muscular effort of the driver) and
– simultaneous or suitably phased braking of the individual units of a vehicle combination.

Non-continuous braking system
Combinations of the braking systems of the vehicles forming a combination which is neither continuous nor semi-continuous.

Braking-system control lines

Wiring & conductors: These are employed to conduct electrical energy.
Tubular lines: Rigid, semi-rigid or flexible tubes/pipes used to transfer hydraulic or pneumatic energy.

Lines connecting the braking equipment of vehicles in a vehicle combination

Supply line: A supply line is a special feed line transmitting energy from the towing vehicle to the energy reservoir of the towed vehicle.
Control line: A control line is a special pilot line by which the energy essential for control is transmitted from the towing vehicle to the towed vehicle.
Common supply and control line: Line serving equally as supply line and as control line (single-line braking system).
Secondary line: Special actuating line transmitting from the towing vehicle to the towed vehicle the energy essential for the secondary braking of the towed vehicle.

Braking mechanics
Mechanical phenomena occurring between the initiation of actuation of the control device and the end of the braking action.

Gradual braking
Braking which, within the normal range of operation of the control device, permits the driver, at any moment, to increase or reduce, to a sufficiently fine degree, the braking force by operation of the control device. When an increase in braking force is obtained by action of the control device, an inverse action shall lead to a reduction of that force.

Braking-system hysteresis: Difference in control forces between application and release for the same braking torque.

Brake-hysteresis: Difference in application force between application and release for the same braking torque.

Forces and torques

Control force F_c: Force exerted on the control device.

Application force F_s: In friction brakes, the total force applied to a brake lining, which causes the braking force by friction effect.

Braking torque: Product of the frictional forces resulting from the application force and the distance between the points of application of these forces and the axis of rotation of the wheels.

Total braking force F_f: Sum of the braking forces at the interfaces between all the wheels and the ground, produced by the effect of the braking system, which oppose the movement or the tendency to movement of the vehicle.

Braking-force distribution: Specification of braking force according to axle, given as % of the total braking force F_f. Example: Front axle 60%, rear axle 40%.

Brake coefficient C^*: Defines the relationship between the total circumferential force of a given brake and the respective brake's application force.

$$C^* = F_u/F_s$$

F_u Total circumferential force, F_s Application force. The mean is employed when there are variations in the application forces at the individual brake shoes.

$$F_s = \sum F_{si}/i$$
i Number of brake shoes

Times (see diagram)

Reaction time
The time which elapses between perception of the state or object which induces the response, and the point at which the control device is actuated (t_0).

Actuating time of the brakes
Elapsed time between the moment when the component of the control device (t_0) on which the control force acts starts to move, and the moment when it reaches its final position corresponding to the applied control force (or its travel). (This is equally true for application and release of the brakes).

Initial response time $t_1 - t_0$
Elapsed time between the moment when the component of the control device on which the control force acts starts to move and the moment when the braking force takes effect.

Buildup time $t_{1'} - t_1$
Period that elapses between the point at which the braking force starts to take effect and the point at which a certain level is reached (75% of asymptotic pressure in the wheel cylinder as per EU Directive 71/320 EEC, App. III/2.4).

Response and buildup time
The sum of the initial response and buildup times is used to assess how the brake system behaves referred to time, until the moment at which the full braking effect is reached.

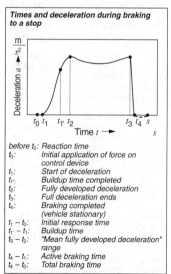

Times and deceleration during braking to a stop

Deceleration $a \rightarrow$ $\frac{m}{s^2}$

Time $t \rightarrow$ s

before t_0: Reaction time
t_0: Initial application of force on control device
t_1: Start of deceleration
$t_{1'}$: Buildup time completed
t_2: Fully developed deceleration
t_3: Full deceleration ends
t_4: Braking completed (vehicle stationary)
$t_1 - t_0$: Initial response time
$t_{1'} - t_1$: Buildup time
$t_3 - t_2$: "Mean fully developed deceleration" range
$t_4 - t_1$: Active braking time
$t_4 - t_0$: Total braking time

Active braking time $t_4 - t_1$
Elapsed time between the moment when braking force takes effect and the moment at which it ceases. If the vehicle stops before braking force ceases, the time of the end of movement is the end of the active braking time.

Release time
Elapsed time between the moment when the actuating time for release starts and the moment when the braking force ceases.

Total braking time $t_4 - t_0$
Elapsed time between the moment when the control device component on which the control force acts starts to move, and the moment when the braking force ceases. If the vehicle stops before the braking force ceases, the time of the end of movement constitutes the end of the total braking time. (See the graph on P. 647)

Braking distance s
Distance traveled by the vehicle during the total braking time. If the time of the end of movement constitutes the end of the total braking time, this distance is called the "stopping distance".

Braking work W
Integral of the product of the instantaneous total braking force, F_t, and the elementary movement, d_s, over the distance travelled during braking, s.

$$W = \int_0^s F_t \cdot d_s$$

Instantaneous braking power P
Product of the momentary total braking force F_t and the vehicle's road speed υ

$$P = F_t \cdot \upsilon$$

Braking deceleration
Reduction of speed obtained by the braking system in the considered time, t. The following can be identified:
Momentary deceleration: $a = d\upsilon/dt$

Mean deceleration: $a_{ms} = \upsilon_0^2/(2 \cdot s_o)$

The mean deceleration value over the stopping distance, whereby υ_0 and s_0 refer to the point t_0.

Mean deceleration a_{mt} within a section of time:
Deceleration between two points in time t_i and t_j. This formula is used for the evaluation of the braking efficiency of retarders.

$$a_{mt} = (\upsilon_i - \upsilon_j)/(t_j - t_i)$$

Mean fully developed deceleration a_{mf}:
Mean value of deceleration (a_{mf}) over subdivision $t_3 - t_2$ of the fully developed deceleration.

$$a_{mf} = \frac{1}{t_3 - t_2} \cdot \int_{t_2}^{t_3} a \cdot dt$$

Braking factor z
Ratio between the total braking force, F_t, and the static weight, G_s, on the axle or the axles of the vehicle:

$$z = F_t/G_s$$

Legal regulations

The testing of braking equipment pursuant to the issuance of the type approval for a vehicle in Germany may take place in accordance with one of the following three groups of regulations as chosen by the vehicle manufacturer. They are:
– National regulations and statutory requirements for the testing of brakes applicable in the country of use,
– Council Directive of the European Communities: Directive 71/320/EEC and the Amending Directives and Annexes or
– ECE Regulation 13, 13H and 78 of the UN Economic Commission in Geneva.

In Europe, the national regulations of individual countries may specify introduction of the EU Directive or ECE Regulations. Essentially, they may be very similar. However, the ECE Regulations 13 and 13H are likely to be more recent and contain, for example, regulations for braking systems with electrical control systems (electronically controlled braking systems).

Braking systems conforming to EU Directives, and ECE Regulations 13 and 78 (for classification refer to P. 717).

Category L vehicles (less than 4 wheels)
Motorized two- and three-wheeled vehi-

cles must be equipped with 2 mutually independent braking systems. In the case of heavy category L_5 3-wheel vehicles, the two braking systems must both act on two wheels. Additionally, these vehicles must be equipped with a parking braking system.

Category M and N vehicles

The categories M and N vehicles must meet the requirements which pertain to the service braking system, secondary braking system and parking braking system. These 3 braking systems may have common components. Such vehicles must have at least 2 mutually independent control devices.

The apportioning of braking force among the individual axles is prescribed. Vehicles in the categories M_2 and N_2 or higher must be fitted with an antilock braking system (ABS) (some exceptions may still apply for older models).

Additional retarding braking systems can be used in order to fulfill braking requirements on long inclines. Vehicles in category M_3 used for local or long-distance duty must be able to meet the requirements for braking on such "descents" using the continuous-operation braking system only.

Category O trailers

Category O_1 trailers are not required to have a braking system, however, there are requirements governing the safety connection to the towing vehicle. Beginning with category O_2, trailers must be fitted with a service braking system and a parking braking system which may have common components. It must be possible for the parking braking system to be operated by a person standing next to the vehicle. The apportioning of braking force among the individual axles is prescribed.

An antilock braking system (ABS) is prescribed for some trailers in Class O_3 and above.

Inertia braking systems are permissible for trailers up to category O_2.

The trailer must brake automatically if it becomes decoupled from the tractor vehicle while moving, or (for trailers < 1.5 t) it must be equipped with a safety connection to the towing vehicle.

Vehicles equipped with antilock braking systems (ABS)

ABS systems must conform to Appendix X of EU Directive 71/320/EEC or Annex 13 of ECE Regulation 13 (on Category 1 vehicles of classes M_2, M_3, N_2 and N_3). The essential requirements are:
– locking of the directly controlled wheels under braking on any road surface at speeds of over 15 km/h must be prevented,
– operating stability and steering control are to be maintained and
– grip on road surfaces offering the same or (in the case of Category 1) different levels of adhesion to wheels on different sides (μ split) must be utilized, and
– there must be a visual warning system for indicating electrical faults.

Only minimum standards are in force for trailer ABS. The ABS on tractor and trailer should be mutually compatible in order to ensure safety and prevent excessive tire wear.

Tractor vehicles and trailers with compressed-air braking systems

The compressed-air connections must be of the two- or multi-line design. When the service brakes on the tractor unit are operated, the service brakes on the trailer must also be operated with a variable degree of force. If any fault occurs on the service brakes of the tractor unit, that part of the system not affected by the fault must be cable of braking the trailer with a variable degree of force. If one of the lines between tractor unit and trailer is separated or develops a leak, it must still be possible to brake the trailer, or it must brake automatically.

The braking efficiency of the vehicle when fully loaded (and when empty for vehicles without ABS) is specified according to the pressure at the control-line coupling head. The service brakes of the trailer must only be capable of operation in conjunction with the service, secondary or parking brake system on the tractor unit.

Requirements of StVZO (Germany), EU Directive 71/320 EEC and ECE Regulations

Vehicle class (For classification, refer to P. 717)		Passenger cars & motor coaches			Commercial vehicles			Trailers			
		M_1	M_2	M_3	N_1	N_2	N_3	O_1	O_2	O_3	O_4
Service braking system		Acting on all wheels Prescribed force distribution to the axles						No braking system or as O_2	Inertia braking system or as O_3		
ABS as per EC Dir, or ECE[1] ($v_{max} \geq 25$ km/h)		–	+	+	–	+	+	–	–	+	+
Type O test (drive disengaged)											
Test speed	km/h	80	60	60	80	60	60	–	60	60	60
Braking distance	≤m	50.7	36.7	36.7	61.2	36.7	36.7		$z \geq 0.50$, Semitrailer $z \geq 0,45$		
Formula for		$0.1v$ $+\dfrac{v^2}{150}$		$0.15v + \dfrac{v^2}{130}$							
Mean fully developed deceleration	≥m/s²	5.8		5.0							
Actuating force	≤n	500		700					at ≤6.5 bar		
Type O test (drive engaged)		Behaviour of vehicle under braking from $30\% - 80\% v_{max}$ and braking efficiency									
Test velocity $v = 80\% \, v_{max}$, but	≤km/h	160	100	90	120	100	90	–	–	–	–
Braking distance	≤m	212.9	111.6	91.8	157.1	111.6	91.8				
Braking distance formula		$0.1v$ $+\dfrac{v^2}{130}$		$0.15v + \dfrac{v^2}{103.5}$							
Mean fully developed deceleration	≥m/s²	5.0		4.0							
Actuating force	≤n	500		700							
Type I test		Repeated braking at 3 m/s² loaded, drive engaged							Continuous braking, loaded 40 km/h 7% downhill gradient 1.7 km $z \geq 0.36$ and $z \geq 60\%$ of figure measured in Type O test at 40 km/h		–
$v_1 = 80\% \, v_{max}$, but $v_2 = {}^1/_2 \, v_1$	≤km/h	120	100	60	120	60	60	–			
Braking cycle repetitions	n	15	15	20	15	20	20				
Braking cycle duration	s	45	55	60	55	60	60				
Effectiveness of hot brakes at end of Type I Test		≥80% of brake efficiency specified for Type O test (drive disengaged) and ≥60% of the brake efficiency achieved in Type O test (drive disengaged)									
Type II Test on long descents		Energy corresponding to 30 km/h, 6% downhill gradient and 6 km, loaded, engine drive engaged, continuous-operation braking system in operation. Measurement as for Type O test (drive disengaged)									at 40 km/h
Effectiveness of hot brakes at end of Type II Test											
Braking distance formula		M_3: $0.15v + \dfrac{1.33v^2}{130}$ N_3: $0.15v + \dfrac{1.33v^2}{115}$						–	–	–	
Braking distance	≤m	–	–	45.8	–	–	50.6				$z \geq$ 0.33
Mean fully developed deceleration	≥m/s²			3.75			3.3				

---

[1] Exceptions may still be allowed for older models.

Vehicle class (For classification, refer to P. 717)			Passenger cars & motor coaches			Commercial vehicles			Trailers			
			M_1	M_2	M_3	N_1	N_2	N_3	O_1	O_2	O_3	O_4
Type IIa Test For continuous-operation braking systems			Energy corresponding to 30 km/h, 7 % downhill gradient, 6 km, loaded, only continuous-operation braking system in operation. Only permitted for M_3[2]) and towing O_4, N_3.									
Type III Test			–						–	–	–	3)
Residual braking effect after failure in the transmission device/circuit failure, engine drive disengaged									The brakes of the trailer must be capable of full or partial operation using variable force.			
Test speed		km/h	80	60	60	70	50	40				
Braking distance, loaded		≤ m	150.2	101.3	101.3	152.5	80.0	52.4				
Braking distance, empty		≤ m	178.7	119.8	101.3	180.9	94.5	52.4				
Mean fully developed deceleration, loaded		≥ m/s²	1.7	1.5	1.5	1.3	1.3	1.3				
empty		≥ m/s²	1.5	1.3	1.5	1.1	1.1	1.3				
Actuating force		≤ n	700	700	700	700	700	700				
Secondary braking system (tested as for Type O Test, drive disengaged)									The brakes of the trailer must be operated using variable force.			
Test speed		km/h	80	60	60	70	50	40				
Braking distance		≤ m	93.3	64.4	64.4	95.7	54.0	38.3				
Braking-distance formula			$0.1v + \dfrac{2v^2}{150}$	$0{,}15v + \dfrac{2v^2}{130}$		$0{,}15v + \dfrac{2v^2}{115}$						
Mean fully developed deceleration		≥ m/s²	2.9	2.5		2.2						
Actuating force, by hand		≤ n	400	600		600						
with foot		≤ n	500	700		700						
Parking braking system (Loaded test)												
Holding stationary on incline (downgrade or upgrade)		≥ %		18			18		–		18	
Together with unbraked vehicle of class O		≥ %		12			12		–		–	
Actuating force, by hand		≤ n	400	600		600			–		600	
with foot		≤ n	500	700		700			–		–	
Type O Test 4) (drive disengaged, loaded)												
Test speed		km/h	80	60	60	70	50	40	–			
Mean fully developed deceleration and deceleration prior to standstill		≥ m/s²		1.5		1.5		–				
Automatic braking system With compressed-air systems, automatic trailer braking in case of pressure loss in supply line												
Test speed		km/h							–		40	
Braking factor		≥ %							–		13.5	

2) Except public transport busses
3) Repeated braking as for Type I test for N_3. Afterwards, braking efficiency ≥ 40 and ≥ 60 % of level achieved in Type O Test.
4) With parking braking system or via auxiliary control device for service braking system.

Design and components of a braking system

Basic components of a braking system:

The braking system consists of:
- Energy supply,
- A control device,
- A transmission device for controlling braking force, and for activating the engine brake, parking brake, and retarder,
- Additional equipment in the towing vehicle for braking the trailer.
- Wheel brakes.

Each of those components affects the braking forces which are decisive for slowing down the vehicle or vehicle combination.

Different ranges of applications for different vehicle types result in highly variegated demands being placed on braking systems. The inescapable result is a multiplicity of highly diversified braking systems, differing from one another in both design and application.

Braking-system applications

Legal regulations stipulate that the braking system on a heavy commercial vehicle will consist of:
- service brakes,
- secondary brakes,
- parking brake, and (in some cases)
- additional retarding braking systems, and
- self-actuated braking system.

The service and parking brakes are equipped with separate individual control and transmission devices. The service brakes are generally applied with the foot, while the parking brake can be actuated with either hand or foot. The secondary braking system frequently shares components with the service or parking brakes. For instance when one circuit in a dual-circuit service-braking system also functions as secondary brake. The additional retarding braking system, which acts as a supplementary, wear-free unit, is especially useful for relieving the service brakes on long downgrades (see "Additional retarding braking system", page 682). Self-actuated (automatic) braking systems apply to trailers only.

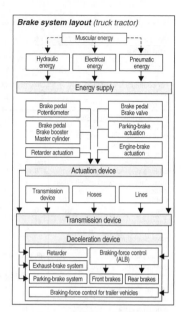

Brake system layout (truck tractor)

Muscular energy

Hydraulic energy — Electrical energy — Pneumatic energy

Energy supply

Brake pedal Potentiometer — Brake pedal Brake valve

Brake pedal Brake booster Master cylinder — Parking-brake actuation

Retarder actuation — Engine-brake actuation

Actuation device

Transmission device — Hoses — Lines

Transmission device

Deceleration device

Retarder — Braking-force control (ALB)

Exhaust-brake system

Parking-brake system — Front brakes — Rear brakes

Braking-force control for trailer vehicles

Type of energy and transmission media

Depending upon the type of energy applied to control the braking system, a distinction is drawn between:
- muscular-energy braking systems,
- energy-assisted braking systems,
- non-muscular-energy braking systems,
- inertia braking systems.

The various systems can also be installed in combination. In contrast to the non-muscular-energy braking system, for instance, the energy-assisted system also depends to some degree on the force exerted at the pedal.

Energy-assisted and non-muscular-energy systems are distinguished not only by energy type, but also by the mediums used to transmit the energy. Pneumatic (vacuum, compressed air) and hydraulic energy are the most common, electrical energy is sometimes also employed.

Type of transmission device

The means employed to transmit energy within the braking system may be me-

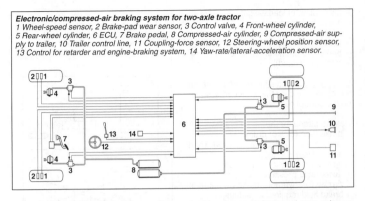

Electronic/compressed-air braking system for two-axle tractor
1 Wheel-speed sensor, 2 Brake-pad wear sensor, 3 Control valve, 4 Front-wheel cylinder,
5 Rear-wheel cylinder, 6 ECU, 7 Brake pedal, 8 Compressed-air cylinder, 9 Compressed-air supply to trailer, 10 Trailer control line, 11 Coupling-force sensor, 12 Steering-wheel position sensor,
13 Control for retarder and engine-braking system, 14 Yaw-rate/lateral-acceleration sensor.

chanical, hydraulic, pneumatic or electric/electronic. Hybrid combinations may also be used in transmitting the force to the wheel brakes. Electric/electronic transmission mechanisms will play an important role in the electronic-pneumatic and electronic-hydraulic braking systems for the next generation of vehicles.

Braking-system design

The braking system is designed with reference to both the requirements of the vehicle and the intrinsic imperatives of the system itself. In the case of the vehicle-oriented design, the vehicle's center of gravity and the specified distribution of braking force to the front and rear axles, determine the amount of braking force which can be applied before the wheels lock at any specific level of adhesion between tire and road surface. The braking-force-distribution diagram is used to illustrate this relationship. The coordinate axes show the braking force at front and rear axles relative to weight. The intersection of the straight lines representing equal adhesion coefficients at front and rear axles form the parabola defining "ideal" braking-force distribution. Lines representing constant braking complete the diagram.

If no braking-force metering device is fitted, then the distribution of the braking force as installed in the unit also forms a straight line. The slope is the ratio of the braking forces at front and rear axles as determined by the dimensions of the brakes. The wheels will always lock on the front axle first as long as the line for as-installed distribution remains below the ideal distribution (stable distribution of braking forces). The point at which the front wheels lock is found at the intersection of "as-installed distribution" and the lines representing the respective coefficient of adhesion.

The essential design criteria are:
- regulations governing minimum braking force required before the onset of lock, and locking sequence,

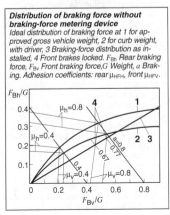

Distribution of braking force without braking-force metering device
Ideal distribution of braking force at 1 for approved gross vehicle weight, 2 for curb weight, with driver, 3 Braking-force distribution as installed, 4 Front brakes locked. F_{Bh} Rear braking force, F_{Bv} Front braking force, G Weight, a Braking. Adhesion coefficients: rear μ_{HFH}, front μ_{HFV}.

- distribution of load weight,
- influence of fading,
- engine braking,
- failure of a brake circuit,
- braking-force metering device (if fitted),
- retarder (if fitted).

<u>System-oriented design</u> concentrates on the dimensions for the wheel brakes and on the control devices.

Design criteria for the wheel brakes:
- brake type (disc or drum),
- endurance (resistance to wear and severe use),
- space available for installation,
- acceptable pressure levels,
- rigidity (on hydraulic brakes: volume of brake fluid required for actuation).

Design criteria for the control device:
- Pedal travel and pedal force for normal braking, emergency braking, and in the event of failure of a brake circuit or the brake servo.
- comfort requirements,
- installation space,
- combination with systems for brake-pressure regulation.

Brake-circuit configurations

Legal regulations stipulate a dual-circuit transmission system as mandatory.

Of the five available options (DIN 74000, see below), versions II and X have become standard. As the brake lines, hoses, connections, and static and dynamic seals remain at a low level of complication, the probability of failure due to leaks is comparable to that achieved with a single-circuit system. The potential response to failure of a circuit due to overheating at one wheel points up a serious weakness in the HI, LL and HH distribution patterns, where loss of both brake circuits on a wheel could lead to total brake-system failure.

Vehicles with a forward weight bias use distribution pattern X to fulfill the regulatory requirements. The II distribution pattern is an excellent solution for vehicles with rear weight bias and mid-range and heavy commercial vehicles.

Brake-circuit configuration: Variants
a) II distribution, b) X distribution, c) HI distribution, d) LL distribution, e) HH distribution.
1 Brake circuit 1, 2 Brake circuit 2.
← Direction of travel.

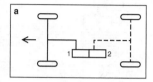

a

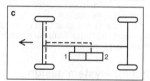

b

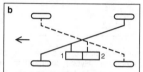

c

d

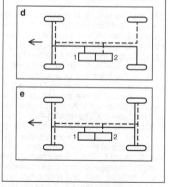

e

II distribution pattern
Front-axle/rear-axle split. One circuit brakes the front axle and the other the rear axle.

X distribution pattern
Diagonal distribution pattern. Each circuit brakes a given front wheel and the diagonally opposite rear wheel.

HI distribution pattern
Front-axle and rear-axle/front-axle split. One circuit brakes the front and rear axles, and one circuit brakes only the front axle.

LL distribution pattern
Front-axle and rear-wheel/front-axle and rear-wheel split. Each circuit brakes the front axle and one rear wheel.

HH distribution pattern
Front-axle and rear-axle/front-axle and rear-axle split. Each circuit brakes the front axle and the rear axle.

Vacuum-operated brake booster
Effect of design parameters.
1 Master-cylinder surface area, 2 Pedal leverage, 3 Boost factor, pedal leverage, 4 Diaphragm surface area, vacuum level, 5 Effect of pedal force, 6 Effect of servo assist, 7 Output point.

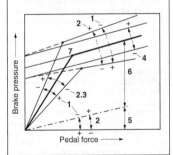

Vacuum-operated brake booster
1 Push rod, 2 Vacuum chamber with vacuum connection, 3 Diaphragm, 4 Piston, 5 Bell valve, 6 Air filter, 7 Piston rod, 8 Rear chamber, 9 Backing plate.

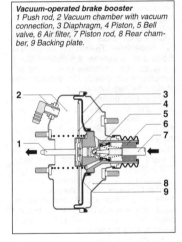

Tandem master cylinder with central valve in secondary circuit
1 Cylinder body,
2 Pressure chamber,
3 Pressure connection,
4 Connection for compensating reservoir,
5 Thrust-rod piston,
6 Secondary piston,
7 Central valve,
8 Stop for central valve,
9 Primary seal,
10 Separating seal,
11 Balancing port.

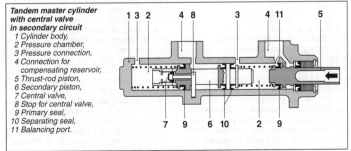

Braking systems for passenger cars and light utility vehicles

Control devices

The control device consists of:
– brake pedal,
– vacuum brake booster,
– master cylinder,
– brake-fluid reservoir,
– device to warn of a brake-circuit failure and/or low brake-fluid level.

In addition to the basic equipment listed above, hydraulic boosters or hydraulic non-muscular-energy braking systems may be used in certain applications. In non-muscular-energy systems, the brake booster and master cylinder are replaced by a brake valve. The force at the pedal is modulated to achieve the desired brake pressure. High-pressure pumps and accumulators are included to generate and to store the requisite energy.

A vacuum brake booster is generally used due to its inexpensive and uncomplicated design. On this type of booster, the force applied at the pedal regulates the amount of outside air which is applied to a diaphragm, while vacuum remains present on the diaphragm's other side. The pressure differential at the diaphragm generates force to supplement that applied at the pedal. The simplified diagram provides a schematic illustration of the main factors which influence the braking pressure; working losses and efficiency levels are not considered:
– Pedal conversion,
– boost factor,
– diaphragm surface area,
– vacuum pressure,
– surface area of master cylinder.

The brake pressure is the result of a combination of the force at the pedal and an auxiliary assist. The proportion represented by the assist increases steadily up to full boost; the designed-in boost factor determines the precise rate. At full boost, the maximum pressure difference between outside air and vacuum has been reached. Additional augmentation of the output force is only possible via an unaccustomed increase in the force applied at the pedal. Thus it is important that the booster be designed to ensure that high rates of deceleration can be achieved without exceeding full boost to any appreciable degree.

The major determinant for output force is the surface area of the diaphragm. Two diaphragms in tandem are employed to satisfy higher pressure requirements. Technical considerations limit the maximum feasible diaphragm diameter to approx. 250 mm. The maximum negative pressure, as obtained at the intake manifold of a spark-ignition engine with the throttle closed, is approx. 0.8 bar. A vacuum pump is required on diesel engines.

As the demand for boost pressure in heavy vehicles is characteristically greater, the logical choice is a hydraulic booster, which can be designed to function on the same principles.

The energy is frequently provided by the power-steering pump, with an intermediate hydraulic accumulator being incorporated in the circuit to reduce the tendency of brakes and steering to influence each other.

A push rod carries the output force directly to the piston in the tandem master cylinder. The hydraulic pressure thus generated is transmitted to the "floating" intermediate piston, resulting in roughly equal pressures in the two chambers which supply the respective circuits.

Failure in one of the brake circuits can have one of two results: Either the push rod comes up against the intermediate piston, or hydraulic force presses the intermediate piston back against the wall of the master cylinder. This condition will be felt at the pedal, which will continue moving with virtually no resistance.

A master cylinder which responds in several stages has proven a useful expedient on vehicles with the II distribution pattern. The intermediate piston, which has a smaller diameter than the push-rod piston, applies pressure to the rear-axle circuit. The system responds to failure in the front-axle circuit by increasing the pressure which is transmitted to the rear circuit at a constant pedal pressure. The degree of pressure increase is based on the ratio of the piston areas of the push-rod and intermediate pistons.

A brake-fluid reservoir is connected to the master cylinder to compensate for the effects of brake-lining wear and leakage. When the brake is released, either a centrally positioned valve in the master-cylinder piston opens or the piston seal opens a balancing port. This arrangement ensures that the brake system is not under pressure when released, while also providing compensation for fluid losses. The chief disadvantage of this simple layout lies in the fact that vapor bubbles in the brake fluid, which have been generated due to overheating, cause the fluid to drain from the affected brake circuit when the brakes are released. This could make it impossible to build up pressure when the brakes are applied again.

In order to prevent complete drainage in the event of a major leak, the brake-fluid reservoir is designed (at least as from a given brake-fluid level) with two circuits. One or two float-actuated switches trigger an optical display once the fluid falls below a certain level. The float-actuated switches can be replaced by differential pressure switches on the master cylinder, these then indicate failure of a brake circuit.

Wheel brakes

The wheel brakes must meet the following requirements:
- uniform effectiveness,
- smooth, graduated response,
- resistance to contamination and corrosion,
- extreme reliability,
- durability,
- resistance to wear,
- ease of maintenance.

Whereas on small passenger cars and commercial vehicles, various types of drum brakes fulfill these demands satisfactorily; disc brakes represent the only means of achieving even response and good control on heavy, high-speed passenger cars.

Gray cast-iron brake discs with bilaterally acting calipers have proven to be the most satisfactory layout. The brake disc is usually located within the well of the wheel rim. An arrangement which makes it necessary to provide for adequate heat dissipation through radiation, convection and thermal conductance. Additional expedients such as internally-ventilated brake discs, air ducts and optimal-flow

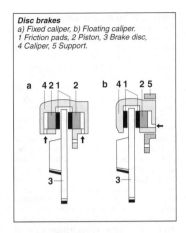

Disc brakes
a) Fixed caliper, b) Floating caliper.
1 Friction pads, 2 Piston, 3 Brake disc,
4 Caliper, 5 Support.

wheel designs are employed to reduce disc temperatures, particularly on high-performance vehicles.

Brake calipers fall into one of two categories: Fixed calipers or floating calipers.

In the case of the fixed caliper, the housing is rigid and "grips" the brake disc from both sides. When the brakes are applied, two pistons in the caliper housing, one on each side of the brake disc, force the brake pads up against the brake disc.

Two basic subcategories of floating caliper have established themselves.
The sliding caliper and the so-called Mark II caliper. With both designs, the piston or pistons act directly against brake pad on the inner side of the disc. The sliding-caliper frame or the caliper then pulls the outer pad against the disc. Compared to fixed calipers, the floating units offer the following advantages:
- Modest space requirement between brake disc and wheel nave (convenient where suspension employs small or negative steering-roll radius),
- Reduced thermal stress on the fluid, as no fluid lines are located in the critical area directly above the brake disc.

Constructive measures effectively alleviate inherent disadvantages (tendency to rattle and squeak, uneven wear of friction pads, corrosion in transmission elements).

Braking-force metering device

The braking-force metering device is not a closed-loop control element, like the brake-pressure regulating valve as used for ABS, but rather an open-loop control element. The individual metering devices differ with respect to their function as braking-force limiters or reducers, or their control parameters, such as brake pressure, axle load or rate of deceleration.

The braking force is apportioned between the front and rear axles in accordance with the dimensions of the particular brakes. It is the job of the metering device to adjust this braking-force apportionment in order to achieve a closer approximation to the ideal distribution, i.e., the parabolic curve. The ideal braking-force distribution is determined solely by the vehicle's center of gravity and the nature of the particular braking maneuver. These relationships can be shown in a dimensionless braking-force-distribution diagram. The weight-related braking forces at the front and rear axles are entered on the coordinate axes. The lines for identical braking appear as straight lines with a negative slope (−1). The ideal braking-force-distribution curves for the vehicle conditions "curb weight" and "approved gross vehicle weight" are in the form of parabolas. Diagram "a" is for a braking-force limiter and diagram "b" a braking-force reducer.

Pressure-sensitive metering valves achieve good approximation of ideal distribution with the vehicle in the "curb weight" state. On the other hand, under "approved gross vehicle weight" conditions (upper parabola), they deviate from the ideal once the limiter or reducer becomes operative (bend in the curve), i.e., the proportion of the total braking force directed toward the rear axle decreases as the rear-axle load increases.

The load-sensitive apportioning valve responds to increased loads by displacing the triggering point upward, allowing a reasonable approximation of ideal braking-force distribution under all load conditions.

The deceleration-sensitive apportioning valve is triggered by a specific rate of deceleration, and is thus basically insensitive to load.

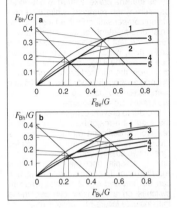

Braking-force-distribution diagram
a) Braking-force limiter, b) Braking-force reducer. F_{Bh} Rear braking force, F_{Bv} Front braking force, G Weight. 1 Loaded, 2 Empty, 3 Loaded, according to load, 4 Empty, according to pressure; empty according to deceleration, and loaded; empty according to load, 5 Loaded, according to pressure.

The metering valve must be designed to ensure that the distribution of braking force remains on or below the ideal curve. The potential effects of fluctuations of the pad friction coefficient, as well as of engine torque and tolerances of the valve itself, must all be considered in preventing over-brake of the rear axle. In practice, this means that actual installed distribution (with bend in curve) should remain well below the ideal.

The criteria according to which the metering valve is designed include the following:
– ABS compatibility,
– Complexity in the case of split rear-axle braking circuits (e.g. X distribution),
– Bypass function for dealing with brake-circuit failure, especially with braking-force limiters,
– Facility for testing of setting and operation.

Vehicles with balanced load conditions are not necessarily equipped with a metering device, as the disadvantages of an undetected defect in the device outweigh its minimal advantages.

ABS antilock braking systems for passenger cars

ABS antilock braking systems are closed-loop control devices within the braking system which prevent wheel lock-up during braking and, as a result, retain the vehicle's steerability and stability. The main ABS components are:

Hydraulic modulator, wheel-speed sensors, and the ECU for signal processing and control and triggering of the signal lamp and of the actuators in the hydraulic modulator.

Basic closed-loop control process

On initial braking, the brake pressure is increased; the brake slip λ rises and at the maximum point on the adhesion/slip curve, it reaches the limit between the stable and unstable ranges. From this point on, any further increase in brake pressure or braking torque does not cause any further increase in the braking force F_B. In the stable range, the brake slip is largely deformation slip, it increasingly tends towards skidding in the unstable range.

Brake slip $\lambda = (v_F - v_R)/v_F \cdot 100\%$
Wheel speed $v_R = r \cdot \omega$
Braking force $F_B = \mu_{HF} \cdot G$
Lateral force $F_S = \mu_S \cdot G$
μ_{HF} Coefficient of friction,
μ_S Lateral-force coefficient.

There is a more or less sharp drop in the coefficient of friction μ_{HF}, depending upon the shape of the slip curve. The resulting excess torque causes the wheel to lock-up very quickly (when braking without ABS); this is expressed as a sharp increase in wheel deceleration.

The wheel-speed sensors monitor the motion of the wheels. If one of the wheels shows signs of lock-up, there is a sharp rise in peripheral wheel deceleration and in wheel slip. If these exceed defined critical values, the controller sends commands to the solenoid-valve unit to stop or reduce the buildup of wheel-brake pressure until the danger of lock-up has passed. The brake pressure must then be built up again in order to ensure that the wheel is not underbraked. During automatic brake control, it is constantly necessary for the stability or instability of the wheel motion to be detected, and the

Forces at the braked wheel
G Force due to weight, F_B Braking force,
F_S Lateral force, v_F Vehicle speed,
α Slip angle, ω Angular velocity, n Caster.

Adhesion/slip curve
The curve shape differs greatly as a function of road surface and tire condition.

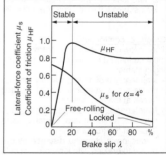

ABS control loop
1 Solenoid-valve unit, 2 Master cylinder,
3 Wheel-brake cylinder, 4 Electronic control unit (ECU), 5 Wheel-speed sensor.

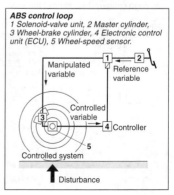

wheel must be kept in the slip range with maximum braking force by a succession of pressure-buildup, pressure-reduction and pressure-holding phases.

<u>Disturbances in the closed control loop</u>
The ABS system must take the following disturbances into account:
– Changes in the adhesion between the tires and the road surface caused by different types of road surface and changes in the wheel loadings, e.g. when cornering,
– Irregularities in the road surface causing the wheels and axles to vibrate,
– Out-of-roundness, brake hysteresis, brake fading,
– Variations in the pressure input to the master cylinder caused by the driver's brake-pedal actuation,
– Differences in wheel circumferences, for instance when the spare wheel is fitted.

<u>Criteria of control quality</u>
The following criteria for control quality must be fulfilled by efficient antilock braking systems:
– Maintenance of driving stability through provision of sufficient lateral guiding forces at the rear wheels.
– Maintenance of steerability through provision of adequate lateral guiding forces at the front wheels.
– Reduction in stopping distance as opposed to braking with locked-up wheels through optimum utilization of the adhe-

sion between tires and road.
– Rapid matching of the braking force to different adhesion coefficients, for instance when driving through deep water or driving over patches of ice or hard snow.
– Guaranteeing low braking-torque control amplitudes to prevent vibrations in the running gear.
– High level of comfort due to silent actuators and low feedback through the brake pedal.

ABS system variants
A variety of versions are available depending upon the braking-force-distribution concept, the type of vehicle drive concerned, functional stipulations, and costs factor. The overview below shows six system variants, which are described in the following according to the number of channels and sensors.

<u>4-channel systems (variants 1, 2)</u>
These systems permit the individual control of the wheel-brake pressure of each wheel for the rear axle/front axle (II) and for the diagonal (X) braking-force-distribution concepts. When braking on split-coefficient road surfaces though, measures must be taken to ensure that the yaw moment (torque around the vertical axis) cannot adversely affect driving stability. The solution here is to control the wheels on the front axle individually and those on the rear axle in accordance with the "select-low" principle (that is, the rear wheel

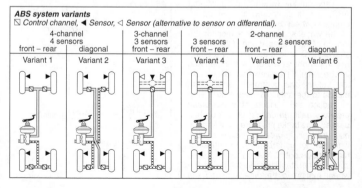

ABS system variants
◻ *Control channel,* ◀ *Sensor,* ◁ *Sensor (alternative to sensor on differential).*

4-channel 4 sensors		3-channel 3 sensors	2-channel 2 sensors		
front – rear	diagonal	front – rear	front – rear	front – rear	diagonal
Variant 1	Variant 2	Variant 3	Variant 4	Variant 5	Variant 6

with the lowest coefficient of friction determines the braking pressure applied to both rear wheels).

3-channel system (variant 3)

The yaw moment when braking on split-coefficient road surfaces is reduced to such an extent (due to the system's operating principle) that passenger cars with a long wheelbase, and a high moment of mass inertia about the vertical axis, are well able to control this braking situation.

In the case of the 3- and 4-channel systems, passenger cars with a short wheelbase and a low moment of mass inertia, however, require electronic delay of the yaw-moment buildup. When braking on split-coefficient road surfaces, this causes a delayed buildup of the braking torque at the front wheel with the high coefficient of friction. As a result, the driver has enough time to correct the yaw by an appropriate steering adjustment.

2-channel systems (variants 4, 5, 6)

The 2-channel systems on the one hand need less components than the 3- and 4-channel versions, and this makes them less costly to manufacture. On the other hand though, this is accompanied by a number of functional limitations.

With variant 4 in the select-high mode (the front wheel with the higher coefficient of friction determines the brake pressure applied jointly to both front wheels), practically every time the driver hits the brakes hard (panic braking), one of the front wheels locks up. This is accompanied by a high level of tire wear and reduced steerability. With version 5, this always occurs when the "sensed" front wheel suddenly encounters a higher level of friction coefficient than the "non-sensed" wheel. Variant 6 can be used only with diagonal braking-force distribution (X). In this version, the brake pressures at the front wheels are controlled individually, while the brake pressures at the rear wheels are jointly controlled. Because the front-to-rear distribution of braking force bears the responsibility for ensuring that the rear wheels do not lock, this system provides somewhat lower deceleration rates than a 3- or 4-channel system.

Note: For some light-truck models with front-rear brake-circuit split in the American market there is a simple system consisting of a sensor on the rear differential and a control channel (without return pump) which prevents the rear wheels locking. The front wheels can lock up with sufficiently high braking pressures with the consequent loss of steering function. This system is not an ABS with the range of functions described at the beginning of this section and is used only for certain specialized types of vehicle.

ABS versions

ABS 2S-3-channel/-4-channel systems (Bosch)

In this system, the ABS and the brake booster are separate units.

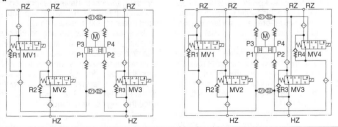

Functional diagrams
a) Three-channel hydraulic modulator, b) Four-channel hydraulic modulator.
D Damper, HZ Master cylinder, M Electric motor, MV Solenoid valve, P Pump, R Control channel,
RZ Wheel-brake cylinder, S Accumulator.

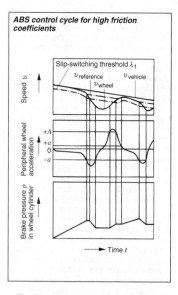

ABS control cycle for high friction coefficients

Slip-switching threshold λ_1

$v_{reference}$ $v_{vehicle}$

v_{wheel}

Speed v

Peripheral wheel acceleration

$+A$
$+a$
0
$-a$

Brake pressure p in wheel cylinder

Time t

The 3-channel hydraulic modulator for the II braking-force-distribution version (front/rear) comprises three solenoid valves with three possible positions, and a return pump with electric drive motor.

In the first, de-energized position, there is an unhindered passage from the master cylinder to the wheel-brake cylinder, with the result that the wheel-brake pressure rises during initial braking and during automatic brake control. In the second, semi-energized position, the passage from the master cylinder to the wheel-brake cylinder is interrupted, with the result that the wheel-brake pressure is kept constant. In the third, fully energized position, the wheel-brake cylinder is connected to the return and the wheel-brake pressure drops.

Pressure dissipation takes only about 20 ms so that the wheel does not lock up; pressure build-up, on the other hand, takes place in several stages with intervening holding phases and typically takes around 200 ms.

The 4-channel hydraulic-modulator valve for diagonal braking-force distribu-

tion calls for four solenoid valves, because the rear-wheel brakes belong to different brake circuits. However, both the rear-wheel valves are jointly energized, so that there is the same pressure in each of the rear-wheel-brakes, and the "select-low" control mode is easy to implement.

The depicted control cycle shows automatic brake control in the case of a high friction coefficient. The change in wheel speed (deceleration) is calculated in the ECU. After the value falls below the $(-a)$ threshold, the hydraulic modulator valve unit is switched to the pressure-holding mode. If the wheel speed then also drops below the slip-switching threshold λ_1, the valve unit is switched to pressure reduction; this is done as long as the $(-a)$ signal is present. During the subsequent pressure-holding phase, the peripheral wheel acceleration increases until the $(+a)$ threshold is exceeded; thereupon, the brake pressure continues to be kept constant. After the relatively high $(+A)$ threshold has been exceeded, the brake pressure is increased, so that the wheel is not accelerating excessively as it enters the stable range of the adhesion/slip curve. After the $(+a)$ signal has dropped out, the brake pressure is slowly raised until, when the wheel acceleration again falls below the $(-a)$ threshold, the second control cycle is initiated, this time with an immediate pressure reduction. In the first control cycle, a short pressure-holding phase was necessary initially for the filtering of disturbances. In the case of high wheel moments of inertia, low friction coefficient and slow pressure rise in the wheel-brake cylinder (cautious initial braking, e.g., on black ice), the wheel might lock-up without the deceleration switching threshold having responded. In this case, therefore, the wheel slip, too, is used in automatic brake control.

Under certain road-surface conditions, passenger cars with all-wheel drive and with differential locks engaged pose problems when the ABS system is in operation; this calls for special measures to support the reference speed, lower the wheel-deceleration thresholds, and reduce the engine drag torque.

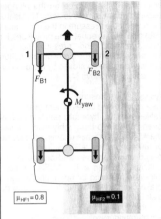

Buildup of yaw moment induced by large differences in friction coefficients
M_{yaw} Yaw moment, F_B Braking-force,
μ_{HF} Coefficient of friction.
1 "High" wheel, 2 "Low" wheel.

$\mu_{HF1} = 0.8$ $\mu_{HF2} = 0.1$

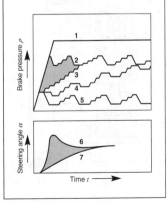

Curves for brake pressure/steering angle with delayed yaw-moment buildup (GMA)
1 Master-cylinder pressure p_{MC}, 2 Braking pressure p_{high} w/o GMA, 3 p_{high} with GMA 1, 4 p_{high} with GMA 2, 5 p_{low} at "Low" wheel, 6 Steering angle α w/o GMA, 7 Steering angle α with GMA.

Brake control with yaw-moment buildup delay

When the brakes are applied on an asymmetrical road surface (for instance, left wheels on dry asphalt, right wheels on ice), the result is vastly different braking forces at the front wheels. This difference induces a turning motion (yaw moment) around the vehicle's vertical axis.

When a heavy passenger car with ABS is braked, the resulting yaw sets in slowly and the driver has time for corrective steering maneuvers. On smaller cars, the ABS must be supplemented by an additional yaw-moment buildup-delay device (GMA) to ensure that control is maintained during panic stops on asymmetrical surfaces. GMA delays the pressure buildup in the wheel cylinder of the front wheel with the higher coefficient of braking force at the road surface ("high" wheel).

The GMA concept is demonstrated in the diagram: Curve 1 represents the master-cylinder pressure p_{MC}. Without GMA, the wheel on asphalt soon arrives at the pressure p_{high} (Curve 2), while the wheel which is running on ice goes to p_{low} (Curve 5); each wheel achieves the maximum retardation available under the given circumstances (individual control).

The GMA 1 System (Curve 3) is suited for use with vehicles with a less critical response pattern, while GMA 2 is designed for cars which display an especially marked tendency toward yaw-induced instability (Curve 4).

In all cases in which GMA comes into effect, the "High" wheel is under-braked at first. This means that the GMA must always be very carefully adapted to the vehicle in question in order to limit increases in stopping distances.

ABS 2E (Bosch)

This economical "full ABS" design (a 3-position solenoid valve with electronic control stage is replaced by a plunger/floating piston arrangement) offers the same safety features and functions as the ABS2S system with only minimal loss of comfort in terms of brake pedal feedback and noise.

Under normal braking, without active ABS, brake fluid flows to the right rear wheel through the rear-axle solenoid valve (4), while the plunger's central valve (6) supplies the left rear wheel.

When the ABS is activated, each of the left-side solenoid valves (2) controls a front brake, while the rear-axle solenoid valve (4) directly controls the rear right wheel (HR). The rear-axle solenoid valve (4) switches to position 3 upon receiving the "pressure-reduce" command from the ECU. In the process, fluid is released from the rear right wheel (HR) into the accumulator chamber (3) via the valve (4) so that the pressure at the wheel brake (HR) is reduced. Since the upper side of the floating piston (7) is hydraulically connected to the wheel brake (HR), this pressure reduction is also applied above the floating piston (7). The underside of the piston (7) is subjected to pressure from the master cylinder (1), and the resulting force on the piston (7) causes the floating piston assembly to move upwards. The upper plunger now comes into contact with the central valve pin (6) so that the central valve closes and volume can be accepted from the rear brake (HL) when

upward movement continues. At the same time, the pressure in the brake (LR) and on the underside of the top plunger also drops as required. The movement of the plunger then comes to a standstill when the resulting force on the plunger assembly has dropped to zero. This is the case when the pressure in the two brakes (HL) and (HR) is equal. The processes for "pressure hold" and "pressure buildup" are analogous to the pressure-reduction process and are controlled by the position of the solenoid valve (4).

ABS5 Family (Bosch)

As a result of the development of solenoid valves with two hydraulic positions it has been possible to thoroughly revolutionize the ABS system while retaining the range of functions of the ABS2S. The ABS5 is based upon the tried and proven return principle as used in the ABS2S. It contains the following components for each brake circuit (with X and II braking-force distribution):
– Return pump,
– Accumulator,

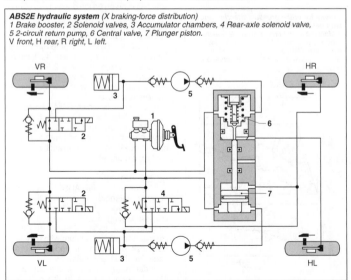

ABS2E hydraulic system (X braking-force distribution)
1 Brake booster, 2 Solenoid valves, 3 Accumulator chambers, 4 Rear-axle solenoid valve,
5 2-circuit return pump, 6 Central valve, 7 Plunger piston.
V front, H rear, R right, L left.

– Damper chamber, and
– 2/2 solenoid valves with two hydraulic positions and two hydraulic connections.

Each wheel (or the rear axle in the case of II braking-force distribution) is allocated a solenoid-valve pair, a solenoid valve (EV – open when de-energized) for the pressure increase (inlet) and a solenoid valve (AV – closed when de-energized) for pressure reduction (outlet). In order to achieve rapid release of pressure at the brakes when the pedal is released, the inlet valves each have a non-return valve which is integrated in the valve body (e.g. non-return valve sleeves or unsprung non-return valves).

Pressure increase and decrease are each allocated a solenoid valve which features only 1 active (energized) position. This leads to compact valve designs with only 2 hydraulic connections, smaller volume, lower weight, and low magnetic forces. The design means that only a single switching transistor is needed for the electrical triggering, with the attendant re-

duced electrical power loss in the solenoid coils and in the ECU. The valve block for mounting the 2/2 solenoid valves results in a smaller and lighter hydraulic modulator and means that the ECU can be attached directly to the hydraulic modulator. This has the advantage that the vehicle's wiring harness needs less lines. Because of their compact design, the 2/2 solenoid valves enable shorter electrical switching times and even pulse-width-modulated cyclic operation which substantially improves function (e.g. adaptation to changes in coefficient of friction) and control convenience (e.g. smaller delay fluctuations with the aid of pressure stages and lower levels of valve noise).

By coordinated development of mechanical valve design and pulse-width-modulated control (mechatronic optimization), it has been possible to produce an ABS system with "quiet" solenoid valves which represents a new milestone in terms of noise generation and pedal feedback.

Electric-motor variants, together with hydraulic throttling (restriction) of the flow

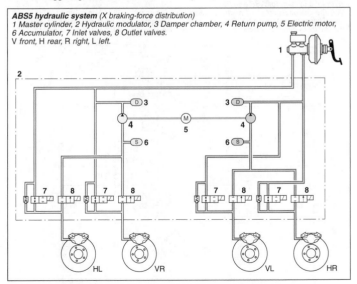

ABS5 hydraulic system (X braking-force distribution)
1 Master cylinder, 2 Hydraulic modulator, 3 Damper chamber, 4 Return pump, 5 Electric motor, 6 Accumulator, 7 Inlet valves, 8 Outlet valves.
V front, H rear, R right, L left.

cross sections in the solenoid valves, and variations in the accumulator volumes, mean that the ABS5-family represents a new generation of ABS systems suitable for installation in all series-production passenger cars.

ABS with TCS (Bosch)

See chapter "TCS traction control system," P. 606

ABS and ESP hydraulics (Bosch)

Proper control of vehicle-handling dynamics by means of ESP Electronic Stability Program (previously known as VDC Vehicle Dynamics Control) requires sufficiently rapid build-up of braking force in the brakes. On the one hand, low temperatures and low coefficients of friction are the conditions under which the ESP is called upon most often. On the other though, at low temperatures the brake-fluid viscosity increases considerably, thus making it necessary to modify the hydraulic concept compared to that used with ABS/TCS. The ABS/TCS5 system as

described in the Chapter "ABS with TCS (Bosch)" was taken as the basic system. Here, the pre-charge pump (VLP) was incorporated to ensure the return-pump delivery capacity when the ESP is needed under cold-weather conditions. The requirement for closed and separate brake circuits meant that this pre-charge pump could not be connected hydraulically directly upstream of the return pump. Instead it is applied to a charge-plunger unit (LKE) connected between the master cylinder and the ABS/TCS hydraulics. As soon as brake pressure is needed, the pre-charge pump switches on (together with the pre-charge valves (VLV) and the changeover valves (USV)) and delivers brake fluid to the charge-plunger unit (LKE) so that the two plungers in the unit move apart.

This mechanically closes the central valves of the LKE and the brake-fluid volume from the two LKE cylinders is forced through the opened pre-charge valves to the return pumps of the ABS/TCS hydraulics. The pre-charging of the return

---

Hydraulic system for ABS and ESP
VLP *Pre-charge pump*, VLV *Pre-charge valve*, RFP *Return pump*, RVR *Non-return valve*, LKE *Charge-plunger unit*, USV *Change-over valve*, D *Damper*, AV *Outlet valve*, EV *Inlet valve*, HZ *Master cylinder*, S *Accumulator*, VA *Front axle*, HA *Rear axle*, V *Front*, H *Rear*, R *Right*, L *Left*.

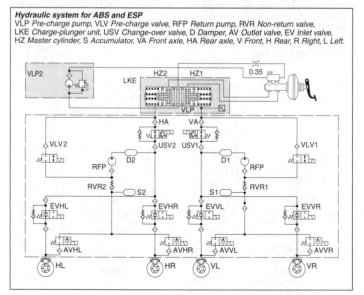

pumps means that sufficiently rapid brake-pressure buildup is ensured at the wheel brakes even at low temperatures. A separate line with a small restriction is provided between the LKE and the reservoir in order that the brake fluid in the pre-charge circuit can be bled, and the LKE plungers return to their initial position when the pre-charge pump is switched off.

By further optimization of the master cylinder and the ABS/TCS5 induction valves with the aim of increasing the hydraulic flow cross-section, it has been possible to produce an ESP hydraulic modulator that enables adequate pressure generation dynamics even without a precharger pump at low temperatures and thus further reduces the number of system components.

MK 2 (Teves)

The hydraulic components – brake booster and ABS – form a compact integrated unit for installation on the firewall. Under normal braking, the booster piston impels brake fluid directly to the rear brakes while pushing the master cylinder piston to the left, supplying brake fluid to the front brakes.

When the ABS is activated, the main valve opens, connecting the booster chamber with the primary side of the master cylinder piston while closing off the connection between the primary side and the reservoir. Brake fluid flows from the booster chamber to the front brakes via the connecting line and seal of the master-cylinder piston. During ABS-controlled braking, booster pressure is exerted against the left side of the positioning sleeve, maintaining master cylinder and booster piston in a middle position. This ensures that sufficient piston travel remains available for front-wheel braking in the event of ABS failure.

The supply and discharge valves provide optimal regulation of the pressures in the wheel cylinders during ABS-controlled braking maneuvers, with the brake fluid which is ejected from the wheel cylinder flowing back to the reservoir.

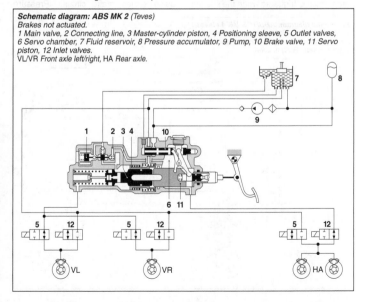

Schematic diagram: ABS MK 2 (Teves)
Brakes not actuated.
1 Main valve, 2 Connecting line, 3 Master-cylinder piston, 4 Positioning sleeve, 5 Outlet valves, 6 Servo chamber, 7 Fluid reservoir, 8 Pressure accumulator, 9 Pump, 10 Brake valve, 11 Servo piston, 12 Inlet valves.
VL/VR Front axle left/right, HA Rear axle.

The front brakes are controlled individually. The rear brakes are regulated together, whereby the wheel with the lower coefficient of traction determines the level of pressure (select low).

MK 4 with TCS (Teves)

This version is used with a conventional vacuum booster to provide "separate ABS". The system can also be extended to include TCS.

When the start of active ABS control makes it necessary to reduce the brake pressure at one of the wheels, the discharge valve is opened while the supply valve remains closed, allowing brake fluid to flow back to the reservoir from the brake. When the supply valve opens to increase the pressure, brake fluid flows from the master-cylinder chamber, and the pedal gives way somewhat. The hydraulic unit must supply new energy, as repeated cycles would otherwise cause the pedal to drop too far.

The ABS hydraulic energy-supply unit employs an electrically-driven, dual piston pump which is triggered when the system recognizes incipient wheel lock. The pump extracts brake fluid from the reservoir and pumps it through the supply-valve orifice and to the brake at a suitably increased pressure.

The excess flow quantity from the pump flows into the chambers of the master cylinder, where it presses back the master-cylinder piston and the brake pedal. The position sensor triggers and switches off the pump so as to ensure that the intermittent flow which it produces results in adequate feel and travel at the pedal.

The hydraulics can be expanded for traction control by adding 2 TCS solenoid valves, which serve to isolate the master cylinder from the TCS, and 2 pressure-relief valves, responsible for regulating pressure in the TCS system.

The rotation sensor is a security device for monitoring the operation of the pump motor.

MK 20 Family (Teves)

In contrast to the MK4, the MK 20 system operates according to the return principle using sealed brake circuits. Pressure

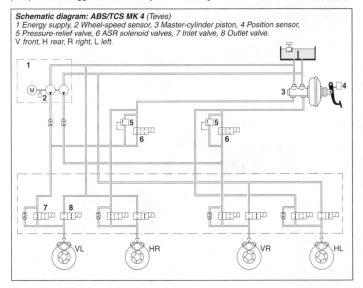

Schematic diagram: ABS/TCS MK 4 (Teves)
1 Energy supply, 2 Wheel-speed sensor, 3 Master-cylinder piston, 4 Position sensor,
5 Pressure-relief valve, 6 ASR solenoid valves, 7 Inlet valve, 8 Outlet valve.
V front, H rear, R right, L left.

modulation is by means of a pair of 2/2 solenoid valves (inlet/outlet) for each wheel and the system can be upgraded to TCS/ESP by the addition of two changeover valves and two induction valves. The hydraulic components thus correspond exactly to the arrangement employed by the Bosch ABS5 Family.

<u>Pumpless ABS</u> (Denso)
For a certain section of the Japanese market, a greatly simplified ABS system was developed which dispenses with damper chambers and return pumps together with their electric motors and control systems. It operates according to the following principle:

If the wheel-speed sensors detect that wheels are about to lock under braking, the appropriate inlet valves are closed in order to prevent further increase of pressure in the wheel cylinders. If this does not succeed in preventing the wheels locking, the corresponding pressure release valve is opened until the wheel stops slipping and is then closed again. The brake fluid that flows out of the wheel

cylinders in the process returns to the reservoir chambers. Once the wheel speed becomes stable again, the inlet valves concerned are opened again. The process described repeats itself continually until the driver stops braking or the vehicle comes to a standstill. When the brake pedal is released by the driver, the brake fluid that has collected in the reservoir chambers flows back through the reservoir-chamber springs and the non-return valves to the master cylinder. The system is then ready for ABS braking again.

The smaller number of components compared with conventional systems offers considerable cost savings but the system has significant functional deficiencies. Among other things, under extended periods of ABS braking (e.g. from high speeds on road surfaces with poor adhesion or in situations where adhesion fluctuates dramatically), the reservoir chambers can reach their capacity while at the same time the brake-pedal travel increases considerably in an unfamiliar way. Apart from the loss in pedal-opera-

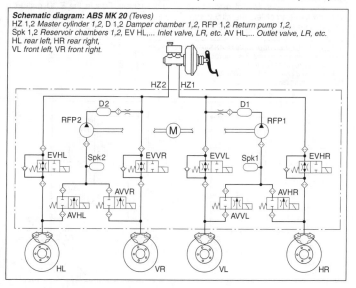

Schematic diagram: ABS MK 20 *(Teves)*
HZ 1,2 *Master cylinder 1,2*, D 1,2 *Damper chamber 1,2*, RFP 1,2 *Return pump 1,2*,
Spk 1,2 *Reservoir chambers 1,2*, EV HL,... *Inlet valve, LR, etc.* AV HL,... *Outlet valve, LR, etc.*
HL *rear left*, HR *rear right*,
VL *front left*, VR *front right*.

tion comfort, this means that the pressure in the wheel cylinders can not be reduced any further with the result that the wheels could lock up. For that reason, this type of system is only used on certain vehicles with limited top speeds and has not as yet become established in the European or American automobile markets.

ABS components (Bosch)

Wheel-speed sensor
The inductive wheel-speed sensor provides the control unit (ECU) with information on wheel speed.

ECU unit with vehicle-specific LSI circuits
The ECU shown in schematic form in a 4-channel system receives, filters and amplifies the speed-sensor signals and ascertains from the degree of wheel slip and the acceleration of the individual wheels as well as the reference speed, which is the best possible calculation of vehicle road speed.

Input circuit:
The input circuit consists of a low-pass filter and input amplifier; the circuit suppresses interference and amplifies the

signals from all wheel-speed sensors (Channels 1...4).

Digital controller:
The digital controller consists in the case of ABS2S of two identical but independent digital vehicle-specific LSI circuits which each process the information from two wheels (channels 1+2 or 3+4) simultaneously and perform the logical processes. Once processed, the wheel frequency data continues in the circuit to a serial arithmetic-logic unit. This logic unit, in turn, uses the data to calculate the values for "wheel slip" and "circumferential deceleration" or "circumferential acceleration" required for closed-loop control. A self-adapting, complex controller logic converts the control signals into position commands for the solenoid valves. A serial interface, connected to the input stage, arithmetic-logic unit and controller logic via data link, maintains data communications between the two digital LSI circuits.

Yet another function block contains the monitoring circuit for error recognition and analysis. Should the ECU malfunction, a warning lamp informs the vehicle operator that the ABS is no longer opera-

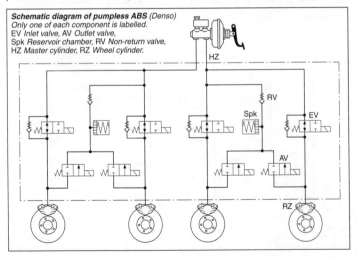

Schematic diagram of pumpless ABS (Denso)
Only one of each component is labelled.
EV *Inlet valve,* AV *Outlet valve,*
Spk *Reservoir chamber,* RV *Non-return valve,*
HZ *Master cylinder,* RZ *Wheel cylinder.*

tional. However, the braking system retains full normal operating capability when the ABS is deactivated.

Output circuits:
Two output circuits function as current regulators for Channels 1 + 2 and 3 + 4 while receiving the position commands employed for solenoid excitation from the LSI circuits.

Output stage:
The output stage employs the input from the current regulators in the two output circuits in providing the excitation current for the solenoid valves.

Voltage stabilizer, fault memory:
This function block stabilizes the supply voltage and monitors it to ensure that it remains within the tolerances required for reliable operation. The block also incorporates undervoltage recognition, which reacts to insufficient on-board voltage by shutting down the unit, as well as relays and the warning-lamp control circuit.

ECU unit with microcontrollers
Instead of the vehicle-specific LSI circuits, this control unit has two microcontrollers which take care of signal processing, "running" the controller program and self-monitoring on the part of the ABS system. The unit also carries out diagnosis in accordance with ISO standards, making it possible to track down defective ABS components with the aid of either the warning lamp or an "intelligent" tester.

The use of microcontrollers could achieve substantial optimization of controller algorithms incorporating customization to vehicle and driver requirements. For example, more precise calculation of wheel slip enables early detection of excessive rear-wheel braking which can then be corrected in time by changes in brake pressure with the result that, on some vehicles, the rear-wheel pressure reducer can be dispensed with. This achieves better overall vehicle braking (electronic brake balancing).

Further hybridization of the electronic components has succeeded in considerably reducing their number and thereby the size of the control unit as well.

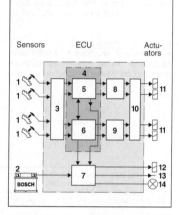

ECU (Bosch, 4-channel layout).
1 Wheel-speed sensors, 2 Battery, 3 Input circuit, 4 Digital controller, 5 LSI circuit 1, 6 LSI circuit 2, 7 Voltage stabilizer/fault memory, 8 Output circuit 1, 9 Output circuit 2, 10 Output stage, 11 Solenoid valves, 12 Safety relay, 13 Stabilized battery voltage, 14 Warning lamp.

Hydraulic modulator (for ABS2S and ABS5S with II and X braking-force distribution)
For each brake circuit, the hydraulic modulator consists of:
– Electric-motor-driven return pump P,
– Accumulator chamber S,
– Damper chamber D, and
– Various solenoid valves.

Return pump P:
The return pump returns the brake fluid from the wheel-brake cylinders to the master cylinder.

Accumulator S:
The accumulators provide temporary storage of the large quantity of brake fluid which accompanies pressure reduction.

Damper chamber D:
The dampers and their downstream throttling devices serve to smooth the high levels of pulsation which occur during the return of brake-fluid to the master cylinder.

They ensure that the noise level is kept to a minimum.

3/3 solenoid valves on ABS2S:
Each wheel is allocated a 3/3 solenoid valve. The valve serves to modulate the pressure in the wheel cylinders during active ABS control. The modulation takes place in 3 modes (build-up, hold, and reduce).

2/2 solenoid valves on ABS5:
Each wheel is allocated an EV/AV valve pair. The same pressure-modulation modes as above can be achieved for each wheel brake by appropriate control of the valves.

In addition to the effect of the damper chambers, PWM control of the 2/2 solenoid valves allows the required pressure changes in the wheel cylinders to be achieved with a greater degree of driver comfort in terms of noise, initiation of suspension vibration and pedal feedback.

Schematic diagram of hydraulic modulator
a) ABS2S system, b) ABS5 system.
HZ *Master cylinder,* M *Electric motor,* P *Plunger pump,* D *Damper,* S *Volume accumulator,*
MV *3/3 solenoid valve,* EV *2/2 inlet valves,* AV *2/2 outlet valve,* RZ *Wheel cylinder.*

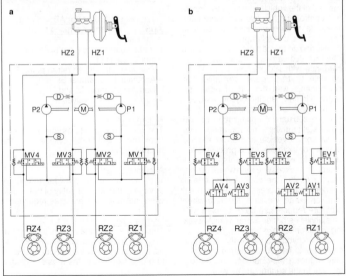

Electrohydraulic Brakes (EHB)

In contrast to antilock braking systems (ABS), the traction control system (TCR) and electronic stability program (ESP) can generate pressure in the wheel cylinders independently of driver action. This capability forms an important basis for electrohydraulic brakes.

Function

In conventional car braking systems, the force applied by the driver is transmitted mechanically by the lever action of the brake pedal to the vacuum brake servo and from there in amplified form to the master cylinder. The pressure thus generated is used to achieve the desired braking effect with the individual brakes on each wheel. With electrohydraulic brakes, that purely mechanical-hydraulic sequence of actions is broken and replaced by sensors, an ECU and a hydraulic pressure supply. Under normal operating conditions, there is no mechanical link between the brake pedal and the wheel brake.

Design

An electrohydraulic braking system consists of the following components (see diagram):
– Actuator unit,
– Hydraulic pressure modulator
– Sensors (e. g. wheel-speed sensor),
– Add-on ECU (at the hydraulic pressure modulator),
– or separate ECU,
– Control and pressure lines.

Mode of operation

For safety reasons, two separate sensors (one on the actuator unit for detecting the pedal travel and a pressure sensor on the hydraulic modulator) are used to detect a "braking request" and transmit it to the ECU. Using software, this ECU also incorporates the brake servo, ABS, TCS and ESP functions. The other sensors in the ABS, TCS and ESP systems provide the ECU with data relating to aspects of vehicle dynamics such as road speed, cornering, and the motion of the wheels. Using this information, the ECU calculates the signals to be sent to the hydraulic modulator which are converted by the wheel pressure modulators into the brake pressures for the individual wheels. An electrically driven hydraulic pump with a high-pressure accumulator and a pressure monitoring device provides the hydraulic pressure supply.

For safety reasons, in the event of a fault in the system it switches to an operating mode in which the vehicle can be braked without power assistance.

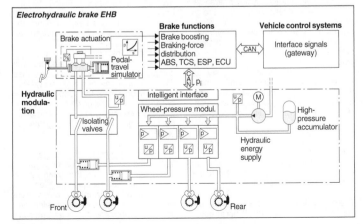

Electrohydraulic brake EHB

Braking systems for commercial vehicles above 7.5 t laden weight

System and configuration
Power-braking systems of medium and heavy-duty commercial vehicles mostly operate with:
– Compressed air (normal pressure level) as a medium for energy supply and as a transmission device.
– Pneumatic-hydraulic power transmission in the service-braking system and pneumatic power transmission in the parking-brake system, or
– Pneumatic high pressure level (Figs. B & C).

<u>Service-braking system for towing (tractor) vehicles</u>
For practical operations, in medium and heavy commercial vehicles, the force exerted by the driver's foot alone is not sufficient to generate adequate braking deceleration. For this reason, compressed-air power-brake systems are principally used; these systems use compressed air as a stored form of energy to control or actuate the service-braking system. Diaphragm actuators create the brake application forces on the wheel brakes. "Air-over-hydraulic" brake systems are becoming less and less common, as the air pressure required to control the wheel brakes must be converted into hydraulic pressure by means of brake servo-unit cylinders, compact brake assemblies or actuating cylinders.

A modern dual-circuit compressed-air brake system with trailer-brake connection, spring-type brake actuator, secondary and parking-brake system consists of the following main components:
– Energy supply,
– Compressed-air reservoir,
– Brake valves,
– Braking-force controller,
– Wheel brakes, and
– Control and air supply for the trailer braking system (diagram D).

The energy supply comprises a compressor and pressure regulator. Where neces-

sary, antifreeze pumps, automatic water drainage, air filters, air dryers and intermediate reservoir are added, providing clean and well-drained air.

As there may be a number of air-consuming installations apart from the braking system in the tractor-trailer combinations used in modern-day commercial-vehicle operations, it is advisable to install considerably more powerful compressors than those, for instance, required by EC/ECE brake regulations.

The four-circuit protection valve is located at the interface point between the energy supply and the compressed air reservoir. In the event of a fault, this protection valve ensures the security and continuing supply of the individual brake circuits and of priority secondary consumers.

The actuating mechanism for the service brakes starts with the brake pedal and ends at the mechanically operated components of the dual-circuit brake valve.

Sometimes, in commercial vehicles, the limited space available makes it necessary to fit the brake valve on the frame behind the cab instead of in the (tipping) cab itself. The problem of left-hand and right-hand drive trucks with the brake valve in the same position on the frame is solved by means of a dual-circuit hydraulic transmission device for the braking-circuit control. In this process an electrical warning system monitors the level of fluid in the compensating reservoirs of both circuits.

Additional installations in towing vehicles for pulling trailers/semitrailers with compressed-air brake systems (see "Basic components of a braking system") help to supply air to the trailer/semitrailer braking system, and provide a controlling function with regard to the braking effect (trailer control valve, coupling heads, etc.).

<u>Two-line braking system for trailers</u>
In the case of the two-line braking system, which is the standard European design version, one line (supply line) connects the energy reservoirs in the towing vehicle with those in the trailer/semitrailer; and this line is permanently under pressure.

The second line (brake line) leads from the trailer control valve in the towing vehicle to the trailer brake valve in the trailer/semitrailer (diagram E). Braking occurs as a result of pressure increase. Automatic braking when the trailer/semitrailer accidentally comes loose from the towing vehicle is ensured in this system by the supply line. If the supply line comes loose or breaks, air flows out of it and the brake valve in the trailer/semitrailer activates the brakes. With the aid of a dual-circuit trailer control valve and the four-circuit protection valve, it is possible to continue the supply of air to the trailer/semitrailer and to control braking, even if one circuit of the dual-circuit braking system in the towing vehicle fails. The standardized coupling heads for "supply" and "brake" are fitted with an automatic shut-off element, which opens during the coupling process.

Automatic load-sensitive device for braking-force metering

The automatic device for correcting braking forces as a function of load (ALB) is a vital element of the braking-system transmission device. With the vehicle partially-loaded or empty, braking-force metering valves permit the braking forces to be adjusted to the reduced axle loading e.g., by sensing of the axle ride clearances) and thus permit a correction of braking-force metering to the vehicle's axles ("kinked load-sensitive braking-force metering"), or they permit a set level of braking (important for vehicles in road train or tractor-trailer operation). There are two kinds of load-sensitive braking-force metering valves (Fig. A):

1. Braking-force limiters
Above a given "switchover point", the braking-force limiter restricts the increase of braking force (e.g., on the rear axle), that is to say there is a "kink" in the braking-force metering characteristic.

2. Braking-force reducers
Even under most unfavorable load conditions, load-sensitive braking-force reducers permit braking-force metering which approaches the parabola of the dynamic (ideal) braking-force metering characteristic (see "Design of a braking system"). In the area above the switchover point the braking forces on the particular axle are reduced with respect to the original braking-force metering level. Here, the installed braking-force metering is dependent on the transmission ratio and on the switchover pressure (which in turn is dependent on axle load) of the braking-force metering valve.

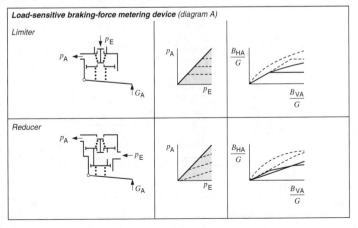

Load-sensitive braking-force metering device (diagram A)

Compressed-air braking systems for trucks

1 Compressor,
2 Pressure regulator,
3 Anti-freeze pump,
4 Four-circuit safety valve,
5 Compressed-air cylinder,
6 Coupling head with automatic shutoff valve,
7 Water drain valve,
8 Non-return valve,
9 Test valve,
10 Parking-brake valve,
11 Trailer-control valve,
12 Coupling head without shutoff valve,
13 Spring-type brake cylinder,
14 Front wheels,
15 Automatic Load-sensitive Braking-force metering (ALB),
16 Rear wheels,
17 Service-brake valve,
18 Brake cylinder,

Dual-circuit two-line power-brake system with pneumatic transmission device *(Fig. B)*

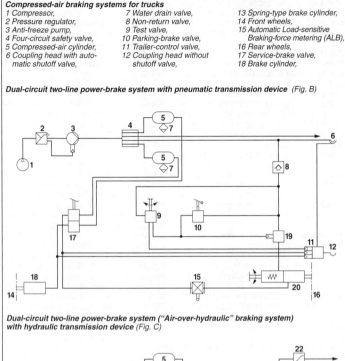

Dual-circuit two-line power-brake system ("Air-over-hydraulic" braking system) with hydraulic transmission device *(Fig. C)*

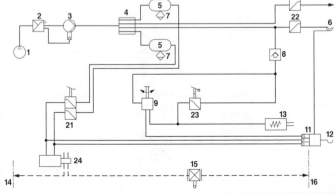

19 Relay valve,
20 Combination brake cylinder,
21 Service-brake valve with
   pressure limiter,
22 Pressure limiter valve,
23 Parking-brake valve with
   pressure limiter,
24 Precharger cylinder, dual-
   circuit,
25 Trailer-brake valve,
26 Loaded/empty valve,
27 Ancillary systems,
   (e.g. Engine braking system).

Main components of a modern compressed-air power-brake system *(Fig. D)*
a) Energy supply device, *b)* Reservoir, *c)* Brake valves, *d)* Trailer control and supply device,
e) Braking-force control, *f)* Wheel brakes.

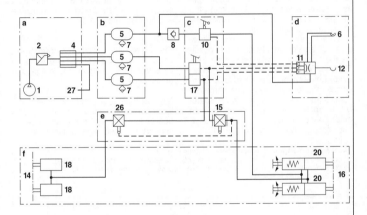

Two-line braking system for trailer/semitrailer *(Fig. E)*

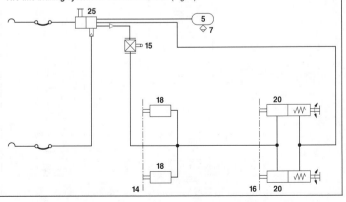

Basic comments on "kinked" braking-force metering

Load-sensitive braking-force metering devices adjust the installed braking-force metering to the dynamic (ideal) metering level and prevent the wheels of a given axle from locking prematurely. However, at low adhesion coefficients and low rear-axle load, it is possible for the wheels to lock. This is because the metering device's switchover point can enter the unstable range of braking-force metering if high engine braking torque (retarder braking torque), tolerance fluctuations in the metering device and/or high fluctuations at the wheel brakes occur.

A braking system which works precisely under all braking conditions is only possible if braking-force metering is optimized. Commercial vehicles with extreme differences between empty and fully laden conditions require braking systems with automatic load-sensitive braking-force control (ALB) on the rear axle together with empty/loaded valves (in order to increase the working range of the ALB, Fig. F).

Wheel brakes

In future, disc brakes will be fitted more and more on medium- to heavy-duty commercial vehicles (at least on the towing-vehicle's front axles). Currently, drum brakes are prevalent worldwide.

The brake factor C^* as an assessment criterion for brake performance, indicates the ratio of braking force to actuating force. This value takes into account the influence of the internal transmission ratio of the brake as well as the friction coefficient, which in turn is mainly dependent on the parameters speed, brake pressure and temperature (Fig. G).

Drum brakes

The actual construction of the drum brake depends upon the requirements imposed by brake-shoe actuation, anchorage, and adjustment.

Simplex drum brakes (Fig. H): These differ in particular according to their type of application (floating, fixed) and type of support or anchorage (rotating shoes,

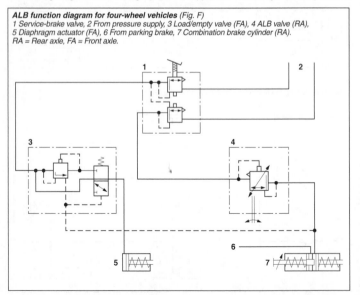

ALB function diagram for four-wheel vehicles (Fig. F)
1 Service-brake valve, 2 From pressure supply, 3 Load/empty valve (FA), 4 ALB valve (RA),
5 Diaphragm actuator (FA), 6 From parking brake, 7 Combination brake cylinder (RA).
RA = Rear axle, FA = Front axle.

sliding shoes). Wheel brakes with floating-brake application and rotating-shoe support are common. In the case of hydraulic braking-force actuation, for instance, the brakes are applied by means of floating pressure pistons whose travel is not fixed, and which develop actuating forces which are equal in both directions. One of the shoes is the leading shoe and the other the trailing shoe. In the former, the frictional forces between the brake lining and the brake drum support the actuating force, whereas in the latter the frictional forces oppose it.

In the case of the Simplex drum brake, C^* is the sum of the values for the individual shoes, and is ≈ 2.0 (referred to a coefficient of friction of $\mu = 0.38$; it always appears in the following C^* observations as the basis value). A disadvantage of this design is the considerable difference in the braking effect between the two brake shoes, and the resulting greatly increased wear on the leading shoe as compared to the trailing shoe.

For this reason, the trailing shoe often has a much thinner lining than the leading shoe.

The simplex drum brake can also be actuated by means of a wedge unit (with integrated adjusting mechanism). This has become more and more prevalent,

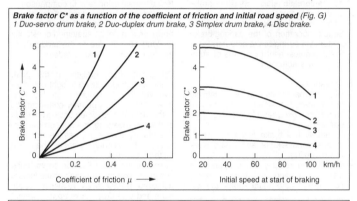

Brake factor C^* as a function of the coefficient of friction and initial road speed (Fig. G)
1 Duo-servo drum brake, 2 Duo-duplex drum brake, 3 Simplex drum brake, 4 Disc brake.

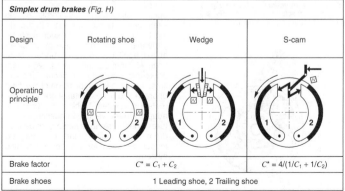

Simplex drum brakes (Fig. H)

Design	Rotating shoe	Wedge	S-cam
Operating principle			
Brake factor	$C^* = C_1 + C_2$		$C^* = 4/(1/C_1 + 1/C_2)$
Brake shoes	1 Leading shoe, 2 Trailing shoe		

particularly in light and medium commercial vehicles with compressed-air braking systems (Figs. H, K).

The type of wheel brake used most often in heavy-duty commercial vehicles is the pneumatic S-cam simplex drum brake with fixed application (Fig. J).

Advantages:
- Uniform lining wear on leading and trailing shoes as a result of fixed application,
- Long lining life,
- An application mechanism which is simple, reliable and insensitive to temperature. It comprises diaphragm cylinder, automatic slack adjuster, brake shaft and S-cams,
- Little change in brake factor C^*,
- Simple operation of the parking-brake system via spring-brake actuators,
- Precise adjustment by means of automatic slack adjusters.

Disadvantages:
- High internal forces and thus relatively heavy brake construction, as unequal cam forces occur and lead to high free bearing forces,
- Relatively low brake factor C^*, which means considerable application work when braking,
- Due to the roughly equal application travel of leading and trailing shoes, compared to individual shoes, the ap-

plication forces behave in the opposite manner.
- For the same coefficient of friction, the brake factor C^* is somewhat lower than that of simplex brakes with hydraulic or pneumatic application.

Duo-duplex drum brakes: The Duo-duplex brake with two leading shoes (for instance with wedge-unit control) (Fig. K) is rarely used nowadays.

This brake features floating application and the resulting sliding shoe anchorage. An advantage of this brake type is the practically equal brake-lining wear on both shoes and the significantly higher internal transmission ratio in comparison to simplex drum brakes. Twin leading shoes achieve characteristics of $C^* \approx 3.0$ which, however, can not be sustained constantly for long periods due to the tendency of this type of drum brake to fade.

Duo-servo drum brakes: In the past, these were widely used in light commercial vehicles (particularly on the rear axle). This brake's primary characteristic is the fact that both when driving forwards and when reversing, the support force of the primary shoe is used as the actuation force for the secondary shoe. The brake factor is $C^* \approx 5.0$.

The popularity of the duo-servo brake lies in the fact that the high brake factors achieved permit even relatively heavy vans and light-duty trucks up to a weight of approx. 7.5 t to be equipped with vacuum-assisted braking systems. At the same time, the manually operated parking brake incorporated in such systems generates a braking torque of considerable magnitude. However, under conditions of high thermal stress, significant brake-factor fluctuations occur. This fact limits the range of application of this type of brake and necessitates a braking-force metering system which is precisely adapted to the vehicle in question. In future wheel-braking systems, duo-servo drum brakes will for the most part no longer be used for the service-braking system.

Simplex drum brake with S-cam (Fig. J)
1 Diaphragm actuator, 2 S-cam, 3 Brake shoes, 4 Return spring, 5 Brake drum.

Disc brakes

Apart from their use in express coaches, disc brakes are currently fitted to medium and heavy commercial vehicles.

The advantages of disc brakes in comparison to drum brakes are:
– Brakes can be applied with far more sensitivity,
– Equal wear of the inboard and outboard brake pads if the appropriate degree of heat dissipation is provided,
– Less tendency to brake noise,
– Relatively constant characteristics with minimal fade tendency.

Disadvantages:
– Shorter brake-lining life,
– Usually higher acquisition and operating costs (in comparison to drum brakes).

The high degree of adaptive braking required at high highway speeds is handled better by disc brakes. The brake discs are less susceptible to cracking than the drums of the drum brakes, apart from which disc brakes are less subject to fading. The brake factor of the disc brake is $C^* \approx 0.76$, referred to the basis value of $\mu = 0.38$.

Floating-caliper disc brakes are currently replacing the fixed-caliper brakes used in the past. This development is the result of efforts to design lighter and cheaper brake assemblies which are more temperature-resistant. Floating calipers have a positive effect on variability and consistency of braking effect.

Automatic adjustment of wheel brakes

Brake-lining wear increases the clearance between brake lining and brake drum, and thus increases the braking distance. If the clearance is not adjusted correctly, in extreme cases the piston stroke in the brake cylinder may increase to such an extent that there is no braking effect. Automatic adjustment to the correct clearance is effected when the wheel brake is released.

When the vehicle is braked, the piston stroke in the brake cylinder necessary to bridge the total clearance can be divided into three sections:
– Preset constructive clearance between brake lining and brake drum/disc,
– Clearance resulting from lining wear,
– Clearance dependent on the elasticity of the brake drum/disc and of the brake linings, as well as on the transmission of force between brake cylinder and wheel brake ("elasticity clearance").

Duo-drum brakes and disc brake (Fig. K)

Design	Duo-Duplex Wedge	Duo-Servo Positive-action adjustment	Disc brake
Operating principle			
Brake factor	$C^* = C_1 + C_2$	$C^* = C_1 + C_2(k_1 + k_2 \cdot C_1)$	$C^* = 2 \cdot \mu$
Brake shoes	1 Leading shoe, 2 Trailing shoe		–

A slack adjuster automatically ensures the correct adjustment (Fig. L).

Parking-brake system
The braking systems with spring-type brake actuators which are usual in commercial vehicles above 7.5 t are a convenient form of parking-brake and service-braking system. In these, in a purely compressed-air braking system, spring-type brake cylinders from the parking-brake system and diaphragm brake cylinders from the service-braking system are combined.

In the disengaged position the four-circuit protection valve and the handbrake valve connect the reservoirs of the service-braking system with the spring compression chamber, and maintain the spring under tension. In vehicles with a connection for the trailer/semitrailer braking system a buffer reservoir is also located in this line. When the handbrake valve is actuated, the pressure in the compression chamber is reduced. Consequently partial braking occurs at first and, with the handbrake valve still actuated, a pressure reduction down to the "surrounding conditions" takes place, and thus full braking of the spring-brake actuator (secondary braking), occurs. Further actuation defines a "Parking setting". With the aid of a further lever setting, in vehicle combinations only the tractor vehicle is braked, and not the entire tractor-trailer

rig. As well as this test setting for checking the efficiency of the mechanical parking brake with a trailer attached, EU/ECE legislation for instance stipulates a safeguard emergency-air supply, as well as a nine-fold actuation and release using the energy reserve, a warning device indicating that the spring-brake is beginning to function, and an auxiliary release device.

Retarder braking systems (additional retarding braking systems)
The wheel brakes used in passenger cars and commercial vehicles are not designed for continued retarding operation. In a prolonged period of braking (e.g., when driving downhill) the brakes can be thermally over-stressed, causing the braking effect to be reduced ("fading"). In extreme cases (particularly if the service-braking system has been badly maintained) this may even lead to complete braking-system failure. In order to permit continuous downhill braking, therefore, particularly vehicles with a high laden weight are frequently fitted with a wear-free supplementary retarding braking system in addition to their normal wheel brakes. This system is independent of the wheel brakes, and is also used for braking the vehicle so as to comply with speed limits.

This reduces brake wear as well as increasing braking comfort for the driver. In commercial vehicles two basic types of

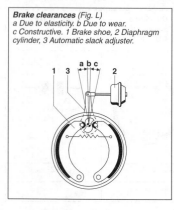

Brake clearances (Fig. L)
a Due to elasticity. b Due to wear.
c Constructive. 1 Brake shoe, 2 Diaphragm cylinder, 3 Automatic slack adjuster.

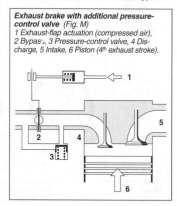

Exhaust brake with additional pressure-control valve *(Fig. M)*
1 Exhaust-flap actuation (compressed air),
2 Bypass, 3 Pressure-control valve, 4 Discharge, 5 Intake, 6 Piston (4th exhaust stroke).

additional retarding braking system are used:

1. Exhaust (engine) braking system

The exhaust braking power is comprised of the drag power together with the braking power (effected by the throttling of exhaust-gas flow in the exhaust stroke). The maximum drag power of standard engines is 5...7 kW/l depending upon engine swept volume. In contrast, standard engines with conventional exhaust brakes ("exhaust-flap brakes") achieve braking powers of 14...20 kW/l. A further increase in exhaust braking power is only possible by means of additional design modification. Decompression exhaust brakes (e.g., "C-brake", "Jake brake", "Dynatard" or "Powertard") as well as the constant-throttle exhaust brake can significantly improve braking power (Fig. P).

Exhaust brake system with exhaust flap:

The exhaust-flap brake is still the most common system in use today. In this system the driver is able to close a butterfly valve in the exhaust tract by means of compressed air (relatively little constructional outlay is involved). As a result, a counterpressure is generated in the exhaust-gas tract which must be overcome by each piston during its exhaust stroke (Fig. M).

Through the use of a pressure-regulator valve in the bypass, in conjunction with an exhaust flap, the braking power can be increased in the engine's lower and medium speed ranges. At higher revs, the pressure-regulator valve prevents pressure increases beyond the limits which could lead to valve or valve-gear damage.

Exhaust brake system with constant throttle:

The conventional exhaust brake with exhaust flap utilizes only the energy available in the engine's gas-exchange process, i.e. during the 4th (exhaust) and 1st (intake) working strokes. Specific decompression during the 2nd and 3rd working strokes releases part of the compression energy. The "pressure-volume" diagrams below show the pressure curves in a cylinder for the "exhaust flap" and "constant throttle" exhaust braking systems as well as for the combination of both systems (Fig. N). The braking power when using the constant throttle system, as opposed to the flap system, is obtained principally in the engine's high-pressure cycle.

The installation of a small restriction valve in the bypass to the exhaust valve permits an increase in braking power. This valve is actuated by compressed air, in the same way as in the servo-cylinder of the exhaust-brake flap. During exhaust-brake operation the valve can remain open, thus providing a constant throttle cross-section (Fig. O).

Principle of operation of exhaust (engine) braking systems as illustrated by "pressure-volume" diagram ($n_M = 1700$ min^{-1}) (Fig. N)
a) Exhaust-brake flap closed, b) Constant throttle actuated,
c) Exhaust-brake flap closed and constant throttle actuated.

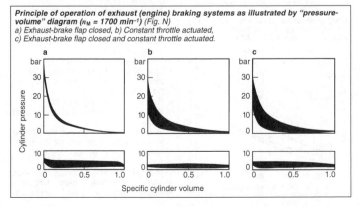

2. Retarders

Retarders are increasingly being used as wear-free additional retarding braking systems in trucks and buses. In this way, the demands of legislation are met, active vehicle safety is increased due to the reduction of the stress placed on the service-braking system, and vehicle economy is increased as a result of higher average speeds and the reduction of brake-lining wear.

Retarders can be fitted between the engine and the transmission (primary retarders) or between the transmission and the driven axle(s) (secondary retarders). The disadvantage of primary retarders lies in the unavoidable interruption of

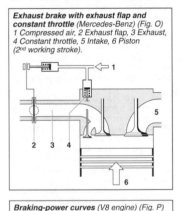

Exhaust brake with exhaust flap and constant throttle *(Mercedes-Benz) (Fig. O)*
1 Compressed air, 2 Exhaust flap, 3 Exhaust, 4 Constant throttle, 5 Intake, 6 Piston (2nd working stroke).

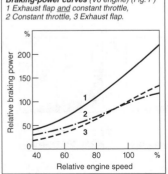

Braking-power curves *(V8 engine) (Fig. P)*
1 Exhaust flap and constant throttle, 2 Constant throttle, 3 Exhaust flap.

power transmission, and thus braking effect, which occurs during gear changing with manual transmissions. Primary retarders can be employed in conjunction with power-shift transmissions, and in the case of steep downhill gradients which are negotiated at low speeds, this provides for a slight advantage in comparison to the secondary-retarder system. (Fig. R)

Currently, two basic design concepts represent the state-of-the-art:

Hydrodynamic retarders: This retarder works in the same way as the Foettinger clutch (Fig. S). The rotor converts the mechanical energy supplied by the drive shaft into kinetic energy of a fluid. This kinetic energy is in turn converted into heat at the stator, which means that the fluid used must be cooled.

A hand lever or the brake pedal (in the case of an integrated retarder) transmits the driver's braking-power requirements. In conjunction with an electronic control circuitry, a defined control air pressure is set. By means of a corresponding quantity of air, this control air pressure then forces a quantity of oil into the retarder's working area between rotor and stator. The flow energy absorbed by the oil as a result of the vehicle speed and the associated rotor motion is braked by the stator's fixed blades. This in turn effects braking of the rotor and thus of the entire vehicle. Characteristics are:

– Adequate cooling-circuit dimensioning is necessary in order to dissipate to the engine cooling circuit the heat generated by braking. An oil/water heat exchanger is used,
– Relatively complex design,
– Low weight of the hydrodynamic retarder which is integrated directly into the transmission,
– High specific braking powers,
– Very sensitive control of applied braking torque,
– Fan losses occurring when the retarder is not running must also be taken into consideration in retarder design.

In the hydrodynamic secondary retarder, an almost constant braking torque is available over a broad propshaft-speed range (Fig. T). Below approx. 1,000 min⁻¹ the braking torque drops steeply. As a result of this characteristic, conventionally designed hydrodynamic retarders are particularly suited to high-speed transport vehicles (overland transport).

Modern retarder designs rectify the unfavorable braking torque characteristic of the secondary retarder design described above by providing high braking torques even at still low propshaft speeds. A spur-gear stage with a transmission ratio of approx. 1 : 2 drives such "boost retarders", which are fitted to the side of the transmission (Fig. S). Even in the propshaft lower speed range, a microprocessor control ensures acceptable braking-torque levels via a proportional valve.

Hydrodynamic retarders can only be used as continuous-operation braking systems in certain situations for limited

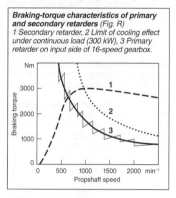

Braking-torque characteristics of primary and secondary retarders (Fig. R)
1 Secondary retarder, 2 Limit of cooling effect under continuous load (300 kW), 3 Primary retarder on input side of 16-speed gearbox.

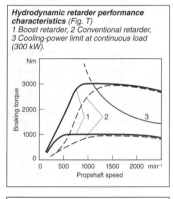

Hydrodynamic retarder performance characteristics (Fig. T)
1 Boost retarder, 2 Conventional retarder, 3 Cooling-power limit at continuous load (300 kW).

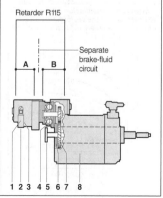

Boost retarder (Fig. S)
1 Transmission, 2 Spur gears (transmission ratio), 3 Gearbox flange, 4 Rotor, 5 Stator, 6 Compressed-air cylinder, 7 Proportional valve, 8 Wiring connector.

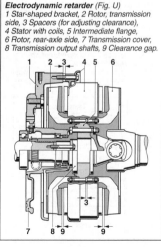

Electrodynamic retarder (Fig. U)
1 Star-shaped bracket, 2 Rotor, transmission side, 3 Spacers (for adjusting clearance), 4 Stator with coils, 5 Intermediate flange, 6 Rotor, rear-axle side, 7 Transmission cover, 8 Transmission output shafts, 9 Clearance gap.

periods. The maximum cooling power of modern diesel engines is approx. 300 kW. Thus, as a result of the coupling of the engine and retarder cooling circuits, there exists a risk for both engine and retarder if additional safety measures are not implemented. For this reason, thermo switches are used to restrict the retarder's braking power so that thermal equilibrium is ensured.

Electrodynamic retarders: Currently common electrodynamic retarders have a mounting in the form of a stator, on which field coils are mounted (Fig. U). The rotors mounted on both sides of the drive shaft are ribbed for better heat dissipation. In order to brake the vehicle, voltage is applied to the field coils (from the battery or alternator) which thus generate a magnetic field which induces eddy currents in the rotors as they pass through the field. This generates a braking-torque level which is dependent on the stator excitation and on the air gap between rotor and stator.

Characteristics are:
– Dissipation to the atmosphere of the heat produced,
– Relatively simple design,
– Relatively heavy construction,
– Trouble-free operation only with adequate current supply,

– Heating of the retarder leads to a reduction in braking torque,
– High braking powers even at low vehicle speeds,
– Braking power influenced by rotor blading, air-flow conditions around the eddy-current brake, and by ambient temperature.

In contrast to the conventional hydrodynamic secondary retarders, electrodynamic retarders provide relatively high braking torques at low driveshaft speeds (Fig. V).

The significant reduction in braking torques of the electrodynamic retarder as the rotor temperature increases result from the thermal safeguard (Fig. W). Vehicle deceleration is reduced as thermal stress on the electrodynamic retarder increases.

In order to prevent temperature-related destruction of the retarder when the vehicle is being braked, a bi-metal switch restricts the current supply to half of the eight coils when the stator temperature reaches approx. 250 °C (Fig. W).

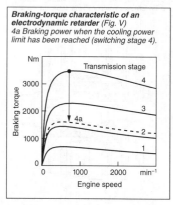

Braking-torque characteristic of an electrodynamic retarder (Fig. V)
4a Braking power when the cooling power limit has been reached (switching stage 4).

Nm

Braking torque

Transmission stage

3000

2000

4a

1000

0

0   1000   2000   min⁻¹

Engine speed

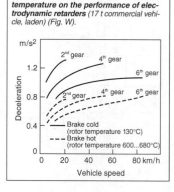

Influence of transmission ratio and rotor temperature on the performance of electrodynamic retarders (17 t commercial vehicle, laden) (Fig. W).

m/s²

Deceleration

1.2

2ⁿᵈ gear   4ᵗʰ gear

6ᵗʰ gear

0.8

2ⁿᵈ gear   4ᵗʰ gear   6ᵗʰ gear

0.4

Brake cold
(rotor temperature 130°C)
Brake hot
(rotor temperature 600...680°C)

0

0   20   40   60   80 km/h

Vehicle speed

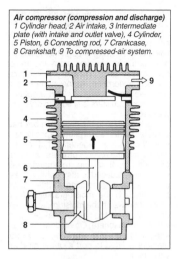

Air compressor (compression and discharge)
1 Cylinder head, 2 Air intake, 3 Intermediate plate (with intake and outlet valve), 4 Cylinder, 5 Piston, 6 Connecting rod, 7 Crankcase, 8 Crankshaft, 9 To compressed-air system.

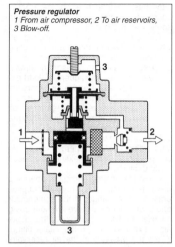

Pressure regulator
1 From air compressor, 2 To air reservoirs, 3 Blow-off.

Components for compressed-air brakes

Energy-supplying device
The energy-supplying device comprises the following:
– Energy source
– Pressure regulator
– Air conditioning
Energy source: The energy source is a continuously running air compressor which is driven by the engine via V-belts or toothed gears. It consists of:
– Crankcase with crankshaft (driver for power-steering pump at the free end of the shaft), bearing assembly and connections for circulating engine lubrication;
– Cylinder with piston and connecting rod;
– Intermediate plate with intake and outlet valves;
– Cylinder cover with suction and pressure connections for air and, if appropriate, the fittings required for liquid-cooled versions.

Energy-economy controls are increasingly being used in order to reduce the losses during idle operation (opening and flow resistances in the valves, lines, and pressure regulator). These are integrated in the valve plate and actuated pneumatically via an actuator. At idle, either a by-pass from the compressor's pressure chamber to the input side is opened, or the intake bore is opened by rotating/shifting the intake valve.

The air compressor is usually mounted on the vehicle engine by means of base or flange attachment. In some cases it is integrated in the engine block.

During its downward stroke, the piston draws in air after the intake valve has automatically opened as a result of the vacuum. The intake valve closes at the beginning of the return movement of the piston. The air is now compressed and, after reaching a set pressure, it is conveyed via the outlet valve, which also opens automatically, into the downstream compressed-air system.

In terms of delivery rate, the aim is a volumetric efficiency of 70 % and in terms of oil consumption a maximum of 0.5 g/h is desirable.

Pressure regulation: The pressure regulator ensures that the desired pressure level is maintained. Two principal types of regulation are used:
1. Regulation in which the pressure regu-

lator has no influence on the energy source (in compressors with maximum speeds >2,500 min⁻¹).

The pressure regulator switches off when the desired maximum operating pressure is reached, and returns the air supplied by the compressor to atmosphere during the subsequent no-load period. If the pressure in the air reservoirs reaches the lower operating-pressure limit the pressure regulator switches on again and supplies the air delivered by the compressor to the air reservoirs.

2. Regulation in which the pressure regulator influences the energy source (in compressors with maximum speeds <2,500 min⁻¹).

When the desired maximum operating pressure is reached, the regulator applies pressure to a plunger in the compressor and opens its intake valve. Without being supplied to the air reservoirs, the intake air is expelled through the intake fitting. When the pressure in the air reservoirs reaches the lower operating-pressure limit, the regulator switches and the intake valve can again automatically open and close, and the air reservoirs are filled.

Pressure level: In towing vehicles, values between 7 and 12 bar (low pressure) and between 14 and 20 bar (high pressure) are used. In the two-line braking system, the pressure in the lines connecting towing vehicle and trailer is between 6 and 8 bar.

<u>Compressed-air conditioning</u>: The air must be conditioned in order to ensure proper operation of the downstream braking-system components. Impurities in the air can cause leaks in the control valves, and water in the compressed air leads to corrosion or icing-up during frost. To combat these problems, an air drier is connected downstream of the air compressor. Such a configuration makes it unnecessary to add antifreeze to the system.

<u>Single-box air drier</u>
Basically, an air drier consists of a desiccant box and a housing. The housing incorporates the air passage, a bleeder valve, and a control element for granulate regeneration. Normally, the granulate is regenerated by switching in a regeneration air reservoir with integral regenerating throttle.

<u>Function</u>: When the bleeder valve is closed, the compressed air from the air compressor flows through the desiccant box and from there to the supply-air reservoirs. When flowing through the desiccant box, water is removed from the moist compressed air by means of condensation and adsorption. At the same time a regeneration-air reservoir with a volume of approx. 4...6 liters is filled with dry compressed air.

The granulate in the desiccant box has a limited water absorption capacity and must therefore be regenerated at regular intervals. In the reverse process, dry compressed air from the regeneration-air reservoir is reduced to atmospheric pressure via the regenerating throttle, flows back through the moist granulate from which it draws off the moisture, and flows as moist air via the opened bleeder valve into the atmosphere. On air driers with an integrated pressure regulator, its control element is fitted to port 4 of the air-drier valve body.

<u>Control device</u>
Normally, the control device comprises the brake pedal and all devices up to the point where influence is exerted on the control units.

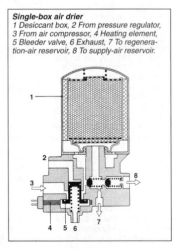

Single-box air drier
1 Desiccant box, 2 From pressure regulator, 3 From air compressor, 4 Heating element, 5 Bleeder valve, 6 Exhaust, 7 To regeneration-air reservoir, 8 To supply-air reservoir.

Transmission device
The transmission device comprises the following:
- Circuit isolation (e. g., multiple-circuit protection valve),
- Energy storage (e. g., air reservoirs),
- Control units (e. g., brake valves),
- Load-sensitive braking-force metering device (e. g., automatic load-sensitive braking-force control), and
- Brake cylinders or servo cylinders.

These components work together as shown in the block diagram below of a power-braking system with dual-circuit service-braking system (see also the braking-system diagram on P. 676). Functions and design of components:
Circuit isolation: Separation of the circuits with respect to one another in the event of damage in one circuit, as well as preservation of the operational integrity of the intact circuits.

Circuit isolation is primarily achieved by a combination of overflow valves grouped together as a unit; the operation of these valves is ensured at both low and high delivery rates.
Energy storage: Provision of the required volume of energy for all circuits in the braking system, including provision of energy in the event of failure of the energy source. Commercially available air reservoirs are used for this purpose; these have corresponding safety allowances for excess pressure and rust.

Control equipment
This equipment is used to control the metering of the required pressure to the corresponding parts of the system. Mechanically, hydraulically or pneumatically actuated or controlled reaction valves are used to control the pressure at the output of each valve as a function of the input variable. Due to the wide range of applications, a correspondingly large number of different components are in use. Dual-circuit control valves are also required for dual-circuit service-braking systems. Proper braking-system operation requires good control behavior, good pressure-metering capability, fast reaction times and low braking-system hysteresis.

Automatic load-sensitive braking-force metering (ALB)
Automatic braking-pressure control as a function of vehicle load. Load is often determined by spring compression (in the case of steel-spring suspension) and bellows pressure (in the case of pneumatic suspension). A control valve with a variable reaction-surface area reduces the output pressure in the valve in relation to the input pressure as a function of spring compression or bellows pressure.

Brake cylinders or servo cylinders
Convert the pressure applied to the braking system into braking force. Both plunger- and diaphragm-type cylinders are used. Diaphragm-type cylinders are primarily used for the service-braking system, while spring-brake actuators are used for the parking system. In the case of axles which are acted upon by both the service-braking system and the parking-brake system, combined single-chamber spring-brake actuators (so-called combination cylinders) are used in braking systems without hydraulic force transmission.

Wheel brakes (see P. 678)

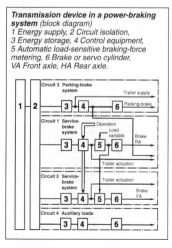

Transmission device in a power-braking system *(block diagram)*
1 Energy supply, 2 Circuit isolation,
3 Energy storage, 4 Control equipment,
5 Automatic load-sensitive braking-force metering, 6 Brake or servo cylinder,
VA Front axle, HA Rear axle.

Service-brake valve

Two tandem-arranged control valves are actuated by a common device (brake pedal with transmission). The synchronized opening of both circuits is ensured by identical spring and valve sealing forces as well as by the mechanical overcoming of the opening forces in both control valves. In the braking position, the rocking piston between the control circuits is subjected at its two ends to the currently applied braking pressure and thus guarantees that the circuits are synchronized. The preloaded travel spring provides small response travels of the service-brake valve. The interaction of the force of the reaction piston with the travel spring enables the system to execute the necessary control travels independently. Dual-circuit sealing of the rocking piston ensures the required safety.

Parking-brake valve

Today's compact design of the parking-brake valve is a direct result of the lack of installation space at the instrument panel (where it used to be fitted). The parking-brake valve always actuates the brake cylinders via relay valves.

A hand lever (actuating lever) adjusts an internal valve seat by means of an ec-centric and a linking strap. In doing so, it controls a double-seat valve in which compressed air from above and the force of compression springs from below act on a valve piston. In the brake position the actuating lever latches into position automatically, and the space above the valve piston is purged of air. As many intermediate settings between the drive and brake settings as desired are possible.

If the actuating lever is moved beyond the brake position, the auxiliary (test) valve is actuated and compressed air flows from the supply-air reservoir into the connecting line to the trailer-control valve. This leads to the towing-vehicle braking effect being retained, although it is cancelled for the trailer.

Automatic load-sensitive braking-force regulator

This device is connected between the service-brake valve and the brake cylinders. Depending on the vehicle load, it regulates the applied braking pressure. The device has a reaction diaphragm with variable active area. The diaphragm is held in two radially arranged and interlocking rakes. Depending on the position of the control-valve seat in the vertical direction, there is a large reaction area

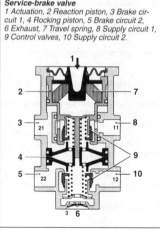

Service-brake valve
1 Actuation, 2 Reaction piston, 3 Brake circuit 1, 4 Rocking piston, 5 Brake circuit 2, 6 Exhaust, 7 Travel spring, 8 Supply circuit 1, 9 Control valves, 10 Supply circuit 2.

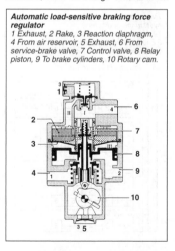

Automatic load-sensitive braking force regulator
1 Exhaust, 2 Rake, 3 Reaction diaphragm, 4 From air reservoir, 5 Exhaust, 6 From service-brake valve, 7 Control valve, 8 Relay piston, 9 To brake cylinders, 10 Rotary cam.

(valve position at bottom) or a small reaction area (valve position at top). Consequently, the brake cylinders are supplied via an integrated relay valve with a pressure which is lower than (unladen), or which is the same as (fully laden), that coming from the service-brake valve. The regulator is mounted on the vehicle frame and senses the compression position of the axle by a rotary lever via linkages. The rotary cam moves the valve rod accordingly in the vertical direction and thus determines the valve position. The pressure limiter which is integrated into the device at the top allows a small partial pressure to flow in on the top side of the diaphragm. Thus, up to this pressure there is no reduction in the brake-cylinder pressure. This results in the synchronous application of the brakes on all vehicle axles. If the rotary lever breaks, the applied pressure flows to the brake cylinders at a ratio of 2 : 1.

Combination brake cylinder for wedge brakes

The combination brake cylinder consists of a single-chamber diaphragm cylinder for the service brakes and a spring-brake actuator for the parking brakes. The cylinder and spring-brake actuator are in tandem and act on a common pressure rod. They can be actuated independently of each other. Simultaneous actuation results in the addition of their forces. The central release screw permits tensioning the spring of the spring-brake actuator without compressed air having to be applied. This is the setting when installed in the vehicle. Following installation, the release screw is screwed into the spring-actuator cylinder, and the spring acts via the piston rod on the wedge mechanism. The entry of compressed air into the spring-actuator cylinder (when parking brake is released) forces the piston back against the action of the spring, loads the spring and releases the brake (position illustrated). When the service brakes are operated, compressed air flows into the diaphragm cylinder, actuating the wedge mechanism by way of the diaphragm and the thrust rod. A drop in air pressure releases the brake.

The principle described above is modified for cam-operated brakes and for disc brakes.

Trailer-control valve

In two-line braking systems, the trailer-control valve which is installed in the towing vehicle controls the trailer's service

---

Combination brake cylinder for wedge brakes
1 Single-chamber cylinder control line,
2 Spring-brake actuator control line,
3 Pressure rod, 4 Piston rod, 5 Release screw.

Trailer-control valve
1 Service-brake circuit 1, 2 Parking-brake circuit, 3 Service-brake circuit 2, 4 Pilot spring, 5 Control piston 1, 6 Control line to trailer, 7 Control-piston unit, 8 Supply line to trailer, 9 Control piston 2, 10 Exhaust.

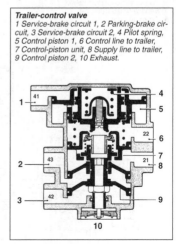

brakes. This multi-circuit relay valve is triggered by both service-brake circuits and by the parking-brake system.

In the driving position, the supply chamber as well as the chamber of the parking-brake circuit are each subjected to equal pressure, and the trailer-control line is exhausted through the central exhaust port. A rise in pressure upstream of the control piston of brake circuit 1 (top) and/or of brake circuit 2 (bottom) leads to a corresponding rise in pressure in the trailer-control line. Brake circuit 1 is equipped with a larger control piston than brake circuit 2, which means that it has priority over the control piston of circuit 2. This priority ends when the pilot pressure is reached (pilot-spring force is exceeded). A reduction in pressure in the service-brake circuits leads to the same reduction in the trailer-control line. The exhausting of the parking-brake circuit (braking) increases the pressure in the chamber to the trailer-control line. The application of air to the parking-brake circuit (releasing) again exhausts the trailer-control line.

<u>Mufflers</u>
Current and future legislation stipulates the reduction of compressed-air valve exhaust noise. Absorption-principle mufflers are used whose size depends on the exhaust-air quantity, air pressure, exhaust duration, and required noise level.

The muffler is a cylinder with radial and axial slits, and is filled with insulating material. Noise damping is due to inflow geometry, the insulation cartridge, and the exhaust slits with spherical exhaust flow. Mufflers are attached to the compressed-air valves via threaded, snap-action, bayonet, or pipe connections. Some versions fulfill the "Low-Noise Vehicle" conditions [72 dB(A)].

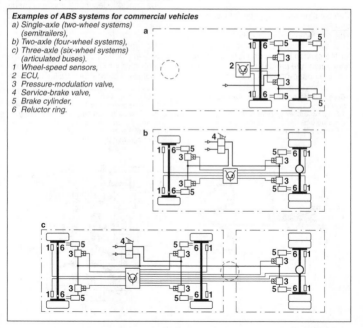

Examples of ABS systems for commercial vehicles
a) Single-axle (two-wheel systems) (semitrailers),
b) Two-axle (four-wheel systems),
c) Three-axle (six-wheel systems) (articulated buses).
1 Wheel-speed sensors,
2 ECU,
3 Pressure-modulation valve,
4 Service-brake valve,
5 Brake cylinder,
6 Reluctor ring.

Antilock braking systems (ABS) for commercial vehicles

The ABS prevents the wheels from locking when the vehicle is overbraked. The vehicle therefore retains its directional stability and steerability even under emergency braking on a slippery road surface. The stopping distance is often shorter than with locked wheels. ABS prevents the danger of jackknifing in the case of vehicle combinations.

In contrast to passenger cars, commercial vehicles have pneumatic braking systems. Nevertheless, the functional description of the ABS control circuits for passenger cars (see P. 659) also applies in principle to commercial vehicles.

The antilock braking system as used in commercial vehicles consists of wheel-speed sensors, an electronic controller (ECU) and pressure-modulation valves. The ABS regulates the brake pressure in each brake cylinder by increasing the pressure, holding it constant or reducing it by exhausting to atmosphere.

Individual control (IR)

This process, which sets and controls the optimum brake pressure individually for each wheel, produces the shortest braking distances. Under μ-split conditions (different friction coefficients between right-hand and left-hand wheels, e.g., black ice at edge of road surface, good grip at center of road surface) braking produces a high yawing moment about the vertical axis of the vehicle, thus making short-wheelbase vehicles difficult to control. In addition, this is coupled with a high steering moment as a result of the positive steering roll radii in commercial vehicles.

Select-low control (SL)

This process reduces the yawing and steering moments to zero. This is achieved by applying the same brake pressure to both wheels on the same axle. This requires only one pressure-control valve for each axle. The pressure applied is chosen to suit the wheel with less grip (select low), the wheel with more grip is braked less heavily compared to the individual control (IR) method. Under

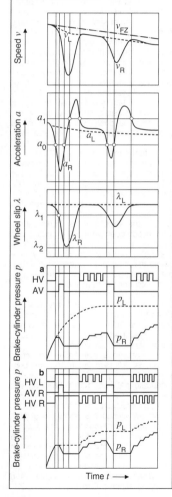

ABS control processes
Example: Braking on μ-split.
a) IR individual control (rear axle), b) IRM individual control modified (steering axle).
HV = Holding valve, AV = Outlet valve.
Subscripts: FZ vehicle, R Right wheel, L Left wheel, 0, 1, 2 thresholds.

μ-split conditions, braking distances are longer but steering control/directional stability of the vehicle is better. If grip conditions (coefficients of friction) are the same on both sides, braking distances, steering control and directional stability are virtually identical with systems which control each wheel individually (IR).

In the case of similar control principles with higher pressure levels than that in the SL method, the wheel running with the lower friction coefficient is forced to run with higher slip until it eventually locks up. Under μ-split conditions, braking distances are shorter compared with pure SL control systems. Steering control and directional stability of the vehicle may be very slightly worse. Normally, due to the lower frictional coefficient, there is no tire damage at the wheel which locks up.

Individual control modified (IRM)

This process necessitates a pressure-modulation valve at each wheel of the axle. It reduces yawing and steering moments only as far as necessary, and limits brake-pressure difference between left and right sides to a permissible level. This leads to the wheel which is running at the high friction coefficient being braked less strongly. This compromise results in a braking distance which is only a little longer than that for individual control (IR), but it does ensure the safe control of vehicles which tend to handle critically.

Commercial-vehicle ABS versions

Since 1 October 1991, within the area covered by the EU member states, ABS has been prescribed by law for the initial registration of commercial vehicles intended for trailer operation, and of semitrailer tractors (> 16t), as well as trailers (> 10t), and busses (> 12t). This regulation has been extended so that since 1/10/1998 all busses and since 1/10/1999 all trucks and trailers (> 3.5t) have had to be fitted with ABS.

The law stipulates 3 categories of ABS which differ from each other with respect to their specifications regarding retardation and the wheel and vehicle behavior on μ-split road surfaces. Most European vehicle manufacturers only use ABS systems in category 1. Only those have to conform to all specifications of Directive 71/320/EEC.

All ABS installations must be equipped with a warning lamp which must light up for at least 2 secs after switching on the driving switch. This lamp is to be referred to by the driver as a form of visual inspection. If it lights up while the vehicle is being driven, this indicates that the installation's continuous self-testing facility has detected a fault. This can result in the ABS being switched off completely.

Towing vehicles and trailers with ABS systems from different manufacturers may be combined as desired provided there is an ABS plug and socket connection between the two vehicles in accordance with ISO 7638.

On all vehicle combinations (semitrailer tractors, truck tractor/trailer combinations), optimum control of braking at the physical limits is only guaranteed when both tractor vehicle and trailer are equipped with ABS. However, even with-

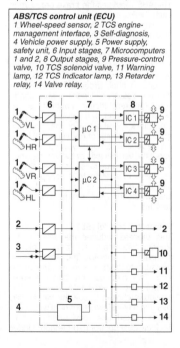

ABS/TCS control unit (ECU)
1 Wheel-speed sensor, 2 TCS engine-management interface, 3 Self-diagnosis, 4 Vehicle power supply, 5 Power supply, safety unit, 6 Input stages, 7 Microcomputers 1 and 2, 8 Output stages, 9 Pressure-control valve, 10 TCS solenoid valve, 11 Warning lamp, 12 TCS Indicator lamp, 13 Retarder relay, 14 Valve relay.

out ABS throughout (only on tractor unit or only on trailer) there are significant improvements compared to a vehicle combination which has no ABS at all.

In order to be able to provide the optimum and cost-effective equipment for the very wide range of commercial vehicles on today's roads, single-axle, 2-axle, and 3-axle ABS systems are available in accordance with the number of axles which are to be controlled. The single-axle systems as used primarily on semitrailers, individually control the wheels on a given axle. The remaining axles are supplied with the same brake pressures as the controlled axle.

2-axle systems are mainly fitted to two-axle buses, trucks, and trailers. Three-axle vehicles can also be equipped with a 2-axle ABS system insofar as two of the axles are in close vicinity to each other and can be provided with the same brake pressure (as for the single-axle ABS systems). The 3-axle systems are mainly intended for installation in long-wheelbase vehicles (e.g. articulated buses). In the case of 2-axle and 3-axle ABS installations, the steered axle uses either the IRM control method or, if this axle is only provided with a single pressure-control valve, the SL control method. Individual control (IR) is always used on commercial-vehicle rear axles.

The range of available ECU's permits further control combinations (not described here in detail). Example: If both axles of a semitrailer have wheel-speed sensors, but each side of the vehicle is only equipped with a single pressure-modulation valve, the wheels of one side of the vehicle are SL-controlled. In this case, one axle may be a lifting axle, which is automatically excluded from the control process when lifted.

All ABS systems can be equipped with single-channel pressure-modulation valves. ABS trailer systems can also be fitted with relay-type pressure-modulation valves (see Fig.).

In light commercial vehicles with pneumatic/hydraulic converters, ABS intervenes in the pneumatic brake circuit via single-channel pressure-modulation valves and defines the hydraulic brake pressure. In other versions, an ABS pressure modulator with integral solenoid valves is connected in parallel to the pneumatic/hydraulic converter. The modulators are controlled by the same ECUs as the single-channel pressure-modulation valves.

When the vehicle is running on a low-friction-coefficient road surface, the operation of an additional retarding brake (engine brake or retarder) can lead to excessive slip at the driven wheels. This would impair vehicle stability. ABS therefore monitors the brake slip and controls it to permissible levels by switching the additional retarding brake on and off.

ABS components

Wheel-speed sensor
For most applications nowadays, an application-engineered inductive sensor attached to the axle tube is used (for description of function, refer to P. 103). In contrast with car applications (rigidly attached sensors), on commercial vehicles the sensor is held in a spring sleeve. When the vehicle is in motion, the action of the wheel-bearing play and the flexing of the axle moves the sensor along its axis, thereby automatically adjusting the clearance between the sensor and the reluctor ring. If, under exceptional circumstances, the clearance gap becomes excessive, the ECU switches off the control for the wheel in question.

In the future, inductive sensors integrated in the wheel bearings and semiconductor speed sensors will be used more and more frequently due to economic considerations.

Electronic control unit (ECU)
The ECU's input stages convert the incoming sinusoidal signals from the wheel-speed sensors into square-wave signals. The wheel speeds are calculated from the frequency of the square-wave signals by (redundant) microcomputers. These speeds are used to estimate a vehicle reference speed. The brake slip for each wheel is calculated using this reference speed and the individual wheel speed. If a wheel has a tendency to lock, this is determined from the "wheel-acceleration" and "wheel-slip signals". In such a case,

Pressure-modulation valve (schematic)
1 Holding valve, 2 Outlet valve, 3 Solenoid valve for "Maintain pressure", 4 Solenoid valve for "Reduce pressure", 5 Control piston, 6 Valve plate, 7 Compression spring, 8 Brake cylinder, 9 Service-brake valve, 10 Supply air, 11 Exhaust.

Single-channel pressure-modulation valve

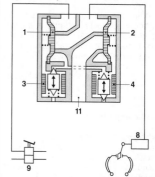

Pressure-modulation valve with relay action

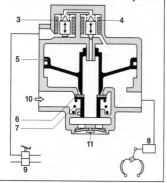

the microcomputer energizes (via the ECU output stages) the solenoids of the pressure-modulation valves which control the brake pressure in the individual wheel-brake cylinders.

The ECU contains a comprehensive program for the detection of faults throughout the entire antilock system (wheel-speed sensors, ECU, pressure-modulation valves, wiring harness). If a fault is detected, the ECU switches off the defective part of the system and stores a code detailing the faulty signal path. That code can be retrieved by a service technician with the aid of the warning lamp (flashing signal) or using an intelligent testing device (e.g. personal computer) via a standardized serial interface.

The ECU's of some European ABS manufacturers include not only the ABS function but also functions for TCS traction control and in some cases for cruise control (see also page 611). The most important factor is that depending upon the model, the ECU automatically configures itself to the required function. In other words, if the vehicle concerned is only ABS-equipped, the ECU only carries out the ABS function; if the vehicle has TCS components the ECU also controls wheel slip automatically.

Pressure-modulation valve

Single-channel pressure-modulation valves are available with and without relay action. The relay-action valves are installed in semitrailers and drawbar trailers. The standard trailer-braking system often includes relay valves which can then be replaced by ABS relay-action valves. Non-relay-action ABS valves are used in all other vehicles, i.e. in buses, trucks and tractor-trailer rigs, as well as in trailers and special vehicles. Both types of valve have 3/2 pilot valves. The non-relay-action valves thereby control 2/2 diaphragm valves, which have a sufficiently large cross-section for almost all applications. In the case of the relay-action valves, the 3/2 solenoid valves affect the pressure in the pilot chamber of a relay valve. The electronics control the solenoid valves in the appropriate combination so that the required function is performed (pressure retention or pressure release). If no pilot-valve actuation takes place, "pressure build-up" is the result.

When braking normally (that is, without ABS response = no locking tendency of a wheel), the air flows through the pressure-modulation valves unhindered in both directions when pressure is applied to or removed from the brake cylinders. This ensures fault-free functioning of the service-braking system.

Electronically controlled braking system (ELB) for commercial vehicles

Assignment

The aim of the electronically controlled braking system (ELB) for commercial vehicles is to optimize the braking process and, in certain cases, the power transmission process. The ELB system also supports the driver and the service technician during monitoring and servicing of the braking system, as well as contributing to an increase in economic efficiency. ELB comprises the areas of ABS (Antilock Braking System), EPB (Electropneumatic Brake), and TCS (Traction Control System). Within an electronic vehicle-management system, the ELB utilizes the information available from the data bus network to produce easy-to-control and

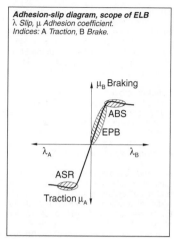

Adhesion-slip diagram, scope of ELB
λ *Slip,* μ *Adhesion coefficient.*
Indices: A Traction, B Brake.

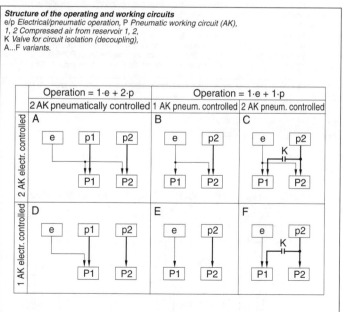

Structure of the operating and working circuits
e/p *Electrical/pneumatic operation,* P *Pneumatic working circuit (AK),*
1, 2 Compressed air from reservoir 1, 2,
K *Valve for circuit isolation (decoupling),*
A...F *variants.*

	Operation = 1·e + 2·p	Operation = 1·e + 1·p	
	2 AK pneumatically controlled	1 AK pneum. controlled	2 AK pneum. controlled
2 AK electr. controlled	A: e, p1, p2 → P1, P2	B: e, p2 → P1, P2	C: e, p2, K → P1, P2
1 AK electr. controlled	D: e, p1, p2 → P1, P2	E: e, p2 → P1, P2	F: e, p2, K → P1, P2

directionally stable braking and power transmission, and to provide information for other systems. Compared with conventional braking systems, an ELB system can be simpler in design. In the ELB, complex functions are processed electronically.

Function blocks

An ELB encompasses at least the following function groups:
– Electropneumatic braking system (EPB),
– Antilock braking system (ABS),
– Traction control system (TCS).

ABS and TCS are already in use on commercial vehicles (see PP. 693 and 610) and in the ELB are up-graded by the availability of additional information such as brake pressures and axle loads. Under stable adhesion/slip range (see Adhesion-Slip Curve) the action of the brakes is controlled electronically by the EPB. In this process, the effect of pressure control on the wheels, axles and the tractor and trailer units over the EPB range as a whole, is designed to comply with a variety of different targets. Thus, for light braking operations, the control-system objective may be even brake-lining wear, for medium to heavy braking it may be precise balancing of braking forces, and for emergency braking the aim may be maximum possible braking effect.

Design

Compressed-air supply, circuit isolation, energy storage and brake cylinders are the same as in conventional braking systems. The additional components include: pressure-control modules in the vicinity of the wheels for adjusting the brake pressure in the wheel cylinders as required, and an ECU. The system may also include a trailer control module the main function of which is to brake a conventional trailer.

Today, ELB systems with pneumatic retention circuits are available in the form of back-up systems at the safety level. Tomorrow's vehicle generations will be able to provide adequate safety while featuring electrically controlled multiple circuits without retention circuits. Normally, the pneumatic working circuits for operation of the brake cylinder in the tractor vehicle are of the dual-circuit design (II braking-force distribution, see P. 654), and in the trailer they are single circuit. The Figure

---

CAN networking of the brake components and their networking to other systems in the vehicle
a) Tractor vehicle, b) Trailer.
1, 2, 3 CAN stations (e.g. information, chassis, drivetrain),
4, 5 CAN stations (ELB control unit),
6 CAN stations (ELB pressure-control module),
7 Plug connection ISO 7638 (7-pole).

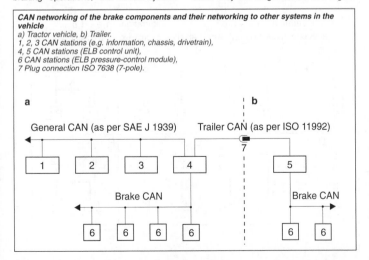

"Structure of the operating and working circuits" shows combinations of electrical and pneumatic control of two working circuits. For example, electrical operation of all axles is possible with Variant A which also features separate pneumatic retention circuits. Trailers are controlled via a standardized CAN data bus (ISO 11 992) (see P. 884). The pneumatic control circuit is retained in order to cope with tractor/ trailer rigs using conventional vehicles and the stipulated control for all braking circuits. However, this function too can be performed by an electronically controlled trailer control module.

Apart from the CAN data bus connecting it to the trailer, an ELB has at least two more: One bus links it to the ECUs for the drivetrain (e.g. EDC and/or retarder ECUs, transmission ECU, etc.) and one internal bus to the system for communicating with the pressure-control modules and the trailer control module (see diagram "CAN Networking"). The ELB is thus able to exchange information with other systems in order to optimize vehicle management functions.

Functional sequence EPB

A single-circuit ELB with 2-circuit reten-

tion circuit (1e + 2p) is shown in the Fig. "Service-brake installation of an ELB". In addition to a conventional pneumatic trailer control, this ELB also features an electrical control.

After the driving switch is turned, the ELB is initialized and subjected to a self-test. If no faults are detected on the ELB, the warning lamps go out and electrically controlled braking can now take place. Redundant principles are applied in the registration of the brake-pedal position. This is used by the ELB control unit to calculate the optimum pressure level for each control channel. The data is transmitted to the pressure-control modules (located near to the wheels) via the braking-system CAN. At the same time, the brake values are sent to the trailer via CAN. The pressure-control modules (DRM) on the tractor unit and trailer automatically adjust the brake pressure to the required level. Sensor signals from the wheels for variables such as wheel speed, brake lining thickness, etc. are sent by the pressure control modules via the CAN to the ELB control unit. The system's rapid reaction with simultaneous pressure regulation on all axles produces a direct braking feel similar to that in a passenger car.

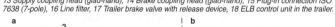

Service-brake installation of an ELB
a) Tractor vehicle, b) Trailer.
1 Four-circuit protection valve, 2 Air reservoir, 3 Service-brake valve with braking-value sensor
(1e+2p), 4 Single-channel pressure-control module (DRM), 5 Wheel-brake cylinder, 6 Wheel-speed
sensor, 7 Lining-wear sensor, 8 ELB control unit in the tractor vehicle, 9 Two-channel pressure-control module (2K-DRM), 10 Pressure sensor, 11 Air-suspension bellows, 12 Trailer control valve,
13 Supply coupling head (glad-hand), 14 Brake coupling head (glad-hand), 15 Plug-in connection ISO
7638 (7-pole), 16 Line filter, 17 Trailer brake valve with release device, 18 ELB control unit in the trailer.

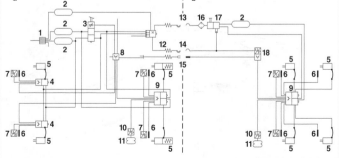

Trailers equipped with ELB which are towed by tractor vehicles having a 5-pole ABS plug-in connection generate their electrical brake value from the pressure in the pneumatic trailer brake line.

When the driving switch is at "Off", or if pressure control is deactivated in the event of a fault, the solenoid valves in the pressure-control modules revert to the mechanically held normal position. In that position, the pneumatic retention circuits from the service brake valve apply the brake pressure to the wheel cylinders unmodified (back up braking).

Extended functions

ELB incorporates EPB, ABS and TCS as standard functions. Other functions for automatic brake balancing and functions which require interaction with other systems are already available for use on production models or are in the course of development.

A few examples are given below:

Brake management

The braking effect desired by the driver can be achieved by means of either the retarder and/or the engine brake and/or the service brakes. The ELB control unit can perform the task of allocating the braking function to the appropriate braking system or systems.

Braking regulation

Vehicle deceleration is performed according to the driver's command, i.e. the position of the footbrake valve, regardless of whether the vehicle is loaded or empty. An automatic brake monitoring system prevents overload.

Brake-lining wear control

The brake-lining thickness is detected by sensors. Under normal braking with low levels of deceleration, the brake-lining

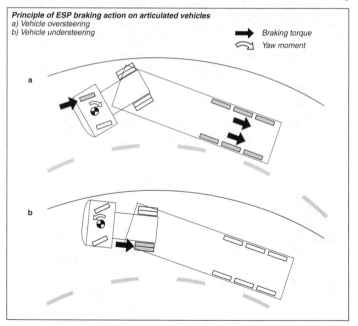

Principle of ESP braking action on articulated vehicles
a) Vehicle oversteering
b) Vehicle understeering

➡ Braking torque
↪ Yaw moment

a

b

wear between the wheels on the same axle is equalized by slight adjustment of the brake balance.

Brake balancing between tractor unit and trailer

The aim of automatic balancing of the braking force of the tractor unit and the trailer is to generate optimum trailer-coupling forces between the two units when braking. For articulated vehicles, the optimum trailer-coupling force is equal to the coupling load; for truck-and-trailer combinations it is zero. Each unit is then braked individually according to its own mass. Assuming appropriate braking-system design and choice of brake linings, this then generally leads to equalization of temperatures and therefore of wear between the brake linings on the tractor unit and the trailer.

Brake monitoring

The energy generated in a brake is dependent on the vehicle's speed and the braking torque, while the temperature of the brakes is also dependent on the dissipation of the heat produced by friction. Using those variables, the ELB can estimate the temperature of the brakes and then take action to prevent overloading.

Inappropriate reduction of braking torque on one or more wheels can be detected by ECU analysis of the vehicle behaviour under braking.

Rollback limiter/"Bus-stop brake"

The use of information that is normally available from other electronic systems via the SAE J1939 CAN enables automatic application of the brakes shortly after the vehicle starts to roll with the drive disengaged, e.g. when stopping at traffic lights. In the same way, the brake is automatically released when the vehicle starts to pull away. On public transport busses, this function can replace the so-called "bus-stop brake".

Electronic stability program (ESP)

ESP is an extension of the ABS system and controls not only longitudinal dynamics (like ABS) but also actively responds to the vehicle's transverse dynamics at the limits of adhesion (e.g. in the event of a skid). This requires a yaw-rate sensor and a lateral-acceleration sensor for determining the actual vehicle behaviour, as well as a steering-angle sensor for detecting the driver's intentions. If there are inconsistencies between the driver's intentions and the vehicle's behaviour, e.g. if the tractor unit starts to understeer or oversteer, the ESP modifies the vehicle behaviour by automatic braking of individual wheels to reflect the intentions of the driver. The physical processes involved are explained in the description of ESP for cars (see P. 704). The same basic principles apply to commercial-vehicle ESP systems with the exception of the braking strategy. This is modified to suit commercial vehicles in their various forms. For example, as well as braking of individual wheels on the tractor unit, correction of oversteer can be assisted by braking the trailer to tension the tractor-and-trailer combination (see diagram "Principle of ESP braking action on articulated vehicles"). The trailers do not normally have sensor systems for detecting handling dynamics and are therefore not involved to any greater degree in the control of vehicle directional stability.

It is clear that the risk of overturning is considerably greater with commercial vehicles than with cars. For that reason, the commercial-vehicle ESP also incorporates functions for reducing the likelihood of vehicle overturn. This applies to ELB systems both on the tractor unit and on the trailer. From the available signals, critical vehicle conditions are detected and the vehicle or vehicle combination automatically braked as required by the particular situation. The behaviour of trailers without ELB is estimated by the tractor unit's ECU. It then instigates appropriate braking operations as required to avert hazardous situations.

Brake test stands

The brakes are of decisive importance in maintaining high technical standards of vehicle safety; it is therefore imperative that the brake system be inspected on a regular basis. The German motor vehicle inspection prescribed by Paragraph 29 of the StVZO Road Licensing Regulations (FMVSS/CUR) employs brake test stands (roller dynamometers) for this purpose, as do automotive service centers for inspections and repairs. The braking forces monitored at the wheel's circumference provide the basis for evaluating the operation and effectiveness of the brake system. Brake stands employed for the inspections stipulated in Paragraph 29 must conform to the "Regulations governing use, design and testing of brake test stands" as administered by the Federal Transport Minister.

Design

The brake test stand's main components are two roller sets, for the left and right sides of the vehicle respectively. The vehicle is driven onto the test stand so that the wheels of the axle being tested rest upon the rollers.

A stable frame supports the roller sets, which assume the form of a drive roller and a secondary roller in a parallel layout, while a drive chain provides the positive dynamic connection between the two rollers. An AC motor powers the drive roller through a gear set with an upward conversion ratio, while the drive unit itself is suspended on an extension of the drive roller's shaft. Pressure exerted against a torque lever flanged onto the gear-drive unit is transferred through the load sensor, with the frame providing positive support for the entire assembly. The braking force F_{Br} is actually measured by monitoring the reaction torque M_R. The electric motors set the rollers in motion and then maintain an almost constant rotational speed against the opposing forces that occur when the vehicle's brakes are applied. The suspended drive unit with torque lever transmits the braking forces to the load-sensing device. The load-sensing device is designed as a flexural sensor with wire strain gauge.

The system's computer employs digital technology in the subsequent evaluation of the various data derived from braking-force testing, such as fluctuations or differences in braking force. Once processed, the information is presented in either analog or digital form, depending upon the specific system, while a printer can be connected to provide a hardcopy test protocol.

Operation

The drive motors for the roller sets may be activated in one of two ways, either by remote control or with an integral automatic on/off switch. An automatic-activation test stand is distinguished by the pressure-sensitive rollers located between the main test rollers on each roller set. When the vehicle is driven onto the test stand, it pushes down the pressure-sensitive rollers and activates the stand. When the vehicle leaves the stand the pressure-sensitive rollers are released and the unit is switched off. Should the applied braking force start to exceed the available traction between tires and test rollers, the wheel will respond by starting to slip and will then lock. Tire slip, however, makes it impossible to perform useful measurements of braking force. Under these conditions, it is the slip resistance between tire and roller (as a function of wheel load) that is measured and this is of no use. Here, assistance is provided by an automatic override device which recognizes this kind of slip by monitoring the test-roller speed, and which responds to it by switching off the test unit when a given maximum figure is exceeded. This avoids both false measurements and possible tire damage. The display, meanwhile, continues to show the maximum braking force achieved before the override device was activated. An electronic memory circuit ensures that the final display remains in place long enough to be recorded by the operator.

In addition, the vehicle and/or axle weight can also be measured at the test stand or entered remotely; the test unit can then use this information to calculate the effective retardation.

The brake test stand employs specific test sequences to provide extremely rationalized examination procedures, allowing the operator to carry out complete testing of both front and rear brakes without leaving the vehicle.

Vehicles with permanent 4-wheel drive and variable torque distribution are tested on special stands, which are constructed to prevent the forces generated at the test axle from being transferred to that axle which is at rest.

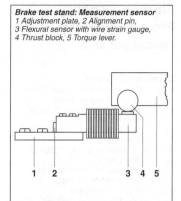

Brake test stand: Measurement sensor
1 Adjustment plate, 2 Alignment pin,
3 Flexural sensor with wire strain gauge,
4 Thrust block, 5 Torque lever.

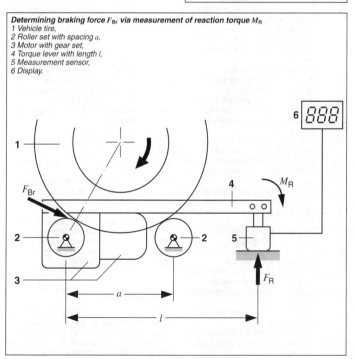

Determining braking force F_{Br} via measurement of reaction torque M_R
1 Vehicle tire,
2 Roller set with spacing a,
3 Motor with gear set,
4 Torque lever with length l,
5 Measurement sensor,
6 Display.

Electronic Stability Program (ESP) for passenger cars

Quantities and terms

a	Distance of front wheels from center of vehicle mass
a_x	Estimated longitudinal acceleration of vehicle
a_y	Measured lateral acceleration of vehicle
A_0, A_1, A_2	Parameters for calculation of tire operating point
c	Distance of rear wheels from center of vehicle mass
C_p	Brake-torque ratio
C_λ	Longitudinal tire stiffness
D_T	Sampling time of the controller
D_λ	Tolerance band of drive-slip difference
F_B	Brake force on the tire
F_{BF}	Steady-state (filtered) brake force on the tire
F_N	Normal force on the tire
F_R	Resultant force on the tire
F_S	Lateral force on the tire
J_{Mot}	Moment of inertia of the engine
J_{Whl}	Moment of inertia of the wheel
$K_p, K_d,$	Controller gains for the P-, D-
K_i	and I-parts
M_{Dif}	Local brake-torque difference between the driven wheels
M_{DR}	Engine torque requested by driver
M_{YwNo}	Nominal yaw moment on the vehicle
ΔM_{YwNo}	Small change in the nominal yaw moment on the vehicle
M_{CaHalf}	Half of the torque on the cardan axle
M_{Ca}	Torque on the cardan axle
M_{Mot}	Actual engine torque
M_{WhlNo}	Nominal brake torque
M_{NoMot}	Nominal engine torque
M_{NoLock}	Nominal brake-torque difference between the driven wheels
M_{NoSPR}	Nominal engine-torque reduction by spark retard
p_{Circ}	Brake circuit pressure induced by the driver
p_{Whl}	Pressure in wheel brake cylinder
p_{WhlPre}	Nominal pressure in wheel brake cylinder

R	Wheel radius
T_{iOFF}	Time during which the fuel injection is shut off
$\ddot{U}_{Tr}$	Transmission ratio
U_{val}	Actuation mode of solenoid valve
v_{CH}	Characteristic velocity of the vehicle
v_{Dif}	Difference between driven-wheel velocities
v_V	Vehicle velocity
v_{Ca}	Cardan-axle speed
v_{Whl}	Measured wheel speed
v_{Whl3}	Measured wheel speed, rear left
v_{Whl4}	Measured wheel speed, rear right
v_{WhlFre}	Wheel speed (free-rolling)
v_{NoDif}	Nominal difference between wheel velocities
v_{NoCa}	Nominal velocity of the cardan axle
v_x	Vehicle speed in the longitudinal direction
v_y	Vehicle speed in lateral direction
x_1, x_2	Parameters of the inverse hydraulic model
α	Slip angle of the tire
α_0, λ_0	Arbitrary operating point of the tire
β	Slip angle of the vehicle
β_{No}	Nominal slip angle of the vehicle
δ	Steering-wheel angle
δ_W	Front-wheel steering angle
λ	Tire slip
λ_{No}	Nominal tire slip
λ_{Ma}	Nominal average drive slip of the driven wheels
μ_{HF}	Coefficient of friction between tires and road
μ_{Res}	Resultant coefficient of friction between tire and road
$\dot{\psi}$	Yaw rate
$\dot{\psi}_{No}$	Nominal yaw rate
m	Minimum value of the nominal driven-wheel brake torque
MIN	Minimum-value operator
SUM	Event-driven integration
ZWV	Spark retard (SPR)

Assignment

The Electronic Stability Program ESP (vehicle dynamics control) system is a closed-loop control system which prevents lateral instability of the vehicle. It is integrated within the vehicle's brake system and drivetrain. While ABS prevents wheel lockup when braking and TCS prevents spin of the driven wheels, ESP prevents the vehicle from "pushing out" of the turn or spinning out of the turn when it is steered.

Further to the advantages inherent in ABS and TCS, ESP improves the active driving safety in the following points:
– Provides the driver with active support, even in laterally critical dynamic situations.
– Enhances vehicle stability and tracking performance even in limit situations in all operating modes such as full braking, partial braking, coasting, accelerating, engine drag, and load shift.
– Enhances directional stability even during extreme steering maneuvers (panic reactions), resulting in a drastic reduction in the danger of skidding.
– Improved handling behavior also in limit situations. For the driver, this behavior becomes predictable as a function of his (or her) experience. The vehicle remains fully under control even in critical traffic situations.
– Depending upon the situation, even better utilization of the friction potential between the tires and the road when ABS and TCS intervene, and therefore improved traction and stopping distances in addition to improved steerability and stability.

Vehicle handling

The vehicle's steering properties are defined in the description of the vehicle's lateral dynamics (P. 350). This description is derived from steady-state cornering and shows the dependence of the tire slip angle α on the lateral vehicle acceleration a_y and therefore on the lateral tire forces. Furthermore, the description of ABS (P. 659) and TCS (P. 606) also underlines the dependence of the lateral tire forces on the tire slip. This means that the vehicle's steering properties can be influenced by means of the tire slip. ESP utilizes this tire characteristic in order to effect servo-control for vehicle handling.

It is important for good vehicle handling that the vehicle remains safely on a track which corresponds as far as possible to the course of the steering-angle (see Fig. "Lat-

eral dynamics of a vehicle", Curve 2). During steering maneuvers, this is the case if the lateral tire forces remain considerably below the friction potential between the tire and the road surface. The yaw-rate curve then corresponds to that of the steering angle.

For ESP though, the mere control of the yaw rate according to the steering angle proves to be inadequate and the vehicle

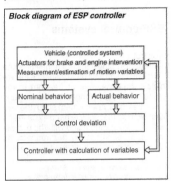

Block diagram of ESP controller

Vehicle (controlled system)
Actuators for brake and engine intervention
Measurement/estimation of motion variables

| Nominal behavior | Actual behavior |

Control deviation

Controller with calculation of variables

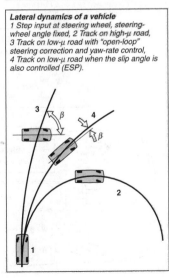

Lateral dynamics of a vehicle
1 Step input at steering wheel, steering-wheel angle fixed, 2 Track on high-μ road, 3 Track on low-μ road with "open-loop" steering correction and yaw-rate control, 4 Track on low-μ road when the slip angle is also controlled (ESP).

can become instable (see Fig., Curve 3). The ESP therefore controls not only the yaw rate but also the vehicle's sideslip angle.

The ESP vehicle-handling control is not restricted to ABS and TCS/MSR operations, but also extends to cover the area in which the vehicle is rolling freely, and also comes into action during partial braking if the vehicle is moving at the physical driving limits.

ESP control systems

Control

The control of the vehicle's behavior at the physical driving limit must influence the vehicle's three degrees of freedom in the plane of the road (longitudinal and lateral velocities, and yaw moment about the vertical axis) so that vehicle handling is in line with the driver's input and with the prevailing road conditions. In this respect, as shown in the block diagram, it must first of all be defined how the vehicle is to behave at the physical driving limit in accordance with the driver's input (nominal behavior), and how it actually behaves (actual behavior). In order to minimize the difference between nominal and actual behavior (deviation), the tire forces must in some way be controlled by actuators.

The overall system (Fig. "Overall control system of ESP" below), shows the vehicle as the controlled system, with sensors (1...5) for defining the controller input variables, and actuators (6 and 7) for influencing the tractive force and the braking force. Also shown are the hierarchically structured controller comprising the higher-level vehicle dynamics controller, and the lower-level slip controllers. The higher-level controllers input the nominal values to the lower-level controllers in the form of a nominal slip. The "observer" determines the controlled state variable (vehicle slip angle β).

In order to determine the desired performance, the signals are evaluated which

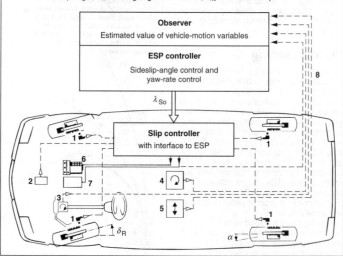

Overall control system of ESP
1 Wheel-speed sensors, 2 Brake-pressure sensor, 3 Steering-wheel sensor, 4 Yaw-rate sensor, 5 Lateral-acceleration sensor, 6 Pressure modulation, 7 Engine management, 8 Sensor signals for ESP. α Tire slip angle, δ_W Steering angle of the wheel, λ_{No} Nominal tire slip.

Observer
Estimated value of vehicle-motion variables

ESP controller
Sideslip-angle control and yaw-rate control

λ_{So}

Slip controller
with interface to ESP

δ_R

α

define the driver's input. These comprise the signals from the steering-wheel sensor (3, driver's steering input), the brake-pressure sensor (2, desired deceleration input), and the engine management (7, desired drive torque). Apart from the vehicle speed, the calculation of the desired performance also takes the coefficients of friction between the tires and the road into account. These are calculated from the signals outputted by the wheel-speed sensors (1), the lateral-acceleration sensor (5), the yaw-rate sensor (4), and the brake-pressure sensor (2). Depending upon the control deviation, the yaw moment which is necessary to make the actual-state variables approach the desired-state variables is then calculated.

In order to generate the required yaw moment, it is necessary for the changes in desired slip at the wheels to be determined by the vehicle dynamics controller. These are then set by means of the lower brake-slip controller and traction controller together

with the "brake-hydraulics" actuator (6), and the "engine-management actuator" (7).

The system relies on tried and proven ABS and TCS components. The TCS hydraulic modulator (6), which is described elsewhere, permits high levels of dynamic braking of all wheels throughout the complete temperature range encountered.

The necessary engine torque can be set by means of the engine management (7) and the CAN interface, so that the traction-slip values at the wheels can be adjusted accordingly.

System components

Vehicle dynamics controller

The relationship between steering angle, vehicle speed, and yaw rate during steady-state driving on a circular course (P. 355), is taken as the basis for the desired vehicle motion during steady-state driving, and when braking and/or accelerating. By applying the "Single-track (bicycle) model": the nominal yaw rate is cal-

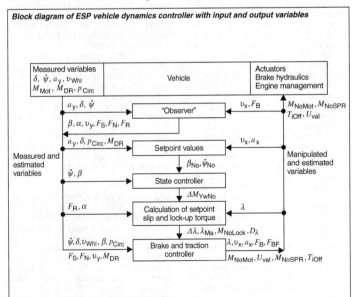

Block diagram of ESP vehicle dynamics controller with input and output variables

culated from the vehicle speed and the steering angle:

$$\dot{\psi}_{No} = \frac{\upsilon_x \cdot \delta_W}{(a + c)\left(1 + \dfrac{\upsilon_x^2}{\upsilon_{CH}^2}\right)}$$

For the sideslip-angle control, this value is first of all limited according to the road-surface coefficient of friction:

$$|\dot{\psi}_{No}| \leq \mu_{HF} \cdot g / \upsilon_V$$

whereby g is the acceleration due to gravity, and the coefficient of friction μ_{HF} and the vehicle speed υ_V are estimated values.

No attempt is made to directly influence the lateral speed, and with it the sideslip angle, by means of changes in the lateral forces. It is better to adjust the lateral motion indirectly by means of changes in the slip angle, whereby the vehicle's rotation is initiated by the generation of yaw moments.

A simplified block diagram is used to demonstrate the structure of the vehicle dynamics controller. Using the measured variables (nominal yaw rate $\dot{\psi}_{No}$, steering-wheel angle δ, and the vehicle lateral acceleration a_y), together with the estimated variables (vehicle longitudinal speed υ_x, and braking forces F_B), a so-called "Observer", using a simple vehicle model, determines the slip angle β, the sideslip angle α, the vehicle lateral speed υ_y, the wheel forces in the lateral and vertical directions F_S and F_N, and the resulting wheel forces F_R in the plane of the road.

The nominal sideslip-angle β_{No}, and the nominal yaw rate $\dot{\psi}_{No}$, are determined from the following driver inputs: steering-wheel angle δ, engine-torque input M_{DR} (accelerator-pedal position), and the brake pressure p_{Circ}, together with the estimated vehicle longitudinal speed υ_x, and the coefficient of friction μ_{HF} which is determined using the estimated longitudinal acceleration a_x and the measured lateral acceleration a_y. In the process, the vehicle's dynamic response, and special situations such as inclinations, banks, and/or μ-split road surfaces (different coefficients of friction between tires and road on the left and right side of the vehicle) are taken into account.

The vehicle dynamics controller is designed as a state controller. The controlled-state variables are the sideslip angle and the yaw rate. The more the sideslip angle increases, the more it is taken into account by the vehicle dynamics controller. The state controller's output variable corresponds to a yaw moment M_{YwNo}.

Together with the actual slip values λ, the resultant wheel forces F_R, and the slip angles α, the linearized vehicle model is now also applied to convert this yaw moment into changes of the nominal slip at the appropriate wheels. For instance, presuming that the vehicle is rolling freely and oversteers in a right-hand bend so that the nominal yaw-rate is exceeded, among other things a nominal brake slip is requested at the front wheel. This subjects the vehicle to a counterclockwise change in yaw moment which reduces the excessive yaw rate. The nominal slip is changed by the lower-level ABS or TCS wheel controller. If the brakes have not been applied, or the driver's brake-pressure input does not suffice to set the required nominal slip (partial-braking range), the pressure in the brake circuits is actively increased.

When TCS is operative, in order to set the vehicle's nominal yaw moment M_{YwNo}, the vehicle dynamics controller outputs a mean absolute drive slip λ_{Ma}, a drive-slip tolerance band D_λ, and a nominal brake locking torque M_{NoLock}. In order to achieve distinct improvements for the ABS and TCS basic functions with regard to their utilization of the adhesion potential in line with the driving situation, all available measurement quantities and estimated values are also applied to the full in the slip controllers.

Lower-level brake-slip controller (ABS) and engine drag-torque controller (MSR)

In order to be able to control the wheel slip to a definite level, it must be possible to evaluate it with an adequate degree of accuracy. The vehicle's longitudinal speed is not measured, but is determined from the wheel speeds υ_{Whl}. To do so, individual wheels are "under-braked" during ABS application. In other words, slip control is interrupted, and the instantaneous wheel brake torque is reduced by a defined amount and held constant for a given period of time. Assuming that the wheel speed is stable toward the end of this period, the zero-slip (free-rolling) wheel speed v_{WhlFre} can be calculated from the momentary braking force F_B and the tire stiffness C_λ.

$$v_{WhlFre} = v_{Whl} \cdot \frac{C_\lambda}{C_\lambda - \dfrac{F_B}{F_N}}$$

Using the yaw rate $\dot{\psi}$, the steering angle δ_W, and the lateral velocity v_y, together with the vehicle geometry, the (free-rolling) wheel speed is transformed into the center of gravity in order to generate the center-of-gravity velocity v_x in the vehicle's longitudinal direction. Finally, v_x is transformed back to the four wheel positions in order to evaluate the free-rolling speed of all four wheels. This enables the actual slip λ to be calculated for the control of the three remaining wheels.

$$\lambda = 1 - \frac{v_{Whl}}{v_{WhlFre}}$$

Starting from the stationary brake force F_{BF}, using a PID control law the nominal torque at the wheel can be calculated as a function of the slip deviation.

$$\begin{aligned} M_{WhlNo} = {} & F_{BF} \cdot R + K_p(\lambda_{No} - \lambda)R \\ & + K_d\left(\frac{d}{dt}v_{Whl} - \frac{d}{dt}v_{WhlFre}\right)\frac{J_{Whl}}{R} \\ & + K_i \cdot C_p \cdot \mathrm{SUM}\left\{(\lambda_{No} - \lambda) \cdot D_T\right\} \end{aligned}$$

In the case of the driven wheels, in order to implement an engine drag torque control (MSR) the nominal braking torque M_{WhlNo} can be partially set by the engine (or completely when the brakes are not applied). The driven wheel with the lower nominal wheel torque is controlled within the permissible limits by engine intervention.

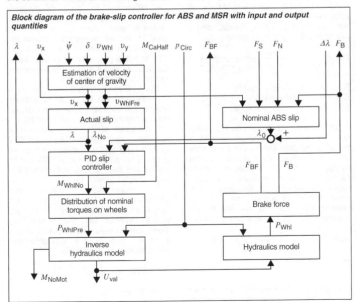

Block diagram of the brake-slip controller for ABS and MSR with input and output quantities

The following applies for rear-wheel drive:

$$M_{NoMot} = -\frac{2m}{\ddot{U}_{Tr}} + \frac{J_{Mot} \cdot \ddot{U}_{Tr}}{R} \cdot \frac{d}{dt} v_x$$

$$m = MIN\,(M_{Whl3}, M_{Whl4})$$

For negative values, the nominal engine torque M_{NoMot} is limited by the maximum engine drag torque, and in the driven case (positive values) it is limited to the maximum dynamic drive torque as permitted by the manufacturer. In case of a positive nominal brake torque M_{WhlNo}, the remaining braking torque must be adjusted through the brake pressure.

$$p_{WhlPre} = \frac{M_{WhlNo} + M_{CaHalf}}{C_p}$$

The pressure p_{WhlPre} applied to the wheel-brake cylinders by the controller, is adjusted by the braking hydraulics and relevant valve-triggering mode U_{val}. The required valve time is calculated using an inverse "hydraulic model", whose parameters x_1, x_2 have been defined beforehand and stored in the controller. Essentially, the model uses the Bernoulli theorem for incompressible media, and a pressure/volume characteristic.

$$U_{val} = \frac{p_{WhlPre} - p_{Whl}}{(x_1 + x_2 \cdot p_{Whl})\sqrt{|p_{Circ} - p_{Whl}|}}$$

$U_{val} > 0$	Build up pressure,
$U_{val} = 0$	Hold pressure,
$U_{val} < 0$	Reduce pressure.

Since the valve-control mode U_{val} is limited by the sampling time and quantified, the adjusted pressure p_{Whl} that has actually been set must be calculated using the hydraulic model. By means of the dynamic wheel equations, taking the known (estimated) wheel brake pressure and the measured wheel speeds, the actual tire braking force F_B and the steady-state braking force F_{BF} can now be calculated:

$$F_B = C_p \cdot \frac{p_{Whl}}{R} - \frac{M_{CaHalf}}{R} + \frac{J_{Whl}}{R^2} \cdot \frac{d}{dt}\, v_{Whl}$$

$$F_B = T_i \cdot \frac{d}{dt} F_{BF} + F_{BF}$$

The steady-state (filtered) braking force F_{BF} now serves as the reference variable

for the PID controller. Using the calculated operating point λ_0, and the change in slip stipulated by the vehicle dynamics controller, the ABS controller calculates the nominal tire slip λ_{No}.

$$\lambda_0 = A_0 \cdot \mu_{Res} + \frac{A_1}{v_{WhlFre}} + A_2$$

$$\mu_{Res} = \frac{\sqrt{F_B + F_S}}{F_N}$$

Traction controller (TCS)

On rear-drive vehicles, the traction controller is used for slip control of the driven wheels only. Active intervention at the front wheels is through the brake-slip controller. Unlike ABS, the traction controller receives from the vehicle dynamics controller the nominal mean traction-slip value λ_{Ma} of both driven wheels and a nominal brake-locking torque value M_{NoLock} to be used as reference variables for directly influencing the yaw moment. The nominal value for the differential speed of the two driven wheels v_{NoDif} is the difference in their (free-rolling) speeds, whereby the vehicle dynamics controller also stipulates a tolerance band D_λ for the difference between the two drive-slip values. This difference represents a dead zone for the control deviation in order that a nominal brake-locking torque M_{NoLock} can be generated.

The TCS module calculates the nominal braking torque M_{WhlNo} for both driven wheels, the nominal engine torque M_{NoMot} to be set by throttle-valve intervention, the nominal value M_{NoSPR} for engine-torque reduction using ignition timing (SPR = spark retard) and, as options, the length of time T_{iOFF} during which the EFI is to be cut off and the number of cylinders this cutoff is to be applied to.

The nominal values for the crankshaft and wheel differential speeds (v_{NoCa} and v_{NoDif}) are calculated from nominal slip values together with the (free-rolling) wheel speeds v_{WhlFre}. The controlled variables v_{Ca} and v_{Dif} are calculated from wheel speeds v_{Whl3} and v_{Whl4}:

$$v_{Ca} = \frac{1}{2}\,(v_{Whl3} + v_{Whl4})$$

$$v_{Dif} = v_{Whl3} - v_{Whl4}$$

The dynamic response depends on the highly differing operating modes of the controlled system. It is therefore necessary to determine the operating mode in order to be able to adapt the controller parameters to the controlled system's dynamic response and to the non-linearities. The large moment of inertia of the complete drivetrain (engine, gearbox, cardan axle, and driven wheels) has an influence on the cardan-axle speed v_{Ca} which is therefore characterized by a relatively large time constant (low dynamic response). On the other hand, the time constant of the wheel differential speed v_{Dif} is relatively small since the dynamic response of v_{Dif} is determined almost completely by the small moments of inertia of the two wheels. Apart from this, v_{Dif} in contrast to v_{Ca} is not directly influenced by the engine. v_{Dif} and v_{Ca} are used therefore as controlled variables because they permit the separation of the drivetrain system (measured wheel speed, rear left and rear right, v_{Whl3} and v_{Whl4} respectively) into two subsystems with distinct dynamic re-

sponse and distinct engine influence. The engine intervention and the "symmetrical" part of the brake intervention represent the controlled variables of the cardan-axle speed controller v_{Ca}. The "asymmetrical" portion of the brake intervention is the actuating signal for the differential wheel-speed controller v_{Dif}.

The cardan-axle speed is controlled by means of a non-linear PID controller, whereby in particular the gain of the I-component (dependent upon operating mode) can vary over a wide range. At steady state, the I-component is a measure for the torque which can be transferred to the road surface. The cardan-axle torque M_{Ca} is the controller output.

A non-linear PI controller is used for controlling the wheel differential speed v_{Dif}, the controller parameters being dependent upon the engaged gear and upon influences from the engine. From the tolerance band D_λ for the differential slip of the driven wheels, which is output by the vehicle dynamics controller, a dead zone is calculated for the control deviation from v_{Dif}. For

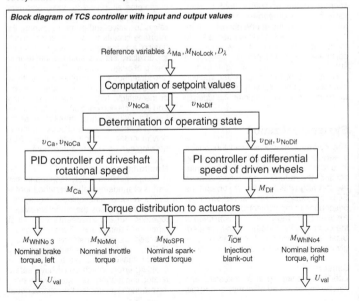

Block diagram of TCS controller with input and output values

Reference variables $\lambda_{Ma}, M_{NoLock}, D_\lambda$

Computation of setpoint values

v_{NoCa} v_{NoDif}

Determination of operating state

v_{Ca}, v_{NoCa} v_{Dif}, v_{NoDif}

PID controller of driveshaft rotational speed   **PI controller of differential speed of driven wheels**

M_{Ca} M_{Dif}

Torque distribution to actuators

$M_{WhlNo\,3}$	M_{NoMot}	M_{NoSPR}	T_{iOff}	M_{WhlNo4}
Nominal brake torque, left	Nominal throttle torque	Nominal spark-retard torque	Injection blank-out	Nominal brake torque, right

U_{val} U_{val}

"μ-split", in order to ensure adequate traction, the vehicle dynamics controller specifies a relatively narrow dead zone. In doing so it increases the sensitivity of the controller for the wheel differential speed v_{Dif}. If the nominal brake-locking torque M_{NoLock} is to be reduced, or in case of the optional Select-Low control, the vehicle dynamics controller defines a wider tolerance band. In these cases, the controller for the differential wheel speed v_{Dif} permits larger differences between the rotational speeds of the rear wheels. The controller output is the differential nominal torque M_{Dif}.

The cardan-axle torque M_{Ca} and the nominal torque differential M_{Dif} are distributed between the actuators. A corresponding valve-triggering mode U_{val} in the hydraulic modulator adjusts the differential nominal torque M_{Dif} via the braking-torque difference between the left and right driven wheels. The nominal cardan-axle torque M_{Ca} is achieved by engine intervention and by means of symmetrical brake intervention. There is a relatively long delay (dead time and transient response of the engine) before throttle-valve intervention comes into effect. For rapid-acting engine intervention, if optionally available, the ignition is retarded, and the fuel injection is cut off. The symmetrical brake intervention provides short-term support for the reduction of engine torque.

By means of this module, the traction controller can be relatively easily adapted to the various engine-intervention types.

System realization

The hydraulic modulator and the wheel-speed sensors are suitable for operation in underhood conditions. The yaw-rate sensor, the lateral-acceleration sensor, the steering-wheel-angle sensor, and the ECU are designed for installation in the passenger compartment or in the trunk. An example of the in-vehicle installation of the components, together with their electrical and mechanical connections, is given on the opposite page.

Sensors

Interface monitoring is a necessity, and can be implemented efficiently and at low cost in modern-day ECUs. It has a decisive effect upon the architecture of the sensor interfaces (for sensors, see P. 94).

The demands reflected in the sensor requirements were ascertained by evaluating simulation studies together with an extensive program of road tests. The consequences of side-effects on ESP operation were also investigated (influence of positioning tolerances, cross-couplings, and other sensor malfunctions). The result was a multi-level, and thus very dense monitoring network which incorporates the aspects of analytical redundancy. In order to be able to master with the necessary reliability those complex systems which are relevant from the safety viewpoint, the aspects of analytical redundancy must be incorporated if reasons of cost forbid the application of redundant sensors.

ECU

The ECU is constructed in conventional (4-layer) pcb technology, and in addition to two partially redundant computers, it incorporates all drivers for valve and lamp triggering, as well as the semiconductor relays for valve and pump triggering, the interface circuits for sensor-signal conditioning, and the appropriate switch inputs for auxiliary signals such as those from the brake-light switch. Furthermore, a CAN interface is integrated in order to facilitate communication with other systems in the vehicle (e.g. engine management and transmission control). The large number of additional signal inputs requires the use of a special plug and socket connection in order that the size of the ECU housing can be kept to a minimum.

Monitoring system

A comprehensive safety-monitoring system is of fundamental importance for the ESP's reliable functioning. The system used encompasses the complete system together with all components and all their functional interactions. The safety system is based on safety methods such as e.g. FMEA, ETA and error-simulation studies.

From these, measures are derived for avoiding errors which could have safety-related consequences. Extensive monitoring programs guarantee the reliable detection of all sensor errors which cannot be prevented completely. These programs are based upon the well-proven safety software from the ABS and ABS/TCS systems which monitor all the components connected to the ECU together with their electrical connections, signals, and functions. The safety software was further improved by fully utilizing the possibilities offered by the additional sensors, and by adapting them to the special ESP components and functions.

The sensors are monitored at a number of stages:

In the first stage, the sensors are continuously monitored for cable open-circuit, and signal implausibility (out-of-range check, detection of interference, physical plausibility).

In a second stage, the most important sensors are tested individually. The yaw-rate sensor is tested by intentionally detuning the sensor element and then evaluating the signal response. Even the acceleration sensor has internal background monitoring. When activated, the pressure-sensor signal must show a pre-defined characteristic, and the offset and amplification are compensated for internally. The steering-wheel angle sensor is provided with "local intelligence" and has its own monitoring functions which directly deliver any error message to the ECU. In addition, the digital signal transmission to the ECU is permanently monitored.

In a third stage, analytical redundancy is applied to monitor the sensors during the steady-state operation of the vehicle. Here, a vehicle model is used to check that the relationships between the sensor signals, as determined by the vehicle motion, are not violated. These models are also frequently applied to calculate and compensate for the sensor offsets as long as they stay within the sensor specifications.

In case of error, the system is switched off either partially or completely depending upon the type of error concerned. The system's response to errors also depends upon whether the control is activated or not.

The ESP system with its electrical connections in the vehicle
1 Wheel brakes, 2 Wheel-speed sensors, 3 Engine-management ECU with CAN interface, 4 Throttle-valve actuator, 5 Precharging pump with admission-pressure sensor, 6 Steering-wheel angle sensor, 7 Brake booster with master cylinder, 8 Hydraulic system with brake-pressure sensor and attached ECU, 9 Yaw sensor with integrated lateral-acceleration sensor.

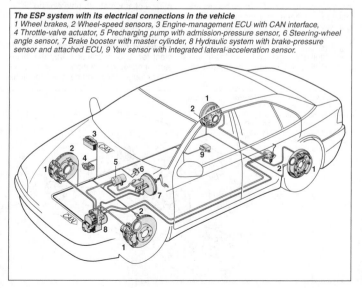

Adaptive Cruise Control (ACC)

Operation
The basic function of Adaptive Cruise Control relies on the conventional cruise-control system (vehicle-speed controller), which maintains a desired speed specified by the driver. In addition, ACC can adapt vehicle speed to changing traffic conditions by means of automatic acceleration, deceleration or braking. This system thus maintains the vehicle's distance to the vehicle driving in front as a function of road speed.

Distance sensor
The most important component in an ACC system is a sensor which measures the distance, the relative speed and the relative position of the preceding vehicles. Maximum performance is achieved – even in poor weather conditions – with a radar sensor.

The radar sensor (P. 101) operates at a frequency of 76 ... 77 GHz which was specially allocated for ACC. Three beams are emitted simultaneously for measurement purposes. The beams reflected by the preceding vehicles are analyzed regarding their propagation time, Doppler shift and amplitude ratio, and from these factors the distance, relative speed, and relative position are calculated (for details, refer to PP. 101 ... 103).

Course setting
To ensure reliable ACC operation, no matter what the situation – e.g. also on curves/bends – it is essential that the preceding vehicles are allocated to the correct lane(s). For this purpose, the information from the ESP sensor system (yaw rate, steering-wheel angle, wheel speeds and lateral acceleration) is evaluated with regard to the ACC-equipped vehicle's actual curve status. Further information on the traffic flow is obtained from the radar signals.

Video imaging and navigation systems are also being considered for future assistance in defining the courses taken by the vehicles.

Engine intervention
Speed control requires an electronic engine-power control system (ETC or EDC). Such a system enables the vehicle to be accelerated to the desired speed or, if an obstacle appears, to be decelerated by means of automatic throttle closing.

Active brake intervention
Experience has shown that deceleration by means of throttle closing is not sufficient for ACC operation. Only the inclusion of brake intervention makes it possible for longer follow-on control operations

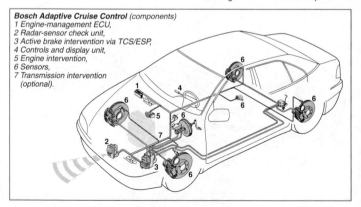

Bosch Adaptive Cruise Control (components)
1 Engine-management ECU,
2 Radar-sensor check unit,
3 Active brake intervention via TCS/ESP,
4 Controls and display unit,
5 Engine intervention,
6 Sensors,
7 Transmission intervention (optional).

with ACC without the need for frequent driver interventions. ESP provides the possibility of braking without driver intervention.

ACC permits only "soft" brake interventions. Emergency braking due to the sudden appearance of obstacles (e.g. the slow-moving vehicle in front suddenly changing its lane) is therefore not possible.

Setting options

The driver inputs the desired speed and the desired time gap; values of 1 ... 2 s are offered for the latter.

Display elements

The driver must be provided with at least the following information:
– indication of the desired speed,
– indication of the switch-on status,
– indication of the desired time gap selected by the driver,
– indication of the follow-on mode, which informs the driver as to whether the system is controlling the distance to a detected target object or not.

Aim of ACC

The aim of ACC is to relieve the driver of the stress associated with "mindless" driving tasks such as maintaining speeds and driving behind other vehicles in heavy traffic. This system helps to improve road safety as well as driver comfort.

System limits

Even with this form of driver support, the driver remains fully responsible for controlling the vehicle. He/she continues to remain responsible for complex decisions relating to straight-ahead driving and control of the vehicle – and obviously for steering as well. The alignment of the functions to emphasize the comfort aspect for the driver, means that a clear boundary has been defined between the tasks which are the responsibility of ACC and those which are the responsibility of the driver. Safety functions such as emergency braking and forced spacing are thus not featured in this system. These functions, together with selecting the desired speed and the desired time gap, are the sole responsibility of the driver.

ACC does not yet permit control operations in urban environments. This system can only be activated at speeds in excess of 30 km/h.

Expanding functions for operation in urban areas would require considerably higher performance on the part of the sensors responsible for monitoring the environment. Such performance cannot be achieved by the 76.5 GHz radar alone.

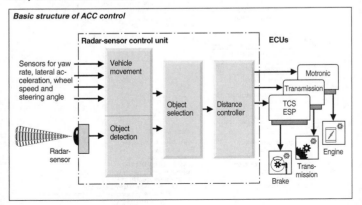

Basic structure of ACC control

Radar-sensor control unit

ECUs

Sensors for yaw rate, lateral acceleration, wheel speed and steering angle → Vehicle movement

Radar-sensor → Object detection

Object selection → Distance controller

Motronic
Transmission
TCS ESP

Engine
Transmission
Brake

Road-vehicle systematics

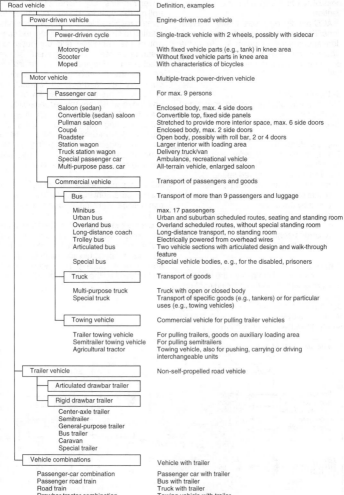

Road vehicle		Definition, examples
	Power-driven vehicle	Engine-driven road vehicle
		Power-driven cycle — Single-track vehicle with 2 wheels, possibly with sidecar
		Motorcycle — With fixed vehicle parts (e.g., tank) in knee area
		Scooter — Without fixed vehicle parts in knee area
		Moped — With characteristics of bicycles
	Motor vehicle	Multiple-track power-driven vehicle
		Passenger car — For max. 9 persons
		Saloon (sedan) — Enclosed body, max. 4 side doors
		Convertible (sedan) saloon — Convertible top, fixed side panels
		Pullman saloon — Stretched to provide more interior space, max. 6 side doors
		Coupé — Enclosed body, max. 2 side doors
		Roadster — Open body, possibly with roll bar, 2 or 4 doors
		Station wagon — Larger interior with loading area
		Truck station wagon — Delivery truck/van
		Special passenger car — Ambulance, recreational vehicle
		Multi-purpose pass. car — All-terrain vehicle, enlarged saloon

Commercial vehicle — Transport of passengers and goods

Bus — Transport of more than 9 passengers and luggage

- Minibus — max. 17 passengers
- Urban bus — Urban and suburban scheduled routes, seating and standing room
- Overland bus — Overland scheduled routes, without special standing room
- Long-distance coach — Long-distance transport, no standing room
- Trolley bus — Electrically powered from overhead wires
- Articulated bus — Two vehicle sections with articulated design and walk-through feature
- Special bus — Special vehicle bodies, e.g., for the disabled, prisoners

Truck — Transport of goods

- Multi-purpose truck — Truck with open or closed body
- Special truck — Transport of specific goods (e.g., tankers) or for particular uses (e.g., towing vehicles)

Towing vehicle — Commercial vehicle for pulling trailer vehicles

- Trailer towing vehicle — For pulling trailers, goods on auxiliary loading area
- Semitrailer towing vehicle — For pulling semitrailers
- Agricultural tractor — Towing vehicle, also for pushing, carrying or driving interchangeable units

Trailer vehicle — Non-self-propelled road vehicle

- Articulated drawbar trailer
- Rigid drawbar trailer
  - Center-axle trailer
  - Semitrailer
  - General-purpose trailer
  - Bus trailer
  - Caravan
  - Special trailer

Vehicle combinations — Vehicle with trailer

- Passenger-car combination — Passenger car with trailer
- Passenger road train — Bus with trailer
- Road train — Truck with trailer
- Drawbar tractor combination — Towing vehicle with trailer
- Articulated road train — Semitrailer towing vehicle with semitrailer
- Double road train — Semitrailer vehicle with trailer
- Platform road train — Truck or towing vehicle with special trailer (dolly), the load forms the connection between the two vehicles

Classification[1])

Category L
Motor vehicles with fewer than 4 wheels, motorized two-wheeled and three-wheeled vehicles.

Category	Design	Piston displacement	Top speed
L_1	two-wheeled	$\leq 50 \text{ cm}^3$	≤ 50 km/h
L_2	three-wheeled	$\leq 50 \text{ cm}^3$	≤ 50 km/h
L_3	two-wheeled	$> 50 \text{ cm}^3$	> 50 km/h
L_4	three-wheeled asymmetrical to longitudinal vehicle axis	$> 50 \text{ cm}^3$	> 50 km/h
L_5	three-wheeled symmetrical to longitudinal vehicle axis	$> 50 \text{ cm}^3$ ≤ 1 t Total weight	> 50 km/h

Category M
Passenger vehicles with at least 4 wheels or with 3 wheels and an overall weight > 1 t.

Category	Driver's seat + passenger seats	Total weight
M_1	$1 \leq 9$	
M_2	> 9	< 5 t
M_3	> 9	> 5t

Category N
Goods transport vehicles with at least 4 wheels or with 3 wheels and a laden weight > 1 t.

Category	Total weight
N_1	≤ 3.5 t
N_2	> 3.5 t ≤ 12 t
N_3	> 12 t

Category O
Trailers and semitrailers

Category	Total weight
O_1 only single-axle trailers	≤ 0.75 t
O_2	> 0.75 t ≤ 3.5 t
O_3	> 3.5 t ≤ 10 t
O_4	> 10 t

---

[1]) Vehicle classification in accordance with the Directives of the European Community (71/320/EEC) and ECE Regulation No. 13 with regard to brake equipment.

Vehicle bodies, passenger cars

Main dimensions

Interior-dimensions

Dimensional layout depends upon body shape, type of drive, scope of aggregate equipment, desired interior size, luggage compartment volume and other considerations such as driving comfort, driving safety and operating safety. Seating positions are designed in accordance with ergonomic findings and with the aid of templates or 3D CAD dummy models (DIN, SAE, RAMSIS): Body template as per DIN 33 408 for men (5th, 50th, and 95th percentile) and women (1st, 5th and 95th percentile). For example, the 5th percentile template represents "small" body size, i.e., only 5% of the population have smaller bodies, and 95% have larger body dimensions.

SAE H-point template in accordance with SEA J826 (May 1987): 10th, 50th and 95th percentile thigh segments and lower leg segments. For legal reasons, motor-vehicle manufacturers in the USA and in Canada must use the SAE H-point template for determining the seating reference point. Body templates in accordance with DIN 33 408 in accelerated form are particularly well suited to the dimensional design of seats and passenger compartments. Most motor-vehicle manufacturers round the world use the 3D CAD dummy model "RAMSIS" in development (RAMSIS: computer-aided anthropological-mathematical system for passenger simulation).

The hip point (H-point) is the pivot center of torso and thigh, and roughly corresponds to the hip joint location. The seating reference point (in accordance with ISO 6549 and US legislation) or R-point (ISO 6549 and EEC Directives/ECE Regulations) indicates the position of the design H-point in the rearmost normal driver seating position in the case of adjustable seats. In determining the design H-point position, many vehicle manufacturers use the 95th percentile adult-male position or, if this position is not reached, the position with the seat adjusted to its rearmost set-

ting. In order to check the position of the measured H-point relative to the vehicle, a three-dimensional, adjustable SEA H-point machine weighing 75 kg is used. The seating reference point, heel point, vertical and horizontal distance between these two points, and body angles specified by the vehicle manufacturer form the basis for determining the dimensions of the driver's seating position.

The seating reference point is used
– to define the positions of the eye ellipse (SAE J941) and the eye points (RREG 77/649) as a basis for determining the driver's direct field of view;
– to define hand reach envelopes in order to correctly position controls and actuators;
– to determine the accelerator heel point (AHP) as a reference point for positioning the pedals.

The space required by the rear axle as well as location and shape of the fuel tank primarily determine the rear seating arrangement (height of the seating reference point, rear seating room, head-room) and thus the shape of the roof rear portion. Depending on the type of vehicle being developed, the projected main dimensions and the required passenger sizes, there are different body angles for the 2D templates or body postures (RAMSIS) and different distances between the seating reference points of the driver's and rear seats. The longitudinal dimensions are greatly influenced by the height of the seating reference point above the heel point. Lower seats require a more stretched passenger seating position and thus greater interior length.

The passenger-compartment width is dependent on the projected exterior width, the shape of the sides (curvature) and the space required for door mechanisms, passive restraint systems and various assemblies (propellor-shaft tunnel, exhaust system etc.).

Luggage-compartment dimensions

The size and shape of the luggage compartment are dependent on the design of the rear of the vehicle, the position of the fuel tank and its volume, the position of the spare wheel and the location of the main muffler.

Typical internal and external dimensions (as per DIN 70 020, Part 1)

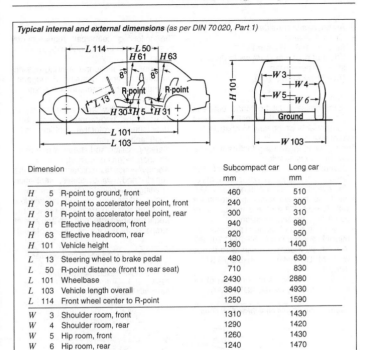

Dimension			Subcompact car mm	Long car mm
H	5	R-point to ground, front	460	510
H	30	R-point to accelerator heel point, front	240	300
H	31	R-point to accelerator heel point, rear	300	310
H	61	Effective headroom, front	940	980
H	63	Effective headroom, rear	920	950
H	101	Vehicle height	1360	1400
L	13	Steering wheel to brake pedal	480	630
L	50	R-point distance (front to rear seat)	710	830
L	101	Wheelbase	2430	2880
L	103	Vehicle length overall	3840	4930
L	114	Front wheel center to R-point	1250	1590
W	3	Shoulder room, front	1310	1430
W	4	Shoulder room, rear	1290	1420
W	5	Hip room, front	1260	1430
W	6	Hip room, rear	1240	1470
W	103	Vehicle width overall	1620	1820

Luggage-compartment capacity is determined in accordance with DIN-ISO 3832 or, more commonly, with the VDA method using the VDA unit module (a right parallelepiped with dimensions of 200 x 100 x 50 mm – corresponds to a volume of 1 dm³).

Exterior dimensions
The following factors must be taken into consideration:
– Seating arrangement and luggage compartment,
– Engine, transmission, radiator,
– Auxiliary and special equipment,
– Space required by sprung and turned wheels (allowance for snow chains),
– Type and size of drive axle,
– Position and volume of fuel tank,
– Front and rear bumpers,

Parameters which determine passenger-car driver's seat location

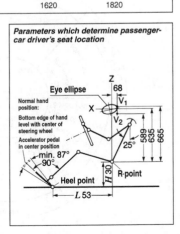

- Aerodynamic considerations,
- Ground clearance
  (approx. 100...180 mm),
- Effect of body structure width on wind-
  shield wiper system
  (ADR 16, FMVSS 104).

Vision

A compromise must be found between optimum vision and the functional layout of components which tend to obstruct the field of vision.

The following influencing factors must be taken into consideration:
- Obscuration by pillars, the roof, the hood and the luggage-compartment lid. The eye ellipse in accordance with SAE J941 and the "eye points" in accordance with RREG 77/649[1]) are the basis for assessing the field of vision,
- Location, size and shape of the rear-view mirror in accordance with RREG 79/795.
- Windshield wiper pattern in accordance with FMVSS 104[2]) and RREG 78/318,
- Windshield curvature,
- View of instruments (obstruction of vision by steering wheel, ADR 18 A[3])).

Body design

The following technical requirements must be met in interior and exterior body design:
- Mechanical functions (lowering of side windows, opening of the hood, luggage-compartment lid and sunroof, positions of lamps),
- Manufacturability and ease of repair (gap widths, bodywork assembly, window shape, protective molding rails, paint feature lines),
- Safety (position and shape of bumpers, no sharp edges or points),
- Aerodynamics (air resistance, dirt on the vehicle body, wind noises, ventilation openings, windshield-wiper operation),
- Optics (distortion caused by window type and slope, glare due to reflection),
- Legal requirements (position and size of lamps, rear-view mirror, license plates),

---

[1]) Directives of the Council of the European Union.
[2]) Federal Motor Vehicle Safety Standard (USA).
[3]) Australian Design Rule.

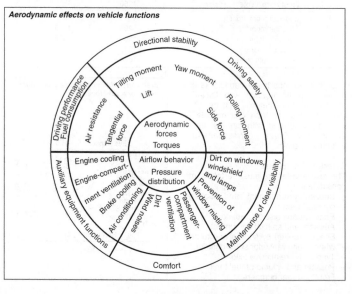

Aerodynamic effects on vehicle functions

– Design and layout of controls (positions, shapes and surface contours),
– Clear layout (parking).

Aerodynamics

Aerodynamics deals with all processes which are observed as air flows through and around a vehicle.

Aerodynamic drag $W = c_W \cdot A \cdot v^2 \cdot \dfrac{\varrho}{2}$

where c_W = drag coefficient,
A = cross-sectional area,
v = driving speed,
ϱ = air density.

Table 1.
c_W **values for various vehicles**

Vehicle (Examples)	c_W –	A m²
Audi A8	0.29	2.25
Porsche 911	0.29	1.95
Mercedes C 200 D	0.30	2.05

The factors to be influenced by the vehicle manufacturer are the drag coefficient c_W as a measure of the aerodynamic quality of the vehicle shape, and the projected vehicle cross-sectional area A.

Attempts to reduce the c_W value by adding spoilers, underbody panels, etc. are not practical, since their effect depends upon the aerodynamic characteristics of the basic vehicle body (see Table 2 for effects of individual modifications on drag coefficient). These types of modifications in optimized form are standard features of modern vehicle design. This means that the fitting of supplementary devices to further improve the c_W value and the axle lifting-force coefficient can only result in very minor improvements. Often, such modifications result in the impairment of the vehicle's day-to-day capabilities due to reduced overhang angle or reduced ground clearance. In other words, such add-on parts serve more for improving the vehicle's appearance than for improving its performance.

The c_W value can be influenced by individual aerodynamic or design measures. Airflow through the vehicle as well as roof-mounted fixtures will always increase the c_W value. Examples (– = better, + = worse). Examples are given in Table 2.

Table 2.
c_W **values for vehicle modifications**

Effect of	Δc_W in %
Lowering vehicle height by 30mm	approx. –5
Smooth wheel covers	–1...–3
Wide tires	+2...+4
Windows flush with exterior	approx. –1
Sealing body gaps	–2...–5
Underbody panels	–1...–7
Concealed headlamps	+3...+10
Outside rear-view mirrors	+2...+5
Airflow through radiator and engine compartment	+4...+14
Brake cooling devices	+2...+5
Interior ventilation	approx. +1
Open windows	approx. +5
Open sunroof	approx. +2
Roof-mounted surfboard rack	approx. +40

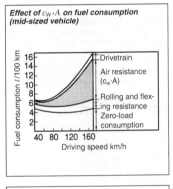

Effect of $c_W \cdot A$ on fuel consumption (mid-sized vehicle)

Drivetrain
Air resistance ($c_W \cdot A$)
Rolling and flexing resistance
Zero-load consumption

Fuel consumption l/100 km — Driving speed km/h

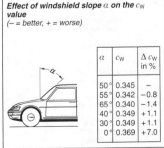

Effect of windshield slope α on the c_W value
(– = better, + = worse)

α	c_W	Δc_W in %
50°	0.345	–
55°	0.342	–0.8
65°	0.340	–1.4
40°	0.349	+1.1
30°	0.349	+1.1
0°	0.369	+7.0

Body structure

Unitized (self-supporting) body
(Standard design)
The conventional unitized (self-supporting) body is built up of hollow sheet-steel components onto which body panels are welded by welding robots or in multispot welding units. Individual parts can also be glued in position.

Depending upon vehicle type, roughly 5000 spot welds must be made along a total flange length of 120...200 m. The flange widths are 10...18 mm. Other parts (front fenders, doors, hood and luggage-compartment lid) are bolted to the supporting structure of the body. Other types of body construction include frame and sandwich designs.
General requirements:

Rigidity
Torsional and bending rigidity should be as high as possible in order to minimize elastic deformation of the apertures for the doors, hood and luggage-compartment lid. The effect of body rigidity on the vibrational characteristics of the vehicle must be taken into consideration.

Vibrational characteristics
Body vibrations as well as vibrations of individual structural components as a result of excitation by the wheels, suspension system, engine and drivetrain can severely impair driving comfort if resonance occurs.

The natural frequency of the body, and of those body components which are capable of vibration, must be detuned by means of creasing and changing the wall thicknesses and cross sections, such that resonance and its consequences are minimized.

Operational integrity
Alternating stresses which can affect the body as the vehicle is driven can lead to incipient structural cracks or weld failure. Areas which are particularly susceptible are the bearing points of the running gear, the steering system and engine units.

Body stresses due to accidents
In the event of a collision, the body must be capable of transforming as much kinetic energy as possible into deformation work while minimizing deformation of the vehicle interior.

Ease of repair
Those components which are most susceptible to damage as a result of minor accidents ("fender-benders") must be easily replaceable or repairable (access

Body structure
1. Cross member under windshield,
2. Roof frame, front,
3. Roof frame, side,
4. Roof frame, rear,
5. C-pillar,
6. Rear-facing panel,
7. Rear floor and spare-wheel pan,
8. Side member, rear,
9. B-pillar,
10. Cross member under rear seat,
11. A-pillar,
12. Cross member under driver's seat,
13. Side member,
14. Wheel well,
15. Engine-support cross member,
16. Side member, front,
17. Cross member, front,
18. Radiator cross member.

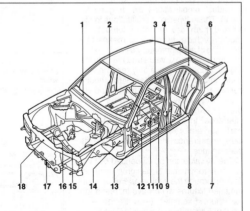

to exterior body panels from inside, access to bolts, favorable location of joints, feature lines for the repainting of individual components).

Body materials

Sheet steel

Sheet steel of various grades (see table on P. 197) is customarily used for the vehicle body structure.

Sheet thicknesses range from 0.6 to 3.0 mm, with most pieces being between 0.75 and 1.0 mm thick. Due to the mechanical properties of steel with regard to stiffness, strength, economy and ductility, alternative materials for the vehicle body structure are not yet available.

High-strength, low-alloy (HSLA) sheet steel is used for highly-stressed structural components. The resulting high strength of these components allows their thickness to be reduced.

Aluminum

In order to reduce weight, aluminum can be used for separate body components such as the hood, luggage-compartment lid, etc.

Since 1994, an aluminum body has been in use for one of the German luxury-class cars. The vehicle's frame is constructed from aluminum extruded sections, and the sheet components are self-supporting in integrated form (ASF Audi Space Frame). The realization of this principle necessitated the employment of suitable aluminum alloys, as well as new production processes and special repair facilities. According to the manufacturers, the rigidity and deformation characteristics are identical to those of steel or are even superior.

Plastics

Plastics as materials for separate body components are used in a limited number of cases in place of steel (see Table below).

Table 3. Examples of alternative materials

Examples of application	Material	Abbre-viation	Processing method
Load-bearing components, e.g. bumper beam	Thermoplastics reinforced by glass-fiber mats	PP-GMT	Injection pressure
Moldings/covers, e.g. front apron, spoiler, front section, radiator grill, wheel-well liners, wheel covers Separate vehicle-body components, e.g. hood, fender, luggage-compartment lid, sunroof	Thermoplastics reinforced by glass-fiber mats	PP-GMT	
	Polyurethane	PUR	RIM (Reaction-Injection-Molding) RRIM (Reinforced-Reaction-Injection-Molding)
	Polyamide Polypropylene Polyethylene Acrylonitrile-butadiene-styrene copolymeres Polycarbonate (with Polybutadiene theraphtha-late mod.)	PA PP PE ABS PC-PBT	Injection-molding, glass-fiber constituent determines elasticity
Protective molding rails	Polyvinylchloride Ethylene-Propylene-Terpolymers Elastomer-modified polypropylene	PVC EPDM PP-EPDM	Injection-molding/extrusion
Energy-absorbing foam	Polyurethane Polypropylene	PUR PP	Reaction foaming

Body surface

Corrosion protection

Allowance must be made for corrosion protection as early as during the body design phase ("Anti-Corrosion Code", Canada). Corrosion protection measures:
– Minimize flanged joints, sharp edges and corners,
– Avoid areas where dirt and humidity can accumulate,
– Provide holes for pretreatment and electrophoretic enameling,
– Provide good accessibility for the application of corrosion inhibitor,
– Allow for ventilation of hollow spaces,
– Prevent the penetration of dirt and water to the greatest extent possible; provide water drain openings,
– Minimize the area of the body exposed to stone-chip throw,
– Prevent contact corrosion.

Precoated sheet steel (inorganic zinc, electrolytically galvanized, hot-dip galvanized) is often used for those components which are particularly endangered, such as doors and load-bearing members at the front of the vehicle. Particularly inaccessible structural areas are coated with spot-welding paste (PVC or epoxy adhesive, approx. 10...15 m seam length per vehicle) prior to assembly.

Painting (P. 228)

Measures subsequent to electrophoretic enameling:
– Covering the spot-welded seams (up to 90...110 m), folds and joints with PVC sealing compound,
– Coating the underbody with PVC underseal (0.3...1.4 mm thick, 10...18 kg per

vehicle) to protect against damage due to stone chips. Plastic trim panels can be used as an alternative.
– Preservation of hollow parts with penetrating, non-aging water-based wax,
– Use of corrosion-resistant, separate plastic components in highly susceptible areas such as the front wheel wells (PVC coating is not suitable here).
– Preservation of underbody and engine compartment after final assembly.

Body finishing components

Bumpers

The front and rear of the vehicle should be protected in such a manner that low-speed collisions will only damage the vehicle slightly, or not at all. Prescribed bumper evaluation tests (US Part 581, Canada CMVSS 215, and ECE-R 42) specify minimum requirements in terms of energy absorption and installed bumper height. Bumper evaluation tests in accordance with US Part 581 (4 km/h barrier collision, 4 km/h pendulum tests) must be passed by a bumper system whose energy absorber is of the no-damage absorber type. The requirements of the ECE standard are satisfied by plastically deformable retaining elements located between the bumper and the vehicle body structure. In addition to sheet steel, many bumpers are manufactured using fiber-reinforced plastics and aluminum sections.

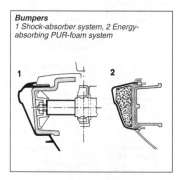

Bumpers
1 Shock-absorber system, 2 Energy-absorbing PUR-foam system

Table 4. Paint/coating thicknesses

Coating system, overall thickness	$\approx 120\ \mu m$
Zinc-phosphate coating Electrophoretic enameling (cathodic) Filler Top-paint coat	$\approx 2\ \mu m$ 13...18 μm $\approx 40\ \mu m$ 35...45 μm
Varnish coat (only for metallic paint)	40...45 μm

Exterior trim, impact strips

Plastics have become the preferred materials for external impact strips, trim, skirts and spoilers, and particularly for those components whose purpose is to improve the aerodynamic characteristics of the vehicle. Criteria used in the selection of the proper material are flexibility, high-temperature shape retention, coefficient of linear expansion, notched-bar toughness, resistance to scratches, resistance to chemicals, surface quality and paintability.

Glazing

The windshield and rear window are usually held in rubber strips and sealed or bonded in place.

The total weight of the windows in a vehicle ranges from 25 to 35 kg. Due to a number of inherent disadvantages, weight considerations have not yet led to plastics (PC, PMMA) being introduced as the substitute for glass. Due to its heat-insulation and noise-damping properties, 2-layer insulating glass has come into use for door windows.

Door latches

Door latches are of great importance with regard to passive accident safety (pertinent regulations: ECE-R 11 and FMVSS 206, among others):
– Fully latched and secondary latched positions,
– Complete integrity under a longitudinal load of up to 12 kN and a transverse load of up to 10 kN (fully latched position),
– Complete integrity under a longitudinal or transverse inertia load of up to 30 · g.
Individual manufacturers have varying solutions with regard to ease of operation, anti-theft protection and child-proof operation.

Seats

The strength requirements which must be met by the seats in a collision pertain to the seat cushion and backrest, the head restraints, the seat adjustment mechanism and the seat anchors (pertinent regulations: FMVSS 207, 202; ECE-R 17, 25; RREG 74/408, 78/932 and others). One component of active safety is seating comfort. Seats must be designed such that ve-

hicle occupants with different body dimensions do not suffer from driving fatigue. Parameters:
– Support of individual body areas (distribution of pressure),
– Lateral support when cornering,
– Seating ambience,
– Freedom of movement so that an occupant can change his/her sitting position without having to readjust the seat,
– Vibrational and damping characteristics (matching of the natural frequency with the excitation frequency band),
– Adjustability of seat cushion, backrest and head restraint.

The above parameters are affected by the following:
– Dimensions and shapes of the upholstery in the seat cushion and backrest,
– Distribution of the spring rates of individual cushioned zones,
– Overall spring rate and damping capacity, of the seat cushions in particular,
– Thermal conductivity and moisture-absorption capacity of the covers and upholstery,
– Operation and range of the seat adjustment mechanisms.

Interior trim

A section of trim consists of a dimensionally stable core (sheet steel, sheet aluminum or plastic) with mounting hardware, and energy-absorbing cushion made of foam material (e.g. PUR) and a flexible surface layer. One-piece plastic trim sections made of injection-molded thermoplastic material are also used.

The headliner is made either as a stretched liner or finished liner. The ma-

Section through an A-pillar with trim
(Principle)
1 Core, 2 Foam, 3 Film, 4 Windshield,
5 Side window, 6 Door frame.

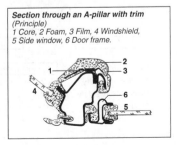

terials used must be flame-retardant and slow burning (FMVSS 302).

Safety

Active safety:
<u>Prevention</u> of accidents
Passive safety:
<u>Reduction</u> of accident consequences

Active safety

<u>Driving safety</u> is the result of a harmonious chassis and suspension design with regard to wheel suspension, springing, steering and braking, and is reflected in optimum dynamic vehicle behavior.

<u>Conditional safety</u> results from keeping the physiological stress that the vehicle occupants are subjected to by vibration, noise, and climatic conditions down to as low a level as possible. It is a significant factor in reducing the possibility of misactions in traffic.

Vibrations within a frequency range of 1 to 25 Hz (stuttering, shaking, etc.) induced by wheels and drive components reach the occupants of the vehicle via the body, seats and steering wheel. The effect of these vibrations is more or less pronounced, depending upon their direction, amplitude and duration.

Noises as acoustical disturbances in and around the vehicle can come from internal sources (engine, transmission, propshafts, axles) or external sources (tire/road noises, wind noises), and are transmitted through the air or the vehicle body. The sound pressure level is measured in dB (A) (see also PP. 52).

Noise reduction measures are concerned on the one hand with the development of quiet-running components and the insulation of noise sources (e.g., engine encapsulation), and on the other hand with noise damping by means of insulating or anti-noise materials.

Climatic conditions inside the vehicle are primarily influenced by air temperature, air humidity, rate of air flow through the passenger compartment and air pressure (see PP. 364 for additional information).

<u>Perceptibility safety</u>
Measures which increase perceptibility safety are concentrated on
- Lighting equipment (see P. 738),
- Acoustic warning devices (see P. 766),
- Direct and indirect view (see P. 720) (Driver's view: The angle of obscuration caused by the A-pillars for both of the driver's eyes – binocular – must not be more than 6 degrees).

<u>Operating safety</u>
Low driver stress, and thus a high degree of driving safety, requires optimum design

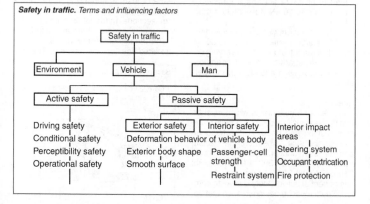

Safety in traffic. Terms and influencing factors

of the driver's surroundings with regard to ease of operation of the vehicle controls.

Passive safety

Exterior safety

The term "exterior safety" covers all vehicle-related measures which are designed to minimize the severity of injury to pedestrians and bicycle and motorcycle riders struck by the vehicle in an accident. Those factors which determine exterior safety are:
– Vehicle-body deformation behavior,
– Exterior vehicle-body shape.

The primary objective is to design the vehicle such that its exterior design minimizes the consequences of a primary collision (a collision involving persons outside the vehicle and the vehicle itself).

The most severe injuries are sustained by passengers who are hit by the front of the vehicle, whereby the course of the accident greatly depends upon body size. The consequences of collisions involving two-wheeled vehicles and passenger cars can only be slightly ameliorated by passenger-car design due to the two-wheeled vehicle's often considerable inherent energy component, its high seat position and the wide dispersion of contact points. Those design features which can be incorporated into the passenger car are, for example:
– Movable front lamps,
– Recessed windshields wipers,
– Recessed drip rails,
– Recessed door handles.
See also ECE-R26, RREG 74/483

Interior safety

The term "interior safety" covers vehicle measures whose purpose is to minimize the accelerations and forces acting on the vehicle occupants in the event of an accident, to provide sufficient survival space, and to ensure the operability of those vehicle components critical to the removal of passengers from the vehicle after the accident has occurred.

The determining factors for passenger safety are:
– Deformation behavior (vehicle body),
– Passenger-compartment strength, size of the survival space during and after impact,
– Restraint systems,
– Impact areas (vehicle interior), (FMVSS 201),
– Steering system,
– Occupant extrication,
– Fire protection.

Laws which regulate interior safety (frontal impact) are:
– Protection of vehicle occupants in the event of an accident, in particular restraint systems (FMVSS 208, ECE R94, injury criteria),
– Windshield mounting (FMVSS 212),

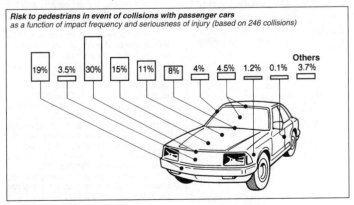

Risk to pedestrians in event of collisions with passenger cars
as a function of impact frequency and seriousness of injury (based on 246 collisions)

19% 3.5% 30% 15% 11% 8% 4% 4.5% 1.2% 0.1% **Others** 3.7%

– Penetration of the windshield by vehicle body components (FMVSS 219),
– Parcel-shelf and compartment lids (FMVSS 201).

Rating-Tests:
– New-Car Assessment Program (NCAP, USA, Europe, Japan, Australia),
– IIHS (USA, insurance test),
– ADAC, ams, AUTO-BILD.

Deformation behavior of vehicle body
Due to the frequency of frontal collisions, an important role is played by the legally stipulated frontal impact test in which a vehicle is driven at a speed of 48.3 km/h (30 mph) into a rigid barrier which is either perpendicular or inclined at an angle of up to 30° relative to the longitudinal axis of the car.

Because 50 % of all frontal collisions in right-hand traffic primarily involve the left-hand half of the front of the vehicle, manufacturers worldwide conduct left asymmetrical front impact tests on LHD vehicles covering 30...50 % of the vehicle width.

In a frontal collision, kinetic energy is absorbed through deformation of the bumper, the front of the vehicle, and in severe cases the forward section of the passenger compartment (dash area). Axles, wheels (rims) and the engine limit the deformable length. Adequate deformation lengths and displaceable vehicle aggregates are necessary, however, in order to minimize passenger-compartment acceleration. Depending upon vehicle design (body shape, type of drive and engine position), vehicle mass and size, a frontal impact with a barrier at approx. 50 km/h results in permanent deformation in the forward area of 0.4...0.7 m. Damage to the passenger compartment should be minimized. This concerns primarily
– dash area (displacement of steering system, instrument panel, pedals, toe-panel intrusion),
– underbody (lowering or tilting of seats),
– the side structure (ability to open the doors after an accident).

Acceleration measurements and evaluations of high-speed films enable deformation behavior to be analyzed precisely. Dummies of various sizes are used to simulate vehicle occupants and provide acceleration figures for head and chest as well as forces acting on thighs.

Head acceleration values are used to determine the head injury criterion (HIC). The comparison of measured values supplied by the dummies with the permissible limit values as per FMVSS 208 (HIC: 1000, chest acceleration: 60 g/3 ms, upper leg force: 10 kN) are only limited in their applicability to the human being.

The side impact, as the next most frequent type of accident, places a high risk of injury on the vehicle occupants due to the limited energy absorbing capability of trim and structural components, and the resulting high degree of vehicle interior deformation.

The risk of injury is largely influenced by the structural strength of the side of the vehicle (pillar/door joints, top/bottom pillar points), load-carrying capacity of floor cross-members and seats, as well as the design of inside door panels (FMVSS 214, ECE R95, Euro-NCAP, US-SINCAP).

In the rear impact test, deformation of the vehicle interior must be minor at most. It should still be possible to open the doors, the edge of the trunk lid should not penetrate the rear window and enter the vehicle interior, and fuel-system integrity must be preserved (FMVSS 301).

Roof structures are investigated by means of rollover tests and quasi-static car-roof crush tests (FMVSS 216).

Distribution of accidents by type of collision
Symbolized by test methods yielding equal results

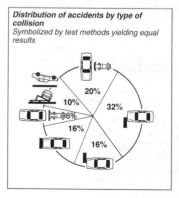

20%
10%
6%
16%
32%
16%

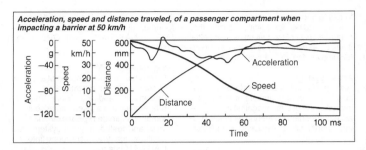

Acceleration, speed and distance traveled, of a passenger compartment when impacting a barrier at 50 km/h

In addition, at least one manufacturer subjects his vehicles to the inverted vehicle drop test in order to test the dimensional stability of the roof structure (survival space) under extreme conditions (the vehicle falls from a height of 0.5 m onto the left front corner of its roof).

Steering system
Legal requirements (FMVSS 203 and 204) regulate the maximum displacement of the top end of the steering column toward the driver (max. 127 mm, frontal impact at 48.3 km/h) and the limit of the impact on the steering system of a test piece (maximal 1111 daN at an impact speed of 24.1 km/h). Slotted tubes, corrugated tubes and breakaway universal joints (among others) are used in the design of the lower section of the steering column spindle so that it can be deformed both longitudinally and transversely.

Passenger restraint systems (P. 803)

Automatic seat belt (manual systems)
The most frequently installed three-point seat belt with retractor mechanism ("automatic seat belt") represents a good compromise between effective safety, ease of buckling, comfort and cost. When a specific vehicle-deceleration value is reached, a built-in, quick-response interlock inhibits the seat-belt roller.

Seat-belt tightener systems
Seat-belt tightener systems represent a further development and improvement of the three-point automatic seat-belt systems. By reducing seat-belt slack, they eliminate excessive forward passenger movement in serious accidents. This in turn reduces the differential speed between the vehicle and passengers, and thus also reduces the corresponding

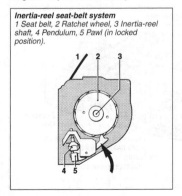

Inertia-reel seat-belt system
1 Seat belt, 2 Ratchet wheel, 3 Inertia-reel shaft, 4 Pendulum, 5 Pawl (in locked position).

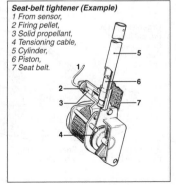

Seat-belt tightener (Example)
1 From sensor,
2 Firing pellet,
3 Solid propellant,
4 Tensioning cable,
5 Cylinder,
6 Piston,
7 Seat belt.

forces acting on the passengers.

Integrated belt-force limiters ensure that controlled give of the belt takes place after it has been tightened, so as to prevent potential overloading in the chest area.

Airbag systems

Airbags (frontal airbags, side bags, window bags) serve to prevent or reduce the impact of the occupant against interior vehicle components (steering wheel, instrument panel, doors, windows, roof pillars).

Calculations

Finite-Element Method

The Finite-Element Method (FEM) can be used to calculate static, dynamic and acoustic characteristics of components and complete bodies. In finite-element analysis, a support structure of any degree of complexity is broken down into simple structural elements (beams, shells and solid elements etc.), of which the elastic behavior is known and can be easily defined. These elements are then assembled to form the overall structure, taking into account compatibility conditions.

This enables a mathematical model to be constructed in such a manner that it sufficiently corresponds to the actual body in terms of its elastic characteristics.

A number of systems are available for practical FE calculation, such as PER-MAS, NASTRAN, ABAQUS and DYNA3D.

Advantages of FEM:
– Characteristics of structures of any level of complexity can be calculated,
– Anisotropic and non-linear material properties can be taken into account,
– Variations can be rapidly examined,
– Tried and tested program systems are available (easy to incorporate into the CAD/CAM chain).

Limits of FEM:
– Accuracy is dependent on element type and precision of element distribution within the structure,
– Changes in sheet-metal thicknesses and material characteristic values resulting from the deep-drawing process are not taken into account,
– Welding joints cannot be precisely replicated in the model.

Complete body calculation

For the calculation, the bodywork structure is broken down into elements with the required level of precision depending on the problem to be solved (as at 1999: up to approx. 300,000 elements with over 1.8 million unknowns). Results under static

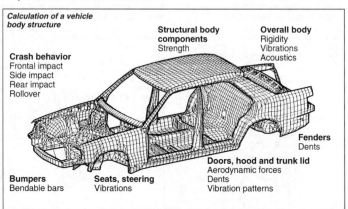

Calculation of a vehicle body structure

Structural body components
Strength

Overall body
Rigidity
Vibrations
Acoustics

Crash behavior
Frontal impact
Side impact
Rear impact
Rollover

Fenders
Dents

Doors, hood and trunk lid
Aerodynamic forces
Dents
Vibration patterns

Bumpers
Bendable bars

Seats, steering
Vibrations

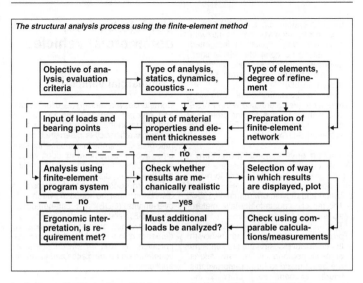

The structural analysis process using the finite-element method

| Objective of analysis, evaluation criteria | → | Type of analysis, statics, dynamics, acoustics ... | → | Type of elements, degree of refinement |

| Input of loads and bearing points | ← | Input of material properties and element thicknesses | ← | Preparation of finite-element network |

no

| Analysis using finite-element program system | → | Check whether results are mechanically realistic | → | Selection of way in which results are displayed, plot |

no — yes

| Ergonomic interpretation, is requirement met? | ← | Must additional loads be analyzed? | ← | Check using comparable calculations/measurements |

load are supplied in the form of deformations, stresses and deformation work.

Strength analysis

Detailed analyses are carried out for individual parts and body sections which are exposed to special stresses caused by factors such as e.g. restraint systems or towed loads. The aim of these analyses is to furnish proof of adequate strength or to reduce unacceptably high stresses by modifying the design.

Analysis of dynamic behavior

Dynamic analyses are carried out both for the complete body and for the individual components. In these analyses, the natural vibration (frequencies, forms of vibration) and the system's response to periodic or generally time-dependent excitation is determined. In this way, critical resonances can be identified and the loads which determine operational integrity can be defined.

For the examination of ride comfort and acoustical behavior in the vehicle interior, FE models of the chassis, engine, doors etc., as well as a model of the interior, are added to the body model.

Analysis of crash behavior

Accident tests carried out by automobile manufacturers (frontal, rear and side impacts, rollover and drop tests) as well as traffic accidents, are dynamic, to a large degree non-linear processes which cannot be described using the current FE programs. Special FE program systems (e.g., DYNA3D, PAM-CRASH) have been developed for numerical simulation of these processes, and are proving successful in the field. These systems include analysis of severe plastic deformations as well as recording of the contact areas arising between various vehicle parts during crash processes.

Analysis of occupant-protection systems

The following main tasks are carried out with the aid of computer simulation:
– Design/optimization of restraint systems with regard to front- and rear-end impacts by means of crash-test sled simulations in the cases in which the interaction between structure and dummy is negligible. The tool for this purpose is a multibody system (e.g. Madymo 3D) in conjunction with an FE

program system (e.g. LS-DYNA-3D).
– Design of protective components with regard to side impacts in integrated simulations, i.e. complete-vehicle simulations with dummy, seat and moldings. Calculation with FE program system (LS-DYNA-3D).
– Design and optimization of cushioning measures (in accordance with FMVSS 201) with regard to satisfying protective criteria. Calculation with FE program system (LS-DYNA-3D).

Recycling, environmental protection
The automobile manufacturers are making progress in their endeavors to maintain clean water and air, prevent noise pollution and recycle raw materials:
– The recycling quota for metallic materials is 95%.
– The recycling quota for plastics is approximately 14%. In cooperation with the chemical industry and the suppliers of plastic components, intensive efforts are being made to further improve this figure.
– Exhaust-gas purification and recovery of high-value catalyst materials.
– Recycling of battery materials.
– Chlorofluorocarbons (CFCs) are no longer used as refrigerants or as expanding agents in the manufacture of plastics.
– Solvents for body degreasing are almost entirely free of chlorinated hydrocarbons; water-based paints are used in dip-priming.
– Water-based paints for top coating are in use.
– Reprocessing of manufacturing agents, e.g. oil, coolant, antifreeze.
– Recycling of some 60% of residual materials (e.g. scrap metal, waste paper, leather, textile and wood waste).

Vehicle bodies, commercial vehicles

Commercial vehicles

Commercial vehicles are used for the safe and efficient transportation of persons and goods. In this respect, the degree of economic efficiency is determined by the ratio of usable space to overall vehicle volume, and of useful load to laden vehicle weight. Dimensions and weights are limited by legal regulations.

From the design-concept viewpoint, a distinction must be made between cab-over-engine (COE) and cab-behind-engine (CBE) vehicles.

A wide variety of vehicle types meet the demands of local and long-distance transportation, as well as the demands encountered on building sites and in special applications.

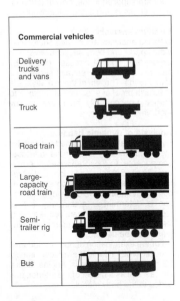

Commercial vehicles

Delivery trucks and vans	
Truck	
Road train	
Large-capacity road train	
Semi-trailer rig	
Bus	

Delivery trucks and vans

These are light-duty trucks (2...7 t) used in the transportation of persons and in local goods distribution. In fulfilling this function stringent demands are made on the vehicle in terms of mobility, maneuverability, performance, operating comfort and safety. The design concepts are based on front-mounted engine, front or rear-wheel drive, independent suspension or rigid axle and, from 3.5 t laden weight, twin tires on the rear axle.

The product range includes enclosed-body multi-purpose vehicles and vans, as well as low-bed and high-bed platform-body vehicles with special superstructures and double cabs.

In small delivery trucks and vans, the bodies form an integral load-bearing unit together with the chassis.

The body and chassis frameworks consist of sheet-metal pressed elements and flanged profiles. Platform-body vehicles have a ladder-type frame with open or closed side members and cross members as the primary load-bearing structure.

Delivery-truck load-bearing unit

Large delivery trucks and vans mostly have their own framework and a separate body.

Medium- and heavy-duty trucks and tractor vehicles

The vehicles in this sector have either a load-bearing chassis or partially load-bearing body. In most cases the engine is at the front. It is seldom fitted as an underfloor engine between the axles. The vehicle is driven via the twin-tire axle(s). In individual cases, the rear axle is fitted with single tires. For building-site (off-road) use with high traction requirements, all-wheel drive with longitudinal and cross-lock technology is applied.

Type of truck undercarriage (see Figure below):
N x Z/L
N = Number of wheels
Z = Number of driven wheels
L = Number of steered wheels

(twin wheels count as <u>one</u> wheel)

Normal chassis have leaf- or pneumatically-sprung rigid front and rear axles. Pneumatic suspension facilitates the simple mounting and removal of interchangeable bodies and unhitching of semi-trailers. Three-axle vehicles (6x2) are fitted with either a leading or a trailing axle (in front of or behind the driven axle) to increase the useful load. High-traction 6x4 vehicles for use on building sites have a twin-axle configura-

Delivery trucks and vans	
Van	
Double-cab low-bed truck	
Platform-type high-bed truck	
Chassis	

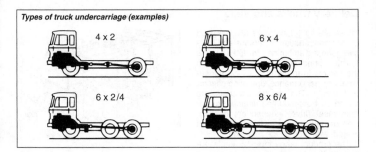

Types of truck undercarriage (examples)

4 x 2

6 x 4

6 x 2/4

8 x 6/4

tion with axle-load compensation and center bearing point or air-sprung single axles.

Chassis frames

The chassis frame is the commercial vehicle's actual load-bearing element. It is designed as a ladder-type frame, consisting of side and cross members. The choice of profiles decides the level of torsional stiffness. Torsionally flexible frames are preferred in medium- and heavy-duty trucks because they enable the suspension to comply better with uneven terrain. Torsionally stiff frames are more suitable for smaller delivery vehicles and vans.

Apart from the force introduction points, critical points in the chassis-frame design are the side-member and cross-member junctions. Special gusset plates or pressed cross-member sections form a broad connection basis. The junctions are riveted, bolted and welded. U- or L-shaped side-member inserts provide increased framework flexural strength and reinforcement at specific points.

Driver's cab

There are a variety of cab designs available depending on the vehicle concept. In delivery vehicles and vans, low, convenient entrances are an advantage, whereas in long-distance transport space and comfort are more important. Modular design concepts allow for short, medium and long cab versions while retaining the same front, rear and doors.

In the case of cab-over-engine (COE) vehicles, the steering system is positioned right at the front of the vehicle. The engine is located under the cab or under

an engine tunnel between the driver and the co-driver. The entrance is positioned in front of or above the front axle. A mechanical (pretensioned torsion bar) or hydraulic cab-tipping mechanism ensures good access to the engine.

In cab-behind-engine (CBE) vehicles, the engine/transmission assembly is mounted ahead of the cab firewall beneath a steel or plastic hood (which is usually tiltable for reasons of accessibility). The driver enters the cab behind the front axle.

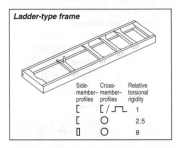

Ladder-type frame

Side-member-profiles	Cross-member-profiles	Relative torsional rigidity
[	[/ ⊓	1
[	O	2.5
⊓	O	8

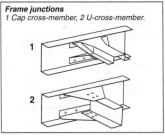

Frame junctions
1 Cap cross-member, 2 U-cross-member.

1

2

Bodies

Specific body structures such as flatbeds, standard vans, box vans, dump-truck deep-beds, tankers, concrete mixers etc. permit the economical and efficient transportation of a wide variety of goods and materials. Connection between body and load-bearing chassis frame is effected in part by means of auxiliary frames with non-positive or positive attachments.

Road trains and semitrailer rigs are used in long-distance transport. As the size of the transportation unit increases, the costs relative to the freight volume decrease.

Load volume is increased by reducing the empty spaces between cab, cargo area and trailer (high-capacity road train). Advantages of semitrailer rigs lie in the greater uninterrupted loading length of the cargo area and the shorter inoperative times of the tractor units. Measures to improve aerodynamics, such as front and side trim on the vehicle and specially adapted air deflectors from the cab to the body, are applied to minimize fuel consumption.

Buses

The bus market offers a specific vehicle for practically every application. This has resulted in a wide range of bus types, which differ in their overall dimensions (length, height, width) and appointments (depending on the application).

Microbuses

Microbuses carry up to approx. 19 passengers. These vehicles have been developed from delivery trucks or vans weighing up to approx. 4.5 t.

Minibuses

Minibuses carry up to approx. 25 passengers. These vehicles have been developed from delivery trucks or vans weighing up to approx. 7.5 t. They are occasionally built on the ladder-type chassis of light-duty trucks. A modified suspension design and special measures carried out on the body result in optimum ride comfort and noise levels.

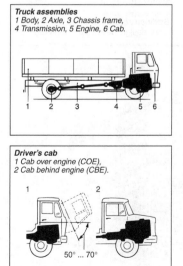

Truck assemblies
1 Body, 2 Axle, 3 Chassis frame,
4 Transmission, 5 Engine, 6 Cab.

1 2 3 4 5 6

Driver's cab
1 Cab over engine (COE),
2 Cab behind engine (CBE).

1   2

50° ... 70°

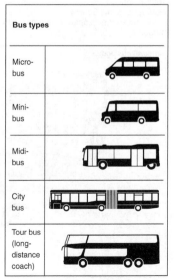

Bus types

Micro-bus	
Mini-bus	
Midi-bus	
City bus	
Tour bus (long-distance coach)	

Midibuses

Depending on the application, midibuses can carry up to approx. 35 passengers (in tour buses) and up to approx. 65 passengers (in city buses). These vehicles weigh up to approx. 12.5 t and are predominantly built on the ladder-type chassis of light-duty trucks. There are also integral-framework designs in operation. A modified suspension design and special measures carried out on the body result in optimum ride comfort and noise levels.

City buses

City buses are equipped with seating and standing room for scheduled routes. The short intervals between stops in suburban passenger transportation operations necessitate a rapid passenger turnover. This is achieved by wide doors that open and close swiftly, low boarding heights (approx. 320 mm) and low floor heights (approx. 370 mm).

Main specifications for a 12 m standard public-service bus:
Vehicle length approx. 12 m,
Total weight 18.0 t,
Number of seats 32...44,
Total passenger capacity approx. 105 persons.

The use of double-decker buses (length 12 m carrying up to approx. 130 passengers), three-axle rigid buses (length up to 15 m carrying up to approx. 135 passengers) and articulated buses (approx. 160 passengers) provides increased transport capacity.

Intercity buses or touring coaches

Depending on the application (standing passengers are not permitted at $v >$ 60 km/h), either low-floor designs featuring the low boarding and floor heights of public-service buses are used, or buses are employed which, with their higher floors and small luggage compartments, are already very much like tour buses. Overland buses come in lengths of 11...15 m as rigid vehicles or in lengths of 18 m as articulated vehicles.

Tour buses (long-distance coaches)

Tour buses are designed to provide comfortable travel over medium and long distances. They range from the low, two-axle standard bus through to the double-decker luxury bus and come in lengths of approx. 10...15 m.

Body structure

Light design based on an integral body.

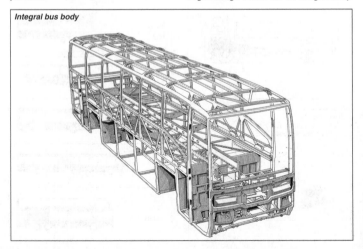

Integral bus body

The body and base frames, which are firmly welded together, consist of pressed grid-type support elements and rectangular tubes.

Undercarriage

The horizontally or vertically mounted engine drives the rear axle. Pneumatic suspension at all axles permits ride-level stabilization and a high degree of ride comfort. Intercity buses and touring coaches are mainly equipped with independent wheel suspension on their front axles. Disk brakes, frequently supported by retarders, are used on all the axles.

Passive safety in commercial vehicles

Passive safety is intended to limit the consequences of accidents and to protect other road users. Systematic recording of accidents, accident tests with complete commercial vehicles and intensive computer optimization help to devise safety measures.

In the event of a collision, the driver's cab and the passenger compartment must maintain the amount of room necessary for occupant survival, while at the same time deceleration must not be excessive. Depending upon vehicle design, there are a variety of solutions to this problem.

In delivery trucks and vans, front-section design is energy-absorbing as in passenger cars. In spite of shorter deformation routes and higher levels of released energy, the physiologically permissible limits are not exceeded in the case of virtually all passenger-car crash-test standards (legal requirements and rating tests).

In the case of trucks, the side members extend up to the front bumper and can absorb high longitudinal forces. Such passive-safety measures are based on accident analyses and are intended to improve the structural design of the cab. Static and dynamic stress and impact tests at the front and rear of the cab, as well as on its roof, simulate the stresses involved in a frontal impact and in accidents in which the vehicle overturns or rolls over, as well as in which the load shifts.

Statistical analyses have proved that the bus is one of the safest means of passenger transportation. Static roof-load tests and dynamic overturning tests provide evidence of body strength. The use of flame-retardant and self-extinguishing materials for the interior of the vehicle minimizes the risk of fire.

Because road traffic involves many different kinds of vehicles, collisions between light and heavy vehicles are unavoidable. As a result of the differences in vehicle weight, and incompatibility in terms of vehicle geometry and structural stiffness, the risk of injury in the lighter vehicle is greater. The formulas below define the change in speed during a normal (non-oblique) plastic impact for frontal or rear collisions between two vehicles:

Vehicle 1 $\Delta c_1 = \dfrac{\mu \cdot \Delta v}{1 + \mu}$

Vehicle 2 $\Delta c_2 = \dfrac{\Delta v}{1 + \mu}$

where $\mu = m_2/m_1$

m_1, m_2 = masses of the vehicles involved, v relative speed prior to impact.

Side, front and rear underride guards help to reduce the danger of the lighter vehicle driving under the heavier vehicle in the event of a collision. In other words, they serve to protect other road users.

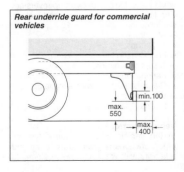

Rear underride guard for commercial vehicles

min.100

max. 550

max. 400

Lighting

Functions

Vehicle front end

The primary function of the headlamps at the vehicle front end is to illuminate the roadway so that the driver can register the traffic conditions and recognize any obstacles and hazards in good time. They also serve to identify and mark out the vehicle to oncoming traffic. The turn-signal lamps serve to show the driver's intention to change direction or to indicate a hazardous situation. The headlamps and lights at the front end include the following:

– Low-/high-beam headlamps,
– Fog lamps,
– Auxiliary driving lamps,
– Turn-signal lamps,
– Parking lamps,
– Side-marker/clearance lamps (wide vehicles) and
– Daytime running lamps (if required by law in individual countries).

Vehicle rear end

Lights are turned on at the vehicle's rear end in accordance with the weather conditions and indicate the vehicle's position. They also indicate how the vehicle is moving and in which direction, e.g. whether it is traveling unbraked straight ahead, or whether the brakes are applied or the driver is intending to change direction, or whether a hazardous situation exists. The backup lamps illuminate the roadway while the vehicle is backing up/reversing. The lamps/lights at the rear end include the following:

– Stop lamps,
– Tail lamps,
– Fog warning lamps,
– Turn-signal lamps,
– Parking lamps,
– Clearance lamps (wide vehicles),
– Backup lamps and
– License-plate lamps.

Vehicle interior

In the vehicle interior, priority over all other functions is given to the ease and reliability with which the switch elements can be reached and operated, and to provide the driver with sufficient information on the vehicle's operating states (while distracting him/her from driving as little as possible). A well-lit instrument panel (P. 783) and discreet lighting of the various functional groups, such as the radio or navigation system, are absolutely essential to ensure relaxed and safe driving. Optical and acoustic signals must be prioritized according to their urgency and then relayed to the driver.

Regulations

Approval codes and symbols

Automotive lighting equipment is governed by national and international design and operating regulations according to which the equipment in question must be manufactured and tested. Each class of illumination device is assigned a specific approval code. The symbol for this code must be legible e.g. on all lenses for headlights and other vehicle lamps. This also applies to approved replacement headlamps and lights.

If a device has one of these approval symbols, this indicates that it has been tested by a technical service body and approved by an official approval authority (in Germany: Federal Motor-Vehicle Agency). All units which are series-produced and assigned an approval symbol must conform in all respects to the approved unit. Examples of approval symbols:

⌒ K   National test symbol D,

ⓔ1   ECE test symbol,

e 1   EU test symbol.

The number 1 following each letter for example indicates that approval has been granted in Germany.

In Europe, installation of all automotive lighting and visual signaling equipment is governed not only by national guidelines but also by the higher European directives (ECE: whole of Europe, EU and Japan). In the course of the ongoing union of Europe, the implementation regulations are being increasingly simplified by the harmonization of directives and legislation.

Bosch headlamps conform to the applicable ECE and EU directives and can therefore be used in all ECE and EU countries regardless of the country in which they were acquired.

In the USA, lighting equipment is governed by regulations that are very different from those in Europe. The principle of self-certification compels each manufacturer as an importer of lighting equipment to ensure and in an emergency to furnish proof that his products conform 100% to the regulations of FMVSS 108 laid down in the Federal Register. There is therefore no type approval in the USA. The regulations of FMVSS 108 are partly based on the SAE industry standard.

Motor vehicles which for instance are reimported into Europe must be refitted to comply with the European directives.

Photometric terms and definitions

Headlamp range
The distance at which the headlamp beam continues to supply a specified luminous intensity: mostly the 1 lux line at the right side of the road (RH traffic).

Headlamp geometrical range
This is the distance to the horizontal portion of the light/dark cutoff line on the road surface. A low-beam inclination of 1% or 10 cm per 10 meters results in a geometric range equal to 100 times the headlamp's installation height (as measured between the center of the reflector and the road surface).

Visual range
Distance at which an object (vehicle, object etc.) within the luminous distribution field is still visible.

The visual range is influenced by the shape, size and reflectance of the objects, road-surface type, headlamp design and cleanliness, and the physiological condition of the driver's eyes. Because of this large number of influencing factors, it is not possible to quantify this range using precise numerical definitions. Under extremely unfavorable conditions (with RH traffic, on the left side of a wet road surface) the visual range can fall to below 20 m. Under optimal conditions it can ex-

tend outward to more than 100 m (with RH traffic, on the right side of the road).

Signal identification distance
Maximum distance at which a visual signal (e.g. fog warning lamp) remains just visible in fog or other inclement weather conditions.

Glare, physiological
This is the quantifiable reduction in visual performance that occurs in response to light sources emitting glare. An example would be the reduction in visual range that occurs as two vehicles approach one another.

Glare, psychological
(discomfort glare)
This condition occurs when a glare source induces discomfort without, however, causing an actual reduction in visual performance. Psychological glare is assessed according to a scale defining different levels of comfort/discomfort.

Reflector focal length
Conventional reflectors for headlamps and other automotive lamps are usually parabolic in shape. The focal length f (distance between the vertex of the parabola and the focal point) is between 15 and 40 mm.

Free-form reflectors
The geometrical configurations of modern reflectors are generated using complex mathematical calculations (HNS, <u>H</u>omo-geneous <u>N</u>umerically Calculated <u>S</u>ur-face). Here, the low mean focal length $\bar{f}$ is defined relative to the distance between

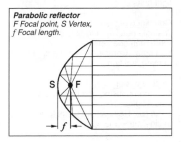

Parabolic reflector
F Focal point, S Vertex,
f Focal length.

the reflector's vertex and the center of the filament. Typical values are between 15 and 25 mm.

In the case of reflectors partitioned with steps or facets (PD2 Partition Design 2), each partition can be created with its own mean focal length f.

<u>Reflector illuminated area</u>
Parallel projection of the entire reflector opening onto a transverse plane. The standard reference plane is vertically perpendicular to the vehicle's direction of travel.

<u>Effective luminous flux, headlamp efficiency ratings</u>
The first of the above is that portion of the light source's luminous flux able to supply effective illumination via its reflective or refractive components (for instance, as projected onto the road surface via the headlamp reflector). A reflector with a short (or limited mean) focal length makes efficient use of the incandescent filament because such a reflector extends outward to encompass the bulb, allowing it to convert a large proportion of the luminous flux into a useful beam of light.

<u>Angles of geometric visibility</u>
Those angles, defined relative to the axis of the lighting device, at which the illuminated surface must be visible.

Definitions of device design

<u>Grouped design</u>
A single housing, but with different lenses and bulbs.
Example: Multichamber rear-lamp assemblies containing different individual light units.

<u>Combined design</u>
A single housing and bulb assembly with more than one lens.
Example: Combined rear lamp and license-plate lamp.

<u>Nested design</u>
Common housing and lens, but with individual bulbs.
Example: Headlamp assembly with built-in side-marker lamp.

Main headlamps, European system

Low beam (dipped beam)
The high traffic density on modern roads severely restricts the use of high-beam headlamps. Under most standard conditions, the low beams are the actual driving lamps. Basic design modifications have allowed substantial improvements in low-beam performance. These include:
– Introduction of the asymmetrical low-beam pattern, characterized (RH traffic) by an extended visual range along the right side of the road,
– Official approval for various types of halogen lamps, making it possible to enhance the luminous intensity at the road surface by 50...80%.
– Introduction of innovative headlamp systems featuring complex geometrical configurations (PES, HNS, PD2) designed to improve efficiency levels by up to 50%.
– The "Litronic" gaseous-discharge headlamp (with luminous arc) supplies more than twice the light generated by comparable halogen units.

Low-beam headlamps require a light/dark cutoff line in the light distribution. This is generated in halogen headlamps with H4 bulbs and in Litronic headlamps with a D2R bulb by reflecting the cap (H4) or the light shield (D2R). In headlamps with all-round use (H1, H7, HB4 bulbs), the light/dark cutoff line is created by

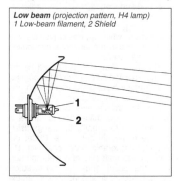

Low beam (projection pattern, H4 lamp)
1 Low-beam filament, 2 Shield

specifically reflecting the filaments.

The "dark above/bright below" distribution pattern resulting from the light/dark cutoff line furnishes acceptable visual ranges under all driving conditions. This configuration holds the glare to which approaching traffic is exposed within reasonable limits while at the same time supplying relatively high levels of illumination in the area below the light/dark cutoff line.

The light distribution pattern must combine maximum visual ranges with minimum glare. These demands are supplemented by other requirements affecting the area directly forward of the vehicle. For instance, the headlamps must provide assistance when cornering, i.e., the light distribution pattern must extend beyond the left and right-side extremities of the road surface.

Automotive headlamp performance is subject to technical assessment and verification. Among the requirements are minimum illuminance levels, to ensure adequate road-surface visibility, and maximum intensity levels, to prevent glare (points for measuring illuminance, P. 742).

Headlamp versions

Conventional headlamps

With conventional headlamp systems, the quality of the low beam increases directly in proportion to the size of the reflector. At the same time, the geometrical range increases as a function of installation height. These factors must be balanced against the aerodynamic dictates according to which the vehicle's front-end profile must be kept as low as possible.

These mutually antagonistic requirements are reconciled by using wider headlamps to accommodate larger reflectors.

Reflectors of a given size, but with different focal lengths, also perform differently. Shorter focal lengths produce wider light beams with better close-range and side illumination. This is of particular advantage during cornering.

Stepped reflectors

Stepped, or graduated reflectors are segmented reflectors consisting of paraboloid and/or parelliptical (combined parabola and ellipse) sections designed to provide various focal lengths. These units retain the advantages of a deep reflector in a shallow unit suitable for compact installation.

Homofocal reflector

The homofocal reflector's supplemental sectors share a single focal point to achieve a shorter focal length than is provided by a basic reflector, thus making a particularly useful contribution to the effective luminous flux. While the light from the supplemental reflectors improves close-range and side illumination, there is no improvement in range.

Multifocal reflector

The principle behind the multifocal reflector is similar to that of its homofocal counterpart. Based on mathematical definitions, the introduction of parelliptical reflector sections, which disperse the light horizontally, produces a large number of focal points.

Variable-focus (stepless) reflectors

Specially designed programs (CAL, Computer Aided Lighting) assist in designing the transitionless VF (Variable Focus Reflector) with its non-parabolic sectors. The focal points of the various reflector zones can change position relative to the light source. This principle can be applied to exploit the entire reflector surface.

Headlamps with clear lenses

Developments in the area of HNS reflector technology (Homogeneous Numerically Calculated Surface) have now made it possible for headlamps to operate at ef-

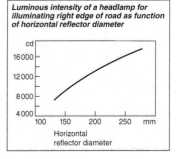

Luminous intensity of a headlamp for illuminating right edge of road as function of horizontal reflector diameter

Perspective illustration with points for measuring illuminance in accordance with ECE Directive 8 and/or 20
Specifications in lx for headlamp with halogen lamp at distance of 25 meters.

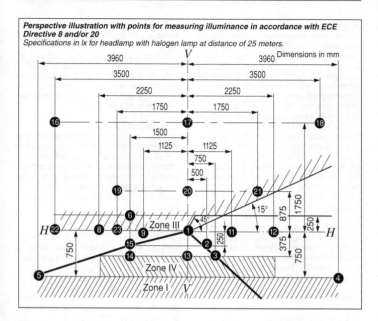

Table 1. Points for measuring low and high beams

Low beam					High beam	
Test points	Specifications in lx	Test points	Specifications in lx		Test points	Specifications in lx
1. E_{HV}	≤ 0.7	14. E_{50L}	≥ 2		7. E_{max}	> 48
2. E_{75R}	≥ 12	15. E_{75L}	≥ 12			< 16 · E_{75R}
3. E_{50R}	≥ 12	16. $E_{8L/4U}$	≥ 0.1; ≤ 0.7			(< 240)
4. E_{25R}	≥ 2	17. $E_{V/4U}$	≥ 0.1; ≤ 0.7		8. $E_{H - 5.15°}$	≥ 6
5. E_{25L}	≥ 2	18. $E_{8R/4U}$	≥ 0.1; ≤ 0.7		9. $E_{H - 2.55°}$	≥ 24
6. E_{B50L}	≤ 0.4	19. $E_{4L/2U}$	≥ 0.2; ≤ 0.7		10. E_{HV}	≥ 0.8 E_{max}
Max. value in Zone I	≤ E_{50R}	20. $E_{V/2U}$	≥ 0.2; ≤ 0.7		11. $E_{H + 2.55°}$	≥ 24
Max. value in Zone III	≤ 0.7	21. $E_{4R/2U}$	≥ 0.2; ≤ 0.7		12. $E_{H + 5.15°}$	≥ 6
Min. value in Zone IV	≥ 3	22. $E_{8L/H}$	≥ 0.1; ≤ 0.7			
13. E_{50V}	≥ 6	23. $E_{4L/H}$	≥ 0.2; ≤ 0.7			

Test figures for test lumens of relevant lamp at approx. 12 V.

ficiency levels of up to 50%. The entire light-distribution pattern is generated on the lens from the reflector surface alone, without additional optical elements. This permits a new, unconventional headlamp design.

<u>Headlamps with facet-type reflectors</u>
The reflector surface is partitioned with facets. The PD2 program provides the CAL and HNS modules for individual optimization of each individual segment. The important feature of surfaces developed with PD2 is that discontinuity and steps are permitted at all boundary surfaces of the partition. This results in freely shaped reflector surfaces with maximum homogeneity and side illumination.

PES headlamps
The PES headlamp system (<u>P</u>oly-<u>E</u>llipsoid-<u>S</u>ystem) employs imaging optics to improve on the technical performance provided by conventional headlamps, making it possible to obtain the light-distribution patterns associated with large-surface conventional lamps from effective projection surfaces as small as 28 cm². This result is obtained using an elliptical (CAL designed) reflector in combination with optical projection technology. A screen reflected with the objective projects precisely defined light/dark cutoffs. Depending upon specific individual requirements, these transitions can be defined as sudden or gradual intensity shifts, making it possible to obtain any desired geometry.

Together with conventional high beams, side-marker lamps and PES fog lamps, PES headlamps can be incorporated in

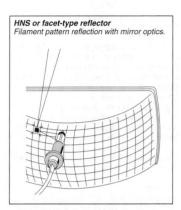
HNS or facet-type reflector
Filament pattern reflection with mirror optics.

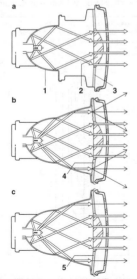
PES reflectors
(reflection and signal patterns)
a) PES, b) PES with ring parabola and lens,
c) PES with ring parabola and partially metallized tube body.
1 Reflector, 2 Objective, 3 Screen,
4 Profiled inner lens,
5 Partially metallized inner lens.

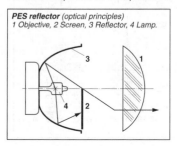
PES reflector (optical principles)
1 Objective, 2 Screen, 3 Reflector, 4 Lamp.

light-strip assemblies to obtain a unit no higher than approximately 80 mm from top to bottom.

In PES headlamps, the beam path can be configured in such a way that the surroundings of the objective are also used in the signal image. This enlargement of the signal image is used above all with small objective diameters to reduce the psychological glare for the oncoming traffic. The annular reflector uses that portion of the light which is not detected by the PES reflector and directs it forward past the objective. An inner screen, which prevents a direct view of the lamp, can be designed as a lens or a partially metallized screen.

Litronic

The Litronic (Light-Electronic) headlamp system with a xenon gaseous-discharge lamp as its central element generates high illumination-intensity levels with minimal front-end surface requirements. This makes it ideal for installation in vehicles with aerodynamic front-end styling exhibiting optimum c_w values.

The 35 W "D2S" bulb's arc generates a luminous flux twice as intense as that pro-duced by the H1 bulb. At 4200 K, the color temperature[1]) is higher, which means it contains − similar to sunlight − larger components of green and blue. Maximum illumination, corresponding to approx. 90 lm/W, is available as soon as the quartz element reaches its normal operating temperature of more than 900 °C. Brief high-power operation at currents of up to 2.6 A (continuous operation: approx. 0.4 A) can be used to obtain "immediate light". The life expectancy of 1500 hours corresponds to the operating time to be anticipated during the vehicle's service life. Failure is not sudden, as with filament bulbs. Instead, gradual dimming facilitates early diagnosis and replacement.

The second generation of these gaseous-discharge lamps for automotive applications features high-voltage-proof sockets and UV glass shielding elements:
– the D2S lamps for PES-design headlamps,

---

[1]) Temperature of the "black beam" which appears to have the same or a similar color when viewed by an observer.

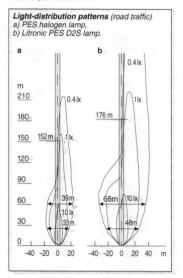

Gaseous-discharge lamp D2S
1 UV inert-gas bulb, 2 Lead-in insulator, 3 Discharge chamber, 4 Electrodes, 5 Lamp holder.

Light-distribution patterns (road traffic)
a) PES halogen lamp,
b) Litronic PES D2S lamp.

Electronic ballast unit (EVG) for 400 Hz alternating current and pulse ignition of the bulb
1 ECU (1a DC/DC converter, 1b Shunt, 1c DC/AC Converter, 1d Microprocessor),
2 Ignition unit, 3 Lamp socket, 4 D2S lamp, U_B Battery voltage.

System components for reflection-type headlamp with integrated dynamic headlight vertical-aim control
1 Lens with or without scatter optics,
2 Gaseous-discharge lamp,
3 Ignition unit,
4 ECU,
5 Stepping motor,
6 Axis sensor,
7 To vehicle electrical system.

System components for PES-design headlamps
1 Headlamp
* (1a Lens,*
* 1b D2S lamp,*
* 1c Screen,*
* 1d Reflector),*
2 Ignition unit,
3 ECU,
4 To vehicle electrical system.

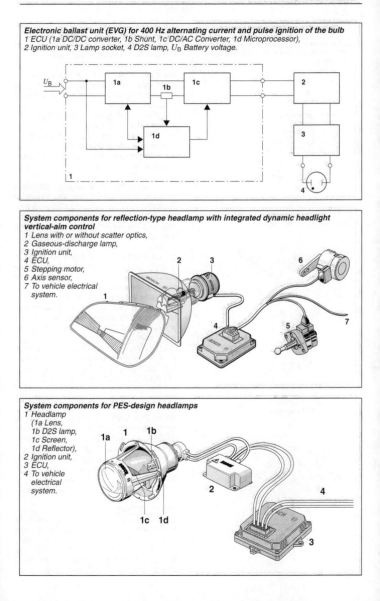

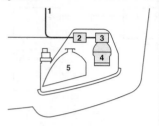

Quad-headlamp system with Litronic
1 Vehicle electrical system, 2 ECU, 3 Ignition unit with lamp connection, 4 Headlamp optics with gaseous-discharge lamp, 5 Halogen high beam.

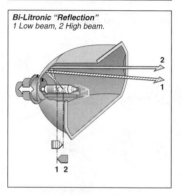

Bi-Litronic "Reflection"
1 Low beam, 2 High beam.

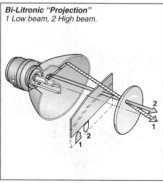

Bi-Litronic "Projection"
1 Low beam, 2 High beam.

– D2R lamps for reflection headlamps; an integral light shield, comparable to the bulb cover used for H4 low beams, generates the light/dark cutoff line.

An integral part of the headlamp is the electronic ballast unit (EVG) responsible for activating and monitoring the lamp. Its functions include:
– Ignition of the gaseous discharge (voltage 10...20 kV)
– Regulated power supply in the cold lamp's warm-up phase and
– Demand-oriented supply in continuous operation.

The system furnishes largely consistent levels of illumination by compensating for fluctuations in the vehicle's electrical system. Should the lamp go out (for instance, due to a momentary lapse in the voltage supply), reignition is spontaneous and automatic.

The electronic ballast unit responds to defects (such as a damaged lamp) by interrupting the power supply to help avoid injury in the event of contact.

Litronic's initial area of application has been as a high-performance low-beam unit in quad headlamp assemblies, where it is designed to operate simultaneously with specially designed halogen high-beam units. This has made it possible to achieve substantially wider road-illumination patterns for lighting the edges of curves and of wide roads as effectively as a halogen unit illuminates straight stretches of road. The driver enjoys substantial improvements in both visibility and orientation in difficult operating conditions and inclement weather. Compliance with ECE-R regulations is achieved by equipping Litronic headlamps with vertical aim control and washer systems to consistently ensure optimal utilization of the extended range while at the same time maintaining excellent beam projection.

Bi-Litronic "Reflection"
Bi-Litronic is a special system. It permits both the low and high beams to be generated by a dual-headlamp system using only one gaseous-discharge lamp. For this purpose, when the high-/low-beam switch is operated, an electromechanical

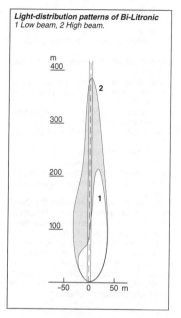

Light-distribution patterns of Bi-Litronic
1 Low beam, 2 High beam.

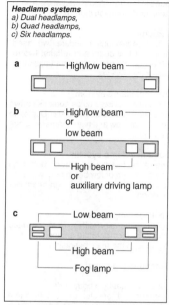

Headlamp systems
a) Dual headlamps,
b) Quad headlamps,
c) Six headlamps.

a High/low beam

b High/low beam
or
low beam

High beam
or
auxiliary driving lamp

c Low beam

High beam

Fog lamp

actuator moves the gaseous-discharge lamp in the reflector into the appropriate position for defining the escape of the light cone for the main and low beams. The essential advantages of Bi-Litronic "Reflection" are:
– Xenon light for high-beam operation,
– Visual guidance through continuous shifting of light distribution from close to long range,
– Clear reduction of required space compared with four-compartment systems,
– Lower cost through use of only one lamp and a ballast unit.

Bi-Litronic "Projection"
Bi-Litronic "Projection" system is based on a PES Litronic headlamp. Xenon light is made available for high-beam operation by shifting a light shield for the light/dark cutoff. With lens diameters of 60 and 70 mm, Bi-Litronic "Projection" enables the presently most compact headlamp design with combined high/low beam and

at the same time outstanding luminous efficiency.

High beam
The high beam is usually generated by a light source located at the focal point of the reflector (see Fig. on P. 739). This causes the light to be reflected outward in the direction of the reflector's axis. The intensity of the high beam projected along the axial plane is largely a function of the reflector's luminous surface area. In four and six-headlamp systems, in particular, purely paraboloid high-beam reflectors can be replaced by units with complex geometrical configurations designed to supply a "superimposed" high-beam pattern.

The calculations employed to design these units seek to achieve a high-beam distribution that harmonizes with the low-beam pattern (simultaneous activation). The pure high beam is virtually "superimposed" on the low-beam projection to do away with the annoying overlap normally found in the transitional area at the front of the light-distribution pattern.

Designs
Global regulations mandate two headlamps for low beam and at least two (or the option of four) high-beam units for all dual-track vehicles.

Dual headlamp system
This design utilizes bulbs comprising two separate light sources (Bilux, Duplo) to project both low and high beams via a single reflector.

Quad headlamp system
Two of the headlamps provide both high and low beam or low beam only, while the second pair only provides high-beam illumination.

Six-headlamp system
This configuration differs from the quad design by incorporating a supplementary fog lamp in the main headlamp.

Component groups:

Lens (adjustable in bodywork)
The lens and reflector are combined in a single headlamp unit. The beam is adjusted by pivoting the complete assembly. Under unfavorable circumstances, this can lead to the lens being at a slight angle relative to the car's bodywork. The headlamp assemblies are generally equipped with seals in the area adjacent to the bulb, and also feature special ventilation systems.

Lens (fixed to the bodywork)
There is no connection between the lens and the reflector which is mounted in a housing designed to move relative to the lens for adjustment (housing type). Because the reflector has no connection to the lens it remains stationary and can be fully integrated into the vehicle's bodywork. The complete headlamp is sealed or provided with ventilation elements.

Components

Reflector
Reflectors are made of sheet metal or plastic.
Sheet-metal reflectors are manufactured as follows:
– Deep-draw processing to obtain a paraboloid or more complex geometrical configuration,
– Galvanization or powder-coating to protect against corrosion,
– Paint application to obtain a smooth surface,
– Evaporative application of aluminum to form the reflective layer, and
– Evaporative application of a special protective layer onto the aluminum substrate.
This process hermetically seals the sheet metal while providing an extremely smooth reflective surface featuring a maximum residual ripple of 1/10,000 mm.

Plastic reflectors are produced by injection molding (duroplastic, thermoplastic); no special anti-corrosion treatment is required. Plastic can be shaped with much greater precision and can also be used to manufacture stepped reflectors.

Lens
A large proportion of lenses is manufactured using high-purity glass (free of bubbles and streaks). During the lens molding process high priority is assigned to surface quality in order to prevent undesirable upward light refraction in the final product – this would tend to blind oncoming traffic. The type and configuration of the lens prisms depend upon reflector size and focal depth as well as the desired light-distribution pattern. With the improvement in calculation methods, it is also possible to develop headlamps where complete light distribution is determined by the reflector. This eliminates all the diffuser elements on the lens, thus producing a "clear lens". The first plastic lens entered series production in 1992. Aside from reduced weight, plastic lenses provide other advantages for automotive applications including greater latitude in headlamp and vehicle design.

Main headlamps, American system

Low beam
The demands placed on light distribution in American motoring differ from those in Europe. Since 1. 5. 1997, however, headlamps with light/dark cutoffs have also been authorized in the USA. These though must be visually adjusted. It is thus now possible to develop headlamps which conform to both legal requirements.

High beam
As with the European system, the light source is usually located at the focal point of the parabolic reflector. Dual, quad and six-headlamp configurations are employed.

Designs

Sealed beam
In this design which is no longer used, the aluminized glass reflector must be sealed gas-tight with the lens on account of the unencapsulated light sources. The whole unit is sealed and filled with an inert gas. Should a filament burn through, the entire unit must be replaced. Units with halogen light sources are also available. The limited range of available sealed-beam headlamps on the market severely restricted the designers' latitude for front-end styling variations.

American sealed-beam headlamps
a) Low beam, b) High beam.
1 Low-beam filament, 2 Focal point,
3 High-beam filament (at focal point).

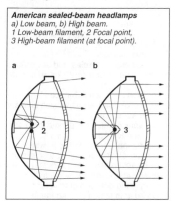

Replaceable Bulb Headlamp (RBH)
European developments based on replaceable bulb technology also had an effect on the American system from 1983 onwards. The headlamps' size and shape can be adapted for improved vehicle design (styling considerations). The RBH design usually features plastic reflectors and lenses.

Vehicle Headlamp Aiming Device (VHAD)
This design involves RBH headlamps which are mechanically adjusted vertically with the aid of a level gauge integrated in each headlamp and horizontally by means of a system comprising needle and dial: This is in fact "on-board aiming".

Headlamp systems
As in Europe, dual-, quad- and six-headlamp configurations are used in North America.

Main headlamps, European regulations

Regulations and directives for main headlamps
<u>76/761/EEC and ECE-R1 and R2</u>:
Headlamps for high and low beam including their bulbs.
<u>ECE-R8</u>: Headlamps with H1, H2, H3, H7, H8, H9, H11, HIR1, HIR2, HB3 and HB4 bulbs.
<u>ECE-R20</u>: Headlamps with H4 bulbs.
StVZO §50: Headlamps for high and low beam.
<u>76/756/EEC and ECE-R48</u>: for installation and application.
<u>ECE-R 98/99</u>: Headlamps with gaseous-discharge lamps.

Low beam, installation
Regulations prescribe 2 white-light low-beam headlamps for multiple-track vehicles.

Low beam, illumination technology
The relevant ordinances governing symmetrical low-beam illumination in Germany are contained in the Technical Requirements (TA) of the StVZO (FMVSS/

CUR; Vehicle Homologation and Licensing Regulations). The only applicable regulations for asymmetrical low beams are international regulations and guidelines containing precise stipulations governing photometric testing of the different low-beam units (with standard or halogen bulb).

Homologation testing is carried out using test lamps manufactured to more precise tolerances than those installed in production vehicles.

Headlamp glare is evaluated based on StVZO §50 (6). Glare is considered to be eliminated when the illuminance at a height equal to that of the center of the headlamp does not exceed 1 lx at a distance of 25 m. This test is carried out with the engine running at moderate speed.

Low beam, switching

All high-beam lamps must extinguish simultaneously when the low beams are switched on. Dimming (gradual deactivation) is permitted, with a maximum dimming period of 5 seconds. A 2-second response delay is required to prevent the dimming feature from activating when the high-beam flashers are used. When the high beams are switched on, the low-beam units may continue to operate (simultaneous operation). H4 bulbs are generally designed for limited use with both filaments in operation.

High beams, installation

A minimum of two and a maximum of four headlamps are prescribed for the high-beam mode.

Prescribed instrument-cluster high-beam indicator lamp: blue or yellow.

High beams, illumination technology

High-beam light distribution is defined in the regulations and guidelines together with the stipulations governing the low beams.

The most important specifications are: symmetrical distribution relative to the central vertical plane, maximum light along the headlamp's center axis.

The maximum approved luminous intensity, a composite of the intensity ratings for all high-beam headlamps installed on the vehicle, is 225,000 cd. The respective ratings are indicated by reference codes located adjacent to the homologation code on each headlamp. 225,000 cd corresponds to the number 75. The luminous intensity of the high beam could be indicated, e.g., by the number 20 stamped next to the round ECE test symbol.

If these are the only headlamps on the vehicle (no auxiliary driving lamps) then the composite luminous intensity is to be in the range of 40/75 of 225,000 cd, viz., 120,000 cd.

High- and low-beam adjustments

Conditions for aiming
– Tire pressures must conform to specifications.
– Vehicle loaded, in accordance with model type:
For passenger cars: one person or 75 kg on the driver's seat.
For trucks: unladen;
For single-track vehicles and single-axle tractors: one person or 75 kg on the driver's seat.
– The vehicle should be rolled several meters to allow the suspension to adapt to the added load.
– The vehicle must be parked on a flat, level surface.
If adjustment is carried out without a headlamp aiming device, a test surface must be set up at a distance of 10 meters from the vehicle so that the center mark is located in the direction of travel in front of the headlamp to be adjusted (see Figs.).

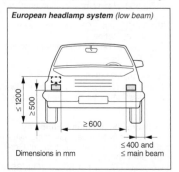

European headlamp system (low beam)

≤ 1200
≥ 500
≥ 600
≤ 400 and
≤ main beam

Dimensions in mm

– The headlamps must be adjusted individually, with all other headlamps covered.
– If the vehicle is equipped with a manual headlamp range adjuster, the switch should be set to the position prescribed by the manufacturer.

Adjustment information:

The adjustment marks and lines are arranged to accommodate main headlamps at a normal installation height, with the center mark set to height H, corresponding to the middle of the headlamp. The adjustment dimension $e = 10$ cm represents the vertical distance between the center mark and the boundary line.

On headlamps with $e > 10$ cm the boundary line is lowered to the required level. Obviously, the center mark will then no longer be level with the center of the headlamp. It can, however, be used to check the position of the high beam (where present).

Table 2. Setting dimension "e" for headlamp adjustment, Europe[1])

Vehicle type	Head-lamp cm	Fog lamp cm
1 Motor vehicles on which the upper edge of the reflector surface is not more than 140 cm above the standing surface.		
1a Pass. cars (also station wagons/estates)	12	20
1b Vehicles with self-leveling suspension or automatic beam adjusters.[2])	10	20
1c Multi-axle tractors and special-purpose machinery.		
1d Single-track vehicles.		
1e Trucks with forward loading area.		
1f Trucks with rear loading area.[3])	30	40
1g Semitrailer tractors.[3])		
1h Buses.[3])		
2 Motor vehicles on which the upper edge of the reflector surface is not more than 140 cm above the standing surface.[4])	$H/3$	$H/3)+7$
3 Single-axle tractors or special-purpose machinery with permanently dimmed headlamps on which the required light beam center inclination is indicated.[5])	$2N$	20
4 Vehicle with homologation in acc. with Directive 76/756/EEC or ECE R48	Reference dimension on vehicle	see above

[1]) The results obtained with the aid of headlamp aiming equipment must correspond to the figures in the table.
[2]) Special attention must be paid to compliance with the manufacturer's instructions.
[3]) Except motor vehicles as defined in 1b.
[4]) H Height of center of headlamp above support surface in cm.
[5]) N Specified figure for inclination of beam center at distance of 5 m.

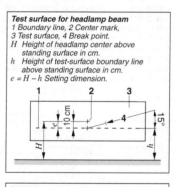

Test surface for headlamp beam
1 Boundary line, 2 Center mark,
3 Test surface, 4 Break point.
H Height of headlamp center above standing surface in cm.
h Height of test-surface boundary line above standing surface in cm.
$e = H - h$ Setting dimension.

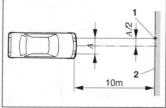

Relative positions of test surface and vehicle's longitudinal axis
1 Center mark
2 Test surface
A Distance between headlamp centers.

Table 3. Geometric range of the horizontal component of the low beam's light/dark cutoff line. Headlamp installed at height of 65 cm

Inclination of light/dark cutoff line in % (1 % = 10 cm/10 m)	1 %	1.5 %	2 %	2.5 %	3 %
Reference dimension e	10 cm	15 cm	20 cm	25 cm	30 cm
Geometric range in m for the horizontal component of the light/dark cutoff line	65 m	43.3 m	32.5 m	26 m	21.7 m

The left-side (horizontal) section of the light/dark cutoff line must be adjusted to the limit line.

Refer to Table 2 for dimension e.

The headlamps must be readjusted following any operations that could affect their height (suspension work, etc.). The procedure is also recommended after bulb replacement.

If the high beam is incorporated in a single unit along with the asymmetrical low beam (Bilux and Duplo bulbs) then it will be aimed automatically when the low beam is adjusted.

Separate individual high-beam units are aimed horizontally and symmetrically using the center of the headlamp and the center mark as references.

Headlamp aiming devices

Function

Correct adjustment of motor-vehicle headlamps should ensure the best possible illumination of the roadway by the low beam while at the same time minimizing dazzle for oncoming traffic. For this purpose, the inclination of the headlamp beams with respect to a level base surface, and their direction to the vertical longitudinal center plane of the vehicle, must satisfy the official requirements.

Equipment design

Headlamp aiming devices are portable imaging chambers which comprise a single lens and a collector screen located in the focal plane of the lens and rigidly connected to it. The collector screen has

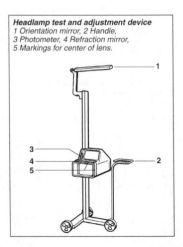

Headlamp test and adjustment device
1 Orientation mirror, 2 Handle,
3 Photometer, 4 Refraction mirror,
5 Markings for center of lens.

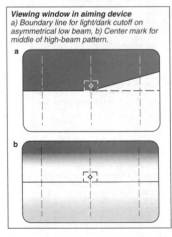

Viewing window in aiming device
a) Boundary line for light/dark cutoff on asymmetrical low beam, b) Center mark for middle of high-beam pattern.

markings to facilitate correct headlamp adjustment, and can be viewed by the equipment operator using suitable appendages such as windows and adjustable refraction mirrors.

The prescribed headlamp adjustment, i.e. the inclination relative to the center line of the headlamp in cm at a fixed distance of 10 m, is set by turning a knob to move the collector screen.

The aiming device is aligned with the vehicle axis using a sighting device such as a mirror with an orientation line. It is turned and aligned so that so that the orientation line uniformly touches two external vehicle-reference marks. The imaging chamber can be moved vertically and clamped at the level of the vehicle headlamp.

Headlamp testing

The headlamp can be tested once the equipment has been correctly positioned at the front of the lens. An image of the light distribution pattern as emitted by the headlamp appears on the collector screen. Some test devices are also equipped with photodiodes and a display to allow measurement of luminous intensity.

On headlamps with asymmetrical low-beam patterns the light/dark cutoff line should contact the marked limits; the point of intersection for the horizontal and vertical components must lie on the center mark of the vertical line. Following adjustment of the low beam's light/dark cutoff line in accordance with the regulations, the center of the high beam (assuming that high and low beam are adjusted together) should be within the corner limits indicated around the center mark.

Main headlamps, North American regulations

Regulations and guidelines

Federal Motor Vehicle Safety Standard (FMVSS) No. 108 and SAE Ground Vehicle Lighting Standards Manual (Standards and Recommended Practices).

The regulations governing installation and control circuits for headlamps are comparable to those in Europe. Since 1.5. 1997, headlamps with light/dark cutoffs have likewise been authorized in the USA.

The main differences were previously in the headlamp systems. Until 1983 the available sealed-beam types in the USA were restricted to the following dimensions:

Dual-headlamp systems:
– 178 mm diameter (round),
– 200 x 142 mm (rectangular).
Quad-headlamp systems:
– 146 mm diameter (round),
– 165 x 100 mm (rectangular).
Since 1983 a supplement to FMVSS 108, has made it possible to use RBH (Replaceable Bulb Headlamps) headlamp inserts of various shapes and sizes.

Headlamps conforming to ECE regulations or EEC directives are not approved for use on dual-track vehicles in the USA, even if they satisfy the American requirements relating to lighting and aimability (visual). They are however approved for use without restriction on motorcycles.

Conditions for aiming

In Europe, headlamps are always adjusted based on visual assessment of the light beam, but the use of mechanical aiming devices has become the most common method of aiming headlamps in the USA. The headlamp units are equipped with three pads on the lens – one for each of the three adjustment planes. A calibrating unit is placed against these pads. The calibration is carried out with spirit levels.

The VHAD (Vehicle Headlamp Aiming Device) method is employed to adjust the headlamps relative to a fixed reference axis defined by the vehicle. This procedure is carried out using a spirit level firmly attached to the headlamp. The three lens pads are no longer required.

Since mid-1997, however, visual (only vertical) aiming authorized as from 1. 5. 1997 has also gained increasing acceptance in the USA. There is no horizontal aiming here.

Headlight leveling control (vertical-aim control)

Table 3 indicates the geometrical ranges at various inclination angles for headlamps installed at a height of 65 cm. The inspection tolerance extends to include inclination angles of up to 2.5% (1.5% below standard setting). According to European Union regulations, the basic setting based on dimension e is (10...15 cm)/10 m with the weight of one person on the driver's seat. The specifications for this setting are provided by the vehicle manufacturer.

Since 1.1.1998, an automatic or manually-operated headlight leveling control (range adjustment) device has been mandatory in Germany for all vehicles registered for the first time, except in those cases where other equipment (e.g., hydraulic suspension control) ensures that the light beam's inclination will remain within the prescribed tolerances. Although this equipment is not mandatory in other countries, its use is permitted.

Automatic leveling
must be designed to compensate for load variations by lowering or raising the low beam's projection by between 5 cm/10 m (0.5%) and 25 cm/10 m (2.5%).

Manual leveling
This device is operated from the driver's seat and must incorporate a detent at the base setting; beam adjustment is also performed at this position. Units with infinitely variable and graduated control, must both feature visible markings in the vicinity of the hand switch which correspond to the vehicle load conditions necessitating vertical-aim adjustment. All design variations employ an adjustment mechanism to provide vertical adjustment of either the headlamp reflector (housing design) or the entire headlamp unit.

Manually operated units employ a switch at the driver's seat to control the setting, while automatic units rely on level sensors on the vehicle axles to monitor suspension compression and relay the corresponding signals to the adjustment actuators.

Hydromechanical systems
This type of system operates by transmitting a fluid through the connecting hoses between the manual switch (or level sensor) and the adjustment elements. The degree of adjustment corresponds to the quantity of pumped fluid.

Vacuum systems
The manual switch (or level sensor) in this type of system modulates vacuum from the intake manifold and transmits it to the adjustment actuators to achieve varying degrees of adjustment.

Electrical systems
These employ electric gear motors as ad-

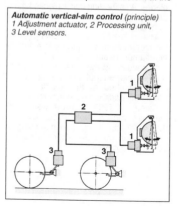

Automatic vertical-aim control (principle)
1 Adjustment actuator, 2 Processing unit,
3 Level sensors.

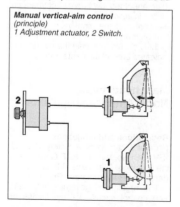

Manual vertical-aim control
(principle)
1 Adjustment actuator, 2 Switch.

justment actuators. These are switched either by the relevant switches in the vehicle or by axle sensors.

Headlamp cleaning systems

Headlamp cleaning systems remove dirt from the lenses of the main headlamps. This ensures unimpaired illumination of the roadway and prevents oncoming traffic from being dazzled. There are two types of cleaning system:

Wipe/wash system
The use of these systems is restricted to glass lenses because plastic lenses, despite having high scratch-resistant coatings, are too sensitive to mechanical cleaning.

High-pressure washer system
High-pressure washer systems (see Fig.) are gaining increasing acceptance as they can be used on both glass and plastic lenses. The cleaning effect is chiefly determined by the cleaning pulse of the water droplets. The decisive factors are:
- the distance between jet nozzle(s) and lens,
- the size, contact angle and contact velocity of the water droplets and
- the amount of water.

As well as fixed nozzle holders on the bumpers, telescopically extending nozzle holders are also used. The telescope significantly improves the cleaning effect because it always assumes an optimal spray position. Furthermore, when not in use, the nozzle holder can be concealed e.g. inside the bumper.

High-pressure washer systems consist of
- water reservoir, pump, hose and non-return valve and
- nozzle holder, which is extended by means of a telescope, with one or more jet nozzles.

Fog lamps

Fog lamps are intended to improve road-surface illumination in fog, snow, heavy rain and dust.

Optical concept

Paraboloid
A parabolic reflector featuring a light source located at the focal point reflects light along a parallel axis (as with the high-beam lamp) and the lens extends this beam to form a horizontal band. A special screen prevents the beam from being projected upward.

Free-form technology
New calculation methods (CAL Computer Aided Lighting) can be used to shape reflectors in such a way that they scatter

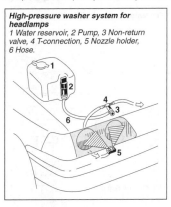

High-pressure washer system for headlamps
1 Water reservoir, 2 Pump, 3 Non-return valve, 4 T-connection, 5 Nozzle holder, 6 Hose.

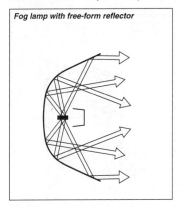

Fog lamp with free-form reflector

light directly (i.e. without optical lens profiling) and simultaneously generate (without separate shading) a sharp light/dark cutoff line.

The fact that the lamp features pronounced envelopment of the bulb leads to an extremely high volume of light combined with maximum dispersion width.

PES fog lamps

In fog, this technology minimizes the glare reflected back to the driver. The screen, the image of which is projected onto the road surface by the lens, furnishes maximum contrast at the light/dark cutoff line.

Designs

DIY and dealer-installed fog lamps are designed as individual projection units in their own housings. These are installed either upright on the bumper, or suspended beneath it.

Stylistic and aerodynamic considerations have led to increased use of integrated fog lamps, designed either for installation within body openings or included as a component within a larger light assembly (with adjustable reflectors when the fog lamps are combined with the main headlamps).

Most fog lamps are designed to project a white beam. There is no substantive evidence that yellow lamps provide any physiological benefits. A fog lamp's effectiveness depends upon the size of the illuminated area and the focal length of the

reflector. Assuming the same illuminated area and focal length, from the lighting-engineering viewpoint the differences between round and rectangular fog lamps are insignificant.

Regulations

Design is governed by ECE R19, installation by EEC 76/756, ECE R48, StVZO (FMVSS/CUR) §52. Two white- or yellow-light fog lamps are permitted. The control circuit for switching the fog lamps must be independent of that used for high and low beams. The (German) StVZO allows fog-lamp installation in positions more than 400 mm from the widest point of the vehicle's periphery provided that the switching circuit is designed to ensure that they operate only in conjunction with the low beams. The adjustment procedures for fog lamps are basically the same as for headlamps. Adjustment dimensions e are provided in Table 2.

Auxiliary driving lamps

Auxiliary driving lamps enhance the high-beam visibility provided by dual, quad and six-headlamp systems. The basic optical principles are similar to those used for fog lamps. The only difference being the lens, which is specifically designed to furnish an extended beam. Auxiliary driving lamps are often identical to fog lamps in

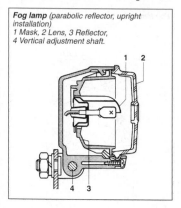

Fog lamp (parabolic reflector, upright installation)
1 Mask, 2 Lens, 3 Reflector,
4 Vertical adjustment shaft.

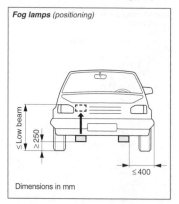

Fog lamps (positioning)

≤ Low beam
≥ 250
≤ 400
Dimensions in mm

shape and size.

Auxiliary driving lamps are mounted and aimed in the same way as standard headlamps, and the underlying lighting concepts are the same. Auxiliary driving lamps are also subject to the cited regulations governing maximum luminous intensity in vehicular lighting systems, according to which the sum of all reference numbers is not to exceed 75. For older lamps without approval number, the number 10 is used for general assessment purposes.

Lights and lamps

Design specifications are contained in ECE R6, R7 and R38, installation is governed by EEC 76/756, ECE R48 and StVZO § 49a (FMVSS/CUR).

These types of lamp are intended to facilitate recognition of the vehicle and to alert other road users to any intended or current changes in direction or motion. Either of two basic concepts can be employed to satisfy the corresponding technical requirements.

Lamps with reflector optics

A reflector in one of various forms (often parabolic) redirects the light emitted by the bulb to obtain a roughly axial projection angle. A lens with optical dispersion elements then determines the beam pattern.

Lamps with Fresnel optics

The light is projected directly against the lens, with no refraction at a reflector. A lens utilizing Fresnel technology then directs the beam in the desired direction.

Fresnel optics devices are usually less efficient than reflector-optics lamps.

Lamps combining reflector and Fresnel optics

Designs combining both the above principles have been used with success. The GP reflector (rotated parabola) is employed to derive undiminished luminous flux from more compact units featuring

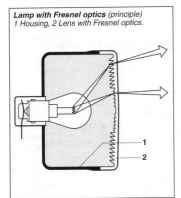

Lamp with Fresnel optics (principle)
1 Housing, 2 Lens with Fresnel optics.

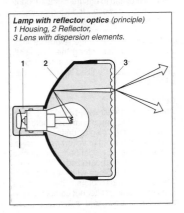

Lamp with reflector optics (principle)
1 Housing, 2 Reflector,
3 Lens with dispersion elements.

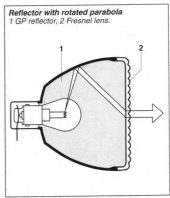

Reflector with rotated parabola
1 GP reflector, 2 Fresnel lens.

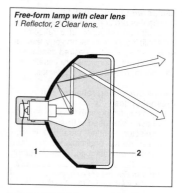

Free-form lamp with clear lens
1 Reflector, 2 Clear lens.

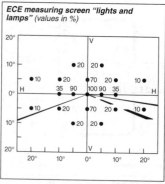

ECE measuring screen "lights and lamps" *(values in %)*

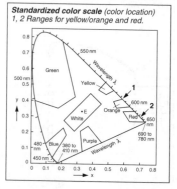

Standardized color scale *(color location)*
1, 2 Ranges for yellow/orange and red.

both shallower reflectors and smaller lenses. These designs employ a specially shaped reflector (rotated parabola) to capture the light beam emanating from the bulb at the largest possible peripheral angle. The Fresnel optics then homogenize the light beam for projection along the desired path. A free-form lamp with Fresnel cap combines excellent luminous efficiency with a variety of stylistic conversion options. The light from the lamp is deflected by the reflector. In the process, the required expansion of light distribution is generated completely or partially by the reflector. The outer lens can thus be designed as a clear lens or supplemented with cylindrical lenses in the horizontal or vertical direction. The Fresnel lens improves the luminous efficiency by deflecting in the desired direction a further part of the light which would not otherwise contribute to the function of the lamp. Both versions are mainly used in the front turn-signal lamps. Which version is actually used depends on the body shape and thus on the available structural space, on the stylistic requirements and on the luminous values required.

Illumination technology, luminous intensities

As projected along the reference axis, minimum and maximum luminous intensities for all lamps must remain within a range calculated to ensure signal recognition without, however, inducing annoying glare for other road users.

Luminous intensity levels to the sides, and above and below the reference axis, may be lower than along the axis itself. This deviation has been quantified on a percentage basis ("unified spatial light distribution").

Color filters

Depending on their application (e.g. stop, turn-signal, fog warning lamps), motor-vehicle lamps must display uniform, distinctive colors in the red or yellow color range. These colors are defined in specific ranges of a standardized color scale (color location). Since white light is composed of various colors, filters can be used to weaken or filter out completely the radiation of undesired spectral regions (colors). The color-filter functions may be performed by either the tinted lenses of the lamp or a colored coating on the glass bulb of the lamp (e.g. yellow lamp in turn-signal lamps with clear lens).

Filter technology can also be used to adapt lamp lenses in such a way that when the lamp is switched off the color is matched to the vehicle's paintwork and nevertheless the existing homologation regulations are complied with when the lamp is on. In the EU region, color locations have been laid down which e.g. correspond to a wavelength of 592 nm for turn-signal lamps that are colored "Yellow/Orange" and to a wavelength of 625 nm for stop and tail lamps that are colored "Red" (see Fig.).

Turn-signal indicators

EEC 76/759, ECE R6, StVZO § 54 (FMVSS/CUR).
Group 1 (front-mounted), Group 2 (rear-mounted) and Group 5 (side) turn-signal lamps are required on dual-track vehicles. Group 2 turn-signal lamps are sufficient for motorcycles and mopeds. The instrument cluster indicator lamp may be in any desired color. The flash frequency is defined as 90 ± 30 cycles per minute.

Front turn-signal lamps
Two yellow turn-signal lamps are stipulated. An indicator is required inside the vehicle.

Rear turn-signal lamps
Two yellow turn-signal lamps are stipulated.

Side-mounted turn-signal lamps
Two yellow turn-signal lamps are stipulated.

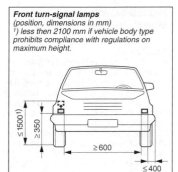

Front turn-signal lamps
(position, dimensions in mm)
1) less then 2100 mm if vehicle body type prohibits compliance with regulations on maximum height.

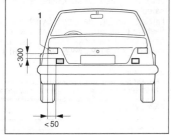

Rear turn-signal lamps
(position, dimensions in mm)
1 Tail lamp. Height and width as for front turn-signal lamps.

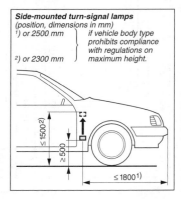

Side-mounted turn-signal lamps
(position, dimensions in mm)
1) or 2500 mm ⎫ if vehicle body type
             ⎬ prohibits compliance
             ⎪ with regulations on
2) or 2300 mm ⎭ maximum height.

Hazard-warning and turn-signal devices

Regulations

Both the StVZO (FMVSS/CUR) and EU Directive EEC 76/756 stipulate that the standard lighting will be supplemented by visual signaling devices for indicating turns and for use as hazard-warning flashers on all vehicles with a top speed exceeding 25 km/h.

Flashing signals: Signals with a frequency of 60...120 pulses per minute and a relative illumination period of 30...80%. Light must be emitted within 1.5 s of initial activation. Should one lamp fail, the remaining lamps must continue to generate visible light.

Turn-signal flashing: Synchronous signal generated by all turn-signal lamps on one side of the vehicle. The lamps are electrically monitored. Malfunctions are indicated.

Hazard-warning flashing: Synchronous flashing of all turn-signal lamps, also operational with the ignition off. An operation indicator is mandatory.

Hazard-warning and turn-signal devices for vehicles without trailer

The electronic hazard-warning and turn-signal flasher includes a pulse generator, designed to switch on the lamps via relay, and a current-controlled monitoring circuit to modify the flashing frequency in response to bulb failure. The turn-signal stalk controls the turn signals, while the hazard flashers are operated using a separate switch.

Hazard-warning and turn-signal devices for vehicles with/without trailer

This type of hazard-warning and turn-signal flasher differs from that employed on vehicles without trailers in the way that turn-signal operation is monitored.

Single-circuit monitoring

The tractor and trailer share a single monitoring circuit designed to activate the two indicator lamps at the flashing frequency. This type of unit cannot be used to localize lamp malfunctions. The flashing frequency remains constant.

Dual-circuit monitoring

Tractor and trailer are equipped with separate monitoring circuits. Localization of malfunction is by means of the indicator

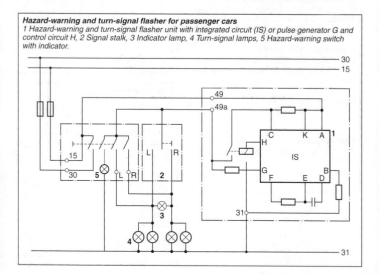

Hazard-warning and turn-signal flasher for passenger cars
1 Hazard-warning and turn-signal flasher unit with integrated circuit (IS) or pulse generator G and control circuit H, 2 Signal stalk, 3 Indicator lamp, 4 Turn-signal lamps, 5 Hazard-warning switch with indicator.

lamp which fails to light up. The flashing frequency remains constant.

Side-marker, clearance and tail lamps

EEC 76/758, ECE R7, StVZO §§ 51 and 53 (FMVSS/CUR). Side-marker lamps (visible from the front) are stipulated on vehicles and trailers with a width exceeding 1600 mm. Tail lamps (at rear) are mandatory equipment on vehicles of all widths. Vehicles wider than 2100 mm (e.g., trucks) must also be equipped with clearance lamps visible from the front and rear.

Side-marker lamps

Two white-light marker lamps are stipulated.

Tail lamps

Two red tail lamps are mandatory equipment.

When the tail and stop lamps are joined in a nested assembly the luminous-intensity ratio for the individual functions must be at least 1:5. Tail lamps are to operate together with the side-marker lamps.

Stop lamps (positions, dimensions in mm)
1 Central high-mounted stop lamp (cat. S3),
2 Stop lamps (cat. S1/S2).
$^1)$ ≥ 400 mm (if width < 1300 mm),
$^2)$ ≤ 2100 mm (if compliance with max. height regulations not possible) or
$^3)$ ≤ 150 mm below lower edge of rear window,
$^4)$ however, the lower edge of the central high-mounted stop lamp must be higher than the upper edge of the (main) stop lamps.

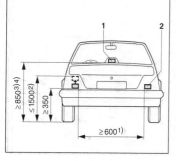

Clearance lamps

Two white-light lamps to be visible from the front, and two red lamps from the rear. Position: As far outward and as high as possible.

Parking lamps

EEC 77/540, ECE R77, StVZO § 51 (FMVSS/CUR).
The vehicle may be equipped with either two parking lamps front and rear or one parking lamp on each side. White light is prescribed at the front and red at the rear. Yellow may also be used at the rear if the parking lamps have been designed as single units with the side turn-signal lamps.

The parking lamps must be designed to operate even when no other vehicle lights (headlamps) are on. The parking-lamp function is usually assumed by the tail and side-marker lamps.

License-plate lamps

EEC 76/760, ECE R4, StVZO § 60 (FMVSS/CUR).
The rear license-plate lamp(s) must be designed to ensure that the rear license plate remains legible up to a distance of at least 25 m by night. Approved are:

The minimum luminance at all points on the surface of the license plate is 2.5 cd/m^2. The luminance gradient of 2 x B_{min}/cm should not be exceeded between any of the test points distributed across the surface of the test plate. B_{min} is defined as the smallest luminance measured at the test point.

Stop lamps

EEC 76/58, ECE R7, StVZO § 53 (FMVSS/CUR).
For each passenger car, two category S1 or S2 stop lamps and one category S3 stop lamp are prescribed as mandatory.

When a nested design with the stop and tail lamps is used, the luminous-intensity ratio between individual functions must be at least 5:1.

The category S3 stop lamp (central high-mounted stop lamp) must not be incorporated in a nested design with another lamp.

Fog warning lamps (rear fog lamps)

EEC 77/538, ECE R38, StVZO § 53d (FMVSS/CUR).
The European Union nations have mandated that one or two red-light fog warning lamps (rear fog lamps) will be installed on all new vehicles.

They must be distanced at least 100 mm from the stop lamp.

The visible illuminated area along the reference axis is not to exceed 140 cm². The electrical switching must be designed to ensure that the fog warning lamp operates only in conjunction with the low beam, high beam and/or front fog lamp. It must also be possible to switch off the fog warning lamps independently of the front fog lamps.

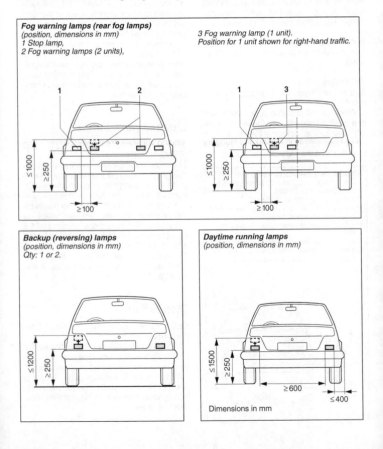

Fog warning lamps (rear fog lamps)
(position, dimensions in mm)
1 Stop lamp,
2 Fog warning lamps (2 units),

3 Fog warning lamp (1 unit).
Position for 1 unit shown for right-hand traffic.

Backup (reversing) lamps
(position, dimensions in mm)
Qty: 1 or 2.

Daytime running lamps
(position, dimensions in mm)

Dimensions in mm

Prescribed indicator lamp: Yellow (green also approved on vehicles initially registered prior to January 1981).

Backup (reversing) lamps

EEC 77/539, ECE R23, StVZO § 52 (FMVSS/CUR).
One or a maximum of two white-light lamps are approved.

The switching circuit must be designed to ensure that the backup lamps operate only with reverse gear engaged and the ignition on.

Daytime running lamps

ECE R87.
ECE R87 authorizes the installation of daytime running lamps in Europe. Their use or the use of low-beam headlamps to generate daytime running light is prescribed as mandatory in Denmark, Norway, Finland and Sweden. "Low beam on" during daytime hours is required by law in out-of-town areas in Poland and Hungary.

Other lighting devices

Identification lamps StVZO § 52 (FMVSS/CUR), ECE R65.
Identification lamps must be visible through 360 degrees from the vehicle, and should be perceived as flashing when viewed from any particular location. The flashing frequency f lies between 2 and 5 Hz. Blue identification lamps are intended for installation on official vehicles. Yellow identification lamps are designed to warn of dangers or dangerous transport.

Spot lamps
Spot lamps generate a narrow beam of light of high luminous intensity, making it possible to illuminate a small area from a substantial distance.

Floodlamps
On a moving vehicle, floodlamps may be switched on only when the vehicle's motion represents an integral part of the operation being performed, for instance, when tractors are used in agriculture and forestry, on self-propelled machinery, on rescue vehicles, etc.

Motor-vehicle bulbs

Bulbs for automotive lighting in accordance with ECE R37 are available in 6 V, 12 V and 24 V versions (see table on following pages). To help avoid mix-ups, different bulb types are identified by different base configurations. Bulbs of differing operating voltages are labeled with this voltage in order to avoid mix-ups in the case of identical configurations. The bulb type suitable in each case must be indicated on the equipment.

The luminous efficiency (lumens per watt) represents the bulb's photometric performance level relative to its power input. The luminous efficiency of vacuum bulbs is 10...18 lm/W. The higher luminous efficiency of halogen bulbs of roughly 22...26 lm/W is primarily a result of the increased filament temperature. D2S and D2R gaseous-discharge bulbs (Litronic) provide a luminous efficiency level in the order of 85 lm/W for substantial improvements in low-beam performance.

Replaceable bulbs must be homologated in accordance with ECE R37. Other light sources which do not conform to this regulation (LED, neon, light bulbs) can only be installed as a fixed component part of a lamp. In the event of repair work, the entire unit must be replaced.

Table 4. Specified minimum flash intensities for identification lamps

Measurement range		Flash intensity cd	
		blue	yellow
Parallel to road surface		> 20	> 40
Within light beam Angle to road surface	± 4°	> 10	
	± 8°		> 30

Table 5. Specifications for motor-vehicle bulbs (2-wheeled vehicles not included)

Application	Category	Voltage rating V	Power rating W	Luminous flux Lumen	IEC Base type	Illustration
High beam/ Low beam	R2	6 12 24	45/40[1] 45/40 55/50	600 min/ 400-550[1]	P 45 t-41	
Fog lamp, High, low beam in 4-HL systems	H1	6 12 24	55 55 70	1350[2] 1550 1900	P14.5 e	
Fog lamp, High beam	H3	6 12 24	55 55 70	1050[2] 1450 1750	PK 22s	
High beam/ Low beam	H4	12 24	60/55 75/70	1650/ 1000[1], [2] 1900/1200	P 43 t – 38	
High beam, Low beam in 4-HL systems, Fog lamp	H7	12	55	1500[2]	PX 26 d	
Fog lamp	H10	12	55	1250(?)	PY 20 d	
Low beam in 4-HL systems	HB4	12	55	1100	P 22 d	
High beam/ Low beam	HIR2	12	55	1875	PX 22 d	
High beam in 4-HL systems	HB3	12	60	1900	P 20 d	
High beam/ Low beam	HIR1	12	65	2500	PX 20 d	
Stop, flasher, rear fog, reversing lamp	P 21 W PY 21 W[6]	6 12 24	21	460[3]	BA 15 s	
Stop lamp	P 21/5 W PY 21 W[7]	6 12 24	21/5[4] 21/5 21/5	440/35[3], [4] 440/35 440/40[3]	BAY 15d	
Side-marker lamp, tail lamp	R 5 W	6 12 24	5	50[3]	BA 15 s	

Table 5. Continued

Application	Category	Voltage rating V	Power rating W	Luminous flux Lumen	IEC Base type	Illustration
Tail lamp	R 10 W	6 12 24	10	125[3])	BA 15 s	
Stop, flasher, rear fog, reversing lamp	P 27 W	12	27	475[3])	W 2.5 x 16 d	
Stop lamp/ tail lamp	P 27/7 W	12	27/7	475/36[3])	W 2.5 x 16 q	
License-plate lamp, tail lamp	C 5 W	6 12 24	5	45[3])	SV 8.5	
Reversing lamp	C 21 W	12	21	460[3])	SV 8.5	
Side-marker lamp	T 4 W	6 12 24	4	35[3])	BA 9 s	
Side-marker lamp, License-plate lamp	W 5 W	6 12 24	5	50[3])	W 2.1 x 9.5 d	
Side-marker lamp, License-plate lamp	W 3 W	6 12 24	3	22[3])	W 2.1 x 9.5 d	
Low beam in 4-HL systems	D1S	85 12[5])	35 approx. 40[5])	3200	PK 32 d-2	
Low beam in 4-HL systems	D2S	85 12[5])	35 approx. 40[5])	3200	P 32 d-2	
Low beam in 4-HL systems	D2R	85 12[5])	35 approx. 40[5])	2800	P 32 d-3	

[1]) High/low beam. [2]) Specifications at test voltage of 6.3; 13.2 or 28.0 V.
[3]) Specifications at test voltage of 6.75; 13.5 or 28.0 V
[4]) Main/secondary filament. [5]) With ballast unit. [6]) Yellow-light version.

Acoustic signaling devices

Regulations
The internationally applicable ECE Regulation No. 28 specifies that the acoustic signals produced by motor vehicles will maintain a uniform sound quality with no perceptible frequency fluctuations during operation. The use of sirens, bells and the like is not permitted, as well as the playing of melodies by means of sound generators operating in a given sequence.

Installation
Elastic couplings must be used to decouple electric horns from the vehicle's body, as the horn would otherwise induce sympathetic oscillations in the adjacent bodywork. The resulting feedback would diminish both volume and tone quality. Both electric and electropneumatic horns are sensitive to resistance in their control circuits. When horns are installed in pairs, they should be triggered by relays.

Horns

Standard horns
The mass of the armature together with the flexible diaphragm forms an oscillating system within the horn. When voltage is applied to the contacts controlling the solenoid coil, the armature impacts against the magnetic core at the horn's fundamental frequency. A fixed tone disk, directly attached to the armature, responds to these intense periodic impacts by radiating harmonic waves. Legal regulations stipulate that the maximum sound energy must lie within a band of 1.8...3.55 kHz. This frequency explains the horn's relatively piercing note. This sound, which is essentially emitted along the horn's axis and out toward the front, can be heard above the background noise in traffic, even over longer distances.

The horn's size is one of the factors which determine the fundamental frequency and volume.

Supertone horns
As well as increased diameters, supertone horns have a higher electrical power input. Their warning signals can therefore still be heard under extreme conditions (truck driver's cab with high noise levels).

Fanfare horns

The electropneumatic fanfare horn employs the same basic actuating system as its standard counterpart, the salient difference being that the armature is allowed to vibrate freely in front of the coil with no impact occurring. The oscillating diaphragm induces vibration of an air column within a tube. The resonant frequency of the diaphragm and the air column are tuned to one another and they determine the pitch of the signal. The tube is in the shape of a funnel, with a wide opening to enhance the efficiency of sound propagation. The funnel tube is generally coiled to minimize the unit's size.

The presence of upper harmonics in the lower range of the frequency spectrum endows the fanfare horn with a rich, melodious sound. The tone is less penetrating than that of a standard horn due to the more consistent distribution of sound energy over a wide spectrum.

Selecting the correct horn
The warning produced by the impact horn is more conspicuous; it thus represents the better choice for vehicles which are frequently used for long hauls on roads with a large amount of truck traffic. Alternatively, the fanfare horn is superior for urban driving, as pedestrians often find the standard horn excessively loud and unpleasant. Both sets of requirements can be fulfilled by installing the two horn types together in a single system with a selection switch for urban or rural traffic. Standard and fanfare horns both operate at standardized frequencies. High and low tones can be combined to produce a harmonious dual-tone sound.

Theft-deterrent systems

Regulations

Theft-deterrent systems (car alarms) installed in motor vehicles must conform to the regulations defined in Paragraph 38 b of the StVZO Road Licensing Regulations (FMVSS/CUR) as well as ECE Directive R18. A primed alarm system responds to attempts at unauthorized vehicle entry by emitting warning signals.

Approved warning signals
– Intermittent audible signals of max. 30 s in length emitted by either the vehicle's own horn or an auxiliary unit.
– Flashing signals of max. 5 min in length using the hazard warning flashers (StVZO), or 30 s flashing of the low beams (ECE).

If the vehicle is repeatedly tampered with, the system may only produce a further acoustic alarm once the previous alarm has

expired. The driver or authorized person must be able to deprime the alarm immediately. It must be impossible for alarm units to become active when the engine is running. The alarm is not to be triggered by vehicle movements (such as tremors etc.) not caused by attempted unauthorized entry.

Automotive alarm systems

Basic system
The schematic diagram below is of an actual unit available on the market. The central ECU evaluates the signals at its input terminals, activates the system and switches on the warning signals (horn and visual signals) via its outputs.

The system is primed and deprimed with an infrared or radio remote-control unit which uses individual codes. This secures the vehicle against unauthorized

Theft-deterrent system (car alarm)
1 Battery, 2 Driving switch, 3 Radio, 4 Ignition, 5 Starting motor, 6 Remote control system (6.1 Transmitter, 6.2 Receiver), 7 Alarm system ECU, 8 Alarm horn, 9 Ultrasonic passenger-compartment protection, 10 Tilt alarm, 11 Interior lighting, 12 Direction indicator, 13 Door contact switch, 14 Contact switches for hood and trunk, 15 Status display.

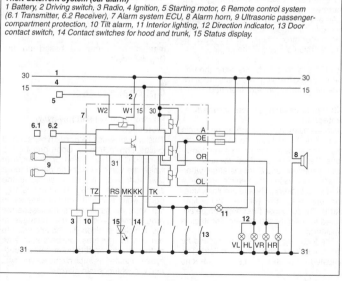

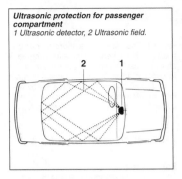

Ultrasonic protection for passenger compartment
1 Ultrasonic detector, 2 Ultrasonic field.

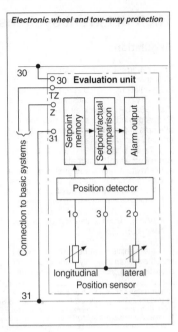

Electronic wheel and tow-away protection

use. The ignition must be off (i.e. engine off) before the system can be primed.

The input terminals TK, MK, KK serve as connections for the door and hood switches. Opening one of these will immediately trigger the alarm. This will also occur when the radio-monitoring loop is open-circuited or the ignition is turned on with the alarm primed. Output Z activates the external ancillaries which trigger the alarm via input TZ.
  All of the mutually independent inputs are able to trigger consecutive alarms. The starter-motor disable facility prevents unauthorized starting of the engine.

An LED at output RS blinks when the unit is primed and in doing so signals the unit's operating status (primed/deprimed).

Ultrasonic passenger-compartment protection

Such installations generate an ultrasonic field inside the vehicle. An ultrasonic detector registers motion or pressure variations that cause the field to fluctuate. Such variations occur, for instance, when a hand reaches into the vehicle or when a window is broken. The electronic evaluation unit responds with an immediate alarm. The response threshold can be adjusted to optimize the system's protective efficiency.
  The following principles are applied for the evaluation of the ultrasonic field: The amplitude method, the pulse-echo method, or a method based on the Doppler effect.

Optional extras

Electronic wheel and tow-away protection

This unit consists of a position sensor and evaluation electronics. Upon priming the alarm unit the inclination or tilt angle at which the vehicle has been parked (on a level surface or on a hill) is stored as the zero reference angle. An alarm is triggered when either the rate of variation in the angle or the angle itself exceeds the programmed limits. Normal changes in the vehicle's position (for instance due to air loss in the tires, deliberate rocking of the vehicle, or settling in soft ground) are recognized as such by the electronics, and do not trigger an alarm.

Vehicle immobilizers

In addition to the ignition and steering-wheel lock, electronic vehicle immobilizers are employed to protect the vehicle against unauthorized use.

After switching off the ignition, and at the latest when locking the doors after leaving the vehicle, the vehicle immobilizer is automatically activated and puts one or more of those major units out of action which are essential to vehicle operation. Systems incorporating interrupter circuits use a relay to immobilize the units. Normally, the following three major circuits are interrupted:

– Starter motor,
– Fuel supply,
– Ignition or diesel fuel-injection pump.

In the case of units featuring coded access, one or more units are blocked or switched into circuit again by entering a code.

The following systems are used for deactivating the immobilizer:

Radio/infrared system

By means of a hand-held transmitter, a coded signal is sent to the immobilizer. The fact that the central-locking system can also be operated with this system represents a further increase in operative comfort for the driver.

Transponder systems

The key is fitted with a transponder which from a short distance transmits a coded signal to a receiver coil (wound around the ignition lock for instance). The system deactivates the immobilizer as soon as the transponder enters the coil's receive area.

Electronic key

The immobilizer is deactivated when conductive coupling takes place between the electronic key and the immobilizer system.

Code keypad

The secret code number to deactivate the system is entered using a keypad.

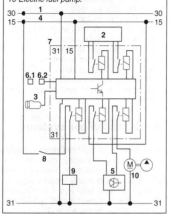

System with interrupter circuits
1 Battery, 2 Central locking system,
3 Display unit, 4 Ignition, 5 Engine ECU,
6 Remote-control system (6.1 Transmitter,
6.2 Receiver), 7 Immobilizer ECU,
8 Starting switch, 9 Starting motor,
10 Electric fuel pump.

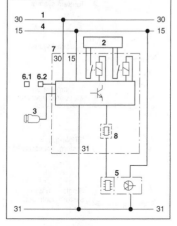

System with coded access
1 Battery, 2 Central locking system,
3 Display unit, 4 Ignition, 5 Engine ECU,
6 Remote-control system (6.1 Transmitter,
6.2 Receiver), 7 Immobilizer ECU,
8 Code unit.

Windshield and rear-window cleaning

Systems for cleaning the vehicle's windshield, headlamps, and rear window are needed in order to comply with legal stipulations for good visibility at all times. Such systems can be subdivided as follows:
– Windshield wiper systems,
– Rear-window wiper systems,
– Headlamp wiper systems
– Headlamp washer systems
– Combination wiper-washer (wipe/wash) systems.

Windshield wiper systems

The following are the most important windshield-cleaning systems, using the passenger car as an example. These systems are based on the legally prescribed areas of vision (Europe, USA and Australia). The wiped areas may be changed by additional controls acting on the wiper blades (parallelogram, general four-bar mechanism).

The windshield wiper system must meet the following requirements:
– Removal of water and snow,
– Removal of dirt (mineral, organic or biological),
– Operation at high temperature (+ 80 °C) and low temperature (– 30 °C),
– Corrosion resistance against acids, alkalis, salts (240 h), ozone (72 h),
– Service life: passenger cars $1.5 \cdot 10^6$ wipe cycles, commercial vehicles $3 \cdot 10^6$ wipe cycles,
– Stall test.

Mechanical wiper mechanism
Series- or parallel-coupled four-bar mechanisms are used, with transversely jointed linkage or additional controlled four-bar linkages also being used for large wipe angles or difficult mechanical transmission configurations.

Optimization of the mechanism is important. Smooth operation can be achieved by matching the maximum values of angular acceleration and/or the force-transmission angles near to the wiper reversal points.

The trend is no longer to allow the crank to rotate fully but to allow it to complete

---

Windshield cleaning systems

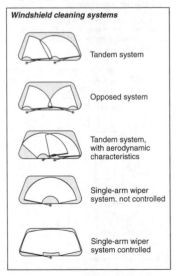

Tandem system

Opposed system

Tandem system, with aerodynamic characteristics

Single-arm wiper system. not controlled

Single-arm wiper system controlled

Principle of the mechanical wiper mechanism
1 Series-coupled, 2 Parallel-coupled,
α Crank angle. β, γ Wipe angle,
v_T Tangential force-transmission angle

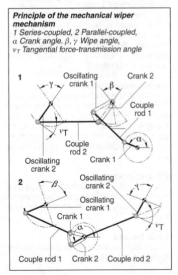

only (barely) a half rotation. This significantly reduces the space needed by the linkage for movement. For this purpose, the drive motor is electronically controlled and its direction of rotation reversed in line with the wiping motion.

It is thus also possible with only minor additional expenditure to achieve an "extended parking position", "protection against snow overload" and, despite varying operating conditions, a relatively constant wiped area.

If problems are experienced in locating the linkage, the above-mentioned technology permits a large linkage to be replaced by 2 significantly smaller units, each with its own (smaller) drive motor.

A second step towards optimization of the wiper mechanism involves the working position of the wiper-blade lip relative to the surface of the windshield or rear-window. By positioning the wiper bearings at the proper angle to the windshield, and by applying additional torsion to the wiper arms, the position of the wiper blades is defined so that at their reversal points they are inclined laterally towards the wiped-area bisector, thus assisting the wiper-blade ele-

Tandem wiper system (series-coupled)
Right-hand part of wiper mechanism designed as:
1 Oscillating crank, 2 Transversely jointed linkage, 3 Additional controlled four-bar linkage, 4 Controlled crank with attached coupling link.

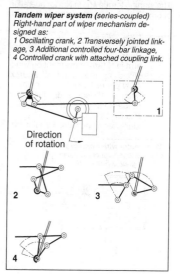

Direction of rotation

ments to swivel into their new working position when reversal takes place.

Wiper blades

Wiper blades are used in lengths of 260...1000 mm. Their dimensions for mounting (e.g., slide-in or hook mounting) are standardized. Minimum-wear operation is achieved by eliminating play in their mountings and joints. The tops of the center brackets are perforated to prevent blade lift-off at high speeds. In special cases aerodynamic deflectors are integrated in the wiper arms or blades to press the blades against the windshield.

Rubber wiper-blade elements

The most important component of a wiper system is the rubber element. It is loaded by the claws of the bracket system, and supported by spring strips. Its double microedge is pressed against the windshield, and at its point of contact has a width of only 0.01...0.015 mm. When moving across the windshield, the wiper-blade element must overcome coefficients of dry friction of 0.8...2.5 (depending upon air humidity), and coefficients of wet friction of 0.6...0.1 (depending upon frictional velocity). The correct combination of wiper-element profile and rubber properties must be chosen so that the wiper lip can wipe the complete wiped area of the windshield surface at an angle of approx. 45°.

Rear-window cleaning systems

These systems perform similar to windshield-cleaning systems. However, service life is limited to $0.5 \cdot 10^6$ wipe cycles.

Rubber wiper-blade element in working position
1 Claw bracket,
2 Spring strip,
3 Lip,
4 Double microedge,
5 Windshield.

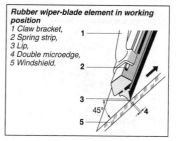

In right-hand traffic vehicles, the wiped area is preferred with parking position on the right-hand side (as viewed in the direction of travel). The 180° system is used when rear-window dimensions permit.

Headlamp cleaning systems

Two systems have been adopted for cleaning headlamps: the wipe/wash system and the wash-only system (P. 773). For the wipe/wash system a wiper arm is driven directly by a motor with a step-down gear unit; the water required to clean the headlamps is taken from the windshield-washer reservoir.

The advantages of the headlamp-wash system lie in its simplicity and often in its easier adaptation to the vehicle styling concept. It is important that the nozzles are positioned correctly so that water jets properly cover the headlamps at all driving speeds.

The law requires that a dirty headlamp whose luminosity has been reduced to 20% must regain 80% luminosity within a

period of 8 seconds. The system must be able to complete at least 50 cycles on one charge of cleaning fluid.

Wiper motors

Permanent-magnet DC motors are used as wiper motors. For normal use in windshield-wiper systems, they incorporate a worm-gear unit, but when used in rear-window and headlamp cleaning systems, they often incorporate an additional gear unit for translating rotary motion into oscillating motion (four-bar linkage, rack-and-pinion mechanism or crank-wheel mechanism).

The output of wiper motors for windshield and window cleaning systems is rated differently from that of common electric drives. Legal regulations and application requirements usually specify that the operating speed of the first wipe frequency be $n_{B1} = 45$ min⁻¹ and for the second wipe frequency $n_{B2} = 65$ min⁻¹. Taking the maximum friction between rubber element and window, this results in a torque for each wiper arm which the wiper motor must produce at a minimum speed of $n_A = 5$ min⁻¹. The starting torque M_{An} in Nm for operation of <u>one</u> wiper arm is calculated as follows:

$$M_{An} = F_{WFN} \cdot \mu_{max} \cdot f_S \cdot f_T \cdot L_A \cdot (\omega_{H\,max}/\omega_{Mot}) \cdot (1/\eta_{Getr}) \cdot (R_{Aw}/R_{Ak})$$

F_{WFN} Downward nominal load of wiper arm in N (arm movement on windshield or rear window, approx. 15 N per m wiper-blade length),

μ_{max} Max. coefficient of dry friction of rubber element (2.5 at $\varphi = 93\%$ relative air humidity),

f_S Multiplier to account for joint fric-

Rear-window wiped areas
The shaded areas (here, LHD vehicle) represent impaired visibility with regard to vehicles which are overtaking.

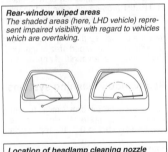

Location of headlamp cleaning nozzle (wash system and wiper blade)

Wiper motor with worm gear
1 Permanent-magnet DC motor,
2 Worm gear, 3 Shaft end.

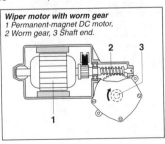

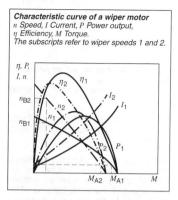

Characteristic curve of a wiper motor
n Speed, I Current, P Power output,
η Efficiency, M Torque.
The subscripts refer to wiper speeds 1 and 2.

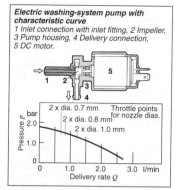

Electric washing-system pump with characteristic curve
1 Inlet connection with inlet fitting, 2 Impeller,
3 Pump housing, 4 Delivery connection,
5 DC motor.

f_T	tion of wiper arm (usually 1.15), Tolerance factor to account for wiper-arm load tolerance (usually 1.12),
L_A	Wiper-arm length in m,
ω_{Hmax}	Max. angular velocity of the wiper arm,
ω_{Mot}	Mean angular velocity of the wiper-motor crank,

$$\omega_{H\,max}/\omega_{Mot} \approx 0.15 \cdot (0.01 \cdot \omega_W)^2 + \sin(\omega_W/2)$$

ω_W = Wiper angle β or γ

η_{Getr} Efficiency of gear unit, usually assumed to be 0.8; must be measured separately when using special mechanism components (e.g. transversely jointed linkage, additional controlled four-bar linkage, multiple O-ring seals),

R_{Aw} Electrical resistance of armature winding heated by nominal operation,

R_{Ak} Electrical resistance of cold armature winding.

(R_{Aw}/R_{Ak}) usually 1.25

The motor's short-circuit strength is another important factor in its design. This is defined as the length of time during which the stalled motor must withstand the full test voltage without short-circuiting its windings (usually specified as $t_K = 15$ min).

Together, the frictional load and the gear ratio result in an operating torque on wet glass which is 0...20% of the tightening torque. In the case of very large wiper

systems operating on nearly vertical windshields (e.g. on buses), the torque of the wiper arm resulting from its own weight must also be taken into consideration (separately calculated allowance).

In the case of drive motors with pendular mechanisms (rear window and headlamp cleaning systems), the required torque is determined at the oscillating shaft.

It is calculated as:

$$M_H = F_{WFN} \cdot \mu_{max} \cdot f_S \cdot f_T \cdot L_A \cdot (R_{Aw}/R_{Ak})$$

Washing systems

To ensure good visibility in the wiped areas, it is imperative that the wiper system is backed by a washing system. Electrical centrifugal pumps of simple design are used (characteristic pump curve) to pump the water through 2 to 4 nozzles and onto the windshield in a narrow spray pattern. The water, to which a cleaning additive is added, is contained in a reservoir of 1.5...2 l capacity. If the same water is used also to clean the headlamps, a larger volume of up to 7 l is necessary. A separate reservoir can be provided for the rear-window cleaning system. The washing system is often coupled to the corresponding wiper system by means of an electronic control so that water is sprayed onto the window or windshield while a pushbutton is pressed, with the wiper system continuing to operate for several additional cycles after the pushbutton is released.

Automotive windshield and window glass

Silica glass is used for automotive windshields and windows. Approximate composition:

72 % SiO_2 as vitrifier
14 % Na_2O as flux
10 % CaO $\left.\vphantom{\begin{matrix}1\\2\end{matrix}}\right\}$ as stabilizer
4 % MgO

Windows are made of flat glass which is poured using the float-glass process. Fusion occurs at a temperature of 1550 °C; the melt then passes through a refining zone of 1500 °C to 1100 °C before being poured onto the so-called float bath (liquid tin) and cooled to a temperature of 600 °C. It is at this stage that the two plane-parallel surfaces of exceptionally high quality are produced (tin-bath surface below, fire-finished surface above). After passing through a cooling zone, the glass is then cut to pieces of 6.10 m × 3.35 m.

The glass can now be further processed in one of two ways:
– as single-pane toughened safety glass (TSG)
or
– as laminated safety glass (LSG), which is primarily used for windshields.

TSG windows differ from LSG windows in that they exhibit higher mechanical and thermal strength as well as different breakage and shattering behavior. TSG panes pass through a toughening process which greatly prestresses the surface of the glass. In case of breakage, these windows break into many small dull-edged pieces.

The LSG window, on the other hand, exhibits a normal shattering pattern. When an LSG window is cracked, it is

Material properties and physical data of automotive glass (finished windshields and windows)

Property	Dimension	TSG	LSG
Density	kg/m³	2500	2500
Surface hardness	Mohs	5...6	5...6
Compressive strength	MN/m²	700...900	700...900
Modulus of elasticity	MN/m²	68 000	70 000
Bending strength			
before prestressing	MN/m²	30[2]	30[1]
after prestressing	MN/m²	50[2]	
Impact-ball strength (DIN 52 306)	Nm	> 7	> 90[1]
(at room temperature)		(227 g ball)	(2.26 kg ball)
Arrow-drop strength			> 18[1]
DIN 52 307 (at room temperature)			
Specific heat	kJ/kgK	0.75...0.84	0.75...0.84
Coefficient of thermal conductivity	W/mK	0.70...0.87	0.70...0.87
Coefficient of thermal expansion	m/mK	$9.0 \cdot 10^{-6}$	$9.0 \cdot 10^{-6}$
Dielectric constant		7...8	7...8
Light transmittance (DIN 52 306), clear	%	≈ 90	≈ 90[1]
Index of refraction		1.52	1.52[1]
Deviation angle of wedging	Angle	< 1.0 flat	≤ 1.0 flat[1]
	minute	< 1.5 bent	≤ 1.5 bent[1]
Dioptric faults (DIN 52 305)	Dptr.	< 0.03	≤ 0.03[1]
Temperature resistance	°C	200	90[1]
			(max. 30')
Resistance to temperature shocks	K	200	

[1] Properties of finished laminated safety glass (LSG). In calculating the permissible bending stress, the coupling effect of the PVB film is to be disregarded.

[2] Calculated values; these values already contain the necessary safety margins.

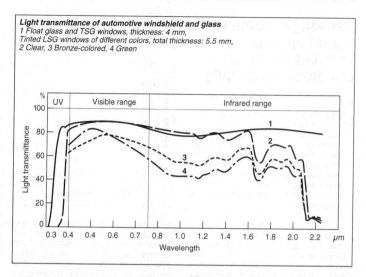

Light transmittance of automotive windshield and glass
1 Float glass and TSG windows, thickness: 4 mm,
Tinted LSG windows of different colors, total thickness: 5.5 mm,
2 Clear, 3 Bronze-colored, 4 Green

easier to see through than a TSG window. Laminated glass is made of two panes of glass bonded to each other by means of an intermediate film of plastic (polyvinyl butyral).

The formation of many small, blunt fragments of glass which are held in position by the plastic film reduces the danger of injury. In the case of the Sekuriflex window (a refinement of the LSG window), an additional plastic film with excellent optical and mechanical properties (e.g., abrasive and scratch resistance) is applied to the inside surface of the window.

Green or bronze-colored windows are used for heat absorption because they block the transmission of infrared light more strongly than light of shorter wave lengths. On the other hand, light transmission in the visual spectrum is reduced from 90 % to 80 %.

Optical properties

The optical properties of TSG and LSG windows are roughly the same, because the optical properties of the PVB film are very closely aligned to those of glass.

Heatable safety glass

In the case of heatable safety glass (TSG), heating conductors are applied to the window (not yet prestressed) using the silk screen process, and are sintered in place during the prestressing process. Subsequent galvanization increases the strength of the heating conductors, tempers them and protects them against environmental influences. Window areas treated in this way can be kept free of mist by heating, and even of ice if the heating power is high enough.

Heated window areas must never be cleaned using caustic or scouring cleansers (e.g. chlorine, ammonia, sand or acids).

In the case of LSG windows, very thin, nearly invisible heating wires are applied in wavy lines to the plastic adhesive film. They are connected in series and/or parallel in order to achieve the intended electrical resistance. The thin wires provide even better heating coverage. The heating power of passenger-car rear window heating systems is approximately 3...5 W/dm^2.

Passenger-compart-ment heating, ventilation and air conditioning (HVAC)

Function

The vehicle's climate-control system provides for the following:
– a comfortable climate for all passengers,
– an environment calculated to minimize driver stress and fatigue,
– more recent units use filters to remove particulate matter (pollen, dust) and even odors from the air,
– good visibility through all windows, and windshield.

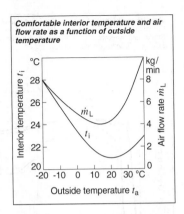

Comfortable interior temperature and air flow rate as a function of outside temperature

In many countries the performance of the heater unit is governed by legal requirements, with emphasis on the defroster's ability to maintain clear windows and windshields (such as EEC Directive 78/317 within the European Community, and MVSS 103 in the USA).

Systems deriving heat from the engine

On vehicles with liquid-cooled engines, the engine heat (by-product of the combustion process) contained in the coolant is used to warm the passenger compartment. With air-cooled engines, engine heat is taken from the exhaust or, in some cases, from the engine's lubrication circuit. The heater core consists of tubes and fins, and has the same basic design as the engine radiator. Coolant flows through the core's tubes while air flows through its fins. Two design concepts are available for regulating the heater's thermal output.

Coolant-side heater control

In these systems, the entire air flow is usually directed through the heater core while a valve controls the heating output by regulating the flow of coolant through the unit. Extreme precision is required from the valves, which must be capable of providing consistent, stable settings for

accurate control at the minimal flow rates necessary for maintaining low heat levels (important between seasons). A disadvantage lies in the fact that the heating output varies according to the coolant's pressure and temperature, meaning that heater performance is affected by engine speed and load.

Air-side heater control

In this type of system the flow of coolant through the heater core is unrestricted. The heat is regulated by dividing the air flow before it reaches the core: A portion of the air flows through the core, while the rest is directed around it. The two currents are subsequently reunited in the plenum chamber. An air flap can be used to regulate the distribution of the two currents, thereby determining the amount of heat taken from the coolant. This type of control arrangement is less sensitive to fluctuations in engine load, and air-temperature adjustments take effect immediately. Water and/or air-side blocks prevent undesirable residual warmth from emerging from the hot core when the heater is not in operation.

One disadvantage of the air-side control layout lies in the larger installation volume required for housing the bypass duct and the plenum chamber.

The air-ventilation current is provided by a constant-speed or adjustable-speed electric blower, whereby aerodynamic pressure can also become a significant factor as vehicle speed increases. The minimum hourly air-flow rate should be 30 m³ per person (figure for reference purposes only). Factors such as passenger-compartment temperature, outside temperature, air flow and (to a certain degree) heat radiation, all affect the process of achieving a comfortable climate (see illustration). Because the precise data on these variables vary substantially from one vehicle to the next, actual figures must be derived empirically.

As motor vehicles have relatively small passenger compartments, drafts and sunlight entering through windshield and windows confront the heating, ventilation and air-conditioning (HVAC) systems with extreme challenges. In order to enhance passenger comfort, an attempt should be made to maintain the temperature in the footwell 4...8 °C above that of the air around the upper body.

Electronic heater control

Variations in outside-air temperature and vehicle speed cause fluctuations in the temperature of the passenger compartment. On standard systems, the heater controls must be constantly readjusted by hand in order to maintain an agreeable temperature. Electronic heater control dispenses with this requirement by maintaining the interior temperature at the desired level automatically.

On heater units featuring water-side regulation, sensors monitor the temperatures of the vehicle's interior and of the emerging air; the control unit processes this information and compares it with the preselected temperature. Meanwhile, a solenoid valve installed in the cooling circuit opens and closes at a given frequency in response to the signals which it receives from the control unit. The adjustments in open/close ratio in the cycle periods regulate the flow rate from the closed position up to the maximum. A servo-actuated adjustment flap is usually employed to provide infinitely-variable temperature regulation in air-side systems (pneumatic linear adjusters are also occasionally used). Sophisticated systems allowing separate adjustment for the left and right sides of the vehicle are also available.

Air conditioners

The heater unit alone is not capable of providing a comfortable environment at all times. When the outside temperature climbs beyond 20 °C, the air must be cooled to achieve the required interior temperatures. Here, compressor-driven refrigeration units with R 134a refrigerant are in use (until 1992, R12 refrigerant).

The engine-driven compressor compresses the vaporous refrigerant, which heats up in the process and is then directed to the condenser where it cools and liquefies. The energy supplied in the compressor and the heat absorbed in the evaporator are dissipated to the environment here.

An expansion valve sprays the cooled liquid into the evaporator where the evaporation process extracts the required evaporation heat from the incoming stream of fresh air, thereby cooling the air.

Air conditioner with electronic water-side control (schematic)
1 Blower, 2 Evaporator, 3 Evaporator temperature sensor, 4 Heater core, 5 Solenoid valve, 6 Air exit-temperature sensor, 7 Setpoint control, 8 Interior sensor (ventilated), 9 Control unit, 10 Compressor; a) Fresh air, b) Recirculated air, c) Defrost, d) AC bypass, e) Ventilation, f) Footwell, g) Condensation drain.

Moisture is extracted from the cooled air as condensation, and the air's humidity is reduced to the desired level. Evaporators and condensers are generally designed as tube-and-fin heat exchangers. The evaporator is located before the heater core in the fresh-air stream and cools the air to approx. 3...5 °C. The dehumidified air is reheated in the heater core to the desired temperature.

Automatic climate control

Automatic climate control is particularly useful for vehicles in which both air conditioner and heater are installed, because the constant monitoring and adjustment required to maintain a temperate climate presents the occupants with a complicated task. This rule applies to bus drivers in particular, as they are exposed only to the conditions at the front of the vehicle. An automatic climate control system in-

corporating a preselection feature can automatically maintain the correct temperature, air flow and air distribution in the passenger compartment. These parameters are mutually interdependent, and changes to one will affect the others. At the center of the system is a temperature-control circuit for interior temperature. The control unit continuously monitors both the preselected temperature and all essential variables which affect the system, using this information to calculate a setpoint t_i. The setpoint is compared with the actual temperature, and the control unit uses the difference between the two as the basis for determining the required heating, refrigeration, and air-flow rate. Another function controls the position of the air-distribution flaps with reference to the program which the occupants have selected. Meanwhile, all control circuits continue to respond to manual inputs.

Coolant circuit of an air-conditioning system
1 Compressor, 2 Electric clutch (for compressor on/off function), 3 Condenser, 4 Auxiliary fan, 5 High-pressure switch, 6 Fluid reservoir with desiccant insert, 7 Low-pressure switch, 8 Temperature switch or on/off control (for compressor on/off function), 9 Temperature sensor, 10 Condensate drip pan, 11 Evaporator, 12 Evaporator fan, 13 Fan switch, 14 Expansion valve.

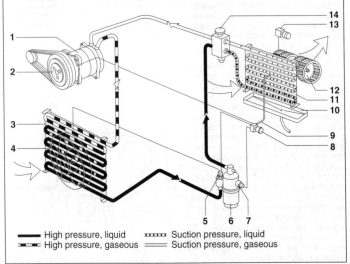

▬▬ High pressure, liquid ▭▭▭ Suction pressure, liquid
▬◼▬ High pressure, gaseous ══ Suction pressure, gaseous

The setpoint temperature determined by the control unit is achieved by means of water or air-side adjustments (as described in "Electronic heater control").

Infinitely-variable or graduated blower control is used to adjust the air flow to the specified level. There is generally no setpoint processing involved in this operation. This type of arrangement is inadequate for dealing with the increases in flow rate caused by aerodynamic pressure at high speeds. Here, a special control function can compensate by responding to increasing vehicle speeds, initially by reducing the blower speed to zero, and then, should the flow continue to rise, by using a restriction flap to throttle the stream of incoming air.

Control of air distribution to the three levels – defroster, upper compartment and footwell – is effected manually, with preselection, or with a fully-automatic program. Especially popular are units featuring program control buttons in which each button provides a specific air-distribution pattern for the three levels.

The defroster represents a special case. In order to clear the windows as rapidly as possible, the temperature control must revert to maximum heat and maximum blower speed while directing the air flow through the upper defroster outlets. On systems with program switches and fully-automatic units, this operating mode is selected with a single button; at temperatures above 0 °C the refrigeration unit is also activated to extract humidity from the air. To prevent the still unheated air giving rise to drafts, the blower is switched off electronically after cold starts in winter, except when "DEF" and cooling are in operation.

The variations described above are used in both passenger cars and trucks. Buses require more complicated layouts. The passenger compartment can be divided into several control zones, in which the temperature is controlled by electronically regulating the speed of the zone's individual water pump.

Auxiliary heater installations

The fuel for units which produce heat without the aid of the engine is supplied either by the standard vehicle tank, or, on large vehicles, by a separate tank. An electric pump supplies the fuel to an injector, which sprays a fuel mist into the combustion chamber; the mist then mixes with the air and burns. The hot exhaust gases are then directed to a heat exchanger. The heat exchanger can function in one of two ways, either warming the interior air directly, or by transferring heat to the engine's coolant circuit. In the latter case, circulation is maintained by a separate electric pump, making it possible to use the standard heating unit to warm the passenger compartment. This type of auxiliary heating for the engine coolant also improves cold-start response in the winter.

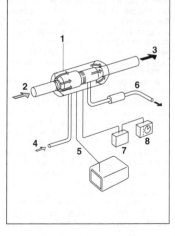

Auxiliary air heater (independent of engine)
1 Air heater with blower for combustion and heating air, combustion chamber and heat exchanger, 2 Hot-air intake, 3 Air outlet to vehicle interior, 4 Combustion-air intake, 5 Fuel supply, 6 Exhaust system, 7 Electronic control unit, 8 Thermostat and timer for pre-selecting switch-on time.

Instrumentation

Drivers have to process a permanently increasing stream of information originating from their own and other vehicles, from roads and from telecommunications equipment. All this information must be conveyed to drivers in the information and communications areas of their vehicles with suitable display and indicating equipment and in compliance with ergonomic requirements. In future, it will increasingly become the norm for cellular phones, navigation systems and ranging systems to join radios and vehicle monitoring systems as standard features in motor vehicles.

Information and communications areas

In any vehicle, there are four information and communications areas, which must satisfy different requirements in terms of their display features:
- the instrument cluster,
- the windshield,
- the center console and
- the vehicle rear compartment.

The display features of these areas are determined by the available range of information and the necessary, useful or desirable information for the occupants concerned.

Dynamic information and monitoring information (e.g. fuel level) to which the driver should respond is indicated in the <u>instrument cluster</u> (i.e. as near as possible to the primary field of vision).

A head-up display (HUD), which reflects the information in the <u>windshield</u>, is especially suited to engaging the driver's attention (e.g. in the case of warnings from a ranging warning radar (ACC) or route directions). The display is supplemented acoustically by voice output.

Status information or dialog prompts are mainly displayed in the vicinity of the operator unit in the <u>center console</u>.

Information of an entertainment nature is featured in the <u>vehicle rear compartment</u>, away from the primary field of vision. This is also the ideal location for the mobile office. The backrest of the front passenger seat is a suitable installation location for the monitor and operator terminal of a laptop computer.

Driver information systems

The driver information area in the vehicle cockpit and the display technologies used have gone through the following stages of development:

Individual and combined instruments
Conventional individual instruments for the optical output of information were initially superseded by more cost-effective instrument clusters (combination of several information units in a single housing) with good illumination and antireflection qualities. The passage of time, with the continual increase in information, saw the creation in the existing space available of the modern instrument cluster with several needle instruments and numerous tell-tale lamps (Fig., no. 1).

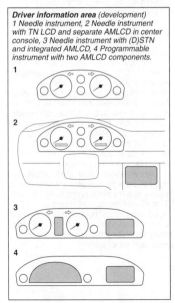

Driver information area (development)
1 Needle instrument, 2 Needle instrument with TN LCD and separate AMLCD in center console, 3 Needle instrument with (D)STN and integrated AMLCD, 4 Programmable instrument with two AMLCD components.

Digital displays

Digital instruments
The first digital instruments used on a large, worldwide scale featuring vacuum fluorescent displays (VFDs) and later liquid-crystal displays (LCDs) can now mainly be found in Japan and the USA in luxury-class cars. These instruments found little favor in Europe and have now virtually disappeared from use. Here the trend towards needle instruments has continued uninterrupted but with a radical technical change in the way in which they are activated (Fig., no. 2).

Central display and operator unit in center console
The introduction of navigation and driver information systems (PP. 796/798) has seen the incorporation of a display monitor and a keypad in the center console. Such systems combine all the additional information from functional units and information components (e.g. cellular phone, car radio/CD, controls for heating/air conditioning (HVAC) and – important for Japan – the "TV" function) in a central display and operator unit. The components are interconnected in a network and are capable of interactive communication.

Positioning this terminal, which is of universal use to driver and passenger, in the center console is effective and necessary from both ergonomic and technical standpoints. The optical information appears in a graphics display. The demands placed by TV reproduction and the navigation system on the image/map display determine the resolution and color reproduction.

Graphics modules
Fitting vehicles with a driver's airbag and power steering as standard has resulted in a reduction in the view through the top half of the steering wheel. At the same time, the amount of information that has to be displayed in the installation space available has increased. This creates the need for additional display modules with graphics capabilities whose display areas are able to show any information flexibly and in prioritized form.

This tendency results in instrumentation featuring a classical needle instrument but supplemented by a graphics display. Even the central display monitor is located at the height of the instrument cluster. What is important to all optical displays is that they can be easily read inside the driver's primary field of vision or in its immediate vicinity without the driver having to divert his eyes from the road for long periods. This is the case for instance when the displays are positioned in the lower area of the center console (Fig., no. 3).

The graphics modules in the instrument cluster permit mainly the display of driver- and vehicle-related functions such as e.g. service intervals, check functions covering the vehicle's operating state and also vehicle diagnostics as needed for the workshop. They can also show route-direction information from the navigation system (no digitized map excerpts, only route-direction symbols such as arrows as turn-off instructions or intersection symbols). It is to be expected that the initially monochrome modules will be succeeded in a second stage by color displays whose reading speed and reliability are increased by color reproduction.

For the central display monitor with an integrated information system, the tendency is now to switch from a 4:3 aspect ratio to a wider format with a 16:9 aspect ratio (cinema-film format), which enables additional route-direction symbols to be displayed as well as the map. More recent developments see the display being split into two separate screens: one screen is only read by the driver and displays driver-related information while the other screen can only be seen by the passenger and shows e.g. a cinema film.

Individual module with computer monitor
By roughly 2003, the remaining mechanical measuring instruments will have disappeared and the entire area of the instrument cluster will have been replaced by a freely addressable graphics monitor (provided the price of LCD computer monitors develops economically). Such a unit module would offer an array of information display options. It is conceivable to have an individually selectable form of display which is geared to the specific needs of individual user groups (e.g. frequent, older or sports car users) (Fig., no. 4).

Instrument clusters

Design

Microcontroller technology and the ongoing networking of motor vehicles have in the meantime transformed instrument clusters from precision-mechanical instruments to electronically dominated devices. A typical instrument cluster (LED-illuminated, with TN-type conductive-rubber-contacted segment LCDs, see Fig.) is a very flat component (electronics, flat stepping motors) and virtually all the components (mainly SMT) are directly contacted on a printed-circuit board.

Operating concept

While the basic functions are the same in most instrument clusters (see typical block diagram), the partitioning of the function blocks into (partly application-specific) microcontrollers, ASICs and standard peripherals sometimes differs significantly (product range, display scope, display types).

Electronic instrument clusters indicate measured variables with high accuracy thanks to stepping-motor technology, and also take over "intelligent" functions such as engine-speed-dependent oil-pressure warning, prioritized fault indication in matrix displays, or service-interval indicator. Even online diagnostic functions are standard and take up a significant part of the program memory.

Because instrument clusters are standard features on all vehicle types and all the bus systems merge here anyway, the former are becoming increasingly established as gateways, i.e. bridges between the different bus systems in the motor vehicle (e.g. engine CAN, body CAN and diagnostic bus).

Measuring instruments

In Europe, manufacturers still tend towards the classical instrument with mechanical needle and dial face. Here, initially the compact, electronically triggered moving-magnet quotient measuring instrument replaced the bulky eddy-current speedometer. Geared stepping motors with very low

Instrument cluster (design)
1 Tell-tale lamp, 2 Printed-circuit board,
3 Stepping motor, 4 Reflector, 5 Plug,
6 View cover, 7 Needle, 8 LED, 9 Dial face,
10 Optical waveguide, 11 LCD.

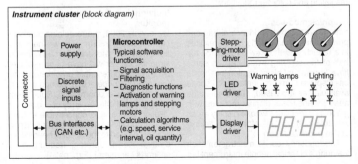

Instrument cluster (block diagram)

overall depth and still higher precision are currently used. Thanks to a compact magnetic circuit and (mostly) 2-stage gearing with a power output of only approx. 100 mW, these motors permit swift and highly accurate needle positioning.

Lighting

Instrument clusters were originally lit by frontlighting technology in the form of electric bulbs. Backlighting technology has in the meantime gained acceptance on account of its attractive appearance. Bulbs have been replaced by long-lasting light-emitting diodes (LEDs, see P. 143). LEDs are also suitable for warning lamps and for the backlighting of scales, displays and (via plastic optical waveguides) needles (refer to table headed "Overview of lighting sources").

Highly efficient InAlGaP-technology LEDs are meanwhile available in the colors yellow, orange and red. The newer InGaN technology is currently producing significant efficiency improvements in the colors green, blue and white. Here the color white is obtained through the combi-

nation of a blue LED chip with an orange-emitting luminescent material (yttrium-aluminum granulate).

However, new technologies are also being used for special configurations:
– CCFLs (Cold Cathode Fluorescent Lamps): mainly for "black screen" instruments, which appear black when they are deactivated. The combination of a tinted view cover (e.g. 25 % transmission) with these very bright lamps (high luminance, high voltage) produces a brilliant appearance with outstanding contrast. Since color LCDs have very low transmission (typically approx. 6 %) it is imperative that CCFLs are used to backlight them in order to obtain good contrast even in daylight.
– EL (electroluminescent) film: AC is applied to this flat film in order for it to light up. It features very uniform light distribution, and has only recently become suitable for automotive applications. It offers extensive freedom of design for color combinations and/or for superimposing dial areas on display surfaces.

Overview of lighting sources

Lighting source	Possible colors	Typical data[1]	Technically suitable for	Conventional ICs	Black-screen instrum.	Service life[2] in h	Activation
Bulb	White (every color possible with filter)	2 lm/W 65 mA 14 V	Dial face Needle Display	+ o +	– – o	$B_3 \approx 4,500$	No special activation required
SMD LED luminescent diode	Red, orange, yellow (InAlGaP)	8 lm/W 25 mA 2 V	Dial face Needle Display	o + +	– + +	$B_3 \gg 10,000$	Series resistors or control required
	Blue, green (InGaN), white (with converter)	2...5 lm/W 20 mA 3.6 V	Dial face Needle Display	o o o	– o o	$B_3 > 10,000$	
EL film electroluminescent	Blue, violet, yellow, green, orange, white	2 lm/W 100 V AC 400 Hz	Dial face Needle Display	+ – –	– – –	approx. 10,000	High voltage required
CCFL cold-cathode lamp	White (every color possible depending on luminescent material)	25 lm/W 2 kV AC 50...100 kHz	Dial face Needle Display	+ – +	+ o +	$B_3 \approx 10,000$	High voltage required

[1] Efficiency in lm/W (lumen per watt), current in mA, voltage in V or kV, activation frequency in kHz.
[2] B_3 Point with 3 % failure probability. Suitability: + preferred, o conditional, – no application.

Display types

TN LCD

With its high status of development, TN-LCD display ("Twisted Nematic Liquid-Crystal Display", see P. 143) is the most commonly used form of display. The term stems from the twisted arrangement of the elongated liquid-crystal molecules between the locating glass plates with transparent electrodes. A layer of this type forms a "light valve", which blocks or passes polarized light depending on whether voltage is applied to it or not. It can be used in the temperature range of −40 °C...+85 °C. The switching times are relatively long at low temperatures on account of the high viscosity of the liquid-crystal material.

TN LCDs can be operated in positive contrast (dark characters on a light background) or negative contrast (light characters on a dark background). Positive-contrast cells are suitable for front- and backlighting while negative-contrast cells can only be read with satisfactory reading contrast when strongly lit from the rear. TN technology is suitable not only for smaller display modules but also for larger display areas in modular or even full-size LCD instrument clusters.

Graphics displays for instrument clusters

Dot-matrix displays with graphics capabilities are needed to display infinitely variable information. They are activated by line scanning and therefore require multiplex characteristics. Under the conditions prevailing in a motor vehicle, conventional TN LCDs can today produce multiplex rates of up to 1:4 with good contrast and up to 1:8 with moderate contrast. Other LCD display technologies are needed to achieve higher multiplex rates. STN and DSTN technologies are now being used for modules with moderate resolution. DSTN technology can be implemented to provide monochrome or color displays.

STN LCD and DSTN LCD

The molecule structure of an STN (Super Twisted Nematic) display is more heavily twisted inside the cell than in a conventional TN display. STN LCDs permit only monochrome displays; usually in blue-yellow contrast. Neutral color can be obtained by applying "retarder film", but this is not effective throughout the entire temperature range encountered in the vehicle.

DSTN LCDs (Double-layer STN) feature considerably improved characteristics, which permit neutral black-and-white reproduction over wide temperature ranges with negative and positive contrast. Color is created by backlighting with colored LEDs. Multicolor reproduction is created by incorporating red, green and blue thin-film color filters on one of the two glass substrates. Under auomotive conditions, shades of gray are only possible to a very limited extent, the result of which is that the range of colors is limited to black, white, the primary colors red, green and blue and their secondary colors yellow, cyan and magenta.

AMLCD

The task of the visually sophisticated and rapidly changing display of complex information in the area of the instrument cluster and the center console with high-resolution liquid-crystal monitors with video capabilities can only effectively be performed by an AMLCD (Active-Matrix Liquid-Crystal Display).

The best developed and mostly widely used are the TFT LCDs (Thin-Film Transistor LCDs) addressed with thin-film

---

Thin-film transistor LCD (TFT LCD)
1 Row circuit, 2 Thin-film transistor,
3 Column circuit, 4 Front-plane electrode,
5 Color layers, 6 Black matrix,
7 Glass substrate, 8 Pixel electrode.

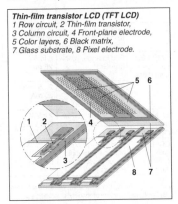

transistors. Display monitors with diagonals of 4″...7″ in the center-console area and an extended temperature range (−25 °C...+85 °C) are available for motor vehicles. Formats of 10″...14″ with a still wider temperature range (−40 °C... +95 °C) are planned for programmable instrument clusters.

TFT LCDs consist of the "active" glass substrate and the opposing plate with the color-filter structures. The active substrate accommodates the pixel electrodes made from tin-indium oxide, the metallic row and column circuits and the semiconductor structures. At each intersecting point of the row and column circuits, there is a field-effect transistor which is etched in several masking steps from a previously applied sequence of layers. A capacitor is likewise generated at each pixel.

The opposite glass plate accommodates the color filters and a "black-matrix" structure, which improves the contrast of the display. These structures are applied to the glass in a sequence of photolithographic processes. A continuous counterelectrode is applied on top of them for all the pixels. The color filters are applied either in the form of continuous strips (good reproduction of graphics information) or as mosaic filters (especially suitable for video pictures).

Head-up display (HUD)

Conventional instrument clusters have a viewing distance of 0.8...1.2 m. In order to read information in the area of the instrument cluster, the driver must adjust his vision from infinity (observing the road ahead) to the short viewing distance for the instrument. This process of adjustment usually takes 0.3...0.5 s. Older drivers find this process strenuous and in some cases, depending on their constitution, even impossible. HUD, a technology involving projection, can eliminate this problem. Its optical system generates a virtual image at such a viewing distance that the human eye can remain adjusted to infinity. This distance begins at approx. 2 m, and the driver can read the information with very little distraction, and without having to divert his eyes from the road to the instrument cluster.

Design
The HUD features an activated display for generating the image, a lighting facility, an optical imaging system and a "combiner", with which the image is reflected into the driver's eyes. The untreated windshield can also take the place of the combiner. Active displays (light emitters) such as CRTs or VFDs and passive displays (light modulators) are used for HUD. PDLC or DSTN displays are suitable but they do need very bright lighting because they absorb approx. 70 % of the transmitted light on account of the required polarizers.

Indication of HUD information
The virtual image should not cover the road ahead so that the driver is not distracted from the traffic or road conditions. It is therefore displayed in a region with a low road or traffic-information content.

In order to prevent the driver from being overwhelmed with stimuli in his primary field of vision, the HUD should not be overloaded with information, and is therefore not a substitute for the conventional instrument cluster. It is however particularly well-suited to displaying safety-related information such as warnings, safety distance and route directions.

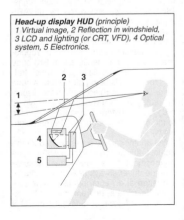

Head-up display HUD (principle)
1 Virtual image, 2 Reflection in windshield, 3 LCD and lighting (or CRT, VFD), 4 Optical system, 5 Electronics.

Automotive sound systems

Reception conditions

Critical FM reception conditions occur e.g. when the transmitter signal is briefly interrupted by a mountain or building (resulting in hiss) or with the delayed reception of broadcast waves which are reflected by these obstructions (resulting in distortion). Other sources of interference: Cross-talk from adjoining high-power transmitters, interference at one frequency emanating from intermodulation products of two other – more powerful – transmitters.

Technical terms

ARI: Autofahrer-Rundfunk-Information (radio information for the driver). This traffic-information system is the product of a cooperative development project involving Blaupunkt, the ADAC (the largest German motorists' association) and the German ARD radio network. It is in active use in Germany, Switzerland, Austria, and Luxembourg:

Those FM broadcasters participating in the traffic-information network constantly transmit a special identification signal (SK), which is recognized by all ARI-equipped radios. If the ARI button has been activated, the channel scanner will pause only at traffic-information stations.

The stations also transmit a supplementary regional identification (BK) code to identify the specific area for which traffic information is being broadcast. A code letter (A through F) appears in the display on radios which are capable of regional recognition (letters correspond to those found on the blue signs on German highways).

Yet another signal is transmitted for the actual traffic announcements: DK, the announcement code. This signal ensures that the driver always hears the traffic information at an appropriate volume (adjustable), quite aside from whether the radio is turned down or a cassette or CD is playing (playback mechanism pauses for the duration of the announcement).

Antenna-diversity recognition: This is a receiver system for vehicles which are equipped with several – usually two – antennas (e.g., window antennas). It's chief function is to alleviate the effects of the multipath distortion induced by reflected radio waves. As multipath interference is characterized by substantial local fluctuations in field strength (within a range of 50...100 cm), at least one of the vehicle's antennas can usually be counted on to be positioned for clear reception, provided that there is sufficient distance between them. The diversity system automatically switches over to the antenna with the best reception. Different systems are characterized by varying degrees of technical complexity.

a) <u>Conventional scanner (1-tuner diversity)</u>: Should the reception quality at antenna "A" fall below a specified level, the unit responds by tentatively switching to antenna "B". If "B" is even worse, then the unit reverts to "A". If "B" is better, the unit remains at "B".

b) <u>Selective process (multi-tuner diversity)</u>: Each antenna feeds to its own tuner. The system compares the reception quality at the respective antennas on a continuous, uninterrupted basis, using this information to select the antenna providing the best signal.

ADA (Auto-Directional Antenna): This is a multi-antenna reception system developed by Blaupunkt which uses a separate tuner with each antenna in a layout similar to that of the "selective process" described above. The salient difference lies in the fact that there is no alternation between antennas with ADA. Instead, the system processes all – up to four – antenna/tuner signals, modifying amplitudes and phase lengths as required for subsequent summation. A special control algorithm automatically processes amplitude and phase to ensure that minimal interference is reflected in the cumulative signal. The system can thus selectively deactivate reception from individual directions, electronically simulating the response of a directional antenna.

ADA has been designed for application

with several window antennas and/or simple wire and foil antennas in bumpers.

ASU: Automatic interference suppression for car radios, suppresses ignition noise in the FM band.

Output power: Amplified output which the car radio or auxiliary amplifier (booster) transmits to the speakers. DIN 45324 distinguishes between sinusoidal output (continuous power with pure tone) and music output (continuous power with complex sample signal) in watts. When units on the market are compared, max. power (brief maximum output power) is generally specified. The relationship between "volume" and "output" is exponential. The increase in volume produced by doubling the output is just barely audible (3 dB). More important is the speakers' efficiency factor (volume in dB/1W/1m). While "output variations in watts" play a secondary role in practice, technical justification for the installation of ultra-high-output systems may well be present in the form of reduced low-frequency distortion (→ Automotive speakers → Subwoofers).

CD (Compact Disc): 12- or 8-centimeter sound-reproduction medium featuring signals stored in digital form and playing time of more than 60 minutes. A laser beam is directed toward a reflective information layer for contactless optical scanning. Variations in this layer (pits) dampen the reflected beam received by the prism. A photo diode monitors this information for binary transmission to a digital-analog converter. A new 16-bit amplitude value is processed 44,100 times per second, providing the D/A converter with the data to reconstitute the original sound signal "bit by bit".

DigiCeiver: New technology developed by Blaupunkt in which the radio receiver digitally processes the signal through to the prestage output. The results in significant advantages in terms of reception performance and sound quality. A constituent part of the DigiCeiver concept is Sharx, a digitally variable filter for optimizing the selectivity. Radio stations which are very close together can thus be crisply picked out from each other.

DPE (Digital Parametric Equalizing): Steep-edged two-stage equalizer with freely selectable operating frequencies and filter levels with which unwanted resonances are effectively suppressed and frequency-response incursions of speakers are linearized. The sound becomes much more homogeneous and coherent.

DSA (Digital Signal Adaptation) comprises a digital 4-channel 9-band equalizer (self-calibrating or manually adjustable) and a DNC component (Dynamic Noise Covering). DNC permanently analyzes the driving noise with an external microphone and adapts the volume and sound of the radio accordingly on a frequency-selective basis. Its operation is adjustable in three stages.

RDS (Radio Data System): Digital data-transmission system for FM broadcasters, who transmit the RDS "data telegram" in a single standardized format throughout Europe. The data, which can be interpreted by car (or home) radios equipped with RDS decoders, include the following:
– The call letters or identity of the station being received (e.g., "BAYERN 3" or "BBC Radio 1") appear on the radio's display (PS Code).
– Also transmitted is a list of alternative frequencies on which the current broadcast can also be received (AF Code). The RDS receiver responds to reductions in the quality of reception from the station to which the radio is tuned by searching through the AF list for alternative frequencies for the same station. If the first alternative provides better reception, then the unit locks onto the new frequency. If it is worse, then RDS continues to the next substitute frequency. The process is virtually inaudible under ideal conditions (depending on individual unit design).
– Each station also has an identification number (PI Code) for backup verification. The PI code must remain constant when the system selects a substitute frequency, otherwise the system registers an impermissible station change.
– Traffic-information and announcement codes (TP and TA Codes). The RDS receiver evaluates TP and TA in a process

comparable to that employed for ARI-SK and DK (→ ARI). As most European countries are still without an ARI traffic-information system, implementation with RDS was a logical step. The present ARI system is expected to remain in place though in A, CH, D, and LUX, operating parallel to RDS, until 2005. In all North, South, and West-European countries, the stations of the national networks and most independent broadcasters can be received with the RDS services listed above.

The RDS format incorporates further options, e. g.:

- PTY Code (Program Type): Classifies up to 16 different program types according to their content, i.e., news, classical music, etc.
- "PTY 31": Control signal for superimposition of civil defense messages for the general population (similar to TA). The PTY 31 function cannot be deactivated.
- EON Code (Enhanced Other Networks): "EON" informs the receiver when a traffic announcement is being transmitted on a parallel program of a chain of stations, and can switch to this parallel broadcast for the announcement's duration.
- TMC Code (Traffic Message Channel): For transmitting standardized information bits, e. g., on traffic congestion. The information bits can be triggered for reproduction – in any language, at any time – via speech synthesizer. Navigation systems can monitor warnings on obstructions for immediate calculation of the best route for the given conditions.
- CT Code (Clock/Time): Time, date.
- RT Code (Radio Text): Text transmission for receiver with suitable display, e.g. display of music track currently being heard.

Auxiliary equipment

- **Amplifier, booster:** Separate auxiliary amplifier (→ Output power).
- **Equalizer:** Equalizers are employed to improve bass and treble response through graduated amplification and/or suppression of individual frequency ranges. The specific acoustical properties of the motor vehicle's interior result in distortions of emphasis (non-linear propagation); an equalizer can compensate for these distortions. Today, it is usually installed as a digital chip in top-line car radios → DPE, DSA.
- **CD changer:** CD player for installation in the luggage compartment/trunk. The CD changer is loaded with a disk magazine which is usually capable of holding up to 10 disks. The CDs and the individual tracks are selected using either a suitably-equipped radio or a separate remote-control unit.

Automotive speakers

The acoustical properties of the vehicle's interior, the speakers' locations and the speakers themselves all influence the quality of reproduction. The larger the speakers, the better the bass response (e. g., four x 160 mm system). Separate subwoofers are becoming popular in sound systems at the higher end of the price range; they can be hidden, e. g. below the rear tray or on the panel between passenger compartment and trunk. For optimal reproduction, subwoofer systems generally require powerful → Amplifiers.

Antennas

The effectiveness of a vehicle's antenna is directly proportional to its distance from the vehicle's major ground masses. Good reception is ensured by the telescoping rod antenna, also available as a motor-driven "automatic antenna". An alternative is the integral window or windshield-mounted antenna which is also available as an aftermarket unit for attaching to the inner surface of windshield or windows. Although it is more sensitive to direction, which puts it at a slight disadvantage relative to the rod-type unit, among its main advantages are the fact that it needs no maintenance and is unaffected by wear: In contrast to the rod antenna, the window unit causes no aerodynamic drag, and it requires no retraction space. A third alternative is a short, flexible whip antenna which is technically a compromise between the other two extremes.

Digital Audio Broadcasting DAB

Features
The new digital broadcasting system DAB is the most significant development in broadcast engineering within the framework of the European EUREKA 147 project since the introduction of FM. It offers the following features:
- safe and interference-free reception for both mobile and portable applications,
- CD-comparable sound quality,
- economical in frequencies due to sound-data reduction and mutual broadcasting networks,
- economical in power due to suitable transmission procedures and coding,
- suitable for international, national, regional and local radio and
- assured future on account of multimedia compatibility.

The system developed by the Eureka 147 DAB project and standardized by the European Telecommunications Standards Institute (ETSI) is up to now the only system which satisfies these requirements and for which the International Telecommunications Union (ITU) has voiced a recommendation.

Typically, 5 ... 7 radio stations and several data channels are combined into an ensemble. A station ensemble, e.g. all the stations of a German ARD broadcasting network (e.g. BR, WDR), is broadcast throughout the country on a mutual network so that the stations can be received everywhere on the same frequency. Band III (175 ... 239 MHz) is designated for national broadcasting while local radio is planned in the L-band (1453 ... 1491 MHz).

Through flexible division of an ensemble, it is possible to transmit other data such as video/television or Internet pages instead of the radio stations. These DAB-system applications have been introduced under the term DMB (Digital Multimedia Broadcasting). Its highly favorable mobile reception characteristics make it possible to provide drivers with intelligent telematics services (DAB/ITS). Under the title MEMO (Multimedia Environment for Mobiles), a return channel via GSM is on

offer for the DAB system. This enables the transmission of the Internet or other data services with high data rates and interactive user operation.

Principles of Eureka 147 DAB system
The DAB system is essentially based on three components:
- the sound-data reduction procedure in accordance with MPEG-1 (ISO 11172-3) or MPEG-2 (ISO 13818-3), Layer II in each case,
- the transmission procedure Coded Orthogonal Frequency Division Multiplexing (COFDM) and
- a flexible division of the transmission capacity into a variety of subchannels which, independently of each other, can transmit sound and data programs with differing data rates and with differing error-protection levels (DAB multiplex).

Audio coders are used for the data reduction of the individual radio stations. Channel coding is then employed to add the redundancy required for error correction in the receiver. Several data services can be combined in a packet multiplexer which is then also submitted to channel coding. The subchannels' channel-coded data are combined with the Fast Information Channel (FIC) data, which contain the multiplex and program-information structure, and are then COFDM-modulated. This generally takes place digitally in the form of a Fast-Fourier Transformation (FFT). The signal is converted from digital to analog, mixed to the corresponding transmit frequency, amplified, filtered and transmitted.

The antenna signal is converted to the intermediate frequency (IF) in the high-frequency stage and then filtered and digitized. The information is then recovered from the individual COFDM carriers (generally by means of an FFT again). Here, in principle only that part of the data which contains the desired programs needs to be evaluated.

After error correction (by Viterbi decoding), the data are either directed to the audio decoder, which recovers the sound signal, or made available for further use at an appropriate data interface. The FIC data are used to control and operate the receiver.

For sound-data reduction, Eureka 147 has settled on the procedure complying with MPEG-1 Layer II and several supplements from the follow-up standard MPEG-2 Layer II, which is sometimes also (although incorrectly) referred to as the "Musicam procedure". The advantage of this procedure is that it permits high compression factors while maintaining manageable complexity and relatively short delays in coding and decoding. With data rates of 160...256 kBit/s, for stereo transmission it provides quality which is comparable to that of a CD.

The COFDM procedure is particularly well-suited to providing reliable multi-channel reception and shared-channel broadcasting by networks. The essential concept of the procedure is to divide the entire data stream into many data sub-streams (192...1536). Each of these sub-streams is transmitted on a subcarrier with a low data rate and thus a long symbol duration (magnitude 100 μs...1 ms). The symbol duration for COFDM is therefore significantly greater than the typical propagation-time differences of the received signal elements (magnitude 10...100 μs). In this way, and due to the additional protection interval, it is even possible to avoid intersymbol interference completely. Error protection coding is used to eliminate remaining bit errors.

A bandwidth of 1.536 MHz has been selected for DAB. There are four parameter records for the COFDM procedure, which facilitate the implementation of both terrestrial common-frequency networks in Band III and the L-band, as well as satellite broadcasting up to 3 GHz. The number of COFDM subcarriers amounts here to 1536, 768, 384 or 192 and the carrier spacing is accordingly 1, 2, 4 or 8 kHz.

On account of the choice of bandwidth, the DAB system offers a considerably higher data rate than is needed to transmit a radio program. For this reason, several programs and data services are combined to form a multiplex which is then transmitted. All the stations transmitted on a DAB multiplex are jointly termed an "ensemble". The ensemble multiplex is flexible, both in terms of the number and data rate of the individual subchannels and also in terms of its error protection, i.e. the redundancy added for transmission. With minimum redundancy, the bit rate of the DAB system can extend to 1.84 MBit/s while it is possible to start out from approx. 1.2 MBit/s for mobile reception.

Because the multiplex is flexible, the receivers must be informed as to how the multiplex of the DAB ensemble that has just been received is configured or when and how it will be reconfigured. This process takes place in the Fast Information Channel (FIC). All other data which is needed to operate and control the receiver, e.g. station names and alternative frequencies, are transmitted on this channel.

The combination described above of sound-data reduction, COFDM, and flexible multiplex, makes DAB an extremely versatile system whose applications can extend far beyond traditional radio broadcasting. In the end, these will lead to digital multimedia broadcasting, which can also be received in cars and with portable devices.

Parking systems

Parking aid with ultrasonic sensors

Introduction

On virtually all motor vehicles, in order to reduce fuel consumption the bodies have been designed and developed in such a way as to achieve the lowest possible drag-coefficient values. Generally speaking, this trend has resulted in a gentle wedge shape which greatly restricts the driver's view when maneuvering. Obstacles can only be poorly discerned – if at all.

Parking aids with ultrasonic sensors provide drivers with effective support when parking. They monitor an area of approx. 30 cm to 150 cm behind or in front of the vehicle. Obstacles are detected and brought to the driver's attention by optical and/or acoustic means.

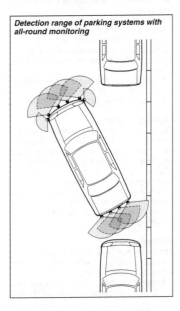

Detection range of parking systems with all-round monitoring

System

The system comprises the following components: ECU, warning element and ultrasonic sensors.

On vehicles with only rear-end protection, usually 4 ultrasonic sensors are installed in the rear bumper.

Additional front-end protection is provided by installing a further 4 to 6 ultrasonic sensors in the front bumper.

The system is activated automatically when reverse gear is engaged or, in a system with additional front-end protection, when the vehicle drops below a speed threshold of approx. 15 km/h. The system's self-test function ensures that all the system components are permanently monitored during operation.

Ultrasonic sensor

Following a principle that is the same as echo depth sounding, the sensors transmit ultrasonic pulses with a frequency of approx. 40 kHz and detect the time taken for the echo pulses to be reflected back from obstacles. The distance of the vehicle to the nearest obstacle is calculated from the propagation time of the first echo pulse to be received back according to the formula:

$$a = 0.5 \cdot t_e \cdot c$$

t_e Propagation time of ultrasonic signal(s)
c Speed of sound in air (approx. 340 m/s)

The sensors themselves consist of a plastic housing with integrated plug connection, an aluminum diaphragm on the inner side of which a piezoceramic water is attached, and a printed-circuit board with transmit and evaluation electronics. They are electrically connected to the ECU by three leads, two of which serve to supply power. The third, bidirectional signal line is responsible for activating the transmit function and returning the evaluated received signal to the ECU. When the sensor receives a digital transmit pulse from the ECU, the electronic circuit excites the aluminum diaphragm with square-wave pulses at the resonant frequency so that it vibrates, and ultrasound is emitted. The diaphragm, which in the meantime has returned to rest, is made to vibrate again by

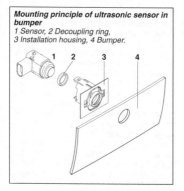

Mounting principle of ultrasonic sensor in bumper
1 Sensor, 2 Decoupling ring,
3 Installation housing, 4 Bumper.

Antenna emitting diagram of an ultrasonic sensor
1 Vertical, 2 Horizontal.

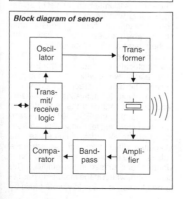

Block diagram of sensor

the sound reflected back from the obstacle. These vibrations are converted by the piezoceramic wafer into an analog electrical signal which is then amplified and converted into a digital signal by the sensor electronics.

In order to be able to cover as extensive a range as possible, the detection characteristic must fulfill special requirements. In the horizontal range, a wide detection angle is desirable. In the vertical range, however, it is necessary to have a smaller angle in order to avoid interference from ground reflections. A compromise is needed here so that obstacles can be reliably detected.

Specifically adapted mounting brackets secure the sensors in their respective positions in the bumper.

ECU

The ECU contains a voltage stabilizer for the sensors, an integrated microprocessor and all the interface circuits needed to adapt the different input and output signals. The software assumes the following functions:

- sensor activation and echo reception,
- propagation-time evaluation and calculation of obstacle distance,
- activation of the warning elements,
- evaluation of the input signals from the vehicle,
- monitoring of the system components including fault storage and
- provision of the diagnostic function.

Warning elements

The warning elements identify the distance to an obstacle. Their design is vehicle-specific, and they usually provide for a combination of acoustic signal and optical display. Both LEDs and LCDs are currently used for optical displays.

In the example of a warning element shown here, the indication of the distance to the obstacle is divided into 4 main ranges (see table).

Protection area

The protection area is determined by the range and number of sensors and by their emission characteristic.

Experience has shown that 4 sensors are sufficient for rear-end protection, and

Range	Distance s	Opt. display LED	Acoustic signal
I	<1.5 m	green	Intermittent
II	<1.0 m	green + yellow	Intermittent
III	<0.5 m	green + yellow + red	Continuous
IV	<0.3 m	All LEDs flash	Continuous

4 to 6 for front-end protection. The sensors are integrated in the bumpers, which means that the distance to the ground is already fixed.

The installation angle of, and the gaps between the sensors are vehicle-specific. These data are taken into account in the ECU's calculation algorithms. At the time of going to press, application engineering had already been carried out on more than 150 different vehicle types. Thus, even older vehicles can be retrofitted.

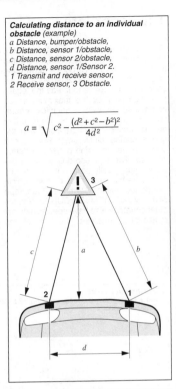

Calculating distance to an individual obstacle (example)
a Distance, bumper/obstacle,
b Distance, sensor 1/obstacle,
c Distance, sensor 2/obstacle,
d Distance, sensor 1/Sensor 2.
1 Transmit and receive sensor,
2 Receive sensor, 3 Obstacle.

$$a = \sqrt{c^2 - \frac{(d^2 + c^2 - b^2)^2}{4d^2}}$$

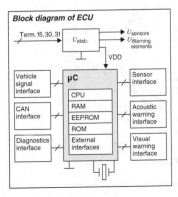

Block diagram of ECU

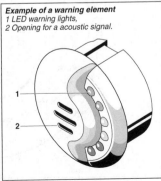

Example of a warning element
1 LED warning lights,
2 Opening for a acoustic signal.

Trip recorders

These devices record the vehicle speed, the distance covered (odometer), and the time. They also incorporate a warning lamp which is triggered when vehicles exceed a preset speed (such as the legally permitted limit, or the maximum speed commensurate with economical operation). The following data is also recorded on the tachograph chart along with the corresponding clock time: Road-speed curve, wheel time and pauses, distance covered. The trip recorder, which is designed specifically so that it can be calibrated, is mandatory for certain vehicle categories within Germany (Paragraph 57b, StVZO (FMVSS/CUR)). Various other countries also have specific national regulations governing the use of trip recorders.

Mode of operation

The EC tachograph is a special form of trip recorder which incorporates an auxiliary feature allowing differentiated recording of wheel time and test periods (time-group monitor); different versions are available, for either one driver or two. The EC tachograph meets all the requirements set forth in EEC Directive 3821/85, i.e., the EC tachograph charts serve as the driver's official daily record. Within the countries of the European Union, the EC tachograph is obligatory equipment on specific types of vehicle, where it monitors compliance with the time behind the wheel and the rest periods prescribed in EEC Directive 3820/85. The supplementary features on the EC tachograph include a clock-function display and an LED which confirms to the driver that the charts are installed and that all styluses are functioning properly.

Some tachographs also display and record engine speed. Operation control and further parameters can also be recorded when the appropriate options

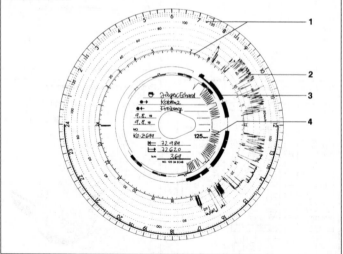

EC tachograph chart
1 Clock time scales, 2 Speed recordings, 3 Driving and stationary times (time group recording),
4 Distance traveled.

are installed. These include the two-stage auxiliary stylus (e.g., for recording fuel consumption) and contacts which trigger other warning and control devices in response to vehicle and engine speed.

Trip recorders and EC tachographs must maintain the strict operating tolerances defined in the German Calibration Regulations, in Paragraph 57b of the StVZO (FMVSS/ CUR) and in EEC Directive 3821/ 85. These regulations also extend to govern periodic inspection of tachograph and related equipment by authorized facilities.

The tachograph chart can be interpreted using any of several methods, including visual, electronic and microscopic evaluation. Visual evaluation is the simplest method, as the chart disk makes it possible to appraise and check an entire day's operation at a glance. Systematic visual evaluation embraces the following individual checks: Written entries, working time, breaks, rest periods, assessment of driving style, fuel consumption and engine speed, as well as manipulated or incorrect recordings. Microscopic examination uses a special microscope to analyze the recording down to a precision range measured in seconds and meters. The data gathered can be entered in a time/distance graph (see illustration) for precise reconstruction, e. g., of the events preceding an accident.

Within the framework of a fleet-management system, tachograph charts can also be subjected to semi- or fully automatic evaluation and the data processed in a computer.

Pulse drive is employed on tachographs featuring electronic monitoring systems. It runs on signals produced by a pulse generator, installed either within the vehicle or at the transmission's speedometer-drive gear, which converts the mechanical rotation of the speedometer pinion into electronic pulses.

The most modern electronic trip recorders and EC tachographs incorporate an integral conversion feature to adapt the unit for variations in the number of pulses per kilometer traveled. No extraneous devices are required. On vehicles with variable-ratio rear axles, a conversion-gear unit modifies the ratio of the tachograph's drive signal to maintain synchronization with vehicle conditions.

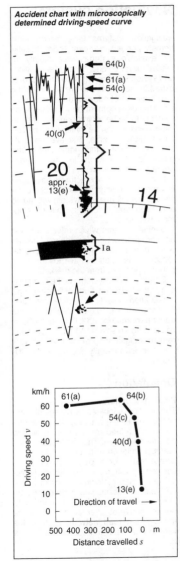

Accident chart with microscopically determined driving-speed curve

Navigation systems

Navigation systems have become extremely popular in recent years. Initially, the available systems were mainly intended for retrofitting. Since then, navigation systems are mainly fitted as optional extras on new cars and are no longer the sole preserve of a few luxury-sedan models. This development has enabled such systems to be better integrated in the vehicle. Sensors can be jointly used by various vehicle systems. Displays in the instrument cluster place important route-guidance information in the driver's primary field of vision.

Some vehicle manufacturers have even incorporated navigation as part of a complete driver information system with audio and telephone functions. This development will continue.

Simple systems which offer the driver no more than a mere indication of his/her position on a card and a straight-line direction to destination, have for the most part disappeared from the market.

Common to all systems is the combination of the basic functions of "positioning", "destination selection", "route computation" and "route guidance". Systems in the upper performance spectrum also offer a color map display. All the functions require a digital map of the road network and this is generally stored on a CD-ROM.

Orientation

Position location

The position is located by means of composite positioning whereby the route elements are added cyclically according to amount and angle. This process involves the accumulation of errors but these are compensated for by permanent comparison of the position with the road in the digital map (map matching). Thanks to the GPS satellite positioning system, the navigation system can still be operated without any problems after short trips outside the digitized road network or after the vehicle has been transported by sea or rail.

Sensors

For positioning purposes, it was frequently the case that two wheel sensors were used to determine the travel and changes of direction, and a geomagnetic sensor was used to determine the absolute direction of travel. Essentially, the GPS positioning system served to correct heavy sensor interference or to locate the correct point of reentry into the stored road network after trips outside the range of the digital map. More modern systems only need a simple travel signal, as is already often available for speed-dependent volume control of car radios. The change of direction is determined by a yaw-rate sensor (gyrometer). The geomagnetic sensor has become superfluous as it has now become possible to determine the absolute direction of travel via the Doppler effect from the GPS signals.

Destination entry

Directories

The digital CD map contains directories so that a destination can be entered as an address. Lists of all the locations (towns, villages) available on the CD are required for this purpose. In turn, all locations are allocated lists containing the names of the stored roads/streets. For further precise pinpointing of destinations, it is also possible to select road/street intersections or street numbers. However, the availability of house numbers is still very limited due to the prohibitive expenditure involved in ascertaining such data. Drivers rarely know the addresses of destinations such as airports, rail stations, service stations, car parks and many more. For this reason, there are classified directories listing these destinations, which are also frequently called points of interest (POIs). With these directories, it is even possible for instance to find a filling station in the vicinity of one's vehicle. Marking a destination in the map display or calling up destinations which were previously stored in a destination memory are further selection options.

Travel guides

As a logical development of selecting POIs, CDs are now available with travel guides as the result of joint cooperation between publishing companies and the manufacturers of the digital maps. For instance, these CDs can be used to look up hotels in the vicinity of the destination. Information on size, prices and facilities of the POIs are also contained on the CDs.

Route computation

Destination selection

It must be possible to adapt the route computation to the driver's wishes. Settings for optimizing the route in accordance with driving time or mileage are available in many systems. Route computation should take care of such assignments as avoiding freeways/motorways, ferry connections and toll roads. Initial computation of the route once the destination has been selected must be completed inside half a minute. If the driver departs from the recommended route, it is critical for the system to recompute the route still more quickly. The option to request an alternative route at the touch of a button is helpful in that it enables the driver to bypass traffic congestion ahead.

Dynamic routing

Automatic bypassing of traffic congestion is already possible through evaluation of RDS-TMC-coded traffic messages. These can be received by way of RDS or GSM.

Route guidance

Determination of route

Route guidance is performed by comparing the present position with the computed route. From the sequence of the road section just covered and the roads still to be covered on the route, the system can decide whether the driver must make a turn-off maneuver or simply continue along the present road.

Route and direction recommendation

The route and direction recommendations are first and foremost issued acoustically. This enables the driver to follow the directions without being distracted from his/her job of driving. Simple graphics, if at all possible in the primary field of

vision (instrument cluster), support the driver in understanding the directions. The conciseness of these acoustic and graphic directions is the decisive factor in the quality of route guidance. Identifying the direction to be taken from a map in the display is not considered a primary option as this distracts the driver.

Dynamic routing

Traffic congestion is automatically bypassed by evaluating the coded traffic messages which are transmitted inaudibly over the Traffic-Message Channel of the Radio Data System (RDS-TMC) parallel to the radio program. They are already available in GSM services.

Map display

Depending on the system, the map can be displayed on a color monitor with a scale ranging between approx. 1:8000 and 1:16 million. It is helpful, depending on the scale, in maintaining an overview of the route in the vicinity or on a more far-ranging scale. Driver orientation is supported by the provision of topographical background information showing such things as lakes, rivers and canals, built-up areas, railroads and forests.

Road-map memory

The CD-ROM has become the primary medium for storing road maps. The structures of the data stored on them represent manufacturer-specific know-how and significantly influence system performance. For this reason, the CDs presently on the market for systems of different manufacturers are not compatible with each other. Efforts are being made however to standardize navigation CDs.

With the size of the digitized areas, the completeness of recording the road network and the increasing wealth of additional information, the capacity of the CD-ROM (which initially seemed so great) will be exhausted in the foreseeable future. The Digital Versatile Disc (DVD), with many times the capacity of the CD-ROM, has already been marked out as its successor.

Traffic telematics

The word "telematics" is derived from the contraction of the words "telecommunications" and "informatics". Accordingly, the transmission of traffic-related information from and to motor vehicles, and its subsequent, mostly automatic evaluation is combined under the term "traffic telematics".

Transmission paths

Today, the main transmission paths for telecommunications are provided by radio and mobile radiocommunications networks.

Radio only allows a path into the vehicle and does not serve to communicate individual messages. With GSM, information can be exchanged in both directions between vehicles and control centers run by service providers. The amount of information exchanged is restricted in each case by the bandwidth of the available transmission channels. It is therefore essential that the coding of standardized message content is as free as possible of redundant information.

Standardization

In the case of reports of traffic holdups, the standardization of content refers for instance to the type of holdup (such as "jam", "road block"), to the causes (such as "accident", "black ice") and to its extent and expected duration. Coding of the location of a traffic holdup is also necessary.

While a person can interpret spoken messages with his/her geographical experience and e.g. the signposts in his/her surroundings, this option is not available for computer-controlled evaluation of information.

The coding of the designations for geographical regions, longer freeway/motorway sections (segments), and individual road points (locations) such as freeway/motorway junctions and intersections, has been standardized to permit transmission over the Traffic Message Channel of the Radio Data System (RDS-TMC).

For traffic-telematics applications using the Short Message Service (SMS) in GSM networks, service providers have drawn up the Global Automotive Telematics Standard (GATS), which is used for breakdown and emergency calls, information services and traffic-data acquisition in accordance with the Floating Car Data principle described below.

Selection

One of the strengths of traffic telematics is its ability to select from a frequently very large stream of information those messages which are of relevance to the driver. For instance, by evaluating the vehicle's position, microcomputers in the vehicle can determine which traffic message could affect the vehicle's route.

Decoding of traffic messages

Decoding and selection of TMC-coded traffic messages are today already integrated features in 1-block car radios, such as the Blaupunkt "VIKING TMC 148". The driver can enter up to 5 freeways/motorways, national highways or regions for which a selection of messages is to be performed. These are then converted by a voice-output chip into audible messages. Because the messages conform to standardized information groups, there is also no problem in converting them into different languages.

Telematics services

Devices such as the Blaupunkt "Gemini GPS 148" have a GSM module and a receiver for the Global Positioning System (GPS). As well as normal telephone functions, the GSM module also facilitates the bidirectional transmission of messages via SMS. The GPS module enables the vehicle's position to be pinpointed to an accuracy of approx. 100 m. Such devices can make use of telematics services such as "traffic information", "breakdown calls" and "calls for assistance".

Traffic messages can be selected as a function of the vehicle's actual location and direction of travel, and also through selection of freeways/motorways and national highways. In the event of a breakdown, the driver can establish a telephone link to a control center at the touch of a button. At the same time, the vehicle's position is transmitted via SMS.

For future GSM services, the functions of the devices can be extended by loading new software.

Dynamic route guidance

The most extensively automated evaluation of traffic information is performed for the purposes of dynamic route guidance. Thanks to standardized coding of locations (see "Standardization"), disturbances and their extent and expected duration, computers in route-guidance systems can assess the effect of a traffic holdup on the driver's route and then assess whether there is a better alternative route.

In this case, the driver is instructed that the route has been recalculated on account of traffic messages. Subsequent route directions follow in accordance with the new route.

For dynamic route guidance, it is necessary for the CDs, which usually carry the digital map for route-guidance systems, to include a reference table covering the locations of the traffic messages.

The traffic messages are received either through an FM receiver with RDS decoder or through SMS from GSM networks.

Systems with dynamic route guidance have been available since 1998, and have rapidly become popular because of their comfort and convenience for the driver.

Information collection

The benefit to drivers presented by traffic telematics can only be as good as the information used. In particular, the up-to-dateness of the messages has not been without problems.

Information collection by way of road infrastructure

For many years now, information about the traffic flow on important stretches of road has been recorded by induction loops inserted in the roads themselves. Using these loops, the number and speed of the vehicles passing over the loops can be ascertained, and the figures used to calculate the traffic density (vehicles per km) and traffic intensity (vehicles per hour). There has been a marked step-up in the installation of such loops in recent years, but this is a time-consuming and expensive process.

Alternatively, GSM service providers install sensors on freeway/motorway bridges. These are powered by solar cells and transmit their information without electric cables. They are simple and cheap to install, but due to their system of measurement they are limited to counting vehicles and roughly classifying their speed.

Floating Car Data

A further option for collecting traffic information involves the Floating Car Data principle.

A car "floats" along in the flow of traffic and transmits its position and speed cyclically to a control center. In the control center, statistical analysis of the individually collected data is employed to generate current messages on the traffic situation. For this method, all vehicles have a bidirectional connection (such as SMS). However, the precondition for the collection of statistically reliable data is that there is a high percentage of appropriately equipped vehicles on the road. Because this is not yet the case, this procedure has up to now only been used in field tests. Since the vehicle percentage was still not high enough in the field tests, final proof of effectiveness is still to come.

Mobile radio

Mobile radiocommunications systems can be divided into two categories: Public radio networks (car phones, etc.) and private mobile radio (or PMR). The public radio networks are – like their land-line counterparts – universal-access systems. In contrast, access to a PMR system is restricted to specific groups. Mobile radio networks consist of mobile transmitter/receiver units (mobile stations) and the requisite infrastructure (system administration, stationary units and base stations). Attempts to economize on the number of necessary frequencies have led to the establishment of cellular networks; these make it possible to use the same frequency repeatedly in numerous cells, provided that the distances between the cells are sufficient. The precise number of stationary transmitters employed in a single network depends upon the size of the area being served and/or the number of subscribers. Mobile radio units fall into three categories: Vehicle units, portable radios and hand-held devices.

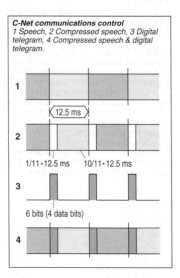

C-Net communications control
1 Speech, 2 Compressed speech, 3 Digital telegram, 4 Compressed speech & digital telegram.

Cellular telephone networks

Communications within the mobile telephone network are always established via a stationary base station; the network is not restricted to providing communications between mobile units, and access to and from the standard land-line telephone system is also possible. At present, there are (technically different) analog cellular telephone networks and digital systems (D-Net: GSM, E-Net) in operation in Europe.

C-Net
This radio-telephone network operates in Germany in the 450 MHz band.

The speech transmission utilizes analog modulation. The communications path between two units is established and monitored with digital telegrams relayed on special organization channels. The system administration facility continually monitors existing communications links on the oral-communications channels by slotting digital telegrams into gaps in the speech transmission. The speech transmission is subdivided into blocks of 12.5 ms. Before transmission, these blocks are compressed into time units of 10/11 x 12.5 ms. The digital telegrams are inserted into the resulting gaps of 1/11 x 12.5 ms. Upon arrival at the receiver, the telegram is filtered from the transmission signal and the speech is re-expanded to its original value of 12.5 ms. In recent years, there has been a drop-off in the number of users in favor of the digital networks.

D- and E-Net
The Europe-wide digitized cellular mobile-telephone system GSM (Global System for Mobile Communications) in the 900 MHz range (E-Nets in the 1.86 GHz range) is intended to overcome the compatibility problems of the various European analog telephone systems. In contrast to the analog telephone networks, in the D- and E-Net the speech is transmitted in digital form. Here, 8 speech channels each with 16 kbit/s, or 16 speech channels with 8 kbit/s, are superimposed upon a high-frequency channel with a bandwidth of 200 kHz. Speech-channel

access inside the high-frequency channel utilizes the TDMA (Time-Division Multiple Access) method.

Private mobile radio systems (PMR)

These are mobile-radio networks designed specifically to meet the individual operational requirements of given customer groups. The essential object is to provide total radio coverage within a specific, well-defined area, thus ensuring consistent access to the mobile stations. For analog PMR systems, the typical times for establishing a link are below 1 second, whereas in special operating modes ("open channel") no time at all is needed to establish a link.

The most important subscriber groups are:
– Electric utilities,
– Public-transport authorities,
– Official agencies and security organizations,
– Common-frequency subscribers,
– Taxi and rental-car agencies.

Various analog and digital signaling procedures are employed to administer the communications links. Selective-call networks allow the user to call a specific individual station. The most important signaling procedures are the 5-tone sequence and the digital calling methods. The five digits of the 5-tone sequence contain the code for the station address of the party being called, with each digit being assigned a value of 0...9. Each number represents a frequency. The transmission time for each number is 70 ms.

Upon receiving and processing the 5-tone sequence, the target station transmits an acknowledge signal in the form of its own 5-tone sequence, while a call tone is also generated to alert the caller. This establishes the communications link.

Systems employing a digital calling system represent a further development of the tone-sequence method. The data in the "call" and "acknowledge" telegrams are contained in binary codes. Frequencies of 1,800 Hz and 1,200 Hz are assigned to the bits "0" and "1" respectively. The advantage over the tone-sequence method lies in the fact that the digital telegram can relay additional status information over and beyond the target address.

Trunked radio networks

In order to eliminate the increasing frequency-crowding which was plaguing the PMR networks, the German Post Office's TELEKOM division set up trunked radio networks in the 400 MHz band. The object is to increase utilization efficiency through common use and administration of several radio channels. Under the same conditions, the system accommodates more users on each channel than a conventional network. It provides good access within the trunked radio network and exclusive communications links. The possibility of dialing from the mobile station into the public land-line telephone system should be mentioned.

The link is administered through a special radio frequency within the frequency group (organization channel), as defined by Specification MPT 1327 (MPT, Ministry of Post and Telecommunications). The digital trunked radio network TETRA-25 (Trans-European Trunked Radio) has been specified by the European Telecommunications Standards Institute (ETSI). This TDMA (Time Division Multiplex Access) procedure uses a channel grid of 25 kHz each with four time slots in the 400 MHz range. The bit rate is 36 kbit/s (overall) per carrier frequency.

Another digital trunked radio network – TETRAPOL – uses the FDMA (Frequency Division Multiplex Access) procedure with a narrow-band channel grid of 10 or 12.5 kHz. The bit rate here is 8 kbit/s (overall) per carrier frequency.

The European railways are planning a radio-transmission procedure based on GSM technology (GSM 2+, GSM-Railway) for their radiocommunications operations.

Vehicle information system

In addition to the display and control elements for the predominantly vehicle-related functions, there is an increasing array of information, communication and comfort applications in a modern-day motor vehicle. The radio is virtually a standard feature, and telephone, navigation system etc. are following this trend. Each of these further applications would normally require its own display, specially configured controls and a different procedure for its operation. This agglomeration of controls and displays would place additional burdens on the driver and, under certain circumstances, would no longer satisfy future requirements for comfort and road safety. The motor-vehicle information system provides the driver with a standardized "user interface" for an assortment of different applications.
This system combines the display and operating elements from several applications within a single display and operating unit. A substantial reduction in the number of input and output elements facilitates implementation of an ergonomically satisfactory control layout. In the face of increasing complexity, the vehicle information system furnishes an opportunity to design clear, convenient vehicle instrumentation, an endeavor in which traffic safety is one of the chief beneficiaries. The display and operating unit maintains mutual (bidirectional) communication with the connected components via a bus system (e.g. CAN) to control and indicate information in the display.

The most important control functions are mainly input via input elements which can be located by the driver "without looking" within his/her immediate reach and also via control elements on the steering wheel. More extensive programming tasks (such as storing automatic-dialing codes for telephone numbers) can be performed by remote control; safety considerations dictate that this type of programming is only carried out with the vehicle stationary.

The central display serves to indicate the most varied of image information such as texts, pictures and videos. Information that is important to the driver while driving (e.g. name of the traffic program station being received, or a direction arrow as a navigation instruction) can be shown in a display in the instrument cluster. A voice-output facility can provide the optical display with additional support. In the future, a voice-input facility will assist the driver in any number of system functions.

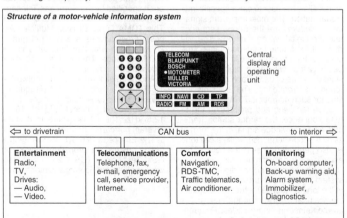

Structure of a motor-vehicle information system

TELECOM BLAUPUNKT BOSCH • MOTOMETER MÜLLER VICTORIA	Central display and operating unit
INFO NAVI CD TP RADIO FM AM RDS	

⇐ to drivetrain   CAN bus   to interior ⇒

Entertainment	**Telecommunications**	**Comfort**	**Monitoring**
Radio, TV, Drives: — Audio, — Video.	Telephone, fax, e-mail, emergency call, service provider, Internet.	Navigation, RDS-TMC, Traffic telematics, Air conditioner.	On-board computer, Back-up warning aid, Alarm system, Immobilizer, Diagnostics.

Safety systems

Safety in motor vehicles

Active and passive safety
Active safety systems help prevent accidents and thus make a preventive contribution to safety in road traffic. One example of an active driving safety system is the Antilock Braking System (ABS) with Electronic Stability Program (ESP) from Bosch, which stabilizes the vehicle even in critical braking situations and maintains steerability in the process.

Passive safety systems serve to protect the occupants against serious or even fatal injuries. An example of passive safety are the airbags, which protect the occupants following an unavoidable impact.

Occupant safety systems

Seat belts and seat-belt tighteners

Function
The function of seat belts is to restrain the occupants of a vehicle in their seats when the vehicle hits an obstacle.

Seat-belt tighteners improve the restraining characteristics of a three-point inertia-reel belt and increase the protection against injury. In the event of a frontal impact, they pull the seat belts tighter against the body and thus hold the upper body as closely as possible against the seat backrest. This prevents excessive forward displacement of the occupants caused by mass inertia (see Fig.).

Operating concept
In a frontal impact with a solid obstacle at a speed of 50 km/h, the seat belts must absorb a level of energy comparable to the kinetic energy of a person in free fall from the 4th floor of a building.

Because of the belt slack, the belt stretch and the delayed effect of the belt retractor ("film-reel effect"), three-point inertia-reel belts provide only limited protection in frontal impacts with solid obstacles at speeds of over 40 km/h because they can no longer safely prevent the head and body from impacting against the steering wheel or the instrument panel. An occupant experiences extensive forward displacement without restraint systems (see Fig. on next page).

In an impact, the shoulder belt tightener compensates for the belt slack and the "film-reel effect" by retracting and tighten-

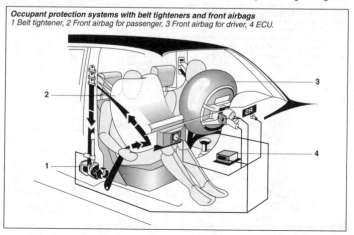

Occupant protection systems with belt tighteners and front airbags
1 Belt tightener, 2 Front airbag for passenger, 3 Front airbag for driver, 4 ECU.

ing the belt strap. At an impact speed of 50 km/h, this system achieves its full effect within the first 20 ms of the impact; and thus supports the airbag which needs approx. 40 ms to inflate completely. The occupant continues to move forward slightly until making contact with the deflating airbag and in this manner is protected from injury.

A prerequisite for optimum protection is that the occupants' forward movement away from their seats remain minimal as they decelerate along with the vehicle. This is achieved by triggering the belt tighteners immediately upon initial impact to ensure that safe restraint of the occupants in the front seats starts as soon as possible. The maximum forward displacement with tightened seat belts is approx. 1 cm and the duration of mechanical tightening is 5...10 ms.

On activation, a pyrotechnic propellant charge is electrically fired. The explosive pressure acts on a piston, which turns the belt reel via a steel cable in such a way that the belt rests tightly against the body (see Fig.).

Variants
In addition to the above-mentioned shoulder-belt tighteners for retracting the belt reel, there are variants which pull the belt buckle back (buckle tighteners) and thus simultaneously tighten the shoulder and lap belts. The restraining effect and the protection afforded against occupants sliding forward beneath the lap belt ("submarining effect") are improved still further by buckle tighteners. The tightening process in these two systems takes place in the same period of time as for shoulder-belt tighteners.

Mechanical belt tighteners are also available in addition to the pyrotechnically triggered versions. In the case of a mechanical tightener, a mechanical or electrical sensor releases a pretensioned spring, which pulls the belt buckle back. The sole advantage of these systems is that they are cheaper.

Further developments
The tightening performance of pyrotechnical seat-belt tighteners is continually being improved: "high-performance tighteners" are able to pull back an extended belt approx. 18 cm in length in roughly 5 ms.

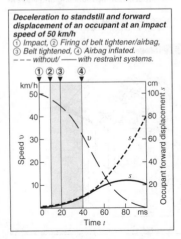

Deceleration to standstill and forward displacement of an occupant at an impact speed of 50 km/h
① Impact, ② Firing of belt tightener/airbag,
③ Belt tightened, ④ Airbag inflated.
– – – without/ —— with restraint systems.

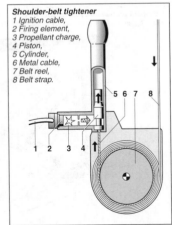

Shoulder-belt tightener
1 Ignition cable,
2 Firing element,
3 Propellant charge,
4 Piston,
5 Cylinder,
6 Metal cable,
7 Belt reel,
8 Belt strap.

Front airbag

Function

The function of front airbags is to protect the driver and the front passenger against head and chest injuries in a vehicle impact with a solid obstacle at speeds of up to 60 km/h. In a frontal impact between two vehicles, the front airbags afford protection at relative speeds of up to 100 km/h. A belt tightener alone cannot prevent the head from hitting the steering wheel in response to severe impact. In order to fulfill this function, depending on the installation location, vehicle type and structure-deformation response, airbags have different filling capacities and pressure build-up sequences adapted to the specific vehicle conditions.

In a few vehicle types, front airbags also operate in conjunction with "inflatable knee pads", which safeguard the "ride down benefit", i.e. the speed decrease of the occupants together with the speed decrease of the passenger cell. This ensures the rotational forward motion of the upper body and head which is actually needed for optimal airbag protection, and is of particular benefit in countries where seat-belt usage is not mandatory.

Operating concept

To protect driver and front passenger, pyrotechnical gas inflators inflate the driver and passenger airbags in pyrotechnical, highly dynamic fashion after a vehicle impact detected by sensors. In order for the affected occupant to enjoy maximum protection, the airbag must be fully inflated before the occupant comes into contact with it. The airbag then responds to upper-body contact with partial deflation in a response pattern calculated to combine "gentle" impact-energy absorption with non-critical (in terms of injury) surface pressures and decelerative forces for the occupant. This concept significantly reduces or even prevents head and chest injuries.

The maximum permissible forward displacement before the driver's airbag is fully inflated is approx. 12.5 cm, corresponding to a period of approx. 10 ms + 30 ms = 40 ms after the initial impact (at 50 km/h with a solid obstacle) (see Fig.

"Deceleration to standstill"). It needs 10 ms for electronic firing to take place and 30 ms for the airbag to inflate.

In a 50 km/h crash, the airbag takes approx. 40 ms to inflate fully and a further 80...100 ms to deflate through the deflation holes. The entire process thus takes little more than a tenth of a second, i.e. the batting of an eyelid.

Impact detection

Optimal occupant protection against the effects of frontal, offset, oblique or pole impact is obtained through the precisely coordinated interplay of electrically fired pyrotechnical front airbags and seat-belt tighteners. To maximize the effect of both protective devices, they are activated with optimized time response by a common ECU (triggering unit) installed in the passenger cell. The ECU's deceleration calculations are based on data from one or two electronic acceleration sensors used to monitor the decelerative forces that accompany an impact. The impact must also be analyzed. A hammer blow in the workshop, gentle pushing, driving over a curbstone or a pothole should not trigger the airbag. With this end in mind, the sensor signals are processed in digital analysis algorithms whose sensitivity parameters have been optimized with the aid of crash-data simulations. Depending on the impact type, the first trigger threshold is reached within 5...60 ms. The acceleration characteristics, which are influenced for instance by the vehicle equipment and the body's deformation performance, are different for each vehicle. They determine the setting parameters which are of crucial importance for the sensitivity in the analysis algorithm (computing process) and, in the end, for airbag and belt-tightener firing. Depending on the vehicle-manufacturer's production concept, the trigger parameters and the extent of vehicle equipment can also be programmed into the ECU at the end of the assembly line ("end-of-line programming" or "EoL programming").

In order to prevent injuries caused by airbags or fatalities to "out-of-position" occupants or to small children in Reboard child seats, it is essential that the front airbags are triggered and inflated in accordance with the particular situations. The following improvement measures are available for this purpose:

1. <u>Deactivation switches</u>. These switches can be used to deactivate the driver or passenger airbag. The airbag function states are indicated by special lamps.

2. In the USA, where there have been approx. 130 fatalities caused by airbags, attempts are being made to reduce aggressive inflation by introducing "<u>depowered airbags</u>". These are airbags whose gas-inflator power has been reduced by 20...30 %, which itself reduces the inflation speed, the inflation severity and the risk of injury to "out-of-position" occupants. "Depowered airbags" can thus be depressed more easily by large and heavy occupants, i.e. they have a reduced energy-absorption capacity. It is therefore essential – above all with regard to the possibility of severe frontal impacts – for the occupants to fasten their seat belts.

3. "<u>Intelligent airbag systems</u>". The introduction of improved sensing functions and control options for the airbag inflation process, with the accompanying improvement of the protective effect, is intended to result in a step-by-step reduction in the risk of injury. Such improvements of function are:

– Impact-severity detection through improvement of the triggering algorithm or through the use of one or two upfront sensors installed in the vehicle's crumple zone (e.g. on the radiator crossmember). These are acceleration sensors which facilitate early detection of impacts that are difficult to sense centrally, e.g. ODB (Offset Deformable Barrier crashes, offset against soft crash barriers), pole or underride impacts. It is also possible to detect the impact energy with these sensors:

– Selt-belt usage detection.

– Occupant presence, position and weight detection.

– Seat-position and backrest-inclination detection.

– Introduction of up to ten and more different triggering thresholds (seat-belt tightener

stage 1 and stage 2; driver's airbag
stage 1, unbelted; driver's airbag
stage 2, unbelted; driver's airbag

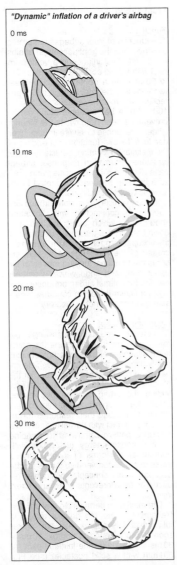

"Dynamic" inflation of a driver's airbag

0 ms

10 ms

20 ms

30 ms

stage 1, belted;   driver's airbag
stage 2, belted;   passenger airbag
stage 1, unbelted;   passenger airbag
stage 2, unbelted;   passenger airbag
stage 1, belted;   passenger airbag
stage 2, belted; rear-end impact stage
1 and stage 2).
– Use of airbags with two-stage gas inflators or with a single-stage gas inflator
  and pyrotechnically activated gas-discharge valve.
– Use of seat-belt tighteners with occu-
  pant-weight-dependent belt-force limitation.
– Including the occupant protection system in a CAN bus network for the communication of data (diagnostic information, warning-lamp activation etc.), and
  for the synergetic use of sensor data
  from other systems (driving-speed,
  brake-actuation, buckle-switch and
  door-contact information).

The "crash output" is used for emergency calls following a crash and to activate "secondary safety systems" (hazard-
warning system, opening of central locking system, shutdown of fuel pump etc.)
(see Fig. "Combined control unit").

Side airbag

Function
Side impacts make up approx. 20 % of all
accidents. This makes the side collision
the second most common type of impact
after the frontal impact. An increasing
number of vehicles are therefore being fitted with side airbags in addition to seat-
belt tighteners and front airbags. Side
airbags, which in order to protect the head
and upper body inflate across the length
of the roof lining (e.g. inflatable tubular
systems, window bags, inflatable curtains) and from the door or the seat backrest (thorax bags), are designed to cushion the occupants gently and thus protect
them against injury in the event of a side
impact (see Fig.).

Operating concept
Due to the lack of a crumple zone, and the
minimum distance between the occupants
and the vehicle's side structural components, it is particularly difficult for side
airbags to inflate in time. In the case of severe impacts, therefore, the time needed
for impact detection and activation of the
side airbags must be approx. 3...5 ms and
the time needed to inflate the approx. 12 l
thorax bags must not exceed 10 ms.

Bosch offers the following option for
satisfying the above requirements: an in-

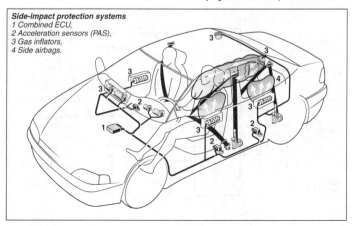

Side-impact protection systems
1 Combined ECU,
2 Acceleration sensors (PAS),
3 Gas inflators,
4 Side airbags.

strument-cluster ECU which processes the input signals of peripheral (mounted at suitable points on the body), side-sensing acceleration sensors, and which can trigger side airbags as well as the belt tighteners and the front airbags.

Components

Acceleration sensors

Acceleration sensors for impact detection are integrated directly in the ECU (belt tightener, front airbag) and mounted at selected points on the left and right body sides (side airbag) or in the vehicle's front-end deformation area (upfront sensors for "intelligent airbag systems"). The precision of these sensors is crucial in saving lives. They are generally surface-micromechanical sensors consisting of fixed and moving finger structures and spring pins. A special process is used to incorporate the "spring/mass system" on the surface of a silicon wafer. Since the sensors only have low working capacitance (≈ 1 pF), it is necessary to accommodate the evaluation electronics in the same housing so as to avoid stray-capacitance and other forms of interference.

Combined ECUs for belt tighteners and front/side airbags

The central ECU, also called the triggering unit, incorporates the following functions (current status):

- Impact detection by acceleration sensor and safety switch, or by two acceleration sensors with no safety switch (redundant, fully electronic sensing).
- Prompt activation of front airbags and belt tighteners in response to different types of impact in the vehicle longitudinal direction (e.g. frontal, oblique, offset, pole, rear-end). Here the acceleration is recorded at a central point in the passenger compartment and evaluated by the triggering algorithm.
- For the side airbags, the ECU operates in conjunction with a central lateral sensor and two or four peripheral acceleration sensors. These are attached to the seat cross-members, to the B-pillars, or to the B- and C-pillars. The peripheral acceleration sensors (PAS) transmit the triggering command to the central ECU via a digital interface. The central ECU triggers the side airbags provided the internal lateral sensor has confirmed a side impact by means of a plausibility check.

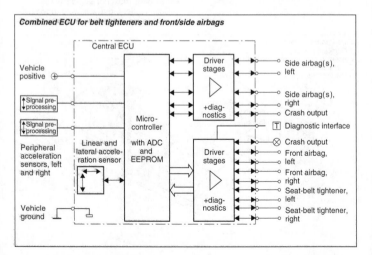

Combined ECU for belt tighteners and front/side airbags

- Voltage transformer and energy accumulator in case the supply of power from the vehicle battery should fail.
- Selective triggering of belt tighteners according to monitored belt-buckle status: firing takes place only when buckle is engaged.
- Setting of up to over ten triggering thresholds for two-stage belt tighteners and two-stage front airbags depending on the status of belt use and seat occupation.
- Adaptation to the different vehicle features (energy absorption and vibrational behavior of the vehicle structure).
- Diagnosis of internal and external functions and of system components.
- Storage of fault types and durations with crash recorder; readout via the diagnostic or CAN-bus interface.
- Warning-lamp activation.

<u>Gas inflators</u>

The pyrotechnical propellant charges of the gas inflators for generating the airbag inflation gas (mainly nitrogen) and for actuating belt tighteners are activated by an electrically operated firing element.

The gas inflator in question inflates the airbag with nitrogen. The driver's airbag integrated in the steering-wheel hub (volume 35...67 l) or the passenger airbag installed in the glovebox (70...150 l) is inflated approx. 30 ms after firing.

<u>AC firing</u>

In order to prevent inadvertent triggering through contact between the firing element and the system voltage (e.g. faulty insulation in the wiring harness), AC firing involves firing by alternating-current pulses at approx. 80 kHz. A capacitor in the firing-element plug incorporated in the firing circuit isolates the firing element from the DC current. This isolation from the system voltage prevents unintentional triggering, even following an accident where the airbag remains untriggered and the occupants have to be freed from the deformed passenger cell by emergency services, whereby it may be necessary to cut through the (permanent +) ignition cables in the steering-column wiring harness.

Rollover protection systems

Function

In the event of an accident where the vehicle rolls over, open-top vehicles such as convertibles, off-road vehicles etc. lack the protecting and supporting roof structure of closed-top vehicles. Initially, therefore, rollover sensing and protection systems were only installed in convertibles and roadsters without fixed rollover bars.

Today, engineers are developing rollover sensing for use in closed passenger cars where there is the danger of nonbelted occupants being thrown through side windows in the event of a crash and crushed by their own vehicle. There is also the danger that body parts of belted occupants, such as arms, head and upper body, can project out of the vehicle and be seriously injured.

To protect against this danger, already existing restraint systems such as belt tighteners and head airbags are triggered in any case, and in convertibles, the extendable rollover bars or the extendable head restraints, are triggered.

Operating concept

The earlier sensing concepts (from mid-1989) started out with an omnidirectional sensing function, i.e. the intention was to detect rollovers in all directions. For this purpose, manufacturers used all-round-sensing acceleration sensors and tilt sensors (AND-wired) with rear-axle switches or level-gauge (spirit-level principle) and gravitation sensors (sensor closes a reed contact with spring support when contact with the ground is lost).

Today's sensing concepts no longer trigger the system at a fixed threshold but rather at one that conforms to a situation and only for the most common rollover situations, i.e. overturning about the longitudinal axis.

The Bosch sensing concept involves a surface-micromechanical yaw sensor (see Fig.) and high-resolution acceleration sensors in the vehicle transversal and vertical directions (y- and z-axes).

The yaw sensor is the primary sensor; the y- and z-acceleration sensors serve primarily to check the plausibility of identified rollover situations. These sensors are incorporated in the airbag triggering unit.

Depending on the rollover situation (rollover on an embankment or slope, or due to an obstacle underneath the vehicle), and on the yaw rate and lateral acceleration, the occupant protection devices are adapted to the situation. In other words, using automatic selection and application of the algorithm module appropriate to the type of rollover, triggering takes place after 30...3000 ms.

Passenger-compartment sensing

Occupant-classification mats, which measure the pressure profile on the seat, are used to identify whether the seat is being occupied by a person or by an object. In addition, the pressure distribution and the pelvic-bone spacing are used to indicate the occupant's size and thus indirectly the occupant's weight. The mats consist of individually addressable force-sensing points which reduce their resistance according to the FSR principle (Force Sensing Resistor) as the pressure increases.

An absolute-weight measurement is also carried out with two to four piezoresistive sensors or wire strain gauges on the seat frame.

Active infrared or ultrasonic sensor arrays are used for "out-of-position" detection with triangulation.

There is as yet no unified standard for interior-compartment sensing. For this reason, occupant classification mats are sometimes also combined with ultrasonic sensors.

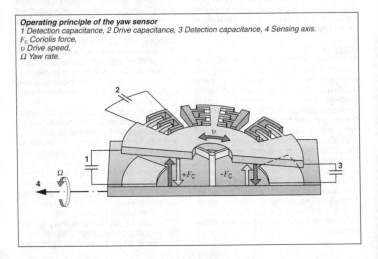

Operating principle of the yaw sensor
1 Detection capacitance, 2 Drive capacitance, 3 Detection capacitance, 4 Sensing axis.
F_c Coriolis force,
υ Drive speed,
Ω Yaw rate.

Outlook

As well as front-airbag switchoff using de-activation switches, in the near future child seats with standardized anchorage, so-called ISOFIX child seats, will come onto the market. Switches integrated in the anchoring locks initiate an automatic passenger-airbag switchoff, which must be indicated by a special lamp.

For further improvement of the triggering function and better advance detection of the type of impact ("precrash" detection), relative speed, distance, and impact angle in a frontal impact, will be detected with microwave radar sensors.

In connection with precrash sensing, reversible seat-belt pretensioners are being developed. They are electromechanically actuated, i.e. they take longer to tighten, and must be triggered earlier, i.e. before initial impact, by precrash sensing alone.

A further improvement in the restraining effect will be provided by airbags integrated in the thorax section of the seat belt ("air belts" or "inflatable tubular torso restraints"); these airbags will reduce the risk of broken ribs in older occupants.

The same path for improving protective functions is being pursued by engineers developing "inflatable headrests" (to prevent whiplash trauma and cervical-vertebra injuries), "inflatable carpets" (prevention of foot and ankle injuries) and two-stage belt tighteners.

In order to reduce wiring-harness thickness and complexity, the firing-circuit network is being developed to include an actuator bus or Firing bus. In this respect, Bosch and Temic are jointly developing "BOTE-ACT", the Bosch-Temic actuator-bus concept. This is a "daisy-chain" principle which e.g. in the event of a short circuit between the two bus lines enables the line section in question to be completely disconnected and all the bus users to function fully thanks to the bus-ring structure. Signals from slow sensors or switches, e.g. the belt-buckle or ISOFIX switches, can also be transmitted with the BOTE-ACT bus.

Efforts are currently being made in the USA to standardize a Firing-bus concept from a range of products from five differ-

ent manufacturers. Standardization is imperative in order to ensure market penetration and because of the potential usability of standardized firing elements with standardized bus-user electronics. Efforts are underway to integrate the receiver electronics in the firing elements, without increasing diameter and while maintaining a maximum cap extension of 5 mm. This would increase the usability of standard gas inflators.

The most promising and economical development is the use of "semiconductor-based bridgewires" (SCBs), i.e. firing resistors incorporated in silicon which are monolithically integrated with the bus-user electronics on a single chip.

In addition to the Firing bus, a "sensor bus" will be introduced – in the longer term – for networking the signals of fast sensors.

Engineers are also developing CMOS-type stereo video cameras for passenger-compartment sensing. This technology will provide an adequate amount of information for ensuring reliable monitoring of the passenger compartment, possibly in conjunction with an additional "auxiliary sensor", the type of which is not yet certain. A video camera also provides for the implementation of numerous comfort functions (this is a question of computer capacity) and thus the required allocation of costs to the various systems.

Because pedestrian protection might possibly be required by law in a few years, work is also being conducted on pedestrian detection and protection devices. Tests are being carried out on a variety of sensing concepts, e.g. foil pressure sensors on the bumpers. Bumper airbags and liftable engine hoods which will cushion the impact of a pedestrian are being considered as protective measures.

Comfort and convenience systems

Power windows

Power windows have mechanisms that are driven by electric motors. There are two types of system in use. The available installation space assumes a prominent place among the criteria applied in determining which system to install.

<u>Regulator mechanism</u> (now declining in popularity):
An electric-motor driven spur pinion transmits the force to a conventional window regulator.

<u>Cable-operated mechanism</u>:
The electric motor transfers the force through a Bowden cable.

Power-window motors
Space limitations inside the door make narrow drive-units imperative (flat motors). The reduction gearing is a self-locking worm-gear design. This prevents the window opening inadvertently of its own accord or being opened by force. Dampers integrated in the gearing mechanism provide for good damping characteristics at the limits of movement.

Power-window control
Window operation is controlled manually by means of a rocker switch. For greater convenience, power windows can be linked to a central or decentralized closing system which, when the vehicle is locked, closes the windows automatically or sets them to a predefined partially-open position for ventilation purposes.

During closing, a force-limitation device (anti-squeeze or finger protection) is in operation. The device serves to prevent human appendages from being caught by the closing window. In Germany, paragraph 30 of the StVZO Road Licensing Regulations stipulates that this protection mechanism remain effective while the window moves upward through a 200...4 mm travel range (as measured from the upper edge of the window opening).

Power-window drives
a) System 1 with regulator,
b) System 2 with flexible Bowden cable.
1 Electric gear motor, 2 Guide rail,
3 Control rod, 4 Lift mechanism,
5 Flexible drive cable.

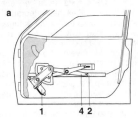

a

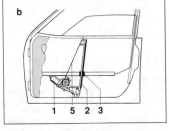

b

Power-window motor with integrated electronics (force limiter)

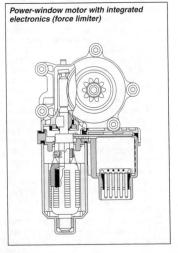

The window drive units include integral Hall sensors to monitor motor speed during operation. If a reduction in speed is detected, the motor's direction of rotation is immediately reversed. The window closing force must not exceed 100 N at a spring rate of 10 N/mm. The unit automatically overrides the anti-squeeze protection immediately before the window enters the door seal, allowing the motor to run to its end position and permitting complete closure of the window. At the same time, the final window position is signalled back to the control unit.

Electronic control may be concentrated in a central control unit, or the control elements may be dispersed among the individual window motors in order to reduce the complexity of the wiring. Those positioners allow multiple use of the wiring (multiplex systems).

Power sunroof

Power sunroofs can combine lifting and tilting-sunroof functions. This requires the use of special control systems that may be electronic or electromechanical in design. With electromechanical control (see illustration), mechanical interlocks on the limit switches a) and b) ensure that the roof can be either slid or tilted open from the closed position, depending on the polarity applied at Terminals I and II. Once the sunroof has been tilted or opened, a polarity shift will initiate the corresponding lowering or closing process. An electronic control unit featuring integral force limitation provides benefits if the sunroof is incorporated in a central-locking system. The electronic control system includes a microcomputer responsible for evaluating incoming signals and monitoring sunroof position. The closed and maximum-opening positions for the sliding action of the sunroof are monitored with the aid of microswitches or Hall-effect sensors. Supplementary functions such as
– preset position control,
– closing via rain sensor,
– motor-speed control, and
– electronic motor protection
can all be included in the package at relatively modest expense.

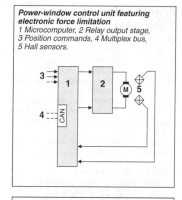

Power-window control unit featuring electronic force limitation
1 Microcomputer, 2 Relay output stage, 3 Position commands, 4 Multiplex bus, 5 Hall sensors.

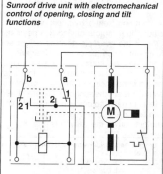

Sunroof drive unit with electromechanical control of opening, closing and tilt functions

Drive for the roof is provided by Bowden cables or other torsion- and pressure-resistant control cables. The drive motor is usually installed in the roof or at the rear of the vehicle (e.g., in the trunk). Permanently energized worm-drive motors with outputs of approx. 30 W are used to drive the sunroof mechanism. They are protected against thermal overload by a thermostatic switch (declining in popularity) or (most frequently) by a software thermoswitch.

Provision must also be made for ensuring that the roof can be closed using the on-board tools (e.g. wheel-nut wrench or similar) in the event of a failure in the electrical system.

Seat and steering-column adjustment

Electric power seats are still essentially restricted to passenger cars of the medium and higher price classes. The primary function of these systems is to enhance comfort, but multiple adjustment options combine with space restrictions and possibly difficult control access to limit the practicality of manually-operated mechanisms. Up to seven motors control the following functions:
– seat-cushion height, front/rear,
– longitudinal travel,
– seat-cushion tilt angle,
– backrest tilt adjustment,
– lumbar support, height/curvature,
– shoulder-support tilt angle,
– head-restraint height adjustment.

A common seat-adjustment system includes four motors driving two gearsets. One of the gearsets governs height adjustment, while the other is designed for combined longitudinal and height adjustment. The unit for adjusting the seat height is not included on simpler seat designs. Yet another concept features three identical gear motors with four height and two linear-adjustment gearsets. The gear motors drive the gearsets via flexible

shafts. This is a highly universal system and can be installed on any seat design. Modern seats (especially for sporting vehicles) do not merely affix the lap belt to the seat frame, they also attach the shoulder strap – together with its height adjuster, inertia reel and tensioner mechanism – to the backrest. This type of seat design ensures optimal belt positioning for a wide range of different-sized passengers at all available seat positions, and thus makes an important contribution to occupant safety. The seat frame must be reinforced for this type of design, while both the gearset components and their connections to the frame must be strengthened.

The optional programmable electric seat adjuster ("memory seat") can recall several previously selected seat positions. Potentiometers or Hall-effect sensors are employed to signal the current seat position. On two-door vehicles a feature designed to slide the front seat to its extreme forward position can be incorporated to ease ingress for rear passengers.

Electrically-adjustable steering columns are also seeing increased use as yet another means of enhancing driver comfort. The adjustment mechanism, consisting of a single electric motor and self-arresting gearset for each adjustment plane, forms an integral part of the steering column.

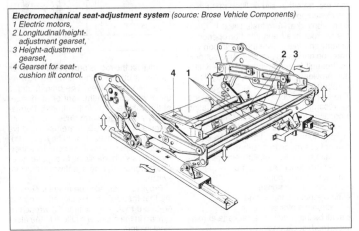

Electromechanical seat-adjustment system (source: Brose Vehicle Components)
1 Electric motors,
2 Longitudinal/height-adjustment gearset,
3 Height-adjustment gearset,
4 Gearset for seat-cushion tilt control.

The gearset for telescopic adjustment must be capable of absorbing any and all impact forces (crash forces) which might be applied to the steering column. The adjustment can be triggered in either of two ways, using the manual position switch or with the programmable seat adjustment. Also available is a provision for tilting the column upward to facilitate driver entry and egress.

Central locking system

Either pneumatic or electric actuators can be used to power central locking systems for vehicle doors, luggage compartments and fuel-filler flaps.

In pneumatic systems, an electric motor drives the reversible dual-pressure pump which provides the required system pressure (positive or vacuum). The system can be switched on and off by a central position switch inside the vehicle and by the ignition switch. As an optional feature, the system can be operated from a number of points (driver door, front-seat passenger door, and trunk lid).

More widespread than the pneumatic systems are those which depend on electric motors for central locking. Although various technologies are used, according to function range and lock type, the basic principle remains constant: a small electric motor featuring a reduction-gear drive unit powers the actuating lever responsi-

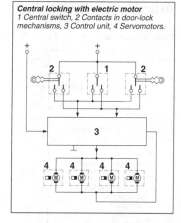

Central locking with electric motor
1 Central switch, 2 Contacts in door-lock mechanisms, 3 Control unit, 4 Servomotors.

ble for opening and closing the lock. Provision must be made to ensure that the door can always be unlocked with the key and the interior handle in the event of a power failure. Central locking systems incorporating special theft-deterrence features must be designed to preclude deactivation of the security system using any means other than the vehicle key.

Ultrasonic or infrared remote control provide increased convenience. Such systems permit remote operation of the central locking system when the driver is still some distance away from the vehicle.

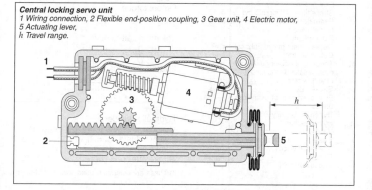

Central locking servo unit
1 Wiring connection, 2 Flexible end-position coupling, 3 Gear unit, 4 Electric motor, 5 Actuating lever,
h Travel range.

Automotive hydraulics

Quantities and units[1])

Symbols		Units
A	Area of flow cross section	cm^2
A_D	Cross-sect. area of restriction	cm^2
A_K	Piston area	cm^2
A_R	Cross-sectional area of line	cm^2
b	Gap width	mm
d	Line diameter	mm, cm
E_{Fl}	Modulus of elasticity, fluid	$N \cdot mm^{-2}$
E_{Oil}	Bulk modulus, oil	$N \cdot mm^{-2}$
e	Eccentricity offset	mm
F	Force	N
g	Gravitational acceleration	$m \cdot s^{-2}$
H	Cylinder stroke length	cm, mm
h	Gap height	μm, mm
l	Gap length, line length	mm, m
l_o	Output length	cm
M_1	Input torque	$N \cdot m$
M_2	Output torque	$N \cdot m$
M_{th}	Theoretical input or output torque	$N \cdot m$
M_{verl}	Torque loss	$N \cdot m$
n	Rotational speed	min^{-1}
P_{an}	Input power	kW
P_{ab}	Output power	kW
p_z	Cylinder pressure	bar
Δp	Pressure difference	bar
Q	Delivery rate of hydraulic pump, or intake rate of hydraulic motor or hydraulic cylinder	$l \cdot min^{-1}$
Q_1	Delivery rate	$l \cdot min^{-1}$
Q_2	Intake rate	$l \cdot min^{-1}$
Q_L	Leakage rate	$l \cdot min^{-1}$
Q_{th}	Theoretical delivery or intake rate	$l \cdot min^{-1}$
Re	Reynolds number	—
r	Line radius	mm
t	Stroke time of hydraulic cyl.	s
U	Perimeter of flow cross section	cm
V_{Fl}	Fluid volume	cm^3
V_H	Displacement of hydraulic cyl.	cm^3
V_o	Output volume	cm^3
V_{th}	Theoretical delivery displacement /intake displacement	cm^3
v	Line flow rate	$m \cdot s^{-1}$
v_1	Stroke rate	$m \cdot s^{-1}$
α_D	Flow coefficient of restrictors, orifices etc.	—
η	Dynamic viscosity	$Ns \cdot m^{-2}$
η_{hm}	Hydromechanical efficiency	—
η_{vol}	Volumetric efficiency	—
λ	Coefficient of flow resistance	—
ν	Kinematic viscosity	$m^2 \cdot s^{-1}$
ϱ	Density	$kg \cdot dm^{-3}$
ω	Angular velocity	s^{-1}

[1]) These are commonly used units, not SI-units.

Calculation of coefficient of flow resistance l

$\lambda = \dfrac{64}{Re}$ for laminar flow and isothermal change of state

$\lambda = \dfrac{75}{Re}$ for laminar flow and adiabatic change of state

$\lambda = \dfrac{0.316}{Re^{0.25}}$ for turbulent flow up to $Re = 80,000$ and smooth lines

$Re = v \cdot D_H / \nu$ where $D_H = A/U$

Terms and formulas
(quantity equations)

Hydraulic pump
Delivery rate
$$Q_1 = V_{th} \cdot n \cdot \eta_{vol}$$
Output power
$$P_{ab} = Q_1 \cdot \Delta p$$
Input torque
$$M_1 = \frac{V_{th} \cdot \Delta p}{2\pi} \cdot \frac{1}{\eta_{hm}}$$
Input power
$$P_{an} = M_1 \cdot \omega$$
Volumetric efficiency
$$\eta_{vol} = \frac{Q_1}{Q_{th}} = \frac{Q_{th} - Q_L}{Q_{th}} = 1 - \frac{Q_L}{Q_{th}}$$
Hydromechanical efficiency
$$\eta_{hm} = \frac{M_{th}}{M_1} = \frac{M_{th}}{M_{th} + M_{verl}}$$

Hydraulic motor
Intake rate
$$Q_2 = V_{th} \cdot n / \eta_{vol}$$
Output power
$$P_{ab} = M_2 \cdot \omega$$
Output torque
$$M_2 = \frac{V_{th} \cdot \Delta p}{2\pi} \cdot \eta_{hm}$$
Volumetric efficiency
$$\eta_{vol} = \frac{Q_{th}}{Q_2} = \frac{Q_{th}}{Q_{th} + Q_L}$$
Hydromechanical efficiency
$$\eta_{hm} = \frac{M_2}{M_{th}} = \frac{M_{th} - M_{verl}}{M_{th}}$$

Hydraulic cylinder
Cylinder pressure $p_z = F/(A_K \cdot \eta_{hm})$
Swept volume $V_H = A_K \cdot H$
Stroke time $t = V_H / Q_1$
Stroke rate $v_1 = Q_1 / A_K$

Flow rates in lines and gaps
Required line cross section
$$A_R = Q_1/\upsilon$$
Pressure loss in straight lines
$$\Delta p = \lambda \cdot \frac{l}{d} \cdot \frac{\varrho}{2} \cdot \upsilon^2$$
Flow through a pipe
(according to Hagen-Poiseuille)
$$Q = \frac{\pi \cdot r^4}{8 \cdot \eta \cdot l} \cdot \Delta p$$
Flow (laminar) through a smooth gap
$$Q = \frac{b \cdot h^3}{12 \cdot \eta \cdot l} \cdot \Delta p$$
Flow (laminar) through an eccentric sealing gap
$$Q = \frac{d \cdot \pi \cdot \Delta r^3}{12 \cdot \eta \cdot l} \cdot \left[1 + 1.5 \cdot \left(\frac{e}{\Delta r}\right)^2\right] \cdot \Delta p$$
$(2 \cdot \Delta r = $ clearance between piston and bore)
Flow through restrictors and orifices
$$Q = \alpha_D \cdot A_D \cdot \sqrt{2 \, \Delta p/\varrho}$$

(α_D at control slide valves: 0.6 to 0.8)

Compressibility of a hydraulic fluid
$$\Delta V_{FI} = A_K \cdot \Delta l = V_0 \cdot \Delta p/E_{FI}$$
where the initial volume is
$$V_0 = A_K \cdot l_0$$
and the bulk modulus for oil is
$$E_{Oil} \approx 1.6 \cdot 10^9 \ N \cdot m^{-2}$$

Gear pumps

Gear pumps are designed either with one external-toothed and one internal-toothed gear or with two external-toothed gears. External-toothed pumps are cheaper to manufacture and are therefore in much more common use. The displacement per revolution is constant, and is determined by the gear diameter, the center-to-center distance and the width of the teeth. The rotating (meshed) gears transport the hydraulic fluid in the spaces between the teeth from the low-pressure to the high-pressure side, and the teeth immersed in the fluid force it into the delivery line. There is almost no clearance between the housing and the tips of the teeth; thus the pump exhibits good radial sealing properties. The pump chamber is axially sealed by plates or bushings which are hydraulically pressed against the gears. These plates or bushings also act as bearings for the gears. This design achieves the high efficiency characteristic of high-pressure pumps. Drive speeds of up to 4000 min⁻¹, maximum pressures of up to approx. 300 bar and high power densities (6 kW/kg) make gear pumps particularly well suited for use in automotive hydraulic systems. The span of delivery rates required, which ranges from 0.5...300 l/min, is covered by a range of 4 to 5 pump sizes.

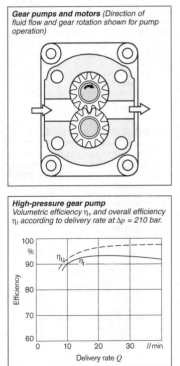

Gear pumps and motors *(Direction of fluid flow and gear rotation shown for pump operation)*

High-pressure gear pump
Volumetric efficiency η_v and overall efficiency η_t according to delivery rate at $\Delta p = 210$ bar.

Gear motors

Like gear pumps, the simplest gear motors are designed to operate in only one direction of rotation. In gear motors, oil flows from the high-pressure to the low-pressure side, and the gears rotate in a direction opposite to the direction in which they would rotate if the device were a pump. Motors suitable for use as vehicle drives, i.e. motors which can be operated in both directions of rotation and which can be loaded in the reverse direction, have also been derived from gear pumps through appropriate design of the axial pressure field and the leakage fluid passages. The advantages of external toothed pumps such as high power density, small installation-space requirements and low manufacturing costs also apply to gear motors. They are therefore chosen for road vehicles, construction equipment and agricultural machinery for driving cooling and cleaning fans, screw conveyors, sweepers, spreading plates, vibrators, etc. The excellent starting behavior of gear motors is utilized in driving pumps and compressors, as well as in motive drives.

Piston pumps and motors

The drive mechanism of hydraulic piston pumps and motors differs significantly from the classical piston-machine design.

The high pressure level (standard pressure for hydrostatic drives 350...400 bar) results in high piston forces which necessitate sturdy and rigid mechanical drive systems. The drive mechanisms of modern machines are nevertheless highly compact, particularly due to the hydrostatic transmission of force between the two primary reciprocating components. The good lubricating and cooling qualities of the hydraulic fluid promote such space-saving designs. Hydraulic piston machines are thus able to achieve a maximum power density of more than 5 kW/kg.

In order to achieve a uniform volumetric flow rate, hydraulic piston machines are designed with an odd number of piston elements. A differentiation is made between radial- and axial-piston machines, depending upon the configuration of the drive mechanism. Both types are available as either pumps or motors with constant or variable displacement, suitable for use in open and closed circuits. Since the phase control of hydraulic machines did not prove itself in practice, continuous control is only possible by varying the piston stroke. Rotating, stroke-generating mechanisms, such as eccentric shaft or crankshaft (radial), and swashplate (axial), are unsuitable for stroke adjustment and are only used in some fixed-capacity machines. All variable-displacement units and many constant-displacement units use other drive mechanisms specific to the hydraulic system. These types incor-

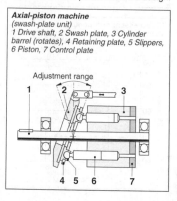

Axial-piston machine
(swash-plate unit)
1 Drive shaft, 2 Swash plate, 3 Cylinder barrel (rotates), 4 Retaining plate, 5 Slippers, 6 Piston, 7 Control plate

Adjustment range

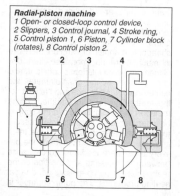

Radial-piston machine
1 Open- or closed-loop control device,
2 Slippers, 3 Control journal, 4 Stroke ring,
5 Control piston 1, 6 Piston, 7 Cylinder block (rotates), 8 Control piston 2.

porate a rotating cylinder assembly. Together with a stationary control plate or control journal, the cylinder assembly forms a rotary slide valve which alternately exhausts and fills the cylinders. Axial-piston machines are designed as swashplate units.

The centrally-ported machine has been adopted as the standard radial design. The cylinder block rotates on the control journal. The bearing forces are supported by hydrostatic pressure fields on the journal. Similar pressure fields transmit the forces between the rotating piston slippers and the stationary cam ring. The ring's variable eccentric position relative to the control journal generates the piston stroke. In the case of pumps in which the delivery direction can be reversed, the stroke ring can be moved in both directions via its adjustment piston. All control elements are located in the stator, allowing rapid and precise adjustments in flow volume using hydraulic or electronic servo elements and controllers. The hydraulic adjustable piston unit can be integrated within the electronic control circuit using either proportional valves in the control circuit or an electrohydraulic adjustment system.

Electrohydraulic pumps and small units

An electrohydraulic pump is a combination of a hydraulic pump and an electric motor. A DC motor is used in most mobile hydraulics applications, however AC and three-phase motors are also used in stationary operation.

Gear pumps are characterized by a low degree of pulsation and quiet operation. As such, these hydraulic components have proven their worth for generating pressure in electrohydraulic pumps. Sizes B and F with capacities of $1...22.5$ cm^3 per revolution are used, and generate operating pressures of up to approx. 280 bar. Together with size I to T electric motors which generate a maximum nominal output of 8 kW, they are used in a number of different mobile-hydraulics applications.

Electrohydraulic pumps are used to supply the hydraulic energy for the "raising/lifting" and "steering" functions in all kinds of vehicles, in particular in industrial trucks (fork-lift trucks and pallet trucks); mobile lifting platforms; trucks; special construction, transport and rescue vehicles; and passenger cars. In passenger cars, electrohydraulic pumps, including increasing numbers of miniaturized versions, are being applied in functions such as ride-level control, and power-assists for steering and parking. Safety-related braking and acceleration control represent a special area of application. A hydraulic unit is at the heart of the ABS and ASR systems, and generates the oil pressure needed when these come into operation.

In addition to electrohydraulic pumps, various valves or valve assemblies must be installed in motor vehicles in order to implement a wide variety of control functions. This has led to the development of small, compact units with outputs of up to 4 kW. In these units, the electric motor and hydraulic pump are supplemented by a valve block, a hydraulic-fluid tank, and fluid and air filters. The design concept accommodates individual modifications for specific control functions. Sleeve and seat valves can be combined in a compact control block or at unions in the system. Small and miniaturized units are used in those applications where high power is required despite limited space being available. Examples include municipal vehicles (street sweepers, rotary snow plows, utility tractors, industrial trucks, special-purpose vehicles, and passenger-transport vehicles with lifts and pivoting equipment for carrying handicapped persons).

Novel applications are found in passenger-vehicle functions. The most advanced convertibles utilize hydraulic mechanisms to operate the folding top; these devices fold the top, stow it in a specified manner, and lock it into place.

Valves

Directional-control valves

OC valves (open-center)
When the valve unit is in the neutral position, the flow from the pump is directed through up to 10 valves (neutral circulation pattern). The fluid flow is restricted when a valve is actuated prior to the opening of the line to the servo unit.
Disadvantages:
– High pressure loss = Energy loss in neutral position,
– Control precision affected by load pressure.

LS Valves (load-sensing)
Used in systems with variable-capacity pumps or constant-capacity pumps and auxiliary pressure compensator. In the neutral position, the LS control line removes the pressure from the pump and pressure compensator. When the valve unit is actuated, the pump controller/pressure regulator maintains the pressure differential at the valve spool at a constant level. The result: The flow of hydraulic fluid to the servo unit is not affected by the load pressure.
Advantages:
– Minimal neutral-position loss,
– Improved precision control independent of load pressure.

Flow-control valves

Throttle valves
Throttle valves are used to adjust the fluid flow rate by altering the cross-sectional area of the flow. According to the laws of rheological science, this flow-limiting function is pressure-dependent; it is therefore used only for simple flow adjustment. Pressure-independent adjustment requires the use of control valves.

Flow-pressure-compensated control valves
In order to be able to set the fluid flow Q independently of the load pressure p_3 at 2-way flow-control valves, the pressure difference at the metering orifice ($p_1 - p_2$) is held constant by a variable restrictor (pressure compensator). The pressure difference $p_1 - p_2$ corresponds to the spring force acting on the pressure compensator. In this type of control, the sur-

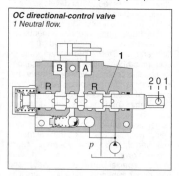

OC directional-control valve
1 Neutral flow.

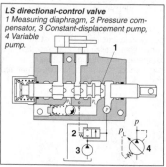

LS directional-control valve
1 Measuring diaphragm, 2 Pressure compensator, 3 Constant-displacement pump, 4 Variable pump.

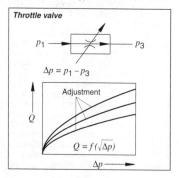

Throttle valve

$\Delta p = p_1 - p_3$

Adjustment

$Q = f(\sqrt{\Delta p})$

plus fluid flows via the pressure-relief valve in the system.

Losses can be reduced by using 3-way flow-control valves which have an additional drain through which the surplus fluid flows back to the tank or to other hydraulic devices.

Pressure-control valves

Pressure-relief valve

Hydraulic circuits incorporate a pressure-relief valve in order to protect the components as well as to ensure the operational safety of the system. If the pressure acting on the seat diameter exerts a force equal to the force exerted by the precompressed spring, the valve cone lifts off its seat and the fluid flows to the tank. Pilot-operated pressure-relief valves are used for greater flow volumes and to achieve valve characteristics which are independent of the flow rate. The pilot valve relieves the spring chamber of the main valve which controls return flow to the tank.

Electric proportional directional-control valves

Nowadays, agricultural and industrial vehicles such as tractors and fork-lift trucks increasingly use electrically operated directional-control valves. The reasons for this are higher productivity, lower demands on the driver and more economical installation costs as a result of the greater scope in the choice of valve location on the vehicle. Electronic circuitry

provides for easy-to-use, safe and reliable control systems which in some cases extend up to automatic movement sequences.

Direct solenoid actuation
In applications involving small to medium

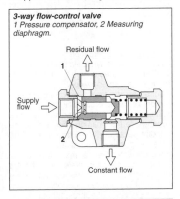

3-way flow-control valve
1 Pressure compensator, 2 Measuring diaphragm.

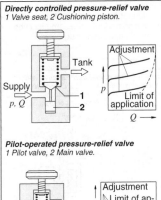

Directly controlled pressure-relief valve
1 Valve seat, 2 Cushioning piston.

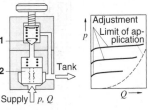

Pilot-operated pressure-relief valve
1 Pilot valve, 2 Main valve.

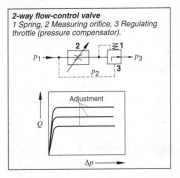

2-way flow-control valve
1 Spring, 2 Measuring orifice, 3 Regulating throttle (pressure compensator).

hydraulic powers (e.g. positioning movements on combine harvesters, tilting function on fork-lift trucks), the directional-control-valve spool is displaced by a solenoid against the action of a spring by an amount proportional to the excitation current. The application limit is determined by the available solenoid force, e.g., 30 l/min, 200 bar. The short stroke of the solenoid limits application of this principle to 3-position valves.

Electrohydraulic actuation

The new "electrohydraulic positioner unit" (EHSe) generates a high actuation force for high-performance control such as is required for the front lifter on agricultural tractors or the jib on a truck loading lift. A positioning piston which moves the valve armature to the position specified by the setpoint generator is used to amplify the force. A position control loop compensates for interference from flow forces thereby providing low hysteresis. The 4/3 pilot-operated directional-control valve with double solenoid is supplied with a control pressure of approx. 20 bar. An inductive travel sensor detects the spool position for the purposes of position control. It also performs the same function for diagnosis and safety purposes.

Electronic control circuitry

The electronic analyzer circuitry of the travel sensor (ASIC) and the digital control electronics with serial CAN bus interface are housed inside the positioner unit casing. The use of a microcontroller with an EEPROM means that the valve characteristics are programmable. The valve and timing characteristics can be chosen and modified according to application. Static characteristics which define the relationship between input signal and flow volume (precision control), and time gradients for defined acceleration and deceleration of hydraulic drive units are stored.

In addition to the primary control option using the CAN bus, control by means of analog or pulse-width-modulated (PWM) voltage signal is also possible. In the event of malfunctions on the part of the directional-control valve, e.g. sticking valve armature, loss of control pressure, etc., depending on the seriousness of the fault it is indicated (coded flashing signal, CAN message) and/or the actuator unit is switched off.

Cylinders

Cylinders convert hydraulic power (pressure, oil flow) into rectilinear motion (force, velocity). They are characterized

---

SB23LS directional-control valve with electrohydraulic positioning unit EHSe
1 Inductive travel sensor, 2 Digital electronics module, 3 Control input: CAN, PWM or potentiometer signal, 4 Diagnostics output: fault signal, 5 Diagnostics output: visual indicator, 6 Pilot valve, 7 Check valve, 8 Pressure compensator.

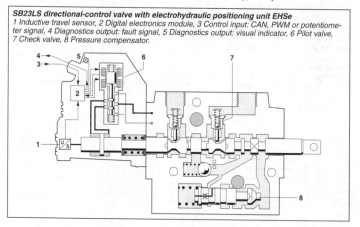

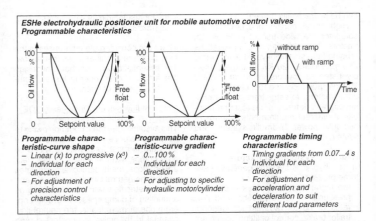

ESHe electrohydraulic positioner unit for mobile automotive control valves
Programmable characteristics

Programmable charac-
teristic-curve shape
– Linear (x) to progressive (x³)
– Individual for each
  direction
– For adjustment of
  precision control
  characteristics

Programmable charac-
teristic-curve gradient
– 0...100 %
– Individual for each
  direction
– For adjusting to specific
  hydraulic motor/cylinder

Programmable timing
characteristics
– Timing gradients from 0.07...4 s
– Individual for each
  direction
– For adjustment of
  acceleration and
  deceleration to suit
  different load parameters

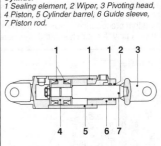

Cylinder
1 Sealing element, 2 Wiper, 3 Pivoting head,
4 Piston, 5 Cylinder barrel, 6 Guide sleeve,
7 Piston rod.

Design	Remarks
Single-acting	Drive possible in only one direction.
Double-acting	Acts in two directions, pressure acts on different surface area on piston and rod sides.
Double-acting	Acts in two directions, both surface areas equal, continuous piston rod.

by high power density and relatively simple design. Cylinder efficiency is determined by the seals, the operating pressure and the piston surface quality. In addition to force and speed, resistance to buckling is also an important design criterion. It determines the dimensions and the extension of the cylinder piston. Types of cylinder mounting at the head and bottom include holes, clevises, pivoting bearings and threads.

Tractor hydraulics

A hydraulic system transforms the tractor into a universal mobile device for agricultural and forestry applications. With the aid of hydraulics, the wide variety of implements used can be quickly mounted to the tractor at the front, rear and between the axles, and moved into their appropriate operating positions by means of open- or closed-loop controls. Quick-disconnect hydraulic couplings are used to control additional linear and rotary motors on the implement itself. Operation of the tractor is facilitated by means of hydraulic power-assisted steering (see also the section on steering systems), brake systems, clutches and gear-shifting systems. Pressure relief valves prevent the tractor from being overloaded. Trailers pulled by the tractor and matched to its brake system can be hydraulically braked.

High power density and flexibility account for the wide use of hydraulics in tractors. The wide variety of applications ranging from small vineyard tractors rated at approximately 20 kW to large center-pivot-steered tractors rated at roughly 300 kW, and including tool carriers, standard tractors, forestry tractors and construction-work tractors, represent a number of different requirements in terms of hydraulic power, hydraulic systems and system operation.

Hydraulic systems for tractors

Tractor hydraulic systems generally have three pressure circuits:
- the high-pressure or work circuit with pressures of up to 250 bar and flow rates of up to 120 l/min for steering, trailer brake, control of lifting equipment and other loads,
- the control circuit which has a pressure of approx. 20 bar and a flow rate of around 30 l/min for power-shift transmission, PTO, locking differential, etc.

- the lubrication circuit with a pressure of approx. 3...5 bar.

There are considerable differences in the high-pressure circuit as described below. The essential criteria for choice of design are function, cost, energy losses, complexity and ease of operation.

Constant flow system/Open center (OC) system (Q constant, p variable)

This system is the most common owing to its favorable price-performance ratio. The pressure is most frequently provided by gear pumps. With all valves in their neutral positions, the hydraulic fluid circulates around the neutral circuit to the tank, and its volumetric flow rate is variable only as a function of pump speed. In order to operate one or more loads, the neutral-flow channel in the valve is constricted, and hydraulic fluid is supplied to the working ports according to the valve-spool displacement. Priority valves are used to ensure that precedence is given to the pressure supply for safety-related functions

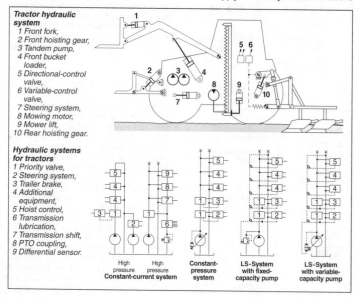

Tractor hydraulic system
1 Front fork,
2 Front hoisting gear,
3 Tandem pump,
4 Front bucket loader,
5 Directional-control valve,
6 Variable-control valve,
7 Steering system,
8 Mowing motor,
9 Mower lift,
10 Rear hoisting gear.

Hydraulic systems for tractors
1 Priority valve,
2 Steering system,
3 Trailer brake,
4 Additional equipment,
5 Hoist control,
6 Transmission lubrication,
7 Transmission shift,
8 PTO coupling,
9 Differential sensor.

High pressure **Constant-current system**

High pressure **Constant-current system**

Constant-pressure system

LS-System with fixed-capacity pump

LS-System with variable-capacity pump

such as steering and trailer-brake operation. The inherent high levels of power loss in the neutral circulation system can be counteracted by appropriate splitting of the work circuit and the use of two or more pumps to provide the pressure.

Constant pressure system/Closed center (CC) system (Q variable, p constant)

A pump with variable volumetric flow rate operates at a regulated constant pressure. When the valves are in their neutral positions, the pump reduces its delivery volume to the rate of leakage loss. When a valve is operated, the pump automatically adjusts its flow volume to that required by the load. Priority valves are used to give precedence to safety-related functions. This type of system is insignificant in terms of automotive hydraulics.

Load-compensating system with constant-displacement pump/Open center load sensing (OCLS) system (Q constant, p variable)

In this type of system, the differential pressure is kept constant with the aid of a control element (pressure compensator) using the variable valve cross-section (measuring diaphragm). Thus, the flow of hydraulic fluid directed to the consumer unit is proportional to the valve opening and unaffected by the load pressure. The highest load pressure within the control system is selected and directed to the pressure compensator by shuttle valves and control lines. The excess pump flow is returned to the tank via the pressure compensator. If load compensation is also to be maintained for all consumer units in parallel operation, a second 2-way flow regulator (individual pressure compensator) is used for each consumer unit.

This system is technically very involved but is becoming increasingly popular in mobile hydraulics (materials flow/agricultural applications) due to its ease of operation. The energy losses are only negligibly lower than with the constant-flow system.

Load-compensating system with variable-displacement pump/Closed center load sensing (CCLS) system (Q variable, p variable)

This system is similar to the OCLS system. The difference, however, is that the pressure is supplied by a variable-displacement pump with regulated pressure and flow, instead of by a constant-displacement pump with pressure compensator. In addition to the gains in convenience, this system also offers substantially reduced energy losses at partial load. This type of system is being increasingly used in applications involving high-power hydraulics (construction machinery, large tractors).

Rear hoisting-gear control

The rear hoisting gear with its standardized 3-point coupling is the most frequently used type of mount for implements. The attached implements can be raised, lowered and held in position. In addition, the tractive force in the hitch linkage can be held constant, or the position of the implement with respect to the tractor can be held constant. Tractive-force regulation is primarily used in working the soil, e.g., plowing (a constant tractive force produces a constant working depth in homogeneous soil). High control quality, i.e. small fluctuations in tractive force, is required for full utilization of engine characteristics and small fluctuations in depth. Because the implements are

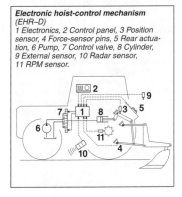

Electronic hoist-control mechanism (EHR–D)
1 Electronics, 2 Control panel, 3 Position sensor, 4 Force-sensor pins, 5 Rear actuation, 6 Pump, 7 Control valve, 8 Cylinder, 9 External sensor, 10 Radar sensor, 11 RPM sensor.

guided and thus largely supported by the hoisting-gear control, the resistance associated with the implement's movement through the soil generates additional downward force at the drive wheels. This reduces wheel slip, and thus energy losses. Position control is used primarily for implements which do not penetrate the ground. In addition, in the case of highly variable soil resistance, a certain percentage of the position control can be mixed with the tractive-force control (mixed control) in order to limit depth fluctuations.

Mechanical hoisting-gear control (MHR)
The sensor signals are monitored and processed as mechanical travel. The tractive force is measured in the form of the spring travel on the upper or lower control arms. The actual position can be read from a cam disc on the lifting shaft. A control rod relays the signals to the control valve according to the selected ratio. At the control valve, the actual values are compared with those selected by the operator. The hoisting mechanism is then raised or lowered to compensate for any control deviations.

Electronic hoisting-gear control (EHR)
The salient feature of EHR lies in the fact that the monitored and control signals are derived, transmitted and processed electronically. The tractive force is measured directly by force-sensor pins at the hitch coupling point. It is possible to supplement position and force control with other functions by expanding the electronic controller and the number of sensors. Rear activation eases attachment of implements. An external sensor can be installed to monitor the travel height of an attached implement (e.g., beet lifter). A speed sensor (radar) and a wheel-speed sensor make it possible to determine slip, providing the basis for a slip-control feature. Active suspension control is useful for enhancing safety and comfort when heavy attachments are being towed.

Hoisting-gear control with hydraulic signal transmission
The basis of this hydraulic signal-transmission system is a hydraulic bridge. The setpoint and actual values of the controlled variable are applied via throttle elements to the bridge's arms and, if the setpoint and actual values do not coincide, this causes the control valve to be shifted against the force of a spring by the diagonally tapped-off differential pressure.

Directional-control valves for tractors
Depending upon the type of hydraulic system, directional-control valves for the high-pressure circuit have either open or closed neutral positions with load sensing. In order to hold heavy loads over a long period of time, as well as for reasons of safety, poppet valves or slide valves (see the section on directional-control valves) are used with downstream mechanically or hydraulically pilot-operated poppet valves in the cylinder port. In addition to the three positions for load extension, retraction and holding, the valves often have a fourth position (free-floating position) in order to permit the implement to be guided on the soil, for example by means of supporting wheels. Detent mechanisms with hydraulic maximum-pressure release automatically reset a valve which has moved past its neutral position in response to overload, or if a cylinder reaches its limit position (operating convenience). Integrated flow regulators allow pressure-independent parallel connections and constant speed of linear and rotary motors. Built-in shock absorbers protect the tractor from overloads if the cylinder port is closed.

Solenoid valves are used to actuate a number of hydraulic functions on the implement, and are controlled from the tractor by means of cables (e.g., beet lifters).

Hydraulic fluid is supplied via hydraulic quick-disconnect couplings or by a separate pump driven by the tractor's power take-off shaft. Electromagnetic switching valves for gear-shifting purposes, and for actuating the various clutches in the tractor, are increasingly being incorporated in the low-pressure circuit.

For trailer braking, a braking valve is included in the high-pressure circuit. It is actuated by the tractor brake, and supplies a correspondingly controlled brake pressure to the trailer.

Hydraulic accumulators

Objectives: Energy storage, impact and pulsation damping, operation as spring element.

The hydraulic accumulator consists of a shell, the interior of which is separated by a solid or flexible barrier. On one side of the barrier is gas, on the other fluid. There are three basic types of units: The bladder, the diaphragm and the piston accumulator.

Nitrogen is employed as the gas medium. During operation, the pressure from the fluid compresses the gas. The minimum operating pressure p_1 should lie at least 10% above the initial gas pressure p_0. The pressure variation between the initial gas pressure and the maximum operating pressure p_2 should not exceed the following: 1:4 in diaphragm and bladder accumulators; 1:10 in piston accumulators. The three operating states illustrated in the diagram are governed by the laws of polytropic changes in state:

$$p_0 \cdot V^n_0 = p_1 \cdot V^n_1 = p_2 \cdot V^n_2$$

For nitrogen, the polytropic exponent for isothermal changes of state is $n = 1$ and for adiabatic changes of state, $n = 1.4$. The available fluid volume between operating pressures is equivalent to the volume difference:

$$\Delta V = V_1 - V_2.$$

Auxiliary drives

Electrohydraulic devices are employed as drive units in numerous automotive applications. The advantages associated with a positive power-to-weight ratio are accompanied by flexibility in installation. Electrohydraulic devices are used to control hoists and trailing axles, and for raising tractor axles. They are also used for controlling the steering and lifting mechanisms on industrial trucks and other vehicles. Platform lifts for loads of 500 to 5,000 kg represent a major area of application for electrohydraulic devices.

The motion of the platform is divided into both lowering and raising. While the upward or downward stroke is controlled

by a single central or two outside cylinders, the tilt function is usually governed by two cylinders. These are either single-action cylinders with return springs, or double-action cylinders. The tilt-control functions are generally governed hydraulically. In addition to the "raise" and "lower" functions, other important features are a "floating" position for loading at fixed-position docks, positioning at an optional height (tilting under full load), and compliance with specified "raising" and "lowering" speeds.

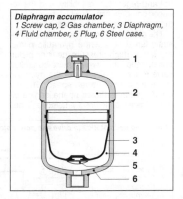

Diaphragm accumulator
1 Screw cap, 2 Gas chamber, 3 Diaphragm, 4 Fluid chamber, 5 Plug, 6 Steel case.

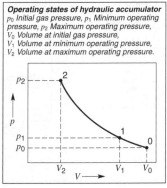

Operating states of hydraulic accumulator
p_0 Initial gas pressure, p_1 Minimum operating pressure, p_2 Maximum operating pressure, V_0 Volume at initial gas pressure, V_1 Volume at minimum operating pressure, V_2 Volume at maximum operating pressure.

Hydrostatic fan drives

Air-cooling of engine coolant is regulated by thermostatic control of radiator-fan speed. In situations which demand greater scope in the siting of the radiator (due to space constraints, engine encapsulation) in positions where it is not in close proximity to the engine, hydrostatic fan drive systems are generally used for higher-power applications (busses, trucks, construction and agricultural machinery, fixed plant). Aside from the flexibility in positioning the radiator, these units also have the advantages of high power-to-weight ratios (low weight, compact component dimensions), uncomplicated control and regulation, reliability, and the reduced component wear which results from the hydraulic fluid's lubrication effect.

The essential components of the hydrostatic fan drive are the hydraulic pump, the motor (high-pressure gear or piston units), and the temperature-controlled valve in the bypass line to the hydraulic motor for controlling fan speed. The hydraulic pump is driven by the engine either directly or indirectly using a V-belt drive (conversion ratio). The pump, in turn, powers the hydraulic motor in the fan assembly. The motor speed depends on the fan's specific response properties ($n_L \sim \sqrt{\Delta p_M}$) and the effective pressure differential (Δp_M). If losses associated with transmitting the power are discounted, the speed will be directly proportional to system pressure (p).

Both continuous-action and discontinuous-action control are employed to govern the engine-coolant temperature. With two-point control (discontinuous), the bypass valve is in the form of an electrically triggered directional-control valve, with actuation controlled by a thermo-switch in the engine's coolant circuit. A pressure valve mounted in a parallel circuit determines the maximum fan speed – and thus cooling power – which will be obtained when the directional-control valve is closed. The precise regulating response is a function of the system pressure to which the valve is set (usually 200 bar). Continuous-control systems feature a bypass valve in the form of a pressure valve or throttle valve with a supplementary bypass-pressure valve for limiting system

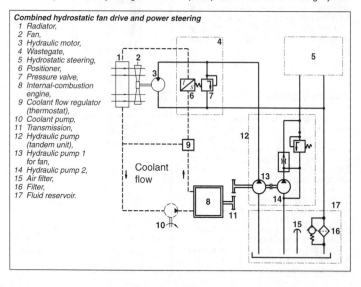

Combined hydrostatic fan drive and power steering
 1 Radiator,
 2 Fan,
 3 Hydraulic motor,
 4 Wastegate,
 5 Hydrostatic steering,
 6 Positioner,
 7 Pressure valve,
 8 Internal-combustion engine,
 9 Coolant flow regulator (thermostat),
10 Coolant pump,
11 Transmission,
12 Hydraulic pump (tandem unit),
13 Hydraulic pump 1 for fan,
14 Hydraulic pump 2,
15 Air filter,
16 Filter,
17 Fluid reservoir.

Coolant flow

pressure. The unit is adjusted by a temperature-sensitive control mechanism with proportional response characteristics. It provides continuous, progressive control of system pressure (in the case of the throttle valve via outgoing bypass flow). The control mechanism can be a thermostatic element (expansion element with wax) located in the coolant stream. Electrohydraulic systems in which the valve is adjusted by a solenoid (proportional solenoid or solenoid with pulse-modulated switching) are becoming increasingly important. This type of solenoid is controlled by the output signal of an electrical temperature sensor located within the coolant stream. This type of unit provides proportional control of the system pressure as a function of temperature. It continually adjusts the fan speed for the required cooling power, remaining within a control range of plus/minus 2.5 °C. The proportion of operating time during which the fan operates at maximum speed is only roughly 5 %, meaning that the fan rotates at reduced speed most of the time. Reductions in fuel consumption and noise emissions are the re-

sult. The inherent system losses with this type of slip regulation, a maximum of roughly 15 %, are commensurate with the requirements of economy. In order to ensure adequate ventilation in the engine compartment beyond the base speed – of particular importance with compartments for encapsulated engines on low-noise vehicles – there is also a limit on minimum system pressure. The control electronics can also be expanded to process additional analog (such as internal and external temperature) and digital input signals. These can serve as the basis for generating output signals to the control solenoid, allowing additional adjustment of fan speed. An example is the combined application of the fan drive to regulate coolant, boost-air, and engine-compartment temperatures, and to switch the fan to maximum min⁻¹ during retarder operation. Electrohydraulic systems can be integrated within the engine-management system. Hydrostatic fan-drive systems can also supply other systems or combine with additional ancillary drive systems such as clutch, transmission, compressor, water pump, alternator, hydraulic power

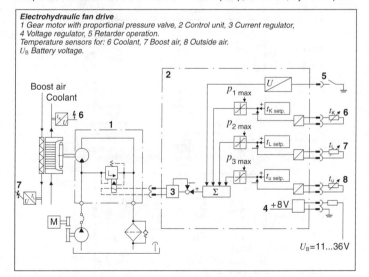

Electrohydraulic fan drive
1 Gear motor with proportional pressure valve, 2 Control unit, 3 Current regulator,
4 Voltage regulator, 5 Retarder operation.
Temperature sensors for: 6 Coolant, 7 Boost air, 8 Outside air.
U_B *Battery voltage.*

steering, rear-axle steering, hydraulic systems for tippers, etc. By means of suitable system design or multiple pump combinations, function prioritization and safety-related demands can be satisfied.

Hydrostatic drives

If the pressure outlet of an adjustable hydraulic pump is connected to a constant-speed or adjustable hydraulic motor (piston or gear motor), the result is an infinitely variable power-transmission device. The mechanical input power (torque × $\min^{-1}$) emerges as mechanical output at another point. The specific conversion ratio is determined by the quotients of the preset pump flow volume and the motor's displacement volume. Parallel layouts incorporating several motors (differential effect) and series layouts (constant velocity) are also possible. However, a basic transmission within an open circuit can neither change direction nor apply braking force without the assistance of auxiliary mechanisms. Nevertheless, this type of layout is well suited to variable ancillary drive systems, such as fans, spreader plates, etc.

Main drives

Hydrostatic drive systems for automotive application must be able to cope with turning under power and with braking. For this reason, it is the closed circuit which has gained predominance. The main (reversible) pump is combined with a charge pump, which is usually flange-mounted. The flow from the charge pump into the low-pressure line compensates for leakage and losses in compression volume. Because there is always pressure on the low-pressure side, the main pump's maximum permissible speed is higher than in suction operation. At a constant conversion ratio, this type of transmission provides almost the same degree of positive drive as a mechanical unit. It is especially well-suited as a device for powering ma-

---

Open-circuit hydrostatic drive system
1 IC engine, 2 Adjustable hydraulic pump, 3 Hydraulic motor, 4 Pressure relief valve, 5 Output, 6 Fluid reservoir.

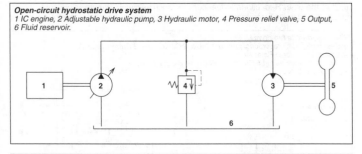

Basic layout for closed circuit
1 IC engine, 2 Adjustable hydraulic pump, 3 Charge pump, 4 Charge-pressure relief valve, 5 High-pressure relief valve, 6 Charge non-return valve, 7 Reversible hydraulic motor, 8 Output.

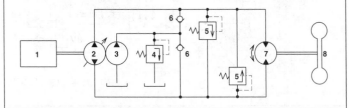

chinery. Meanwhile, "automotive" controls have been developed to provide drive characteristics similar to those of cars (for industrial trucks, etc.). In these, the vehicle's IC engine and the transmission are governed by a single pedal. Most familiar are the circuits in which the operator uses the pedal to control the engine speed only. The engine power is directed through an auxiliary pump and a throttle circuit (generally incorporating several stages) to generate the control pressure which corresponds to the specific engine speed. This pressure, in turn, determines the main pump's flow volume via a control mechanism with proportional pressure response. This control concept is uncomplicated, and prevents the engine from stalling, as the pump responds to losses in input min⁻¹ by switching down to lower flow rates requiring lower torques. However, more complicated circuits are required to satisfy more stringent demands for power control and fuel economy. Elec-

trically adjustable pumps and modern sensor technology provide for elegant solutions using electronics.

Auxiliary drives
Yet another application for hydrostatic drives is as auxiliary units on otherwise free-wheeling truck axles for slow operation in difficult terrain. When required, this unit acts as a hydrostatic substitute for drive shaft and transfer case. For normal road operation, some form of low-loss switchoff is required for the unit. The solution is provided by a constant-displacement pump at the engine; this pump features variable ratios, and can also be disengaged completely. On the auxiliary-drive axle, there are slow-running hub motors whose pistons are retracted by springs when driving on the road. Thus the hydraulic system can be dimensioned for slow vehicle speeds. Neither rotating losses nor substantial friction losses are encountered under normal operating conditions.

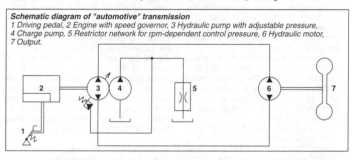

Schematic diagram of "automotive" transmission
1 Driving pedal, 2 Engine with speed governor, 3 Hydraulic pump with adjustable pressure,
4 Charge pump, 5 Restrictor network for rpm-dependent control pressure, 6 Hydraulic motor,
7 Output.

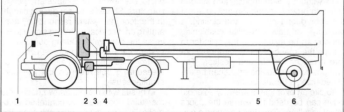

Hydrostatic auxiliary drive
1 Electric control unit for normal/auxiliary drive, 2 Disengageable constant-displacement pump with incremental control, 3 Oil reservoir, 4 Disconnectable hose connections, 5 Hydraulic lines, 6 Hub motors

Automotive pneumatics

Pneumatic systems are used in motor vehicles as sources of energy for
- Opening, closing and locking doors, hatches, etc.,
- Operation and control of brake systems (braking systems) P. 674, and
- Level control P. 613.

Operation of bus doors

Bus doors are operated by double-acting control cylinders. The action of the piston is transmitted to the door leaf. Alternating pressurization and depressurization of the two cylinder chambers opens and closes the door. Three drive systems are in use:
- The working cylinder's piston rod is connected to a lever attached to the door pivot. The door pivot is attached to the door. The extended piston rod responds to cylinder actuation by rotating the spindle to open the door.
- The piston cylinder is axially flange-mounted to the door spindle. The reciprocating motion of the cylinder piston is converted into rotary motion in the door spindle. This rotating motion opens and closes the flange-mounted door by pivoting it outward.
- The control cylinder (rotary drive) is actually a combined cylinder and rotary spindle. The piston stroke is transmitted to the door in the form of a rotating motion at the flange axis.

The doors should reach their travel limits without violent impacts and sudden stops. In order to damp the movement of the door during opening and closing, a pressure- or travel-sensitive cushioning device can be installed in the cylinder to reduce the speed of the door shortly before it reaches either end position. The end-position cushioning effect can be adjusted using a throttle screw.

To cite an example, a 4/2-way solenoid valve can be used to reverse the door's travel as follows. The driver triggers a current pulse by pushing the door-control button, causing the solenoid armature to move the rocker into the opposite position via a rod. The rocker responds by closing the supply valve and opening the discharge on one end of the cylinder, while the discharge is opened and the supply closed on the other end. Additional valve and control functions are specified in Germany by the requirements of the vehicle manufacturers as well as the safety requirements contained in § 35 e of the StVZO Road Licensing Regulations (FMVSS/CUR), the ZH1/494 guidelines for power windows, doors and hatches defined by the professional trade association, and the guidelines of the Association of Public Transport Services (VÖV) for standard city buses.

Power to closing doors must be deactivated or its direction reversed in response to any travel resistance (in Germany, VÖV standard city bus). The opening force must be limited to 150 N or be interrupted upon encountering resistance. After the emergency valve has been operated, the opening or closing force of the door must be canceled, so that the door can be operated by hand. After the emergency valve has been returned to its normal position, door movement must not begin until a separate pushbutton (located on the driver's console or in a box above the door) is pressed or adequate failsafe conditions have been satisfied. Abrupt door movements must be prevented.

Systems in urban buses
The doors in urban buses rely on any of several methods for travel reversal. These include pressure devices in the weather-stripping, differential-pressure switches, photocells, flexible doorshafts and potentiometers. Should a passenger get caught in the door the system responds by generating an electrical switching signal to reverse the door valve. During opening the system can react by depressurizing the control mechanism or, alternatively, by pressurizing both door-control cylinders simultaneously.

In buses with more than two doors, the rear third door must be controlled automatically. The driver only releases the door for operation. Door opening, open time and closing are electronically controlled on the basis of driver and passenger information.

It is often desirable for the front half of the front door to open while the other half remains closed. This function is achieved by a 2/2-way solenoid valve located in the closing line of the cylinder for the second door section.

Systems in touring coaches

Where the emergency valve is located upstream of the door valve (see diagram), the door-control button activates a solenoid to release the pushrod for the return mechanism.

When this power operation is triggered, violent closing is prevented by a flow restrictor. In normal operation the flow restrictor is kept open by secondary pressure.

If the emergency valve is installed downstream of the door valve in the line leading to the closing chamber of the door cylinder, the emergency-valve lock is pneumatically actuated. Once a mean pressure is reached, the control rod is pneumatically released and the valve reverses position.

Door and hatch locking

In large tour-bus doors which swing outward, it is essential that the doors remain locked during the journey. This is done either by lifting the door immediately after the closing process or by additional locking devices, with single-acting actuating cylinders installed in the door frame. At the conclusion of the door-closing process, these are activated by the door itself, for instance by way of a 3/2 shuttle control valve, and thus assist the door drive at the end of the closing process. This closure assistance and locking system is designed in such a way that it unlocks in the event of pressure loss. The door is then held only by the door lock which can be opened by hand in an emergency.

In contrast, springs engage the locking mechanisms for luggage-bay hatches when the control system is depressurized.

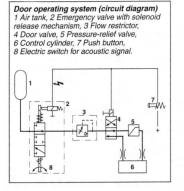

Door operating system (circuit diagram)
1 Air tank, 2 Emergency valve with solenoid release mechanism, 3 Flow restrictor, 4 Door valve, 5 Pressure-relief valve, 6 Control cylinder, 7 Push button, 8 Electric switch for acoustic signal.

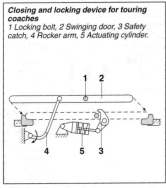

Closing and locking device for touring coaches
1 Locking bolt, 2 Swinging door, 3 Safety catch, 4 Rocker arm, 5 Actuating cylinder.

Symbols used in vehicle electrical systems

Standards: DIN 40900

General symbols (selection from circuit diagrams on P. 839 ff.)

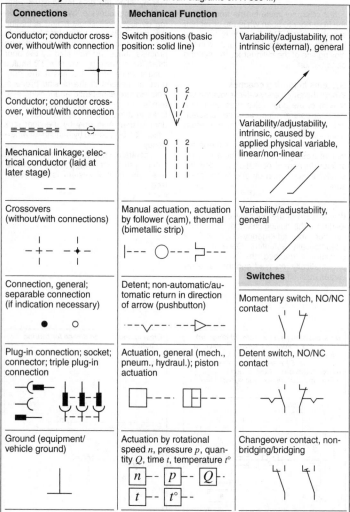

Connections	Mechanical Function	
Conductor; conductor crossover, without/with connection	Switch positions (basic position: solid line)	Variability/adjustability, not intrinsic (external), general
Conductor; conductor crossover, without/with connection		Variability/adjustability, intrinsic, caused by applied physical variable, linear/non-linear
Mechanical linkage; electrical conductor (laid at later stage)		
Crossovers (without/with connections)	Manual actuation, actuation by follower (cam), thermal (bimetallic strip)	Variability/adjustability, general
Connection, general; separable connection (if indication necessary)	Detent; non-automatic/automatic return in direction of arrow (pushbutton)	**Switches**
		Momentary switch, NO/NC contact
Plug-in connection; socket; connector; triple plug-in connection	Actuation, general (mech., pneum., hydraul.); piston actuation	Detent switch, NO/NC contact
Ground (equipment/vehicle ground)	Actuation by rotational speed n, pressure p, quantity Q, time t, temperature $t°$	Changeover contact, non-bridging/bridging

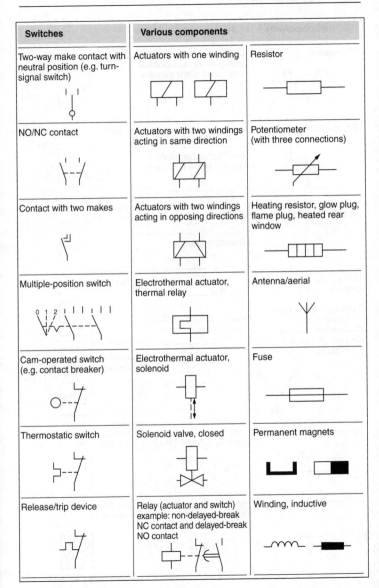

Switches	Various components	
Two-way make contact with neutral position (e.g. turn-signal switch)	Actuators with one winding	Resistor
NO/NC contact	Actuators with two windings acting in same direction	Potentiometer (with three connections)
Contact with two makes	Actuators with two windings acting in opposing directions	Heating resistor, glow plug, flame plug, heated rear window
Multiple-position switch	Electrothermal actuator, thermal relay	Antenna/aerial
Cam-operated switch (e.g. contact breaker)	Electrothermal actuator, solenoid	Fuse
Thermostatic switch	Solenoid valve, closed	Permanent magnets
Release/trip device	Relay (actuator and switch) example: non-delayed-break NC contact and delayed-break NO contact	Winding, inductive

Various components	Devices in motor vehicle	
PTC resistor 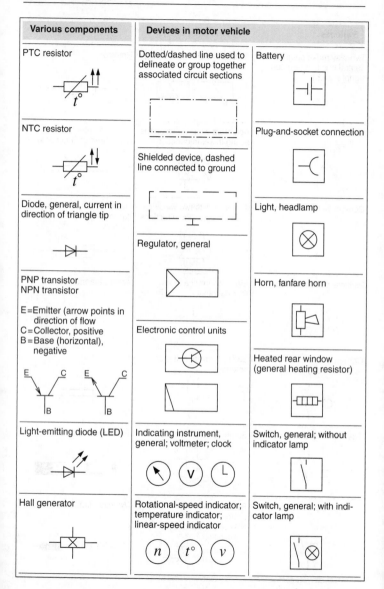	**Dotted/dashed line used to delineate or group together associated circuit sections**	**Battery**
NTC resistor	**Shielded device, dashed line connected to ground**	**Plug-and-socket connection**
Diode, general, current in direction of triangle tip	**Regulator, general**	**Light, headlamp**
PNP transistor **NPN transistor** E=Emitter (arrow points in direction of flow) C=Collector, positive B=Base (horizontal), negative	**Electronic control units**	**Horn, fanfare horn**
Light-emitting diode (LED)	**Indicating instrument, general; voltmeter; clock**	**Heated rear window (general heating resistor)**
Hall generator	**Rotational-speed indicator; temperature indicator; linear-speed indicator**	**Switch, general; without indicator lamp**
		Switch, general; with indicator lamp

Devices in motor vehicle

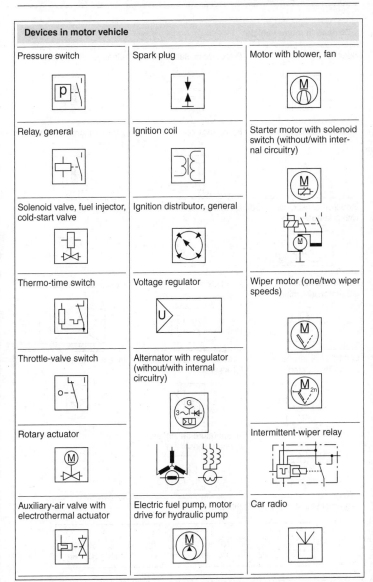

Pressure switch

Relay, general

Solenoid valve, fuel injector, cold-start valve

Thermo-time switch

Throttle-valve switch

Rotary actuator

Auxiliary-air valve with electrothermal actuator

Spark plug

Ignition coil

Ignition distributor, general

Voltage regulator

Alternator with regulator (without/with internal circuitry)

Electric fuel pump, motor drive for hydraulic pump

Motor with blower, fan

Starter motor with solenoid switch (without/with internal circuitry)

Wiper motor (one/two wiper speeds)

Intermittent-wiper relay

Car radio

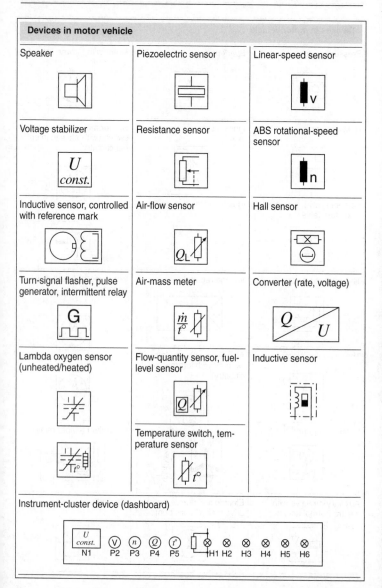

Devices in motor vehicle

Speaker

Piezoelectric sensor

Linear-speed sensor

Voltage stabilizer
U *const.*

Resistance sensor

ABS rotational-speed sensor

Inductive sensor, controlled with reference mark

Air-flow sensor
Q_L

Hall sensor

Turn-signal flasher, pulse generator, intermittent relay
G

Air-mass meter
$\frac{\dot{m}}{t^\circ}$

Converter (rate, voltage)
Q / U

Lambda oxygen sensor (unheated/heated)

Flow-quantity sensor, fuel-level sensor
Q

Inductive sensor

Temperature switch, temperature sensor
t°

Instrument-cluster device (dashboard)

U *const.* — N1 | V P2 | n P3 | Q P4 | t° P5 | H1 | $\otimes$ H2 | $\otimes$ H3 | $\otimes$ H4 | $\otimes$ H5 | $\otimes$ H6

Circuit diagrams

The circuit diagram is a drawn representation of electrical devices by means of symbols, and includes illustrations or simplified design drawings as necessary.

The diagram illustrates the relationship between the various devices and shows how they are connected to each other. The circuit diagram may be supplemented by tables, graphs, or descriptions. The type of circuit diagram actually used is determined by its particular purpose (e.g. illustrating the operation of a system) and by the way in which the circuit is represented.

The circuit diagram must comply with the requirements of the appropriate standards, and deviations are to be explained.

The current paths should be arranged so that signal flow or mechanical action takes place from left to right and/or from top to bottom.

In automotive electrical systems, block diagrams are usually shown with single inputs and outputs, and internal circuitry is omitted.

Schematic diagrams

Assignment
The schematic diagram is the detailed diagram of a circuit. By clearly showing the individual current paths, it explains the operation of an electric circuit. In a schematic diagram, the clear presentation of the circuit's operation, which makes the diagram easy to read, must not be interfered with by the presentation of the individual circuit components and their spatial relationships.

Design
The following schematic diagrams show examples of automotive circuits. They serve only to explain the text and cannot be used as the basis for design or installation.

Examples of identification
G1: Equipment identification (DIN 40 719)
15: Terminal identification (DIN 72 552)
1: Section identification (DIN 40 719)

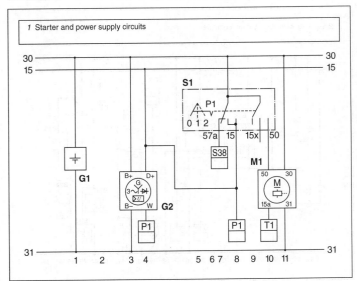

1 Starter and power supply circuits

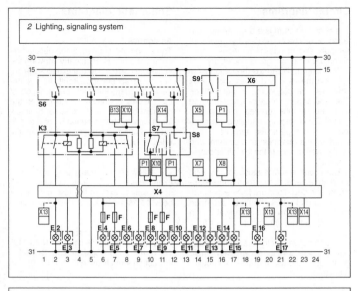

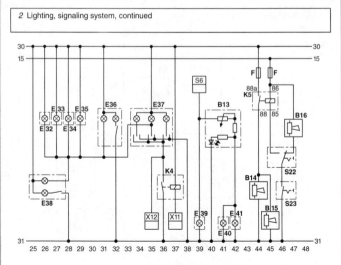

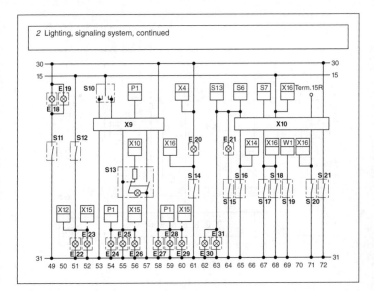

2 Lighting, signaling system, continued

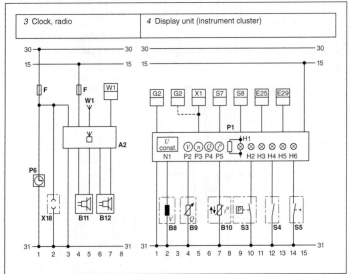

3 Clock, radio

4 Display unit (instrument cluster)

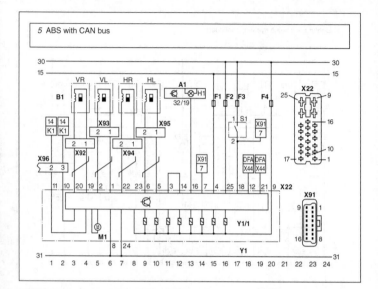

5 ABS with CAN bus

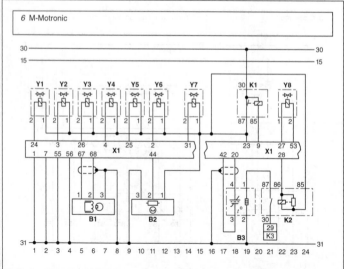

6 M-Motronic

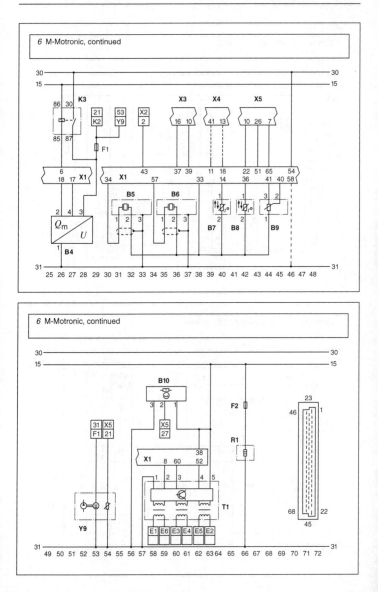

6 M-Motronic, continued

6 M-Motronic, continued

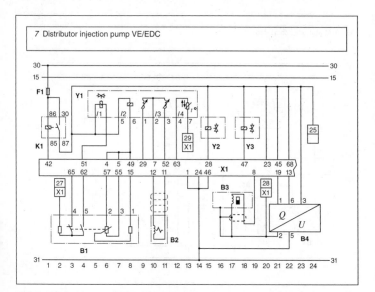

7 Distributor injection pump VE/EDC

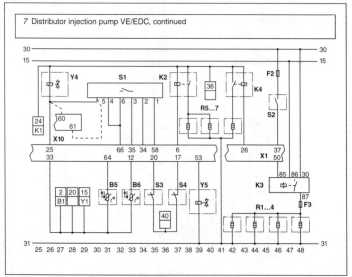

7 Distributor injection pump VE/EDC, continued

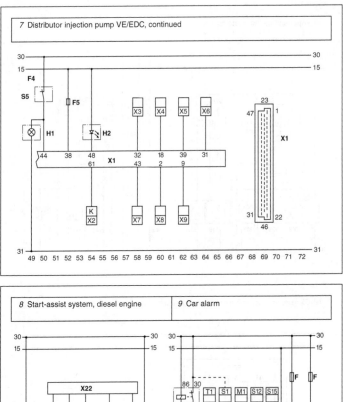

7 Distributor injection pump VE/EDC, continued

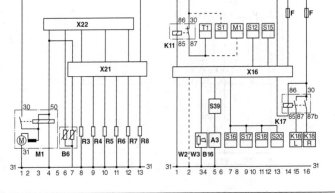

8 Start-assist system, diesel engine

9 Car alarm

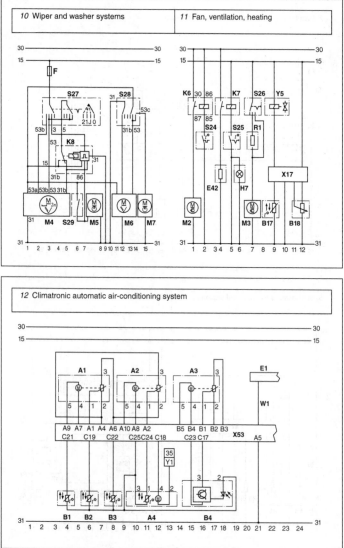

10 Wiper and washer systems

11 Fan, ventilation, heating

12 Climatronic automatic air-conditioning system

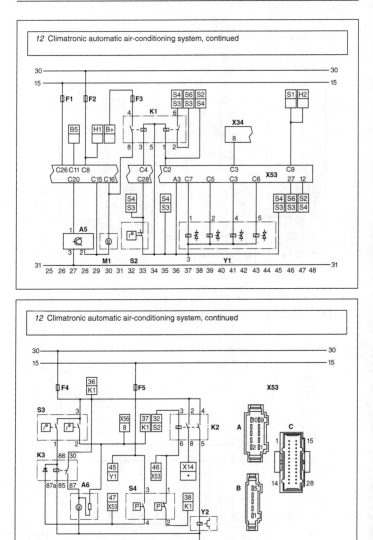

12 Climatronic automatic air-conditioning system, continued

12 Climatronic automatic air-conditioning system, continued

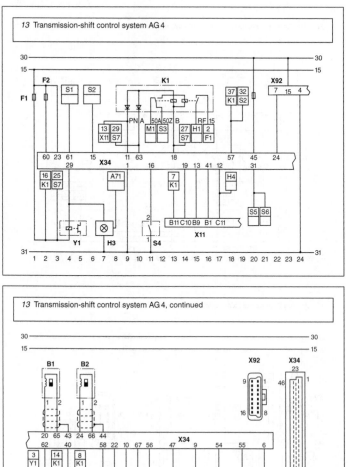

13 Transmission-shift control system AG 4

13 Transmission-shift control system AG 4, continued

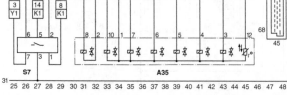

Section designation and device identification

Table 1 details all section designations as listed in "Schematic diagrams" as from P. 839. The sections identify defined areas of the circuit diagrams which represent a particular system.

Table 2 lists electrical devices and their identification codes along with the number of the schematic-diagram section in which they appear.

Table 1 Sections

Section	System
1	Starting and power supply
2	Lighting and signaling system
3	Clock, radio
4	Display unit (instrument cluster)
5	ABS with CAN bus
6	M Motronic
7	Distributor injection pump VE/EDC
8	Start-assist system, diesel engine
9	Car alarm
10	Wiper and washer systems
11	Fan, ventilation, heating
12	Climatronic automatic air-conditioning system
13	AG4 Transmission-shift control system

Table 2 Device identification

ID Code	Device	Section
A1	Display-unit warning lamp	5
A1	Servomotor for center flap	12
A2	Radio	3
A2	Servomotor for dynamic-pressure flap	12
A3	Ignition system with knock control (EZK)	9
A3	Servomotor for temperature flap	12
A4	Instrument-panel temperature sensor and fan	12
A5	Fan control unit	12
A6	Radiator fan	12
A35	Transmission unit, electrical	13
B1	Engine-speed/reference-mark sensor	5, 6
B1	Accelerator-pedal sensor	7
B1	Coolant-temperature sensor	12
B1, 2	Road-speed sensor	6, 13

ID Code	Device	Section
B2	Needle-movement sensor	7
B2	Outside-temperature sensor	12
B2	Transmission input-shaft speed sensor	13
B3	Lambda oxygen sensor	6
B3	Engine-speed/reference-mark sensor	7
B3	Intake-air temperature sensor	12
B4	Air-mass meter	6, 7
B4	Photosensor	12
B5	Knock sensor 1	6
B5, 7	Coolant-temperature sensor	6, 7
B6	Knock sensor 2	6
B6	Fuel-temperature sensor	7, 8
B8	Linear-speed sensor	4
B8	Intake-air temperature sensor	6
B9	Fuel-level sensor	4
B9	Throttle-valve potentiometer	6
B10	Coolant-temperature sensor	4
B10	Cylinder identification sensor	6
B11, 12	Speaker	3
B13	Dimmer for instrument lighting	2
B14, 15	Supertone horn	2
B16	Standard horn	2, 9
B17	Interior-temperature sensor	11
B18	Setting adjuster	11
E1	Climatronic display unit	12
E2, 3	Fog warning lamp, L/R	2
E4, 5	Driving lamp, L/R	2
E6, 7	Fog lamp, L/R	2
E8, 9	Low-beam headlamp, L/R	2
E10, 11	Side-marker lamp, L/R	2
E12, 13	License-plate lamp, L/R	2
E14, 17	Stop lamp L/R	2
E15, 16	Tail lamp L/R	2
E18	Trunk-lid lamp, L/R	2
E19	Trunk lamp	2
E20	Glove-box lamp	2
E21	Engine-compartment lamp	2
E22, 23	Backup lamp, L/R	2
E24, 26	Turn-signal lamp VL/HL	2
E25, 28	Auxiliary turn-signal lamp, L/R	2
E27, 29	Turn-signal lamp VR/HR	2
E30, 31	Ashtray lamp, front/rear	2
E32, 33	Footwell lamp, left front/rear	2
E34, 35	Footwell lamp, right front/rear	2
E36, 38	Rear reading lamp, R/L	2
E37	Front reading lamp	2
E39	Vanity-mirror lamp	2
E40	Instrument lighting	2
E41	Instrument-panel lighting	2
E42	Rear-window heating	11
F..	Fuses	

ID Code	Device	Section
G1	Battery	1
G2	Alternator	1
H1	Charge-indicator lamp	4
H1	ABS-Warning lamp	5
H1	Indicator lamp	7
H2	Oil-pressure warning lamp	4
H2	Brake light	7
H3	Handbrake warning lamp	4
H3	Selector-lever illumination	13
H4	Brake-wear warning light	4
H5	High-beam warning lamp	4
H6	Turn-signal warning lamp	4
H7	Warning lamp for rear-window heating	11
K1	Main relay	6, 7
K1	Air-conditioning relay	12
K1	Starter locking relay	13
K2	Relay for oxygen-sensor heater	6
K2	Relay for small heater filament	7
K2	Air-conditioning compressor relay	12
K3	Side-marker lamp scanning relay	2
K3	Electric fuel pump relay	6
K3	Glow-plug relay	7
K3	Radiator-fan run-on relay	12
K4	Interior-light control relay	2
K4	Heater-filament relay	7
K5	Supertone-horn relay	2
K6	Engine-fan relay	11
K7	Rear-window heating relay	11
K8	Intermittent-wiper relay	10
K11	Starter locking/immobiliser relay	9
K17	Visual alarm relay	9
M1	Starter	1, 8
M1	Pump motor, hydraulic modulator	5
M1, 3	Ventilation-fan motor	11, 12
M2	Cooling-fan motor	11
M4	Wiper motor	10
M5	Windshield-washer motor	10
M6	Engine-fan relay	10
M7	Rear-window washer motor	10
N1	Voltage stabilizer	4
P1	Instrument cluster	4
P2	Electric speedometer	4
P3	Rev-meter	4
P4	Fuel gauge	4
P5	Engine-temperature display	4
P6	Clock	3
R1	Heater resistor	6
R1..4	Glow plugs	7
R1	Blower resistor	11
R5..7	Auxiliary heating (manual gearbox)	7

ID Code	Device	Section
R3..8	Glow plugs	8
S1	Ignition and starting switch	1
S1	Brake-light switch	5
S1	Operating controls for cruise control	7
S1	Lights switch	12
S2	Air-conditioning switch	7
S2	Evaporator temperature switch	12
S3	Oil-pressure switch	4
S3	Brake-pedal switch	7
S3	Radiator-fan temperature switch	12
S4	Handbrake switch	4
S4	Clutch-pedal switch	7
S4	Air-conditioning pressure switch	12
S4	Kick-down switch	13
S5	Brake-wear detector contact	4
S5	Brake-light switch	7
S6	Lights switch	2
S7	Fog-lamp switch	2
S7	Multi-function switch	13
S8	Dipswitch	2
S9	Brake-light switch	2
S10	Turn-signal switch	2
S11	Switch for tailgate lights	2
S12	Switch for backup lamps	2
S13	Hazard-warning and turn-signal switch	2
S14	Switch for glove-box lamp	2
S15	Switch for engine-compartment lamp	2
S16...18	Door position switch, front left, rear right, rear left	2
S19	Impact switch	2
S20	Door position switch, front right	2
S21	Door-handle switch	2
S22	Horn changeover switch	2
S23	Horn button	2
S24	Thermo-switch	11
S25	Rear-window heating switch	11
S26	Fan switch	11
S27	Wiper switch	10
S28	Rear-window wiper/washer switch	10
S29	Washer switch	10
S39	Alarm-system encoding switch	9
T1	Ignition coil	6
W1	Car radio antenna	3
W1	Connector for 16-core ribbon cable	12
W2, 3	Encoding wire	9
X1	ECU connector for Motronic/VE/EDC	6, 7

ID Code	Device	Section
X3	ECU connector for air conditioning	6
X4	Plug, lamp-control module	2
X4	ECU connector for transmission-shift control	6
X5	Connecting plug for instrument cluster	6
X6	Plug, check-control	2
X9	Plug-in base, hazard-warning relay	2
X10	Connector for central body-electronics basic module	2, 7
X11	ECU connector for engine management	13
X16	ECU connector for alarm system	9
X17	ECU connector for air conditioning/heater control	11
X18	Diagnosis socket	3
X21	Connector for glow control unit	8
X22	ECU plug ABS/ABD[1])	5

ID Code	Device	Section
X22	Diagnosis socket	8
X34	ECU connector for transmission-shift control	12, 13
X44	Navigation-system connector	5
X53	Connector for automatic air-conditioning system	12
X91, 92	Diagnosis socket	5, 13
Y1	Hydraulic pressure modulator	5
Y1	Fuel injector 1	6, 7
Y1	Valve block	12
Y1	Disabling solenoid	13
Y2	Air-conditioning output control	7
Y2	Air-conditioning compressor solenoid-operated coupling	12
Y2..5	Injectors 2..5	6, 7
Y5	Hot-water valve	11
Y6	Fuel injector 6	6
Y7	Canister-purge valve	6
Y8	Idle actuator	6
Y9	Electric fuel pump	6

[1]) ABD = Automatic Brake Differential.

Wiring diagram: Detached representation

In the detached method of representation, the continuous connecting lines between the individual devices are omitted. The individual devices are represented by squares, rectangles, circles, symbols or illustrations and designated in accordance with DIN 40719 Part 2. The terminal des-ignation of the device is also indicated. Each outgoing conductor from a device receives a code containing the terminal designation of the destination device as well as the device designation. If necessary, the conductor color is also given.

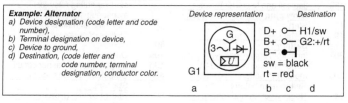

Example: Alternator
a) *Device designation (code letter and code number),*
b) *Terminal designation on device,*
c) *Device to ground,*
d) *Destination, (code letter and code number, terminal designation, conductor color.*

Device representation   Destination

D+ o— H1/sw
B+ o— G2:+/rt
B– •—|
sw = black
rt = red

G1

a   b   c   d

Terminal designation as per DIN 72 552

The purpose of the terminal-designation system for automotive electrical systems is to enable easy and correct connection of the conductors to the various devices, particularly in the event of repairs and equipment replacement.

The terminal designations do not identify the conductors, because devices with different terminal designations can be connected at the two ends of each conductor. For this reason, the terminal des-ignations need not be written on the lines which designate conductors.

In addition to the terminal designations listed, designations according to DIN VDE standards may also be used on electrical equipment.

If in the case of multiple-contact connections the number of terminal designations as per DIN 72552 does not suffice, the terminals are consecutively numbered using numbers or letters whose representations of specific functions are not standardized.

Terminal designations: Examples

Term.	Definition
	Ignition coil, ignition distributor
1	Low voltage
	Ignition distributor with two separate circuits
1a	to contact breaker I
1b	to contact breaker II
	Ignition coil, ignition distributor
4	High voltage
	Ignition distributor with two separate circuits
4a	from ignition coil I, terminal 4
4b	from ignition coil II, terminal 4
	Switched (+) downstream of battery (output of ignition/ driving switch)
15	
	Output on series resistor to ignition coil and to starter motor
15a	
	Glow plug and starter switch
17	Start
19	Preheat
	Battery
30	Input from battery positive (direct)
	Battery changeover 12/24 V
30a	Input from battery II positive
	Return from battery
31	Negative or ground (direct)
	Return to battery
31b	Negative or ground via switch or relay (switched negative)
	Battery changeover relay 12/24 V
31a	Return to battery II negative
31c	Return to battery I negative
	Electric motors
32	Return line[1]
33	Main terminal[1]

Term.	Definition
33a	Self-parking switchoff
33b	Shunt field
33f	For second lower-speed level
33g	For third lower-speed level
33h	For fourth lower-speed level
33L	Counterclockwise rotation
33R	Clockwise rotation
	Starters
45	Separate starter relay, output; starter, input (main current)
	Two-starter parallel operation
	Starting relay for engagement current
45a	Output, starter I, Input, starter I and II
45b	Output, starter II
48	Terminal on starter and on start-repeating relay for monitoring starting procedure
	Turn-signal flashers (pulse generators)
49	Input
49a	Output
49b	Output, second flasher circuit
49c	Output, third flasher circuit
	Starters
50	Starter control (direct)
	Battery changeover relay
50a	Output for starter control
	Starter control
50b	For parallel operation of two starters with sequential control
	Starting relay for sequential control of engagement current for parallel operation of two starters
50c	Input to starting relay for starter I

[1] Polarity reversal terminal 32/33 possible

Term.	Definition
50d	Input to starting relay for starter II
	Start-locking relay
50e	Input
50f	Output
	Start-repeating relay
50g	Input
50h	Output
	Wiper motors
53	Wiper motor, input (+)
53a	Wiper (+), self-parking
53b	Wiper (shunt winding)
53c	Electric windshield-washer pump
53e	Wiper (brake winding)
53i	Wiper motor with permanent magnet and third brush (for higher speed)
	Lighting
55	Fog lamp
56	Headlamp
56a	High beam and high-beam indicator
56b	Low beam
56d	Headlamp-flasher contact
57a	Parking lamp
57L	Parking lamp, left
57R	Parking lamp, right
58	Side-marker lamps, tail lamps, license-plate lamps and instrument-panel lamps
58L	ditto, left
58R	Right, license-plate lamp
	Alternators and voltage regulators
61	Alternator charge-indicator lamp
B+	Battery positive
B−	Battery negative
D+	Dynamo positive
D−	Dynamo negative
DF	Dynamo field
DF1	Dynamo field 1
DF2	Dynamo field 2
U,V,W	Alternator terminals
	Audio systems
75	Radio, cigarette lighter
76	Speakers
	Switches
	NC/changeover switch
81	Input
81a	1st output, NC switch side
81b	2nd output, NC switch side
	NO switch
82	Input
82a	1st output

Term.	Definition
82b	2nd output
82z	1st input
82y	2nd input
	Multi-position switch
83	Input
83a	Output, position 1
83b	Output, position 2
83L	Output, left position
83R	Output, right position
	Current relays
84	Input, actuator and relay contact
84a	Output, actuator
84b	Output, relay contact
	Switching relays
85	Output, actuator (winding end negative or ground)
86	Input, actuator (winding start)
86a	Winding start or 1st winding
86b	Winding tap or 2nd winding
	Relay contact for break (NC) and changeover contacts:
87	Input
87a	1st output (NC switch side)
87b	2nd output
87c	3rd output
87z	1st input
87y	2nd input
87x	3rd input
	Relay contact for make (NO) contact:
88	Input
	Relay contact for make (NO) and changeover contacts (make side):
88a	1st output
88b	2nd output
88c	3rd output
	Relay contact for make (NO) contact
88z	1st input
88y	2nd input
88x	3rd input
	Direction indicators (turn-signal flashers)
C	Indicator lamp 1
C0	Main terminal for monitoring circuits separate from flasher
C2	Indicator lamp 2
C3	Indicator lamp 3 (e. g. when towing two trailers)
L	Turn-signal lamps, left
R	Turn-signal lamps, right

Assembled-representation diagrams

For trouble-shooting on complex and extensively networked systems with self-diagnosis function, Bosch has developed system-specific schematic diagrams. For other systems on a wide variety of vehicles, Bosch provides the assembled-representation diagrams on a "P" CD-ROM. They are fully integrated in ESI, the Electronic Service Information system from Bosch. This provides automotive repair shops with a useful tool for locating faults or connecting up retrofit equipment. An assembled-representation diagram is shown opposite.

In contrast with other schematic diagrams, the assembled-representation diagrams use American symbols that are supplemented by additional descriptions (see below). Those include component codes such as "A28" (Anti-theft system) that are explained in Table 1, and wire color codes (explained in Table 2). Both

those tables are available on the "P" CD-ROM.

Table 1 Explanation of component codes

Code	Description
A1865	Electrically adjustable seat system
A28	Anti-theft system
A750	Fuse/relay box
F53	Fuse C
F70	Fuse A
M334	Fuel-supply pump
S1178	Warning-buzzer switch
Y157	Vacuum actuator
Y360	Actuator, right front door
Y361	Actuator, left front door
Y364	Actuator, right rear door
Y365	Actuator, left rear door
Y366	Actuator, fuel filler flap
Y367	Actuator, trunk lid/tailgate

Table 2 Explanation of wire color codes

Code	Description
BLK	Black
BLU	Blue
BRN	Brown
CLR	Clear
DKBLU	Dark blue
DKGRN	Dark green
GRN	Green
GRY	Gray
LTBLU	Light blue
LTGRN	Light green
NCA	Color not known
ORG	Orange
PNK	Pink
PPL	Purple
RED	Red
TAN	Tan
VIO	Violet
WHT	White
YEL	Yellow

Additional descriptions on assembled-representation diagrams
1 *Wire color code,* **2** *Connector number,*
3 *Pin number (a dotted line between pins indicates that all pins are in the same connector).*

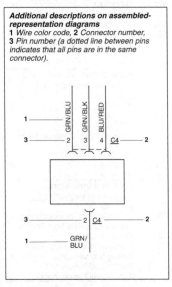

Assembled-representation diagram of a door locking system (example)

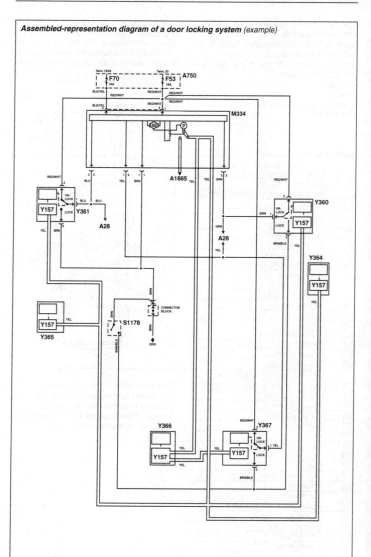

The assembled-representation diagrams are subdivided into system circuits and, if applicable, subsystems (see Table 3). As with other systems in ESI, system circuits are also allocated to one of the four vehicle subassemblies:
– engine,
– body,
– wheels and suspension, and
– drivetrain.

Table 3 System circuits

1	Engine management
2	Starting/charging
3	Air conditioning/heating (HVAC)
4	Radiator fan
5	ABS
6	Cruise control
7	Power windows
8	Central locking system
9	Instrument panel
10	Washer/wiper system
11	Headlamps
12	Exterior lights
13	Electricity supply
14	Grounding
15	Data line
16	Lockout
17	Theft-deterrence
18	Passive-safety systems
19	Power antenna
20	Warning system
21	Heated rear-window/mirrors
22	Supplementary safety systems
23	Interior lighting
24	Power steering
25	Mirror adjuster
26	Soft-top controls
27	Horn
28	Trunk, tailgate
29	Seat adjustment
30	Electronic damping
31	Cigarette lighter, socket
32	Navigation
33	Transmission
34	Active body components
35	Vibration damping
36	Mobile phone
37	Radio/Hi-Fi
38	Immobilizer

It is important to be aware of the grounding points, particularly when fitting additional accessories. For that reason, the "P" CD-ROM includes the vehicle-specific location diagram for the grounding points (see below) in addition to the assembled-representation circuit diagrams.

> **Grounding points**
> **1** *Left front wing*, **2** *Front end*, **3** *Engine*,
> **4** *Bulkhead*, **5** *Right front wing*, **6** *Footwell bulkhead/dashboard*, **7** *Left front door*,
> **8** *Right front door*, **9** *Left rear door*, **10** *Right rear door*, **11** *A pillars*, **12** *Passenger compartment*, **13** *Roof*, **14** *Rear end*,
> **15** *C pillars*, **16** *B pillars*.

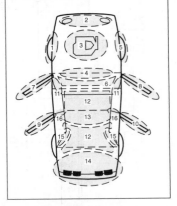

The assembled-representation diagrams use American diagram symbols which are different from the DIN/IEC symbols. A selection of the American diagram symbols is shown on the opposite page.

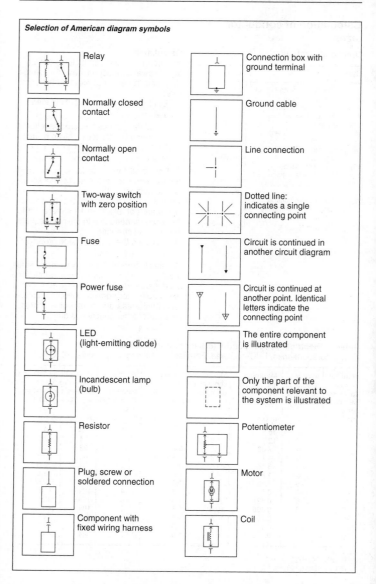

Selection of American diagram symbols

Relay	Connection box with ground terminal
Normally closed contact	Ground cable
Normally open contact	Line connection
Two-way switch with zero position	Dotted line: indicates a single connecting point
Fuse	Circuit is continued in another circuit diagram
Power fuse	Circuit is continued at another point. Identical letters indicate the connecting point
LED (light-emitting diode)	The entire component is illustrated
Incandescent lamp (bulb)	Only the part of the component relevant to the system is illustrated
Resistor	Potentiometer
Plug, screw or soldered connection	Motor
Component with fixed wiring harness	Coil

Calculation of conductor sizes

Units and symbols

Symbol		Unit
A	Conductor cross section	mm²
I	Electric current	A
l	Conductor length	m
P	Power required by load	W
R	Resistance (ohmic) (loads)	Ω
S	Current density of conductor	A/mm²
U_N	Nominal voltage	V
U_{vl}	Permissible voltage drop along insulated wire	V
U_{vg}	Permissible voltage drop across complete circuit	V
ϱ	Resistivity	Ω · mm²/m

Calculations

In determining the conductor cross section, allowance must be made for voltage drop and the effect of elevated temperatures.

1. Determine the current I of the load

$$I = P/U_N = U_N/R$$

2. Calculate conductor cross-sectional area A using figures for U_{vl} given in Table 2 (for copper $\varrho = 0.0185$ Ω · mm²/m).

$$A = I \cdot \varrho \; l/U_{vl}$$

3. Round-off the value for A to the next larger conductor cross section in accordance with Table 1.

Individual conductors with a cross-sectional area of less than 1 mm² are not to be recommended due to their inadequate mechanical strength.

4. Calculate the actual voltage drop U_{vl}

$$U_{vl} = I \cdot \varrho \; l/A \quad \text{and}$$

5. Check current density S to make sure heat generation is within permissible limits (for short-duty operation $S < 30$ A/mm², see Table 1 for nominal conductor cross-sectional areas and permissible continuous currents for continuous duty).

$$S = I/A$$

Table 1. Electrical copper conductors for motor vehicles
Single-core, untinned, PVC-insulated. Permissible working temperature: 70 °C.[2]

Nominal conductor cross-sectional area mm²	Approx. number of individual strands[1]	Maximum impedance per meter[1] at +20°C m Ω/m	Maximum conductor diameter[1] mm	Nominal thickness of insulation[1] mm	Maximum external diameter of insulated wire[1] mm	Permissible continuous current (guide figure)[2] at ambient temperature of +30°C A	Permissible continuous current (guide figure)[2] at ambient temperature of +50°C A
1	32	18.5	1.5	0.6	2.7	19	13.5
1.5	30	12.7	1.8	0.6	3.0	24	17.0
2.5	50	7.60	2.2	0.7	3.6	32	22.7
4	56	4.71	2.8	0.8	4.4	42	29.8
6	84	3.14	3.4	0.8	5.0	54	38.3
10	80	1.82	4.5	1.0	6.5	73	51.8
16	126	1.16	6.3	1.0	8.3	98	69.6
25	196	0.743	7.8	1.3	10.4	129	91.6
35	276	0.527	9.0	1.3	11.6	158	112
50	396	0.368	10.5	1.5	13.5	198	140
70	360	0.259	12.5	1.5	15.5	245	174
95	475	0.196	14.8	1.6	18.0	292	207
120	608	0.153	16.5	1.6	19.7	344	244

[1] To DIN ISO 6722, Part 3.
[2] To DIN VDE 0298, Part 4.

The values given for U_{vl} in Table 2 are used to calculate the dimensions of the main positive conductor. The voltage drop in the ground return is not taken into account. In the case of insulated ground cables, the total length in both directions should normally be used.

The U_{vg} values given in the table are each values and cannot be used for conductor calculations because they also include the contact resistance of switches, fuses, etc.

Notes

1 In special cases where the starter-motor main lead is very long and the minimum starting temperature is reduced, the U_{vl} figure may possibly be exceeded.

2 If the starter-motor main return lead is insulated, the voltage drop along the return lead should not exceed that for the supply lead; the permissible figure is 4 % of the rated voltage in each case and 8 % in total.

3 The U_{vl} figures apply to starter solenoid temperatures of between 50 and 80 °C.

4 Also make allowance for the lead to the starter switch if necessary.

Table 2. Recommended max. voltage drop

Type of conductor	Voltage drop across positive conductor U_v		Voltage drop across complete circuit U_{vg}		Remarks
Nominal voltage U_N	12 V	24 V	12 V	24 V	
Lighting cables From light switch terminal 30 to bulbs < 15 W to trailer socket From trailer socket to lights	0.1 V	0.1 V	0.6 V	0.6 V	Current at rated voltage and rated power
From light switch terminal 30 to bulbs > 15 W to trailer socket	0.5 V	0.5 V	0.9 V	0.9 V	
From light switch terminal 30 to headlamps	0.3 V	0.3 V	0.6 V	0.6 V	
Charging cable From 3-phase alternator terminal B + to battery	0.4 V	0.8 V	—	—	Current at rated voltage and rated power
Starter power cable	0.5 V	1.0 V	—	—	Starter short-circuit current at + 20 °C (Notes 1 and 2)
Starter control cable From ignition switch to starter terminal 50 Solenoid switch with single winding	1.4 V	2.0 V	1.7 V	2.5 V	Maximum control current (Notes 3 and 4)
Solenoid switch with engagement and hold winding	1.5 V	2.2 V	1.9 V	2.8 V	
Other control cables From switch to relay, horn, etc.	0.5 V	1.0 V	1.5 V	2.0 V	Current at rated voltage

Connectors

Function and requirements

Electrical connectors must provide a reliable electrical connection between different system components and thereby ensure safe and reliable operation of the systems concerned under all operating conditions. They are designed to withstand the various stresses they can be expected to be subjected to during the service life of the vehicle. Examples of such stresses are:
- vibration,
- temperature fluctuation,
- extreme temperatures,
- damp and splash-water,
- corrosive fluids and gases, and
- micro-movement between contacts resulting in frictional corrosion.

Such stresses can increase the contact resistance between mating connectors and even cause complete loss of conduction. The insulation resistance can also be reduced, thereby causing short circuits between adjacent conductors.

Electrical connectors therefore must have the following characteristics:
- low contact resistance between current-carrying components,
- high insulation strength between current-carrying components with different electrical potentials,
- high sealing capabilities against water, damp and saline spray.

In addition to their physical properties, connectors must also satisfy other requirements specific to their particular area of application such as:
- straightforward and foolproof connection/disconnection in vehicle assembly/servicing situations, non-reversibility,
- secure and perceptible locking action, straightforward release,
- toughness and suitability for automated wiring-harness manufacture and transport.

Types of design

There is a range of design series spanning the variety of applications for Bosch electrical connectors. The various designs incorporate the types of contact specifically suited to the conditions in which they are used. Below are examples of two types of contact and their characteristics.

Bosch micro-contact

This tin or gold-plated contact which fits a 0.6 mm contact pin has been specially designed for a pin spacing of 2.5 mm, high thermal resistance (155°C) and high resistance to vibration. It is suited to use in multi-pin connectors because it allows very compact connector dimensions.

The contact consists of two parts. One performs the conducting function and the other (steel spring sleeve) provides the contact pressure (normal contact force).

The steel spring sleeve maintains the contact pressure even at high temperatures and for the complete service life of the vehicle. The higher forces that are then necessarily required to connect and disconnect the connector are reduced by a special connector-locating facility. This also ensures the connector is precisely aligned so that the contacts or pins cannot be damaged by twisting or bending.

The complete connector is sealed against the male connector on the ECU concerned by a circumferential radial seal

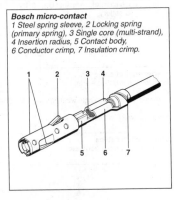

Bosch micro-contact
1 Steel spring sleeve, 2 Locking spring (primary spring), 3 Single core (multi-strand), 4 Insertion radius, 5 Contact body, 6 Conductor crimp, 7 Insulation crimp.

in the connector casing. This, together with three sealing lips, ensures a reliable seal against the ECU sealing collar.

The contacts are protected against the ingress of damp along the cable by a flat seal through which the contacts are passed with the wire crimped to them. The flat seal is made of a silicon gel and replaces the conventional individual core seal while at the same time making it possible to substantially reduce connector size and to vary contact usage (different numbers of contacts used).

The flat seal forms a reliable seal on its inner surfaces against the insulation of the wires.

When the connector is assembled, the contact with the wire attached is pushed through the flat seal that is already in place in the connector and the contact slides home into its position in the contact holder. There, it automatically locks into position by virtue of the locking spring. When all contacts are in position, a sliding pin provides a secondary locking mechanism. This is a supplementary locking facility and increases the security of the connector against inadvertent withdrawal of the wire and contact by force.

Bosch sensor/actuator contact

The Bosch sensor/actuator contact is used for 2...7-pin compact connectors which connect engine-compartment components (sensors and actuators) with the ECU. The pin spacing of 5 mm allows for the physical strength required.

The Bosch sensor/actuator contact has an internal meander-shaped design which reliably prevents vibration transmission from the cable to the contacts. This ensures that there is no relative movement of the contact surfaces that might lead to corrosion.

The compact connector has individual core seals which prevent the ingress of dampness into the contact area. Three sealing lips on the connector casing provide the pressure to ensure there is an adequate seal against splash-water and other sources of damp.

The self-locking snap-on connectors with additional release facility ensure ease of connection and disconnection in vehicle assembly and servicing situations. The connector is released by pressing a point marked by a ribbed surface.

The typical uses for this type of contact include connectors on diesel-engine components (e. g. common-rail pressure sensor, fuel injectors) and gasoline-engine components (e. g. fuel injectors, knock sensor).

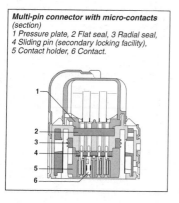

Multi-pin connector with micro-contacts (section)
1 Pressure plate, 2 Flat seal, 3 Radial seal, 4 Sliding pin (secondary locking facility), 5 Contact holder, 6 Contact.

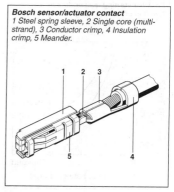

Bosch sensor/actuator contact
1 Steel spring sleeve, 2 Single core (multi-strand), 3 Conductor crimp, 4 Insulation crimp, 5 Meander.

Automotive electrical systems

Energy supply

The vehicle must be able to draw upon sufficient reserves of electrical energy to satisfy a number of requirements. The available current supply must be capable of ensuring that the vehicle can be started and operated at all times. Operation of electrical accessories for a reasonable period of time with the engine off should not make subsequent engine starts impossible. Battery, starter, alternator and the electrical system as a whole must be designed for mutually compatible operation. The optimization criteria for the best possible combination are light weight, small volume and low fuel consumption. Low fuel consumption is generally the prime consideration. The following factors must receive special consideration:

Starting temperature

The lowest temperature at which the engine can be started depends upon a number of factors including the battery (capacity, internal resistance, state of charge, etc.) and the starter (size, with or without intermediate transmission, electrical/permanent-magnet excitation, etc.). If the engine is to be started at a tempera-ture of $-20\,°C$, for example, the battery must have a given minimum state of charge p.

Alternator output

The current output of the alternator varies as a function of engine speed. The alternator can only supply a certain percentage of its rated current at idle n_L. If the current I_V consumed by the loads is greater than the current I_G supplied by the alternator, e.g. when the engine is idling, the battery will discharge. The voltage of the vehicle's electrical system will then drop.

If on the other hand, the current draw I_V is less than the current I_G from the alternator, some of this current difference is used for battery charging I_B.

Driving

The speed at which the alternator turns depends upon the particular type of operation for the vehicle in question. The cumulative speed frequency distribution shows how often a certain speed is achieved or exceeded during vehicle operation.

Owing to traffic congestion or stops at traffic lights, a passenger car driven in commuter traffic is run at idle a high percentage of the time. Under highway driving conditions, on the other hand, the percentage of time the vehicle is run at idle is generally lower. Additional idle time is accumulated by city buses because

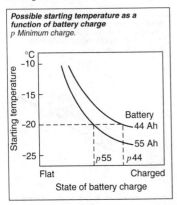

Possible starting temperature as a function of battery charge
p Minimum charge.

Starting temperature (°C): Battery 44 Ah, 55 Ah; $p\,55$, $p\,44$; Flat — Charged
State of battery charge

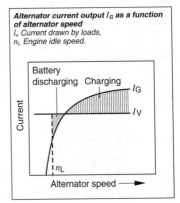

Alternator current output I_G as a function of alternator speed
I_v Current drawn by loads,
n_L Engine idle speed.

Battery discharging — Charging; I_G, I_V; n_L
Current / Alternator speed →

they must make frequent stops. The state of charge of the battery is further reduced when loads must be left on with the engine turned off (e.g., at bus terminals). Long-distance tour buses generally run only a small percentage of the time at idle.

Electrical loads
Electrical loads have different duty cycles. A differentiation is made between continuous loads (ignition, fuel injection, etc.), long-time loads (lighting, heated rear window, etc.) and short-time loads (turn signals, stop lamps, etc.). Use of some electrical loads is seasonal (air conditioners in

summer, seat heaters in winter). The on-time of electrical radiator fans depends upon temperature and driving conditions. In winter, lights are generally used when driving in commuter traffic.

The electrical demands encountered during vehicle operation are not constant. The initial minutes following starting are generally characterized by high demand (for heating or cooling) with a subsequent sharp drop in current draw:

1. In the future, electrically heated catalytic converters will require additional power of 1...4 kW in order to reach operating temperatures of >300 °C within

Equipment power consumption as a function of duty cycle

Load	Power consumption	Average power output
Motronic, electric fuel pump	250 W	250 W
Radio	20 W	20 W
Side-marker lamps	8 W	7 W
Low-beam headlamps	110 W	90 W
License-plate lamp, tail lamps	30 W	25 W
Warning lamp, instruments	22 W	20 W
Heated rear window	200 W	60 W
Interior heating, fan	120 W	50 W
Electric radiator fan	120 W	30 W
Windshield wipers	50 W	10 W
Stop lamps	42 W	11 W
Turn-signal lamps	42 W	5 W
Front fog lamps	110 W	20 W
Fog warning lamp	21 W	2 W
Total Installed loads	1145 W	
Average power consumed by loads		600 W

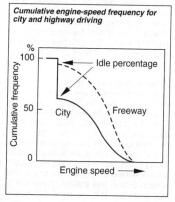

Cumulative engine-speed frequency for city and highway driving

Cumulative frequency (%) — 100, 50, 0
Idle percentage
City
Freeway
Engine speed →

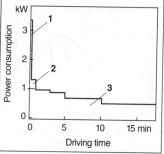

Electrical power consumption as a function of driving time
1 Catalytic-converter heater, 2 Secondary-air pump, 3 Heater, blower, engine management, etc.

Power consumption (kW) — 3, 2, 1, 0
Driving time — 0, 5, 10, 15 min

10...30 s after the vehicle is started (actual figures vary according to engine size and emissions-system design).
2. The secondary-air pump responsible for supplying air immediately downstream of the combustion chambers for exhaust-gas afterburning, can operate for up to 200 s after the engine is started.
3. Other electrical equipment such as heaters (including defrosters, etc.), blowers and lighting systems draw current for various periods, while the engine-management system remains in continuous operation.

Charging voltage

The battery charging voltage must be higher in cold weather and lower in warm weather in order to accommodate the chemical processes which take place inside the battery. The gassing voltage curve indicates the maximum permissible charging voltage at which the battery does not "gas".

Vehicle loads require a voltage which is as constant as possible. The voltage applied to lamp bulbs must have very close tolerances so that lamp-bulb service life and light intensity remain within specified limits. The voltage regulator limits the maximum voltage. It affects the lower voltage limit when the potential alternator current I_G is larger than the system's load-current requirement I_V. The voltage regulator is usually mounted on the alternator.

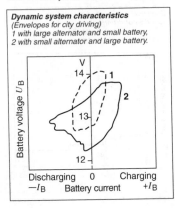

Dynamic system characteristics
(Envelopes for city driving)
1 with large alternator and small battery,
2 with small alternator and large battery.

Battery voltage U_B

Discharging   0   Charging
$-I_B$ Battery current $+I_B$

In the event of significant deviations between the temperature of the voltage regulator and that of the battery electrolyte, it is advantageous to monitor the voltage-regulation temperature directly at the battery. It is possible to compensate for the voltage loss in the charge cable between the alternator and the battery by using a regulator to monitor actual voltage directly at the latter (over a supplementary wire).

Dynamic system characteristics

The interrelationships between the battery, alternator, loads, temperature, engine speed and engine/alternator speed ratio define the system's dynamic response pattern. It is dynamic because it varies along with each combination of parameters and each set of operating conditions. An xy-coordinate graph recorder can be connected to the battery terminals to plot dynamic response patterns.

Charging-balance calculation

The charging-balance calculation must take into consideration the above-mentioned influencing variables. A computer program is used to determine the state of battery charge at the end of a typical driving cycle. A typical passenger-car cycle consists of vehicle operation in commuter traffic (engine speeds are low) combined with winter operation (at which time charging-current consumption by the battery is low). Summer operation may place even greater loads on the system when the vehicle is equipped with an air conditioner (high current draw). The battery's charge at the end of the cycle must – at the very least – be sufficient to allow a subsequent engine start at the temperature in question.

Vehicle electrical system

The voltage level in the vehicle electrical system, and thus the battery charge, are also affected by the wiring between alternator, battery and electrical loads. If all loads are connected on the battery side, the total current in the charging cable is $I_G = I_B + I_V$. The charging voltage is lower owing to the high voltage drop. If all loads are connected on the alternator side, the voltage drop is less and the charging voltage is higher. This could be disadvantageous to loads (such as electronic circuitry) which are sensitive to voltage peaks or high voltage ripple. Those electrical devices which feature high current draw and relative insensitivity to overvoltage should therefore be connected at the alternator, and voltage-sensitive loads with low current draw should be connected at the battery. Voltage drops can be minimized by suitable conductor cross sections and good connections whose resistance remains low even after a long period.

Future automotive electrical systems
Within the standard 12-volt automotive electrical system, the battery represents a compromise between (to some extent) conflicting requirements: its capacity must be selected with reference to starting requirements as well as on-board current supply. During the engine starting sequence, the battery is subjected to high current loads (300...500 A). The associated voltage dip has an adverse effect on certain electrical consumer units (e.g. units with microcontroller). In contrast, current draw in standard operation – where battery capacity is the salient factor – is minimal. It is not possible to optimize both criteria within a single battery.

Future automotive electrical systems will feature two batteries (separate accumulators for starting and other electrical requirements); the "high power for starting" and "general-purpose electrical sup-

ply" functions will be separated. This will make it possible to avoid the voltage collapse that attends the starting process while ensuring reliable cold starts, even with the general-purpose battery discharged to 30 % of its capacity.

Starter battery
The starter battery must supply substantial current, but only for a limited period (during starting). Compact dimensions allow installation in the immediate vicinity of the starter motor with correspondingly short connection cables. Capacity can also be reduced. To ensure consistently high charge factors, this battery features a nominal rating of 10 volts. Because the voltage is lower than the 12 V of the other, general-purpose battery, the starter battery has charging priority.

Charging and isolation module
This module isolates the starter battery with starter from the rest of the electrical system during starting and when the engine is off. This arrangement prevents the on-board voltage collapse associated with starting, while also protecting the starter battery against discharge when electrical systems operate with the engine off.

General-purpose battery
This battery is consigned exclusively to supplying the vehicle's electrical system (excluding the starter). It supplies rela-

---

Vehicle electrical system with loads connected to alternator and battery
1 Alternator, 2 High-draw electrical devices, 3 Low-draw electrical devices, 4 Battery.

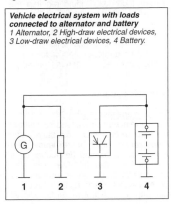

Future electrical system
1 Starter, 2 Charging and insulation module, 3 Starter battery, 4 Alternator, 5 Electrical loads, 6 Engine management, 7 General-purpose battery.

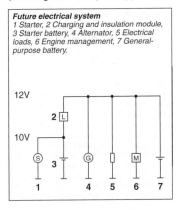

tively low currents (e.g., roughly 20 A for the engine-management system), but is also designed to deal with major cyclical variations; assuming adequate capacity and electrical demand that remains within the discharge range, this unit can store and furnish substantial amounts of energy. Design dimensions are selected based on capacity reserves for electrical equipment (e.g., parking lights, hazard-warning flashers), constant-draw devices and maximum specified discharge level.

Enhanced-performance versions

Progressively more powerful systems are envisaged for vehicles with extremely high power requirements. Among the potential design options could be:
– current supply to the engine-management system is from the starter battery instead of the general-purpose unit, or the system can alternate selectively between the two,
– the starter battery is also a 12 V unit; more complicated design is then needed to ensure that it retains charging priority,
– nominal voltage > 12 V,
– multiple-voltage networks featuring a –12 V (or –24 V) circuit installed parallel to the +12 V supply circuit, providing potential supplementary supplies of 24 V (or 36 V) from the outside conductor sections of the two circuits,
– application of two alternators.

Selection of a particular option will depend upon the precise objectives that the on-board circuit concept is to fulfill (for example, priority on avoiding voltage collapse during starting, weight savings, enhanced starting reliability).

Fuel consumption

A small portion of the fuel used by the vehicle is used to drive the alternator and transport the combined weight of starter, battery, and alternator (approx. 5 % in a medium-sized car).

Average fuel consumption per 100 km: For a weight of 10 kg: approx. 0.1 l; for 100 W of drive power: approx. 0.1 l. Alternators with high levels of efficiency at part load therefore help to reduce fuel consumption despite being slightly heavier.

Starter batteries

Requirements

Modern vehicles are placing increasingly exacting demands on starter batteries: Enhanced cold-starting power (higher currents, especially at low temperatures) is needed with diesel engines, while vehicles equipped with large numbers of sophisticated electrical accessories require large amounts of electrical energy, not only when driving, but also when stationary. Maintaining a positive charging balance is especially difficult with frequent town and commuter driving in winter because these are always accompanied by substantial current consumption.

Within the automotive electrical system, the battery assumes the role of a chemical storage unit for the electrical energy produced by the alternator. The battery must be capable of limited-duration high-current delivery for starting, and it must be able to furnish some or all of the electrical energy for other important system components for limited periods with the engine at idle or off. The lead-acid accumulator battery represents the usual means of meeting these demands. Typical system voltages are 12 V for passenger cars, and 24 V for commercial vehicles (achieved by connecting two 12 V batteries in series).

Batteries must be specifically designed to meet individual system requirements for starting power, capacity and current consumption at temperatures ranging from approx. –30...+70 °C. There are also additional specifications which must be satisfied for particular applications (e.g., maintenance-free batteries, vibration-proof batteries).

Lead-acid batteries

Charging and discharging

The active materials in a lead-acid battery are lead oxide (PbO_2) on the positive plates, spongy, highly porous lead (Pb) on the negative plates and the electrolyte, diluted sulfuric acid (H_2SO_4). The electrolyte is simultaneously an ion conductor for charging and discharging. In juxtaposition with the electrolyte, PbO_2 and Pb

Density and freezing point of diluted sulfuric acid

State of charge	Battery design	Electrolyte density kg/l[1]	Freezing point °C
Charged	standard	1.28	−68
	tropicalized	1.23	−40
Half charged	standard	1.16/1.20[2]	−17 ... −27
	tropicalized	1.13/1.16[2]	−13 ... −17
Discharged	standard	1.04/1.12[2]	−3 ... −11
	tropicalized	1.03/1.08[2]	−2 ... −8

[1] At 20 °C: The specific gravity of the electrolyte decreases as the temperature rises, and increases as the temperature drops at a rate of around 0.01 kg/l per 14 K difference in temperature.

[2] Lower figure: High electrolyte utilization. Higher figure: Low electrolyte utilization.

Element	Charged	Discharged
Positive plate	PbO_2	$PbSO_4$
Electrolyte	$2 \times H_2SO_4$	$2 \times H_2O$
Negative plate	Pb	$PbSO_4$

adopt typical electrical voltages (individual potentials) the magnitudes of which (disregarding polarity) are equal to the sum of the cell voltages measurable from the outside. At rest, the cell voltage is approx. 2 V, increasing during charging and decreasing when the cell is subjected to a load. When the cell discharges, PbO_2 and Pb combine with H_2SO_4 to form $PbSO_4$ (lead sulfate). This conversion causes the electrolyte to lose SO_4 (sulfate) ions, and its density decreases. When the cell charges, the active materials PbO_2 and Pb are reconstituted from the $PbSO_4$.

If the charging voltage continues to be applied after the cell has reached a state of full charge, only the electrolytic decomposition of water occurs, producing oxygen at the positive plate and hydrogen at the negative plate (oxyhydrogen gas). Electrolyte density can be used as an indication of the state of charge of the battery. The accuracy of this relationship depends upon battery design (see table below showing "acidity levels") as well as electrolyte stratification and battery wear with a certain degree of irreversible sulfating and/or a high degree of shedding of the plate material.

Behavior at low temperatures
Basically, the chemical reactions in an accumulator battery take place more slowly at lower temperatures. The starting power even of a fully charged battery therefore decreases as the temperature drops. The more the battery discharges, the more diluted the electrolyte becomes. This means that freezing of the electrolyte in a discharged battery is very likely. Such a battery is only capable of supplying a low current which is not sufficient for starting the vehicle.

Battery characteristics

Designation
In addition to mechanical parameters such as dimensions, mounting and terminal design, batteries are primarily characterized by electrical ratings measured

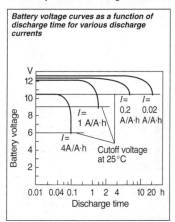

Battery voltage curves as a function of discharge time for various discharge currents

according to specific testing standards (e.g. DIN EN 60096-1, previously DIN 43 539-2). Starter batteries manufactured in Germany are identified by a 9-digit type number, the rated voltage, the rated capacity and the cold-discharge test current as per DIN EN 60095-1/A11.

Example: 555 059 042 indicates 12 V, 55 A·h, a special type designation (059) and a cold-discharge test current of 420 A. In the future, this European standard will become a more widely used battery-identification convention.

Capacity

Battery capacity, rated in A·h, is the current which can be drawn from the battery under specified conditions. Capacity decreases as discharge current increases and temperature decreases.

Nominal capacity K_{20}

As defined by DIN EN, nominal capacity is the charge which the battery can deliver within 20 h at constant discharge current down to a cutoff voltage of 10.5 V (1.75 V/cell). The battery nominal capacity depends upon the quantities of active material used (positive mass, negative mass, electrolyte), and is relatively unaffected by the number of plates.

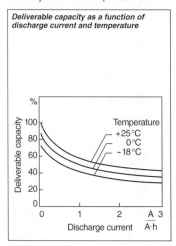

Deliverable capacity as a function of discharge current and temperature

Cold-discharge test current I_{CC} (previously I_{KP})

This figure provides an index of the battery's current-supply capability at low temperatures. According to DIN EN standards, the terminal voltage when discharging at I_{CC} and −18°C must be at least 7.5 V (1.25 V/cell) 10 s after discharge starts. Further details relating to discharge duration are specified in the above standard. The short-time behavior of the battery when discharged at I_{CC} is largely determined by the number of plates, their surface area, and the gap between plates and separator material. Another variable which characterizes starting behavior is internal resistance R_i.

The following equation is true for a fully-charged battery (12V) at −18°C: $R_i \leq 4000/I_{CC}$ (mΩ), where I_{CC} is given in A. The battery internal resistance and other resistances in the starter circuit determine the cranking speed.

Battery design

The 12-volt automotive battery contains six series-connected, individually partitioned cells in a polypropylene case. Each cell consists of a positive and negative plate set. These sets, in turn, are composed of the plates (lead grid and active mass) and the microporous material (separators) which insulates the plates of opposite polarities. The electrolyte is in the form of diluted sulfuric acid which permeates the pores in the plates and separators, and the voids in the cells. The terminals, the cell connectors, and the plate straps are made of lead; the openings in the partitions for the cellular connectors are tightly sealed. A hot-molding process is employed to permanently bond the one-piece cover to the battery case, providing the battery's upper seal. On conventional batteries, each cell is sealed by its own vent plug, which when removed permits initial battery filling and topping-up during service. When screwed in, the vent plugs allow charge gases to escape. Maintenance-free batteries frequently appear to be completely sealed units, but they also require escape vents.

Battery designs

Maintenance-free battery

The maintenance-free battery defined in DIN standards features lead-alloy grids with a low antimony content to reduce gas generation and the attendant water losses during charging. This prolongs the electrolyte check intervals to:

- every 15 months or 25,000 km on low-maintenance batteries, and
- every 25 months or 40,000 km for maintenance-free batteries (as per DIN).

There is never any need (and generally no means provided) to check the electrolyte level on the completely maintenance-free (lead-calcium) battery. With the exception of two extremely small vent orifices, this type of battery is completely sealed. As long as the electrical system is operating normally (U = constant), water decomposition is minimal, and the electrolyte reserves above the plates will last for the life of the battery. A lead-calcium battery of this type also offers the advantage of very low self-discharge. This means that it can be stored for several months provided it is fully charged to begin with. When a maintenance-free battery is recharged remote from the vehicle's electrical system (i.e., with battery charger), the charge voltage is never to exceed 2.3...2.4 V per cell; overcharging at constant currents, or the use of chargers with a W charge curve will always lead to water consumption in the lead-acid battery.

Deep-cycle battery

Due to their particular design characteristics (thin plates, lightweight separator materials), starter batteries are poorly suited for applications in which frequent high levels of discharge occur, as this causes substantial wear at the positive plates (particularly through separation and sedimentation of the active material). In the deep-cycle battery, the separators have fiberglass mats to provide the positive mass with extra support and prevent premature shedding which would otherwise lead to sludge formation. The service life, as measured in charge/discharge cycles, is roughly twice as long as that of a standard battery. Deep-cycle batteries featuring pocket separators and felt layers have an even longer service life.

Vibration-proof battery

In the vibration-proof battery, an anchor of cast resin and/or plastic prevents the

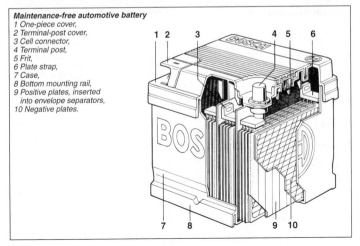

Maintenance-free automotive battery
1 One-piece cover,
2 Terminal-post cover,
3 Cell connector,
4 Terminal post,
5 Frit,
6 Plate strap,
7 Case,
8 Bottom mounting rail,
9 Positive plates, inserted into envelope separators,
10 Negative plates.

plate stacks from moving relative to the battery case. According to DIN requirements, this type of battery must be capable of withstanding a 20-hour sinusoidal vibration test (frequency 22 Hz) and a maximum acceleration of 6 ·g. In other words, the test is roughly 10 times as severe as for a standard battery. Vibration-proof batteries are used primarily in commercial vehicles, construction machinery, tractors, etc. and are identified by the code "Rf".

Heavy-duty battery
The heavy-duty battery combines the attributes of the deep-cycle and vibration-proof units. It is used in commercial vehicles which feature extreme vibration levels, and in which cyclic discharge patterns are commonplace. Designation: "HD".

"Kt" battery
The Kt (or "S") battery shares the basic design of the deep-cycle device, compared to which it has thicker plates, but fewer of them. Although no cold-discharge current is specified for the "Kt" battery, its starting power lies well below (35...40%) that of comparably sized standard units. This battery is used in applications characterized by extreme cyclic variations, e.g., as a drive battery (P. 576, "Lead-acid batteries").

Operating states

Charging
Voltage limiting is applied when the battery is charged in the vehicle. This corresponds to the IU charging pattern, in which the charge current drops automatically in response to increasing battery voltage. The IU method prevents harmful overcharging and ensures a long battery service life.

In contrast, many service-station and home chargers still operate with constant current or with a W-shaped charging curve (see diagram of "W" charging curve). In either case, there is little or no reduction in charge current once the battery is fully charged, resulting in substantial water consumption and corrosion at the positive grid.

Discharge
Soon after the start of the discharge process, the battery's voltage drops by a specific increment; it then remains relatively consistent, falling slowly under continuing load. The ultimate voltage collapse occurs only just before complete discharge, upon exhaustion of one or several active components (positive mass, negative mass, electrolyte).

Self-discharge (see also "Battery maintenance" below)
Batteries discharge themselves continually, even when no loads (electrical de-

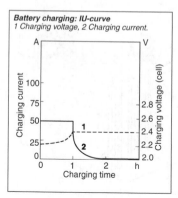

Battery charging: IU-curve
1 Charging voltage, 2 Charging current.

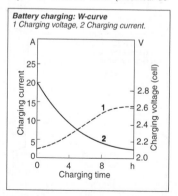

Battery charging: W-curve
1 Charging voltage, 2 Charging current.

vices) are attached. At room temperature, a modern low-antimony battery will lose about 0.1...0.2 % of its total charge each day. As the battery ages, the rate can increase to as much as 1 % per day as a result of antimony transfer to the negative plate, and various other sources of contamination. This phenomenon can ultimately lead to battery failure. Rule of thumb regarding the influence of temperature: The rate of self-discharge doubles with every 10 °C increase in temperature.

The self-discharge rate of the lead-calcium battery is substantially lower (by a factor of 1:5), and it remains virtually constant throughout the life of the battery.

Battery maintenance

On low-maintenance batteries, the electrolyte level should be inspected in accordance with the manufacturer's instructions; when indicated, it should be replenished to the MAX mark with distilled or demineralized water. To minimize self-discharge, the battery should be kept clean and dry. An additional pre-winter examination of the electrolyte's specific gravity – or, should this be impossible, of its open-circuit voltage – is also advisable. The battery should be recharged when the specific gravity is below 1.20 g/ml, or the open-circuit voltage is under 12.2 V. Terminals, terminal clamps and installation clamps should be coated with acid-protection grease.

Batteries temporarily removed from service should be stored in a cool, dry place. The electrolyte's specific gravity and/or the open-circuit voltage should be checked every 3-4 months. The battery should be recharged whenever the figures drop below 1.20 g/ml or 12.2 V. Low-maintenance and maintenance-free batteries are best recharged with the IU method (see "Charging") at a maximum voltage of 14.4 V. This method allows adequate charging times in the order of 24 hours without any attendant risk of overcharging. If a constant-current or W-curve battery charger is used, the current (in A) should be reduced to max. 1/10 of the nominal capacity when gassing is seen to start. That is, for example, 6.6 A for a 66 Ah battery. The battery charger should

be switched off about 1 hour afterwards. Ventilate the charging area (explosive gas formation, risk of explosion, no naked flames or sparks).

Battery malfunctions

Battery failures which are traceable to internal faults (such as short circuits accompanying separator wear or loss of active mass, broken connections between cells and plates) can rarely be rectified by repair. The battery has to be replaced. Internal short circuits are indicated by major variations in the specific-gravity readings between cells (difference between max. and min > 0.03 g/ml). It is frequently possible to charge and discharge a battery with defective cell connectors provided that the currents remain small, but attempts to start the engine will result immediately in total voltage collapse, even if the battery is fully charged.

If no defects can be found in a battery which consistently loses its charge (indication: low specific gravity in all cells, no starting power) or is overcharged (indication: high water loss), this suggests a malfunction in the vehicle's electrical system (alternator faulty, electrical equipment remains on when the engine is switched off due to faulty relays for instance, voltage regulator set too high or too low, or regulator completely inoperative). When a battery remains severely discharged for a relatively long period, the $PbSO_4$ crystals in the active mass become coarse, making the battery more difficult to recharge. Such a battery should be recharged by applying a minimal charge current (approx. 1/40 of the rated capacity in A) for roughly 50 hours.

Safety precautions

Handling
Before fitting a new starter battery, the manufacturer's instructions should be carefully read in order to avoid safety hazards resulting from incorrect handling. The possible dangers originate from the sulfuric acid in the battery and the explosive gas (mixture of hydrogen and oxygen) formed during battery charging. Tipping the battery for extended periods or carelessness during electrolyte checks

can lead to burns from the sulfuric acid. Extra caution should be taken during charging and when connecting and disconnecting jumper cables immediately after charging due to the danger of the oxyhydrogen gas exploding.

The explosive gas mixture created by the charging process can be ignited by a sufficiently high level of thermal energy. For that reason, naked flames must not be permitted in the vicinity of batteries. Spark formation, e. g. by sudden opening or closing of electrical circuits, should be avoided and the generation of static electricity by transfer (carpets) or by rubbing with woolen or artificial fabrics must also be prevented. For the reasons listed above, battery-charging areas should always be well-ventilated, while protective goggles and gloves should be worn when handling the battery.

In order to prevent sparks when the battery is connected or disconnected, all electrical equipment must be switched off, and the terminals must be connected in the proper sequence. The rules are as follows:

– When installing the battery, always connect the positive cable first, and the negative cable last. When removing the battery, first disconnect the negative, and only then the positive cable (assuming that negative is ground).
– When connecting a charger or an external battery to boost a low battery which remains installed in the vehicle, always start by connecting the positive terminal of the battery being charged to the positive terminal of the external booster. Then connect the negative cable from the external charger or booster battery to an exposed metallic surface on the vehicle, at least 0.5 m away from the battery.
– Always disconnect the cable from the negative terminal before commencing work in the vicinity of the battery or on the vehicle's electrical system. Short circuits (with tools) generate sparks, and can also cause injury.

Testing starter batteries

The specifications and test procedures for standard automotive starter batteries are defined in DIN EN 60095-1. Those tests

are suitable for determining and monitoring the quality of new starter batteries but do not claim in any way to fully reproduce the enormous variety of possible demands to which a battery might be subject in practical use.

Battery testers

The purpose of a battery test is to ascertain the starting power, condition, charge level and voltage of a battery. Testers for starter batteries make a distinction between the no-load test and the under-load test.

Under-load test

In the case of the under-load test, the battery is subjected to a current load comparable with that which occurs when starting the engine (up to several 100 A). The voltage dip ΔU while this load is applied, and the voltage rise ΔU during the recovery phase after the load is removed, are criteria for assessing the starting power and the condition of the battery. In order to be able to give a percentage figure for the starting power, the ΔU level measured is compared with the figure specified for a correctly functioning battery. This specified level is dependent on the size of the battery and is preselected by the user by entering the battery capacity or the cold-discharge test current. The charge level is ascertained on the basis of the battery voltage.

The advantage of the under-load test is the reliable detection of even the finest hairline cracks in the battery's cell connectors and lead plates.

The under-load period of around 30 seconds corresponds to the current draw for several starting attempts, and this has a negative effect on the battery charge level.

No-load test

In the no-load test, the battery is subjected for a few seconds only to a low-frequency, square-wave current of between approx. 0.25 A and 2 A. This load superimposes an alternating current in the millivolt range on the battery direct current. An assessment of the starting power and the condition of the battery can then be made on the basis of the signal amplitude and signal wave-form of this alternating current. In order to assess the battery condition and starting power using the no-load test, the cold-discharge test current of the battery being tested must be entered in the tester.

The advantages of the no-load test are minimal discharge of the battery being tested and the speed of the test.

Battery chargers

Charging curves
The most commonly used charging pattern is the "W" curve. The chargers in such cases are generally non-regulated. Due to the battery's and the charger's internal resistances, these chargers respond to increasing battery voltage by steadily lowering the charge current (charging times 12...24 hours).

Because these W-curve chargers do not incorporate any means for limiting the charging voltage, they are only conditionally suitable for use on maintenance-free batteries. For these, chargers should be used which operate according to the IU, IWU, or WU pattern.

With the IU curve, the lead-acid battery (2.4 V per cell) is supplied with constant charging current (to protect the charger against overload) until gassing commences. The charging voltage is then held constant and the charging current reduced sharply (to protect the battery against overcharging). Provided that the initial charging current is high enough, recharging times (to 80 % of full charge) of < 5 hours can be achieved with IU chargers.

Special variations of both the IU and the W charging patterns are available (e.g., Wa, WoW, IUW etc.). These can be applied in combination to meet individual demands for charging time, terminal voltage and freedom from maintenance.

Charging current and voltage settings
On chargers with controlled charging patterns (e.g. IU curve), a regulator continually monitors the momentary actual charging current and voltage levels (and also the ambient temperature if necessary). It compares the monitored (actual-value) data with battery-specific nominal values, and uses a final-control element to reduce the deviation to 0. This type of unit also compensates for fluctuations in its mains input voltage which could otherwise lead to variations in charging current. This has a beneficial effect on, among other things, the battery life and the maintenance intervals.

Charging current
In normal charging ($I_L = 1 \cdot I_{10}$) the battery is supplied with current corresponding to approximately 10 % of its capacity in A·h. Several hours are required to charge the battery completely. Boost charging ($I_L = 5 \cdot I_5$) can be used to bring an empty battery back up to about 80 % of its rated capacity with no damage. Once the gassing voltage is reached, the charging current must either be switched off (e.g., Wa curve) or reduced to a lower level (e.g., IU curve). These current-switching functions are controlled by an adjustable charge limiter or an automatic switchoff device. By the use of special electronic monitoring circuits, the fully charged point can also be determined on the basis of battery-specific voltage patterns in conjunction with the charging period (the battery voltage starts to drop again if it is overcharged).

Alternators

Electrical-energy generation

The alternator must furnish the vehicle's electrical system with a sufficient supply of current under all operating conditions in order to ensure that the state of charge in the energy storage device (battery) is consistently maintained at an adequate level. The object is to achieve balanced charging, i.e., the curves for performance and speed-frequency response must be selected to ensure that the amount of current generated by the alternator under actual operating conditions is at least equal to the consumption of all electrical equipment within the same period.

The alternator actually produces alternating current. The vehicle's electrical system, on the other hand, requires direct current to recharge the battery and operate the electrical equipment. It is thus direct current that must ultimately be supplied to the electrical system.

The essential requirements are:
- Maintenance of a direct-current supply to all electrical equipment in the system,
- Supplementary charging reserves for (re)charging the battery, even with a constant load from electrical devices in continuous operation,
- Maintenance of a constant alternator voltage throughout the entire ranges of engine speeds and load conditions,
- Robust design capable of withstanding externally-imposed stresses such as vibration, high ambient temperatures, pronounced temperature variations, dirt, moisture, etc.,
- Low weight, compact dimensions and long service life,
- Minimal operating noise,
- High level of efficiency.

Design factors

Rotational speed

The alternator's operating efficiency (its power-to-weight ratio expressed as the ratio of energy generated to component mass in kg) increases as a function of rotational speed. This factor alone would dictate as high a conversion ratio as possible between the engine's crankshaft and

the alternator.

The following factors though must also be considered:
- Increasing centrifugal forces at high alternator speeds,
- Alternator and fan noise,
- Efficiency fall-away at high speeds,
- Effect of high speeds on the service lives of the wear components (bearings, collector rings, carbon brushes),
- Mass inertia of the alternator relative to the crankshaft and the resulting load on the belt drive.

Typical conversion factors for automotive applications lie within a range of 1 : 2 to 1 : 3, with ratios of up to 1 : 5 being used in large commercial vehicles.

Engine idle represents roughly a third of the usage pattern of an alternator.

Temperatures

The losses that accompany energy conversion in any machine lead to high component temperatures.

High alternator temperatures are also a result of heat radiation from engine components and ancillaries (such as exhaust systems and turbochargers); the amount of heat depends upon the relative installation positions, and is greatest when the engine operates at high speeds and under high load factors. The supply of cooling air is generally drawn in from the engine compartment.

In view of the trend towards engine-compartment encapsulation which is becoming more and more common as a means of reducing noise, the ducting of fresh air towards the alternator is an appropriate method of reducing component temperatures. For situations where engine-compartment temperatures are extreme, there are liquid-cooled alternators available.

External influences

Installing the alternator on an IC engine means exposing it to extreme mechanical stresses. Depending upon the installation configuration and the engine's vibration characteristics, vibration levels of 500...800 m · s⁻² can occur at the alternator. This subjects the alternator's mountings and components to extreme forces, and it is essential that critical natural frequencies in the alternator assembly are avoided.

Further detrimental influences include spray water, dirt, oil and fuel mist, and road salt in winter. These factors expose all components to the risk of corrosion. It is important that tracking between conducting parts be avoided, as electrolysis could otherwise lead to the early failure of vital operating components.

Characteristics and operation

In order to maintain an adequate charge in 12 V, 24 V or 36 V batteries, automotive alternators are designed to supply charge voltages of 14 V, 28 V for heavy commercial vehicles and in future also 42 V.

As direct current is required for charging the battery, a diode rectifier must be provided to convert the alternator's three-phase alternating current into direct current. The diodes also prevent the battery from discharging when the vehicle is stationary.

The current-generation curve has a sharp bend. There is no current production until after the so-called "0-ampere speed" is exceeded. At high speeds, the effect of the reverse magnetization field generated by the load current prevents

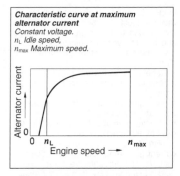

Characteristic curve at maximum alternator current
Constant voltage.
n_L Idle speed,
n_{max} Maximum speed.

the curve from climbing further. This characteristic means that even excessive loading cannot result in further increases in current flow, thereby protecting the alternator from the thermal damage associated with electrical overload.

Alternators are self-excited 12- or 16-pole synchronous devices. The AC winding is wound in the stator's slots, while the excitation winding is housed within the rotor. The DC excitation current required by the excitation winding is conducted to the rotating rotor through sliding contacts (carbon brushes). The current produced

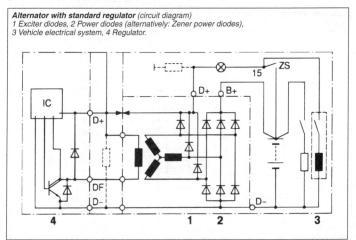

Alternator with standard regulator (circuit diagram)
1 Exciter diodes, 2 Power diodes (alternatively: Zener power diodes),
3 Vehicle electrical system, 4 Regulator.

in the AC winding is channeled in two directions: Most of it flows through the positive diodes of the main rectifier bridge and into the vehicle's electrical system, from where it returns through the negative diodes.

Depending on the design of the alternator and regulator, the excitation current flows
a) through excitation diodes in the case of standard regulators, or
b) directly from the B+ terminal in the case of multifunction regulators.

With standard regulators, some of the current generated acts as excitation current, flowing through the three exciter diodes to terminal D+, through the regulator and collector rings to the rotating field winding and from there, back through the three negative diodes of the main rectifier.

On alternators with multifunction regulators, there are no excitation diodes and the excitation current branches off immediately beyond the main rectifier. The voltage regulator switches on the excitation current only when the engine is started (which it detects by means of alternator rotation), thereby preventing battery discharge when the engine is not running.

The output of the alternator is adjusted

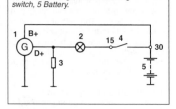

Circuit with fault indication in the event of break in excitation circuit
1 Alternator, 2 Charge-indicator lamp,
3 Resistor R, 4 Ignition and starting switch, 5 Battery.

to suit the demand from the vehicle's electrical system by varying the excitation current. The regulator is controlled by pulse-width modulation on the basis of constant terminal voltage.

The D+ terminal assumes several functions: Firstly, the alternator is pre-excited from battery terminal B+ via the alternator indicator lamp and terminal D+. Secondly, terminal D+ is at a similar voltage level to B+ after excitation of the alternator. Specific consumer groups can be supplied with power via a relay.

The pre-excitation current determines the "on-line" speed at which initial excitation occurs when the engine is started.

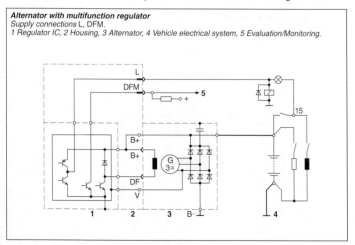

Alternator with multifunction regulator
Supply connections L, DFM.
1 Regulator IC, 2 Housing, 3 Alternator, 4 Vehicle electrical system, 5 Evaluation/Monitoring.

This speed is well above the "zero-ampere speed", with the precise figure being largely determined by the power of the indicator lamp.

The charge indicator lamp should come on when the ignition is switched on prior to starting (monitoring function) and go out as the engine starts to run-up.

Design variations

Claw-pole alternators
The already very familiar mechanical concept embodied in this alternator type has completely replaced the earlier DC generator as the standard design in automotive applications. Based on equal outputs for both concepts, the alternator weighs 50 % less, and is also less expensive to manufacture. Large-scale application only became feasible with the introduction of compact, powerful, inexpensive and reliable silicone diodes.

The leakage flux between the claw poles limits the length – and thus the output – that can be achieved for any given diameter with this type of layout. In order to increase output, two systems can be combined within the same housing in certain cases.

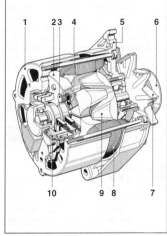

Claw-pole alternator (compact-diode design)
1 Collector-ring end shield, 2 Rectifier heat sink, 3 Power diode, 4 Exciter diode,
5 Drive end shield with mounting flanges,
6 Fan pulley, 7 External fan, 8 Stator,
9 Claw-pole rotor, 10 Transistor regulator.

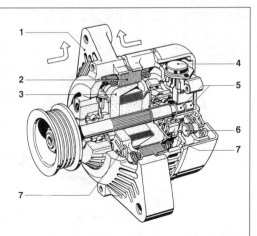

Compact alternator
1 Casing,
2 Stator,
3 Rotor,
4 Electronic voltage regulator with brush holder,
5 Collector rings,
6 Rectifier,
7 Fan.

The <u>classic alternator design</u> is characterized by the external fan providing single-flow axial ventilation (compact-diode design).

Compact alternator (air-cooled)

The compact alternator is a new variant of the claw-pole concept based on dual-flow ventilation with two smaller internal fan elements. The cooling flow is extracted from the surrounding air in the axial plane, and exits the alternator radially in the vicinity of the stator winding heads, at the drive and collector-ring end shields. The major advantages of the compact alternator are:

– Higher maximum operating speeds for enhanced efficiency,
– Smaller fan diameters for reduced aerodynamic noise,
– Substantial reduction in magnetic noise,
– Longer carbon-brush life due to smaller collector-ring diameter.

Salient-pole alternator

Alternators based on the salient-pole concept are required in those special applications which are characterized by extreme power demands (as in touring coaches). The rotor is equipped with individual magnetic poles, each of which is provided with its own field winding. This layout allows the stator to be substantially longer (relative to its diameter) than would be possible with a claw-pole alternator. This means that higher outputs can be achieved without increasing diameter. The maximum speeds achievable, however, are lower than with claw-pole designs. Since the excitation currents required for the salient-pole alternator are substantially higher than those for the claw-pole unit, the attendant higher temperatures mean that the electronic regulator must be mounted in a special housing remote from the alternator.

Alternators with windingless rotors

The windingless-rotor alternator is a special design variation of the claw-pole unit in which only the claw poles rotate, while the excitation winding remains stationary. Instead of being connected directly to the shaft, one of the pole wheels is held in place by the opposite pole wheel via a nonmagnetic intermediate ring. The magnetic flux must cross two additional air gaps beyond the normal working gap. With this design, the rectifier supplies current to the excitation winding directly

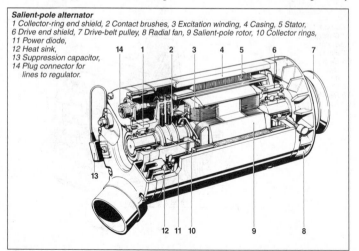

Salient-pole alternator
1 Collector-ring end shield, 2 Contact brushes, 3 Excitation winding, 4 Casing, 5 Stator,
6 Drive end shield, 7 Drive-belt pulley, 8 Radial fan, 9 Salient-pole rotor, 10 Collector rings,
11 Power diode,
12 Heat sink,
13 Suppression capacitor,
14 Plug connector for
lines to regulator.

through the regulator; sliding contacts are not required. This arrangement obviates the wear factor represented by the collector-ring and carbon-brush assemblies, making it possible to design alternators for a substantially longer service life (important for construction equipment and railroad generators). The units weigh somewhat more than claw-pole alternators of comparable generating capacity due to the fact that additional iron is required to conduct the magnetic flux through two additional air gaps.

The windingless-rotor design is also obtainable as a liquid-cooled version (type LIF-B). Engine coolant flows around the complete circumference and rear of the alternator housing. The electronic components are mounted on the drive-end shield.

Operational limits

Ventilation

Air-cooled passenger-car alternators are almost always cooled by a flow of air supplied by an integral or attached radial fan. In certain cases where engine-compartment temperatures are very high, air is ducted in from outside. The dimensions

of the ventilation arrangement must be adequate for ensuring that component temperatures remain below the specified limits under all conceivable operating conditions.

On alternators for heavy-duty vehicles, the entire collector-ring and carbon-brush assembly is usually encapsulated in order to prevent the entry of dust, dirt and water. Fresh-air induction is almost always beneficial, especially with higher outputs. In certain cases, sealed alternators with cooling fins on the outer casing are used. Other special applications may require the use of sealed alternators cooled by a liquid (e.g. oil).

Liquid-cooled alternators with a water jacket around the alternator casing are characterized in particular by
– lack of air-flow noise (−20 dBA),
– suitability for use in engine compartments with high temperatures,
– capability of integration in engine block,
– wading capabilities due to complete encapsulation, and
– contribution to engine warm-up by virtue of the heat dissipated by the alternator to the coolant.

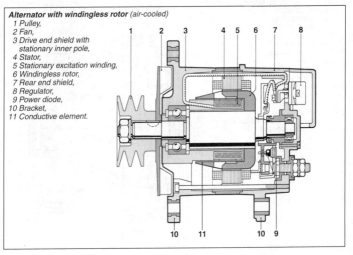

Alternator with windingless rotor (air-cooled)
 1 Pulley,
 2 Fan,
 3 Drive end shield with
   stationary inner pole,
 4 Stator,
 5 Stationary excitation winding,
 6 Windingless rotor,
 7 Rear end shield,
 8 Regulator,
 9 Power diode,
10 Bracket,
11 Conductive element.

In contrast to air-cooled alternators, the external electrical connections are on the drive-pulley end. If a liquid-cooled alternator is fitted to the engine as a separate unit with its own housing, it has to have some means of connecting it to the cooling system (e.g. hoses). The reliable coolant supply must be designed-in during the overall application-engineering work.

Installation in the vehicle

Virtually all those engine-powered alternators which are driven by standard V-belts are installed on bracket assemblies which allow the belt tension to be adjusted by pivoting the alternator. If ribbed V-belts are used (Poly-V-belts), the alternator mounting is generally rigid, and belt tension is maintained by a separate mechanism. Larger alternators can be attached directly to the engine in special cradle-shaped mounts. The load imposed by the drive belt is the decisive factor in selecting the bearing dimensions for the alternator's drive side. The belt forces are determined by both the geometry of the drive layout and the power requirements of all the other devices being driven by the belt. Yet another factor is the effective ra-

dius of the pulley; larger radii can produce a substantial lever effect between the pulley's load-bearing surface and the drive-side bearings. The stresses emanating from these static factors are supplemented by the dynamic forces associated with torque and speed fluctuations.

Belt pulleys with freewheel mechanisms allow the alternator shaft to be isolated from crankshaft vibration, thus making the belt drive substantially smoother for larger alternators with a greater mass inertia.

Drive layout

Although standard V-belts are usually employed to drive the alternator, ribbed V-belts are being increasingly used in automotive applications. Because this design allows tighter bend radii, smaller alternator pulleys and higher conversion ratios can be achieved. Railroad alternators are operated by helical-gear assemblies driven directly from the axle. It is imperative that special precautions be taken to dampen rotary oscillations when direct mechanical drive (without an intermediate belt, e.g., centrally at the crankshaft or via gears) is used to power the alternator.

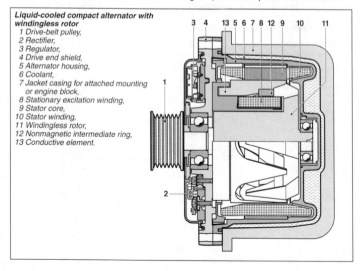

Liquid-cooled compact alternator with windingless rotor
1 Drive-belt pulley,
2 Rectifier,
3 Regulator,
4 Drive end shield,
5 Alternator housing,
6 Coolant,
7 Jacket casing for attached mounting or engine block,
8 Stationary excitation winding,
9 Stator core,
10 Stator winding,
11 Windingless rotor,
12 Nonmagnetic intermediate ring,
13 Conductive element.

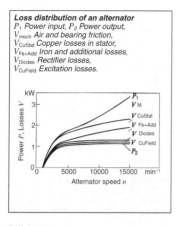

Loss distribution of an alternator
P_1 Power input, P_2 Power output,
V_{mech} Air and bearing friction,
V_{CuStat} Copper losses in stator,
V_{Fe+Add} Iron and additional losses,
V_{Diodes} Rectifier losses,
$V_{CuField}$ Excitation losses.

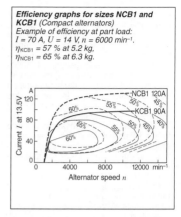

Efficiency graphs for sizes NCB1 and KCB1 (Compact alternators)
Example of efficiency at part load:
$I = 70$ A, $U = 14$ V, $n = 6000$ min^{-1}.
$\eta_{KCB1} = 57$ % at 5.2 kg,
$\eta_{NCB1} = 65$ % at 6.3 kg.

Efficiency

Losses are an unavoidable by-product of all processes in which mechanical or kinetic energy is converted into electrical energy. The efficiency rating is the ratio between the power which is supplied to the unit and that which emerges. Iron losses result from the hysteresis and eddy currents produced by the alternating magnetic fields in the iron of the stator and rotor. Copper losses are produced by resistance in the rotor and stator windings. Their extent is proportional to the power-to-weight ratio, i.e., the ratio of generated electrical power to the mass of the effective components. The mechanical losses include the frictional loss in the roller bearings and at the contact brushes, the air resistance encountered by the rotor and, above all, the fan resistance which rises dramatically as speed increases.

In normal automotive operation, the alternator operates in the part-load range. Efficiency at medium speeds is then around 50%. The use of a larger (and heavier) alternator enables it to be operated in a more favorable partial-load efficiency band for the same electrical load. The efficiency gains provided by the larger alternator more than compensate for the losses in fuel economy associated with the greater weight. However, the higher mass inertia has to be taken into consideration.

The alternator is a typical example of an assembly which is in permanent operation all the time the vehicle is being driven, and when design measures are under consideration regarding maximum fuel economy, more emphasis should be placed on optimization of efficiency than upon optimization of its mass.

Noise

The quieter the modern-day vehicle becomes, the more the noise developed by the alternator becomes noticeable. The alternator's noise is comprised of a magnetic and an aerodynamic component.

The magnetically induced high-pitched noise is audible mainly at low speeds (< 4000 min^{-1}). It can be counteracted by optimizing the alternator's magnetic circuit and its oscillation and radiation characteristics.

The aerodynamic noise occurs for the most part at high speeds. It can be reduced by the use of an optimized (e.g. asymmetrical) fan and optimisation of the air channels.

Alternator (voltage) regulation

Here too, the two options
– standard regulator and
– multifunction regulator

have different basic purposes. The standard voltage regulator serves to keep the alternator voltage approximately constant in the face of wide fluctuations in alternator speed and load. The target level is usually temperature-dependent. The voltage is somewhat higher in winter to compensate for the fact that the battery is then more difficult to charge. In summer, the voltage regulator maintains the system voltage at a lower level to prevent the battery from overcharging. It is also possible for the voltage of the electrical system to drop below the regulation voltage when there is substantial current consumption at low min⁻¹.

Voltage regulators were formerly constructed using discrete components, but today they incorporate hybrid or monolithic circuits. When monolithic technology is applied, the control and regulator IC, the power transistor and the freewheeling diode are all located on a single chip.

Multifunction regulators perform special additional functions apart from the basic task of regulating the voltage.

The "load-response" (LR) function in particular is worthy of mention. It helps to improve the running and exhaust characteristics of the engine by means of a limited rate of output increase over time. A distinction is made between engine-running load response and engine-starting load response (alternator inactive for a defined period after starting).

Voltage regulators with digital interfaces represent a response to the increasing demands for greater mutual compatibility between engine-management and alternator-regulation systems. The interfaces used are chiefly of the bit-synchronous type. Coding is performed by way of the signal duration instead of its amplitude and is stored with a set protocol. The advantages here are the interference immunity and lack of temperature-susceptibility of the interface electronics.

Interface regulators enable the load-response functions to be finely tuned to the engine operating status, the torque pattern to be optimized for the purposes of reducing consumption, and the charging voltage to be adjusted to improve the battery charge level.

Overvoltage protection

The electric strength of alternators and voltage regulators usually suffices to ensure that their semiconductor elements will operate reliably with the vehicle's battery connected. Emergency operation without the battery is characterized by extreme voltage peaks. Especially critical is the load-dump phenomenon in which the current to major consumers is suddenly interrupted. Thus additional measures

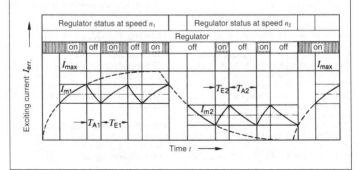

Function of regulator
I_{err} Excitation current, I_m Mean excitation current, T_E Duty period, T_A Off period, n_1 Lower speed, n_2 Higher speed.

are necessary to ensure complete reliability in such cases.

There are three options available for protecting against overvoltage:

Zener diodes

Zener power diodes can be installed in the rectifier in place of the power diodes. Zener diodes limit the high-energy voltage peaks to levels which are harmless for the alternator or the regulator. In addition, Zener diodes can be used to provide remote protection for other voltage-sensitive equipment in the vehicle's electrical system. The response voltage of a rectifier which is equipped with Zener diodes ranges from 25 to 30 V. Compact alternators are 100%-equipped with Zener diodes.

Alternators and regulators with enhanced electric strength

In such alternators and regulators, the semiconductor elements have higher electric-strength ratings. The enhanced electric strength of such alternators and regulators only protects the units themselves; these measures though furnish no additional protection for other electrical equipment in the system.

Overvoltage-protection devices

These semiconductor devices are connected to the alternator's D+ and D– (ground) terminals. The system responds to voltage peaks by shorting the alternator at the excitation winding. The main beneficiaries of these overvoltage protection devices are the alternator and regulator, with only secondary protection being provided for other voltage-sensitive equipment in the electrical system. Overvoltage-protection devices can be combined with other units specially designed to inhibit consequential damage. Such a layout prevents the battery from boiling-off its electrolyte should the regulator malfunction and remain in the "on" position.

Normally, alternators are not provided with reverse-polarity protection. Reversal of battery polarity (e.g. when using an external battery to start the vehicle) leads to destruction of the alternator diodes as well as endangering the semiconductor components of other assemblies in the vehicle.

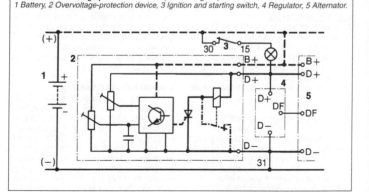

Automatic overvoltage protection device (Circuit diagram)
1 Battery, 2 Overvoltage-protection device, 3 Ignition and starting switch, 4 Regulator, 5 Alternator.

Controller Area Network (CAN)

Present-day motor vehicles are equipped with a large number of electronic control units (ECUs) which have to exchange large volumes of data with one another in order to perform their various functions. The conventional method of doing so by using dedicated data lines for each link is now reaching the limits of its capabilities. On the one hand, it makes the wiring harnesses so complex that they become unmanageable, and on the other the finite number of pins on the connectors becomes the limiting factor for ECU development. The solution is to be found in the use of specialized, vehicle-compatible serial bus systems among which the CAN has established itself as the standard.

Applications

There are four areas of application for CAN in the motor vehicle, each with its own individual requirements:

<u>Real-time applications</u>
Real-time applications, in which electrical systems such as Motronic, transmission-shift control, electronic stability-control systems are used to control vehicle dynamics, are networked with one another.

Typical data transmission rates range from 125 kbit/s to 1 Mbit/s (high-speed CAN) in order to be able to guarantee the real-time characteristics demanded.

<u>Multiplex applications</u>
Multiplex applications are suitable for situations requiring control and regulation of body-component and luxury/convenience systems such as air conditioning, central locking and seat adjustment.

Typical data transmission rates are between 10 kbit/s and 125 kbit/s (low-speed CAN).

<u>Mobile-communications applications</u>
Mobile-communications applications connect components such as the navigation system, cellular phone or audio system with central displays and controls. The basic aim is to standardize control operations and to condense status information so as to minimize driver distraction.

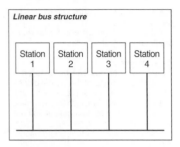

Linear bus structure

| Station 1 | Station 2 | Station 3 | Station 4 |

Data transmission rates are generally below 125 kbit/s; whereby direct transmission of audio or video data is not possible.

<u>Diagnostic applications</u>
Diagnostic applications for CAN aim to make use of existing networking for the diagnosis of the ECUs incorporated in the network. The use of the "K" line (ISO 9141), which is currently the normal practice, is then no longer necessary.

The data rate envisaged is 500 kbit/s.

Bus configuration

CAN operates according to the multi-master principle, in which a linear bus structure connects several ECUs of equal priority rating. The advantage of this type of structure lies in the fact that a malfunction at one node does not impair bus-system access for the remaining devices. Thus the probability of a total system failure is substantially lower than with other logical architectures (such as ring or active star structures). When a ring or active star structure is employed, failure at a single node or at the CPU is sufficient to cause a total failure.

Content-based addressing

Addressing is message-based when using CAN. This involves assigning a fixed identifier to each message. The identifier classifies the content of the message (e.g., engine speed). Each station processes only those messages whose identifiers are stored in its acceptance list (message filtering). Thus CAN requires no station addresses for data transmission, and the nodes are not involved in administering system configuration. This facilitates adaptation to variations in equipment levels.

Logical bus states
The CAN protocol is based on two logical states: The bits are either "recessive" (logical 1) or "dominant" (logical 0). When at least one station transmits a dominant bit, then the recessive bits simultaneously sent from other stations are overwritten.

Priority assignments
The identifier labels both the data content and the priority of the message being sent. Identifiers corresponding to low binary numbers enjoy a high priority and vice versa.

Bus access
Each station can begin transmitting its most important data as soon as the bus is unoccupied. When several stations start to transmit simultaneously, the system responds by employing "Wired-AND" arbitration to sort out the resulting contentions over bus access. The message with the highest priority is assigned first access, without any bit loss or delay. Transmitters respond to failure to gain bus access by automatically switching to receive mode; they then repeat the transmission attempt as soon as the bus is free again.

Message format
CAN supports two different data-frame formats, with the sole distinction being in the length of the identifier (ID). The standard-format ID is 11 bits, while the extended version consists of 29 bits. Thus the transmission data frame contains a maximum of 130 bits in standard format, or 150 bits in the extended format. This ensures minimal waiting time until the subsequent transmission (which could be urgent). The data frame consists of seven consecutive bit fields:

Start of frame indicates the beginning of a message and synchronizes all stations.

The arbitration field consists of the message's identifier and an additional control bit. While this field is being transmitted, the transmitter accompanies the transmission of each bit with a check to ensure that no higher-priority message is being transmitted (which would cancel the access authorization). The control bit determines whether the message is classified under "data frame" or "remote frame".

The control field contains the code indicating the number of data bytes in the data field.

The data field's information content comprises between 0 and 8 bytes. A message of data length 0 can be used to synchronize distributed processes.

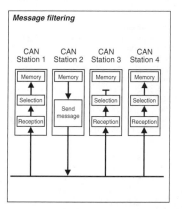

Message filtering

CAN Station 1 | CAN Station 2 | CAN Station 3 | CAN Station 4

Memory — Selection — Reception

Send message

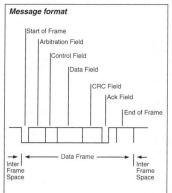

Message format

Start of Frame
Arbitration Field
Control Field
Data Field
CRC Field
Ack Field
End of Frame

Inter Frame Space | Data Frame | Inter Frame Space

The <u>CRC field</u> (Cyclic Redundancy Check) contains the check word for detecting possible transmission interference.

The <u>Ack field</u> contains the acknowledgement signals with which all receivers indicate receipt of non-corrupted messages.

<u>End of frame</u> marks the end of the message.

Transmitter initiative

The transmitter will usually initiate a data transfer by sending a data frame. However, the receiver can also request data from the transmitter. This involves the receiver sending out a "remote frame". The data frame and the corresponding remote frame have the same identifier. They are distinguished from one another by means of the bit that follows the identifier.

Error detection

CAN incorporates a number of monitoring features for detecting errors. These include:
– 15-bit CRC (Cyclic Redundancy Check): Each receiver compares the CRC sequence which it receives with the calculated sequence.
– Monitoring: Each transmitter compares transmitted and scanned bit.
– Bit stuffing: Between "start of frame" and the end of the CRC field, each data frame or remote frame may contain a maximum of 5 consecutive bits of the same polarity. The transmitter follows up a sequence of 5 bits of the same polarity by inserting a bit of the opposite polarity in the bit stream; the receivers eliminate these bits as the messages arrive.
– Frame check: The CAN protocol contains several bit fields with a fixed format for verification by all stations.

Error handling

When a CAN controller detects an error, it aborts the current transmission by sending an error flag. An error flag consists of 6 dominant bits; it functions by deliberately violating the conventions governing stuffing and/or formats.

Fault confinement with local failure

Defective stations can severely impair the ability to process bus traffic. Therefore, the CAN controllers incorporate mechanisms which can distinguish between intermittent and permanent errors and local station failures. This process is based on statistical evaluation of error conditions.

Implementations

In order to provide the proper CPU support for a wide range of different requirements, the semiconductor manufacturers have introduced implementations representing a broad range of performance levels. The various implementations differ neither in the message they produce, nor in their arrangements for responding to errors. The difference lies solely in the type of CPU support required for message administration.

As the demands placed on the ECU's processing capacity are extensive, the interface controller should be able to administer a large number of messages and expedite data communications with, as far as possible, no demands on the CPU's computational resources. Powerful CAN controllers are generally used in this type of application.

The demands placed on the controllers by multiplex systems and present-day mobile communications are more modest. For that reason, more basic and less expensive chips are preferred for such uses.

Standardization

CANs for data exchange in automotive applications have been standardized both by the ISO and the SAE – in ISO 11519-2 for low-speed applications $\leq$ 125 kbit/s and in ISO 11898 and SAE J 22584 (cars) and SAE J 1939 (trucks and busses) for high-speed applications > 125 kbit/s. There is also an ISO standard for diagnosis via CAN (ISO 15765 – Draft) in the course of preparation.

CARTRONIC®

Networked vehicle systems

The continuing development of automotive electronic systems is driven by ever increasing demands. These include: Safety, comfort and environmental compatibility, tougher legal requirements and directives, integration of information and entertainment-system functions ("infotainment") and communication with external computers and data services via mobile telephone.

Under the influence of those demands combined with the unabated downward pressure on prices, individual vehicle systems (fuel injection, ABS, radio) have developed into a networked composite system in which information is exchanged via data busses (e. g. CAN) and reciprocal interaction is possible. Cross-marque standardization of individual components, subsystems and subfunctions within such a composite system is the basic requirement if development times are to be speeded-up. At the same time, reliability and system availability must be increased and, by sharing information between different vehicle systems, a reduction in the number of components required.

Composite systems (examples)

Present-day vehicles already have composite systems such as the traction control system (TCS) and the electronic stability program (ESP) which is an extension of it. The cross-system functions of those two systems are effected by the TCS control unit (ECU) informing the engine-management ECU when the wheels start to spin so that the latter can reduce the engine torque accordingly. Similarly, the air-conditioning system may inform the engine-management system that it is about to switch on, which will result in the need for an increase in engine torque/speed.

Requirements

The implementation of such cross-system functions through the interaction of subsystems requires agreement on the standardization of interfaces and subsystem functions. Definitions must be drawn up which specify what information a subsystem requires and what variables are to be controlled on the basis of that information. This is all the more important in view of the fact that the subsystems are developed separately (often by several different suppliers) and modification to suit a particular vehicle model or the requirements of a specific manufacturer is costly and susceptible to errors.

Concept

The above demands led to the development of the CARTRONIC as a classification and specification concept for all vehicle control and management systems. It contains definite rules for interaction between subsystems as well as expandable modular architectures for "function", "safety" and "electronics" on the basis of these formal rules. It thus provides the means for a description of the vehicle as an overall system. On that basis, suppliers can harmonize interaction between their products without having to be familiar with the internal processes of subsystems and without bringing about large-scale manufacturer- or model-related modifications.

Structuring, architecture

What is required is a universal structuring system and practical implementation of it in an appropriate structure. The function architecture at vehicle level encompasses all control and management tasks that arise within the vehicle. Logical components are defined which represent tasks of the composite system. The links and interfaces between components and the manner of their interaction are specified. The system architecture thus created has to be supplemented by a safety architecture which provides additional elements in order to ensure safe and reliable operation of the system as a whole. The composite system is then created by the transformation of the various logical and functional components into hardware form (electronic circuitry, ECUs, microcomputers). In contrast to the system architecture, the resulting optimized hardware topology is characterized by the specifics of the vehicle model (e.g. specified dimensions and siting of components).

Architecture rules

The rules for the function architecture are designed to create a definition and layout for the composite system that is independent of the specific hardware topology, except from the point of view of logical and functional considerations. For that reason, the rules essentially define components and the permissible interaction in the sense of communication interrelationships.

Functional analysis

Conceptually, the functional analysis of a planned or existing composite system starts with the analysis of the previously autonomous individual systems. As even this takes place at the functional level (as yet separate from practical hardware development and partitioning), the descriptions are still independent of vehicle-specific design variations and therefore largely permit universally valid statements. Basic structuring at this level makes it possible to restrict the diversity of hardware and software and to use identical electronic modules (basic modules) for the basic functions of a large number of vehicle models.

Structural elements

The elements of the architectures are systems, components and communication interrelationships which formally describe a composite system and also include the structuring and modeling rules for designing interaction and defining interdependencies.

Systems, components, interfaces

In those terms, a system is a combination of components that are linked to one another by means of communication mechanisms and which perform a higher-level function beyond their individual functions. The term component is explicitly not limited to interpretation as a physical unit but is understood rather to be a unit of function. CARTRONIC recognizes three types of component:
– components whose function is primarily coordination,
– components whose function is primarily operative, and
– components whose function is exclusively to generate, supply and forward information.

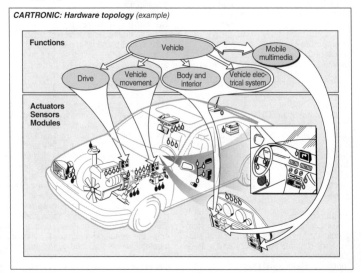

CARTRONIC: Hardware topology (example)

Interfaces on components refer to possible communication interrelationships that can be established with other components. Wherever possible, physical variables are defined as interfaces (e.g. transmission or engine torque).

Description of system
Therefore, a system is described by the representation of all functional components and their communication interrelationships and modes of reciprocal interaction.

Structuring rules
The structuring rules describe permissible communication interrelationships between different components within the system architecture. A hierarchical system concept is created according to the structure which starts from the vehicle as an entity and extends as far as the individual components. Accordingly, there are structuring rules for communication interrelationships between components on the same level and on different levels. There are also structuring rules for the forwarding of communications from one subsystem to another.

Modeling rules
The modeling rules consist of patterns which combine components and communication interrelationships for solving specific tasks which arise more than once within a vehicle system. Those patterns can then be repeated at various points within the structure of the vehicle.

Architectural features
A structure represented by means of the specified structuring and modeling rules displays standardized features and characteristics:
- a hierarchical work flow (jobs are accepted only on the same or a higher level),
- a clear distinction between coordinators and information suppliers (operating controls and sensors),
- clear demarcation between the individual components according to the "black box" principle (as visible as necessary and as concealed as possible).

Consequences
CARTRONIC represents a standardized concept for describing all vehicle functions. By virtue of the facility for defining generic functions, it can describe all commonly used vehicle control and management systems using standardized terminology. New functions will require appropriate extension of those function categories. The next step required is cross-marque definition of interfaces between components/subsystems at the functional and physical levels. This will enable implementation of complex function networks within the vehicle involving collaboration between multiple suppliers.

Outlook
The functional capabilities of present-day vehicle systems are determined to an increasing degree by software, and composite systems are becoming computer networks. The standardization of operating systems is making software applications portable, i. e. they can be used on different ECUs. The software architecture is thus becoming independent of the hardware topology. In order to keep individual software modules interchangeable/re-usable, the CARTRONIC architecture and interface rules will require further refinement and more precise definition. As in the field of computer applications, interfaces between different functions will be defined by "APIs" (application programming interfaces) which will then precisely define the CARTRONIC communication interrelationships. This course requires agreement between the different manufacturers and suppliers on industry standards. CARTRONIC has established the basic foundations for such a development.

Electromagnetic compatibility (EMC) and interference suppression

The expression "electromagnetic compatibility" (EMC) defines an electrical system's ability to remain neutral in the vicinity of other systems. In other words it is compatible, and besides not interfering with other systems it also remains impervious to such interference as may emanate from them. In automotive applications, this means that the various electrical and electronic systems such as the ignition system, the electronic fuel injection, ABS/TCS, airbags, radio, car phone, navigation system, etc. must function in close physical proximity without interfering with each other beyond an allowable level. It also means that the vehicle in its role as a system must remain neutral within its environment; it is not to interfere electrically with other vehicles, and it must not interfere with broadcast or communications transmissions of any kind. At the same time, the vehicle must itself remain fully operational when exposed to strong electromagnetic fields from the outside (e.g., in the vicinity of radio transmitters).

It is in view of these considerations that automotive electrical systems and complete vehicles are designed to ensure electromagnetic compatibility.

Sources of interference

On-board electrical system, ripple

The alternator supplies the vehicle's electrical system with rectified alternating current. Although the current is smoothed by the battery, a residual ripple remains. Its amplitude depends on the electrical system load and the wiring. Its frequency does not change according to alternator or engine speed and the fundamental oscillation is in the kHz range. It can penetrate into the vehicle's sound system – either directly (galvanically) or through inductance – where its presence is heard as a whine in the speakers.

On-board electrical system, pulses

Interference pulses are generated when electrical equipment in the vehicle is switched on and off. They are passed to adjacent systems directly through the power supply (conductive transfer) and indirectly by means of crossover from connecting leads (inductive and capacitive coupling). If the matching between the interference source and the system receiving it is inappropriate, these pulses can cause anything from malfunction to destruction of the adjacent systems.

The wide variety of pulses that occur in the vehicle can be classified in five basic groups. Classification according to amplitude provides the best basis for matching the interference sources and

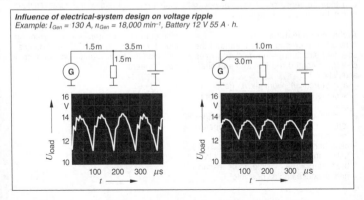

Influence of electrical-system design on voltage ripple
Example: $I_{Gen} = 130$ A, $n_{Gen} = 18,000$ min⁻¹, Battery 12 V 55 A · h.

the potentially susceptible equipment to achieve maximum compatibility between them.

This matching procedure may, for example, entail having all a vehicle's interference sources conform to Class II, while potentially susceptible devices (such as ECUs) can be designed to conform to Class III requirements (taking a safety margin into account). Reallocation to Classes I/II is advisable in cases where suppression at the source is easier than providing the corresponding protection at the susceptible devices.

The principle can also be reversed; if protective measures at the potentially susceptible equipment are easier and less expensive then a move to Classes III/IV is advisable.

On-board electrical system, high-frequencies

High-frequency oscillations are generated inside many electromechanical and electronic components by the switching of voltages and currents (digital circuits, triggering of output stages, commutation). These oscillations travel through the components' circuits – especially the power-supply lines – and back into the vehicle's electrical system, where they arrive at variously attenuated intensities.

Depending upon whether the measured interference voltage's spectrum is

Sources of broad and narrow-band interference
a) Signal progression referred to time $y(t)$,
b) Corresponding spectrum $\tilde{y}(f)$,
c) Observation of spectrum with monitoring device of bandwidth B: with $B \cdot T < 1$ (as shown in diagram) individual bars indicate "narrow-band" interference; $B \cdot T > 1$ continuous curve indicates "broad-band" interference.

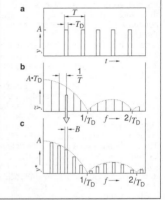

continuous or a collection of individual curves, a distinction is drawn between two kinds of interference source: "broadband" (electric motors, as used for wipers,

Test pulses as per DIN 40839, Part 1 for 12V electrical systems

Test pulses				Classification of permissible pulse amplitudes			
Pulse shape	Source	Internal resistance	Pulse duration	I	II	III	IV
1	Switch-off of inductive loads, e.g. relays or valves.	10 Ω	2 ms	– 25 V	– 50 V	– 75 V	– 100 V
2	Switch-off of electric-motor loads such as fan motor which generate positive overvoltage when running on.	10 Ω	50 µs	+ 25 V	+ 50 V	+ 75 V	+ 100 V
3a	Overvoltages due to switching processes.	50 Ω	0.1 µs	– 40 V	– 75 V	– 110 V	– 150 V
3b				+ 25 V	+ 50 V	+ 75 V	+ 100 V
4	Supply-voltage curve during starting.	10 mΩ	up to 20 s	+ 12 V	+ 12 V	+ 12 V	+ 12 V
				– 3 V	– 5 V	– 6 V	– 7 V
5	"Load dump"[1]	1 Ω	up to 400 ms	+ 35 V	+ 50 V	+ 80 V	+ 120 V

[1] Load dump occurs when the alternator is feeding high current into the battery and the connection between the two is suddenly interrupted.

fans, fuel pump, alternator) and "narrow-band" (ECUs with microprocessors). The classification depends upon the bandwidth of the test instrument being used.

Such high-frequency oscillations can represent a permanent source of interference for communications systems in the vehicle; they are located within the same frequency and amplitude ranges as the transmitted or received signals, and are thus easily able to enter the vehicle's communications system either directly at the sensor (antenna) or through the antenna cable. The narrow-band sources of interference are particularly critical as they have signal characteristics very similar to the spectrum of transmitters.

For broad-band interference sources such as electric motors, fans, etc., the interference output is assessed on the basis of the interference voltages on the supply lines in a defined test setup according to CISPR 25 or DIN/VDE 0879-2. The interference voltage gradings defined by interference-suppression levels simplify the matching of interference sources and devices susceptible to interference at the vehicle's OE-equipment stage.

Should the interference level initially approved for OE purposes prove to be too high upon subsequent installation of an additional communications system, there is a limited range of remedial measures which can be implemented:

- If the source of the interference derives its current directly from terminal 15 or 30, then the interference can be counteracted with suppression capacitors and filters of a type suitable for automotive application. The capacitors are generally connected directly to the source's terminal, with the ground wire being kept as short as possible. Coupling from conductors carrying interference voltage to other conductors can be reduced by passing such wires through a braided metal screen which is grounded as directly as possible at both ends.

- If the interference source is controlled by an ECU, it is generally forbidden to suppress it subsequently by means of suppression components, as this would modify the ECU switching response.

- The clock signals from the microprocessors in the ECUs act as narrow-band interference sources. Subsequent interference suppression is not generally possible with such components. Interference transmission can therefore be minimized as far as possible by appropriate circuitry (e.g. suppression capacitors), and suitable location and routing of components and wiring. If such interference-suppression measures are not sufficient, it is necessary to attempt to achieve satisfactory results by appropriate layout of the electrical system, and the choice of an advantageous antenna position combined with suitable routing of the antenna cable.

In the laboratory, assessment of the interference characteristics of electronic components either also uses line-conducting methods (e.g. measuring the interference voltage level on the supply lines) or antenna measurements in absorber rooms. The final verdict as to whether reception (radio or mobile com-

Permissible radio interference voltage level in dBµV for suppression levels in the individual frequency ranges as per DIN/VDE 0879-2 for broad-band interference (B) and narrow-band interference (S)

Interference-suppression level	Interference level									
	0.15...0.3 MHz (LW)		0.53...2.0 MHz (MW)		5.9...6.2 MHz (SW)		30...54 MHz		70...108 MHz (UHF)	
	B	S	B	S	B	S	B	S	B	S
1	100	90	82	66	64	57	64	52	48	42
2	90	80	74	58	58	51	58	46	42	36
3	80	70	66	50	52	45	52	40	36	30
4	70	60	58	42	46	39	46	34	30	24
5	60	50	50	34	40	33	40	28	24	18

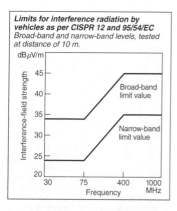

Limits for interference radiation by vehicles as per CISPR 12 and 95/54/EC
Broad-band and narrow-band levels, tested at distance of 10 m.

Broad-band limit value

Narrow-band limit value

creased as appropriate for the vehicle design in order to achieve acceptable reception for an on-board radio, telephone, etc. Ignition systems can be fitted with suitable suppression components such as resistors in the HT connectors and resistor spark plugs to further reduce interference emission. For specialist vehicles (e.g. equipped with two-way radio for emergency services) it can even be necessary to partially or completely shield the ignition system. Such interference-suppression measures can have negative effects on the ignition system's secondary available voltage. In such cases, therefore, a thorough investigation into the permissibility of the measures is necessary.

Potentially susceptible devices

ECUs and sensors are susceptible to interference signals entering the system from outside. The interference signals emanate either from neighboring systems within the vehicle itself or from sources in the immediate vicinity (such as a powerful broadcast transmitter). Malfunctions start to occur at the point where the system loses the ability to distinguish between interference signals and useful signals.

The possibility of taking effective measures depends upon the characteristics of the useful and the interference signals.

The ECU is unable to distinguish between useful and interference signals if their signal characteristics are similar. This is the case for instance, when a pulse-shaped interference signal is similar to the signal from a wheel-speed sensor. Particularly critical here are frequencies in the vicinity of the useful-signal frequency ($f_S \approx f_N$) and in the same range as a few of the useful-frequency harmonics.

Non-modulated (or NF-modulated) sinusoidal HF signals (energy transmitted by interference sources) can be demodulated at the pn junctions in the electronic circuitry. This can lead to the direct components causing level shifts, or to the superimposition of interference signals which fluctuate as a function of time, as a result of the NF component of the interfer-

munications) will be possible in the vehicle depends upon interference-voltage measurements carried out at the receiver end of the antenna cable. This is done with the aid of a suitable testing circuit for matching the input impedance of the test receiver to the input impedance of the receiver unit. In order to obtain realistic results, those tests must if possible be performed using the original antenna in its original installation position. In order to isolate them from the external electromagnetic transmitter and interference signals, such measurements are carried out in shielded EMC chambers equipped with high-frequency absorbers.

The vehicle as an interference source
The ignition system is the major source of interference in the vehicle as a whole. The maximum permissible radiation from motor vehicles is limited by law (EU Directive 95/54/EC) in order to ensure that it does not interfere with the radio and TV reception of other vehicles and roadside residents. Maximum limits are specified for both broad-band and narrow-band interference.

The levels specified in the Directive represent the minimum requirements. Keeping interference to a level only just within the specified limits is not normally sufficient in practice to ensure interference-free reception in the same vehicle. For that reason, suppression has to be in-

$$U_b = \frac{k \cdot R_2 \cdot \sinh(\gamma \cdot l)}{(R_1 + R_2) \cdot \cosh(\gamma \cdot l) + W(k_a + \frac{R_1 \cdot R_2}{W^2} \cdot k_b) \cdot \sinh(\gamma \cdot l)} \cdot (\frac{R_1}{W} \cdot U - W \cdot I)$$

ence signal. Normally, the carrier frequency is a multiple of the useful frequency ($f_{S,HF} >> f_N$). The NF component of the interference signal is particularly critical if it is in the vicinity of the useful-signal frequencies ($f_{S,NF} = f_N$). Unwanted (interference) signals of a far lower frequency ($f_S << f_N$) can also lead to malfunctions due to intermodulations.

The necessary immunity to interference from electromagnetic fields is also defined by the EU Directive 95/54/EC. The field strengths to which a vehicle must be immune as specified by the Directive are, as with the interference emission limits, minimum requirements. In practice, vehicle manufacturers and suppliers provide significantly higher levels of interference immunity.

Interference coupling

Signals from interference sources penetrate susceptible devices in any of three ways:
- Direct (galvanic) coupling occurs when the source and the device affected by the interference share common current paths, a condition which can hardly be avoided with a common voltage source. The vehicle's wiring harness should be

designed with the lowest-possible level of direct coupling in mind. Whether a parallel, serial or multipoint structure is best for the supply lines will depend upon the level of current, the frequency range, the impedance of the components and the general design of the system being connected.
- Coupling occurs on connecting lines when they are laid in parallel between the source and the susceptible device being exposed to the interference. In the model shown at the bottom of page 819, the voltage U_b which is coupled into the device receiving the interference is calculated as shown at the top of the page with the parameters

$k = C/C_0$; $k_a = (C_a + C)/C_0$; $k_b = (C_b + C)/C_0$
$C_0 = \sqrt{C_a \cdot C_b + C \cdot (C_a + C_b)}$

$\gamma \cdot l = j(\omega/c) \cdot l$; $W = 1/(c \cdot C_0)$
$c = 3 \cdot 10^8$ m/s (speed of light)

U_b consists of two parts: a "capacitive" component, which depends on the voltage U, and an "inductive" component, which is a function of the current I. If the wavelength of the interference signal is larger than the geometrical conductor length l, then the formula is simplified as follows:

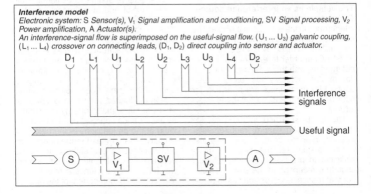

Interference model
Electronic system: S Sensor(s), V_1 Signal amplification and conditioning, SV Signal processing, V_2 Power amplification, A Actuator(s).
An interference-signal flow is superimposed on the useful-signal flow. ($U_1 ... U_3$) galvanic coupling, ($L_1 ... L_4$) crossover on connecting leads, (D_1, D_2) direct coupling into sensor and actuator.

$U_b \approx k \cdot (\gamma \cdot l) \cdot [U(R_1 \cdot R_2)/(R_1 + R_2) - W \cdot I \cdot R_2/(R_1 + R_2)]$

This indicates that coupling can be kept to a minimum the shorter the length l and the lower the standardized coupling capacity k.

k decreases as the distance between the conductors increases, and can be further reduced when a screen connected to ground at both ends.

– Direct interference is possible in cases where sensor S or actuator A (see Figure below) react directly to electromagnetic fields, e.g., if S is a radio antenna, a microphone or the magnetic head on a cassette player. Here the aim is to increase the physical distance between the interference source and the exposed susceptible equipment until the interference disappears.

Electrostatic discharge

The subject of the potential danger to components and electronic circuits from electrostatic discharge (ESD) also falls under the umbrella of EMC. Here, it is a case of protecting components and equipment from damage by static discharge from persons or from machinery on the production line. On the one hand, this involves the adoption of appropriate methods for handling equipment and, on the other, designing units in such a way that the extremely high voltages (several thousand volts) produced by electrostatic charges are reduced to resistible levels.

Measuring techniques

A wide variety of testing methods are in common use for testing the interference signal and the immunity to interference. Depending upon the type of assessment used for the interference phenomena, they can be roughly divided into methods operating in the time range (pulse generators, oscillographs) and those operating in the frequency range (sine-wave generators, measuring receivers, spectrum analyzers).

– In measurement techniques, the interference signals are generally registered as reference values in dB (decibels). The reference quantity for interference voltage is 1 µV; for electric field strength it is 1 µV/m, for power it is 1 mW, thus:

$u^* = 20 \cdot \lg U$
$e^* = 20 \cdot \lg E$
$p^* = 10 \cdot \lg P$

where u^*, e^*, p^* are given in dB; U in µV; E in µV/m; P in mW. In measurement techniques as used for interference-suppression measures, the quantities (pulse amplitude and energy radiated by interference source) are usually given directly (E in V/m; U in V; I in A).

EMC measurements are performed on individual systems in the laboratory and in the vehicle.

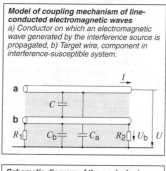

Model of coupling mechanism of line-conducted electromagnetic waves
a) Conductor on which an electromagnetic wave generated by the interference source is propagated, b) Target wire, component in interference-susceptible system.

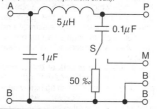

Schematic diagram of the equivalent circuit of an automotive electrical system as per DIN/VDE 0879-2
Connections: P–B Unit being tested, A–B Power supply, M–B Radio-interference monitor, S Switch, B Reference ground (sheet-metal plate, screen for equivalent circuit).

Laboratory test procedures

- Under standardized conditions, artificial networks are used to examine the pulses or high-frequency interference voltages which emanate from a device.
- Immunity to pulse-type interference is tested using special pulse generators which produce test pulses according to DIN 40 839, Part 1, or ISO 7637, Parts 1 and 2.
- Wire-borne interference waves to be injected into the wiring harness of the electrical system under investigation, are produced either with the aid of a stripline, a TEM (transversal electromagnetic field) cell or BCI (bulk current injection). In the case of the stripline, the wiring harness is arranged in line with the direction of propagation of the electromagnetic wave between a strip conductor and a base plate. When the TEM cell is used, the ECU and a section of the wiring harness are arranged at right angles to the electromagnetic waves' direction of propagation. The BCI method involves superimposition of a current on the wiring harness by means of a power clip.
- For higher frequencies (> 400 MHz), the unit being tested and the wiring harness are irradiated by antennas and thereby directly exposed to an electromagnetic field.
- The emitted interference radiation is measured with broad-band antennas in screened measuring cells lined with absorbers.

Vehicle testing procedures

- The electronic system's resistance to the electromagnetic fields radiated by high-power transmitters is tested inside the vehicle which is located in a special anechoic chamber for the purpose. Here, appropriately high electrical and magnetic field strengths can be generated which are applied to the complete vehicle.
- The interference effects of the vehicle electrics and electronics on radio reception are measured using highly sensitive measuring receivers. As far as possible, the original vehicle antenna is left in place, and measurement is carried out at the input to the receiver.

Regulations and Standards

Automotive interference suppression (protection of non-mobile, permanently installed radio reception) has been mandatory in Europe since 1972. (EC Directive ECE10 / EU Directive 72/245/EEC). Since 1.1.1996 binding legal regulations have been in place concerning electromagnetic compatibility (EU/EEC Directive or German EMC laws) for all electrical products and installations which are sold on the market. For motor vehicles, the special EC Directive 95/54/EC, which supersedes the Directive 72/245/EEC, governs the protection of fixed-installation radio reception and the immunity of motor vehicles to interference from electromagnetic fields. In addition to the regulations governing the design of vehicles and components offered for sale to the public, this Directive also specifies the testing methods and maximum allowable limits.

The EMC measurement techniques are defined in a number of German and international Standards. Essentially, the national German Standards (DIN/VDE) agree with the international Standards (ISO/IEC-CISPR) and cover all aspects of automotive EMC.

Standards
Resistance to interference
DIN 40 839, Part 1, ISO 7637-0/-1/-2,
DIN 40 839, Part 3, ISO 7637-3,
DIN 40 839, Part 4, ISO 11451/11452,
ISO/TR 10605.

Interference suppression
DIN/VDE 0879-2.
CISPR 12, CISPR 25.

Alphabets and numbers

German alphabet

Gothic type

𝔄	a	a	𝔍	j	j	𝔖	ſ	s
𝔅	b	b	𝔎	k	k	𝔗	t	t
ℭ	c	c	𝔏	l	l	𝔘	u	u
𝔇	d	d	𝔐	m	m	𝔙	v	v
𝔈	e	e	𝔑	n	n	𝔚	w	w
𝔉	f	f	𝔒	o	o	𝔛	x	x
𝔊	g	g	𝔓	p	p	𝔜	y	y
ℌ	h	h	𝔔	q	q	ℨ	z	z
𝔍	i	i	ℜ	r	r			

Greek alphabet

Letter		Name	Letter		Name
A	α	Alpha	N	ν	Nu
B	β	Beta	Ξ	ξ	Xi
Γ	γ	Gamma	O	o	Omicron
Δ	δ	Delta	Π	π	Pi
E	ε	Epsilon	P	ϱ	Rho
Z	ζ	Zeta	Σ	$\sigma\ \varsigma$	Sigma
H	η	Eta	T	τ	Tau
Θ	ϑ	Theta	Y	υ	Upsilon
I	ι	Iota	Φ	φ	Phi
K	κ	Kappa	X	χ	Chi
Λ	λ	Lambda	Ψ	ψ	Psi
M	μ	Mu	Ω	ω	Omega

Phonetic alphabets

	German	International	2-way radio
A	Anton	Amsterdam	Alpha
Ä	Ärger	–	–
B	Berta	Baltimore	Bravo
C	Cäsar	Casablanca	Charlie
CH	Charlotte	–	–
D	Dora	Danmark	Delta
E	Emil	Edison	Echo
F	Friedrich	Florida	Foxtrott
G	Gustav	Gallipoli	Golf
H	Heinrich	Habana	Hotel
I	Ida	Italia	India
J	Julius	Jerusalem	Juliett
K	Kaufmann	Kilogram	Kilo
L	Ludwig	Liverpool	Lima
M	Martha	Madagascar	Mike
N	Nordpol	New York	November
O	Otto	Oslo	Oscar
Ö	Ökonom	–	–
P	Paula	Paris	Papa
Q	Quelle	Quebec	Quebec
R	Richard	Roma	Romeo
S	Samuel	Santiago	Sierra
Sch	Schule	–	–
T	Theodor	Tripoli	Tango
U	Ulrich	Uppsala	Uniform
Ü	Übermut	–	–
V	Viktor	Valencia	Victor
W	Wilhelm	Washington	Whiskey
X	Xanthippe	Xanthippe	X-Ray
Y	Ypsilon	Yokohama	Yankee
Z	Zeppelin	Zürich	Zulu

Cyrillic alphabet

Letter		Pronun-ciation	Letter		Pronun-ciation
А	а	a	Р	р	r
Б	б	b	С	с	ss
В	в	w	Т	т	t
Г	г	g	У	у	u
Д	д	d	Ф	ф	f
Е	е	je	Х	х	ch
Ё	ё	jo	Ц	ц	z
Ж	ж	sch (soft)	Ч	ч	tsch
З	з	s	Ш	ш	sch (hard)
И	и	i	Щ	щ	schtsch
Й	й	i (short)	Ъ	ъ	hard sign
К	к	k	Ы	ы	ü
Л	л	l	Ь	ь	soft sign
М	м	m	Э	э	ä
Н	н	n	Ю	ю	ju
О	о	o	Я	я	ja
П	п	p			

Roman numerals

I	1	XXX	30
II	2	XL	40
III	3	L	50
IV	4	LX	60
V	5	LXX	70
VI	6	LXXX	80
VII	7	XC	90
VIII	8	C	100
IX	9	CC	200
X	10	CD	400
XI	11	D	500
XX	20	DC	600
XXI	21	M	1000
XXIX	29	MVM	1995

Passenger-car specifications

The following table contains data on selected passenger cars manufactured both inside and outside Germany (Validity: March 1, 1999), Source: "Automobil Revue Katalog 1999". The list is intended only as a representative selection; inclusion in or exclusion from the list is not intended as the reflection of a qualitative judgement of any kind.

Abbreviations

aa	All-wheel drive (AWD)	Lue	Pneumatic suspension, electronically controlled
A	Automatic gearbox/transmission		
ABS	Antilock braking system	Ma	Multi-link axle
ASR	Traction control	Mc	Microcar
		Mm	Mid-engine
Bx	Opposed-cylinder engine	Mv	Microvan
Ca	Convertible	P	Panhard rod
Co	Coupé		
Cp	Compact sedan/limousine	q	Transverse installation
		Qf	Transverse leaf spring
Db	Damper strut	Ql	Control arm
DDQI	Double wishbone	R	In-line engine
De	De-Dion axle	Ra	Multi-link independent-suspension axle (5 control arms per wheel)
DG	Double-link Macpherson-strut suspension		
DQI	A-arm	Ro	Roadster
DQu	Twin control arm	ROZ	Research Octane Number (RON)
Ea	Independent suspension, rear	Sa	Rigid axle
EBV	Electronic brake balancing	Sb	Disc brake
EDS	Electronic differential lock	Sf	Coil spring
El	Electronic gasoline injection	Sl	Semi-trailing arm
Eld	Electronic direct injection	St	Continuously variable transmission (CVT)
EP/CR	Diesel fuel-injection pump, common-rail system, electronically controlled		
		T	Turbocharger
EP/UIS	Unit Injector System UIS	Ta	Torsion crank axle
EP/V	Diesel distributor-type fuel-injection pump	Tb	Drum brake
		Td	Telescopic shock absorber
EP/eV	Diesel distributor-type fuel-injection pump, electronically controlled	Tf	Torsion bar
		Tl	Trapezoidal arm suspension
ESP	Electronic Stability Program	v	Front, on front wheels
F	Spring strut	V	V-engine
		Ve	Valves per cylinder
Ge	Off-road vehicle	Vl	Four-joint trapezoidal-link axle
Gli	High-capacity sedan/minivan	Vla	Trailing-arm torsion-beam axle
h	Rear, on rear wheels	VR	Offset inline engine
H	Manually-shifted transmissions	Wa	Watt linkage
Hf	Hydropneumatic suspension		
Hv	Hydrogas suspension	Ze	Single-point injection (TBI)
		Zl	Supplementary link
Ic	Intercooler	2KE	2 spark plugs per cylinder
Ko	Station wagon	2Tlc	2 turbochargers and 2 intercoolers
Kom	Compressor		
Ku	Anti-roll bar	4Sb	4 disk brakes
Li	Sedan/limousine	–	No details
Ll	Trailing arm		

Explanations

Where available, the following information (lines 1 – 35) is given for each model. Not specifically listed are: Line 16: Mounted longitudinally; Line 20: Front-engined; Line 24: Water-cooled; Line 32: Independent front suspension.

1 **Vehicle body**
Example: 3/5 Ko 5 indicates a three- or five-door station wagon with five seats. The specifications are listed for the first alternative (3>/5 or 5>/3).

2 **Brake horsepower (BHP)**
The net engine output in kW/HP as per DIN 70020. If DIN data are not given, horsepower is referred to ECE (European Commission for Europe), SAE (Society of Automotive Engineers), or JIS (Japan Industry Standard)

4 **Maximum speed**
The maximum speed (in accordance with DIN 70 020) which the vehicle maintains over a measured distance of 1 km.

6 **Curb weight**
The weight of the vehicle when ready for use, excluding the driver.

8 **Weight-to-power ratio**
Calculated from the brake horse-power and weight of the vehicle when ready for use, excluding the driver (curb weight). The smaller the weight-to-power ratio, the greater the acceleration and climbing ability.

9 **Fuel consumption**
As specified by the EU Standard Stage II which is now in force for new vehicles since 1.1.1996, the fuel consumption is determined according to the NEDC (New European Driving Cycle) (P. 336). These tests reflect a certain degree of correspondence with real driving conditions by including "urban" (with cold start) and "out-of-town" components. The figures quoted may also originate from the Environmental Protection Agency in the USA. Some data originate from the ediorial staff (Ed.), or may still be figures determined according to DIN 70030 (90 km/h – 120 km/h – urban).

15 **Specific power output**
Ratio of brake horsepower to swept volume (displacement). Also known as power output per liter. Conversion: 1 kW/l = 1.36 bhp/l.

16 **Engine type**
Order: Engine position, number of cylinders, cylinder configuration.
Examples: q4R indicates a trans-

verse 4-cylinder in-line engine; 4Ve indicates 4 valves per cylinder.

18 **Alternator(14 V)**
Current rating quoted in A or power rating quoted in W.

19 **Battery(12 V)**
Battery capacity quoted in Ah or cold-discharge test current in A.

20 **Engine position/drive configuration**
In the case of mid-engine or rear-engine vehicles, the letters preceding the hyphen indicate the location of the engine, and those following it the location of the driven wheels, e.g., h-h indicates that both the engine and the driven wheels are at the rear of the vehicle. Mm-aa stands for a mid-engine vehicle with all-wheel drive, and v-h signifies a front-engine vehicle with rear-wheel drive.

21 **Transmission step-down ratio**
For the individual gears, transmission step-down ratios between engine and gearbox output shaft (standard equipment). See also line 23.

22 **Final drive ratio**
Conversion ratio between gearbox output shaft and axle drive shaft.

23 **Gearshift**
H indicates the number of forward speeds (gears). (A) indicates the number of automatic-gearbox speeds. Examples: 5 (5) signifies 5 forward gears, 4-speed automatic gearbox. 5/4 (4) signifies 5 or 4 forward gears or 4-speed automatic gearbox. Line 21 (transmission step-down ratio) always lists the first of the available options.

24 **Cooling**
Example: 6.5 means water-cooled, capacity 6.5 l.

32/ **Wheel suspension**
33 Example: QI-F means control arm with MacPherson strut, Sa-Ll-Sf means rigid axle with trailing arm and coil spring.

34 **Tires**
See P. 630 for explanation of tire designations.

35 **Braking system**
Example: Sb-Tb-ABS indicates disk brakes front, drum brakes rear, and antilock braking system (ABS).

	Country		Brazil		Germany		
	Vehicle make Model		Fiat Palio 1.7 TD Weekend 70	VW Gol 1.0	Audi A3 1.6	A3 1.9 TDi	TT 1.8
1	Body Style	–	5 Ko 5	5/3 Li 5	3/5 Li 5	5/3 Li 5	3 Co 2+2
2	Useful power	kW (bhp)	51 (69)	51 (69)	74 (101)	66 (90)	165 (224)
	at engine speed	rpm	4500	5750	5600	3750	5900
3	Max. torque	Nm	134	92	145	210	280
	at engine speed	rpm	2500	4500	3800	1900	2200
4	Maximum speed	km/h	164	161	188	181	243
5	Acceleration from 0 to 100 km/h	s	14.9	14.3	11	12.4	6.4
6	Curb weight	kg	1025	915	1090	1185	1395
7	Gross vehicle weight	kg	1620	1315	1650	1745	1765
8	Weight-to-power ratio	kg/kW	21.8	22.4	14.7	18	8.5
9	Fuel consumption	l/100 km	EU 5.1/8.6	(factory) 6.6/7.8	EU 5.9/10.5	EU 4.1/6.5	EU 7.3/12.3
10	Fuel octane number	RON	Diesel	92	95	Diesel	98
11	Fuel tank capacity	l	51	50	55	55	62
12	Engine swept volume	cm³	1698	998	1595	1896	1781
13	Bore/stroke	mm	82.6/79.2	67.1/70.6	81/77.4	79.5/95.5	81/86.4
14	Compression ratio	–	20.3	10.5	10.3	19.5	8.9
15	Specific power output	kW/l	30	40.1	46.4	34.8	92.6
16	Engine type	–	q 4 R	4 R	q 4 R	q 4 R	4 R 5Ve
17	Fuel management	–	EP/V	Motronic	EI	EP/eV-T-lc	Motronic-T-lc
18	Alternator (14 V)	A	65/85	55	70	70/120	90
19	Battery (12 V)	Ah	60	36	44/60	80	60
20	(Engine pos.)/drive config.	–	v	v	v	v	aa
21	Transmission 1st/2nd gear		3.91/2.24	3.9/2.12	3.46/1.94	3.78/2.12	3.42/2.11
	ratio 3rd/4th gear		1.44/1.03	1.37/1.03	1.37/1.03	1.36/0.97	1.43/1.09
	5th/6th gear		0.8	0.83	0.85	0.76	0.87/0.72
22	Final drive ratio	–	3.77	4.78	4.25	3.39	4.2
23	Gearshift	H (A)	5	5	5 (4)	5 (4)	6
24	Cooling	l	6.9	6	5	6	7
25	Vehicle length	mm	4130	3810	4150	4150	4040
26	Vehicle width	mm	1625	1650	1735	1735	1765
27	Vehicle height	mm	1520	1410	1425	1425	1350
28	Wheelbase	mm	2425	2470	2515	2515	2430
29	Track, front/rear	mm	1390/1385	1390/1380	1515/1495	1515/1495	1530/1505
30	Turning circle diameter	m	10.4	9.7	10.9	10.9	10.5
31	Ground clearance	mm	140	120	140	140	130
32	Suspension, front	–	DQl-F-Ku-Sf-Td	DQl-F	DQl-F-Sf-Ku-Td	DQl-F-Sf-Ku-Td	DQl-F-Sf-Ku-Td
33	Suspension, rear	–	Ll-Sf-Ku-Td	Vla-Ll-Sf-Td	Vla-Sf-Ku-Td	Vla-Sf-Ku-Td	Vla-Sf-Ku-Td
34	Tires	–	175/65 R 14	155 R 13	195/65 VR 15	195/65 VR 15	225/45 ZR 17
35	Braking system		Sb-Tb	Sb-Tb	4Sb-ABS-EBV	4Sb-ABS-EBV	4Sb-ABS-EBV

See PP. 898 for abbreviations and explanations.

	A4 Avant 2.4	S4 Avant 2.7 Biturbo	A6 1.9 TDi	A6 4.2	A8 3.7	A8 2.5 TDi	BMW Z3 1.9
1	5 Ko 5	5 Ko 5	4 Li 5	4 Li 5	4 Li 5	4 Li 5	2 Ro 2
2	121 (165) 6000	195 (265) 5800	81 (110) 4150	220 (300) 6200	191 (260) 6000	110 (150) 4000	103 (140) 6000
3	230 3200	400 1850	235 1900	400 3000	350 3250	310 1500	180 4300
4	222	250	194	250	250	220	205
5							
6	8.6	5.7	12.6	6.9	8.1	9.9	9.5
7	1360	1540	1415	1730	1510	1595	1200
8	1930	2090	1995	2310	2110	2195	1450
9	10.9	7.7	17.5	7.9	8.6	14.5	11.6
10	EU 7.5/14.9	EU 8.7/15.8	EU 4.6/7.5	EU 9.5/19	EU 8.4/16.9	EU 5.5/10.2	EU 6/11.4
11	95	98	Diesel	98	98	Diesel	95
12	62	62	70	82	90	90	51
13	2393	2671	1896	4172	3697	2496	1895
14	81/77.4	81/86.4	79.5/95.5	84.5/93	84.5/82.4	78.3/86.4	85/83.5
15	10.5	9.3	19.5	11	11	19.5	10.0
16	50.6	73	42.7	52.7	51.7	44.1	54.3
17	6 V 5Ve	6 V 5Ve	4 R	8 V 5Ve	8 V 5Ve	6 V 4Ve	4 R 4Ve
18	Motronic	Motronic-T-Ic	EP/eV-T-Ic	Motronic	Motronic	EP/eV-T-Ic	Motronic
19	90	120	120	120	120	120	80
20	70	70	80	92	92	92	70
21	v	aa	v	aa	v-ESP	v-ESP	h
22	3.5/1.94 1.3/0.94 0.79	3.5/1.89 1.23/0.97 0.81/0.68	3.5/1.94 1.23/0.84 0.68	3.57/2.2 1.51/1 0.8	3.67/2 1.41/1 0.74	3.75/2.06 1.32/0.93 0.73/0.6	4.23/2.52 1.66/1.22 1
23	3.89	4.11	3.7	2.91	3.09	3.88	3.45
24	5 (5)	6	5 (4)	(5)	(5)	6 (5)	5 (4)
25	8.5	6	7	11	11	10	6.5
26	4480	4485	4795	4835	5035	5035	4025
27	1735	1735	1810	1850	1880	1880	1690
28	1410	1400	1450	1450	1440	1440	1290
29	2620	2605	2760	2760	2880	2880	2445
30	1500/1480	1500/1490	1540/1570	1580/1590	1540/1580	1595/1585	1410/1425
31	11.1	11.4	11.7	11.7	12.3	12.3	10.0
32	110	110	120	120	120	120	110
33	DQu-Sf-Ku-Td	DQu-Sf-Ku-Td	VI-F-Ku-Td	VI-F-Ku-Td	VI-Sf-Ku-Td	VI-Sf-Ku-Td	DQI-F-Ku-Td
34	VIa-LI-Sf-Ku-Td	DQu-Sf-Ku-Td	VIa-Sf-Ku-Td	VIa-DDQI-Sf-Ku-Td	TI-QI-Sf-Ku-Td	TI-QI-Sf-Ku-Td	SI-Sf-Ku-Td
35	195/65 R 15	225/45 R 17	195/65 VR 15	235/50 R 16	225/60 R 16	225/60 R 16	205/60 R 15
	4Sb-ABS-EBV	4Sb-ABS-EBV	4Sb-ABS-EBV	4Sb-ABS-EBV	4Sb-ABS	4Sb-ABS	4Sb-ABS

Country		**Germany**				
Vehicle make Model		**BMW** (Continued) Z3 3.2	316i Compact	318tds Compact	320d	323i Touring
1	Body style –	3 Co 2	3 Cp 5	3 Cp 5	4 Li 5	5 Ko 5
2	Useful power kW (bhp) at engine speed rpm	236 (321) 7400	77 (105) 5300	66 (90) 4400	100 (136) 4000	125 (170) 5500
3	Max. torque Nm at engine speed rpm	236 7400	165 2500	190 2000	280 1750	245 3950
4	Maximum speed km/h	250	190	175	207	223
5	Acceleration from 0 to 100 km/h s	5.4	11.9	13.9	9.9	8.3
6	Curb weight kg	1390	1175	1215	1375	1365
7	Gross vehicle weight kg	1660	1635	1675	1875	1865
8	Weight-to-power ratio kg/kW	5.9	15.3	18.4	13.8	10.5
9	Fuel consumption *l*/100 km	EU 7.9/16.6	EU 5.8/10.8	EU 4.9/8.5	EU 4.7/7.4	EU 7.3/15
10	Fuel octane number RON	98	95	Diesel	Diesel	95
11	Fuel tank capacity *l*	51	55	55	63	62
12	Engine swept volume cm³	3201	1895	1665	1951	2494
13	Bore/stroke mm	86.4/91	85/83.5	80/82.5	84/88	84/75
14	Compression ratio –	10.5	9.7	22	19	10.5
15	Specific power output kW/*l*	73.7	40.6	39.6	51.2	50.1
16	Engine type –	6 R 4Ve	4 R	4 R	4 R 4Ve	6 R 4Ve
17	Fuel managment –	EI	EI	EP/eV-T	EP/eV-T-lc	EI
18	Alternator (14 V) A	115	80	95	120	80
19	Battery (12 V) Ah	70	50	65	80	65
20	(Engine pos.)/drive config. –	h	h	h	h	h
21	Transmission 1ˢᵗ/2ⁿᵈ gear ratio 3ʳᵈ/4ᵗʰ gear 5ᵗʰ/6ᵗʰ gear	4.21/2.49 1.66/1.24 1	4.23/2.52 1.66/1.22 1	5.43/2.95 1.81/1.26 1	5.09/2.8 1.76/1.25 1	4.21/2.49 1.66/1.24 1
22	Final drive ratio –	3.15	3.23	2.65	2.47	2.93
23	Gearshift H (A)	5 (4)	5	5	5 (54)	5 (5)
24	Cooling *l*	10.75	6.5	7.5	7	10.5
25	Vehicle length mm	4025	4210	4210	4470	4430
26	Vehicle width mm	1740	1700	1700	1740	1710
27	Vehicle height mm	1280	1390	1390	1420	1390
28	Wheelbase mm	2460	2700	2700	2725	2700
29	Track, front/rear mm	1420/1490	1420/1425	1420/1425	1480/1490	1410/1430
30	Turning circle diameter m	10.4	10.8	10.8	10.5	10.8
31	Ground clearance mm	110	108	108	130	110
32	Suspension, front –	DQl-F-Ku-Td	DQl-F-Ku-Td	DQl-F-Ku-Td	DQl-F-Ku-Td	DQl-F-Ku-Td
33	Suspension, rear –	Sl-Sf-Ku-Td	Sl-Sf-Ku-Td	Sl-Sf-Ku-Td	Ma-Sf-Ku-Td	Ql-Ll-Sf-Ku-Td
34	Tires –	¹)	185/65 HR 15	185/60 HR 15	195/65 HR 15	205/60 VR 15
35	Braking system	4Sb-ABS	4Sb-ABS	4Sb-ABS	4Sb-ABS	4Sb-ABS

¹) Front 225/45 R 17; Rear 245/40 R 17
see P. 898 for abbreviations and explanations.

	328i	530d	740d	840Ci	Ford Ka 1.3	Puma 1.4	Fiesta 1.8D	
1	2 Ca 4	4 Li 5	4 Li 5	2 Co 4	3 Li 4	3 Co 2+2	5/3 Li 5	1
2	142 (193) / 5300	135 (184) / 4000	175 (238) / 4000	210 (286) / 5700	44 (60) / 5000	66 (90) / 5500	44 (60) / 4800	2
3	280 / 3950	390 / 1750	560 / 1750	420 / 3900	103 / 2500	123 / 4000	105 / 2500	3
4	230	225	242	250	155	180	158	4
5	7.7	8	6.4	6.6	15.4	11.9	17.6	5
6	1430	1575	1960	1780	890	1035	1015	6
7	1830	2115	2495	2200	1265	1400	1510	7
8	10.1	11.7	11.2	8.5	20.2	15.7	24.2	8
9	EU 6.8/13.5	EU 5.7/9.8	EU 7/14.6	EU 9/19.2	EU 5.5/8.8	EU 5.9/9.5	EU 4.9/6.7	9
10	95	Diesel	Diesel	95	95	95	Diesel	10
11	62	70	85	90	42	42	42	11
12	2793	2926	3901	4398	1299	1388	1753	12
13	84/84	84/88	84/88	92/82.7	74/75.5	76/76.5	82.5/82	13
14	10.2	18	18	10	9.5	10.3	21.5	14
15	50.8	46.1	44.9	47.7	33.9	47.5	25.1	15
16	6 R 4Ve	6 R 4Ve	8 V 4Ve	8 V 4Ve	4 R	4 R 4Ve	q 4 R	16
17	EI	EP/CR-T-Ic	EP/CR-T-Ic	Motronic	EI	EI	EP/V	17
18	70/80	120	150	120	55	55	55	18
19	70	95	110	130	43	43	63	19
20	h	h	h	h	v	v-ASR	v	20
21	4.21/2.49; 1.66/1.24; 1	5.24/2.91; 1.81/1.27; 1	3.55/2.24; 1.55/1; 0.79	4.23/2.51; 1.67/1.23; 1/0.83	3.15/1.93; 1.28/0.95; 0.76	3.15/1.93; 1.38/1.03; 0.76	3.58/1.93; 1.28/0.95; 0.76	21
22	2.93	2.35	2.65	2.93	4.06	4.19	3.84	22
23	5 (5)	5 (5)	(5)	6 (5)	5	5	5	23
24	10.5	9.2	16	12	5.3	6	9.3	24
25	4435	4775	4985	4780	3620	3985	3830	25
26	1710	1800	1860	1855	1640	1670	1635	26
27	1350	1430	1430	1340	1400	1350	1330	27
28	2700	2830	2930	2685	2450	2445	2445	28
29	1410/1420	1510/1525	1550/1570	1555/1560	1395/1410	1450/1410	1430/1375	29
30	10.8	11.3	11.6	11.5	10.3	10.4	10.3	30
31	110	120	120	140	140	–	140	31
32	DQI-F-Ku-Td	DG-Sf-Td	QI-F-Ku-Td	DQI-F-Sf-Ku-Td	DQI-F-Ku-Td	DQI-F-Ku-Td	DQI-F-Ku-Td	32
33	QI-Li-Sf-Ku-Td	Ma-Sf-Td	Ma-Sf-Ku-Td	Ma-Sf-Ku-Td	Vla-Sf-Td	Vla-Li-Sf-Td	Vla-Li-Sf-Td	33
34	205/60 WR 15	225/65 R 15	235/60 WR 16	235/50 WR 16	155/70 R 13	195/50 R 15	155/70 R 13	34
35	4Sb-ABS	4Sb-ABS	4Sb-ABS	4Sb-ABS	Sb-Tb	Sb-Tb-ABS	Sb-Tb	35

Country		Germany				
Vehicle make Model		**Ford** (Continued)				
		Escort 1.6	Focus 1.8	Focus 1.8TD Sedan	Mondeo 2.0	Cougar 2.5i
1 Body style	–	5 Li 5	5/3 Li 5	4 Li 5	4/5 Li 5	3 Co 5
2 Useful power	kW (bhp)	66 (90)	85 (116)	67 (91)	96 (131)	125 (170)
at engine speed	rpm	5250	5750	4000	5600	6250
3 Max. torque	Nm	138	158	200	178	220
at engine speed	rpm	3500	3750	2000	4000	4250
4 Maximum speed	km/h	177	198	184	206	225
5 Acceleration from 0 to 100 km/h	s	12.2	10.2	12.6	9.9	8.1
6 Curb weight	kg	1080	1125	1205	1245	1390
7 Gross vehicle weight	kg	1625	1620	1620	1815	1825
8 Weight-to-power ratio	kg/kW	16.4	13.4	18	12.9	11.1
9 Fuel consumption	l/100 km	EU 6.4/10.7	EU 6/10.3	EU 4/6.7	EU 5.9/11.6	EU 7.3/13.4
10 Fuel octane number	RON	95	95	Diesel	95	95
11 Fuel tank capacity	l	55	55	55	61.5	60
12 Engine swept volume	cm³	1597	1796	1753	1988	2544
13 Bore/stroke	mm	76/88	80.6/88	82.5/82	84.8/88	82.4/79.5
14 Compression ratio	–	10.3	10	19.4	10	9.7
15 Specific power output	kW/l	41.3	47.3	38.2	48.3	49.1
16 Engine type	–	q 4 R 4Ve	q 4 R 4Ve	q 4 R	q 4 R 4Ve	q 6 V 4Ve
17 Fuel managment	–	EI	EI	EP/eV-T-Ic	EI	EI
18 Alternator (14 V)	A	90	90	–	90	90
19 Battery (12 V)	Ah	48	48	–	48	48
20 (Engine pos.)/drive config.		v	v	v	v	v
21 Transmission	1st/2nd gear	3.58/1.91	3.15/1.93	3.66/2.05	3.42/2.14	3.42/2.14
ratio	3rd/4th gear	1.28/0.95	1.28/0.95	1.26/0.86	1.45/1.03	1.48/1.11
	5th/6th gear	0.76	0.76	0.67	0.77	0.85
22 Final drive ratio	–	3.82	4.06	3.56	3.84	3.82
23 Gearshift	H (A)	5	5	5	5 (4)	5 (4)
24 Cooling	l	6.6	6.6	6	6.6	7.5
25 Vehicle length	mm	4140	4150	4360	4560	4700
26 Vehicle width	mm	1700	1700	1700	1750	1770
27 Vehicle height	mm	1400	1480	1480	1420	1320
28 Wheelbase	mm	2525	2615	2615	2705	2705
29 Track, front/rear	mm	1440/1460	1495/1485	1495/1485	1505/1485	1505/1490
30 Turning circle diameter	m	10.5	10.9	10.9	10.9	10.9
31 Ground clearance	mm	–	–	–	120	–
32 Suspension, front	–	DQI-F-Ku-Td	DQI-F-Sf-Ku-Td	DQI-F-Sf-Ku-Td	DQI-F-Ku-Td	DQI-F- Sf-Ku-Td
33 Suspension, rear	–	Vla-Ll-Sf-Td	Ql-Ll-Sf-Td	Ll-Ql-Sf-Td	DQu-Ll-Ku-Td	Ql-Ll-F- Sf-Ku-Td
34 Tires	–	175/70 R 13	185/65 R 14	185/65 R 14	185/65 R 14	205/60 R 15
35 Braking system		Sb-Tb	4Sb-ABS	4Sb-ABS	4Sb-ABS	4Sb

See PP. 898 for abbreviations and explanations.

Galaxy 1.9 TDI	Mercedes-Benz A 140	A 160 CDI	SLK 200	SLK 230 Kompressor	C 240 T	C 220 CDI	
5 Gli 5-8	5 Li 5	5 Li 5	2 Ro 2	2 Ro 2	5 Ko 5	4 Li 5	1
81 (110)	60 (82)	44 (60)	100 (136)	142 (193)	125 (170)	92 (125)	2
4150	5000	3600	5500	5300	5900	4200	
235	130	160	190	280	225	300	3
1900	3750	1500	3700	2500	3000	1800	
172	170	150	208	231	216	198	4
							5
10.8	12.9	18.8	9.3	7.7	9.5	10.5	
1645	1020	1070	1195	1250	1470	1340	6
2400	1480	1530	1530	1585	1970	1890	7
20.2	17	23.9	12	8.8	11.4	14.6	8
EU 5.4/8.7	EU 5.6/9.8	EU 4.3/6	EU 6.9/12.9	EU 7/13.3	EU 7.5/14.3	EU 5/8.2	9
Diesel	95	Diesel	95	95	95	Diesel	10
70	54	54	53	53	62	62	11
1896	1397	1689	1998	2295	2398	2151	12
79.5/95.5	80/69.5	80/84	89.9/78.7	90.9/88.4	83.2/73.5	88/88.4	13
19.5	11	19	10.4	8.8	10	19	14
42.7	42.9	26	50.1	61.9	52.1	42.8	15
4 R	q 4 R	q 4 R 4Ve	4 R 4Ve	4 R 4Ve	6 V 3Ve	4 R 4Ve	16
EP/eV-T-Ic	EI	EP/CR-T	Motronic	Motronic-Kom-Ic	Motronic	EP/CR-T-Ic	17
90	90	90	90	90	115	90/125	18
61	46	62	62	62	74	74	19
v	v-ASR-ESP	v-ASR-ESP	h-ASR	h-ASR	h-ASR	h-ASR	20
3.58/2.05	3.27/1.92	3.63/2.09	3.91/2.17	3.86/2.18	3.86/2.18	4.1/2.18	21
1.35/0.92	1.26/0.88	1.31/0.9	1.37/1	1.38/1	1.38/1	1.38/1	
0.67	0.7	0.72	0.8	0.8	0.8	0.8	
4.36	4.06	3.05	3.91	3.46	3.67	3.07	22
5 (4)	5 (5)	(5) 5	5 (5)	5 (5)	5 (5)	5 (5)	23
11.7	6	6	8	8.5	8.5	8.5	24
4620	3575	3575	4000	4000	4515	4515	25
1810	1720	1720	1720	1720	1725	1725	26
1730	1580	1580	1290	1290	1430	1430	27
2835	2425	2425	2400	2400	2690	2690	28
1520/1505	1505/1450	1525/1470	1490/1470	1490/1470	1500/1465	1500/1465	29
11.7	10.7	10.7	10.6	10.6	10.8	10.8	30
150	–	–	150	150	150	150	31
QI-F-Ku-Td	DQI-F-Sf-Ku-Td	DQI-F-Sf-Ku-Td	DDQI-Sf-Ku-Td	DDQI-Sf-Ku-Td	DDQI-Sf-Ku-Td	DDQI-Sf-Ku-Td	32
SI-Sf-Ku-Td	VIa-Sf-Ku-Td	VIa-Sf-Ku-Td	Ra-Sf-Ku-Td	Ra-Sf-Ku-Td	Ra-Sf-Ku-Td	Ra-Sf-Ku-Td	33
195/65 R 15	195/50 R 15	155/70 R 15	205/60 R 15	205/55 R 16	195/65 R 15	195/65 R 15	34
4Sb-ABS	Sb-Tb-ABS	Sb-Tb-ABS	4Sb-ABS	4Sb-ABS	4Sb-ABS	4Sb-ABS	35

Country		Germany				
Vehicle make Model		**Mercedes-Benz** (Continued) CL 500	E 280 T 4matic	E 430	CLK 200 Kompressor	S 320
1	Body style –	2 Co 4/5	5 Ko 5-7	4 Li 5	2 Co 4	4 Li 5
2	Useful power kW (bhp) at engine speed rpm	225 (306) 5600	150 (204) 5700	205 (279) 5750	141 (192) 5300	165 (224) 3199
3	Max. torque Nm at engine speed rpm	460 2700	270 3000	400 3000	270 2500	315 3000
4	Maximum speed km/h	250	220	250	233	240
	Acceleration from 0 to 100 km/h s	6.5	9.9	6.6	8.4	8.2
6	Curb weight kg	1790	1665	1575	1320	1695
7	Gross vehicle weight kg	2320	2290	2180	1820	2300
8	Weight-to-power ratio kg/kW	8	9.8	7.7	9.4	10.3
9	Fuel consumption l/100 km	EU -/13.4	EU 8.4/16	EU 8.1/16.8	EU 7.2/13.6	EU 8.2/17.1
10	Fuel octane number RON	95	95	95	98	95
11	Fuel tank capacity l	88	65	65	62	88
12	Engine swept volume cm³	4966	2799	4266	1998	3199
13	Bore/stroke mm	97/84	89.9/73.5	89.9/84	89.9/78.7	89.9/84
14	Compression ratio –	10	10	10	8.5	10
15	Specific power output kW/l	45.3	53.6	48	70.6	51.6
16	Engine type –	8 V 3Ve	6 V 3Ve	8 V 3Ve	4 R 4Ve	6 V 3Ve
17	Fuel managment –	Motronic	Motronic	Motronic	Motronic-Kom-Ic	Motronic
18	Alternator (14 V) A	143/150	115	150	90	150
19	Battery (12 V) Ah	100	74	100	62	74
20	(Engine pos.)/drive config. –	h-ASR-ESP	aa	h-ASR-ESP	h-ASR	h-ASR-ESP
21	Transmission 1st/2nd gear ratio 3rd/4th gear 5th/6th gear	3.59/2.19 1.41/1 0.83	3.86/2.18 1.38/1 0.8	3.59/2.19 1.41/1 0.83	3.86/2.18 1.38/1 0.8	3.93/2.41 1.49/1 0.83
22	Final drive ratio –	2.82	3.7	2.82	3.67	3.07
23	Gearshift H (A)	(5)	5 (5)	(5)	5 (5)	(5)
24	Cooling l	15	11	9	8	11
25	Vehicle length mm	4995	4820	4800	4565	5040
26	Vehicle width mm	1855	1800	1800	1720	1855
27	Vehicle height mm	1400	1440	1440	1370	1450
28	Wheelbase mm	2885	2830	2830	2690	2965
29	Track, front/rear mm	1575/1580	1540/1540	1540/1540	1505/1475	1575/1575
30	Turning circle diameter m	11.5	11.3	11.3	10.7	11.7
31	Ground clearance mm	150	160	160	150	150
32	Suspension, front –	DQl-Ql-Ku- Td-Lue	DDQl-Sf-Ku-Td	DDQl-Sf-Ku-Td	DDQl-Sf-Ku-Td	DQl-Ql-Ku- Td-Lue
33	Suspension, rear –	Ra-Ku-Td-Lue	Ra-Ku-Td	Ra-Sf-Ku-Td	Ra-Sf-Ku-Td	Ra-Ku-Td-Lue
34	Tires –	225/55 R 17	215/55 R 16	215/55 R 16	205/55 R 16	225/60 R 16
35	Braking system	4Sb-ABS	4Sb-ABS	4Sb-ABS	4Sb-ABS	4Sb-ABS

See PP. 898 for abbreviations and explanations.

SL 600	ML 230	Opel					
		Corsa 1.0i	Corsa 1.6i	Astra 1.2i	Astra 2.0i	Zafira 1.8i	
2 Ro 2+2	5 Ge 5-7	3/5 Li 5	3/5 Li 5	3/4/5 Li 5	3/4/5 Li 5	5 Gli 5-7	1
290 (394) 5200	110 (150) 5400	40 (54) 5600	78 (106) 6000	48 (65) 5600	100 (136) 5600	85 (116) 5400	2
570 3800	220 3800	82 2800	148 4000	110 4000	188 3200	170 3400	3
250	180	150	192	165	208	184	4
							5
6.1	12.3	18	10.5	16	9	12	
1980	1855	865	980	1035	1170	1320	6
2320	2650	1360	1435	1555	1695	2040	7
6.8	16.2	21.6	12.5	21.6	11.7	11.5	8
EU 10.9/23.3	EU 10/17.1	EU 4.6/7.4	EU 6.1/10.8	EU 5/8	EU 6.6/12	EU 6.8/11.5	9
95	95	95	95	95	95	95	10
80	70	46	46	52	52	58	11
5987	2295	973	1598	1199	1998	1796	12
89/80.2	90.9/88.4	72.5/78.6	79/81.5	72.5/72.6	86/86	80.5/88.2	13
10	10.4	10.1	10.5	10.1	10.8	10.5	14
48.4	47.9	41.1	48.8	40	50	47.3	15
12 V 4Ve	4 R 4Ve	3 R 4Ve	4 R 4Ve	4 R 4Ve	4 R 4Ve	4 R 4Ve	16
Motronic	Motronic	Motronic	EI	Motronic	EI	EI	17
150	90	70	70	70	70	70/100	18
100	62	36	44	36	44	55	19
h-ASR-ESP	aa	v	v	v	v	v	20
3.59/2.19 1.41/1 0.83	3.86/2.18 1.38/1 0.8	3.73/2.14 1.41/1.12 0.89	3.73/2.14 1.41/1.12 0.89	3.73/2.14 1.41/1.12 0.89	3.58/2.14 1.48/1.12 0.89	3.73/2.14 1.41/1.12 0.89	21
2.65	4.73	3.74	3.74	3.94	3.74	4.19	22
(5)	5	5 (4)	5 (4)	5	5 (4)	5 (4)	23
18	8.5	4.3	5.6	5.2	7.2	6.5	24
4500	4590	3740	3740	4111	4111	4320	25
1810	1830	1610	1610	1710	1710	1740	26
1290	1780	1420	1420	1430	1430	1630	27
2515	2820	2445	2445	2610	2610	2690	28
1535/1525	1560/1560	1385/1390	1385/1390	1485/1460	1485/1460	1470/1490	29
11.3	11.9	10.1	10.1	10.8	10.8	11.2	30
150	200	140	140	130	130	150	31
DQl-Db-Sf-Ku-Td	DDQl-Tf-Ku-Td	Ll-Ql-F-Sf-Td	Ll-Ql-F-Sf-Td	DQl-F-Sf-Ku-Td	DQl-F-Sf-Ku-Td	DQl-F-Sf-Ku-Td	32
Ra-Sf-Ku-Td	DDQl-Sf-Ku-Td	Vla-Ll-Sf-Td	Vla-Ll-Sf-Td	Vla-Ll-Sf-Ku-Td	Vla-Ll-Sf-Ku-Td	Vla-Ll-Sf-Ku-Td	33
245/45 R 17	225/75 R 16	165/70 R 13	185/60 R 14	175/70 R 14	195/60 R 15	195/65 R 15	34
4Sb-ABS	4Sb-ABS	Sb-Tb	Sb-Tb	Sb-Tb	4Sb	4Sb-ABS	35

Country		**Germany**				
Vehicle make		**Opel** (continued)				
Model		Vectra 2.5i	Omega 2.5 TD	Sintra 2.2i	Frontera 3.2i	Monterey 3.0 TD
1	Body style –	4/5 Li 5	4 Li 5	5 Gli 5-8	5/3 Ge 5	3/5 Ge 5
2	Useful power kW (bhp)	125 (170)	96 (131)	104 (141)	151 (205)	117 (159)
	at engine speed rpm	5800	4500	5400	5400	3900
3	Max. torque Nm	230	250	202	290	333
	at engine speed rpm	3200	2200	2600	3000	2000
4	Maximum speed km/h	230	200	183	192	160
5	Acceleration from 0 to 100 km/h s	8.5	12	12.7	9.7	15.8
6	Curb weight kg	1355	1550	1655	1780	1965
7	Gross vehicle weight kg	1850	2120	2345	2450	2730
8	Weight-to-power ratio kg/kW	10.6	16	15.9	11.8	16.4
9	Fuel consumption l/100 km	EU 7.3/14.1	EU 6.1/10.9	EU 8.1/12.5	EU 10.1/17	EU 9/14
10	Fuel octane number RON	95	Diesel	–	95	Diesel
11	Fuel tank capacity l	60	75	70	65/75	85
12	Engine swept volume cm^3	2498	2497	2198	3165	2999
13	Bore/stroke mm	81.6/79.6	80/82.8	86/94.6	93.4/77	95.4/104.9
14	Compression ratio –	10.8	22.5	10.5	9.4	19
15	Specific power output kW/l	50	38.4	47.3	47.7	39
16	Engine type –	6 V 4Ve	6 R	q 4 R 4Ve	6 V 4Ve	4 R
17	Fuel management –	Motronic	EP/eV-T-Ic	EI	Motronic	EP/CR-T-Ic
18	Alternator (14 V) A	100	105	105	1013 W	60
19	Battery (12 V) Ah	66	85	54	60	150
20	(Engine pos.)/drive config. –	v	h	v	aa	aa
21	Transmission 1st/2nd gear	3.58/2.02	3.81/2.11	3.67/1.76	3.77/2.25	3.77/2.25
	ratio 3rd/4th gear	1.35/0.98	1.34/1	1.18/0.89	1.4/1	1.4/1
	5th/6th gear	0.81	0.76	0.7	0.81	0.81
22	Final drive ratio –	3.84	3.45	4.05	4.3	4.56
23	Gearshift H (A)	5 (4)	5 (4)	5	5 (4)	5
24	Cooling l	7.7	10.2	8.5	11.1	5.8
25	Vehicle length mm	4495	4785	4670	4660	4795
26	Vehicle width mm	1710	1785	1830	1785	1835
27	Vehicle height mm	1420	1450	1780	1740	1840
28	Wheelbase mm	2635	2730	2850	2700	2760
29	Track, front/rear mm	1465/1470	1515/1530	1560/1610	1515/1520	1515/1520
30	Turning circle diameter m	11.3	11.0	11.4	12.1	12.4
31	Ground clearance mm	140	140	160	230	210
32	Suspension, front –	DQI-F-Sf-Ku-Td	DQI-F-Sf-Ku-Td	DQI-F-Sf-Ku-Td	DDQI-Tf-Ku-Td	DDQI-Tf-Ku-Td
33	Suspension, rear –	DQu-Sf-Ku-Td	QI-Sl-Sf-Ku-Td	Vla-Ll-Sf-Ku-Td	Sa-Li-P-Sf-Ku-Td	Sa-Ll-P-Ku-Td
34	Tires –	195/65 R 15	205/65 R 15	205/65 HR 15	245/70 R 16	215/80 R 16
35	Braking system	4Sb-ABS	4Sb-ABS	4Sb-ABS	4Sb-ABS	4Sb-ABS

See PP. 898 for abbreviations and explanations.

Porsche			VW (Volkswagen)				
Boxster 2.5i	911 Carrera 3.4	911 GT3 3.6	Lupo 1.0	Lupo 1.2 TDI	Polo 1.4	Polo Variant 1.9 TDI	
2 Ca 2	2 Co/Ca 2+2	2 Co/Ca 2+2	3 Li 4-5	3 Li 4-5	3/5 Li 5	5 Ko 5	1
150 (204) 6000	221 (300) 6800	265 (360) 6800	37 (50) 5000	45 (61) 4000	74 (101) 6000	66 (90) 4000	2
245 4500	350 4600	370 5000	86 3000	140 1800	128 4400	210 1900	3
240	280	> 280	152	165	188	180	4
							5
6.9 1250	5.2 1320	4.8 1320	17.9 895	16.5 780	10.5 950	12.5 1135	6
1560	1720	1720	1350	1200	1450	1595	7
8.3	6	6	24.2	17.3	12.8	17.2	8
EU 7.1/14.3	EU 8.5/17.2	(Ed.) 10/22	EU 4.8/7.6	EU 2.7/3.7	EU 5.4/9.6	EU 4.1/6.4	9
98	98	98	95	Diesel	95	Diesel	10
57	64	64	34	34	45	45	11
2480	3387	3600	999	1196	1390	1896	12
85.5/72	96/78	100/76.4	67.1/70.6	76.5/86.7	76.5/75.6	79.5/95.5	13
11	11.3	11.3	10.7	19.5	10.5	19.5	14
60.5	65.2	73.6	37	37.6	53.2	34.8	15
6 Bx 4Ve	6 Bx 4Ve	6 Bx 4Ve	q 4 R	q 3 R	4 R 4Ve	4 R	16
Motronic	Motronic	Motronic	EI	EP/UIS-T-Ic	EI	EP/eV-T-Ic	17
115	120	120	70	70	70	90	18
60/75	70	70	36	36	44	61	19
h	h	h	v	v	v	v	20
3.5/2.12 1.43/1.03 0.79	3.82/2.2 1.52/1.22 1.02/0.84	3.82/2.15 1.56/1.21 0.97/0.75	3.46/1.96 1.36/1.05 0.86	3.46/1.96 1.82/0.81 0.64	3.45/2.1 1.45/1.1 0.89	3.3/1.94 1.31/0.92 0.72	21
3.89	3.44	3.44	4.23	3.33	3.88	3.16	22
5 (5)	6 (5)	6 (5)	5	5	5	5	23
–	22.5	22.5	5	5	5.5	6.5	24
4315	4430	4430	3525	3525	3715	4140	25
1780	1765	1780	1640	1640	1655	1640	26
1290	1300	1270	1460	1460	1420	1460	27
2415	2350	2350	2325	2325	2405	2440	28
1465/1525	1455/1500	1465/1480	1390/1400	1390/1400	1350/1380	1430/1390	29
10.9	12.1	12.1	9.8	9.8	10.4	10.9	30
–	–	–	110	110	110	110	31
Ql-Li-F-Sf-Ku-Td	DQl-F-Sf-Ku-Td	DQl-F-Sf-Ku-Td	DQl-F-Sf-Td	DQl-F-Sf-Td	DQl-F-Sf-Ku-Td	DQl-F	32
Ql-Li-F-Sf-Ku-Td	Ma-Sf-Ku-Td	Ma-Sf-Ku-Td	Vla-Ll-Sf-Td	Vla-Ll-Sf-Td	Vla-Ll-Sf-Ku-Td	Vla-Ll-Sf-Td	33
205/55 ZR 16	205/50 ZR 17	225/40 ZR 18	155/70 R 13	155/65 SR 14	185/55 R 14	185/60 R 14	34
4Sb-ABS	4Sb-ABS	4Sb-ABS	Sb-Tb	Sb-Tb-ABS	Sb-Tb-ABS	Sb-Tb-ABS	35

	Country		Germany				
	Vehicle make Model		**VW (Volkswagen)** (continued) New Beetle 2.0	Golf IV 2.3 VR5	Bora 1.6	Passat Variant 2.8 Syncro VR6	Passat 1.9 TDI
1	Body style		2 Li 4	3/5 Li 5	4 Li 5	5 Ko 5	4 Li 5
2	Useful power at engine speed	kW (bhp) rpm	85 (116) 5200	110 (150) 6000	74 (101) 5600	142 (193) 6000	85 (116) 4000
3	Max. torque at engine speed	Nm rpm	170 2400	205 3200	145 3800	280 3200	285 1900
4	Maximum speed	km/h	185	216	188	238	200
5	Acceleration from 0 to 100 km/h	s	10.9	8.8	11.7	7.6	10.7
6	Curb weight	kg	1230	1245	1185	1495	1320
7	Gross vehicle weight	kg	1650	1800	1720	2040	1880
8	Weight-to-power ratio	kg/kW	14.6	11.3	16	10.2	15.5
9	Fuel consumption	l/100 km	EU 6.9/11.8	EU 7.2/13.2	EU 6/10.6	EU 8/15.2	EU 4.3/7
10	Fuel octane number	RON	95	95	95	95	Diesel
11	Fuel tank capacity	l	55	55	55	62	62
12	Engine swept volume	cm³	1984	2324	1595	2771	1896
13	Bore/stroke	mm	82.5/92.8	81/90.2	81/77.4	82.5/86.4	79.5/95.5
14	Compression ratio	–	10.5	10.1	10.3	10.6	18
15	Specific power output	kW/l	42.8	47.3	46.4	51.2	44.8
16	Engine type	–	q 4 R	5 VR	4 R	6 VR 5Ve	4 R
17	Fuel management	–	Motronic	EI	EI	EI	EP/UIS-T-Ic
18	Alternator (14 V)	A	70/90	70	70	90	120
19	Battery (12 V)	Ah	44/60	60	44/60	320 A	80
20	(Engine pos.)/drive config.	–	v	v	v	aa	v
21	Transmission ratio	1st/2nd gear 3rd/4th gear 5th/6th gear	3.78/2.12 1.36/1.03 0.84	3.3/1.94 1.31/1.03 0.84	3.46/1.94 1.37/1.03 0.85	3.5/1.94 1.3/0.94 0.79	3.5/1.94 1.22/0.88 0.69
22	Final drive ratio	–	4.24	3.94	4.25	3.89	3.56
23	Gearshift	H (A)	5 (4)	5 (4)	5 (4)	5 (5)	5 (4)
24	Cooling	l	5.3	5.2	5.5	6.5	6.5
25	Vehicle length	mm	4080	4150	4375	4675	4675
26	Vehicle width	mm	1725	1735	1735	1740	1740
27	Vehicle height	mm	1500	1440	1440	1500	1460
28	Wheelbase	mm	2510	2510	2515	2705	2705
29	Track, front/rear	mm	1510/1495	1510/1490	1515/1495	1500/1500	1500/1500
30	Turning circle diameter	m	10.9	10.9	10.9	11.4	11.4
31	Ground clearance	mm	130	130	130	110	110
32	Suspension, front	–	DQl-F-Ku-Td	DQl-F-Sf-Ku-Td	DQl-F-Sf-Ku-Td	Ql-Ll-F-Sf-Ku-Td	Ql-Ll-F-Sf-Ku-Td
33	Suspension, rear	–	Vla-Sf-Ku-Td	Vla-Ll-Sf-Ku-Td	Vla-Ll-Sf-Ku-Td	Vla-Ll-Sf-Ku-Td	Vla-Ll-Sf-Ku-Td
34	Tires	–	205/55 R 16	205/55 WR16	195/65 R 15	205/55 R 16	195/65 R 15
35	Braking system		4Sb-ABS	4Sb-ABS	4Sb-ABS	4Sb-ABS	4Sb-ABS

See PP. 898 for abbreviations and explanations.

	France							
		Citroën						
	Sharan 1.8	Saxo 1.0i	Saxo 1.6i	Berlingo 1.4i	Berlingo 1.9D	Xsara 1.8i	Xsara 1.9TD	
	5 Gli 5-7	5/3 Li 5	3/5 Li 5	3/4/5 Ko 5	3/4/5 Ko 5	5 Ko 5	5/3 Li 5	1
	110 (150) / 5700	37 (50) / 6000	66 (90) / 5600	55 (75) / 5500	50 (68) / 4600	66 (90) / 5000	66 (90) / 4000	2
	210 / 1750	74 / 3700	137 / 3000	111 / 3400	120 / 2000	147 / 2600	196 / 2200	3
	194	149	187	150	142	182	178	4
	12	19.1	11.4	14.6	16.3	13.5	12.7	5
	1660	825	920	1125	1185	1120	1140	6
	2400	1240	1360	1780	1840	1650	1690	7
	15.1	21.8	13.9	20.5	23.7	16.2	17.2	8
	EU 7.9/13.9	EU 5.1/8.3	EU 5.8/9.9	EU 5.9/9.2	EU 5.4/8.6	EU 6.2/11	EU 5.2/8.8	9
	95	95	95	95	Diesel	95	Diesel	10
	70	45	45	55	55	54	54	11
	1781	954	1587	1361	1905	1762	1905	12
	81/86.4	70/62	78.5/82	75/77	83/88	83/81.4	83/88	13
	9.5	9.4	9.6	10.2	23	9.5	21.8	14
	61.7	38.8	40.9	40.4	26.2	37.4	34.6	15
	4 R 5Ve	q 4 R	q 4 R	q 4 R	q 4 R	q 4 R	q 4 R	16
	EI-T-Ic	Mono-Motronic	Motronic	EI	EP/V	EI	EP/V-T-Ic	17
	70/90	50	60/70	60/70	70/80	60/70	70/80	18
	280 A	250 A	250 A	200 A	300/400 A	250 A	300/400 A	19
	v	v	v	v	v	v	v	20
	3.58/2.05 / 1.35/0.97 / 0.81	3.42/1.81 / 1.28/0.98 / 0.77	3.42/1.95 / 1.36/1.05 / 0.85	3.42/1.95 / 1.36/1.05 / 0.85	3.42/1.95 / 1.36/1.05 / 0.85	3.45/1.87 / 1.28/0.95 / 0.8	3.45/1.87 / 1.15/0.83 / 0.66	21
	4.06	4.29	3.56	4.54	4.53	3.67	4.05	22
	5 (4)	5	5	5/4	5	5	5	23
	6.5	6.1	6.1	6.5	8.5	7.5	9	24
	4620	3720	3740	4110	4110	4355	4355	25
	1810	1595	1620	1720	1720	1790	1790	26
	1730	1370	1360	1800	1800	1420	1390	27
	2845	2385	2385	2690	2690	2540	2540	28
	1510/1500	1370/1300	1400/1320	1420/1440	1420/1440	1420/1430	1435/1440	29
	11.7	10.0	10.9	10.7	10.7	11.4	11.4	30
	150	120	120	140	140	110	110	31
	DQI-F-Sf-	DQI-F-Ku-Td	DQI-F-Ku-Td	DQI-F	DQI-F	DQI-F-Sf-Ku-Td	DQI-F-Sf-Ku-Td	32
	SI-Sf-Ku-Td	LI-Tf-Ku-Td	LI-Tf-Ku-Td	LI-Tf-Td	LI-Tf-Td	Ea-LI-Tf-Ku-Td	Ea-LI-Tf-Ku-Td	33
	195/65 R 15	155/70 R 13	185/55 R 14	165/70 R 14	165/70 R 14	185/65 R 14	185/65 R 14	34
	4Sb-ABS	Sb-Tb	Sb-Tb	Sb-Tb	Sb-Tb	Sb-Tb	Sb-Tb	35

Country		France				
Vehicle make Model		Citroën (continued)				MCC
		Xsara Picasso 2.0 TDI	Xantia 2.9i	XM 2.5TD	Evasion 1.9TD	Smart 0.6
1	Body style –	5 Gli 5	5 Li 5	5 Li 5	5 Gli 5+3	2 Mc 2
2	Useful power kW (bhp) at engine speed rpm	80 (109) 4000	143 (194) 5500	96 (130) 4300	66 (90) 4000	33 (45) 5250
3	Max. torque Nm at engine speed rpm	250 1750	273 4000	294 2000	196 2250	70 3000
4	Maximum speed km/h	180	230	201	160	135
5	Acceleration from 0 to 100 km/h s	12.5	8.2	12.1	16.8	18.9
6	Curb weight kg	1300	1470	1580	1585	720
7	Gross vehicle weight kg	–	1950	2130	2360	980
8	Weight-to-power ratio kg/kW	16.3	10.5	16.6	24	21.8
9	Fuel consumption l/100 km	(Ed.) 5/8	EU 8/15.9	EU 5.9/10.9	EU 6.7/10.6	(Ed.) 4.8/7
10	Fuel octane number RON	Diesel	95	Diesel	Diesel	95
11	Fuel tank capacity l	–	65	80	80	22
12	Engine swept volume cm³	1998	2946	2446	1905	599
13	Bore/stroke mm	86/86	87/82.6	92/92	83/88	63.5/63
14	Compression ratio –	18	10.5	22	21.8	9.5
15	Specific power output kW/l	40	47.5	38.8	34.6	55
16	Engine type –	4 R	q 6 V 4Ve	4 R 3Ve	q 4 R	3 R
17	Fuel management –	EP/CR-T-Ic	Motronic	EP/eV-T-Ic	EP/V-T-Ic	Motronic
18	Alternator (14 V) A	60/70	90	120	70/80	40
19	Battery (12 V) Ah	250 A	300 A	450 A	300/400 A	35
20	(Engine pos.)/drive config.	v	v	v	v	h-h
21	Transmission 1st/2nd gear ratio 3rd/4th gear 5th/6th gear	–	3.25/1.78 1.19/0.88 0.7	3.42/1.86 1.18/0.86 0.64	3.42/1.94 1.25/0.75 0.67	3.38/2.45 1.76
22	Final drive ratio –	–	4.31	4.06	4.54	4.21/1.67
23	Gearshift H (A)	5	5 (4)	5 (4)	5	2x3 [SOFTIP]
24	Cooling l	6.5	10	13	9	3.5
25	Vehicle length mm	4275	4525	4710	4455	2500
26	Vehicle width mm	1750	1755	1795	1820	1515
27	Vehicle height mm	1640	1400	1390	1710	1529
28	Wheelbase mm	2760	2740	2850	2825	1812
29	Track, front/rear mm	1435/1450	1500/1455	1520/1445	1535/1540	1285/1355
30	Turning circle diameter m	12.0	12.0	12.4	12.3	8.5
31	Ground clearance mm	150	160	140	130	131
32	Suspension, front –	DQl-F-Sf-Ku	Hf-DQl-F-Ku	Hf-DQl-F-Ku	DQl-F-Sf-Td	DQl-Qf-Ku-Td
33	Suspension, rear –	Ea-Ll-Tf-Ku	Hf-Ll-Ku	Hf-Ll-Ku	Vla-Ll-P-Sf-Td	De-Wa-Sf- Ku-Td
34	Tires –	185/65 R 15	205/60 R 15	205/65 R 15	205/65 R 15	1)
35	Braking system	Sb-Tb-ABS	4Sb-ABS	4Sb-ABS	Sb-Tb	Sb-Tb-ABS

1) Front 135/70 R 15; Rear 175/55 R 15
See P. 898 for abbreviations and explanations.

MCC Smart 0.8 TD	Peugeot 106 1.4i	206 2.0i	306 1.8i	306 Break 2.0 TDI	Partner 1.8i	406 Break 2.9i	
2 Mc 2	3/5 Li 5	3/5 Li 5	4/3/5 Li 5	5 Ko 5	3/4/5 Ko 5	5 Ko 5	1
30 (40) 4000	55 (75) 5500	99 (135) 6000	81 (110) 5500	66 (90) 4000	66 (90) 5000	140 (190) 5500	2
100 2000	111 3400	190 4100	155 4250	205 1900	147 2600	267 4000	3
135	178	210	193	181	160	227	4
							5
17.5 720	13.2 815	8.4 1050	11.6 1095	13.2 1200	12.2 1170	8.5 1505	6
980	1315	1560	1560	1655	1780	2175	7
–	14.8	10.6	13.5	17.2	17.7	10.4	8
(Ed.) 3.4/5.5	EU 5.4/9.4	EU 6.2/10.9	EU 6.3/12	EU 4.4/7.2	EU 7.1/11.9	EU 8/15.9	9
Diesel	95	95	95	Diesel	95	95	10
22	45	50	60	60	55	70	11
approx. 800	1361	1997	1762	1997	1762	2946	12
–	75/77	85/88	83/81.4	85/88	83/81.4	87/82.6	13
–	10.2	10.8	10.4	18	9.25	10.5	14
37.5	40.4	49.6	46	33	37.5	47.5	15
3 R	q 4 R	q 4 R 4Ve	4 R 4Ve	4 R	q 4 R	6 V 4Ve	16
EP/CR-T-lc	EI	EI	EI	EP/CR-T	EI	Motronic	17
40	80	70	70	90/120/150	80	157	18
35	200 A	300 A	300 A	300 A	250 A	300 A	19
h-h	v	v	v	v	v	v	20
3.38/2.45 1.76	3.42/1.8 1.28/0.98 0.77	3.46/1.87 1.36/1.05 0.86	3.46/1.87 1.36/1.05 0.79	3.46/1.87 1.15/0.83 0.66	3.42/1.95 1.36/1.05 0.85	3.25/1.78 1.19/0.88 0.7	21
4.21/1.67	3.76	3.79	3.95/3.79	3.68	4.54	4.31	22
2x3 [SOFTIP]	5 (3)	5	5	5	5	5 (4)	23
3.5	6	7.8	6.5	7	7.5	7.8	24
2500	3680	3835	4265	4345	4110	4735	25
1515	1590	1650	1690	1690	1720	1765	26
1529	1380	1430	1380	1410	1800	1500	27
1812	2385	2440	2580	2580	2690	2700	28
1285/1355	1380/1310	1435/1430	1460/1430	1460/1430	1420/1440	1500/1480	29
8.5	11.0	10.2	11.0	11.0	10.7	12.0	30
131	130	110	130	130	140	130	31
DQl-Qf-Ku-Td	DQl-F	DQl-F-Td	DQl-F	DQl-F	DQl-F	DQl-F-Ku	32
De-Wa-Sf-Ku-Td	Ll-Tf-Td	Ll-Tf-Td	Ll-Tf-Td	Ll-Tf-Td	Ll-Tf-Td	Ma-Sf-Ku-Td	33
1)	165/70 R 13	185/55 R 15	185/65 R 14	195/55 R 15	195/65 R 15	205/60 VR 15	34
Sb-Tb-ABS	Sb-Tb	4Sb	Sb-Tb	4Sb	Sb-Tb	4Sb-ABS	35

Country		France				
Vehicle make		Peugeot (continued)			Renault	
Model		406 2.0 TDI	605 2.0i Turbo	806 2.1 TD	Kangoo 1.1i	Clio 1.6i
1	Body style –	4 Li 5	4 Li 5	5 Gli 5-8	4 Ko 5	3/5 Li 5
2	Useful power kW (bhp)	80 (109)	108 (147)	80 (109)	43 (58)	79 (107)
	at engine speed rpm	4000	5300	4300	5250	5750
3	Max. torque Nm	250	235	250	93	148
	at engine speed rpm	1750	2500	2000	2500	3750
4	Maximum speed km/h	191	213	175	140	195
5	Acceleration from 0 to 100 km/h s	12.5	10	14.1	17.2	9.6
6	Curb weight kg	1410	1515	1615	1020	995
7	Gross vehicle weight kg	1950	1935	2385	1600	1515
8	Weight-to-power ratio kg/kW	18.6	14	20.2	23.7	12.6
9	Fuel consumption l/100 km	EU 4.5/7.3	EU 8/14.5	6.1/8.2/9	EU 6.1/8.3	EU 6/9.4
10	Fuel octane number RON	Diesel	95	Diesel	95	95
11	Fuel tank capacity l	70	80	80	52	50
12	Engine swept volume cm³	1997	1998	2088	1149	1598
13	Bore/stroke mm	85/88	86/86	85/92	69/76.8	79.5/80.5
14	Compression ratio –	18	8	21.5	9.6	10
15	Specific power output kW/l	40.1	54	38.3	37.4	49.4
16	Engine type –	4 R	q 4 R	q 4 R 3Ve	q 4 R	q 4 R 4Ve
17	Fuel management –	EP/CR-T-Ic	Motronic-T-Ic	EP/eV-T-Ic	EI	EI
18	Alternator (14 V) A	157	80	70/80/90	60	60
19	Battery (12 V) Ah	300 A	300 A	400 A	40	50
20	(Engine pos.)/drive config. –	v	v	v	v	v
21	Transmission 1st/2nd gear	3.42/1.78	3.17/1.82	3.42/1.78	3.72/2.05	3.36/1.86
	ratio 3rd/4th gear	1.12/0.8	1.25/0.97	1.12/0.8	1.39/1.03	1.32/1.03
	5th/6th gear	0.61	0.77	0.61	0.82	0.82
22	Final drive ratio –	4.06	4.06	4.79	4.21	4.07
23	Gearshift H (A)	5 (4)	5 (4)	5	5	5
24	Cooling l	8.5	7.8	10.5	6.7	6.7
25	Vehicle length mm	4600	4765	4455	3995	3775
26	Vehicle width mm	1765	1800	1835	1660	1640
27	Vehicle height mm	1400	1410	1710	1830	1420
28	Wheelbase mm	2700	2800	2825	2600	2470
29	Track, front/rear mm	1500/1480	1525/1530	1535/1540	1400/1410	1390/1370
30	Turning circle diameter m	12.0	12.0	12.3	10.9	11.1
31	Ground clearance mm	130	100	140	140	120
32	Suspension, front –	DQl-F-Ku	DQl-F-Ku-Td	DQl-F-Sf-Ku-Td	DQl-F-Sf-Ku-Td	DQl-F-Ku-Td
33	Suspension, rear –	Ma-Sf-Ku-Td	DDQl-Ql-Sf-Ku-Td	Vla-Ll-P-Sf-Ku-Td	Ea-Ll-Tf-Sf-Ku-Td	Ta-Sf-Ku-Td
34	Tires –	195/65 HR 15	205/60 VR 15	205/65 R 15	165/70 R 13	165/70 R 13
35	Braking system	4Sb-ABS	4Sb-ABS	Sb-Tb	Sb-Tb	Sb-Tb-ABS

See PP. 898 for abbreviations and explanations.

Clio 1.9 D	Sport Spider	Mégane 1.4i	Mégane Break 1.9 DTI	Mégane Scénic 2.0i	Mégane Cabriolet 2.0i	Laguna Break 1.8i	
5/3 Li 5	2 Ro 2	4/5 Li 5	5 Ko 5	5 Gli 5	2 Ca 4	5 Ko 5	1
47 (64) 4500	110 (150) 6000	70 (95) 6000	72 (98) 4000	84 (114) 5400	103 (140) 5500	88 (120) 5750	2
120 2250	186 4500	127 3750	200 2000	168 4250	200 4250	165 3750	3
161	215	184	183	185	210	203	4
							5
15.4 975	6.9 930	11.8 1015	12.3 1135	11.1 1270	9 1135	11.1 1310	6
1550	1130	1580	1685	1800	1555	2075	7
20.7	7.2	15.6	15.5	15.1	11	14.4	8
EU 4.9/7.9	EU 7.4/9.7	EU 5.2/9.2	EU 4.4/6.8	EU 7.1/12	EU 6.1/10.2	EU 6.5/10.8	9
Diesel	–	95	Diesel	95	95	95	10
50	50	60	60	60	60	66	11
1870	1998	1390	1870	1998	1998	1783	12
80/93	82.7/93	79.5/70	80/93	82.7/93	82.7/93	82.7/83	13
21.5	9.8	10	18.3	9.7	10	9.8	14
25.1	55.1	50.3	38.5	42	51.5	49.3	15
q 4 R	4 R 4Ve	4 R 4Ve	4 R	4 R	4 R 4Ve	q 4 R 4Ve	16
EP/V	EI	EI	EP/eV-T	EI	EId	EI	17
70	70	70	70	70	70	90	18
70	50	50	70	50	50	50	19
v	Mm-h	v	v	v	v	v	20
3.36/1.86 1.32/1.03 0.79	3.36/1.86 1.39/1.09 0.89	3.09/1.86 1.32/1.02 0.79	3.73/2.05 1.32/1.03 0.75	3.37/2.05 1.36/1.1 0.82	3.36/1.86 1.32/1.03 0.82	3.72/2.05 1.39/1.1 0.89	21
3.57	4.06	4.06	3.29	4.06	3.94	3.87	22
5	5	5	5	5 (4)	5	5	23
7.4	5.5	6.5	7.4	7.1	6.5	7.3	24
3775	3795	4400	4440	4130	4030	4630	25
1640	1830	1700	1700	1720	1700	1750	26
1420	1250	1420	1420	1600	1370	1470	27
2470	2340	2580	2580	2580	2470	2670	28
1405/1385	1535/1540	1450/1430	1450/1430	1450/1470	1450/1430	1480/1460	29
10.7	9.8	11.4	11.4	11.4	11.2	11.5	30
120	–	120	120	120	120	120	31
DQI-F-Ku-Td	DDQI-Ku	DQI-F-Ku	DQI-F-Ku	DQI-F-Ku	DQI-F-Ku	DQI-F-Ku	32
Ta-Sf-Ku-Td	DQI-Ku	LI-Tf-Ku	LI-Tf-Ku	LI-Tf-Ku	LI-Tf-Ku	LI-Tf-Ku-Td	33
165/70 R 13	205/50 VR 16	175/65 R 14	175/65 R 14	185/65 R 15	195/50 VR 16	195/65 R 15	34
Sb-Tb	4Sb	Sb-Tb	Sb-Tb	Sb-Tb	4Sb-ABS	Sb-Tb-ABS	35

Country		France		Great Britain		
Vehicle make		**Renault** (continued)		AV	**Aston Martin**	Bentley
Model		Safrane 2.9i	Espace 2.2 TD	Aceca 4.6i	V8 Volante 5.3i Convertible	Arnage 4.4 TI
1	Body style –	5 Li 5	5 Gli 5-7	2 Ca 2	2 Ca 4	4 Li 5
2	Useful power kW (bhp)	140 (190)	83 (113)	240 (326)	261 (355)	260 (354)
	at engine speed rpm	5750	4500	5800	6000	5500
3	Max. torque Nm	267	250	427	500	570
	at engine speed rpm	4000	2000	4600	4300	2500
4	Maximum speed km/h	225	175	250	> 240	240
5	Acceleration from 0 to 100 km/h s	9.5	14.5	5.7	5.9	6.5
6	Curb weight kg	1580	1630	1510	2050	2300
7	Gross vehicle weight kg	2125	2510	–	2370	2750
8	Weight-to-power ratio kg/kW	11.3	19.6	6.3	7.5	8.8
9	Fuel consumption l/100 km	EU 8.7/16.7	EU 6.3/9.6	EU 10.5/15.1	(Ed.) 14/22	EU 13.1/23.4
10	Fuel octane number RON	95	Diesel	98	–	–
11	Fuel tank capacity l	80	78	90	105	94
12	Engine swept volume cm³	2946	2188	4601	5341	4398
13	Bore/stroke mm	87/82.6	87/92	90.2/90	100/85	92/82.7
14	Compression ratio –	10.5	22	9.85	9.75	8.5
15	Specific power output kW/l	47.5	37.9	52.2	48.9	59.1
16	Engine type –	6 V 4Ve	q 4 R 3Ve	8 V 4Ve	8 V 4Ve	8 V 4Ve
17	Fuel management –	EI	EP/eV	EI	EI	Motronic-T-Ic
18	Alternator (14 V) A	75	80	90	75	140
19	Battery (12 V) Ah	300 A	65	60	68	90
20	(Engine pos.)/drive config. –	v	v	h	h	h-ASR
21	Transmission 1st/2nd gear	3.07/1.77	3.91/2.21	3.37/1.99	2.9/1.78	3.55/2.24
	ratio 3rd/4th gear	1.19/0.87	1.39/0.98	1.32/1	1.22/1	1.55/1
	5th/6th gear	0.7	0.76	0.67	0.85	0.79
22	Final drive ratio –	4.73	3.81	3.23	3.54	2.93
23	Gearshift H (A)	5 (4)	5 (4)	5	5/6 (4)	(5)
24	Cooling l	7.8	7.1	16	18	15
25	Vehicle length mm	4770	4515	4420	4945	5390
26	Vehicle width mm	1820	1810	1870	1920	1930
27	Vehicle height mm	1440	1690	1300	1380	1520
28	Wheelbase mm	2770	2700	2470	2810	3115
29	Track, front/rear mm	1530/1490	1535/1540	1590/1570	1510/1550	1610/1610
30	Turning circle diameter m	11.4	11.4	10.5	12.8	12.9
31	Ground clearance mm	120	110	–	100	140
32	Suspension, front –	DQI-F-Ku	DQI-F-Ku	DDQI-Sf-Ku-Td	DQI-Sf-Ku-Td	DDQI-Sf-Ku-Td
33	Suspension, rear –	QI-Sf-Ku	Sa-Ll-P-Ku-Td	Ea-DDQI-Sf-Ku-Td	De-Wa-Ll-Sf-Td	Ea-DDQI-Sf-Ku-Td
34	Tires	205/60 R 15	205/65 R 15	–1)	255/50 ZR 18	255/55 ZR17
35	Braking system	4Sb-ABS	Sb-Tb-ABS	4Sb-ABS	4Sb-ABS	4Sb-ABS

1) Front 235/45 ZR 17; Rear 255/40 ZR 17
See P. 898 for abbreviations and explanations.

	Azure 6.8 TI	Daimler V8 4.0i	Jaguar S-Type 3.0i	XKR 4.0i Supercharged	MG MGF 1.8i	Rolls-Royce Silver Seraph 5.4i	Rover 214 1.4i	
	2 Ca 4	4 Li 5	4 Li 5	2 Co 2+2	2 Ca 2	4 Li 5	5/3 Li 5	1
	286 (389) 4000	216 (294) 6100	179 (243) 6800	276 (375) 6150	88 (120) 5500	240 (326) 5000	76 (103) 6000	2
	750 2000	393 4250	300 4500	525 3600	166 3000	490 3900	127 3000	3
	241	240	235	250	193	225	185	4
								5
	6.7	7.3	7.5	5.4	9.2	7	10.7	
	2610	1730	1630	1640	1060	2300	1000	6
	2980	2260	2030	2010	1320	2750	1480	7
	8.5	8.3	9.3	6.2	12	9.6	13.4	8
	EU 13/25.7	EU 9/16.9	EU 8/14	EU 9.6/16.7	EU 5.7/10.2	EU 12.8/25.4	EU 5.4/9.9	9
	–	95	95	95	95	95	95	10
	108	81	69.5	75	50	94	50	11
	6750	3996	2967	3996	1795	5379	1396	12
	104.14/99.06	86/86	89/79.5	86/86	80/89.3	85/79	75/79	13
	8	10.75	10.5	9	10.5	10	10.5	14
	42.4	52.3	59	66.8	49	44.6	54.4	15
	8 V	8 V 4Ve	6 V 4Ve	8 V 4Ve	4 R 4Ve	12 V	q 4 R 4Ve	16
	El-T-Ic	El	El	El-Kom-Ic	El	Motronic	El	17
	120	140	130	90/140	60	140	65	18
	71	92	72	72/92	45	90	45	19
	h-ASR	h-ASR	h-ASR	h-ASR	h	h-ASR	v	20
	2.48/1.48 1/0.75 –	3.57/2.2 1.51/1 0.8	4.23/2.52 1.67/1.22 1	3.59/2.19 1.41/1 0.83	3.17/1.84 1.31/1.03 0.77	3.55/2.24 1.55/1 0.79	3.42/1.95 1.33/1.05 0.85	21
	2.69	3.06	3.07	3.06	3.94	2.93	3.94	22
	(4)	(5)	5 (5)	(5)	5	(5)	5	23
	18	10	10	12	6	15	5.5	24
	5340	5150	4860	4760	3920	5390	3970	25
	1880	1800	1820	1830	1630	1930	1690	26
	1480	1380	1450	1290	1260	1520	1420	27
	3060	2995	2910	2590	2375	3115	2500	28
	1550/1550	1500/1500	1545/1535	1550/1500	1400/1410	1610/1610	1470/1470	29
	12.9	13.2	12.1	11.0	10.5	12.6	10.2	30
	140	110	140		120	140	120	31
	DQI-Sf-Ku	DDQI-Sf-Ku-Td	DDQI-Sf-Ku-Td	DDQI-Sf-Ku-Td	DQI-QI-Hv	DDQI-Sf-Ku	DQI-Sf-Ku-Td	32
	SI-Sf-Ku	QI-Sf-Ku-Td	Ea-DDQI-Sf-Ku-Td	QI-Sf-Ku-Td	QI-Hv	DDQI-Sf-Ku	VIa-Sf-Td	33
	255/55 WR 17	225/60 R 16	225/55 R 16	1)	205/50 R 15	235/65 VR 16	185/60 HR 14	34
	4Sb-ABS	4Sb-ABS	4Sb-ABS	4Sb-ABS	4Sb-ABS	4Sb-ABS	Sb-Tb	35

1) Front 245/45 ZR 18; Rear 255/45 ZR 18

Country		Great Britain			Italy	
Vehicle make		**Rover** (continued)			**Alfa Romeo**	
Model		420 2.0 TD	75 2.0i	75 2.0 TDI	145 1.6i T.S.	146 1.9 JTD
1	Body style –	4/5 Li 5	4 Li 5	4 Li 5	3 Li 5	4 Li 5
2	Useful power kW (bhp)	77 (105)	110 (150)	85 (116)	88 (120)	77 (105)
	at engine speed rpm	4200	6500	4000	6300	4000
3	Max. torque Nm	210	185	260	144	255
	at engine speed rpm	2000	4000	2000	4500	2000
4	Maximum speed km/h	185	210	193	195	187
5	Acceleration from					
	0 to 100 km/h s	11	10.2	11.7	10.2	10.5
6	Curb weight kg	1220	1370	1410	1165	1245
7	Gross vehicle weight kg	1550	–	–	1685	1765
8	Weight-to-power ratio kg/kW	15.8	12.5	16.6	13.2	15.7
9	Fuel consumption l/100 km	EU 4.3/7.1	EU 7/13.5	(Ed.) 5/7	EU 6.5/11.1	EU 4.7/7.6
10	Fuel octane number RON	Diesel	98	Diesel	95	Diesel
11	Fuel tank capacity l	55	66	66	51	61
12	Engine swept volume cm^3	1994	1991	1951	1598	1910
13	Bore/stroke mm	84.5/88.9	80/66	84/88	82/75.65	82/90.4
14	Compression ratio –	19.5	10.5	19.5	10.3	18.45
15	Specific power output kW/l	38.6	55.2	43.6	55.1	40.3
16	Engine type –	q 4 R	q 6 V 4Ve	q 4 R 4Ve	q 4 R 4Ve	q 4 R
17	Fuel management –	EP/eV-T-Ic	EI	EP/CR-T-Ic	Motronic-2Ke	EP/CR-T-Ic
18	Alternator (14 V) A	65	–	–	75/85	70
19	Battery (12 V) Ah	65	–	–	45/50	60
20	(Engine pos.)/drive config. –	v	v	v	v	v
21	Transmission 1st/2nd gear	3.42/1.95	3.58/2.02	3.58/2.02	3.91/2.24	3.91/2.24
	ratio 3rd/4th gear	1.33/1.05	1.35/1.03	1.29/0.92	1.52/1.16	1.44/1.03
	5th/6th gear	0.85	0.81	0.69	0.97	0.77
22	Final drive ratio –	3.94	4.41	3.74	3.56	3.05
23	Gearshift H (A)	5	5 (5)	5 (5)	5	5
24	Cooling l	8.4	–	–	8.4	8.9
25	Vehicle length mm	4490	4745	4745	4060	4235
26	Vehicle width mm	1700	1780	1780	1710	1710
27	Vehicle height mm	1390	1430	1430	1430	1430
28	Wheelbase mm	2620	2745	2745	2540	2540
29	Track, front/rear mm	1480/1470	1505/1505	1505/1505	1470/1440	1470/1440
30	Turning circle diameter m	10.5	12.0	12.0	10.5	10.5
31	Ground clearance mm	150	120	120	120	120
32	Suspension, front –	DQl-Ql-Ku	DQl-F-Sf-Ku-Td	DQl-F-Ku-Td	DQl-F-Ku-Td	DQl-F-Ku-Td
33	Suspension, rear –	Ll-Ql-Zl-Sf-Td	Ma-Sf-Ku-Td	Ma-Sf-Ku-Td	Ll-Sf-Ku-Td	Ll-Sf-Ku-Td
34	Tires –	175/65 R 14	195/65 R 15	195/65 R 15	185/60 R 14	185/60 R 14
35	Braking system	Sb-Tb	4Sb-ABS	4Sb-ABS	4Sb-ABS	4Sb-ABS

See PP. 898 for abbreviations and explanations.

156 2.5i	166 2.4 JTD	GTV 3.0i Spider	Ferrari 456 GT 5.5i	Fiat Seicento 0.9i	Punto 1.4i.e. Turbo	Coupé 2.0i Turbo	
4 Li 5	4 Li 5	2 Ca 2	2 Co 2+2	3 Li 5	3 Li 5	2 Co 4	1
140 (190) 6300	100 (136) 4000	162 (220) 6300	325 (442) 6250	29 (39) 5500	96 (131) 5600	162 (220) 5750	2
222 5000	304 2000	270 5000	550 4500	65 3000	200 3000	310 2500	3
230	202	250	> 300	140	200	250	4
							5
7.3 1320	9.9 1490	6.7 1350	5.2 1790	18 705	7.9 1000	6.5 1310	6
1820	2000	1610	2200	1190	1450	1720	7
9.4	8.7	8.7	5.5	24.3	10.4	8.1	8
EU 8.4/16.5	EU 5.4/9.3	EU 8.7/16.8	11.6/12.7/29.8	EU 5.1/7.9	EU 6.4/11.7	EU 7.6/14.4	9
95	Diesel	95	98	95	95	95	10
63	72	70	110	35	47	63	11
2492	2387	2959	5474	899	1372	1998	12
88/68.3	82/90.4	93/72.6	88/75	65/67.7	80.5/67.4	82/75.65	13
10.3	18.45	10	10.6	8.8	7.8	8.5	14
56.2	41.9	54.7	59.4	32.2	70	81.1	15
q 6 V 4Ve	q 5 R	q 6 V 4Ve	12 V 4Ve	q 4 R	q 4 R	q 5 R 4Ve	16
Motronic	EP/CR-T-Ic	Motronic	Motronic	EI	Motronic-T-Ic	Motronic-T-Ic	17
120	100	120	140	55/65	65/85	100	18
70	100	70	70	40	40/50	50	19
v	v	v	h-h	v	v	v	20
3.5/2.24 1.52/1.16 0.97/0.82	3.8/2.24 1.36/0.97 0.76/0.61	3.5/2.24 1.52/1.16 0.97/0.82	2.92/1.9 1.37/1.07 0.87/0.74	3.91/2.05 1.34/0.98 0.84	3.91/2.24 1.52/1.16 0.87	3.8/2.24 1.52/1.16 0.91	21
3.94	3.18	3.56	3.64	4.07	3.35	3.11	22
6 (4)	6	6/5	6 (4)	5	5	5/6	23
9.2	9.1	11.7	20	4.8	6	7.2	24
4430	4720	4285	4730	3320	3760	4250	25
1745	1815	1780	1920	1510	1625	1770	26
1420	1420	1320	1300	1440	1450	1350	27
2595	2700	2540	2600	2200	2450	2540	28
1510/1500	1545/1530	1510/1530	1585/1605	1265/1255	1380/1360	1485/1470	29
11.6	11.6	12.0	–	8.8	9.7	11.9	30
140	140	120	130	150	150	150	31
DDQI-Sf-Ku-Td	DDQI-Sf-Ku-Td	DQI-F-Ku-Td	DDQI-Sf-Ku-Td	DQI-F-Td	DQI-F-Ku-Td	DQI-F-Ku-Td	32
DQu-Ll-F-Ku-Td	Ql-Sl-Sf-Ku-Td	Ma-Sf-Ku-Td	Ea-DDQl-Sf-Ku-Td	Ll-Sf-Ku-Td	Ll-Sf-Ku-Td	Ll-Sf-Ku-Td	33
215/60 R 15	205/55 R 16	195/60 R 15	1)	145/70 R 13	185/55 R 14	205/50 R 16	34
4Sb-ABS	4Sb-ABS	4Sb-ABS	4Sb-ABS	Sb-Tb	4Sb-ABS	4Sb-ABS	35

1) Front 255/45 ZR 17; Rear 285/40 ZR 17

Country		Italy				
Vehicle make		Fiat (continued)				
Model		Barchetta 1.7i	Bravo 1.8i	Brava 1.9 JTD	Marea 2.4 TDI	Multipla 1.6i Bipower
1	Body style –	2 Ca 2	3 Li 5	5 Li 5	4 Li 5	5 Gli 6
2	Useful power kW (bhp)	96 (131)	83 (113)	77 (105)	91 (124)	76/68 (103/92)
	at engine speed rpm	6300	5800	4000	4000	5750
3	Max. torque Nm	164	154	200	265	144 (Gas 130)
	at engine speed rpm	4300	4400	1500	2000	4000
4	Maximum speed km/h	200	193	185	195	168 (Gas 157)
5	Acceleration from 0 to 100 km/h s	8.9	10	10.6	10.5	13.5 (Gas 16)
6	Curb weight kg	1060	1100	1180	1280	1300
7	Gross vehicle weight kg	1260	1600	1570	1870	1870
8	Weight-to-power ratio kg/kW	11	14.8	14.9	14.1	17.1
9	Fuel consumption l/100 km	EU 6.5/11.6	EU 6.5/11.3	EU 4.5/7.3	EU 6/10.2	EU 7.2/11.1
10	Fuel octane number RON	95	95	Diesel	Diesel	95 + gas
11	Tank capacity l	50	50	50	63	38 (Gas 164)
12	Engine swept volume cm³	1747	1747	1910	2387	1581
13	Bore/stroke mm	82/82.7	82/82.7	82/90.4	82/90.4	86.4/67.4
14	Compression ratio –	10.3	10.3	18.45	20.7	10.5
15	Specific power output kW/l	54.9	47.5	40.3	38.1	48.1
16	Engine type –	q 4 R 4Ve	q 4 R 4Ve	q 4 R	5 R	q 4 R 4Ve
17	Fuel management –	EI	EI	EP/CR-T-Ic	EP/eV-T-Ic	EI
18	Alternator (14 V) A	75/85	75/85	75	75/85	80/90
19	Battery (12 V) Ah	50	50	60	70	50
20	(Engine pos.)/drive config. –	v	v	v	v	v
21	Transmission 1st/2nd gear	3.91/2.24	3.91/2.24	3.91/2.24	3.8/2.24	3.91/2.24
	ratio 3rd/4th gear	1.52/1.16	1.52/1.16	1.44/1.03	1.36/0.97	1.52/1.16
	5th/6th gear	0.95	0.97	0.77	0.77	0.97
22	Final drive ratio –	3.56	3.35	3.05	3.18	4.07
23	Gearshift H (A)	5	5	5	5	5
24	Cooling l	6.9	6.7	6.1	7.6	7
25	Vehicle length mm	3915	4025	4190	4390	3995
26	Vehicle width mm	1640	1755	1740	1740	1870
27	Vehicle height mm	1270	1420	1410	1420	1700
28	Wheelbase mm	2275	2540	2540	2540	2665
29	Track, front/rear mm	1410/1410	1440/1440	1460/1460	1470/1440	1510/1520
30	Turning circle diameter m	10.5	10.4	10.4	10.7.	11.0
31	Ground clearance mm	120	150	150	120	120
32	Suspension, front –	DQl-F-Ku-Td	DQl-F-Ku-Td	DQl-F-Ku-Td	DQl-F-Ku-Td	DQl-F-Ku-Td
33	Suspension, rear –	Ll-Sf-Ku-Td	Ll-Sf-Ku-Td	Ll-Sf-Ku-Td	Ll-Sf-Ku-Td	Ll-Sf-Ku-Td
34	Tires –	195/55 R 15	175/65 R 14	175/65 R 14	175/70 R 14	185/65 R 15
35	Braking system	4Sb	Sb-Tb	Sb-Tb	4Sb-ABS	Sb-Tb

See PP. 898 for abbreviations and explanations.

	Lamborghini	Lancia					
Ulysse 2.1 TD	Diabolo SV 5.7i	Y 1.2 i.e.	Delta 2.0 i.e. Turbo HPE	Dedra 1.9 TD	Kappa 2.4 JTD	Z 2.0 i.e.	
5 Gli 5-7	2 Co 2	3 Li 5	3 Li 5	5 Ko 5	4 Li 5	5 Gli 5-8	1
80 (109) 4300	390 (530) 7100	63 (86) 6000	142 (193) 5500	66 (90) 4200	100 (136) 4000	97 (132) 5500	2
250 2000	605 5500	113 4500	290 3400	186 2500	304 2000	180 4200	3
175	320	177	225	174	202	186	4
							5
13.3 1615	3.85 1530	10.9 910	7.5 1330	13.9 1285	10 1510	10.1 1555	6
2385	–	1390	1830	1765	2000	2360	7
20.2	3.9	14.4	9.4	18.9	15.1	16	8
EU 6.7/10.8	EU 17.3/37.9	EU 5.1/9.2	EU 8/14.6	EU 5.9/8.8	EU 6.2/10.2	EU 8.5/13.5	9
Diesel	95	95	95	Diesel	Diesel	95	10
80	100	47	61	60	70	80	11
2088	5707	1242	1995	1929	2387	1998	12
85/92	87/80	70.8/78.9	84/90	82.6/90	82/90.4	86/86	13
21.5	10	10.2	8	19.2	18.45	10.4	14
38.3	68.3	50.7	71.2	34.2	41.9	48.5	15
q 4 R 3Ve	12 V 4Ve	q 4 R 4Ve	4 R 4Ve	4 R	5 R	4 R 4Ve	16
EP/eV-T-Ic	EI	EI	EI	EP/V	EP/CR-T-Ic	Motronic	17
90	85	65/75	70	70	100/120	90	18
50/60	55	40	55	60	70	70	19
v	Mm-h	v	v	v	v	v	20
3.42/1.78 1.12/0.8 0.61	2.31/1.52 1.12/0.88 0.68	3.91/2.16 1.48/1.12 0.9	3.8/2.24 1.52/1.16 0.81	3.91/2.24 1.44/1.03 0.79	3.8/2.24 1.36/0.97 0.71	3.25/1.78 1.19/0.9 0.73	21
4.79	4.1	3.73	3.56	3.17	3.56	4.64	22
5	5	5	5	5	5	5	23
9	15	4.5	8.5	8.8	8.3	8.5	24
4455	4470	3725	4010	4345	4685	4470	25
1830	2040	1690	1760	1700	1825	1835	26
1710	1110	1440	1760	1450	1460	1710-1810	27
2825	2650	2380	2540	2540	2700	2825	28
1535/1540	1540/1640	1385/1370	1485/1415	1435/1415	1545/1535	1535/1540	29
11.8	13.0	9.6	11.6	11.4	10.9	11.8	30
130	140	150	150	150	140	–	31
DQI-F-Ku-Td	DQI-Db-Sf-Ku	DQI-F-Ku-Td	DQI-F-Ku-Td	DQI-F-Ku-Td	DQI-F-Sf-Ku-Td	DQI-F-Sf-Td	32
Vla-Sf-Ku-Td	DQI-Db-Sf-Ku	LI-Sf-Ku-Td	LI-Sf-Ku-Td	LI-Sf-Ku-Td	DQu-Sf-Ku-Td	Vla-P-LI-Sf-Ku-Td	33
195/70 R 14	1)	195/50 R 15	215/45 R 16	185/60 R 14	195/65 R 15	205/65 R 15	34
Sb-Tb	4Sb-ABS	Sb-Tb	4Sb-ABS	4Sb-ABS	4Sb-ABS	Sb-Tb	35

1) Front 235/35 ZR 18; Rear 335/30 ZR 18

Country		Italy	Japan			
Vehicle make Model		**Maserati** 3200 GT BiTurbo	**Daihatsu** Charade 1.3i	**Honda** Z 0.7 Ti	Logo 1.3i	Civic Aerodeck 1.5i
1	Body style —	2 Co 2+2	5/3/4 Li 5	3 Mv 4	5/3 Li 5	5 Ko 5
2	Useful power kW (bhp) at engine speed rpm	271 (368) 6250	62 (84) 6500	47 (64) 6000	48 (65) 5000	84 (114) 6500
3	Max. torque Nm at engine speed rpm	491 4500	105 5000	93 3700	108 2500	134 5200
4	Maximum speed km/h	280	170	> 130	152	190
5	Acceleration from 0 to 100 km/h s	5.1	11	–	14.5	11.5
6	Curb weight kg	1590	830	960	940	1135
7	Gross vehicle weight kg	1940	1350	–	1365	1610
8	Weight-to-power ratio kg/kW	5.9	13.2	25.3	19.2	13.1
9	Fuel consumption l/100 km	(Ed.) 11/26	EU 5.6/8.9	(Ed.) 6/10	EU 5.5/7.8	EU 5.7/8.8
10	Fuel octane number RON	95	91	–	95	95
11	Fuel tank capacity l	90	50	35	40	55
12	Engine swept volume cm³	3217	1296	657	1343	1493
13	Bore/stroke mm	80/80	76/71.4	66/64	75/76	75/84.5
14	Compression ratio —	8	9.5	8.5	9.2	9.6
15	Specific power output kW/l	84.2	47.8	57.8	35.7	56.2
16	Engine type —	8 V 4Ve	q 4 R 4Ve	Mm 3 R 4Ve	q 4 R	q 4 R 4Ve
17	Fuel management —	El-2Tlc	El	El-T-lc	El	El
18	Alternator (14 V) A	105	60	35	70	70/75
19	Battery (12 V) Ah	60	36	32	36	36/55
20	(Engine pos.)/drive config. —	h-ASR	v	aa	v	v
21	Transmission 1st/2nd gear ratio 3rd/4th gear 5th/6th gear	4.22/2.51 1.67/1.23 1/0.83	3.18/1.84 1.25/0.86 0.71	2.7/1.55 1.03/0.74	3.23/1.78 1.25/0.94 0.77	3.25/1.78 1.25/0.94 0.7
22	Final drive ratio —	3.23	4.27	3.04	4.06	3.89
23	Gearshift H (A)	6 (4)	5 (4)	(4)	5 (3+St)	5 (4+St)
24	Cooling l	14	4.5	–	4.8	4.8
25	Vehicle length mm	4510	3780	3395	3785	4425
26	Vehicle width mm	1820	1620	1475	1645	1695
27	Vehicle height mm	1310	1390	1680	1520	1440
28	Wheelbase mm	2660	2395	2360	2360	2620
29	Track, front/rear mm	1525/1540	1385/1390	1280/1290	1425/1400	1480/1490
30	Turning circle diameter m	11.5	9.6	9.2	10.2	11.0
31	Ground clearance mm	120	160	200	140	150
32	Suspension, front —	DDQl-Sf- Ku-Td	DQl-F-Sf- Ku-Td	DQl-F-Sf- Ku-Td	Ql-F	DDQl-Sf
33	Suspension, rear —	DDQl-Sf- Ku-Td	Ql-Ll-Sf- Ku-Td	De-P-Ll-Sf-Td	Vla-Sf-Ku-Td	Ql-Ll-Sf
34	Tires —	1)	145 R 13	175 R 15	175/70 R13	175/70 R13
35	Braking system —	4Sb-ABS	Sb-Tb	Sb-Tb	Sb-Tb	Sb-Tb

1) Front 235/40 ZR 18; Rear 265/35 ZR 18
See P. 898 for abbreviations and explanations.

				Lexus		Mazda	
Accord Coupé 2.0i	Capa 1.5i	Odyssey 3.5i	HR-V 1.6i	IS 200 2.0i	GS 300 3.0i	AZ Wagon 0.7 Ti	
2 Co 5	5 Mv 5	5 Gli 7	3 Ge 4	4 Li 5	4 Li 5	3/5 Mv 4	1
108 (147) / 6000	72 (98) / 6300	157 (213) / 5200	77 (105) / 6200	114 (155) / 6200	163 (222) / 5800	44 (60) / 6000	2
184 / 5000	133 / 3500	310 / 4300	135 / 3400	195 / 4400	298 / 3800	83 / 4000	3
208	170	> 190	165	215	230	135	4
10.1	–	–	11.2	9.5	8.2	–	5
1355	1110	1910	1125	1300	1665	750	6
–	–	–	1530	–	2120	–	7
12.5	15.4	12.2	14.6	11.4	10.2	19.7	8
EU 7.1/12.2	(Ed.) 4.5/9	(Ed.) 9/13.1	EU 7.2/9.9	(Ed.) 7/13	EU 8.8/16	(Ed.) 4/8	9
95	95	95	95	95	–	95	10
65	40	75	55	70	75	30	11
1997	1493	3471	1590	1988	2997	657	12
85/88	75/84.5	89/93	75/90	75/75	86/86	65/66	13
10	9.4	9.4	9.6	9.6	10.5	10.5	14
54.1	48.2	45.2	48.4	57.3	56.1	57.8	15
4 R 4Ve	4 R 4Ve	6 V 4Ve	q 4 R 4Ve	6 R 4Ve	6 R 4Ve	3 R 4Ve	16
EI	EI	EI	EI	EI	EI	EI-T-Ic	17
90	75	95	75	–	60	300 W	18
52	36	52	20/45	–	60	36	19
v	v	v	aa (v)	h-ASR	h-ASR	v (aa)	20
3.29/1.96 / 1.34/1.03 / 0.81	2.47-0.45	2.43/1.37 / 0.88/0.58	3.5/1.96 / 1.34/1.07 / 0.87	– / – / –	3.36/2.18 / 1.43/1 / 0.75	3.38/2.06 / 1.28/0.89 / 0.72	21
4.26	5.81	3.94	4.56	–	3.62	5.94	22
5	(St)	(4)	5 (St)	6 (4)	(5)	5 (4/3)	23
–	4.8	7	4.8	–	8.4	4	24
4765	3775	5110	4010	4400	4810	3395	25
1785	1640	1920	1695	1720	1800	1475	26
1400	1650	1730	1590	1410	1450	1690	27
2670	2360	3000	2350	2670	2800	2360	28
1555/1535	1425/1420	1680/1680	1470/1455	1495/1485	1535/1510	1290/1290	29
11.1	9.6	11.5	10.8	–	11.0	8.4	30
150	150	160	190	150	150	–	31
DQl-Ql-Ll-Sf-Ku-Td	DQl-F-Sf-Ku-Td	DQl-Ql-Sf-Ku-Td	DQl-F-Sf-Ku-Td	DQl-Ql-Ll-Sf-Ku-Td	DDQl-Sf-Ku-Td	Ql-F-Ku	32
Ql-Ll-Sf-Ku-Td	Vla-Ll-Sf-Ku-Td	Ql-Ll-Sf-Ku-Td	De-P-Sf-Ku-Td	DQl-DQu-Ll-Sf-Ku-Td	DQl-Ql-Sl-Sf-Ku-Td	Sa-Ll-P-Sf-Td	33
195/65 R 15	175/70 R 13	215/65 R 16	195/70 R 15	215/45 R 17	225/55 R 16	135 R 12	34
4Sb-ABS	Sb-Tb-ABS	Sb-Tb-ABS	Sb-Tb-ABS	4Sb-ABS	4Sb-ABS	Sb-Tb	35

Country		Japan				
Vehicle make		Mazda (continued)			Mitsubishi	
Model		Demio 1.3i	323P 1.5i	626 Wagon 2.0i	Colt 1.6i	Carisma 1.8 GDI
1 Body style	–	5 Ko 5	3 Li 5	5 Ko 5	4/3 Li 5	4/5 Li 5
2 Useful power	kW (bhp)	53 (72)	65 (88)	100 (136)	129 (175)	92 (125)
at engine speed	rpm	5500	5500	5800	7500	5500
3 Max. torque	Nm	105	132	181	167	174
at engine speed	rpm	3500	4000	4500	7000	3750
4 Maximum speed	km/h	158	173	202	> 210	200
5 Acceleration from 0 to 100 km/h	s	13.2	11.8	10.5	7.5	10
6 Curb weight	kg	950	1010	1305	1020	1215
7 Gross vehicle weight	kg	1450	1540	1850	1445	1685
8 Weight-to-power ratio	kg/kW	17.9	16.5	11.8	7.9	13.2
9 Fuel consumption	l/100 km	EU 6/8.7	EU 6.3/9.7	EU 6.7/10.9	(Ed.) 8/14	EU 5/8.4
10 Fuel octane number	RON	95	95	95	91	95
11 Fuel tank capacity	l	43	50	64	50	60
12 Engine swept volume	cm³	1324	1498	1991	1597	1834
13 Bore/stroke	mm	71/83.6	78/78.4	83/92	81/77.5	81/99
14 Compression ratio	–	9.4	9.4	9.7	11	12.5
15 Specific power output	kW/l	40	43.4	50.2	80.8	50.2
16 Engine type	–	q 4 R 4Ve	q 4 R 4Ve	q 4 R 4Ve	4 R 4Ve	4 R 4Ve
17 Fuel managment	–	EI	EI	L-Jetronic	EI	EId
18 Alternator (14 V)	A	70	70	80	50/70	75
19 Battery (12 V)	Ah	50	40	55/75	45/60	50
20 (Engine pos.)/drive config.	–	v	v	v	v	v
21 Transmission ratio	1st/2nd gear	3.42/1.84	3.42/1.84	3.31/1.83	3.07/1.95	3.58/1.95
	3rd/4th gear	1.29/0.97	1.29/0.97	1.31/0.97	1.38/1.03	1.27/0.97
	5th/6th gear	0.82	0.78	0.76	0.77	0.77
22 Final drive ratio		3.85	4.11	4.11	4.63	3.72
23 Gearshift	H (A)	5 (3)	5 (4)	5 (4)	5 (4)	5 (4)
24 Cooling	l	6	6	7	5	6
25 Vehicle length	mm	3810	4035	4660	4290	4435
26 Vehicle width	mm	1670	1695	1710	1690	1695
27 Vehicle height	mm	1540	1410	1520	1390	1400
28 Wheelbase	mm	2390	2505	2670	2500	2550
29 Track, front/rear	mm	1420/1420	1460/1460	1480/1470	1450/1460	1455/1475
30 Turning circle diameter	m	9.4	9.8	10.8	10.6	11.2
31 Ground clearance	mm	150	140	160	120	150
32 Suspension, front	–	QI-F-Ku-Td	DQI-F-Ku-Td	DQI-F-Ku	DQI-F-Ku	DQI-F-Ku
33 Suspension, rear	–	VIa-Sf-Td	QI-LI-F-Ku-Td	QI-LI-Sf-Ku	QI-LI-Sf	QI-LI-Sf
34 Tires	–	165/70 R 13	175/65 R 14	185/65 R 14	185/65 R 14	175/65 R 14
35 Braking system		Sb-Tb	Sb-Tb	4Sb-ABS	Sb-Tb	4Sb

See PP. 898 for abbreviations and explanations.

	Nissan		Subaru	Suzuki		Toyota	
Space Star 1.3i	Almera 1.4i	Terrano II 2.4i	Legacy 2.0i	Wagon R 1.0i	X-90 1.6i	Yaris 1.0i	
5 Gli 5	3/4/5 Li 5	3/5 Ge 5	4 Li 5	5 Mv 4	2 Ge 2	5 Li 5	1
63 (86)	64 (87)	85 (116)	92 (125)	48 (65)	71 (97)	50 (68)	2
6000	6000	4800	5600	6500	5600	6000	
117	116	191	184	181	132	90	3
3000	4000	3200	3600	3500	4000	4100	
170	172	160	188	140	150	156	4
							5
13.4	12.6	13.7	10.8	–	–	12	
1120	1035	1630	1370	845	1100	820	6
1655	1545	2510	1815	1330	1360	–	7
17.8	16.2	18.7	15.7	15.9	15.6	16.4	8
EU 5.6/9	EU 5.8/9.2	EU 10.3/15.8	EU 7.7/12.3	EU 5/7.6	EU 6.7/9.8	(Ed.) 5/8	9
95	95	95	95	95	95	95	10
55	50	72	64	42	42	45	11
1299	1392	2389	1994	997	1590	998	12
71/82	73,6/81,8	89/96	92/75	68/68.6	75/90	69/66.7	13
10	9.5	8.6	10	10	9.5	10	14
48.5	46	35.6	46.1	48.2	44.7	50.1	15
q 4 R 4Ve	q 4 R 4Ve	4 R 3Ve	4 Bx 4Ve	4 R 4Ve	4 R 4Ve	q 4 R 4Ve	16
El	El	El	El	El	El	El	17
50/70	70	50	90	300 W	70	70	18
45/60	55	60	48	26	48	50	19
v	v	aa	aa	v	aa	v	20
3.73/2.05	3.33/1.96	3.59/2.25	3.55/2.11	3.42/1.89	3.65/1.95	3.55/1.91	21
1.32/0.97	1.29/0.9	1.42/1	1.45/1.09	1.28/0.91	1.38/1	1.31/0.97	
0.79	0.73	0.82	0.87	0.76	0.8	0.8	
4.21	4.17	4.63	3.9	4.39	4.3	3.94	22
5	5	5	5 (4)	5 (4/3)	5 (4)	5 (4)	23
5	4	8	6	5	5.3	5	24
4030	4120	4185	4600	3410	3710	3610	25
1700	1690	1755	1700	1575	1695	1660	26
1520	1390	1830	1410	1700	1560	1500	27
2500	2535	2450	2650	2335	2200	2370	28
1475/1470	1470/1435	1455/1430	1460/1455	1360/1355	1425/1430	1450/1430	29
9.6	10.4	10.8	11.1	9.6	9.8	9.8	30
150	140	121	160	150	170	–	31
DQl-F-Ku-Td	DQl-F-Sf-Td	DDQl-Tf-Ku-Td	DQl-F-Sf-Ku-Td	Ql-F-Sf-Ku-Td	DQl-Db-Sf-Ku-Td	DQl-F-Sf-Td	32
Ql-Ll-F-Ku-Td	Ta-Ll-Ql-Sf-Ku-Td	Sa-Ll-P-Sf-Ku-Td	Ma-Sf-Ku-Td	Ta-P-Sf-Td	Sa-Ll-Sf-Td	Vla-Sf-Td	33
175/65 R 14	175/70 R 13	235/75 R 15	195/60 R 15	155/65 R 13	195/65 R 15	175/65 R 14	34
Sb-Tb	Sb-Tb	Sb-Tb-ABS	4Sb-ABS	Sb-Tb	Sb-Tb-ABS	Sb-Tb	35

Country		**Japan**		**Korea**		
Vehicle make Model		**Toyota** (Continued)		**Daewoo**		
		Avensis 2.0 TD-CR	Picnic 2.0i	Matiz 0.8i	Lanos 1.3i	Nubira 2.0i
1 Body style	–	4/5 Li 5	5 Gli 6	5 Li 5	4/3/5 Li 5	5 Ko 5
2 Useful power	kW (bhp)	82 (112)	94 (128)	38 (52)	55 (75)	100 (136)
at engine speed	rpm	4000	5400	5900	5400	5600
3 Max. torque	Nm	250	178	69	113	184
at engine speed	rpm	2500	4400	4600	3400	4000
4 Maximum speed	km/h	180	180	144	170	195
5 Acceleration from 0 to 100 km/h	s	12	10.8	17	15	9
6 Curb weight	kg	1280	1335	725	1005	1285
7 Gross vehicle weight	kg	1830	2010	1210	1595	1860
8 Weight-to-power ratio	kg/kW	18.1	14.2	19.1	18.3	11
9 Fuel consumption	l/100 km	EU 5.2/8.5	EU 7.4/12.3	EU 5.2/8.4	EU 5.9/11.4	EU 7.4/15.1
10 Fuel octane number	RON	Diesel	95	95	91	–
11 Fuel tank capacity	l	62	60	35	48	62
12 Engine swept volume	cm³	1975	1998	796	1349	1998
13 Bore/stroke	mm	86/85	86/86	86.5/72	76.5/73.4	86/86
14 Compression ratio	–	23	9.5	9.3	9.5	9.5
15 Specific power output	kW/l	33.4	47	47.7	40.8	50.1
16 Engine type	–	4 R	4 R 4Ve	q 3 R	q 4 R	q 4 R 4Ve
17 Fuel managment	–	EP/CR-T-Ic	EI	EI	EI	EI
18 Alternator (14 V)	A	70	80	65	75/100	75/85
19 Battery (12 V)	Ah	80	60	35	46/55	55
20 (Engine pos.)/drive config.	–	v	v	v	v	v
21 Transmission	1st/2nd gear	3.54/2.04	3.54/2.04	3.82/2.21	3.55/2.05	3.55/2.16
ratio	3rd/4th gear	1.32/0.95	1.32/1.03	1.42/1.03	1.35/0.97	1.48/1.13
	5th/6th gear	0.73	0.82	0.84	0.76	0.87
22 Final drive ratio	–	3.74	3.94	4.44	4.18	3.55
23 Gearshift	H (A)	5	5 (4)	5	5	5 (4)
24 Cooling	l	6.9	6.7	3.8	7	7
25 Vehicle length	mm	4490	4530	3595	4235	4515
26 Vehicle width	mm	1710	1695	1495	1680	1700
27 Vehicle height	mm	1430	1620	1480	1430	1430
28 Wheelbase	mm	2630	2735	2340	2520	2570
29 Track, front/rear	mm	1480/1450	1470/1450	1315/1280	1405/1425	1465/1455
30 Turning circle diameter	m	11.6	11.0	9.0	9.8	10.6
31 Ground clearance	mm	140	150	140	160	140
32 Suspension, front	–	DQl-F-Ku-Td	DQl-F-Sf- Ku-Td	Ql-F-Sf-Td	Ql-Ll-F-Sf- Ku-Td	DQl-F-Sf- Ku-Td
33 Suspension, rear	–	DQu-Ll-Ku-Td	Vla-Ll-Sf- Ku-Td	Vla-Ll-Sf-Td	Vla-Ll-Sf- Ku-Td	Vla-Sf-Ku-Td
34 Tires	–	185/65 HR 14	195/65 R 14	145/70 R 13	155 R 13	185/65 R 14
35 Braking system		Sb-Tb-ABS	Sb-Tb-ABS	Sb-Tb	Sb-Tb	4Sb-ABS

See PP. 898 for abbreviations and explanations.

			Sweden				
Hyundai		**Kia**	**Saab**				
Atos 1.0i	Coupé 2.0i	Carnival 2.5i	9-3 2.0i	9-3 2.2 TD	9-5 2.0i Turbo	9-5 3.0i Turbo	
5 Mv 5	3 Co 4/5	5 Gli 5-7	5/3 Li 5	3/5 Li 5	4 Li 5	5 Ko 5	1
41 (56) 5500	102 (139) 6000	121 (165) 6500	96 (131) 6100	85 (116) 4300	110 (150) 5500	147 (200) 5000	2
82 3100	182 4900	222 4100	177 4300	260 1900	215 2500	310 2500	3
142	201	185	200	200	215	230	4
15.1	8.6	–	11	10.9	9.8	8.7	5
820	1250	1735	1295	1350	1485	1650	6
1220	1600	2425	1860	1910	–	2180	7
20	12.2	14.3	13.5	15.9	13.5	10.9	8
EU 5.4/8	EU 7.3/11.4	EU 8.9/15.3	EU 6.8/13.1	EU 4.6/8.9	EU 7.2/13.5	EU 8.5/17.2	9
95	95	95	95	Diesel	95	95	10
35	55	75	68	68	75	75	11
999	1975	2497	1985	2172	1985	2962	12
76/73	82/93.5	80/82.8	90/78	84/98	90/78	86/85	13
9.5	10.3	10.5	10.1	19.5	9.3	9.5	14
41	51.6	48.5	48.4	39.1	55.4	49.6	15
q 4 R 3Ve	q 4 R 4Ve	q 6 V 4Ve	4 R 4Ve	4 R 4Ve	q 4 R 4Ve	q 6 V 4Ve	16
El	El	El	Motronic	EP/eV-T-Ic	Ze-T	Ze-T-Ic	17
60	75/90	80	70/130	120	90/130	90/130	18
40/45	68	54	60	85	60	60	19
v	v	v	v	v	v	v	20
3.54/1.95 1.31/0.92 0.78	3.31/1.95 1.39/1.06 0.84	3.75/1.95 1.3/0.94 0.75	3.38/1.76 1.12/0.89 0.7	3.38/1.76 1.12/0.89 0.7	3.38/1.76 1.18/0.89 0.66	2.58/1.41 1/0.74	21
4.53	3.84	4.31	4.45	4.45	4.05	4.28	22
5 (3)	5 (4)	5 (4)	5 (4)	5 (4)	5 (4)	(4)	23
6	6	8	10	10	9	9.7	24
3495	4340	4890	4630	4630	4810	4810	25
1495	1730	1895	1710	1710	1790	1790	26
1610	1300	1730	1430	1430	1450	1450	27
2380	2480	2905	2600	2600	2705	2705	28
1315/1300	1470/1450	1625/1600	1450/1440	1450/1440	1520/1520	1520/1520	29
9.1	10.0	13.0	11.1	11.1	10.8	10.8	30
160	150	170	140	140	–	–	31
QI-F-Sf-Ku-Td	DQI-F-Sf-Ku-Td	QI-F-Ku-Td	DQI-F-Ku	DQI-F-Ku	DQI-F-Sf-Ku-Td	DQI-F-Sf-Ku-Td	32
Ta-QI-LI-Sf-Td	DQu-Sf-Td	Sa-P-LI-Sf-Ku-Td	Vla-Sf-Ku-Td	Vla-Sf-Ku-Td	DQu-LI-Sf-Ku-Td	DQu-LI-Sf-Ku-Td	33
155/70 R 13	205/50 R 15	205/70 R 15	185/65 HR 15	185/65 HR 15	205/65 R 15	205/60 R 15	34
Sb-Tb-ABS	4Sb-ABS	Sb-Tb	4Sb-ABS	4Sb-ABS	4Sb-ABS	4Sb-ABS	35

Country		**Sweden**				
Vehicle make		**Volvo**				
Model		S40 1.8i	V40 1.9 TDI	S70 2.0i	V70 2.4i	S80 2.8 T6
1 Body style	–	4 Li 5	5 Ko 5	4 Li 5	5 Ko 5	4 Li 5
2 Useful power kW (bhp)		92 (125)	70 (95)	93 (126)	125 (170)	200 (272)
at engine speed rpm		5500	5000	6250	6100	5400
3 Max. torque Nm		174	190	170	220	380
at engine speed rpm		3750	2000	4800	4700	2000
4 Maximum speed km/h		200	180	195	210	250
5 Acceleration from						
0 to 100 km/h s		10.5	12.5	11.7	9.2	7.2
6 Curb weight kg		1230	1250	1430	1470	1590
7 Gross vehicle weight kg		1750	1790	1890	1970	2100
8 Weight-to-power ratio kg/kW		13.4	14.4	15.4	11.4	8
9 Fuel consumption l/100 km		5.7/6.9/9.1	5.2/6.3/8.3	EU 8.1/13.4	EU 7.8/15	EU 8/16.4
10 Fuel octane number RON		95	Diesel	95	95	98
11 Fuel tank capacity l		60	60	70	70	80
12 Engine swept volume cm³		1834	1870	1984	2435	2783
13 Bore/stroke mm		81/89	80/93	81/77	83/90	81/90
14 Compression ratio –		12.5	20.5	10	10.3	8.5
15 Specific power output kW/l		50.2	35.3	46.9	51.3	71.9
16 Engine type –		4 R 4Ve	4 R	q 5 R	q 5 R 4Ve	q 6 R 4Ve
17 Fuel management –		Eld	EP/V-T	EI	EI	Motronic-2TIc
18 Alternator (14 V) A		80	80	100	100	120
19 Battery (12 V) Ah		62	72	520 A	520 A	600 A
20 (Engine pos.)/drive config. –		v	v	v	v	v
21 Transmission 1st/2nd gear		3.58/1.94	3.61/1.86	3.07/1.77	3.07/1.77	2.92/1.57
ratio 3rd/4th gear		1.26/0.97	1.32/0.97	1.19/0.87	1.19/0.87	1/0.7
5th/6th gear		0.76	0.76	0.7	0.7	
22 Final drive ratio –		3.72	3.44	4.45	4.00	3.29
23 Gearshift H (A)		5 (4)	5 (4)	5 (4)	5 (4)	(4)
24 Cooling l		5	7.4	7.2	7.2	10.7
25 Vehicle length mm		4480	4480	4720	4720	4820
26 Vehicle width mm		1720	1720	1760	1760	1830
27 Vehicle height mm		1390	1390	1400	1430	1450
28 Wheelbase mm		2550	2550	2660	2660	2790
29 Track, front/rear mm		1450/1470	1450/1470	1520/1470	1520/1470	1580/1560
30 Turning circle diameter m		10.6	10.6	10.2	10.2	10.9
31 Ground clearance mm		150	150	140	140	150
32 Suspension, front –		DQI-F-Sf-Ku-Td	DQI-F-Sf-Ku-Td	DQI-F-Ku	DQI-F-Ku	DQI-F
33 Suspension, rear –		QI-LI-ZI-Sf-Ku-Td	QI-LI-ZI-Sf-Ku-Td	Ma-Sf-Ku-Td	Ma-Sf-Ku-Td	Ma-Sf-Ku-Td
34 Tires –		195/55 VR 15	195/55 VR 15	185/65 R 15	185/65 R 15	205/65 R 15
35 Braking system		4Sb-ABS	4Sb-ABS	4Sb-ABS	4Sb-ABS	4Sb-ABS

See PP. 898 for abbreviations and explanations.

C70 2.3i	Spain				Czech. Rep.	USA	
	Seat				Skoda	Buick	
	Arosa 1.0i	Arosa 1.7 SDI	Ibiza 1.9 TDI	Cordoba 2.0i	Octavia 1.8 T	Le Sabre 3.8i	
2 Ca 4	3 Li 5	3 Li 5	5/3 Li 5	4 Li 5	5 Ko 5	4 Li 5-6	1
176 (239) 5100	37 (50) 5000	44 (60) 4200	81 (110) 4000	110 (150) 6000	110 (150) 5700	153 (208) 5200	2
330 2700	86 3000	115 2200	235 1900	180 4500	210 1750	312 3700	3
250	151	157	193	216	216	200	4
6.9	17.4	16.8	10.2	8.5	9.1	–	5
1560	865	960	1060	1120	1315	1620	6
1970	1265	1360	1520	1580	1830	–	7
–	23.4	21.8	13	10.2	11.8	10.6	8
8.4/11.3/16.3	EU 4.7/7.5	EU 3.6/5.9	EU 3.9/6.4	EU 6.4/11.9	EU 6.2/10.9	EPA 7.8/12.4	9
95	95	Diesel	Diesel	95	95	91	10
68	34	34	45	45	55	66	11
2319	999	1716	1896	1984	1781	3791	12
81/90	67.1/70.6	79.5/86.4	79.5/95.5	82.5/92.8	81/86.4	96.52/86.36	13
8.5	10.5	19.5	19.5	10.5	9.5	9.4	14
75.9	37	25.6	42.7	55.4	61.7	40.4	15
q 5 R 4Ve	4 R	4 R	q 4 R	4 R 4Ve	q 4 R 5Ve	q 6 V	16
El-T	Motronic	EP/eV	EP/eV-T-Ic	Motronic	Motronic-T-Ic	El	17
100	70	70	90	70/90	70/90	120	18
520 A	36	61	61	44/60	44/60	54	19
v-ASR	v	v	v	v-EDS	v	v-ASR	20
3.07/1.77 1.19/0.87 0.7	3.46/2.1 1.45/1.1 0.89	3.46/1.96 1.25/0.93 0.74	3.78/2.06 1.35/0.97 0.74	3.3/1.94 1.31/1.03 0.84	3.3/1.94 1.31/1.03 0.84	2.92/1.57 1/0.7	21
4.00	4.06	3.33	3.3	3.68	3.68	2.86	22
5 (4)	5	5	5	5	5	(4)	23
7	6	6	6.5	6.3	6.3	11	24
4720	3535	3535	3855	4145	4510	5080	25
1820	1640	1640	1640	1640	1730	1865	26
1410	1460	1460	1420	1420	1430	1450	27
2660	2325	2325	2445	2445	2510	2850	28
1520/1520	1370/1400	1370/1400	1430/1395	1430/1395	1515/1490	1580/1580	29
11.7	9.8	9.8	10.4	10.4	10.8	12.3	30
120	110	110	150	130	140	140	31
DQl-F-Sf-Ku-Td	DQl-F-Td	DQl-F-Td	DQl-F-Td	DQl-F-Ku-Td	DQl-F-Sf-Ku-Td	DQl-F-Sf-Ku-Td	32
Vla-Ql-Ll-Sf-Ku-Td	Vla-Sf-Td	Vla-Sf-Td	Vla-Sf-Td	Vla-Sf-Ku-Td	Vla-Ll-Sf-Ku-Td	Ea-Ql-Sl-Sf-Ku-Td	33
225/45 ZR 17	155/70 R 13	155/70 R 13	185/55 R 15	195/45 R 16	175 R 14	215/70 R 15	34
4Sb-ABS	Sb-Tb	Sb-Tb	4Sb	4Sb-ABS	4Sb-ABS	4Sb-ABS	35

Country		USA				
Vehicle make Model		**Cadillac** Catera 3.0i	**Chevrolet** Impala 3.4i	**Chrysler** Stratus 2.5i	Sebring 2.0i	300 M 2.7i
1	Body style –	4 Li 5	4 Li 5-6	4 Li 5	2 Co 5	4 Li 5
2	Useful power kW (bhp) at engine speed rpm	149 (203) 6000	134 (182) 6000	120 (163) 5850	104 (141) 6000	149 (203) 5800
3	Max. torque Nm at engine speed rpm	260 3600	279 4000	214 4400	177 4800	258 4850
4	Maximum speed km/h	200	> 180	210	200	210
5	Acceleration from 0 to 100 km/h s	(0-97 km/h) 8.5	10	10.5	11	10.2
6	Curb weight kg	1710	1540	1435	1335	1610
7	Gross vehicle weight kg	–	–	1930	–	2120
8	Weight-to-power ratio kg/kW	11.5	11.5	12.2	12.8	10.8
9	Fuel consumption l/100 km	EPA 9.4/13.1	(Ed.) 9/15	EU 7.1/15.1	(Ed.) 8/12	EPA 9/11.2
10	Fuel octane number RON	95	91	95	91	92
11	Fuel tank capacity l	60	64.5	60	64	64
12	Engine swept volume cm³	2962	3350	2497	1996	2736
13	Bore/stroke mm	86/85	92/84	83.5/76	87.5/83	86/78.5
14	Compression ratio –	10	9.5	9.4	9.6	9.7
15	Specific power output kW/l	50.3	40	48.1	52.1	54.5
16	Engine type –	6 V 4Ve	q 6 V	q 6 V 4Ve	q 4 R 4Ve	6 V 4Ve
17	Fuel management –	Motronic	EI	EI	EI	EI
18	Alternator (14 V) A	120	105/140	90	90	125
19	Battery (12 V) Ah	300 A	54	60	430 A	60
20	(Engine pos.)/drive config. –	h-ASR	v-ASR	v	v	v
21	Transmission 1st/2nd gear ratio 3rd/4th gear 5th/6th gear	2.86/1.62 1/0.72	2.92/1.57 1/0.71	2.84/1.57 1/0.69	3.54/2.13 1.36/1.03 0.81	2.84/1.57 1/0.69
22	Final drive ratio –	3.9	3.29	3.91	3.94	3.89
23	Gearshift H (A)	(4)	(4)	(4)	5 (4)	(4)
24	Cooling l	10	11.2	10	7	8.2
25	Vehicle length mm	4930	5080	4750	4850	5000
26	Vehicle width mm	1790	1855	1820	1770	1920
27	Vehicle height mm	1430	1460	1380	1340	1420
28	Wheelbase mm	2730	2805	2740	2635	2870
29	Track, front/rear mm	1505/1520	1575/1555	1530/1530	1510/1505	1575/1565
30	Turning circle diameter m	11.0	11.5	11.8	12.2	12.3
31	Ground clearance mm	130	120	140	140	130
32	Suspension, front –	DQI-F-Ku-Td	DQI-F-Sf- Ku-Td	DDQI-Sf- Ku-Td	DDQI-Sf- Ku-Td	QI-Li-F-Sf- Ku-Td
33	Suspension, rear –	QI-SI-Sf- Ku-Td	QI-LI-F-Sf- Ku-Td	Ea-DQI-QI-LI- Sf-Ku-Td	Ea-DQI-QI- Sf-Ku-Td	Ea-QI-LI-F- Sf-Ku-Td
34	Tires –	225/55 R 16	225/60 R 16	185/65 R 15	195/70 HR 14	225/55 R 17
35	Braking system	4Sb-ABS	4Sb-ABS	4Sb	Sb-Tb	4Sb-ABS

See PP. 898 for abbreviations and explanations.

	Dodge Caravan 2.4i	Ford Windstar 3.8i	Lincoln Continental 4.6i	Mercury Cougar 2.5i	Oldsmobile Alero 2.4i	Plymouth Voyager 3.0i	Pontiac Sunfire 2.2i	
	5 Gli 5-8	4 Gli 5-7	4 Li 5-6	3 Co 4	2 Co 5	5 Gli 7	2 Ca 5	1
	112 (152) 5200	149 (203) 4900	205 (279) 5750	127 (173) 6250	112 (152) 5600	112 (152) 5200	86 (117) 5000	2
	226 4000	326 3600	373 4750	224 4250	210 4400	239 4000	183 3600	3
	170	> 175	215	225	200	175	175	4
	–	–	–	8.5	10.5	–	–	5
	1595	1690	1760	1375	1340	1605	1300	6
	–	2440	–	–	–	–	–	7
	14.2	11.3	8.6	11	12	14.3	14	8
	EPA 9.4/11.8	EPA 10.2/13.8	EPA 9.8/13.8	EPA 8.4/12.4	EPA 7.8/11.2	EPA 9.8/12.4	EPA 6.4/10	9
	–	91	–	91	91	87	91	10
	75	95	76	60	57	75	57.5	11
	2429	3797	4601	2544	2392	2972	2190	12
	87.5/101	96.8/86	90.2/90	82.4/79.5	90/94	91.1/76	89/88	13
	9.4	9.3	9.85	9.7	9.5	8.9	9	14
	46.1	39.2	44.6	49.9	46.8	37.7	39.3	15
	q 4 R 4Ve	6 V	8 V 4Ve	q 6 V 4Ve	q 4 R 4Ve	q 6 V	q 4 R	16
	EI	EI	EI	EI	EI	EI	EI	17
	90/120	130	130	130	105	90/120	105	18
	600 A	58	84	68	52	600 A	54	19
	v	v-ASR	v	v	v-ASR	v	v	20
	2.84/1.57 1/0.69	2.77/1.54 1/0.69	2.77/1.54 1/0.69	3.42/2.14 1.45/1.03 0.77	2.96/1.63 1/0.68	2.69/1.55 1	3.91/2.18 1.45/1.03 0.74	21
	3.91	3.89	3.56	4.06	3.42	3.19	3.58	22
	(4/3)	(4)	(4)	5 (4)	(4)	(3/4)	5 (3/4)	23
	10.6	11.9	12.8	7.5	9.8	10.6	9.1	24
	4740	5125	5260	4700	4740	4730	4620	25
	1950	1915	1870	1770	1780	1920	1710	26
	1740	1790	1420	1320	1390	1740	1360	27
	2880	3065	2770	2700	2720	2880	2645	28
	1600/1630	1640/1600	1600/1560	1505/1490	1500/1505	1600/1630	1465/1435	29
	11.5	12.3	12.5	10.9	11.3	11.5	10.9	30
	140	150	150	–	120	140	150	31
	DQI-F-Td	DQI-F-Sf-Ku-Td	QI-F-Ku-Lue	DQI-F-Ku-Td	DQI-F-Sf-Ku-Td	DQI-F-Ku-Td	DQI-F-Sf-Ku-Td	32
	Sa-P-Td	Vla-Sf-Ku-Td	QI-LI-Ku-Lue	QI-LI-F-Sf-Ku-Td	DQu-LI-Sf-Ku-Td	Sa-P-Td	Vla-LI-Sf-Ku-Td	33
	205/75 R 14	205/75 R 15	225/60 R 16	205/60 R 15	215/60 R 15	205/75 R 14	195/70 R 14	34
	Sb-Tb	Sb-Tb-ABS	4Sb-ABS	4Sb	4Sb-ABS	Sb-Tb	Sb-Tb-ABS	35

Index of headings